Sourcebook on Food and Nutrition

Third Edition

Contributing Editors
Ioannis S. Scarpa, Ph.D.
Helen Chilton Kiefer, Ph.D.
Rita Tatum

Marquis Academic Media
Marquis Who's Who, Inc.
200 East Ohio Street
Chicago, Illinois   60611

Copyright (c) 1978, 1980, and 1982, by Marquis Who's Who, Incorporated. All rights reserved. No part of this publication may be reproduced, stored in a retrieval system, or transmitted, in any form or by any means, electronic, mechanical, photocopying, recording, or otherwise, without the prior written permission of the publisher, except in a magazine or newspaper article referring to a specific entry.

Library of Congress Card Number: 82-82014
International Standard Book Number: 0-8379-4503-8
Product Code Number: 031104

Manufactured in the United States of America
1 2 3 4 5 6 7 8 9 10

KIRTLEY LIBRARY
COLUMBIA COLLEGE
COLUMBIA, MO 65216

Sourcebook on Food and Nutrition

Reference books published by
Marquis Academic Media

Annual Register of Grant Support
Consumer Protection Directory
Current Audiovisuals for Mental Health Education
Directory of Certified Psychiatrists and Neurologists
Directory of Publishing Opportunities
Directory of Registered Lobbyists and Lobbyist Legislation
Environmental Protection Directory
Family Factbook
Grantsmanship: Money and How To Get It
Mental Health in America: The Years of Crisis
The Musician's Guide
NASA Factbook
NIH Factbook
NSF Factbook
The Selective Guide to Audiovisuals for Mental Health and Family Life Education
The Selective Guide to Publications for Mental Health and Family Life Education
Sourcebook of Equal Educational Opportunity
Sourcebook on Aging
Sourcebook on Food and Nutrition
Sourcebook on Mental Health
Standard Education Almanac
Standard Medical Almanac
Yearbook of Adult and Continuing Education
Yearbook of Higher Education
Yearbook of Special Education
Worldwide Directory of Computer Companies
Worldwide Directory of Federal Libraries

Preface

Like its predecessors, the third edition of *Sourcebook on Food and Nutrition* is a compendium of dietary information on current topics. It is designed primarily as a reference tool for librarians, dietitians, researchers, biochemists, food scientists, students, physicians and, indeed, anyone interested in the field of nutrition.

In preparing this edition, more than 200 separate research grants for nutritional investigation were analyzed to define important, new dietary directions. From the several hundred thousand articles published in the past five years, a database search yielded 5,000 articles and/or monographs for possible inclusion in this edition. These articles were then evaluated for readability, scientific credibility, medical accuracy, and thematic scope.

From this grouping, the editors selected about 400 articles for thorough analysis. The final selection appears in the first three parts of this book. Each part features a short introduction, followed by a brief listing of other pertinent sections for further information on specific topics.

Part 1, "Dietary Guidelines in the 1980s," begins by discussing the efforts of major governmental groups to develop a national nutrition policy. Essentially, the federal scientists agree in their analyses of the scientific data. However, fully one half of the adult population risks one or more of the diseases that result from affluent diet. Consequently, some dietary guidelines are designed for those with diabetes, obesity, heart disease, cancer, hypertension, and other ailments of a society that is not necessarily well-fed, but one in which food is overabundant. Other guidelines are designed for healthy Americans. As technology advances, new problems surface. Although most Americans no longer need fear gross deficiency diseases such as pellagra or scurvy, scientists are discovering new links to food's direct impact on other human afflictions. Environmental contamination and food safety become important in this regard.

"Nutritive Values" covers the ninth edition of the Recommended Daily Allowances released by the National Academy of Sciences, as well as the measured values of hundreds of food items. "Energy Requirements," "Vitamins," "Minerals," and "Elements" address some of the topical issues on nutrient needs. The emphasis on minerals and trace elements as contributing to good nutrition is also covered.

Because table salt is a frequent mineral in our diet—30 million Americans suffer from hypertension while another 30 million are borderline hypertensives—a subsection of part 1 concentrates on sodium's positive and negative impact on this problem. Technically speaking, dietary fiber has no nutritive value, but it does affect the nutritive value of many other items in our diet, and therefore, is included as a subsection of part 1. Both obese and diabetic patients appear to benefit from increased dietary fiber. And more than one proposed nutritional guideline finds value, for the general population, in increased consumption of dietary fiber. **However, the editors stress that no section of this book should be adapted to an individual's diet without first consulting a nutritional professional or family physician.**

Sugar and a number of its replacements—both good and bad—are addressed in "Sweeteners." Included are fructose, lactose, corn syrups, honey, saccharin, cyclamate, aspartame, and others. The concept of replacing the calories in sweeteners with complex carbohydrates is also addressed.

In the next two parts, the editors grouped life cycle issues. Part 2, "Nutrition from Conception Through Adolescence" begins with the link of the nutritional condition of the mother to the fetus. Caffeine, alcohol, and medical contraindications for the fetus and the breast-fed newborn are discussed in "Pregnancy and Lactation." Next, the nutrients that infants receive from both breast-feeding and supplemental feeding are discussed.

Nutrition has a profound impact on the immunological defenses of the body. Although the development of the immune system begins in childhood, many of the immunological problems of children resurface in geriatrics, when the defense mechanisms in the body begin to break down. Consequently, this section is cross-referenced to the "Geriatric Needs" portion of part 3.

Nationally sponsored nutrition programs for children are also treated in part 2. Highlighted are studies in the very important area of salted snack food consumption. Adolescents also have specific nutritional concerns including the implications of junk food consumption, teenage pregnancy, and the underweight adolescent.

Ideally, physical exercise is a part of the life cycle. However, the editors chose to begin part 3, "Adulthood into the Golden Years," with a positive need. Along with a variety of foods, maintenance of body weight is important for millions of Americans who wish to reduce the potential health problems associated with a sendentary lifestyle. Part 3 then covers dietary influences on the major diseases of adulthood.

"Cardiovascular" covers heart-related aspects of diet, especially the debate whether saturated fats and cholesterol are risk factors or essentials to life. Lipoproteins and the Framingham Heart Study also are highlighted here, along with hypertension.

Cancer is the second leading cause of death in the United States, exceeded only by cardiovascular disease. Actually, cancer is not one disease, but a complex array of disorders. Those cancers that are linked with digestion and diet are touched on here.

Nearly all Americans have had at least one decayed tooth by the time they become adults. Findings that emphasize the relationship of diet to the microbial ecology of the oral cavity are presented.

Adult-onset diabetes is most frequently linked to obesity. A treatment that is increasingly controversial is the use of sugar replacements in the diets of diabetics. Other treatments investigate high-dietary fiber diets for diabetic patients. **The editors stress that diabetics may suddenly precipitate reduced insulin requirements and bring on dangerous hypoglycemic attacks by abruptly introducing large amounts of fiber into their diets. Fiber should be modified only under the direct supervision of a doctor.** Likewise, those diabetics who choose to consume alcoholic beverages, must do so understanding the interaction between insulin and alcohol. This section is very technical because the scientific data are still being tabulated. Dietary changes in diabetics should be made only under the direct supervision of a physician.

"Medical Interactions" covers the interaction of prescribed drugs and other medical treatments with food.

Mental development and learning are linked to nutrition in the section titled "Mental Health." Also of concern is the nutritional demand imposed by stress. For example, mild trauma will elevate energy requirements only slightly, but other reactions to stress, such as overeating or loss of appetite, can derange metabolism far more seriously.

The editors address nutrition in the aged. Statistics show that one out of every nine Americans is a member of that group called the elderly. Every day, about 5,000 Americans celebrate their 65th birthday. By the year 2000, the United States will have approximately 32 million people who will be at least 65 years old. The nutritional needs of this group change as the years add up.

Part 4, "Resources for Further Information," lists associations, colleges and universities with departments in food and nutrition areas, book and magazine publishers, grant support programs, publishing opportunities, and specialized libraries.

Because nutrition today encompasses myriad topics, no single book could begin to cover every topic in depth. However, the editors hope that this edition of Sourcebook on *Food and Nutrition* will provide the reader with a solid, helpful beginning.

About the editors

Ioannis S. Scarpa, Ph.D., is chairman of the Department of Biochemistry, School of Denistry, Loyola University, Chicago. The author of numerous scientific papers, his specialty is in designing and synthesizing polymers to stimulate enzyme-like behavior. Currently, he is researching ways to inhibit the formation of dental plaque.

Helen Chilton Kiefer, M.D., Ph.D., has been involved in biochemical research and the teaching of interrelationships between medical biochemistry and nutrition at Northwestern University and Loyola University, both in Chicago. Currently, she is in postgraduate training in medicine. Dr. Kiefer has held fellowships with the National Science Foundation and the National Institutes of Health.

Rita Tatum is a freelance journalist who has written and edited a number of articles and books. During the past six years, she has specialized in reporting on the latest developments in food processing and nutrition. Recently, she was editor-in-chief of one of the leading food industry magazines. Among her accomplishments is the Jesse H. Neal award granted by the American Business Press for editorial excellence.

Contents

Part 1: DIETARY DIRECTIONS IN THE 1980s 1

National Nutrition Policy

Toward a National Nutrition Policy, by *Nutrition Policy Issues*........3
New Diet-Health Report Causes Confusion, by
  American Medical News..6
Is Obesity a Genetic Disease?, by Gilbert B. Forbes, M.D...............8
Weight Loss Centers a Success, Founders Say, by Sari Staver.........10
'Miracles' of Pritikin Diet Fail to Spur Federal Scientists, by
  Tom Monte, with Phyllis Machta and Patricia Hausman............12
Considerations for a New Food Guide, by
  Jean A.T. Pennington..16
Nutrient Content of the National Food Supply, by
  Ruth M. Marston and Susan O. Welsh..................................19
The Hatch Act: Can the Food Safety Law Finally Be Updated?,
  by Mel Seligsohn..23
The Risk/Benefit Concept As Applied to Food, by the
  Institute of Food Technologists' Expert Panel on Food
  Safety and Nutrition...26

Nutritive Values

The New RDAs: Estimated Adequate and Safe Intake of Trace
  Elements and Calculation of Available Iron, by
  Walter Mertz, M.D..33
Nutritive Value of Foods, by Catherine F. Adams and
  Martha Richardson...40

Energy Requirements

Energy Balance throughout the Life Cycle, by National
  Dairy Council..69
Fats, Cholesterol, and Sodium Intake in the Diet of Persons
  1-74 Years: United States, by Sidney Abraham and Margaret
  D. Carroll, M.S.P.H..75

Vitamins

Encyclopedia of Vitamins, by William Gottlieb.........................85
Vitamin B_{15}—Whatever It Is, It Won't Help, by
  William A. Check...93
Ascorbic Acid and Iron Nutrition, by Sean R. Lynch, M.D...........95
Modern Views of Vitamin D, by Hector F. DeLuca, Ph.D............97
Perspective on Vitamin E As Therapy, by Hyman J. Roberts, M.D..99

Minerals and Elements

Encyclopedia of Minerals, by William Gottlieb........................102
Mineral Elements: New Perspectives, by Walter Mertz, M.D.......110
Fluorine: An Essential Element for Good Dental Health, by
  Durward R. Collier, D.D.S., M.P.H...................................116
Iodine: Going from Hypo to Hyper, by Flora Taylor.................119
Selenium and Human Nutrition, by Orville A. Levander, Ph.D....123
Zinc in Human Nutrition, by Sharon Greeley, Ph.D., and
  Harold H. Sandstead, M.D..125

Salts
Salt Shakes Up Some Of Us, by Louise Fenner............................128
Why Salt? How Much?, by William J. Darby, M.D., Ph.D..........132
Monosodium Glutamate (MSG), by the Institute of Food
    Technologists' Expert Panel on Food Safety and Nutrition........135
The Case for Moderating Sodium Consumption, by
    Roger W. Miller..140

Fibers
Dietary Fiber, by the Institute of Food Technologists' Expert
    Panel on Food Safety and Nutrition......................................144
Plant Fiber in the Pediatric Diet, by the American Academy of
    Pediatrics' Committee on Nutrition......................................149

Sweeteners
Sugar: How Sweet It Is—And Isn't, by Chris W. Lecos...............153
Fructose: Questionable Diet Aid, by Chris W. Lecos...................156
The Sweet and Sour History of Saccharin, Cyclamate, Aspartame,
    by Chris W. Lecos..159
Saccharin Unsafe—Despite the Headlines, by
    Michael Jacobson, Ph.D...163
Saccharin's Influence on Lipid Metabolism Is Related to Dietary
    Fat and Carbohydrate, by Anna Watkins and
    Catherine Carroll, Ph.D. 164

Part 2: NUTRITION FROM CONCEPTION THROUGH ADOLESCENCE............................166

Pregnancy and Lactation
Nutritional Ages of Woman, by William J. Darby.....................168
Caution Light on Caffeine, by Chris W. Lecos...........................172
Anatomy of a Scientific Study: Rodents, Pregnancy, and Distilled
    Water, by *FDA Consumer*...175
Factors Affecting Human Milk Consumption, by
    Stephanie A. Atkinson..177
The Effect of Medications on the Lactating Mother and
    Her Infant, by Watson A. Bowes, Jr., M.D..........................181
The Effect of Maternal Alcohol Ingestion during Pregnancy on
    Offspring, by Eileen M. Ouellette and Henry L. Rosett............185

Infancy
What Nutrients Do Our Infants Really Get?, by Guy H.
    Johnson, Ph.D., George A. Purvis, Ph.D., and
    Robert D. Wallace, M.S..190
Supplementary Foods for Infants, by Calvin W. Woodruff, M.D..202
Infant and Child Nutrition: Concerns Regarding the
    Developmentally Disabled, by the American
    Dietetic Association...204

Immunology
Nutrition and Immunity, by Ronald Ross Watson, Ph.D.............214
Single-Nutrient Effects of Immunologic Functions, by
    William R. Beisel, M.D., Robert Edelman, M.D., Kathleen
    Nauss, Ph.D., and Robert M. Suskind, M.D.........................216

Childhood
Childhood Nutrition Programs, by the National Dairy Council.....222
The Impact of Selected Salted Snack Food Consumption on

    School-age Children's Diets, by Karen J. Morgan, Gilbert A.
        Leveille, and Mary E. Zabik..228
Adolescence
    Dietary Practices in Adolescence, by *Nutrition and the M.D.*.........234
    The Underweight Adolescent, by Harold Meyer, M.D.................238
    Adolescent Pregnancy and Nutrition, by Betty Carruth, Ph.D.......241

Part 3: ADULTHOOD INTO THE GOLDEN YEARS.......243

Athletic Needs
    Nutrition and Human Performance, by the National Dairy Council...245
    Nutrition and Physical Fitness, by the American Dietetic
        Association..250
    Sports Food: A Guide to Nutrition and Exercise, by
        Patricia Cobe..257
    Nutrition for the Athlete, by Laurence Hursh, M.D.....................259

Cancer
    An Update on Nutrition, Diet, and Cancer, by the
        National Dairy Council..262
    Food As a Factor in the Etiology of Certain Human Cancers, by
        Gio B. Gori..269
    New Concepts in Nutrition and Cancer: Implications for Folic
        Acid, by C. E. Butterworth, Jr., M.D....................................278

Cardiovascular
    Diet and Heart Disease, by Consumers Union.............................280
    Cholesterol and Noncardiovascular Mortality, by the
        National Institutes of Health..285
    The Great Cholesterol Debate, by Tim Hackler............................287
    Saturated Fat and Cholesterol: Dietary 'Risk Factors' or
        Essential to Human Life?, by Fred A. Kummerow, Ph.D............289
    Sure Cures, Quick Fixes, and Easy Answers: A Cautionary Tale
        about Coronary Disease, by Thomas N. James, M.D..................292
    Lipoproteins, by David Kritchevsky, Ph.D., and
        Susanne K. Czarnecki..295
    Women, Work, and Coronary Heart Disease: Prospective Findings
        from Framingham, by Suzanne G. Haynes, Ph.D., and Manning
        Feinlieb, M.D., Dr. PH...298
    Nutrition and Hypertension, by S. George Carruthers, M.D............307

Dental Caries
    Bacteria, Diet, and the Prevention of Dental Caries—Part I, by
        Charles F. Schachtele, Ph.D...312
    Bacteria, Diet, and the Prevention of Dental Caries—Part II, by
        Charles F. Schachtele, Ph.D...314

Diabetes
    A Comparison of Carbohydrate Metabolism after Sucrose, Sorbitol,
        and Fructose Meals in Normal and Diabetic Subjects, by
        Suat Akgun and Norman H. Ertel..316
    Effects of Oral Fructose in Normal, Diabetic, and Impaired Glucose
        Tolerance Subjects, by Phyllis A. Crapo, Orville G. Kolterman, and
        Jerrold M. Olefsky..319
    Mineral and Vitamin Status on High-Fiber Diets: Long-Term Studies
        of Diabetics, by J. W. Anderson, M.D., S.K. Ferguson, D.
        Karounos, L. O'Malley, B. Sieling, and W-J L. Chen.................324
    Drinking and Diabetes, by Robert J. Winter, M.D........................326

Medical Interactions
  Interactions between Drugs and Nutrients, by
    Daphne A. Roe, M.D...328
  How to Nourish the Cancer Patient, by Maurice E.
    Shils, M.D., Sc.D..338
  The Interaction of Vitamins with Cancer Chemotherapy, by
    Joseph R. DiPalma, M.D., and Robert McMichael, B.S..............346

Mental Health
  Nutrition, Stimulation, Mental Development, and Learning, by
    Joaquin Cravioto, M.D., M.P.H., D.Sc...................................350
  Nutritional Demands Imposed by Stress, by the
    National Dairy Council...362

Geriatric Needs
  Nutrition in the Aged, by Robert C. Young, M.D., and John
    P. Blass, M.D., Ph.D...368
  Psychosocial Forces that Affect Nutrition and Food Choices, by
    Annette B. Natow, Ph.D., R.D., and Jo-Ann Heslin, M.A., R.D...373
  Nutrition and Aging: Some Unanswered Questions, by Richard
    S. Rivlin, M.D...381

Part 4: RESOURCES FOR FURTHER INFORMATION.................384

  Libraries Specializing in Agriculture, Food, and
    Nutrition Volumes, by Marquis Academic Media....................385
  Food and Nutrition Related Associations in the
    United States, by Marquis Academic Media..........................400
  Colleges and Universities Offering Accredited Courses in
    Agriculture, Food, and Nutrition, by Marquis
    Academic Media..449
  Grant Support Programs in Food Science,
    Agriculture, and Nutrition, by
    Marquis Academic Media...474
  Magazines Covering Food and Nutrition, by *Magazine
    Industry Market Place 1982*...502
  Publishing Opportunities in Food and Nutrition, by
    Marquis Academic Media...512
  Book Publishers of Food and Nutrition, by *Literary Market
    Place 1982*..536

INDEX...540

PART 1

DIETARY DIRECTIONS IN THE 1980s

Since the 1940s—when standards for enriching grain products and magarine were established, and the school lunch program commenced—the United States has been attempting to develop a national nutritional policy. By the end of the 1960s, the first U.S. nutritional status study was showing results and the White House Conference on Food, Nutrition, and Health met.

Following the release of the somewhat controversial *Dietary Goals for the United States* by the Senate Select Committee on Nutrition and Human Needs in December 1977, numerous other scientific and federal groups have issued their own nutritional positions. These groups include the National Research Council—National Academy of Sciences (NAS), the Surgeon General, the U.S. Department of Agriculture (USDA), the Food and Drug Administration (FDA), the Department of Health and Human Services (DHHS, formerly the Department of Health, Education and Welfare), and the Federal Trade Commission (FTC).

In February 1980, the USDA and the DHHS developed their guidelines, *Nutrition and Your Health, Dietary Guidelines for Americans*. Although all officials involved in preparing the Dietary Guidelines stressed that these guidelines represented a consensus among government scientists on the current state of nutritional knowledge, other agencies—most notably, the Food and Nutrition Board of the National Research Council—voiced their concern that consensus in the interpretation of scientific facts may not be appropriate for the public policy decision-making process.

Essentially, however, all of them concur that a variety of foods should be consumed. Similarly, since obesity is linked to increased occurrence of hypertension, diabetes, coronary heart disease, and gall bladder disease, no major group argues that an ideal weight should not be maintained.

There is further agreement in the dietary guidelines developed by each group that if alcohol is consumed, it should be done in moderation. Science links overindulgence in alcohol with a higher incidence of cirrhosis of the liver, certain cancers, and, in pregnant women, defective infants.

Generally, all of the major groups concerned with developing a national nutrition policy also recommend avoiding too much sodium in the diet. But how much is too much depends on the group. NAS suggests 3 to 8 grams of sodium per day would be better than current consumption pattern of between 10 and 12 grams. The Senate Select Committee supports limiting intake to 8 grams per day.

Controversies still entangle three other categories in the dietary guidelines proposed by the various groups. Should a diet high in fat, especially saturated fats and cholesterol, be avoided? Should Americans increase intake of foods with complex carbohydrates and fiber? Should sugar consumption be reduced?

Although these questions remain hotly contested, the disagreements voiced in each of the dietary guidelines rarely rely on interpretations of the scientific facts. Science appears to agree that 50 percent of the adult population risks heart disease, diabetes, hypertension, and cancer—the diseases of an affluent diet. It also agrees that 50 percent of the population is not at risk. As a result, USDA-DHHS formulated its guidelines for the "at-risk" half of this country; NAS addressed its report to the half that is "not at-risk."

Obesity is estimated to plague 10 to 50 million Americans. Excess body fat is associated with the development of such chronic health disorders as cardiovascular disease, hypertension, gall bladder disease, maturity-onset diabetes, and various psychological disturbances, as well as decreased life span. Genetic, psychological, and environmental factors influence both energy intake and energy expenditure. But to control obesity, most experts recommend a conservative weight-reducing approach that combines moderate caloric control with increased physical exercise and behavioral modification.

Truly serious vitamin deficiency diseases are seldom seen in today's U.S. population. Few doctors see cases of scurvy, beriberi, pellagra, or rickets. Those diseases that do occur can frequently be traced to poverty, child abuse or neglect, ignorance and/or indifference in food selection, or bizarre eating patterns. Nonetheless, relative vitamin deficiencies may have an impact on health and well-being, particularly in special health circumstances.

Although vitamins often take center stage in discussions of dietary needs, minerals and trace elements have received accelerated research during the 1970s. The concept of trace elements as biologically active substances was established. Mineral and trace element interactions are recognized as important determinants of metabolism and nutritional status. Also, better determinations of human needs for minerals and trace elements are being developed.

Americans consume the equivalent of between 2 and 2½ teaspoons of sodium daily. Approximately 30 million people in this country suffer from high blood pressure; another 30 million are considered borderline hypertensives. For these people, reducing sodium consumption—when this is combined with a total therapeutic regimen developed with their physician—appears to be extremely beneficial. More complex is the concern that a high sodium intake, particularly in childhood and adolescence, may play a role in the current epidemic of hypertension in America today.

The interpretation of fiber research has been complicated by the lack of a widely accepted definition of the word. Crude fiber is the residue remaining after a food sample has been treated with a solvent, hot acid, and hot alkali. Dietary fiber, however, includes all food components that are not broken down by enzymes in the digestive tract. Although fiber itself has no nutritive value, it interacts with other nutrients, particularly sugars, fats, and vitamins, in some rather and diverse profound ways.

A study released in 1978 by the National Center for Health Statistics indicated that as much as one-third of the U.S. population was overweight. Americans receive as much as 24 percent of their calories from sugar. Three percent of this sugar comes naturally in fruits and vegetables, while another three percent is from dairy products. The rest comes from sugar added to foods. Though some may wish to lower their sugar intake, few Americans, it seems, are willing to sacrifice their taste for sweetness. Alternatives are being touted. Some of them are covered here.

For further information on:

- **Obesity** — See part 3, especially "Cardiovascular" and Diabetes"
- **Energy requirements** — See part 3, "Cardiovascular"
- **Salts** — See part 2, "Children" and part 3, "Cardiovascular"
- **Fibers** — See part 3, "Diabetes"
- **Sweeteners** — See part 3, "Diabetes"

NATIONAL NUTRITION POLICY

Toward a National Nutrition Policy

by *Nutrition Policy Issues*

Preface

The United States Department of Agriculture (USDA) and the Department of Health and Human Services (DHHS, previously known as the Department of Health, Education and Welfare) recently published *Nutrition and Your Health, Dietary Guidelines for Americans*.[1] Although these guidelines are generally consistent with recommendations from other scientific and government bodies, the media has drawn attention to the differences in interpretation. This has resulted in consumer confusion about the function of diet in health and raised Congressional concerns about the direction of a national nutrition policy.

This paper reviews and summarizes the nutritional positions of the National Research Council - National Academy of Sciences (NAS), the Surgeon General, USDA, the Food and Drug Administration (FDA), the Federal Trade Commission (FTC) and the Senate Select Committee on Nutrition and Human Needs.

Background

The United States has been moving toward a national nutrition policy since the 1940s when standards for the enrichment of grains and margarine were established and when the school lunch program began. Since then, many additional steps have been taken. In the 1960s, the first U.S. nutritional status study was conducted and the White House Conference on Food, Nutrition and Health was held. Additional government programs were begun in the 1970s, such as USDA's nutrition education and supplementary feeding program for Women, Infants and Children (WIC) and the congregate dining program for the elderly (TITLE VII); national labeling hearings were held by FDA, USDA and FTC;[2] the Senate Committee on Nutrition and Human Needs published *Dietary Goals for the United States*;[3] and the Surgeon General released his report entitled *Healthy People*.[4]

The 1980s already have yielded Dietary Guidelines which were developed by USDA and DHHS[1] as well as the report *Toward Healthful Diets* from NAS.[5] In response to these more recent publications, several national organizations have released statements dealing with the recommendations.

There is general agreement on most of the recommendations. However, the disagreement among the groups on the interpretation and application of some of the recommendations may cause a delay in the scientific and public policy decision-making process leading toward a national nutrition policy.

Comparison of Opinions

When the USDA-DHHS announced their guidelines in February 1980, Agriculture Secretary Bob Bergland said, "There are no absolutes in our guidelines. It is not a prescription. We are simply trying to advise people how to stay healthy through a proper diet, to dispel some of the misinformation, to give Americans the information they need to make informed decisions about the food they eat."[6] It has been stressed by all the officials involved in preparing the guidelines that these guidelines are a consensus among government scientists on the current state of nutritional knowledge.[6]

The most controversial response to the guidelines is the report *Toward Healthful Diets*, published by the Food and Nutrition Board of the National Research Council in June 1980. The attitude of the Board toward dietary recommendations is summarized as follows in the introduction of their report:

"The Food and Nutrition Board is concerned about the flood of dietary recommendations currently being made to the American public in the hope that a variety of chronic, degenerative diseases may be prevented in some persons.

These recommendations, which have come from various agencies in government, voluntary health groups, consumer advocates and health food interests, often lack a sound, scientific foundation, and some are contradictory to one another.

In an effort to reduce the confusion in the mind of the public that has resulted from these many conflicting recommendations, the Board has prepared [their report]."[5]

Specific Recommendations

The USDA-DHHS Dietary Guidelines are used throughout this paper as the basis for comparison. Comments on them from the various groups are summarized in the chart.
1. Eat a Variety of Foods.
   There is general agreement on this guideline from all major government and scientific groups.
2. Maintain Ideal Weight.
   Since obesity is linked to increased occurrence of hypertension, diabetes, coronary heart disease and gall bladder disease, this recommendation has received unanimous support.
3. Avoid Too Much Fat, Saturated Fat and Cholesterol.
   On this recommendation, there is much disagreement. While there is agreement that high blood levels of cholesterol and certain fats are related to heart disease, the

---

From *Nutrition Policy Issues*, December 1980, No. 9, pp. 1-2. Copyright 1980, General Mills, Inc. Reprinted with permission from *Contemporary Nutrition*, Nutrition Department, General Mills, Inc., Minneapolis, MN.

difference arises on the use of dietary control as a treatment for this condition. Government scientists have taken a public health stance, believing an excess of these substance in the diet may be hazardous since heart disease is a major cause of death; thus they have recommended that all persons reduce their intakes. The Surgeon General, DHHS and USDA believe there is no harm in having the total population reduce its intake of cholesterol and saturated fat.

The NAS has taken a clinical approach, recommending that people with major risk factors (such as diabetes, overweight, cigarette smoking, elevated blood pressure) should have their blood lipid levels determined and then follow the advice of their physicians. Both the NAS and the American Medical Association[7] state that the available evidence is not strong enough to recommend that all healthy adults reduce their intakes of cholesterol, total fat and saturated fat.

4. Eat Foods with Adequate Starch and Fiber.
Although the recommendation to eat adequate starch and fiber was included in the USDA-DHHS *Dietary Guidelines*, no other group supported this recommendation directly. There seems to be some support, however, for the increased intake of complex carbohydrates. The NAS recommends an increase in complex carbohydrates and soluble plant fibers at the expense of simple sugars. In their tentative positions on food labeling announced in December 1979, following closely the USDA - DHHS Guidelines, the USDA-DHHS and FTC did not support fiber labeling since there is a lack of a definition of dietary fiber, methods of analysis and scientific documentation of the significance of fiber in the diet.[2]

5. Avoid Too Much Sugar.
While the NAS does not believe sugar intake for most individuals needs to be reduced, again due to lack of scientific evidence of any harmful effect other than dental caries, most who commented support this recommendation. The recent Federation of American Societies for Experimental Biology (FASEB) review of sucrose essentially states that sugar is safe except for potential dental caries.[8] Dental experts generally believe that the *frequency* of sugar intake is more important in preventing human tooth decay than the *amount* eaten.[9,10]

6. Avoid Too Much Sodium.
Both the NAS and the Surgeon General state that there would be no harm in reducing sodium intake of all individuals and that a reduction may be especially helpful in the prevention of hypertension in susceptible individuals. There is general agreement to a reduction; however, specific suggested levels of sodium intake are given by only two groups. The NAS suggests intake should be limited to 3-8 g salt/day instead of the current intake of 10-12 g. The Senate Select Committee recommends limiting intake to 8 g per day.

7. If You Drink Alcohol, Do So in Moderation.
Again, there is general agreement with this recommendation due to the link of alcohol to cirrhosis of the liver and certain cancers. Also, alcohol is a source of excess calories and therefore a decrease in consumption supports the ideal weight recommendation.

Implications

While the NAS report is not likely to change the USDA - DHHS's position on fat and cholesterol, the lack of consensus among the influential agencies will probably affect the speed with which the agencies make nutrition public policy decisions. Considerable controversy is likely to ensue concerning how the guidelines are to be interpreted and applied. For example, there is already evidence that USDA is interpreting the guideline "Avoid too much sugar" as meaning "eat less sugar." Such interpretations would significantly affect labeling and government feeding programs in the 1980s as well as government nutrition education efforts. The guidelines would thus also have a direct impact on the food industry.

Many other groups commenting on nutritional guidelines frequently mention the need for nutrition education along with a national nutrition policy. In a paper discussing the need for specific dietary guidelines, the National Institute of Health stresses the need to integrate nutrition into a total health curriculum for primary and secondary education.[11] The Board of the National Nutrition Consortium, in their Guidelines for a National Nutrition Policy, strongly supports nutrition education programs.[12] The Surgeon General's Report extensively discusses nutrition education for consumers, school children, health professionals and patients in medical care settings.

Recommendations for All Healthy Americans

USDA-DHHS Dietary Guidelines February, 1980	National Research Council — National Academy of Science June, 1980	Surgeon General's Report July, 1979	Tripartite Agencies' Labeling Positions December, 1979	Dietary Goals of Senate Select Committee December, 1977
1. Eat a Variety of Foods.	Agree.	Agree.	N/A.	Not discussed.
2. Maintain Ideal Weight.	Agree.	Agree.	Support calorie labeling.	Agree.
3. Avoid Too Much Fat, Saturated Fat and Cholesterol.	Disagree.	Agree.	Support total fat labeling, fatty acid labeling and cholesterol labeling.	Agree. Reduce overall fat from 40% to 30%; reduce saturated fat to 10% of total energy intake, balance with polyunsaturated fats; reduce cholesterol to 300 mg/day.
4. Eat Foods with Adequate Starch and Fiber.	Not discussed for general population.	Support increase of complex carbohydrates.	Do not support fiber labeling.	Support increase of complex carbohydrates.
5. Avoid Too Much Sugar.	Disagree.	Agree.	Support sugar labeling.	Agree. Support reducing refined and processed sugars by 45% to 10% of total energy intake.
6. Avoid Too Much Sodium.	Agree. Limit intake to 3-8 g salt/day.	Agree.	Support sodium labeling.	Agree. Support limiting intake to 8 g salt/day.
7. If You Drink Alcohol, Do So in Moderation.	Agree. Limit to no more than the equivalent of three mixed drinks/day.	Agree.	N/A.	Not discussed.

Summary

It seems that the lack of consensus about some of the Dietary Guidelines is based not so much on a controversy about the scientific facts, but rather on what action is to be taken regarding the facts. It is believed by many, including the NAS, that scientific decisions cannot be made by consensus, but rather that the first steps in establishing public policy must be a rigorous and critical examination of the scientific facts. While consensus is the democratically acceptable procedure in decision making, it may not be applicable in the interpretation of scientific facts for public policy. Public policy decisions often bring in other factors, such as political considerations, emotions, moral, ethical and religious beliefs and influence from those who would benefit from that public policy. When USDA - DHHS was formulating their guidelines, they realized that 50 percent of the adult population is at risk from heart disease, diabetes, hypertension and cancer, and thus attempted to deal with these risks. The NAS geared their report to the other 50 percent of the population, those not at risk.

Overall, however, there is general agreement concerning a number of dietary recommendations among the federal government agencies and the cited scientific bodies, which may signal first steps toward the establishment of a national nutrition policy. It is also recognized that any nutrition guidelines need the broad-based support of comprehensive consumer education for implementation.

REFERENCES

1. U.S. Departments of Agriculture and of Health, Education and Welfare, *Nutrition and Your Health, Dietary Guidelines for Americans*, U.S. Government Printing Office, Washington, D.C., 1980.
2. _____, Food Labeling; Tentative Positions of Agencies, *Federal Register*, December 21, 1979.
3. Select Committee on Nutrition and Human Needs, U.S. Senate, *Dietary Goals for the United States*, Second Edition, U.S. Government Printing Office, Washington, D.C., December, 1977.
4. The Surgeon General's Report on Health Promotion and Disease Prevention, *Healthy People*, DHEW (PHS) Publication No. 79-55071, U.S. Government Printing Office, Washington, D.C., 1979.
5. The National Research Council, *Toward Healthful Diets*, National Academy of Sciences, Washington, D.C., 1980.
6. _____, Dietary Guidelines Will Have Marketplace Impact, Officials Predict, *Food Chemical News*, February 11, 1980, p. 17.
7. Statement of the American Medical Association, *Nutrition and Your Health; Dietary Guidelines for Americans*, Chicago, Illinois, April, 1980.
8. Life Sciences Research Office, *Evaluation of the Health Aspects of Sucrose as a Food Ingredient*, Federation of American Societies for Experimental Biology, Rockville, Maryland, 1976.
9. Bureau of Health, Education and Audio Visual Service, *Diet and Dental Health*, American Dental Association, Chicago, Illinois, 1980.
10. Bowen, W.H., "Role of Carbohydrates in Dental Caries." In: *Carbohydrates and Health*, edited by L.F. Hood, E.R. Wardrip and G.N. Bollenback, AVI Publishing Company, Inc., Westport, Connecticut, 1977.
11. Simopoulos, Artemis, P., The Scientific Basis of the "Goals;" What Can Be Done Now? *Journal of the American Dietetic Association* 74:539-542, 1979.
12. The National Nutrition Consortium, Guidelines for a National Nutrition Policy, *Nutrition Reviews* 38(2):96-98, 1980.

NATIONAL NUTRITION POLICY

New Diet-Health Report Causes Confusion

by *American Medical News*

The Food and Nutrition Board of the National Research Council has announced its official assessment of the nutritional status of the American diet, throwing nutrition policymakers into a state of confusion.

Among its conclusions, the board said that the current state of scientific knowledge regarding nutrition is so weak that no general recommendations for the modification of dietary patterns could be made to the public as a whole.

Instead, the board, a part of the National Academy of Sciences, recommended that the one positive way individuals can help themselves to prevent a wide range of diseases (heart disease, hypertension, diabetes and cancer) is to reduce body weight through a well-balanced moderate diet.

In sharp contrast to a spate of recent dietary recommendations coming from various Washington policy groups, the Food and Nutrition Board virtually dismissed the widely accepted belief that low-cholesterol diets will help prevent heart disease. "We think it is important to eliminate cholesterol as a source of worry about disease," said board member Robert E. Olson, MD, of the St. Louis U. School of Medicine.

Echoing this sentiment was board chairman Alfred E. Harper, MD, of the U. of Wisconsin. "Our recommendations are conservative," he said. "They stress moderation and they don't invite undue risk. What we are trying to do is allay some of the apprehension and fear of food that we see is prevalent among the American public at this time."

A report issued by the group, entitled "Toward Healthful Diets," was based on the premise that epidemiological evidence is not sufficient to make recommendations for changes in dietary patterns. Rather, the report relied strictly on data from clinical trials, animal studies, and dose response studies.

The report primarily stressed weight reduction as a preventive influence against disease. In discussing heart disease and cancer, the report said that while there might be some connection with dietary factors, no specific modifications apart from the caloric issue could be reliably made. Regarding diabetes, the report took the traditional path in endorsing the standard exercise, nutrition, and drug management program.

In one area, the question of salt and hypertension, the board did take a strong stand. The report called for a drastic reduction in salt intake to the level of 3-8 mg. a day, a level so low that it would almost prohibit any use of table salt and restrict many pre-salted processed foods.

The report cautioned against "controversial recommendations about nutrition that promise tangible benefits and alter people's lives and habits." This was inferred to include the dietary goals advocated in 1977 by Sen. George McGovern's Senate Select Committee on Nutrition and Human Needs. These urged Americans to reduce consumption of fats, cholesterol, sodium, and sugar and to eat more starches and fiber to protect their health.

Since that time, a fierce debate over nutrition policy and just what should be advocated for the public as a whole has been raging in Washington. The controversy has been punctuated by the introduction of sets of dietary recommendations from various groups, including the Dept. of Agriculture, the Dept. of Health and Human Services, the American Health Foundation, the American Society for Clinical Nutrition, the Institute of Medicine, and the American Medical Association.

According to Philip L. White, ScD, director of AMA's department of foods and nutrition, the AMA has not taken an official position on the Food and Nutrition board report. However, Dr. White said that "the report, if read in proper context, is a good report and not much different from the AMA approach to the subject."

He added, "It is an approach of variety, moderation, constraint, and exercise. The Food and Nutrition Board emphasized the importance of obesity control and indicated that healthy Americans, if eating appropriate

---

From *American Medical News*, June 13, 1980, p. 28. Copyright 1980, American Medical Association. Reprinted with permission.

quantities of fats and cholesterol, have no reason to be concerned."

Said Dr. Olson in evaluating the Food and Nutrition Board's report, "We believe that there has been a general over-perception of the lack of nutritional knowledge on the part of the public. Even if there is a dearth of knowledge, our response must be, 'We're sorry, but at this point we just can't give you all the answers.'"

At a news conference to introduce their report, Drs. Harper and Olson, when asked to catalog the various groups currently involved in nutrition research, noticeably disregarded the Dept. of Agriculture, which supports the majority of such research and has actively endorsed sweeping dietary modifications based on whatever information is available. Concluded Dr. Harper with a grin, "Oh, did we leave out the USDA?"

NATIONAL NUTRITION POLICY

Is Obesity a Genetic Disease?

by Gilbert B. Forbes, M.D.

Obesity is one of the most common "nutritional" diseases in Western society. With rare exceptions, the proximate cause is energy imbalance. It must be admitted that our society fosters such imbalance, for food is abundant, and palatable, and readily obtainable (hence the name "fast foods") for the vast majority of our citizens. The modern situation is compounded by our sedentary life-style and lower energy need of our population with its increasing proportion of elderly. Given this conducive environment, one may well ask why more of us don't get fat. The fact that most of us do not points to some inherent feature of the individual as being of critical importance.

There is a considerable body of data which suggests that a tendency to obesity is inherited. Even the most casual observer cannot fail to notice family resemblances in body size and configuration. Family groups at church picnics, eating in restaurants or attending sports events give a clear indication of "togetherness" for many physical attributes. Then if one considers various mammalian species, it is obvious that body fatness varies: contrast the horse and the pig; the greyhound and the bulldog; the seal and the shark. By determining the body-fat content in 49 species of free-living mammals, previous workers found considerable interspecies variation.[1] Carcass analysis showed that 34 species had less than 11% body fat, 10 had 11-20% fat, and the remainder more than 20%. Another study analyzed a number of newborn animals and here, too, there were species differences, ranging from about 1.5% fat in the rat to 16% in the human, with intermediate values for the pig, cat, rabbit, mouse, seal, and guinea pig (10% fat), the fattest of the sub-human mammals which were studied.[2] It turns out that man ranks among the fattest of mammals!

Young adult males contain 15-20% fat and the females 20-30%. The existence of a sex difference in body fatness, even in the human newborn, points to the influence of the sex chromosomes.[3]

Since animal species breed true, one cannot escape the conclusion that body fatness is inherited. Such is also the case, at least in man, for characteristics as stature, bone cortex thickness[4] and muscle strength.[5] The question of interest, however, is whether obesity *per se*, i.e., supranormal fatness, is inherited. Several lines of evidence can be brought to bear on this question.

Evidence from Animals

A number of hereditary syndromes have been identified in mice and rats. Most are associated variably with hyperphagia, diabetes, inactivity, infertility, hypercholesteremia and poor resistance to cold, in addition to obesity.

The autosomal recessive syndromes include the ob/ob, the db/db, and the ad/ad strains of mice, and the Zucker rat; dominant inheritance occurs in the lethal-yellow, and two viable-yellow mouse mutants, and it is of interest that the degree of obesity is proportional to the number of yellow hairs present.[6,7]

Through selective breeding experiments carried out over many generations in mice, it has been possible to segregate "large" and "small" groups of animals.[8] The former are 1-1½ times larger and 3 to 4 times fatter than the latter group with no difference in food efficiency. When the fertilized egg from animals in one group is transplanted into the other, it turns out that the offspring genotype is more important in determining body size and fatness than is the foster mother's genotype. There are also strain differences in the adipose response of rats to high-fat diets.[9]

Evidence from Man

Family resemblance in body size and adiposity has been noted in the literature. According to one study, in the absence of parental obesity, the incidence of obesity in their children was about 14%; if one parent was obese, this rose to 40%, and if both were obese, it was higher yet (80%).[10] In another, the values were 5%, 19%, and 32% respectively.[11] Still another study found steadily rising values for abdominal skinfold thickness as parental fatness combinations proceeded from lean x lean to obese x obese.[12] The present author's experience (unpublished) with 46 obese children seen in consultation showed that 33 of their 86 parents were obese, and only 8 were slender. Based on triceps skinfold thickness, siblings of obese children tend to be obese themselves, and siblings of thin children tend to be thin.[13]

It must be admitted, however, that such data do not prove the genetic hypothesis since close members of a family share a common environment. Indeed, it has been shown that husband-wife pairs do tend to resemble each other with regard to triceps skinfold thickness; however, the fact that this tendency was also manifest in younger couples indicates that assortative mating may have been as important as a shared environment.[13]

While it is not possible to do the type of breeding experiments in man that have been carried out in animals,

---

From *Contemporary Nutrition*, August 1981, Vol. 6, No. 8, pp. 1-2. Copyright 1981, General Mills, Inc. Reprinted with permission from *Contemporary Nutrition*, Nutrition Department, General Mills, Inc., Minneapolis, MN.

observations on twins and adoptees can provide some insight.

Studies of Twins

Monozygotic twins share common genes, whereas dizygotic twins are comparable to ordinary siblings in this respect. Monozygotic twins (MZ) are more concordant for body size in man than dizygotic twins (DZ) of the same sex[6,14,15] as the elegant photographs by previous workers have clearly shown.[16] In answer to the argument that most pairs of twins share the same environment, MZ twins reared apart are more concordant than DZ twins for body size. One study found that heritability of skinfold thickness was greater for older child twins than for younger.[17] This suggests that environment (household-feeding patterns) played an important role in the younger child, while eventually the child's genotype becomes pre-eminent.

Another way to approach this question is to study *adopted* children: do they resemble their biological parents or their foster parents in body size? Here the evidence is conflicting. One study found that the correlation of child size with that of the biologic parent was significant, while that for the foster parent was not.[18] Another study claimed that infants reared by obese foster mothers were fatter than those reared by nonobese foster mothers, but close inspection of their data shows that this was true only for certain periods of the first year; at one year of age there was no difference.[19]

On the other hand, the abdominal skinfold data from a third study show the same trends for foster parent-child relationships as those for the biologic parent-child: triceps skinfold thickness progressively increases as foster-parental combinations move from lean x lean to obese x obese.[12] However, in this study no data were available on body fatness for the biologic parents of these adoptees, and if perchance the foster parents were selected by the adoption agencies to mimic the biologic parents, the described foster parent-child relationship cannot be used in support of the environmental hypothesis. In a study of 256 families, it was concluded that while height and weight showed significant parent-child correlations, body fatness did not.[20] A later study which purports to show insignificant heritability for percent overweight is marred by reliance on history rather than actual measurement and by lack of distinction between foster and adopted children.[21]

Although published only in abstract form, there is one report of histocompatibility leukocyte antigen types in obese children.[22] HLA B13 antigen was found to be more common in those who had a family history of obesity than in those who did not.

Obesity a Disease of Appetite

Eating behavior can be broken into two components, namely, hunger, a physiological phenomenon, and appetite which is a psychological one.[23] Since obese individuals eat in excess of physiologic need, it is the appetite mechanism which is at fault. Incidentally, the very sedentary life-style of many obese individuals does not invalidate this premise. The frequent claim that obese people do not eat to excess has been nicely put to rest by direct observations of home eating patterns: In two sibling families, the fatter sibling did eat more.[24] Thus one must view obesity as a behavioral disorder and can look for evidence for inherited tendencies of other types of behavior. While an extreme example, schizophrenia is known to be genetic, but the same is true for alcoholism,[25] for depression[26,27] and for disturbed behavior.[28] Indeed, a positive family history is one of the criteria used in the diagnosis of depression. Is it so far fetched, then, to assume that eating behavior is also inherited?

The Hypothesis

The United States produces more food than its citizens can consume, and it is this surfeit which makes possible their generous food intake. For the first time in the history of mankind, Western society has an abundance of palatable food at its disposal. The contribution of palatability is nicely shown by experiments in which laboratory rats did gain weight when given free access to highly palatable foods, only to lose it again upon resumption of a chow diet.[29] Why, then, don't all of us get fat? The present author's thesis is that appetite control is an important factor and that this is faulty for some of us.

Based on the available evidence from animals, including species differences, and from man, it is evident that the tendency to obesity is inherited, and that the gene(s) responsible find expression through modern food abundance. Indeed, "We need not argue any more about whether genes play a significant role. They do."[6]

The mechanism(s) through which the genes (the evidence best fits a polygenic model) exert their influence remains to be elucidated. Does the increased appetite represent a means of coping with the vicissitudes of life – a response to frustration, to feelings of inadequacy? Is eating the prime source of pleasure for some people? Whatever it may turn out to be, the mechanism is obviously a powerful and persistent one, for obesity once established is very resistant to treatment.

Many conditions result from an interaction of genes and environment. Susceptibility to dental caries (a familial trait) is best expressed by frequent consumption of fermentable carbohydrates. Scurvy, which is commonly considered an environmental disease, would not occur were it not that mankind lacks the gene for synthesis of ascorbic acid. Galactosemia, which is classed as a genetic disease, would not occur if our diet did not contain lactose (incidentally, the milk of the sea lion lacks this carbohydrate).

Does the genetic hypothesis of obesity lead to fatalism? We accept the fact that many conditions have a genetic basis – arthritis, diabetes, idiopathic scoliosis, congenital hypertrophic pyloric stenosis, to name but a few – yet this has not forestalled the search for effective treatment and/or amelioration of these conditions. Rather, in the knowledge that we can identify those individuals who are at greatest risk for obesity, we must redouble our efforts to better understand the basic nature of the transmitted influence, and build on this information to hopefully devise better methods of treatment and of prevention.

References

1. Pitts, G.C. and Bullard, T.R. In: *Body Composition in Animals and Man*, Pub. 1958, National Academy of Sciences, Washington, D.C., 1968.
2. Widdowson, E.M., *Nature* 166:626, 1950.
3. Owen, G.M., et al., *J. Pediatr.* 60:858, 1962.
4. Smith, D.M., et al., *J. Clin. Invest.* 52:2800, 1973.
5. Montaye, H.J., et al., *Hum. Biol.* 47:17, 1975.
6. Foch, T.T. and McClearn, G.E. In: *Obesity*, A.J. Stunkard (ed.), W.B. Saunders Co., Philadelphia, pp. 48-71, 1980.
7. Bray, G.A. and York, D.A., *Physiol. Rev.* 51:596, 1971.
8. Sutherland, T.M., *Genetics* 78:525, 1974.
9. Schemmel, R., et al., *J. Nutr.* 100:1941, 1970.
10. Mayer, J., *Ann. NY Acad. Sci.* 131:412, 1965.
11. Davenport, C.B., *Body Build and Its Inheritance*, Carnegie Institute, Pub. No. 329, Washington, D.C., 1923.
12. Garn, S.M., et al., *Ecology Food and Nutrition* 6:1, 1976.
13. Garn, S.M. and Clark, D.C., *Pediatrics* 57:443, 1976.
14. Newman, H.H., et al., *Twins: A Study of Heredity and Environment*, University of Chicago Press, Chicago, 1937.
15. Shields, J., *Monozygotic Twins Brought Up Apart and Brought Up Together*, Oxford University Press, London, 1962.
16. Borjeson, M., *Acta Paediatr. Scand.* 65: 279, 1976.
17. Brook, C.G.D., et al., *Brit. Med. J.* 2:719, 1975.
18. Biron, P., et al., *J. Pediatr.* 91:555, 1977.
19. Shenker, R.I., *J. Pediatr.* 84:715, 1974.
20. Hawk, L.J. and Brook, C.G.D., *Arch. Dis. Child.* 54:877, 1979.
21. Hartz, A., *Ann. Hum. Genet.* 41:185, 1977.
22. Rondanini, G.F., et al., *Pediatr. Res.* 13:1186, 1979.
23. Hamburger, W.W., *Bull. N.Y. Acad. Med.* 33:771, 1957.
24. Waxman, M. and Stunkard, A.J., *J. Pediatr.* 96:187, 1980.
25. Goodwin, D.W., et al., *Arch Gen. Psych.* 28:238, 1973; ibid. 31:164, 1974.
26. Winokur, G., et al., *Arch. Gen. Psych.* 24:135, 1971.
27. Goetzl, U., et al., *Arch. Gen Psych.* 31:665, 1974.
28. Cadoret, R.J., et al., *J. Pediatr.* 87:301, 1975.
29. Sclafani, A. In: *Obesity*, A.J. Stunkard (ed.), W.B. Saunders Co., Philadelphia, pp. 166-181, 1980.

NATIONAL NUTRITION POLICY

Weight Loss Centers a Success, Founders Say

by Sari Staver

"Build a solid future in doctor supervised weight control" invites a large display advertisement that appears regularly in the *Wall Street Journal*.

"Of all the weight loss programs now available," says the ad, "Nutri/System Weight Loss Medical Centers is by far the most successful."

The advertising campaign has been successful as well. In the past eight years, the company has opened more than 230 centers in 27 states; new centers are now opening at the rate of 10 per month.

Headquartered in Melrose Park, Pa., Nutri/System last year grossed over $20 million, with profits of some $5 million. The company says it is the "largest network of comprehensive and medically supervised weight reduction offices in the country."

It all began in 1972, when former salesman Harold Katz established the company, after he watched his mother diet unsuccesfully for years — joining health spas, consulting weight counselors, visiting weight control doctors, shopping at diet food stores, and trying every fad diet that came along.

Katz decided dieters needed a "complete, multi-faceted weight control program that would include medical supervision, exercise, counseling, behavioral education, regular follow-ups and a new approach to diet foods, all in one attractive package," according to company literature.

Katz hired general practitioner Norman Horvitz, DO, to supervise the company's medical program and began to offer franchises to individuals who wanted to go into the diet business. Licensees now pay a minimum of $40,000 in franchise fees and start-up costs to establish a center. To staff the centers, Nutri/System finds local physicians, usually family physicians or internists who have recently completed their residencies. The physicians are hired by Nutri/System medical director Dr. Horvitz but are paid — usually from $25-$60 per hour — by the licensee of the center.

People who enroll in the weight loss program begin with an examination by the physician, either at the weight loss center or at the physician's private office. For a set fee of $90, the patient undergoes a battery of tests, including an electrocardiogram, blood analysis, and urinalysis.

The patient then sees a weight-loss counselor, who uses a computer to set weight loss goals. The fee for the program is based upon the amount of weight the person is targeted to lose: a 30-pound weight loss costs $300, a 50-pound loss costs $460. In addition, patients pay $25 a week for 21 Nutri/System meals (breakfast, lunch, and dinner for seven days), which are purchased at the center.

The Nutri/System foods provide the dieters with 700-1,000 calories daily in pre-packaged, pre-measured form to eliminate any "food decisions" by the patient. There are 38 different foods available, ranging from Nutri Flakes, a breakfast cereal, dehydrated chicken-flavored soup, and such entrees as chicken or beef ragout, brown gravy with veal meatballs, chicken cacciatore, and chicken ala king.

In addition to eating only the Nutri/System foods, the diet program consists of regular visits to a "behavioral counselor" who reviews the dieter's former eating habits and helps the individual to form new eating habits; a regular exercise program; and visits to a staff nurse (three times a week initially, then tapering off), who offers encouragement and support to the dieter. Every two-three weeks, the dieter sees the physician for a check-up.

"I just lost 30 pounds, on the Nutri/System diet," says Dr. Horvitz, whose weight went from 215 to 185 in less than six weeks. Dr. Horvitz says the program "caters to the patient who wants to lose weight quickly . . . who can't emotionally handle taking weight off slowly."

Dr. Horvitz who treated many patients with weight problems during his seven years of private practice before joining Nutri/Systems, says the key to the company's success is "a well organized program."

He explains: "Our average patient is a 45-year-old housewife, who has a husband and a couple of kids at home who are not on a diet. By providing her with all of the foods she needs, the dieter can successfully complete the program without having to really change her family's lifestyle. It's unrealistic to expect her to be able to cook special diet foods for herself and prepare regular meals for the rest of her family. Our plan allows her to keep her family routines intact."

From *American Medical News*, May 2, 1980, p. 18. Copyright 1980, American Medical Association. Reprinted with permission.

According to Dr. Horvitz, some 40 percent of the people who enroll in Nutri/Systems lose weight, with 30 pounds the average weight loss. "It's certainly not uncommon to see a 50-pound loss," he says, "usually in a period of 70-100 days. Of those who have lost weight, Dr. Horvitz believes "a goodly number" have kept the pounds off, although the company has no data on the actual numbers who stay thin.

Dr. Horvitz believes the company's "maintenance program" helps dieters to keep pounds off. "Once the patient loses weight, we wean her off the Nutri/System foods and back onto normal foods, restricted by the number of calories needed to maintain the desired weight. Depending on the patient's metabolism, calories are usually limited to 10 to 15 times the desired weight. So a woman who wants to keep her weight at 120, for example, will be kept on a 1,200 to 1,800 calorie per day diet," he explains.

It takes the average Nutri/System dieter 10-14 weeks to get down to her optimum weight, although the company allows the dieter to visit the center (for no additional charge) for as long as it takes to reach the initially targeted weight.

For one year following the weight loss, dieters continue to come to the center for semi-monthly or monthly check-ups with the staff nurse.

"Initially," says Dr. Horvitz, "some physicians were skeptical of our program. But I believe it was just because we were something new.

"In fact, we're using the accepted medical treatment of obesity. Some doctors think that weight loss should be done slowly. But I feel that under supervision, there's nothing wrong with losing it quickly.

"Right now there are probably 23,000-30,000 patients enrolled in our centers across the country. We must be doing something right."

NATIONAL NUTRITION POLICY

'Miracles' of Pritikin Diet Fail to Spur Federal Scientists

by Tom Monte, with Phyllis Machta and Patricia Hausman

Nathan Pritikin ascends to the stage like a man trying to prove a point. He virtually runs up the stairs to the waiting lectern and, without taking a breath, launches into his presentation, a lecture that might be more accurately described as an assault. The 63-year-old Pritikin is fighting the American diet and much of the scientific and medical establishment, and he wants his audience here at Georgetown University to know he is up to the challenge.

For most of the past decade, Pritikin has been saying that the American diet, a diet high in fat, cholesterol, and simple sugars, is responsible for most of the illnesses that currently beset our society. Although there is growing agreement among many scientists who support this claim, Pritikin has taken it a step further. He maintains that patients with atherosclerosis (arteries clogged with fatty deposits), heart disease, diabetes, and other forms of degenerative illnesses can be "returned to normal function" by eating a diet that is low in fat, cholesterol, protein and high in complex carbohydrates (starch and fiber). That assertion represents the fork in the road for Pritikin and most of the medical and scientific communities.

"There's supposed to be something so sacred about the American diet," said Pritikin, "and the American public is supposed to be so stupid that they would not change one iota of the diet. That's what they [the scientific establishment and food industry] would have us believe, at least."

In 1976, Pritikin, along with a team of physicians, opened what has become known as the Longevity Center, which now makes its home in Santa Monica, Calif. Pritikin and his doctors began treating patients stricken with cardiovascular disease with a diet composed of 10 percent calories from fat, about 10 percent from protein and 80 percent from complex carbohydrates. The diet is made up chiefly of whole grains, vegetables, legumes, and fruits; it prohibits foods high in fat and cholesterol, such as beef and eggs. It also prohibits simple sugars and caffeine. Most dairy products are discouraged and when allowed kept to a strict minimum. Coupled with the diet is an exercise program that includes walking and jogging.

More than 3,000 patients have completed the four-week program since the Longevity Center opened its doors, and by now the stories of patient recovery have become so legendary that they rival those emanating from Lourdes, France. Patients who arrived in wheelchairs, or who previously couldn't walk more than a city block, have left the center walking—indeed running—for miles at a stretch. The average distance patients walk or run each day is six miles, according to statistics compiled by nearby Loma Linda University. Numerous Longevity Center alumni reported that when they got home they cleaned out their medicine cabinets of drugs they had been taking for years.

Loma Linda—which did a statistical analysis on the center's first 900 patients—reported that of the first 111 patients who arrived with blood cholesterol levels between 260 and 279 mg., the average patient left the center with a cholesterol level of 190 mg. On the whole, Loma Linda researchers said the average drop in cholesterol for the first 900 patients was 25 percent. Equally impressive was the fact that half of the people who were taking insulin for diabetes when they arrived left insulin-free. Of the 218 patients who had been treated by their local doctor with anti-hypertension drugs, 186 left the Longevity Center with normal blood pressures and weaned of the medication.

Last Summer, Irvin Rubin, a Washington, D.C. businessman, was overweight, had high blood pressure, and was a diabetic. In August, after being on medication for both his hypertension and diabetes, Rubin went to the Longevity Center to take Pritikin's four-week course. Within three weeks, Rubin was walking and jogging six miles. Before he left, his cholesterol level had dropped from 229 mg to 152, and his blood glucose level was down from 187 to the low 80s. He had been taking six pills a day for his hypertension; when he left the center he was down to two a day. Moreover, Rubin was no longer diabetic.

"The man (Pritikin) is performing a miracle," said Rubin. "My wife was very skeptical, but after we went out there you can't get her to cheat on the diet now." Rubin said that he maintains the diet 90 percent of the time; he says his wife adheres to the diet even more stringently.

A prominent Philadelphia banker, who asked that his name not be used, had had four heart attacks before he went to the Longevity Center in January, 1978. Before he started the program, he tired quickly and needed a nap each afternoon. Strenuous work was out of the question. Today, the banker, who lives on a lush farm within commuting distance of the city, chops wood, takes long walks and jogs each day, and says he has no time for naps. He maintains that after two years, he has complied with the diet 90 percent of the time.

Pritikin has not restricted his efforts to those who come to his center. In an experiment that is impressive in both its size and ambition, Pritikin has asked the town of Natchitoches, La., to adopt his diet for one year. Researchers will determine what effects the diet has on the town's overall mortality rate. Pritikin has stated that he expects a drop in mortality anywhere between 10 and 25 percent.

The University of California at Davis Medical School will soon adopt a Pritikin-program menu for its heart disease patients, according to Pritikin, and United Airlines will offer Pritikin-style meals on all flights.

Pritikin and the Longevity Center have garnered enormous media coverage, which has been overwhelmingly favorable. The CBS news program "60 Minutes" was just one of many major television programs that cast the Pritikin diet and exercise regimen in a very positive light.

Faced with the rising clamor brought about by such claims as those made by the Longevity alumni and by Pritikin himself, one might think that the National Institutes of Health, or the American Medical Association, or some prestigious university medical school would be rushing to verify or disprove the Pritikin hypothesis: that diet can be used as an effective—indeed, preferred—treatment against many diseases that now require either extended drug therapies or expensive and debilitating surgery. Open heart surgery alone often costs more than $10,000.

Unfortunately, as much as the media have lavished attention and praise upon Pritikin, the scientific and medical communities have either ignored or criticized him.

The *Journal of the American Medical Association* recently reviewed Pritikin's bestseller, *The Pritikin Program for Diet and Exercise* and termed the book an unreliable source of nutrition information. According to Frank Chapel, a science writer and public relations official at the AMA's Chicago office, the Pritikin diet is "unbalanced." Chapel would not specify how the diet was unbalanced, but baldly asserted that there "are no dietary diseases in the U.S. today." He went on to state that there is not enough evidence to suggest a link between diet and disease. Chapel called Pritikin's diet "bizarre," another "fad" diet.

The American Heart Association, though more reserved in its criticism, seems equally unimpressed. Said Mary Winston, an AHA nutritionist, "Until he (Pritikin) shows us more than anecdotal evidence, there is nothing to evaluate his work on."

Ironically, the AHA has a diet similar to the Pritikin regimen, which it carts out of the mothballs for patients who don't respond to diets moderately low in fat. "Diet D" is the Heart Association's "extremely low fat" diet, which is used by the heart patients under supervision of a doctor, according to Winston. The diet is made up primarily of grains and vegetables, and low-fat meats. It restricts the use of oils, nuts, butter, olives and avocados; the diet is made up of about 10 to 15 percent calories from fat. According to Winston, studies have shown that Diet D can have a beneficial effect on patients with cardiovascular disease by reducing blood cholesterol levels.

This, however, is not the AHA diet normally prescribed by physicians to anyone interested in cutting down on dietary cholesterol and saturated fat. That diet is composed of 30 to 35 percent calories in fat, and advises patients to reduce simple sugars. Winston was quick to point out that the AHA is currently revising its dietary material and may well do away with Diet D.

The National Heart, Lung, and Blood Institute—this country's most powerful and prestigious heart research institute—is waiting. NHLBI Director Robert I. Levy maintains that so long as Pritikin fails to prove that people will remain on the diet for an extended period of time, then his claims of "return to normal function" or even reversal of atherosclerosis are meaningless.

"How can you have this kind of experiment," said Levy, "if there's not going to be a good percentage of people in the experiment who comply with the diet. It's very hard, if not impossible, to get a free-living population to stay on a diet that is 10 percent calories in fat."

Pritikin says that based on follow-up interviews with former longevity patients, there is an overall compliance rate of about 80 percent. In other words, four out of five ex-patients adhere fairly closely to the diet.

However, this kind of reporting is regarded as anecdotal and carries little weight with the scientific community. Moreover, Levy maintains that the scientific literature is replete with studies that show it is difficult to get people to maintain low-fat diets.

P ritikin is now attempting to raise money in order to document his claims that Longevity alumni are sticking to the diet. He expects the study to begin this year.

However, apart from the argument over whether people will comply with the Pritikin diet requirements, there still exists the unsettling question of what exactly is happening to these people who claim they are rejuvenated once they take up the Longevity regimen. In the past, Pritikin maintained that the diet was actually causing reversal of atherosclerosis; he argued that on a low-fat, low-protein, high-carbohydrate diet, the body can eliminate the fatty deposits that have built up within the walls of the arteries. This reversal of atherosclerosis, Pritikin said, was the reason his patients experienced a drop in blood pressure and hypertension symptoms; it was the reason they were feeling so well.

Many scientists, however, criticized Pritikin for making such a claim, yet failing to show that reversal has actually taken place. As a result, Pritikin then began stating that his patients were "returned to normal function," which he could show by taking their blood pressure, cholesterol levels, and glucose and triglyceride counts. Thus, the question of actual regression of plaque (the fatty deposits in the arteries) was left open. Nevertheless, Pritikin and others have stated for some time that NHLBI should be examining such an issue.

"Regression in man is difficult to demonstrate," said Levy. He said that such an experiment would require a risky procedure called angiography, which amounts to sending a dye into the arteries and then x-raying to find out how much plaque has been built up. There is some risk to the patient. Thus, Levy maintains that there are ethical questions blocking NHLBI from doing such an experiment. Without such a study, however, Levy cannot speculate about the possibility that Longevity patients are or are not experiencing reversal of plaque.

However, based on existing evidence gleaned from animal and human studies, other scientists are not as unwilling to speculate on the possibilities. Dr. William Castelli, director of the long-term Framingham Project, which is following the city of Framingham, Mass., in order to determine the risk factors for heart disease and stroke, maintains that many of Pritikin's patients may indeed be experiencing reversal in arterial plaque. Said Castelli: "My feeling is that if angiograms were performed on his patients, Pritikin would be able to show reversibility."

Castelli points to a period of almost a decade during World War II when rationing forced Europeans to reduce their consumption of foods high in fats and cholesterol. During those years, Castelli said, epidemiological studies show a significant decrease in the number of deaths due to heart disease. Moreover, autopsies done in Europe during those years show that the arteries in the majority of dead were free of plaque. "There wasn't enough atherosclerosis around during those years to show medical school students what it looked like," said Castelli.

Castelli pointed to the work done by Dr. Robert Wissler, professor of pathology at the University of Chicago[1] and Dr. David H. Blankenhorn,[2] at the University of Southern California School of Medicine, as examples of studies where reversal has been shown.

Wissler has demonstrated regression numerous times in rhesus monkeys, while Blankenhorn has demonstrated regression in the femoral arteries (located in the legs) in humans.

"We've seen atherosclerosis turned on and off in monkeys," Castelli said. "The problem is you've got to be a monkey to get proper treatment for heart disease in this country."

When asked if testing the Pritikin hypothesis would be a worthy experiment to perform, Wissler told *Nutrition Action*, "very definitely."

Although Wissler could not comment specifically on Pritikin's diet and exercise progam, he stated that at present there is enough evidence to suggest that regression could take place on such a low-fat diet. Wissler pointed out, however, that an experiment designed to test such a hypothesis would be difficult to perform.

Nevertheless, until Pritikin or someone else proves definitively that enough people have the will power to stick to his diet long enough to conduct a study, or that reversal of atherosclerosis can be accomplished by diet, Levy says NHLBI will not conduct a study examining the Pritikin hypothesis.

Undaunted, Pritikin is now in the process of raising money to conduct his own study on the reversibility of atherosclerosis. The experiment will involve 2,000 patients and span three years. "In three years time, we will know everything there is to know about heart disease," said Pritikin. He said then the taxpayers could stop pouring millions of dollars into NHLBI, an insitutite Pritikin maintains is doing little to bring to an end what he calls the "greatest epidemic in the history of mankind."

The battle between Levy and Pritikin has been a long and bitter one. Levy has on numerous occasions criticized Pritikin for going to the press rather than the scientific establishment with his claims. Moreover, Levy maintains that he has invited Pritikin on numerous occasions to submit a study proposal for possible funding by NHLBI. According to Levy, Pritikin has yet to make such a request.

When asked to comment on NHLBI's director, Pritikin has a terse remark: "Levy is our enemy." Pritikin says that although Levy is the most "powerful heart disease scientist in the world," he nevertheless has done little to educate the public on the risk of a diet high in fat and cholesterol.

Indeed, Levy has come under attack from other quarters for NHLBI's failure to inform the public about a major risk factor in heart disease: namely, diet. Though it has sponsored or assisted a few small-scale pilot education programs, NHLBI has yet to sponsor a nationwide dietary education program that would alert the nation to the dangers of consuming foods high in fat and cholesterol. Ironically, the NIH Task Force on Arteriosclerosis in 1971 recommended that NHLBI undertake such an education program. However, NHLBI decided to reject the recommendation.

As a result, the institute has never advised the public to reduce its intake of fat, cholesterol, and sodium in order to reduce the risk of cardiovascular disease. Nevertheless, in an interview with *Nutrition Action*, Levy said that anyone would be wise to reduce these constituents in their diet.

Still, Levy argued that NHLBI is spending $29 million a year in order to find out what are the risk factors in cardiovascular disease.

NHLBI's principle study is called the Multiple Risk Factor Intervention Trial (MRFIT), which is currently examining the effects of the three major risk factors—smoking, high blood pressure, and high cholesterol levels—on mortality rates of 13,000 males. The group is divided in half; the control group gets the conventional treatment for such problems, including a warning from their doctors to cut down on smoking, as well as the conventional drug therapy to control hypertension. The test group gets an intensive education program on how to quit smoking, reduce blood pressure, and adopt healthful dietary patterns. The goal is to reduce the cholesterol level of the test group by 10 percent and hold it there for six years, and then find out if such a move has had an effect on mortality rates. The total cost of the project is expected to reach $120 million.

Critics have pointed out that if the study proves positive—that is, if reducing blood pressure and smoking and providing information on improving one's diet does have an effect—then scientists will not know which of the three risk factors actually brought about the change in mortality rates. If on the other hand, MRFIT proves negative, and the mortality rates are not affected, many scientists are concerned that the data will be interpreted to mean that diet plays no role as a risk factor in heart disease. These critics point out that such a conclusion would be a grave error, since the men being tested in MRFIT are already in the "11th hour" of the disease; that is, because each man in the test has at least two of the three risk factors, the atherosclerosis may have already reached the point of no return. As a result, the changes in lifestyle enforced by the study may well be "too little, too late." Thus, MRFIT may be unable to test the role of diet as a risk factor in cardiovascular disease.

Levy and other scientists maintain that without the information gleaned by MRFIT and like-experiments, there will not be enough data to provide the public with information on diet.

In his testimony before the Senate Nutrition committee, Dr. Jeremiah Stamler, a heart disease expert at Northwestern University Medical School, stated that "it is entirely unsound and inappropriate to mark time and wait, in the vain hope that additional 'definitive direct' evidence will be forthcoming. In fact, a crucial experiment to produce 'final' proof that 'rich diet' causes epidemic premature coronary heart disease cannot be done."

Stamler went on to encourage the committee to recommend that Americans reduce their intake of red meat, as well as other foods high in fat and cholesterol. Still, before NHLBI and the American Medical Association begin to advocate diet as an important means of prevention and therapy, there must be a thorough reassessment of the role food plays in one's health, said Castelli. "We've got to bring nutrition back into the mainstream of American medicine," he said. "We've abandoned nutrition to people like Pritikin. Now we laugh at vegetarians, but they may be laughing at us all the way to our graves."

In his Washington, D.C., hotel room on the night before he gave his Georgetown University presentation, Nathan Pritikin seemed in perpetual motion. When he was not sitting on the edge of his seat pressing home his points, he was hurrying to various parts of the room to draw from a pile of papers yet another study or anecdote to support his argument. Nathan Pritikin seems forever on the attack, and for this he has paid a price. By going public rather than through scientific channels, and by lobbying Senators and Congresspersons to press NHLBI to be more aggressive in its research and education programs, Pritikin has violated accepted scientific decorum. Said one NIH scientist recently: "Pritikin has offended so many people here, that it is unlikely now that he would be funded by NHLBI even if he did offer a formal protocol."

Another NIH scientist, who requested that his name not be given, elaborated on what Pritikin is up against at this country's foremost research institute. "The psychology that prevades this place is that it's a big club. The club is self-sustaining and there are certain rules that one lives by. To go against those rules is to destroy yourself professionally." Thus, this scientist pointed out, there is little room within such a system for creativity and that a maverick, like Pritikin, will have a long, uphill battle fighting to have his ideas gain acceptance by the club.

1. Wissler, R. W. et al. J. Am. Heart Assoc. 46: 27, (1977).
2. Blankenhorn, D. H. et al. Circulation 57: 355, (1978).

Considerations for a New Food Guide

by Jean A. T. Pennington

A food guide is an instrument which converts the professional's scientific knowledge of food composition and nutrient requirements for health into a practical plan for food selection by those without training in nutrition. Ideally, it should be attractive enough to encourage people to seek more detailed nutrition information. Since 1957, the food guide used most commonly in the United States is the Four Food Groups. This guide suggests a daily food plan that specifically ensures adequate intake of protein, vitamins A and C, and calcium; menus developed from this plan generally are adequate also in thiamin, riboflavin, and niacin, and in iron for males (1). In order to draw attention to foods that people should not overconsume, the U.S. Department of Agriculture added a fifth group (fats, sweets, and alcohol) to the plan in 1979 (2). However, the basic plan still consists of the Four Food Groups because the 1979 guide does not offer specific limitations for the fifth group.

Several factors suggest that now there again may be a need for a new or updated guide. For example, the RDAs for a number of additional vitamins and minerals have been specified (3), the data base for food composition has increased, and analyses of food consumption surveys (4, 5) have identified "problem" nutrients, some of which are not specifically considered in the Four Food Groups. Furthermore, the current food supply is far more complex, especially with respect to refined, processed, and formulated foods, than it was when the Four Food Group concept was initiated. Finally, in order for a nutrition education tool to be useful in combatting nutrition misinformation and to have credibility with the public, it should address the health and nutrition issues that have been presented in recent reports and guidelines (6–8).

There are many different food combinations that provide adequate diets. Any new food guide should accommodate alternative food choice behaviors within the constraint of ensuring adequate intake of essential nutrients while preventing excesses of energy or other food constituents. A food guide, in order to be accepted, should be close to current trends in food consumption but should suggest moderation of those trends believed not to be supportive of health. Specifically, it should encourage consumption of a wide variety of foods in amounts consistent with maintenance of ideal body weight, suggest increased intake of complex carbohydrates, and discourage excessive intake of total fat, saturated fats, cholesterol, sugars, salt, and alcohol. Thus, a food guide must be a compromise between specific nutritional ideals and the realities of the complexity of human food choice behavior. An example of such a compromise food guide is presented in this paper.

A SUGGESTED FOOD GUIDE

The guide herein is not as simple as the Four Food Groups, nor is it sufficiently detailed to meet all contingencies of unique food selection patterns. However, it is flexible, encourages consumption of foods high in nutrient density, and discourages consumption of foods that provide large amounts of constituents believed by many to be detrimental to health. Also, it is visually interesting, and will attract attention, a first step in potential behavior change.

This guide has the shape of a reverse

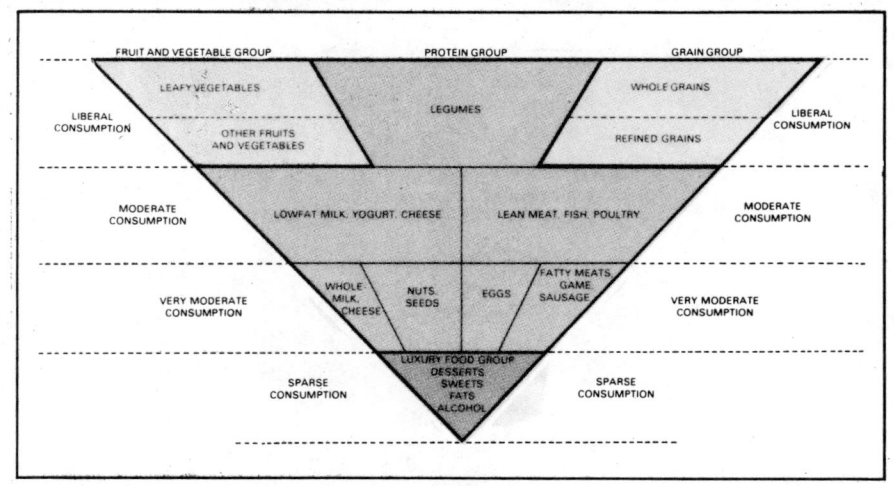

Figure 1 A suggested food guide

pyramid (Figure 1). There are 4 main food groups distributed among 4 levels of recommended consumption. Group I, vegetables and fruits, and Group II, grain products, share the first level. Group III encompasses vegetable, dairy, and meat sources of protein and traverses 3 levels: legumes on the first; skim and lowfat dairy items, lean meat, fish, and poultry on the second; and whole-fat dairy items, nuts, seeds, peanuts, eggs, fatty meats, game, luncheon meats, and sausage on the third level. Group IV consists of luxury foods: desserts, fats, sweets, and alcoholic beverages.

The visual presentation of the guide demonstrates the food selection emphasis, which is to eat liberally from the first level; moderately from the second level; very moderately from the third level; and sparingly from the fourth level. As we look from the top of the reverse pyramid to the apex at the bottom, foods lower down tend to increase in fat content and usually in cost. At the top of the reverse pyramid are foods of plant derivation. At the second level are animal-derived foods which are fairly low in fat. On the third level are the higher-fat animal and plant foods. The fourth level includes both foods that are very high in fat and others that are low in nutrient density (9). Emphasizing foods near the top of the reverse pyramid encourages lower-cost foods of plant origin and may discourage excessive intake of total fat, saturated fat, cholesterol, sugar, and alcohol. The concept of nutrient density is also expressed within consumption levels and groups. Thus, leafy vegetables appear above other vegetables and fruits; whole grains above refined ones; and low-fat dairy items, meats, fish, and poultry above higher-fat (and lower nutrient-density) animal and plant foods.

Suggested servings and portions per day are listed in Table 1. To allow for easy exchange and a wide variety of intake for foods in the protein group, the guide uses small portion sizes that provide 8 to 10 g of protein each. The minimum of 6 portions from the protein group ensures an adequate intake of protein; 2 portions of dairy foods contribute riboflavin, calcium, and phosphorus, and may add vitamin D; 4 portions from meat, legumes, and other protein foods contribute to the intake of vitamin B-6, iron, and zinc, and numerous other vitamins and trace minerals. The maximum of 15 portions may help limit the intake of total fat, saturated fat, and cholesterol and control costs. Vegetarians may use this guide but would require additional information about complementary proteins.

Table 1 Portion sizes and suggested servings per day from the inverse pyramid food guide

Food Group	Example of Portion Sizes	Suggested Servings Per Day Teens and Adults	Children
Vegetables and fruits	¾–1 c raw, ½ c cooked leafy greens ¼–½ c dried fruit ½ c fruit or vegetable juice ¾–1 c other fruits and vegetables	6 or more with at least 1 from leafy greens	4 or more with at least 1 from leafy greens
Grains and grain products	1 slice bread, 1 waffle, 1 tortilla ½ c cooked cereal ½ c rice, noodles, grits ¾–1 c ready to eat cereal	6 or more with at least 3 from whole grains	4 or more with at least 2 from whole grains
Protein foods[a]	1 c milk, yogurt 1 oz cheese, meat, fish, poultry 1 egg ½ c cooked legumes 2 tbsp peanut butter 2 oz seeds, nuts	6 to 15 with at least 2 from dairy foods and at least 4 from others	6 to 15 with at least 3 from dairy foods and at least 3 from others

Luxury foods	Desserts
	  ½ c pudding, ice cream
	  2 cookies
	  small slice cake
	Fats
	  1 tbsp butter, oil
	Sweets
	  1 tbsp sugar, honey
	
	Alcohol
	  1 oz liquor
	  4 oz wine
	  12 oz beer
		Children, Teens, and Adults
		Desserts
		  1 or less
		Fats
		  4 or less
		Sweets
		  4 or less
		
		Adults Only
		Alcohol – 1 or less	

[a] Small portion sizes are specified in order to encourage a wide variety.

Luxury foods are in this food guide because they add flavor to meals and pleasure to eating. However, the quantities are limited. The maximum allowable servings from the luxury food group will supply from 600 to 1,000 kcal, depending upon the choices. Foods from the other 3 groups may provide from 1,000 to 2,000 kcal, again depending upon the selections. People on weight-reducing diets may need further restriction of luxury foods.

DISCUSSION

The time is appropriate for the development of a new or updated food guide which is applicable to U.S. eating habits and the U.S. food supply. The suggested guide is not a drastic departure from the Four Food Groups. It combines the meat and milk groups of the Four Food Groups into one group to allow for meat alternatives on a consistent basis rather than on an occasional basis; it uses the nutrient density approach to emphasize specific food subgroups within the main groups; it deemphasizes luxury foods by setting limits on their consumption; and it increases the suggested servings per day for vegetables, fruits, and grains and thus provides for more essential nutrients and gives less leeway for choices from luxury foods. Overall, this suggested food guide emphasizes plant foods rather than animal products to a greater extent than does the Four Food Groups plan.

The visual presentation of the suggested guide is simple enough to be understood by children and those who are not well educated but is not so simple as to insult moderately or well-educated persons. The visual format and daily serving portions allow for the development of acceptable menus that are adequate in essential nutrients and not excessive in controversial food constituents. It is a framework within which nutrition educators and counselors can deal with the complexities of personal food preferences, individual lifestyles, nutrient requirements of different age groups and physiological conditions, the wide variety of foods available, and other limitations.

The development of a food guide that provides an adequate diet, is applicable to current food consumption habits, and is presented in a manner capable of causing behavioral change is a challenge that will require the input of many nutrition educators. The attempt to ensure the inclusion of essential nutrients and prevent excessive intake of energy, fat, sugar, and sodium is complicated by social, economic, emotional, and availability factors that influence what people consume. A guide that is practical and useful cannot be precise enough to meet the RDAs on a daily basis. To prevent the food guide from being rigid, we must acknowledge that many kinds and combinations of food can lead to a well-balanced diet.

Ultimately, it is important that nutrition educators accept a single guide that they can teach through nutrition education programs in the schools and public health programs. Then one guide could be used consistently and correctly in food ads, promotions, and public health messages in newspapers, magazines, radio, and television. This guide is only an example and perhaps might encourage others to suggest different guides or modifications of this one so that we might adopt an acceptable and usable guide as a nutrition education tool.

NOTE

The views expressed are those of the author and do not necessarily reflect the views or policies of the Food and Drug Administration.

LITERATURE CITED

1. U.S. Department of Agriculture. Agricultural Research Service. *Essentials of an adequate diet . . . facts for nutrition programs,* by L. Page and E. F. Phipard. Home Economics Research Report No. 3. Washington, D.C.: Government Printing Office, 1957.
2. U.S. Department of Agriculture. Science and Education Administration. *Food.* Home and Garden Bull. No. 228. Washington, D.C.: Government Printing Office, 1979.
3. National Academy of Sciences. National Research Council. Food and Nutrition Board. *Recommended dietary allowances.* 9th ed. Washington, D.C.: National Academy of Sciences, 1980.
4. U.S. Department of Agriculture. Science and Education Administration. *Food and nutrient intakes of individuals in 1 day in the U.S., Spring 1977: Nationwide food consumption survey, 1977-78.* Preliminary Report No. 2. Washington, D.C.: U.S. Department of Agriculture, September 1980, 122 pp.
5. U.S. Department of Health, Education, and Welfare. Health Resources Administration. National Center for Health Statistics. *Preliminary findings of the first Health and Nutrition Examination Survey, United States, 1971-1972: Dietary intake and biochemical findings.* Rockville, Md.: U.S. Department of Health, Education, and Welfare, 1974.
6. U.S. Senate. Select Committee on Nutrition and Human Needs. *Dietary goals for the United States.* 2d ed. Washington, D.C.: Government Printing Office, 1977.
7. U.S. Department of Health, Education, and Welfare. Public Health Service. *Healthy people: The surgeon general's report on health promotion and disease prevention.* Washington, D.C.: Government Printing Office, 1979, 177 pp.
8. U.S. Department of Agriculture. U.S. Department of Health and Human Services. *Nutrition and your health: Dietary guidelines for Americans.* Home and Garden Bull. No. 232. Washington, D.C.: Government Printing Office, 1980, 20 pp.
9. Hansen, G., B. Wyse, and A. Sorenson. *Nutritional quality index of foods.* Westport, Conn.: Avi Publishing Co., 1979.

Nutrient Content of the National Food Supply

by Ruth M. Marston and Susan O. Welsh

Over the past year, several small changes have occurred in the nutrient content of the Nation's food supply. Compared with a year earlier, 1980 levels are 1 to 4 percent higher for food energy (calories) and five nutrients—vitamin B_{12}, vitamin A, ascorbic acid, fat, and thiamin; and 1 percent lower for two minerals—calcium and magnesium. Levels for the other seven nutrients remain unchanged.

Vitamin B_{12} shows the largest increase—4 percent. Near-record use of edible offals accounts for almost all of this increase. Offals, which include liver and some other organ meats, are also excellent sources of vitamin A, consumption of which increased 2 percent. Greater consumption of some fruits and vegetables contributed to the rise in total vitamin A; but decreased consumption of sweet potatoes, another excellent source of vitamin A, offset some of the increase in this vitamin.

Ascorbic acid in the food supply is 2 percent higher due to a record-high consumption of frozen orange juice and increased use of fresh oranges. Citrus products are now the leading source of ascorbic acid in the food supply, providing almost 30 percent of the total.

Small (1 percent) increases are indicated for food energy, for fat, and for thiamin—all currently at peak levels—3,520 calories, 168 g, and 2.2 mg per capita per day, respectively. Increases in food energy and fat come from use of 7 percent more pork and slightly higher use of shortening and salad and cooking oils. More calories were also provided by increased use of fruits, grain, and sugar and sweeteners. However, fewer calories came from fresh and frozen potatoes due to their slightly decreased per capita consumption. Pork, a good source of thiamin, was the major contributor to the higher level of this vitamin.

The 1-percent decline in calcium is due to shifts in the use of dairy products, the major source of this mineral. Decreased use of fluid whole milk and nonfat dry milk accounts for this decline despite increased use of fluid lowfat milks. The lower magnesium level is also due to shifts in the use of dairy products, the leading source of magnesium in the food supply. In addition, decreased use of potatoes, chiefly fresh and frozen, and coffee contributed to the decline in magnesium.

For the seven nutrients which remained at 1979 levels, gains from increased use of some foods were offset by decreased use of others. For example, the protein level was increased from the rise in the use of pork and, to a lesser degree, poultry; but was decreased by declines in the use of beef, certain dairy products, eggs, and potatoes.

Greater use of pork and offals contributed to small gains for riboflavin, niacin, vitamin B_6, and iron which were offset by decreased use of other foods, primarily potatoes. More phosphorous was contributed by increases in consumption of pork, offals, lowfat milks, fruits, vegetables (other than potatoes), and grain products. Less phosphorous was contributed by nonfat dry milk, fluid whole milk, and beef which decreased in consumption. The increased amount of carbohydrate provided by use of more fruits, vegetables, and grain products was balanced by decreased use of potatoes.

Since 1967

Current levels for food energy and 12 nutrients are 1-17 percent higher than in 1967, the level for calcium is 6 percent lower, and the level for phosphorous is unchanged.

The ascorbic acid level shows the largest increase, 17 percent. Citrus products, particularly chilled and frozen orange juice, with smaller contributions of ascorbic acid from vegetables and fortification of fruit juices and drinks, account for this large increase.

Higher levels for thiamin, niacin, and riboflavin (16, 15 and 4 percent, respectively), are largely due to the higher standards of enrichment for white flour, set in 1975. A large part of the increase in riboflavin from enrichment was offset by the downward trend in consumption of dairy products, primarily fluid whole milk. Contributions of thiamin, riboflavin, and niacin also came from increased consumption of pork and poultry, which rose 17 and 42 percent, respectively during this period.

Current levels are higher than in 1967 for iron and vitamin B_6 (7 percent), protein (4 percent), and vitamin B_{12} and magnesium (1 percent). Grain products, consumption of which increased 10 pounds per capita since 1967, were the chief sources of the increase in iron and contributed to higher levels for vitamin B_6, protein, vitamin B_{12}, and magnesium as well. Vitamin B_{12} from grain products came solely from enrichment and fortification because this vitamin occurs naturally only in foods of animal origin.

Increased use of pork and poultry also provided iron, but use of these foods primarily accounted for the higher levels of protein, magnesium, vitamin B_6, and vitamin B_{12}. The vitamin A level is 5 percent higher than in 1967 due primarily to the expanded use of some canned tomato products, although offals and poultry also contributed substantially.

The 10-percent higher level for fat resulted chiefly from increased use of salad and cooking oils, with smaller contributions provided by increased pork consumption. The 8-percent higher carbohydrate level is attributed to the sharp increase in use of high-fructose corn sirup (HFCS). Use was first reported in 1970 and now is about 25 pounds per capita per year exceeding that of regular (glucose) corn sirup. Substantially higher levels for two energy-yielding nutrients—fat and carbohydrate—raised the level for food energy 9 percent.

A decline is indicated for only one nutrient—calcium, which is 6 percent lower than in 1967. Consumption of dairy products, in terms of the calcium equivalent of a quart of whole milk, declined from 231 to 204 quarts per capita per year since 1967. Decreased use of fluid whole milk and nonfat dry milk (40 to 60 percent, respectively) was responsible for this decline, despite the more than twofold increase in use of fluid lowfat milk and a two-thirds increase in use of cheese. The decline in use of whole and nonfat dry milk also provided less phosphorus, which was offset by increased contributions from pork, poultry, and some grain products.

Zinc

Estimates of the zinc content of the national food supply are presented for the first time. Since 1909-13, the level of this mineral has fluctuated between 11 and 13 mg per capita per day. The current level of zinc is 12.5 mg per capita per day, approximately the same as at the beginning of the century.

Zinc is a mineral known to be essential for cell growth and repair. The National Academy of Sciences (1980) has recommended a daily allowance (RDA) of 15 mg for children over the age of 10 and adults.

U.S. Food Supply: Contributions of Zinc by Major Food Groups

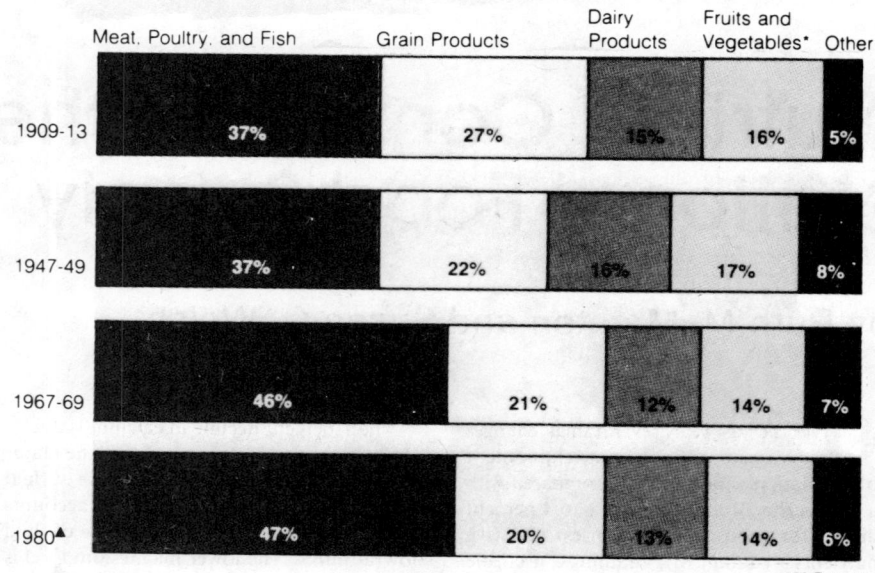

Period	Meat, Poultry, and Fish	Grain Products	Dairy Products	Fruits and Vegetables*	Other
1909-13	37%	27%	15%	16%	5%
1947-49	37%	22%	16%	17%	8%
1967-69	46%	21%	12%	14%	7%
1980▲	47%	20%	13%	14%	6%

▲Preliminary
*Includes Potatoes and Drybeans, Peas, Nuts and Soy Products

Contribution of Major Food Groups to Nutrient Supplies[1]

Food group	Food energy	Protein	Fat	Carbohydrate	Calcium	Phosphorus	Iron	Magnesium	Vitamin A value	Thiamin	Riboflavin	Niacin	Vitamin B6	Vitamin B12	Ascorbic acid
1967						Percent									
Meat (including pork fat cuts), poultry, and fish	20.6	40.5	35.9	0.1	3.7	25.9	31.1	12.6	22.8	28.6	22.4	47.1	39.4	68.4	2.1
Eggs	2.3	5.9	3.4	.1	2.6	6.0	6.3	1.4	6.7	2.6	5.8	.2	2.6	9.6	0
Dairly products, excluding butter	11.8	22.6	13.3	7.3	76.0	36.7	2.3	22.5	12.3	9.7	42.8	1.7	11.8	21.2	4.8
Fats and oils, including butter	16.9	.1	40.3	(2)	.4	.2	0	.4	8.3	0	0	0	.1	0	0
Citrus fruits	.8	.4	.1	1.7	.9	.7	.8	2.0	1.3	2.5	.5	.8	1.4	0	25.8
Other fruits	2.3	.6	.2	5.0	1.2	1.1	3.8	3.9	6.1	1.9	1.6	1.8	6.6	0	10.6
Potatoes and sweetpotatoes	2.8	2.3	.1	5.3	1.0	3.5	4.2	7.1	5.8	5.0	1.6	6.5	10.7	0	16.1
Dark green and deep yellow vegetables	.2	.4	(2)	.5	1.4	.6	1.7	2.0	20.0	.8	1.0	.6	1.9	0	8.5
Other vegetables, including tomatoes	2.5	3.3	.4	4.6	4.7	4.8	9.7	10.3	15.1	6.7	4.5	5.9	10.6	0	30.7
Dry beans and peas, nuts, soya flour and grits	3.0	5.0	3.6	2.2	2.6	5.7	6.8	11.0	(2)	5.4	1.8	6.5	4.9	0	(2)
Grain products	20.1	18.4	1.4	36.5	3.4	12.6	29.6	18.2	.4	36.7	17.3	23.6	9.8	.9	0
Sugar and other sweeteners	16.1	(2)	0	36.0	1.1	.2	.7	.2	0	(2)	.1	(2)	.1	0	(2)
Miscellaneous[3]	.8	.4	1.3	.7	1.0	1.9	2.9	8.4	1.2	.1	.8	5.3	.1	0	1.5

[1]Percentages for food groups are based on total nutrient data in table entitled "Nutrients Available for Consumption."
[2]Less than .05 percent.

However, they have stated that there is evidence suggesting marginal zinc nutrition in segments of the U.S. population. Although not directly comparable to the RDA, the level of zinc in the food supply may provide additional evidence for this statement.

Over the years, the sources of zinc have changed markedly due to changes in the consumption of foods from three major food groups. The meat, poultry, fish group has remained the leading source of zinc in the food supply. It currently provides almost half of all the zinc compared with less than 38 percent before 1947-49. This increase reflects primarily the rise in beef consumption.

Since 1909-13, dairy products have moved from third to second place as a source of zinc in the food supply. They currently provide 20 percent of the zinc, compared with only 15 percent at the beginning of the century. Most of this increase is due to the fourfold increase in cheese consumption.

The third leading source of zinc in the current food supply is the grain products group, providing 13 percent of the total. Grain products accounted for approximately twice as much zinc at the beginning of the century when they were the second leading

Zinc Content of the U.S. Food Supply, Per Capita Per Day Civilian Consumption

Food Group	1909-13	1935-39	1957-59	1967-69	1975	1980[1]
			milligrams			
Meat, poultry, and fish	4.7	3.8	4.8	5.7	5.8	5.9
Dairy products[2]	1.9	2.2	2.7	2.6	2.6	2.5
Grain products	3.3	2.3	1.5	1.5	1.4	1.6
Fruits and vegetables[3]	2.1	2.1	1.8	1.7	1.8	1.8
Other[4]	.6	.7	.9	.8	.8	.8
Total[5]	12.6	11.0	11.6	12.3	12.4	12.5

[1]Preliminary.
[2]Excludes butter.
[3]Includes dry beans and peas, nuts and soy products, and potatoes.
[4]Includes eggs, fats and oils, sugars, coffee, and cocoa.
[5]Components may not add to total due to rounding.

Contribution of Major Food Groups to Nutrient Supplies[1] —Continued

Food group 1980 Preliminary	Food energy	Protein	Fat	Carbohydrate	Calcium	Phosphorus	Iron	Magnesium	Vitamin A value	Thiamin	Riboflavin	Niacin	Vitamin B6	Vitamin B12	Ascorbic acid
								Percent							
Meat (including pork fat cuts), poultry, and fish	21.0	42.9	36.1	.1	4.2	28.6	31.1	14.0	23.9	27.9	23.5	45.4	40.7	71.9	2.1
Eggs	1.8	4.9	2.7	.1	2.4	5.2	5.1	1.2	5.5	1.9	4.9	.1	2.1	8.2	0
Dairy products, excluding butter	9.9	20.2	11.2	5.7	71.6	32.6	2.4	19.8	12.2	7.2	36.3	1.2	10.7	18.4	3.2
Fats and oils, including butter	18.2	.1	43.0	(2)	.4	.2	0	.4	7.8	0	0	0	(2)	0	0
Citrus fruits	1.0	.6	.1	2.1	1.1	.9	.9	2.6	1.7	2.9	.6	.9	1.5	0	29.3
Other fruits	2.3	.7	.3	5.0	1.4	1.3	3.9	4.5	5.9	1.8	1.7	1.7	7.1	0	11.8
Potatoes and sweetpotatoes	2.7	2.3	.1	5.1	1.0	3.6	4.4	7.1	5.0	4.5	1.4	5.9	9.5	0	13.5
Dark green and deep yellow vegetables	.2	.4	(2)	.4	1.5	.6	1.6	2.0	18.5	.7	1.0	.5	1.9	0	9.0
Other vegetables, including tomatoes	2.5	3.3	.4	4.7	5.2	5.1	9.9	10.7	16.7	6.2	4.7	5.7	10.7	0	27.8
Dry beans and peas, nuts, soya flour and grits	3.0	5.5	3.7	2.1	3.1	6.4	6.8	12.3	(2)	5.0	1.9	6.8	5.0	0	(2)
Grain products	19.9	18.8	1.3	36.2	3.8	13.4	31.0	19.1	.4	41.7	23.3	28.4	10.6	1.6	0
Sugar and other sweeteners	17.0	(2)	0	38.1	3.3	.7	.6	.2	0	(2)	(2)	(2)	(2)	0	(2)
Miscellaneous[3]	.6	.3	1.0	.5	.8	1.5	2.1	6.4	2.2	.1	.6	3.3	.1	0	3.3

[3]Coffee, chocolate liquor equivalent of cocoa beans, and fortification of products not assigned to a food group.

source of zinc. Decreased consumption of wheat and corn products has been a primary cause of the decline. ■

Nutrients Available for Consumption, Per Capita Per Day[1]

Nutrient (unit)	1967	1980[2]
Food energy (cal)	3,240	3,520
Protein (gm)	99	103
Fat (gm)	152	168
Carbohydrate (gm)	374	406
Calcium (mg)	947	891
Phosphorus (mg)	1,529	1,528
Iron (mg)	16.4	17.6
Magnesium (mg)	341	343
Vitamin A value (IU)	7,900	8,400
Thiamin (mg)	1.9	2.2
Riboflavin (mg)	2.3	2.4
Niacin (mg)	23.2	26.8
Vitamin B_6 (mg)	1.9	2.0
Vitamin B_{12} (mcg)	9.4	9.5
Ascorbic acid (mg)	105	123

[1] Quantities of nutrients computed by Science and Education Administration, Human Nutrition, Consumer Nutrition Center, on the basis of estimates of per capita food consumption (retail weight), including estimates of produce of home gardens, prepared by the Economics and Statistics Service. No deduction made in nutrient estimates for loss or waste of food in the home, use for pet food, or for destruction or loss of nutrients during the preparation of food. Civilian consumption. Data include iron, thiamin, riboflavin, and niacin added to flour and cereal products; other nutrients added primarily as follows: Vitamin A value to margarine, milk of all types, flavored milk extenders; vitamin B_6 to cereals, meal replacements, infant formulas; vitamin B_{12} to cereals; ascorbic acid to fruit juices and drinks, flavored beverages and dessert powders, flavored milk extenders, and cereals.

[2] Preliminary.

NATIONAL NUTRITION POLICY

The Hatch Act: Can the Food Safety Law Finally Be Updated?

by Mel Seligsohn

Given the Reagan administration's program for rolling back government regulations burdening American industry, it's no secret in Washington that reviewing food safety laws is high on its agenda. Indeed, it now seems likely that the basic food law will be reformulated next year, although strong forces are gathering on various sides of the debate which could swing the outcome either way.

Of course dissatisfaction with the Delaney amendment has been brewing for years. Delaney, it's opponents contend, is too inflexible by today's scientific standards, since it decrees that the Food and Drug Administration must ban from the food supply any substance known to be cancer-causing in any dosage whatsoever. This rigidity created a widely discussed controversy when the agency was forced to consider a ban on saccharin—the country's most widely used artificial sweetener.

The public was baffled by the proposed ban because saccharin had been used for almost 50 years without medical complaint. Further, the food industry was up in arms because saccharin was the only artificial sweetener permitted by FDA and a ban would have created economic chaos. Congress stepped in at the last minute and circumvented the ban with legislation specifically aimed at allowing the sweetener's continued use. The debate over saccharin, however, had an unexpected repercussion: both Congress and the public became aware of the limitations of Delaney and the stage was set for a re-opening of the whole food safety question.

Currently, hearings are being held by both the Senate and House of Representatives on the legislation which has crystallized within it the principle alternatives to Delaney. "The Food Safety Amendments of 1981" (S. 1442) was introduced by Senator Orrin Hatch (R.-Utah), and has emerged as the leading contender in a myriad of legislative proposals and reports whose aim is to reform the current law. Along with general support from the food industry, the "Hatch Act," as it has been dubbed, is raising a storm of opposition from consumer groups.

Although its final shape is not in focus, Hatch would replace Delaney with a highly complicated form of risk/benefit assessment. The assessment would be made as to the safety of a substance in food by a special board of inquiry made up of leading experts in a wide variety of disciplines. Hatch also includes a series of procedures that make it more difficult for FDA to remove a suspect food substance from the market, and less difficult for industry to introduce one.

Consumer response

Despite efforts to downplay the changes the bill seeks, Hatch's bill may be responsible for reviving the moribund consumer movement, which has been waiting quietly for an issue that will bring its troops back out in force. Now they may have just that. In October, 36 organizations announced in letters to President Reagan and to Congress the formation of a Coalition for Safe Food dedicated to opposition to the Food Safety Amendments of 1981.

The Coalition is an combination of old-line consumer advocate groups, labor unions, and a scattering of health groups. Leading the charge is the Community Nutrition Institute, whose head, Ellen Haas, is a founder of the Coalition. Haas says the bill would result in "less regulation and more cancer," and, "Falsely involving the economic health of our economy, they are posing a major threat to the health of the American people."

A release from the Coalition states that the Hatch Act would "gut our nation's food safety laws by redefining 'safe', effectively repealing the anticancer Delaney clause, and undermining the procedural framework to hasten approval and delay removal of unsafe additives." The bill was called "a one-sided 'wish list' for the food industry (that would) ultimately damage public confidence in the safety of American food and contribute to an increase in human disease," by Carolyn Brickey of Congress Watch, a Coalition member.

Other members of the coalition include such groups as: American Federation of State, County and Municipal Employees; American Federation of Teachers; Center for Science in the Public Interest; Federation of Homemakers; Friends of the Earth; National Consumers League; American Medical Student Association; United Food and Commercial Workers; Food and Beverage Trades Department, AFL-CIO; Feingold Associates; and, National Council of Senior Citizens.

Others are cautious

Although the Coalition for Safe Food will undoubtedly make its shrill complaints heard, other, more conservative voices have expressed concern about proposed changes in the food safety laws. For example, in an exclusive interview with this magazine (October, '81, p. 18), FDA Commissioner Dr. Arthur Hull Hayes, Jr., a Reagan appointee, made the following statement in response to a question regarding the prospective changes in the Delaney amendment.

"I think there is no question that the Clause has been overreacted to in some quarters as the item in the food safety laws that is tying everybody's hands. The Delaney clause has only been invoked by the FDA twice, although it has influenced people's thinking as an 'all or nothing' matter.

"The more important underlying issue is what is meant by food safety, and how will science allow us to define it. The current food safety laws provide very little room for judgement or discretion. Still, I'm not ready to say that Delaney has to go and that some sort of risk assessment should take its place."

Another FDA official has directly attacked the Hatch bill. Dr. William Bixler, assistant director of Veterinary Medicine for Program Policy and Communications, said that the bill "debases the Delaney Clause." Referring to the portion of the bill that would refer substances to a standing committee if questions of safety were involved, Bixler said: "The Delaney clause is intended to treat substances presenting a risk of cancer in a manner different from substances presenting other risks. Under the Hatch bill, potential carcinogens and substances presenting other risks would be held to the same 'absence of significant risk standard."

On a more general note, Richard A. Merrill, dean of the University of Virginia School of Law, participating in the National Soft Drink Association's Legal Briefing Conference in October, commented that he believes that changes in food safety legislation should not be too rigidly written, but provide guidance instead of locking in changes that could be disappointing after a few years of experience. He acknowledged, however, that some changes in the current food safety laws are needed, although indicating that the Hatch bill might be too complex, and that some of the regulatory problems faced by industry could be solved through administrative policy changes rather than a total re-write of the food safety law.

Strong attack

In addition to consumer groups, the Hatch bill faces some formidable Congressional opposition. House liberals, in particular, will put up a mighty fight against it. Rep. Robert Gore (D-Tenn.) has already called the bill the "makings of a fraud about to be perpetrated on the American people."

Gore is chairman of the influential House Science and Technology Committee's subcommittee on Investigations and Oversight. Speaking before the Food Marketing Institute's Public Affairs Conference, Gore said the bill would turn one of the strongest consumer protection laws—the Food, Drug and Cosmetic Act—into a "shield behind which toxic substances could hide." Gore is responding to the bill by putting together a series of meetings with the food industry and other affected parties to begin working on the problems of food safety starting with the fundamentals.

Although Gore acknowledged that there is a need to look carefully at the emerging science of risk assessment, he maintained that the Hatch bill would "drive a truck through the food safety provisions of the law." According to Gore:

"It would set a new standard that would permit the introduction of known carcinogens into the food supply, if they presented no 'significant' risk, and it would make it nearly impossible to remove cancer-causing substances from the food supply. To ensure the difficulty of removing problem substances, the proposed statute would not only change the general safety standard of the law, in addition it would introduce a Rube Goldberg-like series of procedural hoops through which the FDA would have to go to remove substances from the market."

Hatch responds

Sen. Hatch has been very low-keyed in his response to criticism of S. 1442, sensing the delicate nature of the issues and fearing, perhaps, to be characterized as a potential polluter of the nation's food supply. Says Hatch:

"Restoring reason to our decision-making process is critical to federal policy-making involving our basic foods. Natural substances found in foods like potatoes, onions and black pepper, have been implicated as potential carcinogens. Essential nutrients such as selenium, vitamin D and calcium—substances required by humans for our diet—act in some doses as carcinogens.

"If FDA were to implement the Delaney Clause as now written, federal inspectors would be banning such traditional foods and essential nutrients. Instead, FDA has wisely chosen to ignore the statute. Yet a failure to now review the law itself would seriously question the legitimacy of our nation's food safety laws and compromise FDA's regulatory authority.

"The law must keep pace with scientific advancements. Scientists can now detect traces of potentially harmful substances at parts per trillion—a million-fold increase in analytic sensitivity compared with the methods available 20 years ago when the law was last examined. . . . Keeping the food supply safe is our highest priority. Yet some degree of risk is inherent. Zero risk is impossible to achieve. FDA must focus its resources on eliminating those risks that have a potential for actually harming humans. Trivial or speculative risks should not be regulated," Hatch contends.

Hatch agrees that "Delaney is essentially good regulatory policy," but that it needs fine-tuning. In a reference to the saccharin episode, he points out that applying a rigid and inflexible rule to a substance that has been in use for decades for which there are no appropriate substitutes will not produce credible results. "While risk-benefit analysis for all substances is impractical, some consideration of the benefits is necessary for those substances to which we have grown accustomed and do not have marketable replacements."

Powerful support

Hatch is far from being a lonely voice in the Senate calling for a "revitalized public debate on food safety." Co-sponsors of S. 1442 include Senators Helms, Huddleston, Jepson, Quayle, Zorinksy, Thurmond, Grassley, Tower, Nickles, Dole and

Hayakawa. In addition, even some Senate liberals have acknowledged that current food safety policy isn't all that it should be.

In 1979, during hearings on saccharin, Senator Ted Kennedy pointed out, "The saccharin controversy is an important one, but it should not be considered in isolation from overall food safety policy. The Congress should not be asked to intervene in the regulatory process on a producty-by-product basis, as is currently the case. If current regulatory statutes do not permit these issues to be fairly resolved, then those statutes should be re-examined. It does no good to have a law which Congress overrules each time its provisions are invoked."

Despite a consensus regarding the need for change and the belief in Congress that some type of risk-assessment might be logical, in the minds of many liberal lawmakers and the consumer organizations the Hatch bill is already unacceptable for one overriding reason: it is perceived to have been drafted by food industry interests with only lip-service being given to consumer-group input. And it is on this point that the bill may stand or fall, and not on the value of its merits or its deficiencies.

Is this perception accurate? To a large extent it is true, but not because of some conspirarcy. The drafting of food law is an extremely technical and complex task. Food law is a highly arcane subject that few lawmakers really understand. In order to formulate S. 1442, Sen. Hatch turned to legal experts in the food field. The final 70-page document—which former FDA chief counsel William Goodrich said "defies reading and understanding"—was put together by lawyers primarily associated with food-industry trade associations. The National Soft Drink Association, still smarting from the saccharin episode, and the American Meat Institute, which had been involved in the debate over the safety of nitrite, dominated the drafting effort.

These groups had their lawyers working with Hatch's legislative committee, which because of the complexities involved had to rely on the lawyers in drafting the bill. However, Congressional staff members claim charges that the bill is lop-sided in favor of industry are unfair. Says one, "If the consumer groups didn't have much input, it's because they weren't willing to work with us. We gave them plenty of chances." The drafting process took about four months.

Interestingly, many of the lawyers involved in drafting the Hatch bill were formerly associated with FDA. Principal among them is the current counsel to the National Soft Drink Association Stuart Pape. Pape had been special assistant to the commissioner of FDA, during which time he wrote a position paper that proposed modifying the nation's food safety standards.

Pape heads the industry ad hoc group that, sensing a more responsive mood in Washington towards relaxing regulations, set out to deal with the new food law issue. Some of the other lawyers in the group include Peter Barton Hutt, former FDA chief counsel; Sherwin Gardner, a former deputy commissioner at FDA and now with the Grocery Manufacturers of America; Howard Roberts, former acting director of FDA's Bureau of Foods; and Richard Silverman, a former FDA associate counsel chief for enforcement. Along with them is former U.S. Representative Paul Rogers, who had a reputation as being a strong advocate for tough health regulations when he was chairman of the House Commerce subcommittee on health and the environment.

According to the *Washington Post*, "Their lawmaking has focused on the same issue that Pape was dealing with at the FDA in the late 1970s. They want to relax what they view as the inflexibility of the Delaney Clause, which bans from the market any food stuff found to contain a carcinogen, no matter how small the quantity."

Despite the agreement about the inflexibility regarding Delaney, which is now 23 years old, it's changing this amendment that will arouse the most passionate debate as the issue of changing the food law is discussed in Congress and around the country in the months ahead. It's going to take a great deal of stamina for the food industry to fight back with logic attacks that are based on pure emotional appeal.

Will Congress and the public listen to reason, or will they listen to Michael Jacobson, executive director of the Center for Science in the public interest when he is quoted in the media across the country as saying about changing Delaney. "It takes the government down the road of allowing a little bit of cancer in the food supply. The only question is how much."

NATIONAL NUTRITION POLICY

The Risk/Benefit Concept as Applied to Food

by the Institute of Food Technologists' Expert Panel on Food Safety and Nutrition

☐ In the last half-century, our society has moved from a largely rural environment to a more urban way of life. Consumers are further away from the farms and ranches where food is actually produced; thus, more processing, storage, and transportation of food are required to provide the urban dweller with his daily diet.

A sophisticated food processing and delivery system has evolved which supplies the consumer with a greater variety of food with a higher level of safety than ever before in history. In spite of this, questions continue to be raised over both the safety and the nutritional value of our food supply. The mere complexity of our present-day food system has led individual scientists and consumers to question various practices and assumptions, raising doubts and concern in the minds of the public.

Consumers Make Daily Risk/Benefit Judgments

The idea of food safety, as viewed by both scientists and government regulators, includes a constant comparison between risks and benefits. Even the consumer, although he or she may not think in those terms, makes many day-to-day decisions on the basis of a judgment of the benefits to be achieved in comparison to the risks inherent in the act being considered. The decisions may be made subconsciously and on the basis of only vague measurements of either the risk or the benefit, but they are real choices nonetheless.

In a few areas, the consumer may define the risks and the benefits fairly easily. For example, clinical and epidemiological studies have enabled investigators to identify a number of activities and conditions that are related to cardiovascular disease, and to estimate their severity. The three major risk factors are heavy cigarette smoking, elevated blood pressure, and elevated blood cholesterol level. Among individuals who don't smoke, and have neither physical condition, i.e., have none of these risk factors, the average death rate per 1,000 from cardiovascular disease is 13. In individuals with any one of the three factors, it is 23; with two of the three, it is 44. With all three risk factors, the rate is 82 deaths per 1,000—more than six times as high as that when none of the three are present. The "risk" side of the equation, then, is fairly well documented.

The individual must decide for himself whether the perceived benefits of smoking outweigh the risks. Similarly, the individual must decide whether the perceived benefits of his other actions that may contribute to high blood pressure and cholesterol levels—e.g., eating an excessively rich diet, not exercising, etc.—outweigh their risks.

Not all human risk/benefit decisions are so easily assessed. For example, one cannot properly calculate the risk of death from human cancer resulting from DDT residues in food, because there has never been a documented case of such cancer. (There is experimental evidence that DDT causes cancer in mice, but none for humans, even for industrial workers exposed for long periods of time to levels much higher than average.) One can, on the other hand, estimate the risk of death from many causes. The accompanying box lists the death rate from such occurrences as automobile accidents, being struck by lightning, etc.

What About Risks from Food?

Risks associated with food are not as obvious. Deaths from food are so rare that they produce headlines instead of being buried in mortality statistics. People are more concerned, however, with risks that fall far short of death. In fact, there is a widespread belief that there should be *no* hazard whatever associated with the food supply.

It should be clear, however, that zero risk or absolute safety in any area, including food, is unattainable. The *goal* of absolute safety is a worthy one, and some industries have approached it. For example, more than 800 billion units of commercially canned food have been produced in North America since 1940, with only five deaths attributable to botulism from that food. This is a remarkable safety record. Yet *achieving* or *proving* absolute safety is somewhat akin to proving that a person is absolutely honest. The *best* we can ever hope for is to show no harm in every situation attempted to date,

---

This Scientific Status Summary first appeared in *Food Technology*, March 1978, published by the Institute of Food Technologists.

or no harm in the situations in which a material is useful.

This leads to the concept of "Risk/Benefit," a phrase which is causing much debate among research scientists and those concerned with regulatory policies today. We can define "benefit" as anything that contributes to an improvement in condition. "Risk" can be subdivided into two categories: "vital" and "non-vital." Vital, by dictionary definition, is "concerned with or manifesting life," and "necessary" or "essential to life." Physicians encounter vital risks relatively often, since many drugs have multiple effects, some of which are undesirable or even dangerous. For example, the treatment of various infectious diseases, such as typhus, with chloramphenicol may be effective, but there is considerable risk of the patient's developing aplastic anemia.

A non-vital risk usually does not involve a threat to life but *may* lead to injury, loss, or damage. The skin of World War II servicemen who took atabrine for malaria turned yellow, but no long-term injury resulted. With foods, for example, non-vital risks could include loss of convenience, reduced satisfaction, increased cost, or total removal from the market. While the difference between vital and non-vital risks is not always clear-cut, most observers would agree that the categories of risks are different.

Since food is necessary to life, its lack is technically a vital risk. This is actually true in undeveloped countries that are chronically short of food. However, in the developed world, food is abundantly available in great variety, and its existence is thus not normally considered to be a vital benefit, since it cannot be traded off against a vital risk. This subconscious thinking has probably led to the belief that food consumption should involve no risks whatever, and indeed, nearly all risks inherent in our food supply today fall into the category of non-vital risks.

Food Legislation Focuses on Risks

The food industry and government regulatory agencies make every effort to ensure that the non-vital risks associated with our food supply are kept as low as possible. However, attempts to simplify scientific concerns in order to write effective legislation have led to some dilemmas. For example, in 1958, the U.S. Congress enacted the Food Additives Amendment to the Federal Food, Drug and Cosmetic Act. Section 409 (c) (3) (A) of this amendment—referred to as the Delaney clause—provides:

"That no additive shall be deemed to be safe if it is found to induce cancer when ingested by man or animal, or if it is found, after tests which are appropriate for the evaluation of the safety of food additives, to induce cancer in man or animal..."

The Delaney clause flatly states that no cancer-causing substance or "carcinogen" shall be added to the food supply. There is no room for scientific judgment as to the risks involved, since a yes or no answer is required to the question as to whether a material is carcinogenic. This clause has received a good deal of publicity, more for its potential than for its actual enforcement. In fact, the only chemical in which the Delaney clause was invoked in a proposal to ban an additive was saccharin. Several other chemicals, such as diethylpyrocarbonate, trichloroethylene, polyvinyl chloride, and acrylonitrile, may have been considered as candidates for banning under the Delaney clause, but in fact, the Delaney clause was not specifically invoked in their regulation.

Most scientists would probably agree that the passage of the Delaney clause was beneficial in 1958, considering the state of development of the science of toxicology at that time. However, as scientific advances have occurred since then, differing views are emerging. In 1962, the Delaney clause was amended by Congress to allow a drug to be used in feed

Some Common Risks to Life in the U.S.[a]

Cause of death	No. of deaths per year	No. of deaths per year per 100,000 people
Heart disease	716,200	336
Cancer	365,700	173
Stroke	194,000	91.9
Auto accidents	45,900	21.8
Suicide	27,100	12.8
Homicide	21,300	10.1
Falls	14,900	7.1
Drowning	8,000	3.79
Poisoning	6,300	2.99
Fires	6,100	2.89
Surgical and medical "complications and misadventures"	3,200	1.52
Inhalation and ingestion of food[b]	2,200	1.04
Airplane travel	1,600	0.76
Struck by falling object	1,100	0.52
Railway accidents	600	0.28
Excessive cold	360	0.17
Electrocution from home wiring and appliances	260	0.12
Suffocation in bed or cradle	210	0.10
Lightning	120	0.06
Cataclysm (tornado, flood, earthquake, etc.)	100	0.05
Bites and stings, venomous animals and insects	50	0.02

[a] Based on 1975 data from the National Center for Health Statistics, Health Services and Mental Health Administration, U.S. Department of Health, Education and Welfare
[b] Does not include food poisoning

for animals destined for human consumption, even when that drug might itself cause cancer in experimental animals. The only proviso was that there should be no detectable residues of the drug in the edible portion of the food animal eating the feed.

The 1962 legislation was inspired partially by the issue of diethylstilbestrol (DES) in food. DES is a synthetic hormone which closely resembles, but is not identical to, the natural female sex hormones. It was being used either as an additive to feed or as an implant in the animal's ear, to improve the feed conversion efficiency in animals. With the addition of 20 mg of DES per day to their feed, steers could be brought to marketable weight (1,000 lb) in 30 days less time, with a saving of about 500 lb of feed for each animal. The Council for Agricultural Science and Technology has estimated that the 10-12% increase in feed efficiency results in a saving of 7.7 billion lb of feed annually, an amount equivalent to the corn grown on 1.7 million acres of farmland (CAST, 1977).

Analytical Improvements Complicate Matters

The 1958 and 1962 legislative actions were based on the analytical capabilities of that time. For example, it was possible at that time to detect approximately 100 parts per billion (0.00001%) of DES, and any amount less than 100 ppb was thus automatically equal to zero. However, detection methods have since been tremendously improved, and it is now possible to detect amounts of DES as low as 2 ppb (0.0000002%), and in some cases in parts per trillion (ppt). It is difficult to visualize these small concentrations, but in one analogy, one part per *million* equals about 1/32 oz (or about one gram) in one ton of food. One part per *billion* is about one drop in a 10,000-gallon tank car. One part per *trillion* is one grain of sugar in an olympic-size swimming pool.

At this point, the ability of scientists to detect minute quantities of chemicals has outstripped their ability to interpret the findings. This may be illustrated using DES as an example. In 1971, regulatory officials launched a concerted effort to look for DES in animal tissues. In 1973, 3,349 livers were analyzed, and DES residues were detected at 0.5-2.0 ppb in ten livers and at concentrations exceeding 2.0 ppb in six livers. From 1973 to 1976, 9,426 samples of liver were analyzed, and 99.4% of the samples were negative for DES (CAST, 1977). No DES was detected in any skeletal meat (muscle meat attached to bones).

In an attempt to visualize the meaning of these small amounts, CAST calculated that if all the liver consumed in the U.S. were contaminated with 2 ppb of DES (which it isn't), the average daily intake would amount to 0.038 micrograms per person—0.014 mg per year—an amount far below the level of natural estrogens produced by the human body. A 120-lb female would have 2,500-25,000 times as much estrogenic activity in her body as she could get from the average daily intake of beef liver containing 2 ppb of DES.

It would also be far below the estrogenic level of foods normally consumed in the daily diet. For example, wheat germ has a DES equivalent of 4,000 ppb; wheat bran has 1,500; soybean oil has 2,200; peanut oil has 1,800. Also, many leafy vegetables and root crops contain estrogenic compounds.

Perhaps we should look at the risk in the above example. Gass et al. (1964) showed that as low as 6.25 ppb of DES consumed in food over a lifetime caused tumors in the C_3H strain of mice. However, this experiment has been disputed because 12.5 and 25 ppb of DES in the same experiment had a lower incidence of tumors. Also, the C_3H strain of mice is particularly susceptible to mammary tumors. Nevertheless, it is generally accepted that 50 ppb of DES will cause tumors in strain C_3H of mice but not in monkeys, even over a prolonged (10-yr) feeding period (CAST, 1977). When one compares the much lower levels of DES in beef liver to the levels in the animal feeding studies, should one conclude that there is a significant risk?

The possible intake of DES from liver is insignificant compared with normal body production and consumption of estrogens from other sources. Yet, in spite of this, several consumer groups have been very vocal in their condemnation of DES, basing much of their objection on the use of economic gain comparisons with even the remotest health risk. The federal government is also reviewing its use.

The ability to detect ever-smaller amounts of a particular substance in foods presents a very real dilemma. Chasing an ever-receding "zero" level with improved analytical instruments could bring you to the ultimate question: "Does the presence of *one* molecule of a carcinogen constitute grounds for removing a food from the marketplace?" There is also the intriguing question as to how one deals with the theoretical presence of a carcinogen in concentrations *below* which it can be detected analytically. Such a situation would seem to lead to a difficult enforcement problem for regulatory officials (Cornfield, 1977), and there seems to be little doubt that the concept of a "tolerance level" or a "calculated-risk level" will have to be adopted eventually.

Difficult to Assess Degree of Risk

The problem of defining the carcinogenic risk of a very low level of a chemical in foods also provides a dilemma for regulatory officials. The present "yes" or "no" legal framework for accepting or rejecting makes the decision process relatively easy. However, many scientists wonder if it is really in the public's best interest, since there is no room for scientific judgment as to the degree of risk vs the overall potential benefit.

It must also be admitted that attempts to assess the degree of risk pose some very difficult scientific questions. For example, some chemicals are thought to cause mutations by altering the structure of DNA in the genes, the molecules that actually govern the inheritance of characteristics. It appears that, in most cases, the human body possesses a repair mechanism which can actually replace the defective portions of DNA, and that only when these repair mechanisms are overwhelmed is there an obviously bad effect. From this type of evidence, one could conclude that there is a "no-effect" or "threshold" level. On the other hand, it is possible that repair mechanisms may not exist for *all* chemicals.

At the practical level, many toxicologists believe that since a no-effect level has never been rigorously established for any known carcinogen, and probably cannot be established by current methodology, we have to assume that there is none, at least for regulatory purposes. Actually, most of the research on mutations has come from studies on radiation done in relation to atomic bombs and nuclear power generation. Most researchers studying radiation-induced mutations agree that there is no no-effect level for radiation mutations, merely an agreement to "live with" a very small risk.

On the other hand, there is good evidence that a no-effect level does exist for estrogenic hormones (NAS, 1966), even though nearly all estrogens, including DES, are carcinogenic. One would expect that many compounds which are essential nutrients in very small concentrations and yet are carcinogenic at high concentrations (e.g., selenium) *must* have a no-effect level. The presence or absence of a no-effect level for carcinogens, and actually for all environmental pollutants, is a subject for high priority research at the present time. This is a difficult question, and the answer may well be different for different chemicals, possibly dependent on a variety of other conditions.

How Substances Are Tested

Even when we set aside the question as to whether a no-effect level exists for a given chemical, we still have to face the questions as to what constitutes an acceptable risk, and how it should be determined.

The present method of determining whether a chemical has any undesirable effects is to feed animals, usually mice or rats, different levels of the chemical in the diet over their entire lifetime and sometimes through three or four generations. The highest level fed is deliberately set high enough to produce a harmful effect. This is almost always possible, since nearly everything, including salt, sugar, starch, some vitamins, and even water, has a harmful effect when fed in high enough concentrations.

After the feeding study is completed, the lowest level having a harmful effect is determined, and the next level below that is designated the "no-effect level." This no-effect level is then divided by 100—sometimes called the "100-fold" safety factor—and that level is often used as the maximum dietary level. The rationale behind the 100-fold factor is that there may be a 10-fold difference in sensitivity between animals and man and a 10-fold difference in sensitivity between individual human beings. However, if any malignant tumors are produced in the test animals at any of the feeding levels of a chemical being tested, the Delaney clause prohibits use of that chemical in any amount in foods.

It is easy to reduce some interpretations of the law to absurd situations. For example, trichloroethylene is a solvent that was formerly used in making decaffeinated coffee. The National Cancer Institute reported that it caused cancer in mice fed large enough amounts. There was a small residue of trichloroethylene in coffee, but translating into human terms the amounts which cause cancer in mice would mean that a person would have to drink 50 million cups of coffee per day for 70 years. Using the now-banned food coloring FD&C Red No. 2 as another example, an adult would have to eat 1,600 lb of food containing 100 ppm of this colorant every day to duplicate amounts used in animal tests. This *reductio ad absurdum* makes people uncomfortable.

One valid objection to such tests is that rats aren't humans, and results cannot be translated directly. To obtain totally valid test results, the substance in question should be absorbed and metabolized in ways that are identical or at least closely similar in both man and the test species, and rats differ from man in many respects. On the other hand, there is no reliable evidence that we cannot extrapolate principles and general effects to humans. And as our knowledge of biochemical mechanisms increases, the extrapolations will be more accurate. Actually, the qualitative extrapolation from rats to humans for prediction of carcinogenicity is on fairly consistent ground. Of the approximately 30 chemicals which have been shown to cause cancer in man, only one—arsenic—does not appear to cause cancer in rats.

A more compelling reason for testing with animals is that it is the only method available. Direct experimentation on humans is, of course, morally unacceptable.

Combining the analytical difficulties in determining exceedingly small quantities of possibly harmful chemicals and the difficulties in interpreting the risks of harm from such minute quantities is a very complex statistical procedure. One possible approach—the Mantel-Bryan concept of virtual safety (Mantel and Bryan, 1961; Mantel et al., 1975)—has been adopted in modified form by the Food and Drug Administration (FDA, 1977a).

What About Natural Toxicants?

It has been suggested that the laws governing the restriction of carcinogens to food should be extended to apply to *all* carcinogens in food. The Delaney clause does not apply to carcinogens naturally present in foods. For example, aflatoxin, produced by a mold which may grow on certain foods, is one of the most potent carcinogens known to man. U.S. laws allow a maximum of 20 ppb of aflatoxin in corn, nuts, and nut products at the present time. Canada allows 15 ppb in nuts and nut products. These levels were set as being obtainable with the best production methods available. Since they were set, however, the technology was improved, and there is every likelihood that these levels will be reduced.

Applying the Delaney clause to naturally occurring carcinogens in food would, in several cases, make specific foods unavailable. In other foods, such as corn contaminated with low levels of aflatoxin from mold during the growing season, the degree of processing required to remove the carcinogen would make that food unacceptable in its natural state. The point is that there *is* ample precedent for setting a tolerance level for a natural carcinogen in food. After a judgment of acceptable risk, the tolerance is set at the lowest level compatible with making the food available to the public. It would seem that similar reasoning could also be applied to foods containing added chemicals, if the risks were judged to be low enough.

One objection raised to this line of reasoning is that although we have to tolerate the carcinogens naturally present in our food, we should not add to the "body burden." All responsible individuals would agree with this and would only advocate a tolerance if the risk were very, very low indeed. An example of an acceptable degree of risk might be the calculation that DES in beef liver (referred to earlier) might cause one case of cancer in the U.S. in 133 years (Jukes, 1976).

If one accepts the concept that some risk is inevitable, the question arises as to who should judge whether a risk is "acceptable." Clearly, the jury should include people competent to judge the scientific issues involved in the very complex field of toxicology, but other disciplines probably should be included also, since there are moral and economic issues involved.

Another objection would be that the human race has had 5,000 years to adapt to problems with food and other environmental factors. However, the human diet has changed appreciably even over the past *300* years, and in view of this relatively short time period, it is hard to take seriously the theory of biological adaptation.

What About Food Additives?

The concept of risk/benefit in foods has raised other dilemmas for food scientists, regulatory officials, and the average consumer. All agree on the goal of a safe, wholesome food supply, continuously available in adequate amounts. However, in discussions as to the *technology* required to achieve this goal, the unanimity disappears. The complex food production and delivery system is not well understood by the average consumer, and it is human nature to fear or distrust what one does not understand.

The scientist would like to employ every conceivable technological advance to ensure the availability of food in safer, more attractive, more nutritious, and less expensive forms. In order to accomplish this, new technologies—and in particular, new additives—have been studied in great detail. In terms of public safety, more information is available for food additives than for many natural foodstuffs. This was pointed out in the recent studies by the Federation of American Societies for Experimental Biology (FASEB) on the status of the additives on the "Generally Recognized As Safe" (GRAS) list. FASEB was asked to establish select committees to review the available information on each additive and place it into one of the following five categories (FASEB, 1977):

1. *Additives for which available information suggests that there is no reason to suspect hazards to the public when used at current levels, or at levels which may reasonably be expected in the future.* Eighty percent of the substances evaluated to date were placed into this category (Anonymous, 1977).

2. *Additives for which available information suggests that there is no reason to suspect hazards to the public when used at current levels. More information is required, however, to determine whether a hazard would exist at higher levels of use.* Fourteen percent of the substances evaluated were in this category.

3. *Additives for which available information demonstrates no hazard at existing levels of use. Sufficient uncertainty, however, exists that additional information is desirable.* Three percent of substances were in this category.

4. *Additives for which information is insufficient to determine that no hazard exists at current levels of use. Pending further information, these substances should be restricted to safe levels of use or banned.* Two percent of substances were in this category.

5. *Additives for which there are no data available, and safety cannot be evaluated.* One percent of substances were in this category.

As the final reports from FASEB become available, it is likely that some of the natural extracts which have been added to foods for a long time will fall into Category 5. This is not to imply that there is a hazard but only that there is insufficient evidence to reach a conclusion; i.e., they have never been tested or have been tested inadequately. The same is true for a number of foods in the diet today. Any logical extension of the risk/benefit concept should be concerned with *all* food in the human diet, regardless of its source. In future years, with a larger world population, this concept will become even more important.

Examples of Risk/Benefit Analysis

This Status Summary has been more concerned with the risk than with the benefit of food additives. While it is sometimes difficult to assess the risk, it is usually possible to describe the benefits. In fact, additives would not be used at all if they did not convey a specific or generalized benefit, although individuals may sometimes debate the necessity or size of that benefit. For example, artificial sweeteners have been very much in the news recently. The banning of cyclamates left the American public with only one non-nutritive sweetener, saccharin, and the FDA recently proposed that it too should be banned. How does one assess the benefits conveyed by a non-nutritive sweetener in relation to obesity and diabetes, when they may be primarily psychological?

Many have questioned whether we really need *any* synthetic colors, in view of studies of the risk factors applying to certain members of the group. If the presence of nitrite in foods is deemed to be too high a risk factor, should we allow bacon, ham, and corned beef to remain on the market? If histamines in red wine are deemed to be too hazardous, do we need red wine? What about arsenic in shellfish or solanine in potatoes or cyanide in lima beans? Elimination of these products would change our present diet and perhaps even our "way of life." When the issues and alternatives are clearly understood, the consuming public may opt for a different concept of risk/benefit in relation to overall food supply. Such decisions are already being made regularly, as when an obese person eats dessert, a diabetic drinks alcohol, or a hypertensive individual adds salt to his food.

So far, we have discussed food additives and food components from the standpoint of their real or imagined health hazards, yet there are other concepts involved in consideration of risk/benefit. While no one would defend a food component that presents an obvious, serious *health* hazard, how does one consider the economic benefits involved? For example, bread produced without additives is a standard food staple in many parts of the world. Paris alone has hundreds of shops where consumers purchase bread for the morning and again for the evening. The bread cannot be kept for more than a day because it loses its delightful aroma and texture as it becomes stale. It is still nutritious but no longer salable as fresh bread.

Bread as usually produced in North America contains various additives that delay spoilage and help to maintain the soft texture for several days. One study by Angelini and Leonards (1973) reported that bread without additives cost 17% more than bread made with additives, mainly because of increased distribution and selling costs. The increased cost is probably even greater today, because of the rise in energy cost. No scientific evidence is available to indicate that the additives used in bread present any health hazard, yet concerns arise because of public fear of the unknown. Bread is only one example.

In addition to economic aspects, the concept of risk/benefit in foods has very real nutritional implications. For example, there is a general concensus that preclinical anemia resulting from inadequate iron intake is widespread in several population groups in the U.S., such as low socio-economic groups. This "iron-deficiency anemia" in recent years has been attributed (in part) to the replacement of iron skillets and cooking pots by stainless steel, aluminum, and plastic-coated utensils. Also, better sanitary conditions have resulted in ingestion of less "dirt" iron. Consumption of eggs, known as a good source of iron, has dropped from 400 per capita in 1940 to about 300 in 1975. On the other hand, consumption of meat, also known as a good source of iron, has been increasing.

However, regardless of the dietary causes, the ingestion of iron has decreased, and most nutrition authorities believe that it would be nutritionally beneficial to fortify the human diet with added iron.

The question is *how* to do this. Should iron be added to bread, pasta, soft drinks, tacos, and enchiladas? The ultimate choice was flour and bread, although the technological and sociological reasons for the choice of a fortification vehicle are beyond the scope of this Status Summary. In Canada, iron enrichment is restricted to flour only, at a level between 13.0 and 16.5 mg/lb of flour. The current regulation for iron enrichment of flour and bread in the U.S. is 12.5 mg/lb of bread and 16.5 mg/lb of flour. A proposal to increase these amounts to 25 and 40 mg/lb, respectively, was made recently by the FDA, with the knowledge that a very small proportion of the population suffers from a condition known as hemochromatosis. This apparently is an inborn error of metabolism which causes some individuals to absorb more iron than they need and actually accumulate iron to the point that they suffer from "iron storage" disease.

A normal male requires approximately 5 mg of iron in his daily diet to absorb the 1 mg he needs. Some nutritionists have commented that the increase from 10 to 25 mg of iron per pound of bread over a period of 20-30 years may push some adult males over the margin from latent to overt hemochromatosis. The disease is very rare at the present time, and only further research over a period of years will settle this question.

The overall question is whether the obvious benefits of reducing the incidence of iron-deficiency anemia for a fairly large segment of the population outweigh the possible increase in hemochromatosis in a small proportion of the population. The FDA has made the decision that they do not, at least for the time being and by the enrichment method suggested (FDA, 1977b).

There may be other ways of dealing with the problem of the small portion of the population who suffer from hemochromatosis. One approach would be to limit the fortification to specific classes of food. People with hemochromatosis could avoid these classes of food. This, however, would also limit the almost automatic intake by the general population using a basic food such as bread. At the very least, adequate labeling should be provided, so that an individual would be able to estimate his intake of iron. This approach has already been adopted, for example, with tartrazine, a yellow food color also known as FD&C Yellow No. 5. A small percentage of the population is known to be allergic to tartrazine, so processors will be required to state it on the label. Many other examples of this type of problem must also exist.

It should be realized that the concepts of risk/benefit as discussed above might prove useful only as a broad reminder to consider all ramifications of a contemplated action. One FASEB committee has concluded that "A rigorous risk/benefit ratio is intrinsically impossible in the state of our present knowledge about GRAS substances" (FASEB, 1977). This may well be true, but we still will have to use the broad concept in everyday life.

More Realistic Approach Needed

The U. S. Department of Agriculture's Economic Research Service has estimated that the world food supply must increase about 2.4% per year if the increased world population is to be fed. Pressure on food production is increasing from year to year, and we will soon reach the point where every technological concept in food availability will be needed to keep up with population growth. The need for a realistic approach to the risk/benefit problem will thus become even more important. The ratio will have to be slanted very heavily toward the lowest possible risk.

Yet risk can never be eliminated entirely. This was recognized in the Yiddish proverb, "Ever since dying became fashionable, life hasn't been safe."

BIBLIOGRAPHY

Angeline, J.F. and Leonardos, G.P. 1973. Food additives—Some economic considerations. Food Technol. 27(4): 40.

Anonymous. 1977. Select Committee on GRAS Substances "White Paper." Food Chem. News, Sept. 26, p. 7.

CAST, 1977. Hormonally active substances in foods: A safety evaluation. Report No. 66. Council for Agricultural Science and Technology, Iowa State Univ., Ames, Iowa.

Cornfield, J. 1977. Carcinogenic risk assessment. Science 198: 693.

FASEB. 1977. Evaluation of health aspects of GRAS food ingredients: Lessons learned and questions unanswered. Select Comm. on GRAS Substances, Federation of Am. Socs. for Exp. Biology. Fed. Proc. 36(11): 2519.

FDA. 1977a. Chemical compounds in food-developing assays for carcinogenic residues. Food and Drug Admin. Fed. Reg. 42(35): 10412, Feb. 22.

FDA. 1977b. Iron fortification of flour and bread. Food and Drug Admin. Fed. Reg. 42(223): 59513, Nov. 18.

Jukes, T.H. 1976. Diethylstilbestrol in beef production. What is the risk to consumers? Prev. Med. 5: 438.

Mantel, N. and Bryan, W.R. 1961. Safety testing of carcinogenic agents. J. Natl. Cancer Inst. 27(2): 455.

Mantel, N., Bohidar, N.R., Brown, C.C., Ciminera, J.L. and Tukey, J.W. 1975. Improved Mantel-Bryan procedure for safety testing of carcinogens. Cancer Res. 35: 865.

NAS/NRC. 1966. Hormonal relationships and applications in the production of meat, milk and eggs. Natl. Acad. of Sciences, Natl. Res. Council, Washington, D.C.

SUPPLEMENTAL MATERIAL

Lowrance, W.W. 1976. "Of Acceptable Risk. Science and the Determination of Safety." Wm. Kaufman, Inc., Los Altos, Calif.

NAS/NRC. 1973. "Toxicants Occurring Naturally in Foods," 2nd ed. Natl. Acad. of Sciences, Natl. Res. Council, Washington, D.C.

NUTRITIVE VALUES

The New RDAs: Estimated Adequate and Safe Intake of Trace Elements and Calculation of Available Iron

by Walter Mertz, M.D.

The dynamic nature of the Recommended Dietary Allowances (RDAs) is evident from their history. Revisions of the original document have appeared at regular intervals, not only changing current levels of recommended intakes, but establishing allowances for an increasing number of nutrients. At the time of publication, a revised edition is as nearly up-to-date as possible in its documentation of human nutritional needs. Yet, at that same time, a new committee of the Food and Nutrition Board is selected for the purpose of again revising and extending the edition that just appeared. The RDAs are neither perfect nor complete; at best, they are an intelligent digest of available knowledge of human nutrient requirements, on which the recommendations are based.

Two major innovations proposed by the RDA Committee for the 1980 edition, the "estimated adequate and safe intakes" and a new method of calculating absorbable iron, will be discussed here. The successful implementation of these proposals for dietary planning and evaluation will depend on their acceptance by the dietetic profession. Implementation of the estimated adequate and safe intakes for six trace elements and the use of the proposed method for calculating available iron impose additional demands of effort and time. However, these efforts will be rewarded by the health benefits to the public that can be derived from substantially improved diets.

The "estimated adequate intakes"

The Committee has proposed the establishment of estimated ranges of "adequate and safe intakes" for three minerals, three vitamins, and six trace elements. The term "estimated adequate and safe intakes" implies that the scientific basis on which these allowances are set is less complete than that for the nutrients with "recommended dietary allowances." Despite this reservation, the estimates reflect the best available modern knowledge and are expected to be useful guidelines as to adequate levels of intakes. Another purpose of the estimated intakes is to warn against excessive intake of minerals and trace elements. Free accessibility to mineral and trace element supplements in drug stores and health food stores and the wide use of these supplements in some parts of the country clearly constitute a danger of nutrient imbalances—and perhaps of chronic and acute toxicity. The estimated ranges of intakes will also be useful in guiding manufacturers of formulated foods to a safe level of the essential trace elements.

Estimates are given for sodium, potassium, chloride, vitamin K, biotin, pantothenic acid, copper, manganese, molybdenum, chromium, selenium, and fluorine; they are presented as "ranges." Although the expression of these estimates as ranges of adequate and safe intakes is a new development which will require re-orientation in the thinking of those who implement them, the concept is well founded and logical.

The least compelling reason for using ranges is the uncertainty of our present knowledge of the human requirement for certain nutrients. Available data do not allow the definition of *one* optimal daily intake for any of these ten nutrients. Future research will provide additional data, but it is doubtful whether new findings will answer the important question of whether there is *one* optimal intake for any nutrient.

This question leads into the second reason to support the concept of ranges of intakes, namely, the organism can maintain optimal nutrient-dependent function within a range of nutrient intakes, the width of which varies from one nutrient to another. This can be illustrated by a biologic dose-response curve, based on Bertrand's mathematical model (1). In this curve (Figure 1), a nutrient-specific biologic function (ordinate) is plotted against nutrient intake (abscissa). The size of the plateau of safe intakes is very small for energy (an intake even slightly in excess of requirement eventually produces harmful effects). It is intermediate for such nutrients as protein or sodium (an intake two- or threefold of the requirement produces subtle, chronic, adverse effects). For most vitamins and trace elements, the plateau is relatively wide (undesirable effects are produced by intakes tenfold or more of the requirement). Within the range of safe intakes, the organism is able to maintain acceptable tissue concentrations by control of absorption or excretion or a combination of both. Control mechanisms in human beings have been described in detail for the metabolism of iron (2) and of manganese (3); it can be inferred from animal experiments that controls also function for other elements.

The third reason for expressing these estimates as ranges is the variability of biologic availability, depending on the chemical form and nutrient interactions. The classical example is the dependence of the apparent copper requirement on the dietary concentration of molybdenum and sulfur, a worldwide problem in animal nutrition (4). Underwood has stated that one concentration of copper in the feedstuff can be deficient, adequate, or toxic, depending on the amount of the other two nutrients present (5). The best known example from human nutrition is the great variability of iron available for absorption, depending on chemical form and on dietary factors that depress or enhance iron absorption. This example will be discussed in detail later.

Substantial differences of biologic availability, influenced by elemental form and dietary composition, are known for zinc, copper, selenium, and chromium (5). In general, diets rich in fiber and phytate tend to decrease the biologic availability of some trace elements significantly (6), and negative balances have been observed in persons consuming these diets, although the trace element concentrations could be considered adequate (7). Conversely, foods of animal origin are usually good sources of biologically available trace elements.

The ranges are given for a mixed U.S. diet, balanced with regard to the major nutrients and with regard to animal and vegetable composition. The habitual consumption of diets rich in fiber and the dependence on foods of vegetable origin as the main sources of trace elements would call for a trace element intake at the higher end of the range. On the other hand, diets providing trace elements from animal sources can be expected to be adequate, even if they furnish amounts near the lower end of the suggested range.

Many mineral and trace element interactions are known from studies of animals, but the amount of information is insufficient for quantitative treatment of these interactions in dietary planning and evaluation. The influences of these interactions can be assumed to be moderate for most balanced diets, but users of the RDAs should be aware that grossly excessive levels of some nutrients can markedly affect biologic availability and, therefore, the requirement for minerals and trace elements.

The estimated ranges of intakes are, in the opinion of the Committee, both adequate and safe (8). If provided by a mixed diet, balanced with regard to the major nutrients, these ranges correspond to the plateau of the biologic dose-response curve discussed above. *All points on this plateau and, correspondingly, all intakes within the suggested range, are considered equivalent; a higher intake should not be considered more desirable than a lower one.* Moreover, occasional or even habitual intakes that fall short of the lower limits should not necessarily be considered deficient; nor should those exceeding the upper limit be regarded as toxic. However, intakes consistently outside the suggested ranges will increase the *risk* of deficiency or toxicity *in a population*. The margin of safety that separates the lower limit from deficiency and the upper limit from toxicity is different for each element. The planning of dietary fluoride intake, for example, does not offer a wide latitude if both dental caries and mottling of the tooth enamel are to be prevented. Manganese, on the other hand, offers a substantial margin of safety, as neither dietary deficiency nor toxicity of this element is known in humans.

The objective of this paper is to discuss recommended estimated safe and adequate intakes of trace elements in context with questions of immediate interest to the dietetic profession.

COPPER. The estimated safe and adequate intake of 2 to 3 mg. for adults is based on balance studies and on the absence of toxicity from much higher intakes. To the dietitian, the implementation of the recommended copper intake might well pose problems similar to those posed by iron and zinc. The recommended range of copper intakes can be obtained from diets furnishing large, perhaps excessive amounts of energy; however, diets furnishing less energy must be carefully planned to supply even the lower limit of 2 mg. In recent analytical studies of diets duplicating exactly what was consumed by subjects, mean intakes were close to 1 mg. copper per day. The discrepancy between the lower end of the range and the actual copper intake is relatively greater than that for iron. The signs and symptoms of copper deficiency in human subjects are well known but are not believed to occur among free-living persons in the United States. It is impossible to state whether short-term balance studies overestimate the human copper requirement, not taking into account a possible gradual adjustment to lower intakes, or whether subtle biochemical or pathologic consequences that might be present

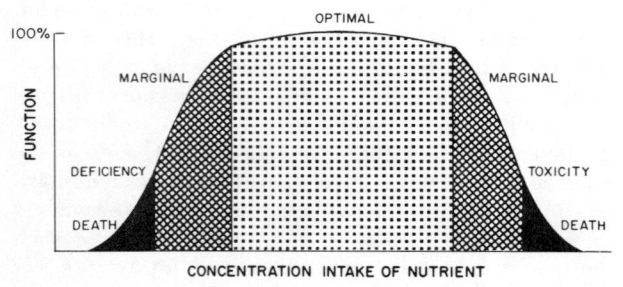

FIG. 1. *Biologic dose-responsive curve, based on Bertrand's mathematical model (1).*

have not yet been identified as a public health problem. In view of this uncertainty, it is prudent to provide a copper intake within the range, particularly at a time when supplements of zinc, a potential copper antagonist, are available and are widely used.

Food composition data on copper are not yet part of the Agriculture Handbook No. 8. However, Schroeder and associates have reported the results of copper analyses of foods (9); and Schlettwein-Gsell and Mommsen-Straub have published (10) their compilation of trace element data from the literature that contains extensive data on copper. In addition, Pennington and Calloway have compiled (11) values for the copper content for over five hundred items. There is some doubt of the accuracy of the analytical copper data for foods, particularly of those based on older methods. However, the range concept offers a latitude of intakes that can accommodate the effects of analytical errors, as long as they are not excessive. The available tables do point out foods that are exceptionally good sources of copper and can be used to increase the intake to the desired levels. In addition, the USDA's Nutrient Composition Laboratory of the Nutrition Institute in Beltsville, Maryland, is determining copper and zinc concentrations in foods with the most modern methods, so that adequate, reliable composition data can be expected in the future.

MANGANESE. Our present knowledge does not suggest a problem of manganese nutrition in the United States. Manganese deficiency is not known to occur in human subjects, even though some dietary intakes may fall somewhat short of the range of 2.5 to 5 mg. per day. Equally unknown is dietary manganese toxicity, even when amounts substantially in excess of the recommended range are consumed. Many foods of vegetable origin are excellent sources of this element; therefore, designing diets that meet the provisional allowances will present no difficulty to the dietitian. Although there are no official food tables for this element as yet, helpful data are available (10).

FLUORIDE. Fluorine differs from other elements in the estimated intakes in several respects. Its safe range of intakes and the margin of safety are smaller than those of other elements included in the table (8). This does not leave the diet planner a margin of error. The risks of dental caries on one hand and of mottling of tooth enamel on the other increase quite sharply with intakes beyond the recommended range. Furthermore, in contrast to the other elements, the total fluoride intake is strongly influenced by the fluoride content of the local water supply, not only due to the water drunk, but also due to the fluoride enrichment of the diet from cooking water. The total fluoride content of the diet, therefore, cannot be planned precisely, nor can it be calculated accurately from the composition of the individual foods of that diet.

However, experience has shown that a safe range of fluoride intakes is furnished by most diets, if the local water supply contains approximately 1 mg. fluoride per liter. In view of the strong influence of the water supply on the amount of fluoride actually consumed, the main concern of the dietitian with regard to this element should be with the desirable levels of fluoride in water. Nutrient compositional data for this element have been published by Spencer and associates (12,13).

CHROMIUM. The implementation of the estimated intakes for chromium of 0.05 to 0.20 mg. per day will be possible by careful planning when adequate food composition tables become available. According to several independent studies, the mean chromium intake from diets lies between 60 and 70 mcg. In the latest, well controlled measurements of chromium in diets designed to meet all the Recommended Dietary Allowances and furnishing 2,800 kcal per day, the mean content of chromium was 76 mcg., with a range of 25 to 220 mcg. The average chromium density of these diets was 22 mcg. per 1,000 kcal (14).

Marginal chromium deficiency is suspected to occur in segments of the American population, and not all diets meet the estimated adequate intakes for this element; therefore, implementation of the desirable ranges of chromium intake should be of concern to the dietitian and nutritionist. Unfortunately, nutrient composition data for chromium are incomplete. The published compilation (10) should provide useful data. The methodology for analysis of chromium in foods has progressed, so that reliable composition information can be expected in the future.

SELENIUM. The estimated adequate intake for selenium of 0.05 to 0.20 mg. should be easy to implement in the United States, as most diets fall within this range. Higher (up to 500 mcg. per day) and lower intakes (as low as 35 mcg. per day) have been reported from Japan and New Zealand, respectively; these were not related to any recognizable adverse health effects. In view of the great differences in the selenium content of foods, it should be easy, if necessary, for the dietitian to adjust the selenium content by proper choice of foods.

Food composition data for selenium were compiled (10), and additional information was published by Morris and Levander (15). Selenium concentrations in soil and water are readily reflected in foods of vegetable origin and, to a lesser extent, in foods of animal origin. Thus, the variability of selenium concentrations reported in foods reflects primarily the origin of the food and not necessarily analytical uncertainties.

MOLYBDENUM. Although the estimated adequate and safe intake for molybdenum (0.15 to 0.5 mg. per day) is larger than that for selenium, both elements have in common that they present no problem to the dietitian and that their concentration in foods is strongly influenced by local soil factors. Diets customarily consumed in the United States are within the estimated range (16). Furthermore, effects of molybdenum deficiency are not known in man, and overt signs of chronic molybdenum toxicity have been reported only with

Table I

Food and Nutrition Board, National Academy of Sciences-National Research Council
RECOMMENDED DAILY DIETARY ALLOWANCES,[a] Revised 1980
Designed for the maintenance of good nutrition of practically all healthy people in the U.S.A.

	Age (years)	Weight (kg)	Weight (lbs)	Height (cm)	Height (in)	Protein (g)	Vitamin A (μg R.E.)[b]	Vitamin D (μg)[c]	Vitamin E (mg α T.E.)[d]	Vitamin C (mg)	Thiamin (mg)	Riboflavin (mg)	Niacin (mg N.E.)[e]	Vitamin B6 (mg)	Folacin (μg)[f]	Vitamin B12 (μg)	Calcium (mg)	Phosphorus (mg)	Magnesium (mg)	Iron (mg)	Zinc (mg)	Iodine (μg)
Infants	0.0-0.5	6	13	60	24	kg x 2.2	420	10	3	35	0.3	0.4	6	0.3	30	0.5[g]	360	240	50	10	3	40
	0.5-1.0	9	20	71	28	kg x 2.0	400	10	4	35	0.5	0.6	8	0.6	45	1.5	540	360	70	15	5	50
Children	1-3	13	29	90	35	23	400	10	5	45	0.7	0.8	9	0.9	100	2.0	800	800	150	15	10	70
	4-6	20	44	112	44	30	500	10	6	45	0.9	1.0	11	1.3	200	2.5	800	800	200	10	10	90
	7-10	28	62	132	52	34	700	10	7	45	1.2	1.4	16	1.6	300	3.0	800	800	250	10	10	120
Males	11-14	45	99	157	62	45	1000	10	8	50	1.4	1.6	18	1.8	400	3.0	1200	1200	350	18	15	150
	15-18	66	145	176	69	56	1000	10	10	60	1.4	1.7	18	2.0	400	3.0	1200	1200	400	18	15	150
	19-22	70	154	177	70	56	1000	7.5	10	60	1.5	1.7	19	2.2	400	3.0	800	800	350	10	15	150
	23-50	70	154	178	70	56	1000	5	10	60	1.4	1.6	18	2.2	400	3.0	800	800	350	10	15	150
	51+	70	154	178	70	56	1000	5	10	60	1.2	1.4	16	2.2	400	3.0	800	800	350	10	15	150
Females	11-14	46	101	157	62	46	800	10	8	50	1.1	1.3	15	1.8	400	3.0	1200	1200	300	18	15	150
	15-18	55	120	163	64	46	800	10	8	60	1.1	1.3	14	2.0	400	3.0	1200	1200	300	18	15	150
	19-22	55	120	163	64	44	800	7.5	8	60	1.1	1.3	14	2.0	400	3.0	800	800	300	18	15	150
	23-50	55	120	163	64	44	800	5	8	60	1.0	1.2	13	2.0	400	3.0	800	800	300	18	15	150
	51+	55	120	163	64	44	800	5	8	60	1.0	1.2	13	2.0	400	3.0	800	800	300	10	15	150
Pregnant						+30	+200	+5	+2	+20	+0.4	+0.3	+2	+0.6	+400	+1.0	+400	+400	+150	[h]	+5	+25
Lactating						+20	+400	+5	+3	+40	+0.5	+0.5	+5	+0.5	+100	+1.0	+400	+400	+150	[h]	+10	+50

a The allowances are intended to provide for individual variations among most normal persons as they live in the United States under usual environmental stresses. Diets should be based on a variety of common foods in order to provide other nutrients for which human requirements have been less well defined. See text for detailed discussion of allowances and of nutrients not tabulated. See Table III (p. 4) for weights and heights by individual year of age. See Table III (p. 4) for suggested average energy intakes.
b Retinol equivalents. 1 retinol equivalent = 1 μg retinol or 6 μg β-carotene. See text for calculation of vitamin A activity of diets as retinol equivalents.
c As cholecalciferol. 10 μg cholecalciferol = 400 I.U. vitamin D.
d α tocopherol equivalents. 1 mg d-α-tocopherol = 1 α T.E. See text for variation in allowances and calculation of vitamin E activity of the diet as α tocopherol equivalents.
e 1 N.E. (niacin equivalent) is equal to 1 mg of niacin or 60 mg of dietary tryptophan.
f The folacin allowances refer to dietary sources as determined by *Lactobacillus casei* assay after treatment with enzymes ("conjugases") to make polyglutamyl forms of the vitamin available to the test organism.
g The RDA for vitamin B12 in infants is based on average concentration of the vitamin in human milk. The allowances after weaning are based on energy intake (as recommended by the American Academy of Pediatrics) and consideration of other factors such as intestinal absorption; see text.
h The increased requirement during pregnancy cannot be met by the iron content of habitual American diets nor by the existing iron stores of many women; therefore the use of 30 - 60 mg of supplemental iron is recommended. Iron needs during lactation are not substantially different from those of nonpregnant women, but continued supplementation of the mother for 2 - 3 months after parturition is advisable in order to replenish stores depleted by pregnancy.

Table II

Estimated Safe and Adequate Daily Dietary Intakes of Additional Selected Vitamins and Minerals[a]

	Age (years)	Vitamin K (μg)	Biotin (μg)	Pantothenic Acid (mg)	Copper (mg)	Manganese (mg)	Fluoride (mg)	Chromium (mg)	Selenium (mg)	Molybdenum (mg)	Sodium (mg)	Potassium (mg)	Chloride (mg)
Infants	0-0.5	12	35	2	0.5-0.7	0.5-0.7	0.1-0.5	0.01-0.04	0.01-0.04	0.03-0.06	115-350	350-925	275-700
	0.5-1	10-20	50	3	0.7-1.0	0.7-1.0	0.2-1.0	0.02-0.06	0.02-0.06	0.04-0.08	250-750	425-1275	400-1200
Children	1-3	15-30	65	3	1.0-1.5	1.0-1.5	0.5-1.5	0.02-0.08	0.02-0.08	0.05-0.1	325-975	550-1650	500-1500
and	4-6	20-40	85	3-4	1.5-2.0	1.5-2.0	1.0-2.5	0.03-0.12	0.03-0.12	0.06-0.15	450-1350	775-2325	700-2100
Adolescents	7-10	30-60	120	4-5	2.0-2.5	2.0-3.0	1.5-2.5	0.05-0.2	0.05-0.2	0.1-0.3	600-1800	1000-3000	925-2775
	11+	50-100	100-200	4-7	2.0-3.0	2.5-5.0	1.5-2.5	0.05-0.2	0.05-0.2	0.15-0.5	900-2700	1525-4575	1400-4200
Adults		70-140	100-200	4-7	2.0-3.0	2.5-5.0	1.5-4.0	0.05-0.2	0.05-0.2	0.15-0.5	1100-3300	1875-5625	1700-5100

a Because there is less information on which to base allowances, these figures are not given in the main table of the RDA and are provided here in the form of ranges of recommended intakes.
b Since the toxic levels for many trace elements may be only several times usual intakes, the upper levels for the trace elements given in this table should not be habitually exceeded.

Table III
Mean Heights and Weights and Recommended Energy Intake

Category	Age (years)	Weight (kg)	Weight (lb)	Height (cm)	Height (in)	Energy Needs (with range) (kcal)	(MJ)
Infants	0.0-0.5	6	13	60	24	kg X 115 (95-145)	kg X .48
	0.5-1.0	9	20	71	28	kg X 105 (80-135)	kg X .44
Children	1-3	13	29	90	35	1300 (900 - 1800)	5.5
	4-6	20	44	112	44	1700 (1300 - 2300)	7.1
	7-10	28	62	132	52	2400 (1650 - 3300)	10.1
Males	11-14	45	99	157	62	2700 (2000 - 3700)	11.3
	15-18	66	145	176	69	2800 (2100 - 3900)	11.8
	19-22	70	154	177	70	2900 (2500 - 3300)	12.2
	23-50	70	154	178	70	2700 (2300 - 3100)	11.3
	51-75	70	154	178	70	2400 (2000 - 2800)	10.1
	76+	70	154	178	70	2050 (1650 - 2450)	8.6
Females	11-14	46	101	157	62	2200 (1500 - 3000)	9.2
	15-18	55	120	163	64	2100 (1200 - 3000)	8.8
	19-22	55	120	163	64	2100 (1700 - 2500)	8.8
	23-50	55	120	163	64	2000 (1600 - 2400)	8.4
	51-75	55	120	163	64	1800 (1400 - 2200)	7.6
	76+	55	120	163	64	1600 (1200 - 2000)	6.7
Pregnancy						+300	
Lactation						+500	

The data in this table have been assembled from the observed median heights and weights of children shown in Table I, together with desirable weights for adults given in Table II for the mean heights of men (70 inches) and women (64 inches) between the ages of 18 and 34 years as surveyed in the U.S. population (HEW/NCHS data).

The energy allowances for the young adults are for men and women doing light work. The allowances for the two older age groups represent mean energy needs over these age spans, allowing for a 2% decrease in basal (resting) metabolic rate per decade and a reduction in activity of 200 kcal/day for men and women between 51 and 75 years, 500 kcal for men over 75 years and 400 kcal for women over 75 (see text). The customary range of daily energy output is shown for adults in parentheses, and is based on a variation in energy needs of ± 400 kcal at any one age (see text and Garrow, 1978), emphasizing the wide range of energy intakes appropriate for any group of people.

Energy allowances for children through age 18 are based on median energy intakes of children these ages followed in longitudinal growth studies. The values in parentheses are 10th and 90th percentiles of energy intake, to indicate the range of energy consumption among children of these ages (see text).

Tables I, II, and III from: *Recommended Dietary Allowances, Revised 1980,* Food and Nutrition Board, National Academy of Sciences-National Research Council, Washington, D.C.

habitual intakes twenty to thirty times the upper limit of the range. Such excessive intakes are known only in regions with soils abnormally high in molybdenum and are no problem in the United States. The molybdenum content of foods is strongly influenced by the molybdenum concentration in the soils where the food was grown. Thus, as for selenium, the variability of compositional data reflects the origin of the foods and not necessarily analytical uncertainties. Data for molybdenum concentration in foods have been compiled (10).

OBSTACLES TO IMPLEMENTING THE ESTIMATED ADEQUATE AND SAFE INTAKES. The implementation of estimated adequate and safe intakes for six new trace elements at first sight appears as a formidable task for the dietitian, particularly in view of the incomplete nutrient analysis data. (The most useful source of such data, the publication by Schlettwein-Gsell [10], is written in German and has not yet been translated into English.) Yet, in the context of the actual concentrations of the six elements in food, it appears that the task is less difficult than it might seem. Three elements—manganese, molybdenum, and selenium—present no nutritional problems; the estimated ranges are easily met by ordinary diets and margins of safety are quite comfortable. Fluoride poses no problem, provided the local water supply contains a desirable fluoride concentration of about 1 mg. per liter.

This leaves copper and chromium, for which undesirably low intakes are not uncommon. Provisional composition data for copper are available and should be used to provide diets that meet the estimated adequate intakes (9-11). The nutrient composition information for chromium is much less complete, but it can be used to avoid dietary patterns extremely low in chromium (10). As analytical information increases and becomes more easily accessible through automatic data processing, dietitians' work with these trace elements will become not only more precise but also more comprehensive. Establishing estimated adequate intakes undoubtedly will help to stimulate the scope and intensity of nutrient composition analysis.

Calculation of available dietary iron

The treatment of the iron problem in previous editions of the Recommended Dietary Allowances was predicated on the assumption of an average 10 per cent iron absorption from the diet (17). On this basis, it was logical to recommend an intake of 18 mg. for women of childbearing age in order to meet the requirements of nearly all healthy individuals in this group. However, this allowance is very difficult to provide with diets that approximate the recommendations for energy intake. In contrast to diets in other countries, where organ meats and foods made from animal blood are perfectly acceptable, diets habitually consumed in this country rarely furnish more than 6 mg. iron per 1,000 kcal. Recent attempts to increase the level of iron enrichment in cereal products have been unsuccessful, leaving the dietetic profession in the difficult situation of not being able to implement the recommended allowance and thus help to alleviate the widespread problem of iron deficiency.

The RDA Committee hopes to offer a solution in the ninth revised edition in the chapter on iron. This chapter outlines a new method for calculating iron that is *available for absorption*. Research in the United States and abroad has clearly demonstrated large differences in the absorbability of this element, depending on form and composition of the diet, which make the previous assumption of an "average availability" for absorption untenable. As the proposed method for calculation of absorbable iron has been described in detail (18), it will be discussed here only briefly.

(a) In view of the interactions of dietary ingredients with iron, to be discussed later, absorbable iron must be calculated for *each meal*. The daily intake can be reconstructed by adding the values of the individual meals.

(b) The iron in a meal must be treated in two categories: Heme iron and non-heme iron; each must be calculated separately. The former category constitutes approximately 40 per cent of the total iron in meat, fowl, and fish; it is highly available for absorption which is independent of influences from other dietary ingredients. The remaining 60 per cent of iron in meat, fowl, and fish and all other dietary iron, including compounds used in enrichment, is termed "non-heme" iron. The availability for absorption of this category is lower than that of the heme category and is subject to influences from dietary constituents. Two such constituents, ascorbic acid and a yet-unidentified factor in meat, fowl, and fish, enhance the availability of non-heme iron significantly, but only *if they are present in the iron-containing meal*.

(c) The amounts of meat, fowl, and fish and of ascorbic acid present in any one meal must be calculated. On the basis of these amounts, the meals are then classified as of high, intermediate, or low availability of non-heme iron, and the amount of non-heme iron available for absorption is calculated.

(d) The amounts of available heme iron and of available non-heme iron are added to give total available iron in that meal.

(e) The available iron per day is the sum of the values from the individual meals.

(f) The results can be related directly to the requirement for absorbable iron as stated in the text of the RDAs (1.5 mg. for females, 1 mg. for males); alternatively, results can be compared with the Recommended Dietary Allowance in the RDA table by multiplying the amount of available iron by ten. (It will be remembered that the iron allowance is based on the assumption of an average 10 per cent absorption of dietary iron.)

OBSTACLES TO IMPLEMENTATION. These calculations for absorbable iron impose a substantial additional work load on the dietitian. They are not complicated, but are more time-consuming than the straight evaluation of total dietary iron. It is expected, however, that computer programs will be available soon to simplify the task.

The poor data base for heme and non-heme iron in foods is another obstacle. Nutrient composition research undoubtedly will provide the needed compositional data in the future. For now, the estimate that 40 per cent of the total iron content of meat, fowl, and fish is present as heme iron is a reasonably satisfactory base for the calculations.

BENEFITS FROM IMPLEMENTATION. The new concept of calculating absorbable iron gives the dietitian a powerful tool with which to influence the amount of absorbable iron by simple dietary means. A food rich in ascorbic acid would have little effect on iron absorption if served with a meal that contains little iron, but would be a powerful stimulator if served with an iron-rich meal. Meals with poor iron availability that previously could not be identified by their total iron content can now be pinpointed and improved. Also, the dietitian can now give judicious counsel to individuals who are in danger of iron overloading and would benefit from meals that are low in available iron.

It is hoped that the members of the dietetic profession will accept the new concept for calculating absorbable iron, in spite of the increased workload. Widespread use of this concept in feeding programs should have a beneficial effect on public health. For maximal impact, however, the concept must be communicated to the public in a readily understandable form. The ultimate benefits of the new concept will depend on the commitment and enthusiasm of the dietetic profession.

Iron is only one of the essential trace elements that present problems of availability for absorption and of interactions with other components of the diet. We can expect difficulties, similar to those for iron with several trace elements. Present knowledge of availability and interactions of these trace elements is inadequate as a basis for exact calculations of availability, but on-going nutrition research should be able to provide this knowledge in the future.

Implementation of the recommendations discussed here will not be easy, but should be feasible, despite several obstacles. With the acceptance of the recommended adequate and safe intakes and with the concept of dietary interactions, the diet planner will have a larger, more complicated but also more effective armamentarium for use in providing more healthful diets.

References
(1) BERTRAND, G.: On the role of trace substances in agriculture. *In* 8th Intl. Congr. Appl. Chem., N.Y., Vol. 28: 30, 1912.
(2) HAHN, P.F., JONES, E., LOWE, R.C., MENEELY, G.R., AND PEACOCK, W.: The relative absorption and utilization of ferrous and ferric iron in anemia as determined with the radioactive isotope. Am. J. Physiol. 143: 191, 1945.
(3) COTZIAS, G.C.: Manganese. *In* COMAR, C.L., AND BRONNER, F., eds.: Mineral Metabolism, An Advanced Treatise, Vol. II, Pt. B. N.Y.: Academic Press, Inc., 1962.
(4) CHAPPELL, W.R., AND PETERSEN, K.K., EDS.: Molybdenum in the Environment. N.Y.: Dekker, 1977.
(5) UNDERWOOD, E.J.: Trace Elements in Human and Animal Nutrition. 4th ed. N.Y.: Academic Press, 1977.
(6) REINHOLD, J.G., FARADJI, B., ABADI, P., AND ISMAIL-BEIGI, F.: Binding of zinc to fiber and other solids of wholemeal bread. *In* PRASAD, A.S., ed.: Trace Elements in Human Health and Disease, VOL. I. Zinc and Copper. N.Y.: Academic Press, Inc., 1976.
(7) KELSAY, J.L., BEHALL, K.M., AND PRATHER, E.S.: The effect of fiber from fruits and vegetables on metabolic responses of human subjects. 2. Calcium, magnesium, iron, silicon, and vitamin A balances. Am. J. Clin. Nutr., in press.
(8) FOOD & NUTR. BD.,: Recommended Dietary Allowances, 9th rev. edition. Washington, D.C.: Natl. Acad. Sci., in press (see J. Am. Dietet. A. 75: 623, 1979).
(9) SCHROEDER, H.A., NASAU, A.P., TIPTON, I.H., AND BALASSA, J.J.: Essential trace metals in man: Copper. J. Chron. Dis. 19: 1007, 1966.
(10) SCHLETTWEIN-GSELL, D., AND MOMMSEN-STRAUB, S.: Spusen elemente in Lebensmitteln. Intl. J. Vit. and Nutr. Res., Suppl. 13, 1973.
(11) PENNINGTON, J.T., AND CALLOWAY, D.H.: Copper content of foods. Factors affecting reported values. J. Am. Dietet. A. 63: 143, 1973.
(12) KRAMER, L., OSIS, D., WIATROWSKI, E., AND SPENCER, H.: Dietary fluoride in different areas in the United States. Am. J. Clin. Nutr. 27: 590, 1974.
(13) OSIS, D., KRAMER, L., WIATROWSKI, E., AND SPENCER, H.: Dietary fluoride intake in man. J. Nutr. 104: 1313, 1974.
(14) KUMPULAINEN, J.T., WOLF, W.R., VEILLON, C., AND MERTZ, W.: Chromium intake in low and high fat diets determined by graphite furnace atomic absorption. J. Agric. Food Chem., in press.
(15) MORRIS, V.C., AND LEVANDER, O.A.: Selenium content of foods. J. Nutr. 100: 1383, 1970.
(16) SCHROEDER, H.A., BALASSA, J.J., AND TIPTON, I.H.: Essential trace elements in man: Molybdenum. J. Chron. Dis. 23: 481, 1970.
(17) FOOD & NUTR. BD.: Recommended Dietary Allowances, 8th rev. ed. Washington, D.C.: Natl. Acad. Sci., 1974.
(18) MONSEN, E.R., HALLBERG, L., LAYRISSE, M., HEGSTED, D.M., COOK, J.D., MERTZ, W., AND FINCH, C.A.: Estimation of available dietary iron. Am. J. Clin. Nutr. 31: 134, 1978.

Nutritive Value of Foods

by Catherine F. Adams and Martha Richardson

NUTRITIVE VALUES

A glass of milk... a slice of cooked meat... an apple... a slice of bread... What food values does each contain? How much cooked meat will a pound of raw meat yield? How much daily protein is recommended for a healthy 14-year-old boy?

Ready answers to questions like these are helpful to homemakers who need the information to plan nutritionally adequate diets and to nutritionists, dietitians, physicians, and other consumers.

The answers will be found in the tables in this publication.

Table 1.—Equivalents by volume and weight

Volume

Level measure	Equivalent
1 gallon (3.786 liters; 3,786 milliliters)	4 quarts
1 quart (0.946 liter; 946 milliliters)	4 cups
1 cup (237 milliliters)	8 fluid ounces ½ pint 16 tablespoons
2 tablespoons (30 milliliters)	1 fluid ounce
1 tablespoon (15 milliliters)	3 teaspoons
1 pound regular butter or margarine	4 sticks 2 cups
1 pound whipped butter or margarine	6 sticks 2 8-ounce containers 3 cups

Weight

Avoirdupois weight	Equivalent
1 pound (16 ounces)	453.6 grams
1 ounce	28.35 grams
3½ ounces	100 grams

Nutritive value of foods—Table 2

Table 2 shows the food values in 730 foods commonly used.

Foods listed.—Foods are grouped under the following main headings:
- Dairy products
- Eggs
- Fats and oils
- Fish, shellfish, meat, and poultry
- Fruits and fruit products
- Grain products
- Legumes (dry), nuts, and seeds
- Sugars and sweets
- Vegetables and vegetable products
- Miscellaneous items

Most of the foods listed are in ready-to-eat form. Some are basic products widely used in food preparation, such as flour, fat, and cornmeal.

---

[1] The authors gratefully acknowledge the assistance of Ruth G. Bowman of this Institute in compiling the data on the subject matter printed here.

From *Nutritive Value of Foods*, published by the U.S. Department of Agriculture's Consumer and Food Economics Institute.

The weight in grams for an approximate measure of each food is shown. A footnote indicates if inedible parts are included in the description and the weight. For example, item 246 is half a grapefruit with peel having a weight of 241 grams. A footnote to this item explains that the 241 grams include the weight of the peel.

The approximate measure shown for each food is in cups, ounces, pounds, some other well-known unit, or a piece of certain size. The cup measure refers to the standard measuring cup of 8 fluid ounces or one-half liquid pint. The ounce refers to one-sixteenth of a pound avoirdupois, unless fluid ounce is indicated. The weight of a fluid ounce varies according to the food measured. Some helpful volume and weight equivalents are shown in table 1.

Food values.—Table 2 also shows values for protein, fat, total saturated acids, two unsaturated fatty acids (oleic acid and linoleic acid), total carbohydrates, four minerals (calcium, iron, phosphorus, and potassium), and five vitamins (vitamin A, thiamin, riboflavin, niacin, and ascorbic acid or vitamin C). Food energy is in calories. The calorie is the unit of measure for the energy furnished the body by protein, fat, and carbohydrate.

These values can be used to compare kinds and amounts of nutrients in different foods. They sometimes can be used to compare different forms of the same food.

Water content is included because the percentage of moisture present is needed for identification and comparison of many food items.

The values for food energy (calories) and nutrients shown in table 2 are the amounts present in the edible part of the item, that is, in only that portion customarily eaten—corn without cob, meat without bone, potatoes without skin, European-type grapes without seeds. If additional parts are eaten—the potato skin, for example—amounts of some nutrients obtained will be somewhat greater than those shown.

Values for thiamin, riboflavin, and niacin in white flours and white bread and rolls are based on the increased enrichment levels put into effect for those products by the Food and Drug Administration in 1974. Iron values for these products and the values for enriched cornmeals, pastas, farina, and rice (except riboflavin) represent the minimum levels of enrichment promulgated under the Federal Food, Drug, and Cosmetic Act of 1955. Riboflavin values of rice are for unenriched rice, as the levels for riboflavin have been stayed. Thiamin, riboflavin, and niacin values for products prepared with white flours represent the use of flours enriched at the 1974 levels and iron at the 1955 levels. Enriched flour is predominantly used in home-prepared and commercially prepared baked goods.

New fatty acid values are given for dairy products, eggs, meats, some grain products, nuts, and soups. The values are based on recent comprehensive research by USDA to update and extend tables for fatty acid content of foods.

Niacin values are for preformed niacin occurring naturally in foods. The values do not include additional niacin that the body may form from tryptophan, an essential amino acid in the protein of most foods. Among the better sources of tryptophan are milk, meats, eggs, legumes, and nuts.

Values have been calculated from the ingredients in typical recipes for many of the prepared items such as biscuits, corn muffins, macaroni and cheese, custard, and many dessert-type items.

Values for toast and cooked vegetables are without fat added, either during preparation or at the table. Some destruction of vitamins, especially ascorbic acid, may occur when vegetables are cut or shredded. Since such losses are variable, no deduction has been made.

For meat, values are for meat cooked and drained of the drippings. For many cuts, two sets of values are shown: meat including fat and meat from which the fat has been removed either in the kitchen or on the plate.

A variety of manufactured items—some of the milk products, ready-to-eat breakfast cereals, imitation cream products, fruit drinks, and various mixes—are included in table 2. Frequently these foods are fortified with one or more nutrients. If nutrients are added, this information is on the label. Values shown here for these foods are usually based on products from several manufacturers and may differ somewhat from the values provided by any one source.

TABLE 2.—NUTRITIVE VALUES OF THE EDIBLE PART OF FOODS

(Dashes (—) denote lack of reliable data for a constituent believed to be present in measurable amount)

Item No.	Foods, approximate measures, units, and weight (edible part unless footnotes indicate otherwise)		Water	Food energy	Pro-tein	Fat	Satu-rated (total)	Oleic	Lino-leic	Carbo-hydrate	Calcium	Phos-phorus	Iron	Potas-sium	Vitamin A value	Thiamin	Ribo-flavin	Niacin	Ascorbic acid
(A)	(B)		(C)	(D)	(E)	(F)	(G)	(H)	(I)	(J)	(K)	(L)	(M)	(N)	(O)	(P)	(Q)	(R)	(S)
		Grams	Per-cent	Cal-ories	Grams	Grams	Grams	Grams	Grams	Grams	Milli-grams	Milli-grams	Milli-grams	Milli-grams	Inter-national units	Milli-grams	Milli-grams	Milli-grams	Milli-grams
	DAIRY PRODUCTS (CHEESE, CREAM, IMITATION CREAM, MILK; RELATED PRODUCTS)																		
	Butter. See Fats, oils; related products, items 103–108.																		
	Cheese:																		
	Natural:																		
1	Blue	1 oz	28	42	100	6	8	5.3	1.9	0.2	1	150	110	0.1	73	200	0.01	0.11	0.3	0
2	Camembert (3 wedges per 4-oz container)	1 wedge	38	52	115	8	9	5.8	2.2	.2	Trace	147	132	.1	71	350	.01	.19	.2	0
	Cheddar:																		
3	Cut pieces	1 oz	28	37	115	7	9	6.1	2.1	.2	Trace	204	145	.2	28	300	.01	.11	Trace	0
4		1 cu in	17.2	37	70	4	6	3.7	1.3	.1	Trace	124	88	.1	17	180	Trace	.06	Trace	0
5	Shredded	1 cup	113	37	455	28	37	24.2	8.5	.7	1	815	579	.8	111	1,200	.03	.42	.1	0
	Cottage (curd not pressed down):																		
	Creamed (cottage cheese, 4% fat):																		
6	Large curd	1 cup	225	79	235	28	10	6.4	2.4	.2	6	135	297	.3	190	370	.05	.37	.3	Trace
7	Small curd	1 cup	210	79	220	26	9	6.0	2.2	.2	6	126	277	.3	177	340	.04	.34	.3	Trace
8	Low fat (2%)	1 cup	226	79	205	31	4	2.8	1.0	.1	8	155	340	.4	217	160	.05	.42	.3	Trace
9	Low fat (1%)	1 cup	226	82	165	28	2	1.5	.5	.1	6	138	302	.3	193	80	.05	.37	.3	Trace
10	Uncreamed (cottage cheese dry curd, less than 1/2% fat)	1 cup	145	80	125	25	1	.4	.1	Trace	3	46	151	.3	47	40	.04	.21	.2	0
11	Cream	1 oz	28	54	100	2	10	6.2	2.4	.2	1	23	30	.3	34	400	Trace	.06	Trace	0
	Mozzarella, made with—																		
12	Whole milk	1 oz	28	48	90	6	7	4.4	1.7	.2	1	163	117	.1	21	260	Trace	.08	Trace	0
13	Part skim milk	1 oz	28	49	80	8	5	3.1	1.2	.1	1	207	149	.1	27	180	.01	.10	Trace	0
	Parmesan, grated:																		
14	Cup, not pressed down	1 cup	100	18	455	42	30	19.1	7.7	.3	4	1,376	807	1.0	107	700	.05	.39	.3	0
15	Tablespoon	1 tbsp	5	18	25	2	2	1.0	.4	Trace	Trace	69	40	Trace	5	40	Trace	.02	Trace	0
16	Ounce	1 oz	28	18	130	12	9	5.4	2.2	.1	1	390	229	.3	30	200	.01	.11	.1	0
17	Provolone	1 oz	28	41	100	7	8	4.8	1.7	.1	1	214	141	.1	39	230	.01	.09	Trace	0
	Ricotta, made with—																		
18	Whole milk	1 cup	246	72	1,790	28	32	20.4	7.1	.7	7	509	389	.9	257	1,210	.03	.48	.3	0
19	Part skim milk	1 cup	246	74	340	28	19	12.1	4.7	.5	13	669	449	1.1	308	1,060	.05	.46	.2	0
20	Romano	1 oz	28	31	110	9	8	—	—	—	1	302	215	—	—	160	—	.11	Trace	0
21	Swiss	1 oz	28	37	105	8	8	5.0	1.7	.2	1	272	171	Trace	31	240	.01	.10	Trace	0
	Pasteurized process cheese:																		
22	American	1 oz	28	39	105	6	9	5.6	2.1	.2	Trace	174	211	.1	46	340	.01	.10	Trace	0
23	Swiss	1 oz	28	42	95	7	7	4.5	1.7	.1	1	219	216	.2	61	230	Trace	.08	Trace	0
24	Pasteurized process cheese food, American	1 oz	28	43	95	6	7	4.4	1.7	.1	2	163	130	.2	79	260	.01	.13	Trace	0
25	Pasteurized process cheese spread, American	1 oz	28	48	82	5	6	3.8	1.5	.1	2	159	202	.1	69	220	.01	.12	Trace	0
	Cream, sweet:																		
26	Half-and-half (cream and milk)	1 cup	242	81	315	7	28	17.3	7.0	.6	10	254	230	.2	314	260	.08	.36	.2	2
27		1 tbsp	15	81	20	Trace	2	1.1	.4	Trace	1	16	14	Trace	19	20	.01	.02	Trace	Trace
28	Light, coffee, or table	1 cup	240	74	470	6	46	28.8	11.7	1.0	9	231	192	.1	292	1,730	.08	.36	.1	2
29		1 tbsp	15	74	30	Trace	3	1.8	.7	.1	1	14	12	Trace	18	110	Trace	.02	Trace	Trace

DIETARY DIRECTIONS IN THE 1980s 43

TABLE 2.—NUTRITIVE VALUES OF THE EDIBLE PART OF FOODS - Continued

(Dashes (—) denote lack of reliable data for a constituent believed to be present in measurable amount)

NUTRIENTS IN INDICATED QUANTITY

Item No.	Foods, approximate measures, units, and weight (edible part unless footnotes indicate otherwise)		Grams	Water Percent	Food energy Calories	Protein Grams	Fat Grams	Fatty Acids Saturated (total) Grams	Unsaturated Oleic Grams	Unsaturated Linoleic Grams	Carbohydrate Grams	Calcium Milligrams	Phosphorus Milligrams	Iron Milligrams	Potassium Milligrams	Vitamin A value International units	Thiamin Milligrams	Riboflavin Milligrams	Niacin Milligrams	Ascorbic acid Milligrams
(A)	(B)			(C)	(D)	(E)	(F)	(G)	(H)	(I)	(J)	(K)	(L)	(M)	(N)	(O)	(P)	(Q)	(R)	(S)
	DAIRY PRODUCTS (CHEESE, CREAM, IMITATION CREAM, MILK; RELATED PRODUCTS)—Con.																			
	Whipping, unwhipped (volume about double when whipped):																			
30	Light	1 cup	239	64	700	5	74	46.2	18.3	1.5	7	166	146	0.1	231	2,690	0.06	0.30	0.1	1
31		1 tbsp	15	64	45	Trace	5	2.9	1.1	.1	Trace	10	9	Trace	15	170	Trace	.02	Trace	Trace
32	Heavy	1 cup	238	58	820	5	88	54.8	22.2	2.0	7	154	149	.1	179	3,500	.05	.26	.1	1
33		1 tbsp	15	58	80	Trace	6	3.5	1.4	.1	Trace	10	9	Trace	11	220	Trace	.02	Trace	Trace
34	Whipped topping, (pressurized)	1 cup	60	61	155	2	13	8.3	3.4	.3	7	61	54	Trace	88	550	.02	.04	Trace	0
35		1 tbsp	3	61	10	Trace	1	.4	.2	Trace	Trace	3	3	Trace	4	30	Trace	Trace	Trace	0
36	Cream, sour	1 cup	230	71	495	7	48	30.0	12.1	1.1	10	268	195	.1	331	1,820	.08	.34	.2	2
37		1 tbsp	12	71	25	Trace	3	1.6	.6	.1	1	14	10	Trace	17	90	Trace	.02	Trace	Trace
	Cream products, imitation (made with vegetable fat): Sweet: Creamers:																			
38	Liquid (frozen)	1 cup	245	77	335	2	24	22.8	.3	Trace	28	23	157	.1	467	[1]220	0	0	0	0
39		1 tbsp	15	77	20	Trace	1	1.4	Trace	0	2	1	10	Trace	29	110	0	0	0	0
40	Powdered	1 cup	94	2	515	5	33	30.6	.9	Trace	52	21	397	.1	763	[1]190	0	[1].16	0	0
41		1 tsp	2	2	10	Trace	1	.7	Trace	0	1	Trace	8	Trace	16	[1]Trace	0	[1]Trace	0	0
	Whipped topping:																			
42	Frozen	1 cup	75	50	240	1	19	16.3	1.0	.2	17	5	6	.1	14	[1]650	0	0	0	0
43		1 tbsp	4	50	15	Trace	1	.9	.1	Trace	1	Trace	Trace	Trace	1	[1]30	0	0	0	0
44	Powdered, made with whole milk.	1 cup	80	67	150	3	10	8.5	.6	.1	13	72	69	Trace	121	[1]290	.02	.09	Trace	1
45	Pressurized	1 cup	70	60	185	1	16	13.2	1.4	.2	11	4	13	Trace	13	[1]330	0	0	Trace	0
46		1 tbsp	4	60	10	Trace	1	.8	.1	Trace	1	Trace	1	Trace	1	[1]120	0	0	0	0
47	Sour dressing (imitation sour cream) made with nonfat dry milk.	1 cup	235	75	415	8	39	31.2	4.4	1.1	11	266	205	.1	380	[1]Trace	.09	.38	.2	2
48		1 tbsp	12	75	20	Trace	2	1.6	.2	.1	1	14	10	Trace	19	[1]Trace	.01	.02	Trace	Trace
49	Ice cream. See Milk desserts, frozen (items 75–80).																			
	Ice milk. See Milk desserts, frozen (items 81–83).																			
	Milk: Fluid:																			
50	Whole (3.3% fat)	1 cup	244	88	150	8	8	5.1	2.1	.2	11	291	228	.1	370	[2]310	.09	.40	.2	2
	Lowfat (2%):																			
51	No milk solids added	1 cup	244	89	120	8	5	2.9	1.2	.1	12	297	232	.1	377	500	.10	.40	.2	2
52	Milk solids added: Label claim less than 10 g of protein per cup.	1 cup	245	89	125	9	5	2.9	1.2	.1	12	313	245	.1	397	500	.10	.42	.2	2
53	Label claim 10 or more grams of protein per cup (protein fortified).	1 cup	246	88	135	10	5	3.0	1.2	.1	14	352	276	.1	447	500	.11	.48	.2	3
	Lowfat (1%):																			
54	No milk solids added	1 cup	244	90	100	8	3	1.6	.7	.1	12	300	235	.1	381	500	.10	.41	.2	2
55	Milk solids added: Label claim less than 10 g of protein per cup.	1 cup	245	90	105	9	2	1.5	.6	.1	12	313	245	.1	397	500	.10	.42	.2	2
56	Label claim 10 or more grams of protein per cup (protein fortified).	1 cup	246	89	120	10	3	1.8	.7	.1	14	349	273	.1	444	500	.11	.47	.2	3
	Nonfat (skim):																			
57	No milk solids added	1 cup	245	91	85	8	Trace	.3	.1	Trace	12	302	247	.1	406	500	.09	.37	.2	2

[1] Vitamin A value is largely from beta-carotene used for coloring. Riboflavin value for items 40–41 apply to products with added riboflavin.
[2] Applies to product without added vitamin A. With added vitamin A, value is 500 International Units (I.U.).

44 DIETARY DIRECTIONS IN THE 1980s

TABLE 2.—NUTRITIVE VALUES OF THE EDIBLE PART OF FOODS - Continued

(Dashes (—) denote lack of reliable data for a constituent believed to be present in measurable amount)

Item No. (A)	Foods, approximate measures, units, and weight (edible part unless footnotes indicate otherwise) (B)		Grams	Water (C) Percent	Food energy (D) Calories	Protein (E) Grams	Fat (F) Grams	Saturated (total) (G) Grams	Oleic (H) Grams	Linoleic (I) Grams	Carbohydrate (J) Grams	Calcium (K) Milligrams	Phosphorus (L) Milligrams	Iron (M) Milligrams	Potassium (N) Milligrams	Vitamin A value (O) International Units	Thiamin (P) Milligrams	Riboflavin (Q) Milligrams	Niacin (R) Milligrams	Ascorbic acid (S) Milligrams
	DAIRY PRODUCTS (CHEESE, CREAM, IMITATION CREAM, MILK; RELATED PRODUCTS)—Con.																			
	Milk—Continued																			
	Fluid—Continued																			
	Nonfat (skim)—Continued																			
	Milk solids added:																			
58	Label claim less than 10 g of protein per cup.	1 cup	245	90	90	9	1	0.4	0.1	Trace	12	316	255	0.1	418	500	0.10	0.43	0.2	2
59	Label claim 10 or more grams of protein per cup (protein fortified).	1 cup	246	89	100	10	1	.4	.1	Trace	14	352	275	.1	446	500	.11	.48	.2	3
60	Buttermilk	1 cup	245	90	100	8	2	1.3	.5	Trace	12	285	219	.1	371	[3]80	.08	.38	.1	2
	Canned:																			
	Evaporated, unsweetened:																			
61	Whole milk	1 cup	252	74	340	17	19	11.6	5.3	0.4	25	657	510	.5	764	[3]610	.12	.80	.5	5
62	Skim milk	1 cup	255	79	200	19	1	.3	.1	Trace	29	738	497	.7	845	[4]1,000	.11	.79	.4	3
63	Sweetened, condensed	1 cup	306	27	980	24	27	16.8	6.7	.7	166	868	775	.6	1,136	[3]1,000	.28	1.27	.6	8
	Dried:																			
64	Buttermilk	1 cup	120	3	465	41	7	4.3	1.7	.2	59	1,421	1,119	.4	1,910	[3]260	.47	1.90	1.1	7
	Nonfat instant:																			
65	Envelope, net wt., 3.2 oz[5]	1 envelope	91	4	325	32	1	.4	.1	Trace	47	1,120	896	.3	1,552	[6]2,160	.38	1.59	.8	5
66	Cup[7]	1 cup	68	4	245	24	Trace	.3	.1	Trace	35	837	670	.2	1,160	[6]1,610	.28	1.19	.6	4
	Milk beverages:																			
	Chocolate milk (commercial):																			
67	Regular	1 cup	250	82	210	8	8	5.3	2.2	.2	26	280	251	.6	417	[3]300	.09	.41	.3	2
68	Lowfat (2%)	1 cup	250	84	180	8	5	3.1	1.3	.1	26	284	254	.6	422	500	.10	.42	.3	2
69	Lowfat (1%)	1 cup	250	85	160	8	3	1.5	.7	.1	26	287	257	.6	426	500	.10	.40	.2	2
70	Eggnog (commercial)	1 cup	254	74	340	10	19	11.3	5.0	.6	34	330	278	.5	420	890	.09	.48	.3	4
	Malted milk, home-prepared with 1 cup of whole milk and 2 to 3 heaping tsp of malted milk powder (about 3/4 oz):																			
71	Chocolate	1 cup of milk plus 3/4 oz of powder.	265	81	235	9	9	5.5	—	—	29	304	265	.5	500	330	.14	.43	.7	2
72	Natural	1 cup of milk plus 3/4 oz of powder.	265	81	235	11	10	6.0	—	—	27	347	307	.3	529	380	.20	.54	1.3	2
	Shakes, thick:[8]																			
73	Chocolate, container, net wt., 10.6 oz.	1 container	300	72	355	9	8	5.0	2.0	.2	63	396	378	.9	672	260	.14	.67	.4	0
74	Vanilla, container, net wt., 11 oz.	1 container	313	74	350	12	9	5.9	2.4	.2	56	457	361	.3	572	360	.09	.61	.5	0
	Milk desserts, frozen:																			
	Ice cream:																			
	Regular (about 11% fat):																			
75	Hardened	1/2 gal	1,064	61	2,155	38	115	71.3	28.8	2.6	254	1,406	1,075	1.0	2,052	4,340	.42	2.63	1.1	6
76		1 cup	133	61	270	5	14	8.9	3.6	.3	32	176	134	.1	257	540	.05	.33	.1	1
77		3-fl oz container	50	61	100	2	5	3.4	1.4	.1	12	66	51	Trace	96	200	.02	.12	.1	Trace
78	Soft serve (frozen custard)	1 cup	173	60	375	7	23	13.5	5.9	.6	38	236	199	.4	338	790	.08	.45	.2	1
79	Rich (about 16% fat), hardened.	1/2 gal	1,188	59	2,805	33	190	118.3	47.8	4.3	256	1,213	927	.8	1,771	7,200	.36	2.27	.9	5
80		1 cup	148	59	350	4	24	14.7	6.0	.5	32	151	115	.1	221	900	.04	.28	.1	1
	Ice milk:																			
81	Hardened (about 4.3% fat)	1/2 gal	1,048	69	1,470	41	45	28.1	11.3	1.0	232	1,409	1,035	1.5	2,117	1,710	.61	2.78	.9	6
82		1 cup	131	69	185	5	6	3.5	1.4	.1	29	176	129	.1	265	210	.08	.35	.1	1

[3]Applies to product without vitamin A added.
[4]Applies to product with added vitamin A. Without added vitamin A, value is 20 International Units (I.I.).
[5]Yields 1 qt of fluid milk when reconstituted according to package directions.
[6]Applies to product with added vitamin A.
[7]Weight applies to product with label claim of 1 1/3 cups equal 3.2 oz.
[8]Applies to products made from thick shake mixes and that do not contain added ice cream. Products made from milk shake mixes are higher in fat and usually contain added ice cream.

DIETARY DIRECTIONS IN THE 1980s 45

(A)	(B)		(C)	(D)	(E)	(F)	(G)	(H)	(I)	(J)	(K)	(L)	(M)	(N)	(O)	(P)	(Q)	(R)	(S)
	DAIRY PRODUCTS (CHEESE, CREAM, IMITATION CREAM, MILK; RELATED PRODUCTS)—Con.																		
83	Soft serve (about 2.6% fat)	1 cup	175	225	8	5	2.9	1.2	0.1	38	274	202	0.3	412	180	0.12	0.54	0.2	1
84	Sherbet (about 2% fat)	1/2 gal	1,542	2,160	17	31	19.0	7.7	.7	469	827	594	2.5	1,585	1,480	.26	.71	1.0	31
85		1 cup	193	270	2	4	2.4	1.0	.1	59	103	74	.3	198	190	.03	.09	.1	4
	Milk desserts, other:																		
86	Custard, baked	1 cup	265	305	14	15	6.8	5.4	.7	29	297	310	1.1	387	930	.11	.50	.3	1
	Puddings:																		
	From home recipe:																		
	Starch base:																		
87	Chocolate	1 cup	260	385	8	12	7.6	3.3	.3	67	250	255	1.3	445	390	.05	.36	.3	1
88	Vanilla (blancmange)	1 cup	255	285	9	10	6.2	2.5	.2	41	298	232	Trace	352	410	.08	.41	.3	2
89	Tapioca cream	1 cup	165	220	8	8	4.1	2.5	.5	28	173	180	.7	223	480	.07	.30	.2	2
	From mix (chocolate) and milk:																		
90	Regular (cooked)	1 cup	260	320	9	8	4.3	2.6	.2	59	265	247	.8	354	340	.05	.39	.3	2
91	Instant	1 cup	260	325	8	7	3.6	2.2	.3	63	374	237	1.3	335	340	.08	.39	.3	2
	Yogurt:																		
	With added milk solids:																		
92	Fruit-flavored[9]	1 container, net wt., 8 oz	227	230	10	3	1.8	.6	.1	42	343	269	.2	439	[10]120	.08	.40	.2	1
93	Plain	1 container, net wt., 8 oz	227	145	12	4	2.3	.8	.1	16	415	326	.2	531	[10]150	.10	.49	.3	2
94	Made with nonfat milk	1 container, net wt., 8 oz	227	125	13	Trace	.3	.1	Trace	17	452	355	.2	579	[10]20	.11	.53	.3	2
	Without added milk solids:																		
95	Made with whole milk	1 container, net wt., 8 oz	227	140	8	7	4.8	1.7	.1	11	274	215	.1	351	280	.07	.32	.2	1
	EGGS																		
	Eggs, large (24 oz per dozen):																		
	Raw:																		
96	Whole, without shell	1 egg	50	80	6	6	1.7	2.0	.6	1	28	90	1.0	65	260	.04	.15	Trace	0
97	White	1 white	33	15	3	Trace	0	0	0	Trace	4	4	Trace	45	0	Trace	.09	Trace	0
98	Yolk	1 yolk	17	65	3	6	1.7	2.1	.6	Trace	26	86	.9	15	310	.04	.07	Trace	0
	Cooked:																		
99	Fried in butter	1 egg	46	85	5	6	2.4	2.2	.6	1	26	80	.9	58	290	.03	.13	Trace	0
100	Hard-cooked, shell removed	1 egg	50	80	6	6	1.7	2.0	.6	1	28	90	1.0	65	260	.04	.14	Trace	0
101	Poached	1 egg	50	80	6	6	1.7	2.0	.6	1	28	90	1.0	65	260	.04	.13	Trace	0
102	Scrambled (milk added) in butter. Also omelet.	1 egg	64	95	6	7	2.8	2.3	.6	1	47	97	.9	85	310	.04	.16	Trace	0
	FATS, OILS; RELATED PRODUCTS																		
	Butter:																		
	Regular (1 brick or 4 sticks per lb):																		
103	Stick (1/2 cup)	1 stick	113	815	1	92	57.3	23.1	2.1	Trace	27	26	.2	29	[11]3,470	.01	.04	Trace	0
104	Tablespoon (about 1/8 stick)	1 tbsp	14	100	Trace	12	7.2	2.9	.3	Trace	3	3	Trace	4	[11]430	Trace	Trace	Trace	0
105	Pat (1 in square, 1/3 in high; 90 per lb)	1 pat	5	35	Trace	4	2.5	1.0	.1	Trace	1	1	Trace	1	[11]150	Trace	Trace	Trace	0
	Whipped (6 sticks or two 8-oz containers per lb):																		
106	Stick (1/2 cup)	1 stick	76	540	1	61	38.2	15.4	1.4	Trace	18	17	.1	20	[11]2,310	Trace	.03	Trace	0
107	Tablespoon (about 1/8 stick)	1 tbsp	9	65	Trace	8	4.7	1.9	.2	Trace	2	2	Trace	2	[11]290	Trace	Trace	Trace	0
108	Pat (1 1/4 in square, 1/3 in high; 120 per lb)	1 pat	4	25	Trace	3	1.9	.8	.1	Trace	1	1	Trace	1	[11]120	0	Trace	Trace	0

[9] Content of fat, vitamin A, and carbohydrate varies. Consult the label when precise values are needed for special diets.
[10] Applies to product made with milk containing no added vitamin A.
[11] Based on year-round average.

46 DIETARY DIRECTIONS IN THE 1980s

TABLE 2.—NUTRITIVE VALUES OF THE EDIBLE PART OF FOODS - Continued

(Dashes (—) denote lack of reliable data for a constituent believed to be present in measurable amount)

Item No. (A)	Foods, approximate measures, units, and weight (edible part unless footnotes indicate otherwise) (B)		Grams	Water Per cent (C)	Food energy Calories (D)	Protein Grams (E)	Fat Grams (F)	Saturated (total) Grams (G)	Oleic Grams (H)	Linoleic Grams (I)	Carbohydrate Grams (J)	Calcium Milligrams (K)	Phosphorus Milligrams (L)	Iron Milligrams (M)	Potassium Milligrams (N)	Vitamin A value International units (O)	Thiamin Milligrams (P)	Riboflavin Milligrams (Q)	Niacin Milligrams (R)	Ascorbic acid Milligrams (S)
	Fats, cooking (vegetable shortenings).																			
109		1 cup	200	0	1,770	0	200	48.8	88.2	48.4	0	0	0	0	0	—	0	0	0	0
110		1 tbsp	13	0	110	0	13	3.2	5.7	3.1	0	0	0	0	0	—	0	0	0	0
111	Lard	1 cup	205	0	1,850	0	205	81.0	83.8	20.5	0	0	0	0	0	0	0	0	0	0
112		1 tbsp	13	0	115	0	13	5.1	5.3	1.3	0	0	0	0	0	0	0	0	0	0
	Margarine: Regular (1 brick or 4 sticks per lb)																			
113	Stick (1/2 cup)	1 stick	113	16	815	1	92	16.7	42.9	24.9	Trace	27	26	.2	29	[12]3,750	.01	.04	Trace	0
114	Tablespoon (about 1/8 stick)	1 tbsp	14	16	100	Trace	12	2.1	5.3	3.1	Trace	3	3	Trace	4	[12]470	Trace	Trace	Trace	0
115	Pat (1 in square, 1/3 in high; 90 per lb)	1 pat	5	16	35	Trace	4	.7	1.9	1.1	Trace	1	1	Trace	1	[12]170	Trace	Trace	Trace	0
116	Soft, two 8-oz containers per lb.	1 container	227	16	1,635	1	184	32.5	71.5	65.4	Trace	53	52	.4	59	[12]7,500	.01	.08	.1	0
117		1 tbsp	14	16	100	Trace	12	2.0	4.5	4.1	Trace	3	3	Trace	4	[12]470	Trace	Trace	Trace	0
	Whipped (6 sticks per lb):																			
118	Stick (1/2 cup)	1 stick	76	16	545	Trace	61	11.2	28.7	16.7	Trace	18	17	.1	20	[12]2,500	Trace	.03	Trace	0
119	Tablespoon (about 1/8 stick)	1 tbsp	9	16	70	Trace	8	1.4	3.6	2.1	Trace	2	2	Trace	2	[12]310	Trace	Trace	Trace	0
	Oils, salad or cooking:																			
120	Corn	1 cup	218	0	1,925	0	218	27.7	53.6	125.1	0	0	0	0	0	—	0	0	0	0
121		1 tbsp	14	0	120	0	14	1.7	3.3	7.8	0	0	0	0	0	—	0	0	0	0
122	Olive	1 cup	216	0	1,910	0	216	30.7	154.4	17.7	0	0	0	0	0	—	0	0	0	0
123		1 tbsp	14	0	120	0	14	1.9	9.7	1.1	0	0	0	0	0	—	0	0	0	0
124	Peanut	1 cup	216	0	1,910	0	216	37.4	98.5	67.0	0	0	0	0	0	—	0	0	0	0
125		1 tbsp	14	0	120	0	14	2.3	6.2	4.2	0	0	0	0	0	—	0	0	0	0
126	Safflower	1 cup	218	0	1,925	0	218	20.5	25.9	159.8	0	0	0	0	0	—	0	0	0	0
127		1 tbsp	14	0	120	0	14	1.3	1.6	10.0	0	0	0	0	0	—	0	0	0	0
128	Soybean oil, hydrogenated (partially hardened).	1 cup	218	0	1,925	0	218	31.8	93.1	75.6	0	0	0	0	0	—	0	0	0	0
129		1 tbsp	14	0	120	0	14	2.0	5.8	4.7	0	0	0	0	0	—	0	0	0	0
130	Soybean-cottonseed oil blend, hydrogenated.	1 cup	218	0	1,925	0	218	38.2	63.0	99.6	0	0	0	0	0	—	0	0	0	0
131		1 tbsp	14	0	120	0	14	2.4	3.9	6.2	0	0	0	0	0	—	0	0	0	0
	Salad dressings: Commercial: Blue cheese:																			
132	Regular	1 tbsp	15	32	75	1	8	1.6	1.7	3.8	1	12	11	Trace	6	30	Trace	.02	Trace	Trace
133	Low calorie (5 Cal per tsp)	1 tbsp	16	84	10	Trace	1	.5	.3	Trace	1	10	8	Trace	5	30	Trace	.01	Trace	Trace
	French:																			
134	Regular	1 tbsp	16	39	65	Trace	6	1.1	1.3	3.2	3	2	2	.1	13	—	—	—	—	—
135	Low calorie (5 Cal per tsp)	1 tbsp	16	77	15	Trace	1	.1	.1	.4	2	2	2	.1	13	—	—	—	—	—
	Italian:																			
136	Regular	1 tbsp	15	28	85	Trace	9	1.6	1.9	4.7	1	2	1	Trace	2	Trace	Trace	Trace	Trace	—
137	Low calorie (2 Cal per tsp)	1 tbsp	15	90	10	Trace	1	.1	.1	.4	Trace	2	1	Trace	2	Trace	Trace	Trace	Trace	—
138		1 tbsp	14	15	100	Trace	11	2.0	2.4	5.6	Trace	3	4	.1	5	40	Trace	.01	Trace	—
	Mayonnaise type:																			
139	Regular	1 tbsp	15	41	65	Trace	6	1.1	1.4	3.2	2	2	4	Trace	1	30	Trace	Trace	Trace	—
140	Low calorie (8 Cal per tsp)	1 tbsp	16	81	20	Trace	2	.4	.4	1.0	2	3	4	Trace	1	40	Trace	Trace	Trace	—
141	Tartar sauce, regular	1 tbsp	14	34	75	Trace	8	1.5	1.8	4.1	1	3	4	.1	11	30	Trace	Trace	Trace	Trace
	Thousand Island:																			
142	Regular	1 tbsp	16	32	80	Trace	8	1.4	1.7	4.0	2	2	3	.1	18	50	Trace	Trace	Trace	Trace
143	Low calorie (10 Cal per tsp)	1 tbsp	15	68	25	Trace	2	.4	.4	1.0	2	3	3	.1	17	50	Trace	Trace	Trace	Trace
	From home recipe:																			
144	Cooked type[13]	1 tbsp	16	68	25	1	2	.5	.6	.3	2	14	15	.1	19	80	.01	.03	Trace	Trace

[12] Based on average vitamin A content of fortified margarine. Federal specifications for fortified margarine require a minimum of 15,000 International Units (I.U.) of vitamin A per pound.
[13] Fatty acid values apply to product made with regular-type margarine.

FISH, SHELLFISH, MEAT, POULTRY; RELATED PRODUCTS

(A)	(B)	(C)	(D)	(E)	(F)	(G)	(H)	(I)	(J)	(K)	(L)	(M)	(N)	(O)	(P)	(Q)	(R)	(S)
	Fish and shellfish:																	
145	Bluefish, baked with butter or margarine.	3 oz	85	68	135	22	4	—	—	—	0	25	244	0.6	—	40	0.09	0.08	1.6	—
	Clams:																		
146	Raw, meat only	3 oz	85	82	65	11	1	0.2	Trace	—	2	59	138	5.2	154	90	.08	.15	1.1	—
147	Canned, solids and liquid	3 oz	85	86	45	7	1	.6	0.4	Trace	2	47	116	3.5	119	—	.01	.09	.9	8
148	Crabmeat (white or king), canned, not pressed down.	1 cup	135	77	135	24	3			0.1	1	61	246	1.1	149	—	.11	.11	2.6	—
149	Fish sticks, breaded, cooked, frozen (stick, 4 by 1 by 1/2 in).	1 fish stick or 1 oz	28	66	50	5	3	—	—	—	2	3	47	.1	—	0	.01	.02	.5	—
150	Haddock, breaded, fried[14]	3 oz	85	66	140	17	5	1.4	2.2	1.2	5	34	210	1.0	296	—	.03	.06	2.7	2
151	Ocean perch, breaded, fried[14]	1 fillet	85	59	195	16	11	2.7	4.4	2.3	6	28	192	1.1	242	—	.10	.10	1.6	—
152	Oysters, raw, meat only (13-19 medium Selects).	1 cup	240	85	160	20	4	1.3	.2	.1	8	226	343	13.2	290	740	.34	.43	6.0	—
153	Salmon, pink, canned, solids and liquid.	3 oz	85	71	120	17	5	.9	.8	.1	0	[15]167	243	.7	307	60	.03	.16	6.8	—
154	Sardines, Atlantic, canned in oil, drained solids.	3 oz	85	62	175	20	9	3.0	2.5	.5	0	372	424	2.5	502	190	.02	.17	4.6	—
155	Scallops, frozen, breaded, fried, reheated.	6 scallops	90	60	175	16	8	—	—	—	9	—	—	—	—	—	—	—	—	—
156	Shad, baked with butter or margarine, bacon.	3 oz	85	64	170	20	10	—	—	—	0	20	266	.5	320	30	.11	.22	7.3	—
	Shrimp:																		
157	Canned meat	3 oz	85	70	100	21	1	.1	.1	Trace	1	98	224	2.6	104	50	.01	.03	1.5	—
158	French fried[16]	3 oz	85	57	190	17	9	2.3	3.7	2.0	9	61	162	1.7	195	—	.03	.07	2.3	—
159	Tuna, canned in oil, drained solids.	3 oz	85	61	170	24	7	1.7	1.7	.7	0	7	199	1.6	—	70	.04	.10	10.1	—
160	Tuna salad[17]	1 cup	205	70	350	30	22	4.3	6.3	6.7	7	41	291	2.7	—	590	.08	.23	10.3	2
161	Bacon, (20 slices per lb, raw), broiled or fried, crisp.	2 slices	15	8	85	4	8	2.5	3.7	.7	Trace	2	34	.5	35	0	.08	.05	.8	—
	Beef,[18] cooked:																		
	Cuts braised, simmered or pot roasted:																		
162	Lean and fat (piece, 2 1/2 by 2 1/2 by 3/4 in).	3 oz	85	53	245	23	16	6.8	6.5	.4	0	10	114	2.9	184	30	.04	.18	3.6	—
163	Lean only from item 162	2.5 oz	72	62	140	22	5	2.1	1.8	.2	0	10	108	2.7	176	10	.04	.17	3.3	—
	Ground beef, broiled:																		
164	Lean with 10% fat	3 oz or patty 3 by 5/8 in	85	60	185	23	10	4.0	3.9	.3	0	10	196	3.0	261	20	.08	.20	5.1	—
165	Lean with 21% fat	2.9 oz or patty 3 by 5/8 in	82	54	235	20	17	7.0	6.7	.4	0	9	159	2.6	221	30	.07	.17	4.4	—
	Roast, oven cooked, no liquid added:																		
	Relatively fat, such as rib:																		
166	Lean and fat (2 pieces, 4 1/8 by 2 1/4 by 1/4 in).	3 oz	85	40	375	17	33	14.0	13.6	.8	0	8	158	2.2	189	70	.05	.13	3.1	—
167	Lean only from item 166	1.8 oz	51	57	125	14	7	3.0	2.5	.3	0	6	131	1.8	161	10	.04	.11	2.6	—
	Relatively lean, such as heel of round:																		
168	Lean and fat (2 pieces, 4 1/8 by 2 1/4 by 1/4 in).	3 oz	85	62	165	25	7	2.8	2.7	.2	0	11	208	3.2	279	10	.06	.19	4.5	—

[14] Dipped in egg, milk or water, and breadcrumbs; fried in vegetable shortening.
[15] If bones are discarded, value for calcium will be greatly reduced.
[16] Dipped in egg, breadcrumbs, and flour or batter.
[17] Prepared with tuna, celery, salad dressing (mayonnaise type), pickle, onion, and egg.
[18] Outer layer of fat on the cut was removed to within approximately 1/2 in of the lean. Deposits of fat within the cut were not removed.

48 DIETARY DIRECTIONS IN THE 1980s

TABLE 2.—NUTRITIVE VALUES OF THE EDIBLE PART OF FOODS - Continued

(Dashes (—) denote lack of reliable data for a constituent believed to be present in measurable amount)

Item No. (A)	Foods, approximate measures, units, and weight (edible part unless footnotes indicate otherwise) (B)	Grams	Water (C) Percent	Food energy (D) Calories	Protein (E) Grams	Fat (F) Grams	Saturated (total) (G) Grams	Oleic (H) Grams	Linoleic (I) Grams	Carbohydrate (J) Grams	Calcium (K) Milligrams	Phosphorus (L) Milligrams	Iron (M) Milligrams	Potassium (N) Milligrams	Vitamin A value (O) International units	Thiamin (P) Milligrams	Riboflavin (Q) Milligrams	Niacin (R) Milligrams	Ascorbic acid (S) Milligrams
	FISH, SHELLFISH, MEAT, POULTRY; RELATED PRODUCTS—Con.																		
	Meat and meat products—Continued																		
	Beef,[18] cooked—Continued																		
	Roast, oven cooked, no liquid added—Continued																		
	Relatively lean such as heel of round—Continued																		
169	Lean only from item 168---- 2.8 oz	78	65	125	24	3	1.2	1.0	0.1	0	10	199	3.0	268	Trace	0.06	0.18	4.3	—
	Steak:																		
	Relatively fat-sirloin, broiled:																		
170	Lean and fat (piece, 2 1/2 by 2 1/2 by 3/4 in). 3 oz	85	44	330	20	27	11.3	11.1	.6	0	9	162	2.5	220	50	.05	.15	4.0	—
171	Lean only from item 170---- 2.0 oz	56	59	115	18	4	1.8	1.6	.2	0	7	146	2.2	202	10	.05	.14	3.6	—
	Relatively lean-round, braised:																		
172	Lean and fat (piece, 4 1/8 by 2 1/4 by 1/2 in). 3 oz	85	55	220	24	13	5.5	5.2	.4	0	10	213	3.0	272	20	.07	.19	4.8	—
173	Lean only from item 172---- 2.4 oz	68	61	130	21	4	1.7	1.5	.2	0	9	182	2.5	238	10	.05	.16	4.1	—
	Beef, canned:																		
174	Corned beef---- 3 oz	85	59	185	22	10	4.9	4.5	.2	0	17	90	3.7	—	—	.01	.20	2.9	—
175	Corned beef hash---- 1 cup	220	67	400	19	25	11.9	10.9	.5	24	29	147	4.4	440	—	.02	.20	4.6	—
176	Beef, dried, chipped---- 2 1/2-oz jar	71	48	145	24	4	2.1	2.0	.1	0	14	287	3.6	142	—	.05	.23	2.7	0
177	Beef and vegetable stew---- 1 cup	245	82	220	16	11	4.9	4.5	.2	15	29	184	2.9	613	2,400	.15	.17	4.7	17
178	Beef potpie (home recipe) baked,[19] (piece, 1/3 of 9-in diam. pie) 1 piece	210	55	515	21	30	7.9	12.8	6.7	39	29	149	3.8	334	1,720	.30	.30	5.5	6
179	Chili con carne with beans, canned. 1 cup	255	72	340	19	16	7.5	6.8	.3	31	82	321	4.3	594	150	.08	.18	3.3	—
180	Chop suey with beef and pork (home recipe). 1 cup	250	75	300	26	17	8.5	6.2	.7	13	60	248	4.8	425	600	.28	.38	5.0	33
181	Heart, beef, lean, braised---- 3 oz	85	61	160	27	5	1.5	1.1	.6	1	5	154	5.0	197	20	.21	1.04	6.5	1
	Lamb, cooked:																		
	Chop, rib (cut 3 per lb with bone), broiled:																		
182	Lean and fat---- 3.1 oz	89	43	360	18	32	14.8	12.1	1.2	0	8	139	1.0	200	—	.11	.19	4.1	—
183	Lean only from item 182---- 2 oz	57	60	120	16	6	2.5	2.1	.2	0	6	121	1.1	174	—	.09	.15	3.4	—
	Leg, roasted:																		
184	Lean and fat (2 pieces, 4 1/8 by 2 1/4 by 1/4 in). 3 oz	85	54	235	22	16	7.3	6.0	.6	0	9	177	1.4	241	—	.13	.23	4.7	—
185	Lean only from item 184---- 2.5 oz	71	62	130	20	5	2.1	1.8	.2	0	9	169	1.4	227	—	.12	.21	4.4	—
	Shoulder, roasted:																		
186	Lean and fat (3 pieces, 2 1/2 by 2 1/2 by 1/4 in). 3 oz	85	50	285	18	23	10.8	8.8	.9	0	9	146	1.0	206	—	.11	.20	4.0	—
187	Lean only from item 186---- 2.3 oz	64	61	130	17	6	3.6	2.3	.2	0	8	140	1.0	193	—	.10	.18	3.7	—
188	Liver, beef, fried[20] (slice, 6 1/2 by 2 3/8 by 3/8 in). 3 oz	85	56	195	22	9	2.5	3.5	.9	5	9	405	7.5	323	[21]45,390	.22	3.56	14.0	23
	Pork, cured, cooked:																		
189	Ham, light cure, lean and fat, roasted (2 pieces, 4 1/8 by 2 1/4 by 1/4 in).[22] 3 oz	85	54	245	18	19	6.8	7.9	1.7	0	8	146	2.2	199	0	.40	.15	3.1	—
	Luncheon meat:																		
190	Boiled ham, slice (8 per 8-oz pkg.). 1 oz	28	59	65	5	5	1.7	2.0	.4	0	3	47	.8	—	0	.12	.04	.7	—
191	Canned, spiced or unspiced: Slice, approx. 3 by 2 by 1/2 in. 1 slice	60	55	175	9	15	5.4	6.7	1.0	1	5	65	1.3	133	0	.19	.13	1.8	—

[18] Outer layer of fat on the cut was removed to within approximately 1/2 in of the lean. Deposits of fat within the cut were not removed.
[19] Crust made with vegetable shortening and enriched flour.
[20] Regular-type margarine used.
[21] Value varies widely.
[22] About one-fourth of the outer layer of fat on the cut was removed. Deposits of fat within the cut were not removed.

DIETARY DIRECTIONS IN THE 1980s   49

(A)	(B)		(C)	(D)	(E)	(F)	(G)	(H)	(I)	(J)	(K)	(L)	(M)	(N)	(O)	(P)	(Q)	(R)	(S)
	Pork, fresh,[18] cooked:																		
	Chop, loin (cut 3 per lb with bone), broiled:																		
192	Lean and fat	2.7 oz	78	42	305	19	25	8.9	10.4	2.2	0	9	209	2.7	216	0	0.75	0.22	4.5	—
193	Lean only from item 192	2 oz	56	53	150	17	9	3.1	3.6	.8	0	7	181	2.2	192	0	.63	.18	3.8	—
194	Roast, oven cooked, no liquid added: Lean and fat (piece, 2 1/2 by 2 1/2 by 3/4 in).	3 oz	85	46	310	21	24	8.7	10.2	2.2	0	9	218	2.7	233	0	.78	.22	4.8	—
195	Lean only from item 194	2.4 oz	68	55	175	20	10	3.5	4.1	.8	0	9	211	2.6	224	0	.73	.21	4.4	—
196	Shoulder cut, simmered: Lean and fat (3 pieces, 2 1/2 by 2 1/2 by 1/4 in).	3 oz	85	46	320	20	26	9.3	10.9	2.3	0	9	118	2.6	158	0	.46	.21	4.1	—
197	Lean only from item 196	2.2 oz	63	60	135	18	6	2.2	2.6	.6	0	8	111	2.3	146	0	.42	.19	3.7	—
	Sausages (see also Luncheon meat (items 190-191)):																			
198	Bologna, slice (8 per 8-oz pkg.).	1 slice	28	56	85	3	8	3.0	3.4	.5	Trace	2	36	.5	65	—	.05	.06	.7	—
199	Braunschweiger, slice (6 per 6-oz pkg.).	1 slice	28	53	90	4	8	2.6	3.4	.8	1	3	69	1.7	—	1,850	.05	.41	2.3	—
200	Brown and serve (10-11 per 8-oz pkg.), browned.	1 link	17	40	70	3	6	2.3	2.8	.7	Trace	—	—	—	—	—	—	—	—	—
201	Deviled ham, canned	1 tbsp	13	51	45	2	4	1.5	1.8	.4	0	1	12	.3	—	0	.02	.01	.2	—
202	Frankfurter (8 per 1-lb pkg.), cooked (reheated).	1 frankfurter	56	57	170	7	15	5.6	6.5	1.2	1	3	57	.8	—	—	.08	.11	1.4	—
203	Meat, potted (beef, chicken, turkey), canned.	1 tbsp	13	61	30	2	2	—	—	—	0	—	—	—	—	—	Trace	.03	.2	—
204	Pork link (16 per 1-lb pkg.), cooked.	1 link	13	35	60	2	6	2.1	2.4	.5	Trace	1	21	.3	35	0	.10	.04	.5	—
	Salami:																			
205	Dry type, slice (12 per 4-oz pkg.).	1 slice	10	30	45	2	4	1.6	1.6	.1	Trace	1	28	.4	—	—	.04	.03	.5	—
206	Cooked type, slice (8 per 8-oz pkg.).	1 slice	28	51	90	5	7	3.1	3.0	.2	Trace	3	57	.7	—	—	.07	.07	1.2	—
207	Vienna sausage (7 per 4-oz can).	1 sausage	16	63	40	2	3	1.2	1.4	.2	Trace	1	24	.3	—	—	.01	.02	.4	—
	Veal, medium fat, cooked, bone removed:																			
208	Cutlet (4 1/8 by 2 1/4 by 1/2 in), braised or broiled.	3 oz	85	60	185	23	9	4.0	3.4	.4	0	9	196	2.7	258	0	.06	.21	4.6	—
209	Rib (2 pieces, 4 1/8 by 2 1/4 by 1/4 in), roasted.	3 oz	85	55	230	23	14	6.1	5.1	.6	0	10	211	2.9	259	—	.11	.26	6.6	—
	Poultry and poultry products:																			
	Chicken, cooked:																			
210	Breast, fried,[23] bones removed, 1/2 breast (3.3 oz with bones).	2.8 oz	79	58	160	26	5	1.4	1.8	1.1	1	9	218	1.3	—	70	.04	.17	11.6	—
211	Drumstick, fried,[23] bones removed (2 oz with bones).	1.3 oz	38	55	90	12	4	1.1	1.3	.9	Trace	6	89	.9	—	50	.03	.15	2.7	—
212	Half broiler, broiled, bones removed (10.4 oz with bones).	6.2 oz	176	71	240	42	7	2.2	2.5	1.3	0	16	355	3.0	483	160	.09	.34	15.5	—
213	Chicken, canned, boneless	3 oz	85	65	170	18	10	3.2	3.8	2.0	0	18	210	1.3	117	200	.03	.11	3.7	3
214	Chicken a la king, cooked (home recipe).	1 cup	245	68	470	27	34	12.7	14.3	3.3	12	127	358	2.5	404	1,130	.10	.42	5.4	12
215	Chicken and noodles, cooked (home recipe).	1 cup	240	71	365	22	18	5.9	7.1	3.5	26	26	247	2.2	149	430	.05	.17	4.3	Trace

[23]Vegetable shortening used.

50 DIETARY DIRECTIONS IN THE 1980s

TABLE 2.— NUTRITIVE VALUES OF THE EDIBLE PART OF FOODS - Continued

(Dashes (—) denote lack of reliable data for a constituent believed to be present in measurable amount)

Item No.	Foods, approximate measures, units, and weight (edible part unless footnotes indicate otherwise)			Water	Food energy	Protein	Fat	Fatty Acids Saturated (total)	Unsaturated Oleic	Linoleic	Carbohydrate	Calcium	Phosphorus	Iron	Potassium	Vitamin A value	Thiamin	Riboflavin	Niacin	Ascorbic acid
(A)	(B)			(C)	(D)	(E)	(F)	(G)	(H)	(I)	(J)	(K)	(L)	(M)	(N)	(O)	(P)	(Q)	(R)	(S)
			Grams	Percent	Calories	Grams	Grams	Grams	Grams	Grams	Grams	Milligrams	Milligrams	Milligrams	Milligrams	International units	Milligrams	Milligrams	Milligrams	Milligrams
	Poultry and poultry products—Continued																			
	Chicken chow mein:																			
216	Canned	1 cup	250	89	95	7	Trace	—	—	—	18	45	85	1.3	418	150	0.05	0.10	1.0	13
217	From home recipe	1 cup	250	78	255	31	10	2.4	3.4	3.1	10	58	293	2.5	473	280	.08	.23	4.3	10
218	Chicken potpie (home recipe); baked,[19] piece (1/3 or 9-in diam. pie)	1 piece	232	57	545	23	31	11.3	10.9	5.6	42	70	232	3.0	343	3,090	.34	.31	5.5	5
	Turkey, roasted, flesh without skin:																				
219	Dark meat, piece, 2 1/2 by 1 5/8 by 1/4 in.	4 pieces	85	61	175	26	7	2.1	1.5	1.5	0	—	—	2.0	338	—	.03	.20	3.6	—
220	Light meat, piece, 4 by 2 by 1/4 in.	2 pieces	85	62	150	28	3	.9	.6	.7	0	—	—	1.0	349	—	.04	.12	9.4	—
	Light and dark meat:																				
221	Chopped or diced	1 cup	140	61	265	44	9	2.5	1.7	1.8	0	11	351	2.5	514	—	.07	.25	10.8	—
222	Pieces (1 slice white meat, 4 by 2 by 1/4 in with 2 slices dark meat, 2 1/2 by 1 5/8 by 1/4 in).	3 pieces	85	61	160	27	5	1.5	1.0	1.1	0	7	213	1.5	312	—	.04	.15	6.5	—
	FRUITS AND FRUIT PRODUCTS																				
	Apples, raw, unpeeled, without cores:																				
223	2 3/4-in diam. (about 3 per lb with cores).	1 apple	138	84	80	Trace	1	—	—	—	20	10	14	.4	152	120	.04	.03	.1	6
224	3 1/4 in diam (about 2 per lb with cores).	1 apple	212	84	125	Trace	1	—	—	—	31	15	21	.6	233	190	.06	.04	.2	8
225	Applejuice, bottled or canned[24]	1 cup	248	88	120	Trace	Trace	—	—	—	30	15	22	1.5	250	—	.02	.05	.2	[2]2
	Applesauce, canned:																				
226	Sweetened	1 cup	255	76	230	1	Trace	—	—	—	61	10	13	1.3	166	100	.05	.03	.1	[2]3
227	Unsweetened	1 cup	244	89	100	Trace	Trace	—	—	—	26	10	12	1.2	190	100	.05	.02	.1	[2]2
	Apricots:																				
228	Raw, without pits (about 12 per lb with pits).	3 apricots	107	85	55	1	Trace	—	—	—	14	18	25	.5	301	2,890	.03	.04	.6	11
229	Canned in heavy syrup (halves and sirup).	1 cup	258	77	220	2	Trace	—	—	—	57	28	39	.8	604	4,490	.05	.05	1.0	10
	Dried:																				
230	Uncooked (28 large or 37 medium halves per cup).	1 cup	130	25	340	7	1	—	—	—	86	87	140	7.2	1,273	14,170	.01	.21	4.3	16
231	Cooked, unsweetened, fruit and liquid.	1 cup	250	76	215	4	1	—	—	—	54	55	88	4.5	795	7,500	.01	.13	2.5	8
232	Apricot nectar, canned	1 cup	251	85	145	1	Trace	—	—	—	37	23	30	.5	379	2,380	.03	.03	.5	[2]36
	Avocados, raw, whole, without skins and seeds:																				
233	California, mid- and late-winter (with skin and seed, 3 1/8-in diam.; wt., 10 oz).	1 avocado	216	74	370	5	37	5.5	22.0	3.7	13	22	91	1.3	1,303	630	.24	.43	3.5	30
234	Florida, late summer and fall (with skin and seed, 3 5/8-in diam.; wt., 1 lb).	1 avocado	304	78	390	4	33	6.7	15.7	5.3	27	30	128	1.8	1,836	880	.33	.61	4.9	43
235	Banana without peel (about 2.6 per lb with peel).	1 banana	119	76	100	1	Trace	—	—	—	26	10	31	.8	440	230	.06	.07	.8	12
236	Banana flakes	1 tbsp	6	3	20	Trace	Trace	—	—	—	5	2	6	.2	92	50	.01	.01	.2	Trace

[19] Crust made with vegetable shortening and enriched flour.
[24] Also applies to pasteurized apple cider.

DIETARY DIRECTIONS IN THE 1980s 51

FRUITS AND FRUIT PRODUCTS—Con.

(A)		(B)	(C)	(D)	(E)	(I)	(G)	(H)	(I)	(K)	(L)	(M)	(N)	(O)	(P)	(Q)	(R)	(S)
237	Blackberries, raw	1 cup	144	85	85	2	1	—	19	46	27	1.3	245	290	0.04	0.06	0.6	30
238	Blueberries, raw	1 cup	145	83	90	2	1	—	22	22	19	1.5	117	150	.04	.09	.7	20
	Cantaloup. See Muskmelons (item 271).																	
	Cherries:																	
239	Sour (tart), red, pitted, canned, water pack	1 cup	244	88	105	2	Trace	—	26	37	32	.7	317	1,660	.07	.05	.5	12
240	Sweet, raw, without pits and stems	10 cherries	68	80	45	1	Trace	—	12	15	13	.3	129	70	.03	.04	.3	7
241	Cranberry juice cocktail, bottled, sweetened	1 cup	253	83	165	Trace	Trace	—	42	13	8	.8	25	Trace	.03	.03	.1	[2][7]81
242	Cranberry sauce, sweetened, canned, strained	1 cup	277	62	405	Trace	1	—	104	17	11	.6	83	60	.03	.03	.1	6
	Dates:																	
243	Whole, without pits	10 dates	80	23	220	2	Trace	—	58	47	50	2.4	518	40	.07	.08	1.8	0
244	Chopped	1 cup	178	23	490	4	1	—	130	105	112	5.3	1,153	90	.16	.18	3.9	0
245	Fruit cocktail, canned, in heavy sirup	1 cup	255	80	195	1	Trace	—	50	23	31	1.0	411	360	.05	.03	1.0	5
	Grapefruit: Raw, medium, 3 3/4-in diam. (about 1 lb 1 oz):																	
246	Pink or red	1/2 grapefruit with peel[28]	241	89	50	1	Trace	—	13	20	20	.5	166	540	.05	.02	.2	44
247	White	1/2 grapefruit with peel[28]	241	89	45	1	Trace	—	12	19	19	.5	159	10	.05	.02	.2	44
248	Canned, sections with sirup	1 cup	254	81	180	2	Trace	—	45	33	36	.8	343	30	.08	.05	.5	76
	Grapefruit juice:																	
249	Raw, pink, red, or white	1 cup	246	90	95	1	Trace	—	23	22	37	.5	399	([29])	.10	.05	.5	93
	Canned, white:																	
250	Unsweetened	1 cup	247	89	100	1	Trace	—	24	20	35	1.0	400	20	.07	.05	.5	84
251	Sweetened	1 cup	250	86	135	1	Trace	—	32	20	35	1.0	405	30	.08	.05	.5	78
	Frozen, concentrate, unsweetened:																	
252	Undiluted, 6-fl oz can	1 can	207	62	300	4	1	—	72	70	124	.8	1,250	60	.29	.12	1.4	286
253	Diluted with 3 parts water by volume	1 cup	247	89	100	1	Trace	—	24	25	42	.2	420	20	.10	.04	.5	96
254	Dehydrated crystals, prepared with water (1 lb yields about 1 gal)	1 cup	247	90	100	1	Trace	—	24	22	40	.2	412	20	.10	.05	.5	91
	Grapes, European type (adherent skin), raw:																	
255	Thompson Seedless	10 grapes	50	81	35	Trace	Trace	—	9	6	10	.2	87	50	.03	.02	.2	2
256	Tokay and Emperor, seeded types	10 grapes[30]	60	81	40	Trace	Trace	—	10	7	11	.2	99	60	.03	.02	.2	2
257	Grapejuice: Canned or bottled	1 cup	253	83	165	1	Trace	—	42	28	30	.8	293	—	.10	.05	.5	[25]Trace
	Frozen concentrate, sweetened:																	
258	Undiluted, 6-fl oz can	1 can	216	53	395	1	Trace	—	100	22	32	.9	255	40	.13	.22	1.5	[31]32
259	Diluted with 3 parts water by volume	1 cup	250	86	135	1	Trace	—	33	8	10	.3	85	10	.05	.08	.5	[31]10
260	Grape drink, canned	1 cup	250	86	135	Trace	Trace	—	35	8	10	.3	88	—	[32].03	[32].03	.3	([32])
261	Lemon, raw, size 165, without peel and seeds (about 4 per lb with peels and seeds)	1 lemon	74	90	20	1	Trace	—	6	19	12	.4	102	10	.03	.01	.1	39
	Lemon juice:																	
262	Raw	1 cup	244	91	60	1	Trace	—	20	17	24	.5	344	50	.07	.02	.2	112

[25]Applies to product without added ascorbic acid. For value of product with added ascorbic acid, refer to label.
[26]Based on product with label claim of 45% of U.S. RDA in 6 fl oz.
[27]Based on product with label claim of 100% of U.S. RDA in 6 fl oz.
[28]Weight includes peel and membranes between sections. Without these parts, the weight of the edible portion is 123 g for item 246 and 118 g for item 247.
[29]For white-fleshed varieties, value is about 20 International Units (I.U.) per cup; for red-fleshed varieties, 1,080 I.U.
[30]Weight includes seeds. Without seeds, weight of the edible portion is 57 g.
[31]Applies to product without added ascorbic acid. With added ascorbic acid, based on claim that 6 fl oz of reconstituted juice contain 45% or 50% of the U.S. RDA, value in milligrams is 108 or 120 for a 6-fl oz can (item 258), 36 or 40 for 1 cup of diluted juice (item 259).
[32]For products with added thiamin and riboflavin but without added ascorbic acid, values in milligrams would be 0.60 for thiamin, 0.80 for riboflavin, and trace for ascorbic acid. For products with only ascorbic acid added, value varies with the brand. Consult the label.

52 DIETARY DIRECTIONS IN THE 1980s

TABLE 2.—NUTRITIVE VALUES OF THE EDIBLE PART OF FOODS - Continued

(Dashes (—) denote lack of reliable data for a constituent believed to be present in measurable amount)

Item No. (A)	Foods, approximate measures, units, and weight (edible part unless footnotes indicate otherwise) (B)		Grams	Water (C) Percent	Food energy (D) Calories	Protein (E) Grams	Fat (F) Grams	Saturated (total) (G) Grams	Oleic (H) Grams	Linoleic (I) Grams	Carbohydrate (J) Grams	Calcium (K) Milligrams	Phosphorus (L) Milligrams	Iron (M) Milligrams	Potassium (N) Milligrams	Vitamin A value (O) International units	Thiamin (P) Milligrams	Riboflavin (Q) Milligrams	Niacin (R) Milligrams	Ascorbic acid (S) Milligrams
	FRUITS AND FRUIT PRODUCTS—Con.																			
263	Canned, or bottled, unsweetened, single strength, unsweetened, 6-fl oz can.	1 cup	244	92	55	1	Trace	—	—	—	19	17	24	.5	344	50	.07	.02	.2	102
264	Frozen, single strength, unsweetened, 6-fl oz can.	1 can	183	92	40	1	Trace	—	—	—	13	13	16	.5	258	40	.05	.02	.2	81
	Lemonade concentrate, frozen:																			
265	Undiluted, 6-fl oz can	1 can	219	49	425	Trace	Trace	—	—	—	112	9	13	.4	153	40	.05	.06	.7	66
266	Diluted with 4 1/3 parts water by volume.	1 cup	248	89	105	Trace	Trace	—	—	—	28	2	3	.1	40	10	.01	.02	.2	17
	Limeade concentrate, frozen:																			
267	Undiluted, 6-fl oz can	1 can	218	50	410	Trace	Trace	—	—	—	108	11	13	0.2	129	Trace	0.02	0.02	0.2	26
268	Diluted with 4 1/3 parts water by volume.	1 cup	247	89	100	Trace	Trace	—	—	—	27	3	3	Trace	32	Trace	Trace	Trace	Trace	6
	Limejuice:																			
269	Raw	1 cup	246	90	65	1	Trace	—	—	—	22	22	27	.5	256	20	.05	.02	.2	79
270	Canned, unsweetened	1 cup	246	90	65	1	Trace	—	—	—	22	22	27	.5	256	20	.05	.02	.2	52
	Muskmelons, raw, with rind, without seed cavity:																			
271	Cantaloup, orange-fleshed (with rind and seed cavity, 5-in diam., 2 1/3 lb).	1/2 melon with rind[33]	477	91	80	2	Trace	—	—	—	20	38	44	1.1	682	9,240	.11	.08	1.6	90
272	Honeydew (with rind and seed cavity, 6 1/2-in diam., 5 1/4 lb).	1/10 melon with rind[33]	226	91	50	1	Trace	—	—	—	11	21	24	.6	374	60	.06	.04	.9	34
	Oranges, all commercial varieties, raw:																			
273	Whole, 2 5/8-in diam., without peel and seeds (about 2 1/2 per lb with peel and seeds).	1 orange	131	86	65	1	Trace	—	—	—	16	54	26	.5	263	260	.13	.05	.5	66
274	Sections without membranes	1 cup	180	86	90	2	Trace	—	—	—	22	74	36	.7	360	360	.18	.07	.7	90
	Orange juice:																			
275	Raw, all varieties	1 cup	248	88	110	2	Trace	—	—	—	26	27	42	.5	496	500	.22	.07	1.0	124
276	Canned, unsweetened	1 cup	249	87	120	2	Trace	—	—	—	28	25	45	1.0	496	500	.17	.05	.7	100
	Frozen concentrate:																			
277	Undiluted, 6-fl oz can	1 can	213	55	360	5	Trace	—	—	—	87	75	126	.9	1,500	1,620	.68	.11	2.8	360
278	Diluted with 3 parts water by volume.	1 cup	249	87	120	2	Trace	—	—	—	29	25	42	.2	503	540	.23	.03	.9	120
279	Dehydrated crystals, prepared with water (1 lb yields about 1 gal).	1 cup	248	88	115	1	Trace	—	—	—	27	25	40	.5	518	500	.20	.07	1.0	109
	Orange and grapefruit juice: Frozen concentrate:																			
280	Undiluted, 6-fl oz can	1 can	210	59	330	4	1	—	—	—	78	61	99	.8	1,308	800	.48	.06	2.3	302
281	Diluted with 3 parts water by volume.	1 cup	248	88	110	1	Trace	—	—	—	26	20	32	.2	439	270	.15	.02	.7	102
282	Papayas, raw, 1/2-in cubes	1 cup	140	89	55	1	Trace	—	—	—	14	28	22	.4	328	2,450	.06	.06	.4	78
	Peaches:																			
283	Raw: Whole, 2 1/2-in diam., peeled, pitted (about 4 per lb with peels and pits).	1 peach	100	89	40	1	Trace	—	—	—	10	9	19	.5	202	[34]1,330	.02	.05	1.0	7
284	Sliced	1 cup	170	89	65	1	Trace	—	—	—	16	15	32	.9	343	[34]2,260	.03	.09	1.7	12
	Canned, yellow-fleshed, solids and liquid (halves or slices):																			
285	Sirup pack	1 cup	256	79	200	1	Trace	—	—	—	51	10	31	.8	333	1,100	.03	.05	1.5	8
286	Water pack	1 cup	244	91	75	1	Trace	—	—	—	20	10	32	.7	334	1,100	.02	.07	1.5	7
	Dried:																			
287	Uncooked	1 cup	160	25	420	5	1	—	—	—	109	77	187	9.6	1,520	6,240	.02	.30	8.5	29
288	Cooked, unsweetened, halves and juice.	1 cup	250	77	205	3	1	—	—	—	54	38	93	4.8	743	3,050	.01	.15	3.8	5

[33] Weight includes rind. Without rind, the weight of the edible portion is 272 g for item 271 and 149 g for item 272.
[34] Represents yellow-fleshed varieties. For white-fleshed varieties, value is 50 International Units (I.U.) for 1 peach, 90 I.U. for 1 cup of slices.

DIETARY DIRECTIONS IN THE 1980s 53

(A)	(B)	(C)	(D)	(E)	(F)	(G)	(H)	(I)	(J)	(K)	(L)	(M)	(N)	(O)	(P)	(Q)	(R)	(S)
	Frozen, sliced, sweetened:																	
289	10-oz container	284	77	250	1	Trace	—	—	—	64	11	37	1.4	352	1,850	0.03	0.11	2.0	[35]116
290	Cup	250	77	220	1	Trace	—	—	—	57	10	33	1.3	310	1,630	.03	.10	1.8	[35]103
	Pears:																		
291	Raw, with skin, cored: Bartlett, 2 1/2-in diam. (about 2 1/2 per lb with cores and stems)	164	83	100	1	1	—	—	—	25	13	18	.5	213	30	.03	.07	.2	7
292	Bosc, 2 1/2-in diam. (about 3 per lb with cores and stems)	141	83	85	1	1	—	—	—	22	11	16	.4	83	30	.03	.06	.1	6
293	D'Anjou, 3-in diam. (about 2 per lb with cores and stems)	200	83	120	1	1	—	—	—	31	16	22	.6	260	40	.04	.08	.2	8
294	Canned, solids and liquid, sirup pack, heavy (halves or slices)	255	80	195	1	1	—	—	—	50	13	18	.5	214	10	.03	.05	.3	3
	Pineapple:																		
295	Raw, diced	155	85	80	1	Trace	—	—	—	21	26	12	.8	226	110	.14	.05	.3	26
	Canned, heavy sirup pack, solids and liquid:																		
296	Crushed, chunks, tidbits	255	80	190	1	Trace	—	—	—	49	28	13	.8	245	130	.20	.05	.5	18
	Slices and liquid:																		
297	Large	105	80	80	Trace	Trace	—	—	—	20	12	5	.3	101	50	.08	.02	.2	7
298	Medium	58	80	45	Trace	Trace	—	—	—	11	6	3	.2	56	30	.05	.01	.1	4
299	Pineapple juice, unsweetened, canned	250	86	140	1	Trace	—	—	—	34	38	23	.8	373	130	.13	.05	.5	[2]80
	Plums:																		
300	Raw, without pits: Japanese and hybrid (2 1/8-in diam., about 6 1/2 per lb with pits)	66	87	30	Trace	Trace	—	—	—	8	8	12	.3	112	160	.02	.02	.3	4
301	Prune-type (1 1/2-in diam., about 15 per lb with pits)	28	79	20	Trace	Trace	—	—	—	6	3	5	.1	48	80	.01	.01	.1	1
	Canned, heavy sirup pack (Italian prunes), with pits and liquid:																		
302	Cup[36]	272	77	215	1	Trace	—	—	—	56	23	26	2.3	367	3,130	.05	.05	1.0	5
303	Portion[36]	140	77	110	1	Trace	—	—	—	29	12	13	1.2	189	1,610	.03	.03	.5	3
	Prunes, dried, "softenized," with pits:																		
304	Uncooked, 4 extra large or 5 large prunes[36]	49	28	110	1	Trace	—	—	—	29	22	34	1.7	298	690	.04	.07	.7	1
305	Cooked, unsweetened, all sizes, fruit and liquid, 1 cup[36]	250	66	255	2	1	—	—	—	67	51	79	3.8	695	1,590	.07	.15	1.5	2
306	Prune juice, canned or bottled	256	80	195	1	Trace	—	—	—	49	36	51	1.8	602	—	.03	.03	1.0	5
	Raisins, seedless:																		
307	Cup, not pressed down	145	18	420	4	Trace	—	—	—	112	90	146	5.1	1,106	30	.16	.12	.7	1
308	Packet, 1/2 oz (1 1/2 tbsp)	14	18	40	Trace	Trace	—	—	—	11	9	14	.5	107	Trace	.02	.01	.1	Trace
	Raspberries, red:																		
309	Raw, capped, whole	123	84	70	1	1	—	—	—	17	27	27	1.1	207	160	.04	.11	1.1	31
310	Frozen, sweetened, 10-oz container	284	74	280	2	1	—	—	—	70	37	48	1.7	284	200	.06	.17	1.7	60
	Rhubarb, cooked, added sugar:																		
311	From raw, 1 cup	270	63	380	1	Trace	—	—	—	97	211	41	1.6	548	220	.05	.14	.8	16
312	From frozen, sweetened, 1 cup	270	63	385	1	1	—	—	—	93	211	32	1.9	475	190	.05	.11	.5	16

[27] Based on product with label claim of 100% of U.S. RDA in 6 fl oz.

[35] Value represents products with added ascorbic acid. For products without added ascorbic acid, value in milligrams is 116 for a 10-oz container, 103 for 1 cup.

[36] Weight includes pits. After removal of the pits, the weight of the edible portion is 258 g for item 302, 133 g for item 303, 43 g for item 304, and 213 g for item 305.

54 DIETARY DIRECTIONS IN THE 1980s

TABLE 2.— NUTRITIVE VALUES OF THE EDIBLE PART OF FOODS - Continued
(Dashes (—) denote lack of reliable data for a constituent believed to be present in measurable amount)

Item No. (A)	Foods, approximate measures, units, and weight (edible part unless footnotes indicate otherwise) (B)		Grams	Water (C) Percent	Food energy (D) Calories	Protein (E) Grams	Fat (F) Grams	Fatty Acids Saturated (total) (G) Grams	Unsaturated Oleic (H) Grams	Linoleic (I) Grams	Carbohydrate (J) Grams	Calcium (K) Milligrams	Phosphorus (L) Milligrams	Iron (M) Milligrams	Potassium (N) Milligrams	Vitamin A value (O) International units	Thiamin (P) Milligrams	Riboflavin (Q) Milligrams	Niacin (R) Milligrams	Ascorbic acid (S) Milligrams
	Strawberries:																			
313	Raw, whole berries, capped	1 cup	149	90	55	1	1	—	—	—	13	31	31	1.5	244	90	0.04	0.10	0.9	88
	Frozen, sweetened:																			
314	Sliced, 10-oz container	1 container	284	71	310	1	1	—	—	—	79	40	48	2.0	318	90	.06	.17	1.4	151
315	Whole, 1-lb container (about 1 3/4 cups)	1 container	454	76	415	2	1	—	—	—	107	59	73	2.7	472	140	.09	.27	2.3	249
316	Tangerine, raw, 2 3/8-in diam., size 176, without peel (about 4 per lb with peels and seeds)	1 tangerine	86	87	40	1	Trace	—	—	—	10	34	15	.3	108	360	.05	.02	.1	27
317	Tangerine juice, canned, sweetened	1 cup	249	87	125	1	Trace	—	—	—	30	44	35	.5	440	1,040	.15	.05	.2	54
318	Watermelon, raw, 4 by 8 in wedge with rind and seeds (1/16 of 32 2/3-lb melon, 10 by 16 in).	1 wedge with rind and seeds[37]	926	93	110	2	1	—	—	—	27	30	43	2.1	426	2,510	.13	.13	.9	30

GRAIN PRODUCTS

	Bagel, 3-in diam.:																			
319	Egg	1 bagel	55	32	165	6	2	0.5	0.9	0.8	28	9	43	1.2	41	30	.14	.10	1.2	0
320	Water	1 bagel	55	29	165	6	1	.2	.4	.6	30	8	41	1.2	42	0	.15	.11	1.4	0
321	Barley, pearled, light, uncooked	1 cup	200	11	700	16	2	.3	.2	.8	158	32	378	4.0	320	0	.24	.10	6.2	0
	Biscuits, baking powder, 2-in diam. (enriched flour, vegetable shortening):																			
322	From home recipe	1 biscuit	28	27	105	2	5	1.2	2.0	1.2	13	34	49	.4	33	Trace	.08	.08	.7	Trace
323	From mix	1 biscuit	28	29	90	2	3	.6	1.1	.7	15	19	65	.6	32	Trace	.09	.08	.8	Trace
324	Breadcrumbs (enriched):[38] Dry, grated	1 cup	100	7	390	13	5	1.0	1.6	1.4	73	122	141	3.6	152	Trace	.35	.35	4.8	Trace
	Breads: Soft. See White bread (items 349-350).																			
325	Boston brown bread, canned, slice, 3 1/4 by 1/2 in.[38]	1 slice	45	45	95	2	1	.1	.2	.2	21	41	72	.9	131	[39]0	.06	.04	.7	0
	Cracked-wheat bread (3/4 enriched wheat flour, 1/4 cracked wheat):[38]																			
326	Loaf, 1 lb	1 loaf	454	35	1,195	39	10	2.2	3.0	3.9	236	399	581	9.5	608	Trace	1.52	1.13	14.4	Trace
327	Slice (18 per loaf)	1 slice	25	35	65	2	1	.1	.2	.2	13	22	32	.5	34	Trace	.08	.06	.8	Trace
328	French or vienna bread, enriched:[38] Loaf, 1 lb	1 loaf	454	31	1,315	41	14	3.2	4.7	4.6	251	195	386	10.0	408	Trace	1.80	1.10	15.0	Trace
	Slice:																			
329	French (5 by 2 1/2 by 1 in)	1 slice	35	31	100	3	1	.2	.4	.4	19	15	30	.8	32	Trace	.14	.08	1.2	Trace
330	Vienna (4 3/4 by 4 by 1/2 in).	1 slice	25	31	75	2	1	.2	.3	.3	14	11	21	.6	23	Trace	.10	.06	.8	Trace
	Italian bread, enriched:																			
331	Loaf, 1 lb	1 loaf	454	32	1,250	41	4	.6	.3	1.5	256	77	349	10.0	336	0	1.80	1.10	15.0	0
332	Slice, 4 1/2 by 3 1/4 by 3/4 in.	1 slice	30	32	85	3	Trace	Trace	Trace	.1	17	5	23	.7	22	0	.12	.07	1.0	0
	Raisin bread, enriched:[38]																			
333	Loaf, 1 lb	1 loaf	454	35	1,190	30	13	3.0	4.7	3.9	243	322	395	10.0	1,057	Trace	1.70	1.07	10.7	Trace
334	Slice (18 per loaf)	1 slice	25	35	65	2	1	.2	.3	.2	13	18	22	.6	58	Trace	.09	.06	.6	Trace

[37] Weight includes rind and seeds. Without rind and seeds, weight of the edible portion is 426 g.
[38] Made with vegetable shortening.
[39] Applies to product made with white cornmeal. With yellow cornmeal, value is 30 International Units (I.U.).

DIETARY DIRECTIONS IN THE 1980s 55

(A)	(B)		(C)	(D)	(E)	(F)	(G)	(H)	(I)	(J)	(K)	(L)	(M)	(N)	(O)	(P)	(Q)	(R)	(S)
	GRAIN PRODUCTS—Con.																		
	Rye Bread:																		
	American, light (2/3 enriched wheat flour, 1/3 rye flour):																		
335	Loaf, 1 lb	1 loaf	454	1,100	41	5	0.7	0.5	2.2	236	340	667	9.1	658	0	1.35	0.98	12.9	0
336	Slice (4 3/4 by 3 3/4 by 7/16 in).	1 slice	25	60	2	Trace	Trace	Trace	.1	13	19	37	.5	36	0	.07	.05	.7	0
	Pumpernickel (2/3 rye flour, 1/3 enriched wheat flour):																		
337	Loaf, 1 lb	1 loaf	454	1,115	41	5	.7	.5	2.4	241	381	1,039	11.8	2,059	0	1.30	.93	8.5	0
338	Slice (5 by 4 by 3/8 in)	1 slice	32	80	3	Trace	.1	Trace	.2	17	27	73	.8	145	0	.09	.07	.6	0
	White bread, enriched:[38]																		
	Soft-crumb type:																		
339	Loaf, 1 lb	1 loaf	454	1,225	39	15	3.4	5.3	4.6	229	381	440	11.3	476	Trace	1.80	1.10	15.0	Trace
340	Slice (18 per loaf)	1 slice	25	70	2	1	.2	.2	.3	13	21	24	.6	26	Trace	.10	.06	.8	Trace
341	Slice, toasted	1 slice	22	70	2	1	.2	.2	.3	13	21	24	.6	26	Trace	.08	.06	.8	Trace
342	Slice (22 per loaf)	1 slice	20	55	2	1	.2	.2	.2	10	17	19	.5	21	Trace	.08	.05	.7	Trace
343	Slice, toasted	1 slice	17	55	2	1	.2	.2	.2	10	17	19	.5	21	Trace	.06	.05	.7	Trace
344	Loaf, 1 1/2 lb	1 loaf	680	1,835	59	22	5.2	7.9	6.9	343	571	660	17.0	714	Trace	2.70	1.65	22.5	Trace
345	Slice (24 per loaf)	1 slice	28	75	2	1	.2	.3	.3	14	24	27	.7	29	Trace	.11	.07	.9	Trace
346	Slice, toasted	1 slice	24	75	2	1	.2	.3	.3	14	24	27	.7	29	Trace	.09	.07	.9	Trace
347	Slice (28 per loaf)	1 slice	24	65	2	1	.2	.2	.2	12	20	23	.6	25	Trace	.10	.06	.8	Trace
348	Slice, toasted	1 slice	21	65	2	1	.2	.2	.2	12	20	23	.6	25	Trace	.08	.06	.8	Trace
349	Cubes	1 cup	30	80	3	1	.2	.3	.3	15	25	29	.7	32	Trace	.12	.07	1.0	Trace
350	Crumbs	1 cup	45	120	4	1	.3	.5	.5	23	38	44	1.1	47	Trace	.18	.11	1.5	Trace
	Firm-crumb type:																		
351	Loaf, 1 lb	1 loaf	454	1,245	41	17	3.9	5.9	5.2	228	435	463	11.3	549	Trace	1.80	1.10	15.0	Trace
352	Slice (20 per loaf)	1 slice	23	65	2	1	.2	.3	.3	12	22	23	.6	28	Trace	.09	.06	.8	Trace
353	Slice, toasted	1 slice	20	65	2	1	.2	.3	.3	12	22	23	.6	28	Trace	.07	.06	.8	Trace
354	Loaf, 2 lb	1 loaf	907	2,495	82	34	7.7	11.8	10.4	455	871	925	22.7	1,097	Trace	3.60	2.20	30.0	Trace
355	Slice (34 per loaf)	1 slice	27	75	2	1	.2	.3	.3	14	26	28	.7	33	Trace	.11	.06	.9	Trace
356	Slice, toasted	1 slice	23	75	2	1	.2	.3	.3	14	26	28	.7	33	Trace	.09	.06	.9	Trace
	Whole-wheat bread:																		
	Soft-crumb type:[38]																		
357	Loaf, 1 lb	1 loaf	454	1,095	41	12	2.2	2.9	4.2	224	381	1,152	13.6	1,161	Trace	1.37	.45	12.7	Trace
358	Slice (16 per loaf)	1 slice	28	65	3	1	.1	.2	.2	14	24	71	.8	72	Trace	.09	.03	.8	Trace
359	Slice, toasted	1 slice	24	65	3	1	.1	.2	.2	14	24	71	.8	72	Trace	.07	.03	.8	Trace
	Firm-crumb type:[38]																		
360	Loaf, 1 lb	1 loaf	454	1,100	48	14	2.5	3.3	4.9	216	449	1,034	13.6	1,238	Trace	1.17	.54	12.7	Trace
361	Slice (18 per loaf)	1 slice	25	60	3	1	.1	.2	.3	12	25	57	.8	68	Trace	.06	.03	.7	Trace
362	Slice, toasted	1 slice	21	60	3	1	.1	.2	.3	12	25	57	.8	68	Trace	.05	.03	.7	Trace
	Breakfast cereals:																		
	Hot type, cooked:																		
	Corn (hominy) grits, degermed:																		
363	Enriched	1 cup	245	125	3	Trace	Trace	Trace	.1	27	2	25	.7	27	[40]Trace	.10	.07	1.0	0
364	Unenriched	1 cup	245	125	3	Trace	Trace	Trace	.1	27	2	25	.2	27	[40]Trace	.05	.02	.5	0
365	Farina, quick-cooking, enriched.	1 cup	245	105	3	Trace	Trace	Trace	—	22	147	[41]113	([42])	25	0	.12	.07	1.0	0
366	Oatmeal or rolled oats	1 cup	240	130	5	2	.4	.8	.9	23	22	137	1.4	146	0	.19	.05	.2	0
367	Wheat, rolled	1 cup	240	180	5	1	—	—	—	41	19	182	1.7	202	0	.17	.07	2.2	0
368	Wheat, whole-meal	1 cup	245	110	4	1	—	—	—	23	17	127	1.2	118	0	.15	.05	1.5	0
	Ready-to-eat:																		
369	Bran flakes (40% bran), added sugar, salt, iron, vitamins.	1 cup	35	105	4	1	—	—	—	28	19	125	12.4	137	1,650	.41	.49	4.1	12
370	Bran flakes with raisins, added sugar, salt, iron, vitamins.	1 cup	50	145	4	1	—	—	—	40	28	146	17.7	154	2,350	.58	.71	5.8	18

[40]Applies to white varieties. For yellow varieties, value is 150 International Units (I.U.).
[41]Applies to products that do not contain di-sodium phosphate. If di-sodium phosphate is an ingredient, value is 162 mg.
[42]Value may range from less than 1 mg to about 8 mg depending on the brand. Consult the label.

TABLE 2.—NUTRITIVE VALUES OF THE EDIBLE PART OF FOODS - Continued

(Dashes (—) denote lack of reliable data for a constituent believed to be present in measurable amount)

Item No. (A)	Foods, approximate measures, units, and weight (edible part unless footnotes indicate otherwise) (B)			Water (C) Percent	Food energy (D) Calories	Protein (E) Grams	Fat (F) Grams	Satu-rated (total) (G) Grams	Unsaturated Oleic (H) Grams	Lino-leic (I) Grams	Carbo-hydrate (J) Grams	Calcium (K) Milli-grams	Phos-phorus (L) Milli-grams	Iron (M) Milli-grams	Potas-sium (N) Milli-grams	Vitamin A value (O) Inter-national units	Thiamin (P) Milli-grams	Ribo-flavin (Q) Milli-grams	Niacin (R) Milli-grams	Ascorbic acid (S) Milli-grams
	GRAIN PRODUCTS—Con.		Grams																	
	Breakfast cereals—Continued Ready-to-eat—Continued Corn flakes:																			
371	Plain, added sugar, salt, iron, vitamins.	1 cup	25	4	95	2	Trace	—	—	—	21	(⁴³)	9	0.6	30	1,180	0.29	0.35	2.9	9
372	Sugar-coated, added salt, iron, vitamins.	1 cup	40	2	155	2	Trace	—	—	—	37	1	10	1.0	27	1,880	.46	.56	4.6	14
373	Corn, puffed, plain, added sugar, salt, iron, vita-mins.	1 cup	20	4	80	2	1	—	—	—	16	4	18	2.3	—	940	.23	.28	2.3	7
374	Corn, shredded, added sugar, salt, iron, thiamin, niacin.	1 cup	25	3	95	2	Trace	—	—	—	22	1	10	.6	—	0	.11	.05	.5	0
375	Oats, puffed, added sugar, salt, minerals, vitamins.	1 cup	25	3	100	3	1	—	—	—	19	44	102	2.9	—	1,180	.29	.35	2.9	9
	Rice, puffed:																			
376	Plain, added iron, thiamin, niacin.	1 cup	15	4	60	1	Trace	—	—	—	13	3	14	.3	15	0	.07	.01	.7	0
377	Presweetened, added salt, iron, vitamins.	1 cup	28	3	115	1	0	—	—	—	26	3	14	⁴⁴1.1	43	1,250	.38	.43	5.0	⁴⁵15
378	Wheat flakes, added sugar, salt, iron, vitamins.	1 cup	30	4	105	3	Trace	—	—	—	24	12	83	(⁴³)	81	1,410	.35	.42	3.5	11
	Wheat, puffed:																			
379	Plain, added iron, thiamin, niacin.	1 cup	15	3	55	2	Trace	—	—	—	12	4	48	.6	51	0	.08	.03	1.2	0
380	Presweetened, added salt, iron, vitamins.	1 cup	38	3	140	3	Trace	—	—	—	33	7	52	⁴⁴1.6	63	1,680	.50	.57	6.7	⁴⁵20
381	Wheat, shredded, plain	1 oblong biscuit or 1/2 cup spoon-size biscuits.	25	7	90	2	1	—	—	—	20	11	97	.9	87	0	.06	.03	1.1	0
382	Wheat germ, without salt and sugar, toasted.	1 tbsp	6	4	25	2	1	—	—	—	3	3	70	.5	57	10	.11	.05	.3	1
383	Buckwheat flour, light, sifted-	1 cup	98	12	340	6	1	0.2	0.4	0.4	78	11	86	1.0	314	0	.08	.04	.4	0
384	Bulgur, canned, seasoned	1 cup	135	56	245	8	4	—	—	—	44	27	263	1.9	151	0	.08	.05	4.1	0
	Cake icings. See Sugars and Sweets (items 532-536). Cakes made from cake mixes with enriched flour:⁴⁶ Angelfood:																			
385	Whole cake (9 3/4-in diam. tube cake).	1 cake	635	34	1,645	36	1	—	—	—	377	603	756	2.5	381	0	.37	.95	3.6	0
386	Piece, 1/12 of cake	1 piece	53	34	135	3	Trace	—	—	—	32	50	63	.2	32	0	.03	.08	.3	0
	Coffeecake:																			
387	Whole cake (7 3/4 by 5 5/8 by 1 1/4 in).	1 cake	430	30	1,385	27	41	11.7	16.3	8.8	225	262	748	6.9	469	690	.82	.91	7.7	1
388	Piece, 1/6 of cake	1 piece	72	30	230	5	7	2.0	2.7	1.5	38	44	125	1.2	78	120	.14	.15	1.3	Trace
	Cupcakes, made with egg, milk, 2 1/2-in diam.:																			
389	Without icing	1 cupcake	25	26	90	1	3	.8	1.2	.7	14	40	59	.3	21	40	.05	.05	.4	Trace
390	With chocolate icing	1 cupcake	36	22	130	2	5	2.0	1.6	.6	21	47	71	.4	42	60	.05	.06	.4	Trace
	Devil's food with chocolate icing:																			
391	Whole, 2 layer cake (8- or 9-in diam.).	1 cake	1,107	24	3,755	49	136	50.0	44.9	17.0	645	653	1,162	16.6	1,439	1,660	1.06	1.65	10.1	1
392	Piece, 1/16 of cake	1 piece	69	24	235	3	8	3.1	2.8	1.1	40	41	72	1.0	90	100	.07	.10	.6	Trace
393	Cupcake, 2 1/2-in diam	1 cupcake	35	24	120	2	4	1.6	1.4	.5	20	21	37	.5	46	50	.03	.05	.3	Trace

⁴³Value varies with the brand. Consult the label.
⁴⁴Value varies with the brand. Consult the label.
⁴⁵Applies to product with added ascorbic acid. Without added ascorbic acid, value is trace.
⁴⁶Excepting angelfood cake, cakes were made from mixes containing vegetable shortening; icings, with butter.

DIETARY DIRECTIONS IN THE 1980s 57

(A)	(B)	(C)	(D)	(E)	(F)	(G)	(H)	(I)	(J)	(K)	(L)	(M)	(N)	(O)	(P)	(Q)	(R)	(S)
	Gingerbread:																	
394	Whole cake (8-in square)------	1 cake	570	1,575	18	39	9.7	16.6	10.0	291	513	570	8.6	1,562	Trace	0.84	1.00	7.4	Trace
395	Piece, 1/9 of cake----------	1 piece	63	175	2	4	1.1	1.8	1.1	32	57	63	.9	173	Trace	.09	.11	.8	Trace
	White, 2 layer with chocolate icing:																		
396	Whole cake (8- or 9-in diam.)-	1 cake	1,140	4,000	44	122	48.2	46.4	20.0	716	1,129	2,041	11.4	1,322	680	1.50	1.77	12.5	2
397	Piece, 1/16 of cake----------	1 piece	71	250	3	8	3.0	2.9	1.2	45	70	127	.7	82	40	.09	.11	.8	Trace
	Yellow, 2 layer with chocolate icing:																		
398	Whole cake (8- or 9-in diam.)-	1 cake	1,108	3,735	45	125	47.8	47.8	20.3	638	1,008	2,017	12.2	1,208	1,550	1.24	1.67	10.6	2
399	Piece, 1/16 of cake----------	1 piece	69	235	3	8	3.0	3.0	1.3	40	63	126	.8	75	100	.08	.10	.7	Trace
	Cakes made from home recipes using enriched flour:[47]																		
	Boston cream pie with custard filling:[47]																		
400	Whole cake (8-in diam.)------	1 cake	825	2,490	41	78	23.0	30.1	15.2	412	553	833	8.2	[48]734	1,730	1.04	1.27	9.6	2
401	Piece, 1/12 of cake----------	1 piece	69	210	3	6	1.9	2.5	1.3	34	46	70	.7	[48]61	140	.09	.11	.8	Trace
	Fruitcake, dark:																		
402	Loaf, 1-lb (7 1/2 by 2 by 1 1/2 in).	1 loaf	454	1,720	22	69	14.4	33.5	14.8	271	327	513	11.8	2,250	540	.72	.73	4.9	2
403	Slice, 1/30 of loaf----------	1 slice	15	55	1	2	.5	1.1	.5	9	11	17	.4	74	20	.02	.02	.2	Trace
	Plain, sheet cake:																		
	Without icing:																		
404	Whole cake (9-in square)-----	1 cake	777	2,830	35	108	29.5	44.4	23.9	434	497	793	8.5	[48]614	1,320	1.21	1.40	10.2	2
405	Piece, 1/9 of cake-----------	1 piece	86	315	4	12	3.3	4.9	2.6	48	55	88	.9	[48]68	150	.13	.15	1.1	Trace
	With uncooked white icing:																		
406	Whole cake (9-in square)-----	1 cake	1,096	4,020	37	129	42.2	49.5	24.4	694	548	822	8.2	[48]669	2,190	1.22	1.47	10.2	2
407	Piece, 1/9 of cake-----------	1 piece	121	445	4	14	4.7	5.5	2.7	77	61	91	.8	[48]74	240	.14	.16	1.1	Trace
	Pound:[49]																		
408	Loaf, 8 1/2 by 3 1/2 by 3 1/4 in.	1 loaf	565	2,725	31	170	42.9	73.1	39.6	273	107	418	7.9	345	1,410	.90	.99	7.3	0
409	Slice, 1/17 of loaf----------	1 slice	33	160	2	10	2.5	4.3	2.3	16	6	24	.5	20	80	.05	.06	.4	0
	Spongecake:																		
410	Whole cake (9 3/4-in diam. tube cake).	1 cake	790	2,345	60	45	13.1	15.8	5.7	427	237	885	13.4	687	3,560	1.10	1.64	7.4	Trace
411	Piece, 1/12 of cake----------	1 piece	66	195	5	4	1.1	1.3	.5	36	20	74	1.1	57	300	.09	.14	.6	Trace
	Cookies made with enriched flour:[50 51]																		
	Brownies with nuts:																		
	Home-prepared, 1 3/4 by 1 3/4 by 7/8 in:																		
412	From home recipe------------	1 brownie	20	95	1	6	1.5	3.0	1.2	10	8	30	.4	38	40	.04	.03	.2	Trace
413	From commercial recipe------	1 brownie	20	85	1	4	.9	1.4	1.3	13	9	27	.4	34	20	.03	.02	.2	Trace
414	Frozen, with chocolate icing,[52] 1 1/2 by 1 3/4 by 7/8 in.	1 brownie	25	105	1	5	2.0	2.2	.7	15	10	31	.4	44	50	.03	.03	.2	Trace
	Chocolate chip:																		
415	Commercial, 2 1/4-in diam., 3/8 in thick.	4 cookies	42	200	2	9	2.8	2.9	2.2	29	16	48	1.0	56	50	.10	.17	.9	Trace
416	From home recipe, 2 1/3-in diam.	4 cookies	40	205	2	12	3.5	4.5	2.9	24	14	40	.8	47	40	.06	.06	.5	Trace
417	Fig bars, square (1 5/8 by 1 5/8 by 3/8 in) or rectangular (1 1/2 by 1 3/4 by 1/2 in).	4 cookies	56	200	2	3	.8	1.2	.7	42	44	34	1.0	111	60	.04	.14	.9	Trace
418	Gingersnaps, 2-in diam., 1/4 in thick.	4 cookies	28	90	2	2	.7	1.0	.6	22	20	13	.7	129	20	.08	.06	.7	0
419	Macaroons, 2 3/4-in diam., 1/4 in thick.	2 cookies	38	180	2	9	—	—	—	25	10	32	.3	176	0	.02	.06	.2	0
420	Oatmeal with raisins, 2 5/8-in diam., 1/4 in thick.	4 cookies	52	235	3	8	2.0	3.3	2.0	38	11	53	1.4	192	30	.15	.10	1.0	Trace

[47] Excepting spongecake, vegetable shortening used for cake portion; butter, for icing. If butter or margarine used for cake portion, vitamin A values would be higher.
[48] Applies to product made with a sodium aluminum-sulfate type baking powder. With a low-sodium type baking powder containing potassium, value would be about twice the amount shown.
[49] Equal weights of flour, sugar, eggs, and vegetable shortening.
[50] Products are commercial unless otherwise specified.
[51] Made with enriched flour and vegetable shortening except for macaroons which do not contain flour or shortening.
[52] Icing made with butter.

TABLE 2.— NUTRITIVE VALUES OF THE EDIBLE PART OF FOODS - Continued

(Dashes (—) denote lack of reliable data for a constituent believed to be present in measurable amount)

Item No. (A)	Foods, approximate measures, units, and weight (edible part unless footnotes indicate otherwise) (B)		Grams	Water Percent (C)	Food energy Calories (D)	Protein Grams (E)	Fat Grams (F)	Saturated (total) Grams (G)	Oleic Grams (H)	Linoleic Grams (I)	Carbohydrate Grams (J)	Calcium Milligrams (K)	Phosphorus Milligrams (L)	Iron Milligrams (M)	Potassium Milligrams (N)	Vitamin A value International units (O)	Thiamin Milligrams (P)	Riboflavin Milligrams (Q)	Niacin Milligrams (R)	Ascorbic acid Milligrams (S)
	GRAIN PRODUCTS—Con.																			
	Cookies made with enriched flour [50][51]—Continued																			
421	Plain, prepared from commercial chilled dough, 2 1/2-in diam., 1/4 in thick.	4 cookies	48	5	240	2	12	3.0	5.2	2.9	31	17	35	0.6	23	30	0.10	0.08	0.9	0
422	Sandwich type (chocolate or vanilla), 1 3/4-in diam., 3/8 in thick.	4 cookies	40	2	200	2	9	2.2	3.9	2.2	28	10	96	.7	15	0	.06	.10	.7	0
423	Vanilla wafers, 1 3/4-in diam., 1/4 in thick.	10 cookies	40	3	185	2	6	—	—	—	30	16	25	.6	29	50	.10	.09	.8	0
	Cornmeal:																			
424	Whole-ground, unbolted, dry form.	1 cup	122	12	435	11	5	.5	1.0	2.5	90	24	312	2.9	346	[53]620	.46	.13	2.4	0
425	Bolted (nearly whole-grain), dry form.	1 cup	122	12	440	11	4	.5	.9	2.1	91	21	272	2.2	303	[53]590	.37	.10	2.3	0
	Degermed, enriched:																			
426	Dry form	1 cup	138	12	500	11	2	.2	.4	.9	108	8	137	4.0	166	[53]610	.61	.36	4.8	0
427	Cooked	1 cup	240	88	120	3	Trace	Trace	.1	.2	26	2	34	1.0	38	[53]140	.14	.10	1.2	0
	Degermed, unenriched:																			
428	Dry form	1 cup	138	12	500	11	2	.2	.4	.9	108	8	137	1.5	166	[53]610	.19	.07	1.4	0
429	Cooked	1 cup	240	88	120	3	Trace	Trace	.1	.2	26	2	34	.5	38	[53]140	.05	.02	.2	0
	Crackers:[38]																			
430	Graham, plain, 2 1/2-in square	2 crackers	14	6	55	1	1	.3	.5	.3	10	6	21	.5	55	0	.02	.08	.5	0
431	Rye wafers, whole-grain, 1 7/8 by 3 1/2 in.	2 wafers	13	6	45	2	Trace	—	—	—	10	7	50	.5	78	0	.04	.03	.2	0
432	Saltines, made with enriched flour.	4 crackers or 1 packet	11	4	50	1	1	.3	.5	.4	8	2	10	.5	13	0	.05	.05	.4	0
	Danish pastry (enriched flour), plain without fruit or nuts:[54]																			
433	Packaged ring, 12 oz	ring	340	22	1,435	25	80	24.3	31.7	16.5	155	170	371	6.1	381	1,050	.97	1.01	8.6	Trace
434	Round piece, about 4 1/4-in diam. by 1 in.	pastry	65	22	275	5	15	4.7	6.1	3.2	30	33	71	1.2	73	200	.18	.19	1.7	Trace
435	Ounce	1 oz	28	22	120	2	7	2.0	2.7	1.4	13	14	31	.5	32	90	.08	.08	.7	Trace
	Doughnuts, made with enriched flour:[38]																			
436	Cake type, plain, 2 1/2-in diam., 1 in high.	1 doughnut	25	24	100	1	5	1.2	2.0	1.1	13	10	48	.4	23	20	.05	.05	.4	Trace
437	Yeast-leavened, glazed, 3 3/4-in diam., 1 1/4 in high.	1 doughnut	50	26	205	3	11	3.3	5.8	3.3	22	16	33	.6	34	25	.10	.10	.8	0
	Macaroni, enriched, cooked (cut lengths, elbows, shells):																			
438	Firm stage (hot)	1 cup	130	64	190	7	1	—	—	—	39	14	85	1.4	103	0	.23	.13	1.8	0
	Tender stage:																			
439	Cold macaroni	1 cup	105	73	115	4	Trace	—	—	—	24	8	53	.9	64	0	.15	.08	1.2	0
440	Hot macaroni	1 cup	140	73	155	5	1	—	—	—	32	11	70	1.3	85	0	.20	.11	1.5	0
	Macaroni (enriched) and cheese:																			
441	Canned[55]	1 cup	240	80	230	9	10	4.2	3.1	1.4	26	199	182	1.0	139	260	.12	.24	1.0	Trace
442	From home recipe (served hot)[56]	1 cup	200	58	430	17	22	8.9	8.8	2.9	40	362	322	1.8	240	860	.20	.40	1.8	Trace
	Muffins made with enriched flour:[38] From home recipe:																			
443	Blueberry, 2 3/8-in diam., 1 1/2 in high.	1 muffin	40	39	110	3	4	1.1	1.4	.7	17	34	53	.6	46	90	.09	.10	.7	Trace
444	Bran, 1 muffin	1 muffin	40	35	105	3	4	1.2	1.4	.8	17	57	162	1.5	172	90	.07	.10	1.7	Trace
445	Corn (enriched degermed cornmeal and flour), 2 3/8-in diam., 1 1/2 in high.	1 muffin	40	33	125	3	4	1.2	1.6	.9	19	42	68	.7	54	[57]120	.10	.10	.7	Trace

[38] Made with vegetable shortening.
[50] Products are commercial unless otherwise specified.
[51] Made with enriched flour and vegetable shortening except for macaroons which do not contain flour or shortening.
[53] Applies to yellow varieties; white varieties contain only a trace.
[54] Contains vegetable shortening and butter.
[55] Made with corn oil.
[56] Made with regular margarine.

DIETARY DIRECTIONS IN THE 1980s 59

(A)	(B)		(C)	(D)	(E)	(F)	(G)	(H)	(I)	(J)	(K)	(L)	(M)	(N)	(O)	(P)	(Q)	(R)	(S)
446	Plain, 3-in diam., 1 1/2 in high.	1 muffin	40	38	120	3	4	1.0	1.7	1.0	17	42	60	0.6	50	40	0.09	0.12	0.9	Trace
447	From mix, egg, milk: Corn, 2 3/8-in diam., 1 1/2 in high.[58]	1 muffin	40	30	130	3	4	1.2	1.7	.9	20	96	152	.6	44	[57]100	.08	.09	.7	Trace
448	Noodles (egg noodles), enriched, cooked.	1 cup	160	71	200	7	2	—	—	—	37	16	94	1.4	70	110	.22	.13	1.9	0
449	Noodles, chow mein, canned	1 cup	45	1	220	6	11	—	—	—	26	—	—	—	—	—	—	—	—	—
450	Pancakes, (4-in diam.).[38] Buckwheat, made from mix (with buckwheat and enriched flours), egg and milk added.	1 cake	27	58	55	2	2	.8	.9	.4	6	59	91	.4	66	60	.04	.05	.2	Trace
.51	Plain: Made from home recipe using enriched flour.	1 cake	27	50	60	2	2	.5	.8	.5	9	27	38	.4	33	30	.06	.07	.5	Trace
452	Made from mix with enriched flour, egg and milk added.	1 cake	27	51	60	2	2	.7	.7	.3	9	58	70	.3	42	70	.04	.06	.2	Trace
	Pies, piecrust made with enriched flour, vegetable shortening (9-in diam.): Apple:																			
453	Whole	1 pie	945	48	2,420	21	105	27.0	44.5	25.2	360	76	208	6.6	756	280	1.06	.79	9.3	9
454	Sector, 1/7 of pie	1 sector	135	48	345	3	15	3.9	6.4	3.6	51	11	30	.9	108	40	.15	.11	1.3	2
	Banana cream:																			
455	Whole	1 pie	910	54	2,010	41	85	26.7	33.2	16.2	279	601	746	7.3	1,847	2,280	.77	1.51	7.0	9
456	Sector, 1/7 of pie	1 sector	130	54	285	6	12	3.8	4.7	2.3	40	86	107	1.0	264	330	.11	.22	1.0	1
	Blueberry:																			
457	Whole	1 pie	945	51	2,285	23	102	24.8	43.7	25.1	330	104	217	9.5	614	280	1.03	.80	10.0	28
458	Sector, 1/7 of pie	1 sector	135	51	325	3	15	3.5	6.2	3.6	47	15	31	1.4	88	40	.15	.11	1.4	4
	Cherry:																			
459	Whole	1 pie	945	47	2,465	25	107	28.2	45.0	25.3	363	132	236	6.6	992	4,160	1.09	.84	9.8	Trace
460	Sector, 1/7 of pie	1 sector	135	47	350	4	15	4.0	6.4	3.6	52	19	34	.9	142	590	.16	.12	1.4	Trace
	Custard:																			
461	Whole	1 pie	910	58	1,985	56	101	33.9	38.5	17.5	213	874	1,028	8.2	1,247	2,090	.79	1.92	5.6	0
462	Sector, 1/7 of pie	1 sector	130	58	285	8	14	4.8	5.5	2.5	30	125	147	1.2	178	300	.11	.27	.8	0
	Lemon meringue:																			
463	Whole	1 pie	840	47	2,140	31	86	26.1	33.8	16.4	317	118	412	6.7	420	1,430	.61	.84	5.2	25
464	Sector, 1/7 of pie	1 sector	120	47	305	4	12	3.7	4.8	2.3	45	17	59	1.0	60	200	.09	.12	.7	4
	Mince:																			
465	Whole	1 pie	945	43	2,560	24	109	28.0	45.9	25.2	389	265	359	13.3	1,682	20	.96	.86	9.8	9
466	Sector, 1/7 of pie	1 sector	135	43	365	3	16	4.0	6.6	3.6	56	38	51	1.9	240	Trace	.14	.12	1.4	1
	Peach:																			
467	Whole	1 pie	945	48	2,410	24	101	24.8	43.7	25.1	361	95	274	8.5	1,408	6,900	1.04	.97	14.0	28
468	Sector, 1/7 of pie	1 sector	135	48	345	3	14	3.5	6.2	3.6	52	14	39	1.2	201	990	.15	.14	2.0	4
	Pecan:																			
469	Whole	1 pie	825	20	3,450	42	189	27.8	101.0	44.2	423	388	850	25.6	1,015	1,320	1.80	.95	6.9	Trace
470	Sector, 1/7 of pie	1 sector	118	20	495	6	27	4.0	14.4	6.3	61	55	122	3.7	145	190	.26	.14	1.0	Trace
	Pumpkin:																			
471	Whole	1 pie	910	59	1,920	36	102	37.4	37.5	16.6	223	464	628	7.3	1,456	22,480	.78	1.27	7.0	Trace
472	Sector, 1/7 of pie	1 sector	130	59	275	5	15	5.4	5.4	2.4	32	66	90	1.0	208	3,210	.11	.18	1.0	Trace
473	Piecrust (home recipe) made with enriched flour and vegetable shortening, baked.	1 pie shell, 9-in diam.	180	15	900	11	60	14.8	26.1	14.9	79	25	90	3.1	89	0	.47	.40	5.0	0
474	Piecrust mix with enriched flour and vegetable shortening, 10-oz pkg. prepared and baked.	Piecrust for 2-crust pie, 9-in diam.	320	19	1,485	20	93	22.7	39.7	23.4	141	131	272	6.1	179	0	1.07	.79	9.9	0

[57]Applies to product made with yellow cornmeal.
[58]Made with enriched degermed cornmeal and enriched flour.

TABLE 2.— NUTRITIVE VALUES OF THE EDIBLE PART OF FOODS - Continued
(Dashes (—) denote lack of reliable data for a constituent believed to be present in measurable amount)

Item No. (A)	Foods, approximate measures, units, and weight (edible part unless footnotes indicate otherwise) (B)		Grams	Water Per cent (C)	Food energy Cal- ories (D)	Pro- tein Grams (E)	Fat Grams (F)	Satu- rated (total) Grams (G)	Oleic Grams (H)	Lino- leic Grams (I)	Carbo- hydrate Grams (J)	Calcium Milli- grams (K)	Phos- phorus Milli- grams (L)	Iron Milli- grams (M)	Potas- sium Milli- grams (N)	Vitamin A value Inter- national units (O)	Thiamin Milli- grams (P)	Ribo- flavin Milli- grams (Q)	Niacin Milli- grams (R)	Ascorbic acid Milli- grams (S)
475	Pizza (cheese) baked, 4 3/4-in sector; 1/8 of 12-in pie.[19]	1 sector	60	45	145	6	4	1.5	1.5	0.6	22	86	89	1.1	67	230	0.16	0.18	1.6	4
	Popcorn, popped:																			
476	Plain, large kernel	1 cup	6	4	25	1	Trace	Trace	.1	.2	5	1	17	.2	—	—	—	.01	.1	0
477	With oil (coconut) and salt added, large kernel	1 cup	9	3	40	1	2	1.5	.2	.2	5	1	19	.2	—	—	—	.01	.2	0
478	Sugar coated	1 cup	35	4	135	2	1	.5	.2	.4	30	2	47	.5	—	—	—	.02	.4	0
	Pretzels, made with enriched flour:																			
479	Dutch, twisted, 2 3/4 by 2 5/8 in.	1 pretzel	16	5	60	2	1	—	—	—	12	4	21	.2	21	0	.05	.04	.7	0
480	Thin, twisted, 3 1/4 by 2 1/4 by 1/4 in.	10 pretzels	60	5	235	6	3	—	—	—	46	13	79	.9	78	0	.20	.15	2.5	0
481	Stick, 2 1/4 in long	10 pretzels	3	5	10	Trace	Trace	—	—	—	2	1	4	Trace	4	0	.01	.01	.1	0
	Rice, white, enriched:																			
482	Instant, ready-to-serve, hot	1 cup	165	73	180	4	Trace	Trace	Trace	Trace	40	5	31	1.3	—	0	.21	(59)	1.7	0
	Long grain:																			
483	Raw	1 cup	185	12	670	12	1	.2	.2	.2	149	44	174	5.4	170	0	.81	.06	6.5	0
484	Cooked, served hot	1 cup	205	73	225	4	Trace	—	.1	.1	50	21	57	1.8	57	0	.23	.02	2.1	0
	Parboiled:																			
485	Raw	1 cup	185	10	685	14	1	.2	.1	.2	150	111	370	5.4	278	0	.81	.07	6.5	0
486	Cooked, served hot	1 cup	175	73	185	4	Trace	Trace	.1	.1	41	33	100	1.4	75	0	.19	.02	2.1	0
	Rolls, enriched:[38]																			
	Commercial:																			
487	Brown-and-serve (12 per 12-oz pkg.), browned	1 roll	26	27	85	2	2	.4	.7	.5	14	20	23	.5	25	Trace	.10	.06	.9	Trace
488	Cloverleaf or pan, 2 1/2-in diam., 2 in high.	1 roll	28	31	85	2	2	.4	.6	.4	15	21	24	.5	27	Trace	.11	.07	.9	Trace
489	Frankfurter and hamburger (8 per 11 1/2-oz pkg.).	1 roll	40	31	120	3	2	.5	.8	.6	21	30	34	.8	38	Trace	.16	.10	1.3	Trace
490	Hard, 3 3/4-in diam., 2 in high.	1 roll	50	25	155	5	2	.4	.6	.5	30	24	46	1.2	49	Trace	.20	.12	1.7	Trace
491	Hoagie or submarine, 11 1/2 by 3 by 2 1/2 in.	1 roll	135	31	390	12	4	.9	1.4	1.4	75	58	115	3.0	122	Trace	.54	.32	4.5	Trace
	From home recipe:																			
492	Cloverleaf, 2 1/2-in diam., 2 in high.	1 roll	35	26	120	3	3	.8	1.1	.7	20	16	36	.7	41	30	.12	.12	1.2	Trace
	Spaghetti, enriched, cooked:																			
493	Firm stage, "al dente," served hot.	1 cup	130	64	190	7	1	—	—	—	39	14	85	1.4	103	0	.23	.13	1.8	0
494	Tender stage, served hot	1 cup	140	73	155	5	1	—	—	—	32	11	70	1.3	85	0	.20	.11	1.5	0
	Spaghetti (enriched) in tomato sauce with cheese:																			
495	From home recipe	1 cup	250	77	260	9	9	2.0	5.4	.7	37	80	135	2.3	408	1,080	.25	.18	2.3	13
496	Canned	1 cup	250	80	190	6	2	.5	.3	.4	39	40	88	2.8	303	930	.35	.28	4.5	10
	Spaghetti (enriched) with meat balls and tomato sauce:																			
497	From home recipe	1 cup	248	70	330	19	12	3.3	6.3	.9	39	124	236	3.7	665	1,590	.25	.30	4.0	22
498	Canned	1 cup	250	78	260	12	10	2.2	3.3	3.9	29	53	113	3.3	245	1,000	.15	.18	2.3	5
499	Toaster pastries	1 pastry	50	12	200	3	6	—	—	—	36	[60]54	[60]67	1.9	[60]74	500	.16	.17	2.1	([60])
	Waffles, made with enriched flour, 7-in diam.:[38]																			
500	From home recipe	1 waffle	75	41	210	7	7	2.3	2.8	1.4	28	85	130	1.3	109	250	.17	.23	1.4	Trace
501	From mix, egg and milk added	1 waffle	75	42	205	7	8	2.8	2.9	1.2	27	179	257	1.0	146	170	.14	.22	.9	Trace

[19]Crust made with vegetable shortening and enriched flour.
[38]Made with vegetable shortening.
[59]Product may or may not be enriched with riboflavin. Consult the label.
[60]Value varies with the brand. Consult the label.

(A)		(B)	(C)	(D)	(E)	(F)	(G)	(H)	(I)	(J)	(K)	(L)	(M)	(N)	(O)	(P)	(Q)	(R)	(S)
	Wheat flours: All-purpose or family flour, enriched:																		
502	Sifted, spooned	1 cup	115	420	12	1	0.2	0.1	0.5	88	18	100	3.3	109	0	0.74	0.46	6.1	0
503	Unsifted, spooned	1 cup	125	455	13	1	.2	.1	.5	95	20	109	3.6	119	0	.80	.50	6.6	0
504	Cake or pastry flour, enriched, sifted, spooned.	1 cup	96	350	7	1	.1	.1	.3	76	16	70	2.8	91	0	.61	.38	5.1	0
505	Self-rising, enriched, unsifted, spooned.	1 cup	125	440	12	1	.2	.1	.5	93	331	583	3.6	—	0	.80	.50	6.6	0
506	Whole-wheat, from hard wheats, stirred.	1 cup	120	400	16	2	.4	.2	1.0	85	49	446	4.0	444	0	.66	.14	5.2	0
	LEGUMES (DRY), NUTS, SEEDS; RELATED PRODUCTS																		
	Almonds, shelled:																		
507	Chopped (about 130 almonds)	1 cup	130	775	24	70	5.6	47.7	12.8	25	304	655	6.1	1,005	0	.31	1.20	4.6	Trace
508	Slivered, not pressed down (about 115 almonds).	1 cup	115	690	21	62	5.0	42.2	11.3	22	269	580	5.4	889	0	.28	1.06	4.0	Trace
	Beans, dry: Common varieties as Great Northern, navy, and others: Cooked, drained:																		
509	Great Northern	1 cup	180	210	14	1	—	—	—	38	90	266	4.9	749	0	.25	.13	1.3	0
510	Pea (navy)	1 cup	190	225	15	1	—	—	—	40	95	281	5.1	790	0	.27	.13	1.3	0
	Canned, solids and liquid: White with—																		
511	Frankfurters (sliced)	1 cup	255	365	19	18	2.4	2.8	.6	32	94	303	4.8	668	330	.19	.15	3.3	Trace
512	Pork and tomato sauce	1 cup	255	310	16	7	4.3	5.0	1.1	48	138	235	4.6	536	330	.20	.08	1.5	5
513	Pork and sweet sauce	1 cup	255	385	16	12	—	—	—	54	161	291	5.9	673	10	.15	.10	1.3	—
514	Red kidney	1 cup	255	230	15	1	—	—	—	42	74	278	4.6	1,163	—	.13	.10	1.5	—
515	Lima, cooked, drained	1 cup	190	260	16	1	—	—	—	49	55	293	5.9	573	30	.25	.11	1.3	—
516	Blackeye peas, dry, cooked (with residual cooking liquid).	1 cup	250	190	13	1	—	—	—	35	43	238	3.3	573	30	.40	.10	1.0	—
517	Brazil nuts, shelled (6-8 large kernels).	1 oz	28	185	4	19	4.8	6.2	7.1	3	53	196	1.0	203	Trace	.27	.03	.5	—
518	Cashew nuts, roasted in oil	1 cup	140	785	24	64	12.9	36.8	10.2	41	53	522	5.3	650	140	.60	.35	2.5	—
	Coconut meat, fresh:																		
519	Piece, about 2 by 2 by 1/2 in	1 piece	45	155	2	16	14.0	.9	.3	4	6	43	.8	115	0	.02	.01	.2	1
520	Shredded or grated, not pressed down.	1 cup	80	275	3	28	24.8	1.6	.5	8	10	76	1.4	205	0	.04	.02	.4	2
521	Filberts (hazelnuts), chopped (about 80 kernels).	1 cup	115	730	14	72	5.1	55.2	7.3	19	240	388	3.9	810	—	.53	—	1.0	Trace
522	Lentils, whole, cooked	1 cup	200	210	16	Trace	—	—	—	39	50	238	4.2	498	40	.14	.12	1.2	0
523	Peanuts, roasted in oil, salted (whole, halves, chopped).	1 cup	144	840	37	72	13.7	33.0	20.7	27	107	577	3.0	971	—	.46	.19	24.8	0
524	Peanut butter	1 tbsp	16	95	4	8	1.5	3.7	2.3	3	9	61	.3	100	80	.02	.02	2.4	0
525	Peas, split, dry, cooked	1 cup	200	230	16	1	—	—	—	42	22	178	3.4	592	150	.30	.18	1.8	—
526	Pecans, chopped or pieces (about 120 large halves).	1 cup	118	810	11	84	7.2	50.5	20.0	17	86	341	2.8	712	—	1.01	.15	1.1	2
527	Pumpkin and squash kernels, dry, hulled.	1 cup	140	775	41	65	11.8	23.5	27.5	21	71	1,602	15.7	1,386	100	.34	.27	3.4	—
528	Sunflower seeds, dry, hulled	1 cup	145	810	35	69	8.2	13.7	43.2	29	174	1,214	10.3	1,334	70	2.84	.33	7.8	—
	Walnuts: Black:																		
529	Chopped or broken kernels	1 cup	125	785	26	74	6.3	13.3	45.7	19	Trace	713	7.5	575	380	.28	.14	.9	—
530	Ground (finely)	1 cup	80	500	16	47	4.0	8.5	29.2	12	Trace	456	4.8	368	240	.18	.09	.6	—
531	Persian or English, chopped (about 60 halves).	1 cup	120	780	18	77	8.4	11.8	42.2	19	119	456	3.7	540	40	.40	.16	1.1	2

62 DIETARY DIRECTIONS IN THE 1980s

TABLE 2.—NUTRITIVE VALUES OF THE EDIBLE PART OF FOODS - Continued

(Dashes (—) denote lack of reliable data for a constituent believed to be present in measurable amount)

Item No. (A)	Foods, approximate measures, units, and weight (edible part unless footnotes indicate otherwise) (B)		Grams	Water (C) Percent	Food energy (D) Calories	Protein (E) Grams	Fat (F) Grams	Fatty Acids Saturated (total) (G) Grams	Unsaturated Oleic (H) Grams	Linoleic (I) Grams	Carbohydrate (J) Grams	Calcium (K) Milligrams	Phosphorus (L) Milligrams	Iron (M) Milligrams	Potassium (N) Milligrams	Vitamin A value (O) International units	Thiamin (P) Milligrams	Riboflavin (Q) Milligrams	Niacin (R) Milligrams	Ascorbic acid (S) Milligrams
	SUGARS AND SWEETS																			
	Cake icings:																			
	Boiled, white:																			
532	Plain	1 cup	94	18	295	1	0	0	0	0	75	2	2	Trace	17	0	Trace	0.03	Trace	0
533	With coconut	1 cup	166	15	605	3	13	11.0	.9	Trace	124	10	50	0.8	277	0	0.02	.07	0.3	0
	Uncooked:																			
534	Chocolate made with milk and butter	1 cup	275	14	1,035	9	38	23.4	11.7	1.0	185	165	305	3.3	536	580	.06	.28	.6	1
535	Creamy fudge from mix and water	1 cup	245	15	830	7	16	5.1	6.7	3.1	183	96	218	2.7	238	Trace	.05	.20	.7	Trace
536	White	1 cup	319	11	1,200	2	21	12.7	5.1	.5	260	48	38	Trace	57	860	Trace	.06	Trace	Trace
	Candy:																			
537	Caramels, plain or chocolate	1 oz	28	8	115	1	3	1.6	1.1	.1	22	42	35	.4	54	Trace	.01	.05	.1	Trace
	Chocolate:																			
538	Milk, plain	1 oz	28	1	145	2	9	5.5	3.0	.3	16	65	65	.3	109	80	.02	.10	.1	Trace
539	Semisweet, small pieces (60 per oz)	1 cup or 6-oz pkg	170	1	860	7	61	36.2	19.8	1.7	97	51	255	4.4	553	30	.02	.14	.9	0
540	Chocolate-coated peanuts	1 oz	28	1	160	5	12	4.0	4.7	2.1	11	33	84	.4	143	Trace	.10	.05	2.1	Trace
541	Fondant, uncoated (mints, candy corn, other)	1 oz	28	8	105	Trace	1	.1	.3	.1	25	4	2	.3	1	0	Trace	Trace	Trace	0
542	Fudge, chocolate, plain	1 oz	28	8	115	1	3	1.3	1.4	.6	21	22	24	.3	42	Trace	.01	.03	.1	Trace
543	Gum drops	1 oz	28	12	100	Trace	Trace	—	—	—	25	2	Trace	.1	1	0	0	Trace	Trace	0
544	Hard	1 oz	28	1	110	0	Trace	—	—	—	28	6	2	.5	1	0	0	0	0	0
545	Marshmallows	1 oz	28	17	90	1	Trace	—	—	—	23	5	2	.5	2	0	0	Trace	Trace	0
	Chocolate-flavored beverage powders (about 4 heaping tsp per oz):																			
546	With nonfat dry milk	1 oz	28	2	100	5	1	.5	.3	Trace	20	167	155	.5	227	10	.04	.21	.2	1
547	Without milk	1 oz	28	1	100	1	1	.4	.2	Trace	25	9	48	.6	142	—	.01	.03	.1	0
548	Honey, strained or extracted	1 tbsp	21	17	65	Trace	0	0	0	0	17	1	1	.1	11	0	Trace	.01	.1	Trace
549	Jams and preserves	1 tbsp	20	29	55	Trace	Trace	—	—	—	14	4	2	.2	18	Trace	Trace	.01	Trace	Trace
550		1 packet	14	29	40	Trace	Trace	—	—	—	10	3	1	.1	12	Trace	Trace	.01	Trace	Trace
551	Jellies	1 tbsp	18	29	50	Trace	Trace	—	—	—	13	4	1	.3	14	Trace	Trace	.01	Trace	1
552		1 packet	14	29	40	Trace	Trace	—	—	—	10	3	1	.2	11	Trace	Trace	Trace	Trace	1
	Sirups:																			
	Chocolate-flavored sirup or topping:																			
553	Thin type	1 fl oz or 2 tbsp	38	32	90	1	1	.5	.3	Trace	24	6	35	.6	106	Trace	.01	.03	.2	0
554	Fudge type	1 fl oz or 2 tbsp	38	25	125	2	5	3.1	1.6	.1	20	48	60	.5	107	60	.02	.08	.2	Trace
	Molasses, cane:																			
555	Light (first extraction)	1 tbsp	20	24	50	—	—	—	—	—	13	33	9	.9	183	—	.01	.01	Trace	—
556	Blackstrap (third extraction)	1 tbsp	20	24	45	—	—	—	—	—	11	137	17	3.2	585	—	.02	.04	.4	—
557	Sorghum	1 tbsp	21	23	55	—	—	—	—	—	14	35	5	2.6	—	—	—	—	—	—
558	Table blends, chiefly corn, light and dark	1 tbsp	21	24	60	0	0	0	0	0	15	9	3	.8	1	0	0	0	0	0
559	Brown, pressed down	1 cup	220	2	820	0	0	0	0	0	212	187	42	7.5	757	0	.02	.07	.4	0
	White:																			
560	Granulated	1 cup	200	1	770	0	0	0	0	0	199	0	0	.2	6	0	0	0	0	0
561		1 tbsp	12	1	45	0	0	0	0	0	12	0	0	Trace	Trace	0	0	0	0	0
562		1 packet	6	1	23	0	0	0	0	0	6	0	0	Trace	Trace	0	0	0	0	0
563	Powdered, sifted, spooned into cup	1 cup	100	1	385	0	0	0	0	0	100	0	0	.1	3	0	0	0	0	0

DIETARY DIRECTIONS IN THE 1980s 63

VEGETABLE AND VEGETABLE PRODUCTS

(A)	(B)		(C)	(D)	(E)	(F)	(G)	(H)	(I)	(J)	(K)	(L)	(M)	(N)	(O)	(P)	(Q)	(R)	(S)
	Asparagus, green: Cooked, drained: Cuts and tips, 1 1/2- to 2-in lengths:																		
564	From raw	1 cup	145	94	3	Trace	—	—	—	5	30	30	0.9	265	1,310	0.23	0.26	2.0	38
565	From frozen	1 cup	180	93	6	Trace	—	—	—	6	40	73	2.2	396	1,530	.25	.23	1.8	41
	Spears, 1/2-in diam. at base:																		
566	From raw	4 spears	60	94	1	Trace	—	—	—	2	13	30	.4	110	540	.10	.11	.8	16
567	From frozen	4 spears	60	92	2	Trace	—	—	—	2	13	40	.7	143	470	.10	.08	.7	16
568	Canned, spears, 1/2-in diam. at base.	4 spears	80	93	2	Trace	—	—	—	3	15	42	1.5	133	640	.05	.08	.6	12
	Beans: Lima, immature seeds, frozen, cooked, drained:																		
569	Thick-seeded types (Fordhooks)	1 cup	170	74	10	Trace	—	—	—	32	34	153	2.9	724	390	.12	.09	1.7	29
570	Thin-seeded types (baby limas)	1 cup	180	69	13	Trace	—	—	—	40	63	227	4.7	709	400	.16	.09	2.2	22
	Snap: Green:																		
571	Cooked, drained: From raw (cuts and French style).	1 cup	125	92	2	Trace	—	—	—	7	63	46	.8	189	680	.09	.11	.6	15
	From frozen:																		
572	Cuts	1 cup	135	92	2	Trace	—	—	—	8	54	43	.9	205	780	.09	.12	.5	7
573	French style	1 cup	130	92	2	Trace	—	—	—	8	49	39	1.2	177	690	.08	.10	.4	9
574	Canned, drained solids (cuts).	1 cup	135	92	2	Trace	—	—	—	7	61	34	2.0	128	630	.04	.07	.4	5
	Yellow or wax: Cooked, drained:																		
575	From raw (cuts and French style).	1 cup	125	93	2	Trace	—	—	—	6	63	46	.8	189	290	.09	.11	.6	16
	From frozen (cuts)	1 cup	135	92	2	Trace	—	—	—	8	47	42	.9	221	140	.09	.11	.5	8
576																			
577	Canned, drained solids (cuts).	1 cup	135	92	2	Trace	—	—	—	7	61	34	2.0	128	140	.04	.07	.4	7
	Beans, mature. See Beans, dry (items 509-515) and Blackeye peas, dry (item 516).																		
	Bean sprouts (mung):																		
578	Raw	1 cup	105	89	4	Trace	—	—	—	7	20	67	1.4	234	20	.14	.14	.8	20
579	Cooked, drained	1 cup	125	91	4	Trace	—	—	—	7	21	60	1.1	195	30	.11	.13	.9	8
	Beets: Cooked, drained, peeled:																		
580	Whole beets, 2-in diam.	2 beets	100	91	1	Trace	—	—	—	7	14	23	.5	208	20	.03	.04	.3	6
581	Diced or sliced	1 cup	170	91	2	Trace	—	—	—	12	24	39	.9	354	30	.05	.07	.5	10
	Canned, drained solids:																		
582	Whole beets, small	1 cup	160	89	2	Trace	—	—	—	14	30	29	1.1	267	30	.02	.05	.2	5
583	Diced or sliced	1 cup	170	89	2	Trace	—	—	—	15	32	31	1.2	284	30	.02	.05	.2	5
584	Beet greens, leaves and stems, cooked, drained.	1 cup	145	94	2	Trace	—	—	—	5	144	36	2.8	481	7,400	.10	.22	.4	22
	Blackeye peas, immature seeds, cooked and drained:																		
585	From raw	1 cup	165	72	13	1	—	—	—	30	40	241	3.5	625	580	.50	.18	2.3	28
586	From frozen	1 cup	170	66	15	1	—	—	—	40	43	286	4.8	573	290	.68	.19	2.4	15
	Broccoli, cooked, drained: From raw:																		
587	Stalk, medium size	1 stalk	180	91	6	1	—	—	—	8	158	112	1.4	481	4,500	.16	.36	1.4	162
588	Stalks cut into 1/2-in pieces	1 cup	155	91	5	1	—	—	—	7	136	96	1.2	414	3,880	.14	.31	1.2	140
	From frozen:																		
589	Stalk, 4 1/2 to 5 in long	1 stalk	30	91	1	Trace	—	—	—	1	12	17	.2	66	570	.02	.03	.2	22
590	Chopped	1 cup	185	92	5	1	—	—	—	9	100	104	1.3	392	4,810	.11	.22	.9	105
591	Brussels sprouts, cooked, drained: From raw, 7-8 sprouts (1 1/4- to 1 1/2-in diam.).	1 cup	155	88	7	1	—	—	—	10	50	112	1.7	423	810	.12	.22	1.2	135
592	From frozen	1 cup	155	89	5	Trace	—	—	—	10	33	95	1.2	457	880	.12	.16	.9	126

TABLE 2.—NUTRITIVE VALUES OF THE EDIBLE PART OF FOODS - Continued

(Dashes (-) denote lack of reliable data for a constituent believed to be present in measurable amount)

Item No.	Foods, approximate measures, units, and weight (edible part unless footnotes indicate otherwise)		Water	Food energy	Protein	Fat	Fatty Acids Saturated (total)	Unsaturated Oleic	Unsaturated Linoleic	Carbohydrate	Calcium	Phosphorus	Iron	Potassium	Vitamin A value	Thiamin	Riboflavin	Niacin	Ascorbic acid
(A)	(B)	Grams	(C) Percent	(D) Calories	(E) Grams	(F) Grams	(G) Grams	(H) Grams	(I) Grams	(J) Grams	(K) Milligrams	(L) Milligrams	(M) Milligrams	(N) Milligrams	(O) International units	(P) Milligrams	(Q) Milligrams	(R) Milligrams	(S) Milligrams
	VEGETABLE AND VEGETABLE PRODUCTS—Con.																		
	Cabbage: Common varieties: Raw:																		
593	Coarsely shredded or sliced- 1 cup	70	92	15	1	Trace	—	—	—	4	34	20	0.3	163	90	0.04	0.04	0.02	33
594	Finely shredded or chopped- 1 cup	90	92	20	1	Trace	—	—	—	5	44	26	.4	210	120	.05	.05	.3	42
595	Cooked, drained- 1 cup	145	94	30	2	Trace	—	—	—	6	64	29	.4	236	190	.06	.06	.4	48
596	Red, raw, coarsely shredded or sliced. 1 cup	70	90	20	1	Trace	—	—	—	5	29	25	.6	188	30	.06	.04	.3	43
597	Savoy, raw, coarsely shredded or sliced. 1 cup	70	92	15	2	Trace	—	—	—	3	47	38	.6	188	140	.04	.06	.2	39
598	Cabbage, celery (also called pe-tsai or wongbok), raw, 1-in pieces. 1 cup	75	95	10	1	Trace	—	—	—	2	32	30	.5	190	110	.04	.03	.5	19
599	Cabbage, white mustard (also called bokchoy or pakchoy), cooked, drained. 1 cup	170	95	25	2	Trace	—	—	—	4	252	56	1.0	364	5,270	.07	.14	1.2	26
	Carrots: Raw, without crowns and tips, scraped:																		
600	Whole, 7 1/2 by 1 1/8 in, or strips, 2 1/2 to 3 in long. 1 carrot or 18 strips	72	88	30	1	Trace	—	—	—	7	27	26	.5	246	7,930	.04	.04	.4	6
601	Grated- 1 cup	110	88	45	1	Trace	—	—	—	11	41	40	.8	375	12,100	.07	.06	.7	9
602	Cooked (crosswise cuts), drained 1 cup	155	91	50	1	Trace	—	—	—	11	51	48	.9	344	16,280	.08	.08	.8	9
	Canned:																		
603	Sliced, drained solids- 1 cup	155	91	45	1	Trace	—	—	—	10	47	34	1.1	186	23,250	.03	.05	.6	3
604	Strained or junior (baby food) 1 oz (1 3/4 to 2 tbsp)	28	92	10	Trace	Trace	—	—	—	2	7	6	.1	51	3,690	.01	.01	.1	1
	Cauliflower:																		
605	Raw, chopped- 1 cup	115	91	31	3	Trace	—	—	—	6	29	64	1.3	339	70	.13	.12	.8	90
	Cooked, drained:																		
606	From raw (flower buds)- 1 cup	125	93	30	3	Trace	—	—	—	5	26	53	.9	258	80	.11	.10	.8	69
607	From frozen (flowerets)- 1 cup	180	94	30	3	Trace	—	—	—	6	31	68	.9	373	50	.07	.09	.7	74
608	Celery, Pascal type, raw: Stalk, large outer, 8 by 1 1/2 in, at root end. 1 stalk	40	94	5	Trace	Trace	—	—	—	2	16	11	.1	136	110	.01	.01	.1	4
609	Pieces, diced- 1 cup	120	94	20	1	Trace	—	—	—	5	47	34	.4	409	320	.04	.04	.4	11
	Collards, cooked, drained:																		
610	From raw (leaves without stems)- 1 cup	190	90	65	7	1	—	—	—	10	357	99	1.5	498	14,820	.21	.38	2.3	144
611	From frozen (chopped)- 1 cup	170	90	50	5	1	—	—	—	10	299	87	1.7	401	11,560	.10	.24	1.0	56
	Corn, sweet: Cooked, drained:																		
612	From raw, ear 5 by 1 3/4 in-- 1 ear[61]	140	74	70	2	1	—	—	—	16	2	69	.5	151	[62]310	.09	.08	1.1	7
	From frozen:																		
613	Ear, 5 in long- 1 ear[61]	229	73	120	4	1	—	—	—	27	4	121	1.0	291	[62]440	.18	.10	2.1	9
614	Kernels- 1 cup	165	77	130	5	1	—	—	—	31	5	120	1.3	304	[62]580	.15	.10	2.5	8
	Canned:																		
615	Cream style- 1 cup	256	76	210	5	2	—	—	—	51	8	143	1.5	248	[62]840	.08	.13	2.6	13
	Whole kernel:																		
616	Vacuum pack- 1 cup	210	76	175	5	1	—	—	—	43	6	153	1.1	204	[62]740	.06	.13	2.3	11
617	Wet pack, drained solids- 1 cup	165	76	140	4	1	—	—	—	33	8	81	.8	160	[62]580	.05	.08	1.5	7
	Cowpeas. See Blackeye peas. (Items 585-586).																		
618	Cucumber slices, 1/8 in thick (large, 2 1/8-in diam.; small, 1 3/4-in diam.): With peel- 6 large or 8 small slices	28	95	5	Trace	Trace	—	—	—	1	7	8	.3	45	70	.01	.01	.1	3

[61] Weight includes cob. Without cob, weight is 77 g for item 612, 126 g for item 613.
[62] Based on yellow varieties. For white varieties, value is trace.

64 DIETARY DIRECTIONS IN THE 1980s

DIETARY DIRECTIONS IN THE 1980s   65

(A)	(B)	(C)	(D)	(E)	(F)	(G)	(H)	(I)	(J)	(K)	(L)	(M)	(N)	(O)	(P)	(Q)	(R)	(S)
619	Without peel---------- 6 1/2 large or 9 small pieces.	28	96	5	Trace	Trace	---	---	1	5	5	0.1	45	Trace	0.01	0.01	0.1	3
620	Dandelion greens, cooked, drained-- 1 cup----------	105	90	35	2	1	---	---	7	147	44	1.9	244	12,290	.14	.17	---	19
621	Endive, curly (including escarole), raw, small pieces. 1 cup----------	50	93	10	1	Trace	---	---	2	41	27	.9	147	1,650	.04	.07	.3	5
	Kale, cooked, drained:																	
622	From raw (leaves without stems and midribs). 1 cup----------	110	88	45	5	1	---	---	7	206	64	1.8	243	9,130	.11	.20	1.8	102
623	From frozen (leaf style)-------- 1 cup----------	130	91	40	4	1	---	---	7	157	62	1.3	251	10,660	.08	.20	.9	49
	Lettuce, raw:																	
	Butterhead, as Boston types:																	
624	Head, 5-in diam--------- 1 head[63]----------	220	95	25	2	Trace	---	---	4	57	42	3.3	430	1,580	.10	.10	.5	13
625	Leaves---------- 1 outer or 2 inner or 3 heart leaves.	15	95	Trace	Trace	Trace	---	---	Trace	5	4	.3	40	150	.01	.01	Trace	1
	Crisphead, as Iceberg:																	
626	Head, 6-in diam--------- 1 head[64]----------	567	96	70	5	1	---	---	16	108	118	2.7	943	1,780	.32	.32	1.6	32
627	Wedge, 1/4 of head--------- 1 wedge----------	135	96	20	1	Trace	---	---	4	27	30	.7	236	450	.08	.08	.4	8
628	Pieces, chopped or shredded------ 1 cup----------	55	96	5	Trace	Trace	---	---	2	11	12	.3	96	180	.03	.03	.2	3
629	Looseleaf (bunching varieties including romaine or cos), chopped or shredded pieces. 1 cup----------	55	94	10	1	Trace	---	---	2	37	14	.8	145	1,050	.03	.04	.2	10
630	Mushrooms, raw, sliced or chopped-- 1 cup----------	70	90	20	2	Trace	---	---	3	4	81	.6	290	Trace	.07	.32	2.9	2
631	Mustard greens, without stems and midribs, cooked, drained. 1 cup----------	140	93	30	3	1	---	---	6	193	45	2.5	308	8,120	.11	.20	.8	67
632	Okra pods, 3 by 5/8 in, cooked---- 10 pods----------	106	91	30	2	Trace	---	---	6	98	43	.5	184	520	.14	.19	1.0	21
	Onions:																	
	Mature:																	
633	Chopped---------- 1 cup----------	170	89	65	3	Trace	---	---	15	46	61	.9	267	Trace[65]	.05	.07	.3	17
634	Sliced---------- 1 cup----------	115	89	45	2	Trace	---	---	10	31	41	.6	181	Trace[65]	.03	.05	.2	12
635	Cooked (whole or sliced), drained. 1 cup----------	210	92	60	3	Trace	---	---	14	50	61	.8	231	Trace[65]	.06	.06	.4	15
636	Young green, bulb (3/8 in diam.) and white portion of top. 6 onions----------	30	88	15	Trace	Trace	---	---	3	12	12	.2	69	Trace	.02	.01	.1	8
637	Parsley, raw, chopped---------- 1 tbsp----------	4	85	Trace	Trace	Trace	---	---	Trace	7	2	.2	25	300	Trace	.01	Trace	6
638	Parsnips, cooked (diced or 2-in lengths). 1 cup----------	155	82	100	2	1	---	---	23	70	96	.9	587	50	.11	.12	.2	16
	Peas, green:																	
	Canned:																	
639	Whole, drained solids--------- 1 cup----------	170	77	150	8	1	---	---	29	44	129	3.2	163	1,170	.15	.10	1.4	14
640	Strained (baby food)--------- 1 oz (1 3/4 to 2 tbsp)--	28	86	15	1	Trace	---	---	3	3	18	.3	28	140	.02	.03	.3	3
641	Frozen, cooked, drained-------- 1 cup----------	160	82	110	8	Trace	---	---	19	30	138	3.0	216	960	.43	.14	2.7	21
642	Peppers, hot, red, without seeds, dried (ground chili powder, added seasonings). 1 tsp----------	2	9	5	Trace	Trace	---	---	1	5	4	.3	20	1,300	Trace	.02	.2	Trace
	Peppers, sweet (about 5 per lb, whole), stem and seeds removed:																	
643	Raw---------- 1 pod----------	74	93	15	1	Trace	---	---	4	7	16	.5	157	310	.06	.06	.4	94
644	Cooked, boiled, drained-------- 1 pod----------	73	95	15	1	Trace	---	---	3	7	12	.4	109	310	.05	.05	.4	70
645	Potatoes, cooked: Baked, peeled after baking (about 2 per lb, raw). 1 potato----------	156	75	145	4	Trace	---	---	33	14	101	1.1	782	Trace	.15	.07	2.7	31
	Boiled (about 3 per lb, raw):																	
646	Peeled after boiling---------- 1 potato----------	137	80	105	3	Trace	---	---	23	10	72	.8	556	Trace	.12	.05	2.0	22
647	Peeled before boiling--------- 1 potato----------	135	83	90	3	Trace	---	---	20	8	57	.7	385	Trace	.12	.05	1.6	22
	French-fried, strip, 2 to 3 1/2 in long:																	

[63] Weight includes refuse of outer leaves and core. Without these parts, weight is 163 g.
[64] Weight includes core. Without core, weight is 539 g.
[65] Value based on white-fleshed varieties. For yellow-fleshed varieties, value in International Units (I.U.) is 70 for item 633, 50 for item 634, and 80 for item 635.

66 DIETARY DIRECTIONS IN THE 1980s

TABLE 2.— NUTRITIVE VALUES OF THE EDIBLE PART OF FOODS - Continued
(Dashes (–) denote lack of reliable data for a constituent believed to be present in measurable amount)

Item No. (A)	Foods, approximate measures, units, and weight (edible part unless footnotes indicate otherwise) (B)		Water (C) Percent	Food energy (D) Calories	Protein (E) Grams	Fat (F) Grams	Fatty Acids Saturated (total) (G) Grams	Unsaturated Oleic (H) Grams	Linoleic (I) Grams	Carbohydrate (J) Grams	Calcium (K) Milligrams	Phosphorus (L) Milligrams	Iron (M) Milligrams	Potassium (N) Milligrams	Vitamin A value (O) International units	Thiamin (P) Milligrams	Riboflavin (Q) Milligrams	Niacin (R) Milligrams	Ascorbic acid (S) Milligrams
		Grams																	
648	Prepared from raw	10 strips — 50	45	135	2	7	1.7	1.2	3.3	18	8	56	.7	427	Trace	.07	.04	1.6	11
649	Frozen, oven heated	10 strips — 50	53	110	2	4	1.1	.8	2.1	17	5	43	.9	326	Trace	.07	.01	1.3	11
650	Hashed brown, prepared from frozen	1 cup — 155	56	345	3	18	4.6	3.2	9.0	45	28	78	1.9	439	Trace	.11	.03	1.6	12
	Mashed, prepared from— Raw:																		
651	Milk added	1 cup — 210	83	135	4	2	.7	.4	Trace	27	50	103	.8	548	40	.17	.11	2.1	21
652	Milk and butter added	1 cup — 210	80	195	4	9	5.6	2.3	0.2	26	50	101	0.8	525	360	0.17	0.11	2.1	19
653	Dehydrated flakes (without milk), water, milk, butter, and salt added	1 cup — 210	79	195	4	7	3.6	2.1	.2	30	65	99	.6	601	270	.08	.08	1.9	11
654	Potato chips, 1 3/4 by 2 1/2 in oval cross section	10 chips — 20	2	115	1	8	2.1	1.4	4.0	10	8	28	.4	226	Trace	.04	.01	1.0	3
655	Potato salad, made with cooked salad dressing	1 cup — 250	76	250	7	7	2.0	2.7	1.3	41	80	160	1.5	798	350	.20	.18	2.8	28
656	Pumpkin, canned	1 cup — 245	90	80	2	Trace	—	—	—	19	61	64	1.0	588	15,680	.07	.12	1.5	12
657	Radishes, raw (prepackaged) stem ends, rootlets cut off	4 radishes — 18	95	5	Trace	Trace	—	—	—	1	5	6	.2	58	Trace	.01	.01	.1	5
658	Sauerkraut, canned, solids and liquid	1 cup — 235	93	40	2	Trace	—	—	—	9	85	42	1.2	329	120	.07	.09	.5	33
	Southern peas. See Blackeye peas (items 585-586). Spinach:																		
659	Raw, chopped	1 cup — 55	91	15	2	Trace	—	—	—	2	51	28	1.7	259	4,460	.06	.11	.3	28
660	Cooked, drained: From raw	1 cup — 180	92	40	5	1	—	—	—	6	167	68	4.0	583	14,580	.13	.25	.9	50
	From frozen:																		
661	Chopped	1 cup — 205	92	45	6	1	—	—	—	8	232	90	4.3	683	16,200	.14	.31	.8	39
662	Leaf	1 cup — 190	92	45	6	1	—	—	—	7	200	84	4.8	688	15,390	.15	.27	1.0	53
663	Canned, drained solids	1 cup — 205	91	50	6	1	2.0	.8	.1	7	242	53	5.3	513	16,400	.04	.25	.6	29
	Squash, cooked:																		
664	Summer (all varieties), diced, drained	1 cup — 210	96	30	2	Trace	—	—	—	7	53	53	.8	296	820	.11	.17	1.7	21
665	Winter (all varieties), baked, mashed	1 cup — 205	81	130	4	1	—	—	—	32	57	98	1.6	945	8,610	.10	.27	1.4	27
	Sweetpotatoes: Cooked (raw, 5 by 2 in; about 2 1/2 per lb):																		
666	Baked in skin, peeled	1 potato — 114	64	160	2	1	—	—	—	37	46	66	1.0	342	9,230	.10	.08	.8	25
667	Boiled in skin, peeled	1 potato — 151	71	170	3	1	—	—	—	40	48	71	1.1	367	11,940	.14	.09	.9	26
668	Candied, 2 1/2 by 2-in piece	1 piece — 105	60	175	1	3	—	—	.1	36	39	45	.9	200	6,620	.06	.04	.4	11
	Canned:																		
669	Solid pack (mashed)	1 cup — 255	72	275	5	1	—	—	—	63	64	105	2.0	510	19,890	.13	.10	1.5	36
670	Vacuum pack, piece 2 3/4 by 1 in	1 piece — 40	72	45	1	Trace	—	—	—	10	10	16	.3	80	3,120	.02	.02	.2	6
	Tomatoes:																		
671	Raw, 2 3/5-in diam. (3 per 12 oz pkg.)	1 tomato[66] — 135	94	25	1	Trace	—	—	—	6	16	33	.6	300	1,110	.07	.05	.9	[67]28
672	Canned, solids and liquid	1 cup — 241	94	50	2	Trace	—	—	—	10	[68]14	46	1.2	523	2,170	.12	.07	1.7	41
673	Tomato catsup	1 cup — 273	69	290	5	1	—	—	—	69	60	137	2.2	991	3,820	.25	.19	4.4	41
674		1 tbsp — 15	69	15	Trace	Trace	—	—	—	4	3	8	.1	54	210	.01	.01	.2	2
	Tomato juice, canned:																		
675	Cup	1 cup — 243	94	45	2	Trace	—	—	—	10	17	44	2.2	552	1,940	.12	.07	1.9	39
676	Glass (6 fl oz)	1 glass — 182	94	35	2	Trace	—	—	—	8	13	33	1.6	413	1,460	.09	.05	1.5	29
677	Turnips, cooked, diced	1 cup — 155	94	35	1	Trace	—	—	—	8	54	37	.6	291	Trace	.06	.08	.5	34
	Turnip greens, cooked, drained:																		
678	From raw (leaves and stems)	1 cup — 145	94	30	3	Trace	—	—	—	5	252	49	1.5	—	8,270	.15	.33	.7	68
679	From frozen (chopped)	1 cup — 165	93	40	4	Trace	—	—	—	6	195	64	2.6	246	11,390	.08	.15	.7	31
680	Vegetables, mixed, frozen, cooked	1 cup — 182	83	115	6	1	—	—	—	24	46	115	2.4	348	9,010	.22	.13	2.0	15

[66] Weight includes cores and stem ends. Without these parts, weight is 123 g.
[67] Based on year-round average. For tomatoes marketed from November through May, value is about 12 mg; from June through October, 32 mg.
[68] Applies to product without calcium salts added. Value for products with calcium salts added may be as much as 63 mg for whole tomatoes, 241 mg for cut forms.

DIETARY DIRECTIONS IN THE 1980s

(A)	(B)		(C)	(D)	(E)	(F)	(G)	(H)	(I)	(J)	(K)	(L)	(M)	(N)	(O)	(P)	(Q)	(R)	(S)
	MISCELLANEOUS ITEMS—Con.																		
	Baking powders for home use:																		
681	Sodium aluminum sulfate: With monocalcium phosphate monohydrate.	1 tsp	3.0	2	5	Trace	Trace	0	0	0	1	58	87	—	5	0	0	0	0	0
682	With monocalcium phosphate monohydrate, calcium sulfate.	1 tsp	2.9	1	5	Trace	Trace	0	0	0	1	183	45	—	—	0	0	0	0	0
683	Straight phosphate	1 tsp	3.8	2	5	Trace	Trace	0	0	0	1	239	359	—	6	0	0	0	0	0
684	Low sodium	1 tsp	4.3	2	5	Trace	Trace	0	0	0	2	207	314	—	471	0	0	0	0	0
685	Barbecue sauce	1 cup	250	81	230	4	17	2.2	4.3	10.0	20	53	50	2.0	435	900	.03	.03	.8	13
	Beverages, alcoholic:																			
686	Beer	12 fl oz	360	92	150	1	0	0	0	0	14	18	108	Trace	90	—	.01	.11	2.2	—
	Gin, rum, vodka, whisky:																			
687	80-proof	1 1/2-fl oz jigger	42	67	95	—	—	—	—	0	Trace	—	—	—	1	—	—	—	—	—
688	86-proof	1 1/2-fl oz jigger	42	64	105	—	—	—	—	0	Trace	—	—	—	1	—	—	—	—	—
689	90-proof	1 1/2-fl oz jigger	42	62	110	—	—	—	—	0	Trace	—	—	—	1	—	—	—	—	—
	Wines:																			
690	Dessert	3 1/2-fl oz glass	103	77	140	Trace	Trace	0	0	0	8	8	—	—	77	—	.01	.02	.2	—
691	Table	3 1/2-fl oz glass	102	86	85	Trace	Trace	0	0	0	4	9	10	.4	94	—	Trace	.01	.1	—
	Beverages, carbonated, sweetened, nonalcoholic:																			
692	Carbonated water	12 fl oz	366	92	115	0	0	0	0	0	29	—	—	—	—	0	0	0	0	0
693	Cola type	12 fl oz	369	90	145	0	0	0	0	0	37	—	—	—	—	0	0	0	0	0
694	Fruit-flavored sodas and Tom Collins mixer.	12 fl oz	372	88	170	0	0	0	0	0	45	—	—	—	—	0	0	0	0	0
695	Ginger ale	12 fl oz	366	92	115	0	0	0	0	0	29	—	—	—	0	0	0	0	0	0
696	Root beer	12 fl oz	370	90	150	0	0	0	0	0	39	—	—	—	0	0	0	0	0	0
	Chili powder. See Peppers, hot, red (item 642).																			
	Chocolate:																			
697	Bitter or baking	1 oz	28	2	145	3	15	8.9	4.9	.4	8	22	109	1.9	235	20	.01	.07	.4	0
	Semisweet, see Candy, chocolate (item 539).																			
698	Gelatin, dry	1 7-g envelope	7	13	25	6	Trace	0	0	0	0	—	—	—	—	—	—	—	—	—
699	Gelatin dessert prepared with gelatin dessert powder and water.	1 cup	240	84	140	4	0	0	0	0	34	—	—	—	7	—	—	—	—	—
700	Mustard, prepared, yellow	1 tsp or individual serving pouch or cup.	5	80	5	Trace	Trace	—	—	—	Trace	4	4	.1	7	—	—	—	—	—
	Olives, pickled, canned:																			
701	Green	4 medium or 3 extra large or 2 giant.[69]	16	78	15	Trace	2	.2	1.2	.1	Trace	8	2	.2	7	40	Trace	Trace	Trace	—
702	Ripe, Mission	3 small or 2 large[69]	10	73	15	Trace	2	.2	1.2	.1	Trace	9	1	.1	2	10	Trace	Trace	Trace	—
	Pickles, cucumber:																			
703	Dill, medium, whole, 3 3/4 in long, 1 1/4-in diam.	1 pickle	65	93	5	Trace	Trace	—	—	—	1	17	14	.7	130	70	Trace	.01	Trace	4
704	Fresh-pack, slices 1 1/2-in diam., 1/4 in thick.	2 slices	15	79	10	Trace	Trace	—	—	—	3	5	4	.3	—	20	Trace	Trace	Trace	1
705	Sweet, gherkin, small, whole, about 2 1/2 in long, 3/4-in diam.	1 pickle	15	61	20	Trace	Trace	—	—	—	5	2	2	.2	—	10	Trace	Trace	Trace	1
706	Relish, finely chopped, sweet	1 tbsp	15	63	20	Trace	Trace	—	—	—	5	3	2	.1	—	—	—	—	—	—
707	Popcorn. See items 476-478.																			
	Popsicle, 3-fl oz size	1 popsicle	95	80	70	0	0	0	0	0	18	0	—	Trace	—	0	0	0	0	0
	Soups:																			
	Canned, condensed: Prepared with equal volume of milk:																			
708	Cream of chicken	1 cup	245	85	180	7	10	4.2	3.6	1.3	15	172	152	.5	260	610	.05	.27	.7	2
709	Cream of mushroom	1 cup	245	83	215	7	14	5.4	2.9	4.6	16	191	169	.5	279	250	.05	.34	.7	1
710	Tomato	1 cup	250	84	175	7	7	3.4	1.7	1.0	23	168	155	.8	418	1,200	.10	.25	1.3	15
	Prepared with equal volume of water:																			
711	Bean with pork	1 cup	250	84	170	8	6	1.2	1.8	2.4	22	63	128	2.3	395	650	.13	.08	1.0	3

[69] Weight includes pits. Without pits, weight is 13 g for item 701, 9 g for item 702.

68 DIETARY DIRECTIONS IN THE 1980s

(A)	(B)		(C)	(D)	(E)	(F)	(G)	(H)	(I)	(J)	(K)	(L)	(M)	(N)	(O)	(P)	(Q)	(R)	(S)
712	Beef broth, bouillon, consomme.	1 cup	240	96	30	5	0	0	0	0	3	Trace	31	.5	130	Trace	Trace	.02	1.2	---
713	Beef noodle	1 cup	240	93	65	4	3	.6	.7	.8	3	7	7	48	1.0	77	50	.05	.07	1.0	Trace
714	Clam chowder, Manhattan type (with tomatoes, without milk).	1 cup	245	92	80	2	3	.5	.4	1.3	3	12	34	47	1.0	184	880	.02	.02	1.0	
715	Cream of chicken	1 cup	240	92	95	3	6	1.6	2.3	1.1	3	8	24	34	.5	79	410	.02	.05	.5	Trace
716	Cream of mushroom	1 cup	240	90	135	2	10	2.6	1.7	4.5	3	10	41	50	.5	98	70	.02	.12	.7	Trace
717	Minestrone	1 cup	245	90	105	5	3	.7	.9	1.3	3	14	37	59	1.0	314	2,350	.07	.05	1.0	1
718	Split pea	1 cup	245	85	145	9	3	1.1	1.2	.4	3	21	29	149	1.5	270	440	.25	.15	1.5	12
719	Tomato	1 cup	245	91	90	2	3	.5	.5	1.0	3	16	15	34	.7	230	1,000	.05	.05	1.2	---
720	Vegetable beef	1 cup	245	92	80	5	2	---	---	---	3	10	12	49	1.0	162	2,700	.05	.05	1.0	---
721	Vegetarian	1 cup	245	92	80	2	2	---	---	---	3	13	20	39	1.0	172	2,940	.05	.05	1.0	
722	Dehydrated: Bouillon cube, 1/2 in	1 cube	4	4	5	1	Trace	---	---	Trace	---	---	---	---	---	4	---	---	---	---	
723	Mixes: Unprepared: Onion	1 1/2-oz pkg	43	3	150	6	5	1.1	2.3	1.0	23	42	49	.6	238	30	.05	.03	.3	6
724	Prepared with water: Chicken noodle	1 cup	240	95	55	2	1	---	---	---	3	8	7	19	.2	19	50	.07	.05	.5	Trace
725	Onion	1 cup	240	96	35	1	1	---	---	---	3	6	10	12	.2	58	Trace	Trace	.02	Trace	2
726	Tomato vegetable with noodles.	1 cup	240	93	65	1	1	---	---	---	3	12	7	19	.2	29	480	.05	.02	.5	5
727	Vinegar, cider	1 tbsp	15	94	Trace	Trace	0	0	0	0	---	1	1	1	.1	15	---	---	---	---	---
728	White sauce, medium, with enriched flour.	1 cup	250	73	405	10	31	19.3	7.8	.8	22	288	233	.5	348	1,150	.12	.43	.7	2
	Yeast:																			
729	Baker's, dry, active	1 pkg	7	5	20	3	Trace	---	---	---	3	3	[70]17	90	1.1	140	Trace	.16	.38	2.5	Trace
730	Brewer's, dry	1 tbsp	8	5	25	3	Trace	---	---	---	3	3	[70]17	140	1.4	152	Trace	1.25	.34	3.0	Trace

[70] Value may vary from 6 to 60 mg.

ENERGY REQUIREMENTS

Energy Balance Throughout the Life Cycle

by National Dairy Council

SUMMARY

The several dietary guidelines recently issued to the American public are consistent in their recommendation to attain and maintain an appropriate body weight for height throughout life. The achievement of this goal requires a balance between energy intake and energy expenditure. Unfortunately, a positive energy balance leading to obesity is a public health problem affecting as many as 10 to 50 million Americans. Excess body fat is associated with decreased longevity, the development of such chronic health disorders as cardiovascular disease, hypertension, gall bladder disease, maturity-onset diabetes, and various psychological disturbances. Much is to be gained by avoiding excess body fat, or if already obese, correcting the condition. Success of treatment is disappointing, and there is a lack of understanding of the complex multifactorial etiology of this condition. Genetic, physiological, psychological, and environmental factors can be shown to influence both sides of the equation: energy intake and energy expenditure. Environmental factors, specifically the unlimited availability of highly palatable foods coupled with physical inactivity, are a pervasive influence in the etiology of obesity. The suggested difference in the efficiency of energy utilization between lean and obese individuals is an area of considerable interest. Treatment modality must be selected on the basis of efficacy in relation to risk. A conservative weight-reducing approach employing moderate energy restriction, increased physical exercise, and behavioral modification is favored. The best approach is avoidance of overweight and obesity at all times throughout the life cycle.

Energy balance throughout the life cycle from infancy through childhood, adolescence, and adulthood depends upon energy intake in relation to energy expenditure. Total energy intake must be adjusted to a level that will prevent overweight or underweight, yet provide essential nutrients. The recommendation to attain and maintain an appropriate body weight for height by controlling energy intake and output is a common denominator of the several recently published U.S. dietary recommendations (1-5). The National Nutrition Consortium Board (6) whose member organizations represent 60,000 trained nutritionists, as well as the American Dietetic Association in a separate position statement (7) likewise endorses this principle.

Obesity (excess body fat above some arbitrary limit) and overweight (excess body weight above some standard weight), conditions resulting from periods of positive energy balance, are considered in this *Digest*. Specifically, the high prevalence, detrimental consequences, complex etiology, and multiple modes of treatment are addressed. Interest in this subject is attested to by the several major international congresses on obesity and energy balance held within the past six years (8-12).

SIGNIFICANCE

Incidence. While overweight/obesity is viewed as a pressing nutritional challenge of public health concern, the precise extent of the problem is unknown. Prevalence data vary according to source of information (e.g., life insurance statistics, national health surveys), techniques used to quantify body fatness (e.g., inspection, anthropometric measurements, body density, isotopic dilution techniques), and the definition of obesity (i.e., the cut-off point between obesity, overweight, and appropriate weight for height).

From *Dairy Council Digest*, Vol. 51, No. 4, July-August 1980, pp. 19-23. Copyright 1980, National Dairy Council. Reprinted with permission.

Based on measurements of skinfold thickness obtained from the U.S. Health and Nutrition Examination Survey (HANES) 1971-1974, conducted by the National Center for Health Statistics, 18% of men aged 20-74 years and 13% of women within the same age range are 10-19% above appropriate weight for height. For those weighing 20% or more above their appropriate weight for height the figures are 14% and 24% for men and women respectively (11,13). Differences in the incidence of overweight are shown to vary according to sex, age, and racial, socioeconomic, and cultural groups (12). More women than men are 20% or more overweight; the reverse holds true for persons 10 to 19% overweight (11,13). Although overweight increases sharply beyond age 30, reaching a peak of 39% of men and 50% of women who are 10% or more overweight, the incidence declines after age 55-65 years (11-13). In terms of actual numbers, an estimated 10-50 million Americans are overweight or obese (12); 2.8 million men and 4.5 million women are severely obese (14). The significance of the problem is portrayed by Hannon and Lohman (15) who have calculated that the energy saved by dieting once Americans have reached their appropriate weight for height is equivalent to 1.3 billion gallons of gasoline or the amount of energy necessary to furnish the annual residential electrical demands of Boston.

Consequences. The effect of excess body fatness on longevity, health, and psychosocial interactions has been well documented (2,9-12, 16-21). Obesity is not a homogeneous entity, and conceivably specific types of obesity as well as the severity could have unique implications for health (11,17). Not all obese individuals will exhibit, or exhibit equally, the negative consequences of excess body weight. Furthermore, obesity rarely exists alone without other changes in lifestyle. Epidemiological evidence and findings from animal and human experimentation, however, indicate an independent role of obesity as a health hazard (16).

According to 1959 and 1979 life insurance statistics, excess body weight correlates with increased mortality rates, and as a corollary, weight reduction prolongs life (12, 17). An 11% decrease in life expectancy is shown in men 10% above average weight; the comparable figure for women is 7% (17). If body weight increases to 20% above average weight, the risk of excess mortality reaches 20% for men, 10% for women (12). The consequences of morbid obesity are even more profound. Drenick et al (22) have demonstrated a 12-fold excess in mortality in morbidly obese men aged 25-34 years and a six-fold excess in the group aged 35-44 years compared with nonobese males in the same age category.

Of note are the differences in minimum mortality risk between the Framingham, Massachusetts prospective study and the life insurance statistics (23). According to the latter, minimum mortality risk occurs among individuals 10% below average weight. By contrast, the Framingham data show minimum mortality around the average weight with increased mortality for persons weighing more or less than average. This finding raises some question as to whether Americans should be encouraged to weigh less than average weights.

Excess mortality associated with overweight is attributed to cardiovascular disease, hypertension, gall bladder disease, and maturity-onset diabetes mellitus (11,12,17,20). Van Itallie (17) has tabulated health disorders and other problems associated with or aggravated by obesity. In addition to the above, musculoskeletal disorders (osteoarthritis), renal disease, liver disease, pulmonary impairment, peripheral vascular disease, gout, cerebrovascular disease, and some forms of cancer (malignancy of the breast and endometrium) are listed. Obese persons experience greater than normal risk from surgery, anesthesia, accidents, and pregnancy and childbirth. The obese individual also can be burdened with psychosocial problems which interfere with the "quality of life." The inability to cope with the cultural environment, an ill-perceived self-image, and the tendency for obese persons to be discriminated against with respect to employment and promotions and in social situations are examples of some of the problems (10,12,16,17). Of interest is the suggestion that obesity acquired between the ages of 20-40 years is more detrimental to health and longevity than either lifelong overweight of moderate severity (17) or obesity in old age (24).

Can the various metabolic alterations and chronic disorders associated with overweight and obesity be corrected with weight loss? Data indicate that obesity is not a major independent risk factor in cardiovascular disease, particularly in women and in persons aged 65-74 years (12,17,21). Nevertheless, reduction of excess body fatness is associated with significant improvements in atherogenic traits such as hypertension, diabetes, hyperlipidemia, and gout (1,17,25,26). According to Reisin et al (27) weight loss significantly reduced elevated blood pressure in more than 50% of patients studied. Similarly, the clinical and chemical manifestations of maturity-onset diabetes tend in most cases to regress with weight reduction (10,12).

Indications are that the incidence of obesity/overweight is high and that the detrimental effects on health, well-being, and longevity are substantial, yet a number of unanswered questions remain. What is the true incidence of obesity? What health risks can be independently attributed to obesity? These and other questions are posed by the Food and Nutrition Board, National Academy of Sciences (20).

COMPLEX MULTIFACTORIAL ETIOLOGY

The statement that obesity results from periods of positive energy balance belies the complexity of the many factors that influence energy intake and energy expenditure (9-12). The precise etiology of obesity is unknown, although possible explanations abound. Genetic, physiological, psychological, and environmental factors have been implicated. The suggestion that obesity or susceptibility to obesity is genetically transmitted is supported by the existence of certain obese strains of laboratory animals (e.g., Zucker obese rat) and human studies involving identical twins who have similar body weights even when raised apart, adopted children who fail to follow their parents' weight as do natural children, and clustering of obesity in families (10,12,21). The difficulty in separating genetic from environmental influences is evident, and it may be that they interact in a way compatible with the development of obesity (12,28,29). Considerable interest is focused on the question of why apparently similar individuals can maintain energy balance on widely differing energy intakes. Is there a difference in the "efficiency" of energy utilization (9-11, 16,29)?

Energy Intake. Regulatory mechanisms to control food intake are ill-defined, but it is hypothesized that their failure could dispose an individual to positive energy balance and hence obesity (12,20,30). The central mechanism by which the body adjusts energy intake to replete or reduce its energy store (i.e., adipose tissue depot) is described as having many features of a negative feedback control system (30). There has been a departure from the previously accepted concept of a dual center in the hypothalamus involved in the central control of food intake: the lateral hypothalamus as a "feeding center" and the ventromedial hypothalamus as a "satiety center" (11,12,30). Van Itallie et al (30) have reviewed numerous experiments, the results of which suggest the presence of diffuse neural pathways in the brain for the excitation and inhibition of feeding. Evidence is accumulating to suggest that brain neurotransmitters, norepinephrine and serotonin which are present endogenously in several major brain pathways, have a central role in eating behavior, either directly or indirectly. Serotonin-depleted rats, for example, exhibit hyperphagia and obesity. However, additional data are needed to confirm whether serotonergic neurons normally inhibit feeding, or conversely whether their depletion leads to overeating and an increase in body weight (30).

It is hypothesized that the neural controller responds to different internal and external satiety signals, the result being expressed by specific meal patterns (e.g., meal size, interval between meals, or both). Probably, both innate and learned mechanisms are involved in meal pattern control. The exact nature of satiety signals is unknown but gastric, intestinal, and postintestinal components have been investigated (30). Signals arising from the gastrointestinal tract, mainly from the small intestine, are emphasized in terms of initiating a satiety response and terminating feeding (negative feedback). Intestinal satiety may be triggered by both humoral satiety signals (e.g., cholecystokinin) and neural signals (30). On the other hand, products of digestion (e.g., hexose sugars, amino acids, some peptides, short- and medium-chain fatty acids and some free glycerol) once absorbed may signal the quantity of stored energy and thus contribute to the maintenance of satiety. Hormones, such as insulin which increases hunger and food intake and glucagon which decreases food intake, as well as growth hormone and cortisol presumably play a role in the short-term control of food intake. In any event, it would appear hypothetically that the neural controller responds to internal signals which reflect energy requirements (i.e., the need to replete or reduce the adipocyte's content of triglyceride) with the result that the pattern of food intake is altered accordingly (30).

External signals also may regulate food intake, and studies have been conducted to ascertain whether the obese are more sensitive to environmental stimuli than normal weight individuals (12). This concept provides a rationale for the behavioral modification technique of weight control (12). The interaction between external and internal food-related cues is complex, thus limiting identification of their relative importance. Environmental or nonhomeostatic factors, as opposed to specific genetic, neural, and hormonal conditions, are favored by a number of investigators as explaining the short-term control of food intake and the occurrence of moderate overweight (9-12,21,29,31-33). The unlimited availability of highly palatable food and beverages coupled with physical inactivity is a pervasive influence in the etiology of obesity (29). This so-called "supermarket" obesity has been demonstrated in both animals and humans, although susceptibility to dietary-induced weight gains is variable, suggesting a genetic component. It is the total intake of food energy that is of importance. There is no evidence that the source of energy-protein, fat, or carbohydrate, or any particular food or combination of foods when consumed in recommended amounts—leads to obesity (16).

Psychosocial factors also may determine an individual's food choices and quantities (10,34-38). For example, some individuals overeat in response to anger, boredom, and stress (34,37). However, a specific personality type characterizing the obese has not been found (34,37).

Energy Expenditure. Differences in energy expenditure, both discretionary (i.e., muscular work) and obligatory (i.e., resting metabolism) between lean and overweight individuals are being elucidated as a result of recent advances in calorimetry which allow more accurate measurement of energy expenditure (10,20). Certainly the discretionary component of energy expenditure, namely physical activity, is highly variable. Physical inactivity, a common feature of modern work and lifestyle, undoubtedly plays an important role in the establishment and perpetuation of obesity, particularly in the case of certain children, adolescents, adults with middle-age spread, and the elderly (12,16,21). For those who already are overweight, it is not always evident whether decreased physical activity is the result or the cause of the condition (16). At both extremely low and high levels of energy expenditure the ability to regulate energy balance precisely may be compromised (20,33).

Obligatory energy expenditure, measured by basal metabolic rate (BMR), is a function of the amount of energy lost as heat due to the performance of chemical and physical internal work and that dissipated from the body due to the requirement to maintain a body temperature different from that of the environment. BMR amounts to about 800 to 900 kcal/meter squared of body surface per day; is lower in females; and declines with age (12,20). A variation of about 15% above and below the mean BMR is shown for individuals matched for age, sex, and surface area (10). The BMR appears to rise and fall with the increase or decrease in food intake, respectively (10,28). Energy utilization is more efficient when energy intake is reduced—a situation which may be a source of frustration for those attempting to lose weight on greatly reduced energy intakes.

Energy stored in the body in the form of adenosine triphosphate (ATP) is used for muscle contraction, biochemical transformations, and heat production. The question is whether obese and lean individuals differ in the efficiency with which they use energy for the above processes (20). Energy required for muscular work is similar for both lean and obese subjects (12). There has been renewed interest in an adaptive change in thermogenesis, specifically diet—induced thermogenesis (the increase in heat production caused by increased food intake) in regulating energy balance (9,10,28,39-43). Some obese subjects may be limited in their ability to produce heat after ingestion of food. This subnormal **thermogenic response** could reduce the maintenance requirement for energy, thereby preferentially shunting **dietary energy to adipose tissue**. However, evidence showing that lean people have a greater thermic response to food and obese individuals a smaller response is equivocal (10,39,40,44). This question is currently under intensive investigation. Mechanisms responsible for the thermic effect of ingested food are not understood, although a genetic basis and various biochemical schemes (e.g., alterations in the rates of substrate or "futile" cycles) are being investigated (41-43). If thermogenesis accounts for the variations in energy expenditure between individuals, it probably is the result of a genetic factor for a high efficiency of food utilization (28). The latter coupled with environmentally induced large intakes of food could lead to marked obesity.

Adipose Tissue Cellularity. Based on adipose tissue morphology three types of obesity have been described: (i) hyperplastic or hypercellular obesity characterized by an increased number and size of fat cells, (ii) hypertrophic obesity in which the number of adipocytes remain normal but the fat cell size is increased, and (iii) a mixed type (9-11,18,21,45). The etiology of adipocyte hypercellularity is unknown but may be partly genetically and partly environmentally determined (10). Hyperplastic obesity most likely begins in childhood, critical periods for cell multiplication being the first two years of life and again between four and 11 years of age (12). Obese individuals whose overweight began in childhood exhibit not only enlarged fat cells but a two-to-four-fold increase in the number of adipocytes (12). Prospective studies of adipose cellularity from childhood into adulthood, however, are needed to substantiate the suggestion that hypercellular obesity is exclusively early-onset (10). Total fat cell number is difficult to quantify by current methodology, and the potential presence of preadipocytes cannot be excluded (10). Hyperplastic obesity is the more severe form of obesity and usually is quite refractory to treatment. With weight loss, the size of the fat cell shrinks but the total number of adipocytes remains the same. Reasons for the poor prognosis are unknown, although both physiological and psychological hypotheses have been advanced. In hyperplastic obesity, regulatory mechanisms of energy balance associated with depot fat storage capacity may be upset, or the overweight child may acquire psychological attitudes about food which lead to obesity in adulthood (21,35). Not all obese children, however, become obese adults, and the obesity is by no means irrevocable, just more difficult to treat (35).

Hypertrophic obesity is primarily adult-onset and characterized by a more moderate increase in body-fat mass than hypercellular obesity. This form of obesity is often associated with hypertension, decreased glucose tolerance, and elevated plasma insulin and triglyceride levels (10,11). It is apparent that there are different forms of obesity, thus confounding the definition and treatment of this condition.

TREATMENT

The numerous approaches to produce negative energy balance include: (1) diet modification (total starvation, very low energy diets(<800 kcal per day), and conventional reducing diets) (46); (2) behavorial modification techniques to repattern dietary and physical activity habits; (3) increased exercise and physical activity (47,48); (4) pharmacological agents (appetite suppressants, calorigenic agents)(49); (5)surgery (gastric bypass, jejunoileal bypass, jaw wiring) (50-54); and (6) various combinations of the above (55,56). These techniques have been reviewed elsewhere (9-12,57,58). In spite of the multiple modes of treatment, several common features are noted. First, in many cases there is no cure for obesity—the various therapeutic modalities listed above tend to treat the symptom, not the cause. There are exceptions, however; if obesity is the result of physical inactivity, treatment with exercise might be said to get at the cause. Second, regardless of the weight-reducing strategy, the prognosis for success, at least in the long-term is generally low. While any one of the above treatments may be effective in eliciting short-term and often rapid weight losses, the long-term success rate has been disappointing, particularly in hyperplastic obesity (59,60). Third, this failure to permanently reduce body weight may be related to an incomplete understanding of the etiology and pathogenesis of obesity (61). And fourth, treatment approaches tailored to the individual, and preventive measures begun early in life to avoid overweight are emphasized (5,9,16,20,21).

While there is no question about the advantages of reducing excess weight if overweight, of great concern is the efficacy of treatment in relation to risk. For example, resorting to surgical intervention carries significant risk of morbidity and mortality, but for some morbidly obese patients for whom such risks are already a reality, surgery may be justified. The most compelling evidence of risk outweighing benefit is the 58 fatalities reported in the U.S. during the late 1970s in persons during or shortly following massive rapid weight reduction by adherence to extremely low-energy (300-500 kcal/day) diets consisting of collagen-or gelatin-hydrolysates (62,63). Investigations conducted by the Center for Disease Control and by the Food and Drug Administration on 17 of the individuals who had been obese but otherwise basically healthy disclosed that death was precipitated by cardiac arrhythmias of unknown cause.

For individuals with mild to moderate degrees of obesity, a conservative weight-reducing approach employing moderate energy restriction, increased physical exercise, and behavioral modification offers the most benefit with the least risk (1-7,16,63). A gradual, steady, weight loss of one-to-two pounds per week until appropriate weight for height is achieved is relatively safe (4). By wise selection of a variety of foods and careful adherence to minimum servings recommended by USDA's Daily Food Guides (USDA, 1957, 1979), 80-120% of the RDA for several selected nutrients can be met by a diet providing only about 1200 kcal daily (5). Increased physical exercise not only increases energy expenditure but improves physical fitness and well-being, helps to mobilize stored fat, and facilitates appetite control (2,5,7). Long-term management of obesity necessitates a basic and permanent change in eating and exercise habits (17). This, in turn, requires a high degree of motivation or long-term discipline. Perhaps, as stated by Garn and Cole (64) "the best way to avoid obesity is to start out lean."

Acknowledgments: National Dairy Council assumes the responsibility for writing and editing this publication. However, we would like to acknowledge the help and suggestions of the following reviewers in its preparation: George A. Bray, M.D., Professor of Medicine, UCLA — Harbor General Hospital, Torrance, California; and T.B. Van Itallie, M.D., Director, Obesity Research Center, St. Luke's-Roosevelt Hospital Center, New York, New York.

REFERENCES

1. Select Committee on Nutrition and Human Needs, U.S. Senate. *Dietary Goals for the United States*. Washington, D.C.. U.S. Government Printing Office, 1977.
2. Council on Scientific Affairs, American Medical Association. JAMA 242: 2335, 1979.
3. Food and Nutrition Board. *Recommended Dietary Allowances, Ninth Revised Edition*. Washington, D.C.: National Academy of Sciences, National Research Council, 1980.
4. U.S. Department of Agriculture, U.S. Department of Health, Education and Welfare. *Nutrition and Your Health. Dietary Guidelines for Americans*. February, 1980.
5. Food and Nutrition Board, National Research Council. *Toward Healthful Diets*. Washington, D.C.: National Academy of Sciences, National Research Council, 1980.
6. National Nutrition Consortium. Nutr. Rev. 38: 96, 1980.
7. The American Dietetic Association. J.Am.Diet.Assoc. 76: 437, 1980.
8. National Institutes of Health. *Obesity in Perspective*. G.A. Bray (Ed). Fogarty International Series on Preventive Medicine, Vol. II, Part 2, DHEW Publication No. (NIH) 75-708, 1975.
9. Garrow, J.S. *Energy Balance and Obesity in Man*. 2nd ed. New York: Elsevier/North-Holland Biomedical Press, 1978.
10. Bray, G.A. (Ed). *Recent Advances in Obesity Research:* II. Proceedings of the 2nd International Congress on Obesity. Westport, Conn.: Food & Nutrition Press, Inc., 1979.
11. National Institutes of Health. *Obesity in America*. G.A. Bray (Ed). DHEW Publication No. (NIH) 79-359, 1979.
12. Bray, G.A. DM; Disease-a-Month 26, 1979.
13. Abraham, S., and C.L. Johnson. *Vital and Health Statistics. Advance Data No. 51*. Hyattsville, MD.: Public Health Service, DHEW. In preparation.
14. Abraham, S., and C.L. Johnson. Am.J.Clin.Nutr. 33 (Suppl. 2): 364, 1980.
15. Hannon, B.M., and T.G. Lohman. Am.J.Public Health 68: 765, 1978.
16. Van Itallie, T.B., and J. Hirsch. Am.J.Clin.Nutr. 32 (Suppl.): 2648, 1979.
17. Van Itallie, T.B. Am.J.Clin.Nutr. 32 (Suppl.): 2723, 1979.
18. Bray, G.A. Int. J. Obesity 2: 99, 1978.
19. Bray, G.A. Food & Nutr. Notes & Rev. (Australia) 36: 130, 1979.

20. Food & Nutrition Board, National Research Council. *Research Needs For Establishing Dietary Guidelines For The U.S. Population.* Washington, D.C.: National Academy of Sciences, 1979, pp. 4-13.
21. Levinson, M.L. Prev. Med. 6: 172, 1977.
22. Drenick, E.J., G.S. Bale, F. Seltzer, and D.G. Johnson. JAMA 243: 443, 1980.
23. Sorlie, P., T. Gordon, and W.B. Kannel. JAMA 243: 1828, 1980.
24. Ostfeld, A.M., and D.C. Gibson. *Epidemiology of Aging.* Washington, D.C.: DHEW Publ. No. (NIH) 75-711, 1975, pp. 217-219.
25. American Council on Science and Health. *Diet Modification: Can It Reduce the Risk of Heart Disease?* January 1980.
26. Simons, L.A. Food & Nutr. Notes & Rev. (Australia) 36: 138, 1979.
27. Reisin, E., R. Abel, M. Modan, D.S. Silverberg, H.E. Eliahou, and B. Modan. N. Engl. J. Med. 298: 1, 1978.
28. Miller, D.S. Bibl.Nutr.Dieta. 27: 25, 1979.
29. Van Itallie, T.B. Food Technol. 33: 43, 1979.
30. Van Itallie, T.B., S.K. Gale, and H.R. Kissileff. In: H.M. Katzen and R.J. Mahler (Eds). *Advances in Modern Nutrition, Vol. 2. Diabetes, Obesity and Vascular Disease, Metabolic and Molecular Interrelationships,* Part 2. New York: John Wiley & Sons, 1978, pp. 427-492.
31. Garn, S.M., P.E. Cole, and S.M. Bailey. Ecol. Food & Nutr. 6: 91, 1977.
32. Durnin, J.V.G.A. Bibl. Nutr. Dieta. 27: 1, 1979.
33. Briggs, G.M., and D.H. Calloway. *Bogert's Nutrition and Physical Fitness.* 10th ed. Philadelphia: W.B. Saunders Co., 1979.
34. Bruch, H. Can. Psychiatr. Assoc. J. 22: 102, 1977.
35. Garrow, J.S. Bibl. Nutr. Dieta 26: 29, 1978.
36. Pudel, V.E., and M. Oetting. Int. J. Obesity 1: 369, 1977.
37. Granat, J.P. Obesity & Bariatric Med. 8: 178, 1979.
38. Keesey, R.E. In: A.J. Stunkard (Ed). *The Psychiatric Clinics of North America, Obesity: Basic Mechanisms and Treatment.* Vol 1. Philadelphia: W.B. Saunders, 1978, pp. 523-543.
39. Kaplan, M.L. and G.A. Leveille. Am.J.Clin.Nutr. 29: 1108, 1976.
40. Glick, Z., E. Shvartz, A. Magazanik, and M. Modan. Am.J.Clin.Nutr. 30: 1026, 1977.
41. Newsholme, E.A. Biochem. Soc. Symp. 43: 183, 1978.
42. Newsholme, E.A. N.Engl.J.Med. 302: 400, 1980.
43. Dauncey, M.J. Br.J.Nutr. 43: 257, 1980.
44. Norgan, N.G., and J.V.G.A. Durnin. Am.J.Clin.Nutr. 33: 978, 1980.
45. Hirsch, J. In: M. Winick (Ed). *Childhood Obesity.* Vol. 3. New York: John Wiley & Sons, 1975, p. 15.
46. Berland, T. *Diets' 80. Rating The Diets.* Consumer Guide, 1980.
47. Allen, D.W., and B.M. Quigley. Med.J.Aust. 2: 434, 1977.
48. Balabanski, L. Bibl. Nutr.Dieta. 27: 33, 1979.
49. Anonymous. FDA Consumer 13: 10, 1979.
50. Bray, G.A., W.T. Dahms, R.L. Atkinson, I. Mena, and A. Schwartz. Am.J.Clin.Nutr. 33: (Suppl. 2): 376, 1980.
51. O'Leary, J.P. Am.J.Clin.Nutr. 33: (Suppl. 2): 389, 1980.
52. Mason, E.E., K.J. Printen, T.J. Blommers, J.W. Lewis, and D.H. Scott. Am.J.Clin.Nutr. 33: (Suppl. 2): 395, 1980.
53. Faloon, W.W., M.S. Flood, S. Aroesty, and C.D. Sherman. Am.J.Clin.Nutr. 33: (suppl. 2): 431, 1980.
54. Jewell, W.R., and J.L. McLean. Am.J.Clin.Nutr. 33: (Suppl. 2): 525, 1980.
55. Blackburn, G.L., and I. Greenberg. Int.J. Obesity 2: 133, 1978.
56. Weltman, A., S. Matter, and B.A. Stamford. Am.J.Clin.Nutr. 33: 1002, 1980.
57. National Dairy Council. Dairy Council Digest 49: 7, 1978.
58. Halsted, C.H., and J.S. Stern. Am.J.Clin.Nutr. 33: 1326, 1980.
59. Bosello, O., R. Ostuzzi, F.A. Rossi, F. Armellini, M. Cigolini, R. Micciolo, and L.A. Scuro. Am.J.Clin.Nutr. 33: 776, 1980.
60. Van Itallie, T.B. Am.J.Clin.Nutr. 33: (Suppl. 2): 358, 1980.
61. Debry, G. Bibl.Nutr.Dieta. 26: 44, 1978.
62. Center for Disease Control, United States Department of Health, Education, and Welfare. Morbid.Mortal. Weekly Rept. 26: 383, 1977.
63. Talbot, J.M. *Research Needs In Management of Obesity By Severe Caloric Restriction.* Prepared for Bureau of Foods, FDA, Bethesda, MD: LSRO, FASEB, December 1979.
64. Garn, S.M., and P.E. Cole. Am.J.Public Health 70: 351, 1980.

ENERGY REQUIREMENTS

Fats, Cholesterol, and Sodium Intake in the Diet of Persons 1-74 Years: United States

by Sidney Abraham and Margaret D. Carroll, M.S.P.H.

Introduction

Several dietary components of the current diet in the United States may be risk factors in the development of major diseases, particularly cardiovascular diseases and cancer.[1-12] Because of the importance of the reported relationship between dietary components and disease patterns, this report provides reference data on the consumption patterns and food groups that are the major sources of these components.

The dietary data were obtained during the first National Health and Nutrition Examination Survey NHANES I. The survey is a program in which measures of nutrition status are collected for a scientifically designed sample representative of the civilian noninstitutionalized population of the United States in a broad range of ages.

Of the 28,043 sample persons selected to represent 194 million persons aged 1-74 years in the U.S. population, 20,749 persons, or 74 percent, were examined. This is an effective response rate of 75 percent when adjustment is made for the effect of oversampling among preschool children, women of childbearing age, the poor, and the elderly.

The NHANES I nutrition examination component included a general medical examination by a physician for indicators of nutritional deficiencies, a skin examination by a dermatologist, and a dental examination by a dentist. Body measurements were taken by a trained technician; a dietary interview, consisting of a 24-hour recall of food consumption and a food frequency questionnaire, was administered by professional dietary staff; and numerous laboratory tests were performed on whole blood, serum, plasma, and urine. A description of the sampling process, NHANES I operations, and response rates has been published.[13]

Estimates in this report were based on weighted observations, i.e., data obtained on examined persons are inflated to the level of the total population using appropriate weights to account for both sampling fractions and response results.

Findings on the consumption patterns and sources of food groups from dietary components will be analyzed and discussed in a future report.[14] Selected data from that report are presented in tables 1-8 and figure 1.

Information on food intake was obtained by the 24-hour recall method for the day, midnight to midnight, preceding the interview and accounted for all regular meals eaten as well as for between-meal foods or snacks. Food recall included foods eaten on Monday through Friday but generally excluded foods eaten on weekends which may pertain to unusual food intakes.

Foods reported by individuals were grouped under 18 main headings (figure 1). Eleven of these food groups were major sources of the nutrients, cholesterol, and sodium intake and are shown in tables 1-7. These 11 food groups and the other 7—sources of only small proportions of nutrients, cholesterol, and sodium—are shown in table 8. Contents of food groups 1-18 referred to in this report are presented in figure 1.

Fat intake

NHANES I provided data on dietary intake of total fat and saturated fat. The data did not permit evaluation of total polyunsaturated and monounsaturated fatty acids, but intake data were available for linoleic and oleic fatty acids.

The quality and kind of fat in the diet affects the serum lipid concentration. Saturated fat tends to elevate and polyunsaturated tends to decrease the serum cholesterol levels. Polyunsaturated fatty acids considered essential for nutrition are linoleic, linolenic, and arachidonic. Of the three, linoleic is relatively more abundant in foods than the other two. Monounsaturated fat, of which oleic acid is the most

---

From *Advance Data*, No. 54, as revised February 27, 1981, pp. 1-10. Published by Vital and Health Statistics of the National Center for Health Statistics, U.S. Department of Health and Human Services.

Figure 1. Food or food groups contributing to fat, cholesterol, and sodium intakes

	FOOD OR FOOD GROUP	EXPLANATION OF FOOD ITEMS
1	Milk and milk products	Includes milk drunk as a beverage or used on cereals; flavored milk drinks; cocoa made with milk; skim milk, yogurt, or buttermilk; ice milk; ice cream or puddings made with milk; cheese and cheese dishes. EXCEPTION: CREAM CHEESE
2	Meat	Includes beef, pork, lamb, veal, luncheon meats, canned meats, frankfurters
	Organ meats	Includes liver, kidney, heart, spleen, etc.
3	Fats and oils	Includes butter, margarine, salad oils, salad dressings, bacon, cream cheese, cream, peanut butter, non-dairy cream
4	Desserts and sweets	Includes cake, pie, cookies, fruit puddings, doughnuts (cake-type and yeast-type), sherbert, sweet snacks. EXCEPTIONS: ICE CREAM, ICE MILK
5	Mixed protein dishes with carbohydrates-starches or vegetables	Includes casseroles, pot pies, pizza, spaghetti with meat, etc. EXCEPTIONS: PLAIN CHEESE DISHES
6	Cereals	Includes breakfast cereals either dry such as cornflakes or cooked such as oatmeal.
7	Poultry	Includes chicken, turkey, duck, game birds, cornish hen, etc.
8	Fish or shellfish	Includes all varieties of fish and shellfish regardless of whether canned, fresh, frozen, dried or salted.
9	Eggs	Includes eggs eaten e.g., fried, boiled, poached, deviled, or egg salad. EXCEPTIONS: EGGS IN COOKED OR BAKED DISHES SUCH AS CUSTARDS, AND PUDDINGS
10	Fruits and vegetables	Includes: a. All kinds: fresh, canned, frozen, cooked or raw; juices, including fruit drinks b. Fruits and vegetables rich in Vitamin A c. Fruits and vegetables rich in Vitamin C
11	Salty snacks	Includes potato chips, corn chips, puffed snacks, cheese snacks, salted popcorn, salted pretzels, etc.
12	Grain products	Includes bread, rolls, biscuits, muffins, cornbread, crackers, unsalted pretzels.
13	Alcoholic beverages	Includes a) beer, b) wine, c) distilled liquors
14	Sugar free and low calorie beverages	Includes coffee (regular, and decaffeinated), tea, bouillion, consomme and diet carbonated drinks
15	Soups	Includes milk and water-based; gravies and sauces (meat and vegetable based)
16	Legumes and nuts	Includes dry beans and peas such as pinto beans, red beans, black-eyed peas, peanuts, soybeans, soy products, etc.
17	Miscellaneous	Includes mustard, gelatin, malt, beverage powders, chili powders, seeds, low fat salad dressings, etc.
18	Sugar and primarily sugar products	Includes candy, soft drinks, lemonade, limeade.

Table 1. Mean daily fat intake and percent of calories provided by fat, by sex and age: United States, 1971-74

Age	Both sexes Mean fat intake (gram)	Both sexes Percent of calories from fat	Male Mean fat intake (gram)	Male Percent of calories from fat	Female Mean fat intake (gram)	Female Percent of calories from fat
1-74 years	83	37	100	37	66	36
1-5 years	63	36	65	36	60	37
6-11 years	83	36	89	37	77	36
12-17 years	96	37	115	37	77	37
18-44 years	90	37	114	37	68	36
45-64 years	75	37	93	37	60	36
65-74 years	61	35	74	36	51	35

common fatty acid, does not elevate or lower the serum lipids.

Findings from NHANES I showed that the average reported consumption of fat was 83 grams on the day of recall. Fat represented 37 percent of the calories consumed daily (table 1). Males reported a higher fat intake, a mean of 100 grams per day, than females (66 grams) did. The percent of calories from fat was 37 percent for males and 36 percent for females.

The daily mean fat intake of females increased with age from 60 grams at the youngest age group (1-5 years) to a maximum of 77 grams at the age group (6-17 years) and then declined in each successively older age group (table 1).

A somewhat similar pattern was found for males. However, the mean fat intake was higher in each age group than that for females (an expected occurrence since the reported food intakes of males provided more calories than the diets of females did).

The major sources of fat in the diet for both males and females aged 1-74 years, in descending order of their percent contribution, were meat, milk and milk products, fats and oils, desserts and sweets, and grain products. These five food groups provided more than 70 percent of the fat for each sex and age group in the population (table 2).

Meat

The meat group includes beef, pork, lamb, veal, luncheon meats, canned meats, frankfurters, and organ meats. For both males and females the percent contribution of meat to the fat value of the diet increased with age from the youngest ages (1-5 years), peaked at the adult ages (18-44 years), and then de-

Table 2. Mean daily fat intake and percent of fat provided by selected major food groups, by sex and age: United States, 1971-74

Sex and age	Mean fat intake (gram)	Meat	Milk and milk products	Fats and oils	Desserts and sweets	Grain products	Other
Male				Percent			
1-74 years	100	25	19	15	8	6	26
1-5 years	65	16	30	14	9	6	25
6-11 years	89	17	28	13	10	7	25
12-17 years	115	21	25	12	10	6	26
18-44 years	114	28	16	15	7	6	27
45-64 years	93	27	14	19	7	7	26
65-74 years	74	24	15	20	8	7	25
Female							
1-74 years	66	21	20	16	8	7	28
1-5 years	60	16	31	13	9	5	25
6-11 years	77	17	29	13	9	7	26
12-17 years	77	21	23	12	9	6	28
18-44 years	68	23	16	17	8	7	29
45-64 years	60	24	15	19	8	7	27
65-74 years	51	21	16	22	8	8	26

clined slightly. Adult males consumed larger percents of fat from meat than adult females did. There was no difference in the percent contributions of meat to total fat intake for males and females ages 1-17 years.

Milk and milk products

The milk and milk products group includes whole milk, skim milk, or buttermilk reported as a beverage or used on cereal, flavored milk drinks, cocoa made with milk, yogurt, ice milk, ice cream, puddings made with milk, and cheese and cheese dishes. Foods from this group supplied more of the fat in the diets of children 1-11 years of age than any other food group did, accounting for roughly 30 percent of the total fat consumed by young boys and girls. The percent contribution of milk and milk products to fat intake for males and females generally declined with age, with the lowest percents falling in the older age groups. This pattern for children was the opposite of that found for the meat group.

Fats and oils

The fats and oils group includes butter, margarine, salad oils and dressings, bacon, cream cheese, creamy peanut butter, and nondairy cream. Gravies and low calorie salad dressings are not included. The largest percent contribution of fats and oils to fat intake was at the oldest age group (65-74 years) of males and females where it accounted for 20 and 22 percent, respectively. However, a smaller percent contribution of fats and oils was in the intakes of children and adolescents.

Desserts, sweets, and grain products

The desserts and sweets and the grain products groups were less important as sources of fat in the U.S. diet. Desserts and sweets, excluding candy, contributed 7-10 percent of the daily fat intake, with the percent contribution about the same in each age group and for both sexes.

Grain products generally contributed a slightly smaller percent of fat to the diet than the desserts and sweets groups did. By age, values ranged from 6-7 percent for males and 5-8 percent for females.

Saturated fat

Table 3 shows that the age patterns described for total fat consumption of males and females were also observed for saturated fat. Table 3 also shows the seven food groups that were the major sources of saturated fat. Altogether, these groups provided 85 percent or more of the saturated fat for each age-sex group. As with total fat intake, the milk and milk products group is the major source of saturated fat for children and adolescents of both sexes. For adults the meat group was the major source.

Other sources of saturated fat were fats and oils, mixed protein dishes, grain products, desserts and sweets, and eggs.

Milk and milk products (table 3) supplied 29 percent of the saturated fat in the food intakes of males and females ages 1-74 years. The age patterns found in percent contributions of these foods to total fat intake for males and females were also found for saturated fat. The largest percent was observed in the lowest age group (1-5 years). After these ages the

Table 3. Mean daily saturated fat intake and percent of saturated fat provided by major food groups, by sex and age: United States, 1971-74

Sex and age	Mean saturated fat intake (gram)	Milk and milk products	Meat	Fats and oils	Mixed protein dishes	Grain products	Desserts and sweets	Eggs	Other
Male					Percent				
1-74 years	37	29	2(	12	5	5	5	4	12
1-5 years	25	43	17	10	5	4	5	5	11
6-11 years	34	41	19	9	6	5	5	3	12
12-17 years	42	36	24	10	6	4	5	2	13
18-44 years	42	24	33	12	6	5	5	4	13
45-64 years	34	21	32	16	4	5	4	5	12
65-74 years	27	23	27	17	4	5	5	7	11
Female									
1-74 years	24	29	25	13	6	5	5	4	13
1-5 years	23	45	17	9	5	4	5	5	11
6-11 years	30	42	19	9	6	4	5	2	13
12-17 years	29	34	24	9	5	4	6	2	15
18-44 years	25	24	27	13	6	5	6	4	14
45-64 years	22	23	28	17	5	5	5	6	12
65-74 years	18	24	25	18	5	6	6	6	12

Table 4. Mean daily linoleic fatty acid intake and percent of linoleic fatty acids provided by major food groups, by sex and age: United States, 1971-74

Sex and age	Mean linoleic fatty acids intake (gram)	Fats and oils	Salty snacks	Fruits and vegetables	Meat	Desserts and sweets	Grain products	Poultry	Other
Male					Percent				
1-74 years	10	38	9	12	10	6	5	4	16
1-5 years	6	38	11	10	8	7	5	4	17
6-11 years	8	37	14	10	7	7	6	4	16
12-17 years	11	31	16	14	7	7	6	3	15
18-44 years	12	38	8	12	11	6	5	4	16
45-64 years	9	44	2	10	11	5	5	5	16
65-74 years	7	45	1	9	11	7	5	5	17
Female									
1-74 years	7	39	9	10	8	6	5	5	17
1-5 years	5	37	14	9	7	6	4	5	17
6-11 years	7	34	17	8	7	6	6	5	17
12-17 years	8	32	18	11	7	7	5	3	17
18-44 years	8	40	7	12	8	6	5	5	16
45-64 years	6	44	3	10	9	6	5	5	17
65-74 years	5	49	2	7	8	6	5	7	16

share of saturated fat from the milk group declined with increased age, falling from 41 and 42 percent, respectively, for males and females ages 6-11 years to about 23 percent in the oldest age group (65-74 years) for both sexes.

The meat group (table 3) supplied 28 and 25 percent, respectively, of the saturated fat in the food intakes of males and females ages 1-74 years. The percent contribution increased from the younger ages for both sexes, peaked at ages 18-44 years for males and at ages 45-64 years for females and then declined.

In the younger ages, both sexes showed a relatively larger share of saturated fat from milk and milk products than from meat products. After ages 12-17 years, the share from meat was relatively higher than that from milk and milk products.

The contribution of fats and oils to saturated fat intake ranged from 9 to 17 percent for males; older males reported the largest percent of their saturated fat from fats and oils. A similar pattern was generally observed for females. The contributions of mixed protein dishes, desserts and sweets, grain products, and eggs to this dietary component were relatively smaller. For each food group, the percents by each sex-age group were fairly constant with no observable age pattern.

Linoleic acids

Fats and oil products were the major sources of linoleic acids for males and females in all age groups (table 4). The largest percent intake from this fatty acid occurred after age 44 years—more than 40 percent for both males and females. At the younger ages this food group contributed more than 30 percent of the daily linoleic acid.

Salty snacks were the second major contributor to linoleic acid for both males and females ages 1-17 years. The percent contribution of salty snacks to linoleic acid decreased rapidly after ages 12-17 years for both males and females. Fruits and vegetables were the second major contributors to linoleic acid for males ages 18-44 years and for females ages 18-64 years, while meat was the second major contributor to linoleic acid for males ages 45-74 years and females ages 65-74 years.

Other major contributors to linoleic acid were desserts and sweets, grain products, and poultry. Generally, the share of linoleic acids from these food groups remained fairly stable with age.

Oleic acids

Meat, milk and milk products, fats and oils, desserts and sweets, grain products, and mixed protein dishes were the major sources of oleic fatty acids, providing about 80 percent of the oleic acids in the intakes of most sex-by-age groups (table 5).

For the population aged 1-74 years, meat was the major source of oleic acids. The percent contributed by those foods peaked at ages 18-44 years for males and at ages 18-64 years for females and then declined slightly.

The share of oleic acids reported from the milk and milk products group was largest among children and adolescents, the pattern previously observed for

Table 5. Mean daily oleic fatty acid intake and percent of oleic fatty acids provided by major food groups, by sex and age: United States, 1971-74

Sex and age	Mean oleic fatty acids intake (gram)	Meat	Milk and milk products	Fats and oils	Desserts and sweets	Grain products	Mixed protein dishes	Other
				Percent				
Male								
1-74 years	37	28	15	15	9	8	6	19
1-5 years	24	18	24	16	10	8	6	18
6-11 years	33	19	23	15	10	9	7	17
12-17 years	41	24	20	13	10	8	7	18
18-44 years	43	31	13	14	8	8	7	19
45-64 years	36	30	11	18	8	9	4	20
65-74 years	29	25	12	20	10	9	4	20
Female								
1-74 years	25	24	16	16	10	8	6	19
1-5 years	22	18	25	15	9	7	6	18
6-11 years	28	20	24	14	9	8	7	17
12-17 years	28	24	19	13	10	8	7	20
18-44 years	26	26	13	16	10	8	7	20
45-64 years	23	26	12	19	9	8	5	20
65-74 years	20	23	12	22	10	9	4	19

other sources of fat. After age 18 the percent contribution of oleic acids from this food group decreased most rapidly with age, declining to about 12 percent in the older age groups.

The third source of oleic acids, the fats and oils group, contributed 13-20 percent of the oleic acids in the daily intake of males with a slight increase for the oldest age group. A similar narrow range of 13-22 percent was noted for females of comparable ages, with a slight increase also noted for the oldest age group.

Desserts and sweets and grain products each contributed about the same percent of oleic acids with no noticeable differences between sex and age groups.

Cholesterol intake

Eggs, meat, and milk and milk products were the major sources of cholesterol, contributing 77 percent of the daily intake of cholesterol for males and 74 percent for females (table 6). The desserts and sweets group and the fats and oils group contributed 3-6 percent and 2-4 percent, respectively, of the cholesterol for all the sex and age groups.

Eggs were the major source of cholesterol for children aged 1-5 years and for adults of both sexes. Each of these subgroups reported more than a third of their cholesterol from this source.

Adolescents aged 12-17 years reported relatively more cholesterol intake from the meat food group—more than one-fourth of their daily intake—than the other major food sources.

Milk and milk products and eggs were the major sources of cholesterol reported by boys ages 6-11 years (about 28 percent) but only milk and milk products were the major sources of cholesterol reported by girls of similar ages (30 percent).

The percent contribution of eggs to cholesterol intake generally declined with age after ages 1-5 years for both sexes to a low at ages 6-11 years for females and at ages 12-17 years for males and then increased with age.

The largest percent of cholesterol intake from meat occurred at ages 18-44 years for males and at ages 12-17 years for females. The share of cholesterol intake from meat then decreased with age, declining to 21 percent for males and 23 percent for females in the oldest age group. The percent contribution of cholesterol from milk and milk products peaked at ages 6-11 years for both sexes with the foods from this group supplying least of the cholesterol intake in the older age groups (table 6).

The mean cholesterol consumption of males increased from age group 1-5 years, peaked at age group 18-44 years, and then declined. The mean cholesterol consumption of females increased with age, peaked at age group 45-64 years, and then declined; the average cholesterol consumption for females was the same for the youngest age group (1-5 years) and the oldest age group (65-74 years).

Sodium intake

NHANES I data on sodium intake were converted to salt intake, assuming a ratio of 1 gram of salt to 400 mg. of sodium. The salt data from NHANES I

Table 6. Mean daily dietary cholesterol intake and percent of cholesterol provided by major food groups, by sex and age: United States, 1971-74

Sex and age	Mean cholesterol intake (mg)[1]	Eggs	Meat	Milk and milk products	Desserts and sweets	Fats and oils	Other
Male				Percent			
1-74 years	445	35	26	16	4	4	16
1-5 years	301	40	15	25	4	3	14
6-11 years	347	28	19	27	5	3	18
12-17 years	410	23	26	25	5	4	17
18-44 years	521	35	28	13	4	3	16
45-64 years	465	39	27	11	3	4	16
65-74 years	411	45	21	11	4	4	14
Female							
1-74 years	303	34	24	16	5	4	18
1-5 years	274	40	15	26	4	2	13
6-11 years	277	21	20	30	5	3	20
12-17 years	291	25	26	23	6	3	18
18-44 years	311	34	25	13	5	4	19
45-64 years	327	40	25	11	4	4	17
65-74 years	274	40	23	11	5	4	17

[1] Milligram

are incomplete because the values cover only naturally occurring sodium in foods and sodium added by processors. Table salt is not included in these data. Males reported an average daily consumption of 2,701 mg. of sodium or about 7 grams of salt and females reported an average daily consumption of 1,850 mg. of sodium or about 5 grams of salt. Among age groups, the differences in reported percent by source of sodium were small (table 7).

Table 7 also shows the seven food groups that supplied 78 percent or more of sodium for all sex and age groups. Foods such as mustard, ketchup, worcestershire sauce, and other condiments, the major sources of sodium, accounted for only 0.2 percent in

Table 7. Mean daily sodium intake and percent of sodium provided by major food groups, by sex and age: United States, 1971-74

Sex and age	Mean sodium intake (mg)[1]	Grain products	Milk and milk products	Mixed protein dishes	Soups	Meat	Fruits and vegetables	Fats and oils	Other
Male					Percent				
1-74 years	2,701	24	13	12	10	9	7	6	19
1-5 years	1,886	20	18	11	12	7	6	6	20
6-11 years	2,532	23	16	13	9	7	6	5	22
12-17 years	2,965	23	15	14	8	8	6	5	21
18-44 years	3,032	23	12	13	9	10	8	6	18
45-64 years	2,540	25	11	8	11	10	8	8	19
65-74 years	2,229	26	11	6	13	9	8	7	21
Female									
1-74 years	1,850	23	14	11	10	8	8	6	19
1-5 years	1,721	20	19	12	11	7	6	6	20
6-11 years	2,238	23	16	12	10	7	7	5	20
12-17 years	2,001	23	16	12	9	8	8	5	19
18-44 years	1,863	23	13	13	10	9	8	7	18
45-64 years	1,702	24	12	8	11	10	9	7	18
65-74 years	1,526	27	13	5	11	7	8	8	21

[1] Milligram

NOTE: HANES sodium intake values converted to salt intake values assuming a ratio of 1 gram of salt to 400 mg of sodium.

Table 8. Percent distribution of dietary components provided by food groups appearing in the 24-hour recall of food consumption and mean intake of dietary components of persons aged 1-74 years: United States, 1971-74

Food or food group	Calories	Protein (gram)	Fat (gram)	Sodium (mg)[1]	Saturated fatty acid (gram)	Oleic acid (gram)	Linoleic acid (gram)	Cholesterol (mg)[1]
				Percent distribution				
Total	100.0	100.0	100.0	100.0	100.0	100.0	100.0	100.0
Skim milk or buttermilk	1.2	2.5	0.4	1.3	0.1	0.1	-	0.2
Cheese and cheese products	1.9	3.5	3.4	4.1	4.9	2.9	1.0	2.4
Milk and milk products excluding cheese	12.9	15.9	15.8	8.2	23.9	12.5	-	13.6
Meat	13.6	29.5	22.9	8.7	26.5	25.7	8.7	22.9
Poultry	2.0	6.6	2.3	0.2	1.9	2.5	4.6	4.1
Organ meats	0.2	0.6	0.4	0.1	0.3	0.4	0.3	2.0
Fish or shellfish	1.1	3.6	1.2	0.7	0.8	1.1	1.4	2.5
Eggs	2.5	4.2	4.6	3.1	4.1	4.9	3.0	34.2
Soups	1.6	1.1	2.0	9.9	1.7	1.7	2.6	0.6
Fats and oils	6.3	2.0	15.6	6.3	12.3	15.5	38.8	3.6
Legumes and nuts	1.7	2.1	1.6	2.0	1.2	1.7	2.2	0.2
Cereals	1.8	1.2	0.4	3.3	0.1	0.1	0.5	-
Grain products	14.7	10.8	6.4	23.4	4.7	8.2	5.1	3.6
Fruits and vegetables	10.8	5.0	5.1	7.6	3.3	3.5	11.1	1.1
Sugar and primarily sugar products	8.8	0.6	1.9	0.5	1.9	2.2	1.6	0.1
Desserts and sweets	8.4	2.9	8.2	6.5	5.0	9.1	6.4	4.3
Miscellaneous	0.6	0.4	0.3	0.3	0.1	0.1	1.2	-
Mixed protein dishes	5.0	6.7	5.4	11.4	5.4	6.3	2.7	4.5
Alcoholic beverages	3.3	0.4	-	0.3	-	-	-	-
Sugar free and low calorie beverages	0.4	0.1	-	0.6	-	-	-	0.1
Salty snacks	1.5	0.5	2.2	1.5	1.6	1.4	8.8	-
Mean	1,989	79	83	2,262	30	31	9	372

[1] Milligram

the 24-hour recall data because of minimal volume consumption. NHANES I data indicate that grain products are the major contributing source of sodium in the 24-hour recall data. Grain products contributed about one-quarter of the sodium intake in all sex and age subgroups, providing 20-27 percent in all groups. The percents are fairly stable throughout the age groups.

The milk and milk products group was generally the second major source of sodium intake. Younger males and females showed a higher percent of sodium intake from milk and milk products than adults did. This pattern is expected because of the higher consumption of milk and milk products by the younger groups. Other major sources of sodium were mixed protein dishes and soups.

Mixed protein dishes contributed 6-14 percent of the daily sodium intake for males and 5-13 percent for females. Both sexes aged 45-74 years showed smaller shares of sodium from this group of foods than those in the younger age group.

The percent contribution of soups to sodium remained fairly stable with age ranging from 8-13 percent for males and from 9-11 percent for females.

Other food groups contributing smaller amounts of sodium in the diets of the U.S. population were meats, fruits and vegetables, and fats and oils. These food groups generally contributed less sodium to the daily intake in all population subgroups than grain products, milk and milk products, and mixed protein dishes did. The differences between sexes in percent of sodium intake were small. For each sex, age was not a factor. The percent of dietary components provided by all food groups appearing in the 24-hour recall of all persons aged 1-74 years in the United States is presented in table 8.

Discussion

Reference data on dietary components implicated in increased risk to disease have been presented and analyzed by sex and age because of the medical interest in such data. These estimates are generalized for the U.S. population and provide cross-sectional data on the consumption of selected dietary components as reported by persons representing different age groups in the U.S. population. The limitations of cross-sectional data should be recognized in considering age group changes. The use of 24-hour recall to estimate dietary habits is also a limitation. Recent food intakes do not necessarily reflect lifetime dietary habits. Since the disease processes of those cited are long-term, it is questionable to relate recent dietary habits to the risk of these diseases. The estimates in this report will be compared with NHANES II data on food consumption patterns which will be available in 1981.

There are limitations to the dietary estimates obtained from NHANES I. The major source of data for the basic nutritional values of food items is from the U.S. Department of Agriculture Handbook No. 8.[15] Because of the introduction of new food items in the market, updated and added values for new foods are made according to information provided by the U.S. Department of Agriculture (USDA), food processors, and manufacturers. With the exception of cholesterol, all nutrient values for chicken, steak, pork chops, and meat loaf were calculated using USDA Handbook No. 456.[16] Cholesterol values were calculated using an article by R.F. Feeley, P.E. Criner and B.K. Watts.[17] However, despite the considerable data on the nutrient composition of foods, information is less than optimal in those areas of the macronutrients whose importance is of immediate interest.

More of the data used in NHANES I, obtained from the USDA data bank, are for commodities than for brand name convenience foods.

Another problem is lack of information on the lipid content of food served by institutions, restaurants, and fast food outlets;[18] the main sources of compiled data have covered only food eaten in the home. The present dietary data bank was compiled mainly for nutrients—e.g., vitamins A and C, calcium, and iron—whose deficiency led to the classical nutritional diseases.

References

[1] American Heart Association: Inter-Society Commission for Heart Disease Resources: Primary prevention of atherosclerotic diseases. *Circulation* 42(6): A55, Dec. 1970.

[2] Turpeinen, O.: Effect of cholesterol-lowering diet on mortality from coronary heart disease and other causes. *Circulation* 59(1): 1-7, 1979.

[3] Keys, A., ed.: Coronary heart disease in seven countries. *Circulation* 41 (Supp. I), 1970.

[4] Wynder, E. L.: Nutritional Carcinogenesis 360-378. Annals of the New York Academy of Sciences. Vol. 300. Food and Nutrition in Health and Disease, 1977. Edited by N. H. Moss and J. Mayer.

[5] McGandy, R. B., Hegsted, D. M., and Stare, F. J.: Dietary fats, carbohydrates and atherosclerotic vascular disease. *New Engl. J. Med.* 277:186, 1967.

[6] Stamler, J.: Diet-related Risk Factors for Human Atherosclerosis: Hyperlipidemia, Hypertension, Hyperglycemia - Current Status. In *Diet and Atherosclerosis*, edited by C. Sirtori, G. Ricci, and S. Gorini, New York Plenum Press, 1973, p. 125.

[7] Diet, Nutrition, and Cancer Program, National Cancer Institute, National Institutes of Health Status Report, 1977.

[8] Harper, A. E.: Dietary goals - a skeptical view. *Am. J. Clin. Nutr.* 31: 310-321, 1978.

[9] American Health Foundation: Position statement of diet and coronary heart disease. *Prev. Med.* I (1,2): 255-286, Mar. 1972.

[10] National Institutes of Health: Atherosclerosis—A report by the National Heart and Lung Institute task force on arteriosclerosis. Vol. II. DHEW Pub. No. (NIH) 72-219. National Institutes of Health, Washington. U.S. Government Printing Office, June 1971.

[11] National Academy of Sciences - National Research Council, Food and Nutrition Board and American Medical Association, The Council on Foods and Nutrition: Diet and Coronary Heart Disease. Washington, D.C. National Academy of Sciences and American Medical Association, July 1972.

[12] Dietary Goals for the United States, Select Committee on Nutrition and Human Needs, United States Senate, 2d edition. Washington. U.S. Government Printing Office, Dec. 1977.

[13] National Center for Health Statistics: Plan and Operation of the Health and Nutrition Examination Survey, United States, 1971-73. *Vital and Health Statistics*. Series 1-Nos. 10a and 10b. DHEW Pub. No. (HSM) 73-1310. Health Services and Mental Health Administration. Washington. U.S. Government Printing Office, Feb. 1973.

[14] National Center for Health Statistics: Consumption patterns in the United States, 1971-1974. *Vital and Health Statistics*. Series 11. Public Health Service, DHEW, Hyattsville Md. To be published.

[15] Watt, B. K., and Merrill, A.: Composition of Foods—Raw, Processed, Prepared. Agriculture Handbook No. 8 (rev.). Washington. U.S. Department of Agriculture, 1963. Revised Data Tape, Expansion (Mar. 1972).

[16] Adams, D. F.: Nutritive Value of American Foods, In Common Units - Agriculture Handbook No. 456, Washington. U.S. Department of Agriculture, November 1975.

[17] Feeley, R. F., Criner, P. E., and Watts, B. K.: Cholesterol Content of Foods, J. American Dietary Association, 61: 134-149, 1972.

[18] Food Quality in Federal Food Programs, Hearings before the Select Committee on Nutrition and Human Needs of the United States Senate. 95th Congress, First Session, Sept. 1977, Part 2. Washington. U.S. Government Printing Office, Statement of Dr. Kent K. Steward, pp. 73-82.

Technical notes

The sampling plan for the 65 examination locations in the National Health and Nutrition Examination Survey (NHANES) followed a highly stratified multistage probability design in which a sample of the civilian noninstitutionalized population of the conterminous United States aged 1-74 years was selected. Successive elements used in the sampling process were the primary sampling unit, census enumeration district, segment (a cluster of households), household, eligible person, and sample person. The sampling design provided for oversampling among persons living in poverty areas, preschool children, women of childbearing age, and the elderly.

The dietary component values are shown as population estimates, i.e., the findings for each individual have been "weighted" by the reciprocal of the probability of selecting the person. An adjustment for persons in the sample who were not examined and post-stratified ratio adjustments were also made so that the final sampling estimates of the population size are brought into closer alignment with the independent U.S. Bureau of the Census estimates for the civilian noninstitutionalized population of the United States as of November 1, 1972, by race, sex, and age.

Symbols

- - -	Data not available
. . .	Category not applicable
-	Quantity zero
0.0	Quantity more than 0 but less than 0.05
*	Figure does not meet standards of reliability or precision

VITAMINS

Encyclopedia of Vitamins

by William Gottlieb

PLEASE NOTE: The editors would like to advise readers that some of the medical effects attributed to specific vitamins in this article are controversial. Articles can be found in the medical literature that support or refute specific claims for the medical effects of certain vitamins.

Linus Pauling thinks you have a birth defect. But don't let that get you down. He thinks everybody has one. This scientist, one of the few people ever to win the Nobel Prize twice (sort of like setting the world high jump record one year and coming out tops at Wimbledon the next), believes that somewhere along the line of evolution our monkey ancestors lost the ability to make vitamin C in their bodies. (Only humans, monkeys, guinea pigs, an Indian fruit-eating bat and the red-vented bulbul bird need to get vitamin C from their diet in order to survive.) Because of this defect, says Pauling, you need to take vitamin C to be at your best. Ten grams of it a day—over 150 times more than the government says you need. Who's right?

Nobody.

Nutrition isn't an exact science, it's a controversial science. Talk to a dietician and you're likely to hear the bland hooey about how most Americans eat a balanced diet and don't need to take vitamins. Talk to a health food store owner and he'll probably try to convince you that you need every pill on the shelves. You're in the middle with an earful, wondering what to think. And more important, what to *do*.

That's what this article is for. As an editor of the country's most-read health magazine, I've spent the last four years *living* vitamins, aware of every single new study and advance in the field of nutrition. And I'm convinced—as are many, many doctors—that if someone tells you that you don't need to take vitamins, he or she has a lot to learn about the subject.

You need to take vitamins if you live in a smoggy city. If you train day after day in the sun. If you eat sugar. If you have an allergy. If you load up on carbohydrates before a race. If you bruise easily. If you're about to compete. Actually, there are no if's about it. To be at the top of your form—in sports and in life—vitamins are a must.

As any athlete knows, life is action. There is nothing static about the body. What sparks and controls that action—the beating of your heart, the steady fire of digestion, your breathing, your moving—are enzymes. Vitamins are a chemical part of your enzymes. Without vitamins, enzymes wouldn't work, and neither would you.

Consider vitamin B-1 (thiamine), for instance. Without thiamine, the enzymes that depend on it are useless; the brain and nervous system collapse. Arms and legs lose their coordination. The eye muscles freeze into paralysis. The mind blackens into amnesia and coma. The heart stretches, swells—and stops.

Not a pretty picture, but not a common one either. With the so-called "fortification" of white flour (which replaces less than half the nutrients stripped from wheat during processing), thiamine deficiency was all but wiped out in America. Or so we're told.

A pediatrician in Ohio found that 20 of his teenage patients had a *relative* thiamine deficiency. Not an out-and-out killing lack, but a low enough level so they were depressed, slept poorly, had chest pains and were tired all the time. When he gave them thiamine supplements their symptoms cleared up.

This type of thiamine deficiency is probably caused by stuffing oneself with sugary foods, which burn up thiamine without replacing it. How many people do you know who are tired and whiny, with vague aches and pains? How many of them eat too many sweets? Or drink too much coffee? Or take the Pill? All these factors destroy thiamine. If you're not careful, it's *easy* to have a deficiency of thiamine, or any other vitamin.

From *Women's Sports* Magazine, pp. 28-42. Copyright 1980, *Women's Sports* Magazine. Reprinted with permission.

But don't tell your doctor that. He'd probably just laugh. When most doctors think about a vitamin deficiency, they think "beriberi" or "rickets" or "pellagra"—diseases caused by complete absence of a vitamin in the body. They're hard put to tell you anything about vitamins beyond that. Doctors receive almost no training in nutrition during medical school, and it shows.

When they prescribe the Pill, how many doctors tell their patients about the serious and very real risk of a deficiency of vitamin B-6—a deficiency that has caused thousands of women who take the Pill to become depressed? How many doctors tell their patients to take zinc and vitamin C before an operation because those nutrients speed healing? How many doctors tell their athletic patients that vitamin E would help them store more of the muscle fuel glycogen? How many—but the list is endless.

What doctors will talk about is the balanced diet. They'll tell you if you eat that diet, you don't need to take vitamins. But a balanced meal, with one item from all four of the major food groups, could consist of a glass of chocolate milk, baloney on white bread and a limp heap of overcooked vegetables. Olga Korbut couldn't balance on that diet.

Even if your diet is truly healthful, with lots of fresh fruits and vegetables, whole grains, lean meats and fish, low-fat dairy products, nuts and seeds and sprouts, you still need vitamins. You need a concentrated extra dose of naturalness to counter the *un*naturalness of modern life.

A researcher I talked to last month said that everybody should take 200 IU (international units) of vitamin E a day to protect his/her lungs from air pollution, even someone living in the Rockies. PCB, a die-hard chemical pollutant that literally saturates every square centimeter of air, soil and water, may be neutralized in your body by vitamins A and C. There are mental pollutants too—overcrowded cities, dismal headlines, a tough day at work—that a maximum level of vitamins helps you deal with. In the long run, vitamins (and minerals, which I'll talk about in a future issue) protect you against serious diseases that could catch up with you later in life: cancer, arthritis, heart disease, diabetes.

Finally, vitamins better your performance. Vitamin C, for example, speeds reaction time, wards off fatigue and helps your body stand up under withering heat or stiffening cold (that last fact has been proven in the sweltering gold mines of South Africa and the sub-zero wastes of the Arctic). So let's look at the vitamins one by one and see how each can help you peak and stay there.

VITAMIN A

If you see polar bear liver on the menu, don't order it. That meat is so high in vitamin A it's poisonous. But it's not polar bear liver that's given vitamin A such bad press. (This is one vitamin a lot of people seem to know a definite fact about: that you can OD on it.) True, your liver stores unused vitamin A, and if it builds up beyond a certain point you're in trouble. But such cases, in which people took over 50,000 IU of vitamin A every day for months, are very rare.

What isn't rare is that people get too *little* vitamin A. A survey showed that over half the people in America aged 18 to 44 take in less than the government's Recommended Dietary Allowance (RDA), and the RDA is too low to start with.

One reason for the lack is that Americans don't eat enough fresh fruits and vegetables, prime sources of vitamin A. Another is that they eat too much fast food, an awful source. (One survey said there was "no good source of vitamin A on the menu.") You can't afford to play fast and loose with vitamin A: It keeps your skin smooth, your vision sharp, your immune system strong and your anti-stress mechanisms on the ball.

Dry, rough or flaky skin may be a sign that you need more vitamin A. Skin is partly made up of epithelial cells, which break down and are replaced constantly. Without enough vitamin A, the new cells are second-rate. Since the scalp's sebaceous glands also depend on vitamin A, a lack could cause dry, brittle hair too.

The epithelial cells aren't only outsiders. They line your throat, nasal passages, bronchial tube, digestive system and genitourinary tract in the form of mucous membrane. Those membranes protect you against cold and flu (and smoke and smog) by ushering germs and dirt out the doors of your body. If vitamin A levels fall, the usher falls asleep on the job and you're more likely to catch cold or be manhandled by pollutants. (There's no question that anyone who has had a fever has burned up 60 percent of his/her vitamin A and needs to replace it.) Since the vagina is lined with mucous membrane, women deficient in vitamin A are more likely to have yeast infections.

Vitamin A also takes the sting out of stress. When life plays rough, the adrenal glands pump out hormones that ready you for action. But too much rough stuff—too much tension, too much bad food, too much dirty air, too much noise—poops out the adrenals and they swell as if bruised. People who live in cities, for instance, have larger adrenal glands than their country cousins.

Vitamin A cuts stress down to size. When you have enough in your system, the adrenal glands cope with stress yet stay normal. Besides that, vitamin A directly short-circuits dangerous, unavoidable pollutants such as PCB, benzene and dieldrin.

As if all that weren't enough, vitamin A can cure heavy menstruation. When women with that problem took 30,000 IU of the vitamin twice a day for 30 days, their periods became normal. In fact, women who begin to menstruate heavily after they stop taking the Pill may have set off a chemical chain reaction that depleted them of vitamin A.

Orange, yellow and green fruits and vegetables such as carrots, sweet potatoes, spinach, apricots and cantaloupe contain a substance called betacarotene (which, by the way, is zapped by overcooking) that changes to vitamin A in the body. A cup of cooked carrots, for instance, has over 16,000 IU of vitamin A.

The most concentrated source of the vitamin, however, is fish liver oil. That doesn't mean you have to relive the childhood horror of cod liver oil. (I can *still* taste it in that grape juice.) Vitamin A supplements, which are virtually tasteless and odorless, are the best source of fish liver oil. A daily supplement of 10,000 IU is enough, but you can take up to 30,000 IU a day without any worry. If you take vitamin E with it, the body's ability to use the vitamin A you take jumps sixfold.

VITAMIN B1 (thiamine)

If things get on your nerves, get them off with the B-complex vitamins. These are often called the "nerve vitamins," and for good reason. You'd be a nervous wreck without them. Symptoms such as depression, irritability, poor concentration, insomnia, forgetfulness, confusion, anxiety and paranoia are all linked in one degree or another with each one of the B-complex vitamins.

They're all similar and, not surprisingly, they like each other's company. You rarely find one without the others. So what's said about nerves goes for the whole bunch, from B-1 to B-12. (The B-15 found in health food stores is a shady character. The discoverer named it B-15 in his patent application; very few reputable scientists think it's a bona fide member of the B-complex family. Recent tests show that a chemical found in some B-15 supplements—they're not all the same because nobody has an exact idea what B-15 is—is mutagenic: It warps cells and may cause cancer. Laetrile or B-17, another trade name, is in the same category, and that's why neither is discussed in this article.)

When it comes to nerves, thiamine is a standout. It's also been dubbed the "tranquility vitamin." (Remember those frazzled teens who were deficient?) Thiamine helps the body turn carbohydrates into glucose which fuels the brain, one reason why a lack of thiamine fogs up thought and emotion.

Glucose also fuels the muscles. That means any athlete who loads up on carbohydrates before a race should take five milligrams (mg.) of thiamine a day. "What's the use of stuffing yourself with pasta," asks one fitness expert who backs the use of thiamine, "if the body can't turn all of it into energy?"

A quirky plus to thiamine is that mosquitos seem to hate it. People report that if they take 100 mg. a day, they don't get bitten. (It's worth a try, at the very least.) Like all the B-complex vitamins, thiamine is water-soluble, which means what you don't use is excreted and there's no risk of an overdose. For most people, the danger is an underdose.

Most people drink coffee, and caffeine and thiamine don't mix. In fact, a case of "coffee nerves" could well be a case of thiamine deficiency. You should take 10 mg. a day if you drink the stuff. In fact, caffeine in any form (coffee, tea, cola, chocolate, cold and headache remedies) does thiamine in. Likewise alcohol; some people have suggested that liquor be supplemented with thiamine. Heavy cooking blasts the nutrient and, as was said before, refined carbohydrates such as sugar use it up without putting it back.

*Un*refined carbohydrates, however, include thiamine in the package. Green, leafy vegetables, whole grains, beans, nuts and seeds are thiamine-rich (and also include plenty of the other B vitamins, except B-12, which is only found in animal products). Other stellar sources of thiamine are brewer's yeast and wheat germ. And if you're one of the few people who like liver, go to it.

Except for special needs, like carbo loading, it's best to take the B-complex together. A good supplement tries to balance them as they're found in nature. For instance, it would include much, much less B-12 than the other B's. The body needs B-12 in *micro*grams, not milligrams. A supplement that gives you 100 mg. of thiamine and most of the other B vitamins is a reasonable choice. Some offer 50 mg. Others 10 mg. In the end, it's a personal matter; experiment and see how you feel. The more unprocessed your diet, the less you're likely to need.

VITAMIN B2 (riboflavin)

The most frequently prescribed drugs are tranquilizers. Second are antibiotics. Both do a number on riboflavin.

That could mean symptoms like teary, bloodshot eyes and oversensitivity to sunlight. (The word on riboflavin has always been that it's "good for the eyes.") Or indigestion, since B-2 helps the digestion of fats. Or cracks at the corner of the mouth and flaky areas around the nose and eyebrows and hairline. Before those signs show up, a person will simply feel ornery—tired, nervous, no appetite.

But that person needs to eat: among vegetables, broccoli and asparagus. Among dairy products, milk and cheese. Among nuts, almonds. Among meats, liver (yes, again). Any whole grain will do, but wild rice is best. And don't leave that food out on the counter. Riboflavin holds up pretty well under cooking but crumbles under the rays of the sun.

VITAMIN B3 (niacin)

When white flour was fortified in the 1940s, a lot of people in mental institutions went home. It must have shocked psychiatrists to see hundreds of thousands of schizophrenic patients suddenly start to behave normally. The catch is that they weren't schizophrenic in the first place. They were suffering from pellagra, the niacin-deficiency disease, which has a host of spooky mental symptoms that mimic schizophrenia. Well, there's no use crying over spilt milk. Unless somebody keeps pouring it on the floor.

"I think there is ample reason to believe that the amount of niacin a person should be getting for good health is not the same amount most Americans are getting on a so-called normal diet," says William Kaufmann, M.D., a medical expert on niacin. Dr. Kaufmann is backed up by a study showing over nine percent of American women between the ages of 19 and 44 had a clinical niacin deficiency. Those women were bone-tired and depressed. How many others, with a less intense deficiency, are cranky a lot, but don't know why?

People fall apart when niacin levels fall because at least 40 biochemical reactions in the body depend on niacin. Perhaps the most important involves the red blood cells, which carry oxygen to all parts of the body. The last stage in their journey is through the capillaries, hair-thin blood vessels connecting to the tissues. The red blood cells line up single file in the capillaries and march in. The only reason they don't bump into one another is that each has a negative electrical charge that forces them apart. Niacin keeps them charged—and you charged up with oxygen.

Niacin comes in two forms: niacin (which, to complicate matters, is also called niacinamide) and nicotinic acid. If you take 100 mg. or more of nicotinic acid all at once, you're in for a slightly bizarre surprise: Your face, neck, shoulders and chest will turn sunburn-red, hot and itchy. You're not sunburned for life. The effect, which is called "flushing," fades in about 20 minutes. If you take that quantity of nicotinic acid every day, the reaction itself will eventually disappear. But why would you want to take nicotinic acid when you could have an easy time of it with niacin? Nicotinic acid lowers cholesterol; niacin doesn't.

Flushing happens because nicotinic acid sparks the release of two chemicals that dilate blood vessels, and a rush of extra blood flows to the skin. The way to avoid it is, of course, to take niacin, or to take no more than 50 mg. of nicotinic acid at any one time.

I was once surprised by a "flush" when I ate a homemade blenderized concoction that contained a lot of super-potency food yeast. To do the same with other niacin-rich foods, you'd probably have to eat a whole turkey, a few pounds of peanuts, an entire tuna or two and ten baby beef livers. The risk, I think you'll agree, is small.

VITAMIN B₆
(pyridoxine)

Do you remember your dreams? If not, you may need more B-6, at least according to some nutrition-minded psychiatrists. This vitamin is a must for the synthesis of serotonin, a brain chemical that regulates memory. If there's too little serotonin in your diet, say these shrinks, you don't bring back any slides from your trip to dreamland.

One thing you should forget is buying processed foods. Canned foods lose over 50 percent of their B-6, frozen foods at least 30 percent. White flour has lost 80 percent and precooked rice has a measly 7 percent left. This is typical of what happens to vitamins by the time processed food reaches the supermarket.

If your period is less than a breeze, low levels of B-6 don't help, though high levels could put you back on top of things. Doctors have found that 50 mg. a day of B-6 clears up the premenstrual acne flares of teenagers. That amount or more has relieved the swollen hands and feet and the headaches and emotional upheavals that preface some women's menstrual periods. It has also eliminated nausea and vomiting during pregnancy. "All pregnant women have an increased need for B-6," says one doctor.

Any woman needs more B-6 as she grows older. A 30-year-old woman has blood levels of B-6 nearly one third lower than a woman of 20; a woman of 60 has dropped by another third, unless she's been taking supplements or eating very, very well. Whole foods are the best source of B-6: organ meats, lean meats and fish, fresh, raw fruits and vegetables (particularly bananas), nuts, buckwheat, soybeans and wheat germ.

VITAMIN B₁₂
(cobalamin)

If you're a vegetarian who doesn't eat dairy products, you already know about B-12. Everybody and his brother has been telling you that you're going to get a deficiency. Maybe. Studies show that vegans (total vegetarians) who eat fermented foods such as tamari or tofu, or who eat a large amount of raw food, have B-12 manufactured right in their own intestinal tracts by good-guy bacteria.

Like the rest of the B vitamins, B-12 helps run the switchboard of the central nervous system, relaying messages between body and brain. But take the Pill for six months and 25 percent of the B-12 operators go on strike. Even a slight deficiency of B-12 can hobble you with fatigue, irritability and some degree of numbness in your arms and legs.

B-12 shots, as you may have heard (or tried), are a popular cure for fatigue. They seem to work even in people who don't have a deficiency. Some mystified experts chalk that up to the "placebo effect": If you think a substance will make you better, you'll get better. Others more realistically believe that scientific knowledge about B-12 isn't complete. (The same goes for all the vitamins.)

Before the nutrient was isolated, people with the disease pernicious anemia had to eat huge quantities of liver to stay alive. Scientists knew that liver contained the "anti-pernicious anemia factor" though they didn't know what that was. Liver is the best source of B-12 but any animal product will do.

FOLATE

If you're anemic you need more iron, right? Not necessarily. A lack of folate can also cause anemia, a disease in which too little oxygen gets to the tissues. Folate helps form genes, the chemicals that blueprint every cell including the oxygen-carrying red blood cells. If the body doesn't have enough folate, the blueprint for the red blood cells looks like it's been drawn up by a two-year-old with a crayon. The cells have a weird shape and they're next to useless. You look pale and feel somewhat weak and irritable.

One doctor claims that a folate deficiency "may affect more people than high cholesterol," and that's millions. Fifty percent of pregnant women, for instance, are somewhat deficient. And since folate helps assemble genes, that deficiency may account for the epidemic of minor and major birth defects (30 percent of all births!). In one study, pregnant women who had low blood levels of folate were compared with pregnant women who had normal levels. The low folate group gave birth to four times more malformed babies than the normal folate group. "Baby blues," the depression that clouds the days of some women after pregnancy, is probably also caused by low levels of folate.

Besides taking supplements, there are some cooking tips to keep your intake high. First, don't use a microwave oven. A microwave destroys 90 percent of the folate in food in 28 minutes; a normal oven set at the same temperature takes 65 minutes. Second, steam rather than boil your vegetables. Eighty-five percent of the folate in cauliflower, for instance, is destroyed after ten minutes of boiling. If you must boil, use that same water to cook rice.

Green, leafy vegetables, particularly from the cabbage family, are the best source of folate. Second best, but far from second-rate, are whole wheat, brewer's yeast, oranges, beets, beans, meat and eggs.

PANTOTHENIC ACID

If you train, compete or even play in cold water, you need more pantothenic acid. A study shows that people immersed in 45-degree water for over ten minutes show much less wear and tear (on a biochemical level) if they've taken pantothenic acid for a few weeks before the dip. In another study, rats were given low, medium and high levels of pantothenic acid and made to swim in cold water until exhausted. The low-level group swam for 16 minutes; the medium group, 29 minutes; the high group, 62 minutes. Would-be Diana Nyads, take note.

The humans fared better and the rats swam longer because adrenal glands contain high levels of pantothenic acid. If you build up that level, your body is steeled against stress and more ready for rugged competition. Roger Williams, PhD, the discoverer of pantothenic acid and a nutrition expert, believes that regular supplements will help you live longer. It is well known that if you react poorly to stress, you shorten your life.

Pantothenic acid is found in all foods; the name is Latin for "from all sides." If you want to keep pantothenic acid on your side, avoid canned and frozen foods, which have lost anywhere from 35 to 75 percent of this vitamin, and anything made with white flour, which may have only 25 percent of its pantothenic acid left.

PABA
(Para-aminobenzoic acid)

PABA is no more a vitamin than a leg is a person. It's *part* of folate. But it steps out on its own too. PABA is the best sunscreen around. It filters out the ultraviolet rays that cause sunburn and skin cancer, a real risk for anyone who lives in a sunny climate and spends a lot of time outdoors. Redheads and blondes claim that PABA is the "anti-freckle" vitamin.

BIOTIN

If Rocky of movie fame had known more about nutrition, he wouldn't have eaten all those raw eggs. A protein in raw egg whites blocks the absorption of biotin. Unless you're an eggnog freak, though, you don't have to worry about a deficiency; biotin will continue to do its thing. Actually, its things, since it's involved on a basic level in many of your body's functions.

CHOLINE, INOSITOL

These two B vitamins are found in lecithin, a substance that's part of the cell walls of plants and animals. They make sure the cells absorb fat, no mean feat since fat is as vital a nutrient as protein or carbohydrate. Choline also turns into the brain chemical acetylcholine. This plays a role in memory function, although scientists have tried to improve the memories of senile patients with choline and lecithin with mixed success.

VITAMIN C

If a heroin addict taking 20 grams of vitamin C every day shot up, nothing would happen. That's right, nothing. It's like shooting up water. Vitamin C is so powerful it immediately detoxifies heroin. Or nicotine. Or alcohol. Or cancer-causing pollutants. Vitamin C is an all-purpose antidote.

But what most people really want to know about vitamin C is: Does it cure the common cold? Yes. You can clear up a cold that's just getting started, or shorten one that's hit full force, by taking one gram every two hours.

Most important, you can prevent colds in the first place. The dosage for that is an individual matter. Some people need as little as 250 mg. a day. Others need two or three grams. One gram (1,000 mg.) may do the trick for most people.

"There is little doubt that the intake of additional vitamin C can lead to a reduced burden of winter illness," says a researcher who conducted studies on vitamin C and the cold. In one of those studies, people who took 500 mg. of vitamin C every day had 38 percent fewer cold symptoms during the winter than those who didn't take the vitamin. Vitamin C strengthens the immune system, your body's protection against the viruses that cause colds.

Winter isn't the only time for runny noses. If you're plagued by hay fever, take heart—and vitamin C.

"Vitamin C almost always alleviates the symptoms of hay fever," says a doctor who uses it in his practice. He gives two grams every three or four hours for a "mild" case (runny nose, itchy eyes) and ten grams every three or four hours for a "severe" case (a lot of mucus, red watery eyes, itchy throat, frequent sneezing). The minimum for anyone with hay fever is four grams a day.

Vitamin C mows down hay fever because it's a natural antihistamine. It's the release of histamine, sparked by pollen, that causes hay fever symptoms. Vitamin C stops that release.

Vitamin C also helps you beat the heat. In a study of people who work in the 100-degree temperatures of a mine, 500 mg. a day of vitamin C increased their ability to work as hard in the mine as they had outside of it. Not that most of us have to work in mines, but increasing your intake of vitamin C a week or so before an event in hot weather will give you the competitive edge. Another study found that 300 mg. of vitamin C a day prevents heatstroke, and a gram a day cures heat rash (prickly heat).

Most athletes have been confronted with the decision of whether or not to take cortisone to relieve a painful swelling or inflammation. Cortisone is a mixed blessing. It works wonders, but it may have a lot of nasty side effects. Vitamin C is a cortisone denastyizer.

VITAMIN	Health Functions	Best Food Sources	Preparation Tips	Deficiency Symptoms	RDA*	Destroyers
A	Smooth, healthy looking skin Resistance to infections and other diseases Normal vision Healthy mucous membranes	Beef liver Spinach Cantaloupe Kale Carrots Broccoli Apricots	Cook or process foods in covered utensils Avoid frying foods at high temperatures Avoid overexposure of food surfaces to air	Night blindness Failures of tear secretion and changes in eyes Susceptibility to respiratory infection Dry, rough skin Changes in mucous membranes	4,000 IU	
B_1 (thiamine)	Emotional stability Energy Memory	Sunflower seeds Brewer's yeast Ham Whole wheat flour Rolled oats Green peas Soybeans	Cook in a minimum of water or steam Avoid high cooking temperatures and long heat exposure Avoid using baking soda with B-1 foods unless used as a leavening agent in baked products	Constipation Depression Loss of appetite Neurological changes Painful calf muscles Beriberi	1.0-1.1 mg.	Caffeine Alcohol Estrogen Aspirin
B_2 (riboflavin)	Enzyme functions in the metabolism of proteins, sugars and fats Essential for growth	Beef liver Milk Brewer's yeast Sunflower seeds Ham Broccoli Beef	Avoid cooking in large amounts of water Cut vegetables into large pieces instead of small Avoid exposure to light Cover pots when cooking	Visual fatigue and sensitivity to strong light Cracks around the mouth Reduced strength Growth retardation Burning and itchy eyes Cracked tongue	1.2-1.3 mg.	Ultraviolet light Water Estrogen Alcohol
B_3 (niacin)	Reduced blood cholesterol levels Mental and emotional health Aids metabolism of carbohydrates, fats and amino acids	Tuna Chicken Turkey Sunflower seeds Halibut Ham Peanuts	Niacin is very stable	Irritability Sleeplessness Headaches	13-14 mg.	Alcohol Sleeping pills Estrogen
B_6 (pyridoxine)	Production of antibodies Emotional stability Healthy skin Central nervous system regulation Rids body tissues of fluid in premenstraul women	Wheat germ Bananas Brewer's yeast Buckwheat flour Sunflower seeds Peanuts Tomatoes	Avoid cooking in large amounts of water Freezing vegetables results in a 30 to 56 percent reduction Canning vegetables results in a 57 to 77 percent reduction	Anemia, weight loss, stomach pains, vomiting Depression, weakness, nervousness Burning, tingling and numbness in the extremities	2.0 mg.	Long storage Alcohol Estrogen Cortisone
B_{12} (cobalamin)	Normal growth Healthy nervous system Normal red blood cell formation	Clams Beef liver Oysters Mackerel Sardines Crab Herring	Avoid extreme heating of meat products	Nervous system damage Raw scarlet tongue with a smooth surface	3.0 mg.	Alcohol Estrogen Sleeping pills

DIETARY DIRECTIONS IN THE 1980s 91

C Teeth and bone formation Bone fracture healing Wound and burn healing Resistance to infections and other disease	Green peppers Honeydew melon Brussels sprouts Broccoli Cantaloupe Strawberries Oranges	Eat foods raw or minimally cooked Shorten cooking time by putting vegetables in very small amounts of water Cut food into large pieces instead of small Avoid prolonged standing of foods at room temperature Avoid overexposure to air and light Don't soak vegetables	Weakness Swollen, tender joints Loose teeth Delayed wound healing	60 mg.	Cooking Smoking
D Facilitates the absorption and utilization of calcium	Cod liver oil Halibut liver oil Eggs Salmon Tuna Milk (vitamin D enriched)	Avoid overexposure to air	Bowleg, knock-knee, curvature of spine, pelvic and chest deformities Softening of bones Excessive tooth decay	200–400 IU	Smog Mineral oil Cortisone
E Healthy heart and skeletal muscles Possible retardation of the aging process Helps fight effects of air pollutants	Oils Almonds Sunflower seeds Whole wheat Wheat germ Peanuts Filberts	Avoid deep-fat frying Avoid freezing	Breakdown of red blood cells	8 IU	Heat Freezing
FOLATE New red blood cell formation Found in the most rapidly growing tissues, such as bone marrow and the lining of the digestive tract	Spinach Broccoli Asparagus Brewer's yeast Wheat germ Liver Orange juice	Avoid high temperatures Avoid cooking in large amounts of water Avoid exposure to light Avoid storing at room temperature	Anemia	400 mcg.	Sunlight Estrogen Aspirin
PANTOTHENIC ACID Strong adrenal glands Converts fat and glucose to energy	Brewer's yeast Beef liver Bran Peanuts Sesame seeds Eggs Soybeans	Avoid extreme heat	Digestive problems Weakness Poor coordination	10 mg.	Food processing Sleeping pills Alcohol Caffeine Estrogen

Don't worry about taking too much vitamin C. It does not cause kidney stones, contrary to what some doctors believe. Excess vitamin C in your urine is more than harmless; it's helpful. It prevents kidney or bladder infections.

Oranges, of course, are rich in vitamin C, as are all citrus fruits. Frozen or bottled orange juice, however, has 100 percent less vitamin C than fresh. Surprisingly, the potato is a fine source. Americans actually get more vitamin C from potatoes than oranges. (But not from potato chips, which have lost 75 percent of their vitamin C.) Green peppers, parsley and broccoli are green pastures for vitamin C. Smokers, especially, should graze there. Pack-a-day smokers have 25 percent less vitamin C in their blood than nonsmokers.

BIOFLAVINOIDS

Bioflavonoids are vitamin C's kissing cousins. The white inner skin of citrus fruits and the white column inside a green pepper are packed with bioflavonoids. And while bioflavonoids work best with vitamin C (most supplements include them together), they've established a reputation of their own, mostly as a cure of gynecological problems.

Thirty-nine out of 40 women who had vaginal bleeding after the insertion of an IUD stopped bleeding when they took bioflavonoids. Women who had an excessive or irregular menstrual flow cleared up their problem with bioflavonoids. The nutrient has cured varicose veins and hemorrhoids during pregnancy. It treats all those problems by strengthening capillaries. My girlfriend bruises easily unless she takes bioflavonoids; then the problem goes away in a day or two. Easy bruising is nothing but a sign of fragile capillaries.

VITAMIN D

Vitamin D is not what you'd call a versatile nutrient. It does one job: It allows the body to absorb calcium. But that's like saying the heart is a second-class organ because it does only one thing: beat. In fact, without vitamin D the heart couldn't beat since calcium regulates muscle contraction. Calcium is crucial; that's why vitamin D is too.

You get very little vitamin D by eating. Sunlight turns a chemical in your skin into vitamin D (which is technically a hormone). So unless you spend most of your time indoors or cover every square inch of your skin when you go outside, there's next to no chance of a deficiency.

VITAMIN E

Curse those pregnant rats! In the early years of scientific study into vitamins, researchers found that vitamin E increased fertility in rats. From that humble beginning, vitamin E has come to be known as the "sex vitamin." Well, improving your sex life is one of the few things vitamin E doesn't do.

It does improve glycogen storage, giving you more fuel for endurance sports. It does improve the tone and strength of your heart muscle. It does protect cells from oxidation (a sort of internal rust). That means it probably lengthens life (more if not better sex) since many scientists theorize that aging is caused by oxidation. If you have breast cysts, 600 IU a day of vitamin E for two months may clear them up, and reduce your risk of breast cancer.

Vitamin E oil is amazing. Chapped lips, surgical incisions, burns (including sunburn), bedsores, warts, athlete's foot, poison ivy—if it's on the skin, vitamin E oil has cleared it up. And when taken as a supplement with vitamin A, it's good for acne.

Processed foods are vitamin E weaklings. Cornflakes have lost all but two percent. Whole wheat bread has seven times more vitamin E than white bread does. Brown rice has six times more than white. The RDA is nine IU which, say experts, is too low to maintain good health. Look for a supplement that has at least 200 IU of vitamin E.

Vitamin B₁₅—Whatever It Is, It Won't Help

by William A. Check

A so-called vitamin sold in health food stores may be giving users cancer rather than prolonging their lives, according to data presented at the recent meeting of the American Society for Clinical Nutrition in Washington, DC.

Neville Colman, MD, of the Hematology and Nutrition Laboratory of the Bronx Veterans Administration Medical Center, New York, told nutrition scientists that one of the components of "vitamin B₁₅," also known as calcium pangamate or pangamic acid, is mutagenic in a widely used in vitro assay.

According to one survey, a chemical that is mutagenic in this test has a 90% probability of being able to cause cancer, Colman pointed out.

Vitamin B₁₅ is promoted as a dietary supplement as well as a drug. According to the Food and Drug Administration, it has been alleged to help heart disease, aging, diabetes, gangrene, hypertension, glaucoma, alcoholism, hepatitis, jaundice, allergies, dermatitis, neuralgia, and neuritis.

Colman and colleagues mixed dimethylglycine hydrochloride (DMG), a compound found in the largest selling formulation of vitamin B₁₅, with sodium nitrite to simulate exposure to saliva. They then incubated the mixture under conditions similar to those found in the human stomach. The investigators expected this procedure to form nitrosamines, many of which previously have been shown to be mutagenic.

When they tested the reaction products in the popular bacterial assay for mutagenesis devised by Bruce Ames, PhD, of the University of California, Berkeley, the results showed the presence of mutagenic chemicals.

Colman concluded that the main component of this vitamin B₁₅ formulation is capable of reacting to form a potential carcinogen under conditions simulating those found in the human digestive tract.

This work is a continuation of the campaign against unscientific health fads being waged by Victor Herbert, MD, JD, chief of the Hematology and Nutrition Laboratory at the Bronx VA and professor of medicine at State University of New York Downstate Medical Center, Brooklyn. Last year Herbert and Colman used the Ames test to show that diisopropylamine-dichloroacetate (DIPA-DCA), a major component of the second-largest selling form of pangamate, is also mutagenic.

For those disturbed by the presence of two different mutagens in these two preparations of vitamin B₁₅, there is worse news: Different brands of this "vitamin" have completely different compositions (Figure). Says Herbert, "The term 'vitamin B₁₅' is chemically meaningless, so producers can throw anything they want into a bottle and label it vitamin B₁₅ or 'pangamic acid.'"

The explanation for this curious situation lies in the history of this substance, explains Herbert. In 1943, Ernst Krebs, Sr and Jr (who gave the world laetrile) announced the discovery of and applied for a patent on pangamic acid, which they said they had isolated from apricot kernels. The name derives from their claim that this material is present in seeds of many fruits (pan-gamete). Following granting of the patent in 1949, the material was heavily promoted as a cure-all under the trade name "vitamin B₁₅."

The Krebses said that pangamic acid was a methylating agent. However, when their co-worker Howard Beard sent a sample to William Darby, PhD, then chairman of the Department of Biochemistry at Vanderbilt University, Nashville, in 1953, Darby found no such activity.

There is no clear chemical identity for pangamic acid. The Krebses defined it as an ester of gluconic acid and DMG. But Paul Sage of the FDA's Bureau of Drugs told JAMA MEDICAL NEWS that "we have never analyzed a batch that contained this formulation."

Recently Darby heard that Herbert was testing modern-day preparations of pangamic acid and asked Herbert if he wanted to test some of the original material, which he (Darby) still had. Herbert obtained a sample, had it analyzed by nuclear magnetic resonance spectroscopy, and found that it was the milk sugar, lactose.

In the eighth edition of *The Merck Index* (1968), "vitamin B_{15}" is identified as a mixture of sodium gluconate, glycine, and DIPA-DCA. The ninth edition lists vitamin B_{15} as the ester of gluconic acid and DMG. In the tenth edition, *JAMA* MEDICAL NEWS learned from one of the index editors, there will be no vitamin B_{15} entry—only one for "pangamic acid." This entry will indicate that the name has been applied to several different substances and mixtures.

The checkered past of vitamin B_{15} has made it easier, however, for its manufacturers to elude the law.

It is illegal to sell any substance under the label "vitamin B_{15}" or "pangamic acid" according to the FDA, which considers it an unsafe food additive. The agency has seized several lots of material labeled "vitamin B_{15}" or "calcium pangamate," and courts have upheld its right to destroy this material. In fact, the FDA is now prosecuting a large suit against Food Science, Inc, of Vermont, distributors of the DMG-containing preparation.

But the attorney for Food Science claims that DMG is a natural food substance. "The FDA wants to classify DMG as a food additive, because then the company would have the burden of proving that it is safe," Robert Ullman told *JAMA* MEDICAL NEWS. "We think that DMG is a food substance and that the FDA should have to prove that it is dangerous."

Even though the FDA has been successful in its suits so far, the essential meaninglessness of the term vitamin B_{15} has made it almost impossible for the agency to keep substances with that name off the market. Pangamic acid is like the mythical Greek god Proteus: When anyone captured this god in his human form, he changed into a snake or a cloud and escaped. When the FDA seizes a wholesale lot of vitamin B_{15} and obtains a court injunction prohibiting its sale, the producer can refill the bottles with some other chemical and put them back in the store.

"The FDA seized some wholesale lots of calcium pangamate marketed by General Nutrition Center (GNC) and brought suit to stop their sale," relates Herbert. "On January 31 of this year, GNC signed a consent decree to stop selling this form of calcium pangamate, which contained DIPA-DCA." This is the material that Herbert and co-workers last year showed to be mutagenic. "But," says Herbert with dismay, "GNC is still selling something in those exact same bottles with the exact same labels. What is it?"

Says Ullman, "I would hope that it's DMG."

VITAMINS

Ascorbic Acid and Iron Nutrition

by Sean R. Lynch, M.D.

Iron is an essential element that plays a vital role in oxygen transport as well as many other metabolic processes. The body of the average man contains about 4 g of iron, 3 g of which is in functionally active compounds; the remainder constitutes the iron store.[1] The major portion of the functional iron is present in the porphyrin complexes of hemoglobin and myoglobin as well as in a variety of heme-containing enzymes. Since iron is carefully conserved and reutilized in the body, the physiological requirement is small. Men need only about 1 mg/day to replace obligatory losses. Women require approximately 1.5 mg/day because of the additional iron losses in menstrual blood and the demands of childbearing and lactation. Despite the relatively small requirement for iron, which is far less than the amount present in the daily diet, nutritional iron deficiency is prevalent throughout the world. This is a consequence of the inefficient absorption of much of the food iron.

Dietary Iron

The varied diet of human beings contains many different forms of iron. Therefore, when considering iron absorption, it is convenient to divide the dietary iron compounds into two classes, those containing heme iron and those containing all other types of iron (nonheme iron). Iron derived from the heme moiety of hemoglobin and myoglobin is found in animal products and it is readily available for absorption while the bioavailability of nonheme iron is much less favorable. For example, in one study Swedish soldiers eating a mixed diet absorbed an average of 34% (0.34 mg) of the 1 mg of heme iron, but only 5% (0.82 mg) of the 16.4 mg of nonheme iron present in their meal.[2] Therefore, they derived 1/3 of their requirements from the heme pool which represented only 6% of the total dietary iron. Meat probably provided man, the hunter, with a very adequate supply of iron. However, as man evolved into a tiller of soil, his meat intake decreased and other less accessible sources of iron became more important. The declining availability of meat and its virtual absence in the diets of many people in developing countries has focused the attention of nutritionists on the less readily available nonheme component of dietary iron.

Nonheme Iron Absorption

Heme iron is absorbed as the iron porphyrin complex and its availability is little affected by meal composition.[1] In contrast, nonheme iron must be released from the parent compound before it can be absorbed. Early studies of nonheme food iron absorption were carried out by using single foods which had been labeled biosynthetically with radioiron.[3] The amount of iron absorbed from different vegetables varied considerably, but depended more on iron availability than on the absolute amount of iron in the particular item. Further investigation demonstrated that availability from any particular food could be altered substantially when it was eaten in a composite meal containing one or more additional foods. For example, soybean iron was much better absorbed than blackbean iron if each was eaten separately, but the percentage absorption from each bean source was approximately equal when they were eaten together.[3] Studies like these have demonstrated that nonheme iron absorption appears to be a property of overall meal composition rather than of the specific food containing the iron.

These observations have led to the conclusion that when several foods are eaten together, nonheme iron destined for absorption behaves as though it is derived from a single common pool.[4,5] This pool comprises vegetable iron, nonheme iron in meat and any soluble inorganic iron salts which may be present in or added to the meal. Since lack of iron is more often the result of poor availability than of inadequate iron intake, an understanding of the dietary components that affect the absorption of nonheme iron is of critical importance to nutritionists.

Ascorbic Acid and Nonheme Iron Absorption

Many chemical ligands in food are known to be powerful inhibitors of absorption. These include carbonates, oxalates, phosphates, fiber components and tannates. Other ligands, such as ascorbic acid, citric acid, tricarboxylic acid, amino acids, meat protein and sugars, promote its absorption.[1] The two factors with the greatest enhancing influence are meat and ascorbic acid.[6] Meat protein improves iron absorption in two ways: first, by providing heme iron and secondly, by enhancing the absorption of nonheme iron in the meal.

However, the properties of ascorbic acid have received most attention since the ascorbic acid content of the diet is more easily modified than is the meat content. Initial evidence suggesting that ascorbic acid would enhance iron absorption from food was obtained in meals eaten with and without citrus fruits.[7] A glass of orange juice containing 50-70 mg ascorbic acid produces approximately a three-fold increase in the nonheme iron absorption from a breakfast meal.[8] The observations with fruit have been amplified by a series of investigations in which the effect of purified ascorbic acid was examined in detail.[7] These studies demonstrated that ascorbic acid exerts an equal influence on all the nonheme iron elements of a meal and therefore appears to act as a ligand for the common nonheme iron pool.[7] The enhancing effect of ascorbic acid is directly proportional to the quantity added to the meal.[6] Moreover, it has been shown to reverse the inhibitory effect of substances such as tea, calcium and phosphate, the degree of reversal of inhibition being directly proportional to the quantity of ascorbic acid in the meal.[6,9] Iron absorption in the presence of ascorbic acid and an inhibitor, such as tea, may therefore exceed the absorption of the basal meal containing neither.

The effect of ascorbic acid depends upon its presence in the meal and is unrelated to the ascorbic acid status of the individual. For example, 500 mg ascorbic acid taken even 4 hours prior to a meal has little effect on iron absorption.[6] Cooking also may alter the influence of ascorbic acid. After baking, virtually no enhancement of iron absorption is seen. When food is boiled, much of the activity is retained.[10]

Ascorbic acid appears to act by increasing the solubility of the nonheme iron at the alkaline pH of the duodenum. Food iron exists predominantly in the ferric form. In an aqueous solution, ferric ions are bound to each other through water bridges. Since increases in pH make more hydroxyl ions available, metallic polymers or precipitated metallic hydroxides are formed and iron becomes unavailable to the mucosal cell. If ascorbic acid is added to a ferric chloride solution at acid pH, hydrogen ions are displaced from ascorbate with the formation of a complex that remains in solution over a pH range of 2-11.[11] Therefore, in the presence of ascorbic acid, ferric iron remains soluble and available for absorption at the alkaline pH in the duodenum.

Iron and Ascorbic Acid Supplementation

Attempts to improve iron nutrition in some populations at risk for iron deficiency by the addition of a soluble iron salt to one of the food components may not be effective. As indicated above, added iron enters the nonheme iron pool in the meal and tends to be relatively unavailable for absorption in diets which consist predominantly of cereals, such as wheat, corn and rice. Although these grains contain iron, they actually are considered poor dietary sources. Such diets are most common among vegetarians and people in less developed countries. For these groups, improvement in iron status may only be possible if the availability of the nonheme pool is increased and the addition of ascorbic acid to the meal is one possible means of achieving this end. However, in lesser developed countries where the problem of anemia is most severe, the relatively high cost of synthetic ascorbic acid and its instability during prolonged food storage and cooking have proven to be major obstacles to its use in fortification programs designed to prevent nutritional iron deficiency. Foods high in ascorbic acid are often grown in the lesser developed countries. Consideration should be given to educating the people to use foods high in ascorbic acid in the same meals as grains.

One further implication of the effect of ascorbic acid on iron absorption merits consideration. While ascorbic acid is important in making iron available for absorption in people who are iron deficient, large quantities of ascorbic acid could lead to excessive iron absorption. This possibility, even if remote, deserves our attention since iron overload results in organ damage and morbidity which is at least as severe or perhaps more severe than that seen in iron deficiency.

Present knowledge of iron overload indicates that the occurrence in the U.S. is relatively rare. Most cases occur in individuals who are genetically predisposed to overabsorption of dietary iron. However, the long-term effects of megadose quantities of ascorbic acid on dietary iron absorption in man are not known, although it has been predicted that people eating 1-2 g each day might increase their iron absorption two to three-fold.[6] If this rate of absorption were maintained over a period of 10 years, severe iron overload could be the consequence. To date, there is no evidence that this does in fact occur and it is possible that adaptive mechanisms would come into play, reducing the rate of iron absorption.

Summary

Iron deficiency anemia is prevalent throughout the world because of the inefficient absorption of nonheme iron which forms the bulk of the iron in the diet. Absorption of this type of iron is impaired by substances in food which reduce its availability. Ascorbic acid reverses the effect of dietary inhibitors and is one of the most powerful known promoters of nonheme iron absorption. It facilitates iron absorption by forming a chelate with the ferric iron in food at the acid pH of the stomach; the chelated iron remains soluble at the alkaline pH of the duodenum. However, the consumption of ascorbic acid with a vegetarian meal containing primarily nonheme iron could improve the absorption of iron for an individual whose diet contains little or no heme iron. Unfortunately, relatively high cost and instability of ascorbic acid during food storage have proven to be major obstacles to its use in combating nutritional iron deficiency in developing countries.

References

1. Bothwell, T.H., et al., *Iron Metabolism in Man*, Blackwell Scientific Publications, Oxford, 1979.
2. Björn-Rasmussen, E.L., et al., Food Iron Absorption in Man, Applications of the Two-Pool Extrinsic Tag Method to Measure Heme and Nonheme Iron Absorption from the Whole Diet, *J. Clin. Invest.* 53:247, 1974.
3. Martinez-Torres, C. and Layrisse, M., Nutritional Factors in Iron Deficiency; Food Iron Absorption, *Clinics in Haematology* 2:339, 1973.
4. Cook, J.D., et al., Food Iron Absorption Measured by an Extrinsic Tag, *J. Clin. Invest.* 51:805, 1972.
5. Björn-Rasmussen, E.L., et al., Food Iron Absorption in Man, II, Isotopic Exchange of Iron Between Labeled Foods and Between a Food and an Iron Salt, *Amer. J. Clin. Nutr.* 26:1311, 1973.
6. Cook, J.D. and Monsen, E.R., Vitamin C, the Common Cold and Iron Absorption, *Amer. J. Clin. Nutr.* 30:235, 1977.
7. Lynch, S.R. and Cook, J.D., Interaction of Vitamin C and Iron, *Ann. N.Y. Acad. Sci*, 1980. In press.
8. Rossander, L., et al., Absorption of Iron from Breakfast Meals, *Amer. J. Clin. Nutr.* 32:2484, 1979.
9. Disler, P.B., et al., The Effect of Tea on Iron Absorption, *Gut* 16:193, 1975.
10. Sayers, M.H., et al., The Effects of Ascorbic Acid Supplementation on the Absorption of Iron in Maize, Wheat and Soya, *Brit. J. Haem.* 24:209, 1973.
11. Conrad, M.E. and Schade, S.G., Ascorbic Acid Chelates in Iron Absorption: A Role for Hydrochloric Acid and Bile, *Gastroenterology* 55:35, 1968.

VITAMINS

Modern Views Of Vitamin D

by Hector F. DeLuca, Ph.D.

Introduction

Vitamin D is unique among the vitamins in several respects. First, it is a steroid and its main active form acts in a manner quite similar to that of other steroid hormones. Second, it is not a dietary requirement when the organisms are subjected to sufficient amounts of ultraviolet light originating from the sun. Third, it is the only vitamin known to be converted to a hormonal form. The full realization of these unique features of vitamin D has led to an explosion of investigation resulting in rapid advances in our understanding of its metabolism and mechanism of action. In addition, these investigations have led to the rapid application of the active forms of vitamin D and our knowledge of the vitamin D endocrine system to the understanding and treatment of metabolic bone disease. This brief review will provide the basic information on the vitamin D endocrine system as it is visualized at the present time and the disturbances in that system in some disease states.

Metabolism of Vitamin D_3

Vitamin D_3 originates from two sources (see Figure 1). It is synthesized in skin under normal conditions. When an organism is subjected to ultraviolet light, an intermediate in the biogenesis of cholesterol, 7-dehydrocholesterol, is converted to previtamin D_3 which then equilibrates slowly to vitamin D_3. The vitamin is then bound to the plasma transport protein and transferred to the liver where it enters the metabolic sequence. Alternatively, vitamin D_3 is absorbed from the small intestine, from the diet or food supplements. Vitamin D is not abundant in the natural food supply, being found only in such sources as liver or fortified foods such as milk. Unfortified milk has about 40 I.U./liter of vitamin D activity despite claims of super active forms of vitamin D in milk. Vitamin D, being lipid soluble, is absorbed primarily with lipids through the lacteal system. Vitamin D_3 from either source is rapidly cleared by the liver.

Fig. 1

Vitamin D_3 Synthesis

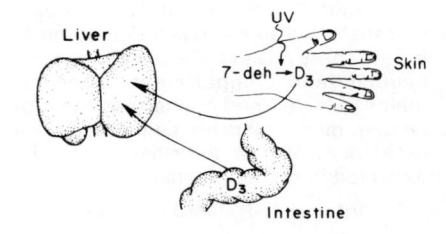

Activation and Functions of Vitamin D_3

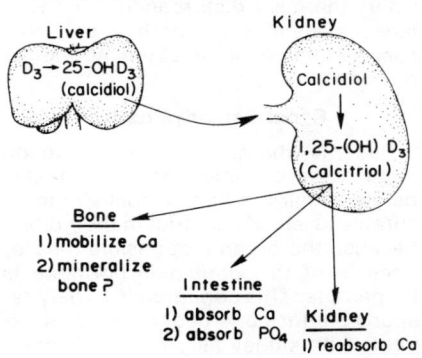

Vitamin D_3 must be metabolically activated before function (Figure 1). The first activation step occurs primarily, but not exclusively, in the liver where it is converted to 25-hydroxyvitamin D_3 (calcidiol) which is the major circulating form of vitamin D_3. Calcidiol also is not active at physiologic concentrations but must be further activated before function. This activation in nonpregnant animals takes place exclusively in the proximal tubule of the kidney where a 1α-hydroxyl group is installed on the molecule giving rise to the final active form of the vitamin D hormone, 1α, 25-dihydroxyvitamin D_3 or calcitriol (see Figure 1). This hormonal form of vitamin D (calcitriol) is then transported to the intestine, bone, kidney, and perhaps other sites, where it initiates the actions of vitamin D. These are a) intestinal absorption of calcium and phosphorus, b) the mobilization of calcium from the bone fluid compartment, and c) renal reabsorption of calcium. This results in an elevation of plasma calcium and phosphorus to levels that will support normal mineralization of bone and neuromuscular activity.

There may be an additional action of one of the vitamin D compounds directly on the mineralization process in the bone. This, however, has not yet been firmly established though clinical evidence is suggestive.

In addition to the metabolic activation of vitamin D to calcitriol, other pathways of vitamin D metabolism are known, but their function remains unknown or controversial. Vitamin D and its metabolites, including calcitriol, are excreted into the feces via the bile with as much as 60-80% of an injected dose appearing in this excretory route. The exact chemical nature of the excretory forms is not known.

In keeping with its hormonal nature, the production of calcitriol is strongly feedback regulated. Perhaps the most important regulating factor is the blood calcium level. Low blood calcium stimulates the parathyroid glands to secrete the peptide hormone, parathyroid hormone. Parathyroid hormone is transported to the kidney where, along with its other functions, it stimulates the 25-hydroxyvitamin D$_3$-1α-hydroxylase that converts calcidiol to calcitriol. Together with the parathyroid hormone, calcitriol stimulates the mobilization of calcium from bone and the renal reabsorption of calcium in the distal tubule. Calcitriol by itself stimulates the intestine to absorb calcium. Calcium from these three sources is then transported into the plasma where the blood calcium level rises to the normal range, thus suppressing the parathyroid glands and thereby shutting down production of calcitriol. It is evident that the vitamin D-based hormonal system is extremely important in the regulation of the blood calcium levels.

It might be expected that under conditions where there are great demands for calcium there is a marked stimulation of calcitriol production. This is clearly the case under conditions of pregnancy and lactation when great demands for calcium are made. In man and animals, calcitriol levels in the blood rise sharply during the terminal stages of pregnancy and rises even more sharply during the periods of lactation. This correlates with both the mobilization of calcium from bone and increased intestinal absorption of calcium. The vitamin D endocrine system therefore reacts in a positive manner to provide calcium under conditions where it is drastically needed. The exact signal involved in stimulating the calcitriol production during pregnancy and lactation is not known although it has been suggested that prolactin may be involved.

A major stimulus of the calcitriol levels in blood is the inorganic phosphorus level. Low blood phosphorus brings about marked elevations of plasma calcitriol levels in both animals and man which markedly stimulates intestinal absorption of phosphorus as well as calcium and also markedly stimulates the mobilization of phosphorus from bone. Thus calcitriol can be regarded as a phosphate-mobilizing hormone as well as a calcium-mobilizing hormone. It is unknown how low blood phosphorus causes the marked elevations in plasma calcitriol levels, although there is no doubt that some of this is the result of a stimulation of the 25-hydroxyvitamin D-1α-hydroxylase system.

Cellular and Molecular Mechanism of Action of Calcitriol

Concentrating on the well-recognized role of calcitriol in stimulating the transfer of calcium and phosphorus across the intestinal mucosa, some idea of how calcitriol functions at the cellular and molecular level can be realized. Calcitriol is transported to the target cells. In the case of the intestine, this is the mucosal villus cell. Here it binds with a specific cytosolic receptor (Figure 2). This receptor-bound calcitriol is transferred

Fig. 2

Mechanism of Calcitriol in Intestine

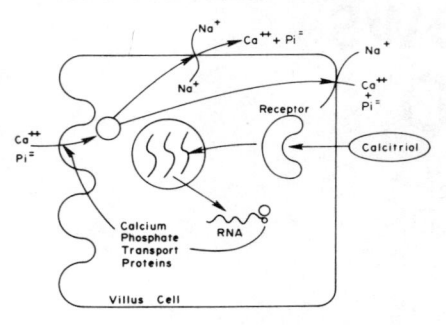

into the nucleus where it initiates a series of events that cause the transcription of specific genetic information. This information, in the form of messenger RNA, makes its appearance in the cytosol and codes for specific calcium and phosphorus transport proteins. The transport proteins are then transferred to the brush border membrane surface where calcium and phosphorus entry into the cell is facilitated. The calcium and phosphorus is transferred to the basal lateral membrane where it is expelled into the extracellular fluid compartment. Much remains to be learned concerning the molecular mechanism of calcitriol and a great deal of new information can be expected in the next decade.

Vitamin D-Related Diseases

Several disease states are now known where there is a disturbance in the vitamin D system. Space permits only cursory mention of some of the more obvious ones.

Renal Osteodystrophy

Patients who have lost renal function and who have glomerular filtration rates below 20 ml/min have virtually unmeasurable levels of calcitriol in their blood because the organ responsible for biogenesis of the vitamin D hormone is inoperable. This condition is largely responsible for bone degeneration in patients with kidney failure. This disorder is treated successfully in 90% of the cases with calcitriol or an analog thereof.

Hypoparathyroidism

Patients without functional parathyroid glands cannot "sense" hypocalcemia and do not secrete parathyroid hormone when required. Thus, calcitriol is not synthesized when needed. Calcium is not mobilized and the sensitive neuromuscular junction reacts in a convulsive or tetanic state. Administration of calcitriol and oral calcium is successfully used to correct this disorder.

Vitamin D-Resistant Rickets

A genetic defect known as vitamin D-dependency rickets type I (autosomal recessive) is in fact a defect in the renal conversion of calcidiol to calcitriol. This disorder is treated with physiologic amounts of calcitriol or pharmacological amounts of other vitamin D analogs. Still other genetically related bone diseases are known to include either primary or secondary disturbances in the vitamin D system.

Osteoporosis

An inability to increase intestinal absorption of calcium when required to meet organismal needs will result in calcium mobilization from bone to maintain blood calcium levels. This results in a chronic loss of bone. There is an age-dependent loss of calcium absorption and of bone mass which correlates with low blood levels of calcitriol. Postmenopausal osteoporotic women have blood calcitriol levels that also correlate with diminished calcium absorption. Administration of calcitriol to osteoporotic post-menopausal women not only increases calcium absorption but also improves calcium balance, an effect that persists for up to two years. Thus, calcitriol appears promising as a therapeutic aid in preventing bone loss of old age and menopause. Definitive studies are now in progress.

Summary

The relatively recent discovery of the vitamin D endocrine system has provided a new dimension in our understanding of metabolic bone diseases. In addition, these investigations have provided new therapeutic tools for management of disorders of calcium and phosphorus metabolism. This area should continue to provide new approaches to the management of bone disorders.

Key References

Deluca, H.F., *Nutrition Reviews* 37:161-193, 1979.

Deluca, H.F., *Nutrition Reviews* 38:169-182, 1980.

Haussler, M.R. and McCain, T.A., *New Engl. J. Med.* 297:974-983 (Part I) and 1041-1050 (Part II), 1977.

Lawson, D.E.M., Editor, *Vitamin D*, Academic Press, London, 1978.

VITAMINS

Perspective on Vitamin E as Therapy

by Hyman J. Roberts

IN A recent editorial on vitamin E therapy, Oski[1] stated: "Fortunately, large doses of this vitamin appear to be tolerated with relative impunity." The purported safety of vitamin E also is repeatedly underscored by physicians in popular health-oriented publications. Wright asserted: "There's never been a case reported of vitamin E toxicity. None of my patients have ever had any problems" (*Prevention*, February 1978, p 74).

This widely held attitude deserves scrutiny because it could pose a major public health concern. I continue to encounter patients with problems that seem to have been caused or aggravated by self-medication with vitamin E (used here to designate the various tocopherols) in high dosages.[2-4] The more serious ones include the following: (1) thrombophlebitis, pulmonary embolism, or both (my series now exceeds 80 such patients, averaging 62 years of age; four had recurrences on resuming vitamin E treatment); (2) hypertension (22 patients), generally with prompt lowering or normalization of the blood pressure on stopping vitamin therapy; (3) severe fatigue; (4) gynecomastia in both men and women; and (5) breast tumors perhaps necessitating biopsy. An estrogenic-like action—also suggested in case reports[6]—might explain the partial relief of menopausal symptoms afforded by vitamin E. Other possible mechanisms for these side effects have been reviewed previously.[3]

The clinical disorders and laboratory abnormalities encountered by me and others in patients with "hypervitaminosis E" are listed in Tables 1 and 2.

These observations have significant implications for our society in light of the considerable and widespread consumption of vitamin E. I frequently obtain a history of the daily ingestion of 800 to 1,600 units from patients seen in consultation. (The same applies to friends who are queried about the matter.) As a frame of reference, these megadoses contrast with the adult requirement of only 8 to 10 mg of D-α-tocopherol recommended by the Food and Nutrition Board of the National Academy of Sciences.[30]

Several factors have influenced such resort to vitamin E:

1. Both the public and many "nutritionists" regard its use as therapeutic or prophylactic for a wide variety of disorders. A partial list includes ischemic heart disease, occlusive peripheral vascular disease, thrombophlebitis, leg cramps, fibrocystic breast disease, the vascular complications of diabetes, various dermatoses, sterility, polymyositis, and the aging process. Some of my patients resumed the use of vitamin E because of its apparent benefit on their leg cramps or other symptoms, even though they risked a recurrence of hypertension or thrombophlebitis (which did occur).

2. Popular writers regard vitamin E as the "granddaddy" of all vitamins because "it puts oxygen quality in each blood cell." Some advocate that it be added to bread and other foods as a mechanism for increasing the life span (based on mice studies) in "project Methuselah."

Table 1.—Clinical Disorders Attributed to Vitamin E

Thrombophlebitis[2-4]
Pulmonary embolism[2-4]
Hypertension[3,4]
Fatigue[5]
Gynecomastia and breast tumors[3]
Vaginal bleeding[5]
Headache[7]
Dizziness[7]
Nausea, diarrhea, and intestinal cramps[3,7-9]
Muscle weakness and a myopathy (accompanied by elevated serum creatinine kinase levels and creatinuria)[7,8,10]
Visual complaints (large doses of vitamin E can antagonize the action of vitamin A)[7]
Hypoglycemia[7]
Stomatitis[7]
Chapping of the lips[7]
Urticaria[3]
Apparent aggravation of diabetes mellitus[3]
Apparent aggravation of angina pectoris[11]
Disturbances of reproduction[8]
Decreased rate of wound healing (in experimental animals)[12]

3. The repletion of antioxidants lost through the refining of natural grains, oils, and other foods is stressed by wellness-oriented periodicals.

Such "treatment" is difficult to reconcile with the fact

that vitamin E deficiency can be demonstrated or induced in adults only with difficulty. This includes elderly persons in whom multiple deficiencies of other vitamins are readily detected.[31] Since vitamin E exists in association with polyunsaturated fatty acids, it is present in adequate amounts in most conventional diets. Moreover, the need for dietary tocopherol seems to decrease with increasing age, as demonstrated in rats.[32]

Admittedly, vitamin E influences "free radicals" and various enzyme systems. *The New England Journal of Medicine* has published information in recent years dealing with its protection of granulocytes in a congenital glutathione synthetase deficiency (one infant),[33] its amelioration of bronchopulmonary dysplasia,[34] and various effects on free radicals.[1] Even so, the wholesale administration of vitamin E cannot be legitimately projected onto the prevention or treatment of most major cardiovascular, pulmonary, metabolic, and neoplastic disorders. *The Medical Letter*[9] has denied such alleged therapeutic efficacy.

Table 2.—Laboratory Abnormalities Induced by Vitamin E

Altered hormone metabolism, especially through an effect on the microsomal enzyme drug hydroxylating complex in the liver[13]
Reduced concentrations of thyroid hormones (triiodothyronine and thyroxine)[3,14]
Altered serum gonadotropins, perhaps owing to an effect on releasing mediators in the hypothalamus
Increased concentrations of the adrenal androgen dehydroepiandrosterone
Potentiation of warfarin sodium action (with potential bleeding)[9,15,16]
Increased levels of serum triglycerides and cholesterol, especially among women taking oral contraceptives[14,17]
Increased level of free cholesterol in low-density and very-low-density lipoproteins[18]
Increased levels of hepatic lipid and cholesterol[19]
Depression of leukocyte bactericidal activity[20]
Decreaed incorporation of tritiated thymidine into peripheral lymphocytes under phytohemagglutinin (mitogen) stimulation[20]
Altered immune reponses[20-25]
The mobilization and increase of platelets[26]
Altered erythrocytes and vascular membrane lipid peroxidation[19,27,28]
Increased erythropoiesis (demonstrated in the monkey) reflecting an enhancement of the androgen effect by vitamin E, and a possible decreased rate of hemolysis[29]

There may be merit in giving judicious amounts of vitamin E to some persons who might benefit from added antioxidant protection. Such circumstances could relate to intrinsic difficulties in metabolizing vitamin E, altered vitamin E receptors, or the ingestion of diets extremely high in polyunsaturated fats. Comparable "dependency" states have been described for other vitamins. In the case of vitamin E, however, I do not know how to define such a condition practically.

There is bound to be considerable controversy as to what constitutes excessive vitamin E therapy. At present, I regard a daily intake of a fully active tocopherol[35] in excess of 100 to 300 units as "megadose." Prasad[20] demonstrated that 300 mg of DL-α-tocopheryl acetate, given daily for three weeks to men and young boys, produced a significant depression in the bactericidal activity of the leukocyte and mitogen-induced lymphocyte transformation.

I have sought explanations for why the cited complications are not more prevalent. One possibility is the observation by Horwitt[35] that *all-rac-α*-tocopheryl acetate (the article of commerce) may have no more than half the biological potency of D-α-tocopheryl acetate when the commercial substance is used as a supplement for vitamin E–depleted adult subjects. The so-called DL-α-tocopherol is a fraction of the commercial mixture of *all-rac-α*-tocopheryl acetate, which includes eight possible stereoisomers in the form of four racemates.

Until these matters are clarified, the following recommendations seem prudent:

1. Megadoses of vitamin E should be used with restraint. This includes sophisticated health-conscious pregnant women seeking to prevent retrolental fibroplasia or bronchopulmonary dysplasia. (Other fat-soluble vitamins are potentially teratogenic in laboratory animals.)[36]

2. Patients taking large amounts of vitamin E should be followed up for the foregoing listed side effects (Tables 1 and 2).

3. Patients with any of these features, especially when unexplained, should be specifically queried about vitamin E intake.

4. The current epidemic status of deep-vein thrombosis and thromboembolism[37-40] warrants formal evaluation of the possible contributory role of vitamin E. Several critical studies have failed to confirm its alleged antiplatelet or antithrombic actions.[41,42]

As early as 1928, Harris and Moore[43] enunciated the concept that fat-soluble vitamins required in small amounts for health can be toxic at high concentrations. This theme has been recently restated by others.

1. *Nutrition Reviews*[44] noted: "The fat-soluble vitamins as a group are two-edged swords, life-saving at physiological levels and dangerous at megavitamin levels."

2. Robert E. Olson, MD, wrote: "I think it's likely that all the fat-soluble vitamins are toxic in high doses. Certainly, vitamin E in doses of 1 gram a day is not innocuous" (written communication, April 23, 1979).

3. London[18] commented:

Right now you can go to the drugstore and buy thousands of grams of vitamin E and take as much as you want, not knowing that it may affect you profoundly. It may change your lipids; it may, and probably will, alter some of your steroid hormones. At least at the dosage levels we prescribed, which weren't all that high, vitamin E is not a benign vitamin that you can take like vitamin C if you think you're getting a cold. It is—and we need to stress this—a pharmacologic agent.

---

1. Oski FA: Vitamin E—a radical defense. *N Engl J Med* 1980; 303:454-455.
2. Roberts HJ: Vitamin E and thrombophlebitis. *Lancet* 1978;1:49.
3. Roberts HJ: Thrombophlebitis associated with vitamin E therapy: With a commentary on other medical side effects. *Angiology* 1979; 30:169-176.
4. Roberts HJ: Is vitamin E 'therapy' innocuous? A plea for restraint. *Tufts Med Alumni Bull*, December 1979, pp 26-27.
5. Cohen HM: Effects of vitamin E: Good and bad. *N Engl J Med* 1973;289:980.
6. Kessler F: Vitamin E does not have estrogenic effects. *JAMA* 1970;214:604.
7. Herbert F: Toxicity of vitamin E. *Nutr Rev* 1977;35:158.
8. Murphy BF: Hypervitaminosis E. *JAMA* 1974;227:1381.
9. Vitamin E. *Med Letter*, Aug 15, 1975, p 69-70.

10. Briggs M: Vitamin E supplements and fatigue. *N Engl J Med* 1974;290:579-580.
11. Caralis DG, cited by *Med World News*, May 2, 1977, p 22.
12. Ehrlich HP, Tarner H, Hunt TK: Inhibitory effects of vitamin E on collagen synthesis and wound repair. *Ann Surg* 1972;175:235-240.
13. Carpenter MP, Howard CN Jr: Vitamin E, steroids, and liver microsomal hydroxylations. *Am J Clin Nutr* 1974;27:966-979.
14. Tsai AC, Kelley JJ, Peng B, et al: Study on the effect of megavitamin E supplementation in man. *Am J Clin Nutr* 1978;31:831-837.
15. Schrogie JJ: Coagulopathy and fat-soluble vitamins. *JAMA* 1975;232:19.
16. Hypervitaminosis E and coagulation. *Nutr Rev* 1975;33:269-270.
17. Nikkilä EA, Pelkonen R: Serum tocopherol, cholesterol, and triglyceride in coronary heart disease. *Circulation* 1963;27:919-928.
18. London RS, cited by González ER: Vitamin E relieves most cystic breast disease; may alter lipids, hormones. *JAMA* 1980;244:1077-1078.
19. Bieri JG: Vitamin E. *Nutr Rev* 1975;33:161-167.
20. Prasad JS: Effect of vitamin E supplementation on leukocyte function. *Am J Clin Nutr* 1980;33:606-608.
21. Beisel WR, Edelman R, Nauss K, et al: Single-nutrient effects on immunologic functions: Report of a workshop sponsored by the Department of Food and Nutrition and its Nutrition Advisory Group of the American Medical Association. *JAMA* 1981;245:53-58.
22. Tengerdy RP, Nockels CF: The effect of the need of vitamin E on egg production, hatchability and humoral immune response of chickens. *Poultry Sci* 1973;52:778-783.
23. Campbell PA, Cooper HR, Heinzerling RH, et al: Vitamin E enhances in vitro immune response by normal and nonadherent spleen cells. *Proc Soc Exp Biol Med* 1974;146:465-469.
24. Harman D, Heidrick ML, Eddy DE: Free radical theory of aging: Effect of free-radical-reaction inhibitors on the immune response. *J Am Geriatr Soc* 1977;25:400-406.
25. Kay MMB: Aging and the decline of immune responsiveness, in Fudenberg HH, Stites DP, Caldwell JL, et al (eds): *Basic and Clinical Immunology*. Los Altos, Calif, Lange Medical Publications, 1976, p 267.
26. Shute E: *The Heart and Vitamin E*. London, Ontario, Shute Foundation for Medical Research, 1969.
27. Bieri JG: Vitamin E, in *Present Knowledge in Nutrition*, ed 4. New York, The Nutrition Foundation, 1976, pp 98-110.
28. Nair EP, Kayden HJ: Vitamin E and its role in cellular metabolism. *Ann NY Acad Sci* 1972;203(special issue):1-247.
29. Solomon D, Strummer D, Nair EP: Relationship between vitamin E and urinary excretion of ketosteroid fractions in cystic mastitis. *Ann NY Acad Sci* 1972;203(special issue):103-110.
30. *Recommended Dietary Allowances*, ed 9, Committee on Dietary Allowances, Food and Nutrition Board. Washington, DC, National Academy of Sciences, 1980.
31. Baker H, Frank O, Thind IS, et al: Vitamin profiles in elderly persons living at home or in nursing homes, versus profile in healthy young subjects. *J Am Geriatr Soc* 1979;27:444-450.
32. Grinna LS: Effects of dietary α-tocopherol on liver microsomes and mitochondria of aging rats. *J Nutr* 1976;106:918-929.
33. Boxer LA, Oliver JM, Spielberg SP, et al: Protection of granulocytes by vitamin E in glutathione synthetase deficiency. *N Engl J Med* 1979;301:901-905.
34. Ehrenkranz RA, Bonta BW, Ablow RC, et al: Amelioration of bronchopulmonary dysplasia after vitamin E administration: A preliminary report. *N Engl J Med* 1978;299:564-569.
35. Horwitt MK: Relative biological values of D-α-tocopheryl acetate and all-rac-α-tocopheryl acetate in man. *Am J Clin Nutr* 1980;33:1856.
36. Sharpe R: Vitamins and neural-tube defects. *Lancet* 1980;1:1301.
37. Moser KM: Pulmonary embolism: Where the problem is not. *JAMA* 1976;236:1500.
38. Dalen JE, Alpert JS: Natural history of pulmonary embolism. *Prog Cardiovasc Dis* 1975;17:259-270.
39. Gould SA, Kerstein MD: The diagnosis and treatment of deep vein thrombophlebitis. *Practical Cardiol*, November 1978, pp 85-95.
40. Roberts HJ: Controversies and enigmas in thrombophlebitis and pulmonary embolism: Perspectives on alleged overdiagnosis. *Angiology* 1980;31:686-699.
41. Olson RE: Vitamin E and its relation to heart disease. *Circulation* 1973;48:179-184.
42. Gomes JACP, Venkatachalapathy D, Haft JI: The effect of vitamin E on platelet aggregation. *Am Heart J* 1976;91:425-429.
43. Harris LJ, Moore T: 'Hypervitaminosis' and 'vitamin balance.' *Biochem J* 1928;22:1461-1477.
44. Vitamin D intoxication treated with glucocorticoids, clinical nutrition cases. *Nutr Rev* 1979;37:323-324.

Encyclopedia of Minerals

by William Gottlieb

You should eat like a pig. Or better yet, a cow.

It's no secret to a veterinarian that farm animals eating food deficient in trace minerals soon become out of sorts, if not downright sick. Cows that graze where the soil is deficient in zinc, for instance, come down with the grass staggers or milk fever (two diseases you needn't worry about). But farmers get around the trace mineral problem by adding those minerals to feed.

"Agricultural experts have known for years that animals need trace minerals for good health and development," says Donald Oberlas, a biochemist from Wayne State University School of Medicine in Detroit. "But this knowledge has never been transferred to human nutrition. In many cases today, animals are better fed than people."

All of the 30-some trace minerals in your body make up only one-one hundredth of one percent of your weight. That's why scientists thought they didn't count for much (at least in us humans; farm animals, on the other hand, are an economic investment and rate more serious attention). But in the last decade or so, research has shown that trace minerals are a very big deal—and the level of trace minerals in the typical American diet is a very raw deal.

For one thing, the type of fertilizers most farmers use actually block out a plant's ability to absorb trace minerals from the soil. Even when roots gorge on the major minerals in those fertilizers, they have a poor appetite for the so-called minor minerals. And to make matters worse, many of those plants are special hybrids, created to suck up large doses of fertilizer minerals and mostly ignore whatever else is in the soil.

The last insult added to this injury is that the trace minerals the plant does use are never returned to the soil as they are in organic farming, which relies on trace mineral-rich fertilizer such as manure and compost. So soil in America is becoming more and more depleted of trace minerals: In over 30 states soil is deficient in zinc, for example.

And when the produce arrives at the processing plant it suffers a fate only slightly better than death. When whole wheat becomes white flour, for instance, 78 percent of the zinc is lost, along with 50 percent of the chromium, 86 percent of the manganese, 89 percent of the cobalt, 48 percent of the molybdenum (those are all trace minerals) *and* 60 percent of the calcium and 75 percent of the phosphorus. (Just to let you know that Americans aren't doing any better in the major-mineral category.)

While those minerals are losing out, others—the bad guys—are gaining the upper hand. Cadmium and lead, trace minerals that were once rare in the environment, are now common because of pollution. These bad trace minerals play a vicious game of "king of the mountain" in your body, stopping some of the good trace minerals from reaching the organs and tissues where they do their job—a crucial job.

"People who are in a state of marginal or poor nutrition with respect to trace minerals are much more susceptible to infectious diseases than are those in an optimal state of nutrition," according to the late Henry Schroeder, M.D., probably *the* expert on mineral nutrition.

Dr. Schroeder knew that people who are easy marks for infection are weak on a very basic level. But not too weak to kick the bucket.

"Nearly 90 percent of the fatal disease in this country involves trace minerals in one way or another," he said. But poor mineral nutrition of both the major and minor minerals is deadly in more ways than one.

Like the vitamins I talked about in the first part of this series (December 1980), minerals are a part of enzymes, those chemical sparks that power the body. Magnesium, which is a mineral you need large amounts of, not trace amounts, is a part of *90* enzymes. A low level of magnesium (a possible problem for anyone involved in endurance sports) could mean tired and tense muscles, nervousness and insomnia, not exactly a plus for training or competition.

From *Women's Sports* Magazine, pp. 1-8. Copyright 1980, *Women's Sports* Magazine. Reprinted with permission.

"For the diet to be balanced," advised Dr. Schroeder, "minerals must come from unrefined food or from a supplement bottle."

But, as I said before, don't try talking to most doctors about supplements. Even if you moo in his ear and graze on his rug, your doctor will probably deny you have any need for minerals beyond those you get in food. He may not have even heard of trace minerals.

"I would venture to say that at any given time, less than one percent of the medical students in the U.S. even know what a trace mineral is," says Robert Henkin, M.D., director of the Center for Molecular Nutrition in Washington, D.C.

I'd venture a large wager that very few medical students, or doctors, could tell you that: Zinc helps rid you of lactic acid; potassium, not sodium, is needed by athletes who train in the heat; calcium uncramps muscles.

CALCIUM

You tote around a load of calcium: three pounds' worth, more than any other mineral in your body. Most of that calcium, of course, is in your bones and teeth, which would be so much jelly without it. But the remaining one-tenth of one percent is no slouch either. Take it away and your muscles couldn't contract.

In fact, the mechanism that regulates the level of that small but precious amount of calcium is so precise that, if the amount drops a couple of micrograms too low, calcium is immediately taken from the bones to make up the difference. (The bones are not a static hunk but living tissue that constantly trades old calcium for new.) So a lack of calcium affects not only your bones and teeth, but your nerves and muscles as well.

That's why you can unknot muscle cramps by taking extra calcium. That includes menstrual cramps: Start the supplements ten days before your period if you usually have cramps. A minor backache will often back off if you use calcium. Some people claim arthritic pain has lessened or vanished when they took calcium.

Even if your bones are hard as hockey pucks and your muscles supple as an old sneaker, you may need more calcium to get the lead out of your system.

You could have a lead problem if you live or work next to a busy highway or in a smoggy town, or near a lead smelter or in a house with peeling flakes of lead-based paint, or if you have a job or hobby that brings you into close contact with lead-based material. One study showed that workers exposed to levels of lead considered "safe" had nerve damage in their arms. Lead had slowed their reflexes so insidiously that they never realized what was happening to them.

Perhaps you don't fit into the above categories. But when so much lead is in the air and food and water, why take any risk of being poisoned? A high level of calcium in your diet stops the absorption of lead. When your calcium intake is high, lead comes in the front door and goes out the back without getting on your nerves.

Women have another reason to take more calcium. Estrogen acts as a chemical dam to keep calcium in the bones but at menopause, levels of estrogen fall. Year by year calcium drifts away from the bones until, weak and riddled with holes, they can break at a slight jostle.

Exercise has been found to decrease the amount of calcium lost, so the sedentary ways most people adopt as they get older don't help matters. The disease called "osteoporosis" hobbles millions of elderly women. "Dowager's hump" is a symptom of osteoporosis: the spinal vertebrae shatter. If your grandmother has broken her hip—a common problem among elderly women—chances are she has osteoporosis. Calcium supplements can stop and reverse the bone loss.

Although bone loss doesn't pick up steam until menopause, it starts much earlier. "Calcium supplements should probably be given from age 25, when bone loss starts," says Jennifer Jowsey, an expert on the problem. "This may seem to be an extraordinary recommendation, but if calcium supplementation is initiated at this early age, by the time the individual is 70, she or he may retain the bone mass and therefore the bone strength of a 40-year-old."

Good news for those of you who have your eye on winning age-group competitions and, more to the point, for any athlete who wants to lessen her risk of a stress fracture.

Most Americans set themselves up for osteoporosis, and other calcium problems, because they eat too much protein. Protein forces calcium out of the body. If you get 100 grams of protein a day in your diet (a typical amount for many Americans), it's impossible to maintain bone strength, unless you also have 1,000 milligrams (mg.) of calcium a day (*not* a typical amount for many Americans).

You could get that amount of calcium from three glasses of milk a day. But that would also mean a bundle of fat and calories. And I'm convinced from talking to doctors who specialize in food allergies that cow's milk is not always a healthful food for humans. Many people cannot digest it properly and react with symptoms from gas to grumpiness.

It's far better, as Dr. Jowsey suggests, to get your extra calcium from a supplement, which should contain at least 800 and as much as 1,500 mg. of calcium. One excellent source of supplemental calcium is bone meal, which is made from sterilized and powdered long bones of cattle.

Dairy products deliver lots of calcium. A cup of cottage cheese has 230 mg.; an ounce of Swiss cheese, 262 mg.; eight ounces of yogurt, 294 mg. Sardines and salmon (with bones) are packed: A three-ounce can of sardines has 372 mg. One cup of collard or turnip greens has more than 250 mg. Tofu is also a fine source. And followers of macrobiotics tout the green tea called "bancha," which they claim has more calcium than milk.

PHOSPHORUS

Phosphorus is in every cell of your body and has a hand in every biochemical reaction. Along with calcium, it keeps your skeleton sturdy. Your heart beats, your meals digest, your kidneys purify and your nerves pass on their messages thanks to phosphorus. In fact, it has more duties than any other mineral.

Where can you get more? You already get too much.

Phosphorus and calcium are partners. Equal partners: The food you eat should have a phosphorus-calcium ratio of one to one. A ratio of any less than that has the same effect as a calcium deficiency.

The average American eats a diet with a phosphorus-calcium ratio of about three to one. Why? We eat too much meat. Beef has a ratio of 209 to 9! So there's no risk of skimping on phosphorus. Just make sure to take your calcium!

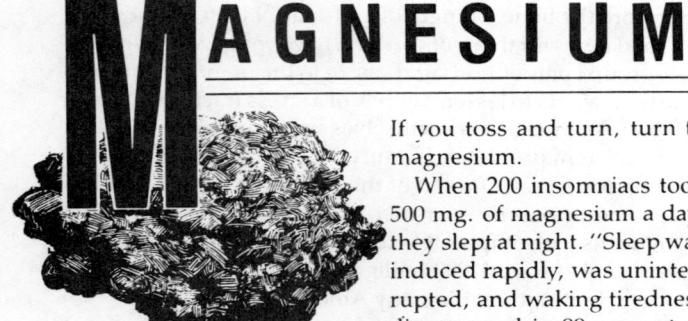

MAGNESIUM

If you toss and turn, turn to magnesium.

When 200 insomniacs took 500 mg. of magnesium a day, they slept at night. "Sleep was induced rapidly, was uninterrupted, and waking tiredness disappeared in 99 percent of the subjects," say the scientists who conducted the study. And, they note, "Anxiety and tension decreased during the day."

August Daro, M.D., a doctor from Maywood, Ill., also finds that uptight patients calm down on magnesium. "I often prescribe magnesium, or magnesium with calcium, as a tranquilizer," he says.

Magnesium is a natural tranquilizer. It also quiets uppity muscles, as well as nerves: Enough magnesium and muscles are relaxed. Too little and they twitch and tremble. Both muscles (including the heart) and nerves depend on magnesium. You also need it for digestion of protein, fat and carbohydrates—in fact, for what one scientist calls "an extraordinary number of metabolic reactions."

If your friends gave you a lot of perfumed soap for Christmas, you might want to consider taking magnesium. "I find that magnesium can lessen body odor in just about any case," says a nutrition-minded doctor.

Teamed up with B-6, magnesium has also been used to prevent "preeclampsia," better known as toxemia of pregnancy. And there are other reasons to baby yourself with magnesium: A study found that women whose active labor went longer than 18 hours were magnesium deficient.

You can put in much less than 18 hours of labor, on a long run, say, or cross-country skiing, and run the same risk. Hours-long endurance activity drains your body of magnesium.

Magnesium also prevents and has cured kidney stones (the dose was 500 mg. a day). From autopsies, researchers have found that heart attack victims have 22 percent less magnesium in their heart muscles than people dying from other causes.

Which may be one reason why Americans have a habit of suffering heart attacks. "We cannot assume that people automatically get as much magnesium in their food as they need," says Roger Williams, a biochemist at the University of Texas. "Mild magnesium deficiency may be widespread, and a disastrous deficiency may not be uncommon among those having heart attacks."

T.W. Anderson, M.D., a magnesium expert from the University of Toronto, seconds the motion. "Highly refined diets may supply barely adequate amounts of magnesium."

A quick look at some refined foods shows why. White flour has 28 percent less magnesium than whole wheat. Canned corn has 60 percent less than fresh corn. Puffed oats have 33 percent less than whole oats. Some chemical additives used to keep frozen vegetables a bright shade of green destroy magnesium completely.

Some good sources of magnesium are whole grains, soybeans, nuts, green, leafy vegetables, fruits and blackstrap molasses. Better than these, however, is dolomite, a preparation from powdered dolomitic limestone. Not only does it have magnesium, it also delivers calcium, and in the exact proportions nature intended. You could also use magnesium oxide supplements. Whatever you decide to take, aim at 350 to 500 mg. a day.

POTASSIUM

Athletes who don't sweat don't need extra potassium. But those who do and take salt tablets need double doses.

James Knochel, M.D., a professor at the University of Texas Southwestern Medical School, found that 50 percent of those hospitalized for "heatstroke" after intense exercise were potassium depleted. Knochel discovered that many of those athletes had taken salt tablets—which forced potassium out of the body. (Like phosphorus and calcium, potassium and sodium are intertwined.)

Add that to the potassium they were already losing through sweating and the bottom line was a severe potassium deficiency and all its symptoms: nausea, muscle weakness, cramps, irritability and, finally, total collapse.

You don't need to replace salt lost in sweat, but you do need to replace the potassium. If anything, you're probably better off sweating out all that salt, because most Americans have too much salt—and too little potassium—in their diets.

Again, processing is the culprit. Whole wheat flour has a potassium-sodium ratio of 360 to 3. White bread has a ratio of 100 to 540. Uncooked peas: 340 to 1. Canned peas: 130 to 230.

If you take diuretics for any reason, such as premenstrual swelling (B-6 is a better remedy), you also run a risk of potassium deficiency.

To replace it, monkey around: a medium-sized banana has 500 mg. of potassium. Other good sources are oranges, tomatoes, cabbage, celery, carrots, grapefruit, apples, beans and fish.

SODIUM

The salt shaker means shaky health.

You need about 2,000 mg. of sodium a day (table salt is sodium chloride). But on a typical American diet you get 10,000 to 12,000 mg. To cut back, fill the salt shaker with natural spices and eat less processed food—a diet of natural foods provides a natural amount of sodium. People who stop salting their food find they start tasting it, and in a few weeks begin to dislike the salty taste they once craved.

Nobody is really sure what all that extra salt does to you, but a good guess is that it pushes you toward high blood pressure. Anyone who already has high blood pressure should swear off salt. And if you train in hot weather, too much salt can derail you.

IRON

If your blood is iron poor, it's not easy to get rich quick.

The type of iron used to "fortify" cereals, baked goods and other processed foods is a rip-off: The body absorbs less than one percent of it. The type of iron your body could absorb would discolor white flour with a grayish tinge and shorten shelf life (which, to food companies, seems more important than lengthening your life). In one study, people who ate iron-fortified bread every day for six months had no boost in their blood-iron levels.

Processed foods also shortchange you if they contain EDTA, a preservative that blocks the absorption of iron. The amount of EDTA in the typical diet cuts iron absorption in half. Phosphates, another common food additive, butcher the iron in your diet. Dairy products latch onto iron and cut down absorption. Lead and cadmium get in the way. The tannic acid in tea muscles iron out of your body. Regular use of aspirin drains you.

No wonder a lack of iron is *the* most common nutritional deficiency. Especially among women: *95 percent of American women between the ages of 18 and 44 get too little iron in their diets.*

Women can't afford that dietary debit, since they need twice as much iron as men to make up for losses during menstruation. Pregnancy, too, depletes women of iron. If you don't get enough, the end result is a bad end: anemia.

Anemia is a form of suffocation. Iron helps form hemoglobin, the substance in red blood cells that snags oxygen and carries it to all parts of your body. When iron and oxygen are low, so are you. Pale, tired, headachy, depressed, but most of all, weak. And there are other, less common, symptoms of anemia: loss of appetite, nausea after meals, diarrhea or stomach pain, constipation or gas, sore tongue, ringing in the ears, dizziness, brittle and ridged fingernails, stiff and numb muscles.

Even if you have none of the symptoms of iron deficiency, you may still need more, and be stronger when you get it. A study of people with normal blood levels of iron showed that adding iron to their diet increased their "work capacity" by four times compared with another normal group which didn't get iron.

Another study, this time of anemic women, showed that peak heart rates during workouts fell from 152 to 123 after the women took iron, and that their pulse rates returned to normal much more quickly after exercise. The doctors found that the women's hearts delivered 15 percent more oxygen with every beat when anemia was cleared up.

There are lots of iron-rich foods: meat, beans, green, leafy vegetables, dried fruits, whole grains, wheat germ, blackstrap molasses.

But the real need is to increase your iron absorption, not just your intake, and for that you need vitamin C.

If you take 1,000 mg. of vitamin C with a meal, you boost your iron absorption tenfold! In one study, eating a papaya with a meal (a papaya has 66 mg. of vitamin C) increased absorption by 500 percent.

Another tip: The type of iron in meat (heme iron) aids the absorption of the type of iron in other foods (non-heme iron). By eating meat with other iron-rich foods, you boost your absorption from those other foods. Vitamin C is the best meal ticket to more iron though, and it wouldn't hurt to take it with an iron supplement. But you don't need more than 20 mg. of iron. As with other trace minerals, too much as well as too little can do some harm.

CHROMIUM

No one looking at a parking lot would think Americans need more chromium. But we do. Not the inorganic kind that coats bumpers but the organic kind your body uses. Americans have less chromium in their bodies than almost any other people in the world. Why? We eat too much sugar.

Chromium helps your body use insulin, the hormone that regulates blood sugar (glucose). But when you eat 120 pounds of sugar a year—the amount the typical American puts away—you need lots of insulin to burn up that sugar, and lots of chromium to lend a hand.

Trouble is, sugar is a refined food, and doesn't put any of that chromium back. By the time you reach middle age, chromium is often so depleted that blood sugar doesn't behave itself. Then you have maturity-onset diabetes: high blood sugar.

The way out (or down) is brewer's yeast, the best food source of chromium. After three months of taking brewer's yeast every day, 27 women with maturity-onset diabetes had normal blood sugar levels. But the time to take care of the problem is now.

"Everybody in this country should be supplementing his or her diet with two tablespoons of brewer's yeast a day," advised the late Richard Doisy, an expert on chromium. If brewer's yeast isn't your cup of tea, try this: a whole wheat pizza with chili peppers and mushrooms washed down with beer. With a dessert of calf's liver, you'll have a meal of every chromium-rich food on nature's menu.

COPPER

If you want to give someone money for his/her thoughts, give a nickel. Not because of inflation but because people get too much copper, from copper pipes, copper cooking utensils, cigarette smoke and car exhaust. Although no one could do without the necessary fraction of an ounce of copper the body needs, too much copper can arrest your health with high blood pressure, bad moods, migraines, even heart disease and senility.

Copper harms you by forcing zinc out of your body. Taking extra zinc turns the tables and lowers copper levels to within reason. In one study, zinc relieved migraines by heading off an overload of copper. To underdose on copper, be sure to take zinc.

ZINC

Zinc is at least one thing we can thank Iran for. If it weren't for a bunch of Iranian dwarfs—teenagers with the sexual equipment of six-year-olds—scientists might never have realized just how important zinc is.

It turned out the dwarfs got that way by eating a diet of almost nothing but a type of bread that stopped zinc absorption. A lack of zinc, the scientists found, stunted their gonads. Replacing the zinc turned little boys into young men. Conclusion: Zinc is a must for normal sexual maturation.

Before that discovery in 1963, zinc was considered about as important as the appendix. Eighteen years later, zinc is in the big leagues. Scientists realize that almost nothing goes on in the body without zinc's say-so. Breathing, digesting, seeing, making new cells all depend on zinc.

Twenty percent of that zinc is stored in the skin, which may be one reason why acne is no match for the mineral. When over 60 people (age 13 to 25) with acne took zinc for four weeks, 65 percent of their pimples cleared. After 12 weeks, 87 percent had cleared.

Zinc also speeds the healing of burns and all kinds of wounds. In one study, researchers divided women who had undergone surgery into two groups and gave one group zinc. That group healed in 46 days, while the non-zinc group took 80 days. Any injury from broken bones to sprained muscles heals faster when you take zinc.

It's smart to take zinc, and zinc may make you smart. Rats given extra zinc found their way out of a maze more quickly than non-supplemented rats, a sign, say the researchers, of a "superior rate of learning." And a study of students showed that those with the highest grade point average had the most zinc in their hair (an indication that more was circulating in their blood and stored in their tissues). You may also be crazy not to take it: Zinc and vitamin B-6 have cured schizophrenia.

Like calcium, zinc also helps stop the absorption of lead. "By increasing zinc," says a nutritionist, "everyone could be better protected against the inevitable lead exposure that is part of modern life."

Zinc also protects against cadmium. This industrial pollutant muscles in on zinc's territory in the body, working over the kidneys in particular and possibly causing high blood pressure. But if you take extra zinc, cadmium is handcuffed to start with, and never has a chance to make trouble.

Although the zinc intake of most Americans is much more than that of an Iranian dwarf, many of us don't get enough. "There is ample reason to suspect that the zinc intake of individuals in this country may be marginal," says one scientist.

The finger of blame points to poor soil and processed food. Alcohol, the Pill, pregnancy and infections chip away at zinc too. If you like oysters, stop worrying about a deficiency. Pearls aren't their only plus; oysters have 100 times more zinc than any other food. Other good sources include red meat, liver, wheat germ and nuts.

Lately some nutritionists have been making a fuss about phytates, a substance in whole grains, beans and nuts that binds with zinc (as well as calcium, magnesium and iron) to form a compound the body can't absorb. For this reason, they suggest people eat *less* whole food. Forget it.

An expert in mineral metabolism at Michigan State University, Pericles Markasis, has this to say about the "problem": "People have been eating beans, grains and nuts for thousands of years. Obviously those foods don't cause mineral deficiencies."

No matter what you eat (unless you're a hopeless oyster freak) you should take extra zinc. Twenty milligrams a day is a good protective level, though people have taken 150 mg. a day for several years with no ill effects.

IODINE

When it rains, it pours—iodine.

The thyroid hormone that paces the body's metabolism depends on iodine. Without the mineral, the gland goes into overdrive in a frantic effort to pump out more hormone, and then it puffs up. This swelling of the thyroid gland is called "goiter."

Goiter is rare today, thanks to iodized salt and the shipping of iodine-rich food into areas where the soil is deficient. But for a tip-top thyroid, include kelp and other seaweeds in your diet. They're the best source of iodine and a fine source of other minerals as well.

SELENIUM

You've heard of the Bible Belt and the Corn Belt, but how about the Stroke Belt? That's a swath of territory in Georgia and the Carolinas where people have more strokes—and less selenium—per capita than anywhere else in the nation.

But those folks shouldn't feel left out. America as a whole ranks behind 26 other countries in selenium intake, perhaps one reason why we outdo most other countries in strokes and heart disease and cancer.

"If we really want to consider nutritional cancer prevention," says Gerald Schrauzer, a selenium expert, "we have to include selenium through a change of diet or supplementation or both."

To do that, eat enough seafood, whole grains, organ meats and brewer's yeast, and make sure selenium is included in your mineral supplement.

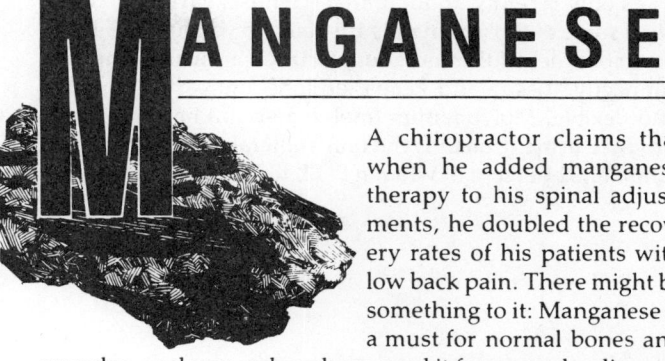

MANGANESE

A chiropractor claims that when he added manganese therapy to his spinal adjustments, he doubled the recovery rates of his patients with low back pain. There might be something to it: Manganese is a must for normal bones and muscles, and researchers have used it for muscular diseases such as myasthenia gravis. It's impossible to say if your muscles will benefit from extra manganese. Probably not—but a lack won't help either. The best manganese foods: beans, peas, spinach, bran, brussels sprouts, blueberries.

FLUORINE

Austria, Italy, Spain, France, Sweden, Denmark, Norway, Switzerland: the itinerary for someone's vacation? No. These are countries that have rejected fluoridated water as unnecessary—and dangerous.

Fluorine (or fluoride) is essential in *very* small amounts. Get much more than you need, and it's one of the most toxic poisons known to man. It warps the bones, wipes out the liver and the nervous system.

"The plain fact that fluorine is an insidious poison, harmful, toxic and cumulative in its effects—even when ingested in minimal amounts—remains unchanged no matter how many times it will be repeated in print that fluoridation of the water supply is safe," says Ludwik Gross, M.D.

As for its beneficial effects, it only works during the years of tooth development and it only delays decay for a few years. Kids in fluoridated areas have as many cavities as kids in non-fluoridated areas by the time they're 16.

Calcium and magnesium protect you against fluoride but have trouble with fluoridated toothpaste. In one study, 65 women (age 20 to 40) with chin pimples completely stopped using fluoridated toothpaste. In every case, the acne cleared up unless they started using the toothpaste again.

If you have pimples at the corners of your mouth and on your chin, stop using fluoridated toothpaste for a month. If the acne goes away, you'll know what caused the problem. You can also try eating brewer's yeast and bee pollen.

YOUR DINNER TABLE ISN'T MUCH DIFFERENT FROM THE periodic table. All those strange-sounding minerals you learned about in high school chemistry—vanadium, silicon, cobalt, molybdenum, to name a few—are found in the earth's crust and in pie crust. And in your body. You need all kinds of minerals, from tin to gold, for health.

It's only recently, though, that scientists have figured out what some of those minerals are doing in your body. Silicon, the most plentiful mineral on earth, is a must for healthy connective tissue and keeps tendons and cartilage strong and flexible. Molybdenum (mol-*ib*-de-num) helps the body produce urine. Cobalt is the only mineral that's part of a vitamin (4.32 percent of vitamin B-12, to be exact). But ask scientists about some of the others and they still draw a blank.

Which is okay. You don't have to know about those minerals; you just have to eat them. If your diet is big on whole, unrefined foods and keeps refined foods to a minimum, chances are your intake of those little-understood trace minerals is good enough. As an athlete, you can rest assured (or run assured) that as more is known about them and their specific health-improving qualities, supplements will appear. Selenium, for example, is a regular in supplements, but a few years ago scientists thought it was poisonous. For now, you'll have to do with winning gold instead of taking it. □

	HEALTH FUNCTIONS	BEST FOOD SOURCES	PREPARATION TIPS	DESTROYERS	DEFICIENCY SYMPTOMS	RDA
CALCIUM	Blood clotting Normal nerve tissue Regular heart beat Iron metabolism Healthy teeth and bones	Almonds, beet greens, brewer's yeast, broccoli, collard greens, dairy products, filberts, kale, salmon, soybeans, tofu, watercress	Don't discard the outer part of vegetables		Muscle cramps Low backache Bones fracture easily Rickets (children)	800 mg.
PHOSPHORUS	Involved in nearly all metabolic reactions in the body	Meat, nuts, seeds, whole grains		Antacids	A deficiency is almost impossible	800 mg.
MAGNESIUM	Conducts nerve impulses Keeps metabolism steady Normal muscle contraction Healthy heart, muscles, brain, kidneys, liver and other organs	Brown rice, green, leafy vegetables, molasses, nuts, peas, soybeans	Avoid peeling foods Avoid cooking in large amounts of water Keep meat drippings and use in gravies	Diuretics Alcohol	Irritability Nervousness Muscle tremors Behavioral disturbances Skin problems Hardening of soft tissues	300 mg.
POTASSIUM	Healthy kidneys, heart and skeletal muscles	Apples, apricots, avocados, bananas, beef, blackstrap molasses, brewer's yeast, broccoli, chicken, halibut, oranges, peanut butter, potatoes, raisins, sesame seeds, sunflower seeds, tomatoes, tuna, wheat germ	Same as magnesium	Alcohol Coffee Sugar Diuretics		
SODIUM	Maintains osmotic pressure of extracellular fluid	Salt	Use less in cooking		A deficiency is unlikely	
IRON	Forms blood Moves oxygen from the lungs to the rest of the body	Apricots, beans, blackstrap molasses, brewer's yeast, eggs, green, leafy vegetables, nuts, organ meats, sunflower seeds, wheat germ, whole grains	Steam vegetables instead of boiling Cook for a short time Avoid excessive water in cooking		Weakness and fatigue Headache Paleness Poor resistance to infection Sore mouth	18 mg.
CHROMIUM	Allows insulin to regulate blood sugar	Beer, black pepper, brewer's yeast, mushrooms		Sugar	Maturity-onset diabetes	
COPPER	Converts iron into hemoglobin Normal skin color Healthy nerve fibers	Almonds, avocado, beans, beef liver, peas, pecans, seafood, walnuts, whole grains			Anemia	
ZINC	Wound healing Healthy skin Activates many enzymes Maintains normal level of vitamin A in the blood	Beef, cheese, eggs, fish, green beans, lamb, lima beans, nuts, wheat germ, whole grains	Avoid cooking in large amounts of water			15 mg.
IODINE	Regulates thyroid function	Kelp, seafood			Goiter	150 mcg.
SELENIUM	Keeps cells from oxidizing	Bran, garlic, onions, tuna, wheat germ			Possibly some forms of cancer	
MANGANESE	Activates several enzymes	Nuts, whole grains			No possibility of a human deficiency	

MINERALS AND ELEMENTS

Mineral Elements: New Perspectives

by Walter Mertz, M.D.

During the 1970s, nutritional research on minerals and trace elements substantially intensified and accelerated, as compared with preceding decades. The results of this research can be summarized in the following three statements:

(a) The concept of the "new trace elements" as biologically active substances has been established and is gaining increasing attention.

(b) Mineral and trace element interactions are now more completely understood and are recognized as important determinants of metabolism and nutritional status.

(c) There has been substantial progress toward a better definition of human requirements for minerals and trace elements.

Some of the new knowledge is of theoretical interest and cannot yet be applied, but other parts concern the nutritionist and dietitian directly. For example, dietary interactions promise to provide a useful tool to improve through dietary means the nutritional status of large population groups (1). Existing recommendations for trace element intake and present knowledge of dietary interactions are difficult to implement because of incomplete background information, such as food tables, exact data on bioavailability, and so forth. Yet, concern for adequate mineral and trace element nutrition is warranted by past and projected changes in man's exposure to dietary and environmental trace elements; by the continuing low food intake in industrial societies resulting in low intakes of minerals and trace elements; and by knowledge of marginal deficiency states for several trace elements (2).

The new trace elements

Proof for an essential function of a nutrient comes from the production of a deficiency, either experimental or furnished by nature, and from the demonstration that the signs and symptoms of deficiency are prevented and/or cured by supplementation in physiologic amounts of the nutrient being investigated, but not by others. Progress in defining essential functions for new trace elements, therefore, depends on the investigator's ability to measure and carefully exclude the nearly ubiquitous contaminations in diet, water, and environment. The discoveries of essential functions for three trace elements during the 1950s—molybdenum, selenium, and chromium—were the last achieved with "traditional" research methods (3).

During the 1960s, two new methods gradually developed into powerful tools of "modern" trace element research. First, atomic absorption spectrometry, originally developed in Australia, became available to the researcher; used in the flame method or in the more sophisticated flameless modification, it greatly extended the detection limits for many trace elements.

The second development resulted in the concept of the "trace element-controlled isolator system" of Smith and Schwarz (4). This concept is based on the maximal possible exclusion of metallic contaminants in diet, water, and air. Animals are raised in metal-free isolator systems, the air going into the isolator is passed through high efficiency filters, and the water is of the highest attainable purity. The ingredients for experimental diets are carefully analyzed and, where necessary, trace element contamination is reduced or removed by washes with acids or chelators, or by crystallization or distillation. Both experimental animals and controls are kept in the isolator system under identical conditions, except for the trace element under investigation.

This new technique was quickly adopted by various investigators who were able to produce deficiencies for the following elements: Nickel, vanadium, tin, silicon, fluorine, arsenic, cadmium, and perhaps lead (5). The results were independently confirmed and extended to two or more animal species for nickel, vanadium, silicon, and arsenic, lending support to the postulate that these four elements may be essential to animals, albeit with very low requirements. Despite much research, the biochemical mode of action of these elements is still unknown.

The implication of these findings for human nutrition

is unknown. The need to employ great precautions when experimental deficiencies are produced could suggest that the very low requirements are easily met by natural contamination of diets, air, and water and that deficiencies in human populations are unlikely. On the other hand, it would be wrong to assume that adequate intakes of man can be taken for granted. Although chromium deficiency is very difficult to produce in experimental animals, it does occur in free-living human populations, particularly in certain areas in children with protein-calorie malnutrition.

Human requirements for the new trace elements are not quantified, and nutrient composition data are not available; for these reasons, the new trace elements are of no immediate, practical concern to the dietitian. Yet, they are of fundamental concern as a reinforcement of the concept that only a varied, balanced diet can furnish all known and potentially essential nutrients.

Concept of interactions
Known interactions among mineral elements (including trace elements) and between these and organic constituents of the diet number in the hundreds, and the number can be expected to increase. Interactions were first defined in animal nutrition, and some of them have assumed great practical importance, particularly in areas with unusual geochemical environments (6). Research during the past decade has expanded the knowledge of interactions from animal to human nutrition. Interactions are of great interest to the dietetic profession, because some determine the nutritional status of individuals more strongly than would the amount of intake of a particular element. At first sight, the multitude of interactions appears confusing and nearly impossible to deal with.

On closer consideration, however, it becomes evident that a few interactions of importance in human nutrition can be singled out and applied. The design and use of suitable computer programs will make this task more manageable. Interactions can be used to improve nutritional status by using dietary factors that either enhance or depress the absorption of particular mineral elements. This is best illustrated by the new proposals for the calculation of absorbable dietary iron which promise to solve the dietitian's dilemma of not being able to implement the Recommended Dietary Allowance of 18 mg. iron for women of child-bearing age (1).

While this is the only interaction that has been quantified so far, others can be expected to follow. Even now, awareness of interactions in a qualitative sense can be of value to the dietetic profession. The following discussion lists interactions of potential interest and importance to the dietitian.

TRACE ELEMENTS AND FOOD. Compounds of iron and zinc taken as supplements are almost always better absorbed when taken between meals than as part of a meal. This suggests that the influence of absorption-depressing factors in foods, such as phytates, fiber, and phosphates, is stronger than absorption-enhancing factors. It is possible, but not yet proved, that other mineral elements are subject to similar influences.

Practical considerations: A person who has a genuine need for supplemental iron or zinc should be advised to take the supplement on an empty stomach; conversely, those who insist on supplements for psychologic reasons only would do best to take them as part of the meal.

IRON, ASCORBIC ACID, AND MEAT. The important interactions among iron, ascorbic acid, and meat have been described, quantified, and recommended for application (1). It is important to realize that the interactions of iron provide a tool not only to increase iron absorption but also to decrease available iron in patients at risk of iron overload.

Practical considerations: The requirement of 1.5 to 1.8. mg absorbable iron in women of child-bearing age can be met from acceptable diets if enough ascorbic acid and/or meat, poultry, or fish products are present in the iron-containing meals. Conversely, subjects at risk of iron overload would benefit from low levels of ascorbic acid in the iron-containing meal, the consumption of tea with the meals, and the avoidance of iron cooking ware.

ANIMAL VS. VEGETABLE SOURCES OF ZINC. It is generally recognized that zinc is better available for absorption from animal than from vegetable products (7). The difference is due to the high phytate contents of many vegetable products, particularly of grains. Dietary fiber is believed to depress the availability of zinc and other trace elements, but there is no firm agreement as yet among different investigators.

Practical considerations: The Recommended Dietary Allowance of 15 mg. zinc per day is based on the consumption of a mixed, American diet. This amount is insufficient when the zinc comes entirely from vegetable products; it may be superadequate when it is derived predominately from animal meat or oysters. When it is not possible to achieve the recommended intake of zinc for a person, for whatever reasons, reliance on animal sources of this trace element will increase the amount available for absorption. Subjects accustomed to a high dietary fiber intake and at risk of low zinc intakes might benefit from the use of dephytinized bran, instead of whole bran. (Dephytinizing is a simple procedure that can be done in the home [8]).

PROTEIN-MINERAL INTERACTIONS. The interactions between protein, calcium, and phosphorus clearly demonstrate the benefits of the interaction concept for the establishment and implementation of dietary recommendations (9). Recommendations for calcium intake always were and remain controversial; this is evident by the spread of 300 mg. between the Recommended Dietary Allowances (10) (800 mg. for adults) and the recommendations for the United Kingdom (11) (500 mg.). There are valid experimental data to justify each level as reasonable, and there are indeed conditions in which 500 mg. calcium per day is more than adequate, and others in which 800 mg. may be barely sufficient. The dietary allowances for Australians (12) took this fact into account by recommending not one intake of calcium but a range of 400 to 800 mg. for adults.

The solution to this problem came from the demonstration that the amount of dietary protein significantly enhances urinary calcium excretion, without proportionally increasing calcium absorption, thus resulting in a decrease of calcium balance (9). The effect is strong; whereas 500 mg. calcium is sufficient at a protein intake of the RDA levels, 800 mg. may be marginal at protein intakes of 100 gm. or more. Such intakes are not uncommon in the United States; the resulting precarious calcium balance in many individuals may be, in part, responsible for the high incidence of osteoporosis in older age.

Shortly after the controversy of calcium requirements appeared to be solved, a new controversy arose with the demonstration of negligible effects on calcium balance in human subjects who consumed their high protein in the form of meat (13). This was resolved when an additional interaction was taken into account, that of phosphorus. In sufficiently high concentrations, this element counteracts the effect of protein on urinary calcium excretion, regardless of whether it is given as a natural constituent in meat or whether it is added as a chemical compound to a diet of purified protein.

These findings have reconciled the previous discrepancies from a theoretical point of view. Practical questions are still unanswered and await clarification by future research—for example, the moderate but distinct negative calcium balance in one study (9) in the presence of high phosphate intake and the question of whether phosphorus in vegetables, which occurs in part as phytate phosphorus, is equivalent in its effects to phosphorus in meat.

The amount of protein in the diet also affects the absorption of trace elements. Whereas protein in the form of meat, poultry, and fish enhances iron absorption markedly, protein from milk, cheese, and egg has the opposite effect (14). In a recent study, doubling the amount of egg albumin in a semi-synthetic meal reduced iron absorption by 40 per cent, and omitting the protein increased absorption by two-and-a-half-fold (15). Protein intake also affects requirements for zinc, copper, calcium, and phosphorus, as determined in a recent balance study. Estimated requirements on high- and low-protein diets (Table 1) show substantial differences, depending on the protein content of diet; for each element, the requirement for balance increases with increasing protein intake (16).

Practical considerations: As most protein sources of animal origin are also good sources of available minerals and trace elements, the increased requirements are usually met by the same foods that cause the increases. Still, the following precautions should be kept in mind: At high-protein intakes, calcium intake should be watched. High-protein intakes predominantly from dairy products can compromise iron absorption. High intakes of protein from vegetable sources will increase the requirement for copper and zinc, while furnishing these elements in a poorly available form. These examples underline the danger of one-sided dietary habits and again emphasize the need for balanced diets.

INTERACTION OF FOODS WITH COOKING WARE. The very significant interaction of foods with iron cooking containers is often overlooked and needs renewed awareness. It can be hypothesized that the diminished

Table 1. Mineral requirements for balance in human subjects*

mineral	requirement		p
	high-protein diet†	low-protein diet‡	
	←—— mg./day ——→		
zinc	12.8	7.3	<0.001
copper	1.27	1.14	<0.05
calcium	941	717	<0.001
phosphorus	1,400	900	<0.02

*Adapted from Sandstead et al. (16).
†15% of energy.
‡8% of energy.

use of iron pots and pans is one contributing factor to the low iron status of American women of child-bearing age.

Moore reported a surprising difference in the calculated iron content vs. the analyzed content of foods served to the military of several countries, in contrast to the usually close agreement between these values in the United States (17). He attributed the differences between the high levels obtained by analyses and the lower levels by calculation to the contribution of iron to the meals from the iron cooking ware. He subsequently investigated this question and demonstrated a very substantial increase of iron concentration of foods cooked in iron containers, particularly of acidic foods (Table 2). The greatest increase found was approximately one hundred-fold, with apple butter cooked for 2 hr., but even the average five-fold increase of the iron in foods, such as gravy, fried potatoes, rice casserole, or beef hash, must be considered nutritionally important.

The aqueous environment and heat during food preparation are conducive to the formation of complexes between iron and some food constituents.

That such complexes are available to the organism and, under extreme conditions, can lead to iron overload is suggested by the high incidence of hemosiderosis in Bantu subjects whose iron intake from their home-brewed beer alone averages 82 mg. per liter (18). This beer is prepared in iron kettles. Similar conclusions may pertain to the contribution of copper containers to the dietary intake; however, except for copper piping and drinking water, such interactions have not yet been quantified.

Table 2. Iron content of foods after cooking in different types of vessels*

food	cooking time	iron content		
		glass dish	iron skillet	increase factor
	min.	←—mg./100 gm.—→		
apple butter	120	0.47	52.5	112
spaghetti sauce	180	3.0	87.5	29
gravy	20	0.43	5.9	14
potatoes, fried	30	0.45	3.8	8
rice casserole	45	1.4	5.2	4
beef hash	45	1.52	5.2	3
scrambled eggs	3	1.7	4.1	2

*From Moore (17).

Practical considerations: The use of iron cooking ware is a simple, practical way of increasing dietary iron when increases are needed. In addition, the effect on dietary iron intake can be somewhat quantified: In cases of small or moderate iron deficits in the diet, the use of iron cookware for non-acidic foods would make a moderate contribution; in cases of large deficits, substantial amounts of iron could be obtained by also preparing acidic foods in iron containers. Conversely, subjects at risk of iron overload should be counseled to use non-iron kitchen utensils. The fact that iron and copper accelerate the destruction of ascorbic acid and other labile vitamins during cooking is well known and need not be discussed.

The interactions discussed here are but a few examples of a very large number. These few are ready for practical application. Unlike food fortification, the use of dietary interactions makes it possible to address small population groups specifically at risk, and even individuals. Except for iron, interactions have not yet been quantified and must be used semiquantitatively; however, incorporation of results of present and future research into effective computer programs will allow quantification of the most important interactions.

Redefining human nutrient requirements
The Committee on Recommended Dietary Allowances has incorporated "ranges of safe and adequate intakes" for two minerals and six trace elements in the ninth revised edition of the Recommended Dietary Allowances. These are: Sodium, potassium, copper, manganese, molybdenum, selenium, chromium, and fluorine. This recommendation is the subject of a detailed publication (19). In brief, safe and adequate intakes are defined as ranges that are considered, in the judgment of the Committee, to meet nutrient requirements and, at the same time, to be safe from even insidious toxicity. The range concept takes into account the homeostatic regulation of trace element levels by the organism, dietary interactions that influence requirements, and incomplete knowledge that does not permit the fixing of one desirable intake. The ranges provide general guidelines for an adequate intake and, at the same time, warn against excessive intakes through trace element supplements. Problems of implementing these guidelines are discussed later.

Researchers on iron metabolism and nutrition have set an example that may point to important new directions for research on other trace elements. They have proposed a new definition of iron deficiency and have proved the validity of extrinsic labeling in determining iron absorption and, therefore, the definition of a dietary iron requirement (20). Iron deficiency is now defined as a reduction or disappearance of the physiologic body stores of iron, regardless of whether this reduction is accompanied by anemia (21). The measurement of serum ferritin reflects the size of the iron stores and allows the detection of even marginal deficiencies.

Similarly, the physiologic importance of a "mobilizable chromium pool" for maintenance of normal glucose metabolism has been proposed for chromium. This pool is the source of acute increases of plasma and urine chromium in response to a glucose challenge. Lack of an acute chromium response suggests insufficient stores; the stores can be replenished by chromium supplementation. The obligatory chromium loss, which is almost exclusively via urine, has been determined and confirmed as less than 1 μg. per day. Assuming an average intestinal absorption efficiency for chromium of approximately 1 per cent, it can be calculated that diets furnishing between 50 and 200 μg. per day meet the adult human requirement (10).

The demonstration of the validity of extrinsic labeling for the measurement of food iron absorption has greatly increased our knowledge of factors that influence biologic availability. Recent work with experimental animals suggests that extrinsic labeling is also valid for measurements of zinc absorption (22); however, this remains to be proven for the human organism.

Implementation
The practical implementation of the range of safe and adequate intakes depends on the availability of accurate data on nutrient composition. Unfortunately, present data are not adequate. Nutrient composition tables for sodium and potassium are mainly restricted to unprocessed foods but are insufficient for pre-processed food items to which salt is usually added during the manufacture. Intensified work on nutrient composition and possibly inclusion of the sodium content on nutritional labels can be expected to improve the situation in the future. A compilation of the trace element content of many foods has appeared (23); unfortunately, it is not yet available in English translation. In short, present composition tables are inadequate as a basis for detailed calculations. The need for such calculations, however, can be expected to be the exception rather than the rule and to be restricted to the long-term feeding of one-sided diets or formulas at the exclusion of a variety of foods. In these cases, information on the trace element content of the formulas by the manufacturer will allow an evaluation of adequacy.

As far as healthy, free-living population groups are

concerned, the consumption of a varied diet, balanced with regard to the major nutrients, will furnish an intake of manganese, molybdenum, and selenium, well within the suggested adequate and safe ranges. The same is true for fluoride in all areas with an adequate fluoride content in the water supplies.

The range of safe intakes for copper is 2 to 3 mg. per day for adults; it is attainable in diets that furnish more energy than is ordinarily consumed in the United States or from foods that are not widely used, such as organ meats or shellfish. Recent surveys suggest an intake from self-chosen diets at close to 1 mg. per day, considerably below the lower end of the safe and effective range (24).

Some concern can also be expressed about the adequacy of dietary chromium intake. A recent study of diets designed to meet all the Recommended Dietary Allowances found an average of 78 μg. chromium in diets furnishing 2,800 kcal, with a low range of only 35 μg. (25). Habitual consumption of diets of low energy content and with a high proportion of refined ingredients may result in undesirably low intakes of chromium. Thus, the adequacy of copper and chromium intakes cannot be taken for granted.

Pennington and Calloway have compiled a list (26) of the copper content of foods and provided an excellent discussion of the many factors that may be responsible for the wide differences of reported values even within one particular food. If the information on the copper content of foods is not very reliable, that on other trace elements is even less so, as ten-fold or greater differences of reported values for one food are not uncommon. These fluctuations make an exact, quantitative evaluation of diets for copper and the other trace elements nearly impossible, but they still permit a qualitative approach to the design and evaluation of diets that can be used to advantage until more reliable data become available. It is possible arbitrarily to establish a mean copper concentration for major food groups, important individual foods, and for foods of outstanding copper content.

The concentration can be expressed on the basis of 1,000 kcal, and the relative contributions of individual foods can be estimated by relating the individual values to the theoretically desirable minimal density of 1 mg. copper per 1,000 kcal. Although this is by no means a quantitative assessment, it may be a useful approach to estimate whether a diet is poor, marginal, or adequate with regard to its copper content. Table 3 shows a representative example of this treatment for copper, based on the compilation of Pennington and Calloway (26). Group A in this table consists of foods that do not furnish copper in proportion to their energy content. The foods of Group B can be considered adequate sources of copper; those of Group C are exceptionally good sources and could be considered as an occasional part of diets which, without these foods, would be unacceptably low.

The food composition data for chromium are even less complete and less reliable, and a quantitative assessment should not be attempted. However, qualitative treatment is still possible: A grouping of foods into one group that supplies a low chromium density, another of

Table 3. Copper density in foods*

food	energy (kcal/100 gm.)	copper p.p.m.	range	mg./1,000 kcal
Low-copper density				
sugar, refined	385	0.2	0 — 5	0.05
oils, fats	800	1.1	0 — 5	0.14
meats	300	1.4	0.1 — 9	0.47
milk	66	0.35	0.02— 4	0.53
wheat flour, patent	360	2.0	0.9 — 4	0.56
eggs	160	1.0	0.2 — 2	0.6
Intermediate-copper density				
bread, white	260	2.5	0.6 — 5	1.0
chicken meat	130	1.6	0.1 — 4	1.2
flour, whole	330	5.0	1 — 10	1.5
fish	100	1.9	0.1 — 5	1.9
nuts and seeds	600	11.3	1 — 32	1.9
fruit, fresh	50	1.0	0.1 — 5	2.0
vegetables, fresh	40	1.0	0.1 — 5	2.5
crab meat	100	9.0	0.1 — 65	9.0
High-copper density				
yeast, dried	280	50.0	30 — 100	18
lobster	90	17.0	3 — 40	19
liver	140	45.0	2 — 290	32
oysters	80	170.0	13 —1,600	212

*Adapted from Pennington and Calloway (26).

Table 4. Relative chromium: energy ratio of foods*

food	relative index
Low-chromium density	
sugar	1
grits	3
butter	4
margarine	5
skim milk	6
corn meal	6
corn flakes	7
spaghetti	8
Intermediate-chromium density	
fish, shrimp, lobster	12
grain, whole	17
flour	14
chicken breast	17
bread	20
fruit, fresh	20
chicken legs	28
cheese	32
bread, whole grain	32
wheat bran	32
vegetables, fresh	35
beef	38
High-chromium density	
oysters	65
potatoes with skin	72
liver	78
yeast, dried	80
egg yolk	104

*Calculated from data in Toepfer et al. (27).

intermediate, and a third of very high, chromium density. The values in Table 4 were derived from a study performed by one investigator using one method (27). The absolute values reported are questionable in the light of recent developments and are, therefore, not given. There is, however, reason to accept the *relative* chromium concentrations as valid, i.e., that one food does indeed contain twice the amount of chromium found in another, regardless of the absolute figures reported for each. The relative chromium ratios in Table 4 are based on the amount of chromium in 1,000 kcal of the food lowest in chromium—refined sugar. This figure is arbitrarily set at 1, and the chromium content per 1,000 kcal of all other foods is expressed on this basis. For example, skim milk and oysters furnish six and sixty-five times more chromium per 1,000 kcal, respectively, than sugar. The foods can be ranked according to their chromium density per 1,000 kcal and, with copper, they can be arbitrarily divided into three groups of low, intermediate, and high chromium value.

No quantitative values should be assigned to these ratios; the latter bear no quantitative relation to a chromium requirement or the "range of safe and effective intakes." They can be used, however, as a first approximation to a qualitative evaluation of dietary adequacy with regard to chromium, assuming that the foods in Group B are most probably adequate and that a pronounced contribution of foods of Group A to the total diet increases the risk of undesirably low intakes. Foods of Group C could serve as occasional supplements to diets that might otherwise furnish undesirably low intakes.

Conclusion

In the past, much of the dietitian's work was concerned with the exact translation of precise Recommended Dietary Allowances into palatable meals. The new perspectives of nutrition research discussed here in relation to the mineral elements cannot be quantified in exact figures. The new concept of "ranges of adequate and safe intakes" for six trace elements is not just an expression of incomplete knowledge of requirements for these nutrients but reflects our increased understanding of nutrient interactions on which the dietary requirement depends. A first step in the quantification of such nutrient interactions has been proposed with the new calculation of absorbable dietary iron; more steps in this direction are expected. The implementation of the recommended ranges of safe and adequate intakes for six trace elements must be based on semi-quantitative, or even qualitative, considerations, until reliable nutrient composition data become available. While such qualitative approaches to implementation may be less than perfect, it is believed that they are necessary and may result in tangible benefits.

References
(1) MONSEN, E.R., HALLBERG, L., LAYRISSE, M., HEGSTED, D.M., COOK, J.D., MERTZ, W., AND FINCH, C.A.: Estimation of available dietary iron. Am. J. Clin. Nutr. 31: 134, 1978.
(2) WHO EXPERT COMM.: Trace Elements in Human Nutrition. WHO Tech. Rept. Series No. 532, 1973.
(3) MERTZ, W.: The newer trace elements. Biol. Trace Element Res. 3: 1, 1979.
(4) SMITH, J.C., AND SCHWARZ, K.: A controlled environment system for new trace element deficiencies. J. Nutr. 93: 182, 1967.
(5) SCHWARZ, K.: Essentiality versus toxicity of metals. *In* Brown, S.S., ed.: Clinical Chemistry and Chemical Toxicology of Metals. N.Y.: Elsevier, North Holland, 1977.
(6) UNDERWOOD, E.J.: Trace Elements in Human and Animal Nutrition. 4th ed. N.Y.: Academic Press, Inc., 1977.
(7) PRASAD, A.S.: Trace Elements and Iron in Human Metabolism. N.Y.: Plenum Press, 1978.
(8) MORRIS, E.R., AND ELLIS, R.: Bioavailability to rats of iron and zinc in wheat bran: Response to low phytate bran and effect of the phytate-zinc molar ratio. J. Agric. Food Chem., in press.
(9) LINKSWILER, H.M.: Interrelationships among protein, calcium, and phosphorus. *In* Beecher, G.R., ed.: Beltsville Symposia in Agricultural Research. IV. Human Nutrition Research. N.Y.: John Wiley & Sons, in press.
(10) FOOD & NUTR. BD.: Recommended Dietary Allowances. 9th rev. ed. Washington, D.C.: Natl. Acad. Sci., 1980.
(11) Recommended Intakes of Nutrients for the United Kingdom. London: Dept. of Health & Social Security, 1969.
(12) NATL. HEALTH & MEDICAL RESEARCH COUNCIL: Dietary Allowances for Use in Australia. Canberra: Australian Govt. Publ. Serv., 1971.
(13) SPENCER, H., KRAMER, L., OSIS, D., AND NORRIS, C.: Effect of a high protein (meat) intake on calcium metabolism in man. Am. J. Clin. Nutr. 31: 2167, 1978.
(14) COOK, J.D., AND MONSEN, E.R.: Food iron absorption in human subjects. 3. Comparison of the effect of animal proteins on nonheme iron absorption. Am. J. Clin. Nutr. 29: 859, 1976.
(15) MONSEN, E.R., AND COOK, J.D.: Food iron absorption in human subjects. 5. Effects of the major dietary constituents of a semisynthetic meal. Am. J. Clin. Nutr. 32: 804, 1979.
(16) SANDSTEAD, H.H., KLEVAY, L.M., JACOB, R.A., MUNOZ, J.M., LOGAN, G.M., JR., RECK, S.J., DINTZIS, F.R., INGLETT, G.E., AND SHNEY, W.C.: Effect of dietary fiber and protein level on mineral element metabolism. ACS Symp. Proc. "Dietary Fibers: Chemistry and Nutrition." N.Y.: Academic Press, 1978.
(17) MOORE, C.V.: Iron. *In* Goodhart, R.S., and Shils, M.E., eds.: Modern Nutrition in Health and Disease. 5th ed. Philadelphia: Lea & Febiger, 1973.
(18) BOTHWELL, T.H., SEFTEL, H., JACOBS, P., TORRANCE, J.D., AND BAUMSLAG, N.: Iron overload in Bantu subjects. Studies on the availability of iron in Bantu beer. Am. J. Clin. Nutr. 14: 47, 1964.
(19) MERTZ, W.: The new RDAs: Estimated adequate and safe intake of trace elements and calculation of available iron. J. Am. Dietet. A. 76: 128, 1980.
(20) COOK, J.D., LAYRISSE, M., MARTINEZ-TORRES, C., WALKER, R., MONSEN, E.R., AND FINCH, C.A.: Food iron absorption measured by an extrinsic tag. J. Clin. Invest. 51: 805, 1972.
(21) JOINT FAO/WHO EXPERT GROUP: Requirements of Ascorbic Acid, Vitamin D, Vitamin B_{12}, Folate, and Iron. WHO Tech. Rept. Series No. 452, 1970.
(22) EVANS, G.W., JOHNSON, E.C., AND JOHNSON, P.E.: Zinc absorption in the rat determined by radioisotope dilution. J. Nutr. 109: 1258, 1979.
(23) SCHLETTWEIN-GSELL, D., AND MOMMSEN-STRAUB, S.: Spurenelemente in Lebensmitteln. Intl. J. Vit. Nutr. Res., Suppl. 13, 1973.
(24) HOLDEN, J.M., WOLF, W.R., AND MERTZ, W.: Zinc and copper in self-selected diets. J. Am. Dietet. A. 75: 23, 1979.
(25) KUMPULAINEN, J.T., WOLF, W.R., VEILLON, C., AND MERTZ, W.: Determination of chromium in selected United States diets. J. Agric. Food Chem. 27: 490, 1979.
(26) PENNINGTON, J.T., AND CALLOWAY, D.H.: Copper content of foods. Factors affecting reported values. J. Am. Dietet. A. 63: 143, 1973.
(27) TOEPFER, E.W., MERTZ, W., ROGINSKI, E.E., AND POLANSKY, M.M.: Chromium in foods in relation to biological activity. J. Agric. Food Chem. 21: 69, 1973.

Fluorine: An Essential Element for Good Dental Health

by Durward R. Collier, D.D.S., M.P.H.

Fluorine and the Fluoridation Process

Fluorine is regarded as an essential trace element. Fluorides are compounds containing the element fluorine. The Food and Nutrition Board of the National Research Council stated in 1968 that fluoride is a normal constituent of all diets and is an essential nutrient (1). In addition, the U.S. Food and Drug Administration has recognized fluorine as an essential mineral in human nutrition (2). In its various forms, fluoride is found in practically all soils, plants and animals, as well as in human blood, bones and teeth. It is also present in at least trace amounts in all natural water supplies; however, its concentration in water varies widely. In the United States, natural fluoride levels range from many parts per million in some areas of the southwest to as little as trace amounts in the northeast.

Fluoridation actually is the redistribution of a natural trace element in accordance with scientific and medical guidelines. The presence of fluorides in the drinking water at a level of about one part per million during tooth development and continuously after tooth eruption prevents dental caries particularly on the smooth surfaces by up to 65% (3, 4, 5, 6, 7, 8, 9, 10, 11). In areas where community water fluoridation can not be achieved, alternative fluoride methods are available, such as school fluoridation (fluorides added directly to the water system of the school), topical fluoride treatments applied professionally and self-administered fluorides, such as mouth rinses and tablets, although these are not as effective as fluoridating the drinking water.

Fluorides provide protection to the teeth through one or more of several mechanisms (12). Although not all of the anti-caries mechanisms of fluorides are fully understood, dental authorities generally agree on three major mechanisms: (1) fluoride ions in low concentrations can increase the formation within the enamel of the stable, relatively insoluble crystallized mineral hydroxyapatite. Hydroxyapatite enables the tooth to resist dissolution by acids during the carious process; (2) fluoride ions in high concentrations can be incorporated into the mineral structure of the tooth enamel either during tooth development or after tooth eruption, and the presence of free fluorides in tooth enamel tends to inhibit dental caries; (3) fluoride also appears to be concentrated in the dental plaque. The fluoride interferes with the attachment of plaque to the teeth. Also, it appears that fluoride may influence the type of extracellular polysaccharide produced by microorganisms, their ability to synthesize intracellular polysaccharide and their capacity to form acid from sugars.

The Dental and Medical Benefits of Fluoridation

Nearly everyone in this country has suffered from dental caries. Much of the pain and experience of dental decay can be prevented through fluoridation. *No other public health measure is as effective in building decay-resistant teeth.* It is available to all without regard to education or socioeconomic background (8). Communities can build a heritage of better dental health through fluoridation at a minimal cost. Depending on the size of the population served, the number of gallons of water pumped and other factors, fluoridation costs betwen $.10 and $.40 a year per capita. It has been estimated that there are one billion untreated carious teeth in the United States; however, by fluoridating a public water system, nearly two out of three caries can be prevented in children with the expectation that they will have far fewer extractions throughout their lifetime and fewer will become endentulous by age 65. By the time children reach their teens, almost six times as many in fluoridated communities are completely free of caries as their counterparts in fluoride-deficient areas (8).

A recent report (13) from the American Dental Association Bureau of Economic Research and Statistics pointed out that the percentage of Americans aged 30 years and older who wear one or two complete dentures has dropped from 35.2% in 1960 to 24.7% in 1975, and one of the preventive procedures credited to the decline in denture wearers is fluoridation. In the State of Tennessee, the dental caries rate for permanent teeth among the school-age population has dropped from an average of 4.6 decayed, missing or filled teeth per child in 1955 to 2.02 decayed, missing or filled teeth in 1979 (5). The number of unfilled, carious permanent teeth per child among the school-age population in Tennessee has dropped from 3.6 in 1955 to 1.04 in 1979 (5). In other words, the unmet need has been reduced by almost 75%. The greatest single factor in bringing about these reductions has been community fluoridation. Purely economic considerations would seem to make fluoridation programs a matter of primary importance.

Americans spend more than eight billion dollars in dental bills during the course of a year and that does not include the rising dental cost in the form of higher taxes to finance dental health programs. It has been estimated that industry loses more than 100 million man hours of production time because of dental ills. Research has shown that fluoridation can cut the professional time needed for children's dental care by one half (14). For every dollar invested in fluoridation, $50 in savings on dental bills can be expected (9). A recent report (20) from the U.S. General Accounting Office quotes Public Health Service officials as estimating that 3.5 billion dollars can be saved in the cost of caries treated during the first 16 years of life for each future generation of children born in fluoridated communities.

In the later years of life, a higher rate intake than normally found of fluoride appears to be necessary to maintain normal calcification of bone. Some experimental studies (15) indicate that the principal action of fluoride on bone is a slowing of the resorptive phase of the remodeling process with an additional promotion of calcification. There are some indications that suitable amounts of fluoride may be helpful in preventing or alleviating osteoporosis in the aging population.

In those areas where community water fluoridation is not possible, alternative fluoridation programs are school water fluoridation which will prevent approximately 40% of dental carious teeth, and self-applied fluoride programs such as fluoride mouthrinse and fluoride tablet programs which will prevent 30 to 35% of the dental caries in a school-age population (6).

One of the big efforts today in a community fluoridation program is maintaining the system at the optimal level after community fluoridation has been accomplished. Continuous surveillance is needed to see that the optimal level is kept within an acceptable range; otherwise, the benefits are reduced drastically.

The Safety of Fluoridation

Over the past 34 years, continuous studies have been made of fluorides and fluoridation by the U.S. Public Health Service, State and Local Health Departments and nongovernmental research organizations. These studies have upheld the effectiveness and safety of fluoridation. In the late 1960's, the World Health Organization (WHO) completed the monumental task of compiling much of the known information about fluoridation. The objective was to provide an impartial review of the scientific literature on fluoridation. Their report "Fluorides and Human Health" came out in 1970 (16). It addressed numerous questions raised about the possible effects of fluoride in different organs and its alleged association to various diseases. The conclusions can be summarized briefly. The study found no reliable evidence that any ill effects or symptoms resulted from drinking fluoridated water at recommended levels. Again in 1975, the World Health Organization stated that the only sign of physiological and pathological change in life-long users of optimally fluoridated water supplies is that they suffer less from tooth decay.

Additional studies by the National Cancer Institute in 1976 (17), the United States Center for Disease Control in 1977 (18), and the National Heart Lung and Blood Institute in 1977 (19), each found no evidence linking fluoride and cancer. Independent investigations by seven of the leading medical and scientific organizations in the English-speaking world have unanimously refuted any claims linking fluoridation to increases in cancer rates.

Fluoridation may well be the most thoroughly studied community health measure of recent history. With the endorsement of fluoridation in 1949, the American Waterworks Association became one of the first organizations to accept a major role in safeguarding the nation's dental health. Since that time, practically every major national health organization in the world has endorsed this measure including the U.S. Surgeon General.

The National and International States of Fluoridation

As of December 31, 1975, approximately 105 million Americans (8), or about 60% of those on public water supplies, consume fluoridated water daily. Some 10 million of these are on naturally fluoridated water supplies. Some 6,795 communities have adjusted the fluoride content of their water and another 2,630 communities receive water naturally fluoridated at optimal or higher levels. Some 24 million people in over 100 cities with populations of 50,000 or more have had adjusted fluoridation for more than 20 years. Approximately 70% of all cities with populations of 100,000 or more have fluoridated water. More than 22 states, the District of Columbia and Puerto Rico provide better dental health through fluoridated water to over one half of their population. Fluoridation is no longer primarily a North American public health measure. It now has been initiated around the world with the results following the pattern discovered and established in the United States. The international acceptance of fluoridation was confirmed in July, 1969, with its approval by the World Health Organization (20). It was estimated that over 110 million people in 32 countries other than the U.S. were drinking fluoridated water.

Fluoridation: A Safe and Effective Public Health Measure

Although 60% of all Americans on a public water system are enjoying the benefits of fluoridation, approximately 40% do not. One of the principal reasons for this is because of the fears raised by opponents of fluoridation. The real goal of some of the anti-fluoridation groups has been to create the illusion of a scientific controversy over fluoridation. The simple truth is *there is no scientific controversy over this measure.* As pointed out, fluoridation is recognized by the scientific world as a safe, economical and beneficial measure to control dental caries. The controversy regarding fluoridation is strictly a political one. Water fluoridation is the only public health measure that many Americans vote on directly. Unfortunately, many times they are misinformed or not informed and therefore deprive themselves of the benefits of fluoridation by electing not to have their public water system adjusted to the optimal level with this essential nutrient.

Summary

Universal water fluoridation will have a positive impact on the oral health of the nation. The ultimate goal is to have every individual's teeth last a lifetime. Fluoridation of community water supplies provides the best cost containment public health measure known for improving the dental health of the nation's citizens.

References

1. National Academy of Sciences, *Recommended Dietary Allowances*, National Research Council, Publication 1694, 1968.
2. *Federal Register*, 38:20713, No. 148, August 2, 1973, Superintendent of Documents, Government Printing Office, Washington, D.C. (FDA Regulation 125:1, para. (C)).
3. American Medical Association, Department of Environmental Health, Division of Scientific Activities, AMA Policy Statement: Fluoridation of Public Water Supplies. Chicago, American Medical Association.
4. *Consumer Reports*, A two-part Report on Fluoridation, July and August, 1978.
5. Statewide Dental Survey, 1979. Division of Dental Health Services, Tennessee Department of Public Health. Unpublished Data.
6. The Relative Efficiency of Methods of Caries Prevention in Dental Public Health: Proceedings of a Workshop at the University of Michigan, June 5-8, 1978.
7. U.S. Department of HEW, Public Health Service Center for Disease Control, Bureau of State Service, Dental Disease Prevention Activity, *Fluoridation Is For Everyone*, DHEW Publication No. (CDC)77-8334.
8. U.S. Department of HEW, Public Health Service Center for Disease Control, *Preventing Disease, Promoting Health, Objectives for the Nation: Fluoridation*, Atlanta, Ga., June 13-14, 1979, p. 17.
9. U.S. Department of HEW, Public Health Services, National Institutes of Health, Bureau of Health Professions Education and Manpower Training, Division of Dental Health, *Fluoridation . . . No Better Health Investment*, DHEW Publication No. 1970-0384-143.
10. U.S. General Accounting Office, Comptroller General. Report to Congress of the U.S. *Reducing Tooth Decay — More Emphasis on Fluoridation Needed*, U.S. Government Printing Office, HRD-79-3, April 13, 1979.
11. Statement of the U.S. Surgeon General, October, 1978.
12. Biggs, John T., Gougler, G.M. and Avery, Kevin, Fluorides and Their Uses in Dentistry, *Oklahoma Dental Association Journal* 69:21-27, Summer, 1978.
13. Percentage of Denture Wearers Over 30 Drops, *ADA News*, August 8, 1977, p. 8.
14. Ast, D.B., Cons, N.C., Pollard, S.T., Jr., et. al., Time and Cost Factors to Provide Regular, Periodic Dental Care for Children in a Fluoridated and Nonfluoridated Area: Final Report. *J. Am. Dent. Assoc.* 80:770-776, 1970.
15. Shambaugh, G.E., Jr., Petrovic, A., Effects of Sodium Fluoride on Bone: Application to Otosclerosis and Other Decalcifying Bone Diseases, *JAMA* 204:969-973, 1968.

16. World Health Organization: *Fluorides and Human Health*. Monograph Series No. 59, 1970.
17. Erickson, J.D., Mortality in Selected Cities with Fluoridated and Nonfluoridated Water Supplies, *New England J. of Medicine*. Vol. 298, May, 1978.
18. Rogot, E., et al., Trends in Urban Mortality in Relation to Fluoridation Status, *Am. J. Epid.* Vol. 107: 104-112, 1978.
19. Upton, Arthur C., Director of National Cancer Institute. Statement on Relationship of Fluoridation of Drinking Water to Cancer. Intergovernmental Relations and Human Resources Subcommittee, House Committee on Government Operations, September 21, 1977.
20. Bernhardt, M.E., Fluoridation International, *J. Am. Dent. Assoc.* 80: 731-734, 1970.

MINERALS AND ELEMENTS

Iodine: Going from Hypo to Hyper

by Flora Taylor

"When It Rains It Pours." So saith the Morton salt box. It's a sentiment echoed by many these days as we find that one food after another contains something we wish it didn't. One of the most disturbing new surprises is that many foods now have too much iodine in them.

It is particularly surprising to find an oversupply of iodine in food, because a lack of dietary iodine was a major public health problem 75 years ago. Iodine is essential for normal nutrition and the consequences of a deficiency can be serious. The thyroid gland uses iodine to make thyroid hormone, which regulates body heat, influences protein synthesis, keeps connective tissues healthy, and promotes physical and mental development. If there isn't enough iodine in the diet, the thyroid gland will enlarge itself so that it can use what iodine is available as efficiently as possible. That enlargement is called goiter. When iodine inadequacy persists, hypothyroidism may also develop, a condition characterized by mental and physical sluggishness and subnormal body temperature. Hypothyroidism in a pregnant woman can result in the mental and physical retardation of her child.

The ultimate source of iodine is the ocean. Seafood is usually rich in iodine, as is food grown on soil that was once covered by the sea. But the effects of glaciers and other weathering of the soil have removed much of the iodine from the soil over large portions of the Earth's surface. Food grown on that soil doesn't contain enough iodine for nutritional needs; the result has been widespread endemic goiter among the natives of those regions. In the United States, endemic goiter was a prevalent public health problem in the early 1900's in the States bordering the Great Lakes and to the northwest. Once it was recognized that goiter was caused by iodine deficiency, the remedy was clear: iodine must be added to food in some way. Iodization of table salt was begun in the State of Michigan in 1924 to prevent endemic goiter in that region, and such salt eventually became available throughout the United States, solving a public health problem of some magnitude. But public health officials were unable to make iodization of salt mandatory, so the fear persisted that some people who weren't using iodized salt might develop deficiencies. For that reason, FDA adopted regulations requiring that salt manufacturers state on the label whether or not the salt supplies iodine, thus warning consumers that if they choose noniodized salt, they are passing up a way of obtaining a necessary nutrient.

But in the early 1970's, it began to appear that iodine deficiency was no longer a public health problem. Physicians noticed that in clinical tests of patients with radioactive iodine, their thyroid glands were taking up less of it, which suggested that their thyroids were already saturated with iodine. Some thyroid specialists became concerned that some people might be getting too much iodine. In 1974, FDA sought more information by including iodine in its Total Diet Study (TDS), which estimates residues of pesticides and certain heavy metals in American diets.

The results were startling. Analysis of the foods sampled revealed that a growing teenage boy consuming 2,850 calories per day received an average of 830 micrograms of iodine. That's about 5½ times the current Recommended Daily Allowance (RDA) of 150 micrograms thought to be needed for normal growth and good nutrition. In the TDS, salt added at the table and used in cooking was not iodized. Thus, use of an average amount of iodized salt would have added another 300 micrograms of iodine per day to the intake.

Iodine in the adult diet decreased in 1975 to 550 micrograms a day (about four times the RDA) in a 2,850 calorie diet and rose again in 1978 to 700 micrograms a day, or about 4½ times the RDA.

The large amounts of iodine weren't the only surprise: the iodine was turning up in unexpected places—for example dairy products contributed up to 38 percent of the iodine. To find so much iodine (about 320 micrograms a day) being furnished by dairy products was also a cause for additional concern, because milk is the dietary staple of babies.

In 1975, FDA expanded its TDS to include the typical American diets for 6-month-old infants and 2-year-old toddlers. The study revealed that iodine intakes of infants and toddlers were even greater than adults in relation to their RDA's. The typical infant diet supplied an average of 380

From *FDA Consumer*, April 1981, pp. 15-18. Published by the U.S. Food and Drug Administration.

micrograms of iodine a day in 1975, although the RDA for 6-month-old infants is only 45 micrograms. In 1976 and 1978 the levels were even higher, 10 and 13 times the RDA, respectively. Typical toddler diets also showed very high levels of iodine (6 to 10 times the RDA) during 1975 through 1978. About one-half to two-thirds of the iodine in the infant and toddler diets was from milk. Preliminary data from the 1979 and 1980 FDA studies indicate that levels of iodine in our food supply, particularly milk, are decreasing, though daily intake still remains several times higher than the RDA.

Iodine can get into milk in a number of ways. Some occurs in milk handling, via use of iodophors, a group of iodine-containing chemicals. Because they kill bacteria, fungi, and viruses, iodophors are used to clean, sanitize, and disinfect. Teat dips used to control mastitis (udder inflammation) sometimes contain iodophors, as may udder salves. Some farmers use iodophors to clean the udders before each milking, or to clean milking machines, refrigerated farm vats, road transport tankers, raw milk tanks, pasteurized milk vats, and bottle filler sealing rubbers.

Indiscriminate use of iodophors can add significant amounts of iodine to milk—up to 740 micrograms per liter according to one study (that's about 180 micrograms per cup, because a liter is just over a quart). But iodophors aren't the major source of iodine in milk. The biggest problem is that cows are being fed too much iodine.

Cows have thyroid glands and, like humans, their bodies need a certain amount of iodine to prevent goiter. Some iodine may occur naturally in cattle feed. Farmers—to be sure their cows will not develop goiter—often provide iodized salt licks, or add iodine to feed in the form of ethylenediamine dihydroiodide (EDDI). Adding about 10 milligrams of EDDI per cow per day will usually prevent iodine deficiency. But many dairy farmers are adding at least five times that much in the belief that the extra iodine will help to prevent a disease known as foot rot—though there is no scientific evidence to support this.

FDA's Total Diet Study assumed that infants were being fed fresh whole milk. Prepared commercial formulas weren't given much weight, and breast milk wasn't included at all. Current data indicate that milk-based infant formulas often contain as much iodine as fresh milk does. The iodine content of breast milk will depend on how much iodine the mother consumes. The few figures available suggest there's an average content of about 139 micrograms per liter in mothers' milk, which is far lower than the 500 micrograms of iodine per liter found in commercial milk.

Dairy products accounted for larger amounts of iodine than any of the other food groups analyzed in the TDS. But other foods were found to contain unexpectedly large quantities. In 1974, grain and cereal-based products accounted for 28 percent of the iodine in the typical adult diet, and sugars and adjuncts (such items as jam, jelly, pudding mixes, and candy bars) supplied another 23 percent.

Iodophors are also widely used in general food processing to clean and sanitize equipment and are probably contributing to the high iodine content in both of these food groups. Many foods in both groups also contain milk and milk-derived products, such as whey. Significant amounts of iodine are probably contributed by the red food color erythrosine (FD&C Red No. 3), which is more than 50 percent iodine. The use of Red No. 3 has almost doubled since two other red food dyes were taken off the market by FDA in 1976. Concentrations of iodine up to 175 micrograms per gram of food, presumably due to erythrosine, have been assayed in dry cereals, fruit cocktails, maraschino cherries, and cake mixes. A single serving of erythrosine-colored dry cereal can increase the daily iodine intake by as much as 400 micrograms. (However, scientists are not sure yet if the iodine in red dye is absorbed and utilized by the body.)

Another possible source for the iodine in grain and cereal products is the iodine found in compounds sometimes used as dough conditioners; these can produce bread containing from 28 to 140 micrograms of iodine per ounce. Most major baking companies have voluntarily switched to other conditioning agents since being made aware of the problem.

Fast foods and many of the highly processed convenience foods of today were not included in the typical daily diets prepared for analysis in FDA's Total Diet Study, but recent research indicates these may contain large amounts of iodine. A typical meal at MacDonald's (a Big Mac, french fries, and a milkshake) contains almost 3 times the RDA of iodine for adults. Frozen fried chicken dinners analyzed in one study contained an average of 970 micrograms of iodine, with a range of up to 4,300 micrograms, or almost 29 times the RDA. Food additives derived from algae, such as carrageenan, contain iodine and are widely used in food processing. Iodine-rich kelp is often used in seasoning mixes; the iodine content of 1 gram of this dried seaweed can be as high as 4,500 micrograms.

Dietary supplements are another possible source. Many multivitamins with minerals supply 100 to 150 micrograms of iodine, but if they are colored with Red No. 3, they will contain more than the label indicates. One brand contained 375 micrograms per tablet.

In some small towns, or farms, and in remote areas of our national forests, iodine is sometimes used instead of chlorine to purify drinking water. This can add another 1,000 to 2,000 micrograms to the daily iodine intake of the people who drink this water. The Environmental Protection Agency has recommended against iodization of drinking water for communities except on a temporary basis.

The American Medical Association's Department of Food and Nutrition Workshop Committee on Current Exposure to Iodine recently stated that current evidence indicates there are no adverse physiologic reactions from iodine intakes up to 2,000 micrograms per day in healthy adults, and 1,000 micrograms per day or more in some children. Average intakes as measured by the TDS are obviously within this range. The AMA committee admits that additional information is needed on the long-term effects of iodine before a maximum "safe" level of intake can be established. Because there has not been enough research, the effects of moderately high levels of iodine in the diet are not known.

Although the usual cause of goiter is inadequate iodine, excessively large intakes can also cause goiter by reducing hormone release from the thyroid gland. Very high levels of iodine (10,000 to 200,000 micrograms per day) among seaweed fishermen in Japan have been found to cause

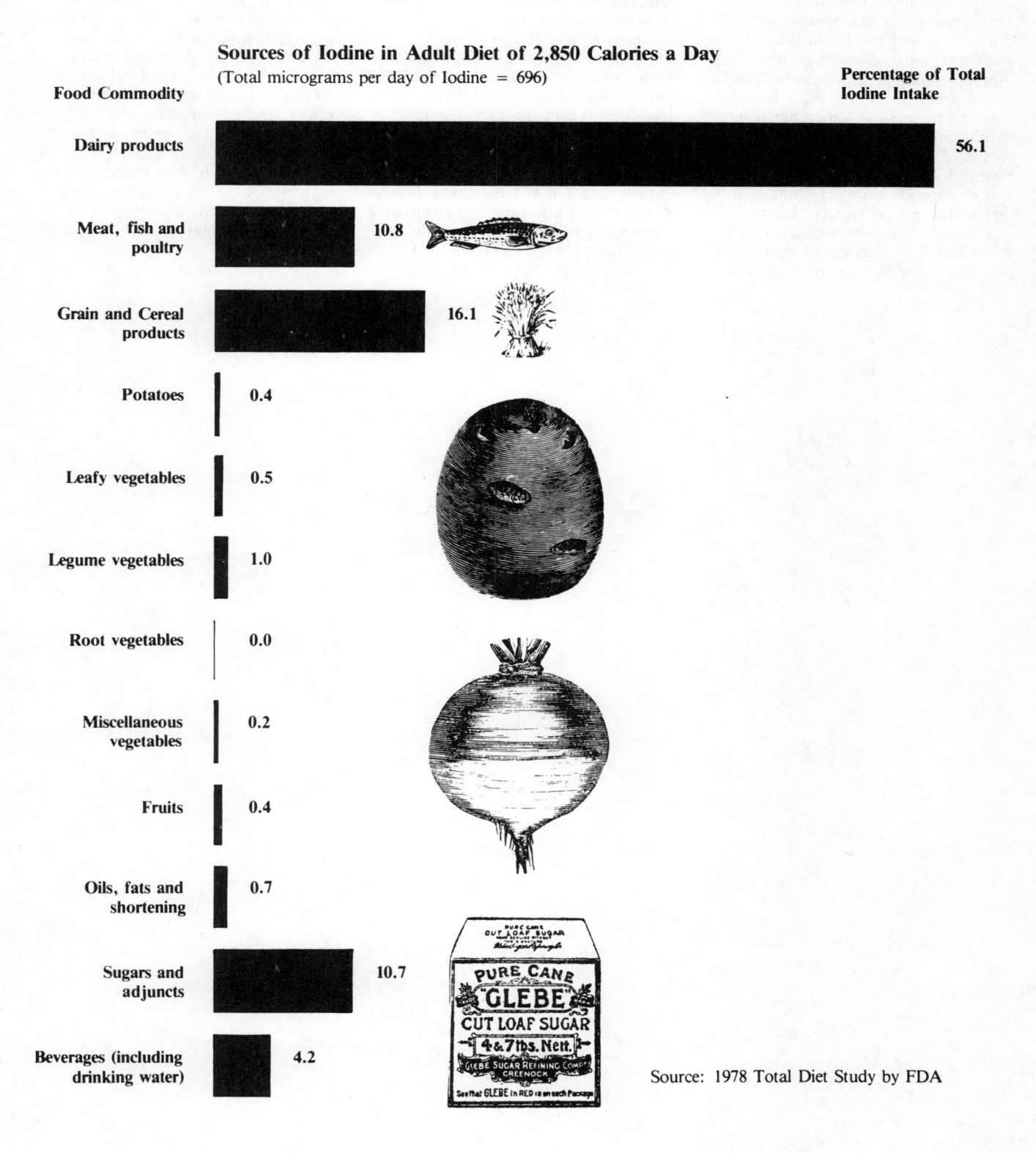

Sources of Iodine in Adult Diet of 2,850 Calories a Day

(Total micrograms per day of Iodine = 696)

Food Commodity	Percentage of Total Iodine Intake
Dairy products	56.1
Meat, fish and poultry	10.8
Grain and Cereal products	16.1
Potatoes	0.4
Leafy vegetables	0.5
Legume vegetables	1.0
Root vegetables	0.0
Miscellaneous vegetables	0.2
Fruits	0.4
Oils, fats and shortening	0.7
Sugars and adjuncts	10.7
Beverages (including drinking water)	4.2

Source: 1978 Total Diet Study by FDA

goiter in 6 to 12 percent of those exposed.

Repeated large doses of iodine-containing medications during pregnancy can cause goiter in newborns. This is particularly dangerous because the goiter can block the airways and cause suffocation. Iodine-containing asthma medications taken by the pregnant mother have been reported to cause goiter in her newborn infant. Those medications may provide daily doses of 12,000 micrograms of iodine.

A disease known as Hashimoto's thyroiditis appears to have become increasingly common in this country in the last few decades. Its yearly incidence is now thought to be 3 to 6 cases per 10,000 people. The higher incidence may be due to increases in dietary iodine, though supporting evidence is circumstantial and incomplete. People suffering from Hashimoto's thyroiditis can be affected adversely by high levels of dietary iodine, which may disturb their hormone synthesis and cause enlargement of the thyroid gland. Daily doses of 2,000 micrograms can block their thyroid function.

Rising iodine intakes may also be responsible for decreased remissions in the treatment of hyperthyroidism with anti-thyroid agents. The rate of therapeutic success reportedly has declined from 60 to 17 percent.

Experts differ as to the need for concern about these hazards. But there is general agreement that we certainly don't need any *more* iodine than we're currently getting. For this reason, in 1977 FDA's Bureau of Foods said it would approve no new iodine compounds for use in foods or food processing. As noted, bureau officials have also urged industry to eliminate indiscriminate use of iodophors, and dairy people and feed manufacturers have been cautioned about the overuse of EDDI. The JOURNAL OF THE AMERICAN MEDICAL ASSOCIATION has asked physicians to be on the lookout for any problems that may be attributable to dietary iodine.

MINERALS AND ELEMENTS

Selenium and Human Nutrition

by Orville A. Levander, Ph.D.

In 1957, Schwarz and Foltz[1] discovered that traces of selenium in the diet prevented nutritional liver necrosis in vitamin E-deficient rats. Very soon thereafter, selenium was found to protect against the development of certain vitamin E-associated animal diseases of practical agricultural importance, such as white muscle disease (nutritional muscular dystrophy) in lambs and calves and exudative diathesis in chicks and turkey poults. More recently, selenium has been shown to have desirable effects even in rats and chicks fed adequate amounts of vitamin E.

These beneficial effects of selenium were a significant "role reversal" for selenium because before these discoveries were made, the element had been regarded only as a poison, responsible for conditions such as alkali disease (chronic selenium toxicity) in livestock. Both selenium deficiencies and toxicities can occur in animals raised under natural conditions because of variations in the amount of selenium in the soil available for uptake by plants.

Biochemical Role of Selenium

For many years, nutritionists puzzled over the close metabolic relationship between selenium and vitamin E, two nutrients that are so dissimilar chemically. Early reserach had demonstrated vitamin E acts as a lipid antioxidant and most workers agreed that selenium must perform some vague antioxidant function in vivo. The situation was clarified considerably when selenium was shown to be a component of glutathione peroxidase, an enzyme known to destroy lipid peroxides.[2] A metabolic scheme was postulated whereby selenium via glutathione peroxidase eliminated any lipid peroxides that escaped the vitamin E antioxidant defense mechanism.[3] No other selenoenzymes have been characterized in mammals, but others have been isolated from microorganisms[4] so metabolic roles for selenium in mammals, in addition to glutathione peroxidase, cannot be ruled out. Since the role of selenium in animal nutrition is so well established, attention has now turned to determining what role it may play in the optimal nutrition of humans.

Evidence That Selenium May Be Nutritionally Essential for Humans

Several lines of evidence suggest that selenium is an essential trace element for humans. For example, the growth of human fibroblasts in culture is stimulated by selenium.[5] Also, the amount of selenium chemically bound to the enzyme glutathione peroxidase isolated from human erythrocytes is similar to that bound to the enzyme isolated from various animal sources.[6] Finally, recent work from both New Zealand and the People's Republic of China shows beneficial effects of small quantities of selenium given to persons thought to be consuming diets deficient in the element.

The New Zealand work[7] concerns a patient from a low-selenium area who had received long-term total parenteral nutrition due to complications after abdominal surgery. The patient developed severe muscular discomfort accompanied by loss of mobility that disappeared after supplemental selenium was added to the intravenous feeding solutions.

The work from China described Keshan disease, a cardiomyopathy that affects primarily children and is characterized by gallop rhythm, heart failure, cardiogenic shock, abnormal electrocardiograms and heart enlargement.[8,9] This disease is distributed in a long region running from northeastern China to the southwest and was shown to be associated with low levels of selenium in the blood and hair. Also, low levels of selenium were reported in several staple foods consumed in the affected areas. A large-scale intervention trial carried out over 4 years and involving more than 12,000 children demonstrated the efficacy of selenium in preventing this disease. However, the Chinese workers interpreted their data conservatively and suggested that factors other than selenium may be involved, since certain epidemiological features were not explainable only on the basis of selenium deficiency.

Dietary Sources of Selenium

The two richest dietary sources of selenium are seafoods and organ meats followed, in decreasing order, by muscle meats, cereals (depending on where grown), dairy products, and fruits and vegetables (reviewed in Reference 10). Several factors can influence the selenium content of a given food commodity but the most dominant factor is the amount of selenium in the soil available for uptake by plants grown in a particular agricultural area. Once taken up by the plants, the selenium is then passed up the food chain to animals and humans. Since crop plants are not known to require selenium, they are more or less passive indicators of the selenium available in the soils of different regions. Thus, the selenium content of wheat, for example, has been shown to vary over almost 3 orders of magnitude depending on where the grain was grown. Such variability in the selenium content of basic food staples makes estimation of the dietary selenium intake in different countries, or even different regions of countries, difficult unless samples representative of the food actually consumed are analyzed.

Limited studies with animal models have shown that there are differences in the nutritional bioavailability of selenium in different foods. The selenium in freeze-dried, water-pack tuna was less readily available to rats than that in beef kidney or wheat grown in a seleniferous area.[11] Selenium has been shown to protect against a toxicity of mercury in tuna,[12] perhaps partially as a result of complex formation with the mercury, and such complex formation may also help to explain the decreased nutritional availability of the selenium observed in the fish.[12]

Dietary Intakes of Selenium

There is a wide range of estimated dietary selenium intakes in various countries because of differences in the selenium content of soils in different parts of the world. In New Zealand, which is known to have selenium-poor soils, intakes as low as 28 µg/day have been reported.[13] On the other hand, intakes as high as 220 µg/day have been calculated in Venezuela,[14] which has an important agricultural production area in a high-selenium zone. Estimates of selenium intakes in the United States and Canada have ranged from 62 to 224 µg/day.[10] In a recent study of the selenium intakes of Maryland residents consuming self-selected diets, the mean intake of selenium was 81±41 µg/day.[15] None of these diets provided less than 20 µg/day, 17% supplied less than 50 µg/day and 3% furnished more than 200 µg/day. The diets that were both highest in selenium and most selenium dense derived more protein and calories from seafoods, while the diets that were both lowest in total selenium and least selenium dense derived more protein and calories from dairy products and processed meats.

Dietary Requirements for Selenium

A "minimum daily requirement" for selenium of 20 µg/day was suggested on the basis of balance studies in New Zealand women consuming low-selenium diets.[16] The Chinese workers reported that no Keshan disease was seen in those areas in which the daily dietary intake of selenium exceeded 30 µg.[9] Long-term daily intakes of 28 to 32 µg have not been associated with any adverse human health effects in New Zealand.[13]

The Food and Nutrition Board has recently set a safe and adequate range of selenium intake of 50 to 200 µg/day for adults.[17] Since there is still uncertainty regarding the exact selenium requirement for humans, a range, rather than a specific level, was established. Most studies of North American diets have reported selenium levels in this range. The safe and adequate range was derived by extrapolation from research with animals since little work to determine requirements has been done with humans.[18] Although the precise level of selenium intake causing toxicity in humans is not clear, the upper limit of the safe and adequate range was set in order to guard against possible selenium overdosing through abuse of nutritional supplements.

A recent depletion/repletion study[19,20] showed that healthy young North American males suffered a 19% drop in plasma selenium levels after 2 weeks on a low-selenium formula diet (19 to 24 µg/day). After 45 days of depletion, the subjects lost about 1 mg of selenium or about 7% of the total body selenium stores. Supplementation with 200 µg/day of selenium as high-selenium wheat resulted in prompt restoration of the original plasma selenium levels.

Selenium and Human Health

The fact that selenium prevents such a diverse array of nutritional diseases in animals has led to considerations about its possible role in the maintenance of human health. Attempts have been made to link selenium with a number of human diseases including cancer and heart disease.

Levels of selenium in excess of the nutritional requirement prevent or delay the onset of chemically or virally induced cancers in laboratory rodents.[21] Also, certain inverse statistical associations have been made between dietary selenium intakes in certain countries or regions of countries and the incidence of cancer.[22] Such results have raised the question whether the optimal levels of selenium in the diet that satisfy the postulated nutritional requirement are the same as those needed for the prevention of cancer.[21] Some workers have advocated increased intakes of selenium (250 to 300 µg/day) either through selenium-rich diets or selenium supplements as a way of decreasing human cancer,[23] but others have concluded that human selenium supplementation is not called for at this time because there are reasonable doubts that selenium has any practical value against human cancer.[21] Moreover, certain studies with rodents suggest that some selenium compounds may cause cancer rather than protect against it.[24]

The Chinese experience with Keshan disease indicates that selenium at very low dietary intakes (about 30 µg/day) is required for proper heart function. As in the case of cancer, low-selenium intakes or blood levels have been associated with an increased incidence of cardiovascular disease.[25] However, in a multinational study, no differences were observed in the selenium concentrations of tissues from patients who died with or without myocardial infarction.[26] Thus, there appears to be little evidence that levels of selenium intake above those furnished by typical North American diets are of any help in counteracting human heart disease.

Summary

Selenium has a well-established role in animal nutrition and is gaining recognition as an essential trace element for humans as well. Its physiological role as a component of the lipid peroxide-destroying enzyme, glutathione peroxidase, explains its close metabolic relationship with the fat-soluble antioxidant vitamin E. Most North American diets furnish quantities of selenium that fall within the safe and adequate range of intake of 50 to 200 µg/day recently established by the Food and Nutrition Board. Some studies with laboratory rodents indicate that levels of selenium in excess of nutritional requirements protect against various forms of experimentally induced cancer, whereas other studies suggest that certain selenium compounds can cause cancer in rodents so the role of selenium in human cancer remains unresolved. Although reports from the People's Republic of China have associated Keshan disease, a juvenile cardiomyopathy, with very low dietary intakes of selenium (less than 30 µg/day), there is little evidence to suggest a role for selenium in human heart disease at more normal levels of intake.

References

1. Schwarz, K. and Foltz, C.M., J. Amer. Chem. Soc. 79: 3292-3293, 1957.
2. Rotruck, J.T. et al., Science 179: 588-590, 1973.
3. Hoekstra, W.G., Fed. Proc. 34: 2083-2089, 1975.
4. Stadtman, T.C., Trends in Biochem. Sci. 5: 203-206, 1980.
5. McKeehan, W.L. et al., Proc. Nat Acad. Sci. 73: 2023-2027, 1976.
6. Awasthi, Y.C. et al., J. Biol. Chem. 250: 5144-5149, 1975.
7. van Rij, A.M. et al., Am. J. Clin. Nutr. 32: 2076-2085, 1979.
8. Keshan Disease Research Group, Chinese Med. J. 92: 471-476, 1979.
9. Keshan Disease Research Group, Chinese Med. J. 92: 477-482, 1979.
10. Levander, O.A., "Selenium in Foods." In: Proc. Symp. Selenium-Tellurium in the Environment, Industrial Health Foundation, Pittsburgh, PA, pp. 26-53, 1976.
11. Douglass, J.S. et al., Federation Proc. 39: 339, 1980.
12. Ganther, H.E. et al., Science 175: 1122-1124, 1972.
13. Thomson, C.D. and Robinson, M.F., Amer. J. Clin. Nutr. 33: 303-323, 1980.
14. Mondragon, M.C. and Jaffe, W.G., Arch. Latinoamer. Nutricion 26: 341-352, 1976.
15. Welsh, S.O. and Levander, O.A., Fed. Proc. 39: 338, 1980.
16. Stewart, R.D.H. et al., Brit. J. Nutr. 40: 45-54, 1978.
17. Food and Nutrition Board — National Research Council, Recommended Dietary Allowances, 9th Revised Edition, National Academy of Sciences, Washington, D.C., 1980.
18. Committee on Animal Nutrition — National Research Council, Selenium in Nutrition, National Academy of Sciences, Washington, D.C., 1971.
19. Levander, O.A. et al., Fed. Proc. 39: 339, 1980.
20. Sutherland, B. et al., Fed. Proc. 39: 435, 1980.
21. Griffin, A.C., Adv. Cancer Res. 29: 419-442, 1979.
22. Shamberger, R.J. et al., Arch. Environ. Health 31: 231-235, 1976.
23. Schrauzer, G.N. and White, D.A., Bioinorganic Chem. 8: 303-318, 1978.
24. National Cancer Institute, Bioassay of Selenium Sulfide for Possible Carcinogenicity, Technical Report 197, National Institute of Health, Bethesda, MD, 1979.
25. Shamberger, R.J. et al., "Selenium and Heart Disease." In: Trace Substances in Environmental Health — XIII, D.D. Hemphill, ed., Univ. of Missouri, Columbia, MO., pp. 59-63, 1979.
26. Masironi, R. and Parr, R., "Selenium and Cardiovascular Diseases." In: Proc. Symp. Selenium-Tellurium in the Environment, Industrial Health Foundation, Pittsburgh, PA, pp. 316-325, 1976.

MINERALS AND ELEMENTS

Zinc in Human Nutrition

by Sharon Greeley, Ph.D., and Harold H. Sandstead, M.D.

Nearly thirty years passed between the study demonstrating that zinc was an indispensable nutrient in experimental animals[1] and the detection of zinc deficiency in a human population[2]. Not until 1974 was zinc included in the Recommended Dietary Allowances although the suggested intake is second only to iron in the trace metal category[3]. Why was there such a long interval? The answer to this question rests with a number of factors.

Prior to the advent of atomic absorption spectroscopy in the late 1960s and its availability to clinical investigators, the analysis of zinc in biological materials was difficult. In addition, the wide distribution of zinc in the environment made the possibility of zinc deficiency in man seem very unlikely. Both the recognition that parakeratosis in pigs was due to zinc deficiency[4] and that zinc metabolism was abnormal in patients with cirrhosis of the liver[5] increased the awareness of the potential importance of zinc in human nutrition. Finally, the description of zinc deficiency in adolescent boys by Prasad, et al.[2] conclusively demonstrated the importance of zinc for man. Since then, there has been an ever increasing research effort and numerous reports of human zinc deficiency.

Level of Zinc Nurture

Today, a major problem is the recognition of mild or marginal zinc nurture. Unless dietary zinc is low or poorly absorbed for a long period of time, plasma zinc tends to stay within the "normal" range[6,7]. Analysis of either plasma or hair in an individual provides the best means of diagnosing marginal zinc consumption. The reported normal range of hair or plasma zinc values is wide and varies with methods used by different laboratories[7]; therefore, cautious interpretation of an individual sample is required. While a low value usually is indicative of zinc deficiency, a normal value does not necessarily rule out the possibility of this deficiency[8].

At present, it appears that people in the United States are more apt to suffer from marginal zinc nurture than from frank deficiency[9]. Hambidge, et al.[7,10] have shown in children in the United States that the effects of dietary zinc deprivation may be particularly striking, resulting in growth failure and loss of taste acuity. Clinicians, dietitians, and nutritionists are therefore faced with the difficult problem of identifying persons at risk of zinc deficiency based on knowledge of economic status, dietary habits and illnesses without the assistance of an absolutely reliable laboratory indicator. In some instances when the clinical setting strongly suggests the possibility of zinc deficiency, a careful therapeutic trial with zinc supplementation may be the only conclusive way of establishing the diagnosis.

Homeostatic adjustments tend to protect individuals from severe zinc depletion and make the diagnosis of marginal states difficult. The adjustments occur in intestinal absorption, distribution and excretion of zinc. Studies in animals suggest that the absorption of zinc from the intestine becomes increasingly efficient as dietary zinc declines[11]. This increased efficiency of absorption presupposes that dietary factors which may have a positive influence on zinc are adequate and factors which may inhibit absorption are not excessive. Homeostatic mechanisms can also induce the transfer of zinc from one tissue to another. During this process, the plasma zinc may be normal while the overall status is deficient[6]. Decreased excretion of zinc through urine, sweat or feces may also be part of an adaptive process to conserve available zinc[12].

Functions of Zinc

Zinc is present throughout the body in every tissue. The role zinc plays is different from tissue to tissue and multifunctional within single cells. We will discuss some general biologic functions attributed to zinc, and cite pertinent examples. At the molecular level, the three most general functional categories for zinc are: (1) as an essential component for metalloproteins, (2) as a cofactor in certain enzyme reactions, (3) as a structural component in macromolecules. These roles for zinc are by no means mutually exclusive and probably overlap in a number of areas.

The enzyme **carbonic anhydrase** was shown to be a zinc metalloprotein in 1940[13]. This enzyme found in red blood cells facilitates the removal of carbon dioxide, as bicarbonate, from tissues and transfers it to the lung where the gas is expired. In the kidney, the carbonic anhydrase is involved in the production of ammonium ion for excretion. A third carbonic anhydrase is found in the parietal cells of the stomach. Here the enzyme functions to produce gastric hydrochloric acid needed to maintain a low pH in the stomach. In the case of **carboxypeptidase A**, a complex enzyme-zinc-substrate has been identified. Carboxypeptidase is a proteolytic zinc metalloenzyme secreted by the pancreas in inactive form. Zinc is required in the actual catalytic reaction in which large peptides are converted into smaller ones. It is interesting that the activity of this enzyme is decreased early when rats are subjected to severe dietary zinc deficiency[14].

Investigations with experimental animals demonstrated that zinc functions as a **cofactor in the synthesis of collagen**[15]. This triple-stranded fibrous protein is produced in connective tissue where it helps to maintain the necessary rigidity of the tissue. Collagen is also found throughout the body where it serves to bind cells together in the formation of tissues. In addition to zinc, ascorbic acid, iron and copper must be present at adequate levels to ensure continued biosynthesis of functional collagen. Zinc may also be involved in the proteolysis of collagen. The neutral protease, **collagenase**, was shown to contain zinc. Furthermore, enzyme activity was depressed in the presence of certain chelating agents[16]. The metabolism of collagen provides an example of a system in which zinc is required for both synthesis and degradation.

Alkaline phosphatase is a zinc metalloenzyme found in various tissues including liver, intestine, bone, kidney, heart and placenta. The catalytic action of the enzyme is to hydrolyze the organic phosphates, but it may also be involved in the transfer of phosphate groups. Isoenzyme forms can be demonstrated electrophoretically or by changing conditions of the assay procedure[17]. Bone phosphatase is required for normal calcification processes but the biological functions of the other isoenzymes are less well-defined.

During the past fifteen years, attention has turned to the role of zinc in replication, transcription and translation of the genetic code. **Nucleotidyltransferases** are classified as enzymes which "polymerize" the appropriate nucleotides to form DNA and RNA. Both DNA and RNA polymerases were reported to contain zinc in certain non-mammalian systems. There is some evidence that the mammalian enzymes also depend on zinc for normal activity. Other investigations suggest that zinc may serve in yet another capacity. The **macromolecules**, DNA and RNA, may depend upon zinc for maintenance of structural integrity. Complex structures such as ribosomes, membranes, and microtubules may also be maintained intact and functional by the presence of zinc[17,18,19].

Populations Potentially at Risk

How do these molecular functions affect the overall well-being of an organism? A sort of biochemical priority system may determine which tissues or processes will be most sensitive to zinc deficiency. Cells which undergo rapid turnover or molecules which do not bind the metal tightly might be expected to relinquish zinc. The physiological state of an individual, such as active growth or tissue repair, may put additional constraints on the system.

Children and teenagers undergoing rapid growth change may be more susceptible to inadequate dietary zinc than adults. At the molecular level, growth involves cell division and protein synthesis. The discovery of hypogonadal dwarfism in the Middle East[2,20] confirms that adequate dietary zinc and its absorption are necessary to support growth and testicular development. The adolescent growth spurt and sexual maturation apparently increases the zinc requirements of these individuals[9] and is in part responsible for the evolution of the zinc deficiency.

Similar reasoning leads us to suspect that **pregnant women** may be at risk of marginal or deficient zinc nutriture. Rapid cell division and growth which accompany embryogenesis and fetal development place an increased burden on homeostasis in women with a limited dietary zinc supply. In experimental animals, zinc deprivation during pregnancy decreases maternal plasma zinc, impairs fetal growth, decreases brain maturation and affects subsequent behavioral performance[21]. In humans, maternal serum zinc has been found to be one of several maternal predictors of the weight of the newborn[22]. **Pregnant teenagers** may be a particularly susceptible group. Zinc is needed for the continued growth of the young mother as well as the developing fetus. Additional roles for zinc during pregnancy have been suggested. Zinc concentrations in plasma taken from Scandinavian women at mid-pregnancy were reported to correlate with the outcome of pregnancy[23]. Women with abnormal labor and difficult childbirth had lower levels of plasma zinc. This observation is consistent with studies in pregnant rats[15,24]. Studies in experimental animals have shown that the zinc requirements of the **suckling infant** must be supplied by the mother[25]. Human infants must also obtain zinc from mothers' milk[26,27] or adequately supplemented formula.

Certain disease conditions and various therapeutic treatments may alter zinc status[28]. Acrodermatitis enteropathica (AE) is a genetic disorder involving zinc metabolism. The symptoms include dermatitis, diarrhea, increased susceptibility to infection, growth failure and death. Infants with the disease respond to human milk or pharmacologic supplements with zinc[26].

Zinc deficiency has been implicated in some taste and appetite disorders. It has been suggested this may involve a zinc-containing protein which has been isolated from human parotid saliva[15]. Some patients with impaired healing and low serum zinc have responded to supplemental zinc with acceleration of wound healing[17]. The response is consistent with the requirement of zinc for nucleic acid and protein synthesis and implies zinc deficiency in such patients. Deficiency can be induced inadvertently when patients are fed parenterally or enterally without sufficient zinc[7,29,30,31].

Zinc Sources and RDA

The ubiquitous nature of zinc deficiency and the disorders associated with it are good evidence for the importance of adequate zinc intake in the diet. Americans are moving towards food with fewer calories and some derive the bulk of their nutrients from vegetables. Zinc is generally considered to be less available from plant sources (beans, nuts, wholegrain cereals and fruits) than from animal sources (organ meats, liver, oysters and muscle meats)[24]. Associated factors such as phytate (an effective chelator for divalent metals) and fiber may be responsible for this relatively lower availability. Bioavailability was taken into account when the World Health Organization suggested provisional dietary requirements for zinc[32]. In the United States the Recommended Dietary Allowances (RDA) for zinc are 10 mg for children ages one through ten years and 15 mg for people eleven years of age or older[3]. Nutritionists and those in the health fields must encourage Americans to select diets which will ensure a proper balance of nutrients and provide adequate zinc[33].

REFERENCES

1. Todd, W.R., et al., *Am. J. Physiol.* 107:146-156, 1934.
2. Prasad, A.S., et al., *J. Lab. Clin. Med.* 61:537-549, 1963.
3. National Research Council, Food and Nutrition Board, *Recommended Dietary Allowances*, 9th edition, National Academy of Sciences, Washington, D.C., 1980.
4. Tucker, A.F. and Salmon, W.D., *Proc. Soc. Exptl. Biol. Med.* 88:613-616, 1955.
5. Vallee, B.L., et al., *New Eng. J. Med.* 257:1055-1065, 1957.
6. Sandstead, H.H., et al., *Clin. Res.* (in press).
7. Hambidge, K.M., *Pediatr. Res.* 6:868-874, 1972.
8. Pekarek, R.S., et al., *Am. J. Clin. Nutr.* 32:1466-1471, 1979.
9. Sandstead, H.H., *Am. J. Clin. Nutr.* 26:1251-1260, 1973.
10. Hambidge, K.M., *Am. J. Clin. Nutr.* 29:734-738, 1976.
11. Weigand, E. and Kirchgessner, M., *Nutr. Metab.* 22:101-112, 1978.
12. Baer, M.T., Experimental Zinc Deficiency in Young Men, Ph.D. Dissertation, University of California, Berkeley, 1979.
13. Keilin, D. and Mann, T., *Biochem. J.* 34:1163-1176, 1940.
14. Mills, C.F., et al., *Am. J. Clin. Nutr.* 22:1240-1249, 1969.
15. U.S. National Research Council, Subcommittee on Zinc, *Zinc*, University of Park Press, Baltimore, 1979.
16. Seltzer, J.L., et al., *Biochim. Biophys. Acta.* 485:179-187, 1977.
17. Sandstead, H.H., Zinc, In: *Present Knowledge of Nutrition*, edited by D.M. Hegsted, Nutrition Foundation, New York, 1976.
18. Kirchgessner, M., et al., Biochemical Changes in Zinc Deficiency, In: *Trace Elements in Human Health and Disease*, edited by A.S. Prasad, Academic Press, New York, 1976.
19. Chesters, J.K., *World Review of Nutrition and Dietetics* 32:135-164, 1978.
20. Sandstead, H.H., et al., *Am. J. Clin. Nutr.* 20:422-442, 1967.

21. Sandstead, H.H., et al., *Teratology* 16:229-234, 1977.
22. Metcoff, J., *Bul. Internatl. Pediatr. Assn.* 3:29-38, 1979.
23. Jameson, S., *Acta Medica Scandinavica* (Suppl.) 593:1-89, 1976.
24. Underwood, E.J., Zinc, In: *Trace Elements in Human and Animal Nutrition*, 4th edition, Academic Press, New York, 1977.
25. Fosmire, G.J., et al., *Pediatr. Res.* 9:89-93, 1975.
26. Neldner, K.H. and Hambidge, K.M., *New Eng. J. Med.* 292:879-882, 1975.
27. Evans, G.W., *Nutrition Reviews* (in press).
28. Sandstead, H.H., et al., Conditioned Zinc Deficiencies, In: *Trace Elements in Human Health and Disease*, edited by A.S. Prasad, Academic Press, New York, 1976.
29. Arakawa, T., et al., *Am. J. Clin. Nutr.* 29:197-204, 1976.
30. Tasman-Jones, C., et al., *Surgery Annual* 10:23-52, 1978.
31. Wolman, S.L., et al., *Gastroenterology* 17:458-467, 1979.
32. Anon., *Trace Elements in Human Nutrition*, World Health Organization Technical Report Series 532, Geneva, 1973.
33. Murphy, E.W., et al., *J. Am. Dietet. Assn.* 66:345-355, 1975.

Salt Shakes Up Some of Us

by Louise Fenner

"Being kissed by a man who didn't wax his mustache was—like eating an egg without salt," said one of Rudyard Kipling's female characters. Although we may puzzle over the difference between mustaches with and without wax, we have no trouble visualizing the blandness of the saltless egg.

Salt—or sodium chloride—was probably the first food additive ever used when man discovered its ability to flavor and preserve meat and fish. Salt is certainly one of the most popular additives, second only to sugar in the total quantity added to food each year.

As with many other spices and flavorings, salt took on a special mystique in man's early days. Greeks and Romans included salt in their offerings to the gods. Covenants were sealed over sacrificial meals that included salt, and in parts of Africa and Tibet cakes of salt were once used as money. Even our word "salary" goes back to the days when the Roman army granted its officers an allowance of salt, called a "salarium." That eventually was converted to an allowance of money the officers could use to buy salt and other necessary items.

Salt is a chemical compound of two substances that are unfriendly to man in their elemental states—sodium, a very reactive, soft, white, silvery metal; and chlorine, a toxic yellow-green gas. Salt is commercially mined from underground and surface deposits of rock salt, and is also obtained by evaporation and crystallization from seawater and other natural brines such as the Great Salt Lake in Utah. Since salt absorbs atmospheric moisture, it is usually combined with anticaking agents to prevent it from becoming a hard mass.

"It has been calculated that there are about 14,000 uses for salt," reports the Salt Institute, a trade organization. Only 5 percent of all the salt used in the United States is food grade, but within the food-processing industry salt is essential to the production of many familiar products. It is a major flavoring ingredient, of course. Salt also helps cure meat and fish, forms the brine for pickles, olives, and sauerkraut, enhances the leavening of bread, and improves the taste of other ingredients. It makes cheeses turn out the way the cheesemaker wants by controlling fermentation. Salt also helps inhibit the growth of harmful bacteria in products such as bacon, sausage, and bread.

The addition of iodine to salt (in the form of cuprous iodide or potassium iodide) was instituted years ago as a public health measure to prevent goiter, an enlargement of the thyroid gland in the neck due to insufficient iodine. Salt manufacturers are not required to add iodine, so consumers should check labels to determine what type of salt they are buying. If the salt is iodized, the label must state: "This salt supplies iodide, a necessary nutrient." Noniodized salt must indicate that no iodine has been added.

Americans like salt. Each of us eats an average of 2 to 2½ teaspoons of it a day—or about 8½ pounds a year. "Not me," you say. "I don't put that much salt on *my* food!"

What comes pouring out of your salt shaker at dinner or during cooking tells only part of the story. It accounts for only about a third of all the salt in your diet. One-fourth to one-half comes from processed food, according to a panel of independent scientists who recently evaluated the use of sodium chloride as a food ingredient for the Food and Drug Administration. The remaining salt you eat occurs naturally in food and in some drinking water.

The panel's evaluation of sodium chloride was part of a continuing review of the safety of substances on FDA's "generally recognized as safe" (GRAS) list. The Select Committee on GRAS Substances of the Federation of American Societies for Experimental Biology (FASEB) is conducting the review for FDA.

In its final report on sodium chloride, published in August 1979, the FASEB committee estimated that Americans consume "not less than" 10 to 12 grams (equivalent to 2–2½ teaspoons) of sodium chloride a day. Since salt is about 40 percent sodium, a daily salt intake of 10 to 12 grams means that Americans are consuming at least 4 to 5 grams of sodium each day.

Many people are confused by the difference between sodium and salt. It is the *sodium* content of foods that is of health concern to some people. Sodium occurs naturally in many foods and is also added via salt and other sodium-containing ingredients.

To keep sodium in perspective, it's important to understand both its positive and negative aspects. Sodium is an essential nutrient—in fact, we could not survive without

---

From *FDA Consumer*, March 1980, pp. 3-7, published by the U.S. Food and Drug Administration.

it. Sodium helps regulate body fluids (including blood) and maintain the balance of fluids and pressure inside and outside the cells. It also plays a major role in nerve impulse transmission, heart action, and the metabolism of carbohydrates and protein.

A daily human requirement for sodium is difficult to establish, because the need fluctuates depending on such conditions as excessive sweating and diarrhea (in which case additional sodium may be called for). Rather than recommending a specific daily amount, the National Research Council (of the National Academy of Sciences) last year issued an estimate of an "adequate and safe" sodium intake: 1,100 to 3,300 milligrams (mg) a day for adults.

Since 1,000 mg = 1 gram, the National Research Council's estimate of "adequate and safe intake" amounts to between 1.1 and 3.3 grams (compared with the 4 to 5 grams per day Americans now consume).

A healthy person's system can normally handle a wide range of sodium by conserving it when it is scarce and excreting any excess through the urine. However, in the past few years, the amount of sodium Americans consume has become a source of increasing concern to nutritionists, health professionals, and others who keep watch on the American diet. More and more evidence is linking excessive sodium intake with hypertension—high blood pressure—a disease that affects 10 to 20 percent of all Americans (estimates vary). Hypertension has been called a silent killer because it rarely produces warning signals, yet it can lead to stroke, heart disease, and kidney failure.

Although the body normally maintains a balance of sodium and other minerals at the proper level, evidence suggests that individuals who are genetically predisposed to hypertension may be increasing their risk by eating a diet high in sodium. Studies in animals and humans seem to support this theory.

As early as 1953, an experiment in which rats were fed various amounts of sodium chloride in their diets showed a positive correlation between the concentration of sodium chloride and the animals' blood pressure. In some well-known studies in the 1960's, a comparison was made between two strains of rats that were fed a diet high in sodium. One strain was genetically predisposed to hypertension and the other strain was resistant. The genetically sensitive group developed hypertension, while the resistant group remained normal. However, neither strain of rats developed high blood pressure on a normal diet.

In humans, it has long been established that a severe reduction in sodium intake will help lower the blood pressure of some individuals with hypertension. As early as 1920, one researcher reported successfully treating 20 patients with a low salt (sodium) diet, and many other reports have appeared in medical literature since then.

A substantial amount of evidence suggesting a relationship between sodium and hypertension comes from studies of populations that have different levels of sodium in their diets. Several geographically diverse populations, varying in size from a few hundred to a few thousand persons, do not exhibit essential hypertension (hypertension that cannot be traced to an underlying disorder). A low sodium intake is often cited as a characteristic of these groups, who range from South Sea Islanders to Brazilian Indians to Alaskan Eskimos. In contrast, some populations with a lot of sodium in their diets, such as the northern Japanese, have a very high incidence of hypertension and death from stroke.

Of course, sodium intake isn't the only difference between these populations. Many other factors are cited as possible contributors to their blood pressure patterns, including stress, age, body weight, genetic factors, chronic kidney infection, and potassium intake (the sodium/potassium balance in the body is very important for proper physiological function). Medical experts recognize hypertension as a complex disease in which a number of factors can operate—not only the foregoing, but also race (Blacks seem to be more susceptible than Whites), obesity, variations in kidney and endocrine function, congenital kidney abnormalities, and others.

From 10 to 30 percent of all Americans are born with a genetic predisposition to hypertension, the FASEB Select Committee on GRAS Substances estimated. Evidence suggests that when this genetic factor is present, a diet high in sodium will increase the risk of hypertension. It is not widely accepted that sodium actually *causes* hypertension. Many experts feel that if sodium consumption is high, the effects of other factors that are associated with high blood pressure might be intensified.

The Harvard Medical School Health Letter last year noted, "Few experts claim that salt [sodium chloride] is the sole cause of hypertension; rather, they describe salt as an important contributing factor in the 10 to 20 percent of Americans who are genetically susceptible to high blood pressure. And for such persons, the hidden salt in processed food of the typical American diet is a real hazard." (Note that this estimate of the percentage of genetically susceptible persons is somewhat lower than the FASEB committee's.)

Sodium restriction and weight loss (if appropriate) may control very mild elevations of blood pressure, the Medical School Health Letter also reported. However, most patients with blood pressure elevated to a certain level (above 160/100) will probably require antihypertensive medication. In these cases, sodium restriction may also be part of the treatment.

The growing evidence about sodium has prompted public health watchers, such as the Surgeon General and the Senate Select Committee on Nutrition and Human Needs, to advise Americans to lower their consumption of salt. The 1979 document, "Healthy People: The Surgeon General's Report on Health Promotion and Disease Prevention," maintained that Americans would "probably be healthier as a whole" if they made several dietary changes, including a reduction in salt.

The Senate Select Committee's "Dietary Goals for the United States," published in 1977, suggested that Americans limit their intake of sodium chloride to about 5 grams a day. Senator George McGovern, chairman of the Senate Select Committee, later indicated in a letter to the Salt Institute that the 5-gram figure referred only to salt added to food commercially and by consumers. "This would be in addition to our nondiscretionary intake of approximately 3 grams of sodium chloride (sodium occurring naturally in foods expressed as sodium chloride)," McGovern stated. Thus, the committee's suggested limit for total salt intake would be about 8 grams a day for adults, or one-third less than current levels.

Echoing the same theme, the FASEB Select Committee on GRAS Substances last year told FDA: "It is the prevalent judgment of the scientific community that the consumption of sodium chloride in the aggregate should be lowered in the United States."

The committee's report on sodium chloride asserted: "The average daily intake of sodium expressed as sodium chloride from all sources . . . exceeds estimates of the amount that may elicit hypertension in susceptible individuals. A lower daily consumption of sodium chloride promises health benefits for the proportion of the population susceptible to hypertension."

To encourage Americans to use less sodium, the FASEB committee called for development of guidelines for restricting the amount of salt in processed foods, "a major contributor of dietary sodium," and for better labeling of how much sodium food contains.

Under current FDA regulations there are relatively few restrictions on the use of sodium chloride in food. General regulations for GRAS substances state that such substances must be used in accordance with "good manufacturing practice." This means that the quantities of sodium chloride used must not "exceed the amount reasonably required to accomplish its intended physical, nutritional, or other technical effect in food."

The recommendation to restrict the amount of salt in processed foods is being evaluated by FDA. The Agency must consider whether such an action would involve a change in the GRAS status of sodium chloride and, if so, what type of change. FDA plans a tentative decision soon, but will make no final decision until industry and the public have the opportunity to express their views.

This year FDA intends to propose that sodium and potassium content be declared on nutrition labeling. Products that make nutritional claims or add nutrients are required to carry nutrition labeling, and many manufacturers provide it voluntarily. Potassium is included because some people, such as those with kidney disease, need to monitor both sodium and potassium in their diets. Regulations to define the terms "low sodium" and "reduced sodium" are also being considered so that label claims will have a standard meaning.

All these changes were described in a tentative policy statement issued by FDA in December 1979 as part of a joint effort between FDA, the U.S. Department of Agriculture, and the Federal Trade Commission to improve food labels.

What will knowing the amount of sodium in foods mean to consumers?

Substantial amounts of sodium are regularly added to processed foods, but not just in the form of salt. Some other common ingredients: sodium nitrite (a curing agent and preservative), sodium benzoate (a preservative), monosodium glutamate (MSG, a flavor enhancer), sodium bicarbonate (baking soda, a leavening agent), and sodium phosphate (a wetting agent for quick-cooking cereals).

For people who are trying to restrict their intake of sodium, eating is somewhat of a guessing game. There is no requirement that labels of food products state how much sodium they contain, except for foods claimed to be "low-sodium" or that are otherwise represented as being useful in sodium or salt-restricted diets.

The "hidden" sodium in processed foods can create difficulties for some people. Consider the predicament of a hypertensive patient who has been told by a physician to keep his or her sodium consumption down to 2,000 mg (2 grams) a day. A single serving of canned chicken noodle soup (about 1¼ cups) would use up over half the day's allowance of sodium. According to information furnished to FDA by one manufacturer, one serving of chicken or turkey noodle, tomato, chunky beef, vegetable beef, or cream of mushroom soup contains over 1,000 mg of sodium—but this fact is not stated on the label.

Besides canned and dried soups, some other processed foods that contain large amounts of sodium are canned vegetables, cheese, tomato juice, dill pickles, olives, canned tuna and crab, sauerkraut, frozen dinners, and condiments such as soy sauce, catsup, and salad dressing. Items such as instant pudding, breakfast cereals, ice cream, cookies, cakes, and bread also contain significant quantities of sodium.

Salt substitutes with little or no sodium are available, but these should be used only under advice of a doctor because they contain potassium or other substances that should not be used by some individuals. Consumers can also buy low-sodium foods that offer enormous reductions in sodium content (for example, most low-sodium versions of the soups mentioned above contain less than 100 mg sodium.) These products are regulated as special dietary foods and must state their sodium content. Consumers should read the labels carefully, because some of these foods may contain more sodium than the purchaser realizes.

There is one drawback to low-sodium foods that most dieters will mention—the taste. There is just no denying it: To most people salt makes food more palatable.

"It took me a year to get used to the taste," recalled Norma Chafe of Los Angeles. She has been restricting her intake of sodium for 7 years because of an intolerance to it. "Low sodium bread tastes like cardboard," she said.

She avoids all processed foods except those labeled as low sodium or reduced sodium. Most of her experience with low-sodium food has been good, although she could recall at least two occasions when such products brought on nausea and swelling, indicating she had consumed a substantial amount of sodium.

Many more low-sodium products are available in America than in her native Canada, she found, but they are more expensive than regular products. Other than these special processed items, all her food has to be prepared from scratch.

"I can't go to any fast-food place, although most other restaurants try their best if I ask them to leave out the salt when they cook," she said. "I can't have Chinese food because of the MSG and the soy sauce, or anything in a can or frozen. They don't tell the amount of sodium, and I'm afraid to try them."

She was asked if food containing significant amounts of sodium now tastes unpleasant to her. "Oh no," she said. "It tastes fantastic."

For Norma and thousands of others on sodium-restricted diets, the addition of sodium content to nutrition labels will make it easier to find foods they can safely eat. And it should do a little to raise consumer consciousness about the amount of sodium in our diet.

"I think labeling and education will eventually act to restrict the amount of sodium that manufacturers put in foods," a nutritionist with FDA commented. "If you want to watch your sodium intake, which product will you buy—the one with 1,000 milligrams of sodium or the one with 500 milligrams?"

Of course, after buying the low-sodium product, the consumer will need to resist the temptation to sprinkle the salt on at the table.

It does taste fantastic.

Why Salt? How Much?

by William J. Darby, M.D., Ph.D.

Salt and Its History
Chemically, salt is sodium chloride (NaCl) with minor admixture of other inorganic chemicals, several of nutritive value such as iodide. Wild animals and early man hunted "licks" as sources of salt. Usefulness of salt for preservation of food and in numerous crafts further enhanced its value. The word "salary" stems from an allowance of salt in payment for services. Today the industrial use of salt far exceeds that for food—of the total of 24.5 million tons produced in 1978, only 4.1% was food grade for all food processing uses.

Physiological Salt Requirements
Sodium is essential in the regulation of body water, maintenance of osmotic pressure of body fluids, the permeability of cell membranes and control of acid-base equilibrium.

The physiologic requirement for sodium in healthy people varies with age, environmental temperature, humdiity and level of physical activity. The estimated safe and adequate levels of dietary intake for *sodium* has been set as 250-750 mg for infants 6 to 12 months of age, 600-1800 mg for children 7 to 10 years of age and 1100-3300 mg for adults.[1] *This is equivalent to a safe and adequate daily intake of 2.8-8.4 g of salt for adults.* An adult under conditions compatible with minimal losses of salt can maintain sodium balance on less than 0.5 g of salt daily.[1]

Salt is readily excreted by the normal kidney, excretion increasing with dietary intake and decreasing during salt restriction. Renal losses by the adult of 2.5-5.0 g of sodium daily (equivalent to about 6.0-12.5 g of salt) are usual; cutaneous excretion varies and is determined by factors that alter sweat losses. Sweat losses of 1 liter/hour for 8-hour periods occur in some heavy industries, and 2 liters/hour may occur in competitive distance runners. Conversely, continuously low-intake levels of salt may result in increased urinary aldosterone levels and conservation of body salt reflected in low urinary loss. Thus, maintenance of salt balance is normally accommodated throughout a wide range of intakes.

Appetite for Salt
The appetite for and behavior toward salt intake suggest a mild aversion in early childhood but not inhibition of salt intake. Studies in children, ages 1-3 years, indicate rejection of salt *per se*, even though the young child's recognition thresholds are comparable to those of adults.[2]

A taste preference study[3] of children 9-15 years of age and adults showed that the majority preferred the mildest salt solution (0.29%), but some twenty percent selected the saltiest sample (2.34%). There were no sex differences for salty taste. In the younger group, more blacks than whites selected stronger salt solutions—thirty percent of young blacks preferring the saltiest sample. A similar trend was present among adults. These observations indicate that populations are not homogeneous in their preferences for saltiness. Whether differences in preference reflect differences in requirements or in experiences and learned preferences is not known. There is much evidence from animal studies that changes in sensitivity to preference and appetite for salt can depend on a variety of endocrinological factors.

Estimates of Salt Intake
Estimates of usual intakes of salt have a reliability similar to estimates of intake of other nutrients, being neither more nor less accurate. Professor E.V. McCollum and associates estimated in 1939[4] that "man consumes 3-6 g of sodium in the ordinary daily diet, the greater part of which is supplied by the sodium chloride added as seasoning." This is equivalent to approximately 8-15 g of NaCl daily. Estimates by the Salt Institute place current average intake at 8-10 g daily;[2] excretion studies indicate it at some 10 g daily.

The Select Committee on GRAS Substances (SCOGS) of the Life Sciences Research Offices of the Federation of American Societies for Experimental Biology reviewed available information on amount and sources of salt in the American diets.[5] They considered evidence of salt usage in the food industry from a 1970 and a 1979 National Research Council Survey, the FDA "market basket" studies, available data on excretion of sodium and data on production and sales of salt. They wrote "...several direct and indirect estimates of discretionary (consumer controlled), nondiscretionary (naturally occurring and added in industrial processing), and total sodium chloride intakes for adults have been examined...these estimates are considered very rough approximations of the national average. The best estimate of sodium intakes by adults based on these data is an average daily intake, expressed as sodium chloride, of not less than 10 to 12 g. Discretionary use accounts for about one-third of this total; estimates vary from about one-fourth to one-half (3.4 to 6.5 g). The nondiscretionary intake is contributed by about 3 g of sodium chloride (sodium occurring naturally in foods expressed as sodium chloride). By difference, the average diet provides the equivalent of about 4 to 6 g of sodium chloride from sodium chloride and other sodium-containing ingredients that were added to foods during commercial processing."[5]

The SCOGS' estimate of salt intake is higher than that of other recent ones but reflects the variation in judgmental factors that enter into such approximations, rather than evidence of increased use of salt. In fact, the SCOGS analysis supports their statement that "the total amount of sodium chloride used by the food industry is decreasing."

Current studies reveal that the salt intake of infants and young children increases about four-fold when the infant ceases to be fed commercially prepared infant foods and begins to eat the family fare as prepared for general consumption. This is because of the *low* content of salt in manufactured infant foods. For over a decade (since 1969) there has been a pronounced reduction in salt added during the manufacture of infant foods and none currently is added by some of the largest processors.[6,7]

Acute Salt Depletion

Symptoms of nausea, vomiting, dizziness, apathy, exhaustion, painful cramps and circulatory failure occurring among workers exposed to elevated temperatures under conditions conducive of extensive sweating have long been termed "miner's cramps." These symptoms are relieved by ingestion of sodium chloride, along with the replacement of water loss. Ingestion of sodium chloride tablets by those engaged in intense physical activity, such as athletes, is *not* currently recommended. Ingestion of water is the most important safeguard of physical status and performance in heavy athletic competition. The dietary intake of salt at mealtimes is adequate for meeting most needs, but if prolonged losses do endanger body salt balance, the salt should be supplied in drinking water as a 0.1% solution, not as salt tablets.

Toxicity of Excessive Salt

The SCOGS Report has reviewed much of the extensive literature on the toxicity of excessive salt intake.[5] It is well established that grossly excessive levels of salt can be acutely toxic and even fatal. For example, instances have occurred in which salt, instead of sugar, was added to infant formulas. Such massive quantities proved fatal.

High levels of feeding sodium chloride (1-2 g/kg body weight daily) in children maintained on a low-potassium diet increased systolic and diastolic blood pressure levels, an effect that could be prevented or greatly lessened by increasing the potassium intake.

Dietary Salt and Hypertension

Efforts to correlate salt intake with incidence of hypertension in homogeneous populations have not provided definitive evidence of a causal relationship. Despite the fact that marked restriction of sodium intake to levels of 200-500 mg often reduces blood pressure, patient compliance with such drastically low-salt diets is rare. Moderate salt restriction is of value as one of a combination of measures in management of hypertensive individuals, but the intake levels should be determined and monitored by a physician.

Very recent studies by Bernard, et al., examined the urinary sodium excretion, plasma renin activity and taste responses of hypertensive and normotensive individuals.[8] Dietary intakes were not estimated. A subgroup of the hypertensive population exhibited higher sodium excretion, lower renin activity and rated sodium chloride solutions significantly more acceptable taste-wise than did a group of normotensive controls, matched carefully for age, sex and race. They have suggested that the combination of high-salt intake, low-plasma renin activity and increased pleasantness of salt taste constitute a form of essential hypertension in which the biological mechanisms that regulate the sodium balance of the body are reset at a higher level. Studies such as these may, in the future, clarify the nature of the defect(s) in sodium metabolism that is (are) associated with so-called essential hypertension.

Controversy on Salt Intake Limitation

Hypertension is a sign, not a disease entity, and may result from a variety of causes through various mechanisms. Epidemiologic studies do not provide decisive evidence of causative relationship between the levels of salt intake widely consumed in the United States and hypertensive disease. Also, a severe decrease in salt intake appears to be necessary to treat the problem of hypertension.

These points are recognized even by those who vigorously advocate reduction in salt intake. For example, the recently published *Dietary Guidelines for Americans*[9] from the U.S. Department of Agriculture and the U.S. Department of Health, Education and Welfare states in part: "The major hazard of excessive sodium is for persons who have high blood pressure; not everyone is susceptible. In the United States, approximately 17% of adults have high blood pressure. The sodium intake is but one of the factors known to affect blood pressure. Obesity, in particular, seems to play a major role...

"At present there is no good way to predict who will develop high blood pressure, though certain groups, such as blacks, have a higher incidence. Low-sodium diets might help some of these people avoid high blood pressure if they could be identified before they develop the condition."

Despite this, several publications including these *Guidelines*, the SCOGS' Report, *Healthy People* from the Surgeon General[10] and *Toward Healthful Diets* from the Food and Nutrition Board of the National Academy of Sciences[11] all recommend a moderate reduction in sodium intake regardless of the individual's habitual dietary salt intake or blood pressure.

Foodstuffs recommended for reduction by the *Guidelines* include cheese, cured meats, potato chips, salted nuts and sauces. It would be useful to look at actual sources of salt in the diet and the nutritional contribution of the foodstuff. In this regard, the SCOGS Report indicates that foods contributing most to the "possible average daily intake" of 7.1 g of salt added to processed foods were meat products (1.9 g), baked goods (1.8 g) and cheese (0.1g), while snack foods contributed less than 0.05 g daily.[5]

Care must be taken when making recommendations for the general public to avoid specific foods on the basis of the amount of salt or other ingredients and not to advise an undesirable reduction in intake of highly nutritious, nutrient-dense foodstuffs. It is also important to recognize the hedonic component of food acceptability can result in elimination of a particular food or a food group from the pattern of consumption.

Summary

Present information concerning dietary salt intake justifies the following conclusions: (1) the estimates of "per capita intake" of salt in the U.S., while clearly above the minimal physiologic need, are within the range of physiologic accommodation by the healthy individual; (2) acute grossly excessive or low levels of salt intake can be toxic; (3) in general, moderate reduction in dietary salt intake cannot predictably be anticipated to decrease the *development* of hypertension; (4) some individuals with hypertension, however, do benefit from limitation of sodium intake at levels appropriate to the therapeutic regimen advised by their physician; and (5) the role of the diet in the cause or prevention of hypertension has not yet been defined.

REFERENCES

1. National Academy of Sciences, National Research Council, Food and Nutrition Board, *Recommended Dietary Allowances*, Ninth Edition, Washington, D.C., 1980.
2. Kare, Morley, R., et al., *Biological and Behavioral Aspects of Salt Intake*, A Nutrition Foundation Monograph, Academic Press, Inc., New York, 1980.
3. Desor, J.A., et al., Preferences for Sweet and Salty in 9 to 15-Year-Old and Adult Humans, *Science* 190:686-687, 1975.
4. McCollum, E.V., et al., *The Newer Knowledge of Nutrition*, Fifth Edition, The MacMillan Company, New York, 1939.
5. Select Committee on GRAS Substances, *Evaluation of the Health Aspects of Sodium Chloride as Food Ingredients*, Life Sciences Research Office, Federation of American Societies for

Experimental Biology, Bethesda, Maryland, 1979.
6. Filer, L.J., Jr., "Availability of Suitable Foods in the Marketplace: a. Are Suitable Low-Salt Foods Available in the Market?" In: *Childhood Prevention of Atherosclerosis and Hypertension*, Edited by R.M. Lauer and R.B. Shekelle, Raven Press, New York, 1980.
7. Institute of Food Technologists, Dietary Salt, A Scientific Status Summary by the Institute of Food Technologists' Expert Panel on Food Safety and Nutrition and the Committee on Public Information, *Food Technology* 34:1, 1980.
8. Bernard, R.A., et al., "Taste and Salt in Human Hypertension." In: *Biological and Behavioral Aspects of Salt Intake*, Edited by Morley R. Kare, et al., Academic Press, Inc., New York, 1980.
9. U.S. Department of Agriculture, U.S. Department of Health, Education and Welfare, *Nutrition and Your Health, Dietary Guidelines for Americans*, U.S. Government Printing Office, Washington, D.C., 1980.
10. U.S. Department of Health, Education and Welfare, *Healthy People, The Surgeon General's Report on Health Promotion and Disease Prevention*, DHEW (PHS) Publication No. 79-55071, U.S. Government Printing Office, Washington, D.C., 1979.
11. National Academy of Sciences, National Research Council, Food and Nutrition Board, *Toward Healthful Diets*, Washington, D.C., 1980.

Monosodium Glutamate (MSG) Scientific Status Summary

by the Institute of Food Technologists' Expert Panel on Food Safety and Nutrition

☐ ONE of the most common natural amino acids, glutamic acid and its salts have a long history of use in foods. The acid itself is used to adjust the acidity in foods and the various salt forms are used to enhance flavor. The sodium salt, usually called MSG (for monosodium glutamate), is by far the most widely used glutamate, although potassium, ammonium, and calcium glutamates have been used in low-sodium formulations as salt substitutes.

The use of MSG in food goes back to the Oriental cooks of antiquity, who used a seaweed called seatangle to make a stock. This stock added a richness to the flavor of foods cooked in it. The link between the seaweed flavor improvement and glutamate (first isolated in 1866) was discovered by Professor Kikunae Ikeda of the University of Tokyo in 1908. He demonstrated that the seaweed *(Laminaria japonica)* contained generous amounts of glutamate and that *it* was the seaweed component responsible for food flavor enhancement. The Japanese began production of glutamate almost immediately, although 30 years passed before it was produced in North America, from corn and wheat gluten. Today, MSG is produced in the United States from sugar beet molasses, in a fermentation process similar to that used in making yeast or sauerkraut. (Kirk-Othmer, 1978). Alternatively, MSG may be extracted directly from sugar beets.

Glutamate is ubiquitous in nature and is present in both food and the human body, either as one of the amino acid building blocks of protein and peptides, or in its free form. The glutamate bound into a protein structure has no flavor enhancing properties—only the free form has that, and then only the "L isomer." Protein-rich foods such as human milk, cow's milk, cheese, and meat have a high content of bound glutamate, while most vegetables contain little, because of their low protein content. However, many of these vegetables—such as mushrooms, tomatoes, and peas—do have high levels of *free* glutamate. In fact, some investigators have suggested that this explains the effectiveness of mushrooms and tomatoes in enhancing the flavor of other foods, in much the same way as seaweed.

In the 1940's, Hac and co-workers (1949) demonstrated that fresh young peas and sweet corn contained more free glutamic acid than more mature vegetables harvested from the same field. They suggested that the amount of glutamic acid present in vegetables was proportional to their rate of growth. Furthermore, they demonstrated that even short cooking times depleted the glutamate in these vegetables.

In addition to being abundantly present in food, glutamate exists as part of the human body itself, in both free and bound form. The human body contains 14 to 17% protein, of which about one-fifth is glutamate. An adult weighing 70 kilograms (156 pounds) contains, on the average, 2 kilograms (4.4 pounds) of glutamate in his protein.

The free form of glutamate is also present in the digestive system, the blood, and other organs and tissues in varying levels. For example, the free glutamate concentration in the brain is about 100 times as high as in the blood. Total circulating free glutamate available for the body's use is about 10 grams (⅓ ounce). Total body turnover in intermediary metabolism is estimated to be 5 to 10 grams per hour.

As previously mentioned, the major use of MSG in food processing or cooking in the western world is as a flavor enhancer—in soups and broths, sauces and gravies, and flavoring and spice blends, as well as in a wide variety of canned and frozen meats, poultry, vegetables, and combination dishes—rather than to add a flavor of its own. Results of taste panel studies on processed foods indicate that a level of 0.2-0.8% of food, by weight, gives the best enhancement of the natural flavor of food. For cooks in home or restaurant kitchens, this translates to about one-half to one teaspoonful per pound of meat or per four to six servings of vegetables, casseroles, soups, etc.

There appears to be some variability from one person to another as to their preferred optimum level of use. Some recipes call for MSG in the food preparation, followed by additional MSG at the time of serving to "season to taste." Since MSG is readily soluble in water,

---

This Scientific Status Summary first appeared in *Food Technology*, October 1980, published by the Institute of Food Technologists.

recipes often call for dissolving it in the aqueous ingredients of products such as salad dressings before they are added to food. In the Orient, MSG is often used in amounts sufficiently large that its own characteristic flavor comes through; the Japanese call this "umami," often translated as meaning "tastiness."

The free glutamate consumed daily as MSG typically equals about 1/1000th of the total glutamate present in the body, including that in the body's protein. Individual consumption ranges from a low of approximately ½ to 1 gram per day in the United States to a high of approximately 3 grams per day in Taiwan (Giacometti, 1979; NAS, 1979). On the average, about 20 additional grams (⅔ ounce) of naturally occurring glutamate are ingested each day as a part of normal food consumption—most of which is bound to protein. The ratio of protein-bound MSG and free MSG ingested each day varies with food habits, of course, depending on protein consumption and MSG use.

The exact mechanism by which MSG exerts its flavor enhancing abilities is not known, despite extensive work. The quality of the taste effect brought about by use of MSG is different from the four basic tastes—sweet, sour, salty, bitter. Also, it does not simply *increase* the intensity of the four basic tastes. Some studies suggest that MSG's effect on food flavor involves two basically different mechanisms: how tightly the flavor enhancer is bound to the taste receptor sites on the tongue, and how accessible these receptor sites are (Cagan, 1979). According to this research, glutamate binds preferentially to the taste receptors and to certain other food-flavor enhancing components. Other studies have shown that MSG has no effect on aroma but tends to enhance perception of a taste, and thus increase its intensity (Yamaguchi and Kimizuka, 1979).

Acute and Chronic Toxicity Studies

Because of its use in food, glutamate's acute and chronic toxicities have been studied extensively. Special toxicological studies have also been done. The acute toxicity of glutamate is low. The LD_{50} for mice—the dose at which half the test animals die—is 19.9 gm/kg body weight for L-MSG when the mice are fed an aqueous solution with a stomach tube (Ebert, 1979b). Translated to a 70-kg man, this dose amounts to more than three pounds.

Chronic feeding studies, which involve feeding the test substance to experimental animals daily for a two-year period of time or longer, have been completed in rodent and non-rodent species (Ebert, 1979a). There was no evidence of chronic toxicity or carcinogenicity (ability to induce cancer) in rats and mice when MSG was fed over a two-year period at dietary levels of either 0.4% or 4% on an "as consumed" basis. Long-term feeding studies on purebred beagle dogs were carried out with diets containing MSG at levels of either 2.5, 5 or 10% by weight (Owen et al., 1978). Two controls were used: the first received a diet with no test compound added, the second received the control diet plus 5.13% sodium propionate to determine the effect of the *sodium* in MSG. The test did not reveal any adverse effect on mortality rate, body weight gain, general behavior, ophthalmological findings, dermatology, blood chemistry, or on gross or histopathologic findings.

Glutamate: The Fetus and Young Child

Placental transfer: The question has been raised as to whether the fetus *in utero* would be exposed to glutamate concentrations higher than those normally found, following ingestion of MSG by the mother.

In one study, enough MSG was administered to pregnant non-human primates to raise the glutamate levels in the maternal blood stream to 40-50 times normal (Pitkin et al, 1979). The primate placenta proved to be a virtually impregnable barrier, apparently capable of metabolizing large amounts of glutamate.

In addition, it is apparently impossible to raise blood glutamate concentrations to those high levels by dietary means alone. Stegink et al. (1975) had to resort to injecting MSG solutions directly into the mother's blood stream to obtain comparable levels when they studied offspring of MSG-treated mothers for brain damage. They looked specifically for lesions in the arcuate nucleus of the hypothalamus, and found that none was present.

In another series of studies on the possible elevation of glutamate levels in mothers' milk following the ingestion of MSG, Stegink and coworkers (1972) administered 0.1 gm. of MSG per kg. body weight. The glutamate level in the lactating mother's *blood plasma* increased almost sevenfold, but the levels in their milk were not significantly affected. Later studies confirmed these results (Baker et al., 1979).

In the late 1960's, the consuming public voiced concern over the possible effects of glutamates fed to infants and small children. At the time, MSG was being added to baby foods in pureed vegetables and meat products, for the same reason as it was used in the adult diet—to enhance their flavor. Because of the concern expressed by the public, baby food manufacturers in both the U.S. and Canada voluntarily stopped using the additive in late 1969. (It was never used in pureed fruits, cereal products, or infant formula.)

Glutamate and the Central Nervous System

Olney and others have demonstrated that glutamate can be markedly toxic to the central nervous system of laboratory animals (Olney et al., 1969, 1970, 1972). In some species, obesity, sterility, and other effects may also result. As with other components in foodstuffs which have been shown to affect the central nervous system and the endocrine glands—such as aspartic acid, cysteine, and related compounds—large doses and high concentrations not common to foods are required. Laboratory animals will usually not eat these large doses voluntarily—they must be administered by injection or tube feeding (gavage). The smallest dose of MSG which will bring about these effects ranges from 0.7 gm/kg in 10-day-old mice to 2 gm/kg in 23-day-old mice, markedly greater than the amounts used in foods eaten by man.

Moreover, the toxic effects appear to apply only to particular species. While the central nervous system findings originally reported by Olney have been corroborated by a number of research laboratories (Lemkey-Johnston et al., 1972), several other laboratories disagree with his findings. They found no evidence of central nervous system damage in the nonhuman primate following oral, subcutaneous or dietary administration of MSG at doses of up to 4 gm./kg. (Abraham, et al., 1971, 1975; Newman et al., 1973; Reynolds et al., 1971; Wen et al., 1973).

Glutamate: Safety on Feeding

A number of laboratories have attempted to explain why different species of animals respond differently to glutamates, as well as why the human being fails to show central nervous system damage. Takasaki and co-workers (1979) concluded that many factors affect the potential damage to the nervous system of even the most sensitive species, the mouse. These factors include the metabolic capacity of the test animal, the dose, the concentration of the dose and the way it is administered. These investigators demonstrated that when glutamate was injected into a mouse, brain damage occurred with smaller doses than when the test animal was tube fed. They also showed that sensitivity decreased as the mice got older.

It is important to note that large doses of MSG were required to induce brain damage. While World Health Organization authorities recommend a maximum daily oral intake of MSG of 0.15 gm/kg body weight for man, the smallest dose which produced negative effects in 10-day old mice was 0.4 gm/kg, using intraperitoneal injection. When force feeding was used instead of injection, 0.7 gm/kg doses were required before damage occurred. When the mice were older—23 days—the doses required to cause central nervous system damage increased to 0.7 gm/kg and 2 gm/kg following subcutaneous injection and forced feeding respectively.

The method of administering MSG doses to mice also affects the peak levels reached in their blood plasma. For example, when infant mice were dosed with an MSG solution by forced tube-feeding, their peak plasma levels of glutamate were only about one-fourth as high as the peaks in mice who were given the same dose by subcutaneous injection (O'Hara, 1979). When a larger dose of MSG was eaten (voluntarily) as part of a commercial laboratory ration, the changes in plasma glutamate levels were minimal.

A number of studies of dietary ingestion of MSG, sometimes in massive doses (up to 46 gm/kg body weight per day), have shown no harmful effects on the hypothalamus (Heywood et al., 1977; Takasaki, 1978; Takasaki et al., 1979). Similarly, fetuses and newborn rodents of *parents* receiving massive doses of MSG in food were unaffected (Semprini et al., 1974), as were several animal species in other tests (Wen et al., 1973).

Stegink and co-workers (1979) measured plasma glutamate levels in humans of varying ages following ingestion of a high protein meal to which MSG had been added, either at the levels actually consumed by 90% of the population, or at the higher "Acceptable Daily Intake" (0.15 gm/kg as defined by FAO/WHO 1979). A control group ate the same high-protein meal with *no* added glutamate. These studies showed that when other foods were eaten with MSG, the peak plasma glutamate levels were drastically reduced. Peak levels reached when WHO's Acceptable Daily Intake was consumed in the high-protein meal were only slightly elevated in comparison to the control meal. When an aqueous solution of MSG *alone* was administered at that dose, however, peak plasma glutamate levels were 12 times as high as those in the control group.

Many other animal studies have shown the importance of considering not only dose but also the concentration of test solution, the route of administration, and the age of the experimental animals in evaluating the safety of glutamate for man.

The "Chinese Restaurant Syndrome"

In addition to the published scientific studies of MSG, a number of anecdotal or case history reports have appeared describing its effects on humans. The effects reported are often tightness, warmth, tingling, and a feeling of pressure in the upper part of the body, sometimes after eating Chinese food (Schaumburg et al., 1969). While many different ethnic foods have been reported as causing reactions, the phrase, "Chinese Restaurant Syndrome," caught on in the general press and with consumers.

Contemporary research on such response to glutamate in individuals with idiosyncracies of metabolism has followed two lines. The first involved the use of survey questionnaires with various groups in an attempt to estimate accurately the overall incidence of glutamate sensitivity in man. The second approach used typical biochemical and physiological studies, in an attempt to determine *how* glutamate might cause a reaction in sensitive humans.

Survey studies by Kerr and co-workers (1979, a,b) showed that some portion of the U.S. population will react adversely to any of a wide variety of ethnic dishes. According to Kerr, one to two percent of the general adult population may react negatively to MSG, compared to previously reported estimates of up to 25 percent of the population. These differences appear to be at least partly related to differences in questionnaire design (Kerr, et al., 1977).

Another study examined the minimum concentrations of MSG needed to induce effects in susceptible people, and concludes that when MSG is added to food at a concentration of 0.75% it is "extremely unlikely that any of the symptoms will be experienced by even a demonstrably sensitive individual" (Kenney, 1979). Furthermore, even doubling the use level to 1.5% resulted in only a few individuals being affected. Kenney postulated that the response to glutamate in sensitive individuals may involve stimulation of receptors in the esophagus, or be linked to reflex esophagitis (similar to heartburn).

Other Dietary Aspects

The presence of MSG in a food is of interest to consumers wishing to control their sodium intake from two standpoints. Since it is the sodium salt of glutamic acid, its sodium content must be considered in evaluating the total amount of sodium ingested from all sources. On the other hand, since MSG's molecule contains only 12 percent sodium (compared to the 40 percent in table salt), its flavor-enhancing properties may sometimes be substituted for salt, with a consequent reduction in total sodium ingested.

If *no* added sodium is permitted in the diet, there are also several commercially available forms of glutamic acid which are derived from non-sodium salts (calcium, potassium or ammonium). For further information on sodium see the IFT Scientific Status Summary on "Dietary Salt."

Regulatory Status

Although glutamate is encountered extensively as a natural component of food and in human metabolic pathways, when it is used as a food additive it is regulated by a variety of government agencies. Because of its efficacy as a food flavor enhancer, MSG is specifically authorized in the Standards of Identity of many foods under Title 21 of the United States Code of Federal Regulations (CFR), but its presence must still be disclosed on the label. Among such foods are mayonnaise, french dressing, canned tuna, and breaded shrimp.

Recently, the Select Committee on GRAS Substances, commissioned by the U.S. Food and Drug Administration, issued a supplement to their report on glutamates. Monosodium glutamate was re-classified to a more liberal status than that originally proposed (from category 3 to 2). The opinion of the Select Committee reads, "there is no evidence in the available information on ... [all common forms of glutamate] ... that demonstrates, or suggests reasonable grounds to suspect, a hazard to the public when they are used at levels that are now current and in the manner now practiced. However, it is not possible to determine without additional data whether a significant increase in consumption would constitute a dietary hazard" (FASEB, 1980).

The report goes on to state that there may be some persons who will react to relatively small doses of MSG because of metabolic idiosyncracies, and that research is underway on this phase of glutamate evaluation.

In Canada, MSG is considered to be a food *ingredient* which has functionality as a seasoning and flavor enhancer. Hence, it may be used at levels consistent with "Good Manufacturing Practises," provided its presence is declared on the label of prepackaged foods.

In short, MSG is a food additive which serves as a useful flavor enhancer. It occurs naturally in a wide variety of foods. In fact, one of its main functions as a food additive may be to restore the natural glutamate lost during storage, processing or cooking. At the levels now used, it has been shown to be safe for use by the general public in places which Professor Ikeda never envisioned.

REFERENCES

Abraham, R., Dougherty, W., Golberg, L., and Coulston, F. 1971. The response of the hypothalamus to high doses of monosodium glutamate in mice and monkeys. Cytochemistry and ultrastructural study of lysosomal changes. Exp. Mol. Pathol. 15:43.

Abraham, R., Swart, J., Golberg, L., and Coulston, F. 1975. Electron microscopic observations of hypothalami in neonatal rhesus monkeys (Macaca mulatta) after administration of monosodium-L-glutamate. Exp. Mol. Pathol. 23:203.

Baker, G.L., Filer, L.J., and Steinink, L.D. 1977. Plasma and erythrocyte amino acid levels in normal adults fed high protein meals: Effect of added monosodium glutamate (MSG) or monosodium glutamate plus Aspartame (APM). Fed. Proc. 36:1154.

Baker, G.L., Filer, L.J., and Steinink, L.D. 1979. Factors influencing dicarboxylic acid content of human milk. In Glutamic Acid: Advances in Biochemistry and Physiology." Raven Press, New York, N.Y.

Cagan, R.H., Torii, K., and Kare, M.R. 1979. Biochemical studies of glutamate taste receptors: The synergistic taste effect of L-glutamate and 5'-ribonuleotides. In "Glutamic Acid: Advances in Biochemistry and Physiology." Raven Press, New York, N.Y.

Ebert, A.G. 1979a. Dietary administration of L-monosodium glutamate, DL-monosodium glutamate and L-glutamic acid to rats. Toxicol. Lett. 3:71.

Ebert, A.G. 1979b. Dietary administration of monosodium glutamate or glutamic acid to C-57 black mice for two years. Toxicol. Lett. 3:65.

FAO/WHO, 1979. "Guide to the Safe Use of Food Additives." (CAC/FAL 5-1979). Food and Agriculture Organization of the United Nations, World Health Organization, Rome, Italy.

FASEB, 1980. "Evaluation of the Health Aspects of Certain Glutamates as Food Ingredients. (Supplemental Review and Evaluation SCOGS-37A). Life Sciences Research Office, Federation of American Societies for Experimental Biology, Bethesda, Md.

Giacometti, T. 1979. Free and bound glutamate in natural products. In "Glutamic Acid: Advances in Biochemistry and Physiology." Raven Press, New York, N.Y.

Glutamate Association, 1978. MSG and sodium in the diet. Atlanta, Ga.

Hac, L., Long, L., and Blish, M.J. 1949. The occurrence of free L-glutamic acid in various foods. Food Tech. 10:352.

Heywood, R., James, R.W., and Worden, A.N. 1977. The *ad libitum* feeding of monosodium glutamate to weanling mice. Toxicol. Lett. 1:151.

International Glutamate Technical Committee. 1974. The remarkable story of monosodium glutamate. Washington, D.C.

Kenney, R.A. 1979. Placebo-controlled studies of human reaction to oral monosodium-L-glutamate. In "Glutamic Acid: Advances in Biochemistry and Physiology. Raven Press, New York, N.Y.

Kerr, G.R., Wu-Lee, M., El-Lozy, M., McGandy, R., and Stare, F.J. 1977. Objectivity of food symptomatology surveys. Questionnaire on the "Chinese restaurant syndrome." J. Am. Diet. Assoc. 71:263.

Kerr, G.R., Wu-Lee, M., El-Lozy, M., McGandy, R., and Stare, F.J. 1979a. Prevalence of "Chinese restaurant syndrome." J. Am. Diet. Assoc. 75:29.

Kerr, G.R., Wu-Lee, M., El-Lozy, M., McGandy, R., and Stare, F.J. 1979b. Food symptomatology questionnaires: Risks of demand—bias questions and population based surveys. In "Glutamic Acid: Advances in Biochemistry and Physiology." Raven Press, New York, N.Y.

Kirk-Othmer—Encycl. of Chem. Tech. (1978), 3rd Edition, Vol. 2, M. Grayson, Ed. John Wiley & Sons, New York, N.Y.

Lemkey-Johnston, N. and Reynolds, W.A. 1972. Incidence and extent of brain lesions in mice following ingestion of monosodium glutamate (MSG). Anat. Rec. 172:354.

National Academy of Sciences 1979. Survey of industry on the uses of food additives (NTIS #PB 80-113418). Food and Nutrition Board, NAS-NRC, Washington, D.C.

Newman, A.J., Heywood, R., Palmer, A.K., Barry, D.H., Edwards, F.P., and Worden, A.N. 1973. The administration of monosodium L-glutamate to neonatal and pregnant rhesus monkeys. Toxicology 1:197.

O'Hara, Y. 1979. Relationship between plasma glutamate levels and hypothalamic lesions in rodents. Toxicol. Lett. 4:499.

Olney, J.W. 1969. Brain lesions, obesity and other disturbances in mice treated with monosodium glutamate. Science 164:719.

Olney, J.W. and Ho, O-L. 1970. Brain damage in infant mice following oral intake of glutamate, aspartate or cysteine. Nature 227:609.

Olney, J.W., Sharpe, L.G., and Feigin, R.D. 1972. Glutamate-induced brain damage in infant primates. J. Neuropathol. Exp. Neurol. 31:464.

Owen, G., Cherry, C.P., Prentice, D.E., and Worden, A.N. 1978. The feeding of diets containing up to 10% monosodium glutamate to Beagle dogs for two years. Toxicol. Lett. 1:217.

Pitkin, R.M., Reynolds, W.A., Stegink, L.D., and Filer, L.J. 1979. Glutamate metabolism and placental transfer in pregnancy. In "Glutamic Acid: Advances in Biochemistry and Physiology." Raven Press, New York, N.Y.

Reynolds, W.A., Lemkey-Johnston, N., Filer, L.J., and Pitkin, R.M. 1971. Monosodium glutamate: Absence of hypothalamic lesions after ingestion by newborn primates. Science 172:1342.

Schaumburg, H.H., Byck, R., Gerstl, R., and Mashman, J.H. 1969. Monosodium glutamate: Its pharmacology and role in the Chinese restaurant syndrome. Science 163:826.

Semprini, M.E., Conti, L., Ciofi-Luzzatto, A., and Mariani, A. 1974. Effect of oral administration of monosodium glutamate (MSG) on the hypothalamic arcuate region of rat and mouse: A histological assay. Biomedicine 21:398.

Stegink, L.D., Filer, L.J., and Baker, G.L. 1972. Monosodium glutamate: Effect on plasma and breast milk amino acid levels in lactating women. Proc. Soc. Exp. Biol. Med. 140:836.

Stegink, L.D., Reynolds, W.A., Filer, L.J., Pitkin, R.M., Boaz, D.P., and Brummel, M.C. 1975. Monosodium glutamate metabolism in the neonatal monkey. Am. J. Physiol. 229:246.

Stegink, L.D., Filer, L.J., Baker, G.L., Mueller, S.M., Wu-Rideout, and M.Y-C. 1979. Factors affecting plasma glutamate levels in normal adult subjects. In "Glutamic Acid: Advances in Biochemistry and Physiology." Raven Press, New York, N.Y.

Takasaki, Y. 1978. Studies on brain lesions by administration of monosodium L-glutamate to mice. II. Absence of brain damage following administration of monosodium L-glutamate in the diet. Toxicology 9:307.

Takasaki, Y., Matuzawa, Y., Iwata, S., O'Hara, Y., Yonetani, S., and Ichimura, M. 1979. Toxicological studies of monosodium L-glutamate in rodents: Relationship between routes of administration and neurotoxicity. In "Glutamic Acid: Advances in Biochemistry and Physiology." Raven Press, New York, N.Y.

Wen, C.P., Hayes, K.C., and Gershoff, S.N. 1973. Effects of dietary supplementation of monosodium glutamate on infant monkeys, weanling rats, and suckling mice. Am. J. Clin. Nutr. 26:803.

Yamaguchi, S. and Kimizuka, A., 1979. Psychometric studies on the taste of monosodium glutamate. In "Glutamic Acid: Advances in Biochemistry and Physiology." Raven Press, New York, N.Y.

The Case for Moderating Sodium Consumption

by Roger W. Miller

Americans consume sodium equivalent to some 2 to 2 1/2 teaspoons of salt a day, and around 60 million Americans suffer from high blood pressure to one degree or another. For many people, there may be a connection. Allan L. Forbes, M.D., associate director for nutrition and food sciences in FDA's Bureau of Foods, discusses the link and efforts to help consumers moderate their salt or sodium intake.

Q. *Dr. Forbes, why is too much sodium a health problem?*

A. The basic reason is that sodium intake is interrelated with hypertensive diseases or high blood pressure. This has been studied for many years and, when you really come down to it, what we know is that population groups around the world who have very low sodium intakes have virtually no hypertension, and population groups that have very high sodium intakes have more hypertension. The thing we don't know with the precision that we wish we did know is if there is an "ideal level" of sodium intake for a population. We certainly know—and we emphasize the point—that very low intakes likely protect against hypertension, and very high intakes tend to predispose some individuals to the development of hypertensive disease. And certainly there is no doubt that, in many individuals with high blood pressure, sodium restriction, best coupled with weight reduction, lowers blood pressure.

Q. *What are some examples of the population groups that you refer to?*

A. Well, for example, in parts of the Orient you find that the biggest killer is hypertension, particularly in northern Japan but also in Thailand and China. There are some population groups scattered around the world—Polynesia, some of the islands off Southeast Asia, northern Brazil and in Africa—where the prevalence of hypertensive disease is very, very low and the salt/sodium intakes are also very low.

Q. *How does hypertension kill?*

A. Hypertension is the most common cause of serious stroke—that is, a hemorrhage into the brain from an artery.

Q. *And pressure on the artery causes it?*

A. We don't fully understand even today what occurs in the wall of the artery. But we know that what happens is that a leak occurs in the artery and a hemorrhage develops into the brain. That is a stroke and a particularly bad type of stroke. Hypertension also is associated with heart attacks. The basic cause of most heart attacks is another disease called atherosclerosis in which there is a blockage inside the artery from cholesterol deposits on the wall of the artery. When an individual has atherosclerosis, with the resulting narrowing of the coronary artery, high blood pressure makes the possibility of having a heart attack even greater. So the two diseases are synergistic in terms of producing adverse effects, particularly relative to the heart. The same is true of kidney disease. When hypertensive disease gets very bad, a lot of troubles arise in the kidneys. Over time, the untreated patient will suffer a decline in kidney function—the ability of the kidneys to clean blood and to excrete products into urine that the body wants to get rid of. So when we're talking about hypertension, we're talking about the possibility of serious brain disease, serious heart disease and serious kidney disease. Hypertension is directly or indirectly contributory to the top four or five causes of death in the United States.

Q. *What does sodium do in the body to cause high blood pressure?*

A. First, I want to stress that sodium is absolutely essential for life itself. In other words, you would not survive on a sodium-free diet. Sodium helps maintain what is called the osmotic pressure of the blood, and therefore is absolutely essential for maintaining blood pressure. Sodium attracts water into the blood vessels, thereby maintaining proper blood volume and keeping the pressure within the blood vessels

---

From *FDA Consumer*, October 1981, pp. 9-13, published by the U.S. Food and Drug Administration.

more or less constant. Sodium also is intimately involved in the production of hormones which regulate blood pressure. Another thing that sodium does—along with other ions like bicarbonate and potassium and chloride—is that it maintains what we call acid-base balance. The body must be adjusted with tremendous precision as to how acid it is and how alkaline it is. This is done, in large measure, by the kidney.

Q. *Do non-hypertensives have to watch their sodium intake?*
A. That is a very good question, and a rather difficult one to answer. We know that there are over 30 million people in the United States who have hypertension, and we know that there are a lot more—perhaps another 30 million—who have what is called borderline hypertension or are in the high normal range. A large proportion of these borderline people are highly likely to develop hypertension later in life, if it goes undiagnosed and untreated. Part of the problem is that there are some people who are particularly sodium sensitive and some people who are not. It is very difficult, given the current state of the medical art, to determine in advance who is and who isn't. So there is a lot of research right now to try to develop methods that will allow the medical profession to determine in advance whether an individual is sodium sensitive or whether he is a part of the population that isn't. The result is that most of the leading health and medical experts in the United States and in a lot of other parts of the world have concluded that it is reasonable to moderate the amount of sodium intake for everybody.

Q. *Aren't some people more likely to be hypertension candidates . . .*
A. Indeed . . .

Q. *. . . blacks, for example?*
A. Indeed, that's absolutely right. It is clearly known that blacks have a higher prevalence of hypertension than whites do.

Q. *Is it known why they do?*
A. This point is not clear. There definitely appears to be a strong genetic component. But that applies to white people as well, and applies to people in general. Exactly why the blacks are somewhat more likely to develop hypertension is still not clear. There have been studies that have demonstrated that it isn't simply because blacks may consume a bit more sodium than whites generally do. So with hypertension, I think we have to emphasize—in communicating to the public—that like so many other diseases, its cause is multi-factorial. Hypertension is due to a number of factors interacting together: sodium intake, genetic susceptibility to the disease, the presence of obesity which aggravates hypertension, smoking, stress and probably other factors that are still unknown.

Q. *When we're talking about sodium aren't we talking mainly about salt, which is 40 percent sodium?*
A. Well, yes, in a way, but I think it is important to point out that sodium comes into our diet in a lot of ways. We don't know for sure how much of our total sodium comes from salt itself, and it varies a lot from person to person. Salt is by far the major source, but I think it is very important to bring to the public's attention that sodium comes from many other sources, including other ingredients added to foods. Baking soda is sodium bicarbonate. Oftentimes vitamin C, which we call ascorbic acid, is added to a food as sodium ascorbate. Lots of people are aware of monosodium glutamate because it has been very much publicized relative to the Chinese restaurant syndrome.

Q. *Known popularly as MSG?*
A. MSG, exactly. About 10 percent of MSG is sodium, so sodium is throughout our food supply. However, much of the sodium in foods is put there by nature. It is present in all parts of plants and animals. So the sodium in foods comes from many sources, and they are all important because they all contribute to the total amount in the diet. And, once it is in the body and circulating in the blood, the body cannot distinguish where the sodium came from.

Q. *And where it comes from is not just the salt shaker or Mother Nature but it is put into food.* *It is processed into food. How much is added in that way?*
A. You know, in this country we have the most extraordinarily diversified diet. There are some 18,000 products in the supermarkets, and practically all of them contain sodium to one degree or another. And dietary patterns are so different between individuals that it is very difficult to say that just this amount comes from salt that you added at the table, this amount from salt that you added while cooking, and that amount was added by the food processor, or put there by nature. I think the rule of thumb, which is never truly accurate because of this tremendous variation in our dietary patterns and the very nature of our food supply, is that about a third of it may come from the food itself in the natural state, a third of it is there because the food processor introduced it, and a third was added in the home or restaurant. The processor puts it into the food for a whole series of reasons, some of which are absolutely essential to the production and preservation of the food.

Q. *Why is sodium such an issue now? Haven't we known these things for years?*
A. We have known an awful lot about this for a long time. The history of a connection between sodium and high blood pressure goes back 50 years or more. However, when dealing with a disease that is multi-factorial, it takes a very long time for the scientific community to unravel enough of the facts to begin to develop clear concepts of what ought to be done. During roughly the last 10 years there has been a gradual development of what I would call a national medical and biological consensus about the association between sodium and blood pressure. That consensus has become national only in the last year or two. I am speaking of groups like the Food and Nutrition Board of the National Academy of Sciences and American Medical Association. Both only recently concluded that the sodium intake of the general public should be moderated. The FDA had a very detailed review of this matter undertaken by another of the most prestigious scientific organizations, the Federation of American Societies for Experimental Biology (FASEB), which reviewed

the matter in great detail and came to the same conclusion. Then two major departments of the government—Health, Education and Welfare (now Health and Human Services) and Agriculture—stated in their published *"Dietary Guidelines for Americans"* that it would be reasonable to moderate the sodium intake in the American diet. The National Heart, Lung and Blood Institute (NHLBI) advisory groups on hypertension in the last several years have been saying the same thing. So that's what I call a gradual development of a national consensus.

Q. *Now that we have this national consensus, what is FDA planning to do?*

A. The basic thrust of FDA's program is aimed at moderation of the sodium content of processed and packaged foods plus a number of initiatives that pertain to labeling to inform consumers on how much sodium is present in the food they buy. We have a five-point initiative concerning sodium. The first is working directly with industry, particularly on moderation of the over-all sodium content of foods as they are processed, packaged and sold to consumers. Second is our labeling proposal. We're asking for comments from everyone—industry, professionals, consumers, the entire population—on having nutrition labels bear sodium labeling in terms of milligrams of sodium per serving. We will also permit, as we have in the past, sodium labeling to appear on a food label by itself without full nutrition labeling so that a manufacturer who decides not to do full nutrition labeling may still put the sodium content in milligrams per serving on the label.

Q. *That won't trigger nutrition labeling?*

A. That's right. It won't trigger full nutrition labeling. Another aspect of the labeling proposal is a series of definitions, so that there is uniformity in the marketplace that makes medical and scientific sense. We're offering definitions of "low sodium," "moderately low sodium," and "reduced sodium." The third part of the FDA program would be new legislation. For example, at the present time, the FD&C (Food, Drug, and Cosmetic) Act does not provide us with clear authority to require sodium labeling on all packaged foods (except under unusual circumstances which do not exist today). We have made a detailed analysis of this and have a whole series of options for consideration. However, for the moment, we wish very much to continue down a voluntary road because we anticipate serious interest by a very large part of the American food processing industry. Step four in our program will be tracking, with considerable care, what is actually happening to the sodium content of the food supply, as well as what is happening to labeling. How much "low sodium" food appears in the marketplace, how much "moderately low sodium" food appears, and how much "reduced sodium" food is getting into the supermarkets. We will watch those things with great care and have a pretty sophisticated system for tracking it. The final part of the FDA initiative is to work with industry, other government agencies and interested non-governmental organizations to help consumers make effective use of the new labeling and to raise consumer awareness of the effects of sodium on health.

Q. *Why three definitions of sodium on labels?*

A. "Low sodium" on the label would mean foods which could be eaten without great concern by individuals who are on sodium-restricted diets. The labeling of "moderately low sodium" foods would help individuals who either are already on a low sodium diet or a sodium-reduced diet. Foods labeled that way could be eaten quite extensively by a person on a low-sodium diet without getting into trouble. It would be very helpful in terms of maintaining good diversity in a sodium-restricted diet. "Reduced sodium" foods would be very useful to consumers who are simply attempting to reduce the sodium in their diets.

Q. *Will FDA's program tie in with what the National Heart, Lung and Blood Institute (NHLBI) is already doing on hypertension?*

A. I want to stress again that the primary focus of FDA in the sodium and hypertension issue pertains to moderation of sodium in the food supply and to labeling. The NHLBI, on the other hand, has a much broader role to play in the picture. The NHLBI has a large scale professional and consumer information and education program already in place. In fact, it has been going on for the better part of a decade. It originally focused on diagnosis because there were so many people in this country who had hypertension but did not know it. That has improved very substantially, so the Institute refocused on proper treatment by drug therapy. The NHLBI program is changing again now to further emphasize the relationship of dietary sodium to hypertension as well as weight control. We're working with the people at the Institute in getting the sodium message across.

Q. *How important is nutrition labeling? How much of the food supply is involved in nutrition labeling?*

A. Excluding fresh produce and fresh meat and poultry, about 40 percent of the food supply has nutrition labeling.

Q. *How much food has sodium labeling?*

A. We have just finished an analysis on that part of the food supply that we call the "core" of the supermarket. It is the part in most supermarkets that is in the middle of the store—foods that are in packages and cans distinct from the fresh produce and refrigerated produce. In this "core" in 1977, a little over 7 percent of the consumer's food dollar went for sodium-labeled foods. By 1979 the figure was 13.4 percent.

Q. *Of the 60 million hypertensives in this country, how many of them can control their hypertension strictly through diet?*

A. I don't think I can answer that question in terms of percentages. I am not sure that anybody knows the answer, but let me try to address it this way. There are a great many individuals with mild hypertension who can be treated initially by non-drug treatment including weight reduction, if necessary, and/or a low sodium diet. There are a great many hypertensives who can readily return their blood pressure to normal by simple drug treatment. Then there is a group of hypertensives who require much more vigorous drug treatment with much more potent drugs. But there is another point I think we ought to mention. Research on hypertension has made it crystal clear that the mild hypertensive should not be ignored. It has been clearly demonstrated that proper dieting and/or medical management of the mild hypertensive markedly reduces the prevalence and occurrence of stroke and high blood pressure-related heart attacks. Therefore, the medical community today is paying a great deal more attention to the mild hypertensive than was true even 5 years ago.

Q. *What has the food processing industry done thus far to make the public more aware of the sodium problem?*

A. The very existence of some sodium labeling out there in the marketplace shows there are major segments of the food industry that are paying particular attention already. Some examples are the ready-to-eat breakfast cereal industry, the baby food industry which voluntarily has greatly reduced the sodium content of baby foods over the past decade, and the shortening and oils part of the industry which has put sodium labeling on a fair number of their products; this also applies to baking mixes. A major manufacturer of soups has a large research program in a number of areas concerning sodium. One is the marketability of low-sodium foods, particularly soups. Another area they're looking into is sodium-reduced products with the best possible retention of flavor and other characteristics.

Q. *Doesn't the public want highly salted foods? Doesn't the public want sodium—like Al Capone said during Prohibition, the public is a guy who wants his beer?*

A. Fair enough. Let me emphasize that it is not the intent of the FDA to revolutionize the nature of our food supply. We are more interested in stimulating readily available choices to the consumer, particularly those individuals who have a medical need to moderate the amount of sodium that is taken in. I absolutely will not pontificate over the lowering of salt content in sauerkraut and dill pickles. I just won't do that. These foods are the way they are and I assume they should stay that way—readily recognizable as being salty. And needless to say, we haven't the slightest intention of castigating the existence of salt in a salt box in the supermarket; that would be patently ridiculous. So our thrust is aimed at choice and moderation where it is reasonable, feasible and marketable to do. But there is another facet to the thing from a medical point of view which has always fascinated me. When a patient is put on a sodium-reduced diet and stays on it for a moderate period of time, an interesting thing often happens. And it's frequently spontaneously offered to the physician as information. The threshold for the perception of saltiness goes down. After some months on a sodium-moderated diet, many patients will say to their doctors—and I have had this experience myself—"That food that I used to really like now tastes so salty that I can't eat it. But the food that I have been eating recently seems to be just about as salty as I really like." So my belief is that there is a high probability that if there was a reasonable moderation of sodium content in our food supply gradually and over time, that the American public will adapt to that quite readily.

144 DIETARY DIRECTIONS IN THE 1980s

Dietary Fiber

by the Institute of Food Technologists' Expert Panel on Food Safety and Nutrition

☐ THE ROLE PLAYED by fiber (or "roughage" as our grandparents called it) in health and disease has recently become the subject of increased public attention. It has gained so much attention, in fact, that a variety of new "high fiber" foods have come on the market, and the retail sale of bran-fortified cereal products increased 20% in a single year. Strange as it may seem, fiber has been largely ignored by nutritionists, who are accustomed to thinking in terms of digestion of foods and subsequent absorption and metabolism of nutrients, whereas fiber, most of which is not digested by humans to absorbable nutrients, is excreted directly in the feces.

Much of the current interest in fiber results from reports by D. P. Burkitt, a British medical researcher and surgeon, who observed that rural Africans—whose diets are high in fiber-containing foods—have a lower incidence of appendicitis, hemorrhoids, diverticular disease, cardiovascular disease, and cancer of the colon than in the United States and other developed countries where diets are low in fiber (Burkitt, 1973).

What is Dietary Fiber?

One of the many factors complicating the interpretation of fiber research lies in the lack of a widely accepted definition of the word. For years, fiber has been discussed in terms of "crude fiber," which is simply the residue after a food sample is treated in the laboratory with a solvent, hot acid, and hot alkali. This chemically inert residue is composed primarily of the lignin and most of the cellulose in the food being analyzed.

"Dietary fiber," on the other hand, is defined as including all the components of a food that are not broken down by enzymes in the human digestive tract to produce small molecular compounds which are then absorbed into the blood stream. Dietary fiber includes hemicelluloses, pectic substances, gums, mucilages, and certain other carbohydrates, as well as the lignin and cellulose. These chemical compounds are found largely in the cell walls of plant tissues, and, as shown in Table I, their total greatly exceeds that expressed as crude fiber.

The use of "crude fiber" in dietary descriptions is thus of limited value, since it may represent as little as one-seventh of the total dietary fiber of the food. The value of fruit is particularly understated by this method. Even the word "fiber" itself may be misleading, since not all the components of "dietary fiber" are fibrous in the usual physical sense, while foods that do contain recognizable fibers, such as muscle meats, do not yield undigestible residue.

Alleged Benefits of Dietary Fiber

Physiological claims for fiber fall into three categories:

1. **Definite value**—relieving constipation problems by increasing the water content of the feces.

2. **Probable value**—treating (or preventing) diverticular disease.

3. **Possible value**—reducing serum cholesterol, prevention of a variety of disorders such as hemorrhoids, varicose veins, ischemic heart disease, colon-rectal cancer, diabetes, appendicitis, obesity, gallstones, phlebitis, dental caries, irritable bowel, ulcerative colitis, and the harmful effects of some ingested toxic substances.

The evidence underlying these claims varies. Some comes from direct human studies, others from animal experimentation. Some observations have been made on different population groups, and attempts made to correlate various disease statistics with local dietary factors. Still other claims are really theoretical hypotheses derived by combining known physical characteristics of foods and physiology. For example:

Constipation: Fiber's value for relieving constipation lies in its ability to increase the water content of the feces, producing bulkier, but soft, well-formed stools. This, in turn, leads to a transit time in the gastrointestinal tract which is intermediate between being too rapid, causing diarrhea, and too slow, causing constipation. It has been proposed that the increased volume and softness of the stools, by reducing straining during defecation, is a factor in preventing hemorrhoids and varicose veins. Experimental evidence

---

This Scientific Status Summary first appeared in *Food Technology*, published by the Institute of Food Technologists.

for this latter claim, however, is limited.

Diverticulosis: Diverticula are outpouchings which develop in weak areas in the bowel wall. When they are numerous and become inflamed, diverticulitis results. This condition is often accompanied by pain on the lower left side, alternating diarrhea and constipation, and flatulence. Diverticulitis was virtually nonexistent in the early 20th century, but its incidence has grown steadily in industrialized countries. Now, an estimated one-fourth to one-third of the middle-aged and older population in the U.S. and other western countries have the condition, although not all suffer from its symptoms. The incidence of the disease has changed little in populations where the diet is high in indigestible residue (e.g. South African Bantus and Chinese).

Until recently, the standard medical treatment for this malady was a low-residue diet, on the presumption that such a diet would allow healing and cause less irritation to the bowel. Now, however, it is treated with a high-fiber diet with good results. This supports the hypothesis that the disease results from a dietary fiber deficiency, although it obviously does not prove it.

Laboratory studies have shown that rats fed a fiber-free diet develop diverticulosis, while those fed a normal, fiber-containing control diet do not. Also, a fiber-containing diet could be used to cure diverticulosis in rats (Carlson and Hoelzel, 1949).

Cardiovascular diseases: A diet high in dietary fiber may lower blood cholesterol levels by reducing the "transit time" through the gastro-intestinal tract, leading to decreased absorption of dietary cholesterol. It may also decrease the reabsorption of bile salts, although evidence is based more on epidemiological studies (comparisons of population characteristics) than on clinical studies. Bile salts are essential in digestion; they emulsify fats and oils, and thus permit their absorption from the intestine. People on certain high-fiber diets excrete more bile acids, sterols, and fat, implying that the fiber compounds "bind" bile acids, and thereby prevent absorption of cholesterol and fat and also the reabsorption of bile acid, derived from the body's cholesterol (Stanley, 1970). The body then draws on its cholesterol stores to synthesize more bile acid, presumably resulting in a lowering of the blood (serum) cholesterol level.

High serum cholesterol levels have been identified as one of the risk factors in atherosclerosis, although there is disagreement as to whether the actual risk can be reduced by lowering cholesterol levels by means of diet or drugs.

Also complicating any resolution of the role of dietary fiber in cardiovascular disease are the inconsistent effects produced by dietary fiber from different foods. For example, studies have shown that adding rolled oats or barley to the diet reduces serum cholesterol levels in rats; the effect of adding whole wheat is variable. Rolled oats has also been shown to have a cholesterol-lowering effect in man (DeGroot, et al, 1963). Pectin (another dietary fiber component) has been shown to have a similar effect in man and experimental animals (Keys, et al, 1961; Leveille and Sauberlich, 1966). Bran does not appear to alter serum lipids, while alfalfa and possibly a lignin component may have a depressing effect (Eastwood, 1977).

Cancer: Some health professionals believe that dietary fiber may provide protection from cancer of the colon and the rectum, based on epidemiological studies of various populations comparing cancer incidence with dietary fiber consumed. The hypothesis relating dietary fiber to cancer presumes that the slow movement of the feces which occurs with a low-fiber diet allows more time for any carcinogens present in the colon to initiate cancer. In addition, according to this hypothesis, the

Table 1—A comparison of crude fiber and dietary fiber in certain foods[a]

Food	Crude fiber g/100 g	Dietary fiber g/100 g
Breads and cereals		
White bread	0.2	2.72
Whole wheat bread	1.6	8.50
All bran cereal	7.8	26.7
Cornflakes	0.7	11.0
Puffed Wheat	2.0	15.41
Puffed wheat, sugar coated	0.9	6.08
Vegetables		
Broccoli tops, boiled	1.5	4.10
Lettuce, raw	0.6	1.53
Carrots, boiled	1.0	3.70
Peas, canned	2.3	6.28
Sweet corn, cooked	0.7	4.74
Fruits		
Apples, without skin	0.6	1.42
Peaches, with skin	0.6	2.28
Strawberries, raw	1.3	2.12
Nuts		
Brazil	3.1	7.73
Peanuts	1.9	9.30
Peanut butter	1.9	7.55

[a] Crude fiber data from U.S.D.A. Handbook 8, Composition of Foods. Dietary fiber data from David Southgate, Medical Research Council, Cambridge, England

extra water, bile acids, salts, and fat bound by added fiber act as solvents to remove a wide variety of chemical factors which might be carcinogenic.

Also, a high-fiber diet may alter the type and number of microorganisms in the colon, and may possibly inhibit their production of potential carcinogens. A diet high in fiber might also contain less of the materials which are converted by microbial action to carcinogens (Leveille, 1976). One study supporting this theory showed that one class of microorganisms, which produce compounds convertible to carcinogens, is present in the feces of Western populations in significantly greater amounts than in feces from populations in the underdeveloped countries (Aries, et al: 1969).

Theories based on correlations of various population characteristics can, of course, be misleading. For example, the incidence of colon cancer in different countries and cultures correlates much better with the consumption of fat in the diet than it does with the consumption of fiber (Carroll, 1975; Chan and Cohen, 1975). Furthermore, there is no proven relationship between bowel transit times and the incidence of colon cancer. Also, no proof exists that constipation leads to cancer, and none that dietary fiber *per se* has a definable effect on the intestinal flora of man (Mendeloff, 1975).

Diabetes: Blood-sugar levels of patients taking insulin were significantly higher on a low-fiber diet than on a high-fiber diet (Miranda and Horwitz, 1978). While this preliminary observation is of interest, clearly diabetics should not change to a high-fiber diet without the advice of a physician.

Appendicitis has been linked to low-fiber diets in some epidemiological comparisons, but other data fail to support this hypothesis. For example, the incidence of appendicitis in the U.S. has decreased by 40% in the last 20 years, while fiber intake has been falling.

Weight loss: Preliminary studies indicate that high-fiber foods, bread, for example, may help promote weight loss, although additional studies are required before firm conclusions can be drawn. Pound for pound, such breads frequently contain fewer calories than normal breads, and they could also simply reduce food consumption because of an increased feeling of satiety (Mrdeza, 1978. One can also envision a mechanism whereby dietary fiber would shorten transit time through the intestine, with consequent decreased absorption of nutrients.

In addition to these major health-related areas, certain plant fibers appear to have an detoxifying effect when fed along with various drugs and chemicals (Ershoff, 1974), but further study is required. On the other hand, there is little evidence to link dietary fiber with such disorders as hiatal hernia, deep vein thrombosis, and phlebitis.

In considering possible relationships between specific diseases and diet or changes in diet, based on epidemiological evidence, one must remember that many changes in lifestyle and the environment occur simultaneously with changes in the diet which might themselves cause or influence the course of these diseases. It must be remembered that epidemiological evidence can never *prove* a causal relationship. It is also dangerous to speculate that a specific dietary factor is most significant. Generally, people eating a low-fiber diet are also consuming increased amounts of refined carbohydrates, fats, and animal products, for example. It is just as logical, epidemiologically speaking, to attribute these diseases to the *presence* of these other materials as it is to the absence of fiber. Furthermore, high-fiber diets also may be high in trace elements and other essential nutrients; thus, it could be *their* presence that produces any beneficial effects (Weininger and Briggs, 1976).

Dietary Fiber Not a Single Entity

As indicated earlier, results of feeding "high-fiber diets" differ from researcher to researcher. One explanation for the conflicting results may be the relatively poor analytical methods available for determining fiber data. Another explanation, however, is that different fiber components have very different physiological functions, and—since fiber composition differs with the food source—the physiological effects noted will depend on the predominant type of fiber used in the experimental diet. Some of the differences are in kind, while others are of degree.

One such example—the effect of fiber on the level of serum cholesterol—has already been mentioned. Pectin, lignin, guar gum, oat hulls, and barley have been shown to have some cholesterol-lowering effect in human and/or animal studies, while bran and cellulose have not. This difference may very well be related to differences in the chemical and physical properties of the various fiber components present. Even the size of the fiber particle being ingested affects the results.

Digestion of some components of dietary fiber, especially the hemicelluloses, takes place in the colon as a result of bacterial action. White flour, for example, is high in hemicellulose. The volatile fatty acids produced from this soluble fiber in the digestive process attract water from the surrounding tissues by osmosis, and thus may have a cathartic effect. Some fibers, such as bagasse from sugar cane, are very sharp and abrasive to the intestinal tract, while others, such as lignin, may actually be constipating.

There are such great differences in the physiological effects of the various constituents of dietary fiber that it is almost meaningless to talk about high-fiber diets in the abstract. This is not to deny that needs may exist for *components* of dietary fiber with specific properties, but rather that these needs may vary with different physiologic states.

Can You Get Too Much Dietary Fiber?

Whenever there is a surge of interest in any dietary component, there is a danger that the significance of laboratory research may be exaggerated relative to everyday dietary decisions. Such a danger exists with respect to fiber. Consumption of as much as 10 tablespoons of bran per day, in addition to the regular diet, has been recommended in some regimes. Such large intakes may cause diarrhea and other digestive complaints.

It has been suggested that too much pectin may cause decreased Vitamin B_{12} absorption. This would be an important concern for certain types of vegetarians, whose diets are already low in this vitamin and high in fiber. There may also be a significant loss of minerals, particularly zinc, iron, calcium, copper, and magnesium, due to binding of these minerals by phytic acid, present in certain plant-based foods.

The high-fiber diets of Africa and India, for example, are associated with a high incidence of such mineral deficiencies and kidney stones, especially in areas where rice is the major calorie source. The rate of stomach cancer in some of these areas is high, which should lead to cautious interpretation of epidemiological studies.

Also, fiber, by its sheer bulk, may reduce the total amount of food consumed, thereby resulting in the deficiency of certain nutrients, and even—in some cases—of needed calories, especially in areas where malnutrition is already existent.

Persons with kidney disease, diabetes, or other disease should, without question, obtain permission from their physician before consuming bran or making other drastic changes in their diet. Very large amounts of fiber could even cause enlargement and twisting (or "volvulus") of the sigmoid colon (Eastwood, 1976) and aggravate ulcerative colitis. Both conditions occur in Africa but rarely in Europe.

Food Sources of Dietary Fiber

A wide variety of foods supply significant amounts of dietary fiber, including all of the various components; Table 2 shows the amounts provided by a selected group of foods. In both fresh vegetables and fruits, the *total* dietary fiber appears to be relatively low, because of their high water content, but it represents a substantial proportion of the solids content. Potatoes and starchy vegetables supply significant amounts of fiber if consumed in fairly large quantities. The lignin content of most vegetables is very low, while that of fruits is highest in those containing lignified seeds, such as the strawberry, or lignified cells in the flesh, such as the pear. The non-cellulosic polysaccharides in these foods are usually rich in pectic substances (uronic acids) and in the so-called 5-carbon sugars (pentoses).

Substitution of whole meal flour for white flour provides increased lignin in the diet, as well as a 3-fold increase in total dietary fiber from that food stuff and a 12-fold increase in non-cellulose pentosans (polymers of 5-carbon sugars).

Consumer interest in this subject has prompted a number of bakeries to develop breads which contain from 6 to 8 percent crude fiber. This is roughly four times as much fiber as is contained in whole wheat bread. Powdered food-grade cellulose is the fiber component added to these products. Cellulose is a recognized food additive often used as a thickener or to decrease the separation of fat and water in other products, although its use in bread is new. When added to bread, it must be listed on the ingredient label. Since cellulose and the water it holds dilute other nutrients in normal bread, fiber-enriched bread is sometimes promoted as a calorie-reduced product.

How Much Is Enough?

While dietary recommendations ranging from 6 to 24 grams of crude fiber per day can be found in popular and scientific literature, almost no detailed information is available to serve as a guide for recommending either the quantity or type of dietary fiber. Trends in fiber consumption that have accompanied increases in the incidence of diseases suspected to be fiber-connected may not be meaningful—they certainly do not *prove* anything.

From 1909-13 to 1965, the daily crude fiber content of the average American diet decreased from approximately 7 grams to about 5 grams. Whether increasing daily consumption of crude fiber by 2 grams to get it back to this earlier level could be expected to have the same effect on health as an increase to the higher levels—25 grams—suggested from the difference between African and American diets, is certainly an unanswered question (McNutt, 1976; Heller and Hackler, 1978).

It may be that the increased consumption of fruits and vegetables, coupled with the decreased intake of cereal in the last 50 years, represents more of a shift in the *type* of fiber than a significant decrease in the amount (Spiller and Shipley, 1976).

Recommendations

Recommendations regarding the consumption of any nutrient must be rational and based on reasonable scientific evidence. In the absence of such evidence, *moderation* should be exercised. A variety of whole grain products, fruits, and vegetables will ensure a good mixture of fiber constituents, and make a positive contribution to the overall nutritional value of the diet.

If there are beneficial effects from dietary fiber, they must stem from more than one component of dietary fiber. Therefore, adding fiber in the form of bran alone, for example, can be expected to have little effect other than on bowel activity. Likewise, the benefits of adding cellulose alone to bread may be limited to reducing calories. Any generalized statements about the use of dietary fiber as a drug to cure specific diseases should be looked at with reservations.

In short, the feeling of urgency about fiber in nutrition prevalent today should not cause investigators to jump to premature conclusions, nor cause the public to make drastic changes in their diets, without thinking through their specific needs and the options open for filling them.

REFERENCES

Aries, V., Crowther, J.S., Drasar, B.S., Hill, J., and Williams, R.E.O. 1969, Gut 10: 334.

Burkitt, D.P. 1973. Some diseases characteristic of modern Western Civilization, British Med. J. 1: 274.

Carlson, A.J. and Hoelzel, F. 1949. Relation of

diets to diverticulosis in the colon of rats. Gastroenterology 12: 108.

Carroll, K.K. 1975. Experimental evidence of dietary factors and hormone-dependent cancers. Cancer Res. 35: 3374.

Chan, P-C, and Cohen, L.A. 1975. Dietary fat and growth promotion of rat mammary tumors, Cancer Res. 35: 3384.

DeGroot, A.P., Lugken, R., and Pikaar, N.A. 1963. Cholesterol-lowering effects of rolled oats. Lancet 2: 303.

Eastwood, M. 1976. Volvulus of the colon, p. 230. In: "Fiber in Human Nutrition," Spillen, G.A., and Amen, R.J., Plenum Publ. Co., New York.

Eastwood, M. 1977. Vegetable dietary fiber. Nutrition and the M.D., 3(11): 1.

Ershoff, B.H. 1974. Anti-toxic effects of plant fiber. Amer. J. Clin. Nutr. 27: 1395.

Heller, S.N. and Hackler, L.R. 1978. Changes in the crude fiber content of the American diet. Am. J. Clin. Nutr. 31 (Sept.): 1510.

Leveille, G.A. and Sauberlich, H. 1966. Mechanism of the cholesterol-depressing effect of pectin in the cholesterol-fed rat, J Nutr. 88: 209.

Leveille, G.A. 1976. Dietary fiber. Food and Nutr. News. 47(3): 1.

Keys, A., Grande, F. and Anderson, J.T. 1961. Fiber and pectin in the diet and serum cholesterol concentration in man. Proc. Soc. Exp. Biol. Med. 106: 555.

McNutt, K. 1976. Perspective—Fiber. J. Nutr. Ed., 8(4): 150.

Mrdeza, G. 1978. Trends in Specialty breads. Cereal Foods World. 29(11): 635.

Mendeloff, A.I. 1975. Dietary fiber. Nutr. Rev. 33(11): 321.

Miranda, P.M. and Horwitz, D.L. 1978. High-fiber diets in treatment of Diabetes mellitus. Ann. Int. Med. 88(4): 482.

Spiller, G.A. and Shipley, E.A. 1976. New perspectives on dietary fiber. Food Prod. Dev., 10(8): 57.

Stanley, M.M. 1970. Quantification of intestinal functions during fasting: estimations of bile salt turnover, fecal calcium and nitrogen excretions, Metabolism 19: 865.

Weininger, J. and Briggs, G.M. 1976 Nutrition update, J. Nutr. Ed., 8(4): 172.

SUPPLEMENTAL MATERIAL

Burkitt, D.P. and Trowell, H.C. 1975. "Refined Carbohydrate Foods and Disease. Academic Press, London and New York.

Hegsted, D.M. (ed.) 1977. "Food and Fiber." Nutrition Reviews 35: 3.

Roth, H.P. and Mehlman, M.A. 1978. "Symposium on the Role of Dietary Fiber in Health." Am. J. Clin. Nutr. (31).

Spiller, G.A. and Amen, R.J. 1976. "Fiber in Human Nutrition." Plenum Publ. Co., New York.

Spiller, G.A. (ed.). 1978. "Topics in Dietary Fiber Research." Plenum Publ. Co., New York.

Plant Fiber in the Pediatric Diet

by American Academy of Pediatrics' Committee on Nutrition

Dietary fiber has been defined as the part of material in foods impervious to the degradative enzymes of the human digestive tract. The dietary fiber of plants is comprised of carbohydrate compounds including cellulose, hemicellulose, pectin, gums, mucilages, and a noncarbohydrate substance, lignin. These substances, which form the structure of plants, are present in the cell walls of all parts including the leaf, stem, root, and seed.[1] Animal tissue also contains indigestible substances.

Crude fiber and dietary fiber are not the same thing. Crude fiber refers to the residue left after strong acid and base hydrolysis of plant material. This process dissolves the pectin, gums, mucilages, and most of the hemicellulose and mainly is a measure of the cellulose and lignin content. Clearly, this method tends to underestimate the total amount of fiber in the food.[1] Most food composition tables give only crude fiber values.

Current interest in fiber was stimulated by the suggestion that it might help to prevent certain diseases common in the United States, namely diverticular disease, cancer of the colon, irritable bowel syndrome, obesity, and coronary heart disease.[2-4] African blacks in rural areas where the fiber intake was high rarely had these diseases; however, during the past 20 years as this population moved to the cities and adopted Western habits (including a Western diet), they began to suffer from the same "Western-type" diseases.

A high-fiber diet increases fecal bulk, produces softer, more frequent stools, and decreases transit time through the intestine.[5] These factors may be responsible for the supposed beneficial effects of fiber. A decreased transit time implies less time for potential carcinogens to be in contact with the intestinal mucosa. The increased bulk would dilute potential carcinogens and produce less straining at stool, a factor implicated by Burkitt and co-workers[5] in the development of diverticulosis.

Obesity is rare in populations eating most carbohydrates as complex carbohydrates, such as rice, beans, lentils, and cereal grains, which contain large amounts of fiber. This could simply be that the increased mastication required for these foods slows caloric ingestion or that the increased bulk acclerates satiety.[6] However, it could also be caused by a lower caloric intake.

Arteriosclerosis and coronary heart disease may also be inversely related to low fiber intake. Trowell[7] suggests that a high fiber intake lowers blood cholesterol by increasing the fecal excretion of bile acids and sterols which are metabolites of cholesterol in man. Human studies have confirmed this. Subjects consuming from 12 to 36 gm of pectin daily for several weeks have shown a significant reduction of total serum cholesterol ranging from 8% to 30%.[1]

The different fractions of fiber have different physiologic effects. Pectin has a cholesterol-lowering effect which may be caused by bile acid sequestration and increased stool-fat content. Lignin has bile acid-binding properties in vitro, but these have not yet been demonstrated in vivo. There are conflicting data about whether it lowers serum cholesterol. Cellulose has been shown to increase output of fecal bile acid. It is not thought to have a hypocholesterolemic effect, although this is questionable. Hemicellulose increases fecal excretion of bile acid, but probably by a mechanism other than adsorption. There is some evidence that it has a hypocholesterolemic effect.[1]

Most evidence for the beneficial effects of fiber is epidemiologic and refers almost entirely to adults, and the diseases mentioned (with the exception of obesity) require years to develop. In addition to fiber intake, there are many variables in the populations studied, such as intake of saturated fats and sucrose, exercise, and stress, all of which are implicated as causative factors in these diseases.

Should a recommendation be made for an increased fiber intake in children? An increase in fiber means an increase in the consumption of fruits, vegetables, legumes, and whole grain cereals and breads. Although survey data are limited, there are some indicators that current intakes of fiber in children are low. In a 2,000-household survey conducted in 1975, the findings were expressed in terms of the number of servings of the four basic food groups suggested by the United States Department of Agriculture (USDA).[8] Seventy-five percent of the children ate less than the recommended daily amounts of fruits and vegetables, and 62% of them ate less than the recommended amount of bread and cereals.[8] HANES (Health and Nutrition Examination Survey) data (C. M. Dresser, J. Habicht, unpublished data, 1977) show that approximately 35% to 50% of children eat one or fewer fruits or vegetables rich in vitamin C per day, that 30% to 40% of children 1 to 5 years old have vitamin C intakes less than two thirds of the recommended daily allowance (RDA), and roughly 20% of them have vitamin A intakes below two thirds of the RDA.[9] Fruits and vegetables (chiefly the deep orange, yellow, and green ones) are important sources of carotenoids, which are precursors of vitamin A. Therefore, in terms of dietary recommendations for nutrients, and without even considering fiber, large numbers of children have low intakes of fiber-containing foods.

Several objections to an increased fiber intake for children have been made. The first is that children have a small stomach capacity and the caloric density of high-fiber foods is low; therefore, children would be unable to ingest adequate calories. This could be a problem in highly restricted vegetarians, although it could be solved easily by including nuts and legumes (which are relatively high in both protein and fat) in the diet.

The second objection is that dietary fiber may influence adversely the absorption of certain essential minerals such as calcium, iron, copper, magnesium, phosphorus, and zinc. One advantage of white flour is that the removal of the husk (bran) means much of the phytate (inositol hexaphosphate) is

TABLE 1. Guide to Usual Food Patterns for Children Aged 1 to 10 Years*

Food	Foods Included	Serving Size	Age Group 1–3 yr	Age Group 4–6 yr	Age Group 7–10 yr
Cereal and bread	Whole grain or enriched and iron-fortified cereals (cooked or ready-to-eat); breads, rolls, muffins; noodles, spaghetti, macaroni, rice; cornmeal, oatmeal, farina, rolled wheat	1 slice bread 1 oz (¾–1 cup) ready-to-eat cereal ½ cup cooked cereal or pasta	4 small (half-sized) servings	4 servings or more	4 servings or more
Fruits	All fruits (fresh, frozen, or canned) and juices. Good sources of vitamin C are citrus fruits (eg, oranges, grapefruit, tangerines), cantalope, strawberries (see also vegetables). Include at least one good source of vitamin C per day	Varies	2 servings or more; fruits with pits not advised this age group	2 servings or more	2 servings or more
Vegetables	All vegetables (fresh, frozen, or canned) and potatoes. Good sources of vitamin C are cabbage, tomatoes, green peppers, white potatoes. Good sources of vitamin A are carrots, yams, sweet potatoes, winter squash, green leafy vegetables, tomatoes. Include one good source of vitamin A at least every other day	1–3 yr: ¼ cup 4–6 yr: ⅓ cup 7–10 yr: ½ cup	2 servings or more	2 servings or more	2 servings or more

* Adapted from *Diet Manual of the Massachusetts General Hospital*. Boston, Little, Brown and Co, 1976.

removed. These minerals may form insoluble compounds with phytate that render them unavailable. If the intake of these minerals is low, and the small amount consumed is chelated, a deficiency state may be produced. This may be a serious problem in developing countries if the main source of zinc is bread. For example, in the rural populations in Iran where zinc deficiency occurs, unleavened whole grain bread accounts for approximately 75% of the energy intake.[10] It is unclear, however, how relevant this observation is to the United States where bread and cereals account for approximately 20% of the zinc intake and the intake of animal protein is high.[10] Also, the phytate in whole wheat can be destroyed by yeast fermentation, and bread in this country is generally made with yeast.[11] Although it is believed that mineral deficiencies are unlikely to develop in children on typical Western diets, even with a reasonable increase in their dietary fiber intake,[12] there is little direct evidence to support this.

However, limited results from metabolic work suggest that moderate amounts of dietary fiber do not significantly affect mineral status. A study was done in 1943 on children 4 to 12 years old who consumed from 4 to 6 gm of crude fiber (cellulose and hemicellulose) per day for periods ranging from 30 to 225 successive days.[13] The authors report that all children enjoyed buoyant health, satisfactory bowel elimination, and no evidence of any untoward effects upon the absorption of nitrogen and the mineral elements. Unfortunately, since no nitrogen or mineral balance studies were actually conducted on the children, this conclusion may not be valid. Based on fecal analysis, the older children also seemed to have an increased ability to decompose cellulose and hemicellulose.

A more recent, rigorously conducted study investigated the effect of three fibers (hemicellulose, cellulose, and pectin) at a level of 14.2 gm/day on copper, zinc, and magnesium utilization by adolescent boys.[14] Some alteration in mineral utilization was found. Hemicellulose supplementation resulted in significantly increased fecal zinc, copper, and magnesium excretions and significantly lowered zinc, copper, and magnesium retentions. Cellulose had a directionally similar approach, but to a lesser degree. Pectin had the least influence on mineral

TABLE 2. Fiber Content of Foods (per 100 gm)*

Food	Little Fiber (0.2 gm)	Low Fiber (0.5 gm; range 0.3–1 gm)	Moderate Fiber (1.5 gm; range 1.1–2.0 gm)	High Fiber (3 gm; range 2.1–4.2 gm)
Bread	White, cracked wheat, rye, pumpernickel bread; white crackers	Whole wheat bread and crackers		
Cereals	Rice, macaroni, noodles, spaghetti	Barley, Cheerios, corn-flakes, farina, oatmeal, puffed rice, brown rice, shredded wheat, Wheaties	40% bran flakes, puffed wheat, raisin bran	All Bran (4.8 gm/cup), wheat germ (2.5 gm/cup)
Vegetables		Asparagus, beets, cabbage, carrots, celery, collards, corn, cucumber, eggplant, lettuce, mushrooms, onions, sweet potato, white potato with or without skin, summer squash, spinach, tomato, white turnip	Green and wax beans, dried beans and peas (kidney, lima, lentils, split pea, soybeans, etc); broccoli; brussel sprouts; cauliflower; dandelion, kale, and mustard greens; fresh or frozen green peas; okra, parsnip, peppers, pumpkin, rutabaga, winter squash	Artichoke, 1 large (2.4 gm), green peas canned only (2.3 gm/½ cup)
Fruits	Juices only	Applesauce, apricots, banana, canned fruit cocktail, cherries, grapefruit, grapes, mango, melon, oranges, papaya, peaches, pears without skin, pineapple, plums, prunes, raisins, rhubarb	Apples, avocado, berries except blackberries, figs, fresh or canned pears with skin	Fresh blackberries (4.1 gm/¾ cup), dried figs (5.6 gm/cup), dried date (2.3 gm/½ cup)

* From *Diet Manual of The Massachusetts General Hospital*. Boston, Little, Brown and Co. Fiber values assigned are based on data in Watt BK, Merrill AL: *Composition of Foods—Raw, Processed, Prepared* (Agriculture Handbook No. 8) Washington, DC, US Department of Agriculture, Agricultural Research Service, 1963.

utilization and retention. This corresponded primarily to losses of these minerals in the feces. Serum levels of zinc, copper, and magnesium were resistant to change. However, each fiber was consumed for only four days, and longer periods may be required before serum changes are detected.

More work needs to be done in this area before any firm recommendations can be made. It is not known whether an increased fiber intake during pregnancy would have any effect on the fetus and newborn infant in terms of vitamin and mineral status, nor is it known what effect the fiber intake of nursing mothers has on the mineral composition of their milk.

Nevertheless, a substantial amount of fiber probably should be eaten to ensure normal laxation. Fiber is probably not needed in infants less than 1 year old. With introduction of solid foods into the diet of the older child, care should be taken to include whole grain cereals, breads, fruits, and vegetables. However, a diet that places emphasis on high-fiber, low-calorie foods, to the exclusion of the other common food groups, would not be recommended for children. Tables 1 and 2 give the fiber content of foods commonly consumed and portions that should be eaten by children.

ACKNOWLEDGMENT

The Committee wishes to thank Deborah Rothman, PhD, for her assistance in the preparation of this paper.

COMMITTEE ON NUTRITION
Lewis A. Barness, MD, Chairman
Peter R. Dallman, MD, Vice Chairman
Homer Anderson, MD
Platon Jack Collipp, MD
Buford L. Nichols, Jr, MD
W. Allan Walker, MD
Calvin W. Woodruff, MD

Liaison Representatives
Betty E. Anderson
Philip L. White, ScD
Mary C. Egan
Margaret Cheney, PhD
Claude C. Roy, MD

Melinda Moore, MD
Joginder Chopra, MD
Myrtle L. Brown, PhD
Herbert P. Sarett, PhD
Thorsten J. Fjellstedt, PhD
L. J. Teply, PhD
Eileen Kennedy, PhD
William J. Darby, MD, PhD
Peter Lewy, MD

Technical Advisory Group
Rudolph M. Tomarelli, PhD
John D. Benson, PhD
George A. Purvis, PhD
Jerome LiCari, PhD
Haines B. Lockhart, PhD
Sidney Saperstein, PhD

REFERENCES

1. Huang CT, Gopalakrishna GS, Nichols BL: Fiber, intestinal sterols and colon cancer. *Am J Clin Nutr* 31:516, 1978
2. Burkitt DP: Some diseases characteristic of modern Western civilization. *Br Med J* 1:274, 1973
3. Burkitt DP: Epidemiology of large bowel disease: The role of fiber. *Proc Nutr Soc* 32:145, 1973
4. Burkitt DP, Walker AR, Painter NS: Dietary fiber and disease. *JAMA* 229:1068, 1974
5. Burkitt DP, Walker AR, Painter NS: Effect of dietary fiber on stools and transit times and its role in the causation of disease. *Lancet* 2:1408, 1972
6. Mendeloff AI: Current concepts: Dietary fiber and human health. *N Engl J Med* 297:811, 1977
7. Trowell H: Fiber: A natural hypocholesteremic agent. *Am J Clin Nutr* 25:464, 1972
8. Celender IM: Food intake of 2000 families. Presented at the General Mills Nutrition Symposium, June 16, 1977
9. *Preliminary Findings of the HANES, United States, 1971–1972: Dietary Intake and Biochemical Findings.* US Departments of Health, Education and Welfare, Public Health Service, 1974
10. Sandstrom B, Arvidsson B, Cederblad A, et al: Zinc absorption from composite meals. I. The significance of wheat extraction rate, zinc, calcium, and protein content in meals based on bread. *Am J Clin Nutr* 33:739, 1980
11. Macdonald I: The effects of dietary fiber: Are they all good?, in Spiller GA, Amen RJ (eds): *Fiber in Human Nutrition.* New York, Plenum Press, 1976
12. Saperstein S, Spiller GA: Dietary fiber. *Am J Dis Child* 132:657, 1978
13. Hummel FC, Shepherd ML, Macy IG: Disappearance of cellulose and hemicullulose from the digestive tracts of children. *J Nutr* 25:59, 1943
14. Drews LM, Kies C, Fox HM: Effect of dietary fiber on copper, zinc, and magnesium utilization by adolescent boys. *Am J Clin Nutr* 32:1893, 1979

SWEETENERS

Sugar: How Sweet It Is—And Isn't

by Chris W. Lecos

Sugar, "that honey from reeds," as one author described it more than 2,000 years ago, has been a part of mankind's diet for as long as anyone cares to remember.

Cave drawings tell us of prehistoric man's taste for honey, figs, and dates. The beekeeping practices of Egyptians are depicted in the artwork in tombs dating around 2600 B.C.

The Bible tells us that the "promised land" flowed with milk and honey. It turned into a flood once sugarcane was discovered.

In the writings of an obscure officer in Alexander's army during its invasion of India, one finds the first written mention of sugarcane. That was around 325 B.C.

Yet, despite this long history, the use of sugar in the diet has become a controversial issue in recent years that has involved doctors, scientists, nutritionists, private citizens, the Government, and the industry itself.

Why all the fuss?

- Because there is a growing body of expert opinion that believes Americans would be healthier if they ate less sugar, not because it's bad for you, but because its only real contribution is taste and Calories.
- Because sugar has become the leading ingredient added to foods in the United States today. That is, most of the sugar consumed is added before it gets to the consumer.
- Because most people don't know how much sugar they eat, and many want to know. This is a principal reason the Food and Drug Administration wants the total amount of all sugars identified on more foods. The total would include both naturally occurring and added sugar.
- Because sugar, though blamed wrongly for many ills, is one of a number of contributors to dental caries. Americans are spending $10 billion a year for dental care.

To most people, sugar is what you find on the kitchen table, put into coffee, or mix in a cake. This, of course, is the sugar refined from cane and beets.

Actually, there are more than a hundred substances that are sweet and which chemists can correctly describe as sugars. Sucrose, or table sugar, is just the most common and abundant of them all.

Industry literature describes sugar as a cheap source of food energy, a major contributor to food processing and general nutrition, and a substance that makes many foods with other nutrients taste better.

"Good nutrition," says a brochure from the Sugar Association, "begins with eating."

Its point, of course, is that if food is sweetened, people will eat the foods with the nutrients they need. However, many nutritionists and others concerned with American eating habits dispute sugar's value.

In a 1976 evaluation of the health aspects of sucrose as a food ingredient, the Federation of American Societies for Experimental Biology (FASEB) stated in a report to FDA: "Unlike most other foods, sucrose furnishes virtually only energy."

Many nutritionists concur and describe sugar as an "empty Calorie." If sugar is to be part of the diet, they say, it is preferable to get it from fruits, vegetables, and other items where it's a natural part of the product.

As it does with most other carbohydrates, the body converts sugar into glucose, the primary fuel of the body. During digestion it is broken down into equal parts of two simple sugars: glucose (dextrose) and fructose (levulose).

These components enter the bloodstream through the walls of the small intestine, and the blood carries the sugars to the tissues and the liver. There it is used or converted into glycogen and stored until the body needs it. The hormone insulin makes it possible for glucose, or blood sugar, to enter nearly all the cells of the body, where it is used as an energy source.

When more energy is needed, the liver converts glycogen into glucose, which is then delivered by the bloodstream to other organs or muscle tissue. Glucose not needed by the cells is metabolized in the liver into fatty substances called triglycerides. The body can call upon this stored energy during dieting and fasting.

Because of these energy reserves, nutritionists discount the argument that sugar is useful for quick energy needs before physical activity.

Americans get about 24 percent of their Calories from sugar—of which 3 percent comes in natural form from fruits and vegetables, 3 percent from dairy products, and the balance from sugar added to foods.

If sugar provides about 20 percent of a person's Calo-

From FDA Consumer, February 1980, pp. 21-23. Published by U.S. Food and Drug Administration.

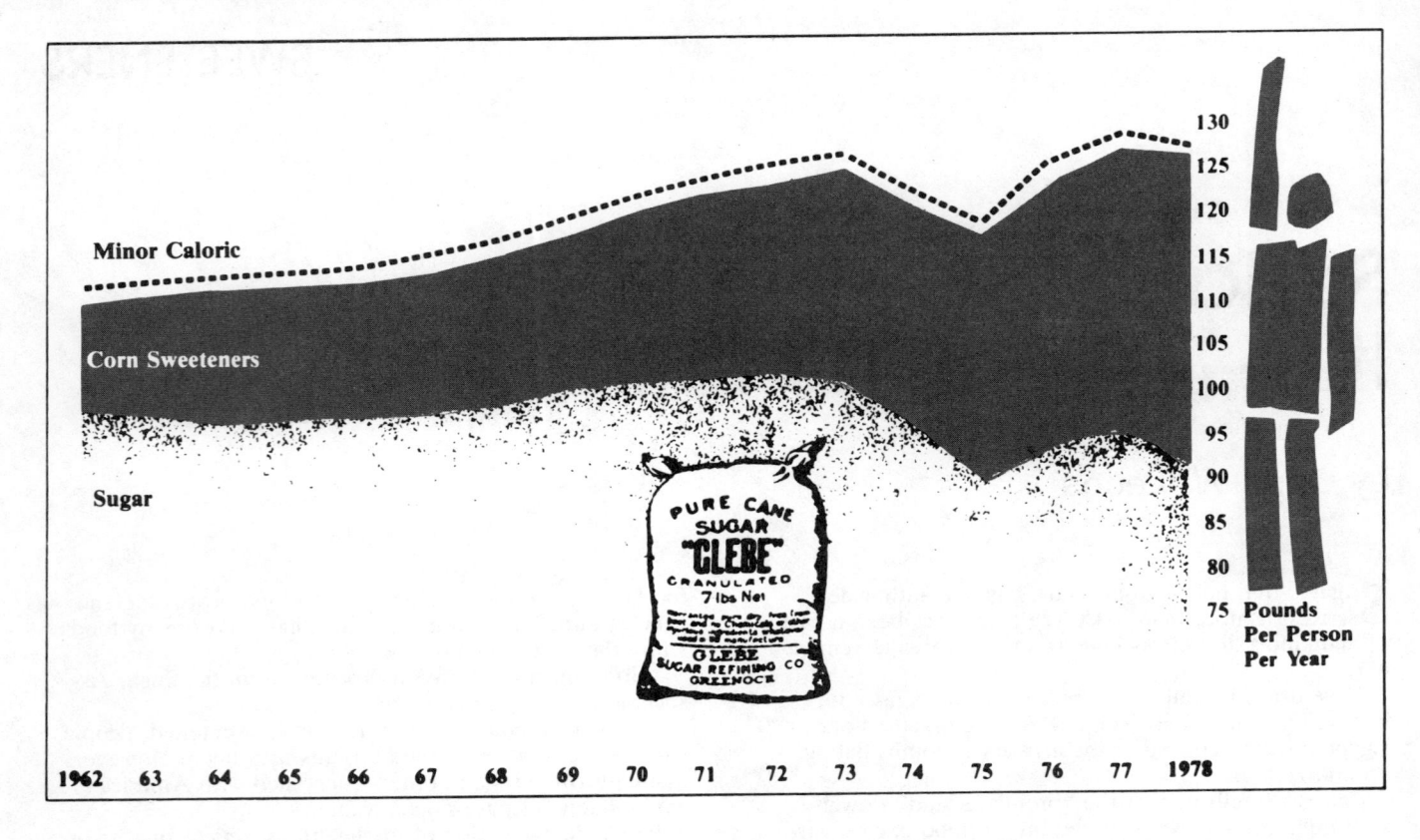

ries, he must get the other 80 percent by selecting foods that supply the other nutrients his body needs—which is not easy to do, say some nutritionists, if one is trying to lose weight.

For many Americans, weight is a problem. A study released in 1978 by the National Center for Health Statistics indicated that one-third of the population was overweight.

In a study of 13,600 people whose weights between 1971 and 1974 were compared with adults of equivalent height a decade earlier, the Center found that men and women under 45 were, on the average, 3.8 and 4.7 pounds heavier, respectively. Those over 45 had gained an average of 4.8 pounds.

There is no accurate measurement of how much sugar the average American eats. The best available barometer of sugar use is the per capita consumption figures of the U.S. Department of Agriculture (USDA).

Although the per capita figures do not tell how much a person actually eats, they do show the amount of sugar that "disappears" into the marketplace—that is, the amount shipped by sugar producers for industrial, home, and other uses.

Citing USDA figures, sugar industry spokesmen maintain that sugar consumption in the United States has been relatively stable for more than 50 years now, at around 100 pounds a year per person.

However, that figure refers only to the consumption of refined cane and beet sugar. It does not reflect the growing impact of a variety of corn sweeteners now in use. The term "corn sweeteners" includes various corn sirups (high fructose corn sirup, glucose) plus other Caloric sweeteners, such as dextrose, that are derived from corn.

Refined sugar, corn sirup, and corn sugar account for the bulk of the sweeteners consumed in this country. Among the remainder are honey, maple, and other edible sirups.

All of these are Caloric, and when all are taken into account, USDA figures show a rise in per capita consumption from 122 pounds in 1970 to 128 pounds in 1978.

Per capita consumption of just refined sugar hovered around the 100 pounds per year level between 1960 and 1974. Since then, the trend generally has been downward, falling below 93 pounds in 1978, according to USDA. Fred Gray, an agriculture economist for USDA, predicted a further drop of several pounds for 1979.

The decline in refined sugar consumption has been more than offset by the steady rise in corn sweetener usage—from a per capita rate of 19 pounds in 1970 to almost 34 pounds in 1978.

Norris Bollenback, scientific director for the Sugar Association, said the primary impetus for the increase has come from the growing industrial use of high fructose corn sirups, especially by soft drink producers.

The use of high fructose corn sirups was negligible—less than a pound per capita, on the average—in the early 1970's. The industry was in its infancy then, and food and beverage manufacturers relied almost entirely on cane and beet sugar for their products because those sugars were cheap and plentiful, selling for about 11 or 12 cents a pound wholesale.

The rapid escalation of sugar prices in 1974—up to around 33 cents a pound wholesale—compelled the food and beverage industries to turn to other sweeteners, and the most attractive of them all was the high fructose corn sirups.

By the end of 1975, USDA figures show that per capita consumption of those corn sirups had risen to 5 pounds and 3 years later up to 11 pounds. Gray predicted that high fructose corn sirup usage would reach 15 pounds in 1979 and 18 pounds by the end of 1980.

Bollenback cited figures that showed that high fructose corn sirup producers have maintained their product's price consistently below that of refined sugar—roughly from 3 to 10 cents a pound less at the wholesale level. Last year, the wholesale price of high fructose corn sirup was around 13 cents a pounds compared to 20 cents for refined sugar.

"If (refined) sugar proponents think things will be back the way they were, they are being unrealistic," Bollenback noted.

Things also aren't the way they used to be in how sugar gets to our stomachs. Fifty years ago, two-thirds of the sugar produced went directly into the home, which meant control was directly in the hands of the housewife or individual who bought it. The balance was used mostly by industry.

Now, the reverse is true. Sixty-five percent of the refined sugar produced today is being consumed by the food and beverage industries and only 24 percent is going for home use.

The beverage industry—comprised of soft drink bottlers and beer and wine producers—is the leading industrial user of refined sugar and of high fructose corn sirups. It used 26 percent of the 9.8 million tons of refined sugar shipped in 1978 and about 40 percent of the high fructose corn sirups.

Although there has been a considerable amount of public controversy over the amount of sugar in cereals, the bakery and cereal industries combined used only 13.4 percent of all the sugar produced for food purposes in 1978. USDA figures did not separate the two.

Producers of confectionery products had the next highest usage at 9.2 percent, followed by 7 percent for the processed food and canning industries, and 5.6 percent for dairy products.

The consumer today is confronted by a wide variety of sugars and other nutritive sweeteners, and there is no significant difference in the amount of Calories each provides.

Below is a brief explanation of the more common sugars and sweeteners:

Sucrose, obtained in crystalline form, from cane and beets, is a double sugar or disaccharide and is composed of two simple sugars, glucose and fructose. It is about 99.9 percent pure and is sold in either granulated or powdered form.

Raw sugar, tan to brown in appearance, is a coarse, granulated solid obtained from evaporation of sugarcane juice. FDA regulations prohibit the sale of raw sugar unless impurities—dirt, insect fragments, etc.—are removed.

Turbinado sugar is sometimes viewed erroneously as a raw sugar. Actually, it has to go through a refining process to remove impurities and most of the molasses. It is produced by separating raw sugar crystals and washing them with steam. It is edible if produced under proper conditions. However, some samples in the past have been found to contain contaminants, the Sugar Association warns.

Brown sugar consists of sugar crystals contained in a molasses sirup with natural flavor and color. However, some refiners make brown sugar by simply adding sirup to refined white sugar in a mixer. It has 91 to 96 percent sucrose.

Total invert sugar, a mixture of glucose and fructose, is formed by splitting sucrose in a process called inversion, which is accomplished by the application of acids or enzymes. It is sold only in liquid form and is sweeter than sucrose. It helps prolong the freshness of baked foods and confections and is useful in preventing food shrinkage.

Honey is an invert sugar formed by an enzyme from nectar gathered by bees. Its composition and flavor depend on the source of the nectar. Fructose, glucose, maltose, and sucrose are among its components.

Corn sirups, produced by the action of enzymes and/or acids on cornstarch, are the result of hydrolysis of starch. High fructose corn sirup is a derivative of corn. The amounts of fructose vary with the manufacturer. One major producer's sirups contain 42 percent, 55 percent, and 90 percent fructose. Dextrose comprises most of the balance.

Levulose, or fructose, is a commercial sugar, considerably sweeter than sucrose, although its sweetness actually depends on its physical form and how it is used in cooking. Fructose, known as a fruit sugar, occurs naturally in many fruits.

Dextrose, or glucose, is also called corn sugar. It is made commercially from starch by the action of heat and acids, or enzymes. It is often sold blended with regular sugar.

Lactose, or milk sugar, is made from whey and skim milk for commercial purposes. It occurs in the milk of mammals. The pharmaceutical industry is a primary user of prepared lactose.

Sorbitol, mannitol, maltitol, and *xylitol* are sugar alcohols or polyols. They occur naturally in fruits but are commerically produced from such sources as dextrose. Xylitol is a sugar alcohol made from a part of birch trees. Sorbitol, mannitol, and maltitol are about half as sweet as sucrose; xylitol has a sweetness about equal to sucrose.

Although fructose and the other sugar alcohols are promoted as suitable substitute sweeteners, especially for diabetics, many health scientists question their supposed advantages pending more research and long-term studies.

SWEETENERS

Fructrose: Questionable Diet Aid

by Chris W. Lecos

Fructose is a sugar that has spawned a number of rapid weight-loss schemes and a lot of misleading ideas about its usefulness in the diets of diabetics and others. It has been ballyhooed as a "natural" replacement for ordinary table sugar and saccharin, as an "elite sweet," as the "newest, most effective diet aid," as a suitable sugar substitute for diabetics, and as a hunger appeaser.

Although the scientific and medical community is by no means unanimous over the merits of fructose as an "ideal substitute" for table sugar, or sucrose, this is how most health professionals respond to such claims:

• The prevailing medical opinion, according to a report prepared for FDA, is that there are no "clinical advantages" in substituting fructose where diabetics are concerned.

• The available scientific data, according to a 1978 report to the Federal agency, is regarded as insufficient "to determine if fructose or any other carbohydrate has beneficial properties for the long-term dietary management of diabetes."

• There is a particular need for scientific studies that evaluate the long-term benefit of fructose when consumed as a part of the regular meal plan of a diabetic. Such studies, said the 1978 report, have not been conducted.

• The claim that fructose is a natural replacement for ordinary sugar can be misleading. Fructose occurs naturally, along with other sugars, in honey and fruits. The pure fructose sold commercially is produced from sucrose (refined sugar), which is comprised of fructose and glucose. Pure fructose should not be confused with high fructose sirups derived from corn.

• Fructose provides the same number of Calories—four per gram—as sucrose. Health experts say there is little if any advantage in using fructose for weight reduction, despite claims that fructose users would consume fewer Calories because they would use less fructose to get the same sweetness as from sucrose.

A number of factors have sparked the public's interest in fructose, and other nutritive sweeteners as well, in recent years. First, is the growing public belief that it would be better for one's health to eat less refined sugar, namely sucrose. Second is the clouded future of saccharin, the only non-Caloric sweetener on the U.S. market today. Saccharin's future is murky because of FDA's proposal to restrict its use in foods based on evidence that it is a weak animal carcinogen. Third is the extensive publicity given to fructose in books, television, and other media.

Diabetologists, such as Dr. John Davidson, professor of medicine at Emory University and director of the Diabetes Unit at Grady Hospital in Atlanta, are particularly concerned about some of the claims being made for fructose.

"I object strenuously to misleading advertising of the type that some of these people have been engaging in, promising this and promising that," he declared. "It burns me up to see the public misled and taken advantage of and promised something that the product is not going to deliver." He is not alone in these concerns.

In recent months, the American Diabetes Association (ADA) has published a number of statements on fructose and other nutritive sweeteners, such as sorbitol, mannitol, and xylitol. All four have these two characteristics in common: They do not contain glucose, a sugar that diabetics should avoid in concentrated amounts to prevent sudden surges in blood sugar levels; and they are not metabolized in the same way as glucose.

During digestion in a normal, healthy individual, sucrose is broken down into equal parts of glucose and fructose. These components enter the bloodstream through the wall of the small intestine and the blood carries the sugars to the tissues and the liver. There they are used or converted into glycogen, which is stored until needed by the body. Insulin makes it possible for glucose, or blood sugar, to enter nearly all the cells of the body, where it is utilized.

The nonglucose sweeteners, such as fructose, are absorbed more slowly than glucose or sucrose and go directly to the liver without insulin. This does not mean, however, that insulin is not needed with fructose. Fructose is absorbed from the intestinal tract into the bloodstream and then transported to the liver. The liver cells transform the major portion to glucose, which does require insulin for use by body cells.

The insulin response is less rapid with fructose than

From FDA Consumer, March 1980, pp. 21-23. Published by U.S. Food and Drug Administration.

with glucose because of the slower intestinal absorption of fructose. It is this slower uptake and more moderate blood glucose response that has led to the claim that fructose is a better and easier sugar for diabetics to digest. Such claims are reinforced by reports that fructose, sorbitol, and xylitol are used widely in some European countries by diabetics. The nonglucose sweeteners generally do not leave the bitter after-taste of artificial sweeteners like saccharin. Studies also indicate that they are less cariogenic than sucrose—that is, contribute less to dental decay.

Xylitol had shown some real promise as a sweetener with a much lower cavity-causing potential. For all practical purposes, however, xylitol is no longer available in the United States. Chewing gum makers and other food manufacturers voluntarily ceased using it after FDA received studies that indicated it could cause tumors. Its status currently is under review by FDA.

Health experts in this country do not always accept the advantages cited for the nonglucose sweeteners. They note that most of the studies and experiments are short-term in duration or lacking in the kind of data considered necessary to demonstrate safety and effectiveness for diabetics.

Of particular importance to the American Diabetes Association and other diabetologists are long-term studies that measure the effects of consuming fructose and the other sweeteners along with the kinds of meals a diabetic would be expected to eat over an extended period. A recent ADA review paper on the nonglucose sweeteners points out that most studies focus on tests of these sweeteners in their pure form with animals and people who had been given no other food. Long-term studies correlating consumption of fructose with the mixed meals of diabetics are needed before firm recommendations can be made, the ADA review paper indicated.

As Davidson, the Atlanta diabetologist, put it:
"I am a hard scientist, and I don't think you should compromise by saying: 'Well, maybe it's all right, and maybe it's not.' Nobody has done anything except short term experiments, mostly on animals and a few humans."

When the Diabetes Association published an update of its 1971 Nutrition and Dietary Guidelines recently, the ADA noted that the amounts of fructose, xylitol, sorbitol, and mannitol acceptable in a food plan for diabetic persons is "uncertain at present" and that there is not enough evidence to accept or reject the use of these substances by diabetics. Dr. Ronald A. Arky, ADA's president, acknowledged that his organization's published comments were aimed, in part, at discouraging the use of the nonglucose sweeteners by diabetics.

"My own feelings are that if you are going to use them, use them in moderation," he added. "But, it's the same old story. How do you get moderation from the public? And how can you be sure the public maintains consumption at a moderate level when you consider both individual eating tastes and needs as well as the volumes of products people can be exposed to with these sweeteners in them."

Dr. Victor Fratalli, assistant to the associate director for nutrition and food sciences at FDA, put it this way:
"You may have some bits and pieces of evidence here and there that some say demonstrate that the nonglucose sweeteners produce a beneficial effect. But let's not try to make any unqualified statements regarding benefits of substances to give people the wrong impression now, and then a couple of years later have to tell them to 'hold the phone' because there are some problems as a result of people consuming them in large amounts.

"It's almost impossible to reverse such trends. Once people get the notion through partly true statements that something may be useful, then they convince themselves that a thing is useful, and there isn't anything in the world that will turn them around."

A report prepared for FDA by the Federation of American Societies for Experimental Biology (FASEB), on the health aspects of fructose, indicated that most diabetologists, in this country at least, are not recommending its use to their patients. FASEB's 1976 study—which is based on a comprehensive review of scientific literature—expressed this conclusion: "It is the prevailing medical opinion that there are no clinical advantages of substituting fructose for glucose either orally or parenterally (intravenously) in any disease state."

The public misunderstanding and lack of unanimity in the medical and scientific community over the merits of fructose led Fratalli to comment:
"You are not dealing with a black-white issue here, and that is the whole problem. There is a difference in the way the body handles these nutritive sweeteners, but, as far as I'm concerned, the difference for diabetics is not so significant as to classify fructose as a substance apart from sucrose."

The same can be said, he added, on the use of the nonglucose sweeteners by nondiabetics. "Any argument one tries to develop that indicates these nutritive sweeteners are beneficial in weight reduction is very tenuous. What you are doing is substituting one carbohydrate for another."

The differences of opinion that may exist over the value of pure fructose are not apparent with high fructose corn sirup. Health experts view it as they do any other sugar that diabetics should restrict from their diet. Not all high fructose sirups are the same either. Some are produced with 42 percent fructose in them, others have 55 percent, still others have 90 percent. The balance is mostly glucose or dextrose as it is sometimes identified on food labels.

Davidson had this comment about the variations by manufacturers:
"Don't you think that's bamboozling the public? They don't tell them they've got glucose in them, yet they push the idea that fructose can be used by diabetics and obese people without telling them the consequences."

For diabetics, Davidson sees little difference between pure fructose and high fructose corn sirups. "Neither one is preferable," he said. "Over 90 percent of the diabetics in this country have what we call obesity-induced diabetes as a result of having ingested too many Calories. They cannot be treated effectively with insulin and pills. The only way they can be treated is to lose weight. Whereas there is a tremendous need by this segment of the population for a non-nutritive sweetener, such as saccharin, there is no need whatsoever for additional nutritive sweeteners, such as fructose, sorbitol, or what have you. These people need less food, not more."

Pure fructose is a dry, crystalline sugar that is produced from sucrose by separating it from the glucose component and then purifying it. To obtain pure fructose from such sources as honey (which is 40 percent fructose) and fruits would be "prohibitively expensive," according to one distributor.

Almost all the high fructose corn sirups are derived from the starch in corn. Extensive milling extracts the starch from the corn. The starch is liquefied and treated with enzymes to convert it into a glucose corn sirup. Further processing converts the glucose into the fructose sirup. The enzymatic transformation of glucose to fructose is known as isomerization.

Fructose can be purchased over the counter at health food stores and some supermarkets in liquid, powder, tablet, or granular form at a price considerably above that paid for regular table sugar. A recent check of four health food stores in the Washington, D.C., area indicated that:

- Granular or crystalline fructose—with 4 Calories per gram—was selling for $3.70 to $4.44 a pound.
- A box of 100 two-gram tablets (8 Calories to the tablet) were priced from $3.95 to $4.15. That's the equivalent of $8.98 to $9.43 a pound.
- A 5-ounce container with 50 packets of powdered fructose (11 Calories to a packet) was priced from $1.90 to $2.20. This amounts to $6.08 to $7.04 a pound.
- Liquid fructose sold for $1.49 for a 16-ounce portion. Other stores sold a 23-ounce container for $2.89 to $3.13. A half teaspoon of the liquid provides 12 Calories. The liquid fructose, however, actually was a corn sirup with 90 percent fructose. On a dry weight basis, this would amount to $3.85 to $4.17 a pound.

The industrial use of fructose-sweetened products is growing and is of concern to many health professionals, particularly since most of the sugar that we consume is added to foods by producers. In other words, the consumer has less control over the amount of sugar in food as industrial use increases. The U.S. Department of Agriculture reports that annual per capita consumption of high fructose corn sirups rose from less than a pound in 1970 to an estimated 15 pounds last year. The soft drink industry is the heaviest user of both high fructose corn sirup and refined cane and beet sugar.

Overconsumption of some of the nonglucose sweeteners also could have an unpleasant side effect, namely diarrhea, according to the ADA and various FASEB reports prepared for FDA. For example, these reports indicated that diarrhea could be induced by consumption, in a day, of 10 to 20 grams of mannitol, 20 to 30 grams of sorbitol, 30 to 40 grams of xylitol, and 70 to 100 grams of fructose. It is considered unlikely that most people would consume this much fructose in a day. However, the potential for the other three sweeteners to cause diarrhea tends to limit their usefulness.

Diabetologists and nutritionists also question whether using fructose as a substitute for sucrose is effective in reducing weight. The argument has been made that since fructose is sweeter than sucrose, one could use less fructose and get the same sweetening effect with fewer Calories.

However, fructose's sweetness depends on how it is used in food and drink. It can be 15 to 80 percent sweeter than sucrose, but its sweetness, according to one FASEB study, decreases as temperature, amount of fructose, and acidity are decreased. This was demonstrated with four prepared products in a 1978 study by Utah State University's Department of Nutrition and Food Sciences.

Sugar cookies, white cake, vanilla pudding, and lemonade were chosen for the study because they represented a wide variety of products, and their degree of sweetness and flavor would not be masked by other ingredients. That study concluded that fructose was not sweeter than sucrose in the cookies, cake, and pudding. Only in lemonade, when compared on an equal weight basis, was fructose considered sweeter by the taste panels who took part in the study.

The updated dietary guidelines of the ADA place much more stress on exercising total Calorie control and sticking to a carefully supervised diet than on which sugar one should use. It warned diabetics against all nutritionally imbalanced "fad" diets, especially the "commercially available, high protein mixtures that contain low quality protein for use in modified starvation diets."

As a general rule, the ADA said, a nutritionally adequate diet should include 12 to 20 percent protein, 50 to 60 percent carbohydrate (with emphasis on complex carbohydrate), and the balance fat. Saturated fatty acids should constitute less than 10 percent of the total Calories and polyunsaturated fats should supply up to 10 percent of intake, it recommended.

Although advocates of low carbohydrate diets believe such diets promote rapid weight loss, FDA nutritionists indicate that any weight loss usually is temporary and that lost pounds return rapidly when regular meal patterns are resumed. FDA's recommendation is that, for long-term reduction in weight, the most successful diet includes regular meals and only small changes in the foods usually eaten.

SWEETENERS

The Sweet and Sour History of Saccharin, Cyclamate, Aspartame

by Chris W. Lecos

Sometimes playing a very vocal role, the American consumer for more than a decade now has been in the middle of a seemingly unending controversy over three well-known artificial sweeteners—saccharin, cyclamate, and aspartame. All have received wide publicity over the years. All have been subjected to long, sometimes tortuous review, scrutiny, and debate by industry, scientists, and Federal regulators.

Saccharin, a sweetener with no calories, has been around the longest. Discovered in 1879, it was used initially as an antiseptic and as a food preservative. Soon diabetics were using it. However, the canning industry showed no strong interest until around 1907—the same year that President Theodore Roosevelt voiced this irate reaction to warnings about its use in canned foods:

"You tell me that saccharin is injurious to health? My doctor gives it to me every day. Anybody who says saccharin is injurious to health is an idiot."

Roosevelt was responding to the concerns of Dr. Harvey W. Wiley, then chief of the Bureau of Chemistry in the Department of Agriculture. Wiley felt that artificial sweeteners like saccharin offered no food value and were used by industry primarily because they were cheaper than regular sugar. Just a year earlier, Wiley had helped win passage of this country's first food and drugs law.

Saccharin dominated the artificial sweetener market for more than 60 years but was supplanted by cyclamate in the 1950's and 1960's. FDA had approved cyclamate for commercial food uses in 1951. Cyclamate, also noncaloric, was used widely in canned fruits, chewing gum, toothpastes, and mouthwashes as well as in other foods. Its use boomed with the diet soda craze that began in the early 1960's. As a table-top sweetener, it was marketed under the trade name "Sucaryl," and was promoted for obese persons and diabetics. Sucaryl actually was a mixture of 10 parts cyclamate and 1 part saccharin. The latter is much sweeter but cyclamate cut the bitter aftertaste of saccharin.

All this halted when questions over the safety and cancer-causing potential of cyclamate surfaced, prompting FDA to ban its continued use in 1970. The artificial sweetener market was again saccharin's. Aspartame—a synthetic compound that has the same food value of four calories to the gram as sugar but which is substantially sweeter—was approved by FDA in 1974. However, the Agency was compelled to withdraw approval of aspartame when questions were raised about its safety and the validity of the animal test data submitted. In July 1981, the Agency again approved aspartame, thereby once again making a choice of sweeteners available to the public.

Here is some further background on the tangled histories of these three compounds:

Saccharin

Today, an estimated 50 to 70 million Americans are considered fairly regular consumers of saccharin, including one-third of the Nation's children under the age of 10, according to a report submitted to Congress in 1978 by the National Academy of Sciences (NAS). Dieters, diabetics, and diet soda drinkers make up a substantial portion of those consumers. It has been estimated that 6 million pounds of saccharin are consumed annually, about three-fourths in soft drinks. The next major use is as a table-top sweetener. The Calorie Control Council, an industry group and an influential proponent of saccharin use, last year estimated that there was a $2 billion annual market for saccharin.

Made from petroleum materials, saccharin is a product of the Sherwin-Williams Paint Company, the sole U.S. producer. More than 2 million pounds is imported annually, mainly from Japan and Korea.

FDA proposed banning most uses of saccharin in 1977 when various studies showed that the chemical caused bladder tumors in rats. However, the public protest was so strong—FDA alone received 100,000 public comments, mostly opposing any ban—that Congress, in November 1977, imposed an 18-month moratorium against any action. The moratorium was extended to June 30, 1981, and most recently to 1983.

What is sometimes a puzzle to the general public is how a product such as saccharin, with a history of more than 100 years of use, can be deemed a hazard to public health. In part, at least, the answer rests with three factors: time, the progress of science, and the demands of law. The status of saccharin, and cyclamate as well,

---

From *FDA Consumer*, September 1981, pp. 8-11. Published by U.S. Food and Drug Administration.

started to change with Congress' passage in 1958 of the Food Additives Amendment to the Food, Drug, and Cosmetic Act. The essence of the 1958 legislation was that it placed upon industry the burden of proving the safety of any new food additive. That proof had to be established before an additive could be marketed. In addition, it provided that no new food additive could be deemed safe by FDA if animal feeding tests showed that the additive caused cancer or if other appropriate tests demonstrated it to be a cancer-producing substance. In effect, FDA was required to prohibit any substance that could cause cancer in animal or man.

The legislation, however, applied to new additives coming on the market. Because of their prior use status, saccharin and cyclamate joined a host of other food compounds and were classified by FDA as substances that were "generally recognized as safe." The classification is commonly referred to as FDA's GRAS list.

In 1968 the Committee on Food Protection of the National Academy of Sciences–National Research Council issued an interim report on the safety of non-nutritive sweeteners, including saccharin. The committee said that although an adult's daily consumption of one gram of saccharin or less probably is no hazard, available studies on the cancer-causing potential of saccharin were inadequate. Additional studies were urged and this recommendation was repeated 2 years later. Pending completion of the ongoing studies, FDA decided in 1972 to remove saccharin from the GRAS list, and established interim limits on the amount of saccharin allowed in processed foods and drinks.

Although concern over the safety of saccharin was growing, as late as 1974 a National Academy of Sciences committee was reporting that the available scientific data had "not established conclusively whether saccharin is or is not carcinogenic when administered orally to the animals."

Despite that position, two studies did raise some troubling questions. One was a 1972 study by the Wisconsin Alumni Research Foundation; the other was an FDA study completed in 1973. In both tests, male and female rats were fed a diet of saccharin from the time of weaning. The offspring of these rats, from the time of pregnancy to growth and death, also were given saccharin diets. The incidence of bladder tumors was considered significant in both tests. But, was saccharin the culprit or was some impurity in it responsible?

In February 1974, Canada's Health Protection Branch, that country's counterpart to FDA, initiated a major study to resolve the uncertainties noted in the 1974 NAS report. The Canadian project focused on the effects of an impurity, orthotoluensulfonamide (OTS). The project was also a two-generation study in which the parent rats and their offspring were fed saccharin. Some groups of rats received different levels of OTS; one group got only purified saccharin; a control group was given neither saccharin nor OTS.

The study concluded in early 1977 that neither the impurity OTS nor bladder parasites, nor bladder stones were causing the cancer in the animals. The carcinogen responsible, the study showed, was saccharin. The study was reviewed by scientific experts in the United States, Canada, Great Britain, and Europe. Soon afterward, FDA reported in the FEDERAL REGISTER: "The findings indicate unequivocally that saccharin causes bladder cancer in test animals."

Despite public protests as clamorous as those in the United States, Canada banned all uses of saccharin except as a table-top sweetener to be sold only in pharmacies, and then only with a warning label.

With the Canadian study now confirming the two earlier studies, FDA announced its intention to prohibit the use of saccharin in foods, and on April 15, 1977, the Agency published its proposal to revoke the interim food additive regulation that allowed saccharin's use in foods, beverages, and cosmetics and in most drugs. The Agency said it was prepared to allow sale of saccharin as an over-the-counter drug (in the form of a table-top sweetener) if its value to diabetics and obese persons could be established. The ensuing public outcry led to Congress' passage of the Saccharin Study and Labeling Act in November of that year.

The law, however, did impose a requirement—still in force—for warning labels on foods containing saccharin and for the display of warning signs in establishments selling products with saccharin. Congress also directed FDA to arrange for further studies and evaluations of carcinogens and toxic substances in foods, including saccharin, and to determine possible health benefits resulting from the use of non-nutritive sweeteners. FDA contracted with the National Academy of Sciences for these studies.

The first NAS report, issued in November 1978, concluded that saccharin was a carcinogen in animals, although of low potency; that it was a potential cancer-causing agent in humans; that the impurities in saccharin were not the carcinogenic agents; that saccharin seemed to promote the cancer-causing effects of other carcinogenic agents.

The second NAS report, sent to Congress in March 1979, called for an overhaul of the entire food safety law—changes that could give FDA a range of options in regulating substances like saccharin. HHS Secretary Schweiker, in a speech before the Food and Drug Law Institute last June 8, said he was working closely with FDA Commissioner Arthur Hull Hayes, Jr. to develop "a reasonable and rational approach to food policy." He also said: "I don't have any preconceived ideas on what kinds of recommendations I expect. But I know we need to shift our thinking away from the notion that we can have a risk-free society. As the case of saccharin demonstrates so vividly, there are few things in our society today that are zero risk. Nearly all products have both a risk and a benefit."

Three human epidemiology studies released in 1980 led to further conclusions and some varying interpretations on the risks posed by saccharin. One study by the National Cancer Institute (NCI) (co-sponsored by FDA) that involved 9,000 people found no added risk to the study population as a whole from artificial sweeteners but a possible risk to some subgroups: heavy users of artificial sweeteners, especially those who consumed diet sodas and sugar substitutes, and heavy smokers who also were heavy users of artificial sweeteners. Women who consumed sugar substitutes or diet beverages at least twice a day had 60 percent greater risk of bladder cancer than women who never used them.

Commenting in an editorial published on March 6, 1980, in the NEW ENGLAND JOURNAL OF MEDICINE, Dr. Robert Hoover, Director of the Environmental Epidemiology Branch at NCI, voiced this view on the NCI-FDA study and the Harvard study:

"... The findings of these studies can be interpreted as being consistent with the laboratory (animal) evidence suggesting that saccharin is a weak carcinogen. On the other hand, the findings can also be interpreted as showing no evidence of carcinogenicity . . . . . The correct or more prudent interpretation will probably be a matter for conjecture and debate for some time . . . ."

But Hoover also added: "... When all the evidence of toxicity is weighed against the lack of objective evidence of benefit, any use (of saccharin) by nondiabetic children or pregnant women, heavy use by young women of childbearing age, and excessive use by anyone are ill-advised and should be actively discouraged by the medical community."

A second study by Harvard University's School of Public Health involved 592 cancer patients and 536 controls. The report said: "The results of this study suggest that, as a group, users of artificial sweeteners have little or no excess risk of cancer of the lower urinary tract." It also said: "The evidence available is consistent with a number of interpretations. One is that the exposures that have been sustained to artificial sweeteners are not carcinogenic for the human bladder . . . . A second interpretation is that artificial sweeteners are carcinogens but weak enough for their effects to be difficult to perceive . . . . A third interpretation is that sufficient time for an obvious carcinogenic effect to appear has not yet elapsed since relatively heavy exposure to artificial sweeteners began in the 1960's. . . ."

The third study by the American Health Foundation involved 367 cancer patients and 367 controls and it found "no association . . . between use of artificial sweeteners or diet beverages and bladder cancer."

Epidemiology studies, however, also have their limitations. They are not always sensitive enough to make accurate estimates of risk to humans and, unless large enough numbers of people are involved, measuring risk is especially difficult in evaluating the effects of substances such as saccharin that are viewed as weak carcinogens.

Cyclamate

Discovered by accident in 1937 by a University of Illinois chemist, cyclamate dominated the artificial sweetener market for nearly 20 years until FDA banned it from foods, beverages, and drugs as of September 11, 1970. The sweetener at one time was so widely used that sales totaled a billion dollars a year and consumption ran as high as 18 million pounds a year.

Its sponsor, Abbott Laboratories, North Chicago, Ill., came back to FDA with a new petition on November 15, 1973, seeking permission for cyclamate as a sweetener in foods for special dietary use and for specific technological purposes. The petition included more than 400 toxicological reports with assessments on its carcinogenicity, mutagenicity (causing genetic damage), and effect on metabolism. All of the material was obtained after 1970.

In March 1976, FDA received a National Cancer Institute report that said that Abbott's evidence did not establish or refute the cancer-causing potential of cyclamate. FDA concurred and informed the company that its evidence did not demonstrate "to a reasonable certainty" that cyclamate was safe for human consumption.

Here again was a situation where, under the law, the burden of proving safety was the company's responsibility, not the Agency's. FDA asked Abbott to drop its petition but the company refused, and in the ensuing years it pressed its case at hearings before an administrative law judge and in Federal courts.

Its fate was not resolved until September 4, 1980, when former FDA Commissioner Jere E. Goyan issued the final decision denying the 7-year-old petition. In brief, FDA took the position that the safety of cyclamate had not been demonstrated, that it had not been shown that cyclamate *would not* cause cancer and *would not* cause inheritable genetic damage. Goyan's decision reaffirmed the earlier rulings of an administrative law judge who had conducted hearings.

Many who followed the cyclamate case closely saw it as a classic example of how complex and subtle the applications and interpretations of the Food, Drug, and Cosmetic Act must be. The wording of the decision is important because the decision, in essence, is based on what the company's evidence did NOT show. In the case of cyclamate, FDA said that safety had not been adequately demonstrated. It did not say that the product could cause cancer. In fact, the Goyan decision noted that the evidence submitted "does not conclusively establish that cyclamate is a carcinogen."

The section of the 1958 legislation that was mainly involved in Goyan's decision was the "general safety clause." This clause applies to a wide range of adverse health effects, including the potential carcinogenicity and mutagenicity of an additive to food. Under this clause, FDA can allow the use of a substance only if the data submitted establish that the proposed use "will be safe."

To determine whether a petitioner has met the requirement, the Goyan decision noted, FDA must arrive at one of three possible conclusions: One, that the evidence establishes the safety of an additive; two, the evidence shows it is unsafe; or three, that the evidence "is such that the safety of the additive is unknown or uncertain." If faced with either the second or third alternative, the Commissioner noted, the Agency must deny the petition.

"Safety" is not defined by the law but, based on what it felt was Congress' intent, FDA interprets it to mean that a food additive is safe if "there is a reasonable certainty in the minds of competent scientists that the substance is not harmful under the intended conditions of use."

In the cyclamate case, Goyan noted that many of the studies contained deficiencies and were inadequate in trying to prove safety of lack or safety. Of the studies given greater weight, "a significant number suggests, though they do not prove, that cyclamate is a carcinogen and a mutagen," he said. And he added:

"Those studies in the record in which no carcinogenic or mutagenic effect was found are either too insensitive to rely on as proof of safety or do not detract sufficiently from the studies which suggest that cyclamate is a carcinogen or mutagen. In these circumstances, the petition must fail, for evidence supporting it does not establish the safety of cyclamate."

Following the decision, a spokesman for Abbott Laboratories announced that the company did not plan to appeal to the Federal courts. The time for doing so has now run out. If the company decides to seek reconsideration of cyclamate, it would have to file a new petition with new supporting data to FDA, an Agency spokesman said.

(A more detailed account on cyclamate appeared in the Dec. 1974–Jan. 1975 issue of FDA CONSUMER.)

Aspartame

Three years after the cyclamate ban, G. D. Searle & Co., Skokie, Ill., petitioned FDA (on March 5, 1973) to approve aspartame's use as a sweetener for table use; as a tablet for hot beverages, for use in cold cereals; as a dry base sweetener for powdered beverages, instant coffee and tea, gelatins, puddings, fillings, and dessert toppings; and as a flavoring agent in chewing gum.

Aspartame also has the same food value—four calories to the gram—as regular sugar, so its main appeal to calorie-conscious Americans lies in the fact that it is about 180 times sweeter than ordinary table sugar. A teaspoon of sugar has 18 calories; aspartame would provide only one-tenth of a calorie for the same amount of sweetness in a teaspoon of sugar. Saccharin, however, is 10 times sweeter than aspartame, but one of aspartame's appeals is that it has no bitter after-taste.

Also discovered accidentally—by a Searle scientist in 1965 who was doing research on new ulcer drugs—aspartame is a synthetic compound comprised of two amino acids, L-aspartic acid and the ethyl ester of L-phenylalanine. Unlike the other two sweeteners, aspartame was a new food additive that came under the full purview of the 1958 food additive legislation and, therefore, required premarket clearance. FDA approved the Searle petition on July 26, 1974, for the uses described above, but challenges over the substance's safety and the validity of the company's data prevented the chemical from ever being marketed. At issue was whether aspartame, either alone or together with glutamate, posed a risk of contributing to mental retardation, brain damage, or to causing undesirable effects on the neuroendocrine (hormone-nerve) systems, and whether the sweetener might cause brain neoplasms (tumors) in rats.

There was agreement among all the parties involved to conduct a formal hearing before a scientific board of inquiry, which would then make a recommendation to the FDA commissioner on whether to approve or disapprove aspartame. But before that board could convene, another problem arose. Questions were raised about the authenticity of certain animal studies conducted for Searle, and FDA wanted to resolve this issue before proceeding with the hearing. The company agreed to fund an independent review of the aspartame data by an outside group of pathologists.

Their report was submitted to FDA in December 1978, and concluded that the data were in fact authentic. The Agency then went ahead with its board of inquiry, which met in January and February 1980. The three university scientists on the board concluded that the evidence did not support the charge that aspartame might kill clusters of brail cells. But the panel recommended that approval be withheld until further, long-term animal tests could be conducted to rule out a possibility that aspartame might cause brain tumors.

On July 15, 1981, the new Commissioner of FDA, Dr. Arthur Hull Hayes Jr., announced the approval of aspartame. He based his approval on the board's findings, recommendations by FDA's Bureau of Foods, and the independent review of Searle's data. Dr. Hayes found the product to be safe at expected levels of consumption, as well as at the highest conceivable levels. (FDA will require the manufacturer to monitor consumption levels.)

The approval of aspartame opened a new chapter in the continuing saga of artificial sweeteners.

SWEETENERS

Saccharin Unsafe—Despite the Headlines

by Michael Jacobson, Ph.D.

"Saccharin Scare Debunked" was the headline in the *Washington Post*. "Harvard Study Fails to Link Saccharin to Risk of Cancer," was the *Wall Street Journal's* headline. Is it true that saccharin, which is loved dearly by many an American, is safe after all, even though FDA has proposed banning it?

Unfortunately, the data are not nearly as rosy as the newspaper headlines would have the reader believe. In fact, the FDA's Associate Commissioner for Public Affairs, Wayne Pines, complained to the *Washington Post,* saying ". . . the headlines were wrong. Your story pointed out that while new studies show no increased risk of bladder cancer among the general public, there is still a risk—among children, youths, heavy saccharin users, users who smoke, and women who are pregnant. It seems to me that's a pretty sizable population."

There were two recent epidemiological studies, one done at Harvard University, the other done at the American Health Foundation (AHF) in New York City. The Harvard study involved 1,128 subjects, while the AHF study involved only 734. Both studies were much smaller—and thus less sensitive—than a 9,000-person study sponsored by the FDA and the National Cancer Institute.

Both the NCI/FDA and Harvard studies gave evidence of an increased risk of bladder cancer for women who did not smoke. Inasmuch as smoking promotes bladder cancer, it is harder to detect an increase in bladder cancer caused by artificial sweeteners in people who smoke. The high rate of cancer caused by smoking tends to obscure the relatively smaller number of cancers that are caused by the artificial sweeteners. In the NCI/FDA study, however, but not the Harvard study, there was evidence of increased risk for heavy smokers (men and women) who were also heavy users of artificial sweeteners.

In both studies, when the bladder cancer rates for the more susceptible and less susceptible segments of the population were combined, no overall risk was seen. This is what the newspaper headlines highlighted.

The least sensitive study (AHF) did not detect an increased risk of bladder cancer in people who consumed artificial sweeteners. However, only 65 women with bladder cancer were studied and only four of these women drank four or more diet beverages a day. Because of the small number of subjects, this study would not detect increased risks due to saccharin unless there was a 50 percent increase in men or 180 percent in women.

All three studies suffered from numerous deficiencies, such as (1) looking only at bladder cancer; (2) not distinguishing between cyclamate and saccharin; (3) not being able to determine exact usage levels of artificial sweeteners; (4) not controlling for all variables, such as drug usage; (5) including a high percentage of old people, who did not consume saccharin from childhood; (6) limited size and sensitivity.

In view of the weaknesses of the epidemiological studies, Dr. Robert Hoover, of the National Cancer Institute, said in an editorial in the *New England Journal of Medicine,* that "the pinpointing of relatively small but potentially important increases in human risk (up to 30 percent) is practically impossible because of the influence of both known and unknown background factors."

Hoover concluded, "When all the evidence of toxicity is weighted against the lack of objective evidence of benefit, any use of nondiabetic children or pregnant women, heavy use by young women of childbearing age, and excessive use by anyone are ill-advised and should be actively discouraged by the medical community."

FDA Commissioner Jere Goyan said in December, "I reiterate my concern about the consumption by so many Americans, especially young people, of large amounts of saccharin. More than half the subjects in the (FDA/NCI) study were 67 years old or older, and therefore consumed much less artificial sweeteners than their children and grandchildren are today. We may have to wait 20 or 30 years to assess the possible effects on our young people of consuming large amounts of a weak carcinogen."

Taken together, the two positive studies and one smaller negative study support the conclusion drawn from earlier animal studies: saccharin is a weak carcinogen. In view of this, Cumberland Packing Company's recent ad for "Sweet 'N Low" (saccharin) in the *Journal of the American Dietetic Association* falls somewhere between the ludicrous and the malevolent. Some of the text reads, "That's why wherever smart people go, they're switching to Sweet 'n Low . . . It makes good sense! . . . Recommend Sweet 'n Low . . .because you care."

From *Nutrition Action*, Vol. 7, No. 4, April 1980, pp. 11-12. Copyright 1980, Center for Science in the Public Institute. CSPI membership is available to the public for $20.00 per year. Reprinted with permission.

SWEETENERS

Saccharin's Influence on Lipid Metabolism Is Related to Dietary Fat and Carbohydrate

by Anna Watkins and Catherine Carroll, Ph.D.

The Food and Drug Administration made plans to ban saccharin from the food supply in March, 1977, when saccharin was found to cause cancer in laboratory animals. Controversy over the proposed ban has been so great that Congress has twice postponed a decision on this matter, leaving saccharin on grocery shelves until at least June 30, 1981.

Meanwhile, an analysis aimed at determining what effects saccharin might have on the body should play a part in this risk-benefit analysis.

This experiment was conducted to study the influence of saccharin on the lipid (fat) contents of liver, serum, and adipose tissue in white rats. When investigating the metabolic effects of a single substance, such as saccharin, it is important to consider other dietary components as well. Previous experiments in this laboratory have shown that the kinds of fat and carbohydrate in the diet make a difference in lipid metabolism.

Young, male rats were fed diets that differed in type of fat (safflower oil or beef tallow) and proportion of sucrose (sugar) and rich starch (20 percent sucrose with 20 percent rice starch and 8 percent sucrose with 32 percent rice starch, by weight). The diets were fed with and without saccharin. The amount of fat and carbohydrate were calculated to be similar to those in the average American diet. When saccharin was fed it made up 0.05 percent of the ration weight, a level that would be considered high for humans, but not excessive. The level that produced cancer in rats was 5 percent of the diet, or 100 times the amount used in this experiment.

We found higher concentrations of total lipid and cholesterol in the liver, and lower levels of triglyceride in the serum, when rats were fed safflower oil (SO) instead of beef tallow (BT) (see table). Both serum cholesterol and serum triglyceride levels were higher when rats were fed diets containing more sucrose.

Saccharin's influence on body lipids was indirect, in the form of interactions with fat. Addition of saccharin to SO diets reduced levels of liver lipid, serum cholesterol, and adipose tissue; however, addition of saccharin to BT diets increased those values.

The results of this experiment indicate that dietary fat and carbohydrate exert stronger influences on lipid metabolism than saccharin does. However, effects of fat were modified when saccharin was added to the diet. It is difficult to determine whether saccharin's influence on lipid metabolism poses a risk or a benefit to health. The effects of fat-saccharin combinations might prove to be better indications of risk or benefit.

In assessing the risks and benefits of the fat-saccharin combinations used in this experiment, two possible applications come to mind. First, the interaction between fat and saccharin, which produced changes in the amount of lipid deposited in liver and adipose tissue, would be of interest to the many people who consume saccharin in order to reduce weight. Second, the changes in serum cholesterol levels due to the fat-saccharin combinations could be linked to coronary heart disease, since elevated serum cholesterol levels are associated with the development of coronary heart disease.

We cannot conclude from this research that saccharin fed with safflower oil would benefit humans by lessening fat deposition in the liver and adipose tissue and lowering serum cholesterol levels; nor can we conclude that saccharin added to beef tallow diets would be a risk because of increased lipid levels. Many other factors must be taken into consideration and more research must be done to see if these effects occur when other variables are introduced.

Lipid Values in Liver, Serum, and Adipose Tissue of Rats Fed Different Fat, Carbohydrate, and Saccharin Combinations

Variables[1]	Liver Total lipid	Liver Cholesterol	Serum Cholesterol	Serum Triglycerides	Adipose tissue, total lipid
	mg/100 mg liver N[2]		mg/100 ml serum[2]		mg/100 g body wt.[2]
Fat					
SO	231 ± 12[a]	21.5 ± 1.3[a]	97 ± 2	105 ± 13[a]	922 ± 53
BT	169 ± 12	10.5 ± 1.3	99 ± 2	256 ± 13	1044 ± 54
Carbohydrate					
20 percent Suc	198 ± 13	15.6 ± 1.3	101 ± 3[b]	211 ± 13[b]	923 ± 55
8 percent Suc	203 ± 12	16.3 ± 1.2	94 ± 2	151 ± 13	974 ± 51
Saccharin					
− Sacc	214 ± 12	17.3 ± 1.3	96 ± 2	166 ± 13	989 ± 54
+ Sacc	186 ± 12	14.7 ± 1.3	99 ± 2	196 ± 13	977 ± 53
Significant fat x saccharin interactions					
SO. − Sacc	271[3]	—	99	—	1019
SO. + Sacc	192	—	94	—	826
BT. − Sacc	158	—	93	—	960
ET. + Sacc	180	—	104	—	1129

[1] Abbreviations: SO. safflower oil: BT. beef tallow: Suc. sucrose: − Sacc. without saccharin: + Sacc. with saccharin.
[2] Mean ± standard error.
[3] Derived mean.
[a] Significantly different from rats fed BT. Data examined by analysis of variance. P less than 0.05 by "F" test.
[b] Significantly different from rats fed 8 percent Suc.

NUTRITION FROM CONCEPTION THROUGH ADOLESCENCE

In the beginning, nutrition is provided by the mother. What she ingests during the nine months of her pregnancy—beyond if she is breast-feeding—can affect her child, sometimes her life.

Recognizing the increased nutritional demands of pregnancy and lactation, the National Academy of Sciences-National Research Council's Recommended Dietary Allowances (RDAs) provide for increases of 30 and 20 grams of protein daily for pregnant and lactating mothers, respectively. Other nutrient percentage increases range from 20 to 100 percent.

For many people, the consumption of caffeine starts early, even before birth. Caffeine is carried in the mother's bloodstream and crosses the placenta to reach the fetus. It also appears in the milk of mothers who breast-feed. In fact, new evidence confirming earlier research that caffeine causes irreversible birth defects in rats has prompted the Department of Health and Human Services (DHHS) to begin a proposal to develop more studies on the drug's health implications.

Many other elements that a mother ingests can also affect lactation and/or her infant, including environmental ones. In fact, most medications can be excreted to some degree in human breast milk. Usually, when a drug is taken for short periods of time under a physician's direction, the drug level remains low enough to pose little hazard to the infant. However, certain drugs should be specifically avoided during lactation.

Few drugs carry the same long-term consequences as maternal ingestion of large quantities of alcohol. Fetal alcohol syndrome has been described as microcephaly, micrognathia, microphthalamia, cardiac defects, and prenatal and postnatal growth retardation (small brain, small nose and chin, and deformed eye development, as well as serious heart deformities). However, alcohol frequently teams with one or more other medical problems including smoking, drug abuse, overall poor nutrtion, and sociological factors. Although it is difficult to define how much is too much, most scientists concur that maternal alcohol consumption contributes to physical abnormalities at birth and in early life, as well as to inadequate mothering practices.

Human milk or prepared formula in amounts producing normal growth patterns contain all the nutrients needed for the first six months of life. When supplementary foods are first introduced, many physicians believe it is important that the infant learn to enjoy foods of differing tastes and colors. General assessments of infant menus are included in this section.

Children with chronic disease and/or developmental disabilities have special nutritional needs. Nutrient-drug interactions must be addressed. Similarly, feeding problems, inborn errors of metabolosm, cerebral palsy, cleft lip and/or palate, congenital heart disease, myelomeningocele, cystic fibrosis, and the newborn in the intensive care unit all require particular nutritional attention.

When compared to adults, newborns and children have greater susceptibility to many diseases because of both an immunological immaturity and lack of previous exposure to microbes. Ironically, the young child and the elderly lack many of the same adequate defense mechanisms. After maturity, some key host defense systems decline, which explains why many senior citizens die from infectious disease rather than old age.

Currently, child nutrition programs have been reduced and/or eliminated in the government's attempt to tighten its fiscal belt. However, the six programs that were available until 1981 should result in some interesting developments among the next generation of adults. A recent survey found that 83 percent of school children consume salted snack foods. The study also found, however, that most children consumed salted snack foods in moderation and had average daily nutrient intakes.

The physiologic and psychologic changes of adolescence can affect nutritional health. While the growth surge of adolescence increases nutrient requirements, psychological demands of maturing—breaking away—may produce behavior that makes it difficult to meet those nutritional needs. Two particular areas of concern are the underweight adolescent and the pregnant teenager.

For further information on:

- **Pregnancy and lactation** — See also "Adolescence" and part 3, "Medicinal Interactions"

- **Infancy** — See part 1, "Vitamins" and "Dietary Fiber"

- **Immunology** — See part 3, "Geriatric Needs"

- **Children** — See part 3, "Athletic Needs"

- **Adolescence** — See also "Pregnancy and Lactation" and part 3, "Athletic Needs"

PREGNANCY AND LACTATION

Nutritional Ages of Woman

by William J. Darby

This monograph concerns the relationship of nutrition to woman's health, the preconceptional nutriture of the mother, the dependence of the fetus and infant on the maternal organism, the subsequent physiologic eras of development and reproduction, and the postreproductive years of the aging woman. The data and interpretations presented are derived from somewhat framentary, albeit extensive, investigations dealing with the more distinct, nonconnected aspects of the nutrition of women. Some of these studies made in the 1940s and early 1950s covered the relationship of nutrition during pregnancy to the outcome of pregnancy and the health of the infant. They include the extensive investigations of Hoobler and Mack in Detroit; Scrimshaw and collaborators in Rochester; Ebbs, Tisdall, and coworkers in Toronto; Burke et al. in Boston; Dieckmann et al. in Chicago; and the Vanderbilt Cooperative Group in Nashville. The physiologic studies by Professor Hytten and his collaborators[6] represent still another aspect of this broad problem. These and related investigations are summarized in a report of the Committee on Maternal Nutrition of the Food and Nutrition Board[7] which provides an extensive bibliography of the literature up to 1970. A prior monograph of the Food and Nutrition Board prepared by Toverud, Stearns, and Macy[15] provides an excellent historical perspective on earlier studies of maternal nutrition and child health.

During the past 25 years, a broader spectrum of workers with everwidening interests and expanded approaches have introduced considerations more comprehensive than those of preceding investigators. Improved, more sensitive techniques have enabled the study of nutrients that previously could not be quantitated. Current journal articles carry exciting findings, such as those from the Human Nutrition Laboratory of the United States Department of Agriculture-Agricultural Research Service on the striking effect of trace element nutriture on pregnancy. An example is the effect of maternal zinc deficiency[8] on the reduction of fetal brain cell size, the complement of DNA, RNA, protein, and lipid in the liver, as well as the reduction of incorporation of thymidine into hepatic DNA. Of startling significance, sociologically, are reports of increased aggressiveness[5] in female offspring of zinc-deficient mothers (i.e., rat dams). Male offspring of these zinc-deficient dams exhibit impaired avoidance conditioning and decreased tolerance to stress. The intensive interest manifest today in the nutrition and metabolism of trace elements[12] was accelerated by human zinc deficiency studies reported by Prasad, Sandstead, and others of the Vanderbilt-NAMRU-3 (U.S. Naval Medical Research Unit Number 3) research group working in Cairo in the 1950s and 1960s.

Society's awareness of the importance of maintaining nutrition and of societal responsibility for assuring that food needs be fulfilled has resulted in new concern for improved understanding of the nutritional needs of the older population. Accordingly, there exists a new interest in the need to define the nutritional requirements of menopausal and postmenopausal woman. Such definition of requirements demands a greater understanding of both the physiologic and the social factors affecting women during the latter part of their life. Similarly, concern for one's exposure to environmental and nonfood influences has directed attention to the effects of smoking, alcohol ingestion, chronic drug therapy, and the use of metabolic regulators such as oral contraceptives. An awareness of the problems of the developing world and a better understanding of the limitations on the rate and type of social development are stimulating the reexamination of many accepted Western diet patterns and attitudes, including those surrounding the practices of breast-feeding and artificial feeding of infants. All of these influences are reflected in the content of this volume.

AGES OF WOMAN, AS MODIFIED FROM SHAKESPEARE

An appropriate classification of the nutritional ages of woman may be provided by taking minor liberties with a brief quotation from Shakespeare's As You Like It — i.e., changing and modernizing the Bard's enumeration of the ages of man to conform to the subject of woman.

> *All the world's a stage,*
> *And all men and women merely players:*
> *They have their exits and their entrances;*
> *And one woman in her time plays many parts,*

From *Nutritional Impacts on Women: Throughout Life with Emphasis on Reproduction*, edited by Kamran S. Moghissi, M.D., F.A.C.O.G., F.A.C.S., and Tommy N. Evans, M.D., F.A.C.O.G., F.A.C.S., pp. 1-9. Copyright 1977, Harper & Row, Publishers, Inc. Reprinted with permission.

*Her acts being five ages.
At first, the infant,
Mewlin and puking in the nurse's arms.
And then the whining school-girl,* with her satchel
And shining morning face, creeping like snail
Unwillingly to school. And then the lover,
*Sighing like furnace, to a woeful ballad
Played on her lover's lute.* And then the wife,
*Her fair round belly with growing fetus lin'd,
With work severe and dress of maternal cut.*
And then the lean and slippered pantaloon,
With spectacles on nose and T.V. on side . . .
With apologies to William Shakespeare

And as "one woman in her time plays many parts" — from infant to "lean and slippered pantaloon" — her nutritional needs change . . . from age to age, and even within an age. Let us briefly overview these nutritional ages.

"AT FIRST, THE INFANT"

During the first year of life, the body weight increases some 7 kg and the body's composition changes from 11 to 14.6% protein.[13] According to Fomon,[4] the increment in body protein is 3.5 g/day during the first 4 months of life and 3.1 g/day during the next 8 months. By the age of 4 years, body protein reaches the adult level of 18-19%. At birth, energy allowances are at a level of 120 kcal/kg/day and decrease to 100 kcal/kg by the end of the first year.

The corresponding need for lesser nutrients is such that food of high nutrient density, *i.e.,* high concentration of essential nutrients per 100 kilocalorie of energy, must be supplied to avoid deficiencies. Two striking consequences of this principle may be be cited. One is the widespread occurrence in the developing world of *kwashiorkor,* with its manifestation of protein deficiency and evidence of associated deficits of other nutrients (vitamin A, folic acid, tocopherol, and zinc, for example). Another consequence more familiar to us in the United States is the appearance of *iron deficiency anemia* as the infant approaches the end of its first year of life, a deficiency that results from the low nutrient density of iron in milk, a deficit that now, fortunately, is widely recognized and compensated for in practice.

Social Conditions and Infant Nutrition

The requirements of the infant and young child for sustenance of high nutrient density cannot be separated from its social implications. These are well considered in scholarly perspective by Aykroyd,[1] the first Director of the Nutrition Division of the Food and Agriculture Organization of the United Nations (FAO), and are worthy of mention here.

Aykroyd quotes Sir John Simon,[14] a great pioneer in public health, who, in 1861, wrote a description of the then existing social conditions and their consequences for infant feeding and health in England:

Factory women soon return to labour after their confinement. The longest time mentioned as the average period of the absence from work in consequence of child-bearing was five or six weeks; many women among the highest class of operatives in Birmingham acknowledged to having generally returned to work as early as eight or ten days after confinement. The mother's health suffers in consequence of this early return to labour . . . and the influence on the health and mortality of children is most baneful. . . . Mothers employed in factories are, save during the dinner hours, absent from home all day long, and the care of their infants during their absence is entrusted either to young children, to hired girls, sometimes not more than eight or ten years of age, or perhaps more commonly to elderly women, who eke out a livelihood by taking infants to nurse. . . . Pap, made of bread and water, and sweetened with sugar or treacle, is the sort of nourishment usually given during the mother's absence, even to infants of a very tender age. . . . Illness is the natural consequence of this unnatural mode of feeding infants. . . . Children who are healthy at birth rapidly dwindle under this system of mismanagement, fall into bad health, and become uneasy, restless and fractious. . . . Abundant proof of the large mortality among the children of female factory workers was obtained.[14]

In 1906, Newman[9] estimated that "hand-fed" infants had a lower chance of survival than did breast-fed infants by a mortality ratio of 3:1. These infants deprived of breast milk were given various substances as the principal article of diet: fresh milk diluted to different degrees; condensed milk, especially skimmed, sweetened, condensed milk; "starchy" foods such as bread, biscuits, oatmeal, and arrowroot; "patent" foods, usually consisting of malted starch, sugar, and some dried milk. All these foods and food mixtures were associated with high infant mortality. The worst were sweetened, skimmed, condensed milk and the starchy foods; diluted fresh milk gave somewhat better prospects of survival, but was usually lethal enough because of pollution and ignorance on the part of mothers of the proper degree of dilution. The "patent" foods varied in their effects; some were rather better than others. The quantities of substitutes for breast milk given to hand-fed infants were often insufficient so that undernutrition as well as malnutrition resulted.

His survey of infant mortality convinced Newman of the extreme importance of suitable infant feeding. "It is not everything," he said, "but a greater factor than any other thing. . . . Even the domestic and social conditions are reducible to terms of nourishment."

Aykroyd[1] notes the similarities of the conditions described in England 50 to 70 years ago with those that pertain to developing countries today: high infant mortality rate, predominating percentage of deaths in the postnatal period, high mortality in the second year of life, weanling diarrhea, measles as a serious disease, and unavailibility of suitable infant foods other than breast milk.

He then observes:

Whereas there may be a few discrepancies, it is reasonable to suppose that something like the complex of malnutrition and infection that we now call protein-calorie malnutrition [PCM] was prevalent in the affluent countries until recently, with disastrous effects on infant and child health. Clinical observations and vital statistics show that it has almost entirely disappeared from these countries. Its disappearance has been hastened by the establishment and development of maternal and child health services and centers (which began between 1900 and 1910), better housing and sanitation, and higher levels of education accompanied by a general rise in living standards.

The most important factor has been improvement in infant and child feeding, associated with the introduction of safe milk, processed infant foods, mixtures based on cow's milk, and the education of mothers in hygienic feeding methods. Greater reliance on breast milk has played no part in reducing infant mortality in the affluent countries [italics added], though it was strongly advocated by Newman and other authorities. In fact breast feeding has declined almost to the vanishing point during the last 40 to 50 years in most of these countries, a period that has seen a transformation in infant and child health.

Experience thus suggests that PCM (protein-calorie malnutrition) can be eliminated in a few decades by the establishment of adequate maternal and child health services, rising standards of living, and hygienic artifical feeding. Examples of this can be found not only in highly developed countries in the temperate zone, but also in poor countries in the tropics, e.g., Barbados and Puerto Rico. In unusual circumstances, the change can actually take place "at one bound," so to speak. With M.A. Hossain,[2] the author showed that when a community from an underdeveloped country was transferred to a well-developed country and adopted the infant feeding practices of the latter, its infant mortality rate immediately fell to something near the level prevailing in the new country. In this instance the fall took place in a Pakistani community that migrated to Bradford in Yorkshire, and affected the first infants born to women who had left home to join their husbands. The infantile mortality rate in the part of Pakistan from which the families came was about 150. In Bradford it was 45. The new environment meant, among other things, an abundance of cheap cow's milk in various forms and an absence of serious intestinal infections. Perhaps the most remarkable thing was the immediate and almost complete abandonment of breast feeding by the immigrant mothers, in spite of the fact that in Pakistan breast feeding is the accepted and traditional infant feeding practice, and an infant who is not breast-fed has little chance of survival.

After further consideration of the alternatives of breast feeding and artificial feeding, Aykroyd concludes:

Given these facts, the best approach to the problem of PCM seems at first sight to be to encourage breast feeding, to promote its retention where it still persists, or to promote a return to the practice where it has been abandoned. This is in line with the teaching of many authorities. But hitherto all attempts to do this have failed everywhere in the world, for reasons that have not been adequately studied. There do not seem to be any real prospects of retaining breast feeding in the spreading urban areas in the tropics where malnutrition is common and serious. Further, in the affluent countries, the virtual disappearance of breast feeding, the general use of processed cow's milk in the feeding of infants and young children, and the elimination of protein-calorie malnutrition have all coincided.

A more promising method of preventing PCM in the developing countries is to encourage the production and use of cheap feeding mixtures, based largely on plant foods that can fulfill the needs of the growing infant. A small percentage of milk powder enhances the nutritive value of such mixtures. Maternal and child health services and centers would, of course, be needed to teach mothers how to handle these mixtures and how to avoid infection. In other words, the aim would be a satisfactory artificial infant food made without cow's milk or with very little of it. The general adoption of this method of infant feeding in developing countries would not prevent the use of processed cow's milk preparations by those who could afford them nor breast feeding by mothers who favored it.

Aykroyd[1] reiterates in his summary:

Experience in the affluent countries has shown that this complex can be rapidly eliminated by efficient health services, rising standards of living, and hygienic artificial feeding. Greater reliance on breast feeding has played no part in its disappearance. The most promising method of attacking PCM in the developing countries is to promote the production and use of cheap feeding mixtures, based on plant foods that fulfill the infant's needs for calories, protein, and other nutrients.

I have quoted this at length because of the apparent lack of perspective manifest by some today who have not troubled to examine how the present state of infant care in our industrialized society has evolved.

"THEN THE WHINING SCHOOL-GIRL"

The velocity of growth of the child decreases from birth to 6-8 years, and nutritional demands are less in proportion to energy needs. The school girl, however, experiences a prepubertal spurt of growth at about 9 or 10 years of age, some 2 years earlier than that of boys. Indeed, she may become taller and larger at that period than a boy of the same age. At this time her energy requirement increases. As growth slows and puberty is followed by menstruation, nutrient demands undergo further alteration.

During subsequent adolescent growth, the energy requirement reaches a plateau, but requirements for protein, calcium, and other essential nutrients increases.[11,13] Hence, there is a greater need for food of high nutrient density. With the onset of menstruation, iron loss markedly increases, and the dietary allowance of this nutrient very nearly doubles, from 10 mg/day to 18 mg/day. It remains at this high level throughout the child-bearing ages — "the lover sighing like a furnace."

"AND THEN THE WIFE"

Woman's requirement of iron as a result of her physiologic loss is in decided contrast to man's need. Her requirement may become greatly exaggerated due to abnormal menstrual losses, common among women until completion of the menopause. These facts account for the prevalence of iron deficiency anemia among women in contrast to its relatively infrequent occurrence in men.

It behooves us to consider a widely misunderstood consequence of this physiologic need of iron by women.[3] Diets in the United States, Sweden, and similar, industrially developed countries supply less than 6 mg iron/1000 kcal, or about 10-12 mg iron, daily for a woman who consumes 2000 calories. The recommended dietary allowance of iron for a woman during the reproductive period is 18 mg/day. This amount cannot be supplied by her diet, which is limited to an intake of some 2000 calories, without the addition or restoration of iron to the food supply. It is not possible for a large proportion of the population with a critical need for iron, i.e., women during the reproductive period, to have an adequate intake of iron as recommended by authorities without enhancing the iron content of our food supply. In the developing countries, the diet contains much larger quantities of iron than in developed countries, as a result of less care in the handling of raw foodstuffs and the opportunity for iron-containing contamination. The major difference is the less rigorous standards exercised for cleaning and storing of raw cereals and the resulting premilling exposure to contamination. This point is obvious from the geographically broad studies made by the Interdepartmental Committee on Nutrition for National Defense (Development), which revealed that the average iron content of diets in country after country — ranging from the lowest in the Philippines (14-39.6 mg daily) to the highest in Ethiopia (98-1418 mg daily) — all well above the levels in the United States. The recommendations relative to increasing the iron content of cereal foodstuffs made by the Food and Drug Administration are well conceived and sound. They should be supported as a means of bringing the American dietary intake of iron to the level that will safely meet the normal needs of women.

"AND THEN THE WIFE, HER FAIR ROUND BELLY WITH GROWING FETUS LIN'D"

The added needs of women during pregnancy and lactation vary from culture to culture, depending upon their size; the level of physical activity maintained; the length of lactation; reserves of nutrients with which they enter pregnancy; concomitant demands of chronic disease states resulting from parasitic infestations such as hookworm or schistosomisis; and a variety of other sociocultural, environmental, and economically related factors.[10]

The magnitude of these needs has been estimated from a variety of studies. The methodologies include direct determination of the composition of fetuses and stillborn infants and placental tissues, the composition and quantitative production of milk, indirect measures of maternal and infant composition, chemical determination of losses and patterns of change in the nutrient levels of body fluids during pregnancy and lactation, as well as direct observation of dietary intakes. Resultant allowances, such as those of the Recommended Dietary Allowances (RDA)[13] or the WHO/FAO Recommended Intake of Nutrients,[11] provide reasoned guidelines to the desirable increments in nutrient intakes during pregnancy and lactation consistent with maintaining a state judged clinically to be healthy.

The RDAs provide[13] for caloric increments of 300 and 500 kcal and increases of 30 and 20 g protein daily, respectively, for pregnancy and lactation. Percentage increments of other nutrients, range from 20-50% for vitamin A, 50% for calcium, and 50-100% for folacin. The increments in most other vitamins and minerals are in the range of 25-40% above those allowances for nonpregnant women. Vitamin D, for which there is no RDA for adults, is needed during pregnancy and lactation in amounts comparable to the recommended intake of growing children. Iron constitutes a special case, in that supplements of 30-60 mg are recommended during pregnancy, an amount that cannot be obtained from the diet in the United States.

Since the recommended increment of energy intake is but some 15%, it is apparent that the diet of the pregnant woman must be carefully planned to provide more foods of higher nutrient density than are required during the nonpregnant state. A corollary is that less of those foods of low nutrient density may be included in her daily fare.

Some aspects of new experimental findings concerning trace elements[12] may have future implications in practice. Worthy of note are the potential implications of recent investigations concerning trace elements and the dependence of the animal organism upon a continuous, almost daily, extrinsic supply to meet high demands of certain localized tissue processes. Interference with such processes may result from a brief period of dietary restriction, lasting only 3-5 days, despite a previously abundant intake of zinc and the absence of measurable changes in the body stores of this element. It appears that mobilization of zinc from body stores is possible, but the rate of mobilization is not sufficiently labile for the intrinsic stores to meet the greatly enhanced localized requirements that may occur as a result of rapid tissue synthesis in processes such as wound healing or crucial periods of rapid fetal development. Studies of this phenomenon during gestation are limited to the lower species at present, but these findings highlight a need to investigate the effect of the relatively short periods of restricted nutrient intake frequently experienced by women early in pregnancy. Investigations of this and the possible roles of other trace elements in the development of the human fetus undoubtedly will receive much attention in the years ahead.

"THE LEAN AND SLIPPERED PANTALOON"

The special requirements of the reproductive-aged woman disappear[11,13] as she reaches the age of "the lean and slippered pantaloon," as her requirements are no longer conditioned by reproduction and her menstrual losses. By this age, her basal metabolic rate has gradually lowered, and her activity often decreases. The "T.V. on the side" is in part responsible for the latter, especially if she is partially incapacitated by any disability or has limited social contacts. Recommended energy allowances are decreased by some 15% in recognition of these changes with age, but there is *no* significant decrease in the estimated allowances of other nutrients except in iron. Accordingly, once more, she has need to include generous proportions of foods of high nutrient density in order to maintain good nutriture.

Other factors may be the older woman's motivation to prepare food and to eat. Without detailing the variants, it is evident that psychologic states of loneliness, dependency, absence of social anticipation, relative immobility, to say nothing of financial limitations, may deter her from partaking of a nutritionally healthy diet — and thus contribute, if not to her exit from the stage, at least to the loss of comfort and well-being as she moves behind the curtain.

This volume brings together aspects of nutrition relative to the health of women which previously have not been assembled in one place. In so doing, it will broaden the understanding of nutritionists and dietitians, gynecologists, obstetricians, pediatricians, and internists about their responsibilities for guiding the nutritionally more vulnerable sex throughout life.

REFERENCES

1. Aykroyd WR: Nutrition and mortality in infancy and early childhood: past and present relationships. Am J Clin Nutr 24:480, 1971.
2. Aykroyd WR, Hossain MA: Diet and state of nutrition of Pakistani infants in Bradford, Yorkshire. Br Med J 1:42, 1967.
3. Darby WJ: The case for the proposed increase in iron enrichment of flour and wheat products. Nutr Rev 30:98, 1972.
4. Fomon SJ: Infant Nutrition. Philadelphia, WB Saunders, 1967.
5. Halas ES, Hanlon MJ, Sandstead HH: Intra-uterine nutrition and aggression. Nature 257:221, 1975.
6. Hytten FE, Leitch J: The Physiology of Human Pregnancy. Oxford, Blackwell, 1964.
7. Maternal Nutrition and the Course of Pregnancy. Washington DC, Committee on Maternal Nutrition, Food and Nutrition Board, National Research Council, National Academy of Sciences, 1970.
8. McKenzie JM, Fosmire GJ, Sandstead HH: Zinc deficiency during the latter third of pregnancy: effects on fetal rat brain, liver, and placenta. J Nutr 105:1466, 1975.
9. Newman G: Infant Mortality, a Social Problem. London, Methuen, 1906.
10. Nutrition in Pregnancy and Lactation. (Tech Rep No. 302). Geneva, 1965.
11. Passmore R, Nicol BM, Narayana Rao M: Handbook on Human Nutritional Requirements. (Monograph No. 61). Geneva, WHO, 1974.
12. Prasad A (ed): Trace elements and human disease, 2 vols. A Nutrition Foundation Monograph, New York, Academic Press (In press).
13. Recommended Dietary Allowances. Committee on Dietary Allowances, Food and Nutrition Board, National Research Council. Washington DC, National Academy of Sciences, 1974.
14. Simon (Sir) J:: Cited by Aykroyd, 1861.
15. Toverud KU, Stearns G, Macy IG: Maternal nutrition and child health, an interpretive review. Bulletin of the National Research Council No. 123. Washington DC, National Academy of Sciences-National Research Council, 1950.

Caution Light on Caffeine

by Chris Lecos

For many people the consumption of caffeine starts at an early age—before birth even—and continues for much of a lifetime. Caffeine is taken up by the bloodstream of the mother and crosses the placenta to reach the fetus. It appears in the milk of mothers who breast feed their newborns while regularly consuming foods, drinks, and drugs that contain caffeine.

Most people probably know there is caffeine in a cup of coffee or tea. Perhaps not as many realize it is also in some soft drinks, and even fewer may know they are taking in caffeine when they sip a cup of cocoa, munch on a chocolate bar, or take some pills for a headache or cold. It is even used in some foods.

In short, caffeine is much a part of the human diet today. It is a natural ingredient in coffee, tea, cocoa, and some cola drinks; FDA requires it as an ingredient in cola and pepper-type beverages and permits it in other soft drinks; it is used in cold, headache, allergy, stay-awake, and other over-the-counter remedies and in some prescription drugs as well; and it is used in some baked goods, frozen dairy products, soft candies, gelatins, and puddings.

Its use in food and drink is hardly new. Tea's origins in China date back to around 4700 B.C. Around 500 A.D., in ancient Abyssinia, in what is now Ethiopia, a curious goatherder's munching on the fruit of an evergreen bush is, according to legend, what got the world started on coffee. America's young soft drink industry was given a real shot in the arm about 90 years ago when an Atlanta, Ga., druggist added a pinch of caffeine to his nonalcoholic mix to give the world Coca-Cola. Cola and pepper-type drinks account for 80 to 90 percent of the caffeine added to foods today.

Consumers are made aware of caffeine by some segments of the coffee industry itself. Actor Robert Young appears on television to extol the virtues of decaffeinated coffee. The technology for drawing most of the caffeine out of a coffee bean results in a valuable product—almost pure caffeine—that is sold to soft drink and drug companies.

One of the newly announced goals of the U.S. Department of Health and Human Services (HHS) and its member agencies—the Public Health Service (PHS) and the Food and Drug Administration (FDA)—is to make Americans, particularly pregnant women, more aware of caffeine and the products in which it occurs. The implications for health of caffeine consumption have been matters of concern and debate for years. This concern has now been heightened by new evidence from animal tests confirming earlier findings that caffeine causes irreversible birth defects and other abnormalities in the fetuses of pregnant rats—adverse effects that also have occurred in experiments with mice and rabbits. But the critical question—still unanswered—is whether this commonly ingested substance poses the same hazards and dangers to unborn children as it does to animals.

Caffeine is a drug, and it acts as a stimulant to the central nervous system, although it does not affect all people the same way. If consumed in large enough doses, it can cause insomnia, nervousness, irritability, anxiety, and disturbances in the heart rate and rhythm. It also seems to have an effect on coronary circulation, blood pressure, the diameter of the blood vessels and secretion of gastric acids. Around 10 grams of caffeine—as much as might be found in 70 to 100 cups of coffee—can be fatal. Its long term effects on people are not clearly known.

The latest evidence comes from a large teratology (birth abnormalities) experiment with pregnant rats completed recently in FDA laboratories. The experiment, which involved the forced feeding of caffeine in various, measured doses to the rats, was done under the direction of Dr. Thomas F. X. Collins, in FDA's Division of Toxicology and leader of its mammalian reproduction teratology team. The study, in part, revealed:

- Complete or partial absence of toes—an irreversible abnormality called ectrodactyly—in nearly one of five of the rat fetuses whose mothers were force fed caffeine at the two highest dosage levels. This was equivalent to the amount of caffeine a human might get from drinking 12 to 24 cups of strong coffee a day.
- Delayed bone development—particularly of the sternebrae or breastbone—was evident in fetuses at all five caffeine dosage levels. This means that the bones of these rat fetuses did not develop or grow as fast as those whose mothers were fed distilled water that did not contain caffeine. Such abnormalities, which may be reversible, were found at caffeine

---

From *FDA Consumer*, October 1980, pp. 6-9. Published by U.S. Food and Drug Administration.

dosage levels equal to what a human might consume from two cups of coffee a day.

Although the Collins teratology study is regarded as an excellent, well-controlled study, one that confirms that caffeine can cause birth defects in rats, FDA officials said they still are uncertain about the relevance and applicability of the study to humans. It is stressed that there is no evidence "caffeine ever caused a birth defect in a human being" and that there are "legitimate questions about whether rats metabolize caffeine the same way people do and whether the rat is the proper experimental subject for such tests."

Although the study's implications for humans are not known, enough concern has been aroused for PHS scientists to advise pregnant women to avoid products containing caffeine or to use them sparingly. The educational program proposed by HHS would be aimed at pregnant women served by various PHS programs, including maternal and child health projects, community health centers, migrant health and Indian health programs, and PHS hospitals and clinics.

In addition, members of health professional organizations, such as the American Medical Association and the American College of Obstetricians and Gynecologists, have been urged by the Surgeon General's office to ask their members to caution pregnant women in use of caffeine. Various FDA publications, including the Agency's DRUG BULLETIN—which is mailed to 967,000 health professionals including 420,000 doctors, 200,000 nurses, and 120,000 pharmacists—would also be used to reach health professionals.

On the regulatory front, FDA proposed actions designed to change the present status of caffeine and to require new, comprehensive studies that may help resolve some of the unanswered issues. One proposed action is to remove caffeine from FDA's list of common substances classified as being "generally recognized as safe," the so-called GRAS list. This status exempts caffeine from regulation as a food additive. Caffeine would instead be placed on an "interim list," which would permit industry to continue using caffeine in its products but would require it to produce acceptable scientific evidence to resolve questions about its use. FDA also proposes changing its present regulation for cola and pepper-type soft drinks to permit industry to market new beverages with even less or no caffeine in them and still allow them to be called a cola. At present, a soft drink cannot be called a cola unless it contains caffeine.

The GRAS list has existed since 1961, 3 years after the adoption of the Food Additives Amendment to the Federal Food, Drug, and Cosmetic Act. The list includes more than 400 substances commonly used in foods—caffeine among them. In 1972, FDA contracted with the Life Sciences Research Office of the Federation of American Scientists for Experimental Biology (FASEB) to undertake a complete review of all substances on the GRAS list. FASEB's review has led to the removal of some substances and affirmed the safe status of others. FDA uses FASEB's recommendations to decide whether it will propose removing a substance from the GRAS list or allow it to remain, whether the substance should remain with certain restrictions, or whether it should be on an interim basis, (a regulatory mechanism to allow FDA, to obtain appropriate studies from industry, to define the nature of the studies to be performed, and to prescribe reasonable schedules and deadlines for their performance; this is what is happening to caffeine).

FASEB's review of caffeine was published in a report released in June 1978, but was limited to caffeine's use as an ingredient in soft drinks. The FASEB scientific committee, with one dissenter, cited these conclusions: (1) that it did not find "clear cut evidence that demonstrated that caffeine was a hazard to the public" when used in beverages; (2) that "uncertainties," however, existed that warranted additional studies for determining the health implications of caffeine; (3) that it was "inappropriate" to permit caffeine to remain on the GRAS list—in effect, that it should be removed from the list.

The FASEB committee expressed concern about the behavioral effects of caffeine on children and on their brain growth and development and that heavy consumption of cola beverages starts at an early age, adding: "It is during this period of plasticity that the developing central nervous system is most sensitive to the effects of all aspects of the environment. The estimated levels of caffeine intake at these ages are near those levels that are known to cause central nervous system effects in adults." The committee qualified this concern, however, by adding it could not state, on the basis of available evidence, whether such stimulation from caffeine was a potential hazard to people—especially children.

The FASEB report was followed by plans for studies by FDA and some outside groups—mainly industry. Collins began two studies in late 1978—the recently completed study in which caffeine was force fed to pregnant rats, and a sipping study, to be finished early next year, in which caffeine at the same five dosage levels is being fed to rats in their drinking water.

Although consumer groups, such as the Center for Science in the Public Interest, a Washington, D.C.-based organization, have petitioned FDA to require warning labels on caffeine-containing products to alert pregnant women to caffeine's possible birth defect potential, FDA decided against the warning label approach because of the lack of documentation that caffeine poses the same risks to humans as it seems to for some animals.

Some of the main challenges to present animal studies have come from such industry groups as the International Life Sciences Institute (ILSI), an industrial consortium supported by the soft drink industry and the National Coffee Association. ILSI has questioned the relevance of the rat as a testing subject, whether rats and other animal species metabolize caffeine in the same manner as humans, and whether Collins' method of feeding caffeine through the mouths of rats is comparable to human consumption of caffeine. One industry contention is that there is no animal that satisfactorily mimics caffeine metabolism in man.

Behavioral studies of children who consume caffeine are now being conducted in laboratories of the National Institute of Mental Health. The coffee association is also involved in a collaborative study with ILSI and is designing a possible epidemiological study of pregnant women, one that would involve 5,500 women and take some 3 years to complete.

About Your Caffeine Intake...

There is no easy way to tell how much caffeine a man, woman, or child consumes from coffee, tea, cocoa, soft drinks, and other products that have caffeine in them. Studies and tests often add to the confusion because the same standards are not always followed.

Some studies are based on a manufacturer's direction for brewing a cup of coffee or tea. In the home, some brew it strong, others brew it weak. Some brew it for a long time, others don't. It is also not easy to compare one study with another because the cup sizes are not always the same.

At the request of the National Coffee Association, Dr. Alan W. Burg, senior biochemist at Arthur D. Little, Inc., Cambridge, Mass., reviewed the scientific literature on coffee and caffeine content and, noting the discrepancies, suggested that the 150-milliliter cup (5 ounces) be considered the average size for technical work.

Basing his data on 29 coffee and 13 tea products, he suggested in a published article in 1975 that there was an average of 85 milligrams (mg) of caffeine in a 5-oz cup of percolated, roasted, ground coffee; 60 mg in instant coffee; 3 mg in decaffeinated coffee; and an average of 30 mg in instant tea.

But these were averages. He also showed a range of 64 to 124 mg of caffeine in percolated coffee; 40 to 108 mg in instant coffee; 2 to 5 mg in decaffeinated coffee; 42 mg (based on one sample tested) in bagged tea; 30 to 48 mg in leaf tea; and 24 to 131 mg in instant tea.

Now, compare this with the findings of the Addiction Research Foundation of Ontario, Canada, which did a caffeine study based on 46 home-brewed coffee samples and 37 tea samples, some of which had cream and other dilutants in the samples. Cup sizes, obviously, also varied.

The foundation's findings were: Percolated coffee: 39 to 168 mg to a cup, with 74 as the median; drip or filtered coffee: 56 to 176 mg, with 112 as the median; instant regular coffee: 29 to 117 mg, with 66 as the median; decaffeinated coffee: 1 to 2 mg; tea: 8 to 91 mg, with 27 as the median.

For other products, other studies indicated cola and pepper-type soft drinks tested at 32 to 65 mg of caffeine in a 12-oz container; cocoa, from 5 to 40 mg; a half-ounce chocolate bar had 10 mg of caffeine; a headache tablet, 65 mg; and some stay-awake tablets, up to 100 mg of caffeine.

Soft drinks, including the cola and pepper-type drinks that have caffeine in them, are the number one beverage of Americans today, with coffee second. According to beverage industry sources, an American consumes on the average of 33.6 gallons of soft drink each year. The average consumption for coffee is 27.8 gallons per person each year, followed next by milk, at 24.8 gallons per person.

Advice On Caffeine

In making the public announcement in September of caffeine's possible dangers to unborn children, FDA Commissioner Dr. Jere E. Goyan urged prudence by pregnant women in the use of caffeine products. He also stressed that further studies, which may take 2 to 4 years, will tell more about the implications of caffeine's effects on people.

Goyan's words to mothers-to-be:

"So while further evidence is being gathered on the possible relationship between caffeine and birth defects, a prudent and protective mother-to-be will want to put caffeine on her list of unnecessary substances which she should avoid. The old saying that a pregnant woman is 'eating for two' has a special meaning in regard to caffeine."

The Commissioner also noted that studies to date support the wisdom passed down from generation to generation that caffeine is not for pregnant women or children. "We hope some day to have better scientific assessments," Goyan said, "but for now adhering to the guidance of our parents seems to be the most prudent course."

Noting that caffeine is also a stimulant and has a definite drug effect, Goyan said, that, as a general rule, pregnant women should avoid all substances that have drug-like effects.

PREGNANCY AND LACTATION

Anatomy of a Scientific Study: Rodents, Pregnancy, and Distilled Water

by *FDA Consumer*

A major experiment of force feeding caffeine to a large population of pregnant rats has accomplished several major objectives for the Food and Drug Administration:

(1) The FDA study clearly demonstrates that caffeine can cause irreversible birth defects in rats at doses not much greater than what many people consume from a fairly heavy intake of coffee, tea, cola, and other products containing the drug. This confirmed earlier studies.

(2) It shows that even low levels of caffeine—the equivalent of what a person might consume in two cups of coffee a day—may have adverse effects on bone and skeletal development of the fetuses of pregnant rats. These are abnormalities that may be reversible—in other words, adverse effects that, in time, may correct themselves.

(3) The study employed a large enough population of animals—2½ to 3 times more than previous teratology (birth defect) studies—to help establish what FDA scientists describe as a "no-effect" level for caffeine—that is, the highest dosage level at which no birth defects were found.

The study, which took 18 months to complete, was done under the supervision of Dr. Thomas F. X. Collins, head of the mammalian reproduction and teratology team at FDA's Bureau of Foods in Washington. The team also included biologists John J. Welsh, Ph.D., and Thomas N. Black, and two biological laboratory technicians, George Gray and James Rorie. All are with the Bureau of Foods' Division of Toxicology.

Earlier studies in the area had been viewed with skepticism because of the limited number of rats used. However, Collins and his staff decided to tackle that issue at the start by using at least 300 rats of the Osborne-Mendel strain, a breed FDA has used in experiments for more than 40 years. Collins actually began the experiment with 366 rats that were believed to be pregnant (based on smear tests). There were 61 rats assigned to each of five dosage level groups and the same number assigned to a control group.

The rats subjected to caffeine were fed it at the rate of 6, 12, 40, 80, or 125 milligrams (mg) a day for each equivalent kilogram of body weight. (A kilogram equals 2.2 pounds.) A syringe with the measured dose of caffeine in distilled water was used to force feed the rats. The control group was given only distilled water, unspiked with caffeine, along with the ground chow that all the rats received as food.

The study ended up with 332 rats, 7 having died during the study and 27 others, when later dissected, found not to be pregnant.

The 332 rats were more than enough to satisfy the study's objectives. The females produced a total of 4,093 living and dead fetuses (a rat litter ranges from 1 to 26 in size, with an 11-fetus average); 3,419 of the fetuses survived the 19-day gestation period during which the mother received either caffeine or, in the case of the control group, unspiked distilled water; 674 fetuses had died before the 20th day. When each pregnant rat reached its 20th day of gestation, it was sacrificed by carbon dioxide asphyxiation and examined by the team.

Around half of the 3,419 fetuses that survived to the 20th day were examined to determine the effects caffeine may have had on such vital organs as the heart, brain, eyes, kidneys, liver, pelvic region, thoracic region, and circulatory system. The other half were examined to determine caffeine's effects on skeletal or bone development. All the surviving fetuses were examined for ectrodactyly, a birth defect characterized by the total or partial absence of digits on the paws. Findings from the experiment were checked, recorded, and checked again, before the data was stored in computers for later tabulation.

The study showed that ectrodactyly occurred among nearly 19 percent (175 of 940) of those fetuses whose mothers had been fed caffeine at the 80 and 125 milligram dose levels. This congenital deformity occurred among 62 out of 544 fetuses produced at the 80-mg level and in 113 out of 396 fetuses at the 125-mg level. In other words, 11 percent of the fetuses suffered birth defects at the 80-mg dosage but the number jumped to more than 28 percent at the highest dosage.

At the two highest dosage levels, irreversible birth defects were more evident among the female fetuses than among the male, with 13.6 percent of the females, and 9.2 percent

From *FDA Consumer*, October 1980, pp. 11-13. Published by the U.S. Food and Drug Administration.

of the males showing defects at the 80-mg level and 31.4 percent of the female and 25.7 percent of the male fetuses at the 125-mg level. The defects occurred mostly in the hind paws of the fetuses; their front paws were minimally affected.

Also evident at the two highest dosage levels was an assortment of skeletal ossification (calcification or hardening) problems including misshapen or poorly developed vertebrae, reduced dorsal arches and pubic bones, missing hind phalanges, and reduced metacarpals and metatarsals (bony portions of the foot).

At all the dosage levels—from 6 to 125 mg of caffeine—a total of 1,146 of the fetuses (nearly 67 percent) displayed at least one or more abnormalities of the sternebrae (or breastbone). In other words, the bones of the offspring did not develop or grow as fast as those whose mothers were not exposed to caffeine.

The number of litters with at least one sternebral problem grew significantly with increases in dosage. At the two highest dosage levels, virtually all the fetuses were affected. At the 6-mg dose level, nearly 51 percent were affected; at the 12-mg level, 52 percent; at the 40-mg level, 77 percent; at the 80-mg level, 98.9 percent; at the 125-mg level, all of the fetuses displayed at least one problem in breastbone development. By comparison, only 39 percent of the fetuses in the control group had one or more such variations.

The number of fetuses with at least two sternebral variations was significant at the three highest dosage levels. Only 7 percent of the fetuses in the control group had two or more sternebral variations compared to more than 50 percent at the 80- and 125-mg dosage levels. The study report also noted that less than 1 percent of the control group had three or more such variations, but at the two highest dose levels, there was a "ten-fold increase" in fetuses with at least that many breastbone abnormalities.

In their examination of the fetuses for other skeletal development problems, the scientists also found significant increases at the three highest dose levels. At the highest dose level, all the fetuses had at least one skeletal variation, 90 percent had four or more, and 32 percent had 10 or more skeletal problems.

The "no-effect" level for the irreversible congenital defects—the level at which none of these defects turned up—was at the rate of 40 milligrams of caffeine a day for each kilogram of body weight. "Our no-effect level compares very favorably with what other investigators determined," Collins said. "The question that we had to ask, as food and drug people, is not whether caffeine is a teratogen (causes birth defects), which we confirmed, but at what level does caffeine stop being teratogenic." Because of the size of the study, it was possible to establish a clear-cut no-effect level as far as ectrodactyly was concerned.

A scientific review on caffeine by the Federation of American Scientists for Experimental Biology (FASEB), released in 1978 stated that many animal tests showed that teratogenic effects were generally absent at caffeine doses of up to 50 mg of caffeine. At doses up to 75 mg, the FASEB report said, the effects were "neither striking nor consistently demonstrated." At doses greater than 75 mg, teratogenic effects were readily apparent.

Other effects of caffeine on the pregnant rats were noted by Collins and his crew. Although the paucity of weight gain was much more apparent at the higher dose levels, the weight gain of the pregnant rats was not as great at any of the dosage levels as the maternal weight gain of the pregnant rats that received only water. Collins said that the caffeine-fed rats also developed anorexia—loss of appetite—during the first week of gestation, but that feeding returned to normal after that.

The study further revealed significant decreases in the fetal weights and size, from the tip of the head to the rump, of both female and male fetuses at the two highest dosage levels. To a lesser extent, both sexes showed similar effects at the 40-mg level although, Collins added, it was more evident among the females.

Caffeine's toxic effects apparently took a toll of some entire litters, Collins said. When the animals were dissected, two entire litters were found dead in the mothers of those fed at the 80-mg level and four litters had died at the 125-mg level.

The examinations made by Collins and his staff of the vital organs and tissues of the fetuses revealed no variations that could be related to caffeine intake.

Collins' study is described as a gavage study because the caffeine dosages were force fed, in controlled amounts. The caffeine was dissolved in distilled water and the solution fed to each pregnant rat daily in carefully calculated amounts. Weights of the pregnant rats were recorded on the first day (called day zero), then on the 7th, 14th, and 20th days.

The results of this study will be compared with another Collins and his staff are doing in which similar caffeine dosages are being given to rats in the distilled water they drink each day. It is commonly referred to as a sipping study and is expected to be finished early next year. "The advantage of the gavage study," he explained, "is that you know how much caffeine you are giving the animals each day and that you will be able to sustain that amount throughout pregnancy."

When the basic findings of the gavage study were announced this summer, FDA officials emphasized that the study—though excellent in its size and methodology—could only be viewed as one that revealed adverse effects to rats, not to humans. Still unanswered is whether rats metabolize caffeine the same as humans, and whether feeding caffeine directly into the stomach of a rat is relevant to the way humans consume caffeine.

Factors Affecting Human Milk Consumption

by Stephanie A. Atkinson

The resurgence of interest in the practice of breast feeding has stimulated biochemists, physicians and nutritionists alike to pursue a re-examination of the biological value of breast milk as the ideal food for the newborn infant. Modern analytical techniques now provide for a more precise biochemical analysis of this age-old biological fluid. Thus recent studies have led to an increasing knowledge of the quantity and quality of the constituents of human milk.

The incidence of breast feeding among Canadian women has significantly increased in recent years. However, many of these mothers demonstrate great concern and anxiety for their ability to produce sufficient milk of good nutritional quality. Evidence of such concern is revealed in data obtained from the recently completed Heinz Infant Feeding Study. Of all women terminating lactation at less than one month postpartum, 51% gave the reason that they felt their milk was of poor quantity or quality. Of those women terminating lactation at three months postpartum 38% gave the same reason. (Dr. D. Yeung, Heinz Co. of Canada, personal communication.)

Because of the concerns of many breast feeding mothers for the quantity and quality of their milk and an apparent lack of information in this area, it seemed timely to review the recent knowledge on the biochemical composition of breast milk and the factors which influence this composition. Where appropriate the practical implications of the affect of specific breast milk constituents on the general health and nutritional well-being of the breast-fed infant will be discussed.

Factors Affecting the Composition of Human Milk

A. Normal Physiological Factors

Hormonal control of milk production is a result of two quite distinct processes: one is the synthesis of milk in the alveolus, predominantly controlled by prolactin; the other is the delivery of milk to the infant by a neuro-hormonal reflex affected by oxytocin (1). Knowledge of the hormonal control of the synthesis of individual nutrients is scanty. Thus it is difficult to explain some of the physiological variations in the constituents of milk which occur between and within well-nourished healthy mothers. For instance, the total fat and calcium content of breast milk is highly variable between mothers. Within the same women variations in concentrations of milk nutrients occur during the course of one feed, in other words from 'fore' to 'hind' milk. Hall (2) demonstrated about a 3-fold increase in total lipid, a 1.3-fold increase in protein concentration and a 1.5-fold increase in the amount of dry weight during the course of a single nursing. Without understanding such physiological variations mothers often become concerned that their milk isn't 'rich enough' or 'looks like skim milk.' Usually the milk which is examined has been expressed prior to a nursing period and thus is representative of low fat 'fore' milk. Diurnal variations have been reported for fat (2) and some minerals such as sodium, potassium (3), copper, iron and zinc (4).

One important and often overlooked variable affecting milk composition is the stage of lactation. 'Early' milk, traditionally referred to as colostrum and 'transitional' milk, is higher in protein, sodium, potassium, chloride (5), copper, zinc, iron (5, 6, 7) and lower in total lipid (5) and lactose (8) than milk produced at a later or 'mature' lactational stage ('mature' milk usually refers to milk produced sometime after 30 days postpartum). Although this variation in milk composition has been recognized since the early analysis of breast milk by Macy (5), no particular physiological significance for the infant has been attached to it. Accordingly, adapted cow's milk formulas for infants have been based on the nutrient composition of 'mature' human milk. For any researcher interested in studying the composition of human milk or the significance of milk composition to early postnatal development, these normal physiological variations must be appreciated. Often it is difficult to compare published reports on specific nutrients in breast milk as stage of lactation, methods of milk collection and biochemical analysis have been so variable as to complex the interpretation of the data.

B. Environmental Factors

1) Maternal Dietary Intake

Energy

According to Thompson and Hytten (9) the energy needs of lactation are derived from two sources. One, from a maternal fat store of about two to four kilograms of adipose laid down during pregnancy and subsequently mobilized to subsidize the energy cost of lactation at the rate of approximately 300 Kcal/day for three to four months (10). The second source is an additional 500 Kcal/day from the diet that the lactating woman nursing one infant should consume in addition to her maintenance energy requirement (9,10). From studies in many under-developed countries of the world, it appears that generally the volume of milk produced by poorly nourished women is somewhat less than that produced by well-fed women (12). Whether this poor milk production is entirely associated with low energy intakes or in combination with other adverse nutritional or social factors has not been clearly established (12). Whichelow (13) in the United Kingdom reported that slimming diets in lactating mothers lead to an immediate reduction in milk supply. Severely limited food supply is unlikely to be the cause of lactation failure in most Canadian women unless they are dieting to lose weight. Therefore, lactating women must be encouraged to eat the recommended extra energy requirement of 500 Kcal/day (11) and not to 'crash' diet while trying to breast feed lest their caloric insufficiency restrict the energy supply necessary to sustain their milk production.

Protein

Milk proteins are synthesized de novo in the mammary gland. Neither protein quantity or quality in human milk has been correlated to maternal protein intake except in cases of severely restricted maternal protein intakes in under-developed countries where the essential amino acids were limiting in both maternal diet and milk (14). The Canadian RDNI for protein for lactating women is 24 grams per day in addition to basal protein requirements (41 grams per day for women 19 to 35 years) (11) but this is probably easily achieved in diets of most women in this society.

Total fat and fatty acid composition

While total fat seems to be the most variable component of milk between women and within women it does not seem to reflect the total amount of fat in the maternal diet. Additionally, lipid class structure does not seem to be affected by maternal diet. The majority of human milk lipid is triglycerides (approximately 98% of total lipid) with less than one per cent contributed by each of diglycerides, free fatty acids, sterols (including cholesterol) and phospholipids (15).

In conditions of energy equilibrium, the fatty acid composition of human milk directly reflects the distribution of fat and carbohydrate calories in the diet and maternal dietary fatty acid composition. Diets high in carbohydrates (about 75% of energy as carbohydrate) result in an increase in the content of saturated fatty acids especially lauric (12:0) and myristic (14:0) acids (synthesized de novo in the mammary gland from carbohydrate metabolites) and a decrease in linoleic acid ($18:2\omega6$) (16). Changes can also be induced in milk fatty acid composition by significantly altering the maternal intake of polyunsaturated fatty acids (PUFA). Potter (17) demonstrated that women on a 40% corn oil diet with a P/S ratio of approximately 1.3 had a greater amount of linoleic and lower amounts of lauric and myristic acids than when on a saturated fat diet (P/S = 0.07). These findings have been confirmed by Mellies and colleagues (18). Such increases in unsaturated fatty acids have also been induced in the milk of a woman on a polyunsaturated, high fat, low-cholesterol diet prescribed for Frederickson type II hyperlipidemia (19). Studies of milk lipids in vegans (pure vegetarians) have also reported higher proportions of linoleic acid and linolenic acid ($18:3\omega3$) and lower proportions of palmitic acid (16:0) and stearic acid (18:0) when compared with the breast milk of a non-vegetarian. It is still speculative as to whether an increase in PUFA content of milk beyond eight to ten per cent of the fat in human milk may have any physiological significance with respect to the essential fatty acid functions in the neonate.

One possibility is that higher polyunsaturates would result in excessive lipid peroxidation in the neonate and thereby increase the requirement for vitamin E that acts as an antioxidant (21). Whether human milk has an increased tocopheral concentration in proportion to increases in the PUFA content is not presently known.

At least two studies have examined the effect of varying levels of linoleate in breast milk on cholesterol levels in the infant. Increasing milk linoleate content by a maternal diet high in PUFA led to a fall in the infants' plasma cholesterol levels over ten to 12 weeks in one study (17). However, a more recent study (18) has been unable to support these findings. Both Potter (17) and Mellies (18) found the cholesterol content of the milk to be independent of maternal dietary intake of PUFA, cholesterol and phytosterols even when maternal serum patterns were altered.

Maternal vitamin intake

The literature suggests that the milk vitamin content directly reflects the vitamin nutriture of the mother (including the vitamins ascorbic acid, nicotinic acid, riboflavin, thiamin, pantothenic acid, cyanocobalmin (B_{12}), pyridoxine (B_6), and folic acid) (22). This is supported by more recent studies on individual vitamins. Maternal consumption of a pure vegan diet deficient in vitamin B_{12} resulted in clinical vitamin B_{12} deficiency (megaloblastic anemia and central nervous system symptoms) in a four month old solely breast-fed infant of this vegan mother (23). The infant's condition was corrected by initial B_{12} injections and then oral supplements to mother and child (23). A report on vitamin B_6 in breast milk observed that by increasing maternal intake of vitamin B_6 two to five fold using supplements there was an increase in the vitamin B_6 content of the breast milk although the increase was not proportional (24). However, a recent report found that moderate vitamin supplementation (i.e. prenatal-type vitamins) in women on already well balanced diets did not change their breast milk content of vitamins B_6, B_{12}, C, folate, thiamin or riboflavin when compared to milk from non-vitamin supplemented well nourished women (25).

Fat soluble vitamin levels in breast milk will be reflective of maternal vitamin stores as well as current vitamin intake. Human milk vitamin A content, present as retinol esters and the precursor carotenes, is influenced by the adequacy of the mother's diet in pregnancy and lactation (26). The effect of long term maternal intakes of mega doses of vitamin A (e.g., 25,000 to 50,000 IU/d) is not yet known. Elevated serum vitamin A levels have been observed in a mother and her premature infant who was fed solely on the mother's milk while the mother was taking 40,000 IU of vitamin A per day (guided by the writings of Adelle Davis). Lactating women should be cautioned against taking mega doses of any vitamins, particularly the fat soluble vitamins.

Vitamin D is normally considered to be low in human milk (22 to 60 IU/litre) irrespective of the vitamin D intake of the mother (27). Reports of vitamin D deficient rickets in solely breast-fed infants who were non vitamin D supplemented and receiving insufficient exposure to sunlight are supportive of this observation (28). Dark-skinned infants in low-income northern urban areas during the winter months are at the greatest risk (28). A 1977 report demonstrated a water soluble vitamin D sulphate to be present in human milk (350 IU/l in mature milk) (27). Subsequent studies by Severs and Jones (personal communication) and Hollis (29) did not detect this vitamin D sulphate. A 25-OHD_3 (hydroxy cholecalciferol)-like compound was quantitated in large amounts in human milk but it is unlikely to have any biological activity. Until the issue of the vitamin D content of human milk is resolved it is probably prudent to supplement solely breast-fed infants with vitamin D until they begin to consume infant formulas or cow's milk fortified with vitamin D or are exposed to sunlight on a regular basis (including winter).

Mineral composition of human milk

Calcium and phosphorus content of milk is not affected by maternal diet. Atkinson and West (30) have shown that healthy lactating women on a low calcium diet mobilize about 2.2% of femoral bone mineral in 100 days representing a daily mobilization of 250 mg of calcium.

Zinc, copper, magnesium and manganese do not appear to vary with maternal intake even when this includes supplements from standard pharmaceutical mineral supplements (31).

Iron is present in human milk in relatively small amounts varying anywhere from 0.1 to 1.6 mg/l, the milk concentration decreasing with progressing lactation (4). Maternal iron supplements of up to 30 mg/day have not been correlated with changes in milk iron concentration (4). No reports on the effects of higher levels of supplements are available. Breast milk iron has a higher bio-availability than the iron of cow's milk or iron fortified infant formulas (32). Based on studies on the hematological status of solely breast-fed full term infants, such infants should not require supplemental iron until about six months of age (33). Recent evidence suggests that solid foods such as vegetables and fruits may have an inhibitory effect on iron absorption from milk, especially breast milk and thus early introduction of such solids may increase the risk of iron deficiency even in breast milk fed infants (34).

Fluorine content of human milk from mothers in fluoridated water areas (1 ppm) and non-fluoridated water areas (0.1 ppm) showed little or no difference (35). The average fluorine concentration of milk was 0.05 ppm (35). The exact amounts of and need for supplemental fluoride during the first months of life of the infant and its effects have not been clearly established. However, it has been recommended by Fomon (36) that solely breast-fed infants receive a 0.25 mg/d fluoride supplement from birth.

2) Maternal Drug Ingestion

Although most every drug may be excreted in breast milk to some degree (usually not exceeding one per cent of the total dose ingested), with only a few is breast feeding contraindicated. However, some maternally ingested drugs may have a pharmacological effect in the infant while others may affect milk production and/or composition.

Oral contraceptive agents (OCAs)

The effect of maternal use of OCAs on milk quality has been examined from the aspect of their pre-conception use and use during lactation. Preconception use (three to six years of use of OCAs within eight months of conception) has been shown to cause a lower milk manganese content when compared to milk of non-OCA users (31). Other minerals (copper, magnesium, zinc, calcium and iron) were not affected. OCAs which contained large doses of both estrogens and progestins have been reported to suppress lactation (37) and thus there would be an inadequate milk supply for the infant. Presently available data is inconclusive as to the effect of varying doses of OCAs on milk nutrient composition (37). More critical is that the hormones in high dose OCAs may pass into the milk in pharmacological quantities which may affect the infant (37, 38). Thus if OCAs must be used during lactation they should be of the lowest possible dose and those which contain progestins alone would be preferable as they seem to have lesser effects (37).

Alcohol

Anecdotal evidence suggests that drinking beer will promote good milk production. Similar evidence states that a glass of wine or beer before breast feeding relaxes the mother sufficiently to facilitate her milk 'let-down' reflex. In contrast, alcohol has been shown to block the reflex response to suckling by inhibiting the release of oxytocin (39). Alcohol from the mother's blood will be secreted in her milk but if alcohol is consumed in moderation it is unlikely to have an adverse affect on the nursing infant. However, excessive internal ingestion of alcohol (50 12 oz. cans of beer plus generous amounts of alcoholic drinks) caused pseudo-Cushing syndrome and delayed growth in a four month old breast-fed infant (40). When the mother ceased drinking the alcohol, the infant's condition resolved and he began to grow normally in length and weight.

3) Maternal Ingestion of Environmental Contaminants

The quantities of lipid-soluble chemical contaminants in human milk are directly reflective of maternal ingestion of such chemicals present in the food supply; maternal body stores of chemicals which may be mobilized from body fat during weight loss; and maternal exposure to contaminants such as PCBs (polychlorinated biphenyls) in an industrial setting.

C. Effect of Premature Birth on Breast Milk Composition

Since mammary gland growth and development is more or less complete by the end of the second trimester of pregnancy it should not be surprising that mothers who give birth as early as 25 or 26 weeks of gestation are perfectly capable of producing adequate quantities of milk by manual or mechanical expression. In our studies, we have observed that mothers giving birth prematurely are capable of expressing quantities of milk up to 1.8 litres per day.

In the interest of assessing the nutritional adequacy of the premature infant's own mother's milk, we are presently examining the nutrient composition of 'pre-term' mothers' milk during early lactational stages. Such information is important in light of the current controversies over the nutritional adequacy of human milk for the small premature infant. Using the nutrient composition of 'mature' milk as a reference standard, Fomon (41) has suggested that the protein and mineral content of human milk would not be adequate to support normal growth and mineral accretion in the premature infant (assuming normal growth is equated with in utero rates of growth and nutrient accretion). A summary of our present investigations on the composition of 'pre-term' mothers' milk suggests that for most nutrients the premature infant's own mother's milk is more appropriate in meeting his nutritional needs than 'mature' milk or formula based on 'mature' milk composition. For example, we have observed that the total nitrogen concentration of 'pre-term' mothers' milk was significantly higher than 'full-term' mothers' milk over the first month of lactation (42). Characterization of the total nitrogen into its protein and non-protein nitrogen fractions determined the 'pre-term' milk to be qualitatively similar to 'full-term' mothers' milk (43). This higher nitrogen content would be important to the premature infant whose protein requirement is estimated to be greater than that of the full-term infant (41). From examination of the mineral composition of 'pre-term' milk we found that the concentrations of sodium, chloride, potassium and calcium were higher during early lactation and then decreased in concentration over the four weeks of lactation studied (44). These observations suggest that 'pre-term' milk would provide adequate amounts of sodium, chloride, potassium and magnesium to meet the predicted requirements of the premature infant during the early weeks of life. Due to the small volumes of milk tolerated by premature infants, calcium and phosphorus intakes from human milk may not be adequate. However, further clinical studies in premature infants must be conducted in order to adequately assess the growth and nutritional health of these small infants when fed their own mother's milk.

Summary

In the absence of maternal stress and anatomical abnormalities of the mammary gland, most adequately nourished Canadian women should be capable of producing sufficient volumes of good quality milk for their infants. Perhaps with more knowledgeable support and information from medical and paramedical personnel on the art of breast feeding and the science of breast milk production, mothers will gain confidence in their own abilities to produce that age-old biological fluid.

Acknowledgements

The author is grateful to Janet Chappell for her interest in reviewing this manuscript and her helpful comments. Special thanks to Carol Sooaar for her assistance in typing the manuscript.

REFERENCES

1. Hytten, F. E., 1976. The physiology of lactation. J. Hum. Nutr. 30:225-232.
2. Hall, B., 1979. Uniformity of human milk. Am. J. Clin. Nutr. 32:304-312.
3. Gunther, M., Hawkins, D. F. and Whyley, G. A., 1965. Some observations on the sodium and potassium content of human milk. J. Obstet. Gynaceol. Brit. Cmwlth. 72:69.
4. Picciano, M. F. and Guthrie, H. A., 1976. Copper, iron and zinc contents of mature human milk. Am. J. Clin. Nutr. 29:242-254.
5. Macy, I. G. and Kelly, H. J., 1961. Human milk and cow's milk in infant nutrition. In: Milk, the mammary gland and its secretion. Vol II (Kon, S. K. and Cowie, A. T., eds.). p. 265, Academic Press, New York.
6. Vuori, E. and Kuitunen, P., 1979. The concentrations of copper and zinc in human milk. Acta. Pediatr. Scand. 68:33-37.
7. Siimes, M. A., Vuori, E. and Kuitunen, P., 1979. Breast milk iron—a declining concentration during the course of lactation. Acta. Pediatr. Scand. 68:29-31.
8. Lonnerdal, B., Forsum, E. and Hambreus, L., 1976. A longitudinal study of the protein, nitrogen and lactose contents of human milk from Swedish well-nourished mothers. Am. J. Clin. Nutr. 29:1127-1133.
9. Thomson, A. M., Hytten, F. E. and Billewicz, W. Z., 1970. The energy cost of human lactation. Br. J. Nutr. 24:565-72.
10. Food and Nutrition Board, 1974. Recommended dietary allowances. Washington, D.C.: Natl. Acad. Sci.—Natl. Research Council.
11. Committee for Revision of the Canadian Dietary Standard, 1975. Dietary Standard for Canada, Department of National Health and Welfare, Ottawa.
12. Jeliffe, D. B. and Jeliffe, E. F. P., 1978. The volume and composition of human milk in poorly nourished communities. A review. Am. J. Clin. Nutr. 31:492-515.
13. Whichelow, M. G., 1976. Success and failure of breast feeding in relation to energy intake. Proc. Nutr. Soc. 35:62A.
14. Wurtman, J. J. and Fernstrom, J. D., 1979. Free amino acid, protein and fat contents of breast milk from Guatemalan mothers consuming a corn-based diet. Early Hum. Dev. 3:67-77.
15. Bracco, U., 1973. Human milk lipids and problems related to their replacement. In: Dietary Lipids and Postnatal Development. p. 23, Raven Press, New York.
16. Insull, W., Hirsch, J. and Ahrens, E. H., 1959. The fatty acids of human milk II Alterations produced by manipulation of caloric balance and exchange of dietary fats. J. Clin. Invest. 38:443.
17. Potter, J. M. and Nestel, P. J., 1976. The effects of dietary fatty acids and cholesterol on the milk lipids of lactating women and the plasma cholesterol of breastfed infants. Am. J. Clin. Nutr. 29:54-60.
18. Mellies, M. J., Iskikawa, T. T., Gartside, P., Burton, K., MacGee, J., Allen, K., Steiner, P. M., Beady, D. and Glueck, C. J., 1978. Effects of varying maternal dietary cholesterol and phytosterol in lactating women and their infants. Am. J. Clin. Nutr. 31:1347-1354.
19. Welby, M., 1973. Maternal diet and lipid composition of breast milk. Lancet, Aug. 25: 458-59.
20. Sanders, T. A. B., Ellis, F. R., Path, F. R. C. and Dickerson, J. W. T., 1978. Studies of vegans: the fatty acid composition of plasma choline phosphoglycerides, erythrocytes, adipose tissue, and breast milk and some indicators of susceptibility to ischemic heart disease in vegans and omnivore controls. Am. J. Clin. Nutr. 31:805-813.
21. Jensen, R. G., Hagerty, M. M. and McMahon, K. E., 1978. Lipids of human milk and infant formulas: a review. Am. J. Clin. Nutr. 31: 990-1016.
22. Deodhar, A. D. and Ramakrishnan, C. V., 1964. Effects of dietary supplementation on vitamin contents of breast milk. Acta. Paediatr. 53:42.
23. Higginbottom, M. C., Sweetman, L. and Nyhan, W. L., 1978. A syndrome of methylmalonic aciduria, homocystinuria, megaloblastic anemia and neurologic abnormalities in a vitamin B_{12} deficient breast fed infant of a strict vegetarian. N. Engl. J. Med. 299-317-323.
24. West, K. D. and Kirksey, K., 1976. Influence of vitamin B_6 intake on the content of the vitamin in human milk. Am. J. Clin. Nutr. 29:961-69.
25. Thomas, M. R., Sneed, S. M., Wei, C., Nail, P. and Wilson, M., 1979. The effects of vitamin supplements on the breast milk and maternal status of well nourished women at six months postpartum. Fed. Proc. 38:610 (2023A).
26. Gebre-Medhin, M., Vahlquist, A., Hofvander, Y., Uppall, L. and Vahlquist, B., 1976. Breast milk composition in Ethiopian and Swedish mothers. 1. Vitamin A and β-carotene. Am. J. Clin. Nutr. 29:441-451.
27. Lakdawala, D. R. and Widdowson, E. M., 1977. Vitamin D in human milk. Lancet, Jan. 22: 167-168.
28. O'Connor, Patricia, 1977. Vitamin D deficiency rickets in two breast fed infants who were not receiving vitamin D supplementation. Clin. Pediatr. 16:361-363.
29. Hollis, B. W. and Draper, H. H., 1978. Vitamin D metabolites in milk. Fed. Proc. 37:1043-(409A).
30. Atkinson, P. J. and West, R. R., 1970. Loss of skeletal calcium in lactating women. J. Obstet. Gynaecol. Brit. Cmwlth. 88:555.
31. Kirksey, A., Ernst, J. A., Roepke, J. L. and Tsia, T. L., 1979. Influence of mineral intake and use of oral contraceptives before pregnancy on the mineral content of human colostrum and of more mature milk. Am. J. Clin. Nutr. 32:30-39.
32. Saarinen, U. M., Siimes, M. A. and Dallman, P. R., 1977. Iron absorption in infants: high bioavailability of breast milk iron as indicated by the extrinsic tag method of iron absorption and by the concentration of serum ferritin. J. Pediatr. 91:36-39.
33. McMillan, J. A., Landaw, S. A. and Oski, S. A., 1976. Iron sufficiency in breast-fed infants and the availability of iron from human milk. Pediatrics, 58:686-691.
34. Saarinen, U. M. and Siimes, M. A., 1979. Iron absorption from breast milk, cow's milk, and iron-supplemented formula: An opportunistic use of changes in total body iron determined by hemoglobin, ferritin, and body weight in 132 infants. Pediatr. Res. 13:143-147.
35. Dirks, O. B., Jongeling-Eijndhouen, J. M. P. A., Flissebaalje, T. D., and Gedalia, I., 1974. Total and free ionic fluoride in human and cow's milk as determined by gas-liquid chromatography and the fluoride electrode. Caries. Res. 8:181-186.
36. Fomon, S. J. and Wei, S. H. Y., 1976. Prevention of Dental Caries In: Nutritional disorders of children. S. J. Fomon (ed.) U.S. Dept. of Health, Education and Welfare. D.H.E.W. Pub. No. (HSA) 76-5612.
37. Vorherr, H., 1974. The Breast Morphology, Physiology and Lactation, p. 113-124. Academic Press, New York.
38. Lonnerdal, B., Forsum, E. and Hambreus, L., 1978. The effect of oral contraceptives on the quality and quantity of human milk. Proc. XI Intern. Cong. Nutr. (Brazil): 150(A193).
39. Fuchs, A. R. and Wagner, G., 1963. Effect of alcohol on release of oxytocin. Nature, London. 198:92.
40. Binkiewicz, A., Robinson, M. J. and Senior, B., 1978. Pseudo-Cushing syndrome caused by alcohol in breast milk. J. Pediatr. 93:965-967.
41. Fomon, S. J., Ziegler, E. E. and Vazquez, H. D., 1977. Human milk and the small premature infant. Am. J. Dis. Child. 131:463-467.
42. Atkinson, S. A., Bryan, M. H. and Anderson, G. H., 1978. Human milk: Difference in nitrogen concentration in milk from mothers of term and premature infants. J. Pediatr. 93:67-69.
43. Atkinson, S. A., Anderson, G. H. and Bryan, M. H., 1978. Human milk: A comparison of nitrogen (N) composition in milk from mothers giving birth prematurely or at term. Pediatr. Res. 12:519(934A).
44. Atkinson, S. A., Bryan, M. H., Radde, I. C., Chance, G. W. and Anderson, G. H., 1978. Effect of premature birth on total N and mineral concentration in human milk. Proceedings of Western Hemisphere Nutrition Congress V: 46-47.

The Effect of Medications On the Lactating Mother And Her Infant

by Watson A. Bowes, Jr., M.D.

> Come to my woman's breasts, and take my milk for gall..."
> MACBETH I:5

Scarcely a day goes by that we do not receive at least one call from a patient or a physician regarding the safety of a medication being taken by a lactating mother. The increasing prevalence of breast-feeding and the frequency of pregnancies in females with chronic medical conditions have increased the number of patients faced with the possible harmful effect on the newborn of a medication excreted in breast milk. It is the purpose of this article to provide patients and practitioners with guidelines for making reasonable judgments in these situations.

GENERAL PRINCIPLES IN COUNSELING BREAST-FEEDING PATIENTS ABOUT MEDICATIONS

1. The advantage of human breast milk for newborns, including preterm infants, is well established. The nutritional, immunologic, antimicrobial, and emotional benefits of breast-feeding are sufficiently important that nursing should be discontinued or discouraged only when there is substantial evidence that the drug taken by the mother will be harmful to the infant.
2. Mothers who are nursing should not be given medications unless there is convincing evidence that the drug will benefit the condition for which it is prescribed. In situations in which there are alternative therapies, the drug least likely to be excreted in the breast milk or the drug with the most extensive use without apparent harm to the newborn should be used.
3. Deterioration of the mother's health in either an acute or chronic illness will be more detrimental to breast-feeding than will the effect of most medical (or surgical) treatments of her condition.
4. In the case of a woman who has been taking a medication throughout pregnancy, e.g., corticosteroids for a collagen disease or anticonvulsants for a seizure disorder, the newborn will have been exposed to higher levels of the drug in utero than it will be during the breast-feeding period. In most situations, drugs are more efficiently transported across the placenta than from the mother to the infant in breast milk.
5. The effect on an infant of a drug taken on a chronic basis by the mother may be quite different (and potentially more dangerous) than that of a drug taken for a short time during an acute illness.
6. The pharmacokinetics of most drugs ingested by breast-feeding women are such that administration of the drug at or immediately after the infant nurses will result in the lowest amount of drug in the milk at the subsequent feeding.

DRUG EXCRETION INTO BREAST MILK

This subject has been summarized in several monographs (3, 8, 28). The amount of a drug or its metabolite that enters the breast milk depends on the extent to which the substance is ionized, lipid soluble, and bound to plasma proteins. In general, drugs known to be extensively protein bound are excreted in breast milk to a lesser extent than drugs that are poorly bound to plasma proteins. Drugs that are nonionized are excreted in the milk in greater amounts than are highly ionized compounds, and low lipid solubility of the nonionized form of the drug or metabolize will diminish its excretion into the milk.

The amount of a drug that will be ingested by a breast-fed newborn can be estimated if one knows the concentration of the drug in the breast milk. For example, a woman being treated with oral chloramphenicol (250 mg every 6 hours) will have a breast milk concentration of the drug ranging from 260 ng/ml to 1.69 μg/ml (15). A 3000-g infant taking 500 ml breast milk per day will then ingest from 0.130–0.845 mg of chloramphenicol in a 24-hour period. While this is far below the recommended therapeutic amount of this drug for an infant (25 mg/kg/day), it is sufficient to initiate the rare, non-dose-related, hyper-sensitivity reaction leading to pancytopenia. With most drugs, a similar calculation will demonstrate insignificant amounts of the drug being ingested by the infants.

REVIEWS ON THE EFFECT OF MEDICATIONS ON THE BREAST-FEEDING INFANT

Several authors have published lists of drugs excreted in breast milk and the dangers (if any) to the infant from ingesting these drugs (4, 19, 22, 31). These summaries have been compiled from the many case reports and studies of specific drug excretion.

The article by Knowles in 1965 (19) was the effort of a practicing pediatrician to summarize the information available at that time about drug excretion in human breast milk. The list of drugs included serum and milk concentrations of the compounds, when such information was available, and the author comments in each case on the reported untoward reactions of the newborn. Some of the information was obtained from pharmaceutical manufacturers when specific data about the drug were not available in the medical literature.

The article by Anderson in 1977 (4), from the Department of Pharmaceutical Services at the University of California Medical Center in San Diego, is a more current listing, provides data about drug levels in milk, and includes an extensive bibliography.

La Leche League International, Inc. in 1977 (31) published a list of drugs and their effect on breast-feeding infants. This list does not include blood or milk levels of drugs, is compiled largely from other review articles, and has a number of references to personal communications. The author's comments and advice tend to be very liberal in reassurances about the lack of documented harm by most of the drugs discussed. This publication is available to breast-feeding women as well as their professional and lay counselors through the La Leche League (9616 Minneapolis Avenue, Franklin Park, IL 60131).

The March 9, 1979, issue of the Medical Letter on Drugs and Therapeutics (22) summarized advice about medications used by breast-feeding mothers. While it is useful and well referenced, it frequently comments about a drug by listing a single reference to an untoward outcome without putting that report into perspective for the reader. This publication also advises against using some drugs because of untoward effects demonstrated in animal experiments.

It is helpful for the practitioner to have at hand copies of these four articles (or at least the three most recent ones). The alphabetized or subject-oriented lists make a drug in question easy to find, and in most cases there is enough information to give a patient reasonable advice (usually reassurance) about the medication. Furthermore, the extensive bibliographies provide a source of references for more specific information about many of the drugs.

Authors of the review articles about the effect of drugs on the breast-fed infant are not unanimous in their advice about those medications that are contraindicated. The following discussion is about those drugs that have been identified by one or more of these authorities as medications to be avoided because of an effect on lactation or because of a potentially untoward drug effect in the infant.

DRUGS THAT MAY HAVE AN ADVERSE EFFECT ON LACTATION

Oral Contraceptive Steroids

The effect on lactation of contraceptive steroids has been the subject of a number of publications, many of which have been summarized in the July 1975 issue of Population Reports (6). A few controlled studies have demonstrated suppression of lactation by the combined type of contraceptive agents containing estrogen and progestin. The progestin-only contraceptive medications appear to have no effect on lactation performance. It has also been shown that there is a decrease in protein, fat, lactose, calcium, and phosphorus in the milk of mothers taking oral contraceptive steroids, but this has not been reflected in a significant impairment of growth of breast-fed infants. Small amounts of steroids can be found in the breast milk, and there is a single case report of a male infant who developed gynecomastia while breast-feeding (10). The breast enlargement resolved when the mother, who was taking 2.5 mg Enovid (norethynodrel and mestranol), stopped nursing. Although oral contraceptive agents are not absolutely contraindicated, it seems wise to advise the use of an alternative method of contraception during nursing.

Ergot Derivatives

Bromocriptine is a well-established inhibitor of prolactin secretion, but it is not likely to be taken by a nursing mother. Although other ergot compounds have been implicated in prolactin inhibition, the short course of therapy of ergonovine maleate (Ergotrate) or methylergonovine (Methergine), frequently prescribed for the control of postpartum bleeding, is unlikely to have a significant influence on milk production (11, 25). It is also unlikely that short courses of ergot-containing compounds used in the treatment of migraine headache will suppress lactation, but there are no specific studies evaluating such medications.

Pyridoxine (Vitamin B$_6$)

There are conflicting reports about the lactation-inhibiting effect of pharmacologic doses (150-200 mg three times a day) of pyridoxine (7, 13). However, there is no evidence to suspect that the relatively small physiologic doses (2-10 mg) contained in multivitamin preparations frequently prescribed for lactating mothers have a significant effect on prolactin secretion or milk production (20).

DRUGS THAT MAY HAVE AN ADVERSE EFFECT WHEN INGESTED BY A BREAST-FED INFANT

Anticancer Drugs

Cyclophosphamide. The advice about this drug is based on two reports. The first is that of a 22-year old woman who was discovered to have lymphosarcoma 8 months after delivery (30). She was breast-feeding, and when vincristine (0.9 mg) and cyclophosphamide (500 mg) were given intravenously, cyclophosphamide could be detected in breast milk samples 1, 3, 5, and 6 hours after the injection. Amato and Niblett (1) reported the case of a woman treated at 2 months postpartum for lymphocytic leukemia with cyclophosphamide, vincristine, and prednisolone. Her breast-fed infant developed an absolute neutropenia, which returned to normal when breast-feeding was discontinued.

Antimicrobials

Chloramphenicol. Small but detectable amounts of this drug are found in breast milk (15). No untoward response in a breast-fed infant has been reported, but because of the rare, non-dose-related, hypersensitivity reaction that results in pancytopenia, it is advised that this medication not be used by a breast-feeding woman.

Metronidazole (Flagyl). The authors of the Medical Letter on Drugs and Therapeutics recommend that this drug not be used by a woman who is breast-feeding (22). This advice is based on reports that metronidazole is mutagenic in bacteria and carcinogenic in rodents taking the compound throughout their lives (21). Based on the same information, these authorities advise against the use of this medication to treat trichomonal infections in any females. Specific untoward effects in a nursing infant as a result of metronidazole ingestion have not been reported.

Without more direct evidence of the harmful effects in humans of short courses of therapy with metronidazole, it seems overly conservative to withhold this drug or discontinue breast-feeding in patients with symptomatic parasite infections (amebiasis, giardiasis, or trichomoniasis) for which metronidazole may be the treatment of choice. This is particularly true if alternative forms of therapy have failed to cure the infection.

Nitrofurantoin (Furadantin, Macrodantin). While there have been no specific reports of untoward reactions in breast-fed infants exposed to these compounds, sufficient amounts of the compounds are excreted into breast milk to result in hemolytic anemia in an infant with glucose-6-phosphate dehydrogenase deficiency (27). The same theoretical problem exists with the sulfonamides. Consequently, alternative drugs should be used unless the infection (usually a urinary tract infection) is not responding to other therapy. If nitrofurantoins or sulfonamides become the drug of choice, the infant should be observed closely for evidence of anemia.

Antithyroid Drugs

Antithyroid drugs of the thioamide type, such as propylthiouracil and methimazole (Tapazole), are said to be contraindicated in mothers who are breast-feeding. This advice is based on a single study by Williams et al, (32) in 1944 in which the breast milk of 2 patients who had each received a single dose of 1 g thiouracil was analyzed. Blood and milk samples collected 2 hours after administration of the drug showed that the concentrations of the drug in the milk (12.0 and 9.2 mg%, respectively) were threefold greater than in the corresponding blood samples. The excretion of propylthiouracil and methimazole in breast milk has not been studied. There have been no reported cases of thyroid suppression in an infant as a result of propylthiouracil or methimazole ingested in breast milk. In fact, there is one reference to a personal communication reporting the treatment of a number of breast-feeding women with propylthiouracil without complications (31). Clearly, this issue needs further study.

Psychotropic Drugs

The information about many of these drugs and their effects on breast-fed infants has been reviewed recently by Anauth (2).

Lithium, widely prescribed for some depressive reactions, is excreted into breast milk. Plasma concentrations of the drug in breast-fed infants have been reported to be one-third to one-half that of the mothers' plasma concentrations. Moreover, there are reports of breast-fed infants with ECG and symptomatic changes compatible with lithium effects.

Diazepam (Valium), one of the most widely used drugs in the United States, is excreted into breast milk, is relatively poorly metabolized by the newborn, and has been associated with lethargy, weight loss, and prolonged hyperbilirubinemia in breast-fed infants.

Because lithium and diazepam are frequently prescribed on a long-term basis and breast feeding infants will, therefore, be exposed to the drugs for prolonged periods, it is advised that when these medications are necessary for treatment of the mother, breast-feeding should be discontinued.

In general, it is not advisable to expose an infant to central nervous system depressants, including those drugs used as "recreational" or "street" drugs, all of which are likely to be excreted in breast milk.

Marijuana excretion in breast milk has not been studied in humans. Tetrahydrocannabinol$_{14}$C has been found in the breast milk of suckling lambs of ewes that were given this compound, and it is assumed from these data that a human breast-fed infant might be exposed to marijuana (17).

Methadone is excreted in breast milk and there are conflicting reports about the safety of breast-feeding during methadone therapy. The only reported catastrophe was the sudden death of a 5-week-old breast-fed infant whose mother was taking methadone (26). Blood levels of 0.04 mg% were found in the infant at autopsy. This level of drug is substantially lower than cord blood levels found in infants of mothers treated during their pregnancies with methadone (5), and the role of methadone in the infant's death is not at all clear.

Radiopharmaceuticals

All diagnostic and therapeutic radioactive substances that have been studied in breast-feeding women have been shown to be excreted in breast milk. The question in each case is the duration of radioactivity in the breast milk and the time during which the patient should discontinue nursing.

Iodine 131 used for lung scans may be found in breast milk for up to 2 weeks after the medication is given to the mother (33). Technetium 99m has a relatively short half-life and breast milk samples studied 48 hours after the mother has been given diagnostic amounts of this agent are usually free of radioactivity.

Miscellaneous Agents

There are a few reports of breast-fed infants responding adversely to breast milk because of specific nutritional deficiencies in the milk (12, 14). Iron deficiency (24), hypophosphatemia (23), vitamin K deficiency (30), and vitamin B$_{12}$ deficiency (31) as a result of breast feeding have been identified, but these are rare situations. There are at least two reports of infant enteropathy related to cows' milk protein secreted in human breast milk (18, 29). The symptoms (colic) in the infants disappeared when cows' milk was removed from the mothers' diets.

Summary

Most drugs have been found to be excreted in human breast milk. Usually when the drug is taken in therapeutic amounts for short periods of time by the mother, the levels of the drug in breast milk are sufficiently low to be of little hazard to the infant. However, if a breast-feeding infant should become ill or fail to thrive and the morbidity cannot be explained, one of the following should be done:

1. Discontinue the drug.
2. Discontinue breast feeding. Frequently this can be accomplished on a temporary basis with the mother pumping her breasts to maintain lactation while the response of the infant is monitored.
3. Collect maternal plasma, breast milk, and infant plasma samples for drug assay. In situations in which this can be accomplished, it may be possible to incriminate (or exonerate) a drug or one of its metabolites as the source of the morbidity on the basis of the amounts of drug found in the milk or the infant's plasma. As tedious and impractical as this approach may seem, it would eventually lead to the

accumulation of a reasonable amount of data from which could be drawn sensible conclusions about the effect of drugs on the breast-fed infant.

ACKNOWLEDGMENTS

The author expresses his appreciation to Robert Peterson, MD, PhD (Assistant Professor of Pediatrics, School of Medicine, University of Colorado Health Sciences Center) for his advice and suggestions and to Christine A. Bowes, RN, MS (Clinical Instructor, School of Nursing, University of Colorado Health Sciences Center) for her help in reviewing the literature and preparing the manuscript.

REFERENCES

1. Amato, D. and Niblett, J.S., 1977. Neutropenia from cyclophosphamide in breast milk. Med J Aust 1:383.
2. Anauth, J., 1978. Side effects in the neonate from psychotropic agents excreted through breast feeding. Am J Psychiatry 135:801.
3. Anderson, P.O., 1977. Drugs and breast feeding: A review. Drug Intell Clin Pharmacol 11:208.
4. Anderson, P.O., 1979. Drugs and breast feeding. Semin Perinatol 3:271.
5. Blinick, G., Inturris, C.E., Jerez, E. and Wallach, R.C., 1975. Methadone assays in pregnant women and progeny. Am J Obstet Gynecol 121:617.
6. Buchanan, R., 1975. Breast-feeding: Aid to infant health and fertility control. Popul Rep JO:49.
7. Canales E.S., Soria, J., Zarate, A., Mason, M. and Molin, M., 1976. The influence of pyridoxine on prolactin secretion and milk production in women. Br J Obstet Gynaecol 83:387.
8. Catz, C.S. and Giacoia, G.P., 1972. Drugs and breast milk. Pediatr Clin North Am 19:151.
9. Cooper, N.A. and Lynch, M.A., 1979. Delayed haemorrhagic disease of the newborn with extradural hematoma. Br Med J 1:164.
10. Curtis, E.M., 1964. Oral-contraceptive feminization of normal term male infant. Obstet Gynecol 23:295.
11. Del Pozo, E., Brun Del Re, R. and Hinselmann, M., 1975. Lack of effect of methyl-erogonovine on postpartum lactation. Am J Obstet Gynecol 123:845.
12. Fomon, S.J. and Strauss, R.G., 1978. Nutrient deficiencies in breast-fed infants. N Engl J Med 299:355.
13. Foukas, M.D., 1973. An antilactogenic effect of pyridoxine. J Obstet Gynaecol Br Commonw 80:718.
14. Gilmore, H.E. and Rowland, T.W., 1978. Critical malnutrition in breast-fed infants. Am J Dis Child 132:885.
15. Havelka, J., Hejzlar, M., Popov, V., Viktorinova, D. and Procházka, J., 1968. Excretion of chloramphenicol in human milk. Chemotherapy 13:204.
16. Higginbottom, M.C., Sweetman, L. and Nyhan, W.L., 1978. A syndrome of methylmalonic aciduria, homocystinuria, megaloplastic anemia and neurologic abnormalities in a vitamin B_{12} deficient breast-fed infant of a strict vegetarian. N Engl J Med 299:317.
17. Jakabovic, A., Tait, M. and McGreer, P.L., 1975. Excretion of THC and its metabolites in ewes milk. Toxicol Appl Pharmacol 28:38.
18. Jakobsson, I. and Lindberg, T., 1978. Cows milk as a cause of infantile colic in breast-fed infants. Lancet 2:437.
19. Knowles, J.A., 1965. Excretion of drugs in milk—a review. J Pediatr 66:1068.
20. Lande, N.I., Rivlin, R.S. and Greentree, L.B., 1979. More on dangers of vitamin B_6 in nursing mothers. N Engl J Med 300:926.
21. Lande, N.I., Rivlin, R.S. and Greentree, L.B., 1975. Metronidazole. Med Lett Drugs Ther 17:53.
22. Lande, N.I., Rivlin, R.S. and Greentree, L.B., 1979. Update: Drugs in breast milk. Med Lett Drugs Ther 21:21.
23. Rowe, J.C., Wood, D.H., Rowe, D.W. and Raisz, L.G. Nutritional hypophosphatemic rickets in a premature infant fed breast milk.
24. Saarinen, V.M., 1978. Need for iron supplementation in infants on prolonged breast feeding. J Pediatr 93:177.
25. Shane, J.M. and Naftolin, F., 1974. Effect of ergonovine maleate on puerperal prolactin. Am J Obstet Gynecol 120:129.
26. Smialek, J.E., Monforte, J.R., Aranow, R. and Spitz, W.V., 1977. Methadone deaths in children. JAMA 238:2516.
27. Varsano, I., Fischal, J. and Schochet, S.B., 1973. The excretion of orally ingested nitrofurantoin in human milk. Pediatrics 82:886.
28. Vorherr, H., 1974. The Breast: Morphology, Physiology and Lactation, New York, Academic Press, pp 107, 124.
29. Walker-Smith, J., Harrison, M., Kilby, A., Phillips, A. and France, A., 1978. Cows milk sensitive enteropathy. Arch Dis Child 53:375.
30. Weirnik, P. and Duncan, J.H., 1971. Cyclophosphamide in human milk. Lancet 1:912.
31. White, M., 1977. Breast Feeding and Drugs in Human Milk. Franklin Park, IL, La Leche League International, Inc.
32. Williams, R.H., Kay, G.A. and Jandorf, B.J., 1944. Thiouracil: Its absorption, distribution, and excretion. J Clin Invest 23:613.
33. Wyburn, J.R., 1973. Human breast milk excretion of radionuclides following administration of radiopharmaceuticals. J Nucl Med 14:115.

PREGNANCY AND LACTATION

The Effect of Maternal Alcohol Ingestion During Pregnancy on Offspring

by Eileen M. Ouellette and Henry L. Rosett

Alcohol, our most widely used drug, may be a major cause of fetal malformations. Excessive alcohol ingestion has long been known to damage the mature nervous system. Despite the historical notation of alcohol as a possible direct toxin to the fetus, the modern view has been that alcohol places the child at risk more in a social and psychologic sense than a direct physical sense. Recently, attention has been directed to the possible teratogenic effects on offspring of chronic maternal alcohol ingestion during pregnancy, the features of which have been grouped under the term *fetal alcohol syndrome*.

DRINKING AMONG AMERICAN WOMEN

According to the most recent report of the National Institute of Alcoholism and Alcohol Abuse to the United States Congress, the proportion of women in the United States who drink heavily is increasing rapidly. The age group from 21 to 29 appears to have the highest proportion of heavy drinkers (23).

Estimates of the ratio of female to male alcoholics range from 1:5 to 1:1. The total population of alcoholics in the United States is estimated to be 9 million, and there may be between 1.5-4.5 million female alcoholics. With changing attitudes toward women drinking and the increased availability of alcoholism treatment programs, more heavy drinkers are being discovered among young females. Belfer et al. (1) stress that alcoholic women have been a largely unknown group in terms of number, psychologic characteristics, and the nature of their drinking patterns. These investigators found that, in 20 of 34 alcoholic women, drinking increased during the premenstrual period. It is very likely that the physiologic changes of pregnancy and the psychologic stress from the demands of motherhood could be additional factors leading to alcoholism.

The increase in alcohol consumption by women during the childbearing years has renewed attention to the possible relationship between alcohol consumption, faulty infant development, and the fetal alcohol syndrome. Maternal alcohol consumption may contribute to physical abnormalities at birth and in early life and to inadequate mothering practices which subsequently retard the growth and development of infants.

MATERNAL DRINKING AND FETAL ABNORMALITIES

Historical Review

Anecdotes concerning the presumed ill effects of parental alcohol ingestion date to antiquity. Both Carthage and Sparta had laws prohibiting alcohol use by newly married couples to prevent conception while intoxicated. Aristotle noted that "foolish, drunken or harebrained women most often bring forth children like unto themselves, morose and languid" (2).

Subsequently, in the eighteenth and nineteenth centuries, substantial literature developed on the harm of maternal alcoholism on children. In England from 1720 to 1750, traditional restrictions on grain distilling were lifted, and the so-called gin epidemic swept the country. A plethora of warnings were published. In 1726, the College of Physicians petitioned Parliament for control of the distilling trade, citing gin as "a cause of weak, feeble and distempered children" (8). In 1834, a select committee of the House of Commons investigating drunkenness indicated that infants born to alcoholic mothers sometimes had a "starved, shriveled and imperfect look" (35).

By the midnineteenth century, reports of abnormalites in offspring of alcoholics began to appear in America. In 1857, Stevens warned that the offspring of such parents inherited "a weak and perverted nervous system overthrown by the least unusual exciting cause, subject to spasms, convulsions, and falling readily into attacks of epilepsy or idiocy" (38). During the late nineteenth and early twentieth centuries, numerous reports in France, Germany, and England cited an increased frequency of abortions, stillbirths, neonatal deaths, retardation of growth and development, epilepsy, and other neurologic disorders in such offspring (4, 16, 44).

Grouping the adverse effects of parental alcoholism without separating paternal from maternal influences, together with a persisting interest in the deleterious influence of acute alcoholic intoxication at the time of conception led to a gradual discreditation of these theories (4, 9). With the advent of prohibition in the United States in 1919, a dramatic decrease in medical articles concerning alcohol and pregnancy occurred, and speculation concerning the teratogenic effects of alcohol disappeared from the English and American medical literature.

From *Nutritional Impacts on Women: Throughout Life with Emphasis on Reproduction*, edited by Kamran S. Moghissi, M.D., F.A.C.O.G., F.A.C.S., and Tommy N. Evans, M.D., F.A.C.O.G., F.A.C.S., pp. 107-120. Copyright 1977, Harper & Row, Publishers Inc. Reprinted with permission.

Modern Clinical Studies

In the French literature, however, reports of a higher incidence of retardation and neurologic disorders in offspring of alcoholics continued to appear (4, 9). In 1951, Desclaux and Morton (4) reported a large group of retarded children of alcoholics with epilepsy and electroencephalographic abnormalities. Rouquette (9) described 100 offspring of alcoholics in whom a high incidence of low birth weight was found and in whom retardation of postnatal growth in height and weight occurred. In 1968, Lemoine et al. (20) reported for the first time a characteristic appearance among 127 offspring of alcoholic mothers: short stature and diminished weight, a peculiar facies, and psychomotor retardation.

In 1972, Ulleland (45) reviewed newborn nursery and delivery records to identify all undergrown infants born in an 18-month period. Personnel of the prenatal clinic were asked to identify, retrospectively, known alcoholics and any women who were intoxicated when seen in the clinic. Eighty-three percent of the infants born to the alcoholic mothers were small for gestational age, compared with 2.3% of the infants of nonalcoholic mothers.

Jones et al. (19), in 1973, described for the first time in the United States a recognizable pattern of multiple congenital anomalies with microephaly, micrognathia, microphthalmia, cardiac defects, prenatal and postnatal growth retardation, and developmental delay in 8 children born to unrelated alcoholic mothers. A few months later, 3 additional cases of this disorder were described by Jones and his associates. The term fetal alcohol syndrome is applied to this constellation of growth and other morphologic abnormalities found among offspring of alcoholic women.

Jones and colleagues (17, 18) reviewed charts from the National Institute of Neurological Diseases and Stroke (NINDS) study of 55,000 pregnancies. Direct questions about alcohol use had not been included when the original data were gathered. The NINDS staff noted grow clinical evidence of maternal alcoholism in 69 charts. Thirty-five of these records had sufficient historical and pathophysiologic data to meet the National Council on Alcoholism's criteria for alcoholism (6). Twenty-three of the 35 mothers continued to drink heavily throughout pregnancy, while 12 reported that they stopped drinking while pregnant. These 23 cases were compared with a matched control group. Four of the 23 infants born to these mothers died during the perinatal period. The mortality rate of 17% contrasted with a 2% mortality rate in the matched control group. Thirty-two percent of the 23 children showed evidence of the fetal alcohol syndrome, while only 1 child born to one of the 12 mothers who stopped drinking while pregnant had signs of the syndrome.

In 1974, we reported familial cases of the fetal alcohol syndrome. Three pregnancies in an alcoholic woman, each by a different father, resulted in offspring with multiple minor congenital anomalies, microcephaly, and developmental delay (28). Since that time we have reported an additional family of three such children, each also fathered by different men (27). In each of two families with 3 children with the fetal alcohol syndrome, each successive child has been more significantly impaired.

To date, autopsy material is available in only 1 recognized human case of the fetal alcohol syndrome (4). This infant died at age 5 days and had a brain weight of 140 g (normal, 400 g) (50). The brain showed lissencephaly (or a smooth appearance), lacked the normal gyration and sulcation pattern, and resembled a fetal brain during the second to fourth gestational months (3, 21). Agenesis of the corpus callosum, which occurs between the first to fourth gestational months, was also present.

PROSPECTIVE STUDY AT THE BOSTON CITY HOSPITAL

Little is known about the frequency and spectrum of the fetal alcohol syndrome. Issues such as the quantity, frequency, and variability of alcohol consumption before conception and during the various phases of pregnancy have not yet been examined systematically. It can be hypothesized that heavy drinking during the first trimester may have the greatest effect on fetal maldevelopment, while heavy alcohol consumption near term may affect nutrition and delivery.

Obviously, not all offspring of alcoholic women are abnormal. If maternal alcohol ingestion during pregnancy is teratogenic to the fetus, many instances of previously unexplained congenital anomalies, especially microcephaly and developmental delay, may be understood.

A pilot prospective study was set up at the Boston City Hospital to study some of these issues. Beginning in May 1974, a random sample of women registering for prenatal care for the first time at the Boston City Hospital were interviewed using a structured interview questionnaire. The interview determined the volume and variability of maternal alcohol intake, as well as the use of other drugs, smoking, and nutritional status. Demographic data also were obtained. Drinking patterns were classified using Cahalan's Volume-Variability Index, which entails a two-step operation (3). Each woman was classified according to her average daily volume, and these groups were divided into sub-groups according to how much the woman's alcohol intake varied from day to day. Separate inquiry was made about the use of wine, beer, and liquor. The monthly volume of alcohol was calculated by multiplying frequency of use of each beverage by the various quantities usually consumed. Division by 30 yielded the daily volume. Variability was established as either high-maximum (5 or more drinks) or low-maximum (fewer than 5 drinks). Women who drank less than once a month were classified as abstinent or rare drinkers; women who drank (at least once a month) up to 2.2 ounces of absolute alcohol daily were defined as moderate drinkers, and were further subdivided according to their average daily volume. Heavy drinkers consumed between 2.3 and 15 ounces of absolute alcohol per day, with a mean of 5.9 ounces.

At the time of delivery, the infants were given detailed pediatric, neurologic, and developmental examinations without prior knowledge of the history of the mother or baby. Additional information concerning pregnancy and delivery history was obtained, but only following coding of the data obtained on the physical examination.

Results

To date, 305 women with a mean age of 23½ years have participated in the study. Fifty-three percent are married or living with the father of the baby; 47% have never been married or are separated or divorced. Their ethnic composition reflects that of the inner city area served by the Boston City Hospital: 52% black, 29% white, 14% Hispanic, and 5% American Indian and Oriental. They are a relatively poor population, with 66% estimating their monthly income under $500.00. Forty-seven percent of these women are primigravidas.

Only 10% of the entire population met the recommended dietary allowance of the National Research Council for at least seven of the nine nutrient categories. In all groups the women's diet contained excess starches and few fresh fruits or vegetables. There was no significant difference in nutrition among drinking and nondrinking women, and none were considered seriously malnourished.

Forty-three percent of the women smoked. Twelve percent stopped smoking with the onset of pregnancy, and 34% abstained from both alcohol and cigarettes. Of the heavy drinkers who also smoked, 78% consumed a package or more of cigarettes per day. Heavy drinking women tended to smoke more than nondrinking women, although 20% of the heavy drinkers did not smoke at all.

Of the 302 women studied, 144 women or 48% were abstinent or rare drinkers; 136 or 45% drank moderately, and 22 or 7% were heavy drinkers. Many of the heavy drinking women reported that they had reduced their alcohol consumption to some extent during this pregnancy. When data on the rare, moderate, and heavy drinkers were compared, no significant differences were found in age, race, religion, income, or nutrition.

Use of psychoactive drugs other than alcohol was reported by less than 10% of our patients. Pregnant heroin addicts, however, are referred to a special methadone maintenance program and are not represented in this study.

Of the 134 babies born to date, 54 or 40% have been born to rarely drinking or abstinent mothers, 65 or 49% to moderate drinkers, and 15 or 11% to heavy drinking women. There have been two therapeutic abortions and no stillbirths or neonatal deaths. Comparing the results of examinations on the offspring of mothers in all drinking groups, no differences were found in 1-minute and 5-minute Apgar scores, nor was there any difference in the frequency of acquired medical illness.

Infants were classified as abnormal if congenital anomalies were present or if the infants showed growth abnormalities, were jittery, or displayed abnormalities of tone. Only 4 of 15 infants born to heavy drinking women or 27% were considered to be normal at the time of the newborn examination, compared with 54% in the moderate drinking group and 60% in the abstinent group. The population at Boston City Hospital is a high-risk group, with 35% of all newborns delivered there admitted to the intensive care unit, which may account for the large number of abnormal infants in the abstinent and moderate drinking groups.

A surprising number of babies in all groups showed hypotonia and/or jitteriness, but again, those signs were more frequent with increasing maternal alcohol intake. Single, minor congenital anomalies were found in all three groups. Only 1 child of the 54 born to mothers in the lowest drinking group had a major anomaly, as did 1 child of the 65 born to moderate drinkers. Congenital anomalies were present in 5 of the 15 babies born to heavy drinking women. Two infants were microcephalic, and 2 had polydactyly. A transverse palmar crease, a minor anomaly, was present in an additional child. One child with microcephaly also displayed a beaked nose, micrognathia, and redundant skin on the neck. Except for 2 cases of microcephaly, no consistent pattern of anomalies was noted.

When growth parameters were compared, the frequency of prematurity differed among the three drinking groups: 7% in the abstinent group, 4% in the moderate group, and 20% in the heavy drinking group. A marked increase in infants found to be small for gestational age was noted with increased alcohol intake, ranging from 5% in infants born to mothers in the abstinent group, to 12% in the moderate group, to 33% in the heavy drinking group.

Major differences were found in growth parameters among the three groups of babies. Birth length was distributed throughout all percentiles among the infants of abstainers and moderate drinkers but was clustered at the lower percentiles among offspring of heavy drinking women. Only 1 child born to a heavy drinker was above the 50th percentile for length.

A similar trend was found when birth weights were compared. No child whose weight was above the 50th percentile was born to a heavy drinking mother, and 3 of 15 or 20% were below the 3rd percentile.

Smaller head circumferences were found more frequently among the offspring of heavy drinking women than in the offspring of the abstinent or moderate drinking groups. No child born to a heavy drinking mother was found to have a head circumference above the 50th percentile, and 2 were microcephalic.

OTHER POSSIBLE TERATOGENIC FACTORS

At the present time, very little more is known about the spectrum of the fetal alcohol syndrome. Issues such as the quantity, frequency, and variability of alcohol consumption before conception and during the various stages of pregnancy have not yet been examined systematically. It can be hypothesized that heavy drinking during the first trimester may have the greatest effect on fetal development, while heavy alcohol consumption near term may affect nutrition and the obstetrical delivery. Continued maternal alcohol consumption during the neonatal period may contribute to child neglect, failure to thrive, and child abuse.

The firm establishment of the teratogenic role of alcohol in the production of these anomalies is critical in view of the fact that malnutrition and vitamin deficiency (particularly of thiamine and folic acid), smoking and drug abuse, hypoglycemia, and deficiency of trace metals may be proposed as alternative etiologic factors. The latter possibilities suggest that there may be a specific intervention or series of interventions which can prevent the syndrome.

Malnutrition

A voluminous literature, from both clinical and experimental studies, has evolved from the study of malnutrition (5, 22, 37, 40, 47-49). Smith studied the effects of acute severe malnutrition on pregnancy in several hundred pregnant women in Holland during the final days of World War II (37). This work demonstrated an increase in small and premature infants, but malformed infants accounted for only 0.5% of the deliveries. More recent work among the poorer people in Latin America demonstrated diminished stature, head size, and intellectual accomplishments in offspring of chronically malnourished mothers, but an increased occurrence of malformations was not noted (5). Stoch and Smythe (39, 40) in South Africa also found that malnutrition in early life impaired body growth, especially body weight, to a greater extent than head growth and psychomotor development. If such children are fed suitable diets postnatally, catch-up growth occurs (22).

By contrast, in infants with the fetal alcohol syndrome, the head circumference and body length are affected more than body weight, and this discrepancy persists postnatally even with an adequate diet. In addition, many mothers of patients with the fetal alcohol syndrome have been carefully followed throughout their pregnancies, and malnutrition has not been noted (4, 19, 28). The present study demonstrated a statistically significant decrease in all growth parameters and in the frequency of congenital malformations in infants of mothers with excessive alcohol intake. There are no significant differences in nutritional intake among all groups in our population to account for these findings.

Vitamin Deficiency

Blood levels of vitamins A and C and folic acid have been measured in several mothers of infants with the fetal alcohol syndrome and found to be normal (4, 28). Possible effects of ethanol on intestinal absorption of folic acid have been reported by Halsted et al. (12). Hematologic response to folic acid therapy was prevented by the concomitant administration of whiskey, wine, or ethanol. Eichner and Hillman (7) found that when a folate-poor diet was given to alcoholics along with ethanol, megaloblastic changes developed much more rapidly than when the same diet was given to these subjects without alcohol. These findings suggest that alcohol administration causes megaloblastic changes only when body vitamin stores are decreased and dietary intake is poor. Under these circumstances, ethanol may act as a weak folate antagonist.

Studies on the effect on the rat embryo of maternal folate deficiency resulting from the administration of folate antagonists have shown that these agents may cause fetal resorption, stillbirths, and congenital malformations (13, 24, 25). In humans, a folic acid antagonist, aminopterin, can produce abortion (42). Recent reports suggest that human fetal malformations may also result from the administration of folate antagonists or from dietary deficiency of folate (10, 14). Therefore, the teratogenic effects of excessive alcohol ingestion during pregnancy may be due in some part to alcohol acting as a folic acid antagonist.

The work carried out by Victor et al. (46) at the Boston City Hospital showed that many of the central nervous system changes seen in adult alcoholics are probably due to thiamine deficiency. Consequently, thiamine deficiency in the mothers must be ruled out as a cause of the anomalies seen in the fetal alcohol syndrome. Neuropathologic changes in thiamine deficiency in adults have been found in the medial thalamic nuclei, mammillary bodies, periaqueductal gray matter and superior cerebellum (46). The clinical syndromes and localization of brain lesions seen in thiamine deficiency in postnatal life, however, bear no resemblance to abnormalities seen in the fetal alcohol syndrome.

Smoking

Although 20% of heavy drinking women in our study do not smoke, many are heavy smokers; however, we lack sufficient data to imply that heavy smoking is a possible contributing factor. Smoking has been associated with lowered infant birth weight (36). Rush and Kass (31) at the Boston City Hospital demonstrated a greater risk of prematurity and infant mortality in offspring of smoking mothers. To date, there is no evidence implicating smoking as a teratogenic influence.

Drug Abuse

Drug abuse was not prominent in any of the three drinking groups and was not reported by any of the mothers of infants with morphologic abnormalities. There are numerous reports of infants with congenital anomalies who were born to addict mothers, but there is no discernible pattern of anomalies in these infants and the incidence of congenital defects is not higher in offspring of addict mothers than in the general population (30).

Hypoglycemia

Hypoglycemia is known to follow ingestion of alcohol, and thus some of the abnormalities seen in the offspring of alcoholic women may be related to hypoglycemia early in the pregnancy. Infants of diabetic mothers have a much higher incidence of major congenital malformations than is seen in the general population, and hypoglycemia may play a significant role in the production of these abnormalities (11).

Deficiency of Trace Metals

Deficiency of trace metals is believed to play a role in the production of many illnesses affecting the nervous system. Magnesium and zinc deficiency are thought to have an effect in the production of Korsakoff syndrome with its attendant memory loss in the adult alcoholic (26, 41, 43). Whether these trace metals may be implicated in the production of the fetal alcohol syndrome is highly speculative in view of the fact that the fetus is often preferentially provided critical nutrients at the expense of the mother.

ANIMAL STUDIES OF EXPERIMENTAL ALCOHOLISM

Experimental work done on a number of pregnant animals given alcohol has resulted in low-birth-weight offspring with a significant number of central nervous system abnormalities.

Papara-Nicholson (29) fed ethanol to pregnant guinea pigs and produced offspring that were of low birth weight and had motor abnormalities, ataxia, and blindness. The brains of these animals showed flattened gyri, shallow sulci, and retarded myelinization. Sandor (32, 34) injected ethanol into chick embryos and noted a high incidence of malformations among the survivors, with defects of neural tube closure and rudimentary deformed brain vesicles. Ho et al. (15) gave radioactive labeled ethanol to pregnant hamsters and monkeys and demonstrated placental transfer of the ethanol with greater concentrations in later pregnancy. In the monkey, high concentrations were seen in the brain, especially in the visual cortex and cerebellum. The only report of experimental fetal alcoholism in the rat is by Sandor (33) who gave ethanol to rats early in pregnancy. Fetuses studied at 19½ days showed retarded skeletal development; there was, however, no description of the nervous system in these animals. Except for Sandor's findings of neural tube closure defects in chick embryos which suggests a teratogenic effect very early in the first trimester of pregnancy, both the clinical features in the human cases and the results of the experimental work in species other than the chick suggest a teratogenic effect somewhat later in the first trimester of pregnancy.

Summary

The fetal alcohol syndrome has been described as microcephaly, micrognathia, microphthalamia, cardiac defects, and prenatal and postnatal growth retardation. In our study, prenatal growth retardation was present, but except for microcephaly in 2 patients, this consistent pattern of malformations was not found in the 15 offspring of heavy drinking mothers. All of the children described to date with the fetal alcohol syndrome have been born to severely alcoholic mothers, and most of these children have been identified only after a retrospective review. Although we identified 6 children in two families with multiple congenital anomalies consistent with the fetal alcohol syndrome and found an additional dozen unrelated cases by retrospective review, we have not demonstrated conclusively a specific pattern of anomalies among the offspring of heavy drinking women in our prospective study. Additional examinations on more infants will be necessary. It is likely that those infants heretofore identified represent the most severely afflicted infants at one end of a bell-shaped curve and that a spectrum of structural, growth, and functional abnormalities will be found in offspring of women with heavy alcohol intake during pregnancy. Because of the complexity of the interrelationships between excessive alcohol intake, smoking, drug abuse, poor nutrition, and other sociologic factors, large well-controlled prospective studies of this problem are essential if a true understanding is to be gained of the effects of maternal alcohol ingestion during pregnancy on the development of the child.

REFERENCES

1. Belfer, M.L., Shader, R.K., Carroll, M. and Harmatz, J.S., 1971. Alcoholism in women. Arch Gen Psychiatry 25:6, 540.
2. Burton, R. The Anatomy of Melancholy, Vol. I. London, William Tegg, 1806, p 890.
3. Cahalan, D., Cisin, I.H. and Crossley, H.M., 1969. American Drinking Practices: A National Study of Drinking Behavior and Attitudes. (Monograph No. 6). New Brunswick, NJ Rutgers Center of Alcohol Studies.
4. Christiaens, L., Miron, L.P. and Delmarle, G., 1960. Sur la descendance des alcooliques. Sem Hop Paris 36:257.
5. Cravioto, J., DeLicardie, E.R. and Birch, H.C., 1966. Nutrition, growth and neurointegrative development: an experimental and ecologic study. Pediatrics 23(2):319.
6. Criteria Committee, National Council on Alcoholism, 1972. Criteria for the diagnosis of alcoholism. Ann Intern Med 77:249.
7. Eichner, E.R. and Hillman, R.S., 1971. The evolution of anemia in alcoholic patients. Am J Med 50:218.
8. Fielding, H. An enquiry into the causes of the late increase of robbers, etc. with some proposal for remedying this growing evil. London, A Millar, 1751.
9. Giroud, A. and Tuchmann-Duplessis, H., 1962. Malformations congenitales, roles des facteurs exogenes. Pathol Biol 10:141.
10. Goetsch, C., 1962. An evaluation of aminopterin as an abortifacient. Am J. Obstet Gynecol 83:1474.
11. Gould, J. Personal communication.
12. Halsted, C.H., Griggs, R.C. and Harris, J.W., 1967. The effect of alcoholism on the absorption of folic acid (H^3-PGA) evaluated by plasma levels and urine excretion. J Lab Clin Med 69:116.
13. Hibbard, B.M., 1964. The role of folic acid in pregnancy, with particular reference to anaemia, abruption and abortion. J Obstet Gynaecol Br Commonw 71:529.
14. Hibbard, E.D, and Smithells, R.W., 1965. Folic acid metabolism and human embryopathy. Lancet 1:1254.
15. Ho, B.T., Fritchie, G.E., Idanpaan-Heikkila, J.E. and McIsaac, W.M., 1972. Placental transfer and tissue distribution of ethanol-1-^{14}C. Q J Stud Alcohol 33:485.
16. Jones, K.L. and Smith, D.W., 1973. Recognition of the fetal alcohol syndrome in early infancy. Lancet 2:999.
17. Jones, K.L., Smith, D.W., Streissguth, A.P. and Myrianthopoulos, N.C., 1974. Incidence of the fetal alcohol syndrome in offspring of chronically alcoholic women. Pediatr Res 8:166.
18. Jones, K.L., Smith, D.W., Streissguth, A.P. and Myrianthopoulos, N.C., 1974. Outcome in offspring of chronic alcoholic women. Lancet 1:1076.
19. Jones, K.L., Smith, D.W. and Streissguth, A.P., 1973. Pattern of malformation in offspring of chronic alcoholic mothers. Lancet 1:1267.
20. Lemoine, P., Harousseau, H., Borteyrn, J.P. and Manure, J.C., 1968. Les enfants de parents alcooliques. Anomalies observees. Quest-Medical 25:476.
21. Miller, J.Q., 1963. Lissencephaly in 2 siblings. Neurology (Minneap) 13:841.
22. Naeye, R.L., Blanc, W. and Paul, C., 1973. Effects of maternal nutrition on the human fetus. Pediatrics 52:494.
23. National Institute on Alcohol Abuse and Alcoholism. Washington DC, US Dept of Health, Education and Welfare, second report to US Congress, 1974.
24. Nelson, M.M., Asling, C.W. and Evans, H.M., 1952. Production of multiple congenital abnormalities in young by maternal pteroylglutamic acid deficiency during gestation. J Nutr 48:61.
25. Nelson, M.M. and Evans, H.M., 1947. Reproduction in rat on purified diets containing succinylsulfathiazole. Proc Soc Exp Biol Med 66:289.
26. Oberleas, D., Caldwell, D.F. and Prasad, A.S. Trace elements and behavior. In Pfeiffer CC (ed): International Review of Neurobiology of Trace Metals Zinc and Copper. New York, Academic Press, 1972, pp 83-103.
27. Ouellette, E.M., 1974. The fetal alcohol syndrome, additional familial cases. Madison, Proc 3rd Natl Meeting Child Neurol Soc.
28. Palmer, R.H., Ouellette, E.M., Warner, L. and Leichtman, S.R., 1974. Congenital malformations in offspring of a chronic alcoholic mother. Pediatrics 53:490.
29. Papara-Nicholson, D. and Telford, I.R., 1957. Effects of alcohol on reproduction and fetal development in the guinea pig. Anat Rec 127:438.
30. Rothstein, P. and Gould, J.B., 1974. Born with a habit: infants of drug-addicted mothers. Pediatr Clin North Am 21:307.
31. Rush, D. and Kass, E.H., 1972. Maternal smoking: a reassessment of the association with perinatal mortality. Am J Epidemiol 96:183.
32. Sandor, S., 1968. The influence of aethyl alcohol on the developing chick embryo. II. Rev Roum Embryol Cytol Ser Embryol 5:167.
33. Sandor, S. and Amels, D., 1971. The action of aethanol on the prenatal development of albino rats. (An attempt of multiphasic screening). Rev Roum Embryol Cytol Ser Embryol 8:105.
34. Sandor, S. and Elias, S., 1968. The influence of aethyl-alcohol on the development of the chick embryo. Rev Roum Embryol Cytol Ser Embryol 5:51.
35. Sedgewick, J. A new treatise on liquors, wherein the use and abuse of wine, malt drinks, water, etc. are particularly considered in many diseases, constitutions and ages; with the proper manner of using them, hot, or cold, either as physick, diet or both. London, Charles Rivington, 1725.
36. Simpson, W.J., 1957. A preliminary report on cigarette smoking and the incidence of prematurity. Am J Obstet Gynecol 73:808.
37. Smith, C.A., 1947. Effects of maternal undernutrition upon the newborn infant in Holland (1944-1945). J Pediatr 30:229.
38. Stevens, J.P., 1857. Some of the effects of alcohol upon the physical constitution of man. South Med Surg J 13:451.
39. Stoch, M.B. and Smythe, P.M., 1963. Does undernutrition during infancy inhibit brain growth and subsequent intellectual development? Arch Dis Child 38:546.
40. Stoch, M.B. and Smythe, P.M., 1967. The effect of undernutrition during infancy on subsequent brain growth and intellectual development. South Afr Med J 41:1027.
41. Sullivan, J.F. and Lankford, H.G., 1965. Zinc metabolism in chronic alcoholism. Am J Clin Nutr 17:57.
42. Thiersch, J.B., 1952. Therapeutic abortions with a folic acid antagonist, 4-aminopterolyl-glutamic acid (4-amino P.G.A.) administered by the oral route. Am J Obstet Gynecol 63:1298.
43. Traviesa, D.C., 1974. Magnesium deficiency: a possible cause of thiamine refractoriness in Wenicke-Korsakoff encephalopathy. J Neurol Neurosurg Psychiatry 35:959.
44. Triboulet, H. Matthieu, F. and Mignot, R., 1905. Traite de l'Alcoolisme. Paris, Masson et Cie.
45. Ulleland, C.N., 1972. The offspring of alcoholic mothers. Ann NY Acad Sci 197:167.
46. Victor, M., Adams, R.D. and Collins, C.H. The Wernicke-Korsakoff Syndrome, Philadelphia, FA Davis, 1971, p 147.
47. Winick, M., 1969. Malnutrition and brain development. J Pediatr 74:667.
48. Winick, M. and Rosso, P., 1969. Head circumference and cellular growth of the brain in normal and marasmic children. J Pediatr 74:774.
49. Winick, M. and Rosso, P., 1969. The effect of severe early malnutrition on cellular growth of human brain. Pediatr Res 3:181.
50. Yakovlev, P.I., 1962. Morphological criteria of growth and maturation of the nervous system in man. Ment Retard 39:3.

What Nutrients Do Our Infants Really Get?

by Guy H. Johnson, Ph.D., George A. Purvis, Ph.D., and Robert D. Wallace, M.S.

It is not generally known that an interest in nutrition actually created a distinguished specialty in the practice of medicine. The specialty is pediatrics. It sets apart those members of the medical profession who confine their practice to the care of children. Providing guidance to their patients and their patient's parents, in what they eat, is, despite all the other services that they render, central to the practice of pediatrics.

Despite all the care that pediatricians take in advising their little patients, they are externally frustrated by the fact that they can never know whether the advice is followed. You can lead a patient to a diet, to paraphrase an old aphorism, but you can't make him eat it, as they say. That was true in yesteryears and may today be little less true now that we are learning to use computers to ferret out facts about the patterns of children's eating habits, and their parents' feeding habits which heretofore eluded us. This is why we can say today that we are closer to learning whether parents are following their pediatrician's advice than we were, say, twenty-five years ago.

Before turning to the findings in the ongoing computer analysis we have been doing in our search for the answer to the question, What nutrients do our infants really get?—the following observations are in order.

The feeding of infants is one of the most interesting applications of modern nutrition science. The past decade has witnessed remarkable changes in infant feeding practices. Breast feeding is enjoying a dramatic resurgence, and the use of evaporated milk formula has been virtually eliminated. In addition, the nutrition composition of many infant foods has changed significantly. Commercially prepared infant foods are now formulated without salt being added. Also, the sugar content of these foods has been significantly reduced.

A number of factors contribute to the great propensity of the infant diet for change. Infants generally consume fewer food items than adults so that changes in the composition of specifically designated foods has a considerable impact on nutrient intake. Also, because energy requirements for each unit of body weight are high during this period, infants normally have excellent appetites. Therefore, the acceptability of foods, which may make modification of the adult diet difficult, has not been a major consideration in infant feeding. In addition, it is relatively easy for "caregiver" to control the infant's menu, so that adherence to a particular regimen does not require a change in established habits, complicating the attempt to modify the daily diet of adults.

Because an adequate diet during infancy is particularly important, and because infant diets are in a constant state of change, if one is to learn what a representative sample of American infants are really consuming, it is necessary to monitor and test all findings periodically. This report compares the average intake of selected nutrients as measured during the first year of our study of a group of 377 infants in 1972. We have now compared these with our latest findings from a group of 154 infants in 1979. The procedures used to collect and analyze dietary information were detailed in our previous report in *Nutrition Today* (N.T. 8 [S/O, 1973] p. 28).

Briefly, parents of babies less than one year of age were selected at random from a birth list. The mothers, a resulting geographically balanced sample of prospective participants, were then contacted by telephone. The aims, purposes and scientific goals we were seeking to achieve were described and each woman was asked if she would care to have more information so she could decide whether she'd like to participate. The response was, with few exceptions, positive. Everyone whose daily routine permitted it, was enthusiastic to join the study.

Having done everything else we could think of to eliminate bias, we also retained a group not identified with any baby food manufacturer to act as a contact with the mothers.

Parents who elected to participate in the study were sent detailed instructions and a form on which to record food intake for a four-day period. The food diaries were recorded beginning on Monday and ending on Thursday so that potentially atypical weekend dietary habits would be avoided. The amount and time at which each food was consumed by the infant was recorded as well as the duration and time of each breast feeding. A questionnaire was also included in the mailing to provide specific demographic information as well as the birth date and weight of the baby.

At the end of the survey period the food diaries and questionnaires were returned by the parents. The raw intake data was translated into a form compatible with data processing capabilities and converted into average daily nutrient intakes. Breast milk consumption was estimated by considering the length and frequency of nursing in conjunction with the weight of the baby according to average intakes reported by Samuel J. Fomon, M.D. (*Infant Nutrition*, 1st ed.: Saunders, 1967).

The nutrient composition of foods used to calculate nutrient intakes was obtained from several sources: commercial manufacturers of infant foods as well as adult foods, nutrient data files maintained by Gerber Products Company, nutrition literature (especially for breast milk composition), USDA Handbook #8, and occasionally by analysis of foods. The data we have now collated and analyzed is presented here. The average daily nutrient intake of infants obtained during both 1972 and 1979 have been displayed graphically in the following comparative atlas of infant nutrient consumption. Nutrient intake, expressed as either percent of the Recommended Dietary Allowances (RDA), or as absolute amount of nutrient, is plotted on the vertical axis, and age in months on the horizontal axis. The contribution of specific nutrients from breast milk, infant formula, cow's milk, commercially prepared baby foods and table foods are each represented by different colored areas on the graphs. Home prepared baby foods are included in the table food category. It is important to note that the values depicted in the figures represent average intakes at each age. In all instances, variation associated with individual intakes was considerable. The average intake of several of these nutrients when expressed as a percentage of the Recommended Dietary Allowances shows a substantial decline for infants at six months of age. This drop in the chart lines is due primarily to an increase in the Recommended Dietary Allowances for this age, and should not be read as an indication of a decline in nutrient intake.

A detailed discussion of the changes that have occurred in nutrient intake between 1972 and 1979 is presented in the text that accompanies each pair of graphs. However, a few trends that have occurred during this period deserve further emphasis.

Although there were marked changes in the relative amounts of food categories provided to infants, the *total energy* content of the diet remained virtually unchanged. One possible explanation for this observation is that normal ad libitum fed infants are able to regulate their energy intake efficiently. Samuel J. Fomon, M.D. of the University of Iowa, fed two groups of female infants formulas of different caloric density. After about six weeks of age, these infants were able to adjust volume intake to achieve the same caloric intakes. If this observation can be applied to the general population of infants, one would not expect the energy intake to change significantly with time.

A marked decrease in the quantity of *iron* supplied to infants occurred between 1972 and 1979. The Committee on Nutrition of the American Academy of Pediatrics recommends that iron supplementation in the form of either iron fortified formula, iron fortified infant cereal or iron drops be provided to the full term infant by four to six months of age. The data presented in this report substantiate the need for this recommendation based on the RDA. However, consideration of this information should include the development and purpose of the RDA, which may be more therapeutic than dietary. The results may, therefore, be somewhat overly pessimistic.

The *sodium* intake of infants has decreased markedly since 1972. An RDA has not been established for sodium, but the National Research Council has established a safe and adequate daily intake of 115-350 mg for infants up to six months of age and 250-750 mg for infants six to twelve months of age. During 1979, 16% of infants received less than this amount. Although there is no evidence to suggest that current low intakes of sodium are harmful, under certain conditions such as high environmental temperatures which increase the requirement for this nutrient, an additional source of sodium may be beneficial. The reduction in sodium has been deliberate since at present salt is not added to manufactured baby foods. A further reduction in electrolyte intake is not recommended during early infancy, and reappraisal of salt usage is clearly in order.

The remaining nutrients examined were generally available in adequate amounts. Since individual dietary intakes vary considerably, some individual infants may be at nutritional risk. Infants who were provided with a diet consistent with recommendations; namely breast milk or iron fortified infant formula supplemented appropriately with a variety of additional foods, received an adequate supply of individual nutrients.

(Charts begin on following pages.)

Average Nutrient Intake for Infants

from age 2 months to age 12 months

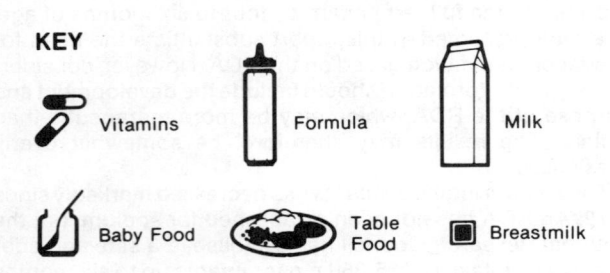

KEY

- Vitamins
- Formula
- Milk
- Baby Food
- Table Food
- Breastmilk

RIBOFLAVIN INTAKE (% RDA)

The average intake of riboflavin was well above the RDA for each month of infancy during both 1972 and 1979. Breast milk and infant formulas provided abundant quantities of riboflavin during the early months of infancy. Cow's milk is a rich source of this vitamin and provided large quantities particularly after the fifth month. The milk component of the diet satisfied the RDA for riboflavin throughout the first year of life during both 1972 and 1979.

Additional sources of riboflavin in the infant diet are baby foods, particularly riboflavin fortified infant cereals and table foods. Riboflavin was also furnished by vitamin supplements, but, as observed for other B vitamins, this source was less important during 1979.

All but one infant of those studied in 1972 received the RDA for riboflavin, and only 11% received less than this amount during 1979.

THIAMIN INTAKE (% RDA)

The average intake of thiamin by infants during 1972 and 1979 exceeded the RDA at each age examined. Breast milk and infant formula supplied quantities of thiamin near the RDA until three months during 1972 and five months in 1979. The trend for extended usage of infant formula in place of cow's milk resulted in a pronounced decrease in the thiamin provided by the latter food. Nevertheless, the total contribution of this vitamin by the milk component of the diet did not change dramatically.

Baby foods supplemented the thiamin provided by the milk component of the diet, and were a substantial source of this nutrient. Infant cereals are fortified with thiamin (as well as riboflavin, niacin and iron), and are the largest baby food source of this nutrient. Table foods also provide thiamin to the diet of infants, but substantial contributions from this source were limited to the later part of infancy. The use of pharmaceutical vitamin preparations containing thiamin decreased during the period between 1972 and 1979, but were still provided at each age. The reduction in thiamin supplementation may be the result of pediatric recommendation which does not indicate universal supplementation with thiamin or other water soluble vitamins.

Twenty-six percent of the infants studied during 1979 received less than the RDA for thiamin. The corresponding value in 1972 was 7%.

NIACIN INTAKE (% RDA)

The niacin intake of infants during the first year of life was generally similar during 1972 and 1979. Breast milk and infant formula, as for most nutrients, make the largest contribution during the early months. As these foods are discontinued, cow's milk becomes a significant source. Although cow's milk is a poor source of preformed niacin, it contains substantial quantities of tryptophan which can be converted to niacin.

Baby foods are an important source of niacin. Fortified infant cereals provided about one-half of the niacin from this category, and meats were another important source. Baby foods were necessary to supplement the milk component of the diet in order to achieve average intakes near the RDA.

Table foods provided increased quantities of niacin during the latter period of infancy, and vitamin supplements supplied a relatively consistent amount of this nutrient during this same period.

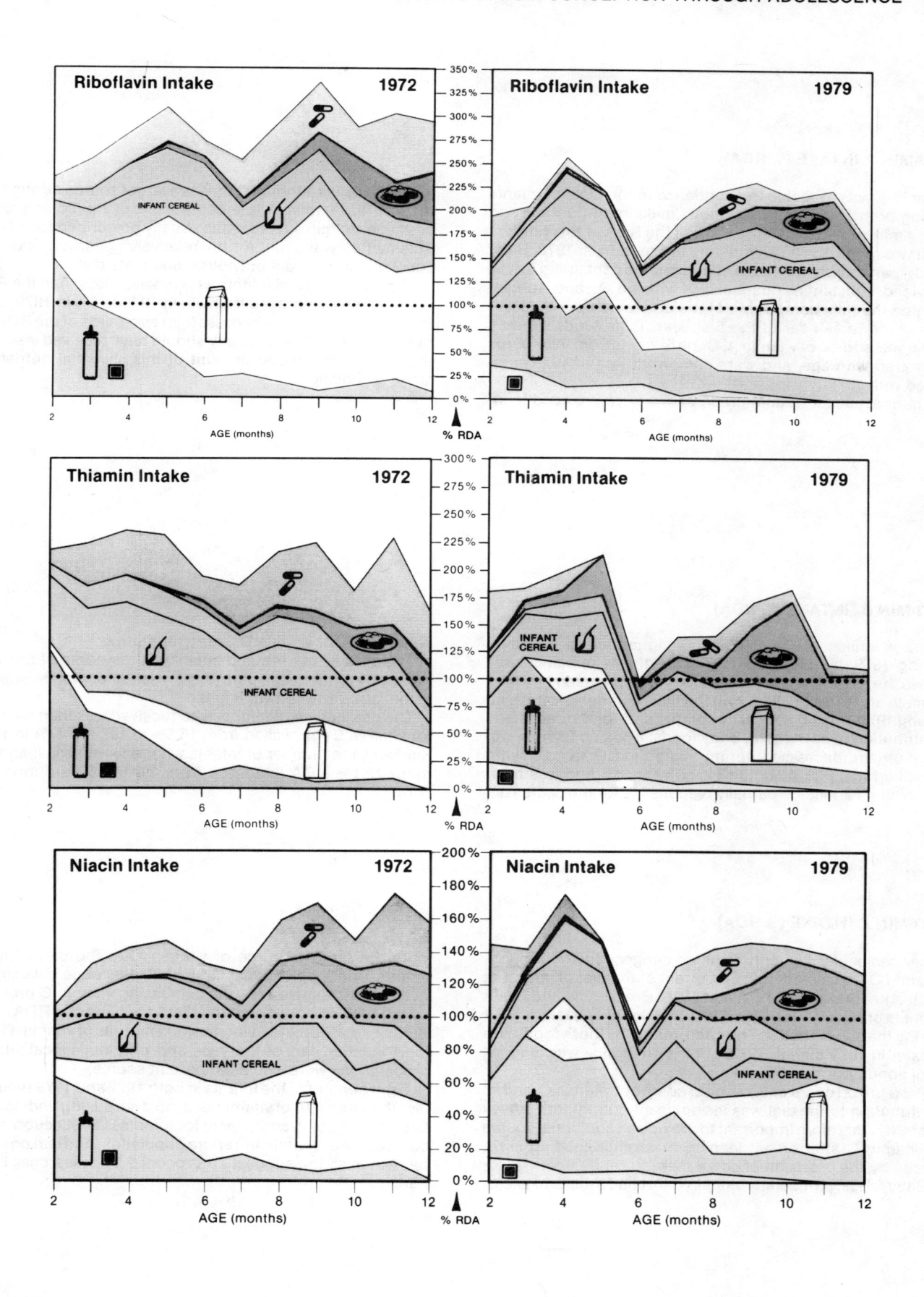

NUTRITION FROM CONCEPTION THROUGH ADOLESCENCE

VITAMIN A INTAKE (% RDA)

Vitamin A was available in abundance in the diets of infants during both 1972 and 1979. Breast milk, infant formula and cow's milk provided at least 100% of the RDA of this nutrient until two months in 1972 and until five months in 1979. Baby foods, particularly vegetable and vegetable containing foods, provided substantial quantities of vitamin A, and supplemented the milk component of the diet to achieve the RDA during the remainder of the first year. Table foods were an additional source of vitamin A. Contributions from this source increased with age, and were somewhat less in 1979 compared with 1972.

Pharmaceutical vitamin preparations were provided to infants at all ages although this was a larger source during 1972 than 1979. Vitamin A is a component of the commercially available vitamin supplements usually prescribed for infants. This fact may account for the relatively generous vitamin A supplementation to a previously adequate diet.

The percentage of infants who received less than the RDA for vitamin A decreased from 8% in 1972 to 5% in 1979. Less than 1% of infants received less than two-thirds of the RDA for this nutrient in 1979. That any should have received less than the full recommended amount of this essential nutrient is alone surprising.

VITAMIN B$_6$ INTAKE (% RDA)

Average intakes of vitamin B$_6$ were higher during 1972 than during 1979, although total average intakes remained well above the RDA. The quantity of vitamin B$_6$ provided by infant formula and breast milk during the first six months increased during 1979, but did not totally compensate for the decreased contribution of cow's milk. Baby foods, also good sources of this nutrient, decreased during this period. A trend toward providing more fruit containing baby foods, and less meat containing varieties is partially responsible for the decreased contribution of vitamin B$_6$ from this source.

Table foods contributed substantial amounts of this nutrient during the latter part of the year, and vitamin supplements also provided vitamin B$_6$.

The percentage of infants who received less than the RDA for vitamin B$_6$ increased from 16.5% in 1972 to 47% in 1979. Similarly, the number of infants who received less than two-thirds of the RDA increased from 3% to 16.5% during this period.

VITAMIN C INTAKE (% RDA)

American babies certainly are in no danger of getting scurvy. Vitamin C was a plentiful component of the diet of infants at each age during both 1972 and 1979. Breast milk and infant formula provided this nutrient in quantities at or near the RDA during the early months. The contribution by these foods was greater in 1979 than in 1972, but the difference was minimal until about four months of age.

Pasteurized cow's milk is a poor source of vitamin C, and its contribution to the diet was insignificant during both survey years. It is therefore important to provide an additional source of vitamin C after breast feeding or formula feeding is replaced by the provision of cow's milk.

Baby foods, particularly vitamin C fortified fruits and juices, were the largest source of vitamin C in the diet of these infants. The supplemental nature of these foods is illustrated in that they complement the decreasing vitamin C provided by the milk component of the diet to achieve the RDA.

Table foods provided increasing amounts of vitamin C during the latter part of the year, and pharmaceutical vitamin preparations were also an important source.

Eight percent of the infants in both 1972 and 1979 received less than the RDA of vitamin C, a most surprising finding. The large intakes of ascorbic acid for infants is a reflection of the consciousness within the entire population, and can possibly be related to the suggestion proposed by researcher Linus Pauling.

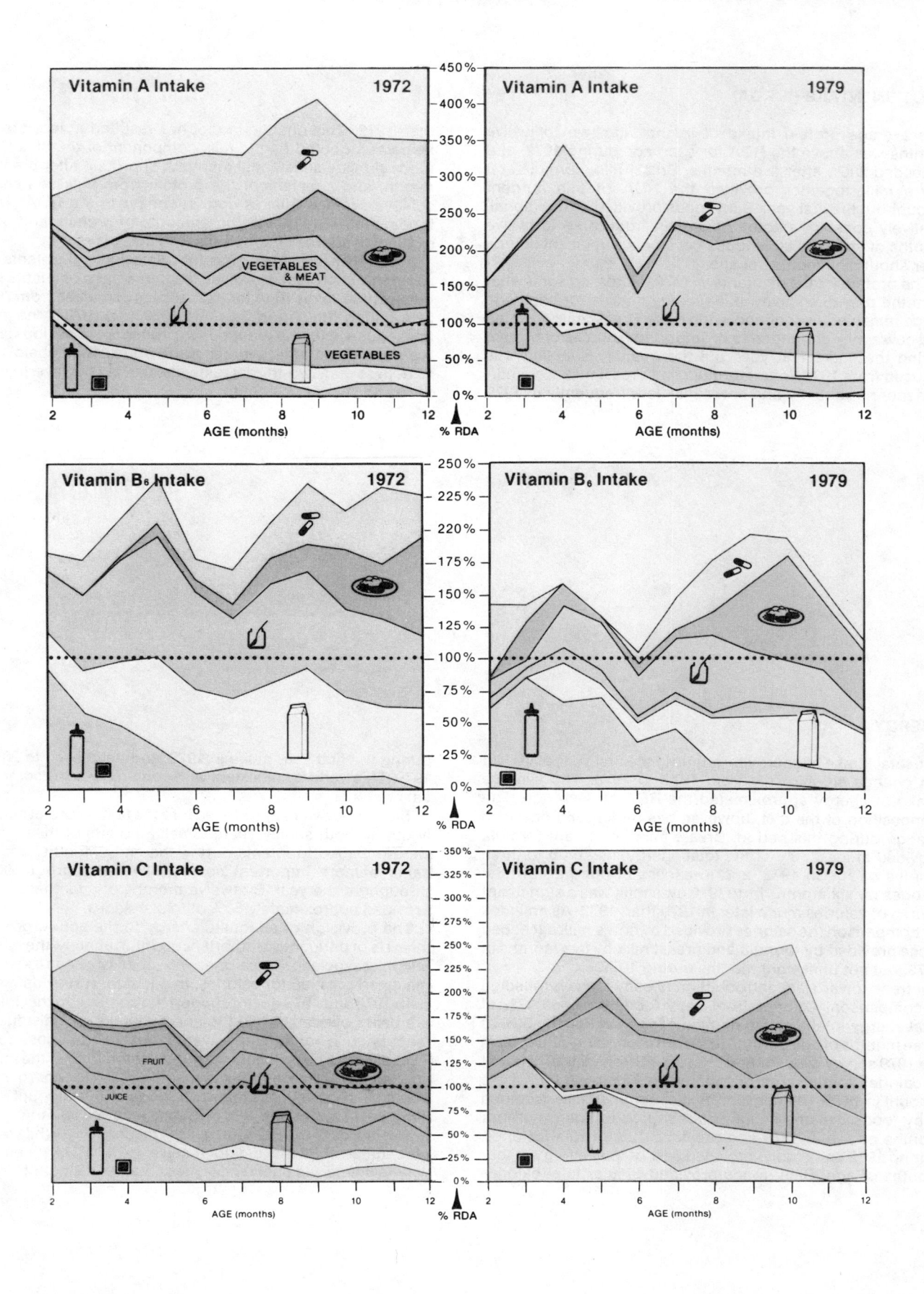

NUTRITION FROM CONCEPTION THROUGH ADOLESCENCE

PROTEIN INTAKE (% RDA)

The average protein intake of infants age two to twelve months was above the RDA for each age during 1972, and exceeded 200% after five months. Breast milk, formula and cow's milk together provided the RDA of this nutrient throughout the first year. Baby foods provided an additional, relatively constant amount of protein from three to twelve months of age, and table foods became a significant source after about nine months of age.

The protein intake of infants in 1979 decreased somewhat from the previous survey, but average intakes for each age range remained near or above the RDA. Breast milk, formula and cow's milk continued to be important sources of protein during the entire first year, but the quantity supplied was reduced from 1972. Infant formula and breast milk were utilized more frequently and cow's milk less frequently in 1979 than 1972. This change in diet has resulted in less protein being contributed by the milk component of the diet. Baby foods provide substantial amounts of protein after the third month, and supplement the protein from milk sources to achieve average intakes corresponding to the RDA. Table foods contribute increasing amounts of protein, and are a significant source after about seven months of age.

A criticism has been that the diets for U.S. infants are excessive in protein. However, the percentage of infants who did not receive the RDA for this nutrient increased from 7% to 29% during the period between 1972 and 1979. A negative consequence for the reduction in protein is not obvious since the percentage of infants receiving substantially below the RDA (less than two-thirds) remained below 7%. Nevertheless, the trend should be noted.

ENERGY

The total intake of energy throughout the first year of life did not change significantly from 1972 to 1979. The average intake of energy approximated the RDA at each age. The composition of the diet, however, has undergone dramatic change during this period. Breast milk and infant formula provided at least 50% of the total energy intake up to three months of age in 1972, and in excess of one-half of total calories for six months in 1979. Cow's milk was a significant source of calories much later in 1979 than 1972. As an index for comparison the calories provided by cow's milk exceeded those provided by formula and breast milk by five months in 1972, but not until eight months during 1979.

A trend toward later introduction of baby foods is reflected in comparison. Calories from baby foods provided 17% of total energy intake at two months of age, and nearly 30% at three months of age during 1972. Corresponding values from the 1979 survey were 9% and 8%, respectively; a total of about 60 calories. Infant cereal accounted for about one-half of this amount in 1979. The consumption of commercially prepared baby foods became a significant source of energy at four months of age in 1979 and provided 22% of total calories. During 1972 baby foods provided 32% of total energy at four months of age. Baby foods provided 27% of total calories during the first year of life in 1972, and decreased to 20% in 1979. This trend is consistent with contemporary recommendation.

Table foods were introduced into the first-year diet similarly during both survey years. Small amounts of these foods were provided to infants during the early months, and became a more important source of energy progressively throughout the year. By twelve months of age, these foods provided approximately 50% of total calories.

The provision of adequate energy to the active, growing infant is of paramount importance. Unfortunately, the misuse and misassociation of calories with obesity often results in a maligned position for calories. In addition, survey data from both 1972 and 1979 do not support the contention that infants are being overfed. While the energy intake of individual infants is quite variable, the average intakes are close to the RDA at each age specified. Although nearly 70% of the infants studied in 1972 received less than the RDA for energy, only about 5% received less than two-thirds of this amount. Similarly, in 1979, 73% and 12% of infants received less than 100% or two-thirds of the RDA for energy, respectively. While a high percentage of infants did not receive the full RDA for energy, very few received substantially less than this amount.

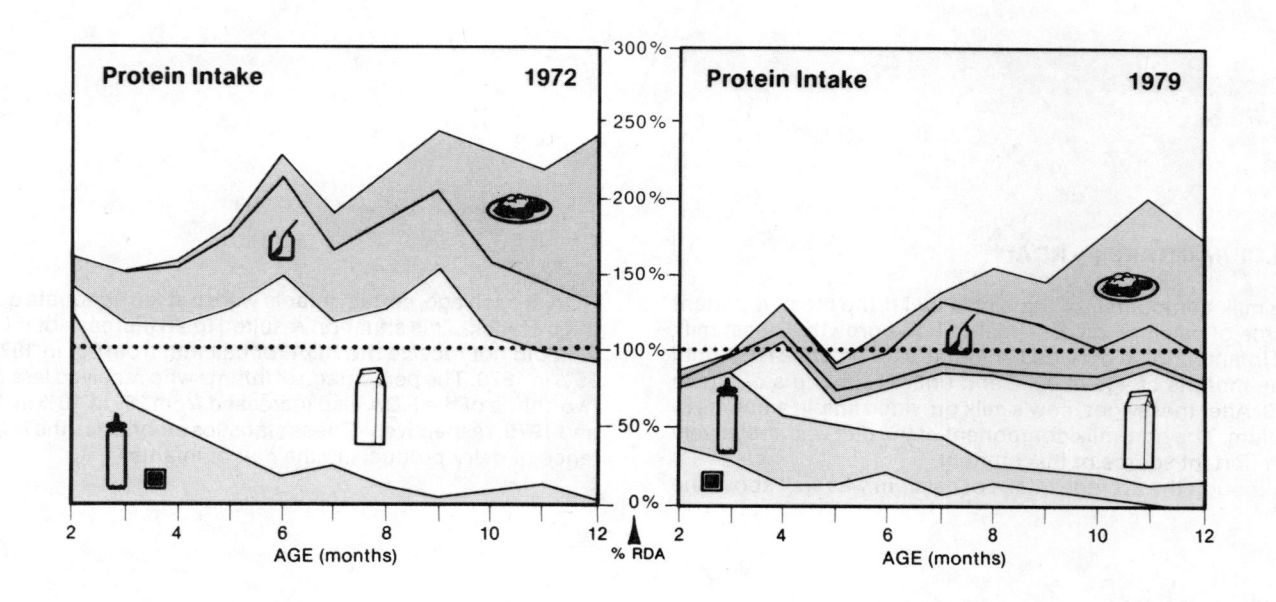

NUTRITION FROM CONCEPTION THROUGH ADOLESCENCE 197

Average Nutrient Intake for Infants

from age 2 months to age 12 months

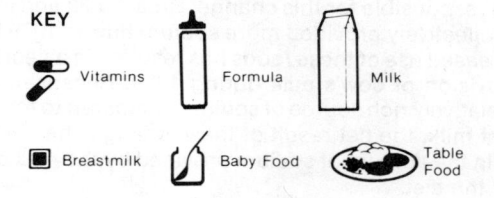

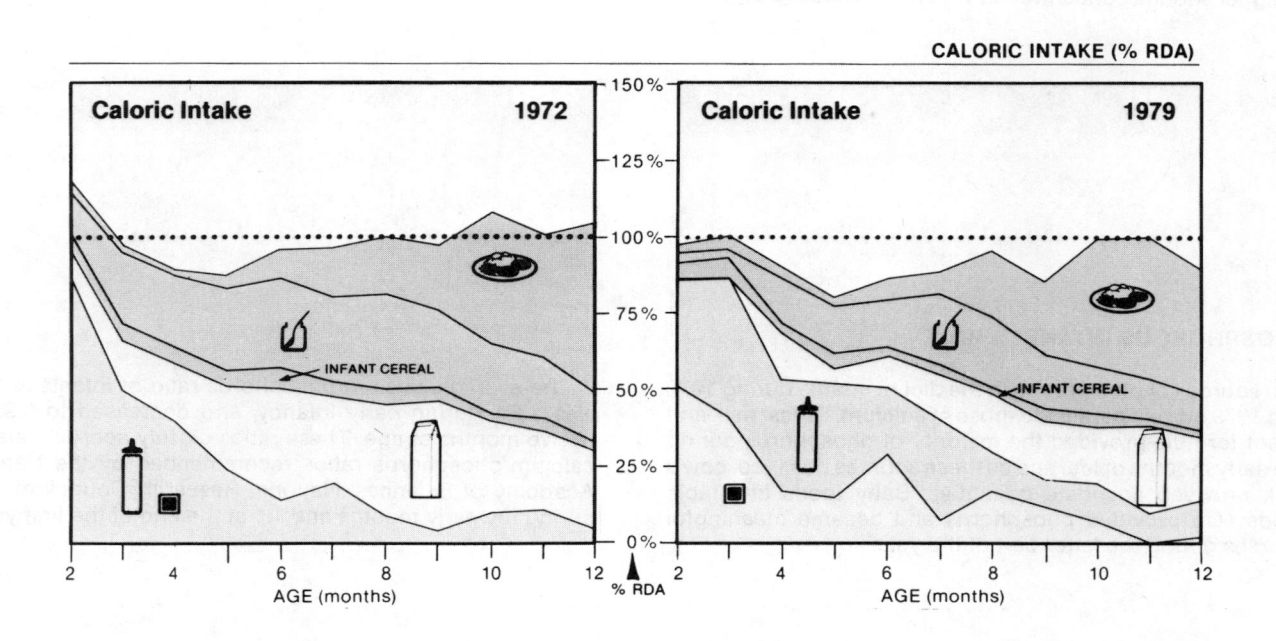

KEY: Vitamins, Formula, Milk, Breastmilk, Baby Food, Table Food

CALCIUM INTAKE (% RDA)

The milk component of the diet is by far the most important source of calcium, an essential to bone growth. Breast milk and infant formula provided amounts at or near the RDA until three months of age in 1972 and until five months of age in 1979. After these ages, cow's milk provided ample amounts of calcium. The non-milk component of the diet was a relatively unimportant source of this nutrient.

Although the average intake of calcium was well above the RDA at each age, certain infants were not fed adequate quantities of milk. This situation resulted in an increase of infants who did not receive the RDA for calcium from 9% in 1972 to 35% in 1979. The percentage of infants who received less than two-thirds of the RDA also increased from 2% to 10% in 1972 and 1979, respectively. These statistics emphasize the importance of dairy products in the diet of infants.

SODIUM INTAKE (mEq/DAY)

The sodium intake of infants has decreased considerably in the period between 1972 and 1979. There are several factors which are responsible for this change. Breast milk and infant formula collectively provided more sodium during 1979 than 1972. Increased use of these foods has resulted in a decrease in the provision of cow's milk during 1979. Because cow's milk is a relatively rich source of sodium compared to formula and breast milk, the net result of these changes has been a decrease in the amount of sodium provided by the milk component of the diet.

The removal of added salt from commercially prepared baby foods has also contributed to the overall reduction in the sodium intake of infants. Also, baby foods of low endogenous sodium content such as fruits have tended to displace those of higher sodium concentration which has added to the effect of salt deletion. Nevertheless, the lower contribution of sodium by baby foods has resulted in a significant change only in infants less than eight months of age due to the large contribution of table foods in the diet of the older infant.

During both 1972 and 1979, the dominant source of sodium in the diet after about eight months of age was table food. These foods provided more sodium than all other sources combined by ten months in 1972 and by nine months in 1979. If the sodium intake of older infants is a concern, prudent selection or delayed introduction of table foods would be the most efficacious dietary change. Many concealed sodium sources are not recognized in the infant's diet; milk and milk products, bread and bakery products, processed meats, canned vegetables and others, are some examples.

PHOSPHOROUS INTAKE (% RDA)

The sources of phosphorus in the diet of infants during 1972 and 1979 closely paralleled those of calcium. Breast milk and infant formula provided the majority of phosphorus during the early months of life, and as these sources declined, cow's milk provided adequate quantities. Baby foods and table foods also provided phosphorus and became meaningful sources during the latter part of the year.

The average calcium/phosphorus ratio of infants in 1979 was 1.5:1 during early infancy, and decreased to 0.9:1 at twelve months of age. These ratios closely approximate the calcium/phosphorus ratios recommended by the National Academy of Sciences' National Research Council of 1.5:1 during the early months and 1:1 at the end of the first year.

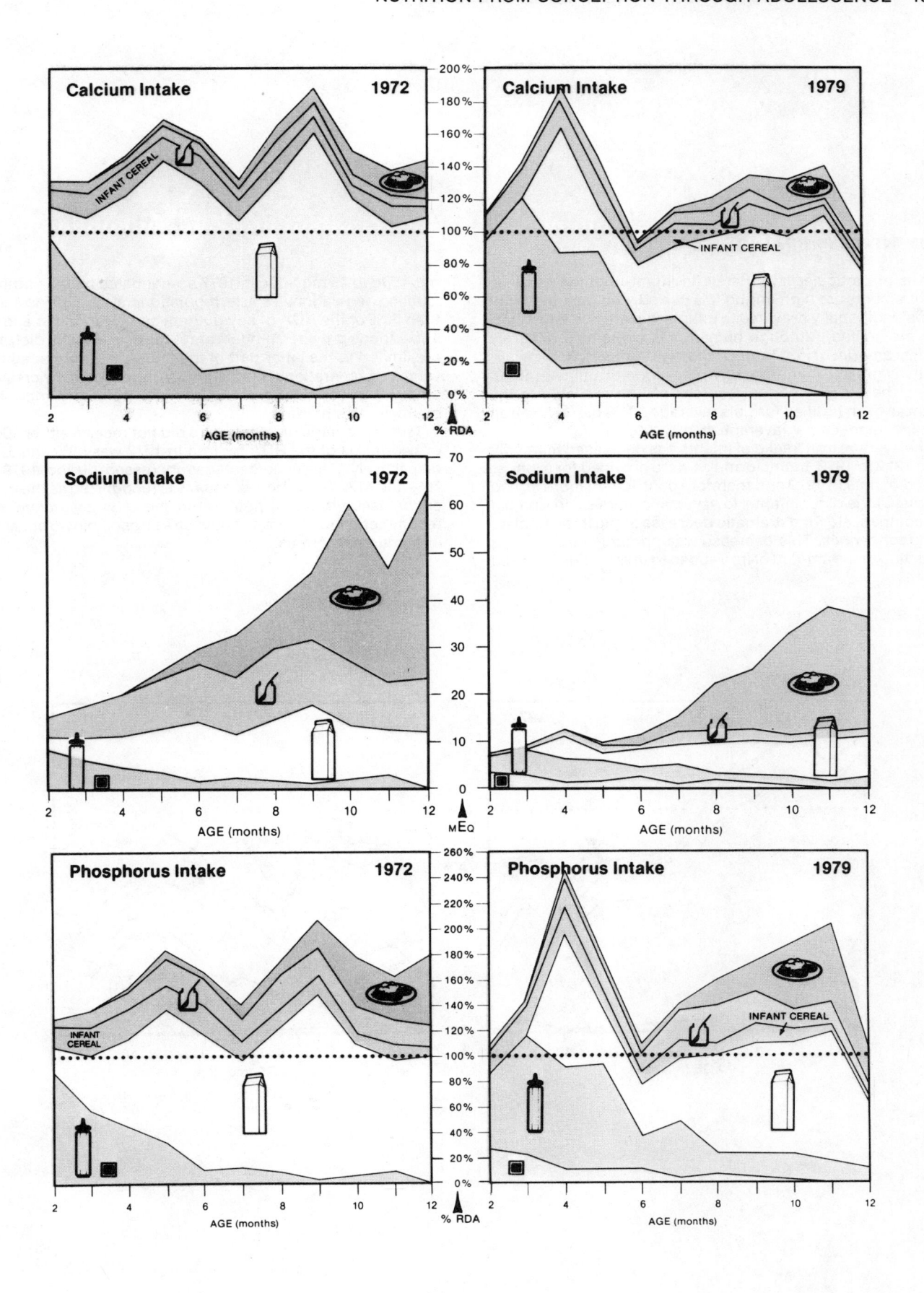

NUTRITION FROM CONCEPTION THROUGH ADOLESCENCE

IRON INTAKE (% RDA)

Iron is of particular importance in infant nutrition because requirements are high during this period, and the number of foods traditionally provided to infants that are rich sources of iron are limited. Although human milk contains a relatively modest amount of iron (approximately 0.5 mg/1), its bioavailability is greater than from any other food examined (about 50%). The other important sources of iron available to the infant are iron fortified formula (average 10-15 mg/1) and iron fortified infant cereal (average 45 mg/100g).

The average iron intake of infants has decreased markedly from 1972 to 1979. Infant formulas were provided for a longer period of time in 1979 and therefore contributed more iron to the diet of the older infant. However, this increase in iron did not compensate for a dramatic decrease in the iron supplied by infant cereals. This decrease was primarily caused by a reduction of the amount of iron added to these foods from 100 mg/100g to 45 mg/100g in 1977 as mandated by the nutrition labeling regulations. These regulations state that no more than 50% of the RDA of any nutrient can be added to a food. Table foods provided modest amounts of iron to the diet, and are limited to the latter part of the first year. Pharmaceutical vitamin preparations containing iron provided increased amounts of iron during 1979, and were a relatively important source of this nutrient.

The percentage of infants who did not receive either 100% or two-thirds of the RDA for iron in 1972 was 58% and 37%, respectively. These percentages increased during 1979 to 70% and 47%. Since iron adequacy is recognized as the most critical issue in infant nutrition in the U.S., assurance and recommendation for iron should be a strong point to consider in nutrition programs.

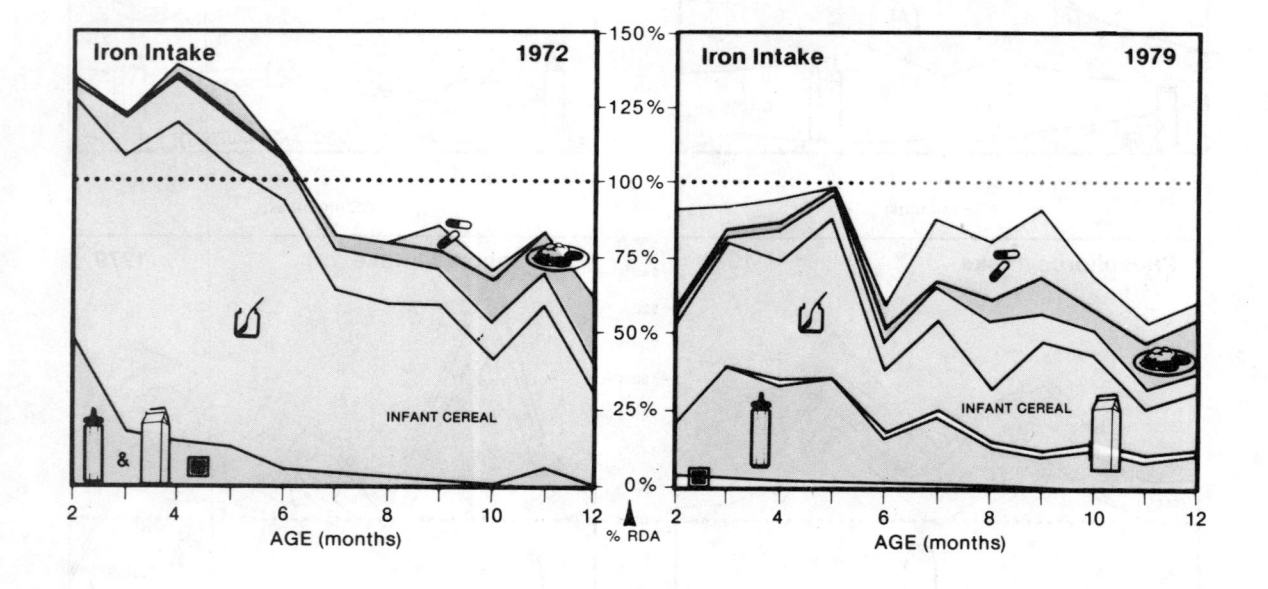

IRON INTAKE (MG/DAY)

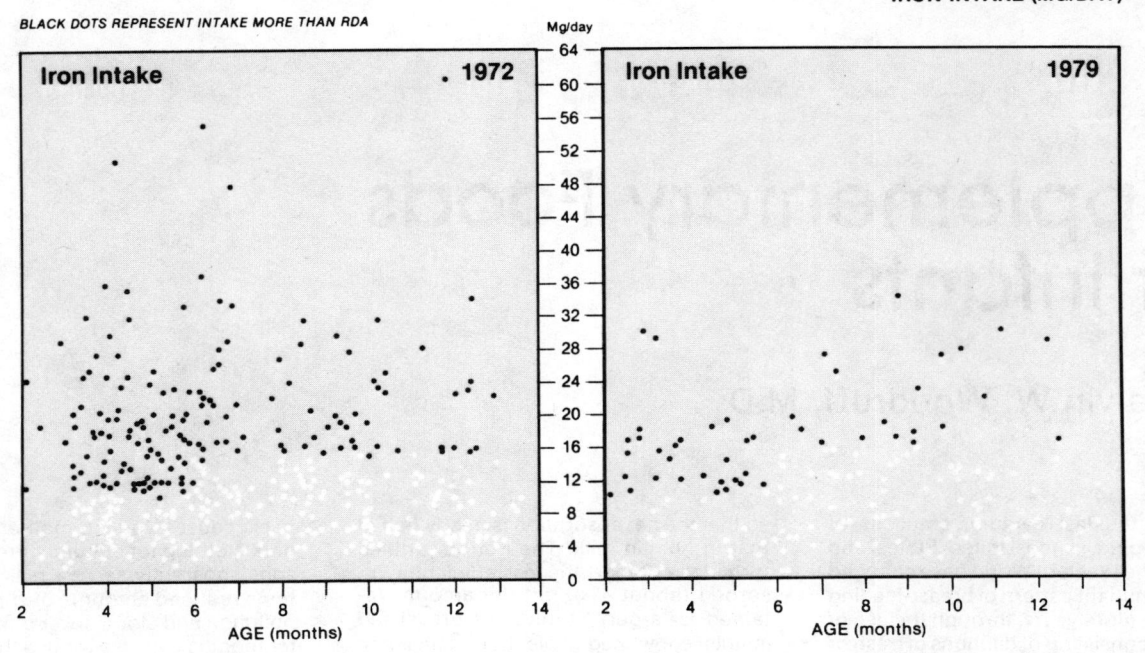

BLACK DOTS REPRESENT INTAKE MORE THAN RDA

Iron Intake — 1972

Iron Intake — 1979

Supplementary Foods for Infants

by Calvin W. Woodruff, M.D.

During the last century, practices of infant feeding in the United States and much of the Western World have changed from a dominant pattern of breast-feeding for one or more years, through the use of formulas consisting of dilutions of fresh or evaporated milk and, most recently, a renewed interest in and a growing scientific rationale for breast-feeding. During this time, practices concerning the supplementation of human milk or its substitutes with other foods and specific essential nutrients have varied from starting such feeding at the age of one year to competition among mothers to begin "solid" foods as early as possible. The purpose of this article is to review the information on which recommendations for supplementary feedings are based.

Human milk or prepared formula in amounts producing normal growth patterns meet all of the nutritional requirements of full-term infants for the first six months of life.[1] Breast-fed infants of healthy mothers have similar weight gains throughout the world until about six months of age when growth may slow if supplementary food is not available to the infant. The exact age at which current prepared formulas need supplementation has not been established but can be assumed to be similar. Before the age of six months, the only supplements which need to be considered are iron, vitamin D and fluoride.

IRON

Milk from either dairy animals or nursing mothers contains little iron. However, the small amount (0.3 to 0.4 mg/L) in human milk is well absorbed by the nursing infant with an average figure being 50%. The specific biochemical factors which are responsible for its high bioavailability are not yet known. Cow's milk-based formula (iron content about 0.8 mg/L) has a bioavailability of about 10% so that the net absorption is nearly half of that in human milk. The iron in fortified formulas (12 mg/L) is less efficiently absorbed (about .4%), but the amount retained is larger. Studies[2] of breast-fed infants show negligible iron deficiency anemia under six months of age; infants fed diluted cow's milk formulas without added iron may develop anemia by the age of four months; and infants fed iron-supplemented formulas rarely become anemic. There is evidence that feeding supplementary foods to nursing infants between four and six months interferes with their iron absorption.

Because some of this information is relatively recent, it has not yet been incorporated into the recommendations of official bodies or individual reviewers. Although the administration of iron to infants is a well-known public health measure,[3] the way in which this type of prevention is applied to individuals should be related to their particular needs. There is general agreement that prepared formulas based upon either cow's milk or soy protein should contain added iron and that iron deficiency is unlikely when this practice is followed. However, the breast-fed infant, especially the exclusively breast-fed infant, does not need an iron supplement before feeding of supplementary food is begun at about six months of age. At this time iron-fortified cereal appears to be an adequate source of iron.

VITAMIN D

Rickets has reappeared in the U.S. population and the question of vitamin D usage needs review. Excluding rickets caused by metabolic disease and an abnormally high requirement of vitamin D, most of the rickets recently reported has been in breast-fed infants.

Much evidence suggests that deprivation of sunlight, rather than failure to administer vitamin D supplements, is the basic cause. Nursing mothers who wear dark clothing for cultural or religious reasons apparently secrete milk which contains reduced amounts of vitamin D.[4] Air pollution and cloud cover during the winter months can also reduce the activation of 7-dehydrocholesterol in the skin by ultraviolet light. Pigmented skin is also a factor and many of the recently reported cases have been in Blacks where a combination of the above factors exists.[4] When sunlight is available to mother and infant, supplementation with vitamin D is unnecessary. Probably for most of the U.S., 300-400 I.U. of vitamin D is supplied by prepared formulas and similar amounts should be given to nursing infants when deprivation from sunlight is suspected.

FLUORIDE

Present recommendations for fluoride supplementation are based upon the amount of fluoride in the water supply and are difficult to extrapolate into the first year of life.[5] Human milk contains little fluoride whether the mother's intake is high or low. Formulas are manufactured with low fluoride water to avoid overdosage when diluted with water of varying fluoride content. Epidemiological studies on the role of fluoride intake in preventing dental caries have not yet been extended into the first year of life. There is some doubt concerning the effect of fluoride before eruption of the teeth. Because of this lack of specific information concerning fluoride in the first year of life, recommendations take different approaches. One is to recommend the routine use of fluoride from birth onwards. Another is to depend on the amount of fluoride in the water supply with supplements used only when the water supply contains less than 0.7 ppm. The intake of water is quite variable during the first year of life. One recent recommendation has compromised on the phrase "soon after birth" which reflects our lack of specific information concerning this question.[6]

When breast-feeding is recommended as the sole source of nutrition for infants, the prescription of supplements of iron, vitamin D and fluoride would not seem necessary except in unusual circumstances.

SUPPLEMENTARY FEEDING

In anticipation of nutritional need and depending on developmental readiness, the infant between 4 and 6 months of age can benefit from beginning to acquire lifelong eating habits.[7] There are two major objectives: to appreciate and enjoy a variety of foods and to learn to keep caloric intake and output in balance. At this age the infant learns to eat from a spoon and to express both eagerness for food and satiety. Although precooked infant cereal fortified with iron is the food usually started first, the order in which strained fruits and vegetables are added is unimportant. Variety in the diet can be thought of in two ways: the basic four food groups or variety in such aspects of food as taste, color, consistency and temperature. Infants consuming diets monotonous in one or more of these attributes are at risk of developing nutritional deficiency. During the period of introduction of supplementary foods, it is more important for the infant to learn to enjoy foods of differing tastes and colors than to have an arbitrary amount of each food since breast milk or formula still supplies the major portion of the calories and essential nutrients. At first the consistency will be that of strained food. As development of motor skills, such as swallowing small particles and a pincer grasp occurs, the infant begins to feed himself and to begin the transition from specially prepared foods to a modified adult diet. Temperature variation, so important to adults, begins. By the age of one year, most infants have completed this transition.

OTHER MILK FEEDINGS

In 1976, the Committee on Nutrition of the American Academy of Pediatrics published standards for infant formula.[8] These standards have been recognized as the best possible estimate of the nutritional requirements of infants during the first year of life. The question often arises concerning the nutritional adequacy of other milk feedings as substitutes for infant formula.

Cow's milk in undiluted form contains amounts of protein and electrolytes which exceed the maximum limits of these standards. When diluted with water and with added carbohydrate, which was a practice widespread a generation ago, cow's milk in either fresh or evaporated form is lacking in ascorbic acid, tocopherol (vitamin E), and essential fatty acids. It also needs to be supplemented with iron. There is increasing evidence that pasteurized, homogenized, fresh cow's milk, particularly when consumed in large amounts, is associated with occult blood loss.[9] Even ordinary amounts (less than one quart daily) have been associated with biochemical iron deficiency when compared with a formula not fortified with iron.[10] Although the mechanism by which fresh cow's milk produces occult blood loss is not yet known in detail, it is most likely due to immunologic immaturity of the infant intestine. Thus, it seems wise to recommend that fresh cow's milk not be used in infant feeding until the intestinal tract reaches immunologic maturity, which probably occurs towards the end of the first year of life.

Skim milk, although cheap, has all the drawbacks of undiluted cow's milk. It does not meet the minimum requirement for fat, even when infant foods make up a significant proportion of the total calories.[11] A study has shown that infants did not gain weight at the expected rate on ad libitum skim milk feedings. Fat calories are needed by infants in addition to their requirements for fat-soluble vitamins and essential fatty acids.

OBESITY

Since the first year of life is a time of rapid development of behavioral patterns including those involved in food intake, achieving a balance between energy intake and energy needs can be part of this developmental process. Monitoring the growth in height and weight is part of health care. The use of growth charts, such as those published by the National Center for Health Statistics, is necessary to relate the growth pattern of the individual infant to the population in which he lives. Although there is considerable variation in size, the rate of growth generally follows the same pattern. An infant who gains at a rate which soon places him above the 95th percentile for weight needs a review of his caloric intake and the circumstances surrounding his feeding. Is food used as a pacifier or as a reward? What does his caretaker(s) know about his individual caloric needs? Although the average caloric requirement for the first year of life is stated to be 100-110 kcal/kg/day, the standard deviation is not well defined. Some infants thrive and grow on intakes less than average, and others eat more without gaining excessive weight. Only individual understanding and management based upon the specific circumstances is effective and may be difficult. Although the evidence linking infantile obesity to obesity in childhood and adulthood is still not conclusive, rapid weight gain in infants should not be ignored.

SUMMARY

Either breast-feeding or the use of an iron-containing infant formula meets all of the nutritional needs of the infant for the first six months of life when available in amounts which result in normal growth. The goal of supplementary feeding is the development of lifelong eating patterns which will maintain optimal health. The introduction of supplementary foods is based upon both nutritional need and developmental readiness.

REFERENCES

1. Woodruff, C.W., The Science of Nutrition and the Art of Infant Feeding, J. Amer. Med. Assoc. 240:657-661, 1978.
2. Dallman, P.R., Siimes, M.A., Iron Deficiency in Infancy and Childhood, International Nutritional Anemia Consultive Group, Nutrition Foundation, New York, 1979.
3. Foman, S.J., Filer, L.J., Jr., Anderson, T.A., et al., Recommendations for Feeding Normal Infants, Pediatrics 63:52, 1979.
4. Bachrach, S., Fisher, J., Parks, J.S., An Outbreak of Vitamin D Deficiency Rickets in a Susceptible Population, Pediatrics 64:871-877, 1979.
5. Committee on Nutrition, AAP, Fluoride Supplementation: Revised Dosage Schedule, Pediatrics 63:150-152, 1979.
6. Amer. Pub. Health Assoc. Position Paper, Infant Feeding in the United States, J. Amer. Pub. Health Assoc, Feb. 1981 (in press).
7. Committee on Nutrition, AAP, On the Feeding of Supplementary Foods to Infants, Pediatrics 65:1178-1181, 1980.
8. Committee on Nutrition, AAP, Commentary on Breast-Feeding and Infant Formulas, Including Proposed Standards for Formulas, Pediatrics 57:278-285, 1976.
9. Wilson, J.F., Lahey, M.E., Heiner, D.C., Studies on Iron Metabolism: V. Further Observations on Cow's Milk-Induced Gastrointestinal Bleeding in Infants with Iron-Deficiency Anemia, J. Pediatr. 84:335-344, 1974.
10. Woodruff, C.W., Iron Deficiency in Infancy and Childhood, Pediatr. Clin. North Am. 24:85-94, 1977.
11. Foman, S.J., Filer, L.J., Ziegler, E.E. et al., Skim Milk in Infant Feeding, Acta. Paediatr. Scand. 66:17-30, 1977.

INFANCY

Infant and Child Nutrition: Concerns Regarding the Developmentally Disabled

by the American Dietetic Association

Part I. Infant and child nutrition

Optimum nutrition is essential for children to achieve their physical and developmental potential. Although studies indicate that many children in the United States are adequately nourished, they have also clearly revealed that there are economically deprived groups of infants and children with a high incidence of malnutrition (1). In addition, some handicapped and developmentally delayed children experience difficulties in consuming an adequate food intake while others, because of inactivity or psychosocial factors, consume excess energy and become obese. The infant, especially the pre-term and small-for-gestational age infant, is at nutritional risk because of size, immaturity, and/or medical complications that often occur and require nutritional therapy.

Dietitians-nutritionists are assuming increasingly important roles in nutritional counseling and education for those who care for infants and children, and in the management of children with health problems amenable to nutritional therapy. Their contribution in preventive and therapeutic pediatrics is becoming better recognized, and through their continuing efforts, better health of infants and children can be promoted. This paper affirms the importance of nutrition for all children and identifies common nutritional problems of normal and developmentally delayed infants and children and of children vulnerable to malnutrition.

Preventive aspects

The provision of adequate nutrients in appropriate amounts is an important factor in preventing developmental disabilities. This is particularly important in relation to inherited metabolic disorders as well as nutritional influences on brain and nervous system growth *in utero* and during the early months of life.

Malnutrition can limit brain and skeletal growth as well as the central nervous system of the fetus or infant. Although controversial, the relationship between malnutrition and intellectual development is becoming clearer. Important considerations include the timing, duration, and severity of the deprivation. Many studies show that children who survive severe malnutrition suffer developmental retardation even after rehabilitation, especially if the malnutrition occurs prior to six months of age. Recent studies indicate that previously malnourished children (particularly those malnourished in late infancy and early childhood) who receive sensory stimulation, along with adequate nutrition, show some evidence of "catch-up" in intellectual development (2-6).

Intrauterine life is most susceptible to nutritional insult. During this period, all fetal organs are in the hyperplastic phase of growth. Fetal malnutrition may result from: (a) reduced maternal circulation, (b) inadequate supply of nutrients from maternal circulation, or (c) faulty placental transport of specific nutrients.

Factors which contribute to a healthy pregnancy and a subsequently healthy infant include adequate weight gain, regular prenatal care, and a diet which meets maternal energy and nutrient needs. Maternal-fetal factors are not sufficiently understood to support restriction of the usual weight gain (10 to 12 kg.) during pregnancy even in the grossly obese. Women who tend to be 10 percent or more underweight have an increased incidence of premature and low-birth-weight infants (7). Of particular concern are teen-age gravidas who are less than three years post-menarche (8). Diet supplementation programs, such as the Supplemental Food Program for Women, Infants and Children (WIC), provide foods which give additional calories and nutrients in conjunction with nutritional education. Prenatal supplementation has improved infant birth weights (9).

Nutrient needs of children

Milk from a healthy mother is the food of choice for healthy newborns and infants. Generally, iron-fortified formula is the best alternative when the mother does not choose or is unable to breast feed, or discontinues breast feeding early. Either human milk or infant formula should be a basic component of the diet throughout the first 12 months of life. Cow's milk in the form of whole, 2 percent, or nonfat milk is inappropriate for young infants. Professional differences exist on whether healthy infants fed human milk should be routinely supplemented with vitamin D, fluoride, or iron, and when this supplementation should occur. The basis for the uncertainty is the lack of sufficient data on human milk composition, the physiologic factors affecting nutrient interaction, and specific absorption rates (10-14). Cases of rickets in children fed human milk have been documented (15). There is lack of conclusive evidence on the optimum time to initiate fluoride supplementation. Infants who do not receive at least 10 oz. daily of fluoridated water (0.3-1 p.p.m.) may benefit from a fluoride supplement introduced soon after birth (16,17). Exclusively breast-fed infants can maintain iron tissue stores for at least six months (18).

Many variables affect the nutritional status of the breast-fed infant. For example, the iron status of exclusively breast-fed infants differs from that of infants who receive food other than milk (19). The decision to give supplements to the breast-fed infant should be based on an individual assessment of the mother's and infant's nutritional status and related infant care practices such as the planned period of exclusive breast feeding and exposure to sunlight. The mother should help make the informed decision on the use and timing of supplements to human milk.

The passage of drugs into human milk is dependent on the concentration gradient established between plasma and milk, which in turn is controlled by the drugs' solubility, pH, dosage, transport mechanisms, and metabolism. Drugs that generally should be avoided during lactation are atropine, anticonvulsants, anti-infective drugs, antimetabolites, antithyroid drugs, cathartics, mercurials, narcotics, oral contraceptives, psychotherapeutic agents, radioactive preparations, sedative-hypnotic drugs, and steroids (20).

Human milk (with possible vitamin-mineral supplements) or iron-fortified formula (with access to fluoride) in adequate amounts provides the energy and nutrients needed by healthy infants until at least four months of age. The rate of growth and development should be closely monitored because either feeding method can be associated with failure to thrive or obesity due to improper feeding techniques. There is no nutritional advantage to the introduction of solid foods prior to the infant's fourth month. Current pediatric practice recommends the introduction of solids between four and six months (21). The timing is influenced by factors including: (a) current weight as related to birth weight; (b) developmental readiness as indicated by head control and ability to sit supported, and the diminishing of the tongue protrusion reflex; (c) feeding satiety as indicated by spacing between nursing periods or consumed formula volume; (d) psychosocial factors; and (e) nutrition needs.

There appears to be a sensitive period in which children are developmentally ready to chew (22). Mashed or chopped table foods of suitable texture should be introduced to the infant by this time, generally at the age of six or seven months.

Between the latter part of the first year and the early months of the second, the child gradually changes to the family's diet. Diets of toddlers and preschool children should provide a variety of nutrient-dense foods divided into four or five feedings. The food habits and related psychologic factors and behaviors associated with food, which are formed during infancy and the first few years of life, may have a lifelong impact.

The rate of growth slows during the first year of life, proceeding erratically until school age. The growth pattern is smoother during the early school age years until the pubertal spurt. Between 5 and 10 years of age, children generally have good appetites, accept a variety of foods, and establish their patterns of exercise, sports, and dental care (22).

Onset of puberty is generally associated with hunger and increasing appetite. The nutritional needs of pre-adolescents and adolescents are ever-changing in relationship to their growth and development patterns.

The energy requirements are dependent on: (a) the nutrient needs for growth, (b) body size and composition, (c) physical activity, and (d) ecological factors. Nutritional requirement data for pubescent and prepubescent children is limited and mainly has been estimated from adult and infant work or from animal studies. We know from experience that children's energy and nutrient needs are highly individual. The energy requirements of a school-aged child or adolescent are not always related to age, size, and physical activity of a reference group.

Children's most prominent nutritional problems are dental caries, iron deficiency anemia (especially between birth and five years, and during adolescence), obesity, and failure to thrive (22). Sociocultural and economic factors (e.g., vegetarianism or poverty) are associated with the nutritional status of children.

Studies of the population's dietary intakes create the concern that present eating habits may not promote health. Low intakes of iron, calcium, and zinc and, in teenage girls, of vitamin B_6, folacin, and magnesium have been reported. Energy intake is lower on the average than the RDAs, yet obesity and overweight are apparent in the childhood population (23). Thus, nutrient density and physical activity must both be addressed.

Nutritional problems of children

ENERGY BALANCE. Achieving an energy intake which supports normal growth and development may be particularly difficult for developmentally delayed children. Obesity occurs commonly in those with Prader-Willi's, Carpenter's, Cohen's, and Laurence-Moon-Biedl syndromes, and myelomeningocele and other syndromes and conditions which limit activity (24). Undernutrition is not unusual in children with neuromotor and psychosocial feeding problems and Cornelia de Lange's syndrome.

Most of these children have energy requirements which deviate from the norm. Individualized therapy and early intervention are important for effective weight control. Periodic anthropometric measurements accurately taken with reliable instruments and concurrent use of growth charts identify children for whom intervention is necessary. When obesity, stunting, or undernutrition is identified, careful evaluation of the child's energy needs should be made prior to implementing a plan of therapy.

IRON DEFICIENCY. Iron deficiency is the most common nutritional deficiency found in children in North America, occurring most often during infancy and early preschool years and the adolescent growth spurt. It is most frequently found in low socioeconomic populations and those who have poor health care (22). Children who consume excessive amounts of milk (more than 36 to 44 oz. per day), who have families that practice dietary extremes or restrictions, or who consume limited amounts of iron-containing foods are at greatest risk. Regular monitoring of iron status should be provided infants, preschoolers, and adolescents. Education about those food sources which provide iron should be furnished for all parents as a preventive measure. Infant formulas with iron or iron supplements containing bioavailable iron should be recommended for high-risk infants and children. When iron deficiency is identified, intensive nutritional education should accompany therapeutic doses of iron.

DENTAL CARIES. A high incidence of dental decay, recurrent dental caries, and periodontal disease are common findings in health surveys of children (22). Children at risk are those with poor dietary and oral health habits. The developmentally disabled child frequently has malformations of the oral area and gingival hyperplasia resulting from anticonvulsant therapy and xerostomia (dry mouth) as a result of other drug therapy (25). Good nutrition, especially adequate protein, vitamins A, C, and D, calcium, phosphorus, and fluoride, during the period of tooth development (in utero to 25 years) is essential to prevent dental problems (26). Oral care (brushing and flossing) during the cavity-prone years is also important (27).

Dietary control of dental caries includes an appropriate diet and restriction of the frequency of the concentrated, sticky, adhesive type of sugar-containing foods. Taking a milk or juice bottle to bed during infancy may contribute to dental caries because it exposes teeth to prolonged contact with fermentable carbohydrate. Fluoride supplementation or topical therapy is recommended for those living in communities without added or naturally occurring fluoridated water or for those consuming less than one quart of fluoridated water (17,18).

Dietitians-nutritionists are urged to look at children's teeth when assessing their nutritional status to identify dental caries. Appropriate referral should be made.

FOOD HYPERSENSITIVITY. Sensitivity to food results in a variety of symptoms that include vomiting, diarrhea, malabsorption, rhinitis, uticaria, eczema, irritability, and hyperactivity. Any food or food component may cause hypersensitivity (commonly called "allergy"). Food hypersensitivities tend to run in families.

During infancy, breast feeding reduces early exposure to cow's milk, one of the most frequent allergens (28). Infants who are not fed human milk and are sensitive to cow's milk should be given a soy-based or protein hydrolysate infant formula. Foods which are associated with family sensitivity should not be given until the latter part of infancy. Suspected single food items should be added slowly (no sooner than every five days) so that any immediate or delayed symptoms of sensitivity can be noted. Sensitivity to a food or food component may occur at any period of childhood, and its identification requires elimination and challenge. Those with multiple food sensitivities require education in nutrition and food composition and monitoring of nutritional status.

Part II. Nutritional problems of children with chronic disease and developmental disabilities

The previous discussion dealt with parameters of nutrition which affect all infants and children. Physically handicapped and developmentally delayed children and those who are chronically ill may have other nutritional concerns resulting from developmental or medical conditions or from the therapy necessary to control a disorder. Part II of the paper focuses on these concerns and Part III makes recommendations for the nutritional health of all children.

Nutrient-drug interactions

Drug therapy has been accepted for children with developmental and behavioral problems and has helped countless individuals. However, it not only causes the desired physical and behavioral changes but may also cause undesirable side effects resulting from drug-drug or drug-nutrient interactions. Some of these changes can be offset by other drugs or dietary modifications.

Drugs commonly used among the developmentally disabled or the mentally or emotionally impaired include: (a) anticonvulsants such as diphenylhydantoin (Dilantin), valproic acid (Depakene), and phenobarbital; (b) central nervous system stimulants such as methylphenidate (Ritalin) and dextroamphetamine (Dexedrine); (c) tranquilizers such as phenothiazine (Thorazine), thioridazine (Mellaril), and diazepam (Valium); (d) antidepressants such as imipramine (Tofranil) and phenelzine (Nardil); and (e) vitamins given in pharmacologic doses.

Anticonvulsants, such as Dilantin and phenobarbital, may precipitate deficiencies in serum folacin and possibly in vitamin B_{12}, abnormalties in vitamin D and bone metabolism, neonatal coagulation defects, connective tissue disorders (gum hypertrophy), endocrine effects (pituitary, adrenal, thyroid, and insulin function), possible deficiencies in pyridoxine, zinc, and copper, and congenital malformations among infants born to mothers on these medications (29-32).

The mechanism producing folacin deficiency following anticonvulsant therapy is still unknown, although many hypotheses have been proposed. The administration of folacin and of vitamin B_{12} to accompany anticonvulsant therapy has been recommended. However, folacin supplementation should not be given *routinely*, as experimental and clinical studies have noted folacin to have potent convulsant properties (33).

In the past decade reports have shown an association between anticonvulsant therapy and a disturbance of bone metabolism. In this country, the incidence of rickets or osteomalacia among persons on anticonvulsants ranged from 8 to 56 percent (34,35). Prophylactic use of vitamin D has produced satisfactory results.

Dietitians-nutritionists are urged to obtain biochemical data to monitor the nutritional status of individuals on anticonvulsant therapy. Supplements should be carefully prescribed and adjusted on the basis of combinations of drugs consumed, the dosages of the drugs, and biochemical data. In light of the many metabolic alterations resulting from anticonvulsants, a trial period to determine the efficacy of the ketogenic diet may be utilized as an alternative to drug therapy (36).

Significant suppression of growth in height and weight has been reported among Ritalin-treated children; a reduction of food intake has also been observed (37,38). Anorexia or appetite suppression may be offset if medication is given during rather than before mealtimes. Monitoring weight, height, and caloric intake is recommended so drug therapy may be regulated.

A dietary alternative to drug therapy proposed by Feingold restricts artificial food colors and flavors, some preservatives, and salicylate-rich foods. Feingold hypothesized that restriction of these additives can prevent hyperactivity (39). Although scientifically designed studies fail to show demonstrable effect of the elimination diet on groups of hyperactive children, some children have shown documentable improvement when on the diet. Additional studies whose design give more attention to the diet-related issues are needed. For parents who insist on following such diets, dietitians-nutritionists are urged to provide professional guidance to ensure nutritional adequacy.

There are few reports on the effects of tranquilizers and antidepressants on metabolism. The commonly prescribed phenothiazine and tricyclic neuroleptic drugs are not associated with abnormal serum vitamin B_{12} and folate levels. Tricyclic neuroleptic drugs, however, cause xerostomia or dryness of the mouth through the drug's cholinergic properties. Because saliva exercises a preventive function in dental cariogenicity, oral hygiene is important during drug therapy. Some antidepressants (phenilzine) inhibit an enzyme, monoamine oxidase, necessary for amine metabolism. Accumulation of amines in the brain may cause headaches, hypertension, and cerebral hemorrhage and could be fatal. Intake of foods such as cheese, alcoholic beverages, soy sauce, and cultured dairy products, rich in amine precursors, is thus restricted (25).

Vitamins in quantities large enough to classify them as drugs have been used therapeutically for more than 20 years. Pharmacologic doses of pyridoxine have been indicated for certain vitamin-dependent genetic disorders such as B_6-dependent infantile convulsions and a folate responsive schizophrenia (40). These metabolic disorders represent a genetic vitamin dependency in which an individual may have a constant life-long requirement for a vitamin in doses which greatly exceed established levels. Vitamins in pharmacologic doses have recently been popularized as "orthomolecular psychiatry" (41). Treatment consists of megadoses of vitamins and minerals and dietary control of sucrose. In 1974 an American Psychiatric Association Task Force rejected this mode of intervention because of lack of supporting controlled experimental studies. The dangers of indiscriminate use of vitamins and minerals in unrestricted quantities cannot be adequately underscored. Although pharmacologic doses of water-soluble vitamins have generally been considered harmless, toxicity and conditioning due to large doses of ascorbic acid have been reported (42). Pathologic changes have also been reported in rats fed high pyridoxine diets (43). Finally, a false sense of security resulting from unprescribed nutrient supplements may result in delay in obtaining critical medical care.

Because of the many metabolic alterations attributed to drug therapy, dietitians-nutritionists should take an active role in facilitating and monitoring appropriate dietary, biochemical, and/or radiologic studies to identify nutritional deficiencies. While additional investigations are needed to determine the type and dose of the supplements, treatment based on current knowledge and assessment findings should be initiated as soon as nutrient deficiencies are identified.

Feeding problems

Feeding problems have been defined "as the inability or refusal to eat certain foods because of neuromotor dysfunction, obstructive lesions or psychosocial factors interfering with eating, or a combination of two or more of these" (44). Several researchers have suggested that at least 25 percent of children (primarily preschoolers) experience feeding problems (45,46).

Neuromotor feeding problems may be identified in infancy. Poor suck, abnormal postural tone during feeding, and the retention of primitive reflexes when they should have faded are all symptoms of central nervous system dysfunction. Eating, chewing, and swallowing problems may in some children be so severe as to compromise the children's nutrient intake (22).

Feeding problems with a psychosocial etiology appear to occur most frequently at two developmental stages: during the first six months of life, and between two and four years of age. Frequently parents consider preschoolers who exhibit normal food behavior such as food jags, erratic appetites, reductions in intake of milk, and disinterest in vegetables to manifest feeding problems. Continually voicing these concerns to the child may turn a transient behavior into an undesirable food habit.

Anticipatory guidance about normal feeding behavior is important for all parents so that appropriate strategies may prevent feeding problems. When feeding problems occur, an interdisciplinary team of a behavior management specialist, an occupational or a physical therapist, a dietitian-nutritionist, a dentist, and a physician is effective in helping parents resolve these problems.

One problem that many who offer food to children report is that milk and acidic fruit juices increase mucous secretions. Most who think this is true restrict intakes of these foods. Controlled studies are needed to confirm or refute the observations. Diets of children who restrict their milk intake should be carefully monitored for calcium, riboflavin, and vitamin D. When dietary intake is inadequate, supplements should be provided. Excessive intakes of high phosphate-containing carbonated beverages should be discouraged to avoid high phosphorus to calcium ratio. If citrus fruit and/or fruit juice is offered in limited amounts, ascorbic acid intakes should be monitored.

Inborn errors of metabolism

Since 1908, when Garrod proposed the concept of hereditary control of metabolic disease, increasing numbers of such disorders have been identified. Presently, dietary treatment is available for disorders of amino acid metabolism such as urea cycle defects, Hartnup's Disease, histidinemia, homocystinuria, hypervalinemia, isovaleric acidemia, maple syrup urine disease, phenylketonuria (PKU), propionic acidemia, tyrosinosis, and methylmalonia aciduria, as well as disorders of carbohydrate metabolism including fructose intolerance, galactosemia, glycogen storage disease, and leucine-sensitive hypoglycemia.

Generally, dietary management of the inherited metabolic disorders involves limiting the nutrient involved, such as phenylalanine in PKU or galactose in galactosemia. In other cases, such as vitamin D-resistant rickets, dietary supplementation may be used. Nutritional status of the child for whom dietary modification is necessary must be closely monitored to ensure adequate growth, appropriate food habit development, and blood levels which will not interfere with normal brain development.

Special dietary formulas are available for the most common inherited disorders. The formulas are designed to provide adequate nourishment with the limiting nutrient absent or reduced. Most formulas are fortified with vitamins and minerals; because these are very expensive, parents may need help in finding programs which may aid in procuring such formulas.

Teaching parents effective nutritional management requires considerable team input. The dietitian is often the case manager because she has special knowledge to meet the critical needs of the family. Considerable time should be spent educating parents on various feeding methods: breast feeding, formula preparation, addition of solid foods, preparation of special recipes, and meal planning. Counseling for dietary restriction should include helping parents realize that consuming a modified diet does not make the child different from other children. Problems can arise, and patients or parents should have access to a dietitian for answers.

The duration of dietary treatment, particularly in PKU, has been the subject of much controversy and discussion. Risks of females with PKU producing defective children appears to be high even with dietary intervention (47).

Cerebral palsy

Nutritional and feeding problems are common in infants and children with cerebral palsy. Children with spasticity often become obese because of limited activity. Those with athetosis may have difficulty consuming adequate energy intakes. Motor incoordination may make self-feeding or normal mastication of food impossible. In addition, children with oral motor problems are often difficult to feed and require many hours daily of patient effort by the feeder.

Prevention and treatment of nutritional problems in these children requires an individualized approach. An interdisciplinary feeding team is the most effective method of evaluating problems and formulating successful plans for therapy.

Cleft lip and/or palate

Most infants and young children with cleft lip and/or palate, a common congenital defect, have problems feeding themselves. Several devices such as the Breck and Beniflex® Feeders are available. Most parents learn how to feed their infants by a trial and error method, experimenting with different devices and/or nipples, until they find a suitable one. Many mothers who have chosen to breast feed their infants with cleft lips and/or palates have been successful. Even so, feeding is usually a slow, laborious, and time-consuming process. With support, parents learn to feed their infants successfully, and the children generally thrive.

The newborn in the intensive care unit

The largest single group of infants with major nutritional concerns are those of low birth weight. Many of these babies have additional serious medical problems which interfere with adequate nutrition (48). Nutritional requirements of sick infants vary considerably, depending upon the type and severity of medical conditions. Advisable intakes of nutrients have been estimated for growing premature infants, utilizing a factorial approach, clinical observations and, in a few cases, experimentally derived data pertaining to a specific nutrient (49). Premature infants seem to have a higher requirement than term infants for protein and minerals (on a per-100-kcal basis) and for vitamins D, C, E and folacin because of a faster rate of growth, lower nutrient stores, and additional stresses or barriers imposed by immaturity.

Differing opinions have been expressed regarding the nutritional management of the premature infant on such issues as the importance of early weight gain, the optimal rate of gain, the chemical composition of growth, and the requirements for several amino acids (e.g., cystine and taurine) (50). Premature infants with complicating disorders may not resume growth for days and sometimes weeks. Water, energy (in the form of glucose), sodium, potassium, and chloride are provided in the first feeding to replace ongoing losses and to maintain homeostasis (49). Although quantitative data do not exist regarding the losses of other body constituents such as protein and calcium, it seems wise to replace the losses, especially if enteral feeding cannot be established within a few days of birth. For infants with birth weights less than 1.5 kg., it may be necessary to provide nutrients parenterally if more conventional methods of feeding are not possible by the fourth day of life (48,51). Depending upon the method of feeding, approximately 60 to 80 kcal per kg. will maintain weight of non-stressed, appropriate-for-gestational-age premature babies. More than 100 kcal per kg. may be needed to simulate weight gains similar to those in utero.

The choice of feedings for a premature infant will be influenced by both nutritional and non-nutritional factors (49-58). The formula should provide adequate, but not excessive nutrients in a digestible form.

The attractiveness of fresh human milk for premature infants is related to immunologic and psychosocial considerations, high digestibility of human milk fat, the amino acid composition of its protein, and the low potential renal solute load. Suspected or demonstrated disadvantages of mature human milk include the possibility that quantities of protein and certain minerals may be inadequate when the low-birth-weight infant is growing (52). Milk from women who deliver prematurely may have higher concentrations of protein and some minerals, and thereby be more suitable for the growing premature infant (53). Further research is necessary to interpret the significance of these data in relation to the nutritional care of small premature infants.

The feeding of the small or sick newborn most often requires some modification of enteral feeding. Coordination of sucking, swallowing, and breathing does not develop until the infant is at about 32 weeks' gestation (approximately 1.5 kg. birth weight). Therefore, alternate methods of tube feeding (continuous or bolus intragastric or transpyloric feedings) have been developed. These techniques have inherent risks from tube passage, including perforations, alterations in bacterial flora, and possibly as yet unrecognized effects of prolonged feeding of premature infants with plastic tubes which bypass the stomach (59-61).

For other infants, provision of nutrients by a peripheral or central vein is necessary to avert undue risks from malnutrition (50,51,62). Total parenteral nutrition (TPN) can support apparently normal growth and development of an infant for an extended period. It is routinely used for infants with intractable diarrhea and for many with surgical anomalies of the gastrointestinal tract. It has been modified for use with sick, premature infants who are unable to tolerate enteral feedings for several days. If there are no contraindications, intravenous fat emulsions should be provided to prevent essential fatty acid deficiency. In general, approximately 1 gm. per kg. per day of Intralipid® infusion is likely to be safe and to meet the essential fatty acid requirements of the premature infant. However, it must be carefully monitored in sick infants, such as those with pulmonary disease, infection, or hyperbilirubinemia, and in those babies who are small for gestational age (50,63,64). Complications from parenteral nutrition can be classified as either catheter-related or metabolic in origin. A competent, trained team, as well as careful surveillance, is essential for successful administration of parenteral nutrition.

Both enteral and parenteral methods of feeding premature and small-for-gestational-age infants have specific indications, contraindications, and complications which should be completely understood by all those providing nutritional care. In any unnatural feeding technique, careful observation and long-term follow-up are necessary to assure that unrecognized complications have not occurred. In every case, the risk of malnutrition must be weighed against the known risks of the feeding techniques which are being used. Parents need a great deal of counseling and reassurance, prior to their infant's discharge, on how to feed their baby appropriately.

Some infants remain at risk for nutritional problems throughout the first year of life for medical reasons (65). Recommendations for three of these entities—congenital heart disease, myelomeningocele, and cystic fibrosis—follow.

Congenital heart disease

Although most babies with congenital heart disease are of normal size at birth, the high frequency of subsequent growth failure has been well documented (66-78). The severity of growth impairment depends upon the hemodynamic effect of the specific lesion (72). In many instances, inadequate energy intake (73,74) resulting from feeding fatigue and labored respiration further compromise the infant's growth. In cases of congestive heart failure, the infant's nutrition may be further jeopardized by increased metabolic requirements and inefficient gastrointestinal absorption (73,75-79). Early recognition of growth failure and nutritional intervention permit surgery to be performed on a child who is better prepared to withstand the procedure.

Many infants with congenital heart disease require more kcal per kg. to gain weight than normal babies of similar age and weight. Some may require as many as 140 to 175 kcal per kg. for sustained growth (80). Because of the infant's ability to take only small volumes, formula and food with high caloric density must often be used. Ideally, caloric intake can be achieved by increasing the caloric density of liquid formulas (81). During the first few months of life, carbohydrate and fat are added to 80 kcal per 100 ml.

(24 kcal per oz.) standard formula to increase the total kilocalories to 100 kcal per 100 ml. (30 kcal per oz.). When formulas are concentrated by adding less water, the renal solute load must be carefully monitored. Limited free water provided by this method may be hazardous if the infant has a low volume of intake or excessive water losses, e.g., evaporation, diarrhea, or emesis (82).

Because of the small amount of formula that many of these babies consume, it may be necessary to supplement their diets with multiple vitamins, iron, calcium, and folacin (80). A high incidence of folacin deficiency has been reported in infants with heart disease (83). When diuretics are used on a regular basis for control of congestive heart failure, potassium losses may need to be replaced by oral supplements.

Routine use of low-sodium formulas by babies who consume small volumes provides adequate sodium neither for growth nor for replacement of obligatory losses. These formulas, therefore, should be offered only during periods of severe cardiac failure or when the infant retains sodium inappropriately. At six to eight months of age, the infant should be offered small amounts of food which require chewing, such as chopped fruits and unsalted vegetables. Meat may be given to the older infant if renal solute load is not considered a problem. When corrective operative procedures are successful, energy and nutrient intake is no longer of major concern.

Myelomeningocele

A congenital defect of the vertebral column and spinal cord may be associated with many factors that influence energy and nutrient needs, such as varying degrees of paralysis of the lower extremities, muscle weakness, constipation, and hydrocephalus (84). Obesity is a frequent complication which can impair the child's ambulation potential (80,85,86). Not only are these children relatively inactive, but they may ingest excessive calories for psychosocial reasons such as overprotective parents or eating out of frustration. Ideally, the concept of obesity prevention should be introduced (80) during the initial hospitalization to operatively close the spinal cord defect. Monitoring nutritional progress (caloric intake, rates of weight gain, skinfold changes) at two- to three-month intervals during the first year of life, and three- to six-month intervals during the preschool years facilitates timely and effective intervention. If an infant's weight for length and skinfold thickness exceed the 75th percentile, it seems reasonable to advise parents to limit high-calorie, low-nutrient foods, substitute lower calorie foods, and, in some cases, limit formula intake. The older infant and child may benefit from low-calorie foods containing dietary fiber to regulate constipation. Infants with minor spinal cord defects may grow satisfactorily with energy intakes equivalent to intakes of healthy infants, whereas infants with more serious defects and more extensive paralysis require fewer calories for appropriate weight gain and maintenance of normal subscapular fatfold thickness. Caloric intakes of infants rarely need to be restricted to less than 90 kcal per kg. (87). Weight reduction as a goal should be reserved for patients who have passed the adolescent growth spurt.

Cystic fibrosis

Although only a few babies present with meconium ileus and cystic fibrosis in intensive care newborn units, many are diagnosed during early infancy with severe growth failure and steatorrhea as primary presenting symptoms (88-91).

Pancreatic insufficiency causes malabsorption and the loss of a variety of essential nutrients, especially fat and nitrogen. Administration of pancreatic enzymes with feeding improves the absorption of fat and reduces steatorrhea but rarely eliminates malabsorption completely (92-95). In order to prevent or reverse malnutrition, a diet that is adequate in calories and protein and as high in fat as can be tolerated or one which provides a readily absorbed fat such as medium-chain triglycerides is generally recommended. Published recommendations for infants suggest 150 to 200 kcal per kg. per day, 4 gm. protein per kg. per day, a water-miscible vitamin preparation twice daily, and, in special circumstances, additional supplements of vitamins K, E, and B complex (96).

Provision of optimal nutrition for the patients with cystic fibrosis may improve their chances for prolonged survival by increasing their immunity to infections and improving their general physical condition.

Part III. Implications and recommendations to attain optimal health of children

The importance of nutrition in disease prevention and health maintenance has been reviewed and documented. The adequately nourished child grows at an expected rate, maintains normal weight for height, is resistant to infectious organisms, and has the energy to take advantage of social and learning opportunities. By means of early nutrition screening, the children "at risk" for malnutrition can be identified for nutritional assessment, and appropriate intervention can be initiated. Anticipatory guidance and nutrition education for families as their children progress through stages of growth and development promote the maintenance of a satisfactory nutritional status. The following are recommendations for policies to support the optimal nutrition of normal and developmentally disabled infants and children.

1. All health care programs should have a visible nutrition component which includes at least: (a) personnel appropriately trained in nutritional screening; (b) interpretation of screening data and early identification of children at risk by use of a

standard protocol; (c) information and education in basic nutrition for client families provided by skilled providers (by adolescence every child should be able to make wise food choices as a result of a formal nutrition and health education curriculum and experience with well prepared foods which provide a variety of nutrients); and (d) nutrition assessment and intervention as needed by an appropriately skilled registered dietitian.

2. At the national level, current and future government sponsored nutrition programs/regulations for children and pregnant women should coordinate information, education, and services among agencies to increase the effectiveness of such programs as Food Stamps; Supplemental Food Program for Women, Infants, and Children; the Expanded Food and Nutrition Education Program; Head Start; Early Periodic Screening, Diagnosis and Treatment, Community Health Clinics; School Lunch and Breakfast; and Nutrition Education and Training Programs. These programs should continue to support optimum nutrition of children.

3. At the community level, food, nutrition, and health program linkages should allow all children access to and coordination of all needed services.

4. Nutrition services for children should be supported by private insurance and other third-party payment mechanisms.

5. Financial assistance in the procurement of special dietary formulations should be continued and expanded to cover all children with special dietary needs whose families cannot afford appropriate nutritional care.

6. All health professionals who work with infants and pregnant women should receive the most up-to-date education on lactation, infant nutrition in relation to growth and development, and suitable alternatives to breast feeding.

7. Specialized training in the nutritional care of high-risk and developmentally disabled infants and children, in adolescent health, and in neonatal/perinatal nutrition is available. Dietitians-nutritionists who are interested in providing nutritional care for one of these groups should seek specialized training and should maintain continuing education to expand their competence.

8. Dietitians-nutritionists who work with infants and children should actively participate in defining quality assurance standards to evaluate professional performance (process criteria) and effectiveness of nutritional care (outcome criteria) within the context of the service delivery continuum.

9. Further clinical research is necessary to augment knowledge of the nutritional care of infants and children at high nutritional risk. Dietitians-nutritionists should become actively involved in applied research through recommending specific needed research, participation in the development of research plans, collection of data, and dissemination of research findings.

References

(1) Owen, G., and Lippman, G.: Nutritional status of infants and young children. Pediatr. Clin. North Am. 24:211, 1977.
(2) Winick, M.: Malnutrition and Brain Development. New York: Oxford Univ. Press, 1976.
(3) Palmer, S.: Normal nutrition, growth and development. *In* Ekvall, S., and Palmer, S., eds.: Pediatric Nutrition in Developmental Disorders. Springfield, IL: Charles C Thomas, 1978.
(4) Winick, M.: Malnutrition and mental development. *In* Alfin-Slater, R.B., and Kortchensky, D., eds.: Human Nutrition. A Comprehensive Treatise. New York: Plenum Press, 1979.
(5) Craviato, J., Birch, H.G., and De Licardie, E.R.: Nutrition, growth and neurointegrative development, an experimental ecological study. Pediatrics 38:319, 1966.
(6) Chavez, A., Martinez, C., and Yaschine, T.: The importance of nutrition and stimuli on child mental and social development. *In* Craviato, J., Hambraeus, L., and Valquist, B., eds.: Symposium of the Swedish Nutrition Foundation. XII. Early Malnutrition and Mental Development. Uppsala: Almquist and Wiksell, 1974.
(7) Task Force on Nutrition: Assessment of Maternal Nutrition. Chicago: American College of Obstetricians and Gynecologists, 1978.
(8) Israel, S.L., and Dentschberger, J.: Relation of the mother's age to obstetric performance. Obstet. Gynecol. 24:411, 1964.
(9) Edozien, J.C., Switzer, B.R., and Bryan, R.B.: Medical evaluation of the special supplemental food program for women, infants and children. Am. J. Clin. Nutr. 32:677, 1979.
(10) Picciano, M.F.: The Volume and Composition of Human Milk. Proceedings of the International Symposium on Infant and Child Feeding, Michigan State University, East Lansing, October 16-17, 1978 (in press).
(11) Committee on Nutrition, American Academy of Pediatrics: Commentary on breast-feeding and infant formulas, including proposed standards for formula. Pediatrics 59:278, 1976.
(12) Lonnerdal, B., Forsum, E., and Hambraeus, L.: A longitudinal study of the protein, nitrogen, and lactose content of human milk from Swedish well-nourished mothers. Am. J. Clin. Nutr. 29:1127, 1976.
(13) McClelland, D.B. L., McGrath, J., and Samson, R.R.: Antimicrobial factors in human milk. Studies of concentration and transfer to the infant during the early stages of lactation. Acta Paediatr. Scand. Suppl. 271, 1978.
(14) National Committee of Canadian Pediatric Society and the Committee on Nutrition, American Academy of Pediatrics: Breast-feeding. Pediatrics 62:591, 1978.
(15) Bachrach, S., Fisher, J., Parks, J.S.: An outbreak of vitamin D deficiency rickets in a susceptible population. Pediatrics 64:871, 1979.
(16) Committee on Nutrition, American Academy of Pediatrics: Fluoride supplementation: Revised dosage schedule. Pediatrics 63:150, 1979.
(17) Driscoll, W.S.: Recommendations for Dietary Fluoride Supplementation. *In* Wei, S.H., ed.: National Symposium on Dental Nutrition. Iowa City: The University of Iowa, 1979
(18) Dallman, P.R., Siimes, M.A., and Stekel, A.: Iron deficiency in infancy and childhood. Am. J. Clin. Nutr. 33:86, 1980.
(19) Picciano, M.F., and Derring, R.H.: The influence of feeding regimens on iron status during infancy. Am. J. Clin. Nutr. 33:746, 1980.
(20) Yaffe, S.J., and Waletzky, L.R.: Drugs and chemicals in breast milk. *In* Symposium on Human Lactation. Rockville, MD: DHEW, 1976.
(21) Committee on Nutrition, American Academy of Pediatrics: On the feeding of supplemental foods to infants. Pediatrics 65:1178, 1980.
(22) Pipes, P.: Nutrition in Infancy and Childhood. 2nd ed. St. Louis: C.V. Mosby Co., 1981.
(23) Lucas, B.: Nutrition and the adolescent. *In* Pipes, P.: Nutrition in Infancy and Childhood. 2nd ed. St. Louis: C.V. Mosby Co., 1981.
(24) Smith, D.W.: Recognizable Patterns of Human Malformation. 2nd ed. Philadelphia: W.B. Saunders, 1976.

(25) Physicians' Desk Reference. 34th ed. Oradell, NJ: Medical Economics Co., 1980.
(26) Navia, J.M.: Nutrition in dental development and disease. *In* Winick, M. ed.: Nutrition Pre- and Postnatal Development. New York: Plenum Press, 1979.
(27) Robinson, L.G., Paulbitski, A., Jones, A., and Roberts, M.: Nutrition counseling and children's dental health. J. Nutr. Educ. 8:33, 1976.
(28) Bock, A.S.: Food sensitivity: A critical review and practical approach. Am. J. Dis. Child 134:973, 1980.
(29) Langhan, P.M., Gold, H., and Vane, J.C.: Phenytoin teratogenicity in man. Lancet 1:70, 1973.
(30) Gurians, S., et al.: Gingival hyperplasia due to Dilantin therapy. J. Acad. Dent. Handicapped. 1:11, 1975.
(31) Reynolds, E.H.: Iatrogenic nutritional effects of anticonvulsants. Proc. Nutr. Soc. 33:225, 1974.
(32) Lowe, C.R.: Congenital malformation among infants born to epileptic women. Lancet 1:9, 1973.
(33) Neubauer, C.: Mental deterioration in epilepsy due to folate deficiency. Br. Med. J. 2:759, 1970.
(34) Tolman, K.G., Jubiz, W., Sannella, J.J., Madsen, J.A., Belsey, R.E., and Goldsmith, R.S.: Osteomalacia associated with anticonvulsant drug therapy in mentally retarded children. Pediatrics 56:45, 1975.
(35) Crosley, C.J., Chee, C., and Berman, P.H.: Rickets associated with long-term anticonvulsant therapy in a pediatric outpatient population. Pediatrics 56:52, 1975.
(36) Janaki, S., Rashid, M.K., Gulati, M.S., Jayaram, S.R., and Barush, J.K.: A clinical EEG correlation of seizures on a ketogenic diet. Indian J. Med. Res. 64:1057, 1976.
(37) Safer, D., Allen, R., and Barr, E.: Depression of growth in hyperactive children on stimulant drugs. N. Engl. J. Med. 287:217, 1972.
(38) Lucas, B., and Sells, C.J.: Nutrient intake and stimulant drugs in hyperactive children. J. Am. Dietet. A. 70:373, 1977.
(39) National Advisory Committee on Hyperkinesis and Food Additives: Final Report to the Nutrition Foundation, October 1980. Washington, DC: The Nutrition Foundation, 1980.
(40) Freeman, J.M., Finkelstein, J.D., and Mudd, S.N.: Folate responsive homocystinuria and schizophrenia. N. Engl. J. Med. 292:491, 1975.
(41) Hawkins, D., and Pauling, L.: Orthomolecular Psychiatry: Treatment of Schizophrenia. San Francisco: W.H. Freeman, 1973.
(42) Stare, F.J., and Hayes, K.C.: Not quite cricket. Nutr. Today 6:20, 1971.
(43) Cohen, P.A., Schneidman, K., Ginsberg-Feller, F., Sterdman, J.A., Knittle, J., and Gavil, G.E.: High pyridoxine diet in the rat: Possible implications for megavitamin therapy. J. Nutr. 103:143, 1973.
(44) Palmer, S., and Horn, S.: Feeding problems in children. *In* Palmer, S., and Ekvall, S., Pediatric Nutrition in Developmental Disorders. Springfield, IL: Charles C Thomas, 1978.
(45) Kanner, L.: Problems of eating behavior. *In* Kanner, L., ed.: Child Psychiatry. Springfield, IL: Charles C Thomas, 1948
(46) Bentovim, A.: The clinical approach to feeding disorders of childhood. J. Psychosom. Res. 14:267, 1970.
(47) MacCready, R.A., and Levy, H.K.: The problem of maternal phenylketonuria. Am. J. Obstet. Gynecol. 113:121, 1972.
(48) Rickard, K., and Gresham, E.: Nutritional considerations for the newborn requiring intensive care. J. Am. Dietet. A. 66:592, 1975.
(49) Ziegler, E., Biga, R.L., and Fomon, S.J.: Nutritional requirements of the premature infant. *In* Suskind, R.M., ed., Symposium on Pediatric Nutrition. New York: Raven Press, 1981.
(50) Nutritional Services in the Neonatal Period. Washington, DC: National Academy of Science (in press).
(51) Brady, M.S., Gresham, E.L., and Rickard, K.: Nutritional care of the low birth weight infant requiring intensive care. Perinat. Press 2:125, 1978.
(52) Fomon, S.J., Ziegler, E.E., and Vazquez, H.D.: Human milk and the small premature infant. Am. J. Dis. Child. 131:463, 1977.
(53) Atkinson, S.A., Bryan, M.N., and Anderson, G.H.: Human milk differences in nitrogen concentration in milk from mothers of term and preterm infants. J. Pediatr. 93:67, 1978.
(54) Raiha, N.C., Heinonen, K., Rassin, D.K., and Gaull, G.E.: Milk protein quantity and quality in low birth weight infants: I. Metabolic response and effect on growth. Pediatrics 57:659, 1976.
(55) Fomon, S.J., and Ziegler, E.E.: Protein intake of premature infants: Interpretation of data. J. Pediatr. 90:504, 1977.
(56) Heird, W.C.: Feeding the premature infant: Human milk or an artificial formula. Am. J. Dis. Child. 131:468, 1977.
(57) Mata, L.J., and Wyatt, R.G.: Human milk: Host resistance to infection. Am. J. Clin. Nutr. 23:976, 1971.
(58) Newton, N.: Psychologic differences between breast and bottle feeding. Am. J. Clin. Nutr. 24:993, 1971.
(59) Boros, S.J., and Reynolds, J.W.: Duodenal perforation: A complication of neonatal nasojejunal feeding. J. Pediatr. 85:107, 1974.
(60) Challacombe, D.: Bacterial microflora in infants receiving nasojejunal tube feeding. J. Pediatr. 85:113, 1974.
(61) Chen, J.W., and Wong, P.W.K.: Intestinal complications of nasojejunal feeding in low birth weight infants. J. Pediatr. 85:109, 1974.
(62) Heird, W.C., and Driscoll, J.M.: Newer methods for feeding low birth weight infants. Clin. Perinatol. 2:309, 1975.
(63) Friedman, Z., Danon, A., Stahlman, M.T., and Oates, J.A.: Rapid onset of essential fatty acid deficiency in the newborn. Pediatrics 58:640, 1976.
(64) Bryan, H., Shennan, A., Griffin, E., and Angel, A.: Intralipid: Its rational use in parenteral nutrition of the newborn. Pediatrics 58:787, 1976.
(65) Rickard, K., Brady, M.S., Hempel, J., and Gresham, E.: Care of patients with pediatric conditions with high nutritional risks. J. Am. Dietet. A. 68:546, 1976.
(66) Feldt, R.H., Stickler, G.B., and Weidman, W.H.: Growth of children with congenital heart disease. Am. J. Dis. Child. 117:573, 1969.
(67) Huse, D.M., Feldt, R.H., Nelson, R.A., and Novak, L.P.: Infants with congenital heart defects. Am. J. Dis. Child. 129:65, 1975.
(68) Naeye, R.L.: Anatomic features of growth failure in congenital heart disease. Pediatrics 39:433, 1967.
(69) Strangway, A., Fower, R., Cunningham, K., and Hamilton, J.R.: Diet and growth in congenital heart disease. Pediatrics 57:75, 1976.
(70) Bayer, L.M., and Robinson, S.J.: Growth history of children with congenital heart defects. Am. J. Dis. Child. 117:564, 1969.
(71) Linde, L.M., Dunn, O.J., Schireson, R., and Rasof, B.: Growth in children with congenital heart disease. J. Pediatr. 70:413, 1967.
(72) Mehrizi, A., and Drash, A.: Growth disturbance in congenital heart disease. J. Pediatr. 61:418, 1962.
(73) Krieger, I.: Growth failure and congenital heart disease. Energy and nitrogen balance in infants. Am. J. Dis. Child. 120:497, 1970.
(74) Puyau, F.A.: Evaporative heat losses of infants with congenital heart disease. Am. J. Clin. Nutr. 22:1435, 1969.
(75) Krause, A.N., and Auld, P.A.M.: Metabolic rate of neonates with congenital heart disease. Arch. Dis. Child. 50:539, 1975.
(76) Lees, M.H., Bristow, J.D., Griswold, H.E., and Olmstead, R.W.: Relative hypermetabolism in infants with congenital heart disease and undernutrition. Pediatrics 36:183, 1965.
(77) Stocker, F.P., Wilkoff, W., Miettinen, O.S., and Nadas, A.S: Oxygen consumption in infants with heart disease. Relationship of severity of congestive failure, relative weight, and caloric intake. J. Pediatr. 80: 43, 1972.
(78) Pittman, J.G., and Cohen, P.: The pathogenesis of cardiac cachexia. N. Engl. J. Med. 271:403 and 453, 1964.
(79) Ehlers, K.H.: Growth failure in association with congenital heart disease. Pediatr. Ann. 7:35, 1978.
(80) Rickard, K., Brady, M.S., and Gresham, E.L.: Nutritional management of the chronically ill child: Congenital heart disease and myelomeningocele. Pediatr. Clin. North Am. 24:157, 1977.

(81) Fomon, S.J., and Ziegler, E.E.: Nutritional management of infants with congenital heart disease, Am. Heart J. 83:581, 1972.
(82) Fomon, S.J.: Infant Nutrition. Philadelphia: W.B. Saunders, Co., 1974.
(83) Rook, G.D., Lopez, R., and Simizu, N.: Folic acid deficiency in infants and children with heart disease. Br. Heart J. 35:87, 1973.
(84) Brockelhurst, G., ed.: Spina Bifida for the Clinician (Clin. Develop. Med.) Philadelphia: J.B. Lippincott Co., No. 57, 1976.
(85) Hayes-Allen, M.C.: Obesity and short stature in children with myelomeningocele. Dev. Med. Child. Neurol. 14:59, 1972.
(86) Hayes-Allen, M.C., and Tring, F.C.: Obesity: Another hazard for spina bifida children. Br. J. Prev. Soc. Med. 27:192, 1973.
(87) Tower, D., and Rickard, K.: Personal communication, 1980.
(88) Chase, H.P., Long, M.A., and Lavin, M.H.: Cystic fibrosis and malnutrition. J. Pediatr. 95:337, 1979.
(89) Lebenthal, E.: Pancreatic function and disease in infancy and childhood. Adv. Pediatr. 25:223, 1978.
(90) Sunshine, P., Sinatra, F.R., and Mitchell, C.H.: Intractable diarrhea of infancy. Clin. Gastroenterol. 6:445, 1977.
(91) Lobeck, C.C.: Cystic fibrosis. *In* Stanbury, J.B., Wyngaarden, J.B., and Fredrickson, D.S., eds. The Metabolic Basis of Inherited Diseases. New York: McGraw Hill Co., 1972.
(92) French. A.B., and Cook, H.B.: Effect of pancreatic replacement therapy on metabolic balance in adolescent fibrocystic disease. J. Lab. Clin. Med. 70:1005, 1967.
(93) Mullinger, M.: The effect of exogenous pancreatic enzymes on fat absorption. Pediatrics 42:523, 1968.
(94) Khaw, K.T., Adeniyi-Jones, S., Gordon, D., Polombo, J., and Suskind, R.M.: Efficacy of pancreatin preparations on fat and nitrogen absorptions in cystic fibrosis patients. Pediatr. Res. 12:437, 1978.
(95) Lapey, A., Kattwinkel, J., di Sant' Agnese, P.A., and Laster, L.: Steatorrhea and azotorrhea and their relation to growth and nutrition in adolescents and young adults with cystic fibrosis. J. Pediatr. 84:328, 1974.
(96) National Cystic Fibrosis Research Foundation: Guide to Drug Therapy in Patients with Cystic Fibrosis. Atlanta: National Cystic Fibrosis Research Foundation, 1974.

Additional references

Elsas, L.D., and Acosta, P.B.: Dietary Management of Inherited Metabolic Disease. Atlanta: Division of Medical Genetics, Department of Pediatrics, Emory University School of Medicine, 1976.
Fireman, P.: Immunologic basis of allergic disease. *In* Kelley, V.C., ed.: Practice of Pediatrics. Hagerstown, MD: Harper and Row, 1978.
Lakdawala, D.R., and Widdowson, E.M.: Vitamin D in human milk. Lancet 1:167, 1977.
Lapatsanis, P., Deliyanni, V., and Doxiadis, S.: Vitamin D deficiency rickets in Greece. J. Pediatr. 72:195, 1968.
Lawrence, R.A.: Breast Feeding: A Guide for the Medical Profession. St. Louis: C.V. Mosby Co., 1980.
McMillan, J.A., Landaw, S.A., and Oski, F.A.: Iron sufficiency in breast fed infants and the availability of iron in human milk. Pediatrics 58:686, 1976.
Saarinen, U.M., Siimes, M.A., and Dallman, P.R.: Iron absorption in infants: High bioavailability of breast milk iron as indicated by the extrinsic tag method of iron absorption and by the concentration of serum ferritin. J. Pediatr. 91:36, 1977.
Saarinen, U.M.: Need for iron supplementation in infants on prolonged breast-feeding. J. Pediatr. 93:177, 1978.
Springer, N.S., and Fricke, N.L.: Nutrition and drug therapy for persons with developmental disabilities. Am. J. Mental Def. 80:317, 1975.
Roe, D.A.: Drug-induced Nutritional Deficiencies. Westport, CT: AVI Publishing Co., 1976.
Woodruff, C.W.: The science of infant nutrition and the art of infant feedings. J.A.M.A. 240:657, 1978.

Nutrition and Immunity

by Ronald Ross Watson, Ph.D.

The nutritional status of the elderly and of children is a major factor affecting host resistance. After maturity, some, but not all, key host defense systems decline in their level of reactivity. It is clear that many people do not die of old age, but rather from infectious diseases.[1,2] Compared to adults, newborns and children have greater susceptibility to many diseases due to a combination of immunological immaturity and lack of previous exposure to microbes.

Malnutrition and Disease

Historically, the association between malnutrition and lowered disease resistance has been recognized by many cultures. It is not merely by chance that famine and pestilence are two of the dreaded "Four Horseman of the Apocalypse." They might well have been depicted riding the same horse, so close is the historical association.[1] The high morbidity and mortality suffered by malnourished populations are caused mainly by nutritional deficiencies which impair immune systems.[1] A major impediment to the study of these problems in human populations lies in the complexity of their nutritional backgrounds and immunological host-defense systems. Undernutrition as well as overnutrition in different populations may exist in a large variety of permuted combinations. These nutritional states may include deficiencies or excesses in protein, calories, vitamins and trace minerals. In addition, the failure to distinguish between these various degrees of malnutrition prevents a critical evaluation of some human studies.

Host defenses include such diverse systems as nonspecific immunity (saliva flow, skin, bactericidal enzymes) humoral immunity (serum antibodies, complement-mediated lysis), cellular immunity (such as phagocytosis, T-lymphocyte "killer cells") and mucosal immunity (antibodies in secretions).[1] These immune systems vary in their response to nutritional stresses, yet their combined functions provide overall host defense.[1,3]

On a worldwide basis, protein-calorie malnutrition is the most common cause of acquired immuno-deficiency.[1] Most human studies to date have focused on severe protein-calorie malnutrition in hospitalized children.[1,3] Although children suffering from marasmus or kwashiorkor represent most dramatically the effects of malnutrition on disease susceptibility, they comprise only 3 to 5% of malnourished children in developing countries. In contrast, up to 60% of all preschool children in many preindustrial societies suffer from the milder forms of malnutrition.[1] Many elderly humans in the United States who are undernourished have contributing factors to nutritional stress including cancer, alcoholism, prolonged hospitalization and other illnesses. In the hospitalized populations of industrialized countries, such as the United States, malnutrition is a major contributing factor to the poor health of these individuals.

Effects of Malnutrition on Humoral Immunity

The humoral immune system is comprised of soluble serum proteins, in particular immunoglobulins (IgG, IgM IgA) and the complement system. The complement system is comprised of eleven protein components (C_1-C_{11}) that act in a coordinated "cascade" sequence in conjunction with IgA, IgG, and IgM antibodies to perform a complex set of host-defense functions. One reaction sequence of the complement system can result in lysis of foreign cells. However, the key role of the complement system in host defense is amplification of other portions of the immune system. These include enhancement of phagocytic cells to engulf pathogens, stimulated attraction of phagocytic cells to the site of infection, and viral neutralization. Almost all studies of severely malnourished children and animals show a significant decrease in total hemolitic complement and an increased incidence of infection.[1] For example, protein-calorie malnourished Thai and Colombian children showed a marked decrease in serum complement component C_3. A total decrease in this complement component has been shown to significantly reduce the efficiency of response by this system. On the other hand, the levels of serum antibodies which must bind to the pathogen before the complement system will function, are generally unaffected by nutritional stresses. Since all complement components react in sequence, anything which significantly reduces the level of activity of even one component affects the function of several aspects of host defense. Complement levels are markedly reduced by dietary protein insufficiency in the young and elderly.[1,3] Hence, persons suffering from prolonged anorexia or surgical trauma which results in negative nitrogen balance would be susceptible to complement suppression and, hence, decreased disease resistance.

Malnutrition and Mucosal Immunity

Although the skin usually acts as an effective barrier to pathogens, there are sites in the body which lack this nonspecific protection. The oral cavity, eye and intestinal tract are frequently exposed to potential pathogens, in addition to those regularly present. To protect these mucosal surfaces from colonization or growth by foreign pathogens, the body has mucosal immune defenses which are susceptible to nutritional stresses.[1,3] These defenses include enzymes (e.g., lysozyme), flow of secretions (IgG and secretory IgA), and cellular defenses in the top cell layers of the mucosal surface.

Recently, moderate and severe protein malnutrition has been shown to significantly suppress the secretion of lysozyme into the tears of children.[3,4] This could result in reduction of host defense against certain bacteria that would normally be destroyed by lysozyme. In addition, the synthesis and secretion of secretory IgA, a principal group of antibodies produced for mucosal defense, was impaired. Many pathogens enter and colonize mucosal surfaces in the intestine, lung or mouth, which are protected by mucosal immunity. In other studies, severely protein-undernourished Thai, Indian and Colombian children had significantly reduced (35-50%) levels of secretory IgA, while IgG levels were unaffected.[1] The levels of nasopharyngeal secretory IgA measles and polio antibodies were also found to be low or undetected in severely protein-calorie, malnourished Indian children following immunization with polio and measles viral vaccines.[5] These suppressed antibody responses are very disturbing since the body relies largely on the immune system to recognize and then respond defensively to pathogens. To the extent that malnutrition impairs immune responses to new pathogens, patients on dietary restriction may be at risk to disease from foreign organisms including those for which vaccines do not exist. Unfortunately, the effects of mild to moderate nutritional stress on secretory immune responses are largely unknown.[1]

Nutritional Suppression of Cellular Immunity

Cellular immunity is produced by a subpopulation of lymphocytes which bind to foreign protein components of microbial pathogens or cancer cells. This binding process can result in direct killing of the pathogen or, more importantly, attraction and activation of macrophages into "killer cells." The macrophages then engulf and destroy the pathogen.

Severe protein undernutrition in children and adults and in young animals frequently is associated with a profound impairment of cell-mediated immune functions.[1,3] Both the number and functional capability of T-lymphocytes are markedly reduced, as is the delayed hypersensitivity response to antigens and sensitizing chemicals. In general, the severity of the impaired immunological response parallels the severity of the protein or calorie nutritional deficiency. Much less is known about the effect of other nutrient deficiencies on cellular immune functions. Severe nutritional deficiencies appear to interfere with production by T-lymphocytes of protein signals to "killer" macrophages resulting in poorer phagocytosis and destruction of pathogens. In addition, the efficacy of vaccines which stimulate cell-mediated immunity may be impaired in severely malnourished individuals.

Studies involving adults and elderly people usually are complicated by surgery, cancer and/or other diseases in addition to malnutrition.[1] For example, patients with adult marasmus with less than 85% of standard weight-height ratio, but with normal levels of serum albumin, showed normal cellular immunity as determined by using in vitro parameters (i.e., complement fixation). On the other hand, in vivo tests of intradermal skin response to candidin and streptokinase-streptodornase was suppressed. In spite of these differences, suppressed cellular immune responses, as determined by either in vivo or in vitro tests, are well recognized signs of immuno-suppression and, hence, increased probability of infections following surgery.[6,7] Indeed, in hospitalized, undernourished patients, presurgical nutritional therapy has been shown to help restore suppressed cellular immune responses. Such therapy may decrease the incidence of morbidity. In fact, measurement of immunological status is becoming a helpful way to assess nutritional status.[7]

Benefits and Problems of Marginal Malnutrition on Host Defenses

Moderate protein malnutrition is clearly associated with important changes in immunological responsiveness. However, the changes observed in certain parameters of cell-mediated immunity may be normal, impaired or sometimes enhanced in moderately malnourished children or animals.[1,3] For example, experiments have recently shown an enhancement of cellular immunities in mature animals fed a moderately low-protein diet.[1,8,9] Marginally malnourished mice fed an 8% protein diet after weaning showed an increase in cellular immunities and their macrophages engulfed pathogenic bacteria at a significantly greater rate than control animals fed a complete protein diet.[10] One postulated explanation may be that macrophages of these mice were activated due to increased immuno-competence of effector T-lymphocytes stimulated by the elevated number of other pathogens found in the malnourished animals. Clearly, protein or calorie intakes which are below normal, but which do not cause severe malnutrition, can produce enhancement in some immune responses in animals.[1,2,3,9] It follows, therefore, that reduced dietary intakes of protein or calories in animals sometimes result in enhanced longevity.[2] For example, female mice nutritionally stressed with a 40% reduction in calories showed a reduced incidence of spontaneous mammary carcinoma and a 70% reduction in tumor incidence compared to well-nourished mice.

Immunological processes which are basic and vital to the living organism can be affected and to a certain extent controlled by nutritional manipulation. Functions such as growth, health, malignancies and tumor development, enzyme activity, longevity and immune response all have been shown to respond to dietary manipulation. The interrelationship between longevity, immunities and diet is very complex. These changes in the host-defense systems appear to be dependent on components of the diet, age at which the animal has started on the diet, and duration of dietary manipulation.

Summary

Severe protein deficiencies such as kwashiorkor result in immuno-suppression of humoral cellular and mucosal immune systems. These suppressions result in a greater incidence of disease in animals and humans and create increased risks of morbidity and mortality due to infectious disease or neoplasias. The effect of moderate protein-calorie deficiency on immuno-competence appears to be highly variable in studies with experimental animals. In young animals, some parts of the host-defense systems are stimulated while others are inhibited. These effects appear to result in long life spans. This may be due to slower maturation and, hence, a slower decline of host-defense systems in the moderately malnourished animals.

References

1. Watson, R. R. and McMurray, D.N., Effects of Malnutrition on Secretory and Cellular Immunity, edited by T.E. Furia, CRC -Critical Reviews of Food and Nutrition, CRC Press, Cleveland, Ohio, 1979.
2. Watson, R. R. and Safranski, D., Dietary Restrictions and Immune Responses in the Aged, CRC Handbook on Aging IV: Immunology, 1981 (In press).
3. Watson, R. R., Nutrition, Disease Resistance and Age, Food and Nutrition News 51:1, 1979.
4. Watson, R.R., et al., Influence of Malnutrition on the Concentration of IgA, Lysozyme, Amylase and Aminopeptidase in Children's Tears, Proc. Soc. Exp. Biol. Med. 157:57, 1978.
5. Chandra, R.K., Reduced Secretory Antibody Response to Live Attenuated Measles and Poliovirus Vaccines in Malnourished Children, Br. Med. J. 2:583, 1975.
6. Bistrian, B.R., et al., Cellular Immunity in Adult Marasmus, Arch. Int. Med. 137:1408, 1977.
7. Miller, C.L., Immunological Assays as Measurements of Nutritional Status: A Review, J. Parent. Enter. Nutr. 2:554, 1978.
8. Copeland, E.M., et al., Nutrition, Cancer and IVH, Cancer 43:2108, 1979.
9. Watson, R.R., et al., Superoxide Dismutase Activity in Polymorphonuclear Leukocytes and Alveolar Macrophages of Protein Malnourished Rats and Guinea Pigs, J. Nutr. 106:1801, 1976.
10. Watson, R.R. and Haffer, K., Modification of Cell-Mediated Immune Responses by Dietary Protein Stress in Immunologically Immature and Mature BALB/c Mice, Mech. Aging Develop. 12:269, 1980.

Single-Nutrient Effects on Immunologic Functions

by William R. Beisel, M.D., Robert Edelman, M.D., Kathleen Nauss, Ph.D., and Robert M. Suskind, M.D.

• Immune system dysfunction can result from single-nutrient deficiencies or excesses, alone or in combination with generalized protein-energy malnutrition. Acquired immune dysfunctions in man occur with deficiencies of iron, zinc, vitamins A and B_{12}, pyridoxine, and folic acid and with excesses of essential fatty acids and vitamin E. Additional micronutrients are important for maintaining immunologic competence in animals. Deficits or excesses of many trace elements and single nutrients thus have potential for causing immune dysfunctions in man. Since nutritionally induced immune dysfunction is generally reversible, it is important to recognize and identify clinical illnesses in which immunologic dysfunctions are of nutritional origin. Correction of malnutrition should lead to prompt reversal of acquired immune dysfunctions.

(*JAMA* 1981;245:53-58)

SEVERE multinutrient deficiencies lead to impaired immunocompetence. Acquired immune system dysfunction can also result from deficiencies, imbalances, or excesses of single nutrients.[1-4] Lymphoid tissue atrophy has long been known to accompany starvation or wasting illnesses. Only during the past decade has much clinical attention been given to the occurrence of impaired immunocompetence in patients who become malnourished.

Generalized malnutrition is most common in underdeveloped nations. It can also arise as a consequence of severe surgical or medical illness. Acquired immune system dysfunction is therefore seen in many hospitalized patients. Impaired immunocompetence increases susceptibility to respiratory, dermal, intestinal, or systemic infections and contributes to high mortality.

When it results from generalized malnutrition, acquired immune dysfunction is relatively easy to diagnose and reverse. Furthermore, simple clinical tests of cell-mediated immunity (such as skin testing with common recall antigens) may have prognostic value in severely malnourished patients.[2,3] The recognition of deficient immunocompetence can thus be important in many clinical fields.

THE ROLE OF SINGLE NUTRIENTS

Most clinical studies of nutritionally impaired immunocompetence involve multiple deficiency states. Far less is known about the contribution of individual nutrients to immune system functions in man. In generalized malnutrition, it is virtually impossible to define causal relationships between individual nutrients and abnormalities in immune responsiveness. Severe deficiencies of protein and other energy sources influence the manner in which body cells use single essential nutrients. However, both animal data and clinical studies suggest that many individual nutrients are important to immune competence.

This workshop was held to assemble information related to single-nutrient effects on the immune system, and to determine clinical applicability of the data. Major gaps exist in current knowledge (Figure); the literature is fragmentary and often limited to single reports. Data from laboratory animals are more complete than data from man, but no individual nutrient has been studied comprehensively for its effects on all measurable immune functions. Many older concepts and techniques are no longer considered valid for evaluating immune system complexities. The interrelationship of single nutrients and immunocompetence must be studied further, for both clinical application and basic knowledge.

Single-nutrient deficiencies, imbalances among individual nutrients, or marked excesses of single nutrients depress some immune functions (although a modest increase in the dietary intake of vitamins A and E and selenium may enhance certain immune functions in animals).

Immunologic changes in man occur with deficiencies of folic acid, iron, and zinc or with excesses of vitamin E or essential fatty acids.[1,2] Scattered clinical reports also document some immunologic changes with vitamin A,

B₁₂, pyridoxine, or pantothenic acid deficiencies, and possibly with hypercholesterolemia.[2-4] Many individual vitamins, minerals, trace elements, amino acids, fatty acids, and cholesterol[1,2] influence immunologic mechanisms in animals.

WATER-SOLUBLE VITAMINS

The most important immunologic effects produced by B-group vitamins are seen with deficiencies of pyridoxine, pantothenic acid, and folic acid.[4] Deficiencies of vitamin B₁₂ in man may be accompanied by defective immune functions. Deficiencies of thiamine, riboflavin, niacin, or biotin have little effect of immunocompetence.[4]

Pyridoxine Deficiency

A deficiency of pyridoxine depresses both cellular and humoral immunity in animals. Lymphoid tissues atrophy, delayed cutaneous hypersensitivity reactions fail to develop, and the expected rejection of skin transplants is inhibited. Impaired humoral responses are evidenced by poor antibody production after either primary or booster immunizations.[2-4] Populations of B lymphocytes and T lymphocytes fail to exhibit normal proliferative responses when stimulated in vitro by test mitogens or antigens. Thymic hormone activity is decreased. Volunteers with short-term experimental pyridoxine deficiency show reduced antibody responses to vaccines.[5]

Pyridoxine deficiency leads to impaired DNA and protein synthesis. The observed abnormalities in lymphocyte multiplication and immunoglobulin production appear to be secondary to these molecular defects.

Pantothenic Acid Deficiency

Pantothenic acid deficiency leads to depressed antibody responses after either primary or booster injections of vaccine antigens or heterologous RBCs. Deficiency of pantothenic acid thus appears to inhibit the stimulation of antibody-producing cells and their ability to produce new immunoglobulins.[4] Experimentally induced, brief pantothenic acid deficiency in man also reduces antibody responses to immunization.[5]

Other B-Group Deficiencies

Lymphocyte responses to mitogens are impaired and a modest reduction in the phagocytic and bactericidal capacity of neutrophils may be found in patients with primary pernicious anemia. Vitamin B₁₂ deficiency cannot be produced in laboratory animals.

Folic acid deficiency depresses immune functions in both animals and man.[1-3] Patients with folic acid deficiency have an impaired ability to respond to skin-test antigens. Peripheral lymphocytes are not triggered by mitogenic stimulation in vitro, but neutrophil functions remain normal.

Guinea pigs and rats are extremely susceptible to folate deficiency. Animals lacking in folate demonstrate lymphoid atrophy, diminished WBC and neutrophil numbers, impaired cell-mediated immunity when tested in vitro, and reduced humoral response to injected antigens.

Isolated deficiencies of methionine and choline depress humoral immune functions in adult animals. Impaired resistance to bacterial infections, atrophy of lymphoid tissue, and defective T-cell–mediated immune function occur also when deprivation is initiated during the prenatal period.

Ascorbic Acid

Despite the popularity of large "prophylactic" doses of vitamin C, there are few data to suggest that ascorbic acid plays a role in lymphocyte function, although it does influence phagocytic cell migration and killing functions, as well as the healing of wounds.[6] The vitamin C content of WBCs may decrease during viral infections, pregnancy, and in elderly persons. Conventional doses of vitamin C may improve phagocytic function in children with congenital neutrophil defects such as the Chediak-Higashi syndrome.[7]

Vitamin C deficiency also reduces delayed cutaneous hypersensitivity responsiveness to skin-test antigens, but this is caused by an inability to develop a local inflammatory response rather than by an immunologic defect in the antigen recognition or processing functions of lymphocytes.

FAT-SOLUBLE VITAMINS
Vitamin A

Modest increases in dietary vitamin A enhance resistance to infection in animals and responsiveness to antigenic stimuli and accelerate the rejection of skin grafts. Vitamin A may also function as an adjuvant, if it is mixed with an antigen before its injection.

Vitamin A deficiency in animals leads to depletion of thymic lymphocytes, depressed lymphocyte responses to various mitogens, and an increased frequency and severity of bacterial, viral, and protozoan infections. The incidence of spontaneous infections is also said to increase in vitamin A–deficient humans.[1] Secretory IgA production may be impaired.[1-3] These effects may be related to the action of vitamin A in maintaining the composition of external cell membranes and surface glycoproteins and in favoring cell differentiation.

Vitamin E

The effect of vitamin E on the immune system has been studied in both farm and laboratory animals.[8] Vitamin E deficiency depresses immunoglobulin responses to antigens, lymphocytic proliferative responses to mitogens and antigens, delayed dermal hypersensitivity reactions, and general host resistance. Attenuated live virus vaccines may become pathogenic in vitamin E-deficient puppies. On the other hand, in doses twofold to tenfold greater than minimal requirements, vitamin E has been found to enhance antibody responses to animal vaccines, to enhance delayed dermal hypersensitivity reactions, to accelerate the clearance of particulate matter by the reticuloendothelial system (RES), and to enhance host resistance and the ability to survive experimental infections.[8] In contrast, megadoses of vitamin E in healthy volunteers inhibit multiple immune functions.[9]

MINERALS

Divalent cations have important regulatory influences on external membrane functions of all body cells. Calcium and magnesium ions also

218 NUTRITION FROM CONCEPTION THROUGH ADOLESCENCE

	Lymphocytes: Lymphoid Anatomy	Total Lymphs in Blood	T and B Cell Differential	Proliferative Response	Splenic PFC Response	Immunoglobulins: Serum Ig Values	Primary Response	Secondary Response	Secretory IgA	Blocking Ig	Other Immune Functions: Delayed Skin Sensitivity	Graft Rejection	PMN Phagocytosis	PMN Bactericidal	Monocyte Function	RES Function	Complement	Inflammatory Response	Host Resistance
Vitamins																			
A, Excess	⇧			⇧		N⇧ N	⇧				N⇩	⇧				⇧ N	⇩	⇩	⇧
A, Deficit	⇩	N⇩	◆⇩ N⇩	⇩			⇩	⇩◆			◆			⇩		⇧		⇩◆	⇩⇩
Thiamine	⇩	⇧		⇩			⇩				⇩								◆
Riboflavin	⇩	⇧					⇩												
Pantothenic Acid	⇩	N	⇩	⇩		◆	◆⇩	⇩											
Pyridoxine	◆⇩ ◆⇩	⇩	⇩	⇩		◆	◆⇩	⇩			◆⇩	⇩			N			⇩	
B₁₂		◆				N			◆		◆	◆							
Folic Acid	⇩	◆⇩ ⇩⇩	⇩			⇩	⇩				◆⇩	N⇩N						⇩⇩	⇩⇩
C, Excess			⇧	N		◆	⇧					⇧ ⇧					◆	◆	⇧
C, Deficit		⇩ N	⇩			N	N⇩				⇩	⇩ ⇩	N	⇩				⇩◆	
E, Excess	⇧		◆⇧	⇧		⇧	⇧	⇧			⇧	⇧◆			⇧				⇧
E, Deficit	⇩	N		⇩	⇩	⇩						⇩						⇩	⇩
Minerals																			
Iron, Excess											⇩							⇩⇩	⇧
Iron, Deficit	⇩⇩	◆⇩	⇩	⇩	⇩	N	N⇩	◆			⇩	N◆⇩⇩	⇩		◆	⇩⇩	⇩⇩		
Zinc, Excess												◆⇩	⇩	⇩	⇩				
Zinc, Deficit	⇩⇩	⇩	⇩⇩	⇩		⇧	⇧	⇩			⇩⇩	⇩ ◆⇧	⇩◆					⇩	⇩
Magnesium, Deficit	⇧			⇩		⇩	⇩	⇩					⇩ ◆		⇩				⇩
Selenium, Excess				⇧			⇧												
Amino Acids																			
Branch Chain	⇩	⇩		⇩	⇩		⇩												
Aromatic	⇩					⇩	⇩		⇩									⇩	
Other	⇩					⇩			⇩									⇩	
Lipids																			
Cholesterol, Excess			⇧			◆⇧						⇩			⇩	⇧	⇩		⇩
Fatty Acids, Excess		⇩	⇩			⇩	⇩					◆ ◆			⇧				⇧
Fatty Acids, Deficit		⇧				⇧	⇧												
Polyunsaturated Fatty Acids, Excess	⇧	◆⇩⇩	⇩			⇩	⇩				◆⇩◆	⇩			◆⇧		◆	⇩	

Any reported change in immune function (top) associated with nutritional variable (left) indicated by direction and length of arrows. Solid arrows indicate human studies; open arrows, animal findings; N, normal findings; PMN, polymorphonuclear leukocyte; PFC, plaque-forming colonies; RES, reticuloendothelial system.

participate in the activation of complement. Iron and zinc help to regulate immune functions in animals and man. Scattered reports indicate that other trace elements may also influence immune responsiveness. These include cadmium, chromium, copper, lead, manganese, and silica. Heavy-metal toxicity depresses immune functions.

Iron

Iron deficiency, often seen as an isolated nutritional problem, causes immune dysfunctions in large numbers of patients. Iron deficiency is accompanied by lymphoid tissue atrophy and impaired in vitro lymphocyte responsiveness to mitogenic stimulation.[10] Iron-deficient humans demonstrate impaired cutaneous hypersensitivity responses and defective macrophage and neutrophil functions. Not all investigators have found the same immunodeficiencies in iron-depleted patients, perhaps because of the coexistence of other deficiency states, concurrent or recent infections, the degree or duration of the iron deficiency in a given subject, or differences in the methods used for collecting samples and performing functional in vitro assays on cultured human cells.[11] Nevertheless, most studies suggest that the immune system of man is exquisitely sensitive to iron availability and responds adversely to deficiencies that are too small to lower hemoglobin values.[10]

Too much iron can also be deleterious and can saturate plasma iron-binding proteins. This increases the availability of iron for uptake by microorganisms and may lead to overwhelming sepsis. Severely malnourished patients with coexisting deficiencies of protein and iron exhibit very low concentrations of iron-binding proteins in plasma; they may experience a clinical activation of intracellular infections, such as malaria, tuberculosis, or brucellosis, during iron repletion therapy.[12]

Zinc

Zinc deficiency causes atrophy of lymphoid tissue and produces abnormalities in both cellular and humoral immunity.[1-3] Lymphocytes demonstrate a decreased in vitro response to mitogens and antigens and depressed T-killer cell activity. Humoral immune responses are inadequate. Delayed cutaneous hypersensitivity reactions and skin graft rejections do not occur in severely zinc-deficient animals, and thymic hormone activity is suppressed. Immature or precursor lymphocytes may be harmed more than the mature cells. Studies of severely zinc-depleted animals are complicated by profound anorexia and early death. However, the immune deficiencies can be reversed by restoring zinc.

Human neutrophilic functions are altered in vitro, if zinc is added to the incubation media. Excess in vitro zinc inhibits the bactericidal and phagocytic function of macrophages and neutrophils. Delayed cutaneous hypersensitivity responses are impaired in zinc-depleted patients. A local application of zinc sulphate to the skin restores responsiveness, apparently by direct absorption.[13] Zinc-deficient patients also show a restoration of immune functions when body zinc is replenished.

Selenium

A modest increase in dietary selenium, alone or in combination with vitamin E, appears to enhance immune responsiveness to vaccine antigens in animals.

Magnesium

Magnesium depletion is not known to produce immunologic impairment in man. However, unusual responses during prolonged magnesium deficiency in animals include hyperemia of the skin, eosinophilia, leukocytosis, degranulation of mast cells with release of histamine, histaminuria, thymic atrophy, and reduced humoral immune response to a variety of antigens.[14] Magnesium-deficient rats are not sensitized by brain-tissue antigens that induce allergic encephalitis in control subjects. Persistent leukocytosis in magnesium-deficient animals is often followed by malignant lymphoma-leukemia, myeloid leukemia, or malignant transformation of the thymus. At the same time, the occurrence of spontaneous or induced tumors is inhibited.

AMINO ACIDS

Dietary deficiencies of many single essential amino acids (phenylalanine, tyrosine, valine, threonine, methionine, cystine, or tryptophan) impair humoral antibody responses in mice but have little apparent effect on cell-mediated immunity. An excessive dietary intake of leucine, if sufficient to cause an amino acid imbalance, reduces the antibody response to immunization in animals. No reports in man document an association of single amino acid deficiency with loss of immune function.[2]

LIPIDS

Abnormalities in lipid intake or metabolism can initiate important changes in immunity. Experimental hypercholesterolemia in animals tends to decrease resistance to bacterial or viral infections or to tumors. Suppression of inflammatory infiltrates and impairment in phagocytic cell and RES functions and in primary antibody responses have been reported.[2] Perturbations in immune function are presumed to be mediated by increases in cell membrane cholesterol content and altered membrane fluidity.

A deficiency of essential fatty acids depresses both the primary and secondary antibody responses to both T-cell dependent and independent antigens in mice. Such an effect has not been reported in man. On the other hand, excess polyunsaturated fatty acids (PUFAs) produce widespread immunologic defects in laboratory animals, including lymphoid tissue atrophy, diminished delayed cutaneous hypersensitivity, and depressed T-cell immune responsiveness to antigenic stimulation. When infused, excess PUFAs cause lymphoid necrosis, impaired RES function, and a depressed rejection response to heterologous grafted tissue. If PUFAs are added in vitro to cell culture media, the phagocytic capacity of neutrophils is impaired and the proliferative responsiveness of lymphocytes is inhibited. However, this inhibition may result from direct toxic effects of PUFA on cultured cells. In patients given conventional immunosuppressive therapy, a high-PUFA diet caused an additional delay in the rejection time of renal transplants.[15]

Saturated fatty acids can serve as adjuvants for a variety of antigens and, in addition, appear to activate macrophages.

DIAGNOSTIC CRITERIA
General Concepts

Immune dysfunction may be present in every wasted or debilitated patient. It is generally more difficult to diagnose single-nutrient malnutrition than generalized protein-energy malnutrition. Although the coexistence of both immunologic and nutritional abnormalities does not mean that a cause-and-effect relationship exists, such would be suggested if an immunologic defect disappeared rapidly following clinical elimination of the nutritional problem. Thus, a therapeutic attempt to correct a nutritional abnormality can also serve as a diagnostic maneuver.

While single-nutrient deficiencies may contribute to generalized malnutrition, they can also lead to immunoincompetence in patients whose general nutritional status seems relatively normal. Single-nutrient deficiencies occur most commonly in patients with chronic anemias, alcoholism, recurrent or chronic diarrhea, chronic renal, liver, or biliary disease, regional enteritis or other malabsorptive states, or after intestinal bypass surgery. Patients receiving long-term hemodialysis or intravenous alimentation may incur unsuspected deficits or excesses of single nutrients. Other "at-risk" groups include the elderly, pregnant women, low-birth-weight infants (both small-for-age and preterm), and children with growth retardation, congenital aminoacidurias, or recurrent bacterial or yeast infections. Surprisingly, obese persons may manifest micronutrient deficiencies, particularly zinc and iron. Drugs and other therapeutic measures may induce single-nutrient abnormalities, such as those caused by folic acid antagonists, phenytoin sodium (folate deficiency), and isoniazid therapy (pyridoxine deficiency).

A single-nutrient deficiency or excess may develop in patients who are food faddists or in those who receive unusual therapeutic diets. Many persons currently consume large quantities of certain vitamins (A, B_{12}, C, E, niacin, or pyridoxine), minerals (zinc or selenium), or other single nutrients, including tryptophan, lecithin, or PUFA. It is therefore important to determine if a patient is following an unusual diet (prescribed or self-imposed) or is ingesting large quantities of a single nutrient.

Single-Nutrient Testing

Confirmation of a single-nutrient deficiency or excess may require reference laboratory facilities. A complete battery of clinical tests for nutrient-related anemias is possible in most major facilities. Iron status may be evaluated by determining hemoglobin level, RBC count, hematocrit reading, serum iron level, total transferrin or iron-binding capacity, and by the presence of iron in marrow cells. Radioimmunoassays of serum ferritin serve to assess tissue iron stores. Vitamin B_{12} can be measured in serum and its absorption evaluated by the Schilling test. Folate measurements can be performed in serum or RBCs.

Easily measured trace elements include zinc and copper; nickel and chromium determinations are more difficult. Most other trace elements can be measured with accuracy only in specialized laboratories. Assays for most vitamins, individual free amino acids, and individual fatty acids usually require specialized laboratory facilities.

Immunologic Evaluation

Some immunologic studies can be performed easily. Normal adults demonstrate delayed cutaneous hypersensitivity to skin tests with many ubiquitous antigens, such as monilia, phytohemagglutinin, streptokinase-streptodornase, or trichophyton. In some populations, mumps and tuberculin sensitivities are also common. Anergy exists if none of the common recall antigens elicits a delayed cutaneous hypersensitivity reaction. An anergic patient could be studied further by purposeful dermal sensitization with an unfamiliar new antigen, dinitrochlorobenzene, to test cell-mediated immunity. An initial application evaluates the ability to generate a localized inflammatory response, to become sensitized (ie, to develop immunologic memory), and a second application quantitatively tests recall.[3] While these studies can have diagnostic value, appropriate nutrient therapy should not be withheld simply to achieve research goals.

Measurements of total IgG, IgM, IgA, IgE, or complement concentrations in serum tell little about nutritionally induced immunoincompetence. On the other hand, a depressed IgA content in body surface fluids and secretions (eg, saliva or milk) can be an important finding. The enumeration of subsets of human lymphocytes may also assist in evaluating immune status. This is done by determining if there are immunoglobulins on their surface membranes, if sheep RBCs adhere to form rosettes, or if they can kill foreign cells.

Lymphocyte proliferative responses to mitogens or test antigens can now be measured in many laboratories. Such assays require that lymphocytes from the peripheral blood be gathered, cultured in vitro, and tested over a period of several days to determine whether appropriate mitogens or antigens will stimulate them. Proliferative responses are quantified by determining the uptake of radiolabeled thymidine, a nucleic acid precursor. In vitro assays can be performed in specialized laboratories to determine the chemotactic, phagocytic, and bactericidal capacities of neutrophils, as well as the ability to activate their hexosemonophosphate shunts.

Other participants in the workshop were Abraham E. Axelrod, PhD; Surendra Baliga, PhD; Ranjit K. Chandra, MD; Gabriel Fernandes, PhD; Allan L. Forbes, MD; Pamela J. Fraker, PhD; Philip Frost, MD, PhD; Raymond M. Galt, MD; George M. Hass, MD; Grant H. Laing, MD; Roger M. Loria, PhD; Margarita Nagy, MS, RD; Cheryl F. Nockles, PhD; Ronald D. Schultz, PhD; Gloria J. Troendle, MD; and Joseph J. Vitale, ScD, MD.

References

1. Dreizen S: Nutrition and the immune response—a review. *Int J Vitam Nutr Res* 1978;49:220-228.
2. Beisel WR: Malnutrition and the immune response, in Neuberger A, Jukes TH (eds): *Biochemistry of Nutrition I*. Baltimore, University Park Press, 1979, pp 1-19.
3. Edelman R: Cell-mediated immune response in protein-calorie malnutrition—a review, in Suskind RM (ed): *Malnutrition and the Immune Response*. New York, Raven Press, 1977, pp 47-75.
4. Axelrod AE: Immune processses in vitamin deficiency states. *Am J Clin Nutr* 1971;24:265-271.
5. Hodges RE, Bean WB, Ohlson MA, et al: Factors affecting human antibody response: V. Combined deficiencies of pantothenic acid and pyridoxine. *Am J Clin Nutr* 1962;11:187-199.
6. Thomas WR, Holt PG: Vitamin C and immunity: An assessment of the evidence. *Clin Exp Immunol* 1978;32:370-379.
7. Boxer LA, Watanabe AM, Bister M, et al: Correction of leukocyte function in Chediak-Higashi syndrome by ascorbate. *N Engl J Med* 1976;295:1041-1045.
8. Nockels CF: Protective effects of supplemental vitamin E against infection. *Fed Proc* 1979;38:2134-2138.
9. Prasad JS: Effect of vitamin E supplementation on leukocyte function. *Am J Clin Nutr* 1980;33:606-608.
10. Chandra RK, Au B, Woodford G, et al: Iron status, immune response and susceptibility to infection, in Kies H (ed), *Iron Metabolism*, Ciba Foundation symposium 51. Amsterdam, Elsevier/Excerpta Medica/North-Holland, 1977, pp 249-268.
11. Buckley RH: Iron deficiency anemia: Its relationship to infection susceptibility and host defense. *J Pediatr* 1975;86:993-995.
12. Murray MJ, Murray AB, Murray MB, et al: The adverse effect of iron repletion on the course of certain infections. *Br Med J* 1978;2:1113-1115.
13. Golden HN, Golden BE, Harland PSEG, et al: Zinc and immunocompetence in protein-energy malnutrition. *Lancet* 1978;1:1226-1228.
14. Bois P: Effect of magnesium deficiency on mast cells and urinary histamine in rats. *Br J Exp Pathol* 1963;44:151-155.
15. McHugh MI, Wilkinson R, Elliott RW, et al: Immunosuppression with polyunsaturated fatty acids in renal transplantation. *Transplantation*, 1977;24:263-267.

Child Nutrition Programs

by National Dairy Council

SUMMARY

Six child nutrition programs administered by the Food and Nutrition Service (FNS) of the United States Department of Agriculture (USDA)—National School Lunch Program (NSLP), School Breakfast Program (SBP), Special Milk Program (SMP), Child Care Food Program (CCFP), Summer Food Service Program for Children (SFSPC), and Special Supplemental Food Program for Women, Infants and Children (WIC)—are reviewed with respect to legislative and regulatory amendments shaping their current status, Federal costs, and changes in meal pattern requirements during the past six years. Included among the latter are the following:

• NSLP—elimination of the butter/fortified margarine requirement; introduction of the "offer versus serve" provision; deletion of the traditional "Type A lunch" terminology; expansion of the bread alternates and an increase in the number of bread servings specified on a weekly rather than a daily basis; the requirement that schools serve unflavored fluid lowfat milk, skim milk, or buttermilk as the lunch beverage and if they choose to offer another type of milk (e.g., whole or chocolate flavored), then they must also offer one of the above forms of milk as the beverage choice (in contrast to the previous less restrictive provision that allowed the same variety of milks in the NSLP that is indicated for the other programs); the requirement that schools involve students and parents toward improving acceptability of their lunch program; the suggestion that schools serve specified minimum quantities or portion sizes of food for four age/grade groups with maximum quantities specified for a fifth group and a provision for children 12 years and older to request smaller portion sizes; the encouragement of schools with State approval to serve lunch in two portions to children ages 1-5 years at two service periods; and an increase in the required portion sizes of certain meat alternates (eggs, cooked dry beans, peas).

• SBP—expansion of the grain requirement; and the suggestion to include a protein-rich food.

• CCFP and the SFSPC—elimination of the butter/fortified margarine requirement; and the stipulation that "juices shall not be served when milk is served" as part of the supplemental food pattern.

• WIC—an increase in the number of different food packages from three to six; specification of a maximum sugar limit for cereals; deletion of the flavored milk provision; a limit on the amount of cheese that can be substituted for milk and an expansion of the variety of domestic cheeses allowed; deletion of the authorization for whole cow's milk and evaporated milk in food packages for infants (previously these milks were allowed for infants beginning at six months of age); and inclusion of additional foods (peanut butter and mature dry beans or peas) in the food packages for children and pregnant and breastfeeding women.

• Other developments—(a) Alternate Foods—introduction of "cheese alternate products" in the lunch and supper requirements, an addition to the other alternate foods already allowed by USDA (e.g., textured vegetable protein products and enriched macaroni products with fortified protein); approval, and subsequent removal, of permission to use a "formulated fortified milk-based product" in the SFSPC; and an unsuccessful attempt to cancel or restrict the use of "formulated grain-fruit products" in the SBP. (b) Competitive Foods—restriction on the sale of specific categories of "foods of minimal nutritional value" from the beginning of the school day to the end of the last lunch period. Prior to the current regulation the State or local school system defined foods which were competitive.

The Food and Nutrition Service (FNS) of the United States Department of Agriculture (USDA) administers several Federally supported child nutrition programs, the general purpose of which is to improve the health and well-being of the nation's children by providing nutritious meals or food. Four of these programs — 1.) National School Lunch Program (NSLP); 2.) School Breakfast Program (SBP); 3.) Special Milk Program (SMP); and 4.) Special Food Service Program for Children (now the Child Care Food Program [CCFP] and the Summer Food Service Program for Children [SFSPC]) — were previously reviewed in a 1974 *Digest* (1). In the intervening six years, additional legislative and regulatory changes have occurred in these five programs, particularly in the meal pattern requirements. These major changes, as well as those related to the Special Supplemental Food Program for Women, Infants and Children (WIC), established since our previous publication (1), are summarized and reviewed in this *Digest*. Background information on the programs including their original purpose and objectives can be found in the 1974 *Digest* (1) and in reviews by Longen (2) and Owen et al (3). Complete details of the purpose and full requirements of the program changes can be obtained in the referenced documents.

For participating schools and service institutions to receive Federal reimbursement and donated foods for meals served under the programs, meals must meet specific requirements in terms of quantities of certain types of food. Changes in the meal requirements reflect efforts to combat traditional problems of hunger and malnutrition, to increase participation in the programs, to reduce plate (food) waste, to cut costs, to increase flexibility, and to meet current nutritional concerns, namely, the role of diet in health promotion and prevention of chronic degenerative diseases.

NATIONAL SCHOOL LUNCH PROGRAM (NSLP)

As the largest and most comprehensive of the child nutrition programs, the NSLP has increased in participation from 6.6 million children (24% of eligible school children) in its first year of operation (4) to 27.4 million children (61% of the eligible school enrollment) in Fiscal Year (FY) 1979 (5). Today, over 90% of the nation's schools participate in the NSLP (5). Federal expenditures for this program have increased from $1.1 billion in FY 1974 to $2.0 billion in FY 1979 (2).

Since 1974, program changes have been made with the primary purpose of increasing participation, particularly of children most in economic need. Prior to 1975, schools were permitted, but not required by law, to offer reduced-price meals to eligible children; and States were permitted to increase their free meal eligibility guidelines up to 25% above the income poverty guidelines. With enactment of Public Law (PL)94-105 on October 7, 1975, however, reduced-price meals were required by law, and the eligibility ceiling for such meals was increased from 175% to 195% of income poverty guidelines, thus making more children eligible for reduced-price meals (6). This ceiling remains in effect for reduced-price meals served under the SBP, CCFP, and NSLP (7). Any child whose family size and income, less an annually adjusted standard deduction, is under 125% of the poverty guidelines is eligible to receive and must be served free meals; children from families with incomes above 195% of the poverty line are referred to as "paying students"(8). PL94-105 also made a major administrative change which modified the number and types of schools participating in the school food service programs — the definition of school was broadened to include licensed public or nonprofit private residential child care institutions such as hospitals, juvenile detention centers, halfway houses, orphanages, and homes for the mentally retarded (9). And, effective June 29, 1979, the program definition of "child" was clarified to include physically or mentally handicapped persons regardless of age enrolled in non-residential schools participating in the NSLP (10).

The NSLP is unique in that it has a published, up-to-date, defined nutritional objective in terms of furnishing nutrients which, on an average over a period of time, provides a specified percentage of the Recommended Dietary Allowances (RDA) for children in various age groups. The quantities and kinds of foods planned for the NSLP are those that would yield approximately one-third of the 1980 RDA (11) for children in each of five age/grade groups (12,13).

The current meal pattern for the NSLP differs in many respects from the Type A lunch of 1974 which contained milk (pasteurized fluid types of unflavored or flavored whole milk, lowfat milk, skim milk, or cultured buttermilk), meat or meat alternate, vegetables and/or fruits, bread, and butter or margarine (1). The portion requirements of the Type A lunch pattern were established for only one age category (children 10-12 years), although there were provisions for decreasing and increasing the amounts served to younger and older children.

On June 11, 1976, the butter/fortified margarine requirement was eliminated from the lunch meal pattern (14). One of the next changes was the legislated "offer versus serve" provision, required in senior high schools (14) and permitted, at the option of local officials, in junior high and middle schools (15), that allows students the option of choosing less than the complete NSLP meal pattern (i.e., any three of the five food items comprising the lunch meal pattern).

Among the most recent meal pattern changes are those included in the final regulations of 1979 and 1980, published in two parts by USDA (12,13). With these regulations the "Type A" terminology was deleted and the following additional changes have taken place: 1.) the bread alternates have been expanded to include enriched or whole-grain rice, macaroni, noodles, other enriched or whole-grain pasta products, and other cereal grains such as bulgar and corn grits; and the number of servings required has been increased and is specified on a weekly as opposed to a daily basis; 2.) schools are required to serve unflavored fluid lowfat milk, skim milk, or buttermilk; and if they choose to offer another form of milk (e.g., whole or chocolate flavored), then they must offer unflavored fluid lowfat milk, skim milk, or buttermilk as a choice; 3.) schools must promote activities that involve students and parents toward improvements in the program; 4.) schools are encouraged to serve minimum quantities or portion sizes of food for children in the following four age/grade groups: I (age 1-2; preschool), II (age 3-4; preschool), III (age 5-8; grades K-3), and IV (age 9 and older; grades 4-12), and a fifth (V) group (12 years and older; grades 7-12) for which maximum servings are recommended; 5.) schools, if they elect to serve the group V portions, are allowed to permit children 12 years and older to request smaller portion sizes; 6.) schools can choose to serve lunch with State approval to children ages 1-5 years in two portions at two service periods; and 7.) the required quantities of certain meat alternates (eggs, cooked dry beans, peas) are increased to be nutritionally comparable to meat and the other meat alternates.

SCHOOL BREAKFAST PROGRAM (SBP)

The SBP, a program primarily benefiting needy children, has realized a significant but still disappointing increase in participation—from 330,000 school children in 1969 to 3.4 million in FY 1980 (4,5). The magnitude of participation in this program is approximately 12% of that of the NSLP. About one-third of the nation's schools now participate, and the program serves about 24% of the participating schools' enrollment (5). Federal expenditures for the program have increased from $59 million in FY 1974 to $224 million in FY 1979 (2). The suggestion has been made that expansion of the SBP may be one of the most cost effective means to increase the amount of nutritious food available to children (5). The General Accounting Office has reviewed major factors contributing to the less than expected expansion of this program and has recommended several actions to increase program participation (16).

Due to expire June 30, 1975, the program was expanded and given permanent authorization with passage of PL 94-105 in October 1975 (6). As in the NSLP, the SBP definition of "school" now includes licensed public or nonprofit private residential child care institutions (9). Eligibility and Federal reimbursement for breakfasts are based on the same income guidelines used in the NSLP, except for the "severe need" category which provides significantly higher than the average SBP reimbursement to economically needy schools (17).

Although no nutritional goals are set forth for the SBP, it is widely assumed that school breakfast is intended to provide one-fourth of the RDA. A breakfast eligible for Federal reimbursement must contain a minimum of the following three components in the amounts indicated: 1.) one-half pint fluid milk (pasteurized fluid types of unflavored or flavored whole milk, lowfat milk, skim milk, or cultured buttermilk meeting State and local standards for such milk); 2.) one-half cup serving of fruit or vegetables or both or full-strength fruit or vegetable juice; and 3.) one slice of whole-grain or enriched bread, or three-quarters cup enriched or fortified cereal, or equivalent (18). It also is suggested that for children over one year of age, breakfasts include, as often as practicable, protein-rich foods such as one ounce servings of meat, poultry, fish, cheese, or one egg, or two tablespoons of peanut butter, or equivalent. This meal pattern, like that of the NSLP, reflects changes. For example, the grain requirement has been expanded to include more items, and the suggestion to include a protein-rich food has been added (19).

SPECIAL MILK PROGRAM (SMP)

On an average day in 1975, about 9.2 million children received milk served through the SMP (20). In FY 1980, the SMP subsidized the milk served to over 8 million children (5). Participation in this program has been hampered by the move in 1974 to limit the milk program in schools without food service, even though this restriction was subsequently removed (1). Cost-wise, the Federal government expended $49.2 million in FY 1974, $141.1 million in FY 1979 (2).

Following in a similar pattern to that prior to 1974, legislation has continued to both expand and constrict this program which serves milk in addition to that served with school meals. For example, legislation enacted in 1975 expanded the SMP, making it available to Puerto Rico, Virgin Islands, American Samoa, and the Pacific Trust Territories (21). But, with implementation of PL 95-166 in 1977, children who qualified for free lunches were eligible for free milk *only* when SMP milk was made available at times other than Federally assisted meal service periods (22). That is, eligible children were unable to receive a second half-pint of milk free in addition to that served with their free meal. Eligible children, however, who did not take their free lunch under the NSLP (such as children who brought a bag lunch from home) were eligible for free milk during the lunch period. While this restriction on the service of free milk was rescinded in 1978 by PL 95-627 (23), availability of free SMP milk is now optional with local school or district officials. Federal funds are provided to States to assist participating schools and institutions in paying the cost of all half-pints of fluid milk consumed by children other than the first half-pint served as part of Federally assisted meals. The minimum rate of reimbursement per half-pint of milk which was previously adjusted annually, based on changes in the food away from home series of the consumer price index (CPI) (24) has, since 1978, been adjusted to reflect changes in the producer price index of fresh processed milk (23). While this adjusted rate is paid to all schools and institutions that operate only the SMP, those which also provide meals under the NSLP, SBP, or CCFP are reimbursed five cents for each SMP half-pint served (8).

One-half pint fluid milk (i.e., pasteurized types of unflavored or flavored whole milk, lowfat milk, skim milk, or cultured buttermilk which meet State and local standards for such milk) continues to be allowed under the current SMP.

CHILD CARE FOOD PROGRAM (CCFP) AND SUMMER FOOD SERVICE PROGRAM FOR CHILDREN (SFSPC)

Participation in the CCFP, formerly the year-round portion of the Special Food Service Program for Children, increased from 40,000 children in 1969 to 713,000 children in the first quarter of 1980 (2,4,21). Likewise, the number of program outlets has grown: from 2,200 in 1970 to 29,000 in FY 1979 (5,21). Participation in this program has not been as large as expected, and many eligible centers have not joined the program.

In October 1975, with PL 94-105, the Special Food Service Program for Children was changed into two independent programs: 1.) CCFP and 2.) SFSPC. Basically, the CCFP provides financial and commodity assistance for meals served to children in eligible nonresidential public or private institutions. Scheduled to terminate in 1978, the program was revised and made permanent by the Child Nutrition Amendments of 1978 (PL 95-627 enacted November 10, 1978). Significant revisions in the CCFP included easing of certain licensing requirements governing institutional eligibility for aid and reworking the formula for determining Federal assistance. In recognition of the three distinct types of operations in the CCFP—child care centers, family day-care homes, and outside-school-hours care centers—separate administrative and operational requirements recently have been authorized (25).

The SFSPC, which served fewer than 100,000 children in 1969, reached approximately 2.4 million children in about 22,700 feeding sites in July, 1979 (5,21,24). Federal expenditures for both the CCFP and the SFSPC have increased from $61.8 million in FY 1974 to $281.3 million in FY 1979 (2).

The SFSPC, primarily directed toward children from needy areas (in which at least one-third of the children are eligible for a free or reduced-price meal under the National School Lunch Act), focuses on assisting States to provide nutritious meals to preschool and school-aged children in recreation centers, summer camps, or during vacations in areas operating under a continuous school calendar or where poor economic conditions exist (21). The program was scheduled to expire in 1977, but PL 95-166 (November 10, 1977) extended it through 1980 and issued major reforms and administrative controls. Amendments issued January, 1980 emphasized changes directed at reducing mismanagement, waste, and abuse in the program (26). PL 96-499, enacted on December 5, 1980, extends the program authorization through September 30, 1984, and also limits daily meal service at food service sites (8).

Breakfast, lunch, supper, and between-meal supplements, or any combinations of these types of meals are provided under the CCFP and the SFSPC (18). The meals offered must meet minimum standards established by USDA. Supplemental food, which only is approved for reimbursement if the institution does *not* participate in the SMP, must contain two of the following four components: 1.) one-half pint of milk; 2.) one ounce of meat or meat alternate; 3) six fluid ounces of full-strength fruit or vegetable juice (juice cannot be served when milk is served) or three-quarters of a cup of fruit or vegetables; and 4.) one slice of whole-grain or enriched bread, or an approved substitute (18). The lunch and supper patterns differ from those originally required for the SFSPC. For example, on May 6, 1974, the butter/fortified margarine requirement was eliminated (27). And under the original meal requirements for the CCFP and the summer programs, both milk and fruit juice could be served. In 1978, USDA stipulated that "juices shall not be served when milk is served" as part of the supplemental food pattern (28).

SPECIAL SUPPLEMENTAL FOOD PROGRAM FOR WOMEN, INFANTS AND CHILDREN (WIC)

WIC, a program specifically targeted to nutritionally vulnerable groups, is the second largest and fastest growing program (5). It has expanded from serving 87,700 low-income women, infants and children with special nutritional needs in FY 1974 to serving about 2.2 million in FY 1980 (2,4,5). Federal expenditures for the program have increased from $10.4 million in FY 1974 to $530.9 million in FY 1979 (2).

Authorized by PL 92-433, WIC began on September 26, 1972 as a two-year pilot program for each of FYs 1973 and 1974 (5,21,24). The aim was to provide supplemental nutritious foods as an adjunct to good health care to pregnant and lactating women, infants and children up to four years of age, who, as judged by competent health professionals, were at nutritional risk due to low income and/or inadequate nutrition. Eligibility at this time was not based on national income limits and, as such, varied from State to State. Unlike other child nutrition programs that are carried out through State education agencies, the WIC program is financed by cash grants from the Secretary of Agriculture to State health departments or comparable agencies. Supplemental food packages containing specified amounts of certain foods are provided for all eligible participants. These are distributed via three general types of food delivery systems: 1.) retail purchase by food vouchers; 2.) home delivery; and 3.) direct distribution by local WIC clinics.

In November, 1973 (PL 93-150), Congress authorized the extension of the WIC program through 1975 and allowed recognized Indian tribes to be included in the program. Subsequent legislation from 1974 through 1978 (i.e., PL 93-326 in 1974; PL 94-105 in 1975; PL 95-627 in 1978) further extended, expanded, clarified, and revised the WIC program, doubling authorized funds and providing nutrition education monies (24). Nutrition education is an integral component of the WIC program. In fact, unless States receive a waiver, they are required to spend at least one-sixth of the administrative funds on nutrition education (29). Eligibility for the program was expanded by including non-nursing mothers up to six months postpartum, nursing mothers up to one year, and infants and children up to five years of age. PL 95-627 in 1978 extended the WIC program through FY 1982 and outlined specific changes including national income limits for participation in the program (29). And the most recent legislation, PL 96-499 enacted on December 5, 1980, extends WIC authorization through FY 1984 with funds to be appropriated in amounts necessary to operate the program (8).

Requirements for providing supplemental foods for WIC recipients are set forth as maximum monthly quantities of foods as opposed to minimum requirements per meal (18). Requirements as stated August 26, 1977 (30) have been updated and must be implemented by November 12, 1981 (31). Six food packages, designed to furnish nutrients deficient in the diets of the WIC program target population (i.e., protein, iron, calcium, vitamins A and C) are specified for: 1.) infants through 3 months; 2.) infants 4 through 12 months; 3.) children/women with special dietary needs; 4.) children 1 to 5 years; 5.) pregnant and breastfeeding women; and 6.) non-breastfeeding postpartum women (31). Types of foods included in the food packages are as follows: iron-fortified infant formula; infant cereal high in iron; cereal high in iron and limited in sugar (a maximum of six grams of sugar per ounce of dry cereal); fruit juice or vegetable juice high in vitamin C; pasteurized fluid unflavored whole milk, skim milk, or lowfat milk or cultured buttermilk, or evaporated (whole or skimmed) milk, or dry milk (whole, nonfat or lowfat) fortified with vitamin D (400 I.U.) and vitamin A (2000 I.U.) where indicated; domestic cheese (pasteurized process American, Monterey Jack, Colby, Natural Cheddar, Swiss, Brick, Muenster, Provolone, and Mozzarella); eggs; and peanut butter or mature dry beans or peas (31).

In contrast to previous requirements, these most recent regulations for the WIC food packages are specified for six as opposed to three groups; a maximum sugar limit for cereals is stipulated; the provision allowing flavored milk has been eliminated; a limit has been placed on the amount of cheese that can be substituted for milk; the variety of domestic cheeses allowed has been expanded; whole milk and evaporated milk in the infant food package have been deleted (previously whole milk, evaporated milk, and in some areas whole dry milk were allowed for infants beginning at six months of age); and additional foods (peanut butter or mature dry beans or peas) have been included in the food packages for children and for pregnant and breastfeeding women.

OTHER DEVELOPMENTS

Alternate Foods. Use of alternate foods in child nutrition programs continues to be a controversial issue. From the early 1970s, there has been a slow but steady increase in the introduction of these foods which substitute for all or part of a required meal component. Since authorization of the alternate foods, enriched macaroni with fortified protein, formulated grain-fruit products, and textured vegetable products, as reviewed in the previous *Digest* on child nutrition programs (1), "cheese alternate products" and a "formulated fortified milk-based product" have been introduced (32,33).

In 1974, USDA authorized use of "cheese alternate products" as an alternate food for the meat/meat alternate components specified in the lunch and supper requirements for the child nutrition programs (32). Cheese alternate products, available in forms similar to Mozzarella and American processed cheese, can be used to extend and partially replace natural or processed cheese. The products, which must be mixed and melted with at least 50% real cheese, can be used in cooked items such as cheese sandwiches, pizza, and macaroni and cheese. On July 13, 1976, a "formulated fortified milk-based product" was introduced as a one-component alternate food for the supplemental food pattern of the SFSPC (33). Due to a number of concerns related to the product and USDA's position that "a properly balanced diet of conventional foods is the preferred source of adequate nutrition," authorization for this product was withdrawn (34).

In line with the policy that conventional foods are the preferred source of adequate nutrition, USDA proposed on August 12, 1977, to withdraw authorization for use of "formulated grain-fruit products" (i.e., cake or doughnut-type products fortified with nutrients) in the SBP effective June 30, 1978 (35). The proposal did not prohibit schools from serving the formulated product, but rather, required that a fruit/juice/vegetable component also be served. USDA was required to take into consideration the findings and recommendations of a study conducted by the Comptroller General (36) before making a final decision.

Competitive Foods. Until recently, competitive foods sold in schools included items of varied nutritional value such as soups, sandwiches, fruits, candies, potato chips, and soda pop (37). Authority for regulating the sale of competitive foods was previously with State and local education agencies (1). Subsequently, in 1977, the U.S. Congress through PL 95-166 (38) restored the authority to regulate the sale of competitive foods to the Secretary of Agriculture. To implement the appropriate provision of the law, USDA proposed on April 25, 1978 to prohibit the sale of certain competitive foods to children on school premises until after the last lunch period (39). This was followed by withdrawal of the proposal and public hearings on the issue of competitive foods (40), development of a second proposed rule in July, 1979 (41), and in January, 1980, publication of final regulations restricting the sale of categories of "foods of minimal nutritional value" from the beginning of the school day to the end of the last lunch period (37). The four restricted categories of "foods of minimal nutritional value" (i.e., foods that "—provide less than 5% of the USRDA for each of eight specified nutrients per 100 calories and per serving.") include: soda water, water ices, chewing gum, and certain candies (37). This final rule was amended in November 1980 to provide that no food can be exempted from the restricted sale requirements by virtue of fortification with nutrients (42).

REFERENCES

1. National Dairy Council. Dairy Council Digest 45: 1, 1974.
2. Longen, K. *Domestic Food Programs: An Overview.* U.S.D.A. Economics, Statistics, and Cooperatives Service: ESCS-81, August 1980.
3. Owen, A.L., G.M. Owen, and G. Lanna. In: *Costs and Benefits of Nutritional Care, Phase 1.* Chicago, Illinois: The American Dietetic Association, 1979, pp 67-79.
4. Austin, J.E., and C. Hitt. *Nutrition Intervention in the United States Cases and Concepts.* Cambridge, Mass.: Ballinger Publishing Company, 1979.
5. Congressional Budget Office. *Feeding Children: Federal Child Nutrition Policies in the 1980's.* Washington, D.C.: U.S. Government Printing Office, May, 1980.
6. Public Law 94-105, Enacted October 7, 1975.
7. Child Nutrition Program. Determining Eligibility for Free and Reduced Price Meals and Milk in Schools. Fed.Regist. 44: 33048, June 8, 1979.
8. Public Law 96-499. The Omnibus Reconciliation Act of 1980. December 5, 1980.
9. National School Lunch Program. Child Nutrition Programs. Fed.Regist. 41: 18426, May 4, 1976.
10. National School Lunch Program. Final Rule. Fed.Regist. 44: 37896, June 29, 1979.
11. Food and Nutrition Board. *Recommended Dietary Allowances, Ninth Revised Edition.* Washington, D.C.: National Academy of Sciences, National Research Council, 1980.
12. National School Lunch Program. Nutritional Requirements. Final Regulation. Fed.Regist. 44: 48149, August 17, 1979.
13. National School Lunch Program. Nutritional Requirements. Final Regulation. Fed.Regist. 45: 32502, May 16, 1980.
14. National School Lunch Program. Implementation. Fed.Regist. 41: 23695, June 11, 1976.
15. National School Lunch Program. Requirements: Type A Lunches. Fed.Regist. 43: 25990, June 16, 1978.
16. Report by the Comptroller General of the United States. *Major Factors Inhibit Expansion of the School Breakfast Program.* CED-80-35. Washington, D.C.: General Accounting Office, June 16, 1980.
17. School Breakfast Program. Fed.Regist. 44: 48157, August 17, 1979.
18. Code of Federal Regulations. 7 Agriculture Parts 210 to 299, Revised as of January 1, 1980. Chapter II—Food and Nutrition Service, Department of Agriculture. Subchapter A—Child Nutrition Programs. Part 210-246.
19. School Breakfasts and Nonfood Assistance Programs and State Administrative Expenses. Fed.Regist. 40: 2697, January 15, 1975.
20. United States Department of Agriculture. Food and Nutrition Service. *Special Milk Program Evaluation and National School Lunch Program Survey.* FNS-167, June 1978.
21. Food and Nutrition Service, United States Department of Agriculture: *Annual Statistical Review—Preliminary Report, Food and Nutrition Programs, Fiscal Year 1976.* FNS-161. Washington, D.C.: U.S. Department of Agriculture, November, 1976.
22. Special Milk Program for Children. National School Lunch, School Breakfast or Child Care Food Programs. Fed.Regist. 43: 1059, January 6, 1978.
23. Special Milk Program for Children; Free Milk Option in the Special Milk Program. Fed.Regist. 44: 33046, June 8, 1979.
24. Report by the Comptroller General of the United States. *Federal Domestic Food Assistance Programs—A Time for Assessment and Change.* CED-78-113. Washington, D.C.: General Accounting Office, June 13, 1978.
25. Child Care Food Program. Fed.Regist. 45: 4960, January 22, 1980.
26. Summer Food Service Program for Children. Fed.Regist. 45: 1843, January 8, 1980.
27. Special Food Service Program for Children. Administration. Fed.Regist. 39: 15756, May 6, 1974.
28. Summer Food Service Program for Children. Final Rule. Fed.Regist. 43: 13020, March 28, 1978.
29. Special Supplemental Food Program for Women, Infants and Children. WIC —Legislation. Fed.Regist. 44: 44422, July 27, 1979.
30. Special Supplemental Food Program for Women, Infants and Children. Fed.Regist. 42: 43206, August 26, 1977.
31. Special Supplemental Food Program for Women, Infants and Children. Final Rule. Fed.Regist. 45: 74854, November 12, 1980.
32. National School Lunch Program, Appendix A: Alternate Foods for Meals: Cheese Alternate Products. Fed.Regist. 39: 31514, August 29, 1974.
33. Summer Food Service Program for Children. Alternate Food Proposal. Fed.Regist. 41: 28796, July 13, 1976.
34. Summer Food Service Program for Children. Fed.Regist. 42: 23606, May 10, 1977.
35. Formulated Grain-Fruit Products. Fed.Regist. 42: 40911, August 12, 1977.
36. Report by the Comptroller General of the United States. *Formulated Grain-Fruit Products: Proposed Restrictions on Use in School Breakfast Program Should be Reevaluated.* CED-79-12. Washington, D.C.: General Accounting Office, December 26, 1978.
37. National School Lunch Program and School Breakfast Program; Competitive Foods. Fed.Regist. 45: 6758, January 29, 1980.
38. PL 95-166, Enacted November 10, 1977.
39. National School Lunch Program. Fed.Regist. 43: 17476, April 25, 1978.
40. National School Lunch Program Regulation of Competitive Foods; Withdrawal of Proposed Rule; Meetings. Fed.Regist. 43: 58780, December 15, 1978.
41. National School Lunch Program and School Breakfast Program. Fed.Regist. 44: 40004, July 6, 1979.
42. National School Lunch Program and School Breakfast Program; Competitive Foods. Fed.Regist. 45: 76937, November 21, 1980.

… CHILDHOOD

The Impact of Selected Salted Snack Food Consumption on School-age Children's Diets

by Karen J. Morgan, Gilbert A. Leveille, and Mary E. Zabik

Abstract

Seven-day food diaries of a cross-sectional sample of United States children ages five to 12 years (n=657) were used to assess the role of selected salted snack foods in children's diets. Results indicated that these foods were consumed by 83 percent of the children and were, in general, consumed in moderation. Most children who consumed selected salted snack foods had an average nutrient intake comparable to that of children not consuming these foods. Five of the children were found to have consumed amounts of snack foods that could be considered excessive. These had average daily nutrient intakes that were inadequate for some vitamins and minerals. An education program was recommended to inform children how to incorporate these well-liked foods into their diets appropriately, without compromising the nutrient quality of their diets.

INTRODUCTION

There is currently concern about the possible negative impact of the consumption of salted snack foods, as well as other foods, on the nutritional adequacy of the United States diet (1). Public policy makers and the mass media have expressed particular concerns about diets of school children ages five to 12 years. Yet, to date, appropriate surveys have not been conducted to provide reliable empirical data on the use of such foods and of their impact on children's diets.

Data presently available consists of information on the disappearance of food from the marketplace. For example, the United States Department of Agriculture (USDA) has projected that 0.9 billion pounds of potato chips will be sold in 1981 (2). In view of this projected potato usage, it is not surprising that some nutritionists have expressed concern about abusive usage of salted snack foods such as potato chips. Other nutritionists, however, contend that specific foods in the diet, including salted snack foods, are neither good nor bad. The important element in a high quality diet is balance among a variety of foods that provide the nutrients and energy required by the body (3).

In order to evaluate these two viewpoints, it is imperative that data be examined to reveal whether or not such foods impair the quality of diet. Thus, the objective of the research reported in this paper was to examine food consumption patterns of five to 12 year-old children as they relate to the intake patterns of selected salted snack foods and to determine whether consumption of such foods leads to dietary inadequacies.

METHOD

Data Collection. Market Facts of Chicago, Ill., gathered the data used in this investigation during the third week of September, 1977. The firm's Consumer Market Panel II, consisting of 2,000 families, was provided with seven-day food diaries and were requested to complete the diaries for each family member presently living in the household. The households selected by Market Facts were balanced for geographic area, population density, degree of urbanization, and income and age of panel member. Diaries from 1,434 families were returned and considered to be in usable form. From these diaries food intake observations of children ages five to 12 years (657 children from 404 families) were coded for computerized analyses. A complete description of the instrument used for data collection has been reported by Cala et al. (4).

The type of data collection employed in this study may have questionable reliability and validity for being an absolute measurement of nutritional intake. As indicated by Madden et al. (5), however, reliability and validity of data collection techniques are of lesser importance when estimating differences in mean nutrient consumption between the means of two or more groups from the same population than when estimating the mean for an entire sample group to compare with results of another study. The objective of this study reported was to make within sample population comparisons of the impact of various food consumption patterns on nutrient intake levels.

Indepth descriptions of the socioeconomic and demographic characteristics of this cross-sectional sample of 404 families containing one or more children ages five to 12 years has been reported by Morgan et al. (6). The authors concluded that the sample was representative of a cross-sectional sample of middle to upper-middle class, two parent families composed of four to six members with parents who had attained an educational level somewhat higher than the general United States population.

Data analysis. Each child's seven-day food diary was coded to use the Michigan State University Nutrient Data Bank that allowed calculation for 24 nutrients on a meal, daily, and weekly basis. The percentage of National Research Council-Recommended Dietary Allowances (NRC-RDA) (7) was calculated for appropriate nutrients. These calculations were based on the age and sex of each child, as well as kilocalories consumption for thiamin, niacin, and riboflavin and utilized the standards set in 1974. The average nutrient intake for the sample population, as well as the percentage of sample population whose daily nutrient intake fell below 100 percent, 66 percent, and 33 percent of the NRC-RDA for one, two, three . . . seven days during the assessment period, has previously been reported by Morgan et al. (5). This report indicated that, in general, the nutrient intakes of this sample population were acceptable.[1]

The total sample was first assessed for its average consumption level of selected salted snack foods (SSFs). SSFs included potato chips, popcorn, corn chips, pretzels, tortilla chips, cheese twists, potato sticks, and bacon rinds. Data were analyzed for total consumption of all SSFs in one week as well as by average consumption per week and per

---
[1]Although information was collected pertaining to consumption of vitamin supplements, this data was not included in the analysis because the primary objective of the study was to assess the nutrient intake of children via their food consumption patterns.

Table 1. Average Daily Nutrient Intake of Various Groups of Children Classified According to the Percentage of Caloric Intake from the Consumption of Selected Salted Snack Foods.

	Percentage of Calories from Selected Salted Snack Foods					
	>10 (n=16)			5.0 to 9.9 (n=65)		
Nutrient	Ave.	Std. Dev.	Ave. %RDA	Ave.	Std. Dev.	Ave. %RDA
Calories	2220 [1,2]	529	92 [1,2]	2136 [1,2]	566	87 [2]
Total Protein, g	70 [2]	19	176 [2]	72 [2]	19	188 [2]
Total Fat, g	102 [1]	27		92 [1]	31	
Total Carbohydrate, g	264 [1,2]	67		264 [1,2]	68	
Total Sugar, g	123 [2]	41		134 [1,2]	42	
Cholesterol, mg	282 [1,2]	83		271 [2]	106	
Crude Fiber, g	3.2 [1,2]	1.5		3.1 [1,2]	0.9	
Ascorbic Acid, mg	124 [1]	107	302 [1]	102 [1]	52	248 [1]
Thiamin, mg	1.23 [2]	0.39	113 [1]	1.29 [1,2]	0.33	116 [1]
Niacin, mg	17.3 [1]	4.5	119 [1]	17.2 [1]	4.3	117 [1]
Riboflavin, mg	1.71 [2]	0.60	129 [3]	1.94 [2]	0.57	144 [2,3]
Pyridoxine, µ	1186 [2]	326	93 [2]	1302 [1,2]	377	108 [1,2]
Vitamin B$_{12}$,[2] µ	3.84 [2]	2.72	169 [2]	3.84 [2]	2.02	185 [2]
Folacin,[4] µ	219 [1,2]	81	71 [1]	202 [2]	62	69 [1]
Total Vitamin A, IU	5006 [2]	3003	147 [2]	5065 [2]	1874	150 [2]
Vitamin D, IU[5]	143 [2]	95	36 [2]	186 [1,2]	112	47 [1,2]
Iron, mg	12.6 [1,2]	3.9	103 [2]	12.7 [1,2]	3.5	111 [1,2]
Calcium, mg	892 [2]	404	97 [3]	992 [2]	345	112 [3]
Phosphorus, mg	1228 [2]	372	132 [2]	1276 [2]	364	144 [2]
Sodium, mg[6]	3098 [1]	786		2907 [1]	769	
Potassium, mg	2546 [2]	860		2534 [2]	672	
Magnesium, mg	235 [2]	76	90 [2]	235 [2]	60	92 [2]
Copper, µ	1482 [1,2]	540		1329 [2]	578	
Zinc, mg	10.7 [1,2]	5.1	90 [2]	10.4 [1,2]	4.7	95 [1,2]

[1,2,3]Means in a row sharing a common superscript ([1,2,3]) are not significantly different (P ≤ 0.05) using Duncan's multiple range test (9).
[4]Folacin data are underestimated because analytical data are insufficient (11).
[5]Vitamin D data inaccurate as fortification of skim and 2% milk not indicated (12); also it is synthesized from the sun.
[6]Sodium consumption is underestimated because added table salt not included in calculation.

230 NUTRITION FROM CONCEPTION THROUGH ADOLESCENCE

day of the eight individual snack items. Data were examined through cross tabulations and chi-square tests (8) to determine if any relationship existed between consumption levels and socioeconomic characteristics of the children.

Following analyses of the total sample, the sample was partitioned to reflect groups of children who consumed various amounts of SSFs. Initially the sample was divided into five groups. Group one (n=16) consisted of all children who obtained greater than 10 percent of their average daily caloric intake from the consumption of SSFs. Those children who obtained less than 10 but greater than 5 percent of their average daily caloric intake from the SSFs eaten were placed in another group (n=65). This classification procedure was followed for dividing remaining children into categories that reflected their consumption levels of SSFs as greater than 3 percent but less than 5 percent of total caloric intake (n=104), greater than zero but less than 3 percent of total caloric intake (n=361), or as zero, i.e., no SSFs consumed during the one week surveyed (n=111). For each of the five classified groups of children, average daily intake of 24 dietary components was calculated as well as standard deviations and average percentage NRC-RDA. Each set of mean intakes was analyzed for statistically significant differences using general linear model (8). Where significant differences were observed using means, Duncan's multiple range test (9) was utilized to pinpoint the differences among the five groups tested.

It is often implied that individuals who consume these selected snack foods derive excessive amounts of sodium and fat from these foods. The impact of the consumption of these foods, on sodium[2] and fat intake of the sample children, therefore, was examined by determining what percentage contribution SSFs made to total intake of these two dietary components.

In an attempt to examine the effect of high intakes of SSFs closely, the nutrient intake of the child having the highest consumption to SSFs, amounting to 36 percent of caloric intake, and the intake of those children consuming 20 percent or more of their calories from SSFs (n=4), were tabulated and compared to children who consumed no SSFs (n=111). Because sample sizes were very unequal (10), no statistical analysis was performed on these data.

RESULTS AND DISCUSSION

Consumption Patterns for SSFs. Approximately 83 percent of all children in the sample consumed SSFs. Those children who consumed SSFs consumed an average of 3.3 ounces per week. Average consumption per week for all five to 12 year-olds in the sample was 2.5 ounces. Analysis revealed an increase in the amount of SSFs consumed as the age of the children increased, i.e., the average intake for five and six year-old children was 2.0 ounces per week and 3.1 ounces per week for 11 and 12 year-olds.

Cross-tabulation of consumption data with regard to geographic location, family income, and both father's and mother's education levels showed no trends of relation for

---

[2]Average sodium consumption reported here does not include added table salt.

	3.0 to 4.9 (n=104)			0.1 to 2.9 (n=361)			0 (n=111)		
Ave.		Std. Dev.	Ave. %RDA	Ave.	Std. Dev.	Ave. %RDA	Ave.	Std. Dev.	Ave. %RDA
2121 [1,2]		476	88[2]	2239 [1]	581	100[1]	2051 [2]	560	92[1,2]
74 [2]		17	194[2]	80 [1]	21	220[1]	76 [1,2]	21	211[1,2]
92 [1]		23		96 [1]	29		87 [1]	24	
259 [1,2]		61		274 [1]	71		248 [2]	80	
132 [2]		43		145 [1]	48		130 [2]	54	
316 [1]		116		328 [1]	132		325 [1]	123	
2.9 [2]		1		3.3 [1]	1.3		2.7 [2]	1.1	
98 [1]		48	238[1]	113 [1]	64	274[1]	99 [1]	65	241[1]
1.24[2]		0.26	113[1]	1.36[1]	0.38	117[1]	1.27[2]	0.40	116[1]
16.7 [1]		3.7	113[1]	17.7 [1]	5.1	115[1]	16.8 [1]	5.1	114[1]
2 [2]		0.50	148[2]	2.22[1]	0.69	157[1]	2.01[2]	0.57	150[1,2]
1263 [2]		326	106[1,2]	1381 [1]	456	115[1]	1266 [2]	432	108[1,2]
4.21[2]		2.14	206[2]	5.23[1]	4.56	255[1]	4.33[2]	2.39	218[1,2]
214 [1,2]		136	74[1]	227 [1]	88	79[1]	203 [2]	77	72[1]
5316 [2]		2938	158[2]	6359 [1]	3843	190[1]	5792 [1,2]	3091	176[1,2]
209 [1,2]		113	52[1,2]	220 [1]	131	55[1]	198 [1,2]	96	49[1,2]
12.5 [2]		2.7	109[2]	13.5 [1]	3.8	119[1]	12.5 [2]	4.0	111[1,2]
1035 [2]		306	117[2,3]	1147 [1]	381	131[1]	1055 [2]	324	122[1,2]
1327 [2]		319	150[2]	1452 [1]	412	165[1]	1349 [2]	366	156[1,2]
2830 [1]		733		2923 [1]	819		2636 [1]	764	
2621 [2]		636		2856 [1]	862		2580 [2]	825	
247 [2]		81	97[2]	286 [1]	123	113[1]	239 [2]	72	96[2]
1423 [1,2]		512		1548 [1]	637		1354 [2]	464	
9.9 [2]		2.9	89[2]	11.4 [1]	4.5	103[1]	10.2 [2]	3.7	93[2]

these elements. Figure 1 shows the consumption patterns of specific snack foods.[3] A large proportion of the children consumed potato chips with the average amount consumed in one week being 1.9 ounces. Similar data are shown for each of the snack foods studied. These average data show SSFs were, in general, consumed in moderation by the sample children.

Figure 1. Average Number of Ounces of Selected Salted Snack Foods Consumed by Five to 12 year-old Children in One Week and During One Day.

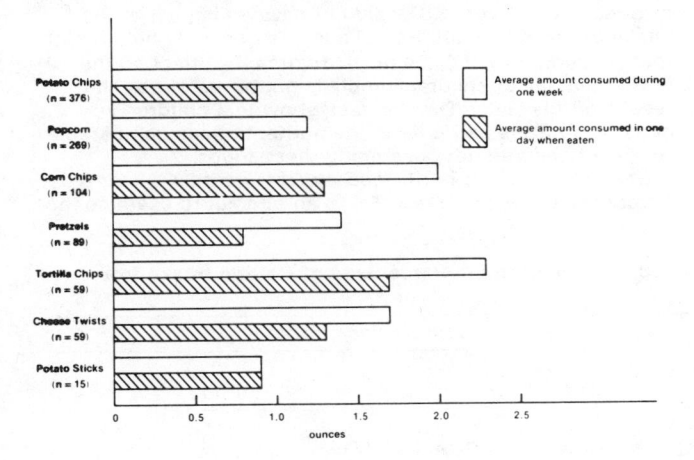

Figure 2. Average Daily Intake of Sodium by Various Groups of Five to 12 year-old Children and Average Proportion of Sodium Obtained from the Consumption of Salted Snack Foods (Tabulated Sodium Consumption Does Not Include Added Table Salt).

Average Daily Nutrient Intake of Children Consuming Various Amounts of SSFs. Table 1 displays the average daily nutrient intake of groups of children who consumed greater than 10.0 percent, 5.0 to 10.0 percent, 3.0 to 4.9 percent, and 0.1 to 2.9 percent of calories from SSFs and finally, those children who consumed no SSFs. Only 2.4 percent of the children studied obtained more than 10 percent of their calories from SSFs. The majority of children who consumed SSFs derived less than 3 percent of their calories from these items.

As shown in Table 1, statistical comparisons of mean intakes of the various groups of children revealed no significant differences ($p \leq 0.05$) among the groups' intakes for total fat, vitamin C, niacin, and sodium.[4] It is generally implied that individuals consuming SSFs derive excessive amounts of sodium and fat from these foods. Although this allegation was not borne out in statistical analysis of the data, the impact of the consumption of SSFs on sodium and fat intake was further investigated.

Figure 2 shows the amount of sodium[5] consumed by individuals classified relative to the proportion of calories derived from SSFs and the average amount of sodium each obtained from eating SSFs. Not surprisingly there was an increase in sodium intake as the proportion of calories from SSFs increased. This increase, however, was not found to be statistically significant and, further, the total amount of sodium derived from SSFs does not appear to have been excessive. In the very highest group, deriving greater than 10 percent of calories from SSFs, 19 percent of the sodium ingested was derived from SSFs.

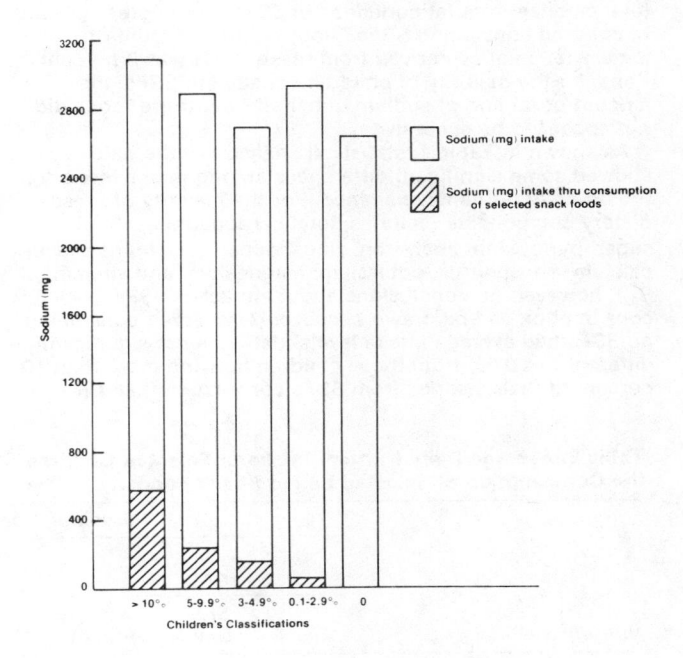

Figure 3. Average Percentage of Calories Obtained by Various Groups of Five to 12 year-old Children from Dietary Fat and Average Proportion of Percentage Fat Calories Obtained from Consumption of Salted Snack Foods.

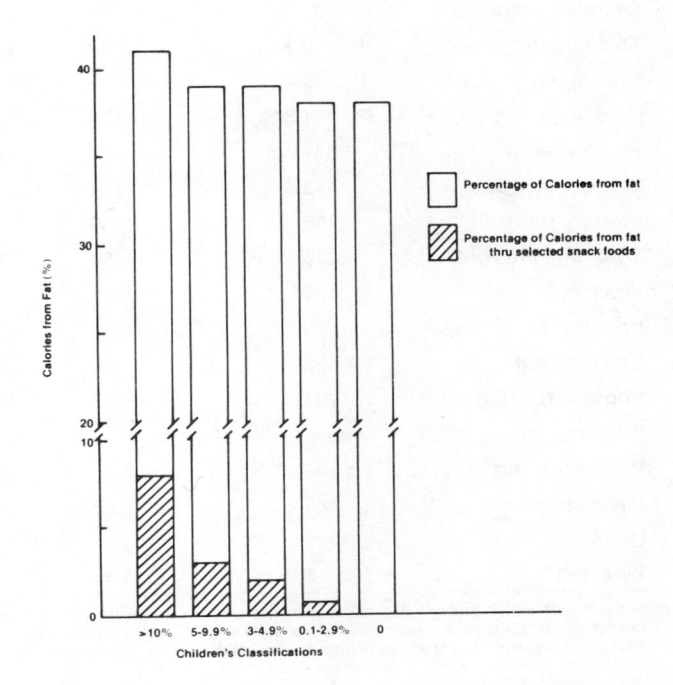

[3]Bacon rinds were consumed by only two children, each of whom consumed 1.3 ounces in one day.

[4]Average sodium consumption reported here does not include added table salt.

[5]Average sodium consumption reported here does not include added table salt

Figure 3 shows similar data for total fat. There was a trend to an increasing proportion of calories derived from dietary fat as the proportion of calories derived from SSFs increased. This increase, however, was not found to be statistically significant. The group deriving more than 10 percent of their calories from SSFs obtained 8 percent of its total calories from fat contained in SSFs. In the other groups of children consuming SSFs, the maximum amount of dietary fat calories derived from these foods was 3 percent. Thus, for the majority of children consuming SSFs, the amount of fat and of sodium obtained from these foods did not appear to be excessive.

As shown in Table 1, statistical analyses of the data showed some significant differences among intake levels for the other 20 nutrients examined. For the majority of these dietary components (calories, total carbohydrates, total sugar, pyridoxine, fiber, iron, zinc, copper, folacin, riboflavin, calcium, phosphorus, potassium, magnesium, and vitamin B_{12}), however, no conclusions about impact of SSFs consumption can be drawn because: (a) children consuming no SSFs had average intake levels that were not significantly different ($p \leq 0.05$) from those children deriving more than 10 percent of their calories from SSFs consumption, and (b) children consuming no SSFs had significantly lower ($p \leq 0.05$) average nutrient intake than children deriving from 0.1 to 2.9 percent of their calories from SSFs consumption. There was a suggested trend toward a lower intake of protein, vitamin A, and thiamin for children consuming the greater quantities of SSFs. In no case, however, were the average intake levels of these three nutrients below recommended dietary allowances (7).

These data demonstrate that the consumption of varying proportions of energy from SSFs has little impact on the average daily nutrient intake of children five to 12 years old. In general, the intake of all nutrients[6] was adequate with the possible exceptions of magnesium and zinc, which were marginal. It should be noted, however, that the proportion of calories derived from SSFs did not have an impact of the intake of these two nutrients. Thus, the generally held notion that consumption of SSFs has a detrimental effect on the nutrient intake of children simply is not borne out by the results of this study. Data, in fact, show that children consuming SSFs had an average nutrient intake comparable to that of children not consuming these foods.

Daily Nutrient Intake of Children Obtaining 36, 20, or 0 Percent of Calories from SSFs. In an attempt to examine the

Table 2. Average Daily Nutrient Intake of Selected Children Classified According to the Percentage of Caloric Intake from the Consumption of Selected Salted Snack Foods.

	\multicolumn{9}{c	}{Percentage of Calories from Selected Salted Snack Foods}
	36 (n=1)			36<20 (n=4)			0 (n=111)		
Nutrient	Ave.	Std. Dev.	Ave. %RDA	Ave.	Std. Dev.	Ave. %RDA	Ave.	Std. Dev.	Ave. %RDA
Calories	2224	—	88	2098	292	78	2051	560	92
Total Protein, g	57	—	125	61	18	130	76	21	211
Total Fat, g	110	—		106	16		87	24	
Total Carbohydrate, g	259	—		234	25		248	80	
Total Sugar, g	109	—		89	17		130	54	
Cholesterol, mg	298	—		287	36		325	123	
Crude Fiber, g	3.1	—		3.1	1.0		2.7	1.1	
Ascorbic Acid, mg	31	—	70	56	23	132	99	65	241
Thiamin, mg	0.93	—	90	0.98	0.15	102	1.27	0.40	116
Niacin, mg	15.4	—	125	16.6	4.6	128	16.8	5.1	114
Riboflavin, mg	1.32	—	115	1.17	0.22	102	2.01	0.57	150
Pyridoxine, μ	871	—	54	950	277	73	1266	432	108
Vitamin B_{12}[1], μ	3.4	—	114	3.4	1.7	146	4.33	2.39	218
Folacin, μ	156	—	39	171	28	56	203	77	72
Total Vitamin A, IU	2015	—	50	3672	2168	105	5792	3091	176
Vitamin D, IU[2]	123	—	31	105	31	26	198	96	49
Iron, mg	10.1	—	56	10.8	2.6	80	12.5	4.0	111
Calcium, mg	653	—	82	547	115	68	1055	324	122
Phosphorus, mg	987	—	123	933	183	117	1349	366	156
Sodium, mg[3]	3547	—		3250	603		2636	764	
Potassium, mg	2181	—		2294	523		2580	825	
Magnesium, mg	188	—	63	197	30	76	239	72	96
Copper, μ	1103	—		1143	226		1354	464	
Zinc, mg	8.0	—	53	13.1	8.1	104	10.2	3.7	93

[1]Folacin data are underestimated because analytical data are insufficient (Perloff and Butrum, 1977).
[2]Vitamin D data inaccurate as fortification of skim and 2% milk not indicated (USDA, 1974); also it is synthesized from the sun.
[3]Sodium consumption is underestimated because added table salt not included in calculations.

effect of high intakes of SSFs more closely, the nutrient intake of a child who had the highest consumption of SSFs (36 percent of caloric intake), as well as those consuming 20 percent or more of their calories from SSFs (n=4), were compared to the average nutrient intake of children who consumed no SSFs. As shown in Table 2, caloric intakes were not excessive for any of the three groups. The consumption of fat was greater for the higher consumers of SSFs as contrasted to those consuming none of these foods, whereas the cholesterol intake was lower for those children consuming SSFs. Protein, niacin, riboflavin, phosphorus, and vitamin B_{12} intake levels were adequate for all three classifications of children.

Sodium[7] intakes were higher for children consuming the greater quantities of SSFs; however, total sugar intakes were lower for these children than for those consuming no SSFs. The intake of all vitamins except niacin, riboflavin, and vitamin B_{12} and of all minerals except phosphorus fell below the standard for the one child deriving 36 percent of calories from SSFs. The average intakes of pyridoxine, iron, calcium, and magnesium were inadequate for the four children consuming 20 percent or more of their calories from SSFs. Children consuming none of the SSFs had marginal intakes of magnesium and zinc.

These data demonstrate that excessive intakes of SSFs can compromise the nutritional quality of the diet. These very high intakes, however, were consumed by only a very small proportion of the children, i.e., less than 1 percent of the total sample. As shown previously, children consuming more reasonable quantities of these foods had adequate nutrient intakes. These data indicate what already is well known—any food, including snack foods, can be abused.

CONCLUSION

In general, these data fail to support the widely held beliefs that a large proportion of children in the United States consume inordinate amounts of salted snack foods. In fact, a significant proportion of children in the United States consumed none of these foods and most of the children who consumed these foods did so in moderation.

The nutrients and energy needed by individuals should be provided by a balance of a wide variety of foods. Specific foods, such as snack foods, can be incorporated into a diet without compromising the nutritional quality of the diet. These snack foods should be consumed in moderation and eaten in addition to numerous other foods. Educational programs are needed to inform children how to incorporate these foods into their diets appropriately, thereby deriving the advantages of convenience and sensory qualities that these foods can contribute without compromising the nutrient quality of their diets. Such a program could be included in the nutrition education programs now provided in many elementary schools. Research is needed to examine how important nutrition information, such as moderate usage of many well-liked foods, can be taught to children effectively.

---

[6]The lack of adequate food composition analyses for folacin (11) is believed to distort data for the nutrient. The absence of standardized fortification of skim and low-fat milk across the United States (12) necessitated that even when such items were consumed by children, they did not contribute to their nutrient profile of vitamin D consumption. Further, vitamin D is synthesized in the presence of sunlight.

[7]Average sodium consumption reported here does not include added table salt.

[8]The 1974 RDA was used because analyses were complete before 1980 RDA was available. Because level of intake and unit measures is given in tables, this information was deemed adequate.

References

(1) Parrish, J.B. 1971. Implications of changing food habits for nutrition educators. *J. Nutr. Educ.* 2:140.

(2) U.S. Department of Agriculture. Spring, 1980. *Potato facts report.* National Economic Division; Economics, Statistics, and Cooperative Services, USDA. Washington, D.C.

(3) Leveille, G.A. 1980. Eating on the run—fast foods and snack foods in our diet. *Practical Gastroenterology* (in press).

(4) Cala, R.F.; Zabik, M.E.; and Morgan, K.J. 1980. Snacking and its nutrient contribution to the diet of school-age children. *School Food Service Res. Rev.* 4(2):113.

(5) Madden, J.P.; Goodman, S.J.; and Guthrie, H.A. 1976. Validity of the 24-hour recall. *J. Am. Dietet. Assoc.* 68:143.

(6) Morgan, K.J.; Zabik, M.E.; Cala, R.F.; and Leveille, G.A. 1980. Nutrient intake patterns of children ages 5 to 12 years based on seven-day food diaries. Res. Report No. 406. Michigan State Univ. Agric. Exp. Stat., East Lansing.

(7) Natl. Res. Council. 1974. Recommended dietary allowances. Eighth rev. ed. Washington, D.C.: Natl. Academy of Sciences.[8]

(8) Barr, A.J.; Goodnight, J.H.; Sall, J.S.; and Helwig, J.T. 1976. *A user's guide to SAS 76.* Raleigh, N.C.: Sparks Press.

(9) Duncan, D.B. 1957. Multiple range test for correlated and heteroscidastic means. *Biometrics.* 13:164.

(10) Snedecor, G.W., and Cochran, W.G. 1972. *Statistical methods,* 6th ed. Ames, Iowa: The Iowa State University Press.

(11) Perloff, B.P., and Butrum, R.R. 1977. Folacin in selected foods. *J. Am. Dietet. Assoc.* 70:161.

(12) U.S. Department of Agriculture. 1974. *Federal and state standards for the composition of milk products.* Agric. Handbook, No. 51. Washington, D.C.

Dietary Practices in Adolescence

by *Nutrition & the M.D.*

The busy schedules of teenagers combined with their newly-acquired feelings of independence result in more time and meals away from home and more decision-making about food choices. Often this results in irregular eating patterns.

Food choices are likely to be made on the basis of peer pressure, sociability, status, and enjoyment, rather than on the basis of nutrient content or health reasons. Teenagers may adopt extreme diets as a means of expressing their independence. Furthermore, adolescents often do not relate the effects of suboptimal dietary practices with future health.

Eating Patterns

The most striking changes in teenage eating habits are meal skipping, between-meal-snacking, and more frequent meals away from home.

Breakfast and lunch appear to be the most frequently missed meals. School activities, social events, and part-time jobs may cause a teenager to eat little or nothing during the day and then 'catch up' in the evening.

Snacking is a characteristic adolescent food habit. Surveys have confirmed that teenagers tend to eat more often, up to six times a day. Frequent intake of snacks of limited nutritional value may contribute to dietary deficiencies. However, snacking can also add greatly to total nutrient intake.

Since adolescents tend to eat whatever is most readily available, parents can help by keeping nutritious, easy-to-prepare snacks on hand—such as fruit, juices, milk, cheese and crackers, yogurt, and nuts. 'Empty-calorie' foods don't need to be eliminated from the diet, provided high quality foods that meet nutrient needs are consumed concurrently.

Eating meals and snacks at franchised fast food outlets is especially popular with busy adolescents. Such foods tend to be high in calories, fat, protein, sugar and sodium, and low in fiber. Carbonated drinks often replace milk, resulting in lower intakes of calcium, riboflavin, and vitamins A and D; the few fruits and vegetables eaten provide insufficient fiber.

Unusual Eating Patterns

For various social, health, and religious reasons, an increasing number of young people are becoming vegetarians. Lacto-ovo-vegetarians include eggs and dairy products in their diets and generally have adequate nutrient intakes. However, strict vegans, who eat no animal protein, are at particular risk of developing protein, vitamin B_{12}, calcium, iron, and possibly zinc deficiency. A strict vegetarian diet can be adequate only if it is carefully planned. Professional advice may be needed.

JUNK FOODS—A SCIENTIFIC EVALUATION

Helen A. Guthrie, PhD, RD • Head, Nutrition Program • Professor of Nutrition • College of Human Development • Pennsylvania State University • University Park.

Although the term 'junk food' defies definition, it is used frequently by professionals and consumers alike. Health professionals should assess all possible meanings and avoid indiscriminate use of this expression.

According to Webster, junk is defined as 'meaningless' and 'of no worth.' The widely accepted roles of food are primarily as sources of carbohydrates, fats, and proteins, which serve as sources of energy, and secondarily as sources of minerals, vitamins, and amino acids, which support growth and maintenance of tissue. If we accept that, we must concede that there is no food that is totally worthless under all circumstances.

If one superimposes the concept that food also fulfills social and psychologic needs, then it is even more difficult to agree that any food is worthless. How can health professionals deal with the widely-held notion that some foods are worthless, junk?

'Junk Diets'

The concept that there are junk diets is much more viable. Any food or any diet, no matter how poorly constructed, has *some* nutritional merit, even if only to provide calories. We must, however, encourage consumption of nutritious diets that provide energy and nutrients in the amounts and proportions close to those suggested in the Recommended Dietary Allowances.

Additionally, diets should not provide an excessive amount of any single nutrient nor any one food, as this will usually result in a lack of nutrients that would normally be provided by a more varied diet. It may lead to consumption of too much of some dietary components which, in excess, may have

---

From *Nutrition & the M.D.*, Vol. 7, No. 2, pp. 1-5. Copyright 1981, PM, Inc. Reprinted with permission.

undesirable sequelae—saturated fat, cholesterol, salt.

Diets that fall slightly short of the RDA may be completely adequate for those people who, for a variety of genetic, environmental, and physiologic reasons, do not need as high a level as recommended in the RDAs. Diets that fall far short of these standards, while not necessarily 'junk', must be considered of 'limited nutritional value'.

INQ and NCBR

What is a food of 'limited nutritional value'? In general they are foods that by themselves do not make a significant contribution of nutrients in relation to calories, or foods that do not provide the nutrients needed to supplement the rest of the diet. Thus, while certain foods may provide large amounts of some nutrients, they must be balanced by other foods that help to satisfy nutritional needs. In that context, a given food may be virtually worthless.

The contribution of a food to the nutrient needs in relation to caloric needs is most easily expressed as an INQ (Index of Nutrient Quality) or an NCBR (Nutrient Calorie Benefit Ratio). Both of these are represented by the formula:

$$\frac{\% \text{ of requirement of nutrient}}{\% \text{ of requirement of energy}}$$

for any unit of that food—a cup, a pound, or a serving.

The INQ or NCBR for a particular food varies, depending on the nutrient and the caloric needs of any particular individual. It is customary to use the US RDA for the nutrient in calculating the numerator of the INQ formula, and 2,000 kcal in calculating the denominator.

A food with an INQ of 1 or more for a nutrient is 'carrying its weight' for that nutrient. If it has an INQ of 1 or more for four nutrients or an INQ of 2 or more for two nutrients, it may be considered 'nutritious'. Examples of INQ profiles for six foods are given in the table.

No matter what its nutrient profile, a food is nutritious in the context of a diet only if it provides some needed nutrients. Thus if a diet has adequate calcium but lacks vitamin C, then milk (which is devoid of vitamin C) is not a nutritious food in that diet, but oranges are considered nutritious. Conversely, milk is nutritious in a diet needing calcium but is not nutritious in a diet needing vitamin C or iron.

Important Vs. Limited Usefulness

It is obvious that a food that makes an important contribution to one diet may be of limited usefulness in another—but it is still not 'junk', unless its use raises the caloric intake above that needed to meet energy expenditure.

By the same token, if a diet provides recommended levels of all nutrients except calories, then a food that provides only calories is meeting a need and in that context is not 'junk', even though it would be considered worthless in a diet low in other nutrients.

A food that is eaten in amounts that exceed the energy needs leading to 'fat' gain, or one that contributes excessive sodium for a hypertension-prone individual, or one that provides a between-meal snack of sticky carbohydrate which contributes to tooth decay, must be considered to make negative nutritional contribution for that individual on that day. The same foods in relation to another diet may make a much more positive contribution or at least have a less negative impact.

Correcting Misbeliefs

Any clinician who allows his/her patients to persist in using the term 'junk' to describe foods such as pizza, ice cream, hamburgers, french fries, and granola—all of which have significant nutrient content—is helping to perpetuate a growing distrust of our food supply. Such beliefs must be corrected.

In summary, individual foods are neither nutritious nor of limited nutritional value when considered by themselves. They must be considered in relation to the total diet. We may indeed have 'junk diets' if we allow certain foods of low nutritional value to constitute a large part of that diet. These must then be considered nutritionally limited—and conceivably 'junk', especially if they also have negative qualities for individuals with predisposition to certain risk factors.

Suggested Reading

Guthrie HA: "Junk Foods"—a scientific evaluation. *Prof Nutritionist* 12:12, 1980.

Hansen GR: An index of food quality. *Nutr Rev* 31:1, 1973.

THE ADOLESCENT ATHLETE

Increased physical activity, such as that associated with participation in sports activities, accentuates the increased energy requirements of adolescents. The best training diet for the adolescent athlete is one that contains foods from each of the four major food groups in quantities sufficient to meet energy demands and nutrient requirements.

There is no evidence that consumption of large amounts of specific foods or nutrients has specific benefits on athletic performance. In particular, protein supplements are not necessary for the adolescent athlete, and may even be detrimental. While some additional protein may be needed for lean tissue synthesis during training, these needs can be easily met by a diet providing 1 gm of protein per kg body weight.

Sodium and potassium may become depleted during exercise. Replacement can usually be met by eating a balanced diet. Salt tablets and special electrolyte-rich beverages are unnecessary.

Sweat losses must be replaced by frequent intake of small amounts of fluid during the exercise period. The myth that water intake harms athletic performance has led some coaches to restrict water during periods of prolonged exercise. This dangerous practice can lead to heat stroke and death. Thirst is the best guide to water intake.

Water and food restriction and induced sweat losses are dangerous and undesirable ways to make a lower weight classification (as in boxing or wrestling). Lean body tissue loss, electrolyte imbalances, and dehydration may actually decrease athletic performance. In some states, the specific gravity of athletes' urine is measured prior to an athletic event; if very high, the officials may disqualify the athlete because of presumed dehydration.

Nutrient profiles of representative foods

	Cheddar Cheese	Broccoli	Eggs	Bananas	Enriched White Bread	Brownies
Protein	2.2	3.8	2.7	0.4	1.1	0.4
Vitamin A	1.5	46.0	3.4	1.1	—	0.1
Vitamin C	—	84.3	—	4.6	—	—
Thiamin	0.1	3.5	1.0	0.9	1.4	0.5
Riboflavin	1.5	6.2	2.5	1.0	1.0	0.3
Niacin	—	2.3	—	0.9	1.1	0.1
Calcium	4.3	4.8	0.8	0.2	0.7	0.2
Iron	0.3	3.5	1.7	1.0	1.2	0.6

NUTRITION NEEDS DURING ADOLESCENCE

About 15% of an adult's height and as much as 48% of the skeletal mass is accrued during and immediately after the adolescent growth spurt. Both males and females gain appreciable weight. However, the rate, amount, and composition of this weight gain differs between the two sexes.

Males experience an increase in the percentage of muscle mass with concomitant decrease in total body fat, while females gain both muscle and adipose tissue. By age 20, women have about twice as much adipose tissue as men but only about two-thirds as much lean tissue. However, male energy requirements increase even in proportion to other nutrient requirements, because of the high activity level of most healthy adolescent boys. Average intakes of protein usually exceed the RDA, supplying a constant 12-16% of the energy intake through childhood and adolescence.

The RDA (see table) for protein and all non-calorie nutrients include a 'fudge factor', so that the needs of virtually all normal adolescents are met. However, the energy recommendations for adolescents do *not* include this safety factor, but instead are considered to approximate average needs.

Recommended Dietary Allowances for adolescents

	Males		Females	
Age (yrs):	11-14	15-18	11-14	15-18
Weight, kg	45	66	46	55
Energy, kcal	2700	2800	2200	2100
Protein, gm	45	56	46	46
Vitamin A, mcg (R.E.)*	1000	1000	800	800
Vitamin D, mcg	10	10	10	10
Vitamin E, mg (a-T.E.)**	8	10	8	8
Vitamin C, mg	50	60	50	60
Thiamin, mg	1.4	1.4	1.1	1.1
Riboflavin, mg	1.6	1.7	1.3	1.3
Niacin, mg	18	18	15	14
Vitamin B_6, mg	1.8	2	1.8	2
Folacin, mcg	400	400	400	400
Vitamin B_{12}, mcg	3	3	3	3
Calcium, mg	1200	1200	1200	1200
Phosphorus, mg	1200	1200	1200	1200
Magnesium, mg	350	400	300	300
Iron, mg	18	18	18	18
Zinc, mg	15	15	15	15
Iodine, mcg	150	150	150	150

* = Retinol equivalents
** = Alpha-tocopherol equivalents

Minerals most likely to be in inadequate supply in the adolescent's diet are calcium, iron, and zinc *(Ped Clin NA 27:125, 1980)*. Compared to the preadolescent period, the need for these three minerals increases substantially during the growth spurt: calcium, for the increase in skeletal mass; iron, for the expansion of muscle mass and blood volume; and zinc, for the generation of both skeletal and soft tissues.

The recommendation for calcium—1,200 mg per day for both boys and girls—is designed to meet the needs of the fastest growing adolescents.

Boys require more iron per kg weight gain than girls, but adolescent girls have additional iron losses from menstruation. The recommended daily intake for both sexes is 18 mg.

Zinc is essential for growth as well as for sexual maturation. To provide for these needs, a daily intake of 15 mg of zinc is recommended. This is easily obtained from the average American adolescent diet.

Because of greater energy demands during adolescence, more thiamin, riboflavin, and niacin are necessary for the metabolism of carbohydrates. The increased rate of tissue synthesis during the adolescent growth spurt also increases the demands for folacin and vitamin B_{12}, which are required specifically for normal DNA and RNA synthesis.

The requirements for vitamins A, C, and E are similarly increased, compared to the preadolescent period. These vitamins participate in the preservation of the structural and functions properties of the new cells attained during growth.

Body size and rates of growth differ from one adolescent to another. The RDA provides only estimates for the entire population. When the growth spurt fails to progress normally in an individual, dietary intake should be reviewed as a possible contributor to the altered growth pattern.

NUTRITION AND COMMON ADOLESCENT DISEASES

Anemia • Most of the iron-deficiency anemia in childhood occurs during two periods of most rapid growth—infancy and adolescence. Muscle mass and blood volume increase greatly at these ages. In adolescence, the red cell mass increases, both with increasing blood volume and increasing hematocrit. If the growth spurt is rapid, available iron may be insufficient to prevent anemia.

Adolescent girls are affected more often than boys, due to poor iron intake and menstrual blood losses. Iron-deficiency anemia may be suspected in an adolescent by a dietary history reflecting inadequate iron intake, by the presence of pallor, or by low hemoglobin or hematocrit levels.

Inflammatory bowel diseases • In teenagers, these produce recurrent or chronic problems and interfere with the life style of this age group. Ulcerative colitis involves the rectum and the colon, while Crohn's disease usually occurs in the ileum with occasional involvement of the jejunum and colon. Initial manifestations include malabsorption and weight loss, weakness, anemia due to bloody diarrhea, abdominal pain, or growth failure.

Inflammatory intestinal diseases can be associated with malnutrition or anemia secondary to anorexia, blood loss, or malabsorption. Parenteral nutrition may be required in the acute phase of inflammatory bowel disease. Supplementation with iron, folate, and vitamin B_{12} also may be necessary. Restriction of dairy products and dietary fiber may also prove helpful.

Obesity • Obese adolescents often try to minimize the deleterious role their excess weight plays in their lives. When the body becomes sufficiently unattractive and unwieldy to impose social restriction, psychologic damage may ensue. However, once established, moderate to severe obesity in the adolescent is often resistant to medical or psychologic therapy.

Whether or not the adolescent is actually obese depends on the proportion of the body weight that is fat. This distinction is important because increased muscle mass and skeletal size are not indications for weight loss.

An obese adolescent tends to eat more when food is readily accessible. They often initiate eating as a result of such external cues as time of day, they combine eating with other behavior such as talking on the telephone or doing homework, and they seek or accept food just before and just following a meal. They also tend to eat less early in the morning and to eat more later in the day. The foods preferred by obese adolescents tend to have little variety and are high in caloric density. Obese adolescents usually are less physically active than their normal-weight counterparts.

The recommended management for obese adolescents is counseling and a well-balanced diet taken in frequent small portions and eliminating most fats and desserts. This should allow the adolescent to grow normally without excess accumulation of body fat. Unfortunately, this therapy is usually ineffective unless the patient is highly motivated.

Dental caries • The incidence of tooth and gum disease among adolescents in recent decades has directly paralleled their consumption of sugary baked goods and confections between meals. Adolescents who snack frequently on such cariogenic foods have a greater risk of dental problems than those who eat similar quantities of such food only once during the day. While snacks can and do contribute substantially to the nutrient quality of adolescent diets and should not be eliminated, they must be carefully selected.

Adolescents may need to be reminded about the importance of brushing their teeth after meals and before bedtime, and flossing should be introduced as a valuable adjunct to brushing. Body-conscious adolescents may be motivated to improve their dental health practices by discussing with them the effects of poor dental hygiene on their appearance.

The Underweight Adolescent

by Harold Meyer, M.D.

A brief review of the causes of underweight in adolescence is presented to help the practitioner determine the cause of underweight in his patient. Poor nutrition is determined by several key observations: (1) history; (2) physical examination; (3) anthropometric measurements—height, weight, triceps skinfold thickness (TSF), mid-arm circumference (MAC), and mid-arm muscle circumference (MAMC). Causes of the underweight state may be divided into three categories: disease states; environmental conditions; and factors peculiar to the adolescent.

Very little can be found in the literature about the underweight adolescent. It is possible to find "underweight" discussed under various disease headings, as part of the symptomatology, but nowhere is it discussed as a problem itself. The literature is filled, of course, with articles on obesity, the concept being that fat is bad, and thin is good.

It is my intention to outline an approach for the evaluation of the underweight patient. No attempt is made to list and discuss all possible etiologies, but rather to give the practitioner a method that may make arriving at a solution to the problem somewhat easier.

Determination of Poor Nutrition

In office practice, the determination of poor nutrition is made by the use of several key observations: (1) history of the type and quantity of food ingested; (2) physical signs of chronic disease and/or signs of nutritional deficiency; and (3) anthropometric measurements—height, weight, triceps skin-fold thickness (TSF), mid-arm circumference (MAC), and mid-arm muscle circumference (MAMC).[1-3] The value of these anthropometric measurements may be greater than expensive laboratory tests. Because adolescents enter puberty at varying chronologic ages, weights for stature charts are not available for this group.

The most convenient way to assess the amount of body fat, the principal energy source of the body, is by anthropometric measurement. Parizkova[4] has demonstrated that skin-fold thickness alone relates very closely to determinations of body fat. However, because the size of the muscle mass is an indirect indicator of protein reserve, it is recommended that MAC and MAMC measurements also be made. The method for determining these measurements is as follows:

For TSF thickness,[5] the Lange caliper is used. (This is the one most commonly used in the United States. The Harpenden caliper made in England is also available.) A mark is made halfway between the tip of the olecranon and acromial process. The posterior plane is marked vertically across the arm midpoint mark. The arm should be hanging relaxed at the side at the time of measurement. The examiner's left forefinger and thumb then pick up the skin and subcutaneous tissue just proximal to the mark made on the arm. The tissue is pulled away from the bulk of the underlying triceps muscle and is held firmly between the fingers while the measurements are being made. The calipers are applied to the fold just below the fingers, being sure the pressure on the fold is being made by the calipers and not the fingers. The reading is made 3 seconds after applying the caliper. For accuracy the reading should be made twice.

To measure mid-arm circumference, a tape is passed around the arm at the mark previously made with the arm hanging relaxed at the side. From the TSF and MAC measurements the MAMC can then be calculated, using the following formula:

$$\text{MAMC (CM)} = \text{MAC (CM)} - [3.14 \times \text{TSF (CM)}]$$

The values obtained are compared with standards.[3,5-7] For adolescents, adult standards are used. The percentage deviation from the standard values is determined. Patients with values within 60 to 90 per cent of the standard are considered to be moderately malnourished, and those with values less than 60 per cent of the standard are considered severely malnourished.

The causes of the underweight state may be divided into three categories (Table 1): (1) disease states; (2) environmental conditions; and (3) factors peculiar to the adolescent.

Discussion

For the purposes of this paper, the more frequently involved *Disease States* are merely listed in Table 1, since underweight is a secondary symptom of each of these disease complexes. Discussion of each of the disease states may be found in any standard pediatric text. They must, of course, be considered seriously in any underweight individual.

TABLE 1. Causes of Underweight in Adolescents

I. Disease States
   Gastrointestinal
      Crohn's disease
      Ulcerative colitis
      Irritable bowel syndrome
      Malabsorptive states
   Endocrine
      Juvenile diabetes mellitus
      Hyperthyroidism
   Malignancy
      Leukemia
      Hodgkin's disease
      Late stages of all others
   Genetic
      Cystic fibrosis
      Hemoglobinopathies
   Chronic Infection
      Urinary tract infection
      Bacterial infection
      Kartagener's syndrome
   Collagen
      Juvenile rheumatoid arthritis
      Systemic lupus erythematosus
   Other Chronic Disease
      Pulmonary disease
      Renal disease
      Cardiac disease
II. Environmental Conditions
   Emotional stress
   Nutrition, socioeconomic status, race
   Constitutional
   Exposure to toxic agents
III. Problems peculiar to the adolescent
   Body perception
   Drugs
   Food fads
   Sports programs
   Anorexia nervosa

Environmental Conditions

As the child enters adolescence, he becomes subject to the *emotional stresses* implicit in the process. The usual stresses of adolescence may be worsened by conflicts within the house, at school or among the adolescent's peers. Depression, conversion reactions, and chronic anxiety are not uncommon to this age group, and may be important contributing factors to an underweight state. Therefore, it is necessary to establish early in the interview process of the adolescent and his family the emotional-physical interaction that may contribute to ill health.

The ten-state nutritional survey of 1968-1970[8] provides important data relating to thinness in adolescents as it relates to *socioeconomic groups and race*. Those of the lower socioeconomic group were leaner than those of the upper socioeconomic group. In comparing black and white adolescents (male and female), blacks were leaner than whites in all socioeconomic groups.

Familial *constitutional* factors may cause a predilection for the adolescent to be underweight. Lean mothers and father (at or below the 15th percentile for skin-fold thickness) give rise to lean children. Children of lean parents usually do not gain an appreciable amount of fat during adolescence. As one might expect, obese parents are more likely to have obese children. It would appear that the apparent attraction of a thin man to a thin woman and vice-versa gives rise to husband/wife similarity (thin wife-thin husband; obese wife-obese husband). This may be an expression of common attitudes toward food, eating and exercise. The fact that their children are thin or obese is, therefore, most probably due to what psychosomaticists term "pseudo-heredity."

Marston et al.[9] demonstrated eating behaviors in obese and non-obese subjects, and their observations revealed that thin subjects take fewer bites and smaller mouthfuls of food within a given period of time. Thin subjects hesitate more often and for longer periods between bites. They also tend to toy with food and the utensils between bites.

During vocational training,[10] adolescents may be exposed to *toxic materials*. Toxicity may not be detected until symptoms and physical findings are present. Weight loss because of illness due to the toxic substances may be a presenting symptom.

Problems Peculiar to the Adolescent

One of the major areas of adjustment concerning physical growth and bodily changes in the adolescent is the development of *an image of one's physical self*. It is, therefore, important to know how adolescents see themselves. In the National Health Survey,[11] 96 per cent of the youths described themselves as being in good to excellent health. Only 13 per cent considered themselves underweight.

As a reflection of the male "macho" and female "Twiggy" syndrome seen in this country, boys were twice as likely as girls to consider themselves underweight, and girls twice as likely as boys to consider themselves overweight.

At 17 years of age, one-half of all girls would like to be thinner than they are, while only 18 per cent of the boys would like to be thinner. This fact probably explains the difficulty one has in attempting to get underweight girls to gain weight. Most girls who consider themselves thin prefer to remain so or to be even thinner; most thin boys would prefer to be heavier.

When adolescents were asked about various conditions for which they would definitely see a doctor, only 19 per cent indicated that "loss of appetite" would be cause for them to seek medical attention. Perhaps this is an indication of lack of concern with weight loss, among girls particularly.

The *drug subculture* is probably the greatest source of chemical contact by the teenager, and any effect on growth and development can be assumed to be due to the chemical used.[12] Examples of effects of drugs on the teenage user are: amphetamines lead to loss of appetite, with resultant weight loss; angiitis occurs after prolonged use and will give rise to chronic illness and weight loss. Peptic ulcer, probably histamine-induced, frequently develops in heroin addicts. They may also develop pulmonary symptoms, hepatitis, and local and systemic infections, which contribute to poor health and weight loss.

Imipramine HCl, used as a therapeutic agent in enuretic adolescents, and methylphenidate HCl, used in management of hyperactivity, may cause wakefulness, loss of appetite and weight loss. Prolonged use may give rise to abnormal loss of weight.

Adolescents are prone to being caught up in *food fads*. There is danger in following unsupervised diets because of the lack of knowledge of what constitutes a nutritious diet program. Some adolescents tend to become underweight by following a trendy fad which does not provide sufficient calories or nutritional balance.

The emphasis on control of serum cholesterol and lipoproteins[13] has led to minimization of saturated fats in the diet.

Is the exclusion of saturated fatty acids by normal individuals correct? More information is needed concerning the long-term effects on the rapidly growing adolescent.

The effect of malnutrition on menarche has been the subject of some debate since Frisch and Revelle[14] proposed that menarche in girls tends to occur at a critical body weight. It has long been noted that obese girls enter puberty earlier than their thin counterparts, and that girls who are markedly underweight may tend to stop menstruating. Glass et al.,[15] experimenting with rats, found that the onset of puberty was a function of growth rate rather than a particular fixed weight. Poorly nourished rats growing at a slow rate had a later onset of puberty than well nourished rats growing at a more rapid rate. However, malnourished rats entered puberty at a greater weight but later age than well nourished rats.

Participation in *sports programs* in high school has increased greatly in the past few years. Long-distance running and wrestling are sports where weight, or rather lack of weight, create the most concern. Carrying less weight is important to the long-distance runner. As physicians to these patients, we should be sure that they do not become malnourished.

Many youngsters on the wrestling team are asked to lose as much as 12 to 15 per cent of their body weight. As has been noted, malnutrition (many of these youngsters so restrict their intake that they are indeed malnourished) prevents proper cell turn-over of actively metabolic organs—bone marrow, liver and gastrointestinal tract. Adolescents have been seen in our clinic who have so injured the gastrointestinal tract as to develop a disaccharidase deficiency and symptoms mimicking granulomatous colitis.

An adolescent in training may be considered to have about 12 per cent of his body weight as fat. As a rule of thumb, they should not be allowed to lose more than one-half of this amount, equivalent to about 6 per cent of their body weight. The physician has the responsibility not to sign a petition form in athletics when the suggested weight reduction exceeds this estimate.

Many observers have noted an increased prevalence of *anorexia nervosa*. Physically there is severe weight loss, 40 per cent on the average, occurring without organic explanation. The problem occurs mostly in females, a ratio of 10:1.

Bruch[16] describes the typical adolescent with this disease as having a preoccupation with food and eating. They consider self-denial and the discipline of not eating the highest virtue. She also describes excessive concern with the body and its size. The patients feel enslaved and exploited and not competent to lead a life of their own. It is against this background that they develop the preoccupation with controlling the body and its demands. These patients are defiant, stubborn and manipulative, and difficult to deal with in therapy.

Many of these patients express a dissatisfaction with self, which is a core issue in anorexia nervosa.

In her book, *The Golden Cage,* Bruch[16] emphasizes the psychic consequences of starvation: hyperacuity, a continuous state of tension which interferes with concentration, irritability, disorganized thinking, and a dissociation from their own physical feelings. Better nutrition is, therefore, a precondition for the patients' understanding of their psychological problems. Effective therapy should correct malnutrition, clarify underlying family issues, and correct self-concept.

Summary

An approach to the problem of the underweight adolescent has been presented that may serve the physician in determining the basis of either weight loss or failure to gain weight.

REFERENCES

1. Hodges, R.E. and Adelman, R.D. Evaluation of nutritional status of patients, Nutrition in Medical Practice. Edited by R.E. Hodges. Philadelphia, WB Saunders, 1980.
2. Zerfas, A.J., Schorr, I.J. and Neumann, C.G., 1977. Office assessment of nutritional status. Pediatr Clin North Am 24:253.
3. Blackburn, G.L., et al., 1977. Nutritional and metabolic assessment of the hospitalized patient. J Parent Enteral Nutr 1:11.
4. Parizkova, J., 1961. Total body fat and skinfold thickness in children. Metabolism 10:794.
5. Tanner, J.M. and Whitehouse, R.H., 1962. Standards for subcutaneous fat in British children. Br Med J 1:446.
6. Frisancho, A.R., 1974. Triceps skin fold and upper arm muscle size norms for assessment of nutritional status. Am J Clin Nutr 27:1052.
7. Gurney, J.M. and Jeliffe, D.B., 1973. Arm antropometry in nutritional assessment: Nomogram for rapid calculation of muscle circumference and cross-sectional muscle and fat areas. Am J Clin Nutr 26:912.
8. DHEW: Ten State Nutritional Survey 1968-1970: DHEW Publ. No. (HMS) 72-8130 to 72-8134, 1972.
9. Marston, A.R., et al., 1977. In vivo observation of the eating behavior of obese and non-obese subjects. J Consult Clin Psychol 45:335.
10. Giguz, T.L., 1968. Effect of low concentrations of ammonia and nitrogen oxides on adolescents undergoing vocational training in the chemical laboratory. Hyg Sanit 33:431.
11. National Health Survey: Series 11, No. 147, DHEW Publ. No. (HRA) 75-1629. Self-reported health behavior and attitudes of youths 12-17 years, United States.
12. Cohen, M.F., 1974. Environmental exposures and biologic considerations of the adolescent in relation to chemical pollutants. Pediatrics 53:845, (part II).
13. Kannel, W.B., Dawber, T.R., 1972. Atherosclerosis as a pediatric problem. J Pediatr 80:544.
14. Frisch, R.E. and Revelle, R., 1970. Height and weight at menarche and a hypothesis of critical body weights and adolescent events. Science 169:397.
15. Glass, A.R., et al., 1976. Effect of undernutrition and amino acid deficiency on the timing of puberty in rats. Pediatr Res 10:951.
16. Bruch, H. The Golden Age. Cambridge, Harvard University Press, 1978.

ADOLESCENCE

Adolescent Pregnancy and Nutrition

by Betty Ruth Carruth, Ph.D.

Changes in the sexual behavior of teenagers in the United States in recent decades involve all segments of the population and the consequences of these behaviors are having an impact on the health care system and the health professional who provides services. Zelnik, et al., reported that one in five females have intercourse by age 16 and one in ten get pregnant before age 17. Over one-third of the females who are sexually active premaritally have a premarital pregnancy before reaching age 19, with one-quarter becoming pregnant by age 17.[1]

For the years 1957 to 1974, the overall fertility rate decreased for females ages 15-17 years; however, the number of adolescent girls almost doubled in that period so the actual number of live births to that age group has changed little.[2] The fertility rates for females less than 15 years have risen. As could be anticipated, 85 percent of the births to girls 15 years and younger were illegitimate as compared to 23 percent of those born to girls age 19. Live births to girls ages 15-17 years increased by more than 20 percent during the years 1966-1975.[3,4]

Sociological Implications

The pregnant teenager has less opportunity to develop self-esteen, gain skills for economic independence, and to separate from the family unit or environment which contributed to behaviors that resulted in a pregnancy.[5] Sugar described a syndrome of failures characteristic of many pregnant adolescents who become more dependent on the family, welfare systems and child-care assistance, and who are frequently abandoned by the putative father or husband.[6]

Health Implications of Adolescent Pregnancy

In terms of health risks, the younger the mother the greater the risk of having a low birth-weight infant with the sequela of possible abnormalities of development, inadequate bonding of mother and child, and potential for child abuse and neglect.[5] In 1979, the Committee on Adolescence of the American Academy of Pediatrics published a "Statement on Teenage Pregnancy."[7] The main complications of teenage pregnancy were considered to be pre-eclampsia and low birth-weight infants. The time interval between onset of menses and conception was a risk factor because conception two years or less after onset of menses was associated with a higher incidence of low birth-weight infants, irrespective of social class. The etiology of pre-eclampsia is unknown and develops as the onset of hypertension, albuminuria or edema between the 20th week of pregnancy and the first week postpartum.

Other factors, smoking, alcohol and drug use, socio-economic status and nutrition, influenced the pregnancy outcome in all age groups. In addition, early and adequate prenatal care, as well as an absence of pre-existing chronic health problems, enhanced pregnancy outcome. Generally, teenagers seek prenatal care later and have fewer total visits than older women of childbearing age. Therefore, the biological maturity, the amount and frequency of prenatal care, as well as the overall life-style of adolescents, place them at a greater risk than women in the 20-24 age group.

Nutrient Needs During Pregnancy

Both pregnancy and adolescence are periods of increased requirements for energy and for some 40 essential micro- and macronutrients. The most rapid rate of skeletal and muscle growth for adolescents is prior to menarche. Following menarche, the rate of tissue synthesis rapidly declines, reaching adult levels within two to three years.[8] Thus, if a teenager has good nutritional practices prior to pregnancy, the health risks are reduced for both her and the infant.[9]

Recommended Dietary Allowances (RDAs)

The RDAs represent a norm for estimating nutrient allowances of groups. They are often applied improperly to food intake records of individuals. They also are based on chronological age rather than maturity. A review of the 9th edition reveals the limited scientific data upon which allowances for nonpregnant and pregnant adolescents are based.[10] Epidemiological surveys describe practice but do not establish nutrient requirements. Thus, in most part, the RDAs are extrapolations from infant data and/or adult values. Energy and nutrient allowances for pregnancy are additive to those for the nonpregnant female.

In estimating nutrient needs, there is evidence that protective and unexplained mechanisms are involved in regulating both energy stores and plasma levels of most nutrients during pregnancy. According to Hytten,[11] the mechanisms are unknown and are not explained on the basis of dietary deficiencies or malabsorption, e.g., the fetus may be protected from vagaries associated with maternal diet except in extreme malnutrition. However, if a diet inadequate in calories and other nutrients is supplemented, the result is bigger infants and thus reduction of the incidence of low birth-weight infants.

Prepregnancy Weight and Gain During Pregnancy

Low maternal weight gain during pregnancy correlates with a higher incidence of low birth-weight infants and higher mortality rates among neonates born to teenagers.[12] In a study of the relationship between weight gain and perinatal mortality, the optimal weight gain for an overweight mother was about half that for a very thin mother.[13] A total weight gain of 24 pounds is essential to adequate fetal development[9] with a recommended weight gain of about 20 pounds occurring in the last half of pregnancy.[12]

Adolescents may diet in order to minimize the obligatory gain associated with the increasing maternal and fetal weight gain of pregnancy. Restrictive calorie intakes may result in ketonemia with subsequent ketosis, a condition ill-tolerated by the fetus and which may result in impaired neurological development.[12] Emphasis should be placed on the value of a good diet during pregnancy and the modification of food choices to contribute to better health postnatally.

For the pregnant teenager who is physically immature or is underweight, the rate and total amount of weight gain is greater than for the more mature female and energy costs are additive to those of pregnancy. In a controlled study, Blackburn and Calloway compared energy intake and expenditure of pregnant and nonpregnant girls. They estimated expenditures of sedentary pregnant adolescents as about 2300 Kcal/day.[14]

In a review of reported energy intakes of pregnant women in the United States, Australia and the Soviet Union, it was found that (1) energy intake was frequently less than recommended, and (2) energy intake tended to remain constant throughout gestation.[15]

Comparing these findings to data from the Health and Nutrition Examination Survey (HANES) for United States teenagers shows similar results.[16] Females ages 12-14 consumed about 1,900 Kcal/day and ages 15-17 consumed about 1,750 Kcal/day. An addition of 300 Kcal/day for pregnancy to the usual energy intake of 1,750 results in 2,050 Kcal/day. This is far below the recommended energy allowances of 2,700 Kcal/day for pregnant girls ages 11-14 and 2,400 Kcal/day for ages 15-18.[9] If energy intakes tend to remain constant throughout pregnancy, a low initial intake provides inadequate calories for fetal and maternal needs. Early evaluation of prepregnancy weight and calorie balance are essential factors of a nutritional assessment.

Dietary Deficiencies

The most frequently reported deficiencies are calcium, iron and vitamin A,[17] as well as folacin, riboflavin (B_2) and pyridoxine (B_6) in some groups. Most of the calcium consumed during pregnancy is accumulated in the fetus. During pregnancy, iron, vitamin A and folacin are essential for hematopoiesis. In addition, tissue synthesis requires energy and vitamins B_2 and B_6.

Recent surveys indicate that girls ages 12-14 years consume on the average about 75 percent of RDAs for calcium and older teens ages 15-17 about 66 percent. A daily intake of 1200-1600 mg/day of calcium is recommended.[9]

Iron and folacin supplementations have changed very little in the past decade. The increased requirements for iron during pregnancy cannot be met by the iron content of diets eaten by most teenagers. Thus, 30-60 mg/day of elemental iron and 300-500 mg/day of folacin are usually prescribed.

Inadequate dietary protein is uncommon unless the diet is also inadequate in calories and other nutrients. Many of the fast foods consumed by adolescents are relatively high in protein. An analysis of four fast-food meals for protein, vitamins A and C and iron indicated the following: 16-43 g of protein, 21-725 I.U. vitamin A, 12-29 mg vitamin C, and 3-7 mg iron.[18] A fast-food meal could provide over one-half of the protein allowance. Allowances for pregnancy should equal the nonpregnant allowances plus 30 g/day, which is about 75 g/protein/day.

Vegetarianism

Teenage vegetarians may be at a risk for deficiencies of intake for energy, protein, iron and vitamins D, B_2, B_{12}. In addition, calcium, zinc, magnesium and iodine may be inadequate for the increased needs of pregnancy.[19] It is reported that naturally occurring phytates and oxalates found in cereals, fruits and vegetables bind iron, zinc and chromium and reduce the bioavailability;[20] however, this is a controversial issue and many studies are in progress.

These pregnant adolescents may be especially susceptible to zinc deficiencies because of maternal and fetal needs. Studies in human and experimental animals indicate that abnormal labor and difficult childbirth were associated with lower levels of plasma zinc.[21] The rapid pre-menses growth spurt and sexual maturation increases zinc requirements[22] and are in part responsible for subsequent development of zinc deficiencies during pregnancy.

Conclusions

The incidence of teenage pregnancies is increasing. The major risks of these pregnancies are low birth-weight infants and pre-eclampsia and their related problems. To reduce these risks, emphasis should be placed on providing optimal energy and nutrient intakes to promote adequate material weight gain and fetal development. Known dietary deficiencies should receive special emphasis in counseling the pregnant adolescent.

Key References

1. Zelnik, M., et al., *Fam. Plann. Perspect.* 11:177-183, 1979.
2. National Center for Health Statistics, *Fertility Tables for Birth Cohorts by Color*, United States 1979-1973, U.S. Government Printing Office, Washington, D.C., 1976.
3. Natality Statistics, Teenage Childbearing, United States 1966-1975, *Monthly Vital Statistics Report*, National Center for Health Statistics, Vol. 26 No. 5 (suppl.), 1977.
4. Trends in Illegitimacy, United States 1940-1965, *Vital and Health Statistics*, National Center for Health Statistics, Series 21, No. 15, 1968.
5. Lorenzi, M., et al., *Adolescence* XII: 14-22, 1977.
6. Sugar, Max, *J. of Youth and Adol.* 5:251-269, 1976.
7. Committee on Adolescence, *Pediatrics* 63:795-797, 1979.
8. McGanity, W.J., In: *Nutritional Impacts on Women*, edited by K.S. Moghissi and T.N. Evans, Harper and Row, Hagerstown, 1977.
9. Task Force on Adolescent Pregnancy of the American College of Obstetricians and Gynecologists, *Adolescent Perinatal Health*, 1979.
10. Food and Nutrition Board, *Recommended Dietary Allowances, 9th edition*, National Academy of Sciences, 1980.
11. Hytten, F.E., *Postgrad. Med.* 55:259-302, 1979.
12. _____, Maternal Weight Gain and the Outcome of Pregnancy, *Nutr. Rev.* 37:318-320, 1979.
13. Naeye, R.L., *Am. J. Obstet. Gynecol.* 135:3-9, 1979.
14. Blackburn, M.L. and Calloway, D.H., *J.A.D.A.* 65:24-30, 1974.
15. Appel, J.A. and King, J.C., *Family and Community Health* 1:7-18, 1979.
16. Dietary Intake Findings, United States 1971-1974, *Vital and Health Statistics*, Series 11, No. 202, DHEW Pub. No. (HRA) 77-1647, U.S. Government Printing Office, Washington, D.C., 1977.
17. *Food Consumption Profiles of White and Black Persons Aged 1-74 Years*, United States 1971-1974, DHEW Pub. No. (PHS) 79-1658, U.S. Government Printing Office, Washington, D.C., 1979.
18. Kresina, M., *J. Curr. Adol. Med.* 2:26-28, 1980.
19. Dwyer, Johanna, Vegetarianism, *Contemporary Nutrition*, Vol. 4, No. 6, General Mills, Inc., Minneapolis, MN, 1979.
20. Mertz, Walter, Trace Elements, *Contemporary Nutrition*, Vol. 3, No. 2, General Mills, Inc., Minneapolis, MN, 1978.
21. Underwood, E.J., In: *Trace Elements in Human and Animal Nutrition*, 4th edition, Academic Press, New York, 1977.
22. Butrimoritz, G.P. and Purdy, W.C., *Am. J. Clin. Nutr.* 31:1409-1412, 1978.

PART 3

ADULTHOOD INTO THE GOLDEN YEARS

Depending on the source cited, half of this country's adult population faces one or more of the well-fed society's diseases—cancer, cardiovascular problems, diabetes, hypertension, obesity. Much of part 3 addresses these topics.

Ideally, physical exercise is an integral element of the life cycle. In particular, the sedentary lifestyle of most Americans can benefit from some form of athletics. Articles in the section on "Athletic Needs" discuss the increased energy and water requirements associated with more activity, glycogen loading, and "sports foods."

The section that addresses "Cardiovascular" topics treats heart-related aspects of diet, especially the debate whether saturated fats and cholestrol are risk factors or essentials to life. The editors selected articles that present both views. Lipoproteins and the famous Framingham Heart Study are also highlighted here. Hypertension is addressed in a separate article. (The sodium controversy is covered in part 1, under "Salts.")

Exceeded only by cardiovascular disease, cancer is the second leading cause of death in the United States. Actually, cancer is not one disease but many diseases with a complex array of disorders. The etiology of certain cancers linked to dietary patterns is discussed here. The actual needs of the cancer patient are addressed in "Medical Interactions."

Nearly all Americans have had at least one decayed tooth by the time they become adults. In "Dental Caries," the contribution of diet to the microbial ecology of the oral cavity is discussed. Readers are also reminded of the fluorine article in part 1, under "Minerals and Elements," as well as the section on "Sweeteners."

Adult-onset diabetes is most frequently linked to obesity. Some scientists emphasize the relationship by referring to "diabesity." Whatever the label, discussions of proper weight maintenance and the consumption of a variety of foods in moderation can be found throughout the first three parts of this book. This section presents new techniques in dietary treatment. For example, one article discusses incorporating sugar replacements into the diet of diabetic subjects. Other researchers are investigating high-fiber diets and their effects in reducing insulin requirements. **However, any dietary changes made by diabetics should be done only under the direct supervision of a physician.** The editors stress that certain dietary changes may precipitate dangerous hypoglycemic attacks by abruptly reducing insulin requirements.

"Medical Interactions" covers the interaction of prescribed drugs and other medical treatments with food and drink. Of particular concern is the maintenance of good nutrition for cancer patients. The systemic effects of the cancer itself may directly affect the digestive tract. Various treatments can significantly alter the dietary requirements of cancer patients. In addition, research is analyzing the role that vitamins play in a cancer cell's growth and development. However, because vitamins can be quite toxic in high doses, they cannot be used indiscriminately.

Mental development and learning are linked to nutrition in the section titled "Mental Health." For adults, the nutritional demands posed by stress are discussed.

Statistics show that every ninth American is a member of the group labeled the elderly. Every day, about 5,000 Americans blow out the candles on their 65th birthday cake. By the year 2000 there will be approximately 32 million people in the United States who will be at least 65 years old. These people have specific nutritional needs. Readers are reminded of the "Immunology" section in part 2 for mention of the host-defense system breakdown of aging. For specific areas that address health problems also found in adulthood, the reader is referred to earlier sections in this part.

"Geriatric Needs" emphasizes the psychosocial and physical forces that affect the nutritional requirements of the elderly and make them the major age grouping in our society that risks being profoundly malnourished.

For further information on:

- **Cancer** — See also "Medical Interactions"
- **Cardiovascular** — See part 1, "Energy Requirements"
- **Dental caries** — See part 1, "Minerals and Elements" and "Sweeteners"
- **Diabetes** — See part 1, "Fibers" and "Sweeteners"
- **Medical interactions** — See part 1, "Vitamins"
- **Geriatric needs** — See part 2, "Immunology"

ATHLETIC NEEDS

Nutrition and Human Performance

by National Dairy Council

SUMMARY

For optimal physical performance individuals must establish and maintain an appropriate body weight with a desired level of body fat, be well nourished, and well hydrated. In general, the nutritional needs of the physically active person are similar to those of the more sedentary individual, the difference being the increased energy and water requirements associated with more activity. Dehydration is a major factor limiting physical work capacity. As the duration and intensity of physical work increase, dietary carbohydrate is emphasized. Glycogen loading, a dietary manipulation used to increase muscle glycogen stores, improves performance in certain activities such as long distance running—its technique, selective application, and possible risks are reviewed. Undesirable nutritional practices associated with the timing and composition of the pre-event meal, intake during competition, and the means to lose and gain body weight can interfere with physical performance. Unfortunately food faddism is widespread among athletes or those seeking to attain a competitive advantage. There is no scientific foundation to support the claims that special ergogenic dietary aids (wheat germ oil, honey), massive doses of protein, vitamins, and minerals, and/or restriction of highly nutritious foods such as milk, improve physical performance.

Within the past several years there has been a promising resurgence of interest in physical performance (1). According to a 1977 Gallop Poll almost half of American adults exercise regularly to keep fit. Tennis, bicycling, swimming, calisthenics, walking, and running are among some of the more popular forms of exercise (1). For persons engaged in normal activities or light to moderate exercise, for athletes who train and compete, for military recruits, and for those in occupations such as mining or heavy construction, nutrition is an important, although certainly not the only factor affecting the individual's overall physical performance (2).

As reviewed in a previous *Digest* (3) and supported by most authorities (4-15), a nutritionally balanced diet based on the four food groups with sufficient calories to meet energy demands will satisfy all the nutritional requirements of most active persons. For those involved in activities of high intensity or prolonged duration (e.g., distance running) special nutritional needs appear to be indicated (2, 13, 16, 17). Such needs can be met by modifying the diet, as opposed to ingestion of special ergogenic "work producing" dietary aids which may prove detrimental. This *Digest* reviews some of the more recent findings and recommendations regarding dietary intake in relation to physical performance.

DIET GUIDELINES

The Basic Diet. The diet that will provide the best performance for athletes must contain adequate quantities of water, energy, protein, fat, carbohydrate, vitamins, minerals, and electrolytes in suitable proportions (3). A nutritionally balanced diet not too dissimilar from what the average American eats each day is recommended (14, 18). According to the results of a U.S. household food consumption survey conducted in the Spring of 1977, 14% of food energy was supplied by protein, 43% by fat, and 42% by carbohydrate (19). For athletes in training, greater emphasis is given to carbohydrates, with dietary energy derived as follows: 10—20% protein, 30—35% fat, and 50—55% carbohydrate (14, 20). And for athletes who train exhaustively on successive days and/or compete in prolonged endurance events, a diet containing more than 70% carbohydrate has proven beneficial to enhance performance (4, 6).

More so in the past (4) but even recently (20), large amounts of protein have been considered necessary to improve performance, hence the popularity of highly promoted protein formulations of various types. Fifty-one percent of 75 coaches and trainers recently surveyed believed that protein was the most important factor to increase muscle mass (21). This misconception has been difficult to dissipate. Muscle mass can be increased only by appropriate exercise. The weight of scientific data suggests that muscular activity does not increase the body's need for protein (0.8 g/kg body weight/day) beyond the amount consumed in a normal diet (4, 5). A diet containing as much as 2.8 g protein per kg body weight does not enhance physiological work performance during intensive physical training (22). Furthermore, contraindications to a high-protein diet include possible ketosis, dehydration, and hyperuricemia with the threat of gout (3, 18, 20). Protein, while essential to build and repair tissues, is the least important nutrient as an energy source (4, 20, 23).

Results of early analyses of respiratory exchange ratios and more recent sensitive analytical methods substantiate that both fat and carbohydrate are the major fuels for muscular activity (4, 16, 23-29). The metabolism of fat and carbohydrates (and to a minor degree, proteins) generates adenosine triphosphate (ATP) which is the ultimate source of energy for working muscle cells. The relative contribution of each of these fuels depends on the duration and intensity of work, the individual's total work capacity or maximal oxygen uptake (VO_2 max), and diet. Fat (triglycerides in muscle cells and free fatty acids derived from triglycerides stored in adipose tissue) is the primary fuel for muscle activity in mild to moderate aerobic activities (e.g., walking at 20 to 30% VO_2 max). As performance increases in intensity (70% VO_2 max) and oxygen availability to the working muscle becomes more limited, the body's fuel supply switches to more carbohydrate (muscle and liver glycogen and blood glucose). Less oxygen is required to metabolize carbohydrate than fat (4). If submaximal (aerobic) work continues in duration, fat becomes a prevalent fuel source; during sustained high level activity, carbohydrate utilization is greatly increased (4).

Because fat is a less readily-available source of energy, and it has almost unlimited storage in the body, there is no rationale for increasing the fat content of the diet. In fact, high-fat diets, by creating a condition of acidosis, adversely affect performance (4, 6). On the other hand, carbohydrate, stored as glycogen in muscle and liver, can become depleted during repeated bursts of intense activity (e.g., sprinting) or during long, exhaustive exercise (e.g., distance running, cross-country skiing). Strauzenberg et al (25) have shown that when glycogen falls below 5 g/kg wet muscle, efficiency and performance rapidly deteriorate. Thus, the length of time an athlete can sustain physical work of high intensity depends in part on the content of muscle glycogen (16, 25-29). In terms of diet, it has been repeatedly demonstrated that inclusion of carbohydrate in the diet increases utilization of blood glucose, storage of muscle and liver glycogen, and ultimately endurance performance (16, 27-29). Conversely, a low-carbohydrate diet (i.e., fad weight-reducing regimens) would, by leading to depletion of carbohydrate in muscles and liver, render it difficult for the individual to participate in vigorous physical activities or training (4).

As energy expenditure is increased by work, physical exercise, and athletic performance, the quantity of the basic diet consumed should be compatible with maintaining an efficient body weight and meeting the increased energy requirements of the activity (4, 6, 20). Excess body fat decreases mechanical work efficiency; that is, more energy and oxygen are required to produce a given amount of physical work (8). For highly-trained male athletes in top condition, the ideal fat content for some sports is five to eight percent of body weight; for females it is nine to ten percent (20). This compares with a fat content of 10 to 15% body weight in well-nourished non-athletic males and 20 to 25% in females (14).

Several factors influence the energy cost of exercise. These include the individual's age, sex, size (body weight and height), and metabolic rate, and the type, intensity, frequency, and duration of the activity (6). For example, a heavier person expends more energy than a lighter-weight person for a given activity, and the energy cost of short-distance racing is less than marathon races (4, 6, 30). Energy turnover among athletes varies from about 3,000 to 5,000 kcal daily, increasing an additional 500 to 1500 kcal during training (14). Normally, appetite and satiety are sensitive regulators automatically adjusting energy intake to meet the increased energy requirements (4, 6, 8, 14, 20). However, under the emotional stress of training and competition, the athlete may fail to consume sufficient energy or alternatively, eat excessively. The increased energy demands should be accommodated by greater intake of high quality carbohydrate foods (e.g., enriched grain products).

Body fluid balance is of utmost importance in attaining maximal physical performance (4, 5, 13, 15-17, 31-34). Dehydration is one of the major limiting factors in physical work capacity. Water requirements are significantly increased under conditions of heavy work in warm environments. When more than two to three percent of the body's weight is acutely lost by exercise-induced sweating, circulatory and thermoregulatory functions are diminished (4, 5, 8, 13, 32). Individuals who have low fitness levels and who are not acclimatized to the environmental heat tolerate fluid losses less well than athletes in better condition. Dehydration, by decreasing blood volume, limits the circulatory system's capacity to transport blood to the skin where body heat can be dissipated and to the working muscles where essential nutrients are needed. In severe cases this can lead to heat exhaustion and even death. The need for adequate fluid replenishment before, during, and after physical performance cannot be overemphasized. There is no basis for restricting water intake of athletes. In fact, the American College of Sports Medicine, recognizing the dangers of dehydration, published a position paper on this very subject, outlining guidelines to prevent heat injuries during distance running (34).

Although sweat loss can be substantial, the loss of electrolytes and minerals in sweat is relatively small (16). A bodyweight loss of 5.8% by dehydration can decrease total exchangeable sodium and chloride by six to eight percent, and potassium and magnesium by about one percent (13, 16). Renal conservation of electrolytes (principally sodium), consumption of regular meals, and adequate fluid intake are sufficient, in all but the most exceptional circumstances, to maintain electrolyte homeostasis. Despite the suggestion of large deficits of potassium stores with concomitant muscular weakness in individuals who train exhaustively on repeated days (35), Costill and Miller (16) and Costill (17) present evidence indicating that this is not the case, even when dietary potassium intake is extremely low.

The Pre-event Meal. The timing and composition of the meal consumed prior to an athletic event or competition have elicited much controversy (4). This overrated meal has been readily manipulated, often based on unsound nutritional principles, in hopes of attaining a competitive advantage. Although the pre-event meal is unlikely to influence performance, at least in short duration events, most authorities recommend the following practices (4, 13, 16, 17, 20).

In terms of timing, the object is to ensure that the stomach and upper bowel are empty at the time of the event. As gastrointestinal motility may be reduced by emotional tension, this meal should be consumed three to four hours prior to the event (4, 16). For endurance events, a light carbohydrate meal (500 kcal) low in protein and fat is recommended (16). Protein and fat (as in steak and fried potatoes) are digested slowly and are not utilized readily as fuels during the event (16). Concentrated sugars (honey, candy, soft drinks) have been promoted for athletes the hour preceding endurance exercise. However, their consumption may result in gastrointestinal distress and impaired performance or earlier exhaustion (4, 16). For long distance runners or persons in training who may become susceptible to dehydration, ingestion of 400 to 600 ml of cold water 10 to 15 minutes prior to performance is advisable (14).

During Performance. As thirst is not a sensitive indicator of fluid needs for athletes during training and prolonged periods of competition in warm environments, athletes should force themselves to drink fluids in excess of their perceived needs (4, 16). Even partial rehydration can minimize the risks of overheating and stress on the circulatory system. One investigator has noted that a psychological "lift" is given to athletes who consume liquids during exercise (36). To be readily available, ingested fluids must quickly leave the stomach. Thus factors which affect gastric emptying such as the volume, temperature, and osmolarity of the replacement fluid, are of significance. While large volumes (up to 600 ml) of fluid empty rapidly from the stomach, they cause gastric distress for the athlete. Therefore, it is preferable to drink small volumes of fluid more frequently (200 to 300 ml every 15 minutes). Cold drinks offer the advantages of emptying more rapidly from the stomach and at the same time enhancing body cooling. Sugars and electrolytes should be used sparingly, if at all, in replacement fluids as they elevate the osmolarity of the drink and impair gastric emptying. In most situations plain water is preferred.

Glycogen Loading. Initial stores of muscle and liver glycogen play a large part in determining success or failure in endurance-type activities lasting 60 minutes or longer (e.g., distance running, long duration cycling, cross-country skiing) (4, 16, 17, 27-29, 37). Glycogen loading or "muscle glycogen supercompensation" is a dietary regimen known to increase muscle glycogen storage well above normal levels. There have been slight modifications, but basically the procedure, initiated about a week prior to competition, involves exercising the athlete to the point of exhaustion during which time muscle glycogen levels are significantly decreased. This also stimulates the muscle's glycogen synthetase activity which facilitates muscle glycogen storage once a high carbohydrate diet is fed. A mixed diet based on the four food groups is fed during these first three days. For the remaining days of the week, a high carbohydrate (75 to 90%) diet is consumed, and exercise/training is drastically reduced to spare glycogen stores. The result, which is localized in the exercising muscles, is about a two-to three fold increase in muscle glycogen storage compared with that of the unexercised muscle (16). Application of glycogen loading also benefits performance at high altitudes (8,000 feet) such as mountain climbing where oxygen is less available and greater demands are placed on the anaerobic metabolism of carbohydrate (glycogen storage). The procedure is of no value for short (or intermittent) strenuous events such as football (38).

The type of carbohydrate (simple versus complex) fed during the glycogen loading procedure makes little difference to the rate and quantity of muscle glycogen stored (16). However, complex carbohydrates (pasta, bread) may be preferred as they produce a longer lasting insulin stimulation and blood glucose elevation. Glycogen storage in an athlete can be monitored by the temporary change in body weight (1 to 2 kg) as 2.7 g of water are stored with each gram of glycogen (4). The procedure is to be used cautiously and selectively with consideration of possible metabolic and nutritional side-effects (3, 4, 16, 20, 39). Electrocardiographic changes have been shown in at least one participant, and therefore glycogen loading is potentially harmful for the cardiac rehabilitation type runner (3, 15).

Weight Gain/Loss. To effectively compete, athletes must attain their appropriate weight, and simultaneously be well nourished, well hydrated, and have a healthy minimum energy reserve as fat (40). In certain athletic events such as heavyweight wrestling and some positions in football, an increase in body weight may optimize performance. In other sports such as gymnastics or long distance running a leaner body weight may confer greater efficiency of movement (4, 10, 41, 42). For the athlete, like the non-athlete who wishes to change his or her body weight, a well-planned and supervised weight control program is emphasized. Weight change should be accomplished gradually (± 1 to 2 lb per week) by moderately adjusting energy balance: energy intake in relation to energy expenditure. Diet modifications for either gaining or losing weight should be based on the four food groups to assure an optimal intake of all essential nutrients (6, 8, 40).

The aim of a weight-gaining program should be to increase lean body mass, i.e., muscle, as opposed to body fat. Muscle mass can be increased only by muscle work supported by an appropriate increase in dietary intake, not by any special food, vitamin, drug, or hormone (40).

An estimate of existing and desired body fat should be a prerequisite of the athlete's weight reduction program. In sports such as wrestling, gymnastics, and distance running, about five percent of body weight as fat is considered a healthy minimum. Body fat can be reduced by a modest decrease in food intake and an increase in energy expenditure. One hour of appropriate conditioning can increase energy expenditure by 250 to 750 kcal (6, 40). Unfortunately, starvation, semi-starvation, and dehydration are all-too-common practices among high school and college wrestlers attempting to abruptly reduce body weight to make a lower weight classification (4, 7, 10, 43, 44). Such practices will not only impair performance (i.e., endurance) but also may endanger health. Dehydration resulting from any means (ketogenic diet, water deprivation, salt deprivation, or diuretics) impairs circulatory function and eventually physical work capacity (4). Starvation and semi-starvation cause weight loss at the expense of lean body tissue rather than fat. This is particularly serious in highly-trained wrestlers who already have a low body fat content. For young competitors, such practices could compromise normal growth (4, 40).

SPECIAL CONCERNS

Sports Anemia. This appears to be a transient condition of borderline low hemoglobin levels sometimes observed in athletes during the early stages of a strenuous physical training program (4, 20, 45). Theoretically, as total body hemoglobin is related to maximal oxygen uptake, muscular endurance of an individual participating in aerobic type activities could be compromised by low hemoglobin levels. However, its cause and significance are unknown (4). Various hypotheses have been advanced with respect to its etiology. Perhaps it is a physiological adaptation to training (20). An increased susceptibility of red blood cells to lysis during exercise which in turn is related to the quality and quantity of dietary protein has been proposed (4, 45-47). And loss of iron in sweat has been presented as an explanation (14). Whether or not the condition affects physical working capacity is unknown.

Of more serious consideration is the dietary iron intake of women during childbearing years and teenage boys, both of whom have high iron requirements (4, 7). Iron deficiency anemia will adversely affect performance as the oxygen carrying capacity of the blood is reduced. In most cases, iron needs can be met by diet, or by iron supplements for those clinically diagnosed as iron deficient. Unless there is actual measureable iron deficiency, large doses of iron supplements are contraindicated (4).

Food Faddism. A discussion of nutrition and performance would be incomplete without mention of food faddism. Unfortunately, misconceptions and ignorance concerning food selections among athletes are widespread (7, 21). Darden (48) gives two basic reasons for this. First, coaches and athletes are under great pressure to win at all costs; and second, athletes have a tremendous desire to believe in almost anything that will turn them into champions.

Popular among athletes are various ergogenic or work-enhancing dietary aids: glucose and dextrose, honey, gelatin, lecithin, wheat germ oil, yeast powder, phosphates, and vitamins (4). While it is recognized that any one of the above may confer psychological benefits to the athlete, the vast majority of claims regarding their ergogenic effect is without scientific documentation. Furthermore, their indiscriminate use may impede performance and create unnecessary health problems.

Deficiencies of vitamins can be damaging to work performance due to their role in metabolic pathways. However, this does not mean that vitamin supplementation for athletes who already are well nourished will further improve performance. In particular, vitamin C, vitamin E, and the B-complex vitamins have been studied in this respect. There is a general consensus among investigators that if the athlete consumes a nutritionally balanced diet, vitamin supplements are unnecessary, do not enhance performance, and in the case of fat-soluble vitamins A, D, and E which are stored in the body, may lead to toxic effects (4, 17, 20, 49).

While certain foods and food constituents have been overemphasized on the alleged basis of improving performance, use of other foods has been discouraged (4). Milk fits into this latter category. Coaches and trainers have restricted athletes' milk consumption during training and before an athletic event on the supposition that milk contributes to cottonmouth (a dryness or discomfort in the mouth due to decreased activity of salivary glands), cuts speed and wind, and causes stomach upset due to curdling in the stomach. Studies show that there is no basis for restricting milk and milk products for the athlete (4). Cottonmouth appears to be due to emotional stress and fluid loss; performance is not reduced when milk is included in the diet; and milk curdling which is a natural and necessary part of digestion, does not cause stomach upset. More importantly, milk supplies the athlete with valuable nutrients such as calcium, good quality protein, vitamin A, and riboflavin (4).

Acknowledgments: National Dairy Council assumes the responsibility for writing and editing this publication. However, we would like to acknowledge the help and suggestions of the following reviewers in its preparation: D. L. Costill, Ph.D., Professor and Director, Human Performance Laboratory, Ball State University, Muncie, Indiana; N. J. Smith, M.D., Professor, Department of Pediatrics and Sports Medicine, University of Washington, Seattle, Washington; and D. S. Wiggans, Ph.D., Professor, Department of Biochemistry, University of Texas, Southwestern Medical School, Dallas, Texas.

REFERENCES

1. U.S. Department of Health, Education, and Welfare. *Healthy People. The Surgeon General's Report On Health Promotion And Disease Prevention.* DHEW (PHS) Publ. No. 79-55071, 1979.
2. Hanley, D. F. Nutr. Today 14:22, 1979.
3. National Dairy Council. Dairy Council Digest 46:7, 1975.
4. Williams, M. H. *Nutritional Aspects Of Human Physical And Athletic Performance.* Springfield, Illinois: Charles C. Thomas, 1976.
5. Parizkova, J., and V. A. Rogozkin (Eds.). *Nutrition, Physical Fitness, And Health.* Baltimore, MD.: University Park Press, 1978.
6. Katch, F. I., and W. D. McArdle. *Nutrition, Weight Control, and Exercise.* Boston, Mass.: Houghton Mifflin Co., 1977.
7. Smith, N. J. *Food For Sport.* Palo Alto, CA.: Bull Publ. Co., 1976.
8. Briggs, G. M., and D. H. Calloway (Eds). *Bogert's Nutrition and Physical Fitness.* 10th ed. Philadelphia: W. B. Saunders Co., 1979, pp. 527-539.
9. Lincoln, A. *Food For Athletes.* Chicago, Illinois: Contemporary Books, Inc., 1979.
10. Smith, N. J. In: *Pediatric Nutrition Handbook.* American Academy of Pediatrics. Evanston, Illinois: American Academy of Pediatrics, 1979, pp. 427-435.
11. Darden, E. *Nutrition and Athletic Performance.* Pasadena, CA: The Athletic Press, 1976.
12. Young, D. R. *Physical Performance Fitness and Diet.* Springfield, Illinois: Charles C. Thomas, 1977.
13. Higdon, H. *The Complete Diet Guide for Runners and Other Athletes.* Mountain View, CA.: World Publ., 1978.
14. Buskirk, E.R. Postgrad. Med. 61:229, 1977.
15. The American Dietetic Association. J. Am. Diet. Assoc. 76:437, 1980.
16. Costill, D.L., and J. M. Miller. Int. J. Sports Med. 1:2, 1980.
17. Costill, D.L. *A Scientific Approach To Distance Running.* Los Altos, CA.: Tafnews Press, 1979.
18. Hursh, L.M. Nutr. Today 14:18, 1979.
19. Cronin, F. J. Family Economics Rev. Spring: 10, 1980.
20. Vitousek, S. H. Nutr. Today 14:10, 1979.
21. Bentivegna, A., E. J. Kelley, and A. Kalenak. Phys. Sports Med. 7:99, 1979.
22. Consolazio, C. F., H. L. Johnson, R. A. Nelson, J. G. Dramise, and J. H. Skala. Am. J. Clin. Nutr. 28:29, 1975.
23. Felig, P., and J. Wahren. N. Engl. J. Med. 293:1078, 1975.
24. Hanley, D. F. Nutr. Today 14:5, 1979.
25. Strauzenberg, S. E., F. Schneider, R. Donath, H. Zerbes, and E. Kohler. Bibl. Nutr. Dieta. 27:133, 1979.
26. Koivisto, V., V. Soman, E. Nadel, W. V. Tamborlane, and P. Felig. Fed. Proc. 39:1481, 1980.
27. Consolazio, C. F., and H. L. Johnson. Am. J. Clin. Nutr. 25:85, 1972.
28. Lewis, S., and B. Gutin. Am. J. Clin. Nutr. 26:1011, 1973.
29. Martin, B., S. Robinson, and D. Robertshaw. Am. J. Clin. Nutr. 31:62, 1978.
30. Harger, B. S., J. B. Miller, and J. C. Thomas. J.A.M.A. 228:482, 1974.
31. Consolazio, C. F. In: *Nutrient Requirements in Adolescence.* McKigney, J. I., and H. N. Munro (Eds). Cambridge, Mass.: MIT Press, 1976, pp. 203-221.
32. Claremont, A. D., D. L. Costill, W. Fink, and P. Van Handel. Med. Sci. Sports 8:239, 1976.
33. Consolazio, C. F. In: *Symposia of the X International Congress of Nutrition.* Japan:Victory-Sha Press, 1976, pp. 183-185.
34. American College of Sports Medicine. Med. Sci. Sports. 7:7, 1975.
35. Lane, H. W., G. S. Roessler, E. W. Nelson, and J. J. Cerda. Am. J. Clin. Nutr. 31:838, 1978.
36. Johnson, D. J. J. Sports Med. 15:138, 1975.
37. Bergstrom, J., L. Hermansen, E. Hultman, et al. Acta. Physiol. Scand. 71:140, 1967.
38. MacDougall, J. D., G. R. Ward, D. G. Sale, and J. R. Sutton. J. Appl. Physiol. 42:129, 1977.
39. Jette, M., O. Pelletier, L. Parker, and J. Thoden. Am. J. Clin. Nutr. 31:2140, 1978.
40. Smith, N. J. J.A.M.A. 236:149, 1976.
41. Freyschuss, U., and A. Melcher. Scand. J. Clin. Lab. Invest. 38:753, 1978.
42. Niinimaa, V., M. Dyon, and R. J. Shephard. Med. Sci. Sports 10:91, 1978.
43. Sproles, C. B., D. P. Smith, R. J. Byrd, and T. E. Allen. J. Sports Med. 16:98, 1976.
44. Vaccaro, P., C. W. Zauner, and J. R. Cade. J. Sports Med. 16:45, 1976.
45. Consolazio, C. F., and T. Takahashi. In: *Symposia of the X International Congress of Nutrition.* Japan: Victory-Sha Press, 1976, pp. 174-176.
46. Shiraki, K., T. Yamada, T. Ashida, and H. Yoshimura. In: *Symposia of the X International Congress of Nutrition.* Japan: Victory-Sha Press, 1976, pp. 181-182.
47. Shiraki, K., T. Yamada, and H. Yoshimura. Japan J. Physiol. 27:413, 1977.
48. Darden, E. J. Home Econ. 69:40, 1977.
49. Lawrence, J. D., R. C. Bower, W. P. Richl, et al. Am. J. Clin. Nutr. 28:205, 1975.

ATHLETIC NEEDS

Nutrition and Physical Fitness

by the American Dietetic Association

With industrialization and mechanization, many individuals in the United States have become more sedentary. The decrease in physical activity and an abundant food supply have contributed to wider prevalence of obesity and reduced physical fitness. In turn, the risk of chronic disease, such as cardiovascular disease and diabetes mellitus, is increased. Members of The American Dietetic Association are obligated to influence a change in the fitness of the American public.

In our professional affiliations, it is our responsibility to promote programs that incorporate concepts of good nutrition and physical fitness. This statement by The American Dietetic Association is intended as a guideline to help dietitians and nutritionists achieve these goals. Recommendations are made for two levels of physical fitness: (a) For the general public and (b) for the more intense level of performing athletes.

Part I. Recommendations for the general public

The American Dietetic Association maintains that a nutritionally adequate diet and exercise are major contributing factors to physical fitness and health.

With a nutritionally adequate diet and an increase in the level of exercise, most persons will improve in their physical capacities until they reach a genetically predetermined level. The nutritionally adequate diet is one that provides sufficient nutrients and energy to meet the metabolic needs for optimal functioning of the body. In addition, substantial evidence indicates that individuals who avoid excessive intakes of energy, fat, cholesterol, sugar, salt, and highly refined foods lacking in fiber can maintain better health and may reduce their risk of developing chronic diseases.

The many benefits of physical conditioning include: Development of muscular strength, muscular endurance, and cardiovascular endurance; improved work capacity; increased muscle efficiency in handling oxygen; better muscle tone; greater flexibility and agility; and an improved sense of well-being. Also, blood pressure, pulse rate, and percentage of body fat may be modified. Aerobic exercise is one of many factors that may alter the lipid profile of the blood (1,2) and reduce the risk of coronary artery disease.

In addition to appropriate diet and exercise, physical fitness and health are influenced by other interdependent factors: Genetic variables; endocrine balances; psychologic and emotional status; sleep; and the use of alcohol, drugs, and tobacco.

The American Dietetic Association recommends that weight maintenance and weight loss be achieved by a combination of dietary modification, change in eating behavior, and regular aerobic exercise.

The key to weight control is a balance of energy intake and energy output. Individuals must learn to adjust their energy intakes throughout life to correspond to their changing metabolic needs. Customarily, some reduction in caloric intake is recommended during the middle and later years of adult life to correspond to the generally reduced energy requirements for the maintenance of desirable body weight and body fatness. For the obese, a low-calorie diet will bring about weight loss. However, with dietary adjustments alone, the recidivism rate has been high.

Behavioral modification of food habits is based on the premise that food intake is a learned response that can be changed. The individual learns to focus attention on the environmental factors that influence his/her food intake and to modify them gradually so that desirable changes in eating behavior occur.

An increase in physical activity can be as important as a decrease in the caloric intake to enable an individual to maintain desirable weight with the advancing years or to reduce weight if obese. Energy expenditure varies from one individual to another, depending on body weight, efficiency of movement, and training. The energy equivalents of many kinds of exercise have been determined, and convenient guidelines are available (1,3,4). With exercise, there is a slight increase in lean body mass which may result initially in a small increase in body weight since muscle tissue is heavier than fat tissue. Exercise will gradually reduce the percentage of body fat, even with weight maintenance, and to a greater extent with weight loss. When exercise is interrupted for an extended period, the percentage of body fat again increases (5).

Individuals are likely to achieve a higher success rate for long-term weight maintenance or weight loss if they take a three-phase approach: (a) Adjustment of the caloric intake to lose or maintain weight, (b) modification of inappropriate eating behavior, and (c) an increase in energy expenditure through regular aerobic exercise.

The American Dietetic Association recommends that skinfold measurements be used to determine the level of body fatness.

Traditionally, standard height-weight tables have been used to determine desirable body weight. However, individuals who conform to these standards actually vary widely in the proportions of lean and fatty tissue; that is, some persons who fall within the defined height-weight standards may have excessive deposits of fatty tissue.

Body composition is a better indicator of leanness than is body weight. A number of techniques have been used by investigators to determine body composition, including underwater weighing (body density), considered the most accurate technique; multiple isotope dilution (total and extracellular body water); total body potassium, using a whole body scintillation counter (lean body mass); and soft tissue roentgenography (width and thickness of adipose pads) (6,7).

Acceptable levels of body fat range from 7 to 15 per cent for men and from 12 to 25 per cent for women (8). A fat content in excess of 20 per cent for men and 30 per cent for women is regarded as obesity (9). With aging, total body fat for both sexes gradually increases, with the greater increase occurring in women (10,11).

None of the techniques used in research laboratories lends itself to clinical practice. Skinfold measurements with calipers applied at constant pressure at selected body sites—triceps, subscapular, abdominal, supriailiac crest, pectoral, and thigh and calf areas—are practical, reliable predictors of body fatness (12-14). Changes occur with aging in the subcutaneous tissues. Occasionally, large errors in estimation of body fat can occur, especially with a single measurement, because of unusual fat distribution. Such errors are reduced with multiple measurements (15). Tables based on several measurements show the interpretation of skinfold measurements of men and women in terms of percentage of body fat (8,14).

The triceps skinfold is a single measurement readily used for the estimation of body fatness, but, as mentioned, it does have limitations. The individual does not need to undress, as is necessary when several sites are measured. A table is available showing minimum values for skinfold thickness for men and women of various ages; above these levels, obesity is present (13).

The American Dietetic Association maintains that the generally healthy individual who regularly consumes a diet that supplies the Recommended Dietary Allowances receives all necessary nutrients for a physical conditioning program.

The Recommended Dietary Allowances (16) for each age/sex category afford a margin of safety for most individuals and will furnish the needs of persons entering on a physical conditioning program. Adjustments for energy intake are made to effect weight maintenance, weight loss, or weight gain as individually determined. For pre-adolescent and adolescent youth, the energy intake must be sufficient to cover growth needs.

A slight increase in the body's muscle mass occurs during the training period. Consequently, there is a small addition to the body's content of protein and water. Once the muscle mass has been developed, little addition to body protein and no increased catabolism of body tissues with continuing exercise occur. The recommended allowances for protein fully cover the increment to body tissues during the training period. Moreover, most Americans consume protein in excess of the recommended allowances. This additional protein consumption is not harmful and may be desirable, because many of the protein-rich foods are also excellent sources of the B-complex vitamins, iron, and other trace minerals.

The percentage of calories from protein varies somewhat with the level of caloric intake. For low-calorie diets, the protein intake may account for 20 per cent, and occasionally more, of total caloric intake. On maintenance diets, a protein intake representing 10 to 15 per cent of calories is customary. Nutritionally adequate diets can be planned with widely varying proportions of carbohydrate and fat. Many nutritionists, physicians, and athletic coaches recommend that the fat intake be kept to from 30 to 35 per cent of calories, with a corresponding increase in carbohydrate intake. The use of complex-type carbohydrates should be emphasized.

The new "Dietary Guidelines for Americans,"[1] developed by the Departments of Agriculture and of Health, Education, and Welfare, together with the food groups published in 1979 by the Department of Agriculture in the booklet, *Food*[2], are useful for planning the diet. One of the food groups, namely "Fats, Sweets, and Alcohol," includes foods that are generally low in nutrient density. If these foods are used in moderation and within the nutrient and caloric requirements of the individual, they

---

[1] USDA and DHEW: Nutrition and Your Health. Dietary Guidelines for Americans, 1980. (Available from: Off. of Governmental and Public Affairs, USDA, Washington, D.C. 20250.)
[2] Food. USDA Home & Garden Bull. No. 228, 1979.

may enhance the palatability of the diet. If the fat intake is restricted to 35 per cent of calories or less, food choices from the milk and meat groups should be modified and those from fats sharply restricted. Persons who have increased caloric requirements should give preference to additional servings from the bread-cereal and vegetable-fruit groups.

Protein, mineral, and/or vitamin supplements do not enhance physical performance or well-being if the healthy individual consumes a diet that meets the Recommended Dietary Allowances. For some individuals with chronic conditions, the physician may prescribe supplements to meet specific deficiencies or increased metabolic needs.

The American Dietetic Association recommends that the intensity, duration, and frequency of exercise should be determined according to the age, physical condition, and health status of the individual.

Before starting any exercise program, the individual should be advised to consult a physician. This is especially important for individuals over thirty-five years of age and for all persons in whom risk factors for cardiovascular disease, such as hypertension, smoking, or elevated blood lipids, are present (1). When an individual enters into an exercise program, his/her cardiovascular fitness can be assessed by an electrocardiogram and by oxygen uptake levels during maximal and submaximal stress tests administered and interpreted by a cardiologist or physiologist (with a physician present for persons over thirty-five years of age).

The capacity of a person's body to take in, deliver, and use oxygen is measured by *maximum aerobic power* (abbreviated VO_2-max.). It is expressed as milliliters of oxygen consumed per kilogram body weight per minute (ml. O_2 per kilogram per minute) (4). The VO_2-max. for women is from 70 to 85 per cent of that for men.

On the basis of the individual's medical history, physical examination, and stress tests, a planned program should be worked out for each person. The duration and intensity of each exercise period are increased gradually until the prescribed goal is reached. The goal for intensity is from 60 to 80 per cent of the person's VO_2-max. Below 60 per cent, there is little cardiovascular benefit; above 80 per cent, there is little added benefit and possible excessive stress. The goal should be from 15 to 60 min. of continuous aerobic activity three to five days a week. Low- to moderate-intensity exercise of longer duration is recommended for the non-athletic adult (17).

Aerobic exercises promote the improved utilization and consumption of oxygen in the body. The exercise should be continuous and of sufficient duration and intensity to condition muscles and the cardiovascular system without being excessively strenuous. Jogging, brisk walking, swimming, skating, cross-country skiing, cycling, jumping rope, aerobic dancing, rowing, and jumping on a trampoline are examples of aerobic exercises. Walking can be recommended for persons of all ages. Jogging may increase the risk of foot, leg, and knee injury in some individuals (17). Such exercises as handball, tennis, squash, and volleyball are not considered aerobic for most people and may promote overexertion (18). Golf and bowling are not effective aerobic exercises.

The heart rate provides a guide to aerobic activity. Each individual entering on a physical conditioning program should be taught how to measure the pulse rate *immediately* on beginning exercise, at the peak period, and at the end of each exercise period. Since the maximum heart rate declines with age, an appropriate guide to the maximum heart rate is to subtract the age in years from 220. Exercise that achieves 70 per cent of the maximum heart rate is likely to be accompanied by from 55 to 60 per cent oxygen utilization. An intensity of exercise that achieves 85 per cent of maximum heart rate results in an aerobic response of from 75 to 80 per cent (1). Within this range of response, improvement in physical conditioning can be expected.

The American Dietetic Association recommends that habits for a nutritionally balanced diet and physical fitness be established during childhood and maintained throughout life.

Food habits and patterns of activity are set in childhood. The establishment of good food habits requires consideration of the physical needs of the individual and the socioeconomic environment that pertains. Food habits are also affected by psychologic, ethnic, cultural, and religious factors. Desirable patterns of food behavior are fostered by nutrition education in the school and by continuing nutrition education throughout adult life.

Physical education in the schools can introduce the child to activities that may be pursued on an individual as well as a group basis throughout a lifetime. If physical fitness is to become a lifetime goal, the activities to achieve it must be enjoyable and adaptable to a variety of environments. Activities appropriate for a lifetime should be promoted by the schools, at camps and playgrounds, and in the home.

An integrated nutrition/physical fitness approach can be achieved in the elementary and secondary schools through the cooperation of classroom teachers, health and physical education teachers, school physicians and nurses, school foodservice dietitians, and nutrition specialists.

Part II. Recommendations for athletes involved in training or competition

The American Dietetic Association recommends that the athlete meet increased caloric and nutrient needs by increasing the number of selections from the "calories-plus-nutrients"[3] foods.

Athletes usually expend from 3,000 to 6,000 kcal per

---

[3] Food. USDA Home & Garden Bull. No. 228. 1979.

day. With the increased energy requirement, there is a proportionate increase in the need for thiamin (0.5 mg. per 1,000 kcal). The recommended allowances for riboflavin and niacin intake are also based on caloric intake (16).

The athlete can best meet the higher caloric requirement by increasing the number of servings from the "calories-plus-nutrients" food groups. Liberal intake of carbohydrates from the bread-cereal and fruit-vegetable groups should be emphasized. Moderate amounts of fats and sugars may be used to furnish energy and to enhance the palatability of the diet. When caloric requirements are from 5,000 to 6,000 kcal per day, five or six meals may be preferred to three.

The protein needs of performing athletes include tissue maintenance requirements, allowances for growth by adolescent athletes, and small increments for the development of muscle mass during the conditioning period. No satisfactory evidence exists that additional protein improves work performance or that activity leads to increased cellular destruction of protein (19-21). Although the recommended allowances for protein are appropriate for the athlete in training, they may not be sufficient to cover the significant losses of nitrogen that occur from the skin during vigorous activity accompanied by profuse sweating in a hot, humid environment. Balance studies have shown that 100 gm. protein per day is adequate to cover all needs of men performing heavy work and perspiring profusely (19). If protein furnishes from 10 to 12 per cent of the total caloric intake, it will be more than sufficient to cover the losses through the skin.

The American Dietetic Association recommends that athletes maintain a hydrated state by consuming fluid before, during, and after exercise.

Water is the substance of primary concern when profuse sweating accompanies prolonged strenuous exercise. Some individuals may lose as much as 2 to 4 liters of sweat (from 6 to 8 lb. body weight) per hour when competing in endurance events (22-25). In addition, with heavy exercise, the respiratory loss of water may exceed 130 ml. per hour, compared with a normal loss of 15 ml. per hour (26).

The effects of dehydration are: Fatigue; deterioration in performance; an increase in body temperature; reduced volume of extracellular fluid; reduced urinary volume; and a decline in circulatory function, including lower blood volume, lower blood pressure, increased pulse rate, and if the dehydration is severe enough, circulatory collapse (27,28). A 3 per cent weight loss leads to impaired performance; a 5 per cent loss can result in some signs of heat exhaustion; a 7 per cent loss may produce hallucinations and put the individual in the danger zone (28). A 10 per cent weight loss can lead to heat stroke and circulatory collapse.

Dehydration to accomplish weight loss prior to an event, as for wrestlers and boxers, is never acceptable (28,29). When such athletes must lose weight, the loss should result from a caloric deficit so that body fat, not body water, is lost.

Ordinarily, thirst is a reliable guide to the need for water. But, because of tension and anxiety and because of large sweat losses, thirst is an inaccurate indicator of water need during competition. Athletes should be encouraged to weigh themselves before and after an event to determine the amount of fluid that needs to be replaced. Some forced drinking of fluid is essential.

About 2 hr. before an event, the athlete in endurance competition should try to drink about 600 ml. (21 oz.) fluid. Then 10 to 15 min. before the event, he/she should drink about 400 to 500 ml. (14 to 17 oz.) water. Small amounts of water—100 to 200 ml. (3 to 7 oz.)—at 10- to 15-min. intervals are better than copious amounts of water every hour or so. The maximum fluid intake is about 1 liter per hour, because this is the limit of gastric emptying time (22,23). Cold drinks (5°C. or 41°F.) leave the stomach more rapidly than warm drinks (35°C. or 94°F.) (30).

Fluid taken before and during the event will not fully replace fluid losses, but partial replacement reduces the risk of overheating. After the event, the athlete should continue to drink water at frequent intervals until the weight has been regained. If the weight loss is from 4 to 7.5 per cent, up to 24 to 36 hr. are required for complete rehydration (26).

The glycogen stores built up with carbohydrate loading prior to endurance competition are a potential source of water to the body. With the breakdown of 1 gm. glycogen, 2.7 gm. associated water are released. Also, each gram of glycogen aerobically metabolized forms 0.6 gm. water. Thus, for each gram of glycogen released, more than 3 gm. water are available that can partially compensate for evaporative water loss (22,27).

The American Dietetic Association recommends that athletes meet their needs for additional electrolytes from the foods they ordinarily consume.

Sodium and chloride are the principal electrolyte deficits that must be corrected following profuse sweating. On occasion, potassium may also require replacement.

The concentration of electrolytes in sweat and the total losses that occur during an event vary widely from one individual to another, according to the degree of acclimatization, adrenal cortical activity, environmental temperature, and humidity (31). The range of electrolyte concentrations in sweat is great: Sodium, from 12 to 120 mEq; potassium, from 5 to 30 mEq; and chloride, from 8 to 80 mEq (32). Sodium losses of 350 mEq per day are not uncommon as a result of profuse sweating (33). With acclimatization, the losses are lower.

The precise requirements for sodium and chloride are not known. A suggested "safe and adequate intake" of sodium by adults is from 1,100 to 3,300 mg. (48 to 144 mEq) and of chloride, from 1,700 to 5,100 mg. (48 to 144 mEq) (16). Typical mixed diets furnish from 6 to 18 gm. salt (100 to 300 mEq sodium and chloride) (33). The production of 5 to 8 liters of sweat may necessitate an intake of from 13 to 15 gm. salt daily (26). Athletes do not need to replace salt losses hour by hour but can correct these losses in the foods they consume following the event (26,27,34,35). They may use more salt at the table and eat foods that have been prepared with a high salt content. One-half tsp. salt contains approximately 1 gm. sodium. Liberal amounts of fluid should accompany sodium replacement. *Caution:* Excessive sodium intake leads to potassium depletion.

A "safe and adequate intake" of potassium for adults is from 1,875 to 5,625 mg. (48 to 144 mEq) (16). Typical mixed American diets furnish from 1,950 to 5,850 mg. (50 to 150 mEq) per day (33). Acclimated athletes who perspire profusely need more than 3,000 mg. potassium daily, while those who are not acclimated require up to 5,000 to 6,000 mg. (36). If the athlete selects foods to meet his additional energy requirements from foods that are also rich sources of potassium, he/she should be able to replace all but the most exceptionally heavy losses. With the substantial metabolism of glycogen during endurance competition, considerable amounts of potassium are released to help meet body needs. Each gram of glycogen metabolized releases 16.6 mg. (0.45 mEq) potassium (22,32).

The American Dietetic Association recommends that electrolyte supplements should be used only on the advice of the team physician.

Generally, the losses of sodium chloride and potassium can be made up at meals following the competition. If sweat losses exceed 4 liters, some electrolyte replacement during the competition may be indicated (33). The team physician is best qualified to evaluate the conditions of temperature, humidity, and activity that require such supplementation.

Gastric emptying is controlled by the volume and osmolarity of the fluid administered. Hypertonic solutions should be avoided because they exert an osmotic effect, forcing water into the stomach. They can thus accentuate dehydration and cause a feeling of gastric fullness and distress. Gastric emptying will not occur until the stomach contents are isotonic. Not more than 20 to 30 mEq sodium chloride per liter and 50 to 60 gm. glucose per hour are well tolerated (22). A solution that contains less than 10 mEq sodium per liter, less than 5 mEq potassium per liter, and up to 2.5 per cent of glucose is recommended (23).

Salt tablets are not recommended because they frequently cause nausea, vomiting, and gastric distress (37). Excessive salt intake increases the load on the kidney, and without adequate fluid intake, a state of dehydration can be further aggravated.

The American Dietetic Association recognizes that a high carbohydrate intake prior to competition can be beneficial to some athletes engaging in endurance events.

It is generally agreed that the availability of muscle glycogen is the limiting factor in endurance competition (20,38-40). When the muscle glycogen is exhausted, the athlete can no longer perform. Carbohydrate loading or glycogen loading is a dietary procedure whereby high-carbohydrate diets are used to build up muscle glycogen stores. A store of liver glycogen is also necessary to reduce the likelihood of hypoglycemia (22).

When muscles are first depleted of glycogen and then replenished by consumption of a high-carbohydrate diet, the glycogen content of muscle is about twice that achieved with a normal mixed diet (39,41). The endurance time correlates with the glycogen content of the muscle. Carbohydrate loading entails these steps: (a) Depleting the muscle glycogen one week before the event by exercising to exhaustion, using the same type of activity that will occur in the competition; (b) consuming a high-protein, high-fat, low-carbohydrate (100 gm.) diet for three days; (c) consuming a moderate-protein, low-fat, high-carbohydrate (250 to 525 gm.) diet for three days immediately preceding the event (38,40-43). The small amount of carbohydrate recommended during the depletion phase is necessary to prevent the effects of ketosis. During the repleting phase, complex carbohydrates are preferred since they are also useful sources of minerals and vitamins and are more gradually absorbed. Excessive amounts of sugar, candy, soft drinks, and honey are not needed (43).

Carbohydrate loading must not be used indiscriminately (4). It is of no advantage to the athlete in short-time, high-intensity competition (4,22). Because water is held with the glycogen that is stored, the weight gain may be as much as 2.5 to 3.5 kg. (27). This can lead to a feeling of stiffness and heaviness that is a distinct disadvantage to the athlete in competition.

Carbohydrate loading should be used very selectively for high school and college athletes, and rarely, if ever, for early adolescent or pre-adolescent athletes (42). Some athletes do not tolerate carbohydrate loading very well and should not attempt it for the first time prior to a competition. Probably the full loading sequence should be used no more than two or three times a year (43).

An athlete with diabetes or hypertriglyceridemia should consult his physician before adopting a carbohydrate loading program (43). Occasional health impairments have been observed, including chest pains, changes in the electrocardiogram (44), and myoglobinuria, following persistent glycogen loading (45). Although these changes are uncommon, athletes should seek medical advice if they encounter symptoms.

The American Dietetic Association does not recognize any unique ergogenic values of products, such as wheat germ, wheat germ oil, vitamin E, ascorbic acid, lecithin, honey, gelatin, phosphates, sunflower seeds, bee pollen, kelp, or brewer's yeast.

An ergogenic aid is any substance that can increase the ability to work. Many athletes claim that one reason for a successful performance was the inclusion of a particular food or food supplement. This type of testimonial is purely anecdotal and is not supported by scientific studies (4,34,40). Investigations with vitamin E supplementation (46,47) and ascorbic acid supplementation (48) showed that performance was no better with the supplement than with the placebo.

For those engaging in athletic events, The American Dietetic Association does not advocate the use of beer, wine, or distilled alcoholic beverages as a source of calories, as a muscle relaxant, or as an ergogenic aid.

Although alcohol is a ready source of energy for muscular work, its use by athletes is not recommended. Alcohol is a depressant of the central nervous system. It accentuates fatigue by increasing the production of lactate (49). It interferes with the nervous system by slowing the reaction time; interfering with voluntary and involuntary reflexes; and reducing the responsiveness, reaction time, and coordination (49,50). Alcohol has a diuretic effect that increases the loss of body water, thus contributing to dehydration.

The American Dietetic Association maintains that future research is needed on the usefulness of caffeine as a stimulus to fatty acid mobilization.

Initially, in endurance competition, carbohydrate furnishes about 90 per cent of the energy, and fat about 10 per cent. As the competition continues, less energy is derived from carbohydrate and more from free fatty acids. By the end of the competition, most of the energy is derived from free fatty acids (24).

With improved fat utilization, the depletion of glycogen is retarded, and endurance is enhanced (20). Some claims have been made that caffeine ingested 1 hr. prior to exercise stimulates the release of free fatty acids (8,51), thus sparing glycogen; others do not support the use of caffeine (4).

The suggested intake is from 4 to 5 mg. per kilogram body weight. For a 70-kg. person, this is equivalent to about two cups of coffee (approximately 150 mg. caffeine per cup). For most persons, such moderate consumption probably has no harmful effect (4).

Some persons are more sensitive than others to the effects of caffeine. When a person ingests 1 gm. caffeine (six to seven cups coffee) or more, effects on the central nervous system and circulatory system include insomnia, excitement, restlessness, ringing of the ears, tachycardia, extrasystoles, and quickened respiration. Gastric irritation often occurs, and muscles become tense. Diuresis can accentuate losses of body fluids (49).

The American Dietetic Association recommends that a light pre-game meal be eaten 3 to 4 hr. prior to the competition.

The stomach should be empty at the time of competition. If an athlete begins to exercise immediately after ingesting food, he/she may experience gastrointestinal distress, including nausea, vomiting, stomach fullness, or cramping. The digestion of food and absorption of nutrients competes with muscle metabolism for the blood supply. The result may be a diminished blood supply to the working muscle. A 3- to 4-hr. interval between meal time and training or competition will minimize any gastrointestinal discomfort.

Athletes vary in their assimilation and tolerance of foods. These differences are accentuated during physical and mental stress. Thus, the best pre-game meal is one with familiar foods that the athlete tolerates well and is convinced will help him/her to win (4,8). Some athletes experience discomfort when they eat foods that are gas-producing or that are highly spiced.

The pre-game meal should include some protein, a minimal amount of fat, and a liberal level of complex carbohydrates. It might include moderate amounts of lean meat, poultry, or fish, vegetables, fruits, and bread. Milk—long tabooed in the past—may be drunk (4). There is no evidence that liquid meals are tolerated better than solid meals.

Small amounts of carbohydrate taken up to an hour before competition are not harmful but probably do no good. Large amounts of simple sugars are not recommended, for they may cause a surge in the release of insulin and subsequent hypoglycemia.

The American Dietetic Association recommends that athletes not currently involved in training or competition should reduce their caloric intake to balance their energy expenditure.

Caloric expenditure is substantially reduced when the athlete is not involved in training or competition. To maintain desirable body weight and levels of body fatness, the caloric intake must be substantially reduced. The recommendations made for diet and for exercise for the general public are appropriate during the interim or off-season period.

References

(1) Fox, S.M., Naughton, J.P., and Haskell, W.L.: Physical activity and the prevention of coronary heart disease. Ann. Clin. Res. 3: 404, 1971.
(2) Gyntelberg, F., Brennan, R., Holloszy, J.O., Schonfeld, G., Rennie, M.J., and Weidman, S.W.: Plasma triglyceride lowering by exercise despite increased food intake in patients with type IV hyperlipoproteinemia. Am. J. Clin. Nutr. 35: 716, 1977.
(3) Passmore, R., and Durnin, J.V.G.A.: Human energy expenditures. Physiol. Rev. 35: 801, 1955.
(4) Jensen, C.R., and Fisher, A.G.: Scientific Basis of Athletic Conditioning. 2nd ed. Philadelphia: Lea & Febiger, 1979.
(5) Pařízková, J.: Impact of age, diet and exercise on man's body composition. Ann. N.Y. Acad. Sci. 110: 661, 1963.
(6) Keys, A., and Grande, F.: Body weight, body composition and calorie status. In Goodhart, R.S., and Shils, M.E., eds.: Modern Nutrition in Health and Disease. 5th ed. Philadelphia: Lea & Febiger, 1973, pp. 1-27.
(7) Pike, R.L., and Brown, M.L.: Nutrition: An Integrated Approach. 2nd ed. N.Y.: John Wiley & Sons, Inc., 1975, pp. 757-813.
(8) Fox, E.L.: Sports Physiology. Philadelphia: W.B. Saunders Co., 1979.

(9) DAVIDSON, S., PASSMORE, R., BROCK, J.F., AND TRUSWELL, A.S.: Human Nutrition and Dietetics. 6th ed. London: Churchill Livingstone, 1975, p. 289.
(10) YOUNG, C.M., BLONDIN, J., TENSUAN, R., AND FRYER, J.H.: Body composition of "older" women. J. Am. Dietet. A. 43: 344, 1963
(11) KEYS, A., AND BROZEK, J.: Body fat in adult men. Physiol. Rev. 33: 245, 1953.
(12) EDWARDS, D.A.W., HAMMOND, W.H., HEALY, M.J.R., TANNER, J.M., AND WHITEHOUSE, R.H.: Design and accuracy of calipers for measuring subcutaneous tissue thickness. Br. J. Nutr. 9: 133, 1955.
(13) SELTZER, C.C., AND MAYER, J.A.: A simple criterion of obesity. Postgrad. Med. 38: A101 (Aug.), 1965.
(14) DURNIN, J.V.G.A., AND WOMERSLEY, J.: Body fat assessed from total body density and its estimation from skinfold thickness: Measurements on 481 men and women aged from 16 to 72 years. Br. J. Nutr. 32: 77, 1974.
(15) YUHASZ, M.S.: Assessment of Percentage Body Fat from Skinfold. Physical Fitness and Sports Appraisal. A Laboratory Manual. London, Ont., Canada: Univ. of Western Ontario.
(16) FOOD & NUTR. BD.: Recommended Dietary Allowances. 9th rev. ed. Washington, D.C.: Natl. Acad. Sci., 1980.
(17) AM. COLL. SPORTS MED.: Position paper: The recommended quantity and quality of exercise for developing and maintaining fitness in healthy adults. Med. Sci. Sports, 10: vii (3), 1978.
(18) VAN HUSS, W.D.: Physical activity and aging. In Strauss, R.H., ed.: Sports Medicine and Physiology. Philadelphia: W.B. Saunders Co., 1979.
(19) CONSOLAZIO, C.F.: Protein metabolism during intensive physical training in the young adult. Am. J. Clin. Nutr. 28: 29, 1975.
(20) LEWIS, S., AND GUTIN, B.: Nutrition and endurance. Am. J. Clin. Nutr. 26: 1011, 1973.
(21) IRWIN, M.I., AND HEGSTED, D.M.: A conspectus of research on protein requirements of man. J. Nutr. 101: 385, 1971.
(22) BERGSTROM, J., AND HULTMAN, E.: Nutrition for maximal sports performance. J.A.M.A. 221: 999, 1972.
(23) AM. COLL. SPORTS MED.: Position statement: Prevention of heat injuries during distance running. Med. Sci. Sports 7: vii (1), 1975.
(24) COSTILL, D.L.: Physiology of marathon running. J.A.M.A. 221: 1024, 1972.
(25) WILLIAMS, M.H.: Nutritional Aspects of Human Physical and Athletic Performance. Springfield, Ill.: Charles C Thomas, 1976.
(26) COSTILL, D.L.: Water and electrolytes. In Morgan, W., ed.: Ergogenic Aids and Muscular Performance. N.Y.: Academic Press, 1972, pp. 293-320.
(27) OLLSON, K., AND SALTIN, B.: Diet and fluids in training and competition. Scand. J. Rehab. Med. 3: 31, 1971.
(28) COMM. ON NUTRITIONAL MISINFORMATION, FOOD & NUTR. BD.: Water deprivation and performance of athletes. Nutr. Rev. 32: 314, 1974.
(29) SMITH, N.J.: Gaining and losing weight in athletics. J.A.M.A. 236: 149, 1976.
(30) COSTILL, D.L., AND SALTIN, B.: Factors limiting gastric emptying during rest and exercise. J. Appl. Physiol. 37: 679, 1974.
(31) CONSOLAZIO, C.F., MATOUSH, L.O., NELSON, R.A., HARDING, R.S., AND CANHAM, J.E.: Excretion of sodium, potassium, magnesium and iron in human sweat and the relation of each to balance and requirements. J. Nutr. 79: 407, 1963.
(32) WEST, E.S., TODD, W.R., MASON, H.S., AND VAN BRUGGEN, J.T.: Textbook of Biochemistry. 4th ed. N.Y.: Macmillan Publishing Co., 1966, p. 686.
(33) FOOD & NUTR. BD.: Recommended Dietary Allowances. 8th rev. ed. Washington, D.C.: Natl. Acad. Sci., 1974, pp. 89-91.
(34) MAYER, J., AND BULLEN, B.: Nutrition and athletic performance. Physiol. Rev. 40: 369, 1960.
(35) MURPHY, R.J.: Heat illness and athletics. In Strauss, R.H., ed.: Sports Medicine and Physiology. Philadelphia: W.B. Saunders Co., 1979, pp. 320-26.
(36) LANE, H.W., AND CERDA, J.J.: Potassium requirements and exercise. J. Am. Dietet. A. 73: 64, 1978.
(37) SHILS, M.E.: Food and nutrition relating to work and environmental stress. In Goodhart, R.S., and Shils, M.E., eds.: Modern Nutrition in Health and Disease. 5th ed. Philadelphia: Lea & Febiger, 1973, pp. 722-24.
(38) BERGSTROM, J., HERMANSEN, L., HULTMAN, E., AND SALTIN, B.: Diet, muscle glycogen and physical performance. Acta Physiol. Scand. 71: 140, 1967.
(39) CONSOLAZIO, C.F., AND JOHNSTON, H.L.: Dietary carbo'ydrate and work capacity. Am. J. Clin. Nutr. 25: 85, 1972.
(40) HORSTMAN, D.H.: Nutrition. In Morgan, W., ed.: Ergogenic Aids and Muscular Performance. N.Y.: Academic Press, 1972, pp. 343-397.
(41) KARLSSON, J., AND SALTIN, B.: Diet, muscle glycogen and endurance performance. J. Appl. Physiol. 31: 203, 1971.
(42) SMITH, N.J.: Nutrition and the athlete. In Strauss, R.H., ed.: Sports Medicine and Physiology. Philadelphia: W.B. Saunders Co., 1979, pp. 271-81.
(43) FORGAC, N.T.: Carbohydrate loading. A review. J. Am. Dietet. A. 75: 42, 1979.
(44) MIRKIN, G.: Carbohydrate loading. A dangerous practice (letter). J.A.M.A. 223: 1511, 1973.
(45) BANK, W.J.: Myoglobinuria in marathon runners. Possible relationship to carbohydrate and lipid metabolism. Ann. N.Y. Acad. Sci. 301: 942, 1977.
(46) LAWRENCE, J.D., BOWER, R.C., RIEHL, W.P., AND SMITH, J.L.: Effect of α-tocopherol acetate on the swimming endurance of trained swimmers. Am. J. Clin. Nutr. 28: 205, 1975.
(47) SHARMAN, I.M., DOWN, M.G., AND SEN, R.N.: The effects of vitamin E and training on physiological function and athletic performance in adolescent swimmers. Br. J. Nutr. 26: 265, 1971.
(48) GEY, G.O., COOPER, K.H., AND BOTTENBERG, R.A.: Effect of ascorbic acid on endurance performance and athletic injury. J.A.M.A. 211: 105, 1970.
(49) GOODMAN, L.S., AND GILMAN, A., ED.: The Pharmacological Basis of Therapeutics. 5th ed. N.Y.: Macmillan Publishing Co., 1975, pp. 137, 373.
(50) HANLEY, D.F.: Drug use and abuse. In Strauss, R.H., ed.: Sports Medicine and Physiology. Philadelphia: W.B. Saunders Co., 1979, pp. 396-404.
(51) COSTILL, D.L., DALSKY, G., AND FINK, W.J.: Effects of caffeine ingestion on metabolism and exercise performance. Med. Sci. Sports 10: 155, 1978.

Reading list

ASTRAND, P., AND RODAHL, K.: Textbook of Work Physiology. N.Y.: McGraw-Hill Book Co., 1970.
DARDEN, E.: Nutrition and Athletic Performance. San Marino, Calif.: Athletic Press, 1976.
MATHEWS, D.K., AND FOX, E.L.: The Physiological Basis of Physical Education and Athletics. Philadelphia: W.B. Saunders Co., 1976.
Nutrition for Athletes. A Handbook for Coaches. Washington, D.C.: Am. Assoc. for Health, Physical Education & Recreation (with cooperation from The Am. Dietet. Assoc. and The Nutr. Foundation), 1971.
SMITH, N.F.: Food for Sport. Palo Alto, Calif.: Bull Publishing Co., 1976.
WILLIAMS, M.H.: Nutritional Aspects of Human Physical and Athletic Performance. Springfield, Ill.: Charles C Thomas, 1976.
ZOHMAN, L.R.: Beyond Diet . . . Exercise Your Way to Fitness and Heart Health. Englewood Cliffs, N.J.: Best Foods, 1974.

ATHLETIC NEEDS

Sports Food: A Guide to Nutrition and Exercise

by Patricia Cobe

To pitch a perfect game or score the winning point, professional athletes have to be in top physical condition. What do they eat to keep fit? To find out, FORECAST asked a group of sports people to tell us.

Put all the joggers, cyclists, hikers, and other exercise enthusiasts together and it soon becomes apparent—*getting into shape* is a popular sport today. All across America, people of all ages are working harder and harder at keeping fit. Since exercise and eating go hand in hand, food plays an important part in this fitness trend. But even though serious and casual athletes alike are watching their diets, some are not too sure what they're looking for.

We're about to help you and your students gain an understanding of the eating-exercise relationship. Over the years, many tall tales have been told around the training table concerning food and sports. To try to set the record straight, we have compiled the most popular of these myths and their truthful counterparts. Be sure to pass along the information to the active sportsmen and women in your classes.

GETTING DOWN TO BASICS

Whether one is a weekend or full-time athlete, eating a varied diet from the Basic Four food groups is very wise. That means two servings from the dairy group, two from the protein group, and four each from the grains/cereals and fruits/vegetables groups. Vegetarian athletes should follow the same basic plan, choosing combinations of dried beans, nuts, eggs, and dairy products, along with grains for their protein quota. A strict vegetarian diet (minus the eggs and dairy foods) should be avoided; it is deficient in Vitamin B_{12}, and can possibly cause the development of anemia and muscle weakness.

Once the basic nutrient needs have been met, foods should be added, and portions increased, to meet the increased caloric demands of the athlete. As one engages in more exercise, more calories can be taken in; some athletes in training need 5000 calories per day, while others require only 1200.

FACT AND FANTASY

Is it possible that eating steak before a game will give a football player a winning edge? Can oranges improve a runner's performance? Parents, coaches, and amateur and professional athletes alike believe that eating certain foods can help an athlete win a game or meet. Let's see how these beliefs hold up.

MYTH: Protein is the most essential of all nutrients for the athlete.

FACT: Of the six classes of nutrients—proteins, fats, carbohydrates, vitamins, minerals, and water—water is really the most essential! This important fluid is the medium for all chemical processes, including the production of energy. The evaporation of water through perspiration serves as a means of controlling body temperature and eliminating waste. Therefore, the body's supply of water must be constantly replenished, especially during sweat-producing activities. (More about this later.) However, all the nutrients are equally important for maintaining health.

MYTH: Protein is necessary for meeting the energy demands of heavy exercise, and it is the athlete's best energy source.

FACT: Muscular activity does not increase the need for protein. However, small additional amounts may be needed by growing athletes and those involved in sports where trauma may occur (i.e. football). Actually, carbohydrate foods, at four calories per gram, are the most efficient and readily available sources of energy. Protein foods are the least efficient. Although some of the amino acids in protein do play important roles in energy production, they must first be converted to carbohydrates. Excess protein can even cause dehydration.

MYTH: Eat a candy bar or sweet food to give you an energy boost before or during exercise.

FACT: Although sugary foods provide carbohydrates for energy, it is nutritionally better to eat complex carbohydrate foods. These include potatoes, beans, bread, rice, corn, and other whole-grain products. Along with fruits and vegetables, these complex carbohydrate foods should comprise at least 50 percent of the diet. As a bonus, fruits and vegetables are valuable sources of water.

MYTH: High-fiber vegetables—including celery, lettuce, and cabbage—are valuable foods in the athlete's diet.

FACT: These foods provide mostly bulk to the diet, contributing very little energy. Athletes with high-energy demands can include small amounts of these foods, but should concentrate on other sources of complex carbohydrates.

MYTH: Swimming and football are the activities that burn up the most calories per minute.

FACT: The amount of energy expended, or calories burned in an activity depends upon the person's size and the effort with which the exercise is performed. Smaller people usually expend less energy than larger ones. Check this chart to see the approximate number of calories burned per minute in the following activities:

ACTIVITY	CALORIES PER MINUTE
Climbing	11-12
Cycling (5 mph)	4-5
(13 mph)	11
Dancing	4-7
Football	10
Golf	5
Jogging	11
Jumping Rope	15-20
Running (10 mph)	18-20
Skiing	15
Swimming	7-11
Tennis	7-10
Walking (3 mph)	3-5
Volleyball	3-7

MYTH: All athletes perform best on a balanced diet.

FACT: Different types of activity rely on different energy-producing systems and foods. While most physically active people can get immediate energy from the muscle cells, this supply is often exhausted through long-term exercise. Therefore, endurance athletes must draw from a second energy source called "glycogen," which is stored in the muscles and liver. Glycogen is actually made in the body from glucose, the simple sugar.

MYTH: Therefore, all endurance athletes should build up their glycogen supply before competition.

FACT: Sports that demand intense muscle exertion for periods of time, such as wrestling, marathon running, and middle-distance swimming, are especially dependent on muscle glycogen stores. Dr. Nathan Smith of the University of Washington, and other athletic-nutrition specialists, have found that these stores can be increased significantly if a high-carbohydrate regimen is introduced during the week preceding competition. This is often referred to as the "High Performance Diet" or "Carbohydrate Loading." Basically, this diet consists of eating mostly proteins and fats for the first 2½ days during the week before a competition, accompanied by exercising the specific muscles involved in the sport. Beginning on the third day, a high-carbohydrate, low-salt, low-fiber diet is followed until the day of competition. (For more details, see Dr. Smith's book, *Food for Sport*, Bull Publishing, 1976). It is very important to follow this regimen under a coach's supervision, and it should be tried by endurance athletes only.

MYTH: Athletes should fast on the day of competition.

FACT: Fasting is never recommended. However, since it is easier to compete on an empty stomach, it is advisable to eat lightly about 2½ hours before a competition. Again, nonbulky, starchy foods will provide the most efficient source of energy and the least chance of stomach upset; fatty foods stay in the digestive tract too long and high-protein foods tend to dehydrate the system.

MYTH: Coffee and tea prevent dehydration and maximize athletic performance.

FACT: Keeping the body full of fluids (hydrated) is very important to both the casual and competitive athlete. But coffee and tea contain caffeine—a substance that can overstimulate the young athlete. Two to three glasses of some beverage should be included in the pregame meal—water, fruit juice, and fruit-flavored drinks are recommended. Juicy fruits such as peaches, plums, and nectarines can be eaten as well. All these liquids maintain an adequate supply of body water to regulate temperature.

MYTH: Thirst is a good indicator of the need for water.

FACT: A competitive athlete in training might be in real need of body water but not be thirsty. Aside from perspiration and urination, there is a constant water loss through the skin and normal breathing. To keep check on this subtle water loss, all athletes should consume plenty of water before, during, and after a workout.

MYTH: Athletes should take salt tablets to replace the salt lost in perspiring.

FACT: Even during heavy perspiring, salt replacement is rarely needed. Normally, we get enough salt in our food supply to compensate for this loss. In fact, too much salt might prevent the availability of water needed during vigorous exercise. If water loss should exceed 5 to 10 pounds in one period of time, however, Dr. Smith suggests drinking one quart of water to which 1/3 teaspoon salt has been added for replacement. *Always* take plenty of water along with the extra salt, and avoid salt tablets.

MYTH: Vitamin and protein supplements help athletes perform better.

FACT: As long as athletes eat a wide variety of foods, they do not need to take vitamin supplements. And contrary to popular belief, vitamins do not contribute energy to the diet. Protein supplements are worthless in this respect as well.

ATHLETIC NEEDS

Nutrition for the Athlete

by Laurence Hursh, M.D.

There are few reasons for the athlete to deviate from a regular diet based on age, height, ideal weight, and activity. The average diet pattern is 15 percent protein, 40 percent fat, and 45 percent carbohydrate. Athletes remain in good physical and clinical condition on this diet.

Diets higher than 15 percent protein may result in osmotic problems, especially in hot weather or when water is limited. More than 45 percent carbohydrate in the diet results in an osmotic deficit so the athlete has difficulty retaining water. Diets containing more than 40 percent fat lead to ketosis—which may not interfere with performance, but is an abnormal state. Improved athletic performance has not been demonstrated when a liquid rather than a solid diet is used.

Glycogen Loading

Oxygen from the blood stream is delivered to muscles and tissues and assists in converting chemical energy into mechanical energy for muscle movement. In prolonged exhausting exercise, there is a decreased supply of oxygen to the muscles.

Carefully controlled studies of energy and physical performance permit several valid conclusions: 1) Protein is not used as a source of energy during any kind of exercise; 2) fats are the primary source of energy during light to moderate exercise, 3) carbohydrates are the primary energy source in vigorous prolonged exercise.

The determining factor as to whether fats or carbohydrates will be utilized is the amount of oxygen available to the muscle. When plenty of oxygen is present, fats are used. The greater the oxygen debt of the muscle, the more likely carbohydrates will be used as the source of energy.

Another conclusion also is valid. The higher the glycogen stores in the muscle, the greater the ability to perform heavy, prolonged exercise. When the glycogen stores of the muscles are exhausted it is impossible to continue to work at the same rate as when glycogen stores are available. Finally, the level of glycogen stores can be altered by the type of diet consumed.

The recommended regime for any endurance event exceeding 30 to 60 minutes is as follows:

1. One week prior to the "event" (day 1—Saturday), exercise those same muscles to be used in the event to exhaustion, thus depleting the muscles of all glycogen.
2. For the next three days (Sunday, Monday, and Tuesday) the diet should be fat and protein exclusively, thus keeping the glycogen content low. Sunday exercise should be a light to moderate workout. Monday and Tuesday should include a heavy workout.
3. For the next three days (Wednesday, Thursday, and Friday) the athlete should continue to eat the same amount of fat and protein but add large quantities of carbohydrates (so the composition of the diet consists of 68 percent carbohydrates). Wednesday's exercise may be a moderate workout, but Thursday and Friday should be very light.
4. On the day of competition (day 8—Saturday) the athlete should eat whatever he desires, whatever he thinks will help him to win.

Eating and Game Time

What about the breakfast, lunch, game interval? Consensus is that performance is more comfortable when the athlete's stomach is empty. In general, a three-hour interval from time of consumption is adequate to accomplish this goal. The player follows a fairly predictable schedule five days a week. He eats breakfast at 7:00 to 8:00 a.m., lunch at noon, and he is on the field at 3:00 to 4:00 p.m. Saturday, however, is never the same as the other five days. Saturday, the player becomes a prima donna. He is wined and dined on steak, honey, and you name it. He doesn't play at 4:00 p.m., but at 2:00 p.m. and sometimes as early as 1:00 p.m.

While I have no solid data, it is my belief that if the player observed the same time interval between breakfast and lunch that he did during the week, he would provide the same performance on Saturday as he did the other days of the week. The time to treat him as a prima donna (win or lose) is after the game, not before. What I am proposing is that on the day of competition, he have his usual or desired breakfast at, for example, 6:00 a.m., lunch as desired at 10:00 a.m. if the game is at 1:00 p.m. or at 11:00 a.m. if the game is at 2:00 p.m.

Psychological Aspects of Food

When athletes win, they often attribute it to a certain sequence of events such as the type of meal that preceded the event. They then have a tendency to follow the same routine for the next event. While we know of no reason why a special food provides this kind of benefit, we also know that the

---

From *School Foodservice Journal*, Vol. 32, No. 9, October 1978, pp. 61-63. Copyright 1978, American School Food Service Association. Reprinted with permission.

power of the mind or the strength of one's convictions is such that if we deprive athletes of a food they believe is essential to performance, chances are they will lose the contest.

Height-Weight Tables

A cautionary note about the hazard of using the standard desirable height and weight tables to determine if an athlete is under or over weight is in order. Many athletes are classified as being overweight when fatness is determined by specific gravity. Allow a "fudge factor" so you do not penalize the athlete who is really lean. In general, athletes will consume only enough calories to maintain their weight when on a vigorous physical conditioning program.

Likewise, the same type of physique does not lend itself to all types of performance. The long distance runner who does best is a lean, thin, wiry individual who has little weight to carry and an efficient muscular system. The weight lifter is one who is usually overweight by the usual standards of the height and weight tables. The long distance runner probably would do poorly at weight lifting, while the weight lifter would do poorly at long distance running. It is as equally erroneous to try to put weight on the underweight miler as it is to take weight off the weight lifter.

Coaching is an art in which only a few are sufficiently versed to be outstanding. It's the same as in any other profession. It is the coach's responsibility to determine where a particular athlete functions best. For too long a time we've had an armchair philosophy that the athlete who is all muscle without an ounce of fat is the athlete who performs best. This is fallacious. The only way to determine who performs best is to play the game; the proof of the pudding is in the eating.

Water Discipline

To get the best performance from athletes they must drink more water than their thirst demands and at as frequent intervals as possible. I know it's not easy to do this as many people have been brought up under the concept that too much water in the belly will water log the athlete and adversely affect his performance. This is utter nonsense.

Ingestion of 1.0 to 1.5 liters of water five minutes before exercise had no adverse effect on heart rate and minute volume of ventilation during mill running nor on performance time in swimming and track events. It is suggested that, except in the case of the occasional athlete who suffers nausea, there is no physiological justification for rigid restrictions of water intake in athletic contests.

Because under the most favorable circumstances man tends to voluntarily dehydrate, athletes should be encouraged to drink more water than they want, especially during periods of prolonged activity. Dehydration places stress on the circulatory system, partly because of the decrease in blood volume. This stress is reflected in rises in pulse rate and body temperature. External symptoms include generalized discomfort, fatigue, apathy, low morale, and unwillingness and inability to undertake strenuous activity. These symptoms become evident after the dehydration has reached 2 percent of the body weight.

As soon as a person loses 2 percent of his body weight in perspiration performance declines. For a 200-pound football player, this is only four pounds. A player putting out any effort at all has lost four pounds by the end of the first half of a football game. You expect this athlete to perform the same in the second half, but in this case he doesn't have enough blood volume.

What happens when an athlete is perspiring profusely and takes salt tablets? He normally takes only a small amount of water to swallow the tablets so he has hyperosmotic solution of salt in the gut. The salt cannot be absorbed (nor can the water for that matter) until the osmotic pressure of the solution in the gut is equal to that of the blood. The gut must, therefore, get more water to dilute this solution. The only place it has to get water is from the vascular tree that is already depleted because of heavy perspiration.

Accordingly, more water is pulled out of the vascular tree compromising the cardiovascular system even more, so the athlete is now in real trouble. Forget the salt tablets; water is all that is needed and lots of it. The squirt bottle will never get the job done. Offer the athlete 16 to 32 ounces at a time and do so frequently, every 30 to 60 minutes. Let them drink all they can hold, then ask them to drink a little bit more.

Some have raised the question of adverse effects from drinking cold water when overheated. There have been few controlled studies on this matter, but of those reported, no adverse effect has been demonstrated. There is no special cooling effect to be gained by drinking cold water, but there is some evidence that consumption of cold water will reduce the rate of perspiration so the overall balance is to raise the body temperature. Accordingly, there may be some minor benefit in drinking warm water. My personal opinion is that the temperature of the water is inconsequential other than that it is refreshing and the players have a strong desire for it.

Heat Exhaustion

Antihistamines have been blamed in the past for contributing to heat exhaustion and heat stroke. I have had no personal experience with this, but believe it is a possibility even though it is somewhat remote. Most antihistamines have the ability to block cholinergic nerve impulses that result in perspiration. They also have a tendency to be antagonistic to the anticholinesterases that also would result in reducing perspiration.

I think that neither of these actions are of any major concern except in the rare case where the player is unusually sensitive to these actions of the medication. Trainers and coaches, however, should be aware of all players who might be taking antihistamines for whatever reasons (allergies, poison ivy, etc.) and be alert to the greater possibility of heat exhaustion in these players.

Summary

In general, the diet providing the best performance for the athlete contains 15 percent protein, 40 percent fat, and 45 percent carbohydrate. There are two possible exceptions to this rule. One is when exercise is to be exhausting and prolonged (30 to 60 minutes), and the other is when one is performing at high altitude (14,000 feet). In these two instances, there is now sufficient data to suggest that performance will be improved if the athlete consumes a diet composed of at least 68 to 70 percent carbohydrate according to the following schedule:
- Day 1: Exhaust the muscles of all glycogen.
- Day 2: Regular diet, low in carbohydrate; heavy exercise.
- Days 5, 6, and 7: 68 percent carbohydrate diet; very light exercise.
- Day 8: Eat as desired prior to contest.

At the same time one should not disregard the athlete's food preferences that may play a decisive psychological role in his performance. Breakfast, lunch, and performance intervals should be similar on the day of the event to what they are during the days of practice.

Remember, standard desirable height-weight tables were not designed for the athlete and should be used with caution, recognizing that many athletes will rank in the overweight category erroneously. The idea that the athlete who is all muscle without an ounce of fat does best is not necessarily true for all events.

Finally, don't forget the importance of water. The athlete must drink more water than his thirst demands because man has a tendency to dehydrate himself voluntarily. As soon as an athlete loses 2 percent of body weight by perspiring, a stress is placed on the circulatory system that is reflected by rise in pulse rate and body temperature. External symptoms then include generalized discomfort, fatigue, apathy, low morale, and an unwillingness and inability to undertake strenuous activity. The concept that water intake prior to or during an event is harmful to the athlete is erroneous. Likewise the use of salt tablets is more likely to be harmful than beneficial. Special drinks on the market for athletes have nothing more to offer than plain water. Finally, the temperature of the drinking water is immaterial. Simply insist and require the players to drink more water than they require.

Dr. Hursh's presentation was given at the March 1978 "Nutrition for the Athlete" symposium sponsored by the Bismarck-Mandan (N.D.) Nutrition Council, North Dakota State Department of Health, and North Dakota Dietetic Association.

CANCER

An Update on Nutrition, Diet, and Cancer

by National Dairy Council

SUMMARY

The relationships of nutrition, diet, and cancer can be viewed from three perspectives: (1) diet as a factor in cancer causation; (2) the effect of cancer and its treatment on nutritional status; and (3) nutritional management of the cancer patient. Various types of studies (epidemiologic, animal, case control) have described a number of highly suggestive associations between diet and cancer in humans, but there is as yet no absolute proof of a direct cause/effect relationship. The role that ingestion of food-borne carcinogens or carcinogen precursors has in causing major human cancers remains to be determined. It is likely that diet has an indirect role, modifying carcinogenesis. Several mechanisms are advanced to explain this effect. For example, it is theorized that excess dietary fat may promote carcinogenesis via its influence on altering bile acid production and/or gut microflora development in colon cancer, and secretion of endocrine glands in breast cancer. Although there is probably no specific "preventive" diet for cancer, it may be advisable to eat a variety of foods, adjust energy intake to energy expenditure, and avoid moldy food, a deficiency of certain nutrients (e.g., vitamin A) and known dietary carcinogens such as alcohol. Cancer per se exerts both systemic effects (e.g., cachexia) and localized effects (e.g., malabsorption due to pancreatic insufficiency) which can lead to profound nutritional problems for the cancer patient. In addition, specific treatment modalities (e.g., surgery, radiotherapy, and chemotherapy), used singly or in combination, may compromise the patient's nutritional status. Malnutrition need not be a necessary condition for the cancer patient. Advantages of nutritional intervention via oral, enteral, or intravenous hyperalimentation include improved well-being, enhanced weight gain, improvement in immunocompetence, and potentially a better response of the tumor to oncologic treatment. The effect of nutritional support on the overall outcome for the cancer patient is unknown. A concern is the possibility that nutritional support may harm the host by promoting tumor growth. Consequently, it is recommended that nutritional intervention be accompanied by adequate antitumor treatment. To date, there is insufficient evidence to support the suggestion that megadoses or reduced amounts of any essential nutrient, or removal of any normal dietary component, prevents cancer or has a useful role in its treatment in human beings.

Cancer (i.e., malignant tumors or neoplasms) is the second leading cause of death in the United States, exceeded only by cardiovascular disease (1). In 1980, all cancers are expected to claim the lives of 405,000 individuals (1,2). Although the age-adjusted mortality rate from lung cancer (the most prevalent type) has been increasing, that from colon-rectum and breast cancers (the next most common types) has leveled off (2). Carcinogenesis (or tumorigenesis) is a multifaceted process, its initiation and promotion influenced by genetics, life-style, cultural patterns, health status, exposure to specific carcinogens and other unknown factors (3). As such, it is no longer viewed as a single disease with a single etiology (4). Of great interest, and an area of active research, is the relationship between the incidence of cancer at particular sites and certain nutritional imbalances (3-12). It is emphasized, however, that a direct cause/effect relationship between diet and cancer in humans has not been firmly

---

From *Dairy Council Digest*, Vol. 51, No. 5, pp. 25-30. Copyright 1980, National Dairy Council. Reprinted with permission.

established (13,14). It is the purpose of this *Digest* to update information presented in the previous *Digest* (15) on the role of nutrition and diet in the etiology of cancer. In addition, nutritional problems induced by cancer per se and its treatment modalities, as well as the nutritional management of the cancer patient will be discussed.

NUTRITION, DIET, AND CANCER ETIOLOGY

Types of Evidence. Sources of information implicating diet in specific forms of cancer include epidemiological surveys, experiments using animal models, and, to a lesser extent, case control studies in humans (5). According to some epidemiologists, 80 to 90% of cancer incidence in the United States can be attributed to specific environmental factors, and diet and nutrition are related to 60% of all cancers in women and over 40% in men (6, 9-11,16,17). Correlations between cancer incidence and dietary habits are evident from migrant population studies in which cancer incidence patterns of migrants change from that of their native country to that common to the population of the host country (e.g., Japanese who migrate to the U.S.A.); special population groups that live in the same environment but adhere to different dietary habits (e.g., Seventh-Day Adventists in California who follow a unique vegetarian diet); geographical or world-wide high/low correlations; and trends in incidence over time (9,10,16,18-20). Epidemiologic correlations, however, do not establish causation (16). Furthermore, epidemiological studies do not pinpoint carcinogenic agents, particularly as a long latent period prior to the onset of cancer may be apparent. While laboratory work with animals allows strict control of dietary factors and the findings tend to corroborate epidemiological data, such findings cannot be extrapolated with assurance to man (5). Different species may respond in unique ways to the same dietary stimuli, and spontaneous tumors may react unlike those of experimentally induced tumors (12). Animal studies do, however, help to elucidate mechanisms by which environmental factors contribute to carcinogenesis.

Speculated Mechanisms of Carcinogenesis. Various hypothetical mechanisms by which diet and nutrition might influence human carcinogenesis have been reviewed (5,9,10,12,18,19,21-24). Current evidence reveals that dietary patterns or certain nutritional deficiencies or excesses, as opposed to ingestion of specific carcinogens or carcinogen precursors (either naturally occurring in food or present as additives) are more important in the diet: cancer relationship (5,9). In terms of the latter, however, saccharin and sodium nitrite are of special concern (13,25).

Saccharin, the only nonnutritive artificial sweetener approved for use in the United States, has been demonstrated to cause malignant bladder tumors in rats fed high doses. According to findings of a National Academy of Sciences (NAS) study, saccharin is a carcinogen of low potency relative to other carcinogens in rats and a potential carcinogen in humans but of unknown risk (26). And the National Cancer Institute (NCI) and FDA concluded, on the basis of a large-scale epidemiologic study, that there was no increased risk of bladder cancer among users of artificial sweeteners in the study population. The sweetener, however, was hazardous for persons who were both heavy smokers and heavy users of saccharin (27). Some industries, organizations such as the American Diabetes Association (28), and consumer groups, insist that saccharin is essential for use in diabetes, obesity, and other health problems. As it stands, the moratorium on the saccharin ban has been extended until June 30, 1981 (25) with the need to find a substitute for saccharin emphasized (28).

The question of banning sodium nitrite, an additive used to preserve, flavor, and color foods such as cured meats, continues to be debated (13,25). Nitrosamines, formed under certain conditions from the combination of nitrite (either added to food or produced by the bacterial reduction of nitrates in the body) with naturally occuring secondary amines, are potent carcinogens for laboratory animals (29). Direct evidence that nitrosamines are carcinogenic for humans is lacking (30). Moreover, the importance of sodium nitrite for preventing botulism is well recognized (25). Nevertheless, FDA and USDA favor a gradual phasing out of nitrites in certain products, the timing dependent on how soon a chemical substitute can be found (25). Of note is the possible anticarcinogenic potential of antioxidants such as vitamin C (5,24). As an active reducing agent, it has been shown to interact with nitrates (the main sources being vegetables and drinking water) or nitrites inhibiting nitrosamine formation. In fact, the steady decline in stomach cancer in the United States over the past 50 years has been hypothesized to be due to the year-round availability of vitamin C-rich foods and refrigeration of foods which both inhibits reduction of nitrate to nitrite and lessens the amount of sodium nitrite preservative needed in foods (5,13,22).

Foods and nutrients appear to modify rather than to initiate the carcinogenic process (5,12,21). Also, the way in which diet affects carcinogenesis may differ for distinct types of cancer (22). The presence or absence of specific dietary constituents has been shown to influence carcinogenic activity (5,12). Restriction of energy intake or underfeeding decreases the development of spontaneous and transplanted tumors in experimental animals (3,5,9,31,32). This raises the question of whether obesity, the converse of undernutrition, augments carcinogenesis. Obesity seems to be associated with only two types of human cancer, endometrium and kidney cancer in women (21). Breast cancer may also be associated but the evidence is less clear. Other dietary deficiencies (e.g., vitamin A, riboflavin, protein, iodide, pyridoxine, magnesium, and iron) augment specific types of chemically-induced tumors in experimental animals (5,6). And increased amounts of dietary fat have been positively correlated with the development of colonic and mammary tumors on exposure to certain carcinogens (5,9,21).

Dietary and nutritional factors may protect against tumorigenesis by inactivating carcinogens or inhibiting early stages of carcinogenic activity (5). For example, various indoles present in vegetables of the Brassicaceae family (e.g., Brussels sprouts, cabbage, broccoli) induce drug metabolizing (microsomal oxidase) enzymes located in the epithelium of the gastrointestinal tract, lungs, and skin, thereby inactivating primary carcinogens (3,5,9). On the other hand, specific nutrient deficiencies may depress these enzymes, reducing the body's defense against chemical carcinogens (33). Nutrients which have antioxidant properties (e.g., vitamins E and C) may inhibit carcinogens. The value of vitamin E in this respect is unknown (5). Of special interest is the potential protective role of vitamin A and related compounds in inhibiting tumor growth (3,5,7a,33-37). Fat-soluble vitamin A, which plays an important role in epithelial cell differentiation, is toxic at pharmacologic doses, therefore synthetic retinoid analogs have been developed. These are more effective in preventing precancerous lesions, less toxic, and have a different tissue distribution than natural retinoids with greater concentration in epithelial tissues. The efficacy of synthetic retinoids in preventing environmentally induced epithelial cancers in humans is an area of active research.

Another important way in which nutrition and specific dietary constituents may influence cancer incidence is via the immune system (3,5). Immune processes, which are affected by nutrition, appear to be involved in removal of precancerous and cancerous cells, and in the resistance of concurrent infection (3,5). Other possible mechanisms are reviewed in the following discussions of colon and breast cancers.

Colon Cancer. Colon and rectal carcinomas, collectively, are the second most frequently diagnosed cancer by site in the United States, excluding common skin cancers (1). Epidemiological data reveal that environmental factors, in particular a Western-type diet high in fat and protein and low in fiber, is involved in the etiology of colon cancer (as distinct from cancer of the rectum) (5,7b). Worldwide, colon cancer incidence and mortality display wide geographical variations. With the exception of Japan and to a lesser extent Finland, the more economically developed a society (e.g., United States, Canada, Western Europe), the greater the incidence of colon cancer (7b). Developing countries such as Africa and Asia show relatively low incidence rates. Migrant studies also support an environmental influence. Colon cancer mortality progressively increases in a population within a relatively short time (i.e., in first generation migrants) in Japanese born and living in Japan, those migrating to Hawaii, and those of Japanese descent born in Hawaii (5,24,38). Also, an increasing trend in colon cancer in Japan is attributed to a general increase in the Westernization of that country's diet (7b,22). There is also an associated fall in gastric cancer at the present time in Japan (5). The above correlations suggesting a strong environmental influence in the etiology of colon cancer have led to numerous epidemiological and experimental studies designed to identify specific dietary constituents (5,7b). Geographical correlations between increased colon cancer frequency and mortality and high dietary fat consumption have been observed (39,40). Also, Seventh-Day Adventists in California whose diet contains little fat experience a colon cancer incidence 50 to 70% of that of the general American population (41). Mormon and non-Mormons in Utah likewise show a lower colon cancer incidence (42), but little difference in fat and fiber consumption is evident between the Utah population and the United States as a whole (43). The relationship of specific dietary components to colon cancer etiology remains unsettled (44).

If diet (in particular, fat) has a role in colon cancer etiology, an important question concerns its mode of action. The current working hypothesis is that high dietary fat intake (i) increases bile secretion and hence bile acids and neutral steroids in the large bowel, and (ii) influences the composition and metabolic activity of the intestinal microflora such that the latter contains an increase in anaerobic clostridia capable of converting bile acids and neutral sterols (primary bile acids) by dehydrogenation to carcinogen or cocarcinogen compounds (secondary bile acids) (7b). Although a specific carcinogen has not been identified for colon carcinogenesis in humans (4), experimental studies in animal models and metabolic studies in man have been carried out to examine the above hypothesis (7b). Substantial support for dietary fat and for the colon cancer-enhancing effects of secondary bile acids (e.g., deoxycholic acid and lithocholic acid) has come from a variety of animal studies (7b).

In humans, the relationship between diet and bile acids and neutral steroids is less clear. On the one hand, significant increases are reported in the fecal concentration of bile acids and neutral sterols and fecal bacterial flora in various populations with high colon cancer mortality; in populations consuming a high-fat mixed Western-type diet versus a vegetarian diet; and in volunteers receiving a high-fat diet versus a low-fat diet. Similarly, in patients with colon cancer, these fecal constituents are elevated. These findings have been reviewed in detail elsewhere (5,7b,45-47). In contrast, other investigators (48-52) have not shown a significant change in the fecal microflora content and composition with diet, or in patients with carcinoma of the colon or in persons at risk of colon cancer compared with controls. Assessment of the total metabolic activity of the intestinal microflora may be a better means of determining relative risk of colon cancer (50). Diet and other environmental factors can modify the metabolic activity of fecal flora (50). Specific bacterial enzymes (e.g., B-glucuronidase, nitroreductase, and 7-alpha-dehydroxylase), known to catalyze reactions that result in the formation of proximal carcinogens, can be elevated by a Western-type diet, and decreased by dietary supplements of *Lactobacillus acidophilus* (47,53-56). It is suggested that the lower colon cancer incidence in Finland (where fat intake is relatively high) may be due to the Finns' higher consumption of dairy products and the greater numbers of lactobacilli harbored in their fecal microflora (4,56). Other investigators place emphasis on the high dietary fiber intake by the Finnish population as a factor contributing to their lower risk of colon cancer (4,57). Several mechanisms by which dietary fiber may exert a protective role in colon cancer have been advanced (13,58-62). However, study of the effect of dietary fiber in colon cancer etiology is complicated by the complex nature of this dietary component (i.e., not all types of fiber have the same biological properties) (63-65).

Breast Cancer. Breast cancer, a hormone-dependent malignant tumor of mammary tissue, is the leading cause of cancer mortality among women in industrialized countries (Japan being an exception) (1). Similar to colon cancer, indirect evidence is available from epidemiologic and animal studies showing an association between the environment and risk of breast cancer (5,7c,24,66-69). Unlike other major cancers, change in incidence of breast cancer upon migration from a low-risk country (e.g., Japan) to a high-risk country (e.g., United States) is not apparent until the second generation (i.e., children of the immigrants) as opposed to being evident in the immigrants themselves (70). This suggests that mammary tissue may be more sensitive to etiologic factors of breast cancer at times of active cell proliferation (i.e., time of puberty or during teenage years) (22,66,68).

Both the amount and type of dietary fat are of importance in promoting mammary tumors in experimental animals (71,72), but conclusions cannot be drawn as to what type of fat (i.e., saturated versus unsaturated) is a more potent stimulus of tumor genesis (66,67). A certain amount of polyunsaturated fatty acids as well as a high level of dietary fat appears to be necessary to enhance mammary tumorigenesis in rats exposed to a carcinogen (71). This finding deserves further investigation.

Greater risk of breast cancer has been associated with conditions influencing endocrine status — increased body height and weight, first pregnancy after 30 years of age, early menarche, and late menopause (5,66,67,73). Gray et al (73) propose that some of the effects of diet on breast cancer may be mediated through the influence of diet on these known risk factors. Diet also may promote or inhibit breast cancer by modifying hormones (e.g., androgens, prolactin, estrogens, and possibly other hormones), particularly as hormone patterns are determined in part by diet (18,66,67,73). One theory proposed is that a high-fat diet increases serum prolactin, or more specifically the prolactin: estrogen ratio which in turn promotes mammary tumors (74,75). While it has been reported that a high-fat diet elevates plasma prolactin in experimental animals exposed to a carcinogen, and that a vegetarian diet decreases the nocturnal release of prolactin in women (76,77), the relation of diet modification to hormone activity and to the development or promotion of breast cancer remains unclear (66). There is little evidence to suggest that hormones, particularly prolactin, are primary carcinogens for human breast cancer (67). Not unlike colon cancer, evidence relating diet to breast cancer is circumstantial (67,78).

Prevention. The suggestion has been made, similar to that for prevention of cardiovascular disease, that modification of our present dietary intake might decrease cancer incidence. Unfortunately, this suggestion has given rise to a number of food fallacies and quackery with extravagant claims regarding cancer preventive, curative, and causative properties of various dietary constituents (79).

Adoption of a "prudent" diet, one low in energy, total fats (not to exceed 35% of total energy intake), saturated fat (not to exceed 10% of total energy intake), and cholesterol (not to exceed 300 mg daily) has been recommended to lessen the risk of cancer (4,7b,18,21,24). An even stricter type of a "prudent" diet — cholesterol intake not to exceed 100 mg daily and total fat intake to constitute no more than 20% of total energy intake — is recommended to prevent those cancers in which dietary fat is implicated (7b,18,21).

Presently, information is incomplete to predict the efficacy of major changes in food habits and dietary composition in terms of cancer prevention (9). Of more serious consideration is the possibility that such changes may potentiate carcinogenesis. Preliminary findings from four epidemiologic studies have disclosed an association between low blood cholesterol levels (below 180 mg/dl) and increased mortality from various types of cancer (80). Confirmation of this cholesterol/cancer connection is being actively pursued by the National Heart, Lung and Blood Institute and the NCI (80). Guidance on this issue of diet and cancer prevention is provided by the Food and

Nutrition Board, NAS: "Clearly, a nutritious diet providing adequate amounts of all nutrients and the proper energy content to achieve desirable weight is important for general health and for vigorous defense mechanisms against cancer as well as other diseases" (14).

NUTRITIONAL IMPACT OF CANCER AND ITS TREATMENT

Cancer per se and its various treatments can have profound negative effects on the nutritional status of the cancer patient (7,81-88). Malnutrition can be a most disabling aspect of this disease, not only reducing the patient's quality of life, but contributing to morbidity and mortality (88,89).

The interrelation of cancer and nutrition has been described in terms of both systemic effects of cancer and localized tumor effects (81-83). Cancer cachexia is a most frequent accompaniment of late, advanced cancer, affecting one-third to two-thirds of cancer patients (7d, 83,84). This complex metabolic problem of uncertain etiology is characterized clinically by marked anorexia (decrease or lack of appetite), early satiety, weight loss, wasting, and weakness (81,84). In patients with advanced malignant disease it is a major cause of mortality. Cancer itself and its treatment contribute to this syndrome (84).

Neoplasms exert a number of localized effects resulting in nutritional problems (81-86). These are tabulated by Shils (81). Interference with food intake, due to partial or complete obstruction of one or more sites of the gastrointestinal tract, is viewed as the most common cause of malnutrition in this general category (81). Maldigestion or malabsorption associated with various conditions (e.g., pancreatic insufficiency) concomitant with neoplastic diseases can lead to deficiencies of a variety of nutrients (81,85,86).

Although a tumor "toxin" has not been unequivocally identified, tumors may secrete a number of potent pharmacologic substances (ectopic hormones) such as hormone peptides, kinins, and prostaglandins (81-83). These, in turn, may produce systemic effects that disturb the patient's nutritional status (81,82). Other localized tumor effects evident in advanced cancer include fluid and electrolyte disturbances (generally due to vomiting and diarrhea), hypoalbuminemia and anemia, and depressed serum and tissue levels of vitamins and minerals (81,83).

Specific treatment modalities (e.g., surgery, radiotherapy, and chemotherapy), used singly or in combination to eradicate the tumor, may predispose, by way of their effects on normal tissues, to various nutritional problems. Effects of surgery are numerous and varied (7e,81,82). Ensuing nutritional problems depend both on the site and extent of the surgical intervention. Radical surgical operations on the head and neck region, for example, may contribute to malnutrition via interference with mastication and swallowing (7e,81,83). Radiotherapy likewise can compromise the patient's nutritional status, the nutritional sequelae dependent on dose and region irradiated (7f,90). Without specific dietary intervention, 88 to 92% of patients receiving high-dose radiation experience significant weight loss (7f,82,83). Mucosal surfaces of the head and neck region are sensitive to radiation, thus radiotherapy to this area leads to loss of taste sensation ("mouth blindness"), xerostomia (dry mouth), loss of teeth and worsening of dental caries, and difficulty in chewing and swallowing (dysphagia) (7f,81,82).

Most chemotherapeutic agents, while effective against various malignancies, adversely affect dietary intake as a result of anorexia, nausea, vomiting, mucositis, and, to a lesser extent, diarrhea (7f,82,83,90). The effect depends on the type of drug or combination of drugs used, duration of treatment, rates of metabolism, and individual susceptibility (90). Some chemotherapeutic agents are antimetabolites, and some, like 5-fluorouracil, produce a sprue-like syndrome and increase the requirement for certain vitamins such as thiamin (81,90,91). If chemotherapy is prolonged, as is often the case, weight loss and progressive debility may be severe (81). Although only limited data are available, nutritional complications may be magnified by a combination of treatments (e.g., chemotherapy-radiotherapy) (82,90).

NUTRITIONAL MANAGEMENT

Due to effective antitumor treatments, cancer is increasingly becoming a chronic or protracted illness (81). As such, correction of malnutrition and its consequences is of utmost importance to improve the cancer patient's quality of life (81,92,93). Shils (81,94), summarizing principles of nutritional therapy, states foremost that malnutrition need not be a necessary condition for the cancer patient. Nutritional therapy is described as being supportive, adjunctive, or definitive (81,94). Preliminary evidence indicates some advantages of nutritional support for the cancer patient, including improved sense of well-being and better preservation of tissue function and repair, and improvement in immunocompetence. Also, the well nourished patient may be better able to undergo pharmacological, radiological and surgical therapies when compared to his/her malnourished counterpart (12,89,92-97). However, whether nutritional support results in an overall improvement in outcome for the cancer patient is not proven. A concern which has been expressed is that nutritional support might harm the host by promoting growth of the tumor (81,83,98). Tumors have been shown to grow slowly in malnourished animals (83). And while patients do not generally exhibit explosive tumor growth during periods of improved nutrition, it is likely that tumor cells, like non-tumor cells, depend on good nutrition (81). Therefore, it is recommended that nutritional support be accompanied by adequate antitumor treatments (81,90).

A variety of nutrition intervention techniques, both oral and enteral, are available. Their advantages, contraindications, and methods of delivery are reviewed elsewhere (7e,96,99,100). Nutritional assessment is seen as the first step in the nutritional management of the patient presenting with cancer (81,83,87-89,96,101). Based on results of the nutritional assessment, a nutritional therapeutic program can be tailored to each individual's needs. Continual follow-up of the patient's nutritional status is emphasized (81).

The preferred route for nutritional support is the alimentary tract (i.e., oral feeding), although this often necessitates manipulation of diets to account for various eating problems of the patient such as anorexia and taste aversions (102,103). When oral feeding is contraindicated (e.g., ineffective alimentary tract or severe anorexia) two alternatives are available: tube feeding (chemically defined diets) and parenteral feeding (intravenous hyperalimentation [IVH]). Recent attention has centered on the use of IVH as a viable clinical procedure of delivery of adequate nutrition (81,87,89,104-106). There is increasing evidence that for cancer patients receiving IVH as adjunctive nutrition therapy, risk of sepsis is low and nutrition replenishment may be rapid (often within 10-20 days). Furthermore, tumor growth has not been stimulated by nutritional repletion in human beings (83,89,93,104-106). However, it should be emphasized that patient selection is an important factor in determining the success or failure of IVH (107), and the cost and requirement for a well-trained hyperalimentation team must be considered (83).

Unfortunately, a number of non-medical cancer treatments, many based on myths, and most unsupported by scientific evidence, are being practiced by those with cancer. Included in this category are megavitamin therapy (e.g., vitamin C), laetrile, pangamic acid, starving the tumor by starving oneself, and use of natural foods (79,108-111). At this time, there are many suggestive leads but still no conclusive evidence to indicate that reduced or excess amounts of any nutrient have a beneficial role in the treatment of cancer in humans (93,109,111).

Acknowledgments: National Dairy Council assumes the responsibility for writing and editing this publication. However, we would like to acknowledge the help and suggestions of the following reviewers in its preparation: E. M. Copeland, III, M.D., Professor, Department of Surgery, Texas Medical Center, Houston, Texas; R. S. Rivlin, M.D., Professor of Medicine and Chief of Nutrition, Memorial Sloan-Kettering Cancer Center and New York Hospital—Cornell Medical Center, New York, New York; and Staff of the Diet, Nutrition, and Cancer Program, National Cancer Institute, Bethesda, Maryland.

REFERENCES

1. USDA. *Healthy People. The Surgeon General's Report On Health Promotion And Disease Prevention.* USPHS, DHEW Publ. No. 79-55071, 1979.
2. American Cancer Society. *Cancer Facts & Figures 1980.* New York: American Cancer Society, Inc., 1979.
3. Petering, H.G. In: *Inorganic And Nutritional Aspects Of Cancer.* G.N. Schrauzer (Ed). New York: Plenum Press, 1978, pp. 207-223.
4. Wynder, E.L. Cancer *43:* 1955, 1979.
5. Shils, M.E. Med.Clin. North Am. *63:* 1027, 1979.
6. Rivlin, R.S. Cancer Res. *33:* 1977, 1973.
7. Winick, M. (Ed). *Nutrition And Cancer.* New York: John Wiley & Sons, 1977, (a) Sporn—p. 119; (b) Wynder and Reddy—p. 55; (c) Carroll—p. 25; (d) Theologides—p. 75; (e) Shils—p. 155; (f) Donaldson—p. 137.
8. Weisburger, J.H., B.S. Reddy, P. Hill, L.A. Cohen, E.L. Wynder, and N.E. Spingarn. Bull. N.Y. Acad. Med. *56:* 673, 1980.
9. Gori, G.B. Food Technol. *33:* 48, 1979.
10. Gori, G.B. Cancer *43:* 2151, 1979.
11. Wynder, E.L., and G.B. Gori. J. Natl. Cancer Inst. *58:* 825, 1977.
12. Alcantara, E.N., and E.W. Speckmann. Am.J.Clin.Nutr. *29:* 1035, 1976.
13. Upton, A.C., and D.J. Fink. *Statement on Diet, Nutrition and Cancer.* Hearing before the Subcommittee on Nutrition of the Committee on Agriculture, Nutrition, and Forestry, United States Senate. Oct. 2, 1979. Washington, D.C.: U.S. Gov't. Printing Office, 1980.
14. Food and Nutrition Board. *Toward Healthful Diets.* Washington, D.C.: National Academy of Sciences, National Research Council, 1980.
15. National Dairy Council. Dairy Council Digest *46:* 25, 1975.
16. Gori G.B. Nutrition and Cancer *1:* 5, 1978.
17. Wynder, E.L. Nature *268:* 284, 1977.
18. Wynder, E.L. J.Am.Diet.Assoc. *71:* 385, 1977.
19. Gori, G.B. Bull. Cancer (Paris) *65:* 115, 1978.
20. Gori, G.B. J.Am.Diet.Assoc. *71:* 375, 1977.
21. Wynder, E.L. Fed.Proc. *35:* 1309, 1976.
22. Weisburger, J.H. Cancer *43:* 1987, 1979.
23. Modan, B. Cancer *40:* 1887, 1977.
24. McMichael, A.J. Food & Nutr. Notes & Rev. *36:* 187, 1979.
25. Levey, B. National Food Review *8:* 44, 1979.
26. Assembly of Life Sciences, National Research Council and the Institute of Medicine. *Saccharin: Technical Assessment of Risks and Benefits—Part 1.* Washington, D.C.: National Academy of Sciences, 1978.
27. National Cancer Institute. *Progress Report to the Food and Drug Administration from the National Cancer Institute Concerning the National Bladder Cancer Study.* Bethesda, MD: NCI Office of Cancer Communications, 1980.
28. American Diabetes Association. Diabetes Care *2:* 380, 1979.
29. Newberne, P. Science *204:* 1079, 1979.
30. Fraser, P., C. Chilvers, V. Beral, and M.J. Hill. Int.J.Epidemiol. *9:* 3, 1980.
31. Tannenbaum, A. Cancer Res. *5:* 616, 1945.
32. Tannenbaum, A. In: *Physiopathology of Cancer.* F. Homburger (Ed). New York: Hoeber-Harper, 1959, pp. 517-562.
33. Calabrese, E.J. *Nutrition and Environmental Health.* Vol. 1. *The Vitamins.* New York: John Wiley & Sons, 1980.
34. Sporn, M.B., N.M. Dunlop, D.L. Newton, and J.M. Smith. Fed.Proc. *35:* 1332, 1976.
35. Anonymous. Nutr.Rev. *37:* 153, 1979.
36. Sporn, M.B., and D.L. Newton. Fed.Proc. *38:* 2528, 1979.
37. Mettlin, C., and S. Graham. Am.J.Epidemiol. *110:* 255, 1979.
38. Correa, P., and W. Haenszel. Adv. Cancer Res. *26:* 1, 1978.
39. Wynder, E.L. Cancer Res. *35:* 3388, 1975.
40. Armstrong, B., and R. Doll. Int.J. Cancer *15:* 617, 1975.
41. Phillips, R.L. Cancer Res. *35:* 3513, 1975.
42. Lyon, J.L., M.R. Klauber, J.W. Gardner, and C.R. Smart. N.Engl.J. Med. *294:* 129, 1976.
43. Lyon, J.L., and A.W. Sorenson. Am.J.Clin.Nutr. *31:* S227, 1978.
44. Enstrom, J.E. Br.J.Cancer *32:* 432, 1975.
45. Reddy, B.S., A. Mastromarino, and E. Wynder. Cancer *39:* 1815, 1977.
46. Hill, M.J. Surg.Annu. *10:* 135, 1978.
47. Reddy, B.S., and E.L. Wynder. Cancer *39:* 2533, 1977.
48. Goldberg, M.J., J.W. Smith, and R.L. Nichols. Ann.Surg. *186:* 97, 1977.

49. Moskovitz, M., C. White, R.N. Barnett, S. Stevens, E. Russell, D. Vargo, and M.H. Floch. Dig.Dis.Sci. *24:* 746, 1979.
50. Mastromarino, A.J., B.S. Reddy, and E.L. Wynder. Cancer Res. *38:* 4458, 1978.
51. Mower, H.F., R.M. Ray, R. Shoff, G.N. Stemmermann, A. Nomura, G.A. Glober, S. Kamiyama, A. Shimada, and H. Yamakawa. Cancer Res. *39:* 328, 1979.
52. Mower, H.F., R.M. Ray, G.N. Stemmermann, A. Nomura, and G.A. Glober. J.Nutr. *108:* 1289, 1978.
53. Ayebo, A.D., I.A. Angelo, K.M. Shahani, and C. Kies. J.Dairy Sci. *62* (Suppl. 1): 44, 1979.
54. Goldin, B.R., and S.L. Gorbach. Cancer *40:* 2421, 1977.
55. Goldin, B.R., L. Swenson, J. Dwyer, M. Sexton, and S.L. Gorbach. J.Natl. Cancer Inst. *64:* 255, 1980.
56. Goldin, B.R., and S.L. Gorbach. J.Natl.Cancer Inst. *64:* 263, 1980.
57. Reddy, B.S., A.R. Hedges, K. Laakso, and E.L. Wynder. Cancer *42:* 2832, 1978.
58. Burkitt, D.P. Am.J.Clin.Nutr. *31:* S58, 1978.
59. Walker, A.R.P. Am.J.Clin.Nutr. *29:* 1417, 1976.
60. Cummings, J.H. J.Hum.Nutr. *32:* 455, 1978.
61. Cummings, J.H., M.J. Hill, E.S. Bone, W.J. Branch, and D.J.A. Jenkins. Am.J.Clin.Nutr. *32:* 2094, 1979.
62. Modan, B. Israel J.Med.Sci. *15:* 301, 1979.
63. Spiller, G.A. Am.J.Clin.Nutr. *31:* S 231, 1978.
64. Maclennan, R., and O.M. Jensen. Lancet *2:* 207, 1977.
65. Miller, A.B. Can.J.Surg. *21:* 209, 1978.
66. MacMahon, B. Nutrition and Cancer *1:* 38, 1979.
67. Hankin, J.H., and V. Rawlings. Am.J.Clin.Nutr. *31:* 2005, 1978.
68. Miller, A.B. Cancer *39:* 2704, 1977.
69. Cole, P., and D. Cramer. Cancer *40:* 434, 1977.
70. Wynder, E.L., and T. Hirayama. Prev.Med. *6:* 567, 1977.
71. Hopkins, G.J., and K.K. Carroll. J.Natl. Cancer Inst. *62:* 1009, 1979.
72. Hillyard, L.A., and S. Abraham. Cancer Res. *39:* 4430, 1979.
73. Gray, G.E., M.C. Pike, and B.E. Henderson. Br.J. Cancer *39:* 1, 1979.
74. Chan, P.C., and L.A. Cohen. J.Natl.Cancer Inst. *52:* 25, 1974.
75. Chan, P.C., and L.A. Cohen. Cancer Res. *35:* 3384, 1975.
76. Hill, P., and E.L. Wynder. Lancet *2:* 806, 1976.
77. Hill, P.B., and E.L. Wynder. Cancer Letters *7:* 273, 1979.
78. Miller, A.B. Cancer Res. *38:* 3985, 1978.
79. Young, V.R., and D.P. Richardson. Cancer *43:* 2125, 1979.
80. Anonymous. JAMA *244:* 25, 1980.
81. Shils, M.E. Med.Clin. North Am. *63:* 1009, 1979.
82. Shils, M.E. Nutrition and Cancer *1:* 9, 1978.
83. Costa, G., and S.S. Donaldson. N.Engl.J.Med. *300:* 1471, 1979.
84. Theologides, A. Cancer *43:* 2004, 1979.
85. Lawrence, W., Jr. Cancer *43:* 2020, 1979.
86. Shils, M.E. Cancer Res. *37:* 2366, 1977.
87. Van Eys, J., M.S. Seelig, and B.L. Nichols, Jr. (Eds). *Nutrition And Cancer.* New York: SP Medical & Scientific Books, 1979.
88. Harvey, K., A. Bothe, and G. Blackburn. Cancer *43:* 111, 1979.
89. Copeland, E.M., III. J.Fla.Med.Assoc. *66:* 373, 1979.
90. Donaldson, S.S., and R.A. Lenon. Cancer *43:* 2036, 1979.
91. Dickerson, J.W.T. J.Hum.Nutr. *33:* 17, 1979.
92. Theologides, A. Minn.Med. *62:* 547, 1979.
93. Drasin, H., E.H. Rosenbaum, C.A. Stitt, and I.R. Rosenbaum. West.J.Med. *130:* 145, 1979.
94. Shils, M.E. Cancer *43:* 2093, 1979.
95. Theologides, A. Postgrad.Med. *61:* 97, 1977.
96. Wollard, J.J. (Ed). *Nutritional Management of the Cancer Patient.* New York: Raven Press, 1979.
97. Ota, D.M., E.M. Copeland, III., J.N.Corriere, Jr., and S.J. Dudrick. Surg. Gynecol.Obstet. *148:* 104, 1979.
98. Munro, H.N. J.Am.Diet.Assoc. *71:* 380, 1977.
99. Johnston, I.D.A. J.Hum.Nutr. *33:* 189, 1979.
100. Soukop, M., and K.C. Calman. J.Hum.Nutr. *33:* 179, 1979.
101. Dwyer, J.T. Cancer *43:* 2077, 1979.
102. De Wys, W.D., and S.H. Herbst. Cancer Res. *37:* 2429, 1977.
103. De Wys, W.D. JAMA *244:* 374, 1980.
104. Dudrick, S.J., B.V. MacFadyen, Jr., E.A. Souchon, D.M. Englert, and E.M. Copeland, III. Cancer Res. *37:* 2440, 1977.
105. Copeland, E.M., III., J.M. Daly, and S.J. Dudrick. Cancer Res. *37:* 2451, 1977.
106. Anonymous. Br.Med.J. *1:* 912, 1979.
107. Elliott, J. JAMA *243:* 1610, 1980.
108. Herbert, V. Am.J.Clin.Nutr. *32:* 96, 1979.
109. Basu, T.K. Oncology *33:* 183, 1976.
110. Darby, W.J. Cancer *43:* 2121, 1979.
111. Creagan, E.T., and C. Moertel. N.Engl.J.Med. *301:* 1399, 1979.

CANCER

Food as a Factor in the Etiology of Certain Home Cancers

by Gio B. Gori

☐ UNTIL A FEW YEARS AGO, the role of nutrition in disease was recognized only for certain specific deficiency syndromes, such as beri-beri, scurvy, and rickets, for which rapid nutritional therapies were found. Until recently, many eyebrows would have been raised by suggesting that an imbalance of normal dietary components could predispose to cancer and cardiovascular diseases.

Today, the accumulation of epidemiologic and laboratory evidence in man and animals makes this notion not only possible but certain. Anthropological studies have shown that man has slowly adapted to changing environmental conditions throughout his evolution, and the technological change in the last 2,000 years has been so rapid that we have not had enough time for genetic selection and adaptation to occur. This is most evident for changes in food consumption, and variations in food use within a wide range of environments (Sussman, 1977). The resulting nutritional imbalances have put different stress on the expression of human disease.

There are populations in which dietary habits appear to inhibit disease incidence (Doll et al., 1970), and cancer is one of the diseases that has been found to be in lower incidence among primitive populations (Leaf, 1973). Populations in transition represent baselines from which change can be measured, and have proved to be some of the most fertile groups in studying the relationship of nutrition and disease.

RELATIONSHIP BETWEEN NUTRITION AND DISEASE

Diet appears to determine the secondary and tertiary physiological changes that predispose individuals within a population to chronic diseases, including cancer. Although the scientific evidence relating nutrition and disease remains unclear, chronic disorders such as heart disease, stroke, cancer, diabetes, arthritis, and dental caries have been associated with dietary and nutritional factors.

Some of the best evidence links excessive caloric intake with obesity (Mann, 1974 a;b), hypertension (Ahrens, 1974), and atherosclerosis (Stamler et al., 1972). Nutrition education and eating-behavior modification have proved effective in prevention of obesity (Tullis, 1973). Excessive intake of dietary fats—particularly saturated fats—leads to increased risk of atherosclerosis (Levy, 1973; Reiser, 1973); a reduc-

tion of fat intake is followed by a reduction in risk (Dayton and Pearce, 1969; Malmros, 1973). The same appears true for cholesterol (Kritchevsky et al., 1974; Frederickson and Levy, 1972).

The role of excessive sucrose intake in the etiology of dental caries is well documented in both animals and man (Makinen and Philosophy, 1972; Brown, 1974). It has also been implicated in the causation of diabetes (Brown, 1974; Cohen et al., 1972).

Alcoholism is probably the most common disease of undernutrition in the United States adult population (Popper, 1974). Alcoholics generally consume an inadequate diet with a number of vitamin and mineral deficiencies (Vitale and Coffey, 1971; Leevy et al., 1965).

Studies of nutrition in women during pregnancy have shown a definite relationship between the diet of the mother and the condition of the baby at birth (NAS/NRC, 1975). Infancy is one of the most critical periods in the life cycle because of the rapid growth rate and high nutritional requirements. Malnutrition during this period can directly influence physical growth and maturation (Aykroyd, 1971; Chase and Martin, 1970).

Studies on effects of malnutrition in mental development indicate a close association between severe protein-calorie malnutrition and impaired brain and behavioral development and depressed cognitive development in children (Scrimshaw and Gordon, 1968; Winick, 1976; Latham, 1974). Undernutrition of infants is a worldwide problem, whereas in certain segments of the U.S. population, overnutrition is also a problem. Overfeeding babies in early infancy may lead to obesity-related diseases in later life (Anonymous, 1973; Kennel and Dawber, 1972).

In the developed countries, protein-calorie malnutrition in adults is not a serious problem, except in hospitals and nursing homes where nutritional support of medical and surgical patients has been neglected. The syndrome of acute adult malnutrition in semi-starved patients with wasting illness develops rapidly in 10-50% of patients in many hospital wards (Bistrian et al., 1974). This iatrogenic, hospital-based malnutrition impairs wound healing, recovery of strength, and well-being and leads to superimposed infections and increased morbidity and mortality (Bistrian et al., 1975). Greater emphasis on nutritional training of

---

From *Food Technology*, December 1979, pp. 48-56. Copyright 1979, Institute of Food Technologists. Reprinted with permission.

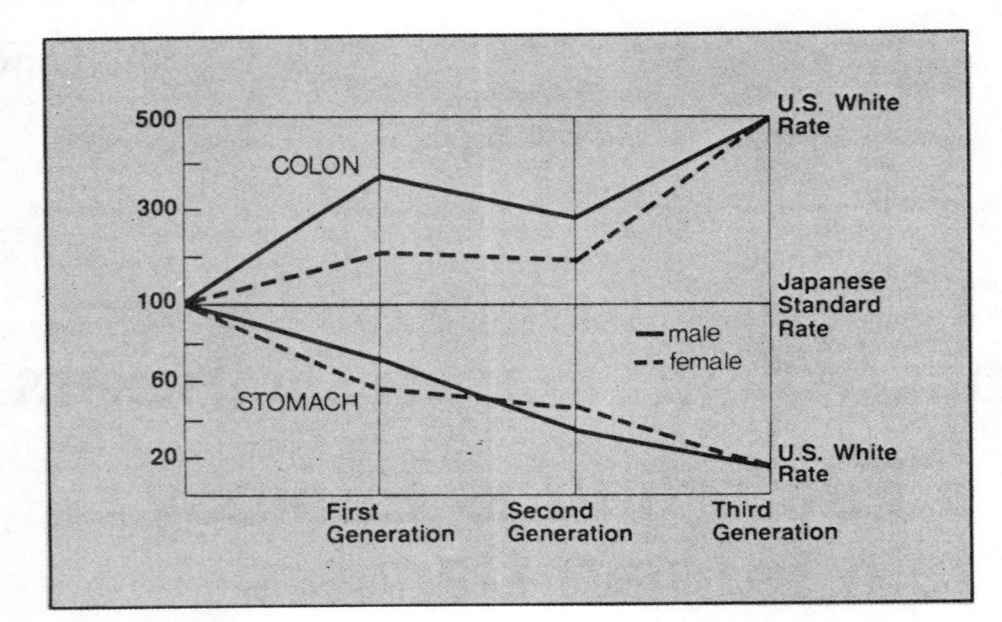

Fig. 1—**MORTALITY TRENDS** among Japanese migrants to the U.S. (from Haenszel and Kurihara, 1968)

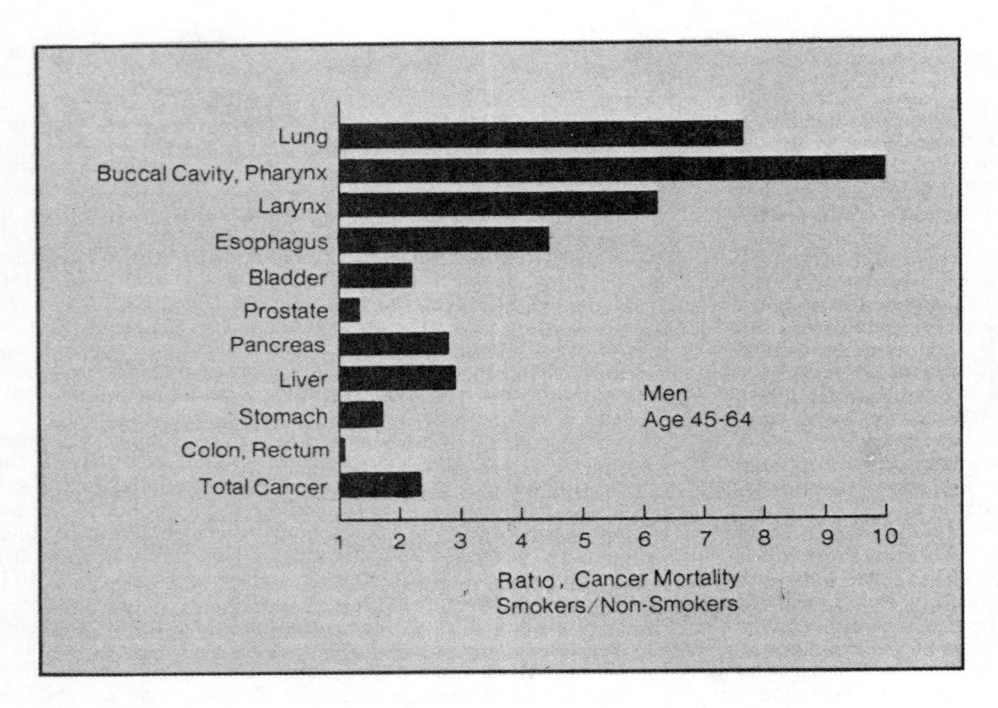

Fig. 2—**RELATIVE RISK OF CANCER MORTALITY** among smokers compared to non-smokers (from NCI, 1966)

physicians to recognize and deal with this serious problem is urgently needed.

EPIDEMIOLOGIC STUDIES ON CANCER

Epidemiologic and laboratory data suggest that diet is an important factor in the causation of various forms of cancer, and that it is correlated to more than half of all cancers in women and at least one-third of all cancers in men (Wynder, 1975a).

Some of the best evidence comes from migrant populations, which rapidly change their original cancer experience to that common to the population of the host country. Colon and breast cancer are low and stomach cancer is high in the Japanese population (Doll et al., 1970); the reverse is true in the U.S. Within two or three generations, Japanese migrants to the U.S. show a shift of cancer incidence patterns from those common in Japan to those prevalent in the U.S. (Staszewski and Haenszel, 1965); this is shown in Figure 1. These shifts take a few generations because dietary habits learned in the country of origin are slowly changed in the process of acculturation to the American way of life.

The observations on stomach cancer are not confined to migrants to the U.S. The cancer registry in Cali, Colombia, has described similar marked differences for stomach cancer among migrants within that country (Correa et al., 1970). Parallel observations for breast cancer and other forms of cancer have been noted in Israel among immigrant Jewish populations of different origin (Shani et al., 1966), and among Polish immigrants in the U.S. (Staszewski and

Haenszel, 1965).

One could argue that the environment of different countries could explain the observed differences in cancer incidence between populations. However, the general pollution and food contamination is similar in Japan and the U.S. (Sawicki et al., 1960); therefore, it is not likely to be responsible for the cancer incidence differences between these countries, or for the shifting of patterns of incidence observed in migrant populations.

To further support that diet rather than environment is an etiologic factor in the incidence of certain cancers, it has been observed that, within a given population, groups having different exposures to environmental contaminants show similar rates of cancer. Smokers are exposed to enormous quantities of carcinogenic substances similar to, but far in excess of, what is normally found in air, water, or food pollution (HEW, 1976). If these carcinogenic substances had a role in the causation of cancer of the colon, breast, stomach, and some other forms of cancer, then one would expect these types of cancers to be exceedingly common among smokers. In fact, as shown in Figure 2, smokers do not have an excess of these cancers (NCI, 1966). Therefore, it is reasonable to surmise that the types of carcinogens present in smoke, and which are commonly found in air, water, and food contaminants, are not likely to play a causative role for cancer of the colon, breast, and stomach.

Thus far, there is no epidemiologic evidence that the presence of such agents as DDT in food has affected the cancer experience in man. Several groups of people have been exposed to high doses of DDT for more than 30 years, and these people do not experience an excess of cancer over the non-exposed population (Jukes, 1973). Other studies indicate that heavy users of saccharin and cyclamates (e.g., diabetics) also do not show an excess of bladder cancer incidence over the general population (Armstrong and Doll, 1975) (Figure 3).

Based on this evidence, potential carcinogens present in

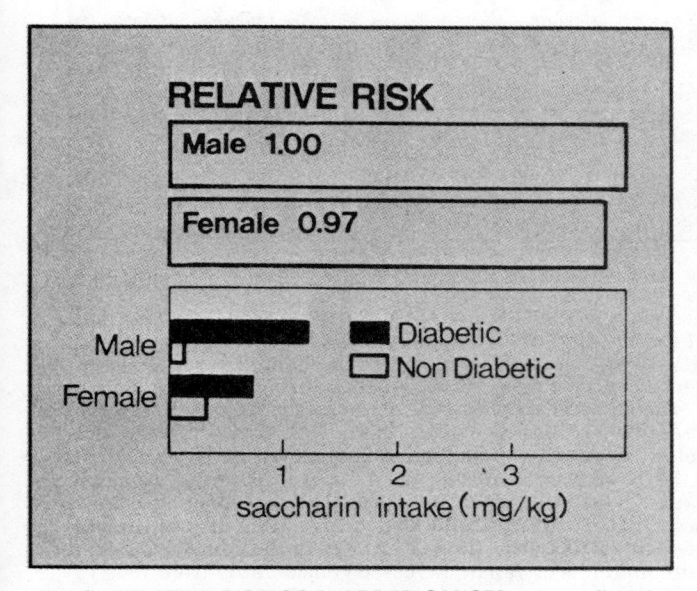

Fig. 3—RELATIVE RISK OF BLADDER CANCER among diabetics and usage of saccharin by diabetics and non-diabetics (from Armstrong and Doll, 1975)

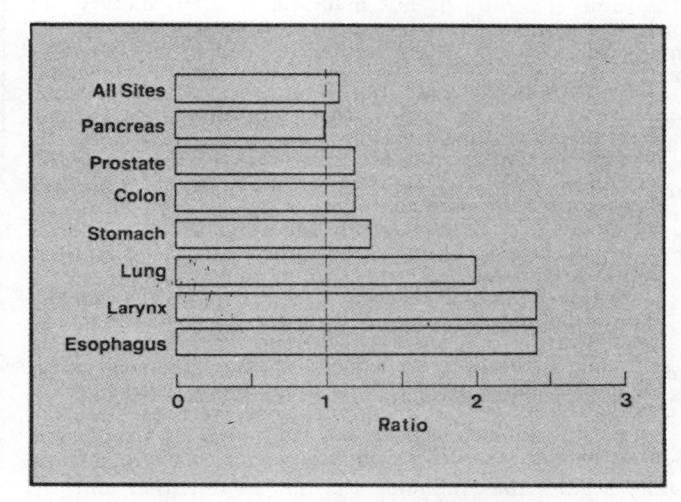

Fig. 4—RELATIVE RISK OF CANCER INCIDENCE among non-Mormon males in Utah compared to Mormon males (from Lyon et al., 1976)

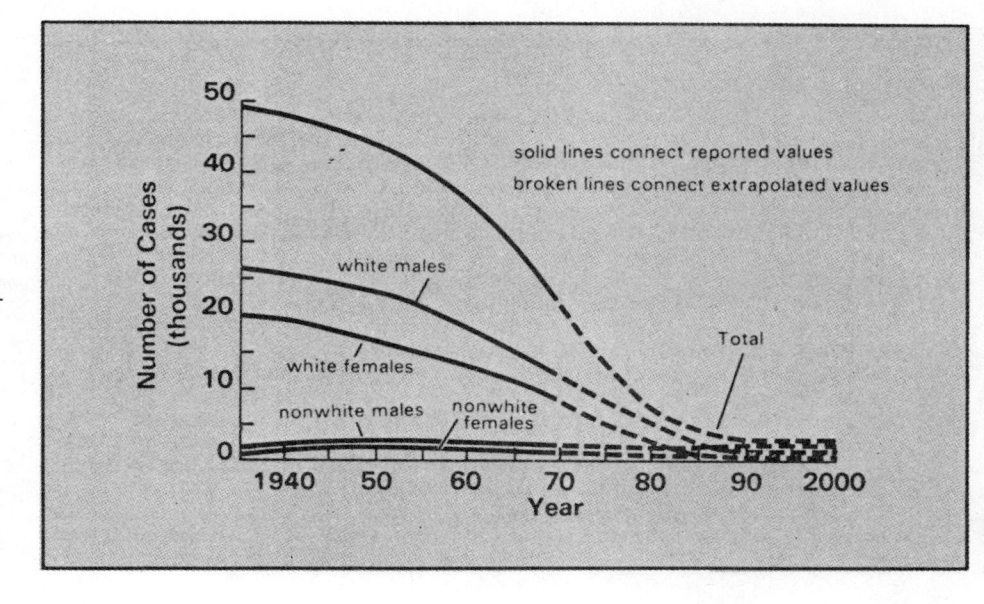

Fig 5—INCIDENCE OF STOMACH CANCER in the U.S.

272 ADULTHOOD INTO THE GOLDEN YEARS

Table 1—SELECTED FOODS THAT POSE A HIGH RISK of stomach cancer for Japanese migrants (from Haenszel et al., 1977)

Japanese-style foods	Western-style foods
Dried fish	Coffee
Salted fish	Candy
Shoyu	Cherries
Pickled radish	Butter
Sake	Beer

the environment or as food contaminants do not appear likely to play a significant role in the relationship of nutrition and certain forms of cancer, particularly colon, stomach, and breast cancer. Rather, it is plausible that nutritional deficiencies and/or excesses influence metabolic processes that, after many years of insult, result in the appearance of certain forms of cancer.

The hypothesis that different diets rather than other environmental contaminants are important in the causation of certain forms of cancer is sustained by the significant differences of cancer incidence among populations that live in the same environment but maintain different dietary habits. This is true of the Seventh-Day Adventist population in California and the Mormon population in Utah. Existing data document that mortality rates among Seventh-Day Adventists are substantially less than the general population rates for cancer sites related to nutrition (Phillips, 1975). Mormons in Utah are reported to have lower rates of stomach and colon cancer than non-Mormons (Fig. 4) and female Mormons experience lower rates of breast, uterine, and other cancers than their non-Mormon counterparts (Lyon et al., 1976).

Ethnic differences also provide insights into the probable role of diet in the causation of cancer. For instance, Jewish people in the U.S. show a higher incidence rate than the general population for cancer of the stomach, colon, pancreas, and kidney (MacMahon, 1960). Epidemiologic studies of different ethnic groups show considerable differences for stomach and breast cancer among populations with similar genetic and environmental background, but with sharply different dietary habits (Higginson and Muir, 1973).

Other studies that reinforce the link of nutrition and certain forms of cancer have noted changes in cancer rates over time. The sharp decrease in stomach cancer in the U.S. in the last 20 years (Fig. 5) suggests the likely introduction of protective factors in the diet. Gortner's (1975) study on nutrition in the U.S. indicates changes in the consumption of specific dietary components during this same time period that may explain the decrease in stomach cancer incidence.

The same phenomenon is observed in Japan (Hirayama, 1975), where during the previous 10 years, stomach and colon cancer rates changed. These changes can be correlated to the introduction of Western dietary habits into Japan. Gastric cancer in Japan has been found to be negatively correlated with the consumption of raw vegetables and milk (Oiso, 1975). The consumption of milk and milk products in Japan increased considerably from 1949 to 1971 (Fig. 6), and a decrease of stomach cancer was observed. Hirayama (1967) found that among cancer cases, milk drinking became less frequent and consumption of salted foods increased over the observation in control

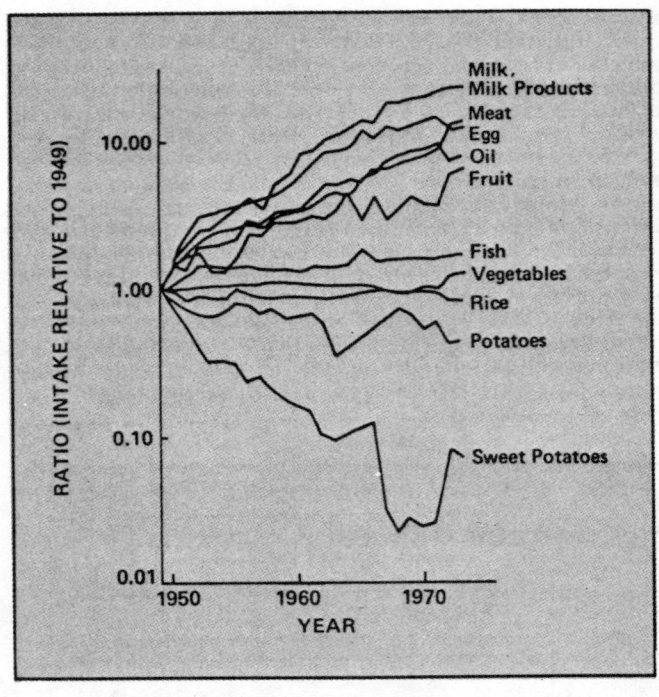

Fig. 6—CHANGES IN AMOUNT OF INTAKE of selected foods in Japan since 1950 (from Wynder, 1975a)

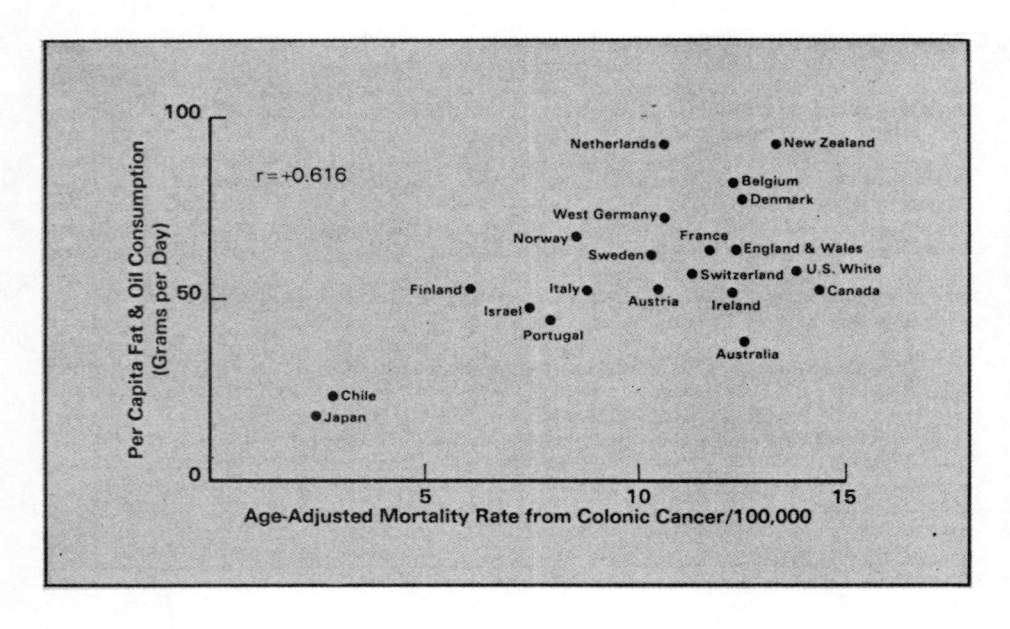

Fig. 7—CORRELATION BETWEEN BOWEL CANCER MORTALITY and dietary fat and oil consumption (from Wynder, 1975b)

subjects. Haenszel et al. (1972) have identified certain high-risk foods for Japanese migrants to the U.S.; these include both Japanese- and Western-style components (Table 1).

Epidemiologic studies of various populations have correlated specific dietary components with certain forms of cancer (Howell, 1974). There exists a worldwide correlation between bowel cancer and fat consumption, as shown in Fig. 7 (Wynder, 1975b). The difference between high incidence of colon cancer in the U.S. and low incidence in Japan is consistent with the differences in fat intake between the two countries. Also, the greater incidence of colonic cancer in Japanese migrants to the U.S. reflects an increase of fat intake from their native habits to Western dietary habits (Hankin et al., 1975). And colon cancer seems to be increasing in Japan, a finding consistent with an increasing Westernization of its diet and an increased intake of fat (Correa and Haenszel, 1975).

Colon cancer has also been shown to correlate highly with the consumption of meat (Haenszel et al., 1973), even though it is not clear whether the meat itself or its fat content is the real correlating factor. Mortality rates from colonic cancer are high in the U.S., Scotland, and Canada, which are high meat-consuming countries. Other populations where meat consumption is low, such as in Japan and Chile, also experience a low incidence of colon cancer. Seventh-Day Adventists have a restricted fat and meat intake compared to other populations living in the same district (Fig. 8), and they suffer considerably less from some forms of cancer, notably breast and colon (Phillips, 1975).

Other observations have resulted in the postulation that a low fiber intake in Western countries may be responsible for a high incidence of colon cancer (Burkitt, 1971). Indeed, the Japanese diet is high in fiber content, and several observations indicate that African populations with high fiber intake in their diet experience, like the Japanese, a low incidence of colon cancer. The same appears true for the Seventh-Day Adventists.

If we consider alcohol as an abnormal dietary component, it is also clear that its excessive consumption is a very significant causative factor, particularly for cancers of the upper alimentary tract (Graham et al., 1967).

ANIMAL STUDIES ON CANCER

It is important to note that laboratory work in animals parallels and strongly confirms the results of epidemiologic studies in man. Various manipulations of nutritional components of the diet have been tested in animals for their effect on cancer development. Of all dietary modifications, caloric restriction has had the most regular influence on tumor formation (Tannenbaum and Silverstone, 1957). With few exceptions, caloric restriction generally inhibits tumor formation. In mice, a decreased incidence of spontaneous neoplasms of the breast are noted with caloric restriction. Furthermore, even within a group of animals being fed identical diets, the incidence of tumors tends to be consistently greater in heavier rats than in lean rats (Ross and Bras, 1971).

Amino acids, the component parts of protein, have also been noted to influence cancer development in animals (Shils, 1975). Low levels or even deficiencies of certain amino acids seem to have a therapeutic effect on cancer.

Chemicals such as polycyclic hydrocarbons, many of which are carcinogenic, have been found to be moderated by administration of vitamin A. In hamsters, administration of vitamin A appears to inhibit the induction of cancer of the stomach and cervix which is otherwise caused by carcinogenic hydrocarbon compounds (Maugh, 1974).

Both the amount of fat in the diet as well as the degree of saturation of the fat tend to influence tumor incidence. Increased amounts of fat in animal diets have resulted in an increased incidence of certain tumors—notably breast tumors—and the tumors have also occurred earlier in the life of the animal (Carroll, 1975). Furthermore, animals consuming a diet containing polyunsaturated fat had a higher incidence of colonic tumors, compared to a group consuming saturated fat (Reddy et al., 1975b).

THEORIES ON THE ROLE OF DIET AND NUTRITION

Despite the epidemiologic evidence and animal studies, the specific role of diet and nutrition in cancer etiology is still unclear. Theories on the relationships between diet, nutrition, and cancer are not lacking, and are occasionally advanced as the sole causative link. It is unlikely, however, that the interrelationships are as simple and unconfounded as any one of these theories suggests. At the same time, it is likely that they all reflect occurrences in a far more complex chain of causative events. The brief summary of some of these theories provided here will perhaps serve to indicate the extraordinary diversity of relationships which have already been identified.

- **Bile Acids.** The metabolic derivatives of bile acid degradation by intestinal microorganisms are thought to act as direct carcinogens in the etiology of large bowel cancer (Reddy et al., 1975a). In addition, the levels of specific bile derivatives may be affected by the functioning metabolic pathways of endogenous microorganisms, which in turn are affected by psychological stress, diet, and other factors (Moore and Holdeman, 1975). Bile production is directly affected by diet. A diet high in fat content stimulates increased bile production, thus increasing the risk of these carcinogenic processes' occurring.

- **Protease Inhibitors.** These compounds inhibit enzymes which catalyze the hydrolysis of peptide bonds (Troll et al., 1978). Protease enzymes act at the extracellular level in promotion of malignant transformations and may do so by inhibiting an anti-inflammatory response such as that found for glucocorticoids (Belman and Troll, 1972), by interfering with mechanisms for repressing abnormal cell growth (Giraldi et al., 1977), or by directly promoting tumor cell growth (Schnebli and Burger, 1972; Burger, 1970). At the extracellular level, protease inhibitors oppose these processes. It has also been suggested that the inhibitors may be absorbed intact through pinocytosis and exert their anti-tumor effects intracellularly through inhibition of gene activation (Hodges et al., 1973; Troll et al., 1975). Experimental studies indicate that leupeptin and other protease inhibitors do have anti-tumor activity (Matsushima et al., 1975; Troll, 1976; Troll et al., 1975). Because seed foods such as soybeans and lima beans are rich natural sources of protease inhibitors, they have been suggested as a possible factor in the lowered cancer incidence among vegetarian populations.

- **Antioxidant Deficiency.** A number of natural and artificial dietary antioxidants—vitamin E, selenium, BHT, BHA, and ethoxyquin—are known to negatively affect chemically induced tumor incidence (Griffin and Jacobs, 1977; Harber and Wissler, 1962; Harman, 1961). They may affect the mixed-function oxidase system and thereby have an indirect mode of action, or they may act directly by combining with free-radical carcinogens, thereby preventing tumorigenic cellular reactions. Recent studies of ultraviolet-light-induced tumor formation suggest that antioxidants can also affect this process (Black and Chan, 1975; Black et al., 1978). In contrast to earlier studies, these findings imply a common etiologic mechanism for both chemical- and ultraviolet-induced carcinogenesis.

- **Dietary Fiber.** Fiber is thought to exert its effect on the carcinogenic process in several ways. First, it increases fecal bulk, thereby reducing the concentration of carcinogens in the intestinal tract. This, then, would reduce carcinogenic exposure of the intestinal epithelium and could also reduce carcinogenic and precarcinogenic absorption. It may also affect the metabolic processes of endogenous microflora, as well as their population per se. Increased fecal bulk also decreases intestinal transit time, thereby shortening potential contact time with epithelial cells and absorptive surfaces (Ward et al., 1973; Leveille, 1974; Burkitt et al., 1972; Harvey et al., 1973).

- **Hormone Production.** Nutrient intake and dietary components, along with nutritional status, play a major role in determining an individual's hormone profile. Significant alteration of hormone profiles is known to increase the likelihood of cancer development in laboratory animals (Belman and Troll, 1972). This theory appears to be potentially viable with respect to the development of hormone-tissue-specific tumors such as breast, uterine, testicular, or prostate. Altered hormone profiles may also repress tumors whose growth is affected by the anti-inflammatory hormones (Viaje et al., 1977).

- **Excess Nutrient and Caloric Consumption.** Excessive consumption of a variety of nutrients and excessive caloric intake have been linked to cancer incidence in both animal and human epidemiologic studies. Animals on calorie-restricted diets are known to have a reduced cancer incidence for both spontaneous and chemically induced tumors (Tannenbaum, 1959; Ross and Bras, 1971).

Excessive protein may exert tumorigenic actions through metabolic by-products which may be mutagenic, such as ammonia (Topping and Visek, 1976). Excessive lipid consumption may affect hormone profiles (Benson et al., 1975; Carroll and Khor, 1970; 1971; Tannenbaum, 1942). In addition, fat or cholesterol metabolites, e.g., epoxides of unsaturated fatty acids, may be either carcinogenic or precarcinogenic (Kotin and Falk, 1963). Several of the minor nutrients, including selenium, may be carcinogenic per se at high-enough dosage levels (Shapiro, 1972; Anonymous, 1972; Sunderman, 1978). Actually, most minerals appear to have an optimum range for dietary consumption, and intake above or below this range may increase susceptibility to tumorigenesis.

- **Deficient Nutrient Consumption.** Nutrient deficiencies, especially of the trace elements, have been linked to cancer etiology. Both animal and epidemiologic studies have linked a selenium deficiency with an increased cancer incidence. Chronic deficiencies of vitamins A, C, and E, as well as most of the B-complex vitamins, have been shown to increase susceptibility of animals to chemically-induced tumors (Hancock and Dickie, 1969; Sporn et al., 1976; Chu and Malmgren, 1965; Maugh, 1974; Raineri and Welsburger, 1975; Mirvish, 1975; Kamm et al., 1975; Cameron and Pauling, 1973; Tannenbaum and Silverstone, 1952; Anonymous, 1974; Rivlin, 1973). Overt deficiencies in animal studies are usually associated with reduced caloric intake, so that starvation or other complications of malnutrition claim the animal before alterations in spontaneous tumor incidence can be observed.

- **Carcinogenic Absorption.** Certain dietary components may enhance or inhibit absorption of carcinogens. Among the strongest evidence for this specific role of diet is the increased incidence of upper alimentary tract cancers among persons who both smoke and drink. Alcohol and cigarette smoke appear to have a synergistic effect on the development of cancers of the mouth, pharynx, and larynx. Only a relatively small risk increase for these forms of cancer is experienced among nonsmokers who drink alcohol, suggesting that the alcohol acts as a cocarcinogen rather than the primary causative agent (Wynder et al., 1957; Vincent and Marchetta, 1963; Keller and Terris, 1965; Wynder et al., 1956; Rothman and Keller, 1972). Other dietary constituents or imbalances may also affect absorption; the possible role of fiber in this respect has already been mentioned.

- **Food-Borne Carcinogens.** The theories presented thus far have dealt primarily with metabolic and hormonal processes, and nutrient excesses and deficiencies which can have cancer-promoting or -inhibitory effects. Directly carcinogenic or precarcinogenic substances are present in foods as well. These substances may be classified in the following way: natural inherent (e.g., cycasin); natural contaminant (aflatoxins, molds); condiments (saffrole, chili powder); food additives (aniline dyes); metabolites of additives (nitrosamines); metabolites of nutrients (epoxides); compounds used in food production (herbicides, pesticides, fertilizers); and residues of food processing and preparation (benzo(a)pyrenes, the mutagens in meats identified by Sugimura et al., 1977, Commoner et al., 1978, and Dolara et al., 1979).

Amazingly little research has been conducted in this area, although food additives have been tested for toxicity and carcinogenicity for some time. More recently, potential food contaminants introduced in food production, processing, and preparation have been investigated—in some cases by accident. Comparatively few studies have looked at the safety of endogenous but exotic chemical constituents of foods, although food technologists have often exploited these constituents in food processing and chemical production procedures (Gross and Newberne, 1977; Miller, 1973; Shank et al., 1972a; b; Boffey, 1976; Shubik, 1975; Miller and Miller, 1976; Issenberg, 1976; Grover, 1973; Stout, 1968; Rice, 1976; Marx, 1977).

With the exception of food additives, little effort has been made to identify the levels of risk associated with any one of the above categories of substances. Appropriate risk/benefit analysis procedures will also need to be developed to guide recommendations and decision-making regarding the use of some of the substances. For example, how does one weigh the benefits in increased food production against the possible dangers posed by certain pesticides and fertilizers?

- **Dietary Inducers of the Mixed-Function Oxidase System.** Chemical compounds occurring naturally in some foods—but having no known nutritive role—have been shown to inhibit carcinogenesis. They appear to achieve this effect by increasing activity of the mixed-function oxidase system, which metabolizes many known chemical carcinogens. Plants of the *Cruciferae* genus, such as brussel sprouts, cabbage, cauliflower, and broccoli, contain specific indoles which have been associated with increased aryl hydrocarbon hydroxylase (AHH) activity. In turn, this increased AHH activity from exogenous food sources has been demonstrated to protect against chemical induction of mammary tumors and forestomach neoplasia (Wattenberg and Loub, 1978). The inclusion in the diet of foods in which these compounds are present may therefore modulate the effect of environmental carcinogens (McLean and Drives, 1977).

DIETARY GUIDELINES

It is probable that all these theories, and more, contain elements of truth which can contribute to our understanding of the overall process of human carcinogenesis. That process is complicated by the interaction of nutrients and dietary compounds with each other, the many factors affecting metabolic processes, and both dietary and nondietary carcinogens. For example, studies of radiation-induced tumors (Pajeau and Bounous, 1976) showed that irradiated mice consuming a purified diet had a significantly increased tumor incidence compared to those maintained on a natural food stock diet. Nonirradiated mice fed either diet were virtually free of tumors. Caution in releasing results of this type of research is well-advised, proper, and ethical. But there would be little justification for extending such caution to the recommendation of prudent dietary practices (Table 2) such as those contained in the Dietary Goals for the United States (Senate Select Committee, 1977).

While it is true that we cannot guarantee the efficacy of these dietary guidelines in disease prevention, neither can we guarantee the results of most modern medical and public health practices. The line of demarcation between research findings which should responsibly be withheld, and those which should be released in the public interest, is not always as sharp and well-defined as one might wish. Yet to abdicate responsibility in providing guidance on important health-related issues may well lead to public reliance on less scientifically sound and frequently less scrupulous sources of information. In nutrition, as in other areas where research and experimentation constantly produce new insights and information, one must rely on one's best judgment in applying the knowledge available, and do so in a manner which maximizes health-promoting effects while minimizing associated risk factors.

We must also maintain an awareness of the dynamic context within which dietary goals evolve—age, genetics, physical activity, environment, and other demographic and lifestyle factors influence each individual's nutritional status and requirements. A given individual could safely consume a diet that would be unwise for another based on a number of genetic, somatic, behavioral, or environmental variables. Furthermore, current prudent dietary recommendations are based in large part on epidemiologic data amassed over the past 50 or 60 years, and consequently reflect conditions that may be unique to the 20th century rather than fundamental to man's physiology. If environmental, lifestyle, or dietary changes occurred, nutritional requirements and dietary goals undoubtedly would be affected.

For example, changes in consumption levels of a specific nutrient or foodstuff might well influence metabolic processes and other nutritional requirements in a way that is not altogether predictable at this time. Increased fiber intake is a case in point. Such an increase would likely affect the current prudent-diet message regarding fat, vitamins, minerals, and perhaps even cholesterol (Eastwood, 1977).

Reduction in stress levels, cessation of smoking, and increased physical exercise may all have influences on nutritional status. For instance, the anorectic effects of smoking are popularly recognized, and gaining weight is much feared by smokers who consider quitting, women in particular (Blitzer et al., 1977). At the same time, smoking may also influence the utilization of some nutrients.

The beneficial effects of exercise would likely go beyond caloric consumption and affect dietary requirements in other ways. The modification of blood lipids is but one of the more likely consequences (Holloszy et al., 1964; Kahn, 1963; Werko, 1971).

In addition, dietary patterns are not formed on the basis of nutritional needs alone. Preferences in food, methods of food preparation, and the ritual surrounding mealtime are all part of our individual social and cultural heritage. The alteration of eating habits—even when such alterations are considered desirable—is not always easy to achieve, as evidenced by the constant struggle against overweight among a large number of Americans. And, as conditions in some Third World countries make all too abundantly clear, dietary patterns may also be economically determined. Even were we able to accurately predict the nutritional consequences of a prescribed diet, under controlled conditions, the influence of culture, habit, and economic necessity could not be readily or easily overcome.

It is obvious that dietary requirements—and therefore dietary goals—are as plastic as the many factors that affect them. Equally obvious is the fact that dietary habits do not lend themselves to rapid change. But while such changes may occur slowly, they do take place. Indeed, American dietary patterns are now changing. Evidenced by the increasing popularity of restaurants and stores promoting "natural" and "health" foods, and subtle shifts in marketing by the food industry, much of this change reflects an interest in developing healthier eating habits.

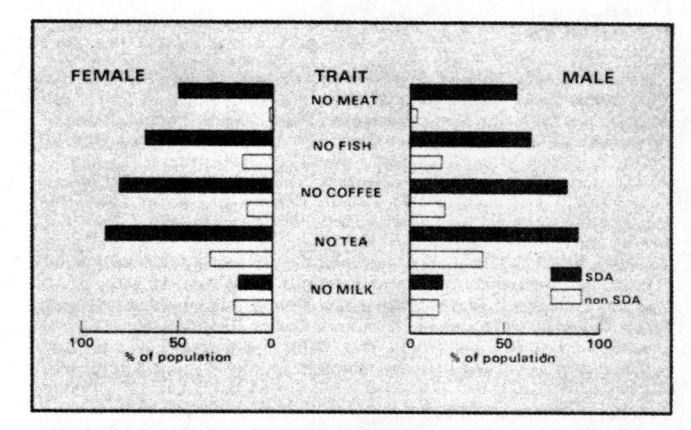

Fig. 8—SELECTED DIETARY TRAITS of Seventh-Day Adventists (from Phillips, 1975)

Table 2—A SUGGESTED PRUDENT AMERICAN DIET, similar to the Dietary Goals proposed by the Senate Select Committee (1977)

Category	Reduce	Substitute/Increase
Calories, Protein	Fats Fatty meats Whole-milk products Refined flours Sugar	Lean meat Lean poultry Lean fish Vegetable protein[a] Skim milk products Unprocessed flours[a]
Cholesterol	Eggs Organ meats	
Salt	Salt	
Bulk Vitamins, Minerals, Micronutrients		Unprocessed flour[a] Raw or cooked vegetables and fruits[a]

[a]Increase variety of food sources in these categories

As one continues to search for new knowledge on the role of diet and nutrition in health and disease, the information currently available should be utilized in a wise and judicious manner. The prudent application of this knowledge by an informed public is not likely to produce radical and abrupt shifts in eating habits, with undesirable nutritional and economic consequences. Rather, important steps toward the implementation of prudent dietary practices should take place, and a favorable environment created for continued efforts to monitor nutritional processes and develop more precise and individualized recommendations for a healthy diet.

FOOD TECHNOLOGISTS HAVE KEY ROLE

The food industry and food technologists in particular have a key role in improving general dietary habits. Sudden and sweeping changes in the food supply are neither desirable, safe, nor feasible, and better dietary habits are likely to follow many years of patient and prudent educational efforts.

Yet, the food industry has consistently displayed remarkable inventiveness in the pursuit of successful marketing. This ought to be applied, as a responsible commitment to public health, in the exploration of new product lines that can be profitable and which can offer healthier options to a better-informed consumer.

REFERENCES

Ahrens, R.A. 1974. Sucrose, hypertension and heart disease: An historical perspective. Am. J. Clin. Nutr. 27: 403.

Anonymous. 1972. The selenium paradox. Food Cosmet. Toxicol. 10: 867.

Anonymous. 1973. Overfeeding in the first year of life. 1973. Nutr. Rev. 31: 116.

Anonymous. 1974. Riboflavin metabolism in cancer. Nutr. Rev. 32: 308.

Armstrong, B. and Doll, R. 1975. Bladder cancer mortality in diabetics in relation to saccharin consumption and smoking habits. Brit. J. Prev. Soc. Med. 29: 73.

Aykroyd, W.R. 1971. Nutrition and mortality in infancy and early childhood: Past and present relationships. Am. J. Clin. Nutr. 24: 480.

Belman, S. and Troll, W. 1972. The inhibition of croton oil-promoted mouse skin tumorigenesis by steroid hormones. Cancer Res. 32: 450.

Benson, J., Lev, M., and Grand, C.G. 1975. Enhancement of mammary fibroadenomas in the female rat by a high fat diet. Cancer Res. 16: 135.

Bistrian, B.R., Blackburn, G.L., Hallowell, E., and Heddle, R. 1974. Protein status of general surgical patients. J. Am. Med. Assn. 230: 858.

Bistrian, B.R., Blackburn, G.L., and Scrimshaw, N.S. 1975. Cellular immunity in semistarved states in hospitalized adults. Am. J. Clin. Nutr. 28: 1148.

Black, H.S. and Chan, J.T. 1975. Suppression of ultraviolet light-induced tumor formation by dietary antioxidants. J. Invest. Dermatol. 65: 412.

Black, H.S., Chan, J.T., and Brown, G.E. 1978. Effects of dietary constituents on ultraviolet light-mediated carcinogenesis. Cancer Res. 38: 1384.

Blitzer, P.H., Rimm, A.A., and Giefer, E.E. 1977. The effect of cessation of smoking on body weight in 57,032 women: Cross-sectional and longitudinal analyses. Great Britain, J. Chron. Dis. 30: 415.

Boffey, P.M. 1976. Color additives: Botched experiment leads to banning of red dye No. 2. Science 191: 450.

Brown, A.T. 1974. In "Sugars in Nutrition," ed. H.L. Sipple and K.W. McNutt, p. 689. Academic Press, New York.

Burger, M.M. 1970. Proteolytic enzymes initiating cell division and escape from contact inhibition of growth. Nature 227: 170.

Burkitt, D.P. 1971. Epidemiology of cancer of the colon and rectum. Cancer 28: 3.

Burkitt, D.P., Walker, A.R., and Painter, N.S. 1972. Effect of dietary fiber on stools and transit-times and its role in the causation of disease. Lancet 2: 1408.

Cameron, E. and Pauling, L. 1973. Ascorbic acid and the glycosaminoglycans: An orthomolecular approach to cancer and other diseases. Oncology 27: 181.

Carroll, K.K. 1975. Experimental evidence of dietary factors and hormone-dependent cancers. Cancer Res. 35: 3374.

Carroll, K.K., and Khor, H.T. 1970. Effects of dietary fat and dose level of 7,12-dimethylbenz(a)anthracene on mammary tumor incidence in rats. Cancer Res. 30: 2260.

Carroll, K.K. and Khor, H.T. 1971. Effects of level and type of dietary fat on incidence of mammary tumors induced in female Sprague-Dawley rats by 7,12-dimethylbenz(a)anthracene. Lipids 6: 416.

Chase, H.P. and Martin, H.P. 1970. Undernutrition and child development. New Eng. J. Med. 282: 933.

Chu, E.W. and Malmgren, R.A. 1965. An inhibitory effect of vitamin A on the induction of tumors of forestomach and cervix in the Syrian hamster by carcinogenic polycyclic hydrocarbons. Cancer Res. 25: 884.

Cohen, A.M., Teitelbaum, A., and Saliternik, R. 1972. Genetics and diet as factors in development of diabetes mellitus. Metabolism 21: 235.

Commoner, B., Vithayathil, A., Dolara, T., Nair, S., Madyastha, P., and Cuca, G. 1978. Formation of mutagens in beef and beef extract during cooking. Science 201: 913.

Correa, P. and Haenszel, W. 1975. Comparative international incidence and mortality. In "Cancer Epidemiology and Prevention," ed. D. Schottenfeld, p. 386. Charles C. Thomas, Springfield, Ill.

Correa, P., Cuello, C., and Dugue, E. 1970. Carcinoma and intestinal metaplasia of the stomach in Colombian migrants. J. Natl. Cancer Inst. 44: 297.

Dayton, S. and Pearce, M.L. 1969. Prevention of coronary heart disease and other complications of atherosclerosis by modified diet. Am. J. Med. 46: 751.

Dolara, P., Commoner, B., Vithayathil, A., Cuca, G., Tuley, E., Madyastha, P., Nair, S., and Kriebel, P. 1979. The effect of temperature on the formation of mutagens in heated beef stock and cooked ground beef. Mutat. Res. 60: 231.

Doll, R., Muir, C., and Waterhouse, J. 1970. In "Cancer Incidence in Five Continents," Vol. II. Intl. Union against Cancer, Springer-Verlag, New York.

Eastwood, M.A. 1977. Fiber and enterohepatics circulation. Nutr. Rev. 35: 42.

Frederickson, D.S. and Levy, R.I. 1972. Familial hyperlipoproteinemia. In "The Metabolic Basis of Inherited Diseases," ed. J.B. Stanbury, J.B. Wyngaarden, and D.S. Frederickson. McGraw Hill, New York.

Giraldi, T., Kopitar, M., and Sava, G. 1977. Anti-metastatic effects of a leukocyte intracellular inhibitor of neutral proteases. Cancer Res. 37: 3834.

Gortner, W.A. 1975. Nutrition in the United States, 1900 to 1974. Cancer Res. 35: 3246.

Graham, S., Lilienfeld, A.M., and Tidings, J.E. 1967. Dietary and purgation factors in the epidemiology of gastric cancer. Cancer 20: 2224.

Griffin, A.C. and Jacobs, M.M. 1977. Effects of selenium on azo dye hepatocarcinogenesis. Cancer Letters 3: 177.

Gross, R.L. and Newberne, P.M. 1977. Naturally occurring toxic substances in foods. Clin. Pharmacol. and Therap. 22(5): 680.

Grover, P. 1973. How polycyclic hydrocarbons cause cancer. New Scientist 58: 685.

Haenszel, W. and Kurihara, M. 1968. Studies of Japanese migrants. I. Mortality from cancer and other diseases among Japanese in the United States. J. Natl. Cancer Inst. 40: 43.

Haenszel, W., Kurihara, M., Segi, M., and Lee, R.K.C. 1972. Stomach cancer among Japanese in Hawaii. J. Natl. Cancer Inst. 49: 969.

Haenszel, W., Berg, J.W., Segi, M., Kurihara, M., and Locke, F.B. 1973. Large bowel cancer in Hawaiian Japanese. J. Natl. Cancer Inst. 51: 1765.

Haenszel, W., Kurihara, M., Segi, M., and Lee, R.K.C. 1977. Stomach cancer among Japanese in Hawaii. J. Natl. Cancer Inst. 49: 969.

Hancock, R.L. and Dickie, M.M. 1969. Biochemical, pathological, and genetic aspects of a spontaneous mouse hepatoma. J. Natl. Cancer Inst. 43(2): 407.

Hankin, J.H., Nomura, A., and Rhoades, A.G. 1975. Dietary patterns among men of Japanese ancestry in Hawaii. Cancer Res. 35: 3259.

Harber, S.L. and Wissler, R.W. 1962. Effect of vitamin E on carcinogenicity of methylcholanthrene. Proc. Soc. Exp. Biol. Med. 111: 774.

Harman, D. 1961. Prolongation of the normal lifespan and inhibition of spontaneous cancer by antioxidants. J. Gerontol. 16: 247.

Harvey, R.F., Pomare, E.W., and Heaton, K.W. 1973. Effects of increasing dietary fibre on intestinal transit. Lancet 1: 1278.

HEW. 1976. Toward less hazardous cigarettes. Report No. 1, Pub. No. (NIH) 76-905. Dept. of Health, Educ. and Welfare, Washington, D.C.

Higginson, J. and Muir, C.S. 1973. Epidemiology in cancer. In "Cancer Medicine," ed. J.F. Holland and E. Frei III. Lea and Febiger, Philadelphia.

Hirayama, T. 1975. Epidemiology of cancer of the stomach with special reference to its recent decrease in Japan. Cancer Res. 35: 3460.

Hirayama, T. 1967. The epidemiology of cancer of the stomach in Japan with special reference to the role of diet. Unio. Intern. Contra Cancrum Monograph Ser. 10: 37.

Hodges, C.M., Livingston, D.C., and Franks, L.M. 1973. The localization of trypsin in cultured mammalian cells. J. Cell Sci. 12: 887.

Holloszy, J.O., Skinner, J.S., Toro, G., and Cureton, T.K. 1964. Effects of a six month program of endurance exercise on the serum lipids of middle-aged men. Am. J. Cardiol. 14: 753.

Howell, M.A. 1974. Factor analysis of international cancer mortality data and per capita food consumption. Brit. J. Cancer 29: 328.

Issenberg, P. 1976. Nitrite, nitrosamines and cancer. Fed. Proc. 35: 1322.

Jukes, T.H. 1973. The Delaney 'Anti-cancer' clause. Prev. Med. 2: 133.

Kahn, H.A. 1963. The relationship of reported coronary heart disease mortality to physical activity of work. Am. J. Public Health 53: 1058.

Kamm, J.J., Dashman, T., Conney, A.H., and Burns, J.J. 1975. Effect of ascorbic acid in amine-nitrate toxicity. Ann. New York Acad. Sci. 258: 169.

Keller, A.Z. and Terris, M. 1965. The association of alcohol and tobacco with cancer of the mouth and pharynx. Am. J. Public Health 55: 1578.

Kennel, W.R. and Dawber, T.R. 1972. Atherosclerosis as a pediatric problem. J. Pediatr. 80: 544.

Kotin, P. and Falk, H.L. 1963. Organic peroxides, hydrogen peroxide, epoxides, and neoplasia. Radiation Res. Suppl. 3: 193.

Kritchevsky, D., Davidson, L.M., Shapiro, I.L., Kim, H.K., Kitigawa, M., Mahotra, S., Nair, P., Clarkson, T.B., Bersohn, I., and Winter, P.A.B. 1974. Lipid metabolism and experimental atherosclerosis in baboons: Influence of cholesterol-free semisynthetic diets. Am. J. Clin. Nutr. 27: 29.

Latham, M.C. 1974. Protein-calorie malnutrition in children and its relation to psychological development and behavior. Physiol. Rev. 54: 541.

Leaf, A. 1973. Observations of a peripatetic gerontologist. Nutr. Today 8(5): 4.

Leevy, C.M., Cardi, L., Frank, O., Gellene, R., and Baker, H. 1965. Incidence and significance of hypovitaminemia in a randomly selected municipal hospital population. Am. J. Clin. Nutr. 17: 259.

Leveille, G.A. 1974. Importance of dietary fiber in food. Presented at meeting of Chicago Section of Inst. of Food Technologists and meeting of Mid-West Section Am. Assn. Cereal Chemists

Levy, R.I. 1973. Triglycerides as a risk factor in coronary artery disease. J. Am. Med. Assn. 224: 1770.

Lyon, J.L., Klauber, M.P., Gardner, J.W., and Smart, C.R. 1976. Cancer incidence in Mormons and non-Mormons in Utah, 1966-1970. New Eng. J.

Med. 294(3): 129.
MacMahon, B. 1960. The ethnic distribution of cancer mortality in New York City, 1955. Acto Unio Intern. Contra Cancrum 16: 1716.
Makinen, K.K. and Philosophy, L. 1972. The role of sucrose and other sugars in the development of dental caries. Intl. Dent. J. 22: 363.
Malmros, H. 1973. Primary dietary prevention of atherosclerosis. In "Clinical Nutrition," ed. J.C. Somogy. Bibliotheca 'Nutritio et Dieta,' No. 19 Karger, Basel.
Mann, G.V. 1974a. The influence of obesity on health (Part 1). New Engl. J. Med. 291: 178.
Mann, G.V. 1974b. The influence of obesity on health (Part 2). New Eng. J. Med. 291: 226.
Marx, J.L. 1977. Drinking water—Getting rid of the carbontetrachloride. Science 196: 632.
Matsushima, T., Kaziko, T., Kawachi, T., Hara, K., Sugimura, T., Takeuchi, T., and Umezawa, H. 1975. Effects of protease-inhibitors of microbial origin on experimental carcinogenesis. In "Fundamentals in Cancer Prevention," ed. P.N. Magee, S. Takayama, T. Sugimura, and T. Matsushima, p. 57. Univ. of Tokyo Press, Tokyo, and Univ. Park Press, Baltimore.
Maugh, T.H. 1974. Vitamin A: Potential protection from carcinogens. Science 186: 1198.
McLean, A.E.M. and Drives, H.E. 1977. Combined effects of low doses of DDT and phenobarbital on cytochrome P450 and amidopyrine demethylatin. Biochem. Pharm. 26: 1299
Miller, J.A. 1973. Naturally occurring substances that can produce tumors. In "Toxicants Occurring Naturally in Foods," 2nd ed. Natl. Acad. of Sciences, Washington, D.C.
Miller, J.A. and Miller, E.C. 1976. Carcinogens occurring naturally in foods. Fed. Proc. 35: 1316
Mirvish, S.S. 1975. Blocking the formation of N-nitroso compounds with ascorbic acid in vitro and in vivo. Ann. New York Acad. Sci. 258: 169.
Moore, W.E.C. and Holdeman, L.V. 1975. Discussion of current bacteriological investigations of the relationship between intestinal flora, diet, and colon cancer. Cancer Res. 35: 3326.
NAS/NRC. 1975. Nutritional supplementation and the outcome of pregnancy. Comm. on Maternal Nutrition, Food and Nutr. Board, Natl. Acad. of Sciences, Natl. Res. Council, Washington, D.C.
NCI. 1966. Epidemiological approaches to the study of cancer and other chronic diseases. Monograph 19. Natl. Cancer Inst., Washington, D.C.
Oiso, T. 1975. Incidence of stomach cancer and its relation to dietary habits and nutrition in Japan between 1900 and 1975. Cancer Res. 35: 3254.
Pajeau, R., and Bounous, G. 1976. Systemic protection against radiation. II. Effects of protein and lipid concentration of diet. Rad. Res. 66: 267.
Phillips, R.L. 1975. Role of lifestyle and dietary habits in risk of cancer among Seventh-Day Adventists. Cancer Res. 35: 3513.
Popper, H. 1974. Alcoholic hepatitis—An experimental approach to a conceptual and clinical problem. New Eng. J. Med. 290: 159.
Raineri, R. and Welsburger, J.H. 1975. Reduction of gastric carcinogens with ascorbic acid. Ann. New York Acad. Sci. 258: 181.
Reddy, B.S., Mastromarino, A., and Wynder, E.L. 1975a. Further leads on metabolic epidemiology of large bowel cancer. Cancer Res. 35: 3403.
Reddy, B.S., Narisawa, T., Maronpot, R., Weisburger, J.H., and Wynder, E.L. 1975b. Animal models for the study of dietary factors and cancer of the large bowel. Cancer Res. 35: 3421.
Reiser, R. 1973. Saturated fat in the diet and serum cholesterol concentration: A critical evaluation of the literature. Am. J. Clin. Nutr. 26: 524.
Rice, J.M. 1976. Environmental factors: Chemicals. In "Prevention of Embryonic, Fetal and Perinatal Disease," ed. R.L. Brent and M.I. Harris, p. 163. Pub. No. (NIH) 76-853, Natl. Inst. of Health, Bethesda, Md.
Rivlin, R.S. 1973. Riboflavin and cancer: A review. Cancer Res. 33: 1977.
Ross, M.H. and Bras, G. 1971. Lasting influence of early caloric restriction on prevalence of neoplasms in the rat. J. Natl Cancer Inst. 47: 1095.
Rothman, K.J. and Keller, A.Z. 1972. The effect of joint exposure to alcohol and tobacco on risk of cancer of the mouth and pharynx. J. Chron. Dis. 25: 711.
Sawicki, E., Elbert, W.C., Hauser, T.R., Fox, F.T., and Stanley, T.W. 1960. Benzo(a)pyrene content of the air of American communities. Am. J. Industrial Hygiene Assn. 21(6): 443.
Schnebli, H.P. and Burger, M.M. 1972. Selective inhibition of growth of transformed cells by protease inhibitors. Proc. Natl. Acad. Sci. 69: 3825.
Scrimshaw, N.S. and Gordon, J.E. 1968. "Malnutrition, Learning and Behavior." MIT Press, Cambridge, Mass.
Senate Select Committee on Nutrition and Human Needs. 1977. Dietary Goals For the United States, 2nd ed. U.S. Govt. Print. Office, Washington, D. C., February.
Shani, M., Modan, B., Steinitz, R., and Modan, M. 1966. The incidence of breast cancer in Jewish females in Israel. Harefuah 71: 337.
Shank, R.C., Gordon, J.E., Wogan, G.N., Nondasuta, A., and Subhamani, B. 1972a. Dietary aflatoxins and human liver cancer. III. Field survey of rural Thai families for ingested aflatoxins. Food Cosmet. Toxicol. 10: 71.
Shank, R.C., Bhamarapravati, N., Gordon, J.E., and Wogan, G.N. 1972b. Dietary aflatoxins and human liver cancer. IV. Incidence of primary liver cancer in two municipal populations of Thailand. Food Cosmet. Toxicol. 10: 171.
Shapiro, J.R. 1972. Selenium and carcinogenesis: A review. Ann. New York Acad. Sci. 192: 215.
Shils, M.E. 1975. Nutrition and cancer: Dietary deficiency and modifications. In "Cancer Epidemiology and Prevention," ed. D. Schottenfeld. Charles C. Thomas, Springfield, Ill.
Shubik, P. 1975. Potential carcinogenicity of food additives and contaminants. Cancer Res. 35: 3475.
Sporn, M.B., Dunlop, N.M., Newton, D.L., and Smith, J.M. 1976. Prevention of chemical carcinogenesis by vitamin A and its synthetic analogs (retinoids). Fed. Proc. 35: 1332.
Stamler, J., Berleson, D.M., and Lindberg, H.A. 1972. Risk factors: Their role in the etiology and pathogenesis of the atherosclerotic diseases. In "The Pathogenesis of Atherosclerosis," ed. R.W. Wissler and J.C. Geer, p. 41. Williams and Wilkins, Baltimore.
Staszewski, J. and Haenszel, W. 1965. Cancer mortality among the Polish born in the United States. J. Natl. Cancer Inst. 35: 291.
Stout, V.F. 1968. Pesticide levels in fish of the northeast Pacific. Bull. Environ. Contam. Toxicol. 3: 240.
Sugimura, T., Kawachi, T., and Nagao, M. 1977. Mutagenic principles in tryptophan and phenylalanine pyrolysis products. Proc. Japan. Acad. 53: 58.
Sunderman, F.W. 1978. Carcinogenic effects of metals. Fed. Proc. 37(1): 40.
Sussman, R. 1977. Foraging patterns of non-human primates and the nature of food preferences in man. Presented at the 61st Ann. Meet., Federation of American Societies for Experimental Biology, Chicago, Ill.
Tannenbaum, A. 1942. The genesis and growth of tumors. III. Effects of a high-fat diet. Cancer Res. 2: 468.
Tannenbaum, A. 1959. Nutrition and cancer. In "Physiopathology of Cancer," 2nd ed., ed. F. Homburger, p. 517. Hoeber-Harper, New York.
Tannenbaum, A. and Silverstone, H. 1952. The genesis and growth of tumors. V. Effects of varying the level of B vitamins in the diet. Cancer Res. 12: 744.
Tannenbaum, A. and Silverstone, H. 1957. Nutrition and the genesis of tumors. In "Cancer," Vol. 1, ed. R.W. Raven, p. 305. Butterworth and Co., Ltd., London.
Topping, D.C. and Visek, W.J. 1976. Nitrogen intake and tumorigenesis in rats injected with 1,2-dimethylhydrazine. J. Nutr. 106(11): 1583.
Troll, W. 1976. Blocking tumor promotion by protease inhibitors. In "Fundamentals in Cancer Prevention," ed. P. Magee, S. Takayama, T. Sugimura, and P. Matsushima. p. 41. Univ. of Tokyo Press, Tokyo, and Univ. Park Press, Baltimore.
Troll, W., Meyn, M.S., and Rossman, T.G. 1978. Mechanisms of action in carcinogenesis. In "Carcinogenesis: A Comprehensive Survey. Vol. II. Mechanism of Tumor Promotion and Cocarcinogenesis," ed. T.S. Slaga, A. Sivak, and R.K. Boutwell. Raven Press, New York.
Troll, W., Rossman, T., Katz, J., Levitz, M., and Sugimura, T. 1975. Proteinases in tumor promotion and hormone action. In "Proteases and Biological Control," ed. E. Reich, D.B. Rifkin, and E. Shaw, p. 977. Cold Spring Harbor Laboratory, Cold Spring Harbor, New York.
Tullis, I.F. 1973. Rational diet construction for mild and grand obesity. J. Am. Med. Assn. 226:70.
Viaje, A., Slaga, T.J., Wigler, M., and Weinstein, I.B. 1977. Effects of anti-inflammatory agents on mouse skin tumor promotion, epidermal DNA synthesis, phorbol ester-induced cellular proliferation and production of plasminogen activator. Cancer Res. 37: 1530.
Vincent, R.G. and Marchetta, F. 1963. The relationship of the use of tobacco and alcohol to cancer of the oral cavity, pharynx or larynx. Am. J. Surg. 106: 501.
Vitale, J.J. and Coffey, J. 1971. Alcoholism and vitamin metabolism. In "Biochemistry," Vol. I, ed. B. Kissin and H. Begleiten, p. 327. Plenum Press, New York.
Ward, J.M., Yamamoto, R.S., and Weisburger, J.H. 1973. Brief communication: Cellulose dietary bulk and azoxymethane-induced intestinal cancer. J. Natl. Cancer Inst. 51: 713.
Wattenberg, L.W. and Loub, W.D. 1978. Inhibition of polycyclic aromatic hydrocarbon-induced neoplasia by naturally occurring indoles. Cancer Res. 38: 1410.
Werko, L. 1971. Can we prevent heart disease? Ann. Int. Med. 74: 278.
Winick, M. 1976. "Malnutrition and Brain Development." Oxford Univ. Press, New York.
Wynder, E.L. 1975a. Introductory remarks in nutrition in the causation of cancer. Cancer Res. 35: 3238.
Wynder, E.L. 1975b. The epidemiology of large bowel cancer. Cancer Res. 35: 3388.
Wynder, E.L., Bross, I.J., and Day, E. 1956. Epidemiological approach to the etiology of cancer of the larynx. J. Am. Med. Assn. 160: 1384.
Wynder, E.L., Bross, I.J., and Feldman, R. 1957. A study of etiological factors in cancer of the mouth. Cancer 10: 1300.

CANCER

New Concepts in Nutrition and Cancer: Implications for Folic Acid

by C. E. Butterworth, Jr., M.D.

INTRODUCTION

A great deal of interest has developed in the subject of nutrition and cancer in recent years both on the part of the general public and professional scientists. Indeed, *Nutrition and Cancer*, an international journal, has been established to deal exclusively with the subject and has been available since 1979.

It is now generally recognized that cancer is not one disease, but a complex array of disorders with widely varying etiologies and treatments. In view of the known complexities and broad scope of nutrition sciences, it would seem an almost hopeless task to find meaningful interrelationships between the two topics! Yet, some order seems to be emerging from the seeming chaos of this unwieldy pair of topics.

SOME MECHANISMS BY WHICH DIET AND NUTRITION MAY BE RELATED TO THE ETIOLOGY OF CANCER

It will not be possible, due to limitations of space, to discuss all of the possible mechanisms by which diet and nutrition may be related to the etiology of cancer. Some of them are presented in Table I.

Table I

1. Carcinogens (and pro-carcinogens) in food,
2. Oxidant damage to cells; lack of antioxidant substances in the diet,
3. Excessive intake of certain nutrients (e.g., animal fat, selenium, iron, alcohol, vitamin A),
4. Altered solubility, adsorption, absorption of nutrients and/or carcinogens due to dietary factors (e.g., fiber),
5. Altered enteric bacterial population due to dietary factors,
6. Chromosome damage due to nutrient deficiency,
7. Abnormal repair of chromosome damage,
8. Altered metabolism of hormones (e.g., in obesity),
9. Impaired immunity to tumor cells and viruses, and
10. Genetic "susceptibility" plus dietary factors.

It may be seen that some of the mechanisms are not strictly independent. Many seem to share, as a common denominator, some sort of genetic or chromosomal injury which may, in turn, be conditioned by nutritional factors. For example, healthy immune systems are thought to be capable of recognizing and destroying certain deviant cells which might arise from a chemical or viral mutagen. In other situations, chromosome damage could occur as a result of either primary nutritional inadequacy or an abnormal repair mechanism. It has, moreover, been known for many years that certain tumors are hormone dependent and it is well known that the action of hormones and nutrients are intricately intertwined.

Three new concepts seem to be emerging which have great promise for understanding relationships between nutrition and cancer; these are: (1) the concept of hormonally induced *localized nutrient deficiency*, (2) the concept of nutritionally dependent, *fragile sites on human chromosomes*, and (3) the concept of altered pathways of nutrient metabolism induced by oncogenic viruses. Since these seem to be unifying concepts which are likely to have considerable influence on future research, they merit careful study. The following paragraphs are offered as a brief, general introduction to the subject.

THE CONCEPT OF LOCALIZED NUTRIENT DEFICIENCY

It has been traditional to think of nutrient requirements in terms of the whole organism and relatively little attention has been paid to the requirements of individualized tissues. Of course, the importance of nutrient requirements during pregnancy, infancy, lactation and even in response to trauma have been recognized. However, the role of nutrients in the maintenance of structure and function in individual tissues has received scant attention. Moreover, it has been tacitly assumed that the nutrient content of a tissue is somehow a constant property related in some way to its structure and function. But, relatively little is known about the dynamic changes that may occur normally in either animal or human tissues over short periods of time.

It seems important now to consider the *fluctuations* that may occur in nutrient content of tissue as the result of intake patterns, hormonal stimulation and various other stresses. Folic acid may be regarded as a model nutrient to illustrate some of these concepts.

It has been known for many years that folic acid plays a key role in the expression of steroid hormone effects on target tissue.[1,3] For example, when chicks and monkeys are grown on a folic acid-deficient diet, the female genital tract fails to develop normally in response to estrogen stimulation. In 1973, Whitehead et al.[4] observed megaloblastic features in cervical epithelial cells from a group of women who were using steroid hormones as oral contraceptive agents (OCA's). Although the cytologic changes were not associated with evidence of systemic vitamin deficiency, they disappeared with oral folate supplementation, leading the authors to postulate the existence of *localized* folate deficiency in the cervix.

Subsequently, Krumdieck et al.[5] demonstrated in laboratory tests that cyclic variations normally occur in the content and nature of folate coenzymes in the rat uterus during successive stages of the reproductive cycle. During proestrus the activity of the enzyme pteroyl polyglutamyl hydrolase ("conjugase") doubled, and the total folate content was nearly doubled. There was a relative decline in the polyglutamate form and an increase in the coenzymes having a shorter chain length. These changes were interpreted as being associated with the cyclic "burst" of mitotic activity needed to regenerate the endometrium in preparation for possible implantation of fertilized ova during the subsequent stage of estrus. In this connection, it is of interest to note that the risk of developing endometrial cancer is increased 4-fold to 15-fold in women who have been long-term users of estrogens.[6] It is also of interest that many papers have called attention to the association of obesity with endometrial cancer. It has also been shown[7] that there is an increased conversion of a naturally occurring androgen to an estrogen in obese subjects. Thus, individual differences in hormone metabolism could affect the nutrient content of specific tissues. In 1976, a clinical trial began to test the hypothesis that cervical dysplasia is associated with localized folacin deficiency and that the deficiency can be corrected by an oral supplement of the vitamin.

Forty-seven young women with mild or moderate dysplasia have now received oral supplements of either folic acid 10 mg daily, or a placebo, under strict double-blind conditions for 3 months while continuing their established use of a combination-type OCA.[8,9] There was significant improvement in the final cytology scores of the supplemented subjects, whereas the placebo group showed no change. In addition, biopsies obtained under colposcopic guidance were significantly better among supplemented than unsupplemented subjects. There were 4 cases of apparent regression to normal among subjects receiving folic acid supplementation, but none in the unsupplemented group. There were 4 cases of apparent progression to carcinoma *in situ* among the unsupplemented subjects, but none in the group receiving folic acid supplementation. The data is interpreted as indicating that oral folate supplementation may prevent the progression of early cancer to a more severe form and in some cases promote reversion to normalcy.

THE CONCEPT OF FRAGILE SITES AND SOMATIC MUTATIONS

It has recently been demonstrated that human chromosomes tend to break at certain specific locations under certain specific conditions and that the tendency is a heritable trait demonstrable in family pedigrees. In a recent series of papers, Sutherland[10,11,12] has described the occurrence of fragile sites in at least 7 different human chromosomes in lymphocytes and fibroblasts grown under chemically defined conditions. Manifestations of fragile sites include nonstaining gaps at exactly the same point on a given chromosome, acentric fragments, deleted chromosome, sister chromatid exchange and related phenomena. It seems highly significant that the nutrient content of the culture medium is a key factor in demonstrating the presence of a fragile site. Many of them can be demonstrated by growing in tissue culture medium that is relatively deficient in folic acid. Expression of the phenomenon can be blocked by providing an excess of folic acid, citrovorum factor or thymidine in the medium.

So far, there is no clear evidence that fragile sites are involved in cancer formation in humans or animals. However, their existence offers a mechanism whereby specific mutations could occur in target tissue if folic acid or some other essential nutrient is in relatively short supply. In addition, they would help explain how a family tendency toward cancer could exist in a dormant state until exposure to nutritional stress or perhaps an environmental mutagen brought forth a full blown malignant transformation. Indirect support of this concept may be seen in a report by Branda et al.[13] of a family with an inherited defect of cellular folic acid uptake. Among four generations of this family, there were 34 cases of proven or suspected serious hematologic disease, including 5 cases of acute leukemia. In another report, Marinello et al.[14] described the occurrence of "double minute" chromosomes in 40 of 320 patients with hematologic disease. The abnormal chromosomes resemble and are compatible with fragments arising from chromosome breaks at a fragile site.

VIRAL ONCOGENESIS

There is considerable circumstantial evidence that cervical cancer is related in some way to the herpes simplex virus,[15] a DNA-containing virus. The "retroviruses," which contain RNA, are proven tumor-inducing agents in certain species; they cause RNA-directed synthesis of DNA by reverse transcriptase.[16] There would be good reason to suspect that folic acid-containing coenzymes play important roles in this DNA synthesis just as they do elsewhere.

It is relevant to note that another virus, the even-numbered T-bacteriophages of *E. coli*, contains pteroyl hexaglutamate as an essential component of the tailplate in the region of attachment of the 6 tail fibers.[17] Treatment of phage particles with conjugase renders them noninfectious but does not alter their morphologic appearance by electron microscopy. It is believed that the folacin component is essential for the recognition of and attachment to specific binding sites on the bacterial cell membrane. If these observations apply, as a matter of general biological principle to human oncogenic viruses, several important questions are raised:

1. Is the site of viral modification of chromosomal DNA unusually susceptible to damage or breakage?
2. Do human oncogenic viruses pass from cell to cell by means of receptors intended for nutrient uptake?
3. Does viral-induced synthesis of a coenzyme (e.g., a folacin-containing polyglutamate) "trigger" cell division and malignant transformation?
4. Since nutrients required for viral proliferation may be different from those of the host, can viruses be attacked by specific metabolic inhibitors without affecting normal pathways?
5. Do viruses and steroid hormones share any common biochemical mehanisms for affecting nuclei (i.e., chromosomal DNA) of target tissues?

SUMMARY

From the foregoing discussion, it is apparent that important new leads are developing which may help explain relationships that were heretofore considered obscure between cancer, nutrition, hormones and viruses. New concepts are emerging and new techniques are being applied. The 1980s promise to be a decade of intense, exciting and fruitful research in man's battle to conquer cancer — or at least some forms of it.

REFERENCES

1. Hertz, R., Sebrell, W.H., Impairment of Response to Stilbestrol in the Oviduct of Chicks Deficient in L. Casei Factor, Science 100:293-294, 1944.
2. Hertz, R., Dietary Impairment of Estrogen Response in the Immature Monkey, Proc. Soc. Exp. Biol. Med. 67:113-115, 1948.
3. Kline, I.T. et al., Estrogen Stimulation of the Oviduct in Vitamin-Deficient Chicks, Endocrinology 48:345-357, 1951.
4. Whitehead, N. et al., Megaloblastic Changes in the Cervical Epithelium: Association with Oral Contraceptive Therapy and Reversal With Folic Acid, JAMA 226:1421-1424, 1973.
5. Krumdieck, C.L. et al., Cyclic Variations in Folate Composition and Pteroylpolyglutamyl Hydrolase (Conjugase) Activity of the Rat Uterus, Am. J. Clin. Nutr. 29:288-294, 1976.
6. Gusberg, S.D., Current Concepts in Cancer: The Changing Nature of Endometrial Cancer, New Engl. J. Med. 302:729-731, 1980.
7. Rizkallah, T.H. et al., Production of Estrone and Fractional Conversion of Circulating Androsteneione to Estrone in Women with Endometrial Carcinoma, J. Clin. Endocrinology 40:1045-1056, 1975.
8. Butterworth, C.E., Jr. et al., Folate-Induced Regression of Cervical Intraepithelial Neoplasis (CIM) in Users of Oral Contraceptive Agents (OCA), Am. J. Clin. Nutr. 33:926, 1980.
9. Butterworth, C.E., Jr. et al, Improvement in Cervical Dysplasia Associated with Folic Acid Therapy in Users of Oral Contraceptives (submitted for publication).
10. Sutherland, G.R., Fragile Sites on Human Chromosomes: Demonstration of Their Dependence on the Type of Culture Medium, Science 197:265-266, 1977.
11. Sutherland, G.R., Heritable Fragile Sites on Human Chromosomes, I. Factors Affecting Expression in Lymphocyte Culture, Am. J. Hum. Genet. 31:125-135, 1979.
12. Sutherland, G.R., Heritable Fragile Sites on Human Chromosomes, II. Distribution, Phenotypic Effects and Cytogenetics, Am. J. Hum. Genet 31:136-148, 1979.
13. Branda, R.F. et al., Folate-Induced Remission in Aplastic Anemia with Familial Defect of Cellular Folate Uptake, New Engl. J. Med. 298:469-475, 1978.
14. Marinello, M.J. et al., Double Minute Chromosomes in Human Leukemia (letter to the editor), New Eng. J. Med. 704-705, 1980.
15. Rotkin, E.D., A Comparison Review of Key Epidemiological Studies in Cervical Cancer Related to Current Searches for Transmissible Agents, Cancer Res. 33:1353-1367, 1973.
16. Bishop, J.M., The Molecular Biology of RNA Tumor Viruses: A Physician's Guide, New Eng. J. Med. 308:675-682, 1980.
17. Kozloff, L.M. et al., Bacteriophage Tail Components, I. Pteroylpolyglutamates in T-even Bacteriophages, J. Virol 5(6):726-739, 1970.

CARDIOVASCULAR

Diet and Heart Disease

by Consumers Union

In the aftermath of World War II, alert scientists made an intriguing discovery. During the wartime food shortages, cardiovascular death rates in Northern Europe plummeted. When hostilities ceased and food became ample, the death rates reverted to prewar levels.

Subsequent studies couldn't establish whether the dramatic changes in mortality were directly related to diet—especially the shortages of meat, butter, and other staples rich in fat or cholesterol—or whether the events were largely coincidental. But, coincidence or not, the provocative observation focused attention on the possible role of diet in heart and blood-vessel diseases. Although earlier experiments with animals had hinted that diet might be important, the wartime experience stimulated the first genuine hope that dietary changes might reverse the epidemic rise of cardiovascular deaths in the 20th century.

That goal still remains elusive. Nearly two generations since the war, a crossfire of debate still rages among scientists, politicians, consumer activists, and food producers about what dietary advice, if any, to offer the public. At one end of the spectrum, some argue that a shift away from meat, eggs, and dairy foods will virtually assure a reduction in heart disease. At the other end are those who insist that any dietary approach is nonsense.

Between those extremes are two more moderate viewpoints. One holds that the public should be encouraged to follow specific dietary guidelines on fat and cholesterol to reduce the risk of heart disease. The other contends that such advice is premature and that dietary measures should be directed mainly to people with known risk factors and should be individualized to fit each case. Most medical scientists, physicians, and nutrition specialists tend to subscribe to one or the other viewpoint. Both viewpoints have important elements in common as well as points of difference.

Common ground

The main goal of most dietary advice regarding the heart is to prevent or retard the development of atherosclerosis, a buildup of fatty deposits or "plaques" on the inner walls of major arteries. Atherosclerosis can reduce or cut off the blood flow in arteries serving major organs such as the heart or brain. When it affects the coronary arteries nourishing the heart, it can lead to impaired heart function and heart attacks.

The complex process that produces atherosclerosis is still only dimly understood, and intensive investigation around the world is trying to shed light on its causes. It's well known, though, that cholesterol is an important component of arterial plaque. A fatty alcohol found in all body cells, cholesterol serves as a building block for cell components and hormones and shares in other essential processes. Its exact role in plaque formation is unclear, however.

Nevertheless, most experts agree that elevated levels of serum cholesterol (cholesterol in the blood) are associated with an increased risk of heart attack in men. Many men with high serum cholesterol don't suffer heart attacks, and some men with low levels do. But, on average, the risk increases with increasing serum-cholesterol levels. In the Framingham Heart Study, a long-term study of residents of Framingham, Mass., men with an average serum cholesterol of 260 milligrams (per 100 milliliters of blood) have had a heart-attack rate three times as high as men with levels below 195 milligrams.

Since diet can affect serum cholesterol, many physicians prescribe dietary changes for people at risk—especially those with elevated serum cholesterol who smoke, have high blood pressure or diabetes, are obese, have a family history of premature heart attacks, or have known coronary heart disease. Even though the efficacy of diet therapy is unproved, most experts feel that reasonable measures that may reduce risk are justified in such patients. When it comes to healthy people without known risk factors, however, the experts part company.

The diet-heart theory

For years the American Heart Association (AHA) has advised the public to cut its intake of saturated fats and increase that of polyunsaturated fats. Saturated fats, which come primarily from animal products, tend to raise serum cholesterol. Polyunsaturated fats, which come mainly from vegetable sources, tend to lower serum cholesterol. (Mono-unsaturated fat, another major type of dietary fat, has a neutral effect on serum cholesterol.)

Americans were also encouraged to maintain an ideal body weight and reduce their consumption of cholesterol, which is found solely in animal products, especially eggs. Like the dietary prescriptions for heart patients, the recommendations were based on what is known as the diet-heart theory—that reducing the level of serum cholesterol through diet will reduce the risk of developing coronary heart disease.

In practical terms, that meant cutting back on dairy foods and eggs and favoring poultry and fish over red meat. It also meant substituting margarine for butter and using vegetable oils for cooking, thereby raising intake of polyunsaturated fats at the expense of saturated ones.

Copyright 1981 by Consumers Union of United States, Inc., Mount Vernon, N.Y. 10550. Reprinted by permission from CONSUMER REPORTS, May 1981.

While meat, egg, and dairy-food producers gagged on the AHA's advice, some food companies were quick to exploit public concern about cholesterol. The term "no cholesterol" was advertised as though it meant "germ-free," while margarine and vegetable oils were often promoted as if they were drugs.

Currently, the AHA urges people to reduce total fat to between 30 and 35 percent of daily calories, compared to the present national average of about 40 percent. The difference would be made up by eating more vegetables, fruit, and grain products.

Saturated fats should be trimmed to about 10 percent of daily calories, says the AHA, and polyunsaturated fats increased to the same level. In effect, it means eating roughly one-third less saturated fat than Americans average today and about 50 percent more polyunsaturated fat. (The remaining part of dietary fat would be mono-unsaturated.)

As for cholesterol, the AHA advises a daily limit of 300 milligrams, or slightly more than the amount in an egg. Americans currently consume an average of 450 milligrams daily (roughly 350 among women and 550 among men).

In 1979, the U.S. Surgeon General announced nutrition recommendations similar to those of the AHA. The following year, the Department of Agriculture and the Department of Health, Education and Welfare (now Health and Human Services) issued a joint policy on nutrition that agreed in most respects with the Surgeon General and the AHA.

Neither set of Federal recommendations endorses an increase in polyunsaturated fat. But their overall thrust clearly supports the AHA's dietary view. At least 17 other major health organizations concur with the AHA's stand on fat and cholesterol, according to a New York Times editorial last year. A show of hands doesn't prove a theory, but many Americans have come to accept the AHA's advice as a prudent health measure.

It's not surprising, then, that a report issued last spring by the Food and Nutrition Board of the National Research Council/National Academy of Sciences set pots rattling in the nation's kitchens. The board, a group of 15 scientists who establish the recommended dietary allowances (RDA's) for Americans, said it had found no persuasive evidence to indicate that healthy people should restrict their intake of cholesterol. Nor was there any proved benefit in restricting fat intake, said the board, except to reduce obesity and achieve weight control.

The board also concluded that "it does not seem prudent at this time" to advise an increase in the proportion of polyunsaturated fat consumed, "except for individuals in high-risk categories."

Reaction to the report ranged from confusion among the public to attacks on the objectivity and integrity of the board itself. Some politicians and consumer groups charged that the report was tainted because several members of the board had previously received consulting fees or research funding from meat, egg, and dairy interests. The acrimonious debate that ensued over the charges has tended to obscure a more immediate issue: Was criticism of the report justified on scientific grounds, or does the diet-heart theory rest on shakier foundations than people have come to believe?

Support for the theory

The most provocative evidence linking diet to heart disease comes from epidemiology, the medical specialty that investigates the incidence and potential causes of diseases in different populations. Since World War II, studies of populations around the world have shown strong associations between dietary fat, serum cholesterol, and cardiovascular disease.

In one of the most notable studies in epidemiology, Dr. Ancel Keys of the University of Minnesota and associates on three continents investigated 16 population groups in seven countries. Nearly 12,800 men between 40 and 59 years of age entered the study, which examined dietary intake, smoking habits, and other suspected risk factors in heart disease.

Over the ensuing 10 years, heart-disease rates were found to vary as much as fourfold between countries, with Finland and the U.S. experiencing the highest incidence and Japan the lowest. Among the major findings was that saturated-fat intake, serum cholesterol, and heart-disease rates were significantly associated with one another.

Epidemiologic studies of migrant populations also suggest that diet affects heart-disease rates. Dr. Keys summarized one of the early studies in a recent issue of The Lancet, a British medical journal. "Over 20 years ago we studied Japanese [men] in Japan and their countrymen who had migrated to Hawaii and then to California," said Keys. "With each move, they became more Americanized in the diet, serum cholesterol rose, and the incidence of coronary heart disease increased." Nearly two decades after Keys's initial investigation, an independent study reported similar findings.

In general, studies comparing different populations have produced strong associations between diet and heart disease. But statistical associations aren't capable of proving a cause-and-effect relationship. Heart-disease rates have been associated positively or negatively with many factors, ranging from smoking and national income to wine consumption and the number of cars per 100 persons. Accordingly, even a highly plausible association requires confirming evidence from other research.

Experimental evidence

Next to population studies, the most significant evidence implicating diet in heart disease has come from animal experiments. Diets high in cholesterol and fat have produced a form of atherosclerosis in many species, including primates such as rhesus monkeys.

What the results mean for humans is uncertain, because there's no consistency of effect from species to species. Animals vary widely in their response to such diets, with rabbits showing the greatest sensitivity and carnivores the least. Where humans fit on the scale is unclear. Nevertheless, the fact that cholesterol and fat can induce a form of atherosclerosis in some animals suggests that they might be able to do so in humans.

The experiments show conclusively that taking in large amounts of cholesterol and fat raises serum cholesterol in susceptible animals and eventually leads to effects on the arteries. In turn, rigidly controlled studies conducted in hospital or institutional settings suggest that a similar progression is possible in humans. Using formula diets and precise quantities of pure cholesterol or egg yolk, researchers demonstrated that variations in cholesterol or fat intake can affect serum-cholesterol levels in humans.

In those human experiments, which are known as metabolic-ward studies, ethical and practical considerations naturally preclude long-term tests to determine whether atherosclerosis can be induced. But the studies add another important link to the chain of evidence implicating specific dietary components in the genesis of coronary heart disease.

The decline in death rates

Many authorities believe the chain of evidence is strong enough to warrant changes in what Americans eat. Lending support to that view is the steady decline in heart-disease mortality rates since the late 1960's, which followed a change in American dietary habits that began several years earlier.

According to recent studies, the death rate for coronary heart disease declined 27 percent in the U.S. from 1968 to 1977, the latest year for which figures are available. That period also witnessed a shift away from some of the foods commonly considered part of a rich diet. Last December, Surgeon General Julius Richmond reported that per-capita consumption of milk, cream, eggs, and butter had fallen significantly since 1965. Milk and cream declined 21 percent; eggs, 10 percent; and butter, 28 percent.

Richmond also noted a decline in the number of people with elevated serum cholesterol. Between the early 1960's and the mid-1970's, the number of adults with serum cholesterol of 260 milligrams or higher fell 12 percent among men and 22 percent among women.

Whether such changes affected coronary death rates is uncertain. Many factors influence serum cholesterol besides the intake of dairy foods and eggs. And many factors besides serum cholesterol might influence coronary mortality.

Since the mid-1960's, for example, coronary-care units and other advances in treatment have reduced hospital deaths among cardiac patients by about one-third. Although most fatal heart attacks occur away from the hospital, improvements in hospital care and other medical treatment have probably contributed somewhat to the declining death rates.

During roughly the same period, moreover, other important changes have taken place regarding major coronary risk factors. The estimated percentage of Americans 20 years of age or older who smoke cigarettes has dropped 13 percent among women and 28 percent among men. Treatment for high blood pressure has also improved, and the number of people under treatment has increased by several million.

Unidentified factors might also be involved. Some experts have speculated, for example, that the infrequency of severe influenza epidemics since 1968 may have reduced the stress of respiratory infections on heart patients.

Most experts agree that the decline in coronary death rates, which has occurred in several countries besides the U.S., is still not clearly understood. Whether diet is a major factor is debatable. Switzerland, for instance, has experienced a major, long-term decline in deaths from all types of heart disease despite a concurrent rise of 20 percent in animal-fat consumption. Researchers have associated the decline with the growth of economic prosperity. In Japan, the already-low coronary death rate continues to fall, although intake of saturated fats has soared more than 200 percent. Here, better recognition and control of high blood pressure may be a factor in the decline.

Meanwhile, as the Surgeon General's report disclosed, many Americans appear to be heeding advice to eat less fat and cholesterol. The nation has become cholesterol conscious, and there's little doubt that Americans are consuming less animal fat and much more polyunsaturated fat than they did a generation ago. Accordingly, the Food and Nutrition Board's report last spring came as a shock to many people.

Grounds for skepticism

Essentially, the board's viewpoint reflects a frustrating fact about the diet-heart theory: What one would expect to happen on the basis of population comparisons and laboratory evidence has yet to be demonstrated in practice.

For one thing, the distinct differences that emerge when one population is compared to another tend to vanish among people *within* a population. The Japanese, for example, will show marked differences from Americans in fat intake, serum cholesterol, and heart-disease rates. But when Japanese are compared to other Japanese (in Japan), or Americans to other Americans, differences in fat intake or dietary habits show no consistent relationship to either serum-cholesterol levels or heart-disease incidence. In part, this is because the range of dietary variation within a country tends to be relatively narrow. Countries, on the other hand, may vary greatly from one another in eating habits and lifestyles.

Most studies that have examined the relationship of dietary components to heart disease among Americans have found no consistent association. One exception involves vegetarian groups such as Seventh-Day Adventists, where studies have noted a positive association between low intake of saturated fat and cholesterol and low rates of heart disease. However, these groups also differ substantially from most Americans in smoking habits, alcohol intake, and other important aspects of lifestyle. Consequently, the independent role of diet has been hard to assess.

The only other exception is a report recently published in The New England Journal of Medicine and widely covered in the press. Known as "The Western Electric Study," it investigated the diets and subsequent coronary-death incidence of 1900 middle-aged men selected at random from Western Electric Co.'s Hawthorne Works near Chicago.

In 1957, each man received an examination and dietary interview, which was supplemented by data from other sources. The entire process was then repeated a year later. Twenty years after the initial examination, the health status or death records of all participants were obtained and analyzed.

On the basis of the results, the researchers concluded that the overall fat composition of the diet "affects serum cholesterol concentration and the risk of coronary death in middle-aged American men." They also reported that high intake of cholesterol was associated with increased risk of coronary mortality.

A close examination of the study, however, raises doubts about its validity. Experts whom CU consulted judged its methodology to be questionable. The method for collecting dietary data was less than reliable, they said, and the lack of follow-up to check dietary changes over the years made the results suspect.

Among those who consider the study unpersuasive is Dr. Edward H. Ahrens Jr., an authority on fat metabolism at Rockefeller University in New York City and a pioneer in diet-heart studies. "One doesn't know how many dietary changes might have occurred since the interviews were taken," says Ahrens regarding the lack of follow-up. "It's hard to imagine that their eating habits wouldn't have been affected by all the publicity about diet and heart disease over the course of 20 years."

Meanwhile, some of the specific data reported in the study raised eyebrows. Intake of saturated fat, which tends to have the greatest effect on serum cholesterol, wasn't associated with risk of coronary death. And the group with the lowest cholesterol intake had a higher coronary-death rate than the group with a moderate cholesterol intake. Finally, the investigators later reported that a mistake had been made in calculating one of the two main dietary scores. The score was no longer statistically associated with the risk of coronary death.

In short, the Western Electric study offers little evidence that diet affects the risk of heart attack among Americans.

'Free-living' people

Most data showing the effects of dietary cholesterol or fats on serum cholesterol come from metabolic studies. As some scientists point out, however, people don't live in metabolic wards. Nor do they eat formula diets laced with precise amounts of pure cholesterol. They eat ordinary food on free-choice diets.

Among nutrition scientists, people living their usual lives on free-choice diets are called "free-living" people. One of the weak links in the diet-heart chain is that free-living people don't respond to variations in fat and cholesterol intake the way subjects in metabolic wards do. For example, no study conducted among groups of free-living Americans has been able to show that changes in cholesterol intake affect serum-cholesterol levels.

One explanation for those results is that a mixed diet contains a variety of compounds that have different effects on serum cholesterol. What effect a food will have may not depend solely on the amount of fat or cholesterol in it.

Fat-controlled diets have reduced serum cholesterol in clinical trials. But the ultimate test of the diet-heart theory is whether it reduces total mortality. Thus far, the results have been discouraging.

Eight large-scale clinical trials have been conducted in Australia, England, Finland, Norway, and the U.S., using dietary intervention to reduce the incidence of heart disease and mortality in middle-aged men. Approximately 3500 men were studied for 2 to 10 years, and serum-cholesterol reductions of 7 to 16 percent were achieved. In most of the studies, there was only a marginal decrease in coronary disease incidence and no effect on overall mortality. The design of each of these studies has been criticized on various grounds, however, so the results are not considered conclusive. In one of the better-designed studies, which was conducted in Finland, there was a significant decline in heart-attack deaths and a borderline decrease in total mortality. In short, the overall results of the eight studies have been mixed and largely inconclusive.

Accordingly, although elevated serum cholesterol is a risk factor for coronary heart disease, there is still insufficient proof that lowering serum cholesterol through diet reduces the risk. Most scientists are unwilling to abandon the dietary theory, however, partly because they believe it hasn't been definitively tested.

Complicating factors

Many things tend to complicate the search for a clear-cut result. High serum cholesterol, for instance, is only one of several factors believed to influence the risk of heart attacks. Cigarette smoking and high blood pressure are also major risk factors. Other influences include increasing age, male sex, maturity-onset diabetes, family history of heart disease, a sedentary lifestyle, and possibly personality characteristics or emotional stress. Furthermore, all the known risk factors combined account for only about 50 percent of the overall risk. Other important influences are unknown.

Another difficulty in assessing the role of diet is that individuals differ in the way their bodies respond to particular foods. In metabolic-ward studies, for example, most subjects experience only a slight increase in serum cholesterol after a cholesterol-rich meal. But some individuals seem particularly sensitive to dietary cholesterol; they experience a striking rise in serum cholesterol after eating cholesterol-rich foods. There is no way to predict how each person will respond.

The body, in fact, produces cholesterol on its own, about 800 to 1500 milligrams daily. The liver is the primary source, but most tissues—including the artery walls—can synthesize cholesterol from substances derived from carbohydrate and protein foods as well as from fat. Generally, when a person eats more cholesterol, the body produces less. When a person eats less cholesterol, the body produces more. That "feedback" process helps to regulate serum-cholesterol levels. How efficiently it operates, though, varies from one individual to another.

Within the last several years, moreover, scientists have learned that a formerly discarded theory about serum cholesterol may be crucial to understanding its role in heart disease. Certain cholesterol-carrying proteins in the blood, called high-density lipoproteins (HDL), appear to protect against coronary atherosclerosis. Others, called low-density lipoproteins (LDL), seem to promote the disease process. Yet both HDL and LDL contain cholesterol. Thus, **the relative distribution of cholesterol into the two types of lipoproteins may be as important as the serum cholesterol level.**

Studies indicate that women, lean people, nonsmokers, moderate drinkers, and people who exercise have relatively higher HDL levels, respectively, than men, obese people, smokers, nondrinkers, and sedentary people. As yet, the effect of diet on HDL and LDL levels isn't clear. What is clear, though, is that people vary widely not only in their coronary risk factors, but also in blood composition and in their response to diet.

Too little, too late?

Some scientists believe that such wide individual differences among people make blanket dietary advice concerning heart disease inadvisable for the general public. They argue that any decision about changing the diet of healthy people should await the outcome of studies now in progress.

Other scientists contend that the host of complicating factors may preclude ever reaching a clear answer about diet. They point out that most of the men in the clinical trials were either middle-aged or confirmed heart patients, and that the disease process was probably too far advanced for diet to do much good. It offered too little, too late. For diet to be of value, they say, it should begin earlier in life, before atherosclerosis is already advanced.

Organizations espousing action assume that enough is known about food to offer practical guidelines to the public—and that the advice proposed is safe. Some evidence suggests, though, that neither of those assumptions is beyond debate.

Take, for example, the standard admonition to cut back on dairy foods. For years, it has been assumed that milk, cream, cheese, and especially butter should be eaten sparingly, if at all, by those trying to **reduce saturated-fat intake and serum cholesterol. But part of that assumption may be mistaken.**

Since 1977, reports have appeared in The Lancet, Atherosclerosis, and The American Journal of Clinical Nutrition indicating that milk may actually *lower* blood cholesterol slightly rather than raise it. According to the investigators, there appear to be substances in milk that tend to inhibit cholesterol production by the liver. The cholesterol-lowering effect has been observed with yogurt as well.

The number of participants in the reported studies is relatively small, and the design of each study can be criticized on other grounds as well. So the findings require further confirmation. But it appears that a closer look at milk products is warranted before applying uniform advice to all dairy foods.

Eggs and shellfish

Under current AHA guidelines, people are advised to limit cholesterol intake to 300 milligrams daily. In effect, that relegates the egg, which contains about 250 milligrams, to the status of an occasional treat. Is that status deserved?

In metabolic-ward studies, patients or volunteers who ate moderate to large amounts of egg yolk experienced variable increases in serum cholesterol. Several recent studies among free-living people, however, have reported no significant increases in serum cholesterol when one or two eggs daily were added to the diet for several weeks or months.

Overall, the studies CU has reviewed suggest that most healthy people experience no significant rise in serum cholesterol with moderate egg consumption. As noted earlier, though, some people are sensitive to dietary cholesterol and may need to treat eggs as occasional fare. Scientists are currently trying to develop a practical way to identify such people.

Meanwhile, eggs are relatively low in

calories and high in important nutrients, making them especially suitable for diets to reduce obesity. Weight loss among people who are overweight is often one of the most effective ways to reduce serum cholesterol, and recent estimates indicate that as many as 80 million Americans are overweight. So, a policy that discourages egg consumption to reduce serum cholesterol may be self-defeating.

Shellfish are another food often limited in cholesterol-lowering diets. The "high-cholesterol" label was affixed to shellfish soon after a 1963 study reported that a shrimp diet produced atherosclerosis in rabbits. Actually, shrimp are higher in cholesterol than most other shellfish. British tests of local shellfish disclose cholesterol levels only slightly higher than in other fish. The effects on serum cholesterol from eating various shellfish are unknown, largely because tests in humans are lacking.

Hard or soft fat?

The gaps in current knowledge about diet aren't limited to the effects of specific foods. There are unanswered questions as well about the overall diet that the AHA and Federal agencies are urging the public to follow.

Since the diet is relatively low in fat and high in carbohydrates, it tends to produce body tissues rich in saturated fatty acids, or "hard fat." One of the diets previously tested in clinical trials was moderate in total fat but much higher in polyunsaturated fat, tending to produce body tissues rich in unsaturated fatty acids, or "soft fat."

Both diets, if conscientiously followed, are capable of reducing serum cholesterol. But which is preferable for overall health, including possible reduction of heart disease? Addressing that question in The Lancet in December, 1979, Ahrens of Rockefeller University emphasized that the issue has not been adequately studied. He and his associates are only now beginning to investigate whether the fatty-acid composition of body tissues affects cholesterol transport, immune response of white blood cells, aging of cells, and the like. Such processes might conceivably be affected by the "hardness" or "softness" of body fat, says Ahrens. "How can we make the choice now, in the face of the unanswered questions, to request the general public to adhere to a low-fat diet?"

The cancer question

Another unanswered question is now drawing increasing attention. Several studies, including one conducted recently by the National Heart, Lung, and Blood Institute, have found a significant association between low serum cholesterol and increased cancer mortality, particularly colon cancer.

The surprising association first came to light in 1969, following a clinical trial in Los Angeles to test the effects of diet on heart disease. Since then, a total of 10 studies have examined the question among various groups. Four have found no association, and six have reported a positive one.

Thus far, scientists believe the evidence does not prove that either cholesterol-lowering diets or low serum cholesterol itself increases the risk of cancer. In fact, one analysis concludes that the relation may be reversed: Cancer undetected at the time of initial examination may have reduced serum-cholesterol levels.

But the issue still requires more study, and the National Heart, Lung, and Blood Institute has scheduled a conference of experts this month to explore the matter further. In the meantime, the institute cautions heart patients on fat-controlled diets not to abandon the regimen. The risk of heart attack is still far greater than the uncertain risk of cancer.

Some scientists believe that risks from dietary changes are minimal, while others are concerned that unsuspected problems may occur. Even for the AHA, the issue of risk remains an active one, especially concerning preventive diets for children in high-risk families. At a recent AHA meeting, according to a report in Science magazine, the current and past presidents of the association "privately expressed opposite views" on the issue.

Dr. James Schoenberger, the current president, reportedly felt strongly that "prudent" diets should be advised for everyone, including children. He stressed that there was more than enough evidence to support such action.

Dr. Thomas N. James, the immediate past president, disagreed. He was concerned over possible long-term effects on children of a diet that was still unproved. "Their brains are developing, their muscles are developing, their bones are growing. And the prudent diet is still pushing *increased* amounts of unsaturated fats, whose effects are unknown," says James. "Do we really know enough about the long-range consequences of such dietary advice to be confident of its merit?"

Recommendations

Since the safety and efficacy of fat-controlled diets have yet to be proved and perhaps never will be, CU's medical consultants cannot recommend such a dietary policy to the entire population. Its implications for women have not been studied, nor is anything known about the long-term effects of such diets begun in childhood or adolescence.

Meanwhile, the protective role of HDL cholesterol in heart disease—and how diet might influence it—is only now being explored. What is eventually learned may have an important bearing on dietary advice for individuals.

CU's medical consultants believe that people with serum-cholesterol levels judged to be a risk factor for coronary heart disease would be the target population most likely to benefit from changes in diet. And among those people, dietary manipulation should not be applied in a vacuum. Elimination of cigarette smoking, control of hypertension and diabetes, avoidance of a sedentary lifestyle, and attainment of an ideal body weight should all be part of a comprehensive program to reduce the incidence of coronary heart disease.

CARDIOVASCULAR

Cholesterol and Noncardiovascular Mortality

by National Institutes of Health

Of potential medical interest is a meeting recently held at National Institutes of Health (NIH) under National Heart, Lung, and Blood Institute (NHLBI) sponsorship to review data from eight epidemiologic studies relating serum cholesterol levels and mortality from noncardiovascular causes.

Data from four of these studies suggest that very low cholesterol levels (below approximately 180 mg/dL), while associated with very low mortality from coronary heart disease, may be associated with some increase in subsequent risk of mortality from various types of cancer.

An inverse statistical relationship between naturally occurring serum cholesterol levels and cancer risk (lower levels being associated with higher cancer mortality) has been observed among men (but not women) in the Framingham Heart Study and among the men participating in the Puerto Rico Heart Study and the Honolulu Heart Study. Previous studies by Kark et al[1] in Evans County, Georgia, and by Beaglehole et al,[2] among New Zealand Maoris, had also suggested such an inverse relationship.

However, though the inverse relationship reached statistical significance ($P=.05$) in the Framingham, Puerto Rico, and Honolulu studies, it apparently is not a constant one. In several other large population studies reviewed by the panel, which included experts in epidemiology, nutrition, gastroenterology, lipid metabolism, and pathology, there was no significant association between cholesterol levels and cancer mortality.

The panel agreed that available data are insufficient to conclude that there is a causal relationship between low cholesterol and cancer risk. The data may instead be reflecting effects on blood lipids of inapparent or silent malignant disease, a conclusion reached by Rose and Shipley[3] in a recent study among London civil servants.

But the panel also agreed that the preliminary finding in some studies of a significant association between very low cholesterol level and increased cancer risk required further investigation to ascertain whether the association is valid and, if so, to determine reasons for it.

The panel believed that further detailed laboratory study should await validation and clarification of existing epidemiologic data, including reexamination of data from other ongoing population studies for evidence in support or in refutation of any cholesterol-cancer connection. Toward this end epidemiologists from NHLBI and the National Cancer Institute (NCI) will continue to review data from studies in progress, and investigators in the United States and abroad who are working in related areas are being asked to analyze their data with regard to whether or not similar cholesterol-cancer relationships are suggested.

The panel and the NCI conclude that physicians should continue treating elevated cholesterol levels when encountered in their patients, since the risk of mortality from coronary heart disease posed by elevated cholesterol levels far exceeds the small and uncertain increase in risk of malignant neoplasms associated with very low cholesterol levels in some of these studies. They also think it still desirable for the average person to follow prudent patterns of diet if his blood cholesterol level tends to be high.

It is a common observation in medicine that physiological measures have particular ranges of values that correlate with health and longevity, whereas values greatly above or below that range are accompanied by pathological correlates of various kinds. For example, body weight has a healthful range, with excessive overweight or underweight being disadvantageous and often accompanied by different diseases. There are numerous other instances of excess or deficiency states resulting in illness: iron deficiency anemia and hemochromatosis, hyperthyroidism and hypothyroidism, and vitamin deficiencies and vitamin A or D toxic reaction, to name only a few. It may turn out that the lowest end of the blood cholesterol distribution (levels below 180 mg/dL) may not be optimal from the standpoint of overall mortality, even as the upper end of the distribution is disadvantageous from the standpoint of cardiovascular disease mortality. The former remains to be demonstrated; however, the latter is well documented.

A second meeting of experts will be convened next

spring to assess the additional data relating to blood cholesterol levels and cancer risk.

1. Kark JD, Smith AH, Hames CG: The relationship of serum cholesterol to the incidence of cancer in Evans County, Georgia. *J Chronic Dis*, to be published.

2. Beaglehole R, Foulkes MA, Prior IA, et al: Cholesterol and mortality in New Zealand Maoris. *Br Med J* 1:285-287, 1980.

3. Rose G, Shipley MJ: Plasma lipids and mortality: A source of error. *Lancet* 1:523-526, 1980.

CARDIOVASCULAR

The Great Cholesterol Debate

by Tim Hackler

Last spring, the Food and Nutrition Board of the National Research Council stirred up a storm of protest by questioning the conventional wisdom that a diet high in cholesterol promotes coronary heart disease. The reaction was swift and vitriolic as critics of the board accused its members of everything but buying egg futures. Now that the dust has settled, what have we learned about the link between cholesterol and coronary heart disease — still the number-one killer in the United States?

For thirty years a growing number of doctors advised their patients at risk for coronary heart disease — mostly middle-aged men — to cut down on their intake of cholesterol. And the message got through: between 1965 and 1979 the consumption of cholesterol-rich eggs dropped by nearly 20 percent. The advice was based on impeccable reasoning, given the information available at the time. A number of studies had shown that individuals who had higher-than-average amounts of cholesterol in their bloodstream had higher-than-average chances of developing coronary heart disease.

As a result of these studies, it was assumed that coronary heart disease was caused by high concentrations of cholesterol in the blood, and that high concentrations of cholesterol in the blood were caused by high levels of cholesterol in the diet. These assumptions are now in question.

Cholesterol is a fat and as such does not mix with liquids. Therefore, to move cholesterol through the bloodstream, the body produces substances called lipoproteins. For two decades, American research was focused on low-density lipoproteins (LDLs), which pick up excess cholesterol and deposit it on the interior linings of coronary arteries. Newer research, however, has demonstrated the existence of another kind of lipoprotein — high-density lipoproteins (HDLs), which work in the opposite direction: they float around in the bloodstream, pick up excess cholesterol and carry it back to the liver for excretion from the body. According to some researchers, the key to the causation of coronary disease is not so much the total amount of cholesterol in the blood as it is the ratio of LDLs to HDLs. Even if your total cholesterol level is high, you may have little risk of heart disease if your HDL-LDL ratio is high. This ratio is probably determined at least in part by heredity.

While some researchers are questioning whether a high level of cholesterol is itself a causative agent — as opposed to a *sign* — of coronary heart disease, others are questioning the theory on even more fundamental grounds. They say that even if high cholesterol in the blood does cause coronary heart disease, there is no proof that a high level of cholesterol in the diet translates into a high level of cholesterol in the blood.

In a diet too *low* in cholesterol (not a common situation in any industrial country), it will be manufactured in the liver, because cholesterol — in spite of its bad press — *does* have its functions to perform. It is a necessary ingredient in pituitary, adrenal and gonadal hormones; it helps emulsify fats, and it is a conductor of nerve impulses.

A case defending cholesterol in diets has been put forth by Dr. Norman Spritz, chief of medicine at the Veterans Administration Medical Center in New York and a recognized expert on nutrition: "It turns out that our bodies manufacture much of our cholesterol" and that the effect of diet is "relatively small." He has also said that "there is no direct data to support the contention" that lower dietary cholesterol would lead to fewer heart attacks.

Why, then, did the Food and Nutrition Board's report raise such a fuss? Part of the explanation will have to be left to sociologists and historians, for the reaction in many circles was curiously emotional. Yet, even though many respected organizations have accepted the cholesterol theory and recommended diets accordingly, the opinion has been by no means unanimous. "It is becoming increasingly apparent . . . that widely accepted coronary-risk factors and dietary regimens for their correction may be due for reassessment," wrote Dr. Samuel Vaisrub in 1977 in the *Journal of the American Medical Association*. Dr. Vaisrub, a senior editor of *JAMA*, was reflecting the judgment of the AMA.

Still, critics of the report did make some provocative points. In the first place, the Food and Nutrition Board was heavily weighted with biochemists and other researchers from the "hard" sciences. It did not contain any epidemiologists — statisticians who draw conclusions about the origins of diseases from studying incidence rates among large population groups.

Critics also note that the board does recommend that persons "with a positive family history of heart disease and other risk factors, such as obesity, hypertension and diabetes" should consult a physician in regard to the possibility of going on a low-cholesterol diet. Critics point out that these categories make up half the population and suggest that a policy of cholesterol reduction among the entire population would be prudent.

The fundamental disagreement on how to interpret the tan-

Reprinted courtesy *Mainliner* magazine, carried aboard UNITED AIRLINES. Copyright 1980, East/West Network, Inc., publisher.

talizing but contradictory evidence available is illustrated by the conclusions reached by two doctors associated with the Framingham (Massachusetts) Heart Study, which monitored the health of 5,127 people for twenty-eight years. Dr. William B. Kannel concluded in his final report that there is "no discernible association between the amount of cholesterol in the diet and the level of cholesterol in the blood. No matter how much or how little animal fat there is in the diet, some people will have low levels of cholesterol in their blood; others will have moderate levels and others high levels." Yet his coworker from the study, Dr. William P. Castelli, has said that "it appears that a low-fat, low-cholesterol diet can have almost the same effect on preventing coronary disease as a favorable HDL-LDL ratio."

In the face of such contradictory conclusions, what should you do, if anything, about your own diet? For one thing, you can consult your doctor and get a blood test that will reveal the concentration of cholesterol and lipoproteins. If cholesterol or LDLs are abnormally high, then you almost certainly will want to reduce your dietary cholesterol. In addition, your doctor may prescribe drugs, such as cholestryamine, nicotine acid and clofibrate, which lower cholesterol concentration. A new drug called L-prostacyclin may be even more effective when it is approved.

Perhaps, then, the final word should go to the advocates of erring-on-the-side-of-caution. One doctor who believes that "the relationship between high-cholesterol foods and arteriosclerosis is not nearly as well substantiated as many doctors have led the general public to believe" nevertheless found himself cutting back. Dr. William Nolan says, "My personal approach to cholesterol-rich foods has changed since my heart surgery two and a half years ago for arteriosclerotic disease. I am not as rigid in my diet as I initially was. However, I do not often eat extremely high-cholesterol foods — partly because they are often loaded with calories and partly because, as a physician, I have been influenced, perhaps 'brainwashed' — by the anti-cholesterol thesis. I find it difficult, after twenty-five years, to shed this thesis emotionally even though, intellectually, I find it far from compelling."

CARDIOVASCULAR

Saturated Fat and Cholesterol: Dietary 'Risk Factors' or Essential to Human Life?

by Fred A. Kummerow, Ph.D.

The current view on dietary "risk factors" is so overwhelmingly focused on saturated fat and cholesterol that it may have hindered a clear understanding of the pathology that evolves in the development of atherosclerosis, the underlying cause for 90% of all coronary heart disease (CHD).

Blackburn[1] stated recently in *Heartbook,* a publication of the American Heart Association, "The surest and in fact the only way to produce fatty arteries in animals is to feed them diets high in cholesterol." He overlooked the fact that the coronary arteries from weanling swine fed a low fat cholesterol free diet can be 90% occluded (damaged by cholesterol deposits) by the simple addition of an excess amount of cholecalciferol (vitamin D_3) to the diet for a short period of time in a life span of six months[2].

Furthermore, the aortae (the main blood vessel) from humans subjected to elective coronary bypass surgery exhibited the same type of pathology as swine that had never been fed cholesterol or saturated fat[3-5]). This pathology seems to be due to the natural consequence of "aging." The key question to ask is, Do the saturated fat and cholesterol in the American diet accelerate the "aging" of arteries?

This focus on saturated fat and cholesterol has resulted from a seemingly logical interpretation of studies with either animal or human models fed diets imbalanced with excessive calories from saturated fats or excessive amounts of cholesterol. The incidence of atherosclerosis increased in animal models fed 1-2% cholesterol (the equivalent of the level of cholesterol in 80 eggs or more/day)[6-8]. Also, the serum cholesterol level increased in human subjects fed artificial diets in which polyunsaturated fats, as the only source of fat, were replaced by saturated fats[9-11].

The incidence of atherosclerosis can be lower in populations which consume 900 mg/day, such as Eastern Europeans, rather than 600 mg/day of cholesterol, such as Western Europeans. Both populations consume a mix of polyunsaturated and saturated fat rather than one fat at the exclusion of the other[12]. Furthermore, the serum cholesterol level of human subjects on nutritionally balanced diets did not decrease when a highly polyunsaturated fat was included in their diet[13].

Risk Factors or Essential Factors?

As the average dietary cholesterol intake of Americans is no more than 600 mg/day, and as they consume both polyunsaturated and saturated fats, neither cholesterol nor saturated fatty acids should be considered "risk factors" in such diets. In fact, they should be considered "essential factors" to human life.

Saturated fatty acids and cholesterol are so essential to life that they are synthesized *in vivo* from carbohydrate, polyunsaturated fatty acids (PUFA) or protein so as to assure adequate levels for tissue structure and function. Their structural role is vital to the structure of the phospholipids in every cell membrane and to the triglycerides in cell tissue.

As polyunsaturated fatty acids increase the "fluidity" of phospholipids, the presence of PUFA in high concentrations in marine mammals must be important to their survival in cold water[14]. Dolphins and whales contain over 25% of long chain C_{20} and C_{22} polyunsaturated fatty acids with four to five double bonds or points of unsaturation and less than 25% saturated fatty acids.

Terrestrial mammals contain less than 1% of C_{20} and C_{22} (PUFA) fatty acids, and more than 25% saturated fatty acids[14]. The need for less fluidity in the phospholipids of the cell membranes in terrestrial mammals requires the presence of more saturated fatty acids[15,16].

Essential Need for Saturated Fatty Acids

All vegetable-source fats (margarine, shortening, frying fats, salad oils) and all animal-source fats (butter, lard, tallow) as well as human milk and human body fat contain saturated fatty acids (Table 1). Furthermore, no significant difference is evident in the fat composition of people consuming different diets. Lipids in the erythrocytes (red blood cells—RBC's) from human populations on largely vegetarian diets (Japanese) contain as high a percentage of saturated fatty acids as those from human populations on largely nonvegetarian (American) diets (Table 2).

The saturated fatty acids in human back fat provide a plastic cushion of fat in which the kidneys are imbedded, and they form a layer of fat of varying thickness under the skin which insulated the body against extremes in environmental temperature. As the unsaturated fatty acids are all liquid at body temperature (37°C), they cannot substitute for saturated fatty acids in either capacity.

The saturated and unsaturated fatty acids that are present in the phospholipids help to bridge the gap between water insoluble and water soluble compounds in the body, and they form cholesterol esters which are present in nerves and brain tissue in high concentration. Both saturated and unsaturated fatty acids can serve as energy sources in the body.

Mechanisms in the body decide which fatty acid in a dietary fat is to be deposited in the tissue stores and which is to be "burned away" or metabolized. For example, an analysis of the fat depots of animals fed butter indicate that the major share of the short chain saturated fatty acids in butter (butyric, caproic, caprylic, and capric acids) are lengthened or used as energy (17).

Human adipose tissue fat contains only traces of these saturated fatty acids which are present in butterfat to a total concentration of almost 10%. Butterfat contains 2.8% lauric acid and 10.1% myristic acid, human tissue fat contains only 1.1% and 3.6% of these saturated fatty acids, respectively (Table 1).

Palmitic acid, the saturated fatty acid which many cardiologists are most concerned about, is present in approximately the same concentration in human fat as in lard and beef tallow. Vegetable oils contain three times more linoleic acid (the main PUFA) than human tissue fat. Due to the increased consumption of such oils, the linoleic acid content of human tissue has more than doubled in the last 30 years—from 8% in 1943 to 18.2% in 1975[18]. This increase was at the expense of oleic, palmitic, and stearic acid.

Studies with animal models have shown that excess amounts of linoleic are "burned up." The amount that is burned up, however, depends on body needs[19]. Radioactively tagged linoleic was rapidly metabolized to carbon dioxide combined with glycerol, phosphoric acid derivatives, other fatty acids, and even synthesized into cholesterol. When radioactively tagged linoleic acid was fed to rats kept on a diet containing corn oil, more of it was metabolized in a 24-hour period than when it was fed to rats kept on a diet containing coconut oil[20].

When greatly in excess of body need, however, the linoleic acid in corn oil displaced oleic acid, and more saturated stearic and palmitic acid were then synthesized in the body to keep the body's unsaturated fat content as normal as possible[21]. When fed diets in which hydrogenated vegetable fat was substituted for beef tallow, swine had higher serum cholesterol levels although there was no apparent influence on lipoprotein levels or lipoprotein composition[22].

Salad oils such as corn and sunflower seed oil are excellent sources of the essential linoleic acid and vitamin E, but they do not contain fewer calories than butterfat, lard, or beef tallow. The fats in milk, cheese, eggs, and meat contain less linoleic acid than in corn oil, but they more than compensate for their lack of linoleic acid by the protein, vitamins, and minerals they contain, all essential to optimum nutrition. High polyunsaturates are not an adequate dietary trade-off for other nutrients essential to health. Animal models fed all of the essential nutrients develop atherosclerosis at a slower rate than those on high calorie *imbalanced* diets[12].

Rhesus monkeys fed a diet of commonly available food items in an amount 200 Calories/day higher than the amount considered prudent (for monkeys) had higher serum cholesterol levels and a greater incidence of atherosclerosis than those on nutritionally optimum diets[23]. The prudent diet was identical to the nutrient requirement of the rhesus monkey as suggested for this animal model by the Food and Nutrition Board, National Academy of Science[24].

Essential Need for Cholesterol

Cholesterol, as well as the saturated fatty acids, serves as a structural component and as a functional component in every cell in the body. It serves as a structural component in the skin and provides it the properties to shed water. It also insulates brain and nerve cells in an aqueous system so that stimuli can be carried from nerve endings for interpretation by the brain. It is an essential structural component in the thin layer of membrane that surrounds every one of the ten trillion specialized cells in the heart, liver, kidney, muscles, brain, nerves, veins, arteries, eyes, intestines, and the various glands and other organs of the body.

Plants have no need for cholesterol for their structure or function and therefore do not synthesize it in their tissue, whereas every animal cell must have cholesterol to exist.

Cholesterol serves as a functional component by providing specialized glands the starting structure for the making of hormones which regulate and act much like the conductor of a symphony orchestra, directing all of the specialized cells in unison so as to provide life.

Phospholipid and protein combine with cholesterol to act as lipoprotein "carriers" of the fat absorbed in the intestinal tract from the fat in the diet. The lipoproteins are heterogeneous in composition varying from 90% fat (very low density lipoproteins—VLDL), 75% fat (low density lipoproteins—LDL) and 50% fat (high density lipoproteins—HDL). They "carry" the energy-yielding fat to the fat storage (adipose tissue) from which it is released as a fatty acid protein complex as needed[25]. Because the diet may not furnish enough cholesterol to satisfy the need for optimum lipoprotein synthesis, cholesterol must be "made" in the body, i.e., synthesized from fat, carbohydrate, or protein in the diet. Approximately 1500 mg of cholesterol is synthesized every day, most of it in the liver. It is believed that normal subjects maintain a plasma LDL cholesterol of approximately 120 mg/dl. There are approximately 1/250 to 1/500 "heterozygous" people with a serum LDL cholesterol level that is elevated two- to threefold and 1/1,000,000 "homozygous" people with a serum LDL cholesterol level that is elevated sixfold[26]. These people develop coronary heart disease at an earlier age than "normal" people.

Cholesterol gradually accumulates in the arteries of all people during a lifespan, especially in the coronary arteries which supply blood to the heart. Some researchers believe that the cholesterol in foods derived from animal tissues, such as meat, dairy products, and eggs, adds unnecessarily to the cholesterol that is made in the body every day[11,23]. Others believe that only a fraction of the cholesterol in these animal food products is absorbed from the intestinal tract and finds its way into the blood[8,26].

No one to date has proven that this exogenous (source outside the body) cholesterol adds to the cholesterol that normally accumulates in the arteries of Americans consuming the average 600 mg/day of cholesterol from meat, dairy products, and eggs "balanced" with fruits, vegetables, and cereals to furnish all of the essential nutrients.

A low serum cholesterol level and the least amount of lipid deposits in the arteries (atherosclerosis) have always been noted in the "control" animal models fed a diet which contains all of the essential nutrients. When such a diet is "imbalanced" with added calories from either vegetable or animal fat, both the serum cholesterol level and the incidence of atherosclerosis in animal models increases. An analogous situation exists in Americans eating too many calories from fat and sugar.

Serum cholesterol levels can be lowered by decreasing the caloric intake, by decreasing the level of dietary fat, by balancing protein intake, and by exercising to "burn off" calories.

Adjustments in metabolic levels may reduce the hereditary heterozygous and homozygous type of dangerously high cholesterol levels. This requires further research. The serum cholesterol level varies from one individual to another and is often considered the warning tip of the iceberg. On the other hand, the coronary arteries can be occluded in human subjects exhibiting below "normal" cholesterol level without the "warning tip."

Those researchers and advocates for change to a cereal-type diet to reduce dietary cholesterol intake from meat, milk, and eggs from 600 to 300 mg/day have not considered how such a change could imbalance the American diet. Hundreds of millions of Chinese, Indians, Africans, and Latin Americans fill their stomachs with little else than cereals every day of the year. However, they have neither excessive fat nor excessive sugar in their diet. Americans need foods which are "nutrient packed" to balance out their daily caloric intake from the nutrient-deficient fat and sugar sources in their diet.

In moderation, fat and sugar sources can be economical and are pleasant to eat. Balanced out with nutrient-packed meat, milk, and eggs, this combination has provided the most nutritious diet available to man to date. Along with fruits, vegetables, and cereals, this diet has increased life expectancy to at least ten years longer than for people on largely cereal diets[12].

Cereals are a modest source of protein, vitamins, and minerals. Combined with meat, milk, eggs, fruits, and vegetables and consumed in balance, without excess nutrient-deficient food (junk food), this diet provides for maximum health and an increased life span.

Meat, eggs, and dairy products furnish the major required nutrients to most easily attain the daily recommended dietary allowances (RDA). These nutrient sources do not alter tissue lipid structure or function in human subjects. Saturated fat and cholesterol are not "risk factors" in balanced diets.

REFERENCES

1. *The American Heart Association Heartbook.* Eds. E.P. Dutton, New York, N.Y. 1980.
2. Taura, S., Taura, M., Imai, H. and Kummerow., F.A., 1978. Coronary atherosclerosis in normocholesterolemic swine artery. *Arter. Wall* 4:395.
3. Taura, S., Taura, M., Tokuyasu, K., Kamio, A., Kummerow, F.A. and Cleveland, J.C., 1978. Human arterio- and atherosclerosis: Identical to that in a 6- and 36-month-old swine fed a corn soy diet free of cholesterol and saturated fat. *Artery* 4:100.
4. Kamio, A., Kummerow, F.A. and Imai, H., 1977. Degeneration of aortic smooth muscle cells in swine fed excess vitamin D_3. *Arch. Pathol. Lab. Med.* 101:378.
5. Taura, A., Taura, M., Tokuyasu, K., Kamio, A. and Kummerow, F.A., 1977. Ultrastructure of aortic intima obtained as a by-product of coronary bypass surgery. *Artery* 3:529.
6. Imai, H., Lee, S.K., Pastori, S.J. and Thomas, W.A., 1970. Degeneration of arterial smooth muscle cells: Ultrastructural study of smooth muscle cell death in control and cholesterol-fed *animals. Virchows Arch. Pathol. Anat.* 350:183.
7. Imai, H. and Thomas, W.A., 1968. Cerebral atherosclerosis in swine. Role of necrosis in progression of diet induced lesions from proliferative to atheromatous stage. *Exptl. Molec. Pathol.* 8:830.
8. Imai, H., Werthessen, N.T., Taylor, C.B. and Lee, K.T., 1976. Angiotoxicity and arteriosclerosis due to contaminants of USP-grade cholesterol. *Arch. Pathol. Lab. Med.* 100:565.
9. Ahrens, E.H., Jr., Insull, W., Jr., Blomstrand, R., Hirsch, J., Tsaltas, T.T. and Peterson, M.L., 1957. The influence of dietary fats on serum-lipid levels in man. *Lancet* 1:943.
10. Kummerow, F.A., Ueno, A., Nishida, T. and Kokatnur, M., 1960. Unsaturated fatty acids and plasma lipids. *Am. J. Clin. Nutr.* 8:62.
11. Connor, W.E., Stone, D.B. and Hodges, R.E., 1964. The interrelated effects of dietary cholesterol and fat upon human serum lipid levels. *J. Clin. Invest.* 43:1691.
12. Kummerow, F.A., 1979. Nutrition imbalance and angiotoxins as dietary risk factors in coronary heart disease. *Am. J. Clin. Nutr.* 32:58.
13. Emken, E.A. and Dutton, H.J., eds. Geometrical and positional fatty acid isomers. *Am. Oil Chem. Soc.*, Champaign, Ill., 1979.
14. Hilditch, T.P. *The chemical constitution of natural fats,* 2nd ed. John Wiley and Sons, Inc. New York, N.Y., 1947, p. 55.
15. Chapman, D. *Biological membranes physical fact and function.* Academic Press, New York, N.Y. 1968.
16. Van Deenen, L.L.M. In *Molecular basis of membrane function,* ed. D.C. Testeson. Prentice Hall, Englewood Cliffs, New York, N.Y., 1969.
17. Egwin, P.O. and Kummerow, F.A., 1972. Influence of dietary fat on the concentration of long-chain unsaturated fatty acid families in rat tissues. *J. Lipid Res.* 13:500.
18. Witting, L.A., Ph.D., Lok Lee, M.S., 1975. Recommended dietary allowance for vitamin E: Relation to dietary, erythrocyte and adipose tissue linoleate. *Am. J. Clin. Nutr.* 28:577.
19. Sgoutas, D.S. and Kummerow, F.A. The influences of the major fatty acids in milk fat on serum cholesterol levels. From: *Symposium: Dairy Lipids and Lipid Metabolism,* eds. M.F. Brink & D. Kritchevsky. The Avi Publishing Co., Inc., Westport, Conn., 1968, p. 116.
20. Sgoutas, D.S., Moon Ja Kim and Kummerow, F.A., 1965. Radiohomogineity of ^{3}H and ^{14}C labeled linoleic acid in vivo. *J. Lipid Res.* 6:383.
21. Chu, T.K. and Kummerow, F.A., 1950. The deposition of linolenic acid in chickens fed linseed oil. *Poultry Sci.* 29:846.
22. Jackson, R.L., Morrisett, J.D., Pownall, H.J., Gotto, A.M., Jr., Kamio, A., Imai, H., Tracy, R. and Kummerow, F.A., 1977. Influence of dietary trans-fatty acids on swine lipoprotein composition and structure. *J. Lipid Res.* 18:182.
23. Wissler, R. Development of the atherosclerotic plaque. In: *The myocardium: Failure and infarction,* ed. E. Braunwald, H.P. Publishing Co., N.Y., 1974, p. 155.
24. *Nutrient Requirements of Laboratory Animals,* 2nd ed., Number 10, National Academy, Washington, D.C.
25. Jackson, R.L., Morrisett, J.D. and Gotto, A.M., Jr., 1976. Lipoprotein structure and metabolism. *Physiol. Rev.* 56:259.
26. Lauer, R.M. and Shekelle, R.B., eds. *Childhood prevention of athersclerosis and hypertension.* Raven Press, New York, N.Y., 1980.

CARDIOVASCULAR

Sure Cures, Quick Fixes and Easy Answers: A Cautionary Tale About Coronary Disease

by Thomas N. James, M.D.

In a country craving for simple solutions to complex problems it is dangerously tempting to promise more than can be delivered. Yet, history teaches us that citizens deal harshly with false prophets. Today I want to share with you my growing concern about overpromise in coronary disease. My remarks will be centered about the matter of credibility, both of the American Heart Association and of medical science in general.

For over three decades now dietary cholesterol has been one of the most intensely studied subjects in science, especially as it may or may not relate to the development of coronary disease. Despite this remarkable concentration of scientific talent and fiscal resources, the terms "diet-lipid hypothesis" and "the cholesterol controversy" have become commonplace even in nonmedical publications. If something remains hypothetical and controversial over so long a time and despite intensive research, surely it is time that we take a different look at the subject. My own interest in the matter was wonderfully focused within the past year by the report of the National Research Council (NRC) which has stimulated so much anguish and even some angry confrontation.

Most of the NRC report dealt with subjects such as the prudence of maintaining normal weight, with which almost no one will quarrel. Two components of the NRC report differed somewhat from American Heart Association advice. The NRC recommended more salt restriction for all Americans than we believe is prudent, and in fact could be dangerous. But where the real debate emerged was between the more liberal advice of the NRC who said that only some people need be concerned with fats and cholesterol while the American Heart Association recommendations are much broader and apply to virtually everyone. I wish to express some personal concern about our nonexceptional advice, which is taken by the public as meaning that everyone should be deeply concerned about their dietary cholesterol. It is not overstating the matter to say that the public thinks cholesterol causes heart attacks, although most of them are not clear just how that happens.

In a nation of over a quarter of a billion people we are an enormously heterogeneous lot, and in truth there are no two of us alike. Those with low cholesterols as a group seem to have less coronary disease than those with high cholesterols, but this is too often extrapolated to apply directly to one individual. Let us look for a moment at the components in this loop of logic. Epidemiologists have long recognized and publicly deplored the soft nature of the clinical data obtained from masses of people, data which they then subject to increasingly complex and sophisticated mathematical analysis. But no matter how marvelous such an analysis may be, there is no escaping the fact that the entire initial basis so often is less exact, less reproducible and less reliable than any of us would wish. This flaw is sometimes addressed by demands for an increase in the sample size, extensive lengthening of observation time, or the utilization of mathematical smoothing maneuvers and creation of comparability indices, as if any of these could somehow strengthen the original weakness. But no chain can be stronger than its weakest link.

The other end of the loop in this logic may be even more flawed, and that is in the applicability of mass data to one person. In a study to be presented at these scientific sessions, Naito and his colleagues from the Cleveland Clinic have found that a low level of high density lipoprotein can be considered a risk factor for coronary disease based on population data, but that it is not a dependable clinical diagnostic aid for predicting the severity of coronary disease in one person. There is no physician in this audience who has not treated patients with terrible coronary disease but no cholesterol problem and, conversely, patients with unequivocal abnormalities of cholesterol but who have no coronary disease. Whether these are frequent or infrequent exceptions to the rule is not the point. The point is that every patient is unique, that cholesterol may or may not be a true risk factor in that one person, and that there are indisputably other important risk factors.

BASIS FOR ADVICE

In considering our dietary advice for entire populations four things merit particular concern. First, we should be more explicit in telling the public when our advice is based on factual evidence, when it is from logical deductions, and when it is actually conjectural, no matter how reasonable that conjecture may be. Second, we should be more honest about the difference between risk reduction and true prevention, a fundamental difference too often rhetorically blurred. Third, we had better be concerned about how much of our advice and possibly subsequent regulation is good for society, independent from what health benefits may or may not accrue from such regulations. Put another way, we are coming closer to 1984 all the time, both chronologically and philosophically. Fourth, in our growing trend to think of atherosclerosis as beginning in childhood, an appealing but possibly treacherous concept, we had better think very carefully about possibly harmful long-term side effects from dietary manipulations in children.

Dealing with my first expressed concern, when we advised the public that they should eat less saturated fat and cholesterol, it is seldom made sufficiently clear that this advice is based on reasonable deductions rather than absolute proof, that such advice may or may not be helpful to everybody or could even be harmful to some, or that dietary modifications without due consideration of other risk factors may be of little avail. Given the soft nature of much of the relevant evidence, would it not be better to advise the public that it is unhealthy to be fat, that the surest way to control one's calories is to reduce dietary fat intake, that the cholesterol content may or may not be independently important in dietary fat reduction and if any one person has a question about that, it would be wise to consult a physician for specific personal advice?

MEANS FOR PREVENTION

My second concern stems from hearing and reading repeated claims about preventing coronary disease. Now no one, and almost certainly no one here, is likely to speak against the value of preventing heart disease. The American Heart Association is fully committed to doing everything possible for such prevention and shares with many others a great pride in seeing what happened in preventing rheumatic heart disease. But much as any of us may want to believe so, we do not yet have the means of preventing coronary disease. We may have the means of reducing the incidence of coronary disease in large masses of people, but that is not the same thing as telling one person that you can prevent coronary disease.

When we talk about prevention we must not succumb to sloganeering. Many of these banner cries by legislators, news reporters, and others with true social conscience arise from epidemiological studies. Somehow we must separate the almost synonymous apposition of epidemiology and prevention, that has now become a standard term for councils, symposia, task forces and the like. Separating the two is necessary not because epidemiology is not a valuable science—which it most certainly is—nor because prevention is not a worthy goal—it may be the most worthy of all—but because of the unavoidable implications that epidemiology is the main or perhaps only basis for prevention, or conversely, that prevention is of interest only to epidemiologists. Epidemiologists can indeed contribute useful information—just as pharmacologists, immunologists, pathologists, and others can, although probably no more than the others. Both risk reduction and prevention are everybody's responsibility.

EFFECTS OF REGULATION

My third concern deals with the coercive nature of public advice, and the real hazard of resultant legislation and regulations. Suppose laws were passed which limited the butterfat content of all milk, prohibited the sale of eggs for dietary consumption, and mandated the substitution of polyunsaturated oleomargarines for butter. Given the evangelistic fervor of advice offered by some, those are not impossible nightmares. While I abhor as much as any of you the growing bureaucratic regulations of so much of our lives, I am just as concerned by the weaknesses of the evidence upon which such laws would be based.

A corollary to this regulatory concern comes from common sense about human nature. If people are told that they cannot eat butter, we know that they will eat something else, and the same can be said for eggs, whole milk, red meat, and all the other frequently proscribed foods. What else will they eat, exactly, and how safe is that? Many of you may be familiar with the rapeseed oil controversy, which illustrates the point. Rapeseed oil has been a major source for manufacture of oleomargarine, especially in the Scandinavian countries. Some years ago it was found that rapeseed oil fed to young rats caused serious and prompt degeneration of myocardium, and this finding has now been extended to some other species. Whether this problem exists for man is an understandably pressing question being actively investigated in Norway and other Scandinavian countries where rapeseed oil products are eaten, and in Canada, where the growth of rapeseed is a major industry. We are not only woefully ignorant about the possible harmful effects of food substitutes of natural origin, such as rapeseed oil margarine, we are even more ignorant about the potential immediate and long-range harm which may come from eating some synthetic foods now being popularized.

DANGERS TO CHILDREN

My fourth concern is about the future health of children. Even if the theory that coronary disease begins in childhood is correct, and there is much yet to be learned about that, what are some of the possible harms to children by dietary manipulation to reduce their intake of saturated fats and cholesterol? Suppose that children were taught not to eat any butter or eggs and not to drink whole milk, and suppose that while such avoidance perhaps did reduce their risk of getting coronary disease it also increased their chance of getting some type of cancer or gallbladder disease, or suppose that their developing brains or muscles did not grow as well. Do we really know enough about the long-range consequences of such advise to be confident of its merit?

All of us have recently been cheered by the evidence for steadily declining mortality from heart attacks. But a closer look at the nature of this declining mortality raises more questions than it answers. For example, the proper classification of a cause of death can be so arbitrary in these graphs as to weaken its meaning. If a patient with hypertension and a recent acute myocardial infarction then dies of a stroke (not a rare clinical course), where should he be classified? Any possible answer is less important than the realization that multiple classification is not permitted.

Furthermore, the heart attack graph only plots deaths and only those clinically diagnosed as due to heart attack. It is not necessary to belabor what a spectrum of accuracy this represents, ranging from confirmation at autopsy to clinical impression by inexperienced observers. The question of accuracy of the diagnosis may not even be the major question, for it tells us nothing about non-fatal heart attacks nor about the existence of coronary disease in the asymptomatic population. Yet there is a growing public belief and even claim by some physicians and scientists that we are reducing the incidence of coronary disease. These are such separate subjects and their inter-relation is so complex that we must be more explicit and accurate in public statements about this graph and what it means.

So here I will conclude. Some will say it has been simply a jeremiad, a curmudgeonly glance at the necessary complexity of science today. For those and all others let me close with the brighter side. There have been astonishing advances recently in our knowledge about the pathogenesis of coronary disease.

Rediscovery of the platelet has revolutionized our thinking about the morphogenesis of endothelial and medial lesions. New knowledge about lipoproteins, both high and low density, and of their cellular receptors grows daily. Coronary angiography has taught us more accurate ways to assess spasms of coronary arteries, where platelets may be very important. We have come to accept the near ubiquity of electrical instability of the heart as the major mechanism underlying sudden coronary death. And the surgical triumphs of today would have staggered the imagination little over one decade ago. These few examples do not do full justice to a long list of comparable discoveries.

In our zeal to prevent coronary disease immediately, we must not lose sight of two things, that we are not truly able to do that yet, but that promising new possibilities are emerging. I firmly believe that the American people can and will continue to support medical research for the conquest of coronary disease, but that they will do this best and most enthusiastically when we level with them, do not dissemble, do not overpromise, and restrain ourselves from shrill postures and polemical diatribes. The truth is exciting enough.

Lipoproteins

by David Kritchevsky, Ph.D., and Susanne K. Czarnecki

The relationship of plasma cholesterol and triglyceride levels to atherosclerosis is ultimately related to the plasma lipoproteins. The lipoproteins, first described by Macheboeuf in 1929, are the vehicle for transporting insoluble lipids from their site of origin to their site of utilization. In the past decade, much has been learned about analysis, synthesis, structure and function of these substances.

Separation of the Various Lipoproteins

The lipoproteins are polydisperse macromolecules which vary in size, hydrated density and chemical composition. Table 1[1] presents the characteristic chemical composition of the four principal classes of lipoproteins of human serum.

The lipoproteins may be separated by electrophoresis, which is usually carried out at a basic pH and which separates the molecules by their electrical charge. They may also be separated and classified by their rates of flotation in a dense salt solution (S_f rates by analytical ultracentrifugation). The S_f rates are a function of lipoprotein shape, size and density. Recently, Rudel et al. have developed an effective method of separation based on particle size rather than hydrated density. Circulating lipoproteins can also be separated by polyanion-metal precipitation techniques which permit separation of lower density lipoproteins as a precipitate and leave the higher density lipoproteins in solution. The usual precipitants are heparin or dextran sulfate and the ions most commonly used are Mn^{++} or Ca^{++}.

With the increasing importance of high density lipoprotein (HDL) levels as possible predictors of coronary disease, the availability of simple analytical techniques becomes important.

Functional Relationship of Lipoproteins

In the body, lipoproteins form a dynamic system in which both exchange and net transfer of protein and lipid occur. Catabolism of lipoproteins within the circulation produces new lipoproteins altered in chemical composition and molecular properties.

The functional relationship among lipoproteins is typified by the conversion of very low density lipoproteins (VLDL) to low density lipoproteins (LDL). VLDL transport endogenous triglyceride from the small intestine and they carry about 10% of the total plasma cholesterol. VLDL breakdown occurs in a series of steps during which triglyceride is removed progressively by tissue lipoprotein lipase. The free cholesterol, phospholipid and

Table 1[1]
Characteristics of Serum Lipoproteins

	Chylomicrons	VLDL[a]	LDL[b]	HDL[c]
Chemical composition (%)				
Protein	2	10	23	55
Triglyceride	85	50	10	4
Free cholesterol	1	7	8	2
Esterified cholesterol	3	12	37	15
Phospholipid	9	18	20	24
Physical Characteristics				
Diameter (nm)	75-1000	30-80	19-25	4-10
Mol. wt. x 10^{-6} (dalton)	$>4 \times 10^2$	5-6	2.3	0.18-0.36
Density	< 1.006	0.95-1.0006	1.006-1.063	1.063-1.21
Electrophoresis	Origin	pre β	β	α
S_f (ultracentrifuge)	400-10[6]	20-40	0-20	HDL

[a] VLDL, very low density lipoprotein
[b] LDL, low density lipoprotein
[c] HDL, high density lipoprotein

Table 2[2]
Total Cholesterol (mg/dl) and Cholesterol (mg/dl) Distribution Among Plasma Lipoproteins of Normal Subjects*

Age	Total Male	Total Female	VLDL Male	VLDL Female	LDL Male	LDL Female	HDL Male	HDL Female
20-24	162	162	14	12	103	98	45	52
25-29	179	174	17	12	117	106	45	56
30-34	193	174	21	11	126	109	46	55
35-39	201	188	24	14	133	119	43	55
40-44	205	196	26	14	136	125	44	57
45-49	213	205	24	17	144	130	45	58
50-54	213	222	27	17	142	145	44	60
55-59	215	231	22	21	145	150	48	60

*Sample size: 2450 white males and 1640 white females not on hormones.

Table 3
Characteristics of Apolipoproteins

Apolipoprotein	Density Class	Mol. Wt.	Function
AI	HDL	28,000	LCAT Activator*
AII	HDL	17,000	—
B	VLDL, LDL	250,000	—
CI	VLDL, HDL	6,500	LCAT and Lipase Activator
CII	VLDL, LDL(?), HDL	~10,000	Lipase Activator
CIII	VLDL, HDL	10,000	Lipase Inhibitor (?)
D	HDL₃	~20,000	Cholesterol Ester Transport
E	VLDL, LDL, HDL	32-3,900	Cholesterol Transport (?)

*LCAT, lecithin-cholesterol acyltransferase

apoprotein (apo C) are transferred to HDL.

The normal distribution of cholesterol among the plasma lipoproteins is given in Table 2[2].

The lipid-free protein portions of lipoproteins, the apoproteins of the major lipoprotein classes, possess distinct chemical and metabolic features, some of which are summarized in Table 3. Although each apoprotein functions as a lipid transport protein, they differ in lipid-binding properties and in ability to function as cofactors for the lipolytic enzymes responsible for lipoprotein metabolism.

Characteristics of the Hyperlipoproteinemias

In 1967, Fredrickson, Levy and Lees[3] reviewed a systematic approach to diagnosis of hyperlipidemias which they had been exploring for several years. Based on the appearance of plasma and its electrophoretic characteristics, they were able to describe five different types of hyperlipoproteinemia.

The typing of lipoproteinemias (Table 4) permitted a classification based on elevation of specific lipoprotein classes or specific lipids; it also made for a rationalization of treatment since some hyperlipoproteinemias responded to dietary intervention and others to drug treatment. In addition to the primary hyperlipoproteinemias, there are a number of secondary lipoproteinemias due to excess caloric intake, alcoholism, diabetes, nephrosis, myxedema, obstructive liver disease and pancreatitis.

Dietary regimen, as part of the total treatment of the hyperlipoproteinemias, is determined by the Type:

Type I.
The defect appears to be inability to clear fat from the blood, hence reduced fat intake.
- Limit fat intake (25-35 g/day)
- No alcohol

Type IIA.
High cholesterol content of blood is symptomatic of this defect.
- Increase polyunsaturated fat
- Reduce cholesterol
- Limit alcohol

Type IIB.
Both cholesterol and triglycerides are elevated in Type IIB.
- Maintain ideal weight
- Limit carbohydrate (40% of calories)
- Normal fat (40% of calories)
- Increase polyunsaturated fat
- Reduce cholesterol
- Limit alcohol

Type III.
As in Type IIB. Maintain ideal body weight.

Type IV.
Synthesis of triglycerides must be reduced.
- Maintain ideal weight

Table 4[3] Primary Hyperlipoproteinemias

Type	Lipoprotein Elevation	Appearance of Plasma	Plasma Cholesterol	Lipids Triglycerides
I	Chylomicrons +++	Creamy layer over clear or slightly turbid infranatant	Normal to +	+++
IIA	LDL +++	Clear	+	Normal
IIB	LDL +++ VLDL +	Slightly to moderately turbid	+	++
III	Floating β*	Turbid to opaque	+	++ to +++
IV	VLDL +++	Turbid to opaque	Normal to +	++ to +++
V	Chylomicrons ++ VLDL +++	Creamy layer over turbid or opaque infranatant	++	+++

*Abnormal lipoprotein of density < 1.006 g/ml with β mobility; a pre-β migrating lipoprotein is also present. Elevation: +, slightly; ++, moderately; +++, markedly.

- Limit carbohydrate (35-40% of calories)
- Increase polyunsaturated fat
- Normal cholesterol (up to 500 mg/day)
- Limit alcohol

Type V.
Synthesis of triglycerides must be reduced.
- Maintain ideal weight
- Normal carbohydrate (48-53% of calories)
- Reduce fat (25-30% of calories)
- High protein (21-24% of calories)
- Limit cholesterol (300-500 mg/day)
- No alcohol

In addition to diet, cholesterol-lowering drugs, such as bile acid-binding resins (cholestyramine, colestipol), D-thyroxine, nicotinic acid, probucol, atromid-S (clofibrate) and β-sitosterol have been used in the treatment of Type II-V hyperlipoproteinemias. The effectiveness of these drugs has been variable.

Lipoproteins and Heart Disease

In the early 1950s, Barr and his co-workers examined the relationships between the major lipoproteins of plasma and susceptibility to coronary disease. They found that the ratio of α/β lipoprotein [(HDL/LDL by today's nomenclature) was higher in the plasma of young women (18-35 years) than in that of young men even though their cholesterol levels were quite similar. The young women were at much lower risk of coronary disease. Barr et al. also found that the ratio of α/β lipoprotein was much lower in plasma of subjects with diabetes, nephritis or coronary disease than in normal subjects. Olson reflected on the observation that the susceptibility of animal species to experimental atherosclerosis was more a function of their α/β ratios than of their normal cholesterol levels.

A few years ago, Miller and Miller reassessed the data concerning coronary disease and HDL/LDL levels and reached a conclusion similar to that of Barr. In the ensuing years, much had been learned of HDL and LDL structure and metabolism. Tissue culture experiments suggested that LDL essentially caused entry of cholesterol into the cell and HDL enhanced egress. Other studies showed that very old people exhibited increased HDL levels, some hypolipidemic drugs raised HDL levels and exercise, such as jogging, increased HDL levels as did moderate drinking.

Despite these encouraging data, it is too early to conclude that the HDL/LDL ratio is the ultimate diagnosis or that increasing HDL is the simplest therapeutic modality. Much has yet to be learned about the mechanisms by which HDL is elevated (liver toxins such as chloroform or dioxin also elevate HDL levels). Furthermore, HDL can now be subfractionated into HDL_2, which is more prevalent in female plasma, and HDL_3, which is found in male plasma. HDL_2 is larger, lighter and carries more lipid and less protein than HDL_3. At this writing, there are few data concerning the effects of exercise, alcohol or drugs on HDL_2 or HDL_3 levels.

We have entered an era in which we are learning about cellular mechanisms of LDL uptake. Work on HDL metabolism is not as well delineated but it, too, is making great strides. The use of simple methodologies to give accurate assessments of circulating lipoproteins and their diagnostic interpretations may not be too far in the future.

REFERENCES*

1. Lewis, B., *The Hyperlipidemias*, Blackwell Scientific Publications, Oxford, 1976.
2. Heiss, G., Tamir, I., Davis, C.E., Tyroles, H.R., Refkend, B.M., Schonfeld, G., Jacobs, D. and Frantz, I.D., Jr., Lipoprotein-Cholesterol Distributions in Selected North American Populations: The Lipid Research Clinics Program Prevalence Study. *Circulation* 61:302-315, American Heart Association, Dallas, Texas, 1980.
3. Fredrickson, D.S., Levy, R.I., Lees, R.S., Fat Transport in Lipoproteins — an Integrated Approach to Mechanisms and Disorders, *New England J. Med.* 276: 34-44, 94-103, 148-156, 215-225, 273-281, 1967.

4. Dietschy, J.M., Gotto, A.M. Jr., Ontko, J.A. (eds), *Disturbances in Lipid and Lipoprotein Metabolism*, American Physiological Society, Bethesda, Maryland, 1978.
5. Felts, J.M., Rudel, L.L., Mechanisms of Hyperlipidemia, Kritchevsky, D. (ed), *Hypolipidemic Agents*, Springer Verlag, Berlin, 1975, pp 151-190.
6. Peeters, H. (ed) *The Lipoprotein Molecule*, Plenum Publishing Company, New York, 1978.
7. Eisenberg, S., Levy, R.I., Lipoproteins and Lipoprotein Metabolism, Kritchevsky, D. (ed), *Hypolipidemic Agents*, Springer Verlag, Berlin, 1975, pp 191-215.
8. Gotto, A.M., Jr., Miller, N.E., Oliver, M.F. (eds), *High Density Lipoproteins and Atherosclerosis*, Elsevier-North Holland, Amsterdam, 1978.
9. Day, C.E., Levy, R.S. (eds), *Low Density Lipoprotein*, Plenum Publishing Company, New York, 1976.
10. Rifkind, B.M., Levy, R.I. (eds), *Hyperlipidemia, Drugs and Therapy*, Grune and Stratton, New York, 1977.
11. Greten, H. (ed) *Lipoprotein Metabolism*, Springer Verlag, Berlin, 1976.

*The material on which this publication is based can be found in one or more of these references.

Women, Work, and Coronary Heart Disease: Prospective Findings from Framingham

by Suzanne G. Haynes, Ph.D., and Manning Feinlieb, M.D., Dr.PH.

Abstract: This study examined the relationship of employment status and employment-related behaviors to the incidence of coronary heart disease (CHD) in women. Between 1965 and 1967, a psychosocial questionnaire was administered to 350 housewives, 387 working women (women who had been employed outside the home over one-half their adult years), and 580 men participating in the Framingham Heart Study. The respondents were 45 to 64 years of age and were followed for the development of CHD over the ensuing eight years. Regardless of employment status, women reported significantly more symptoms of emotional distress than men. Working women and men were more likely to report Type A behavior, ambitiousness, and marital disagreements than were housewives; working women experienced more job mobility than men, and more daily stress and marital dissatisfaction than housewives or men. Working women did not have significantly higher incidence rates of CHD than housewives (7.8 vs 5.4 per cent, respectively). However, CHD rates were almost twice as great among women holding clerical jobs (10.6 per cent) as compared to housewives. The most significant predictors of CHD among clerical workers were: suppressed hostility, having a nonsupportive boss, and decreased job mobility. CHD rates were higher among working women who had ever married, especially among those who had raised three or more children. Among working women, clerical workers who had children and were married to blue collar workers were at highest risk of developing CHD (21.3 per cent.) (*Am J Public Health* 70:133-141, 1980.)

During the past 30 years, the number of women participating in the United States labor force has risen sharply. In this period, the proportion of women in the labor force has increased from 28 per cent in 1950 to 42 per cent in 1978.[1,2] Most of this growth has resulted from an influx of married women into the labor force.[3]

The growing participation of women in the work place has brought fears that women will lose their survival advantage over men, and will have increasingly higher mortality rates from chronic diseases such as coronary heart disease (CHD). Contributing to these fears is an unsubstantiated assumption that men live fewer years than women because they work outside the home.

At the present time, there is no evidence from mortality statistics to suggest that women are losing their survival advantage over men because of their increased participation in the labor force. On the contrary, in the last 10 years, mortality rates from coronary heart disease have been declining in both men and women at all ages,[4] with greater percentage declines seen among women than men.

Since mortality rates may not reflect trends in illness or disability, morbidity rates among men and women should also be examined. Unfortunately, morbidity statistics are usually collected in cross-sectional surveys. Since these surveys do not follow populations over time, they are not useful in determining whether working women have incurred higher rates of CHD over time than working men or housewives.

In order to examine the effect of employment on the cardiovascular health of women, the present study followed working women, housewives, and men participating in the Framingham Heart Study over an eight-year period for the development of coronary heart disease. In addition, the behaviors and family responsibilities associated with employment outside the home were examined in relation to CHD incidence.

Materials and Methods

Between 1965 and 1967, an extensive psychosocial

questionnaire was administered to a sample of men and women in the Framingham cohort undertaking their 8th or 9th biennial medical examinations. The present analysis includes the 350 housewives, 387 working women, and 580 men, aged 45 to 64 years, who were free of coronary heart disease at the time of the examinations. Although persons 65 years of age and over were also included in the original study, the present analysis was restricted to individuals in their employment years. A comprehensive description of the characteristics of this sample of the Framingham cohort has been reported previously. In most respects, the sample under study appears representative of the entire study population. The questionnaire, also described previously, assessed employment and occupational status as well as personality types, situational stress, reactions to anger, somatic strains, sociocultural mobility, and family responsibilities.[5]

Women who indicated they had been employed outside the home for over one-half their adult years (age 18+) were designated "working women"; otherwise they were classified as "housewives." Thus, a working woman 50 years of age would have worked the full-time equivalent of at least 15 years outside the home. Although complete work histories were not available for the Framingham population for the period prior to the first examination in 1950, calculation of the number of years worked was possible between 1950 and 1967. Using a 10 per cent random sample of women, single working women were found to have worked outside the home at least two-thirds of their adult years. In contrast, working women who had ever married were employed about one-half and housewives were employed less than 10 per cent of their adult years.

In addition, working women were separated into those who were currently employed, unemployed, or retired at the time of the study. Housewives included only women who had ever been married. Twelve women, including two nuns and one single housewife, were excluded from the study population because of inappropriate or missing data on employment status.

Occupation, as defined by one's usual lifetime work, was grouped into the following six categories according to the Warner index of status characteristics:[6] professionals, proprietors and managers, businessmen, clerks and kindred workers, manual workers, and protective and service workers. The first three groups were designated white-collar occupations, the last two groups were blue-collar occupations, and clerical jobs were considered separately.

Twenty psychosocial scales were examined in this study. A complete description of their content, including reliability coefficients and interscale correlations, may be found in a previous publication.[5] The scales were grouped in five categories: behavior types, situational stress, anger reactions, somatic strains, and sociocultural mobility.

The behavior types studied included the Framingham Type A behavior, ambitiousness, emotional lability, and non-easygoing scales. Several validation studies[7] on the Framingham Type A scale have found it to be measuring some, but not all, aspects of the Type A behavior pattern* described by Rosenman and Friedman.[8] The situational stress scales represented situations in marriage, work, or life that posed a potential threat to the respondent. These scales included measures of work overload, nonsupport from one's boss, marital disagreements and dissatisfaction, aging and personal worries.

Two scales assessed educational and occupational mobility as compared to one's father, and another scale measured social class incongruity as compared to one's acquaintances. The mobility scales were scored as upwardly mobile (3), stable (2), or downwardly mobile (1). Finally, a family responsibility scale was developed to account for marital status and the number of children in family. Respondents were scored as single (1); ever-married, no children (2); ever-married, 1–2 children (3); or ever-married, 3+ children (4).

The entire study group was followed for the development of coronary heart disease over an eight-year period. Coronary heart disease was diagnosed if, upon review of all clinical and examination data, a panel of investigators agreed that a myocardial infarction, coronary insufficiency syndrome, angina pectoris, or CHD death had occurred. Definitions of these clinical manifestations of CHD have been presented elsewhere.[7]

Statistical differences in demographic characteristics and coronary incidence rates were determined by a two-sided Chi-square test. To test whether the psychosocial scales and coronary risk factors varied across employment groups, mean scores among working women, housewives, and men were compared using Student's t-test. The direct method of age-adjustment, using all Framingham men and women (ages 45–54 and 55–64 years) in this study as the standard population, was used to test whether observed differences in mean scale scores, CHD risk factors, and CHD rates were due to differences in the age distributions between groups. With one exception (marital status), the associations were unaffected by the adjustment for age. Thus, unless otherwise stated, unadjusted incidence rates and mean levels of psychosocial and coronary risk factors for the entire age group 45–64 years will be presented throughout the analysis.

Results

Demographic characteristics

Table 1 summarizes selected demographic characteristics of the working women and housewives examined in this study. There were no significant differences between working women and housewives according to age or educational level. Significant differences in marital status and number of children were observed since almost 20 per cent of working women were single (i.e., never married) and almost 25 per cent of ever married working women had no children. Working women were also less likely to have husbands employed in white collar jobs (13 per cent) than were housewives (26 per cent).

Over one-third of all working women had been employed in clerical and kindred occupations during their working years. Secretaries, stenographers, bookkeepers, bank clerks and cashiers, and sales personnel made up the majority of

---

*Aggressiveness, competitiveness, ambition, restlessness and a chronic sense of time urgency (associated with high CHD rates).

these positions. Although equal proportions of working women and men were employed in white-collar jobs (20 per cent), more women (37 per cent) were employed in clerical occupations than men (18 per cent), and fewer women (43 per cent) were employed in blue collar jobs than men (62 per cent) (p = .000, comparing occupations of men with women). The majority of men with white collar occupations were graduate degree professionals (lawyers, doctors, dentists,

TABLE 1—Demographic Characteristics of Working Women and Housewives in the Framingham Cohort Aged 45 to 64 Years at their 8th or 9th Biennial Medical Examinations

Selected Characteristics (%)	Working Women (N = 387)	Housewives (N = 350)	Significance
Age			
45–49 years	21.0	25.6	
50–54 years	33.5	30.4	N.S.
55–59 years	27.5	24.1	
60–64 years	17.9	19.9	
Education[1]			
≤8 years	20.4	16.6	
9–12 years	54.3	54.3	N.S.
13+ years	25.3	29.1	
Marital Status[1]			
Single	18.6	—	
Married	62.0	87.9	p = .000
Divorced, widowed, or separated	19.4	12.1	
Number of children among the ever married			
0	24.8	5.7	
1–2	46.2	48.9	p = .000
3+	29.0	45.4	
Husband's occupation among the ever married			
White-collar	12.8	25.9	
Clerical and kindred	19.1	17.5	p = .000
Blue-collar	68.1	56.6	

1) Since the age distributions of working women and housewives were similar, age-adjusted proportions were identical to the unadjusted proportions shown in the Table.

etc.) or business managers, while most women professionals were teachers, nurses, or librarians.

Behavioral Differences by Sex and Employment Status

Mean scores on the 20 psychosocial scales used in this study were compared among working women, housewives, and men. Table 2 summarizes the results of these comparisons, listing only those scales which varied according to sex and employment status. Since the age distributions were similar among the three employment groups, unadjusted mean scores for the age group 45–64 were identical to the age-adjusted mean scores.

Sex differences are reported for scales in which scores among working women and housewives were similar, but significantly different from scores among men, a pattern suggesting that women, regardless of employment status, differed from men on these characteristics. Sex differences were found for scales dealing with symptoms reflecting emotional distress, such as tension, anxiety, anger and emotional lability. For example, women regardless of employment status scored higher on the tension scale than men (about .40

and .25, respectively). Women were also more likely to exhibit anger-in and to have experienced less educational mobility than men.

Behaviors related to employment are also summarized in Table 2. Here scale scores among working women and men were similar, but significantly different from those of housewives, suggesting that the differences were related to employment per se. That is, these behaviors were either the result of working outside the home or the result of self-selection into the work force. Employed persons, regardless of sex, were more likely than housewives to score higher on the Framingham Type A behavior, ambitiousness, and marital disagreement scales. For example, mean scores on the Type A scale were similar for working women and men (.38 and .39, respectively), although both were significantly higher than the mean score for housewives (.31).

Several scales appeared to reflect the specific role of being an employed woman. On these scales, working women scored significantly higher or lower than both men and housewives. Working women experienced more daily stress, marital dissatisfaction, and aging worries and were less likely to show overt anger (as measured by a low score on the anger-out scale) than either housewives or men. In addition, working women had considerably more occupational mobility and more job and line of work changes than men, but received fewer promotions than men in the 10 years before the survey.

TABLE 2—Mean Psychosocial Scores among Housewives (HW), Working Women (WW), and Mean Aged 45–64 Years at their 8th or 9th Biennial Medical Examinations

Psychosocial Scales Grouped according to Differences by	Housewives (350)	Working Women (387)	Men (580)
Sex[1]			
Emotional lability	.36	.37	.30
Tension	.36	.40	.25
Anxiety symptoms	.21	.20	.11
Anger symptoms	.30	.31	.18
Anger-in	.51	.54	.47
Educational mobility	2.38	2.37	2.53
Employment[2]			
Framingham Type A	.31	.38	.39
Ambitiousness	.37	.48	.51
Marital disagreement	.14	.18	.17
Sex and Employment[3]			
Daily stress	.27	.33	.29
Anger-out	.13	.10	.12
Marital dissatisfaction	.22	.27	.19
Aging worries	.16	.19	.15
Occupational mobility	1.80	2.02	1.81
Job changes in past 10 years	—	.51	.36
Line of work changes in past 10 years	—	.33	.25
Times promoted in past 10 years	—	.46	.57

1) For these six variables, comparisons were statistically significant (p ≤ .05) for HW vs men and WW vs men.

2) For these three variables, comparisons were statistically significant (p ≤ .05) for WW vs HW and men vs HW. For the ambitiousness scale, comparison of WW vs men was also significant at the .05 < p ≤ .10 level.

3) For the first five variables (except anger-out), comparisons were statistically significant (p ≤ .05) for WW vs HW and WW vs men. For the anger-out scale, comparisons between WW vs men were significant at the .05 < p ≤ .10 level. In the last three variables, comparisons were significant (p ≤ .05) for WW vs men.

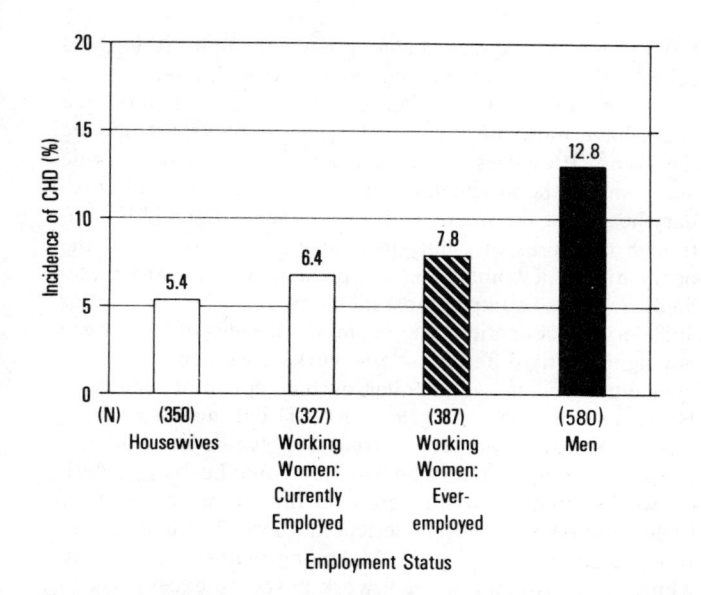

FIGURE 1—Eight Year Incidence of Coronary Heart Disease by Employment Status among Men and Women Aged 45–64 Years

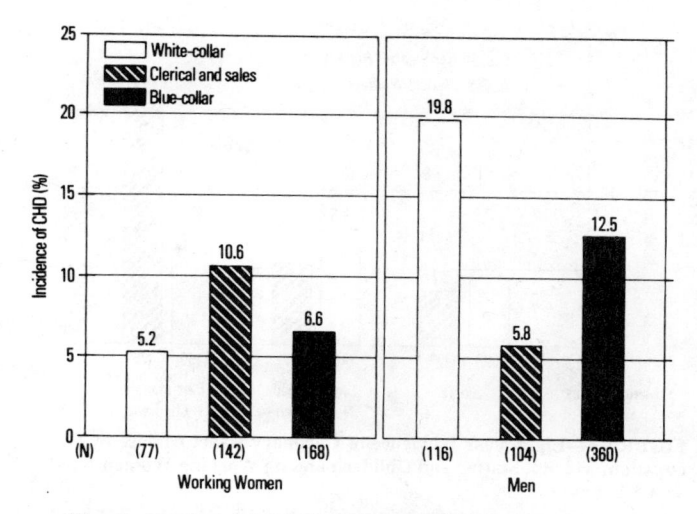

FIGURE 2—Eight Year Incidence of Coronary Heart Disease by Occupational Status among Working Women and Men Aged 45–64 Years

White-collar occupations include professionals, managers, and business men
Blue-collar occupations include manual, protective, and service workers

Incidence Rates of Coronary Heart Disease

Figure 1 presents incidence rates of coronary heart disease over the eight-year period among housewives, working women, and men aged 45–64 years. Data were also analyzed separately for working women, as previously defined, who were currently employed at the time of the study. All working women were included in the ever-employed group.

Employment status did not significantly affect the risk of developing CHD in women. Incidence rates were only slightly higher among the ever-employed working women than among housewives (7.8 vs 5.4 per cent, respectively). The incidence rate of CHD among these working women was lower than the rate for men, which was about 13 per cent (p = .02).

Likewise, employment status at the time of the study did not affect these associations. Although CHD rates were generally lower among workers employed at the time of the study, currently employed working women had lower incidence rates of CHD than currently employed men (6.4 vs 12.4 per cent, respectively). As expected, working women and men who were unemployed or retired at the time of the study had the highest rates of CHD (13.8 and 24.0 per cent, respectively, for women and men).

Figure 2 shows incidence rates of CHD among working women and men according to the usual occupation held during the working years. Among women, clerical workers were almost twice as likely to develop coronary disease as either white- or blue-collar workers. The incidence rate of CHD among women clerical workers (10.6 per cent) was higher than the rate among housewives (5.4 per cent, p = .06).

Among men, an entirely different pattern was observed, with higher rates occurring among white-collar workers (19.8 per cent) and lower rates occurring among clerical (5.8 per cent) and blue-collar (12.5 per cent) employees (p = .01). Only among clerical workers were the rates of coronary disease greater in women than in men, although this difference did not achieve statistical significance.

Age-adjusted coronary rates were examined among working women and housewives according to marital status. No significant differences were observed among housewives who were married and housewives who were widowed, divorced, or separated (WDS) (4.6 vs 6.9 per cent, respectively). Married and WDS working women had similar age-adjusted rates of CHD (8.1 and 8.5 per cent, respectively), while single working women exhibited the lowest rate of coronary disease (4.2 per cent).

Since women who had ever married were at greater risk of developing CHD than single women, the effect of having children on CHD was also examined. Among working women, the incidence of CHD rose as the number of children increased (Figure 3). Working women with three or more

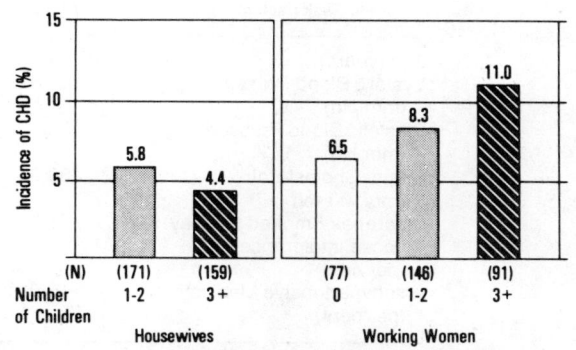

FIGURE 3—Eight Year Incidence of Coronary Heart Disease by Number of Children among Women Aged 45–64 Years

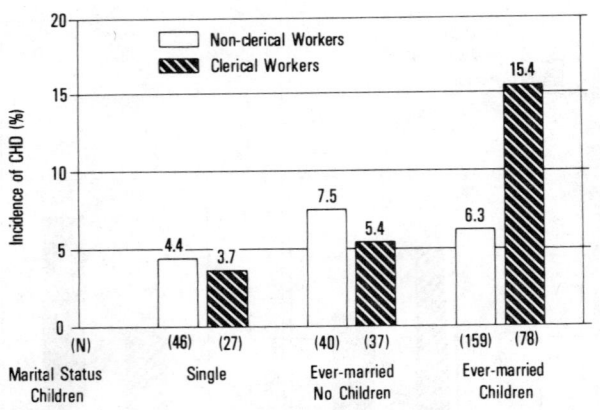

FIGURE 4—Eight Year Incidence of Coronary Heart Disease by Occupation, Marital Status, and Children among Working Women Aged 45–64 Years

children (11.0 per cent) were more likely to develop CHD than working women with no children (6.5 per cent) or than housewives with three or more children (4.4 per cent, p = .08). Although there were not enough childless housewives for comparison (n = 20), CHD rates were similar among housewives with 1–2 or 3+ children.

Although one would expect working women to be equally affected by family responsibilities, the relationship of these responsibilities to CHD incidence was examined among clerical and non-clerical working women (Figure 4). Surprisingly, single or married clerical workers without children were at no greater risk of developing CHD than other workers. However, clerical workers who had ever married and had children were over twice as likely to develop CHD than non-clerical workers in the same situation (15.4 and 6.3 per cent, respectively, p = .04). Thus, the excess risk of CHD previously observed among women employed in clerical jobs occurred only among women with children.

Economic pressures due to an increased family size could have motivated women to seek employment outside the home. Pressures associated with a low socioeconomic status might then explain the higher incidence rate of coronary heart disease among working women with children. Although measures of family income were not available, the occupation of a woman's past or present husband was examined. For these comparisons, men employed in white-collar and clerical occupations were combined. Rates of CHD were not significantly different among working women married to men employed in white-collar or blue-collar occupations. However, the risk of developing CHD did increase among clerical working women married to blue-collar workers. Among working women who had blue-collar husbands, clerical workers with children were over three times more likely to develop CHD than non-clerical mothers (21.3 and 6.0 per cent, respectively) (p = .004). Among mothers married to white-collar workers, clerical work posed no excess risk of CHD. The incidence rates of CHD among non-clerical mothers, employed in either white- or blue-collar occupations, were not affected by the husband's occupation.

Standard Coronary Risk Factors

Table 3 presents mean levels of the standard coronary risk factors measured between 1965–1967 among the various employment groups. The risk factors included age, systolic and diastolic blood pressure, serum cholesterol, cigarette smoking, and glucose intolerance. The proportion of persons on antihypertensive medication was also compared.

Mean levels of all six risk factors examined were similar among working women and housewives. Likewise, no significant differences were observed between housewives and white-collar, clerical, or blue-collar working women. Preva-

TABLE 3—Mean Levels of Coronary Risk Factors among Housewives, Working Women, and Men Aged 45–64 Years at their 8th or 9th Biennial Medical Examinations

		Working Women				
Risk Factors	Housewives (350)	Total (387)	White-Collar (77)	Clerical (142)	Blue-Collar (168)	Men (580)
Age (years)	54.1	54.1	54.9	53.5	54.2	53.6
Systolic Blood Pressure (mm Hg)	135.8	135.4	134.5	135.2	135.9	136.0
Diastolic Blood Pressure (mm Hg)	82.1	82.0	81.9	81.7	82.2	83.6*
Serum Cholesterol (mg/100 ml)	238.9	242.2	243.9	241.2	242.4	229.0*
Cigarettes Smoked per Day	7.6	7.5	8.6	7.9	6.7	12.3*
Glucose Intolerance (per cent)	5.1	5.5	2.6	5.0	7.2	5.5
Anti-hypertensive Medication (per cent)	15.0	15.5	9.3	17.7	15.8	8.5*

*p ≤ 0.5 when comparing men with working women and housewives. Comparisons of working women with housewives were not statistically significant.

TABLE 4—Mean Scale Scores for CHD Cases and Non-cases among Women, Aged 45-64 Years, in Clerical Occupations

	Clerical occupations	
Psychosocial Scales	Cases (15)	Non-Cases (127)
Behavior Type		
Framingham Type A	.41	.37
Emotional lability	.34	.33
Ambitiousness	.54	.45
Non-easygoing	.18	.23
Reactions to Anger		
Anger-in	.64	.52*
Anger-out	.02	.12***
Anger-discuss	.38	.63**
Situational Stress		
Nonsupport from boss	.38	.13***
Marital dissatisfaction	.24	.23
Marital disagreement	.16	.19
Aging worries	.14	.21
Personal worries	.09	.15**
Sociocultural Mobility		
Job changes in past 10 years	.13	.77***
Line of work changes in past 10 years	.26	.38
Times promoted in past 10 years	.71	.95
Educational mobility	2.17	2.35
Occupational mobility	2.13	1.97
Social class mobility	2.07	2.02
Somatic Strain		
Tension state	.47	.36
Daily stress	.37	.30
Anxiety symptoms	.21	.18
Anger symptoms	.23	.30

*.05 < p ≤ .10
**.01 ≤ p ≤ .05
*** p < .01

lence rates of hypertension (SBP ≥ 160 or DBP ≥ 95) among women did not vary by employment or occupational status.

Men, on the other hand, had significantly higher levels of cigarette consumption and lower levels of serum cholesterol than working women or housewives. Mean levels of diastolic blood pressure were also significantly higher among men than women. This finding may be partially explained by the lower proportion of men on antihypertensive medication.

Psychosocial Risk Factors among Women

In a previous report from Framingham,[7] several psychosocial scales were associated with the development of CHD in women, depending upon employment status. Controlling for the standard risk factors, Framingham Type A behavior and suppressed hostility (not discussing anger) were significant predictors of CHD incidence among all working women aged 45-64 years. In contrast, being easygoing, showing tension symptoms, and the Framingham Type A behavior were associated with CHD among housewives of the same age.[7]

Since clerical workers had a greater risk of CHD than other workers or housewives, the psychosocial risk factors for CHD were examined separately in this group (Table 4). Clerical workers who developed CHD were more likely to suppress hostility (in terms of the anger-in, anger-out, anger-discuss scales), to have a nonsupportive boss, to report fewer personal worries, and to experience fewer job changes over a previous 10-year period than clerical workers remaining free of CHD. Similar associations were observed among clerical women who had ever married and raised children.

In order to determine the independent effect of these scales, each was included, along with the standard coronary risk factors and a measure of family responsibility, in a multivariate logistic regression analysis.[9] As seen in Table 5, the anger-discuss, nonsupport from boss and family responsibility scales remained independent predictors of CHD. Infrequent job changes were also associated with the incidence of CHD in the multivariate analysis, but the association did not reach statistical significance (p = .11). None of the standard coronary risk factors included in the analysis (age, systolic blood pressure, serum cholesterol, or cigarette smoking) were associated with CHD in this group of 125 women. Thus, remaining in a job with a nonsupportive boss while not discussing one's anger increased the risk of coronary heart disease among clerical working women. This risk was further increased with the size of the family.

Discussion

The present study has shown that employment by women, per se, is not related to an increased risk of coronary heart disease. In fact, women who were employed the longest period of time, i.e., single working women, had the lowest rate of CHD. The lack of association between employment status and CHD in women is not surprising. Although previous research has not examined the effect of employment on the incidence of CHD, three prevalence surveys found that working women were no more likely to have had CHD than housewives.[10-12] In the 1960-1962 U.S. Health Examination Survey, prevalence rates of definite coronary heart disease, myocardial infarction, and angina pectoris were greater among women (aged 18-79 years) keeping house than among women who usually worked.[10] In the 1972 Health Interview Survey, the prevalence of coronary heart disease was similar among women (aged 45-64 years) who usually worked or who usually kept house.[11]* Prevalence rates of CHD among Framingham working women (currently or ever-employed) and housewives aged 45-64 were comparable to those of the Health Interview Survey (35.6, 39.9 and 27.6 per 1000, respectively).[12]

The tendency for housewives to have similar or higher prevalence rates of CHD as compared to working women

---

*In both national surveys, women who usually worked included those whose usual activity during the preceding 12-month period was paid employment. Women usually keeping house included women whose major activity over the same period was described as keeping house.[10]

TABLE 5—Multiple Logistic Regression of the 8 Year Incidence of Coronary Heart Disease among Clerical Working Women Aged 45-64 Years†

Variables	Standardized Coefficient	T
Age (years)	.06	.12
Systolic Blood Pressure (mm Hg)	.34	.84
Serum Cholesterol (mg/100 ml)	.46	1.22
Cigarettes Smoked per Day	−.19	−.51
Anger-discuss	−1.32	−2.70*
Nonsupport from Boss	.92	2.56*
Job Changes in past 10 Years	−1.96	−1.58
Family Responsibility	1.27	2.69*

†Analysis based on 125 women
*P < .01

may reflect the healthy worker effect,[13] i.e., the selection of certain women into the labor force because of relatively good health, while women in poor health who are unable to seek, obtain, or hold jobs become or remain housewives.[14] The National Health Survey[14] found higher rates of disability due to cardiovascular-renal and most other chronic diseases among housewives as compared to working women at all ages.

Although CHD incidence was similar in working women and housewives in this study, some groups of working women were more susceptible to the development of CHD than others. In particular, women clerical workers who had ever married and had children experienced coronary rates that were twice as great as those of other comparable non-clerical workers or housewives.

The higher incidence rate of CHD among working women who had ever married appears to contradict the general pattern of increased CHD death rates among single rather than married persons. However, close examination of published morbidity and mortality data in the U.S. shows that single white women have CHD rates that are lower than or equivalent to married or ever-married women.[10, 15-17]

Age-adjusted death rates from arteriosclerotic heart disease in the U.S. were lower among single as compared to ever-married white women in 1959-61 and mortality rates from CHD were quite similar among single and married women.[15] Married women had lower age-specific death rates from CHD than single women between the ages of 20 and 54, while for the ten-year age groups 55-64 and 65-74, the reverse was true.[15] The prevalence of definite coronary heart disease among women aged 18-79 in the Health Examination Survey was lowest among single women (.6 per cent), followed by the married, divorced, and widowed women (1.5, 3.7 and 6.1 per cent, respectively).[10]

Moriyama, et al, have suggested that the biologic function of childbearing or the psychologic and socioeconomic correlates of childbearing may provide a mortality advantage before age 50.[16] Selection of healthier women for marriage could also be a factor. After age 50, one would expect the effect of selection on marriage to decline. Reasons for the shift in favor of single women past the 50th year are unknown. Zalokar has postulated that, despite the advantages of ever-married women in selection and environment, childbearing may produce a more severe strain on the circulatory system, although the effects do not culminate in increased mortality until the end of the childbearing period.[17]

That prior childbearing may produce increased risks of CHD past age 50 was borne out among working women, but not among housewives in Framingham. Women who had worked outside the home and had raised three or more children were twice as likely to develop CHD as housewives with the same family responsibilities. Bengtsson, et al, found that Swedish women aged 50-54 with four or more children were more likely to have had a myocardial infarction than women in the general population.[18] Approximately two-thirds of the Swedish women had been employed outside the home.

These findings suggest that the dual roles of employment and raising a family may produce excessive demands on working women. Perceived demands on time (at home and in general) and psychiatric symptoms have been shown to increase monotonically among employed women with an increase in the number of children.[19] However, since this trend was also observed among housewives, it does not explain the differences in coronary rates between working women and housewives with three or more children noted in the present study. Perhaps demands on the job, coupled with demands at home, explain the high incidence of CHD among working women with several children.

Of the occupations examined in this study, clerical work was associated with the greatest risk of CHD among women. Since over one-third of the female workers in the U.S. are employed in clerical jobs,[20] reasons for this excess risk require further examination. Unfortunately, few epidemiologic data are available on cardiovascular morbidity or mortality among women according to occupation.

The association between occupational status and CHD incidence in women could be explained, in part, by the distribution of standard coronary risk factors by employment and occupational status. However, mean levels of blood pressure, serum cholesterol, cigarette smoking, and glucose intolerance in Framingham were similar among housewives and working women, regardless of occupation. These findings are consistent with other national and population-based surveys.[21-25] Using Framingham data, Johnson has also shown that sex differences in the standard risk factors do not explain the sex differential in CHD incidence past age 54.[26]

In previous reports from Framingham, two of the strongest psychosocial predictors of CHD among all working women and while-collar men were Type A behavior and suppressed hostility.[7] Of further note in the present study was the finding that suppressed hostility predicted CHD incidence among working women with the greatest risk of CHD, i.e., clerical employees. For female clerks, having a nonsupportive boss and few job changes were also associated with the incidence of CHD.

Many of these behaviors appear to be related to employment, i.e., the result of working outside the home or the self-selection of certain persons into the work force. Support for this interpretation comes from several studies which have shown Type A behavior[27] and need for achievement[28-29] to be higher among employed women than among housewives. Working men and women aged 45-64 in the Chicago Heart Association Detection Project also had similar scores on the Jenkins Activity Survey Type A scale.[30] Studies by Harburg, et al, among employed persons in Detroit, showed that white women were more likely than white men to suppress hostility (more anger-in and less anger-out) when confronted with an arbitrary boss.[31]

In Framingham, suppression of hostility coupled with a nonsupportive boss and a lack of job mobility were associated with the incidence of coronary heart disease among clerical working women. These findings are consistent with observations that women clerical workers may experience several forms of occupational stress, including a lack of autonomy and control over the work environment, underutilization of skills, and lack of recognition of accomplishments.[20]

The excess risk of CHD observed among women employed in clerical jobs occurred only among women with children and among women married to blue-collar workers, suggesting that economic pressures may also have affected the decision or necessity to work. Since the risks of CHD did not increase among white- or blue-collar working mothers with blue-collar husbands, the exact meaning of these results is unclear. The occupational status of one's spouse reflects not only an economic status, but also certain life style behaviors and attitudes, not measured in this study.

In conclusion, although employment, per se, was not associated with the incidence of coronary heart disease in women, behaviors and situations related to employment were associated with CHD among some working women. Working women who had ever married, had raised children, and had been employed in clerical work were at increased risk of developing CHD. The risk factors for CHD among clerical women included suppressed hostility, a non supportive boss, few job changes over a 10-year period, and family responsibilities. These risk factors may be the product of one or more of the following factors: the particular working environment for clerical occupations, self-selection of certain personalities into the labor force, or economic stress. Whatever the origins of these risk factors, the findings suggest that interpersonal relationships, coping styles, and the occupations of some employed women, coupled with family responsibilities, may be involved in the development of coronary heart disease.

REFERENCES

1. U.S. Dept. of Labor, Women's Bureau: Changes in Women's Occupations 1940-1950. Washington, DC: U.S. Govt Printing Office, Women's Bureau Bulletin 253, 1954.
2. U.S. Dept. of Labor, Bureau of Labor Statistics: Employment and Earnings. Washington, DC: U.S. Govt Printing Office, December 1978.
3. Lipman-Blumen J: Demographic trends and issues in women's health. In Olesen V., (ed): Women and Their Health: Research Implications for a New Era. Washington, DC: U.S. Govt Printing Office, DHEW Publication No (HRA) 77-3138, 1977.
4. U.S. Dept. of Health, Education, and Welfare, Public Health Service, National Center for Health Statistics: Chartbook for the Conference on the Decline in Coronary Heart Disease Mortality. Hyattsville, MD: August 1978.
5. Haynes SG, Levine S, Scotch N, et al: The relationship of psychosocial factors to coronary heart disease in the Framingham Study I. Methods and risk factors. Am J Epidemiol 107:362-383, 1978.
6. Warner WL, Meeker M, Eells K: Social Class in America. New York: Science Research, 1949.
7. Haynes SG, Feinleib M, Kannel WB: The relationship of psychosocial factors to coronary heart disease in the Framingham Study III. Eight year incidence of coronary heart disease. Am J Epidemiol, 111, 1980.
8. Rosenman RH, Friedman M, Straus R, et al: A predictive study of coronary heart disease: the western collaborative group study. JAMA 189:15-22, 1964.
9. Walker SH, Duncan DB: Estimation of the probability of an event as a function of several independent variables. Biometrics 54:167-179, 1967.
10. U.S. Dept. of Health, Education, and Welfare, Public Health Service, National Center for Health Statistics: Coronary Heart Disease in Adults—United States, 1960-1962. Vital and Health Statistics, Series II, No. 10. Washington, DC: U.S. Govt Printing Office, 1965.
11. U.S. Dept. of Health, Education, and Welfare, Public Health Service, National Center for Health Statistics: Prevalence of chronic circulatory conditions—United States, 1972. Vital and Health Statistics, Series 10, No. 94. Washington DC: U.S. Govt Printing Office, DHEW Publication No. (HRA) 75-1521, 1975.
12. Haynes SG, Feinleib M, Kannel WB, et al: The relationship of psychosocial factors to coronary heart disease in the Framingham study II. Prevalence of coronary heart disease. Am J Epidemiol 107:384-402, 1978.
13. McMichael AJ, Haynes SG, Tyroler HA: Observations on the evaluation of occupational mortality data. J Occup Med 17:128-131, 1975.
14. U.S. Dept. of Health, Education, and Welfare, Public Health Service: The Prevalence of Disabling Illness Among Male and Female workers and Housewives. Washington DC: U.S. Govt Printing Office, Public Health Bulletin No. 260, 1941.
15. U.S. Dept. of Health, Education, and Welfare, Public Health Service, National Center for Health Statistics: Mortality from Selected Causes by Marital Status—Part A. Vital and Health Statistics, Series 20, No 8a. Washington, DC: U.S. Govt Printing Office, 1970.
16. Moriyama IM, Krueger DE, Stamler J: Cardiovascular Diseases in the United States. Massachusetts: Harvard University Press, 1971.
17. Zalokar JB: Marital status and major causes of death in women. J Chronic Dis 11:50-60, 1960.
18. Bengtsson C, Hallstrom T, Tibblin G: Social factors, stress experience and personality traits in women with ischemic heart disease, compared to a population sample of women. Acta Med Scand (Suppl) 549:82-92, 1973.
19. Gove WR, Geerken MR: The effect of children and employment on the mental health of married men and women. Soc Forces 56:66-76, 1977.
20. Stellman JM: Occupational health hazards of women: an overview. Prev Med 7:281-293, 1978.
21. U.S. Dept. of Health, Education, and Welfare, Public Health Service, National Center for Health Statistics: Hypertension and Hypertensive Heart Disease in Adults—United States, 1960-1962. Vital and Health Statistics, Series 11, No. 13. Washington, DC: U.S. Govt Printing Office, 1966.
22. Hauvenstein LS, Kasl SV, Harburg E: Work status, work satisfactions, and blood pressure among married black and white women. Psychol Women Q 1:334-349, 1977.
23. Mushinski MH, Stellman SD: Impact of new smoking trends on women's occupational health. Prev Med 7:349-365, 1978.
24. Sterling TD, Weinkam JJ: Smoking characteristics by type of employment. J Occup Med 18:743-754, 1976.
25. Slack J, Noble N, Meade TW, et al: Lipid and lipoprotein concentrations in 1604 men and women in working populations in northwest London. Br Med J 2:353-356, 1977.

26. Johnson A: Sex differentials in coronary heart disease: the explanatory role of primary risk factors. J Health Soc Behav 18:46-54, 1977.
27. Waldron I: The coronary-prone behavior pattern, blood pressure, employment and socioeconomic status in women. J Psychosom Res 22:76-87, 1978.
28. Baruch R: The achievement motive in women: implications for career development. J Pers Soc Psychol 5:260-267, 1967.
29. Kriger SF: N Ach and perceived parental child-rearing attitudes of career women and homemakers. J Voc Behav 2:419-432, 1972.
30. Waldron I, Zyzanski S, Shekelle RB, et al: The coronary-prone behavior pattern in employed men and women, J Hum Stress 3:2-18, 1977.
31. Harburg E, Blakelock EH, Roeper PJ: Resentful and reflective coping with arbitrary authority and blood pressure. Psychosom Med 41: 189-202 1979.

ACKNOWLEDGMENTS

This paper was presented in part at the 1978 American Psychological Association meetings and the 1979 American Psychosomatic Society meetings.

CARDIOVASCULAR

Nutrition and Hypertension

by S. George Carruthers, M.D.

Hypertension is a complex disorder of almost epidemic proportions in Western society. It is a major risk factor in the development of atherosclerosis and exerts its principal morbid effects on the brain (thrombotic stroke, hemorrhagic stroke and encephalopathy), on the kidneys (progressive renal failure) and on the heart (angina pectoris, myocardial infarction and congestive cardiac failure).

No single etiological factor for hypertension has as yet been determined. Recognized causes include adrenal cortical tumors (Conn's syndrome), adrenal medullary tumors (pheochromocytoma), coarctation of the aorta, renal artery stenosis and chronic kidney disease. Physicians spend a great deal of time, effort and laboratory expense in searching for these causes which contribute a mere 0.5% to 5% of all known hypertensive patients. The remaining 95 to 99.5% of hypertensive patients are classified as suffering from "essential" hypertension, a term which reveals our initial misconceptions rationalizing the elevation in blood pressure, conceals our present ignorance of the etiology of the condition and protects our professional pride by avoiding the term "hypertension of unknown cause"!

A simplistic approach to understanding the pathogenesis of any disease is the assessment of the contribution of genetic factors, environmental factors and the interaction between these forces. Unfortunately, much of the epidemiological evidence relating diet to hypertension and information describing the genetic contribution to blood pressure elevation has been mutually exclusive. The probability that the etiology of hypertension is multi-factorial has been considered for several years. It is important that we remember this as we consider the role of a single aspect, that of nutrition.

Salt Intake and Hypertension

Ambard and Beaujard (1) surmised that salt intake and salt restriction influenced arterial pressure. By modern standards, their scientific techniques must be considered less than perfect, yet their observations especially with respect to diet make fascinating reading. Their dietary manipulations revolved around the use of a bouillon (containing 10.5 g of salt per liter!) which they used to provoke hypertension and a lacto-vegetarian diet containing only 3 to 6 g of salt which they employed when they wished to control hypertension.

The American physician Allen (2-4) emphasized the role of sodium restriction in the management of hypertension and kidney disease. This message was taken up by Kempner (5, 6), whose clinic in Durham, North Carolina still attracts hypertensive and overweight patients to its spartan routine of exercise and a dietary consisting of boiled, unsalted rice and fruit juices. It is perhaps ironic, that 33 years after Kempner reported the life-saving effects of his diet on two seriously ill male patients, the Senate Select Committee on Nutrition and Human Needs (7) published its dietary goals for the United States which are summarized: (1) a reduction in caloric intake, (2) an increase in the consumption of complex carbohydrates and naturally occurring sugars, (3) a reduction in the consumption of refined and processed sugars, (4) reduced fat intake, (5) reduced cholesterol intake and (6) a limitation of salt intake to about 5 grams daily (approximately 85 millimoles Na^+). Kempner's diet certainly excelled in each of these areas, containing 15-25 g protein, 4-6 g fat, 460-470 g carbohydrate, 0.25-0.4 g sodium, 0.1-0.15 g chloride. The rice diet included 700-1000 ml of fruit juice daily and had a nutritional value of 1800-2000 calories. The diet, unfortunately, suffers from lack of variety and taste. Its demands on self-discipline are strict and unlikely to appeal to many people for prolonged periods of time.

The advent in the 1950s, 1960s and 1970s of effective diuretics and other antihypertensive medications, and the development of dialysis and transplantation for patients with renal failure, have unfortunately obscured the significant contribution of these early workers to our understanding of the association of salt intake and hypertension. Physicians and their patients have accepted too readily the option of long-term medication rather than the option of review and revision of nutritional habits. I would submit that until we have antihypertensive drugs which are absolutely safe, extremely inexpensive and invariably effective, that this totally medication-oriented approach is no more or less rational than the extreme dietary regulation proposed by Kempner.

We should examine some of the scientific requirements of any hypothesis which attributes a causal role for sodium chloride in the pathogenesis of hypertension.

1. A consistent biological model should demonstrate that excessive use of salt produces hypertension and its complications. In addition, the model should demonstrate (a) failure to develop hypertension when salt is withheld and (b) reduction of blood pressure after its development when salt is withdrawn from the diet. The model should clearly exclude any other dietary manipulation as the factor re-

sponsible for the changes in blood pressure.
2. There should be epidemiological evidence of between-population and within-population association of salt intake and blood pressure in man.
3. There should be experimental evidence that established hypertension in man is indeed reversible by salt restriction, otherwise a dietary change in already hypertensive patients has no scientific foundation.
4. There should be evidence that dietary salt restriction enhances the antihypertensive effect of drug therapy, otherwise the imposition of diet and drug therapy has no basis.

Animal model for hypertension

In a series of elegant experiments, Dahl and his associates (8-10) demonstrated that rats became hypertensive when subjected to a large salt intake in their diets. The rats demonstrated considerable biological variation, in that some colonies remained normotensive despite the excessive salt intake, whereas others died within a few months from fulminant hypertension. Careful cultivation of these distinctive colonies has succeeded in producing a strain of rats which is exquisitely sensitive to the effects of salt and a strain which is extremely resistant.

The Dahl-sensitive strain has played an important role in the evaluation of antihypertensive therapy, both drugs and dietary. Remarkably, after hypertension is produced by feeding salt to these rats, their blood pressures remain elevated even when salt intake is subsequently reduced. The life span of hypertensive rats deprived of salt is appreciably longer than other rats which continue to receive excessive amounts of salt in the diet. This animal model fails to demonstrate an antihypertensive effect of salt restriction on established hypertension, even though life is prolonged. The relevance of this observation in the treatment of humans is presently uncertain.

Between-population epidemiological studies

The literature is replete with numerous observations relating sodium intake and blood pressure in populations throughout the world. These data have been extensively reviewed by Page (19) and Stamler (20). In summary, there is unequivocal evidence of a clear correlation between the average daily sodium chloride intake of a population and the prevalence of hypertension in that population. In general, populations with a low salt intake are unacculturated, but differ widely in their geographic location, racial origins, altitude and climate. Their dietary habits range from completely vegetarian to largely carnivorous. Groups which have been studied in detail include the native Greenlanders, the Fijians, Cook Islanders, Easter Islanders, Solomon Islanders, African bushmen of Botswana, Samburu of Kenya and Tarahumara Indians of Mexico. There are occasional exceptions to the association between unacculturation and low sodium diet of less than 70 millimoles per day. The Qashqa'i nomads of Southern Iran ingest 150-200 millimoles of sodium daily and demonstrate the common Western tendency to develop a marked increase in blood pressure with increasing age and a high frequency of hypertension. The Lau, unlike other Solomon Island communities, cook their food in salt water and have salt intakes and blood pressures considerably in excess of other groups. Since their ancestral roots are common to other Solomon Island groups, it is unlikely that differences in their blood pressures can be accounted for by genetic variation.

Within-population epidemiological studies

The possibility that genetic variation rather than dietary variation accounts for the observed differences between populations can be assessed more critically when the salt-ingesting habits and blood pressures are studied within a population of genetically similar individuals. The most celebrated and controversial study in Western man is that of Dahl and Love (21). These investigators studied the salt intake of 547 American adults undergoing annual physical examination at the Brookhaven National Laboratory, Upton, New York. In 65 persons who never used salt at the table, there was not a single case of hypertension, in 243 persons who sometimes added salt after tasting their food, there were 17 cases of hypertension and in the 239 persons who routinely added salt to their food without prior tasting, there were 24 cases of hypertension. Their data demonstrate a clear correlation between salt intake and hypertension, but the hypertensive patients were more often overweight than their normotensive counterparts.

The usually normotensive Samburu become hypertensive within 2 years of joining the Kenyan army (22). Their elevation in blood pressure is associated with a change in their diet from milk and meat containing approximately 50 millimoles of sodium per day to a salted maize gruel containing over 250 millimoles of sodium daily.

The Chicago School Children Study on salt and blood pressure (20) demonstrated a significant correlation between sodium intake and blood pressure, second only to the relationship between weight and hypertension (a topic which will be discussed later).

Sasaki (23) is one of several Japanese workers to relate the higher incidence of hypertension in the north of his country to the heavier salt use in Northern Japan. This may relate to the greater use of salt as a preservative in the climatically harsher north which has less ready access to fresh fish during the winter months than the south of Japan.

Does sodium restriction reduce blood pressure?

The work of Kempner (5, 6) indicates that extreme reduction of sodium chloride intake is effective in controlling hypertension. Other investigators have, in general, been less successful and their negative results have tended to diminish enthusiasm for this strict dietary approach. The reason for their relatively poor results is apparent in critical analysis of their data. Morgan and his colleagues (24, 25) demonstrated average reductions in diastolic blood pressures of approximately 7 mmHg with salt restriction, but their intakes show that most patients did not achieve optimal reduction of salt intake. Although they were provided with a diet that should have reduced sodium intake to 70-100 mmol/day, urinary sodium in 24 hour samples averaged 157 mmol compared with the control average of 191 mmol/day. The results bear testimony to (a) the apparent unwillingness of patients to accept a diet even richer in salt than the U.S. Senate Committee recommendations and (b) the fact that a modest reduction in blood pressure was achieved even with minimal reduction in salt intake!

Salt restriction—adjunct to antihypertensive drugs?

Morgan and his colleagues (24, 25) also demonstrated that the antihypertensive effects of thiazides could be potentiated by the concurrent (admittedly slight) reduction in salt intake.

Amery and his colleagues in Belgium (26) have related a

reduction in mean blood pressure from 167/113 mmHg to 159/109 mmHg when salt was restricted from 170 mmol/day to 70 mmol/day. The effect of salt restriction was similar to that of a diuretic given in conjunction with a regular high salt diet (152/106 mmHg). Combined sodium restriction is a useful adjunct to the antihypertensive effects of diuretics and other antihypertensive medications. There is evidence that the converse is also true, i.e., the use of excessive amounts of salt (>200 mmol/day) is capable of negating the antihypertensive effects of thiazide diuretics. In addition, Kaplan and his colleagues at the University of Texas (27) have shown an inverse relationship between salt intake and potassium loss in patients receiving thiazide diuretics (personal communication). In summary, the hypertensive patient on thiazide diuretics can improve the likelihood of response in three ways if salt intake is also reduced (1) the thiazide is more likely to exert an antihypertensive effect, (2) there is likely to be summation of antihypertensive effect of salt restriction and diuretic and (3) with less potassium loss, complications of hypokalemia and the need for potassium supplementation may be avoided.

Mathematical correlations of salt intake and hypertension

The numerical relationships between salt use and blood pressure have intrigued some investigators. Joossens (28) investigated the relationship between blood pressure and 24 hour urinary sodium excretion in 2027 Belgian men and women. A significant correlation was found between the mean systolic blood pressure within each of 20 sub-groups and the sodium chloride excretion as follows:

$$y = 132 + 0.97x$$

where y = systolic blood pressure in mmHg and x = sodium excretion expressed in g sodium chloride/1.7 g creatinine.

Joossens' work was investigated further at Amery's Laboratory (26). An average 7.7fi 4.4 mmHg reduction in blood pressure was associated with a reduction of 24 hour urinary sodium excretion from 191.1 ± 61.2 mmol to 92.8 ± 41.9 mmol. These workers developed an equation relating the decrease in systolic blood pressure produced by the sodium restriction and the decrease in 24 hour urinary sodium excretion as follows:

$$y = 6.58 + 0.163x$$

where y = reduction in systolic BP (mmHg) and x = decrease in 24 h urinary sodium excretion (mmol).

They concluded that the average patient could expect a decrease in blood pressure of about 10/5 mmHg if daily sodium chloride intake were reduced from 10 g to 5 g.

Obesity and Hypertension

To incriminate excessive weight as a possible contributing factor to elevation of blood pressure, a number of criteria should be established.
1. There should be evidence of a relative increase in blood pressure and prevalence of hypertension with increase in weight in all age groups.
2. An increase in weight in a given individual or population should be associated with an increase in blood pressure.
3. Weight loss in a given individual or population should be associated with a reduction in blood pressure.
4. The effect of weight should be dissociated from other risk factors, e.g., salt intake, and should not be an alternative manifestation of other risk factors.

Epidemiological studies of weight and blood pressure

Stamler and his associates (29) have published the weight and blood pressure findings in one million Americans of all age groups and ethnic backgrounds. Their data demonstrated a clear distinction between the prevalance rates of hypertension in underweight, normal weight and overweight individuals of both sexes and all ages. A white male aged 20-39 years who is underweight (39 cases of hypertension per 1000 population) has approximately half the risk of hypertension as males of the same age who are normal in weight (72/1000) and less than one quarter the risk of males of his own age group who are overweight (176/1000). Overweight white women in the age group 20-39 years have the greatest relative risk (111 cases per 1000 population), compared with women of the same age and normal weight (41/1000). The relative risk factor for overweight young white women is therefore 2.7 (111/41). The relative risk factors for obesity in black and white males and females of different age groups are shown in Table 1. It appears that obesity is relatively less important as a risk factor in black or elderly persons and relatively more important in younger white individuals.

A follow up study of men 22-31 years after college admission found that relative weight at the time of college entrance correlated significantly to the risk of developing hypertension (Table 2). Those in the highest quintile of weight at the time of college admission had an 11.7% rate of hypertension in middle age compared with a 7.6% hypertension rate for the leanest quintile at the time of admission (30).

A study of tenth grade school children determined a strong correlation between relative obesity and both systolic and diastolic blood pressures (31). Not all overweight individuals develop hypertension nor are all hypertensive individuals overweight, but these and several other studies are in close agreement in correlating weight with blood pressure. There are no clear explanations for the phenomenon. Excessive amounts of salt may be consumed in conjunction with excessive amounts of food. Adiposity increases the vascular bed and peripheral resistance. Obese individuals tend to exercise less. Perhaps there are even factors related to the metabolic activity of fat cells.

Effects of increasing weight

A study of adolescents in Evans County, Georgia (32) showed that young people who gained most weight in a seven year period demonstrated a higher rate of development of sustained hypertension. The numbers in this study are quite small and the risk of gaining weight has been assessed in conjunction with the risk of initial overweight, but the data reflect the relative risk of increasing body weight, whether the individual was initially normal weight or overweight.

Effects of losing weight

The Chicago Coronary Prevention Evaluation Program established a nutritional program and encouraged exercise in overweight individuals. The study demonstrated a significant correlation between weight reduction and decrease in blood pressure over a five year period (33).

A study at the Glasgow Blood Pressure Clinic in Scotland (34) allocated 49 hypertensive individuals who were overweight to one of three strategies for attaining weight reduction over a one year period. Individuals referred to a dietitian for guidance lost an average of 5.1 kg in weight, those given a diet sheet lost an average of 2.64 kg, while those advised by a physician simply to lose weight without additional support lost an average of 2.15 kg. These workers demonstrated a highly significant correlation between weight loss and improvement in blood pressure control, noting that this was more likely when a dietitian was consulted. They also noted that patients whose weight was successfully controlled required less frequent increases in antihypertensive therapy.

Effect of weight loss without salt restriction

Dahl (35) has argued that the fall in blood pressure with weight loss is due entirely to the concomitant reduction in salt intake. To determine the validity of this claim, Reisin and his colleagues (36) undertook an evaluation of 107 hypertensive patients. Blood pressure control was unsatisfactory in all patients at the beginning of the study. Group I consisted of 24 patients who did not take any medications but underwent a weight reduction program. Group IIa consisted of 57 patients who continued on drug therapy and also underwent a weight reduction program. Group IIb consisted of 26 patients who continued on their usual drug therapy and their usual dietary. The sodium intake in all 3 groups was essentially the same, i.e., Group I 165.3 ± 51.7, Group IIa 184.7 ± 42.8 and Group IIb 154.8 ± 79.0 mmol/24 h.

The study concluded that those patients who lost weight showed a normalization of blood pressure, whereas those patients who were not on the weight reduction program had no significant change in blood pressure or weight. These authors conclude that weight reduction has an independent effect on hypertension, completely unrelated to dietary salt intake. They argue that weight control offers an efficient, low-cost means of blood pressure control that is free of side effects. Weight reduction may make it unnecessary for some patients to require medications and limit or reduce the amount of antihypertensive drugs required by other overweight patients.

Vegetarian or mixed diet?

A study of vegetarians living in the Boston area (37) suggested that blood pressure elevation might be related to habitual high intake of animal protein. In contrast to this evidence, the bulk of epidemiological data from unacculturated people does not distinguish between those that are predominantly vegetarian, those who have a mixed diet and those that are predominantly carnivorous. In all of the studies which have been discussed earlier, the common denominator in diet appeared to be the sodium chloride content rather than the fraction of plant or animal protein. Indeed, anthropological data go further in suggesting that man's first major use of salt was associated with his trend towards an agricultural society from his primeval hunting life style. The individual experience of the Samburu discussed earlier certainly suggests that a highly salted vegetarian diet is more likely to be associated with hypertension than a no added-salt meat and milk diet. It is neither relevant nor appropriate to discuss other aspects of vegetarian diet at this point.

Alcohol intake and blood pressure

From analysis of alcohol intake in their Chicago population studies, Stamler and his colleagues (38) concluded that habitual intake of five or more alcoholic drinks per day was associated with increased prevalence of hypertension. They defined an alcoholic drink as 12 ounces of beer, 6 ounces of wine or 1.5 ounces of distilled liquor. Remarkably, they saw a threshold phenomenon at this level of alcohol intake, rather than a gradual increase in blood pressure with increasing alcohol consumption. It is difficult to understand these data completely without some further knowledge of differences between the socio-economic groups, dietary habits, salt intake and weight of these heavy alcohol users and individuals who consume less alcohol or are totally abstinent.

Dietary management of hypertension—how feasible in 1980?

Critics of epidemiological data are always eager to cite the individual cases which, they claim, entirely refute the hypothesis in question. The obese individual who habitually consumes large amounts of salt in his diet yet remains normotensive is clear evidence, they say, of the irrelevance of weight or salt intake in the development of hypertension. Their negative approach towards altering the patient's life style is rationalized by claiming that weight loss and salt restriction are difficult, unpopular procedures which impair the quality of life, are unlikely to succeed and should not therefore be attempted. In any case, they argue that the availability of effective antihypertensive drugs makes it necessary to interfere with the patient's life style, apparently neglecting the interference of labelling the patient and prescribing prolonged drug therapy.

The cost of detecting, investigating and treating all currently known and unknown hypertensives would place an intolerable financial and resource burden on our health care system. It is obvious, therefore, that preventive health measures must play a major role in the control of hypertension. Unfortunately, the only popular health care measures are those which increase our personal comfort such as better housing and sanitation. Those measures which demand a measure of self-discipline are less likely to succeed.

As health professionals, I believe we should not be defeatist in our approach. The problem should be addressed at several levels. Society is, in general, aware of the risks of obesity and individuals are often willing to attempt to lose weight because the "body beautiful" attitude is an important peer pressure in our society. Excessive salt intake is a more pernicious prob-

Table 1 Prevalence of hypertension (DBP ≥ 95mm Hg) according to age, sex, weight and colour in one million Americans. The figures in parenthesis indicate the relative risk for an individual within each subgroup (Ref. 20, 28)

Prevalence of Elevated Blood Pressure per 1,000

	WHITES				BLACKS			
	20-39 Years		40-64 Years		20-39 Years		40-64 Years	
Weight	M	F	M	F	M	F	M	F
Underweight	39 (0.54)	39 (0.95)	182 (0.75)	173 (0.78)	88 (0.72)	89 (0.87)	300 (0.8)	377 (0.92)
Normal Weight	72 (1.0)	41 (1.0)	244 (1.0)	222 (1.0)	123 (1.0)	102 (1.0)	375 (1.0)	412 (1.0)
Overweight	176 (2.44)	111 (2.71)	361 (1.48)	353 (1.59)	260 (2.11)	201 (1.97)	519 (1.38)	539 (1.31)

Table 2 Weight at college entrance (quintile 1 represents lowest group, quintile 5 heaviest group) and risk of hypertension in middle age. (Ref. 29)

Weight Group	Number	% Hypertensive
1	2210	7.6
2	1731	7.7
3	1542	8.7
4	981	9.6
5	902	11.7

lem. So much of the process of food preparation is outside the control of the individual that one might despair of controlling sodium intake, even with a high level of motivation. Salt content of prepared food should be clearly labelled. Restaurants and fast food outlets especially should allow the customer to determine his individual salt preference, rather than indiscriminantly salting all food. The traditional central position of the saltcellar at the family table is to be deplored. Salting food encourages the expectation of saltiness and gives the unfortunate impression of blandness to unsalted or lightly salted food.

As a clinical pharmacologist involved in the treatment of hypertension, my major interest is in the drug management of these patients. To ignore these other aspects would be a disservice to my patient, but I am conscious that I may be asking too much of a patient if demands are placed on altering dietary habits. Only education of society in general can make that task easier for me and for my individual patient.

"It (salt) is fit neither for the land nor the dunghill; men throw it way" (Luke 14, verse 35).

REFERENCES

1. Ambard, L. and Beaujard, E., 1904. Causes de l'hypertension arterielle. Arch. Gen. Med. 193:520-533.
2. Allen, F. M., 1920. Arterial hypertension. JAMA 74:652-654.
3. Allen, F. M., 1922. Treatment of arterial hypertension. Med. Clin. N. Am. 6:475-481.
4. Allen, F. M., 1925. Treatment of Kidney Diseases and High Blood Pressure. Morristown, New Jersey: The Physiatric Institute.
5. Kempner, W., 1944. Treatment of kidney disease and hypertensive vascular disease with rice diet. N. Carolina Med. J. 5:125-133.
6. Kempner, W., 1948. Treatment of hypertensive vascular disease with rice diet. Am. J. Med. 4:545-577.
7. Senate Select Committee on Nutrition and Human Needs, 1977. Dietary Goals for the United States, 2nd Edition. Washington D.C., U.S. Govt. Printing Office.
8. Dahl, L. K., Heine, M. and Tassinari, L., 1962. Role of genetic factors in susceptibility to experimental hypertension due to chronic excess salt ingestion. Nature, 194:480-482.
9. Dahl, L. K., Heine, M. and Tassinari, L., 1965. Effects of chronic excess salt ingestion. Further demonstration that genetic factors influence the development of hypertension: evidence from experimental hypertension due to cortisone and to adrenal regeneration. J. Exptl. Med. 122: 533-545.
10. Dahl, L.K., Knudsen, K. D., Heine, M. A. and Leitl, G. J., 1968. Effects of chronic excess salt ingestion. Modification of experimental hypertension in the rat by variations in the diet. Circulation Res. 22:11-18.
11. Maddocks, I., 1961. Possible absence of essential hypertension in two complete Pacific Island populations. Lancet, 2:396-399.
12. Maddocks, I., 1967. Blood pressure in Melanesians. Med. J. Aust. 1:1123-1126.
13. Oliver, W.J., Cohen, E. L. and Neel, J. V., 1975. Blood pressure, sodium intake, and sodium-related hormones in the Yanomamo Indians, a "no-salt" culture. Circulation, 52: 146-151.
14. Page, L. B., 1976. Epidemiologic evidence on the etiology of human hypertension and its possible prevention. Am. Heart J. 91:527-534.
15. Page, L. B., Damon, A. and Moellering, R. C., Jr., 1974. Antecedents of cardiovascular disease in six Solomon Islands societies. Circulation, 49:1132-1146.
16. Page, L. B., Vandervert, D. and Nader, K., 1978. Blood pressure, diet and body form in traditional nomads of the Qashqa'i tribe, Southern Iran. Acta Cardiologica, 33:102-103.
17. Prior, I. A. M., Grimley-Evans, J. and Harvey H. P. B., 1968. Sodium intake and blood pressure in two Polynesian populations. NEJM, 279:515-520.
18. Shaper, A. G., Wright, D. H. and Dyobe, J., 1969. Blood pressure and body build in three nomadic tribes of Northern Kenya. E. Afr. Med. J. 46: 273-281.
19. Page, L. B., 1979. Hypertension and atherosclerosis in primitive and acculturating societies. Hypertension Update Volume 1. Cardiovascular risk factors and consequences of hypertension. Health Learning Systems Inc., Bloomfield, N.J.: 1-12.
20. Stamler, J., 1979. Hypertension: Aspects of risk. Hypertension Update Volume I. Cardiovascular risk factors and consequences of hypertension. Health Learning Systems Inc., Bloomfield, N.J.: 22-37.
21. Dahl, L. K. and Love, R. A., 1954. Evidence for relationship between sodium (chloride) intake and human essential hypertension. Arch. Int. Med. 94:525-531.
22. Shaper, A. G., Leonard, P. A. and Jones, K. W., 1969. Environmental effects on the body build, blood pressure, and blood chemistry of nomadic warriors serving in the army in Kenya. E. Afr. Med. J. 46:282-289.
23. Sasaki, N., 1964. The relationship of salt intake to hypertension in the Japanese. Geriatrics, 19:735-744.
24. Carney, S., Morgan, T., Wilson, M., Matthews, G. and Roberts, R., 1975. Sodium restriction and thiazide diuretics in the treatment of hypertension. Med. J. Aust. 1:803-807.
25. Morgan, T., Gilles, A., Morgan, G., Adam, W., Wilson, M. and Carney, S., 1978. Hypertension treated by salt restriction. Lancet, 1:227-230.
26. Parijs, J., Joossens, J. V., Van der Linden, L., Verstreken, G. and Amery, A. K. P. C., 1973. Am. Heart J. 85:22-34.
27. Ram, C. V. S., Garrett, B. N. and Kaplan, N. M., 1980. Moderate sodium restriction and various diuretics in the treatment of hypertension: Effects on potassium wastage and blood pressure control. Archives of Internal Medicine (in press).
28. Joossens, J. V., Williems, J., Claessens, J., Claes, J. and Lissens, W., 1971. Sodium and hypertension in Fidanza, F., Keys, A., Ricci, G. and Somogyi, J. C., editors: Nutrition and cardiovascular diseases, Rome, Morgagni Edizioni Scientifiche.
29. Stamler, R., Stamler, J. and Riedlinger, W.F., 1978. Weight and Blood Pressure: Findings in hypertension screening of 1 million Americans. JAMA, 240:1607-1610.
30. Paffenbarger, R. S., Thorne, M. C. and Wing, A. L., 1968. Chronic diseases in former college students. VIII. Characteristics in youth predisposing to hypertension in later years. Am. J. Epidemiol. 88:25-31.
31. Miller, R. A. and Shekelle, R. B., 1976. Blood pressure in tenth-grade students. Results from the Chicago Heart Association Pediatric Heart Screening Project. Circulation, 54:993-1000.
32. Heyden, S., Bartel, A. G., Hames, C. G. and McDonough, J., 1969. Elevated blood pressure levels in adolescents, Evans County, Georgia. JAMA, 209:1683-1689.
33. Stamler, J., Farinaro, E., Mojonnier, L. M., Hall, Y., Moss, D. and Stamler, R., 1980. Prevention and control of hypertension by nutritional-hygienic means: Long-term experience of the Chicago Coronary Prevention Evaluation Program. JAMA, 243:1819-1823.
34. Ramsay, L. E., Ramsay, M. H., Hettiarachchi, J., Davies, D. L. and Winchester, J., 1978. Weight reduction in a blood pressure clinic. Br. Med. J. 2:244-245.
35. Dahl, L. K., 1972. Salt and hypertension. Am. J. Clin. Nutr. 25:231-244.
36. Reisin, E., Abel, R., Modan, M., Silverberg, D., Eliahou, H. E. and Modan, B., 1978. Effect of weight loss without salt restriction on the reduction of blood pressure in overweight hypertensive patients. NEJM, 298:1-6.
37. Sacks, F. M., Rosner, V. and Kass, E. H., 1974. Blood pressure in vegetarians. Am. J. Epidemiol. 100:390-398.
38. Dyer, A., Stamler, J. and Paul, O., 1977. Alcohol consumption, cardiovascular risk factors, and mortality in two Chicago epidemiologic studies. Circulation, 56:1067-1074.

DENTAL CARIES

Bacteria, Diet and the Prevention of Dental Caries— Part I

by Charles F. Schachtele, Ph.D.

Hardly a month goes by where the news media does not present some release on the prevention of human tooth decay (dental caries). Why the increase in publicity related to this disease? A response to this question requires an appreciation for the extent and consequences of this public health problem and an understanding of the status of research on this disease. Virtually all Americans have decayed teeth by the time they become adults. The average 15-year-old has ten decayed, filled or missing teeth and approximately six billion dollars per year are spent in this country to repair the damage caused by this disease.[1] In addition, caries can cause appreciable pain and loss of time.

Dental caries has been neatly defined[2] as "localized, progressive decay of the teeth, initiated by demineralization of the outer surface of the tooth due to organic acids produced locally by bacteria that ferment deposits of dietary carbohydrates." During the past decade, dental researchers have been able to uncover many of the microbiological and biochemical details important for caries development. In the first part of this article, we will discuss dental caries as an infectious disease and summarize some of the exciting progress which has been made in determining how unique oral bacteria interact with components in the diet to enhance caries formation. In part II of this article, we will discuss how this new information is being used to develop caries control measures which have great potential for disease prevention.[2]

Oral Bacteria and Diet

Greater than 60 different types of bacteria reside in the human oral cavity. Each type has characteristics which allow it to survive in the mouth and to elude both the flushing and antibacterial influences of saliva. Saliva contains approximately 100 million viable bacterial cells per milliliter, and the surfaces of teeth accumulate bacterial mats or masses (dental plaque) with a density of approximately 200 billion cells per gram of wet material. It is important that we consider these bacteria as our friends and realize that the symbiotic relationship we have with them may be critical to our health. Members of our oral flora have the potential to contribute to our nutrition, to induce the production of protective antibodies, and to influence the development of various organs and tissues.[3] We are just beginning to appreciate the developmental and immunological consequences of the several grams of oral bacteria we swallow each day.

Unfortunately, specific types of bacteria can rapidly become dominant at certain sites in the mouth and turn from friend to foe. In the case of dental caries, this transition appears to be primarily related to diet.

If we compare the mouth to other microbial niches in nature, it is clear that the oral cavity is a nutritionally rich environment. Indeed, the host can contribute so effectively that a complex bacterial flora exists and plaque accumulates on the teeth of human subjects who receive all of their food by stomach tube.[4] Plaque formed in this way has a diminished capacity to produce acid and, therefore, caries when supplied with fermentable carbohydrate. At this time the whole story on the effect of various diets on the oral flora is not available, but it is known that alterations in the ingested levels of carbohydrates can dramatically influence the concentration of certain bacteria. These findings emphasize the contribution of the diet to the microbial ecology of the oral cavity and indicate that the diet may significantly influence the bacteria which reside on the teeth. Specifically, *Streptococcus mutans* levels in plaque can be markedly elevated by increasing the quantity of carbohydrate in the diet. It is essential to realize that the importance of this response can only be evaluated in light of what we have recently learned about the cariogenic potential of *S. mutans*.

Streptococcus mutans

Current excitement in caries research stems from our growing knowledge of *S. mutans*.[5] This unique microorganism has characteristics which indicate that it is responsible for a major portion of the carious lesions which develop in humans. Arguments for treating caries as an infectious disease caused by a specific pathogen have been clearly presented.[6] Since the degree of infection by *S. mutans* and the extent of the disease is related to the level of fermentable carbohydrate in the diet, it is important to understand what is known about the interaction of these two factors. Initially, we must evaluate what is known about the ecology of *S. mutans* and how this can be related to disease development.

The only natural habitat of *S. mutans* is the mouth of humans and some animals. Specifically, this bacterium is primarily found as a part of plaque on the surfaces of teeth. The bacterium does not colonize the mouth of children prior to tooth eruption and disappears from the oral cavity after complete loss of the teeth. Reservoirs of *S. mutans* in parents appear to be the source of infection for infants whose erupting teeth are being colonized for the first time. The complexity of the caries process is reflected by the findings that the interoral spreading of *S. mutans* can be influenced by the frequency of exposure to the bacterium, the dose received, the nature and levels of antibacterial substances in saliva, the saliva flow rate, the nature of the other bacteria at the sites of initial contact, and other factors related to the specific adherence mechanisms of S. mutans.

It is important to note that S. mutans colonizes teeth in a very localized pattern and that the sites which harbor high concentrations of S. mutans are those sites which most rapidly become diseased. Recent studies have strongly implicated S. mutans in lesions which develop in the pits and fissures of the teeth[7] and on the smooth surfaces.[8] Another critical point is that when S. mutans is localized on the tooth surface, its ability to spread to adjacent sites is limited.[9] Fortunately, there are strong inhibitors, such as factors in saliva, which prevent S. mutans from spreading in a manner analogous to more rapidly disseminating bacterial infections.

Caries development is dependent on the presence of dental plaque. During the formation of plaque, S. mutans and the disaccharide sucrose have a unique relationship. Sucrose is made up of the monosaccharides glucose and fructose, and S. mutans utilizes the energy in the bond between these sugars to synthesize polymers of glucose (glucans) on the tooth surface. The production of these glucans is considered to be the critical reaction for the oral accumulation and cariogenicity of S. mutans. The enzyme responsible for glucan formation is a glucosyltransferase. Research has shown that mutants of S. mutans which produce elevated or reduced levels of this enzyme initiate correspondingly higher or lower levels of caries when tested in an animal model system with sucrose.[10] Consequently, this enzyme has been proposed by many researchers as the prime candidate antigen for an anticaries vaccine. Crude enzyme preparations have been shown to be effective immunogens when tested in animal models.[11]

Part of the glucan produced by S. mutans contains chemical bonds which decrease the solubility of the polysaccharide. This adds unique physical characteristics to colonies of S. mutans within plaque. Localized, glucan-coated colonies of S. mutans adjacent to the enamel surface might limit access to helpful buffering entities in saliva and block diffusion of harmful acid away from the teeth. Finally, the aggregated and compact colonies of S. mutans might be less susceptible than plaque, in general, to disruption and removal. This could be a great problem in retentive areas which have limited accessibility. This could be a major factor in the efficiency of certain oral hygiene procedures and emphasizes the need for proper and thorough periodic cleaning of the teeth by a professional.

A logical prediction from our brief survey of sucrose metabolism by S. mutans would be that samples of dental plaque from carious lesions should have a higher concentration of this bacterium and metabolize sucrose in a definable manner. Recent studies[12] have demonstrated that there is a marked difference in sucrose metabolism by plaque from a lesion and plaque removed from a noncarious surface on the same tooth. In contrast to the plaque from noncarious sites, the plaque from the diseased sites contained high levels of S. mutans and metabolized sucrose to lactic acid at a faster rate. These results support the concept that S. mutans is metabolically dominant in plaque associated with carious lesions and strengthen the argument for a key role for this bacterium and sugar metabolism in human caries formation.

Although we have emphasized the importance of sucrose in the cariogenicity of S. mutans, it is important to realize that other components of the human diet can be readily utilized for acid production by this bacterium. Strains of S. mutans also have been shown to efficiently transport and metabolize glucose, fructose, lactose, and the polyols sorbitol and manitol.[12] In addition, starch may be degraded to glucose and be rapidly metabolized by S. mutans. This ability to utilize a variety of potential substrates from the diet may partially explain the great cariogenic potential of S. mutans and its capacity to respond to the complexity of foodstuffs which enter the mouth.

As discussed previously, acid production by S. mutans is critically involved in dental enamel modification and consequent caries development. It is important that another unique aspect of S. mutans is its ability to survive and grow in acidic environments. Acid production from fermentable carbohydrates in the diet gives S. mutans a great advantage in the oral cavity since more acid-sensitive bacteria cannot survive and S. mutans can become the predominant organism at specific sites.

Summary

Tooth decay in humans results from acid produced by bacteria during fermentation of dietary carbohydrate. Recent findings on the details of this process have shown: that of the very many bacteria in the mouth, Streptococcus mutans appears to be the primary culprit in caries formation; that S. mutans infects the mouth after transfer from parents and other people; that S. mutans lives and eventually can predominate at unique (caries-prone) sites on the teeth; that the level of infection by S. mutans is increased by the quanitity and frequency of fermentable carbohydrate consumption, and; that S. mutans has a unique ability to utilize dietary sucrose to enhance its cariogenic potential. The ability to focus on S. mutans as the infectious agent in human dental caries has opened up several new approaches to disease prevention. These approaches are presented in Part II of this article.

References

1. Sanders, H.J., Tooth Decay, Chem. Eng. News, pp. 30-42, Feb. 25, 1980.
2. Scherp, H.W., Dental Caries: Prospects for Prevention, Science 173: 1199, 1971.
3. Gibbons, R.J., Significance of the Bacterial Flora Indigenous to Man. Am. Inst. Oral Biol. Symp. 26:27, 1969.
4. Bowen, W.H., Effect of Restricting Oral Intake to Invert Sugar or Casein on the Microbiology of Plaque in Macaca fascicularis (Irus), Arch. Oral Biol. 19:231, 1974.
5. Hamada, S. and Slade, H.D., Biology, Immunology and Cariogenicity of Streptococcus mutans. Microbiol. Rev. 44:331, 1980.
6. Loesche, W.J., Chemotherapy of Dental Plaque Infections. Oral Sci. Rev. 9:65, 1976.
7. Loesche, W.J. and Straffon, L.H., Longitudinal Investigation of the Role of Streptococcus mutans in Human Fissure Caries, Infect. Immun. 26:498, 1979.
8. Duchin, S. and van Houte, J., Relationship of Streptococcus mutans and Lactobacilli to Incipient Smooth Surface Dental Caries in Man, Arch. Oral Biol. 23:779, 1978.
9. Svanberg, M.L. and Loesche, W.J., Intraoral Spread of Streptococcus mutans in Man, Arch. Oral Biol. 23: 557, 1978.
10. Michalek, S.M., et al., Virulence of Streptococcus mutans: Biochemical and Pathogenic Characteristics of Mutant Isolates, Proc. Soc. Exp. Biol. Med. 150:498, 1975.
11. Taubman, M.A. and Smith, D.J., Effects of Local Immunization with Glucosyltransferase Fractions from Streptococcus mutans on Dental Caries in Rats and Hamsters, J. Immunol. 118:710, 1977.
12. Maryanski, J.H. and Wittenberger, C.L., Mannitol Transport in Streptococcus mutans, J. Bacteriol. 124: 1475, 1975.

Bacteria, Diet, and the Prevention of Dental Caries—Part II

by Charles F. Schachtele, Ph.D.

In part I of this article,[1] human dental caries (tooth decay) was discussed as an infectious disease resulting from specific interactions between cariogenic oral bacteria, such as *Streptococcus mutans*, and the fermentable carbohydrates which are found in the diet. From our increasing knowledge of the details of the formation of carious lesions in teeth, three main approaches to disease control have evolved. In addition, good oral hygiene practices, such as brushing and flossing, continue to be extremely important in helping to prevent dental caries. Each of these approaches contains several new and exciting potential means for caries prevention.

Caries Control: Protecting the Teeth

Water fluoridation, salt fluoridation and fluoride containing tablets, dentrifices, mouth rinses and gels are all capable of preventing caries to some degree.[2] Fluoride can suppress sugar metabolism by bacteria, make enamel more resistant to acid and stimulate remineralization of the teeth. "...optimal level fluoridation of drinking water can prevent 65 percent of decay that would otherwise occur."[3] Three new approaches to deliver fluoride to the tooth surface and ensure adequate exposure time are being studied.[4] Sodium fluoride has been incorporated into capsules which, when chewed, release 10 to 15 percent of the fluoride. When the capsule is swallowed, the remaining fluoride is released in the gastrointestinal tract from where it is absorbed and slowly returned to the mouth via saliva. A second related approach involves an aerosol which causes fluoride-containing microcapsules to adhere to the teeth where enhanced fluoride uptake by plaque and enamel could occur. A third approach involves attaching to the teeth a small device consisting of an inner core of a fluoride-containing material surrounded by a membrane. Fluoride is released from the device at a predetermined rate for at least six months.

It is important to note that fluoride is most effective in reducing caries on the smooth surfaces of teeth, but it is less effective on the biting surfaces. Since caries on these latter surfaces account for approximately 40 percent of all carious surfaces in six and seven-year-old children, it must be pointed out that sealant materials have been developed which are ideal for protecting these areas of the teeth. These polymers must be carefully applied in a dental office.

Caries Control: Diet Modification

Dental caries is associated with both the frequency of ingestion of fermentable carbohydrate and the duration of time the substrate is retained in the mouth.[5] Few clinical trials to determine the cariogenicity of various sugars have been performed. One important study was performed in Turku, Finland.[6] In this experiment caries formation was monitored in subjects ingesting foods containing a normal level of sucrose, foods with fructose in place of sucrose, and foods with xylitol in place of sucrose. After two years it was determined that the group consuming sucrose had an average caries index of decayed, missing and filled teeth of 7.2. The indices of the fructose and xylitol groups were 3.8 and 0.0, respectively. Since oral bacteria can not ferment xylitol, this study demonstrated the role of fermentable carbohydrate in human caries formation. It is important that this study does not allow a prediction as to what might be the effect of partial substitution of fructose for sucrose in the diet.

It has been proposed that caries could be prevented by altering the diet through replacement of sucrose or by reducing the frequency of sucrose consumption. The unique physical and chemical properties of sucrose have made attempts to develop and substitute other agents in many foodstuffs extremely difficult. Artificial sweeteners and other sugar substitutes have been extensively evaluated.[7,8] In developing an appropriate substance, one must carefully consider the metabolism and safety of the substitute, practical problems in using the compound, and the regulatory aspects of its utilization. As with xylitol, evaluation of the cariogenic potential of a substitute can be upstaged by an evaluation of its carcinogenicity.[9]

As mentioned previously,[1] an important aspect of *S. mutans* metabolism is that this bacterium has the ability to efficiently transport and metabolize not only sucrose but glucose, fructose, lactose, mannitol and sorbitol.[10] The latter two compounds are sugar alcohols which meet many of the criteria for sugar substitutes. Although there are problems in their utilization in a wide range of foodstuffs, they have been accepted in chewing gums. Some manufacturers of these products have used the label "Does not promote tooth decay." It is true that in animal model systems sorbitol and mannitol are markedly less cariogenic than sucrose and that dental plaque produces little acid when incubated with these polyols. Few bacteria in plaque are capable of fermenting sorbitol or mannitol. However, *S. mutans* can grow rapidly and produce acid when incubated *in vitro* with sorbitol or mannitol as its primary carbon source.[10] Ingestion of these sugar alcohols between meals could enhance the ability of *S. mutans* to compete with other oral bacteria. Within plaque, *S. mutans* has the potential to metabolize the polyols when they are supplied in the absence of other fermentable carbohydrates. Work should be performed to determine if, by supplying these compounds, we are inadvertently aiding a bacterium with documented cariogenic potential.

There is no experimental support for a direct correlation between the total intake of sugar and the incidence of caries. One of the dietary guidelines from the U.S. Department of Agriculture (USDA) and the U.S. Department of Health, Education and Welfare (DHEW) suggests a reduction in the consumption of refined and other processed sugars. With regard to dental caries, it is difficult to project any change in disease level with this decrease in consumption.

Indeed, a strong controversy exists concerning the relative cariogenicity of different carbohydrates. In general, it appears that monosaccharides and disaccharides are more cariogenic than starch, and sucrose is considered the most cariogenic sugar.[11] However, there are conflicting data on this subject and some animal studies indicate that *there is little difference in the cariogenicity of sucrose, glucose and fructose.*[12]

It can not be too strongly emphasized that one must carefully monitor *which* surfaces and sites on the teeth are being attacked in such studies and also the *type* of bacterial flora that is present before, during and at the termination of the study. Since *S. mutans* can readily transport and metabolize the predominant sugars found in the human diet, a great deal of caution should be used when attempting to evaluate studies where multiple types of fermentable carbohydrate are available. Only very low levels of sucrose may be needed to stimulate rapid decay when other fermentable carbohydrates are available in the diet. It is not unlikely that a subject with high or moderate levels of *S. mutans* might develop significant caries after shifting to a diet free of sucrose if the new diet contained available carbohydrate. Clearly, there are no simple answers when discussing the cariogenicity of various fermentable carbohydrates.

Fermentable carbohydrates are eaten as an ingredient of food or are added by the user. Unfortunately, *the fermentable carbohydrate content of a foodstuff can not be used to predict its cariogenic potential.* If a food is rapidly cleared from the mouth or enhances saliva flow, its cariogenicity will be reduced. If there are components in the food which bind the carbohydrate, inhibit its metabolism, or buffer the acid which is produced, the foodstuff might be less cariogenic. These complications make it critical that methodology be developed which will allow confident statements concerning the relative cariogenic potential of a particular foodstuff. In response to this need, the Health Foundation Research Institute of the American Dental Association has initiated a collaborative program to develop suitable systems to measure the paramaters relating food to caries formation.[13] The methods being analyzed include caries formation in rat model systems, acid production by human dental plaque and *in vitro* caries models. This program could be a step forward in attempts to reduce caries formation in humans.

Caries Control
Combating Cariogenic Bacteria

Progress in caries control could be made by specifically suppressing *S. mutans* infections. Prophylaxis of a subject's teeth followed by three topical applications of an iodine solution has recently been shown to significantly reduce the levels of *S. mutans* in plaque for prolonged intervals.[14] In light of the localized nature of *S. mutans* infections, iodine may be a useful adjunct in attempts to prevent caries.

Bacterial infections may theoretically be controlled by allowing the host to be colonized with nonvirulent variants of the pathogenic bacteria. Mutants of *S. mutans* have been obtained which produce minimal acid from carbohydrate.[15] Replacement therapy might involve supplying the mutants to subjects either during tooth eruption or after a thorough cleaning of the teeth. By filling specific ecological niches, the mutants might reduce the ability of pathogenic strains of *S. mutans* to infect an individual's teeth.

It is known that the external secretions of the body, including saliva, contain secretory immunoglobulin A (sIgA) as their predominant immunoglobulin. These fluids bathe the mucous membranes of the body and their antibodies are involved in "first-line defenses," such as the coating of bacteria and inhibition of their adherence. Since colonization of teeth by *S. mutans* involves production of glucan from dietary sucrose, *it is possible that inhibition by antibodies of the enzyme involved in glucan synthesis could prevent S. mutans-initiated caries.* Recent excitement in vaccine development stems from the observation that ingestion of antigens results in the appearance of corresponding sIgA antibodies in saliva. It has been proposed that antibody-producing lymphoid cells are stimulated in the gut-associated lymphoid tissue. The cells then migrate through the lymphatic system and blood stream to secretory tissues in various parts of the body. In these tissues the lymphocyts differentiate and produce antibody directed to the original antigen. These ideas stimulated a study[16] where four adults ingested capsules filled with nonviable *S. mutans* for several weeks. After one week antibodies to the *S. mutans* strain could be detected in the saliva of the subjects. Immunization with a pill is an exciting concept and further studies on this problem will be of great interest.

Summary

Recent research on the bacterial and nutritional causes of human dental caries has revealed new and exciting approaches for prevention of this disease. In addition to brushing and flossing, the teeth may be protected by supplying fluoride in new ways. The diet may be modified as new methods for testing the cariogenic potential of foods are perfected. Cariogenic bacteria may be suppressed by utilization of selective agents, replacement with noncariogenic bacteria and by immunization. The multifactorial etiology of caries makes it likely that a combination of treatments will be required for complete prevention of this disease.

References

1. Schachtele, C.F., Bacteria, Diet and the Prevention of Dental Caries, Part I, *Contemp. Nutrition* Vol. 5, No. 7, 1980.
2. Cariostatic Mechanisms of Fluorides, Edited by W.E. Brown and K.G. Konig, *Caries Res.* 11, Supplement 1, S. Karger, Basel, 1977.
3. The Surgeon General's Report on Health Promotion and Disease Prevention, *Healthy People*, DHEW (PHS) Publication No. 79-55071, U.S. Government Printing Office, Washington, D.C., 1979.
4. Mirth, D.B. and Bowen, W.H., "Chemotherapy: Antimicrobials and Methods of Delivery." In: *Microbial Aspects of Dental Caries*, Edited by H.M. Stiles, et al., pp. 249-262, Information Retrieval, Washington, D.C., 1976.
5. Gustafson, B.E., et al., The Vipeholm Dental Caries Study, The Effect of Different Levels of Carbohydrate Intake on Caries Activity in 436 Individuals Observed for Five Years, *Acta Odont. Scand.* 11:232, 1954.
6. Scheinin, A. and Makinen, K.K., Turku Sugar Studies I-XXXI, *Acta Odont. Scand.* 33:1, 1975.
7. Shaw, J.H. and Roussos, G.G., *Sweeteners and Dental Caries*, Information Retrieval, Washington, D.C., 1978.
8. Guggenheim, B., *Health and Sugar Substitutes*, S. Karger, Basel, 1979.
9. Xylitol: Another Sweetener Turns Sour, *Science* 199:670, 1978.
10. Brown, A.T. and Bowles, R.D., Polyol Metabolism by a Caries-Conducive *Streptococcus*: Purification and Properties of a Nicotinamide Adenine Dinucleotide-Dependent Mannitol-1-Phosphate Dehydrogenase, *Infect. Immun.* 16: 163, 1977.
11. Bowen, W.H., "Role of Carbohydrates in Dental Caries". In: *Sweeteners and Dental Caries*, Edited by J.H. Shaw and G.G. Roussos, pp. 147, Information Retrieval, Washington, D.C., 1978.
12. Colman, G., et al., The Effects of Sucrose, Fructose and a Mixture of Glucose and Fructose on the Incidence of Dental Caries in Monkeys (*M. fascicularis*), *Brit. Den. J.* 142:217, 1977.
13. Cooperative Program on Foods, Nutrition and Dental Health, *J. Amer. Dent. Assoc.* 97:239, 1978.
14. Caufield, P.W. and Gibbons, R.J., Suppression of *Streptococcus mutans* in the Mouths of Humans by a Dental Prophylaxis and Topically Applied Iodine, *J. Dent. Res.* 58:1317, 1979.
15. Hillman, J.D., Lactate Dehydrogenase Mutants of *Streptococcus mutans*: Isolation and Preliminary Characterization, *Infect. Immun.* 21:206, 1978.
16. McGhee, J.R., et al., Induction of Secretory Antibodies in Humans Following Ingestion of *Streptococcus mutans*, *Adv. Exp. Biol. Med.* 107:177, 1978.

A Comparison of Carbohydrate Metabolism after Sucrose, Sorbitol, and Fructose Meals in Normal and Diabetic Subjects

by Suat Akgun and Norman H. Ertel

Sucrose, sorbitol, and fructose (35 g) were fed to normal and diabetic subjects as a component of a 400-calorie breakfast. In both normal and diabetic subjects, the mean peak increment in plasma glucose was highest after the sucrose meals (44.0 mg/dl for normal subjects; 78.0 mg/dl for diabetic subjects); lowest after sorbitol meals (9.3 mg/dl for normal subjects; 32.3 mg/dl for diabetic subjects); and intermediate after the fructose meals (29.0 mg/dl for normal subjects; 48.0 mg/dl for diabetic subjects). In normal subjects, the mean peak increment of plasma immunoreactive insulin followed a similar pattern, but in diabetic subjects there was no significant difference between the three groups. We conclude that fructose or sorbitol, given as part of a meal, results in lower glucose levels in both normal and diabetic subjects, but that the latter is not related to a difference in insulin release.
DIABETES CARE 3:582-585, SEPTEMBER–OCTOBER 1980.

Interest in the use of sugars other than sucrose as a component of the diabetic diet stems from the earliest days of diabetes research. In 1874, Külz initially suggested that diabetic patients were able to metabolize oral fructose better than other sugars.[2] Fructose, but not glucose, was found to partially replete the hepatic glycogen stores of diabetic depancreatectomized dogs by Minkowski in 1893,[3] and Elliott Joslin published on the clinical usefulness of fructose in 1915.[4] Other nonsucrose sweetening agents used include sorbitol and xylitol, but they have not been investigated as extensively as fructose.[5]

Several groups have established a decreased plasma glucose and insulin rise after oral and i.v. administration of fructose and other sweetening agents compared with glucose in normal and diabetic subjects.[6] Bohannon and colleagues have also described the decreased reactive hypoglycemia after fructose.[7] Most studies used the pure sugar as a test substance. However, in analogy with the problems posed in interpreting the oral glucose tolerance test, it is clear that most patients do not consume large quantities of pure sugar. In a report prepared for the Food and Drug Administration in May 1978 by the Federation of American Societies for Experimental Biology, it was pointed out that adequate studies of the clinical effectiveness of fructose, xylitol, and sorbitol as part of mixed meals have not been conducted.

This report presents data on changes in glucose and insulin in normal and diabetic subjects after standardized meals containing fixed amounts of either sucrose, fructose, or sorbitol.

MATERIALS AND METHODS

Ten nondiabetic and six diabetic subjects participated in the study. The protocol was approved by the Human Safety Committee of the East Orange Veterans Administration Medical Center and written informed consent was obtained from each individual. No more than two tests were carried out in 1 wk, and the interval between any two tests was at least 3 days.

Studies in nondiabetic subjects. Ten nondiabetic males, aged 19-62 yr (mean age 43 yr) participated in the study. None of the subjects had a history of diabetes mellitus or chronic illness. Ten individuals were given a sucrose meal, six a sorbitol meal, and five received a fructose meal. Usually the sucrose meal was given first, although some patients received the meals in random order. All the nondiabetic volunteers underwent oral glucose tolerance testing (OGTT) with 100 g of dextrose after ingestion of at least 300 g of carbohydrates for 3 days. Fasting plasma glucose ranged between 71 and 93 mg/dl with a mean of 80 mg/dl. Each test meal, consisting of a scrambled egg, farina, low fat milk, and 120 mgs of decaffeinated coffee, was given after an overnight fast. Of the 400 calories, 140 calories were comprised of 35 g sucrose, sorbitol, or fructose. A reason for choosing 35 g of various sugars is related to the fact that Adcock and Gray [9] showed that 35 g ^{14}C-sorbitol is almost completely absorbed, and administration of more than this quantity would result in diarrhea in many patients. The first bite was considered zero time, and each subject finished the entire test meal in 5 min. Blood samples were drawn into heparinized tubes every 15 min up to 2 h, then at 150 and 180 min. Plasma glucose (PG) determinations were usually performed on the day of the test using the Beckman Glucose Analyzer. Pure solutions of either sorbitol or fructose were not detected by the analyzer. Determinations for plasma immunoreactive insulin (IRI) and growth hormone (GH) were performed by radioimmunoassay. All the determinations on one subject were carried out in the same assay to prevent interassay variability. All data were analyzed as the change from the mean of two baseline values. The paired Student's *t* test was used for statistical analysis in all tests except for comparison of sorbitol with fructose in normal subjects. In the latter, the *t* test for independent data was used.

Studies in diabetic subjects. Six male individuals with non-insulin-dependent diabetes mellitus (NIDDM), aged 52-59 yr, participated in this study. Three patients exceeded ideal body weight (IBW) by 23%, 30%, and 35%; the other three were normal in weight. All patients met the criteria of the National Diabetes Data Group for the diagnosis of diabetes mellitus (fasting PG > 140 mg/dl on at least two occasions).[10] Fasting PG ranged between 90 and 197 mg/dl with a mean of 162 ± 15.4 (SEM ± mg/dl). Two patients had been taking oral hypoglycemic agents, which were discontinued at least 1 wk before the study was carried out. One patient had diabetic neuropathy but had no clinical evidence of enteropathy. The same format as in the control subjects was followed, with the exception that they did not have an OGTT. Since each diabetic patient received each of the three sweeteners with a test meal, the paired Student's *t* test was used uniformly.

RESULTS

Nondiabetic Subjects

Plasma glucose. The mean peak change in PG concentration (ΔPG) after sucrose, fructose, and sorbitol meals was reached at 30 min, with mean values of 44 ± 5.4 (SEM) mg/dl, 29.0 ± 4.6 mg/dl, and 9.3 ± 2.3 mg/dl, respectively. When sucrose versus sorbitol meals were compared at individual times, statistically significant differences were noted at 15, 30, 45, and 60 min. When sucrose versus fructose meals were compared, ΔPG was significantly higher after sucrose at 15 and 30 min, and lower at 150 and 180 min.

An analysis of mean ΔPG by computing the areas under the curves by planimetry reveals a major and significant difference when sucrose is compared with sorbitol. There is no such difference in mean ΔPG for the entire sucrose versus fructose study, but when the total curve is separated into early (hyperglycemic) and late (reactive) phases, significant differences in opposite directions are noted.

Plasma IRI. The mean peak ΔIRI after a sucrose meal was seen at 30 min with a mean of 55.6 ± 10.0 μU/ml; at 60 min after a fructose meal with a mean of 36.2 ± 10.6 μU/ml; and at 15 min after a sorbitol meal with a mean of 18.6 ± 6.0 μU/ml. When ΔIRI after sucrose and sorbitol meals were compared, there was statistical significance at 15, 30, 45, 60, 75, and 90 min. When ΔIRI after sucrose and fructose meals were compared, ΔIRI was significantly higher after a fructose meal at 120, 150, and 180 min.

When areas under the curves of mean ΔIRI after sucrose versus fructose or sorbitol meals are compared, results similar to mean ΔPG were obtained.

Diabetic Subjects

Plasma glucose. The mean peak ΔPG after sucrose meals was 78.0 ± 12.0 mg/dl, after fructose meals 48.0 ± 11.0 mg/dl, and after sorbitol meals 32.3 ± mg/dl. There was a statistically significant difference between paired ΔPG after sucrose versus sorbitol meals at every individual point in time between 15 and 150 min. When ΔPG after sucrose was compared with ΔPG after fructose, significant differences were noted at 15, 30, 45, 75, 105, and 120 min. Lastly, comparison of fructose versus sorbitol yielded statistical significance only at 90 min. An analysis of mean ΔPG by examining areas under the curves revealed significant differences when sucrose, fructose, and sorbitol meals were compared with each other.

Plasma IRI. The mean peak ΔIRI after sucrose meals was 21.9 ± 6.8 μU/ml at 60 min, after fructose meals 18.0 ± 3.2 at 45 min, and after sorbitol meals 16.2 ± 3.6 at 90 min. Comparison of ΔIRI after the three types of meals revealed no statistical significance whether one looks at individual points in time or areas under the curve.

DISCUSSION

The presence of obesity and/or diabetes mellitus does not seem to decrease the desire for sweets in the diet. In the United States, 80% of diabetic patients use dietetic foods.[11] The need for dietetic foods in diabetes has been questioned on the basis of cost versus nutritional benefits,[12] but there is little doubt that such products will continue to be used in great volume. Since the disapproval of cyclamates, there has been a growing interest in the nonsucrose nutritive sweeteners, fructose and sorbitol.

Studies using the pure carbohydrate showed lower levels of PG after ingestion of both fructose and sorbitol compared with sucrose or glucose in normal and diabetic subjects.[6] Bohannon and colleagues confirmed these findings in normal subjects using fructose and also showed a lesser insulin increase.[7] Despite these studies, little scientific work has been performed looking at the effects of fructose and sorbitol as components of meals. Arvidsson-Lenner[13] has been cited in many reviews as showing no significant differences among sucrose, fructose, and sorbitol meals with respect to blood glucose levels or glycosuria. However, this study was performed in diabetic and healthy subjects over the age of 60 yr, without prior carbohydrate feeding and without standardized meals between subjects. In addition, she used relatively small quantities of sweeteners (14–21 g) and did not perform insulin determinations. The metabolic effects of 75 g of fructose compared with an equal amount of dietary starch was studied in two insulin-dependent diabetic patients.[14] Fructose feeding did not alter blood glucose levels or urinary excretion of glucose; insulin values were not measured. In an acute study, fructose was given to 26 hospitalized diabetic children by isocalorically substituting 1.0 g/kg fructose for other carbohydrates at breakfast.[15] Blood glucose values from 30 to 120 min after ingestion were significantly lower on fructose days. A longer 4 wk trial of fructose, compared with isocaloric sugar-free diets, did not result in impaired control of diabetes, and it was concluded that fructose could be used as a sweetening agent in such patients. Steinke, et al., gave sorbitol (up to 40 g in three divided doses) during meals for 8–48 days to diabetic children at camp.[16] When compared with control periods without sweetening agents, sorbitol resulted in no significant variation in either glycosuria or daily insulin dose. Shuman et al., also evaluated sorbitol and found no alteration of diurnal blood glucose values when sorbitol was added to the usual diets.[17]

While the current studies do not answer the question of long-term effects of nonglucose nutritive sweeteners as a substitute for glucose and sucrose in diets of patients with diabetes mellitus, they do provide information that is more useful than that obtained by administration of the pure sugars fructose and sorbitol. In normal subjects, both fructose and sorbitol meals resulted in lower PG and IRI levels than corresponding amounts of sucrose also given as parts of a meal, with sorbitol resulting in lower PG levels during the first hour. The patients did not describe any difference in sweetness between the three meals, but half of the patients eating the sorbitol meals complained of either mild abdominal cramps or diarrhea. These side effects, while mild, led to better acceptance of fructose as a sweetening agent.

The changes in PG in diabetic patients followed the same relative patterns as in nondiabetic subjects, but both the absolute levels and differences from baseline were greater. The achievement of peak levels of PG was delayed after the ingestion of all three sugars. In the nondiabetic subjects, the peak levels of PG were seen at 30 min in 18 of 22 studies. In the diabetic subjects, the peak PG was seen at 60 min in 9 of the 18 studies, at 75 min in 2 studies, and at 45 min in the remaining 7 tests. The delayed peak is in agreement with other studies.[18] The mean baseline plasma IRI concentration was higher in diabetic subjects compared with control subjects (19.3 ± 1.8 μU/ml versus 12.9 ± 2.4 μU/ml). This is compatible with the higher fasting PG in this group with NIDDM.[19] Insulin secretion in the diabetic subjects was markedly impaired in response to sucrose and fructose meals, but there were no significant differences in either peak insulin values or integrated insulin secretion when the three sugars were compared. Therefore, the difference in PG after the various meals cannot be attributed to differences in insulin secretion.

It is clear from our studies that both fructose and sorbitol in meal form result in lower PG levels when compared with sucrose in normal and diabetic subjects. Many investigators currently believe that prolonged elevations of PG play a role in the development of the vascular complications of diabetes.[20] Although our experiments do not address the problem of long-term effects of fructose and sorbitol on plasma glucose and insulin values, it is possible that such agents may be advantageous in the diabetic diet when sweeteners are desired.

ACKNOWLEDGMENT

This work was supported, in part, by a grant from the American Diabetes Association, New Jersey Affiliate, Incorporated.

REFERENCES

1. Ertel, N. H., Akgun, S. and Haim, A., 1979. A comparison of fructose, sorbitol and sucrose meals in diabetic subjects. Diabetes, 28:384.
2. Külz, E., 1874. Beitrage zur Pathologie und Therapie des Diabetes Mellitus. Marburg, Elwert Verlag, pp. 130-46.
3. Minkowski, O., 1893. Untersuchungen über den Diabetes Mellitus nach estirpation des Pankreas. Arch. Exp. Pathol. Pharmakol. 31:85-189.
4. Joslin, E. P., 1915. Carbohydrate utilization in diabetes. Arch. Intern. Med. 16:693-732.
5. Talbot, J. M. and Fisher, K. D., 1978. The need for special foods and sugar substitutes by individuals with diabetes mellitus. Diabetes Care, 1:231-40.
6. Haslbeck, M., Bachmann, W. and Mehnert, H., 1978. Zucker, Zuckeraustauschstoff und Sübstoff in der Diatetik von Stoffwechselstörungen. Aktuel. Ernahrung, 2:53-57.
7. Bohannon, N. V., Karma, J. H. and Forsham, P. H., 1978. Advantages of fructose ingestion over sucrose and glucose in humans. Diabetes, 27(Suppl. 2):438.
8. Moskowitz, O., 1971. The sweetness and pleasantness of sugars. Am. J. Psychol. 84:387-405.
9. Adcock, L. H. and Gray, C. H., 1957. The metabolism of sorbitol in human subjects. Biochem. J. 65:554-60.
10. National Diabetes Data Group, 1979. Classification and diagnosis of diabetes mellitus and other categories of glucose intolerance. Diabetes, 28:1039-57.
11. Bender, A. E., 1973. Nutrition and Dietetic Foods, 2nd edit. New York, Chemical Publishing Co., pp. 49-64.
12. Wunschel, I. M. and Sheikholtslam, B. M., 1978. Is there a role for dietetic foods in the management of diabetes and/or obesity? Diabetes Care, 1:247-49.
13. Arvidsson-Lenner, R., 1976. Specially designed sweeteners and food for diabetics—a real need? Am. J. Clin. Nutr. 29:726-33.
14. Pelkonen, R., Aro, A. and Nikkilä, E. A., 1972. Metabolic effects of dietary fructose in insulin dependent diabetes of adults. Acta. Med. Scand. (Suppl.)542:187-93.
15. Akerblom, K. H., Siltanen, I. and Kallio, A., 1972. Does dietary fructose affect the control of diabetes in children? Acta. Med. Scand. 542:195-202.
16. Steinke, J., Wood, F. C., Domenge, L., Marble, A. and Renold, A. E., 1961. Evaluation of sorbitol in the diet of diabetic children at camp. Diabetes, 10:218-27.
17. Shuman, C. R., Kamp, R. L., Coyne, R. and Wohl, M. G., 1956. Clinical use of sorbitol as a sweetening agent in diabetes mellitus. Am. J. Clin. Nutr. 4:61-67.
18. Molnar, G. D., Taylor, W. F. and Langworthy, A., 1974. On measuring the adequacy of diabetes regulation: comparison of continuously monitored blood glucose patterns with values at selected time points. Diabetologia, 10:139-143.
19. Genuth, S. M., 1973. Plasma insulin and glucose profiles in normal, obese, and diabetic persons. Ann. Intern. Med. 79:812-22.
20. Bloodworth, J. M. B., Jr., 1973. Diabetes mellitus and vascular disease. Postgrad. Med. 53:84-89.

Effects of Oral Fructose in Normal, Diabetic, and Impaired Glucose Tolerance Subjects

by Phyllis A. Crapo, Orville G. Kolterman, and Jerrold M. Olefsky

We studied the acute effects of oral ingestion of 50 g loads of dextrose, sucrose, and fructose on postprandial serum glucose, insulin, and plasma glucagon responses in 9 normal subjects, 10 subjects with impaired glucose tolerance, and 17 non-insulin-dependent diabetic subjects. The response to each carbohydrate was quantified when the respective carbohydrate was given alone in a drink or when given in combination with protein and fat in a test meal. The data demonstrate that (1) fructose ingestion resulted in significantly lower serum glucose and insulin responses than did sucrose or dextrose ingestion in all study groups, either when given alone or in the test meal; (2) although fructose ingestion always led to the least glycemic response compared with the other hexoses, the serum glucose response to fructose was increased the more glucose intolerant the subject; (3) urinary glucose excretion during the 3 h after carbohydrate ingestion was greatest after dextrose and least after fructose in all groups. In conclusion, fructose ingestion results in markedly lower serum glucose and insulin responses and less glycosuria than either dextrose or sucrose, both when given alone or as a constituent in a test meal. However, as glucose tolerance worsens, an increasingly greater glycemic response to fructose is seen. DIABETES CARE 3:575-582, SEPTEMBER-OCTOBER 1980. *

The role of fructose in the dietary treatment of diabetes has been debated for many years. Fructose is used in a number of European countries, but to date, has not been widely accepted or used in the United States. However, the ban of cyclamates by the U.S. Food and Drug Administration, the questionable future of saccharin, and increased commercial fructose availability have renewed interest in the use of fructose as an alternative sweetener for individuals with diabetes. In spite of the long history of fructose research, major questions about the use and metabolism of oral fructose still remain unanswered.[1,2]

Fructose has been commonly compared with glucose[3-12] and starch[6,12,13] but not with sucrose (50% glucose and 50% fructose), which is one of the sugars most commonly excluded from the diabetic diet. Also, studies of fructose substitution into meals containing a variety of carbohydrates have not allowed for the calculation of the contribution of fructose to the results compared with other carbohydrates.[14] In addition, comparative insulin values following glucose and fructose have only been reported in normal individuals.[10,11] We therefore studied and quantified the postprandial effects of dextrose, sucrose, and fructose on serum glucose, insulin, and glucagon responses in normal subjects and a broad range of non-insulin-dependent diabetic patients. These responses to the various sugars were investigated when the sugars were given alone as drinks or in combination with protein and fat in a liquid formula meal.

MATERIALS AND METHODS

We studied 9 normal subjects, 10 subjects with impaired glucose tolerance,* and 17 non-insulin-dependent diabetic subjects with fasting hyperglycemia (>140 mg/dl). The clinical characteristics of the study groups are displayed in Table 1. No subject was ingesting any drug known to affect glucose or insulin metabolism during the course of the study. None of the diabetic subjects had been treated with insulin. Those diabetic subjects on oral hypoglycemic agents had discontinued the drug 2 wk before testing. Each person consumed a weight-maintenance, solid food diet that contained at least 150-200 g of carbohydrates each day throughout the period of investigation. Three sugars (dextrose, sucrose, and fructose) were tested alone (drinks) and in combination with other nutrients (meals). The compositions of the test loads are outlined in Table 2. All tests were conducted after an overnight fast, and their order was randomized for each subject. At 8 a.m. the subject was given one of the solutions to drink over a 15-min period. Blood samples were timed from the initiation of consumption. Three-hour urine samples for determining urinary glucose excretion were obtained during each of the studies in nine of the subjects with impaired glucose tolerance and five of the diabetic subjects.

---
*Seven of the 10 subjects had chemical diabetes as previously defined by the criteria of the American Diabetes Association.[15] The remaining 3 had impaired glucose tolerance by previously published criteria,[16] i.e., a 1-h serum glucose >165 mg/dl and/or a 2-h value >135 mg/dl after the oral ingestion of 50 g dextrose.

---
* Only major tables and figures have been included. The publisher apologizes for any inconvenience this may cause.

Analytic methods. Samples for serum and urinary glucose were measured by the glucose oxidase method using a Beckman Glucose Analyzer (Beckman Instruments, Fullerton, California). This method measures glucose specifically and does not register increases in serum fructose levels. Serum immunoreactive insulin was measured by the method of Desbuquois and Aurbach.[17] Plasma glucagon was collected in Traysolol on ice and determined in duplicate by radioimmunoassay using antibody G1-5.[18] Statistical analysis was carried out utilizing the Student's *t* test for dependent and independent means as indicated.

RESULTS

In Figure 1 the serum glucose and insulin responses of the normal individuals to the drinks and meals can be seen. Dextrose and sucrose drinks or meals resulted in similar serum glucose responses, whereas the fructose elicited flat response curves. Likewise, the serum insulin responses to dextrose and sucrose were comparable, but the insulin response to fructose was reduced.

In Figure 2 the serum glucose and insulin responses to the carbohydrate drinks and meals in the subjects with impaired glucose tolerance are shown. It can be seen in Figure 2A that the serum glucose responses to the dextrose and sucrose drinks are significantly greater than the flattened response to fructose. Additionally, the responses to dextrose are somewhat greater than the response to sucrose. Serum insulin responses (Figure 2B) are greater after the dextrose and sucrose drinks than after the fructose drink, while the serum insulin responses to dextrose and sucrose are not significantly different from each other. Fructose meal ingestion leads to flattened and significantly lower serum glucose responses (Figure 2C) compared with dextrose and sucrose meals. The serum insulin responses to the meals (Figure 2D) show that similar responses are elicited by dextrose and sucrose, while the fructose meal insulin response is flattened.

The mean Δ serum glucose and the insulin responses of the non-insulin-dependent diabetic patients to the carbohydrate drinks and meals are shown in Figure 3. Twelve of the 17 patients had only the dextrose and fructose drink tests, whereas 5 participated in all six tests. The values plotted in Figure 3 and statistical analysis are from the 5 subjects who completed all the tests. Since fasting serum glucose values differed among the individual diabetic patients, the Δ serum glucose responses were plotted. The actual fasting glucose values and the peak serum glucose values during each test are shown in Table 3. It can be seen in Figure 3A that the mean serum glucose responses to dextrose and sucrose drinks were similar, whereas the response curve to fructose was much lower. The serum glucose response to the sucrose meal (Figure 3C) was lower than that to the dextrose meal at 60 and 120 min, but the dextrose and sucrose meal responses are both signficantly greater than the fructose meal responses.

Since subjects with fasting hyperglycemia are usually characterized by decreased postprandial insulin responses, the curves in Figures 3B and 3D are all essentially flat. Although few significantly different values can be seen, no obvious trends are apparent.

The comparative Δ serum glucose responses to the fructose drinks in the normal, impaired glucose tolerance, and diabetic (NIDDM) groups are shown in Figure 4. Normal individuals have a flat response to the fructose, which dips slightly below baseline at 2 and 3 h. The peak Δ glucose response in the impaired glucose tolerance group is 3.3 times greater than in the normal group and the peak Δ glucose response of the diabetic (NIDDM) group is 1.7 and 5.6 times greater than in the impaired glucose tolerance and normal groups, respectively. The Δ serum glucose responses of the three groups to the fructose meals show similar but somewhat attenuated differences (data not shown). The diabetic (NIDDM) group's Δ peak glucose response to the fructose meal is 1.6 times greater than the response of the impaired glucose tolerance group and 4.7 times greater than the response of the normal group. The Δ peak serum glucose response to the fructose meal in the impaired glucose toler-

TABLE 1
Clinical characteristics of the study groups

	No. Men	No. Women	Age (yr)*	Relative weight*†	Fasting serum glucose* (mg/dl)
Normal	2	7	56 ± 2 (24 – 66)	1.18 ± 0.07 (0.78 – 1.76)	90 ± 3 (74 – 100)
Impaired glucose	2	8	51 ± 3 (28 – 64)	1.19 ± 0.08 (0.89 – 1.67)	106 ± 5 (81 – 130)
Fasting hyperglycemia	6	11	42 ± 5 (30 – 69)	1.13 ± 0.10 (0.76 – 1.77)	250 ± 21 (144 – 453)

*Values represent mean (±SE), and the numbers in parentheses indicate the ranges.
†Relative weight was determined according to the Metropolitan Life Tables.

FIG. 1. Mean (±SE) serum glucose and insulin responses to the dextrose, sucrose, and fructose drinks and meals in the nine normal individuals.

	Serum glucose				Serum insulin			
	Sucrose:fructose		Dextrose:fructose		Sucrose:fructose		Dextrose:fructose	
	Drinks	Meals	Drinks	Meals	Drinks	Meals	Drinks	Meals
Time								
F	NS	NS	NS	NS	NS	NS	NS	NS
15	P<0.01	P<0.05	P<0.05	P<0.025	P<0.005	P<0.025	P<0.025	NS
30	P<0.001	P<0.005	P<0.005	P<0.0005	P<0.025	P<0.025	P<0.01	P<0.05
45	P<0.0001	P<0.0005	P<0.0005	P<0.0005	P<0.025	P<0.025	P<0.005	P<0.025
60	P<0.005	P<0.025	P<0.0001	P<0.0005	P<0.05	P<0.05	P<0.005	P<0.005
120	NS	NS	P<0.05	NS	NS	NS	P<0.025	NS
180	P<0.025	NS	P<0.005	NS	NS	NS	NS	NS

TABLE 2
Composition of tolerance tests

	Dextrose (g)	Sucrose (g)	Fructose (g)	Corn oil (g)	Egg albumin (g)	Lemon flavoring (ml)	Total Volume (ml)
A. Dextrose (drink)	50					15	500
B. Sucrose (drink)		50				15	500
C. Fructose (drink)			50			15	500
D. Dextrose (meal)	50			20	20	15	500
E. Sucrose (meal)		50		20	20	15	500
F. Fructose (meal)			50	20	20	15	500

ance group is 2.8 times greater than the response of the normal group. Therefore, although the serum glucose response to fructose is flattened in all groups compared with dextrose and sucrose, fructose causes an increasingly greater glucose excursion as glucose tolerance worsens.

Urinary glucose excretion over the 3-h test period in the subjects with impaired glucose tolerance and the patients with NIDDM was greatest after dextrose consumption and least after fructose ingestion either when given alone or when given in a meal.

Fasting and postprandial plasma glucagon values in 12 of the diabetic subjects after ingestion of oral dextrose and fructose drinks are presented in Table 4. As can be seen, glucagon levels are relatively nonsuppressible after glucose and increase somewhat ($P < 0.05$ at 15 and 180 min and $P < 0.025$ at 30, 45, and 120 min) after fructose. Therefore, on the basis of the data in the diabetic subjects, it can be concluded that changes in the glucagon level cannot explain the markedly lower glycemic response to fructose compared with dextrose.

DISCUSSION

We studied the effects of orally administered 50 g loads of dextrose, sucrose, and fructose on the postprandial serum glucose and insulin and plasma glucagon responses when given alone in a drink, or when given in combination with protein and fat in a liquid test meal, to normal individuals, individuals with impaired glucose tolerance, and diabetic (NIDDM) subjects. The results show that the serum glucose responses to oral fructose are significantly lower than the responses to dextrose and sucrose, when given alone and when given in a formula meal with other nutrients. The serum insulin responses to fructose are also significantly lower than the responses to dextrose and sucrose in the normal and

TABLE 3
Individual fasting serum glucose levels and peak serum glucose responses in the five patients with non-insulin-dependent diabetes mellitus* during each of the tests.

	Patients				
	1	2	3	4	5
Dextrose					
Fasting glucose	468	289	278	146	268
Peak glucose	573	398	418	261	417
Sucrose					
Fasting glucose	441	267	274	152	266
Peak glucose	606	394	403	264	349
Fructose					
Fasting glucose	438	259	263	141	248
Peak glucose	519	388	299	196	283
Dextrose meal					
Fasting glucose	414	289	274	146	251
Peak glucose	564	432	426	260	370
Sucrose meal					
Fasting glucose	381	230	251	136	208
Peak glucose	525	360	333	212	325
Fructose meal					
Fasting glucose	375	388	267	147	223
Peak glucose	465	448	292	168	279

*In these five patients who completed all the tests, the relative weights were 1.30, 0.91, 1.08, 0.99, and 1.42; ages were 69, 48, 50, 62, and 62 yr; and duration of diabetes was 14, 6, 7, 1, and 1 yr for patients #1-5, respectively.

FIG. 2. Mean (±SE) serum glucose and insulin responses to the dextrose, sucrose, and fructose drinks and meals in the 10 subjects with impaired glucose tolerance.

	Serum glucose				Serum insulin			
	Sucrose:fructose		Dextrose:fructose		Sucrose:fructose		Dextrose:fructose	
	Drinks	Meals	Drinks	Meals	Drinks	Meals	Drinks	Meals
Time								
F	NS	NS	NS	NS	NS	NS	NS	NS
15	P<0.025	P<0.025	P<0.025	P<0.025	NS	P<0.05	NS	NS
30	P<0.0005	P<0.005	P<0.0005	P<0.01	P<0.005	P<0.025	P<0.01	P<0.025
45	P<0.0005	P<0.005	P<0.0005	P<0.005	P<0.005	P<0.05	P<0.01	P<0.025
60	P<0.0005	P<0.005	P<0.0005	P<0.005	P<0.005	P<0.025	P<0.01	P<0.05
120	NS	P<0.01	P<0.0005	P<0.005	P<0.025	NS	P<0.05	P<0.05
180	NS	NS	P<0.05	P<0.05	NS	NS	P<0.05	NS

impaired glucose tolerance groups. In the diabetic group, insulin responses to all three sugars are flat and not significantly different from each other.

These results correspond to previously published acute and chronic studies of fructose consumption. Thus, in acute comparisons of pure dextrose to fructose, significantly lower plasma glucose levels,[6-11] lower plasma insulin levels,[10-12] and less glycosuria[8] have been described in diabetic[6-9] and nondiabetic[7,8,10,11] individuals.

In short-term feeding studies, reductions in blood glucose, glycosuria, and ketonemia following the isocaloric substitution of fructose for glucose in diets of controlled diabetic subjects have been shown.[3-5] In addition, the isocaloric substitution of fructose for starch in the diets of moderately controlled insulin-dependent diabetic subjects[13] or diabetic children[6] did not alter diurnal blood glucose levels[13] or urinary glucose output.[6,13] However, beneficial effects are not seen in severe or uncontrolled diabetes.[3,4] The reason for this is most likely an accelerated rate of hepatic conversion of fructose to glucose and hepatic glucose release.

Fructose is more slowly absorbed from the gastrointestinal tract than glucose[19] and is primarily and rapidly taken up by the liver.[20] Consequently, blood fructose levels rise only minimally after fructose ingestion.[21-23] The entry of fructose into liver cells and its initial steps of metabolism are insulin independent. It is converted predominantly into glucose or triglyceride by the liver and, in normal animals and man, most of the glucose formed is stored as glycogen, resulting in only a modest increase in the blood glucose concentration.[24] However, with insulin deficiency glycogen synthesis is impaired, and the fructose, which is converted to glucose in the liver, is rapidly released, leading to a considerable rise in plasma glucose concentration. This has been demonstrated after 2 h of intravenous fructose administration (1.2 g/kg body wt/min) in insulin-dependent diabetes.[25] The degree of insulin deficiency necessary to impair glycogen synthesis is not known. Our data in Figure 4 show substantial increases in serum glucose response in non-insulin-dependent diabetic subjects as well as smaller but notable increases in the subjects with impaired glucose tolerance after fructose ingestion. Thus, it is possible that this moderate or relative degree of insulin deficiency is enough to impair glycogen synthesis and cause a rise in serum glucose. Alternatively, gastrointestinal conversion of fructose to glucose (10-20% in normal individuals[26]) could be increased in these subjects, or decreased peripheral glucose disposal rates could be responsible for the greater serum glucose responses to fructose.

On the basis of some animal experiments, it has been suggested that fructose ingestion can lead to hypertri-

TABLE 4
Mean (±SE) △ plasma glucagon responses in 12 patients with non-insulin-dependent diabetes mellitus to dextrose and fructose drinks*

Time	△ Plasma glucagon (pg/ml)		
	Glucose	Fructose	
15	−21 ± 10	19 ± 11	($P<0.025$)
30	−7 ± 13	37 ± 12	($P<0.005$)
45	2 ± 16	26 ± 11	(NS)
60	2 ± 21	18 ± 12	(NS)
120	−17 ± 24	36 ± 15	($P<0.05$)
180	−10 ± 20	35 ± 19	($P<0.05$)

*Statistical comparisons indicate the significant differences between glucose and fructose. The mean fasting plasma glucagon level was 166 ± 21 pg/ml before the dextrose drink and 147 ± 18 pg/ml before the fructose drink.

glyceridemia. However, studies in man have not supported this notion. When normal or hypertriglyceridemic individuals, diabetic or nondiabetic, are fed moderate amounts of fructose in their daily diet for periods ranging from 2 wk to 2 yr, no increase in plasma triglyceride level has been detected.[27-29] On the other hand, little or no data are available regarding postprandial triglyceride levels with fructose feeding in diabetic individuals.

Studies involving the use of fructose in combination with varying kinds and amounts of other carbohydrates, proteins and fats in normal food products and normal meals must be performed before the daylong quantitative reduction of hyperglycemia, which may result from substitution of fructose into the diet, can be established. Since it is possible that adaptation to fructose may occur, further studies are also needed to define the long-term effectiveness on reduction of hyperglycemia that may result when fructose is substituted into the diet for other sugars or nonnutritive sweeteners.

Fructose appears to be an acceptable nutritive sweetener for mild or moderately well-controlled diabetic patients in whom further control of hyperglycemia is felt to be of therapeutic importance. Indeed, fructose may provide some advantages in the dietary management of these patients. Fructose is, of course, a nutritive sweetener, and thus provides calories. This must be recognized when incorporating fructose in the diet. It should also be recognized that, like all sugars and highly refined carbohydrates, fructose is not nutritionally comparable to natural foodstuffs in terms of vitamin and mineral content.

FIG. 3. Mean (△SE) serum glucose and mean insulin responses to the dextrose, sucrose, and fructose drinks and meals in five subjects with non-insulin-dependent diabetes.

	Serum glucose				Serum insulin			
	Sucrose:fructose		Dextrose:fructose		Sucrose:fructose		Dextrose:fructose	
	Drinks	Meals	Drinks	Meals	Drinks	Meals	Drinks	Meals
Time								
F	NS	NS	NS	NS	NS	NS	NS	NS
15	$P<0.05$	NS	NS	$P<0.025$	NS	NS	$P<0.025$	NS
30	$P<0.025$	NS	$P<0.005$	$P<0.025$	NS	NS	NS	NS
45	$P<0.025$	$P<0.025$	NS	$P<0.025$	NS	NS	NS	NS
60	$P<0.005$	$P<0.025$	$P<0.025$	$P<0.0005$	NS	NS	NS	NS
120	NS	$P<0.005$	$P<0.05$	$P<0.005$	NS	NS	NS	NS
180	NS	$P<0.01$	NS	NS	$P<0.05$	$P<0.025$	NS	NS

Time	Normal:impaired glucose tolerance	Normal:diabetes	Impaired glucose tolerance:diabetes
15	NS	P<0.025	NS
30	NS	P<0.05	NS
45	P<0.005	P<0.01	NS
60	P<0.005	P<0.0005	P<0.025
120	P<0.05	P<0.005	P<0.025
180	NS	NS	NS

FIG. 4. Mean (±SE) Δ serum glucose responses to fructose drinks in 9 normal individuals (▲), 10 subjects with impaired glucose tolerance (○), and 17 subjects with non-insulin-dependent diabetes (●). Statistical analysis was carried out by Student's test for two means.

ACKNOWLEDGMENTS

This work was supported in part by National Institute of Arthritis, Metabolism, and Digestive Diseases grant 5-R01-AM-25240 and General Clinical Research Centers grant RR-00051 from the Division of Research Resources, National Institutes of Health, Bethesda, Maryland 20014. We wish to thank the staff of the General Clinical Research Center for their invaluable technical assistance.

REFERENCES

1. Sestoft, L., 1979. Fructose and the dietary therapy of diabetes mellitus. Diabetologia 17:1-3.
2. Kimura, K. K. and Carr, C. J., 1976. Dietary sugars in health and disease. I. Fructose. Prepared for the Bureau of Foods, Food and Drug Administration, Department HEW, Washington, D.C. Contract No. FDA 223-75-2090, pp. 1-37.
3. Moorhouse, J. A. and Kark, R. M., 1957. Fructose and diabetes. Am. J. Med. 23:46-58.
4. Hiller, J., 1955. Die Laevalose verwertung des acidotishen Diabetes mellitus. I. M. Heilung, Zur Analyse der Acetonurie und der Glucosurie. Z. Klin. Med. 153:388-96.
5. Felber, J. P., Renold, A. E. and Zahno, G. R., 1959. The comparative metabolism of glucose, fructose, galactose and sorbitol in normal subjects and in disease states. Med. Probl. Paediatr. 4:482.
6. Akerblom, H. K., Siltanen, I. and Kallio, A. K., 1972. Does dietary fructose affect the control of diabetes in children? Acta. Med. Scand. (Suppl.) 542:195-202.
7. Metz, R., Mako, M., Stevens, T. and Franklin, J., 1967. The metabolism of fructose in diabetes mellitus. J. Lab. Clin. Med. 69:494-503.
8. Lamar, C. P., 1959. Comparative oral glucose and fructose tolerance tests in normal subjects and in diabetic patients. J. Fla. Med Assoc. 46:180-186.
9. Brinck, U. C., Wubbens, D., Oelgeschlager, W. and Otto, H., 1973. Blood glucose response to glucose, fructose, and sucrose in patients with subclinical diabetes mellitus. In Diatetik bei Diabetes Mellitus. Otto, H. and Spaethe, R., Eds. Bern, Stuttgart, and Wein, Verlag Hans Huber, pp. 150-53.
10. Swan, D. C., Davidson, P. and Albrink, M. J., 1966. Effect of simple and complex carbohydrates on plasma non-esterified fatty acids, plasma-sugar, and plasma-insulin during oral carbohydrate tolerance tests. Lancet, 1:60-63.
11. McDonald, I., Keyser, A. and Pacy, D., 1978. Some effects, in man, of varying the load of glucose, sucrose, fructose, or sorbitol on various metabolites in blood. Am. J. Clin. Nutr. 31:1305-11.
12. Schauberger, G., Brinck, U. C., Guldner, G., Spaethe, R., Niklas, L. and Otto, H., 1977. Exchange of carbohydrates according to their effect on blood glucose. Diabetes 26 (Suppl. 1):415.
13. Pelkonen, R., Aro, A. and Nikkila, E. A., 1972. Metabolic effects of dietary fructose in insulin dependent diabetes of adults. Acta. Med. Scand. (Suppl.) 542:187-93.
14. Arvidsson-Lenner, R., 1976. Studies of glycemia and glucosuria in diabetics after breakfast meals of different composition. Am. J. Clin. Nutr. 29:716-25.
15. Committee on Statistics of the American Diabetes Association, 1969. Standardization of the oral glucose tolerance test. Diabetes, 18:299-310.
16. Reaven, G. M. and Olefsky, J. M., 1977. Relationship between heterogeneity of insulin responses and insulin resistance in normal subjects and patients with chemical diabetes. Diabetologia 13:201-06.
17. Desbuquois, B. and Aurbach, D. F., 1971. Use of polyethylene glycol to separate free and antibody bound peptide hormones in radioimmunoassays. J. Clin. Endocrinol. Metab. 33:732-38.
18. Sperling, M. A., Delamater, P. V., Kazenelson, M., Fisher, R. H. and Fisher, D. A., 1974. Development and application of a radioimmunoassay for plasma glucagon. Clin. Chem. 20:566-70.
19. Dehmel, K. H., Foster, H. and Mehnert, H., 1969. Absorption of xylitol. In International Symposium on the Metabolism, Physiology, and Clinical Use of Pentoses and Pentitols. Horecker, B. L., Lang, K. and Takagi, H., Eds. New York, Springer-Verlage, pp. 177-81.
20. Mendeloff, A. I. and Weichselbaum, T. E., 1953. Role of the human liver in the assimilation of intravenously administered fructose. Metabolism, 2:450-58.
21. Grace, N. D., Castelle, D. O. and Wenner, M. H., 1969. A comparison of the oral fructose and ammonia tolerance tests in cirrhosis. Arch. Intern. Med. 124:330-35, 1969.
22. Bohannon, N. J., Karam, J. K. and Forsham, P., 1977. Comparison of prolonged responses to fructose, sucrose and glucose feeding. Abstracts of the 60th Annual Meeting of the American Dietetic Association, p. 20.
23. Miller, M., Drucker, W. R., Owens, J. E., Craig, J. W. and Woodward, H., Jr., 1952. Metabolism of intravenous fructose and glucose in normal and diabetic subjects. J. Clin. Invest. 13:115-25.
24. Nilsson, L. and Hultman, E., 1974. Liver and muscle glycogen in man after glucose and fructose infusion. Scand. J. Clin. Lab. Invest. 33:5-10.
25. Bergstrom, J., Hultman, E. and Roch-Norland, A. E., 1968. Lactic acid accumulation in connection with fructose infusion. Acta. Med. Scand. 184:359-64.
26. Cook, G. C., 1969. Absorption products of D-fructose in man. Clin. Sci. 37:675-687.
27. Huttenen, J. K., Karro, K., Makinen, K. and Scheinin, A., 1975. Effects of sucrose, fructose and xylitol in glucose, lipid and urate metabolism. Acta. Odontol. Scand. (Suppl.) 70:239-45.
28. Nikkila, E. A. and Kekki, M., 1972. Effects of dietary fructose and sucrose on plasma triglyceride metabolism in patients with endogenous hypertriglyceridemia. Acta. Med. Scand. (Suppl.) 542:221-27.
29. Turner, J. L., Bierman, E. L., Brunzell, J. D. and Chait, A., 1979. Effect of dietary fructose on triglyceride transport and glucoregulatory hormones in hypertriglyceridemia man. Am. J. Clin. Nutr. 32:1043-50.

Mineral and Vitamin Status on High-Fiber Diets: Long Term Studies of Diabetics

by J. W. Anderson, S.K. Ferguson, D. Karounos, L. O'Malley, B. Sieling, and W-J L. Chen

High-fiber diets have a beneficial impact on glucose metabolism of selected persons with diabetes mellitus. A major concern is the long-term effects of fiber intake on mineral and vitamin status. We measured serum concentrations of selected minerals and vitamins and also assessed three fat-soluble vitamins in 15 patients fed high-fiber diets for an average of 21 mo. Average values for serum calcium, phosphorus, alkaline phosphatase, iron, total iron-binding capacity, magnesium, and hemoglobin values were normal. Vitamin B_{12} and folic acid concentrations in serum were also normal. Indirect assessment suggested that these patients had adequate intakes of the fat-soluble vitamins A, D, and K. These preliminary observations suggest that high-fiber diets containing a wide variety of natural foods are well tolerated for up to 51 mo; we failed to detect evidence suggesting mineral or vitamin deficiency in these patients. DIABETES CARE 3: 38-40, JANUARY-FEBRUARY 1980.

High-fiber diets may be useful in the treatment of selected patients with diabetes mellitus.[1-4] However, a major concern is that long-term use of high-fiber diets may lead to mineral or vitamin deficiencies.[5,6] Short-term studies have demonstrated variable changes in mineral balance after high-fiber diets[5-8] and decreases in serum folate levels.[9,10] Unfortunately, the chronic effects of high-fiber diets on mineral and vitamin status have not been well evaluated. Because diets containing large amounts of fiber may have beneficial effects in diabetic control, we have examined over a 21-mo period, in a preliminary fashion, the long-term effects of high-fiber diets on serum levels of minerals, folic acid, and vitamin B_{12} and indirectly assessed three fat-soluble vitamins in 15 diabetic patients.

METHODS

Patients. Fifteen patients with diabetes mellitus were studied. They averaged 50 yr in age with an average of 8-yr duration of diabetes. Eleven patients were lean (10 men and 1 woman) and 4 men were obese. Initially, 12 patients were receiving insulin, 2 were on sulfonylurea agents, and 1 was on no antidiabetes medication.

Diets. All patients were admitted to a metabolic ward and baseline measurements were made while on a control diet.[4] Subsequently, all patients were fed high-carbohydrate, high-fiber (HCF) diets[4] and received detailed instruction in high-fiber maintenance diets,[2] which provide 55%-60% of energy as carbohydrate and 25-35 g of plant fiber/1000 kcal.[11] These high-fiber maintenance diets provided approximately the following percentages of the recommended daily allowances (RDA): vitamin A, 402; B_6, 97; B_{12}, 51; C, 781; niacin, 109; riboflavin, 109; thiamine, 138; calcium, 102; phosphorus, 185; magnesium, 119; and iron, 174.[12]

After discharge from the hospital the patients were seen at 3-8 wk intervals, adherence to the diet was encouraged, and food intake was estimated from multiple 24-h diet recalls and diet diaries maintained by the patients. Three patients were taking one multivitamin capsule per day before admission to the hospital. They were maintained after discharge on these vitamin supplements, which provided 100% of the RDA for vitamins A, B_{12}, D, and folate. None of the other 12 patients received vitamin or mineral supplements before these follow-up measurements.

Measurements. On the control and high-fiber diets, measurements of hemoglobin, serum calcium, phosphorus, and alkaline phosphatase were obtained. After an average of 21 ± 3 mo (mean ± SEM, range 5-51) on the high-fiber diets, prothrombin and partial thromboplastin times, serum folate, vitamin B_{12}, carotene, iron, total iron-binding capacity, and magnesium were measured. Body weights and fasting plasma glucose values were measured at each visit. All studies on blood were performed in the clinical laboratory by conventional analytic techniques.

RESULTS

Body weights and glucose metabolism. Lean individuals maintained their body weights well on the high-fiber diets whereas four obese patients lost an average of 10 lb. While on the HCF or high-fiber diets, insulin therapy was discontinued in eight patients and sulfonylurea therapy in two. Despite lower doses or no medication, fasting plasma glucose values were lower by an average of 12 mg/dl on the high-fiber diets than on the control diets in the hospital.

Dietary compliance. Most patients followed the high-fiber maintenance diets remarkably well. Compared with their prescribed diet, carbohydrate intake averaged 97%, protein intake 113%, fat intake 96%, and plant fiber 103%. Despite the intake of an average of 50 g/day of plant fiber, no adverse gastrointestinal side effects were observed.

Mineral values. After an average of 21 mo, hemoglobin values were stable and there were no significant alterations in serum calcium, phosphorus, or alkaline phosphatase. Average values for serum iron, total iron-binding capacity, and magnesium were within the normal range, with only a few individual values outside.

Vitamin assessment. Serum folate and vitamin B_{12} values were measured in the 12 patients who were not receiving vitamin supplements and all values fell within the normal range (Figure 1). The availability of vitamin D was assessed by measuring serum calcium phosphorus and alkaline phosphatase, and we have no evidence of vitamin D deficiency. Vitamin A levels were estimated by serum carotene measurements; all values were either normal or high (Figure 1). Vitamin K availability was assessed by measuring prothrombin and partial thromboplastin times; all these values were normal.

DISCUSSION

Using serum levels to assess the status of selected minerals and vitamins, we failed to detect any deficiencies in patients who had received high-fiber diets for an average of 21 mo. Serum measurements may not have the sensitivity to detect minor inadequacies of these minerals and vitamins. Subtle deficits of trace minerals are especially difficult to detect clinically. Iron was the only trace mineral we evaluated. Despite these limitations, our study indicates that these diabetic patients tolerated high-fiber diets for up to 51 mo without evidence of calcium, iron, or magnesium deficiency.

Multiple mineral deficiencies have been observed in Iranian children who consume large quantities of whole-wheat bread.[13] However, only a limited number of investigators have evaluated prospectively the long-term effects of high-fiber diets on mineral status in adults. Vegetarians who have high-fiber intake usually maintain normal serum mineral levels if they carefully select their food.[14,15] Two long-term studies,[16,17] like ours, failed to detect evidence of mineral depletion. When wheat-bran supplements (24 g/day) were provided for over a minimum of 6 mo for 40 patients with diverticular disease, there were no significant changes in serum calcium, phosphorus, iron, or hemoglobin.[16] When two healthy subjects ate large quantities of whole-meal bread, transient negative balances of calcium and zinc were noted shortly after beginning the high-fiber diet; however, these imbalances returned to normal over a 21-mo span.[17] These observations[17] suggest that adaptive mechanisms may intervene to restore normal mineral homeostasis with long-term use of high-fiber diets. Although hypomagnesemia is fairly common among patients with diabetes,[18,19] none of our patients had subnormal serum magnesium levels despite their high fiber intake.

Only limited information is available about the long-term effects of high-fiber diets on vitamin metabolism. Several studies[9,10] have suggested that high-fiber diets might lead to a fall in serum folate levels. No abnormally low serum folate levels were observed in our patients. Diets that are restricted in animal products, as are ours, usually are somewhat deficient in vitamin B_{12} content. Despite a low intake of vitamin B_{12}, surprisingly few vegetarians develop vitamin B_{12} deficiency.[15] Serum vitamin B_{12} levels were normal in all our patients, including those followed for as long as 36-51 mo.

Our observations suggest that normal mineral and vitamin levels were maintained over the 21-mo duration of this study. Thus, our data on 15 patients treated for diabetes indicate that a high-fiber diet can be formulated that supplies an adequate nutrient intake to prevent any discernible nutritional deficits. However, long-term studies will be necessary to determine the impact of high-fiber diets on trace mineral metabolism.

ACKNOWLEDGMENTS

This work was supported by the Veterans Administration and by a grant (1-RO1-AM20889-01) from the National Institutes of Arthritis, Metabolism and Digestive Diseases.

REFERENCES

1. Kiehm, T.G., Anderson, J.W. and Ward, K., 1976. Beneficial effects of a high carbohydrate, high fiber diet on hyperglycemic diabetic men. Am. J. Clin. Nutr. *29:* 895.
2. Anderson, J.W. and Ward, K., 1978. Long-term effects of high carbohydrate, high fiber diets on glucose and lipid metabolism: a preliminary report on patients with diabetes. Diabetes Care *1:* 77.
3. Jenkins, D., Wolever, T.M.S., Nineham, R., Taylor, R., Metz, G.L., Bacon, S. and Hockaday, T.D.R., 1978. Guar crispbread in the diabetic diet. Br. Med. J. *2:* 1744.
4. Anderson, J.W. and Ward, K., 1979. High carbohydrate, high fiber diets for insulin-treated men with diabetes mellitus. Am. J. Clin. Nutr. *32:* 2190.
5. Kelsay, J.A., 1978. A review of research on effects of fiber intake on man. Am. J. Clin. Nutr. *31:* 142.
6. Kay, R.M. and Strasberg, S.M., 1978. Origin, chemistry, physiological effects, and clinical importance of dietary fiber. Clin. Invst. Med. *I:* 9.
7. Reinhold, J.C., Faradji, B., Abaidi, P. and Ismail-Beigi, 1976. Decreased absorption of calcium, magnesium, zinc, and phosphorous by humans due to increased fiber and phosphorous consumption as wheat bread. J. Nutr. *106:* 493.
8. McCance, R.A. and Widdowson, E.M., 1942. Mineral metabolism of healthy adults on white and brown bread dietaries. J. Physiol. *101:* 44.
9. Luther, L., Santini, R., Brewster, C., Petez-Santizgo, E. and Butterworth, C.E., 1965. Folate binding by insoluble components American and Puerto Rican diets. Ala. J. Med. Sci. *3:* 389.
10. Russell, R.M., Ismail-Beigi, F. and Reinhold, J.G., 1976. Folic contents of Iranian breads and the effects of their fiber content on the intestinal absorption of folic acid. Am. J. Clin. Nutr. *29:* 79.
11. Anderson, J.W., Lin, W.J. and Ward, K., 1978. Composition of foods commonly used in diets for persons with diabetes. Diabetes Care *I:* 293-302.
12. International Dietary Information Foundation, Inc.: Extended Table Nutrient Values. International Dietary Information Foundation, Inc., P.O. Box 38143, Atlanta, Georgia 30334.
13. Prasad, A.S., Halstead, J.A. and Nadimi, M., 1961. Syndromes of iron deficiency anemia, hepatosplenomegaly, dwarfism, hypogondism and geophagia. Am. J. Med. *31:* 532.
14. Harland, B.F. and Peterson, M., 1978. Nutritional status of lacto ovo vegetarian Trappist monks. J. Am. Diet. Assoc. *72:* 259.
15. Anonymous, 1979. Nutrition and vegetarianism. Dairy Council Digest. *50:* 1-6.
16. Brodribb, A.J.M. and Humphreys, D.M., 1976. Diverticular disease: three studies. Br. Med. J. *1:* 424-30.
17. Campbell, B.J., Reinhold, J.G., Cannell, J.J. and Noumand, I., 1976. The effects of prolonged consumption of wholemeal bread upon metabolism of calcium, magnesium, zinc and phosphorous of two young American adults. Pahlavi Med. J. *7:* 1-7.
18. Stutzman, F.L. and Amatazio, D.S., 1953. Blood serum magnesium in portal cirrhosis and diabetes mellitus. J. Lab. Clin. Med. *45:* 215-19.
19. Jackson, C.E., Meier, D.W., 1968. Routine serum magnesium analysis. Correlation with clinical state in 5100 patients. Ann. Internal. Med. *69:* 743-48.

Drinking and Diabetes

by Robert J. Winter

You have diabetes and are receiving insulin. Can you drink? Should you drink? When and if you do, what will happen? What precautions should you take? If you have ever asked any of these questions, or think you ever will, read on.

Little straightforward information concerning the relationship between drinking (alcohol) and diabetes has been readily available to individuals with diabetes or to their physicians, for that matter. This addition to the Youth Education Series will provide you with some information to make that relationship better understood and to find an intelligent approach to answer the above questions. The following discussion of drinking deals with the relationship of alcohol to insulin-dependent diabetes. Special considerations of individuals on oral hypoglycemic agents are beyond the scope of this discussion, as are the moral, legal, and ethical considerations of drinking.

First, some definitions and disclaimers. Drinking refers to alcohol; alcohol refers to ethyl alcohol or ethanol, the intoxicant present in virtually all commonly available alcoholic beverages. A calorie (cal) is a unit measure of heat produced when a substance is fully metabolized or burned. Common alcoholic beverages contain a certain number of calories, depending on the alcoholic content and the materials with which the alcohol is mixed.

For someone with diabetes, there are two basic concerns about alcohol. One deals with its metabolic effects or how alcoholic beverages can be incorporated into the diet. The other concern relates to the physical or mental effects of alcohol as a drug and how these "drug effects" may influence diabetes.

To understand how drinking alcohol affects diabetes, a brief discussion of its metabolism is necessary. You know that insulin is required for the metabolism of most food that you eat or drink, but pure ethanol is metabolized without the need for insulin. An ounce of a standard alcoholic beverage (bourbon, scotch, gin, vodka, etc.) contains approximately 75-90 cal. These calories have no true food value or any beneficial metabolic effect in the body. In people with and without diabetes, therefore, there is little if any change in blood sugar when alcohol in this form is consumed.

Even though the above is true, the story doesn't end there. The calories in alcohol are "utilized" by the body for energy or stored as fat. Hence, a steady intake of alcohol along with the usual diet has the potential of increasing body weight. The typical "beer belly" is a testament to that fact and also introduces a further reality for those who imbibe. Beer and most mixed drinks also contain sugar or carbohydrate. Hence these drinks contain "insulin-dependent" calories in addition to calories derived solely from alcohol. The total caloric content, and that portion due to carbohydrate, varies from drink to drink. A 12-oz can of standard beer, for example, contains approximately 75 cal as carbohydrate (roughly equivalent to a slice of bread) and 75 cal as alcohol. The new "light" beers have reduced the total caloric content by about one-third, primarily by reducing the carbohydrate content. The caloric value of the usual whiskey sour is approximately 150 cal, of which about one-third is derived from carbohydrates and therefore dependent on insulin for metabolism. It should be clear that when these sorts of alcohol are consumed, the balance between insulin and diet can be quickly disrupted.

As a rule of thumb, a jigger (1½ oz) of most standard liquors has about 125 cal and is therefore equivalent to about three fat exchanges. By subtracting that figure from the total caloric value of the mixed drink (obtainable from most pocket-sized calorie counting books), you can estimate the number of calories that are from carbohydrates. A screwdriver made with 6 oz of unsweetened orange juice and a jigger of vodka is equivalent in total calories to approximately three fat exchanges (the alcohol) and 1½ fruit exchanges (the orange juice). Calculations of this sort can become very imprecise, however, because the alcohol and carbohydrate content depends on what the drink is and how it is mixed. Drinks made with cream, sweet liqueurs, sweetened fruit juices, or sweet wines will require more complicated approaches to estimating calories. Obviously, the less complicated the drink, the easier it is to guess what its "worth."

There are several additional considerations for the person with diabetes who drinks. Alcohol ultimately acts as a depressant to the brain, although many people initially are "turned on" by alcohol as evidenced by its reputation as an "icebreaker" or "social lubricant." The effects of alcohol can mimic some of the symptoms of an insulin reaction (hypoglycemia). Because alcohol may cloud thinking, the diabetic person may not perceive the warning signs of hypoglycemia and may be unable to differentiate the effects of alcohol from the early symptoms of hypoglycemia. In addition, many cocktail and dinner parties occur at times much later than one's "normal" mealtime, and this may make hypoglycemia more likely. If an insulin reaction occurs and is inadequately treated, it may be assumed by the partygoers that the person with diabetes is "just" drunk and acting strangely for that reason. Severe hypoglycemic reactions can result. By contrast, another effect of drinking in most people is appetite stimulation. Because hors d'ouevres and "munchies" are frequently present in abundance at such parties, the diabetic person may lose restraint while "under the influence." This, followed closely by a "big" dinner, may upset diabetes for many days unless precautions are taken.

Everything discussed so far deals with realistic, everyday-type problems that can and do occur. In addition, it is important to be aware of two less frequent problems. If alcoholic consumption continues unrestrained ("out on a binge") to the point of unconsciousness and/or vomiting, the stress of this "illness" can easily result in ketosis or ketoacidosis. On the other hand, if alcoholic intake is excessive, hypoglycemia reactions can occur many hours after the drinking has stopped, or the next morning, because of certain metabolic effects of alcohol.

After having been told of all these potential effects, one might assume that the next step in this discussion is a firm admonition not to drink. Not so. The decision whether or not to drink must be a personal one, even though you might wish to discuss it with family members and your physician. Indeed, many people with insulin-dependent diabetes drink and regulate both their drinking and their diabetes very successfully. The reason for their apparent success is a knowledge of how drinking and diabetes mix. An excessive amount of alcohol may distort your perception of the world around you and make it more difficult to cope with daily stresses. Exactly what is "excessive" depends on how the body and mind respond to the alcohol you drink and may vary from person to person, time to time, etc. Drinking on an empty stomach, when excessively tired, or when ill may change one's response.

Can you drink? Yes, if you are properly informed and prepared. Should you drink? Only if you have made an intelligent decision to do so, weighing the facts and the social pressures as you know them. What will happen when and if you do? Probably nothing you cannot cope with, if you keep your wits about you and drink only in moderate amounts. What precautions should you take? Keep your diabetes under good control, so that you can better anticipate how schedule changes might affect it. Develop a taste for liquor itself, do not cling to the sugary, sweet drinks that provide a substantial carbohydrate load as they "hide" the taste of alcohol. You will be better off if you stick to drinks mixed with water, club soda, or diet soda. Go slowly with these, though. When you start "feeling" your liquor, slow down. Avoid drinking on an empty stomach. And most important, discuss all this with your doctor. Drinking and diabetes require knowledge and planning for each individual, because each individual and his/her diabetes may respond differently to alcohol. Your doctor knows you and your diabetes and can help keep all the surprises to a minimum.

If you decide that drinking is not for you, there are many ways to participate socially without feeling, or being, ostracized. Club soda or diet tonic water, with a lemon or lime, Perrier water, or club soda and bitters all have the "look" of a mixed drink without alcohol or appreciable calories.

Cheers! (Whether that's hard, soft, or in the middle.)

MEDICAL INTERACTIONS

Interactions Between Drugs and Nutrients

by Daphne A. Roe, M.D.

Nutrient and non-nutrient constituents of foods and beverages can interact with drugs such that the predictable effect of the drug is modified. Outcome of drug-food, drug-alcohol, and drug-nutrient interactions include a change in the rate or level of drug absorption, change in the rate of drug metabolism, drug-food or drug-alcohol incompatibilities, as well as drug-induced nutritional deficiencies. Megadoses of vitamins can alter drug responsiveness. Nutrients, particularly vitamins, can be used as drugs, not only in the treatment of nutritional deficiency disease, but also for their pharmacological effects in disorders that may not be due to nutritional factors.

EFFECTS OF FOOD ON DRUGS

Effects of Food on Drug Absorption and Bioavailability

Absorption of drugs may be increased or decreased by physiological changes which occur in the gastrointestinal tract in the fed versus the fasting state.[122] Nutrients in foods can promote drug absorption. Non-nutrient components of the diet, including specific forms of dietary fiber, may adsorb drugs, producing a transient or net reduction in drug absorption. Delayed absorption of common drugs such as digoxin occurs when the drug is taken at the same time as food. Delayed absorption of drugs, brought about by food, does not imply that less drug is totally absorbed, but rather that the time for a drug to reach peak blood levels after a single dose is lengthened.[62] Little is known about the specific components of food which delay drug absorption. Studies do indicate that the delaying effect of food on absorption of acetaminophen may be due to the pectin content.[50] Reduced absorption of drugs may be due to eating at the same time or close to the time when the drug is taken.[57] Drugs which are more slowly or less efficiently absorbed when taken with food are shown in Table 1. The absorption of other drugs such as nitrofurantoin, hydrochlorothiazide, and griseofulvin is promoted by food intake. Drugs and nutrients which are better absorbed after food are griseofulvin,[23] nitrofurantoin,[6] riboflavin,[59] riboflavin-5'-phosphate,[52] propranolol,[72] metoprolol,[72] hydralazine,[70] spironolactone,[71] carbamazepine,[60] and propoxyphene.[124] Known mechanisms whereby food or nutrients promote drug absorption or bioavailability are as follows:

1. Food enhances absorption of dosage forms of drugs with the poorest in vitro dissolution characteristics. It is believed that delayed gastric emptying time caused by the presence of food in the stomach allows for disintegration and dissolution of these drug formulations.[55] On the other hand, macrocrystalline nitrofurantoin in capsule form is much better absorbed after food and it is believed that this is a specific example of a drug requiring prolonged residence in the stomach for dissolution.[6]

2. Delayed gastric emptying time may allow metering out of a drug (or nutrient) solution from the stomach to the optimal saturable absorption site in the small intestine. It has been demonstrated that absorption of riboflavin or riboflavin-5'-phosphate is enhanced by intake of food,[52,59] particularly of food containing fiber,[103] and also by intake of carbonated beverages.[48] The latter effect has been attributed to a decrease of gastric emptying rates induced by carbohydrates (sugar) and phosphoric acid present in the beverage. It has been suggested that it may be through this mechanism that food promotes absorption of drugs such as hydrochlorothiazide.[49] The absorption of propoxyphene is better after a carbohydrate meal (this may also be an effect of gastric emptying time).[124]

3. Nutrients may promote drug absorption. The antifungal agent, griseofulvin, is better absorbed when taken with a meal containing fat, probably because it is a lipid-soluble drug and because bile flow may enhance absorption. Therapeutic diets

Table 1. *Drugs for Which Absorption is Delayed or Reduced by Food**

DELAYED	REDUCED
Amoxicillin	Penicillin G
Cephalexin	Penicillin V (K)
Cephradine	Phenethicillin
Sulfanilamide	Ampicillin
Sulfadiazine	Amoxicillin
Sulfamethoxine	Tetracycline
Sulfamethoxypyridazine	Demethylchlortetracycline
Sulfisoxazole	Methacycline
Sulfasymazine	Oxytetracycline
Aspirin	Aspirin
Acetaminophen†	Propantheline
Digoxin	Levodopa
Furosemide	Rifampicin
Potassium ion	Doxycycline
	Isoniazid
	Phenobarbital

* References 9, 21, 22, 37–39, 55, 61, 62, 79, 108, 115, 123
† Probable pectin effect

may produce or alter the efficiency of griseofulvin absorption. For example, low fat diets prescribed for patients with hyperlipidemia, atherosclerotic heart disease, and diabetes mellitus may significantly reduce the absorption of griseofulvin. When low fat diets have been prescribed and it is necessary to administer griseofulvin, then a micronized or ultramicronized form of the drug should be used, or it should be given in suspension in a small volume of corn oil.

4. Food increases splanchnic blood flow and hence enhances drug absorption.[65]

5. Food enhances the bioavailability of certain drugs. Oral bioavailability of a drug is defined as the fraction of unchanged drug reaching the systemic circulation after oral intake compared to that following intravenous administration. Melander[69] has suggested that since absorption of both propranolol and metaprolol is complete under fasting condition, food (or food components) cannot actually promote absorption but that food intake may reduce first pass extraction and hence hepatic metabolism of these drugs.

Absorption of ethanol from alcoholic beverages is slowed by intake with food.[109] The tradition of drinking milk before liquor or other alcoholic beverages has a sound physiological basis.[73] The delaying effect of food on ethanol absorption may be explained by slower absorption of ethanol via the gastric absorption site because of altered diffusion rate in a filled stomach, and delayed gastric emptying so that less alcohol reaches the area of maximal absorption in the small intestine.

Alcohol taken with slow-release drug formulations may produce untoward effects. For example, if alcoholic beverages are drunk at or close to the same time that slow-release antihistamine capsules are taken, dissolution of the preparation is more rapid than intended, and the patient may rapidly become somnolent. Patients who are not appraised of this effect could be involved in auto accidents when falling asleep at the wheel of the vehicle.[89]

Diet and Drug Metabolism

In animals as well as in human studies, it has been shown that changes in diet may affect the rate of drug metabolism. Drugs may be metabolized faster when patients are on high protein-low carbohydrate diets rather than high carbohydrate-low protein diets. Kappas et al.[53] reported that change in the ratio of carbohydrate to protein in the diet can alter the elimination rate of model drugs including antipyrine and theophylline.

Indolic compounds present in cabbage and Brussels sprouts can speed up the rate of drug metabolism.[85] Cooking methods may also alter the rate of drug metabolism. Charcoal-broiling promotes hepatic drug metabolism.[54]

Changes in the intestinal microflora produced by diet, as for example, alterations in dietary fiber source or level or change in the level of dietary protein, may influence intestinal drug metabolism.[107]

Adverse Drug Reactions Caused by Food

Adverse reactions to drugs can be precipitated by intake with specific foods or alcoholic beverages. Reactions vary greatly in intensity, some being unpleasant enough to prevent the person from wishing to go through the episode again, while other reactions are life-threatening. The major types of drug-food and drug-alcohol incompatibilities are summarized in Table 2.

Tyramine Reactions

Tyramine reactions have been recognized since 1961 when it was first observed that patients receiving drugs which are monamine oxidase inhibitors may develop acute hypertensive attacks.[99] Monamine oxidase inhibitor drugs presently available in the United States include phenelzine (Nardil), isocarboxazid (Marplan), and tranylcypromine (Parnate). These drugs were introduced into therapeutic use as mood elevating agents for the treatment of severe depression.[42] Whereas use is now limited by knowledge of potential side effects, monamine oxidase inhibitor drugs are presently recommended for the treatment of selected patients with psychotic depression and patients with phobic anxiety. These drugs elevate levels of norepinephrine and serotonin in the central nervous system and potentiate the cardiovascular effect of simple phenylethylamines such as tyramine.[90] Asatoor et al.[4] not only showed that toxic reactions might occur when cheese was eaten by patients on these drugs, but also observed that the reactions resembled those associated with paroxysmal release of catecholamines from a pheochromocytoma. The attacks are characterized by hypertension of short duration, headaches, palpitations, nausea, and vomiting. In some instances, major cerebrovascular accidents have been documented. The severity of the attack has been related both to drug dosage and also to the level of tyramine in particular foods or food samples. Foods which have been demonstrated to cause hypertension crises in patients receiving monamine oxidase inhibitor drugs are those high in tyramine or in dopamine.[11,45,83]

Cheeses which have been allowed to mature have a high tyramine content. Intake of unmatured cheeses by people receiving these drugs offers a much lower risk of tyramine reactions and may be entirely innocuous. Blackwell and Mabbit measured the tyramine content of a number of cheeses and found the highest values among cheddar cheeses for those with acid or rancid flavors.[10]

Other foods and beverages which have been shown to produce hypertensive attacks in patients on monamine oxi-

Table 2. *Drug-Food and Drug-Alcohol Incompatibilities*

CLASSIFICATION	REACTANTS 1	REACTANTS 2	EFFECT
1. Tyramine reactions	MAO Inhibitors Antidepressants, e.g., phenelzine Procarbazine Isoniazid INH, Isonicotinic acid hydrazide)	High tyramine/dopamine foods Cheese Red wines Chicken's liver Broad beans Yeast extracts	Flushing Hypertension Cerebrovascular accidents
2. Disulfiram reactions	Aldehyde dehydrogenase inhibitors Disulfiram (Antabuse) Calcium carbimide Metronidazole Nitrofurantoin C. atramentarius* Sulfonylureas	Ethanol Beer Wine Liquor Foods containing alcohol	Flushing, headache Nausea, vomiting Chest and abdominal pain
3. Hypoglycemic reactions	Insulin releasers Oral hypoglycemic agents Sugar (as in sweet mixes)	Ethanol	Weakness Mental confusion Irrational behavior Loss of consciousness
4. Flush reactions [see 2]	Miscellaneous Chlorpropamide [+diabetes] Griseofulvin Tetrachlorethylene	Ethanol	Flush Dyspnea Headache

*Coprinus Atramentarius = Inky cap mushroom

dase inhibitor drugs are pickled herring, chicken livers, broad beans, Chianti wines, and beers.[47] In broad beans, the amino acid dopa or its amine derivative dopamine triggers attacks.[12] Both tyramine and dopa, or dopamine, which escape oxidative deamination, are believed to enter the systemic circulation, release norepinephrine from local stores in nerve endings, and so prolong the action of this catecholamine on adrenergic receptors. These drugs inhibit monamine oxidase either in the intestine or in the liver, or in both of these sites. Reactions usually occur within 30 to 60 minutes after ingestion of the particular food or beverage.[66]

The interaction between tranylcypromine and cheddar cheese has actually been utilized to treat patients with severe postural hypertension. When this drug was given at a dose of 70 mg per day and 90 gm of cheddar cheese, equivalent to 26 mg of tyramine per day, was also given daily, the blood pressure in a hypotensive patient rose so that she was able to stand up without developing symptoms.[28] The tyramine content of foods which commonly evoke hypertensive tyramine reactions are shown in Table 3.

Other monamine oxidase inhibitor drugs which may evoke a tyramine reaction are used for quite other therapeutic purposes than the treatment of depression. Kent Smith and Durack[56] reported tyramine reactions from ingestion of cheese with isoniazid. Procarbazine, used in the treatment of Hodgkin's disease, is a mild monamine oxidase inhibitor and is also capable of causing hypertensive attacks when taken with foods containing high levels of tyramine.[116]

Disulfiram Reactions

The acute reactions which occur when people receiving the drug disulfiram (Antabuse) drink alcoholic beverages or consume foods containing alcohol begin about 15 minutes after the alcohol-containing food or drink is taken. Flushing and headache are followed by nausea, vomiting, and a variable degree of chest and/or abdominal pain. Symptoms are very unpleasant, and the drug has therefore come to be used as a deterrent to drinking for alcoholics. Disulfiram reactions are caused by drugs that are aldehyde dehydrogenase inhibitors. Drugs, other than disulfiram (Antabuse) itself, which have been documented as causing disulfiram reactions, are: calcium carbimide, used in Canada as an aversion drug for alcoholics; metronidazole, chlorpropamide, furazolidone, griseofulvin, quinacrine, tolazoline, and procarbazine.[35,42,76,88,110] The inky cap mushroom *Coprinus atramentarius* contains an aldehyde dehydrogenase inhibitor. When thse mushrooms are eaten with or followed by alcoholic beverages, including beer, disulfiram reaction occurs.[15,96]

Hypoglycemic Reactions

Drugs and/or foods having the property of inducing rapid release of insulin can cause hypoglycemia when taken with alcoholic beverages. Thus hypoglycemia may develop when diabetic patients receiving oral hypoglycemic agents ingest alcohol. Reactions are characterized by weakness, mental confusion, irrational behavior and, if untreated, loss of consciousness. Milder hypoglycemic reactions have been identified when sweet or semi-sweet drinks such as gin and tonic are ingested on an empty stomach. A warning has been given that hypoglycemic attacks following the drinking of alcohol with sweet mixes in the fasting state could very easily lead to automobile accidents.[84]

Flush Reactions

Flush reactions have been described when patients on a variety of drugs also have a drink of a beverage containing alcohol. The flushing appears rapidly after ingestion of the drink and may be accompanied by dyspnea and headache. Chlorpropamide is known to induce the flush reaction in certain diabetics. Pike and Leslie[93] have described a distinctive syndrome in diabetics or prediabetics, inherited as an autosomal dominant trait, which is associated with chlorpropamide-alcohol flush reaction. These authors have found that this syndrome can be detected with a single dose of chlorpropamide before the onset of glucose intolerance and that therefore a "flushing test" could be used as a genetic marker for the syndrome.

Other drugs which may induce a flush reaction are griseofulvin, in which the reaction is usually confined to the period soon after the initiation of treatment, and tetrachlorethylene. The etiology of the griseofulvin and tetrachlorethylene flush reactions is not well understood. Tetrachlorethylene also potentiates the sedative effects of alcohol.[64]

When central nervous system depressant drugs including hypnotic sedatives, antihistamines, phenothiazines, and narcotic analgesics are taken with alcoholic beverages, drug effects which may cause loss of consciousness are potentiated.[110]

EFFECTS OF DRUGS ON FOOD INTAKE AND ABSORPTION OF NUTRIENTS

Effects of drugs on Appetite, Food Intake, and Body Weight

Numerous drugs in common therapeutic use alter appetite.

Table 3. *Tyramine Content of Foods and Beverages**

FOODS/BEVERAGES	TYRAMINE CONTENT ($\mu g/g$)
Cheese	
Cheddar	120-1500
Camembert	20-2000
Emmenthaler	225-1000
Stilton	466-2170
Processed	26-50
Brie	0-200
Gruyere	516
Gouda	20
Brick, natural	524
Mozzarella	410
Roquefort	27-520
Parmesan	4-290
Romano	238
Provolone	38
Cottage	5
Fish	
Salted, dried	0-470
Pickled herring	3000
Meat	
Meat extracts	95-304
Beef liver (stored)	274
Chicken liver (stored)	100
Vegetables	
Avocado	23
Fruit	
Banana	7
Alcoholic Beverages	
Beer and ale	1.8-11.2
Wines	0-25
Chianti	25.4
Sherry	3.6

*Adapted from Lovenberg, W.: Some vaso- and psychoactive substances in food. *In* Natural Toxicants in Food. National Academy of Science, Washington, D.C., 1973, Table 1, p. 172, Table 2, p. 174.

Drugs which promote appetite may be used intentionally for this purpose, or enhanced desire for food in general or for certain foods may be considered as an undesirable side effect of such drugs. Despite the obvious connection between stimulation of appetite, increased food intake and weight gain, these causal associations cannot be assumed.

Hyperphagic Agents

Antihistamines. Appetite can be stimulated intentionally in debilitated children or adults by administration of cyproheptadine hydrochloride (Periactin), which is both an antihistamine and a serotonin antagonist. Increased hunger with administration of cyproheptadine occurs largely when anorexia previously existed. Cyproheptadine may be considered as a rational therapy for treatment of anorexia except when distaste for food is associated with weight phobia (as in anorexia nervosa) or with disease in which food intake causes pain or discomfort.[30] Asthmatic children treated with cyproheptadine experience increased appetite and gain weight.[5] Cyproheptadine has also been shown to improve appetite and cause significant weight gain in underweight adults.[117] Mainguet[64] also found that cyproheptadine is a nontoxic appetite stimulant.

Psychotropic Drugs. Appetite promoting effects of psychotrophic drugs have been recognized, particularly in psychiatric patients on prolonged high dosage therapies.[86] Chlorpromazine (Thorazine) and other phenothiazines can improve appetite in agitated patients. Benzodiazepines including chlordiazepoxide (Librium) and diazepam (Valium) stimulate appetite and increase food intake, both in people and in experimental animals. In rats it has been demonstrated that diazepam promotes food intake under conditions of conflict and it has been hypothesized that this may also be the case in human subjects.[51] Meprobamate has appetite-stimulating properties when given to disturbed patients. Hydroxyzine hydrochloride (Atarax, Vistaril), a mild tranquilizer with antiemetic and antihistaminic properties, may also increase the desire for food. Patients with long-standing dermatoses are particularly likely to experience increased appetite with intake of hydroxyzine, probably because of associated relief from itching (personal observation).

Whereas tranquilizers given to disturbed psychotic patients often effect a marked increase in food intake such that patients become obese, these same drugs given to geriatric patients may have an opposite effect. When phenothiazines or benzodiazepines are given in high dosages to elderly patients whose rate of drug metabolism is slowed, somnolence and disinterest in food, as well as in surroundings in general, may be responsible for diminished food intake.

Tricyclic antidepressants, like the tranquilizers, may promote appetite. Specific drugs in this class are recognized as having a very marked effect on the desire for food. Amitriptyline (Elavil) increases appetite and food intake and may cause massive weight gain.[3] Patients receiving this drug often describe a craving for sweets.[87] Combined tricyclic and monamine oxidase inhibitor antidepressants have been found to induce weight gain in a high percentage of patients with depressive illness.[37a]

Tranquilizers such as chlorpromazine have been used in the management of anorexia nervosa. However, it is to be questioned whether the beneficial effects of the drug on the disease result from stimulation of appetite. Evidence suggests that chlorpromazine given to patients with anorexia nervosa may reduce resistance to counseling.[20a]

Hypoglycemic Agents

In diabetics and nondiabetics, injections of insulin in the fasting state induce a sensation of hunger. Insulin-induced hypoglycemia, however, may be associated with nausea and a sensation of weakness, rather than a desire for food. The sulfonylurea tolbutamide and chlorpropamide increase appetite in certain diabetic patients, and may induce weight gain. Pawan has suggested that these drugs may stimulate appetite through pancreatic release of insulin.[86]

Steroids

Anabolic steroids including methandrostenolone (Dianabol), nandrolone phenproprionate (Durabolin), and norethandrolone (Nilevar) increase appetite in debilitated patients. Appetite may also be stimulated by testosterone. Weight gain associated with administration of these drugs promotes nitrogen retention with increase in lean body mass.

Glucocorticoids may stimulate appetite, leading to weight gain. The appetite-stimulating effects of glucocorticoids are most notable in patients with chronic adrenal insufficiency or anterior pituitary insufficiency. When corticosteroids are used in the treatment of leukemia, appetite and weight gain improve only if the appetite depressant effects of chemotherapeutic drugs such as methotrexate do not outweigh the effects of the glucocorticoids.

Increased appetite with improved food intake and weight gain may occur with administration of anti-infective drugs, particularly tuberculostatic drugs in tuberculosis. Altered responsiveness to food under these circumstances is a sign of improved well-being.[86]

Hypophagic Agents

Amphetamines and Related Stimulant Drugs. Unsubstituted amphetamines and related drugs have been and are still used as anorectic agents in the treatment of obesity. Alteration of appetite by unsubstituted amphetamines may be due to catecholamine-dependent mechanisms.[13] In obese people, anorectic effects of these drugs are significant on initial administration. However, for chronic management of obesity, these drugs are unsatisfactory, both because of adverse side effects and because efficacy in reducing body weight is limited since hyperphagic obese people tend to eat in response to sensory appeal of food rather than in response to appetite.[74,119]

Fenfluramine (Pondimin), a trifluoromethyl-substituted amphetamine which is also widely used as an appetite suppressant, has a central effect which occurs through activity of the drug on serotonin-dependent pathways.[25]

Hyperactive children receiving amphetamines such as dextroamphetamine or the related stimulant drug, methylphenidate, exhibit growth retardation. Slow weight gain and height gain is associated with diminished food intake. Effects are dose-dependent. When these drugs are discontinued in these children, growth rebound occurs and is proportional to the previous growth depressant. It is believed that the growth rebound is associated with increase in food intake.[104-106]

Cancer Chemotherapeutic Drugs

Antineoplastic drugs including methotrexate as well as purine and pyrimidine derivatives frequently induce anorexia as well as nausea and vomiting in cancer patients. Aversions to food, particularly to meat, may arise as a result of the primary disease or may be associated with the chemotherapy. In children with leukemia it has been shown that foods given during the period of chemotherapy may become distasteful. Anorexia followed by return of appetite occurs with antileukemia multidrug regimens. Methotrexate, particularly when given when the patient is in relapse, will frequently cause anorexia in association with adverse gastrointestinal symptoms. Administration of corticosteroids with this regimen may promote appetite. Abnormalities in taste including aversion to meat associated with the presence of malignant primary or secondary neoplasms may be normalized by cancer chemotherapeutic agents.[27,75]

Other Agents

Chelating Agents. D-Penicillamine, used in the treatment of Wilson's disease, cystinuria, heavy metal poisoning, and rheumatoid arthritis, may produce loss of taste. Loss of taste is most likely to occur in patients who are receiving this drug for a prolonged period of time, as is the case with penicillamine management of rheumatoid arthritis. Loss of taste has been attributed to zinc deficiency, which is induced by the drug. Recent studies indicate that copper deficiency may be a contributory factor. Loss of taste in these patients is frequently associated with diminished food intake and weight loss.[63]

Alcohol. Alcohol abuse can cause anorexia and diminished food intake. Causes of anorexia in alcoholics are inebriation, gastritis, lactose intolerance, pancreatitis, hepatitis, cirrhosis, ketoacidosis, alcoholic brain syndromes, and withdrawal syndromes. Anorexia in alcoholics can also be due to thiamine deficiency, zinc deficiency, or protein deficiency.[97]

Bulking Agents. Methyl cellulose and guar gum have been shown to reduce food intake if given to healthy normal weight volunteers.[32] These agents, however, offer little for the management of obesity.

Cardiac Glycosides. Digitalis and related cardiac glycosides in high dosage produce anorexia which is usually accompanied by nausea. Vomiting may occur. Digitalis cachexia may result from intoxication with these drugs and mimics cachexia associated with internal malignancy. Rapid return of appetite occurs when drug dosage is adjusted.[5]

EFFECTS OF DRUGS ON ABSORPTION OF NUTRIENTS

Drugs Which Promote Absorption of Nutrients

Cimetidine, a potent gastric antisecretory drug, has been shown to be effective in controlling malabsorption and maldigestion associated with the short bowel syndrome. Among patients with this syndrome, those responding to cimetidine have been persons who shortly after massive bowel resection develop maldigestion and malabsorption in association with increased duodenal acid and high volume loads. These pathophysiological changes may impair digestion and absorption in the proximal intestine. High fecal nitrogen losses, steatorrhea, and diarrhea associated with impaired protein and carbohydrate absorption, as well as malabsorption of other nutrients, ensue. Cimetidine has been shown in these patients to reduce gastric acid output, to reduce gastric volume output, to lower duodenal acid load and volume, to prevent a fall in jejunal pH, and to reduce jejunal flow, to decrease fecal fat and nitrogen, as well as fecal volume, and to improve absorption of protein and carbohydrate.[18,34,77]

Drugs Which Decrease Absorption of Nutrients

Numerous drugs have been shown to induce malabsorption, which may be primary or secondary. Primary drug-induced malabsorption is here defined as being due to the direct effects of a pharmacologic agent on luminal events or on the intestinal mucosa. Secondary malabsorption occurs when a drug interferes with the absorption, disposition, or metabolism of one nutrient, which in turn leads to malabsorption and deficiency of another nutrient.

Causes and consequences of primary drug-induced malabsorption are summarized in Table 4.

Drugs which cause secondary malabsorption are those which (a) suppress vitamin D absorption or metabolism, leading to malabsorption of calcium; and (b) cause malabsorption or impair utilization of folacin and malabsorption of other nutrients. Chesney et al.[16] found that serum concentrations of 1,25-dihydroxycholecalciferol were reduced in children who were being treated with a corticosteroid (prednisone) for renal disease. Other children with renal disease who were not receiving corticosteroids had normal serum 1,25-dihydroxycholecalciferol levels. Effects were dose-dependent and there was a relationship between the decrease in serum 1,25-dihydroxycholecalciferol levels and the amount of corticosteroid given. These effects could partially explain steroid-induced osteopenia. It was suggested that steroid-induced osteopenia has several etiologic components, among which the reduced serum level of the renal vitamin D metabolite may be most significant. No explanations of the steroid-induced fall in 1,25-$(OH)_2$-D_3-dihydroxycholecalciferol is presently available.[16]

Table 4. *Primary Intestinal Absorptive Defects Caused by Drugs**

DRUG	USAGE	MALABSORPTION OR FECAL NUTRIENT LOSS	MECHANISM
Mineral oil	Laxative	Carotene, vitamins A, D, K	Physical barrier, nutrients dissolve in mineral oil and are lost; micelle formation decreased
Phenolphthalein	Laxative	Vitamin D, Ca	Intestinal hurry; K depletion; loss of structural integrity
Neomycin	Antibiotic to "sterilize" gut	Fat, nitrogen, Na, K, Ca, Fe, lactose, sucrose, vitamin B_{12}	Structural defect; pancreatic lipase lowered; binding of bile acids (salts)
Cholestyramine	Hypocholesterolemic agent; bile acid sequestrant	Fat, vitamins A, K, B_{12}, D, Fe	Binding of bile acids (salts) and nutrients, e.g., Fe
Potassium chloride	Potassium repletion	Vitamin B_{12}	Ileal pH lowered
Colchicine	Anti-inflammatory agent in gout	Fat, carotene, Na, K, vitamin B_{12}, lactose	Mitotic arrest; structural defect; enzyme damage
Biguanides: Metformin Phenformin	Hypoglycemic agents (in diabetes)	Vitamin B_{12}	Competitive inhibition of B_{12} absorption
Para-amino salicylic acid	Anti-tuberculosis agent	Fat, folacin, vitamin B_{12}	Mucosal block in B_{12} uptake
Salicylazosulfapyridine (Azulfidine)	Anti-inflammatory agent in ulcerative colitis, and regional enteritis	Folacin	Mucosal block in folate uptake
Methyldopa	Antihypertensive agent	Folacin, vitamin B_{12}, iron	Autoimmune mechanism?

*Adapted from Roe, D.A.: Effects of drugs on nutrition. Minireview. Life Sciences, 15:1219-1234, 1974.

Drugs commonly causing secondary malabsorption, together with their known or proposed mode of action and nutritional consequences, are listed in Table 5. Both primary and secondary drug-induced malabsorption are due to intraluminal events which inhibit digestion. Drug-induced malabsorption is reversible. A recently described cause of reversible malabsorption is that associated with intake of methyldopa. Intestinal villous atrophy and inflammatory changes in the gut wall were seen in a jejunal biopsy specimen. It was suggested that these changes could be due to an immune mechanism similar to that causing hemolytic anemia and cirrhosis with methyldopa "hypersensitivity." However, the Coombs' test was negative, and the hypothesis was therefore not supported.[114]

Supportive evidence that nutrient malabsorption induced by a drug can produce malabsorption of other nutrients is from reports of methotrexate-induced malabsorption found in children with acute lymphoblastic leukemia. A significant degree of malabsorption has been found in children who had had methotrexate within the previous seven days and the degree of malabsorption is dose-dependent over time. Methotrexate, which functions as an anti-folate drug, impairs intestinal absorption of calcium.[19]

ROLE OF DRUGS IN MINERAL DEPLETION

Mineral depletion or deficiency may be induced by drugs of varying therapeutic and social use (Table 6). Drugs may induce renal hyperexcretion of minerals or minerals may be lost via the gastrointestinal tract. Whereas diuretics are intentionally used for removal of sodium, diuretic-induced loss of other minerals may be considered as an undesirable side-effect. Oral diuretics such as furosemide, ethacrynic acid, and triamterene cause significant hypercalciuria. Renal clearance of calcium is increased by intravenous furosemide, intravenous ethacrynic acid, or oral triamterene. Oral furosemide decreases the renal tubular reabsorption of calcium and indeed this drug has been used as a temporary measure to control symptoms of hypocalcemia. Thiazide drugs, on the other hand, may cause a transient hypercalcemia.[31,118]

Potassium depletion is a special risk with prolonged or high dosages of oral diuretics including thiazides, furosemide, and ethacrynic acid. Triamterene and spironolactone are potassium-sparing diuretics. Potassium depletion also occurs with laxative abuse because large amounts of potassium are lost into the lumen of the large intestine. Body deficits of potassium are reflected by hypokalemia. Drug-induced causes of hypokalemia, in addition to diuretics and laxatives, include antibiotics (carbenicillin and penicillin), glucocorticoids, outdated tetracycline which is nephrotoxic, and licorice.[78]

Factitious hypokalemia can occur by self-administration of diuretics, laxatives, and licorice, as well as self-induced vomiting. Persons who induce hypokalemia by these means usually have underlying psychiatric problems such as anorexia nervosa.[36]

Potassium deficiency is manifested by weakness, anorexia, nausea, vomiting, listlessness, apprehension, sometimes diffuse pain, drowsiness, stupor, and irrational behavior. However, marked hypokalemia can occur without abnormal clinical findings. In the elderly, clinical signs may be limited to muscle weakness and electrocardiographic changes.[125] In elderly patients, potassium depletion and hypokalemia are commonly the result of low potassium intake, renal wasting of potassium by use of diuretics, and gastrointestinal loss of potassium by misuse of laxatives. Potassium depletion sensitizes patients to digitalis intoxication. Potassium deficiency also causes structural and functional impairment of the kidney.

Magnesium and zinc are hyperexcreted by patients on oral diuretics as well as by those receiving cardiac glycosides. There has been some debate as to whether the magnesium and zinc deficiencies induced by these drugs are sufficient to induce severe deficits.[70]

Penicillamine, which chelates metals, will induce depletion of zinc and copper with chronic administration, and may cause loss of taste because of zinc deficiency or possibly copper deficiency.[26,41]

Alcohol induces excessive losses of potassium, magnesium, and zinc. Excessive alcohol intake may have an added effect with therapeutic drugs in inducing clinical deficiencies of these minerals.[113]

A phosphate depletion syndrome is known to occur in patients on heavy doses of antacids. Antacids producing phosphate depletion are those containing aluminum and/or magnesium hydroxide. Dietary phosphate combines with these antacids to form insoluble aluminum and magnesium phosphates which are excreted by the gastrointestinal tract. The risk of acute phosphate depletion is greatest when there is an interactive effect with a low phosphate diet. Symptoms of phosphate depletion are profound muscle weakness which may be limited to proximal limb muscles, malaise, paresthesia, anorexia, and convulsions. In some patients, phosphate depletion leads to osteomalacia or hemolytic anemia.[94,113]

Iron deficiency may be induced by chronic intake of aspirin and/or other salicylates or other non-narcotic analgesics such as indomethacin. These drugs cause erosions in the stomach and intestine which are associated with blood loss.

Table 5. Drugs Causing Secondary Malabsorption*

DRUG	USAGE	MALABSORPTION	MECHANISM
Prednisone (other glucocorticoids)	Used in allergic and collagen	Calcium	Calcium transport ⇓
Phenobarbital	Anticonvulsant	Calcium	Accelerated metabolism of vitamin D
Diphenylhydantoin	Anticonvulsant	Calcium	
Primidone	Anticonvulsant	Calcium	
Glutethimide	Sedative	Calcium	Impaired Ca transport
Diphosphonates	Paget's disease	Calcium	1,25-(OH)$_2$-D$_3$ formation ⇓
Methotrexate	Leukemia	Calcium	Acute folacin deficiency

*Adapted from Roe, D. A.: Effects of drugs on nutrition. Minireview. Life Sciences, 15:1219-1234, 1974.

Table 6. Mineral Depletion Induced by Drugs

Diuretics	Calcium (not thiazides)
	Potassium
	Magnesium
	Zinc
Laxatives (Laxative abuse)	Potassium
	Calcium
Glucocorticoids	Calcium
	Potassium
Chelating agents (penicillamine)	Zinc
	Copper
Ethanol	Potassium
	Magnesium
	Zinc
Antacids	Phosphates
Non-narcotic analgesics (aspirin, indomethacin)	Iron (by GI blood loss)

Chronic blood loss into the gastrointestinal tract causes iron deficiency anemia.[14,58]

DRUGS AND VITAMINS

Effects of Drug-Vitamin Interactions on Drug Efficacy

Pharmacologic doses of vitamins can lower blood levels of drugs when these vitamins undergo drug interaction. In these circumstances, the desired therapeutic effects of the primary drug may not be obtained. High doses of folic acid or vitamin B_6 given to patients receiving diphenylhydantoin and/or phenobarbital for seizure disorders may reduce blood levels of these drugs and thereby reduce their therapeutic efficacy.[7,43,68]

Hypotheses have been put forward to explain these nutrient-drug interactions. Whereas it has been suggested that both folic acid and pyridoxal phosphate could alter the rate of metabolism of diphenylhydantoin and/or phenobarbital, there are no experimental data to support such a hypothesis. Another possibility as yet untested is that high intakes of folic acid or pyridoxine could inhibit absorption of anticonvulsants.

Vitamin Antagonists

Vitamin antagonists with well-established therapeutic efficacy include coumarin anticoagulants, cancer chemotherapeutic drugs such as methotrexate, and the antimalarial drug, pyrimethamine.

Vitamin K is required for carboxylation of glutamic acid residues in precursor proteins of clotting factors. The storage form of vitamin K in the liver is vitamin K 2,3-epoxide. Matshiner et al.[67] showed that when coumarin or indandione anticoagulants are administered, vitamin K 2,3-epoxide accumulates in the liver. This finding led to a working hypothesis for the mode of action of these anticoagulants. It has been proposed that they function by inhibiting regeneration of vitamin K from the epoxide.[67,111]

Ren et al.[95] tested this hypothesis in rats by studying effects of nine coumarin and indandione anticoagulants on prothrombin synthesis and on the conversion of vitamin K_1 epoxide to vitamin K. A high degree of correlation was obtained between inhibition of prothrombin synthesis and the level of vitamin K, epoxide in the rat liver. Similar effects were observed both in vivo and in vitro.

Biochemical effects of methotrexate include multiple antagonistic actions on folacin metabolism. The drug in the tissues binds firmly to the dihydrofolate reductase enzyme and the enzyme that is bound to the drug decays more slowly than the free enzyme. Utilizable folacin is displaced from the dihydrofolate reductase enzyme and excreted in the urine. Methotrexate polyglutamates are formed, and there is a reduction in the synthesis of polyglutamates derived from folacin. Thymidylate synthetase is inhibited. DNA, RNA, and protein synthesis are inhibited. Cytotoxic effects are selective according to the rate of cell reproduction and self-limiting methotrexate is more effective when cell populations are in the log phase of growth.

The potential of methotrexate as an antitumor agent has been greatly increased since citrovorum factor rescue was introduced into treatment protocols. Citrovorum factor (folinic acid, 5-formyl tetrahydrofolate) can be utilized in the presence of methotrexate-inhibited reductase enzyme, thus reducing methotrexate toxicity with some retention of antitumor activity.[2,29,46,121] Enhanced bioavailability of methotrexate may result from dietary manipulation which alters intestinal microflora because intestinal methotrexate metabolism is decreased. However, the use of poorly absorbable antibiotics such as neomycin decreases the bioavailability of this drug.[1122] Reversal of antifolate effects of pyrimethamine can be accomplished with folic acid. Citrovorum factor may, however, be required as "rescue" in high dosage pyrimethamine therapy. Binding of pyrimethamine to the dihydrofolate reductase enzyme is less than methotrexate which accounts for the therapeutic efficiency of folic acid supplements.

Antivitamin properties of other drugs are recognized as an avoidable side effct. Isoniazid, cycloserine, levodopa, and penicillamine inhibit the normal metabolism of vitamin B_6 by formation of both drug-vitamin complexes and by inhibition of the pyridoxal kinase enzyme (Table 7).[100]

Vitamins as Rational Therapeutic Agents for Drug Intoxication

Riboflavin and Boric Acid Poisoning. A new use for riboflavin may be in the treatment of boric acid poisoning. Boric acid combines with the ribityl side chain of riboflavin and induces massive riboflavinuria. It has further been suggested that in boric acid poisoning, formation of flavin coenzymes may be depressed or the binding of flavin coenzymes to their respective apoenzymes may be impaired. Animal studies indicate that riboflavin has a protective effect against boric acid toxicity.[91,102]

Vitamin E and the Prevention of Bronchopulmonary Dysplasia in Infants. In rats vitamin E has been shown to combat pulmonary oxygen toxicity, while rats deficient in vitamin E are vulnerable for oxygen damage to the lungs.[2,17,92]

Chronic lung disease in premature infants treated by mechanical ventilation and with increased concentrations of oxygen in inspired air have developed a severe respiratory distress syndrome designated bronchopulmonary dysplasia. Disease is believed to result from the toxic effects of excess oxygen. In a study by Ehrenkranz,[32] infants at risk for the development of bronchopulmonary dysplasia were protected by administration of vitamin E during the acute phase of the respiratory distress syndrome that required oxygen administration.

Hypovitaminoses and Other Nutritional Changes in Oral Contraceptive Users

Biochemical evidence of vitamin depletion or deficiencies has been obtained among women on oral contraceptives. Whereas subclinical deficiencies of folacin, riboflavin, vitamin B_6, vitamin B_{12}, and vitamin C may be found by laboratory tests, physical signs of these deficiencies can seldom be linked to the oral contraceptive. Whereas depression occurring in women on these drugs has been attributed to vitamin B_6 deficiency, the association cannot be generalized. It is

Table 7. *Vitamin Antagonists*

Folacin antagonists	Methotrexate
	Pyrimethamine
	Triamterene
	Trimethoprim
Vitamin B_6 antagonists	Isoniazid
	Hydralazine
	Cycloserine
	Levodopa
Vitamin K antagonists	Coumarin anticoagulants

assumed that if depression is due to vitamin B_6 deficiency, it would be reversed by administration of pyridoxine.[1]

We have shown that in women taking the pill, and in non-users, red cell folacin values are highly correlated with intake of dietary folacin. The risk of serious folacin depletion with megaloblastic anemia developing in pill users is related to inadequate dietary intake of this vitamin, to alcohol abuse, to malabsorption syndromes, and to use of other drugs such as anticonvulsants which elevate folacin requirements.[101]

In a study of the nutritional status of women attending family planning clinics which serve a low income population, we found plasma folacin was correlated positively with age and education and negatively with weight for height for age and triceps skinfold thickness. Findings suggested that in the sample population plasma folacin was an indicator, as was obesity, of poor dietary habits which may be influenced by youth and lack of education. Plasma folacin levels were not affected by intake of the pill; however, women on the pill in these clinics had lower red cell folacin levels than non-users. Both plasma and red cell folacin values increased when physiological vitamin supplements containing folic acid were given.

In this study, women on the pill also tended to show reduced riboflavin status as indicated by red cell glutathione reductase assay.[98]

Newman et al.[82] showed that riboflavin deficiency is common in women of low socioeconomic status in the reproductive period of life. Use of the pill increases the incidence of riboflavin deficiency.

In a 1978 review of the risks and benefits of the pill,[120] a decreased incidence of iron deficiency anemia is cited as a noncontraceptive benefit. Reduced menstrual blood flow in pill users reduces physiological iron losses and improves iron status. Serum iron may be increased but total iron binding capacity is more uniformly elevated.

Changes in composition of contraceptive steroids with reduction in estrogen content suggests a need for re-evaluation of any adverse nutritional effects. It is perhaps significant that in the last two years the numbers of publications on nutrition and the pill has declined.

CONCLUSIONS

Drugs may be discontinued prematurely for many reasons. The drug may have been ineffective or nutrients may have caused an adverse effect on drug bioavailability. Adverse drug reactions may be due to drug-nutrient, drug-food, or drug-alcohol incompatibility, or to drug-induced nutritional deficiencies. A lack of drug efficacy or unwanted drug effects of nutritional etiology related to food or nutrient interaction are predictable and preventable provided that the risk is understood and the patient's diet as well as drug regimen is known to members of the health care team including the physician, nurse, and pharmacist.

REFERENCES

1. Adams, P.W. Rose, D.P., Folkar, D.J., et al., 1973. Effect of pyridoxine hydrochlorode (vitamin B_6) upon depression associated with oral contraception. Lancet, 1:897.
2. Aler, D.W., 1953. Effects of vitamin E deficiency on oxygen toxicity in the rat. J. Physiol., 121:47P-48P.
3. Arenillas, L., 1964. Amitriptyline and body weight. Lancet, 1:432-433.
4. Asatoor, A.M., Levi, A.J. and Milne, M.C., 1963. Tranylcypromine and cheese. Lancet, 2:733-734.
5. Banks, T. and Nayab, A., 1974 Letter. Digitalis cachexia. New Eng. J. Med., 290-746.
6. Bates, T.R., Sequiera, J.A. and Tembo, A.V., 1974. Effect of food on nitrofurantoin absorption. Clin. Pharmacol. Therap., 16:63-68.
7. Bayless, E.M., Crowley, J.M., Preece, J.M., et al., 1971. Influence of folic acid on blood phenytoin levels. Lancet, 1:62-64.
8. Bergen, S.S., 1974. Appetite-stimulating properties of cyproheptadine. Amer. J. Dis. Child., 108:270-273.
9. Berlin, H and Bante, G. Studies on oral utilization of penicillin V. Antibiotics Annual, Med. Encycl. Inc., pp. 149-157, 1959.
10. Blackwell, B. and Mabbit, L.A., 1965. Tyramine in cheese related to hypertensive crisis after monamine oxidase inhibition. Lancet, 1:938-940.
11. Blackwell, B., Marley, E. and Mabbit, L.A., 1965. Effects of yeast extract after monamine exidase inhibition. Lancet, 1:940-943.
12. Blomley, B.J., 1964. Monamine oxidase inhibitors. Lancet, 2:1181-1182.
13. Blundell, J.E., Latham, C.J. and Leshem, M.B., 1976. Differences between the anorexic actions of amphetamine and fenfluramine—possible effects on hunger and satiety. J. Pharm. Pharmac., 28:471-477.
14. Boardman, P.L. and Hart, E.D., 1967. Side effects of indomethacin. Ann. Rheum. Dis., 26:127-132.
15. Buck, R.W., 1961. Mushroom toxins—brief review of the literature. New Eng. J. Med., 265:681-686.
16. Chesney, R.W., Hamstra, A.J., Mazees, R.B., et al., 1978. Reduction of serum-1, 25-dihydroxy vitamin-D in children receiving glucocorticoids. Lancet, 2:1123-1125.
17. Clark, J.M. and Lambertson, C.J., 1971. Pulmonary oxygen toxicity: A review. Pharmacol. Rev., 23:38-133.
18. Corto, T.A., Fleming, C.R. and Malageldad, J-R., 1978. Improved nutrient absorption after cimetidine in short-bowel syndrome with gastric hypersecretion. New Eng. J. Med., 300:79-80.
19. Craft, A.W., Kay, A.G.M. Lawson, V.N., et al., 1977. Methotrexate induced malabsorption in children with acute lymphoblastic leukemia. Brit. Med. J., 2:1511-1512.
20. Crane, G.E., 1973. Clinical psychopharmacology in its 20th year. Science, 181:124-128.
20a. Crisp. A.H., 1965. A treatment regime for anorexia nervosa. Brit. J. Psychiatry, 112:505-512.
21. Cronk, G.A., Naumann, D.E., Albright, H., et al. Laboratory and clinical studies with potassium penicillin-152 (potassium (α-phenoxyethyl)-penicillin). Antibiotics Annual, 1959-1960. Med. Encycl. Inc., pp. 133-145, 1960.
22. Cronk, G.A., Wheatley, W.B., Fellers, G.F., et al., 1960. The relationship of food intake to the absorption of potassium alpha-phenoxyethyl penicillin and potassium phenoxymethyl penicillin from the gastrointestinal tract. Amer. J. Med. Sci., 240:219-225.
23. Crounse, R.G., 1961. Human pharmacology of griseofulvin: the effect of fat intake on gastrointestinal absorption. J. Invest. Dermat., 37:529-533.
24. Crisp. A.H., 1970. Anorexia nervosa—"feeding disorder," "nervous malnutrition" or "weight phobia?" World Rev. Nutr. Dietet., 12:452-504.
25. Datey, K.K., Kelar, P.N. and Pandya, R.S., 1973. Fenfluramine in the management of obesity. Brit. J. Clin. Pract., 27(10):373-375.
26. Day, A.T., Golding, J.R., Lee, P.N., et al., 1974. Penicillamine in rheumatoid disease: A long-term study. Brit. Med. J., 1:180.
27. DeWyss, W.D., 1974. Abnormalities of taste as a remote effect of a neoplasm. Ann. N.Y. Acad. Sci., 230:427.
28. Diamond, M.A., Murray, R.H. and Schmid, P., 1969. Treatment of idiopathic postural hypertension with oral tyramine (Ty) and monamine oxidase inhibitor (MI). J. Clin. Res., 17:237.
29. Djerassi, I., 1975. High-dose methotrexate (NSC-740) and citrovorum factor (NSC-3590) rescue: Background and rationale. Cancer Chemotherap. Rep., Part III, 6:3-6.
30. Drash, A., Elliott, J., Langs, H., et al. Effect of cyproheptadine on carbohydrate metabolism. Clin. Pharm. Therap., 7:340-346.
31. Duarte, G.C., Winnacker, J.L., Becker, K.L., et al., 1971. Thiazide-induced hypercalcemia. New Eng. J. Med., 284:828-830.
32. Ehrenkranz, R.A., Bonta, B.W., Ablor, R.C., et al., 1978. Amelioration of bronchopulmonary dysplasia after vitamin E administration. A preliminary report. New Eng. J. Med., 299:564-569.
33. Evans, E. and Miller, D.S., 1975. Bulking agents in the treatment of obesity. Nutr. Metab., 18:199-203.
34. Finkelstein, W. and Isselbacher, K.J., 1978. Drug therapy: Cimetidine. New Eng. J. Med., 299:992-996.
35. Fitzgerald, M.G., et al., 1962. Alcohol sensitivity in diabetics receiving chlorpropamide. Diabetes, 2:40.
36. Fleming, B.J., Genuth, S.M., Gould, A.B., et al., 1975. Laxative-induced hypokalemia, sodium depletion and hyperreninemia. Effects of potassium and sodium replacement on the renin-angiotensinaldosterone system. Ann. Intern. Med., 83:60-62.
37a. Gander, D.R. and Lond, M.B., 1965. Treatment of depressive illnesses with combined anti-depressants. Lancet, 2:107-109.
37. Gibaldi, M. and Grundhofer, B., 1975. Biopharmaceutic influences on the anticholinergic effects of propantheline. Clin. Pharmacol. Ther., 18:457-461.

38. Gill, C.V., 1976. Rifampicin and breakfast. Lancet, 2:1135.
39. Gillespie, N.G., Mena, I., Cotzias, G.C., et al., 1973. Diets affecting parkinsonism with levodopa. J. Amer. Diet. Assoc., 62:525-528.
40. Gander, D.R., 1965. Treatment of depressive illnesses with combined antidepressants. Lancet, 2:107.
41. Gordon, M.H. and Ahrlich, G.E., 1974. Penicillamine for treatment of rheumatoid arthritis. J.A.M.A., 229:1342-1343.
42. Griffin, J.P. and D'Arcy, P.F. A Manual of Adverse Drug Reactions. John Wright & Sons, Ltd., Bristol, England, pp. 60-61, 1975.
43. Hansson, O. and Sillanpan, A.M., 1976. Doxine and serum concentrations of phenytoin and phenobarbitone. Lancet, 1:256.
44. Hansten, P.D. Drug Interactions. Philadelphia, Lea and Febiger, 2nd ed., pp. 214, 1973.
45. Hodge, J.V., Nye, E.R. and Emerson, G.W., 1964. Monamine oxidase inhibitors, broad beans and hypertension. Lancet, 1:1108.
46. Hoffbrand, A.V. Synthesis and breakdown of natural folates (folate polyglutamates). In Progress in Hematology, IX. New York, Grune & Stratton, pp. 85-105, 1975.
47. Horwitz, D., Lowenberg, W., Engelman, K., et al., 1964. Monamine oxidase inhibitors, tyramine and cheese. J. Am. Med. Assoc., 188:1108-1110.
48. Houston, J.B. and Levy, G., 1975. Effect of carbonated beverages and an antiemetic containing carbohydrate and phosphoric acid on riboflavin bioavailability and salicylamide biotransformation in humans. J. Pharm. Sci., 64:1504-1507.
49. Hunt, J.N., 1963. Gastric emptying in relation to drug absorption. Amer. J. Digest Dis., 8:885-894.
50. Jaffee, J.J., Colaizzi, J.L. and Barry, H., 1971. Effects of dietary components on GI absorption of acetaminophen tablets in man. J. Pharm. Sci., 60:1646-1650.
51. Johnson, D.N. Effect of diazepam on food consumption in rats. Psychopharmacology, 56:111-112.
52. Jusko, W.J. and Levy, G., 1967. Absorption, metabolism and excretion of riboflavin-5'-phosphate in man. J. Pharm. Sci., 56:58-62.
53. Kappas, A., Anderson, K.E., Conney, A.H., et al., 1976. Influence of dietary protein and carbohydrates on antipyrine and theophylline metabolism in man. Clin. Pharmacol. Therap., 30:643-653.
54. Kappas, A., Alvares, A.P., Anderson, K.E., et al., 1978. Effect of charcoal-broiled beef on antipyrine and theophylline metabolism. Clin. Pharm. Therap., 23:445-450.
55. Kelly, M.R., Cutler, R.E., Forrey, A.W., et al., 1974. Pharmacokinetics of orally administered furosemide. Clin. Pharmacol. Ther., 15:178-186.
56. Kent Smith, C. and Durack, D.T., 1978. Isoniazid and reaction to cheese. Ann. Intern. Med., 88:520-521.
57. Koch-Weser, J., 1974. Bioavailability of drug. New Eng. J. Med., 291:233-237.
58. Leonards, J.R. and Levy, G., 1973. Gastrointestinal blood loss during prolonged aspirin administration. New Eng. J. Med., 289:1020-1022.
59. Levy, G. and Jusko, W.J., 1966. Factors affecting the absorption of riboflavin in man. J. Pharm. Sci., 55:285-289.
60. Levy, R.H., Pitlick, W.H., Troupin, A.S., et al., 1975. Pharmacokinetics of carbamazepine in normal man. Clin. Pharmacol. Therap., 17:657-688.
61. McCarthy, C.G. and Finland, M., 1960. Absorption and excretion of four penicillins; penicillin G, penicillin V, penethicillin and Phenymercaptomethyl penicillin. New Eng. J. Med., 263:315-326.
62. MacDonald, H., Place, V.A., Falk, H., et al., 1967. Effect of food on absorption of sulfonamides in man. Chemotherapia, 12:282-285.
63. MacFarlane, M.D., 1974. Penicillamine and zinc. Lancet, 2a:962.
64. Mainguet, P., 1972. Effect of cyproheptadine on anorexia and loss of weight in adults. Practitioner, 208:797-800.
65. Mao, C.C. and Jacobson, E.D., 1970. Intestinal absorption and blood flow. Amer. J. Clin. Nutr., 23:820-823.
66. Marley, E. and Blackwell, B., 1970. Interactions of monamine oxidase inhibitors, amines and foodstuffs. Adv. Pharmacol. Chemotherap., 8:185-239.
67. Matschiner, J.T., Bell, R.G., Amelotti, J.M., et al., 1970. Isolation and characterization of new metabolite of phylloquinone in the rat. Biochem. Biophys. Acta, 201:309-315.
68. Mattson, R.A., Gallagher, B.B., Reynolds, G.H., et al., 1971. Folate therapy in epilepsy. A controlled study. Arch. Neurolog. (Chicago), 29:78-81.
69. Melander, A., 1978. Influence of food on the bioavailability of drugs. Clin. Pharmacokinet., 3:337-351.
70. Melander, A., Danielson, K., Hanson, A., et al., 1977. Enhancement of hydralazine bioavailability by food. Clin. Pharmacol. Therap., 22:104-107.
71. Melander, A., Danielson, K., Schersten, B., et al., 1977. Enhancement by food of canrenone bioavailability from spironolactone. Clin. Pharmacol. Therap., 22:100-103.
72. Melander, A., Danielson, K., Schersten, B., et al., 1977. Enhancement of the bioavailability of propranolol and metoprolol by food. Clin. Pharmacol. Therap., 22:108-112.
73. Miller, D.S., Sterling, J.L. and Yudkin, J., 1966. Effect of ingestion of milk on concentrations of blood alcohol. Nature, 212:1051.
74. Modell, W., 1960. Status and prospect of drugs for overeating. J.A.M.A., 173(10):1131-1136.
75. Morrison, S.D., 1978. Origins of anorexia in neoplastic disease. Amer. J. Clin. Nutr., 31:1104-1107.
76. Murdoch Ritchie, J. The aliphatic alcohols. In Goodman, L.S. and Gilman, A., eds.: The Pharmacological Basis of Therapeutics. Macmillan Co., New York, 3rd ed., pp. 155-156.
77. Murphy, J.P., Jr., King, D.R. and Dubois, A., 1978. Treatment of gastric hypersecretion with cimetidine in the short-bowel syndrome. New Eng. J. Med., 300:80-81.
78. Nardone, D.A., McDonald, W.J. and Girard, D.E., 1978. Mechanisms in hypokalemia: Clinical correlations. Medicine, 57:435-446.
79. Neuvonen, P.J., Gothini, G., Hackman, R., et al., 1970. Interference of iron with the absorption of tetracyclines in man. Brit. Med. J., 4:532-534.
80. Neuvonen, P., Matilla, M., Gothini, G., et al., 1971. Interference of iron and milk with absorption of tetracycline. Scand. J. Clin. Lab. Invest. (Suppl.), 27:76.
81. Neuvonen, P.G. and Turakka, H., 1974. Inhibitory effect of various iron salts on the absorption of tetracycline in man. Eur. J. Clin. Pharmacol., 7:357-360.
82. Newman, L.J., Lopez, R., Cole, A.S., et al., 1978. Riboflavin deficiency in women taking oral contraceptive agents. Amer. J. Clin. Nutr., 31:247-249.
83. Nuessle, W.F. and Norman, F.C., 1965. Pickled herring and tranylcypromine reaction. J.A.M.A., 192:726-727.
84. O'Keefe, S.J.D. and Marx, V., 1977. Lunch-time gin and tonic: A cause of reactive hypoglycaemia. Lancet, 1:1286-1287.
85. Pantuck, E.J., Hsiao, K.C., Loub, W.D., et al., 1976. Stimulatory effect of vegetables on intestinal drug metabolism in the rat. J. Pharmacol. Exper. Therap., 198:278-283.
86. Pawan, G.L.S. Drugs and appetite. Proc. Nutr. Soc., 33:239-244.
87. Paykel, P.S., Mueller, P.S. and De La Vergne, P.M., 1973. Amitriptyline, weight gain and carbohydrate craving; a side effect. Brit. J. Psychiat., 123:501-507.
88. Penick, S.B., et al., 1969. Metronidazole in the treatment of alcoholism. Amer. J. Psychiat., 125:1063.
89. Petrie, J.C., Durno, D. and Howie, J.G.R. Drug interaction in general practice. In Cluff, L.E., and Petrie, J.C., eds.: Clinical Effects of Interaction Between Drugs. Amsterdam, Exerpta Medica, pp. 237-253, 1974.
90. Pettinger, W.A. and Oates, J.A., 1968. Supersensitivity to tyramine during monamine oxidase inhibition in man. Mechanism at the level of the adrenergic neuron. Clin. Pharmacol. Therap., 9:341.
91. Pinto, J., Huang, W.P., McConnell, R.J. et al., 1978. Increased urinary riboflavin excretion resulting from boric acid ingestion. J. Lab. Clin. Med., 22:126-134.
92. Polin, R.L., Bolliner, R.O., Bozynski, M.E., et al., 1977. Effect of vitamin E deficiency on pulmonary oxygen toxicity, Pediatr. Res., 11:577.
93. Pyke, D.A. and Leslie, R.D.G., 1978. Chlorpropamide-alcohol flushing: A definition of its relation to non-insulin-dependent diabetes. Brit. Med. J., 2:1521-1522.
94. Ravid, M. and Robson, M., 1976. Proximal myopathy caused by iatrogenic phosphate depletion. J.A.M.A., 236:1380-1381.
95. Ren, P., Stark, P.Y., Johnson, R.L. and Bell, R.G., 1977. Mechanism of action of anti-coagulants: Correlation between the inhibition of prothrombin synthesis and the regeneration of vitamin K, from vitamin K, hypoxide. J. Pharmacol. Exper. Therap., 201:541-546.
96. Reynolds, W.A. and Lowe, S.H., 1965. Mushrooms and a toxic reaction to alcohol. Report of 4 cases. New Eng. J. Med., 272:630-631.
97. Roe, D.A. Alcohol and the Diet. Westport, Connecticut, AVI Publ. Co., in press.
98. Roe, D.A. Assessment of Need for Nutritional Counselling as a Component of Family Planning Information and Education Services. Final Report, HSA 240-BCHS-106(6)DE, Washington, D.C., 1977.
99. Roe, D.A. Diet-drug interactions and incompatibilities. In Hathcock, J.N., and Coon, J., ed.: Nutrient and Drug Interactions. New York, Academic Press, pp. 319-345, 1978.
100. Roe, D.A. Drug-Induced Vitamin Deficiencies. Westport, Connecticut, AVI Publ. Co., 1976.
101. Roe, D.A. Nutrition and the contraceptive pill. In Winick, M., ed.: Nutritional Disorders of American Women. New York, John Wiley and Sons, pp. 37-49, 1977.
102. Roe, D.A., McCormick, D.B. and Linn., R-T., 1972. Effects of riboflavin on boric acid toxicity. J. Pharm. Sci., 61:1082.
103. Roe, D.A., Wrick, K., McLain, D., et al., 1978 (Abstract). Effects of dietary fiber sources on riboflavin absorption. Fed. Proc., 37:756.
104. Safer, D.J. and Allen, R.O., 1973. Factors influencing the suppressant effects of two stimulant drugs on the growth of hyperactive children. Pediatrics, 5:660-667.
105. Safer, D., Allen, R. and Barr, E., 1972. Depression of growth in hyperactive children on stimulant drugs. New Eng. J. Med., 287:7-20.

106. Safer, D.J., Allen, R.P. and Barr, E., 1975. Growth rebound after termination of stimulant drugs. Pediat. Pharm. Therap., 86:113-116.
107. Schelme, R.R., 1973. Metabolism of foreign compounds by gastrointestinal microorganisms. Pharmacol. Rev., 25:451-523.
108. Schreiner, J. and Altemeier, W.A., 1962. Experimental study of factors inhibiting absorption and effective therapeutic levels of declomycin. Surg. Gynec. Obstet., 114:9-14.
109. Sedman, A.J., Wilkinson, P.K., Sakmar, E., et al., 1976. Food effects on absorption and metabolism of alcohol. Quart. J. Stud. Alc., 37:1197-1214.
110. Seixas, F.A., 1975. Alcohol and its drug interactions. Ann. Intern. Med., 83:86-92.
111. Shearer, M.J., McBurney, A., Breckinridge, A., et al., 1976. Dose-response relationships between warfarin and the metabolism of phylloquinone (vitamin K) in man. Int. J. Vitamin. Nutr. Res., 46:215-219.
112. Shen, D.D. and Azarnoff, D.L., 1978. Clinical pharmacokinetics of methotrexate. Clin. Pharmacol. Kinet., 3:1-13.
113. Shields, H.M., 1978. Rapid fall of serum phosphorus secondary to antacid therapy. Gastroenterology, 75:1137-1141.
114. Shneerson, J.M. and Gazzard, D.G., 1977. Reversible malabsorption caused by methyldopa. Brit. Med. J., 2:1456-1457.
115. Spiers, A.S.D. and Malone, H.R., 1967. Effect of food on aspirin absorption. Lancet, 1:440.
116. Spivack, S.D., 1974. Procarbazine. Ann. Intern. Med., 81:795-800.
117. Stiel, J.N., Liddle, G.W. and Lacy, W.W., 1970. Studies on mechanism of cyproheptadine-induced weight gain in human subjects. Metabolism, 19:192-200.
118. Suki, W., Yium, J.J., VonMinden, M., et al., 1970. Acute treatment of hypercalcemia with furosemide. New Eng. J. Med., 283:836-840.
119. Van Praag, H.M. Abuse of, dependence on and psychoses from anorexigenic drugs. In Meyler, L., ed.: Drug-Induced Diseases. New York, North Holland Publ. Co., pp. 281-294, 1968.
120. Vessey, M.P., 1978. Contraceptive methods: risks and benefits. Brit. Med. J., 2:721-722.
121. Wan, S.H., Hoffman, D.H., Azarnoff, D.L., et al., 1974. Effect of route of administration and infusions on methotrexate pharmacokinetics. Cancer Res., 34:3487-3491.
122. Welling, P.G., 1977. Influence of food and diet on gastrointestinal absorption: A review. J. Pharmacokinet. Biopharm., 5:291-334.
123. Welling, P.G., Huang, H., Koch, P.A., et al., 1977. Bioavailability of ampicillin and amoxicillin in fasted and nonfasted subjects. J. Pharm. Sci., 66:549-552.
124. Welling, P.G., Lyons, L.L., Tse, F.L.S., et al., 1975. Propoxyphene and norpropoxyphene: Influence of diet and fluid on plasma levels. Clin. Pharmacol. Therap., 19:559-565.
125. Zintel, H.A. Nutrition in the care of the surgical patient. In Wohl, M.G., and Goodhart, R.S., eds.: Modern Nutrition in Health and Disease. Philadelphia, Lea and Febiger, 1968.

MEDICAL INTERACTIONS

How to Nourish the Cancer Patient

by Maurice E. Shils, M.D., Sc.D.

The thirty year incidence trends of the ten most frequent sites of cancer in the United States indicate a remarkable variable picture. The number of cases of cancer of the uterus, stomach and rectum have been declining appreciably, those of the bladder, intestines and breast are essentially stable while the incidence of lung cancer, particularly, is increasing at a great rate not only among men but now also among women. (fig. 1) It can be expected that the total number of patients developing cancer will increase in the next decade if these trends persist, if the number of elderly people continues to rise, and if the mortality rate from coronary artery disease continues to fall. In the future cancer will be the way of dying for more and more people. We wish to make this point at the outset because such a trend will certainly impose new obligations on physicians, dietitians and other health professionals to gain a better understanding of the very special nutrition requirements of the cancer patient.

Cancer must be viewed as being an increasingly protracted disease for many patients for the following reasons: It is being diagnosed earlier; it is being treated more aggressively; and, the treatments, especially radiation and chemotherapy are more effective. This combination results in a prolonged survival by patients suffering from certain types of tumors, even though these may be in an advanced state. Present trends in cancer chemotherapy involve high dose, multiple combinations given in cycles, often over many months or years with chronic or intermittent side effects. Furthermore, even though the disease may be considered arrested or even "cured," the long-term effects of certain surgical procedures, radiation therapy and even chemotherapy may produce physiologic and nutrition problems which persist for many years or for the life of the patient. The need for continuing chemotherapy or the chronic undesirable effects of previous radiation or surgery impose certain psychological stress situations for the patient which add to the uncertainty that the tumor persists. There is a need for recognition by the patient, the physician, dietitian and other health personnel that there must be a continuing concern for all aspects of the individual's welfare in order to maintain and improve the quality of life under circumstances that can be difficult. A major factor in maintaining an optimum quality of life for a given patient is the maintenance of good nutrition status. We hope to provide some pointers how this might be achieved.

One should not think of "the cancer patient" as though each cancer patient has similar kinds of problems. One must consider the individuality of each patient and understand the cause and severity of the nutrition problems that have developed or which are likely to arise. Before one can rationally prevent or treat nutrition deficiencies in cancer patients, one must have a firm understanding of the factors inducing or likely to induce such nutrition problems and the degree to which malnutrition has already occurred. A treatment plan must then be developed which meets the requirements of the individual in the best possible way.

NUTRITION PROBLEMS CAUSED BY CANCER

Cancer may adversely affect the nutrition status of the patient through one or more of three avenues: 1) the systemic effects of cancer itself, 2) the local effects of cancer, and 3) the effects of the various treatments of cancer. Understanding how each of these factors influences nutrition status is essential to developing principles of treatment.

Systemic Effects

A striking and presently unexplained effect of active neoplastic disease in a significant number of patients is the marked loss of appetite which, if prolonged, will lead to wasting of body mass ("cancer cachexia"). This anorexia is often not directly attributable to intestinal obstruction, sepsis, endocrine disorder or other causative anatomical lesions. Although anorexia is not unique to cancer, its high incidence and prolonged and deleterious effect make it of special concern. It is manifested most commonly and noticeably in patients with cancer in one or more areas of the alimentary tract including liver and pancreas and in those with widely disseminated disease. Its etiology is not understood although it has been the subject of many publications and conferences.

The weight loss experienced by many cancer patients is, for the major part, attributable to inadequate food intake resulting from anorexia. It is common for such hospitalized patients to ingest breakfast fairly well and then to eat progressively less of each succeeding meal throughout the day. Our on-going studies with outpatients on cancer chemotheraphy suggest that a different pattern may exist, particularly in women homemakers. They eat breakfast poorly and their "best" meal is usually dinner.

Often the loss of appetite is associated with alterations in taste, leading patients to ascribe their diminished appetite to the unpleasant taste of one or more foods. Efforts have been made to begin to dissect out the prevalence and types of taste alterations in cancer patients. It is the opinion of this author that available data must be viewed as preliminary and variable to the point of being of questionable value. More precise studies are essential before we can be certain of the patterns (if any) that occur in relation to the type and stage of various malignancies. Alterations in taste are probably not primary factors in anorexia but are associated with more basic changes initiated by tumors in association with psychosomatic factors.

It has been suggested by various investigators that cancer per se, not only dampens the desire for food but paradoxically alters energy metabolism so that requirements are increased beyond those of normal individuals. The results of various investigations on this subject have been inconsistent, the cases relatively few, and the available information limited. However, the majority of studies have indicated a tendency toward elevation of energy output especially in patients with leukemia and Hodgkins disease. In a recent study, energy intake although varying greatly in cancer patients was not significantly different from that of controls without malignancy. Both the daily energy expenditure and the resting metabolic rate were significantly greater in the cancer patient than in the controls. The variabilities of energy intake and expenditure of the cancer patient were great and there was a cluster of cancer patients with expenditure similar to that of controls.

While more data are needed, there is reasonable evidence that some cancer patients do have increased resting metabolic expenditure occurring often in a setting of decreased energy intake. Obviously, the anorexia is working against the nutrition interest of the patient by limiting caloric intake during a period of normal or increased expenditure. In the latter case, the patient is at increased risk of depletion during periods of impaired food intake.

There are a number of metabolic changes which may occur in cancer patients which can modify energy expenditure. Fever, surgery and other causes of stress with increased corticosteroid and catecholamine production are not uncommon and these increase protein catabolism with increased gluconeogenesis. However, in addition to such known stimulatory effects on energy requirements, consideration must be given to the effects of the malignancy, per se, on metabolic changes. It has been proposed that the increased rate of resynthesis of glucose in the liver from lactate (Cori cycle) produced by the tumor results in a significant energy drain on host tissues. Cori cycle activity has been measured in a heterogeneous group of patients with metastatic carcinoma and it was found to be increased in those experiencing progressive weight loss. It has been pointed out, however, that increased Cori cycle activity does not appear to account for a significant fraction of daily energy expenditure. The disappearance rate of intravenous glucose is significantly lower in cachectic cancer patients as compared to cancer patients who do not show outward signs of malnutrition and wasting, and normal healthy individuals. Cachectic subjects did not respond normally to glucagon; this suggests an impairment of insulin release with cachexia. It has been proposed also that cancer patients have increased energy cost as the result of increased conversion of glucose to fat before being metabolized but the significance of this is unknown. In summary, it can be stated, however, that there are systemic effects of cancer which lead to increased catabolism of lean body mass and negative energy balance with resultant body wasting.

Malnourished patients with extra-alimentary tract malignancies often have abnormalities of mucosal histology, increased epithelial cell loss and decreased lactose utilization. However, it should be noted that similar changes also are to be seen in seriously malnourished patients without cancer. The data suggest that such mucosal changes are the result of malnutrition rather than the direct cause of cachexia or the direct effects of malignancies outside of the gastrointestinal tract. Once present, of course, impaired mucosal function can contribute further to malnutrition by depressed efficiency of absorption.

"Localized" Tumor Effects

In addition to the systemic effects of cancer that lead to nutrition problems there are a number of more localized ef-

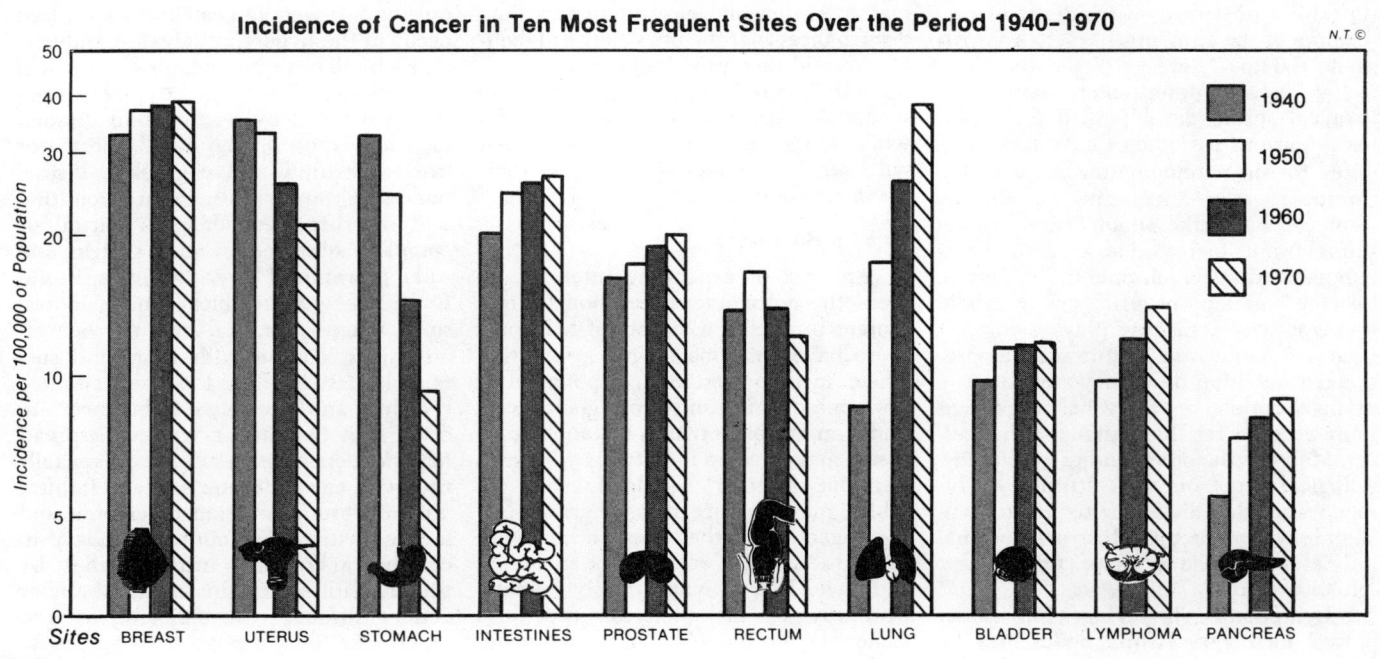

Incidence of Cancer in Ten Most Frequent Sites Over the Period 1940-1970

Figure 1.

fects of various neoplasms that also result in the cancer patient being something less than well nourished.

By far the most common causes of malnutrition in this general category are interferences with food intake as a result of partial or complete obstruction of some portion of the gastrointestinal tract. Relief of the obstruction by surgical or other treatment is necessary to restore normal function. Nutrition support by tube feeding into a site distal to the obstruction or, usually more effectively, by intravenous alimentation may be very useful in sustaining such patients until normal oral feedings can be reinstituted following surgical or other therapy.

Involvement of the pancreas, pancreatic duct or common bile duct by a malignant tumor impairs pancreatic and biliary secretion and may lead to impaired digestion and absorption of fats and fat-soluble vitamins. The resulting decrease in fat absorption soon leads to increased excretion of calcium and magnesium in the feces. With the interference of the normal function of the pancreas, proteins are likely to be much less efficiently absorbed. One should take special note that pancreatic insufficiency may be associated with impaired vitamin B_{12} absorption. The use of parenteral vitamin K and other fat-soluble vitamins is also often helpful in restoring the patient to the best possible nutrition state for surgical procedure in such situations.

Patients suffering with afflictions that promote long-standing intestinal mucosal abnormalities are more inclined to exhibit an increased incidence of carcinoma of the alimentary tract. Approximately 6 to 7 percent of patients with celiac disease (gluten enteropathy, nontropical sprue) develop such malignancies. Various hypotheses have been suggested for the carcinomatous involvement in these patients including possibilities that the abnormal small bowel epithelium permits increased absorption of carcinogens, that the chronic inflammation of the lamina propria or lymphoid hyperactivity somehow plays a role, or that environmental factors such as prolonged nutrition deficiency secondary to malabsorption or intestinal organisms may account for the malignant changes. Many of the older studies had no histological proof of villus atrophy by biopsy and the diagnosis of celiac syndrome was made by history or abnormal fat absorption and/or in response to gluten-free diets.

Lymphoma involving the small bowel mesentery lymph nodes may be present as malabsorption. Because of this relationship lymphoma should be suspected with the onset of the celiac syndrome in middle age especially, but also in young people particularly with certain racial backgrounds. Males above forty years of age with long-standing celiac syndrome who are not on a gluten-free diet are a major risk group.

The mechanisms for the development of malabsorption with intestinal lymphoma are several. The intestinal epithelium may be disrupted by the generalized villus atrophy found in association with lymphomatous involvement. Infiltration of the lamina propria and draining lymph nodes can lead to obstruction of mesenteric lymph channels and dilation of lymphatics within the intestinal villi which in turn can lead to development of a protein-losing enteropathy with hypoalbuminemia, hypoglobulinemia, and lymphocytopenia. Protein-losing enteropathy has also been described with cases of gastric carcinoma.

The blind loop syndrome in the upper small bowel secondary to partial obstruction with bacterial overgrowth may also result in steatorrhea and vitamin B_{12} deficiency. The blind loop syndrome involves not only direct interaction of bacteria with certain nutrients but it also results in the development of abnormalities of the intestinal epithelium and accounts for associated malabsorption common to this condition.

Bypass of small bowel as a result of gastro-colic and jejuno-colic fistulas may also occur in the course of abdominal cancer. These usually lead to significant malabsorption and electrolyte and fluid disturbances that the physician and dietitian should be on the lookout for.

Nutrition replacement and support in such malabsorption syndromes are useful while direct antineoplastic treatment with surgery, radiation and chemotherapy are undertaken.

Ectopic Hormones

An area of expanding interest concerns the autonomous secretion by malignant tumors of a variety of hormones that have pharmacologic properties. These include steroid and polypeptide hormones, kinins and prostaglandins. A wide variety of nutrition-metabolic problems may develop in patients with such hormone-secreting neoplasia, some of which may produce more than one active agent. Diarrhea may occur with gastrin-secreting islet cell adenomas (Zollinger-Ellison syndrome) by tumors, primarily of the pancreas (but also tumors of the bronchus and ganglioneuroblastoma), which secrete vasoactive inhibitory peptide (VIP) and other hormones (Verner-Morrison syndrome or "pancreatic cholera"), by malignant carcinoid tumors of the intestine, by medullary carcinoma of the thyroid, by villus adenoma and ganglioneuroma. Losses of potassium and fluid with Verner-Morrison syndrome and villus adenoma may be severe. Steatorrhea occurs in Zollinger-Ellison syndrome; this has been attributed partly to inactivation of pancreatic lipase by excessive acid production in the stomach and partly to villus damage. While the diarrhea of carcinoid is usually of the watery type, cases of steatorrhea have been reported.

Lowered levels of sodium in the blood, fluid retention and increased urinary sodium losses attributable to inappropriate antidiuretic hormone secretion have been described, most commonly in association with, but not restricted to bronchogenic and oat cell carcinoma, a small anaplastic cellular malignancy frequently found in the bronchi. Medullary carcinoma of the thyroid gland (generally part of multiple endocrine adenomatosis, type III) secretes excessive amounts of calcitonin as well as prostaglandins and histamine and may be associated with pheochromocytoma. Calcitonin induces secretion of water and electrolytes by the jejunal mucosa, thereby explaining the diarrhea. There are reports of malabsorption and diarrhea occurring in patients with systemic mastocytosis, a disease associated with increased secretion of histamine from the mast cells.

Electrolyte disturbances and increased nitrogen and calcium losses often occur in the hyperadrenal state, induced either by the secretion of adrenal cortical carcinoma, or less frequently, by corticotropin secreted by certain solid tumors, especially those in the lung. The major causes of fluid and electrolyte disturbances in cancer patients are vomiting and diarrhea, secondary to partial or complete obstruction, and gastric and small bowel fluid losses through a fistula. Losses of sodium, bicarbonate, potassium, magnesium, and zinc may be serious in association with large and sustained intestinal fluid losses.

Fluid and electrolyte imbalances are often seen in patients with widespread hepatic metastases, ascites and liver failure, with cardiac metastases and failure, with metastatic ovarian carcinoma and ascites, with renal failure secondary to obstruction of the urinary tract by tumor, with obstruction of lymphatic or venous drainage in major areas and other situations described above.

Hypoalbuminemia and anemia are

also frequently noted in advanced cancer cases. The depressed albumin levels are usually secondary to either

• an inability to produce sufficient albumin as a result of serious protein-calorie deficiency, of the metabolic effects of certain tumors or of hepatic insufficiency associated with parenchymal cell damage or replacement by tumor; and/or
• losses of albumin from the body in excess of synthetic capacity, e.g., protein-losing enteropathy or nephrotic syndrome; and/or
• dilution of albumin into abnormally large extra-cellular compartments (e.g., ascites and edema).

Hypoalbuminemia will respond to appropriate nutrition therapy when malnutrition is the primary or an important contributory factor. Antitumor therapy is obviously indicated to treat the direct effects of neoplastic growth.

The etiology of an existing anemia must be evaluated appropriately. The physician is cautioned that it may be secondary to insufficiency of hematopoietic nutrition factors; if so, it should be treated with the necessary nutrient. On the other hand, a normochromic normocytic anemia is not infrequently associated with cancer and does not respond to nutrition factors. Radiation and chemotherapy may also be contributing factors by virtue of their depressive effects on bone marrow. Hemolytic anemia or that secondary to erythrocyte sequestration in hypersplenism are other potential causes of anemia.

Vitamins

Vitamin levels may be low in cancer patients for reasons already explained. However, much of the depletion is secondary to poor intake and this is exacerbated in some people by losses through abnormal alimentary tract and renal function. Abnormalities in folate metabolism may occur in acute and chronic leukemias. Patients with leukemias, disseminated lymphomas and various metastatic carcinomas tend to have low serum folate levels. It has been known for some time that serum vitamin B_{12} levels are elevated when body neutrophils are increased, e.g., chronic myelogenous leukemia and in the presence of metastatic liver disease. The rise results from an increase in transcobalamins I and III. The high serum levels do not necessarily mean that tissue levels are not depleted.

Any interference in the complex digestive and absorptive mechanisms can depress vitamin nutrition as well as that

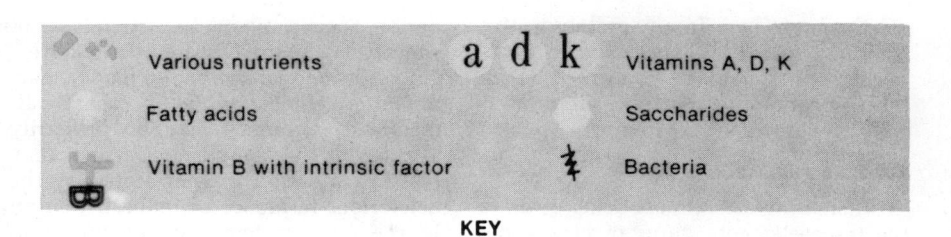

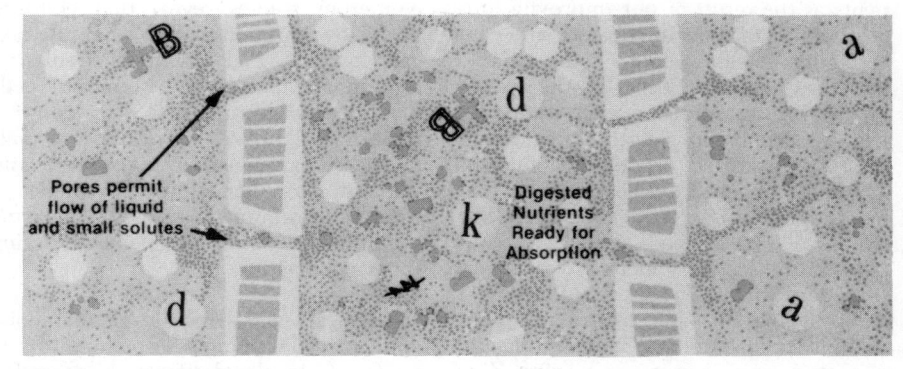

KEY

Various nutrients
Fatty acids
Vitamin B with intrinsic factor
a d k Vitamins A, D, K
Saccharides
Bacteria

NORMAL ABSORPTION

MALABSORPTION AND BACTERIA BUILDUP

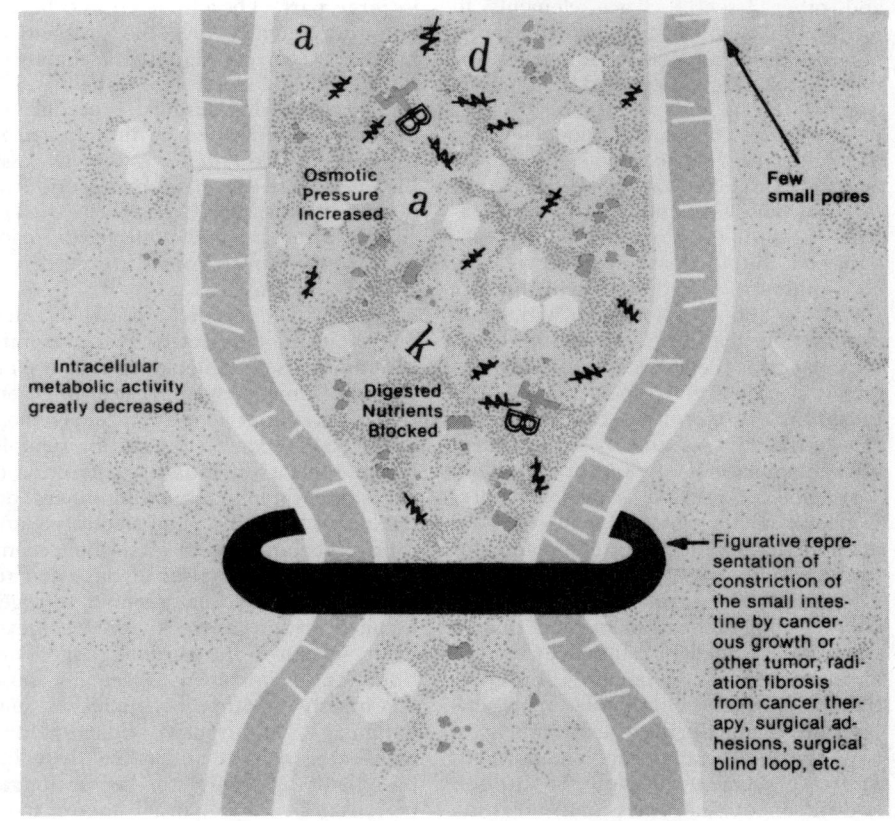

Diagram of the mechanism of the *Blind Loop Syndrome*. A constriction of the small intestine causes the passage of the chime to slow and the jejunum above the stricture to distend. In the semi-stagnant chime, the bacteria multiply enormously, damaging the jejunal mucosa and consuming Vitamin B_{12}; transport of nutrients through the cell membrane is impaired by reduction of the pores' size and number and reduction of metabolic activity.

of other nutrients. In any malabsorptive state resulting from cancer and its treatments, one should be concerned about the absorption of fat-soluble vitamins as well as water-soluble vitamins.

Minerals and Trace Elements

Increasing attention is being given to the trace elements status of cancer patients as the result of our improving understanding of their importance and ease of clinical measurement. The available data are primarily those of the survey type of serum and urine levels and some tissue concentrations with little knowledge of associated or etiologic factors. The levels of certain mineral ions such as magnesium and trace elements reflect the intake, basic needs, and losses. Impaired intake and/or increased excretion secondary to organ disease will lower serum values of key electrolytes, e.g., sodium, potassium and magnesium and of certain trace elements, e.g., zinc. Zinc losses are particularly significant in small bowel drainage and this is reflected in low serum levels. Failure to provide this and other essential trace elements in intravenous or tube feedings will exacerbate the problem. Serum copper, on the other hand, is often elevated in malnourished cancer patients and those with liver disease. Since copper and manganese are dependent on bile secretion as a major avenue of elimination, increased serum levels of these elements occur with intrahepatic and extrahepatic biliary obstruction. Rapid tissue breakdown with chemotherapy or radiation will increase excretion, and, in association with renal dysfunction, lead to rises in serum levels of those trace elements ordinarily excreted into the urine. Since zinc is bound to certain serum proteins, its level will be affected by disease and by drugs which affect the levels of binding proteins.

A note of caution is in order here. Cancer is such a profound, consequential disease that patients often reach for straws. This makes them vulnerable to promises of easy cure. This is the reason why a strong element of medical quackery has developed in relation to the use of trace elements in cancer. Unsubstantiated claims are being made for the importance of measuring trace elements in hair with associated recommendations for trace element therapy. So little is known about the roles and nutrition needs of certain trace elements, e.g., manganese and selenium, that caution must be advised in suggesting supplementation for the cancer patient.

It is well established that immune responses are often depressed in a number of cancer patients. In certain types of cancer, Hodgkins Disease is a good example, hormonal antibodies may be particularly deficient while in others cell-mediated immunity may be primarily affected as the complement system may be. The situation is complicated by the deleterious influence of malnutrition on host defense systems against infection. Numerous studies reveal that children with low protein-calorie malnutrition can have normal or high circulating immunoglobulins but impaired cell-mediated immunity and low complement levels. Improved nutrition of malnourished animals or man with and without malignancies usually results in improved immune responses. That rule should be kept in mind when considering the cancer patient.

Treatment

Reversal of the undesirable metabolic and nutrition changes secondary to systemic and localized effects of cancer for any significant period depends primarily upon how successful the cancer team is in eliminating the malignancy entirely or in large part. The physician and his dietitian frequently face the problem of having to correct significant malnutrition, fluid and electrolyte imbalances in patients requiring surgical procedure or in those who need to be maintained in the best possible state for as long as possible in order to permit a therapeutic trial of radiation and/or chemotherapy. The careful attention and positive approach of these two professionals are needed to correct abnormalities.

As with all chronic, wasting diseases, one should not expect to restore significant amounts of depleted tissue in a short period of time. Urgent surgical intervention often cannot wait upon achievement of the goal of complete nutrition rehabilitation. In such a situation correction of acute or chronic vitamin and mineral deficiencies, blood loss, and electrolyte and fluid imbalances can often be accomplished within a matter of days and reversal of negative caloric and nitrogen balance within a week. This achievement improves the surgical risk. Continuation of intravenous feeding postoperatively is often beneficial in such patients. When surgery is indicated for a debilitated patient and when there has been and is likely to be prolonged periods of little or no oral intake of food, prompt initiation of procedures to improve nutrition and metabolic status by adequate parenteral or tube feeding may be an aid to survival or to decreased morbidity and possibly a shortened period of convalescence.

NUTRITION PROBLEMS CAUSED BY CANCER TREATMENT

Significant nutrition problems may arise as the result of a specific treatment instituted in an effort to eradicate or palliate the neoplastic disease. This section discusses briefly some of the more common problems in this area.

Radiation

Radiation therapy is a valuable treatment modality. Improvements in radiation sources, ports and shielding have increased tumor responsiveness and decreased the period a patient is ill. However, the need to provide effective radiation dosage and different ways in which a patient may respond to radiation therapy may induce a variety of serious, acute and chronic effects on the patient's nutrition status that must be dealt with. Serious psychological, physiologic, and nutrition after-effects may result from radiation (often combined with surgery) of the head and neck.

The resulting loss of taste sensation— some patients call it "mouth blindness" —or xerostomia (dry mouth) consequent to decreased salivary secretion and damage to alveolar bone and teeth make chewing and swallowing more difficult. These effects may combine to create a potentially serious situation since the patients often have depressed appetites. When all food becomes tasteless, appearance and aroma become much more important. Chewing and swallowing of dry foods is assisted by use of gravies and salad dressings. Supplementary liquid formulas improve total intake. Some patients find it easier to swallow soft foods than liquids. Education and testing of foods and techniques to minimize aspiration are important. Where aspiration during swallowing is a chronic problem, tube feeding is indicated as a preventive measure or the patient may have to undergo a laryngectomy (with resulting loss of voice) separating the alimentary and respiratory tracts.

Radiation to the lower neck and mediastinum may induce esophagitis after several weeks of therapy but this usually disappears following cessation of the treatment. A delayed effect which may occur is fibrosis resulting in esophageal stricture with dysphagia and difficulty in swallowing.

Radiation damage to the small and large bowel occurs in a small but significant number of patients receiving external and/or internal radiation therapy. The epithelium of the small bowel is second only to bone marrow in its sensitivity to radiation. Acute radiation effects may occur with altered intestinal function during therapy manifested by diarrhea or nausea; these usually disappear within a period after terminating radiation. Some patients may then go on to develop "late" radiation changes after a brief period or later. The interval may, on occasion, be many years. Flattening and ulceration of the mucosa, telangiectasis, fibrosis, endarteritis of small vessels and stenosis of the bowel may develop and these changes are often progressive. Obstruction and fistula formation may occur and require bowel resection. While the presence of adjacent radiation-damaged tissue may make surgery more difficult, the obstructive symptoms are often remediable. Consequently exploratory laparotomy is recommended before malnutrition increases the risk. Obstruction or fistula may recur necessitating further surgical intervention. In our experience, patients with severe radiation damage and previous resection are more difficult to manage than patients with massive small bowel resection alone. Intermittent obstruction, diarrhea, malabsorption and chronic intestinal and bladder blood loss create a multitude of problems in nutrition and electrolyte balance. However, with close follow-up and attention to nutrition requirements utilizing enteral or parenteral routes of feeding, these patients may do very well.

Surgery

The effects of surgery for the removal of organs or parts of the body are varied and many. Most of these procedures and their sequelae are, of course, not peculiar to surgery for cancer. However, certain resections—extensive resection of the head and neck or total gastrectomy, to name but a few—are much more common or limited almost entirely to patients with cancer.

Surgery of the Head and Neck

Radical surgery of the head and neck region, often includes partial or total removal of the tongue, resection of muscles and salivary glands and varying degrees of mandibulectomy. Naturally, these extensive amputations lead to difficulties with mastication and swallowing. Where prolonged tube feeding may be required, patients or family members can be taught to insert a nasopharyngeal tube so that patients can avoid the psychologic trauma and throat irritation associated with an indwelling tube. For those unable to pass the tube, its insertion via an esophagostomy or gastrostomy is recommended.

Surgery of the Digestive Tract

Esophagectomy often induces gastric stasis, diarrhea, and significant malabsorption of fat. The cause of these dysfunctions appears to be bilateral vagotomy inherent in the procedure. However, the precise mechanisms for the diarrhea and steatorrhea are unknown. Carbohydrate absorption is normal. The use of medium-chain triglycerides (MCT) as a major portion of fat intake diminishes the steatorrhea. Since the stomach (with its proximal resection) is often pulled up into the chest and since gastric emptying may be delayed, frequent small meals are more acceptable to the patient than are large meals.

Gastrectomy

The physiologic and nutrition consequences of subtotal and total gastrectomy are multiple as a result of the loss of the reservoir, titurating, diluting, enzymatic and other functions of the stomach and the accelerated flow of undigested food into the jejunum. Clinical problems increase proportionately to the extent of the resection. In addition to the well-known occurrences of dumping syndrome, with its discomforting flushing, sweating, dizziness, weakness and, frequently, vasomotor collapse, hypoglycemia, steatorrhea, afferent loop syndrome with its pain and distension after eating and followed usually by vomiting of pure bile, and the loss of intrinsic factor, there may be the insidious development of various vitamin and mineral deficiencies. The dumping syndrome may be so severe and unpleasant that the patient may be afraid to eat. Serious and continuing attention by the physician to prevent and ameliorate patient's nutrition problems is essential for long-term health when the underlying disease is benign or when the malignancy is believed to have been eradicated or controlled by chemotherapy.

Intestinal Resection

Clinical studies in normal subjects and in those in whom varying portions of small intestine have been removed indicate that all nutrients, with the exception of vitamin B_{12}, are most efficiently and (in the usual dietary amounts) rather completely absorbed in the proximal small bowel, the jejunum. The small amount of undigested food passing through the jejunum is then absorbed in the upper ileum. Following jejunal resection for any reason, the ileum, with its reserve absorptive capacity, can absorb these nutrients in good degree if adequate nutrition status, that permits maximal hyperplasia with an increase in the size of the villi, is maintained.

When the terminal ileum has been removed, bypassed or damaged, there will be decreased absorption of both vitamin B_{12} and conjugated bile salts since this is the site of their physiologic absorption. Provision of vitamin B_{12} intramuscularly in doses of 100 mcg every month will prevent the development of a vitamin B_{12} deficiency.

Failure to reabsorb conjugated bile salts in the normal efficient manner will result in one of several problems. If the ileum resection is not extensive, (say it is usually less than 100 cm), sufficient bile salts enter the large bowel to induce a brown water diarrhea, a condition which may be very distressing to the patient. Cholestyramine can be dramatically effective in controlling such a choleric diarrhea by its mechanism of binding bile salts. With more extensive resection, the loss of bile salts may be such that the limited capacity of the liver to synthesize sufficient new bile salts may be exceeded and their concentration in the intestinal lumen will fall below the critical micellar level. Consequently, fat absorption will be depressed and steatorrhea will ensue. In such a situation, the patient will be helped by a diet low in long-chain fats and supplemented with medium-chain triglycerides (MCT), which do not require bile salts for their absorption. The use of water-soluble forms of vitamin K and more of the other fat-soluble vitamins is indicated to prevent deficiency of these nutrients. Sufficient polyunsaturated fats should be fed to assure an adequate essential fatty acid intake.

Another consequence of ileum resection is hyperoxaluria which poses the risk of renal oxalate stone formation. This is due to the fact that the normal precipitation of oxalate ion by intestinal calcium ions is prevented by a shortage of such free calcium ions because of their binding to fatty acids present in increased amounts in the remaining small bowel and colon by the steatorrheic ileectomized patients. The soluble oxalate is then absorbed in the colon. It appears in the urine in increased concentrations with resultant probability of precipitation as calcium oxalate in the renal tubule. On the basis of the explanation a reduced fat intake appears advisable together with an increased intake of calcium salts.

Malabsorption may also be associated with magnesium depletion and decreased citrate concentration in the urine. Deficiencies of these substances in the urine contribute to the likelihood of oxalate stone formation. Consequently, they should be provided.

Massive small bowel resection, with a residual of less than three feet (especially in older individuals) presents very serious and long-term problems in maintaining adequate nutrition, including water and electrolytes. If there is some radiation damage to the remaining bowel or loss of ileocecal valve and portions of the colon, the problems are intensified. However, the application of present knowledge of how to care for these patients will often permit a successful outcome.

Pancreatic Insufficiency

Pancreatic insufficiency is a result of the surgical treatment of cancer of the pancreas. Pancreatectomy with consequent loss of digestive enzymes leads to loss into the stool not only of fats and of protein, but also of significant amounts of various vitamins and minerals. Pancreatectomy necessitates partial gastrectomy and duodenectomy with a gastrojejunal anastamosis and this is a complicating factor predisposing to additional malabsorption.

The situation is further complicated by the fact that even subtotal pancreatectomy with anastomosis of the duct of the remaining portion of the pancreas to the jejunum is associated fairly frequently with both exocrine and endocrine pancreatic insufficiency. Total pancreatectomy, of course, promptly induces diabetes mellitus. The diabetic state occurring in conjunction with impaired carbohydrate, protein and fat digestion further complicates the nutrition management of such patients. The use of MCT, hydrolyzed protein and oligosaccharides may be beneficial since these do not require pancreatic enzymes for further digestion of absorption.

Pancreatic enzyme insufficiency may be effectively replaced by potent pancreatic extracts given with meals or at two-hour intervals. An important factor is adequate dosage of the extract with meals. The use of antacids or the histamine H_2 receptor antagonist, cimetidine, is often beneficial when gastric secretion is normal or high since the latter may inactivate the pancreatic enzymes. There may be impaired vitamin B_{12} absorption with pancreatectomy and this is improved by administration of pancreatic extract. The diabetes mellitus following the resection is usually of the "brittle" type, requiring relatively small amounts of insulin and is rather difficult to control with precision. Hence, tolerance of some glycosuria is safer than the hypoglycemic episodes which may occur with achievement of glucose-free urine.

Major Hepatic Resection

The liver has a remarkable ability to regenerate by cellular hypertrophy and hyperplasis following massive resection. Immediate postoperative problems are met by glucose and albumin infusions and adequate replacement of electrolytes including phosphate.

Chemotherapy

As a result of new drug development and better understanding of therapeutic application, significant and, in some cases, dramatic improvement in the treatment of a number of types of cancer has occurred. Most of the present chemotherapeutic agents exert this effectiveness by inhibiting one or more key phases in the intermediary metabolism of cells —normal as well as neoplastic—particularly those reactions involving the syntheses of purines, pyrimidines, DNA and RNA. Since the epithelial cells of the small intestine move along the villi rapidly before being shed into the lumen, it is to be expected that many of these drugs will adversely affect intestinal functions to some degree depending upon the drug dosage, the duration of treatment, the rates of metabolism and individual susceptibility. The epithelium of the mouth and large bowel can also be affected and so can other organs.

Adrenocortico-steroids are commonly used in treatment of certain types of cancer. They have metabolic effects and influence nutrition status in ways which are well known; they include depletion of nitrogen from muscle and loss of calcium and potassium from the body. Such effects may be significant to the patient depending on the type of steroid, dosage, and duration of treatment.

There has been increasing use of multi-combination, high-dose, cyclical chemotherapy as the result of

• the frequent occurrence of resistance of malignant cells to a single drug,
• the realization of the need to kill the entire population of neoplastic cells in order to obtain a "cure," and
• improved understanding of the sites in DNA and RNA synthesis at which various chemotherapeutic agents have their effect.

These treatment programs, while increasingly effective against various malignancies, also result in prolonged periods of anorexia and nausea because of the way such drugs affect the alimentary tract and impair food intake. Since treatments may be prolonged, weight loss and progressive debility is frequently severe. These undesirable reactions are intensified when radiation therapy to the abdomen or surgery of the intestinal tract further decreases appetite or impairs intestinal function. Adequate nutrition support with nutrient mixtures specifically formulated for such occasions makes a major contribution in permitting patients on these regimens to maintain weight and strength.

Prolonged inadequate intake or utilization of food for any of the reasons discussed above will lead to advanced malnutrition.

NUTRITION THERAPY IN THE CANCER PATIENT

With the exceptions of certain resistant leukemias, cancer is usually a lingering illness. It is rarely abruptly fatal. Now, with the discovery and use of more effective treatments it has become an affliction that is even more chronic, more protracted. It is, consequently, a condition that is more demanding of attention to nutrition by the physician and dietitian than ever before. More successful palliation or potential "cure" of cancer is associated often with a requirement for variably long-term chemotherapy treatment schedules. Years must elapse before the patient and physician are willing to admit that the disease may be "cured." The physician and patient are faced, each in his own way, with the effects of the disease process, the psychological impact of its presence, and the long-term problems of treatment modalities and their side effects. These factors often combine to adversely affect the quality of life of the patient. Add to this the demands of proper nutrition that these circumstances impose and it is easy to see that the problems are accentuated and there is increased morbidity and mortality. If the physician undertakes current treatment modalities, a sincere effort should be made to improve or maintain the quality of life because this makes for a reasonably comfortable and functioning individual. Concern for patient status should begin with the initial treatment and continue through to the hoped for long-term survival.

Various principles of nutrition therapy in the cancer patient are summarized here as follows:

• Malnutrition is not an obligatory response of the host to cancer. It is relatively uncommon to find a cancer patient who cannot be either maintained in

good nutrition status or improved when previously malnourished by means of appropriate therapeutic modalities (i.e., oral, tube or intravenous feeding).
- A rational nutrition therapeutic program for a patient requires analysis of the factors inducing depletion in that patient. Every patient should have an initial and then periodic follow-up assessments of nutrition status so that the already malnourished patients or those at risk of developing malnutrition are detected as early as possible.
- Nutrition therapy should be instituted early when the patient is deemed to be at risk for malnutrition since it is much easier to maintain a reasonably good state of nutrition than it is to try to rehabilitate the already debilitated.
- It is essential that the patient who has had improvement in nutrition status in the hospital be followed after discharge in such a manner that the nutrition therapy program is not neglected.
- Who is to be given aggressive nutrition therapy? If antitumor therapy of one type or another is to be undertaken, the patient deserves nutrition therapy so long as the treatment is applied and is being evaluated. If, on the other hand, the patient is not considered a suitable candidate for any further type of treatment, nutrition therapy is not to be stressed except in rare instances.
- Nutrition therapy can be divided into: a) supportive, b) adjunctive, and c) definitive. Supporting therapy is exemplified by the patient with bowel obstruction who is deemed a poor surgical risk because of malnutrition and who will be clinically improved by nutrition means to the point where surgery can be undertaken at appreciably lower risk. Adjunctive nutrition therapy is the type where nutrition becomes a part of the therapeutic program. Examples of this are: a) improving resistance to infection by improving immune status, b) permitting more rapid application and better adherence to a proposed antitumor therapeutic regimen by improved nutrition, or c) inducing spontaneous closure of an intestinal fistula as a result of nutrition therapy. Definitive nutrition therapy is defined as that where the therapy becomes the modality upon which the longer term existence of the patient depends, i.e., when the nutrition program permits survival of a patient in good condition who has had a massive bowel resection or severe radiation enteritis, or both, and where debility or death will result without such therapy. This may be a short or long term endeavor. The therapeutic modalities necessary to achieve these objectives should be available for inpatients and outpatients.
- Nutrition status, tumor growth, and antitumor treatment are intimately related. Many of the most potent cytoxic agents used in antitumor therapy have optimum activity against cells that are in the process of division. Hence, malignancies are most susceptible to chemotherapeutic measures where a high percentage of cells are in that stage. Nutrition plays a role in the rate of cell growth and mitosis. Improved nutrition by mouth or by parenteral feeding of experimental animals with transplanted tumors results in improved weight of the host; tumor weight may increase proportionately or to a greater extent. Clinical experience indicates it is a rare patient who has marked acceleration of growth of tumor during a period of improved nutrition. Increased residual tumor growth would be expected in patients given more adequate nutrition since tumor cells have a dependency on good nutrition as do host cells. However, improved nutrition may be a therapeutically useful occurrence since actively dividing tumor cells are more likely to be more sensitive to radiation therapy and chemotherapy than are slowly dividing cells. It is my opinion that it is not in the interest of the tumor-bearing patient who is a candidate for treatment to be carried on nutrition therapy without at the same time having institution of adequate antitumor therapy.

WHAT CAN BE DONE

This brief review indicates the complexity of the factors that may intervene to place the cancer patient at serious risk for developing malnutrition. The numerous possibilities that may affect one or another individual make it clear that a simplistic non-analytical approach will fail to meet specific needs and may, in fact, do harm. A thorough understanding is essential of 1) the patient's status, 2) his or her requirements, and 3) the techniques of various feeding modalities which may be employed in order to institute a rational therapeutic regimen.

It has been emphasized that a very significant number of cancer patients present either short-term or long-term nutrition problems as the result of their disease and/or of its treatment. While an adequate oral intake (regular foods with supplements as indicated) is highly desirable, it is often not achievable in the anorectic or malabsorbing patient. If the individual is under active treatment or post-treatment and doing reasonably well except for prolonged anorexia, and if he or she has a functioning intestinal tract, tube feeding with up-to-date techniques is often very beneficial. When the alimentary tract cannot be used, intravenous feeding is obviously essential. Discussion of specific aspects of the alternative techniques is beyond the scope of this paper but their competent use is another facet of the adequate nutrition management of the cancer patient.

The Interaction of Vitamins with Cancer Chemotherapy

by Joseph R. DiPalma, M.D., and Robert McMichael, B.S.

The role that vitamins play in the growth and development of the cancer cell is understood only in certain instances. For example, methotrexate—which is actually a folate antivitamin—is effectively used as a chemotherapeutic agent and its toxic actions are well controlled by leucovorin, a folate vitamin.[1] However, there is conflicting evidence and relatively little known about the importance of such critical vitamins as cholecalciferol, ascorbic acid, niacin, pyridoxine, thiamine and riboflavin, to mention only a few. Many studies on nutrition in cancer make special efforts to relate the protein content of the diet to cancer growth and immune capacity of the host, but fail to investigate the specific influence of vitamin content or deficiency, which may be of equal importance.[2] (There are those who invent dubious vitamin substances or are advocates of "megavitamin therapy" for cancer without firm scientific or clinical basis.[3]) In the past ten years impressive experimental data have accumulated relating vitamins to the induction of cancer by carcinogens and the course of malignant disease.[4-7]

The great improvement in the technology of performing vitamin serum level assays—mostly as a result of the development of radioimmune assays—has placed a powerful tool in the hands of clinicians and researchers. It is now possible to assay serum levels of vitamins present in only minute amounts, such as B_{12}. This provides exact informtion on the presence of deficiency or excess.

The purpose of this article is to report on the role of vitamins in: (1) the induction of cancer by carcinogens; (2) the enhancement or inhibition of chemotherapy; and (3) the course of malignant disease. Contrary to popular opinion, vitamins can be quite toxic and cannot be used indiscriminantly.[8] In cancer chemotherapy their use is especially critical and we need more information.

Vitamin A

Because vitamin A has a natural role in the preservation of the function of cell membranes—particularly epithelium—it and other retinoic acid analogues have been widely used with some success in the therapy of such diseases as leukoplakia.[9] More recently retinoic acid has been used topically in skin diseases such as acne, psoriasis and icthyosis. Promising results have been obtained in cystic and anglobate acne with 13-cis-retinoic acid.[10] However, caution is necessary because it has been demonstrated that in nude mice retinoic acid causes sensitization of the skin to ultraviolet light and an increased susceptibility to epidermal cancers.[11]

Far more important is the development of a concept of "chemoprevention," which involves certain lung neoplasias and vitamin A analogues, or retinoids.[4] (See also Sporn MB: Retinoids and Cancer Prevention. CA: 29:120-125, 1979). This therapy attempts to block key metabolic pathways during the period of preneoplasia rather than attempting to destroy developed and established cancer cells. There is a balance between the induction of neoplasia by carcinogens and its inhibition by nutritive agents. The problem becomes one of "selective toxicity," a familiar one in pharmacology.[12,13] Additional data come from an epidemiological study of 8,000 male smokers in Norway that relates the incidence of lung cancer to a low dietary intake of vitamin A.[14]

Considerable experimental evidence clearly demonstrates that retinoids, like hormones, control cell differentiation and growth in target organs such as bronchi, trachea, stomach, intestine, uterus, kidney, bladder, testis, prostate, pancreatic ducts and skin.[15] In organ cultures of prostate glands, hyperplastic and anaplastic epithelial lesions induced by chemical carcinogens can be reversed by retinoids.[16,17] Retinoid deficiency may enhance the binding of the carcinogens or their metabolites to epithelial DNA.[18]

Unfortunately, vitamin A itself cannot be used in large enough doses for a sufficient period of time to be therapeutically effective without causing hypervitaminosis A.[8] Fortunately, synthetic retinoids that modify the basic molecule, either in the hydrocarbon ring, the side chain or the polar terminal group, retain their antineoplastic properties and are much less toxic systemically.[4] Some of these derivatives show great promise experimentally and it is likely that controlled human studies will be undertaken (at least one is underway now in the study of bladder cancer) with the best available compounds.

Vitamin C

The so-called "Orthomolecular Therapy" of cancer with "megadoses" of vitamin C (up to 10 grams a day) has received a great deal of popular attention. The beneficial actions claimed are:

- relief of pain from skeletal metastases;
- reduction of opiate dosage;

- correction of high urinary hydroxyproline;
- tumor regression and prolonged life expectancy.[19-22]

However, evidence for benefit is based on uncontrolled and non-randomized clinical trials. While therapeutic actions remain unconfirmed by other researchers or by a well-conducted clinical trial, there has been considerable effort expended to discover a secure experimental basis. It is claimed that vitamin C either slows down or stops the growth of malignant cells by inhibiting the action of hyaluronidase, the substance necessary for cell division, proliferation and migration.[23] Recently, all the possible mechanisms of potential beneficial action have been reviewed.[24]

In lung cultures, the addition of either L-cysteine or ascorbic acid to the medium protects against the abnormal growth and malignant transformation induced by exposure to smoke from tobacco or marijuana cigarettes. This protection was afforded to both young and old cultures.[25] Decrease of DNA synthesis and neoplastic cell proliferation have been observed for ascorbic acid in tumor cell lines in culture.[26] A mutagenic action of vitamin C has been demonstrated in fibroblast cultures.[27] Tumor bearing guinea pigs require ascorbic acid for tumor growth.[28] Thus, it is seen even in this brief review that at least experimentally there is ample evidence of an interaction of vitamin C with both neoplastic cells and carcinogenic agents.

It is not entirely true that vitamin C therapy is without risk. When taken in daily gram amounts for prolonged periods, vitamin C can be toxic.[8] Perhaps its most serious reaction is the depression of B_{12} serum levels that may lead to bone marrow changes.[29-31] The utilization and distribution of B_{12} is a factor in carcinogenesis. Consequently, the effect of vitamin C upon Vitamin B_{12} may be indirectly involved in the problem of carcinogenesis.

The relationship of vitamin C therapy to the radiosensitivity of neoplastic tissues is also significant because inhibition of cellular oxidation protects tumors against radiation to a considerable degree. The chemical reaction of ascorbate with radiation induced radicals and the resulting additional oxygen consumption may produce a greater degree of hypoxia and subsequent radioprotection. Drugs such as metronidazol and Flagyl (which inhibit cellular oxygen consumption) cause reoxygenation of tumor tissue and hence increase radiosensitivity.[32] Obviously, patients taking large amounts of ascorbic acid are subject to an inhibiting interaction with radiosensitizing drugs and this should be guarded against.

Vitamin B_{12}

In rat leukemia therapy with cis-diammine-chloroplatinum, the addition of vitamin B_{12} and the citrovorum factor greatly increased the life span of the animals.[33] In humans it has been found that a high serum B_{12} level usually implies a poor prognosis in a patient with hepatic cancer.[34] In hepatocellular carcinoma, serum B_{12} unsaturated binding capacity provides a simple method of following the course of chemotherapy. This is related to the production of high serum levels of a B_{12} binding glycoprotein by such tumors as malignant hepatoma.[35,36]

In the experimental production of hepatic tumors with aflatoxins there is some evidence that B_{12} potentiates chemical carcinogenesis and tumor formation.[37] Of greater importance in this study was the protein level of the diet. B_{12} increases the excretion of urinary N-formino-L-glutamic acid, as do several chemical carcinogens (e.g., diethylnitrosamine), which similarly interfere with enzymes involved in the metabolism of carbon compounds.[38] This may partially explain the results of the study.

While the exact role of vitamin B_{12} in chemical carcinogenesis is still obscure, there is little doubt that it is involved. In hepatocellular carcinoma, B_{12} is clinically useful as a diagnostic and prognostic tool in the form of serially followed serum levels. In some instances, its administration may accelerate the course of the disease, while in others it may increase survival time.

Pyridoxine, B_6

Pyridoxal phosphate is the essential co-enzyme for biosynthetic reactions concerned with antibody production and cell-mediated immunity. In advanced metastatic carcinoma of the breast and other tissues, there is a substantially lower pyridoxal phosphate level as compared to normal controls. It is still unknown whether the anergic state of advanced breast cancer patients is due to B_6 deficiency or if it can be reversed by B_6 therapy.[39]

A comparative study of the effectiveness of placebo, topical thiotepa and pyridoxine in preventing recurrence of stage 1 bladder cancer showed that oral pyridoxine was significantly more effective than the placebo. Indeed, it equaled local thiotepa in effectiveness.[40] In the therapy of primary and metastatic liver carcinoma with intrahepatic arterial infusion of Mitomycin-c and 5-fluorouracil, the addition of pyridoxine led to a lower incidence of toxicity.[41]

There have been attempts to produce B_6 antivitamins such as 4-halovinyl and 4-ethinyl-4-diformyl-pyridoxal derivatives. These do inhibit mouse mammary carcinoma in cell culture and in some instances the inhibition may be reversed by pyridoxine.[42]

Vitamin E

The exact requirements for this fat soluble vitamin in human metabolism and its mechanism of action remain an enigma. Most explanations of its action are based on the fact that it is an antioxidant and the belief that it is a general protector of structural lipoproteins or of oxidizable lipid components. Recent work considers selenium an essential component of glutathione peroxidase, which destroys H_2O_2 and organic hydroperoxides, which in turn protects cell membranes against oxidative damage. Selenium works in conjunction with vitamin E; the latter prevents the formation of liquid hydroperoxides.[43]

The drug andriamycin (doxorubicin) is an effective chemotherapeutic agent whose mechanism of action is suppression of DNA synthesis. Unfortunately, it also causes peroxidation of cardiac lipids and as a result, along with its other toxic side-effects, it is specifically cardiotoxic. Prior therapy of mice with alpha tocopherol greatly reduces the cardiac toxicity of adriamycin without inhibiting its anti-tumor effects.[44] The administration of selenium-vitamin E to weanling rabbits treated chronically with adriamycin results in decreased incidence of cardiomyopathy and increased survival time.[45] Clinical studies are now in progress that indicate that vitamin E does afford protection against adriamycin cardiotoxicity. However, this does not obviate the need for careful monitoring and follow-up of the cardiac status of patients receiving adriamycin.

Vitamin K

It is now known that vitamin K is a component of a microsomal carboxylase system. Studies of this system have uncovered a new amino acid, gamma carboxyglutamic acid (Gla), which is a component of prothrombin and phylogenetically related proteins that are found in bone and renal tissue. It is suspected that vitamin K dependent proteins—which have strong calcium and phospholipid binding properties—are involved at the membrane level in the metabolism of calcium.[46]

The carcinogen 4-nitroquinoline-1-oxide and its metabolites have properties similar to vitamin K at the subcellular level.[47] The mean number of spontaneous lung metastases from Lewis lung carcinomas was reduced in three groups of C57BL mice when vitamin K deprivation was induced by adding the vitamin K antagonist phenprocoumon to the drinking water.[48] It is believed that fibrinolysis and prevention of platelet aggregation are important elements in preventing metastasis; in light of this, intravenous chemotherapy with adjunctive coumadin anticoagulants may represent a new approach to the prevention of metastases.[49,50] There is growing evidence and conviction that vitamin K has a role in chemical carcinogenesis.[51-53] Vitamin K antivitamins may prove beneficial clinically, especially in the prevention of metastasis.[49]

Miscellaneous Vitamins

Riboflavin deficiency has been shown to stimulate azo dye carcinogenesis and to inhibit tumor growth in man and animals. Other work with riboflavin demonstrates an inhibition of uptake of methotrexate by neoplastic cells and also a slight inhibitory effect in 3, 4-benzopyrene-induced skin tumors.[54,55]

About one-third of patients receiving 5-fluorouracil therapy were found to have thiamine deficiency as compared to normal controls. When the thiamine was replaced there was rapid progression of the tumor and such therapy may be detrimental.[56]

Niacin is crucial to the function of the pyridine nucleotides NAD and NADP and could be expected to have a significant role in carcinogenesis but this relationship has not been thoroughly studied. However, in one of the few studies that have been conducted niacin appeared to promote the development of kidney neoplasias induced by diethylnitrosamine. It is known that niacin will increase the incidence of pancreatic islet-cell tumors after the administration of streptozotocin. On the other hand, niacin will prevent the depletion of NAD coenzymes by alkylating agents.[57] Thus, the role of niacin in chemical carcinogenesis remains obscure and requires further inquiry.

Comment

It is obvious that no blanket recommendations can be made with respect to the use of either vitamins or antivitamins as adjunctive cancer therapy, except where the clinical therapeutic benefit has been substantiated. However, this subject has been neglected too long and what is needed are more accurate and detailed observations of carcinogenesis and its course in humans, with particular emphasis on diet and crucial dietary factors such as vitamins and the quality of protein intake. There are areas in which further study of the interaction of vitamins with cancer chemotherapy may bring improvement to what is currently a bleak therapeutic outlook:

- Smokers may be able to protect themselves with vitamin A derivatives.
- There may be dietary factors in the development of stomach cancer that interact with environmental carcinogens to either enhance or prevent the disease.
- The incidence of metastatic disease may perhaps be minimized by dietary manipulation.

Examination of most patient charts shows little or no reference to detailed and accurate dietary history; a more thorough approach to the dietary history of cancer patients is urgently needed. Are we missing important clues to the causation or prevention of cancer that could be discovered if more attention was paid to a thorough documentation of the intake of vitamins?

REFERENCES

1. Meyers, C., Brooks, A. and Chabner, B. The value of monitoring plasma methotrexate concentrations during antineoplastic therapy, in Brodsky I, Kahn SB, Conroy JF (eds): Cancer Chemotherapy III. New York, Grune & Stratton, 1978, pp 25-33.
2. Copeland, E.M., III., 1978. Intravenous hyperalimentation as an adjunct to cancer patient management, CA 28:322-330.
3. Greenberg, D.M., 1975. The vitamin fraud in cancer quackery. West J Med 122:345-348.
4. Sporn, M.B., et al., 1976. Prevention of chemical carcinogenesis by vitamin A and its synthetic analogs (retinoids). Fed Proc 35:1332-1338.
5. Basu, T.K., et al., 1976. Plasma vitamin A in patients with bronchial carcinoma. Br J Cancer 33:119-121.
6. Chopra, D.P. and Wilkoff, L.J., 1977. Reversal by vitamin A analogues (retinoids) of hyperplasia induced by N-methyl-N-nitro-N-nitrosoguanidine in mouse prostate organ cultures. J Natl Cancer Inst 58:923-930.
7. Hilgard, P., 1977. Experimental vitamin K deficiency and spontaneous metastases. Br J Cancer 35:891-892.
8. DiPalma, J.R. and Ritchie, D.M., 1977. Vitamin toxicity. Ann Rev Pharmacol Toxicol 17:133-143.
9. Schettler, D. and Koch, H., 1976. Long-term follow-up after vitamin A acid therapy of leukoplakia of the buccal mucosa. Fortschr Kiefer Gesichtschir 21:179-180.
10. Peck, G.L., et al., 1979. Prolonged remissions of cystic and conglobate acne with 13-cis-retinoic acid. N Engl J Med 300:329-333.
11. Forbes, P.D., Urbach, F. and Davies R.E. Enhancement of experimental photocarcinogenesis by topical retinoic acid, (written communication, to be published).
12. Auerbach, O., Stout, A.P., Hammond, E.C. and Garfinkel, L., 1962. Bronchial epithelium in former smokers. N Engl J Med 267:119-125.
13. Plamenac, P., Nikulin, A., Pikula, B., 1972. Cytology of the respiratory tract in former smokers. Acta Cytol 16:256-260.
14. Bjelke, E., 1975. Dietary vitamin A and human lung cancer. Int J Cancer 15:561-565.
15. Moore, T. Effects of vitamin A. Deficiency in animals. Pharmacology and toxicology of vitamin A, in Sebrell WH, Harris RS (eds): The vitamins, ed 2. New York, Academic Press, 1967, vol 1, pp 245-266, 280-294.
16. Lasnitzki, I., 1955. The influence of A hyper-vitaminosis on the effect of 20-methylcholanthrene in mouse prostate glands grown in vitro. Br J Cancer 9:434-441.
17. Chopra, D.P. and Wilkoff, L.J., 1975. Inhibition and reversal of carcinogen-induced lesions in mouse prostate in vitro by all trans-retinoic acid. Proc Am Assoc Center Res 16:35.
18. Genta, V.M., et al., 1974. Vitamin A deficiency enhances binding of benzoapyrene to tracheal epithelial DNA. Nature 247:48-49.
19. Cameron, E. and Campbell, A., 1974. The ortho-molecular treatment of cancer. II. Clinical trial of high-dose ascorbic acid supplements in advanced human cancer. Chem Biol Interact 9:285-315.
20. Cameron, E. and Baird, G., August, 1973. Ascorbic acid and dependence on opiates in patients with advanced disseminated cancer. Res Commun Systems.
21. Cameron, E., Campbell, A. and Jack, T., 1975. The orthomolecular treatment of cancer. III. Reticulum cell sarcoma: double complete regression induced by high-dose ascorbic acid therapy. Chem Biol Interact 11:387-393.
22. Basu, T.K., et al., 1974. Leucocyte ascorbic acid and urinary hydroxyproline levels in patients bearing breast cancer with skeletal metastasic. Eur J Cancer 10:507-511.
23. Cameron, E. and Pauling, L., 1973. Ascorbic acid and the glycosaminoglycans. An ortho-molecular approach to cancer and other diseases. Oncology 27:181-192.
24. Cameron, E., Pauling, L. and Leibovitz, B., 1979. Ascorbic acid and cancer: a review. Cancer Res 39:663-681.
25. Leuchtenberger, C. and Leuchtenberger, R., 1977. Protection of hamster lung cultures by L-cysteine or vitamin C against carcinogenic effects of fresh smoke from tobacco or marijuana cigarettes. Br J Exp Pathol 58:625-634.
26. Bishun, N., Basu, T.K., Metcalfe, S. and Williams, D.C., 1978. The effect of ascorbic acid (vitamin C) on two tumor cell lines in culture. Oncology 35:160-162.
27. Stitch, H.F., et al., 1976. Mutagenic action of ascorbic acid. Nature 260:722-724.

28. Migliozzi, J.A., 1977. Effect of ascorbic acid on tumor growth. Br J Cancer 35:448-453.
29. Herbert, V. and Jacob, E., 1974. Destruction of vitamin B_{12} by ascorbic acid. JAMA 230:241-242.
30. Hines, J.D., 1975. Ascorbic acid and vitamin B_{12} deficiency, letter. JAMA 234:24.
31. Herbert, V., et al., 1978. Low serum vitamin B_{12} levels in patients receiving ascorbic acid in megadoses: studies concerning the effect of ascorbate on radioisotope vitamin B_{12} assay. Am J Clin Nutr 31:253-258.
32. Biaglow, J.E. and Jacobson, B., 1977. The reaction of hypoxic cell radio-sensitizing drugs with vitamin C, letter. Br J Radiol 50:844-846.
33. Kovarik, J., Svec, F. and Zemonová, D., 1977. Experimental chemotherapy of rat leukemia RBA-Le with cis-diamminedichloroplatinum. Neoplasma 24:475-486.
34. Carmel, R. Eisenberg, L., 1977. Serum vitamin B_{12} and transcobalamin abnormalities in patients with cancer. Cancer 40:1348-1353.
35. Kane, S.P., et al., 1977. Vitamin B_{12} binding protein in hepatocellular carcinoma: value in monitoring therapy, meeting abstract. Gut 18:A985.
36. Waxman, S., et al., 1977. The clinical and physiological implications of hepatoma B_{12}-binding proteins. Cancer Res 37:1908-1914.
37. Poirier, L.A., 1974. Vitamin B_{12} acceleration of hepatocarcinogenesis. Proc Am Assoc Cancer Res 15:51.
38. Temcharoen, P., Anukarahanonta, T. and Bhamarapravati, N., 1978. Influence of dietary protein and vitamin B_{12} on the toxicity and carcinogenecity of aflatoxins in rat liver. Cancer Res 38:2185-2190.
39. Potera, C., Rose, D.P. and Brown, R.R., 1977. Vitamin B_6 deficiency in cancer patients. Am J Clin Nutr 30:1677-1679.
40. Byar, D. and Blackard, C., 1977. Comparisons of placebo, pyridoxine and topical thiotepa in preventing recurrence of stage I bladder cancer. Urology 10:556-561.
41. Misra, N.C., Jaiswal, M.S.D., Singh, R.V. and Das, B., 1977. Intrahepatic arterial infusion of combination of mitomycin-C and 5 fluorouracil in treatment of primary and metastatic liver carcinoma. Cancer 39:1425-1429.
42. Korytnyk, W. and Potti, P.G., 1977. 4-Halovinyl and 4-ethynyl-4-diformyl-pyridoxal derivatives and related analogues as potentially irreversible antagonists of vitamin B_6. J Med Chem 20:567-572.
43. Holkstra, W.G., 1975. Biochemical function of selenium and its relations to vitamin E. Fed Proc 34:2083-2088.
44. Myers, C.E., et al., 1977. Adriamycin: the role of lipid peroxidation in cardiac toxicity and tumor response. Science 197:165-167.
45. Van Vleet, J.F., Greenwood, L., Ferrans, V.J. and Rebar, A.H., 1978. Effect of selenium-vitamin E on adriamycin-induced cardiomyopathy in rabbits. Am J Vet Res 39:997-1010.
46. Stanflo, J. and Suttie, J.W., 1977. Vitamin K dependent formation of γ-2-carboxyglutamic acid. Am Rev Biochem 46:157-172.
47. Hadler, H.I. and Cao, T.M., 1978. Vitamin K and chemical carcinogenesis, letter. Lancet 1:397.
48. Hilgard, P. and Thomas, R.D., 1976. Perspectives in cancer research. Anticoagulants in the therapy of cancer. Am J Cancer 12:755-762.
49. Ambrus, J.L. and Ambrus, C.M. Anticoagulants, fibrinolytic enzymes and platelet aggregation inhibitions in cancer chemotherapy, in Brodsky I, Kahn SB, Conroy JR (eds): Cancer Chemotherapy III. New York, Grune & Stratton, 1978. pp 97-109.
50. Hilgard, P., 1977. Cancer and vitamin K, letter. Lancer 2:403.
51. Kummer, D. and Kraml, F., 1977. Studies on thymidine triphosphate synthesis in malignant tumors II: effect of hyperthermia, vitamin K and cytoxic agents. Krebsforsch 88:145-156.
52. Egilsson, V., 1977. Cancer and vitamin K, letter. Lancet 2:254-255.
53. Bell, R.G., 1978. Vitamin K and chemical carcinogenesis, letter. Lancet 1:1161.
54. Roe, F.J., 1962. Effect of massive doses of riboflavin, and other vitamins of the B group, in skin carcinogenesis in mice. Br J Cancer 16:252-257.
55. Rivlin, R.S., 1973. Riboflavin and cancer: a review. Cancer Res 33:1977-1986.
56. Soukop, M. and Calman, K.C., 1978. Thiamine vitamin B_1 status in cancer patients and the effect of 5-fluorouracil therapy, meeting abstract. Br J Cancer 38:180.
57. Schoental, R., 1977. The role of nicotinamide and of certain other modifying factors in diethylnitrosamine carcinogenesis: fusaria mycotoxins and 'spontaneous' tumors in animals and man. Cancer 40:1833-1840.

Nutrition, Stimulation, Mental Development, and Learning

by Joaquin Cravioto, M.D., M.P.H., D.Sc.

In the second half of the twentieth century, there has been an increasing interest in the ways through which environment can affect man. Health, growth and development have become a major topic of interest for an increasing number of persons and institutions dealing with social, political and economic policies. This, in turn, has led to the consideration of unfavorable environment as an important factor in the life of the individual from the time of conception to socially functioning adulthood.

Among the many features of the child's environment, nutrition has been accepted almost as a prerequisite for optimal growth and development. Nowadays nobody denies that a diet adequate in quantity and quality is a relevent factor in the life of man and, perhaps, the most ubiquitous factor affecting growth, health and development.

NOT BY BREAD ALONE

It is of the utmost importance to realize that even if at first appearance nutrition is primarily related to physical environmental factors such as climate, weather, topography, and geological structure, and to the biologic component of human environment represented mainly by its food chains, the primordial determinant of the nutritional status of a population is the social environment.

Malnutrition at the community level is a man-made disorder characteristic of the underprivileged segments of society. This is particularly true of the pre-industrial societies, characterized by a social system which consciously or unconsciously creates malnourished individuals generation after generation through a series of social mechanisms such as limited access to goods and services, limited social mobility, and restricted experiential opportunities at crucial points in life.

The understanding of malnutrition in man thus requires an ecological frame of reference in which the social, psychological and cultural aspects of human behavior are appropriately related to the biological nature of man and to the physical environment in which he lives. Nutrition is above all an important focus on organized human behavior.

Nutrition inadequacy in pre-industrial societies and in underprivileged segments of affluent societies is manifested by a series of disease states, which, although usually affecting a large proportion of those populations, are particularly prevalent in the vulnerable groups: infants and young children, and lactating and pregnant women. This is due to the influence of the social milieu on individuals whose physiological requirements for nutrients are the highest.

In the fight against malnutrition, survival was our primary concern. Better knowledge of the difference in homeostatic responses to noxious agents in well-nourished and malnourished children, a more detailed knowledge of the biochemical pathology of malnutrition[1] together with better means for the prompt diagnosis and treatment of electrolyte disturbances and infections played a major role in reducing lethality. From a fifty-fifty chance of death, survival went up to more than 95 percent of severely malnourished preschool children treated in the pediatric wards.[2] In spite of these spectacular advances it was of importance to bear in mind that the problem of severe malnutrition in infants and children would not end when a low lethality rate had been achieved. Precisely the fact that the majority of malnourished children would not die and the fact that in vast regions of the world the majority of living adults have experienced at least one episode of malnutrition in childhood, led us to the consideration of the possible consequences of early malnutrition on later mental development and learning.

Rather than starting with the question of the impairment of mechanisms of brain functioning which may result from deficient nutrient intake, our strategy was to attempt first to answer the practical question of whether the more readily noted reductions in somatic growth and biochemical development were associated with reduced mental performance.[3-5] If mental lags were found we would then try to document if they represent permanent changes in functional effectiveness or are merely transient phenomena. This approach was based on the consideration that a negative finding would indicate that the lower performance found in malnutrition was a transient phenomenon which disappeared with nutritional rehabilitation. On the other hand, if after successful dietary treatment the children still exhibit significant lags the implications for policy making and national economic planning would be of such an importance that a systematic investigation should be carried on in order to define, through research, the causal relationship between malnutrition and mental development, and the interaction of deficient nutrient intake with other adverse social, cultural and educational circumstances affecting the child, since inadequate nutrition, except under highly special conditions such as those of war or of natural catastrophe, is a characteristic of children living

---

From *Nutrition Today*, Vol. 16, No. 5, September/October 1981, pp. 4-15. Copyright 1981, *Nutrition Today*, Inc. Reprinted with permission.

under conditions of social, cultural and stimuli deprivation.

POOR FOOD: POOR PERFORMANCE

Studies of mental performance of kwashiorkor patients during the period of rehabilitation have shown that as children recover from malnutrition, developmental quotients increase in most cases. The magnitude of the increment was in direct relation to the age at which the children suffered the disease. Therefore, with successful treatment, the difference between chronological and mental age progressively diminished in all children except in those who were stricken by severe malnutrition below the age of six months[6-8] (figs. 1 and 2).

Research conducted on infants recovering from nutritional marasmus has also disclosed that basal intelligence and psychomotor activity, as judged by the Bayley Scales,[9] remain severely retarded despite apparent somatic recovery. These studies extend the results found in children recovered from kwashiorkor and point out the fact that both extremes of chronically severe protein-calorie malnutrition behave in a similar way, giving marked retardation in mental development which is present even after physical and biochemical rehabilitation.

The association between malnutrition in preschool children and low levels of mental performance has been amply documented in several regions of the world where malnutrition is prevalent. A direct association between deficits in height and weight of severely malnourished children and retardation in psychomotor, adaptive, language and social-personal behavior has been reported from several countries.[10-16]

Another approach being followed in the assessment of the later effects of malnutrition has been the study of survivors several years after discharge from the hospital. Two main strategies have been used for this purpose. The first one compares the mental performance of children with documented past histories of severe malnutrition with the mental performance of children living in the same community, but without the antecedent of severe malnutrition. Since all investigators are well aware that severely malnourished children live in environments conducive, in many ways, to lower intellectual performance they have tried to match index cases with comparison children for those variables considered as capable of playing an important role.

The second strategy involves the use of siblings as controls. The assumption behind this type of research design is that siblings as controls cancel out the majority of the demographic or macro-environmental factors leaving those related to the specific microenvironment of each child within his own family to be accounted for by other means or in another study.

Seven studies employing the first strategy, and two studies that have used siblings as controls have been published in the available literature. These reports deal with children living in quite different cultural settings, with geographical representations for Europe, Asia, Africa, the Caribbean, and Latin America.[17-25]

The results of all these studies show that the environment in which children at risk of malnutrition live is highly negative in its effects on mental development. Irrespective of the presence or absence of a previous admission to a hospital because of severe malnutrition, children developing in this milieu have a high probability of showing poor performance on intelligence testing. The presence of a superimposed episode of malnutrition occurring early in life, and of enough severity to force the child into a hospital, increases his chances of scoring at values even lower than those characteristic of his social class.

In spite of the methodological errors that many of these studies have in regard to a number of aspects such as sample size, psychological tests employed, lack of documented nutritional history, etc., etc., it is clear that even after a period of several years, children who have been successfully treated for severe malnutrition and are considered as cured, still show developmental lags. These occur not only in motor behavior, but in other areas, including hearing and speech, socio-personal behavior, problem solving ability, eye and hand coordination, and categorization behavior.

With the demonstration that survivors of malnutrition perform at a lower level than either children of the same ethnic and socioeconomic class or siblings, we had to consider the degree to which this handicap represents permanent changes in the child's capacity or whether the negative outcomes are reversed by appropriate modification of other non-nutritional factors present in the environment of the child.

RESEARCH STRATEGIES

Because of the intimate association between nutritional status and socioeconomic level in almost all societies, children who have been at greatest and most persistent nutritional risk tend to cluster most heavily in the lowest social and economic segments. Such segments of any population differ from the remainder not only in their increased exposure to nutritional stress but also in a host of other variables. They tend to have poorer housing, higher infection rates, lower levels of educational accomplishment, greater degrees of attachment to outmoded patterns of child care, and in general to live in circumstances which are less conducive for the development of

Figure 1. Evolution of the Development of motor behavior.

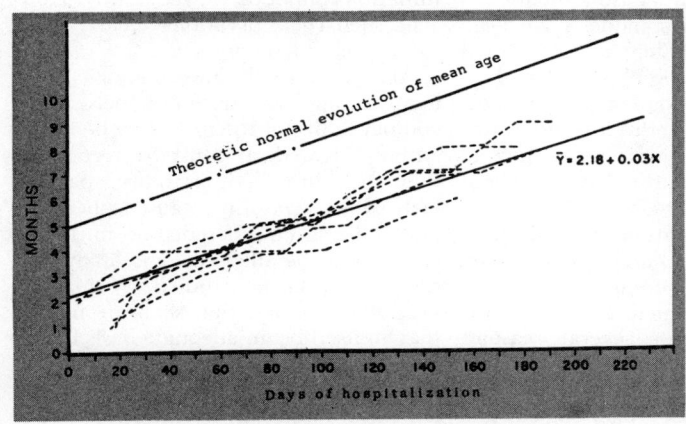

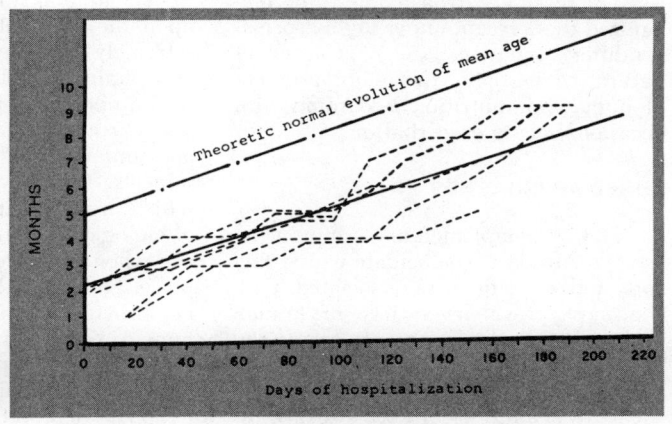

Figure 2. Evolution of the development of adaptive behavior.

technologic and educational competence.

Given these facts and associations, it is of course inevitable that any consequences for physical or mental growth deriving from nutritional conditions of risk will be associated with social status and the variables attaching to it. There has been some tendency to view this relationship circularly and to conclude that social status *per se* is capable of accounting for the disturbed outcomes in development. This is unfortunate, since it substitutes a truism for an analysis. Given the associations between depressed social standing and undesirable physical and mental outcomes, the task of analysis is to tease out the effective variables which mediate these outcomes. Clearly, social class as such does not determine physical stature. Rather, individuals are stunted when their social positions provide a general environment in terms of nutrition, infection, habits, and housing which influence the biologic processes involved in growing. Similarly, mental growth is modified to the degree to which conditions of life associated with depressed social position function directly, to modify the growth and differentiation of the central nervous system, and indirectly, to affect the opportunities for obtaining and the motives for profiting from experience.

The strategies with which investigators have approached the study on the effect of malnutrition on development were derived in the first place from the investigators' views of human malnutrition. One group has been dominated by certain aspects of the Indian experience and has considered malnutrition an acute disorder of severe degree more or less sharply delimited in time. Another attitude views malnutrition as a chronic state of affairs, which may or may not have acute exacerbations, related both to social conditions and to the age and physiologic stage of the individuals at risk. Increasingly it has come to be recognized that, except under highly special conditions such as those of war or of natural catastrophe, the major problem of human malnutrition is chronic with occasional acute exacerbation.

THREE APPROACHES

Three complementary approaches have been taken to elucidate causal factors and consequences associated with the most prevalent variety of human malnutrition. In each of these approaches there has been general agreement that the young organism should be the focus of study—both because of transiency of consequences attaching to even severe degrees of malnutrition in adults and because of the various findings on the vulnerability of the young brain even to mild dietary restrictions. Against this general agreement on focus, the three major strategies of research have been the deprivation model, the intervention model and the natural history of ecologic model. Investigations within any of these frameworks have included case studies, the comparison of populations, and the analysis of special conditions of risk and of replacement and rehabilitation.

Animal investigations have for the most part taken place within the framework of deprivation models. Experimental animals have been used not so much to replicate the most common human conditions of chronic and moderate deprivation but rather to examine the effects of severe degrees of food deprivation similar to that found under episodic famine conditions. Animals have been nutritionally deprived both in a qualitative and quantitative sense, and the effects of such nutritional lacks upon growth and development have been reported. These studies in their totality provided clear evidence for at least three developmental consequences of severe malnutrition. In the first place, animals exposed to the experimental conditions, particularly when exposure had occurred early in life, exhibited growth failures which were not fully repaired by a subsequent presentation of an adequate diet, even when this was accompanied by supplementations. Second, such early severe malnutrition resulted in lags in maturation accompanied by the development of abnormal metabolic and enzymatic patterns. Third, in almost all instances in which behavior as well as central nervous system structure and composition have been carefully studied, the exposure to malnutrition resulted in central nervous system abnormality and some degree of behavioral incompetence.

The animal studies basing themselves upon the deprivation model have been extremely valuable. They have permitted an examination of the effects of malnutrition upon the biology of the organism under controlled conditions impossible and immoral to achieve with human subjects. They have provided data about which organs, systems, and mechanisms of biological organization risk most damage when exposure to malnutrition takes place. However, the animal studies have not provided a complete analogy to the human condition for several reasons. First, the organisms studied have no social substrate against which human nutritional deprivation takes place and with which it interacts. Second, the effects on behavior have necessarily been limited to the simple types of behavioral adaptation of which the lower animal is capable. Therefore, the effects of malnutrition on complex behavioral and social functions could not be studied, and the analogy, though useful, is incomplete and a complement to rather than a substitute for the study of the effects of malnutrition in man.

COIN'S OTHER SIDE

The interventionist approach represents the other side of the deprivation coin. Through its use the investigator wishes to assess the conjoined effects of nutrition, infection, and familial and social circumstances by systematically altering each of the relevant variables. In practice, this has meant the differential application of food supplementation, infectious disease control, improved housing, education, economic support, and increased opportunities for social learning in presumably equated communities or population samples. The method has appeal in that it apparently separates influential variables and cross-compares them in a manner similar to that used in the standard experiment. However, the similarity is perhaps more formal that it is real. It is extremely difficult to achieve comparability of groups and to prevent effects spreading when subsections of a single population are being differentially supplemented. Moreover, each time a single variable is affected the danger of ecologic rearrangement exists.

Moral problems, too, attach to the use of food supplementation in studies based upon the intervention model. Perhaps the principal one of these is the recognition that such supplementation will in most instances be terminated at the end of the period of study. The effect of the supplementations on food ecology and the potentially disastrous consequences of termination cannot be viewed lightly. However, such a consideration is clearly moral rather than methodological.

The crux of the methodologic problem in supplementation models is the comparability of the groups to be differentially treated. It must be recognized that to ensure comparability, particularly when a multiple caused phenomenon is being considered, one must first carry out a detailed ecologic analysis of the groups to be studied. It may be argued, therefore, that such an analysis may in itself be an adequate basis for the identification of determinative variables, if sufficient natural intragroup variability exists to permit systematic internal cross comparisons. This set of considerations leads one to the second major approach—ecology. It is this approach that we believe to be the first essential form of study, and it is the one we have used in our longitudinal investigation in "the Land of the White Dust."

The ecologic approach is a particular form of the natural history method. It seeks to determine the nature of effective variables through a consideration of their interrelations in a single population. When applied to the problem of malnutrition, it attempts to tease out patterns of cause and consequence by considering the interrelations among food, health, and social factors. By orienting itself longitudinally, the ecologic approach can identify age-specific conditions of risk, relate antecedents to consequences at different developmental stages, and integrate biologic and social time scales. It can consider both the general and the microenvironment of the developing individual and deal with the interaction of biologic and social variables. Perhaps most important for its usefulness is the fact it uses uncontrolled variation as the fact of study. A basic requirement for the use of the ecologic method is, therefore, sufficient variation in the attributes to be considered in the population studied. If such variation is present, associative analysis can serve to identify, to segregate, and to interrelate the factors influential in affecting the consequences.

TRANSIENT OR PERMANENT SEQUELAE

In the attempt to find out if the mental lags present in survivors of early malnutrition are or could be reversible, we started our analysis contrasting a series of macroenvironmental features present in a group of children who developed protein-calorie clinical severe malnutrition and in a group of children selected from the same birth cohort, who were never diagnosed as severely malnourished and who were matched at birth with the malnourished for sex, gestational age, season of birth, body weight, total body length, and sensorimotor performance.[26]

It seems important to emphasize that the cases of severe clinical malnutrition occurred despite the fact that all children in the cohort were medically examined every two weeks, who failed to grow normally were identified, their infectious illnesses were treated, and their parents were given advice (which they did not follow) on the appropriate feeding and management of children who fail to thrive. In contrast to its lack of influence on the incidence of clinically severe malnutrition, this medical attention decreased the infant mortality rate from a figure of 96 per thousand to 46 per thousand, and also reduced the preschool mortality of the cohort by one-half. These data point out once again that traditional medical care can strongly influence mortality while having minimal or no effect on morbidity.

The factors of the macroenvironment considered related first, to the parents as biological and social organisms. Second, to the family structure and third, to objective circumstances such as source of family income, income per capita and sanitary facilities in the household.

Differences in age, weight or height of the parents, differences in the number of pregnancies or in the number of live children were not significant enough to distinguish the families of the controls from the families of the future malnourished children. No significant associations were also found between the presence or absence of clinical advanced malnutrition or in the variables related to personal cleanliness, literacy and formal education of the parents.

Neither the size of the family nor its type (nuclear or extended) were factors that could separate the homes of malnourished children from those of the controls without malnutrition.

The socioeconomic status of the families was estimated through the use of four indicators: principal source of family income, sanitary facilities present in the home, annual per capita income and percentage of total expenditures used for food. None of these four indicators was significantly associated with the presence or absence of children with advanced malnutrition in the family.

THE MEDIA AND MALNUTRITION

Contact with mass media was explored through radio listening and in literate parents through newspaper reading. The number of mothers or fathers of malnourished children who were regular newspaper readers was not significantly different from the number of the matched control group. Similarly, the number of fathers who listened regularly to the radio was similar in both the malnourished and the control groups.

The situation with the mothers was different. There were almost equal numbers of radio listeners and nonlisteners in the malnourished group, but the number of listeners among the matched control group was more than three times the number of nonlisteners. The difference was significant at the 0.05 level of statistical confidence.

In summary, from all features of the macroenvironment the only differential

TABLE 1
Aspects of Test Situation to Which Mothers of "Future" Severely Malnourished Children and of Controls Showed Significantly Different Behavioral Responses. ("Land of the White Dust")

ASPECT OF TEST SITUATION	"t" Test (SEPARATED)	p
Reaction when child performs easily	4.03	0.000
Response to interview	3.61	0.001
Sensitivity to child	3.51	0.001
Interest in child's test performance	3.19	0.003
Responses to child's needs	3.09	0.004
Mother's view of her role	2.92	0.006
Emotional involvement with child	2.79	0.009
Amount of verbal communication with child	2.57	0.015
Expressions of affection toward child	2.54	0.016
Reaction when child performs extremely well	2.33	0.027
Status consciousness	2.18	0.036
Cooperation with examiner during testing	2.11	0.042

between severely malnourished children and controls matched at birth for gestational age, body weight and total body length was the mother's contact with the world outside the village through regular radio listening. None of the other characteristics of the parents (biological, social, or cultural) of family circumstances (including per capita income, main source of income, and family size) was significantly associated with the presence or absence of severe malnourishment.

Because of the lack of association between the features of the macro-environment and the presence of severe malnutrition, attention was directed toward the analysis of the micro-environment of the two groups of children. The potential stimulation of the home, as a general indicator of the quality of child care, and the mother's psychological characteristics as the principal stimulating agent for the child, were selected as the focus of the analysis. The instrument used for estimating home stimulation was the inventory developed by Betty Caldwell[27] designed to sample certain aspects of the quantity and/or quality of social, emotional, and cognitive stimulation available to a young child within his home. Recording and scoring of the maternal transactions with her child was done by an adaptation of the Maternal Behavior Profile developed by Nancy Bayley, Laboratory of Psychology, National Institute of Mental Health. The profile contains 20 variables comprising the majority of transactions occurring during a test situation. Each variable consists of seven scaled steps, each designating a relative point of degree or type of manifestation of that variable. Each step is defined as a statement of behavior. The statement that most closely portrayed the reaction of the mother, as her habitual response during the first 12 consecutive monthly examinations was taken as her rating on that particular aspect of behavior.

THE HOME STIMULUS COUNTS

When the group of severely malnourished children was compared with the control group it was evident that even before the appearance of the first case of severe malnutrition, available home stimulation scores were markedly different. Thus, at six months of age on a range of 27 to 41 scoring points, one of every four "future malnourished" children had 30 or fewer points and none scored higher than 36 points. None of the control children had a home with a score of less than 32 points, and at least one of every four homes scored above 36 points. Similarly, at 58 months of age, when the malnourished children had been rehabilitated, in a range of scores from 55 to 124, almost one-half of the survivors of severe malnutrition were in homes with scores below 104 points and one-fourth of their homes did not exceed 84 points. As a contrast, the homes of the control children had a minimum of 100 points, with almost one-half above 110 points.

The behavioral responses of mothers of infants who later developed severe malnutrition also were different from the responses observed in the mothers of the control children.[28] The highest levels of statistical significance of the difference among the two groups were obtained in the behavior of the mother when, in a test situation, her child performed adequately and easily; in the overt signs of sensitivity toward her child; and the mother's response to the interview.

Significant differences were also observed for: interest in the child's performance, response to child's needs, mother's view of her role in the test situation, and emotional involvement of the mother with her child (p less than 0.01). The amount of verbal communication and the expressions of affection toward the child showed differences between the two groups at the 0.02 level of statistical confidence. Mother's reaction when her child performed extremely well, her status consciousness and her cooperation with the examiner during the test gave differences in behavioral responses significant at the 0.05 level. A significance level of 0.10 or less was obtained for the mother's behavioral responses when the child had difficulty with a test item, her affective response to the entire situation, and her control of the child during the test (table 1).

The amount of physical contact with the child, mother's overall general evaluation of the child, tolerance of child's behavior, type of physical contact with child, and hostility toward child were the fine aspects of behavior during the test situation in which responses from mothers of malnourished children and control children did not show statistically significant differences even at the 0.10 level of confidence (table 2).

MOTHER'S REACTIONS

Srikantia and Sastry[29] have shown that mothers of children with or without kwashiorkor, even when matched for most variables like age, parity, family size, income, religion, caste, urban or rural, etc. differ not only in specific knowledge of food values for children, concepts regarding weaning practices and timing of supplementary foods, but also in their attitudes on general health care, and in their concern for their child's health. The mothers of kwashiorkor children also performed at a lower level on a battery of intelligence tests. A low level of measured intelligence was also found by Martinez et al[30] in a group of mothers of severely malnourished children in Mexico.

In a study conducted in a pre-industrial bilingual village of Guatemala[31] it was observed that besides radio listening by the mother, the lan-

TABLE 2
Aspects of Test Situation to Which Mothers of "Future" Severely Malnourished Children and of Controls Did Not Show Significantly Different Behavioral Responses. ("Land of the White Dust")

ASPECT OF TEST SITUATION	"t" Test (SEPARATED)	p
Reaction when child had difficulty on an item	1.81	0.079
Mother's affective response to entire situation	1.74	0.092
Control of child during test situation	1.70	0.098
Amount of physical contact with child	1.59	0.121
Mother's overall general evaluation of child	1.34	0.192
Tolerance of child's behavior	1.14	0.262
Type of physical contact with child	0.34	0.736

guage spoken to the child at home could separate infants with significantly different weight increments in the first six months of their lives. Mothers who addressed their children in the local dialect of the village had infants whose weight increments were significantly lower than the increments on infants whose mothers talked to them in the national language.

One could entertain the hypothesis that listening regularly to the radio, as well as the use of the national language in preference to the local dialect are indicators of a behavioral pattern breaking away from the traditional. Along this line of thinking, this kind of mother may take more chances at innovative ideas, be more prone to provide her child with a more diversified and stimulating home environment, and to view her mother's role as a series of affective, engaging and gratifying transactions between mother and child and not simply as one of passive traditional status to be taken for granted and carried on with a minimum of gratifying interaction and novelty.

It becomes clear that a low level of home stimulation and a passive traditional mother unaware of the cognitive needs of her child and responding to him in a minimal way as if unable to decode the infant's signals, are two features of the poor microenvironment of the potentially malnourished child which are in themselves capable of influencing mental growth and development.

It has been correctly stated that in most of the studies dealing with mother-child interactions, a model that evaluates the influence of the behavior of the mother on the child but not of the influence of the child's behavior on that of the mother has been implicitly or explicitly employed.[32] In the field of nutrition, Pollitt[33] has emphasized the discussion of a multifactorial etiology of malnutrition, pointing out that the study of the host is generally superficial and segmented. The danger of this unidirectional focusing is the lack of capacity to judge the possibility that the socializing behavior of the parents could be partially dependent on the temperamental or constitutional characteristics of the child as has been described by Bell and others.[34-36]

In our studies, an analysis of the scales employed clearly shows that our interest is precisely the observation of the behavior of the mother during a situation created by the testing of her child. In other words, we wish to analyze the reaction of the mother confronted with a variation in a reactive stimulus, for example, when changing the efficiency with which her child performs something that is asked from him; the reaction of the mother towards the changing necessities of her child during the test; her cooperation with the examiner to evaluate if her behavior is dependent on the stimulus or if it constitutes a pattern of behavior that is only slightly dependent on a specific stimulus, as seems to be the case with our group of low socioeconomic rural mothers.

TABLE 3

Efficiency of Food Utilization by Normal, Inactive and Active Rats Fed on Adequate Diet Either "ad libitum" or in Restricted Quantities.

FOOD INTAKE	GROUPS	EFFICIENCY OF FOOD UTILIZATION (g. of food intake per g. of weight gain in 32 days)	EFFICIENCY (% of normal)
Ad libitum	Normal	30	100
Ad libitum	Active	32	94
Ad libitum	Inactive	39	77
73% of Ad libitum	Active	27	111
73% of Ad libitum	Inactive	54	56
49% of Ad libitum	Active	36	83
49% of Ad libitum	Inactive	77	39
33% of Ad libitum	Active	46	65

(taken from Viteri et.al.)

In the interpretation of the data presented it is interesting to point out that the level of attention, the ease with which the children became interested in the way the different stimuli were handled during the test, and their somatometric measurements were not different at birth in the two groups examined[37] nor at any other age before the appearance of malnutrition, just as there were no differences between these groups and the cohort as a whole.

It must be remembered that in the studies reported here we are referring to clinical severe malnutrition that appeared with one exception during the second and third years of life. Even the cases of marasmus were diagnosed after the children were one year old.

In marasmic cases of the "Monckeberg type," that is, small infants that at four to six months of age have practically the same body measurements that they had at birth, it is possible that certain maternal attributes such as age, multiparity, short spacing pregnancies and certain characteristics of the child such as low birth weight, early weaning, immature suction behavior and lethargy could be significantly associated with marasmus. At other ages these associations are not apparent and children show no differences in behavior as long as they are not malnourished. Contrary to this, the behavior of the mother towards the child and other characteristics of the microenvironment showed significant differences even before the time of appearance of severe malnutrition. It is not surprising that dealing with diseases of children, at a certain age the characteristics of the host are the most important, while at another age the characteristics of the environment may play a major role in the production of the disease.

Within the context of stimulation and nutrition or rather the lower level of available stimulation and its association with severe clinical malnutrition, the studies of Viteri on the effect of physical inactivity on growth retardation of young rats,[38] and a review of some important dimensions of food and feeding in human children appear as relevant.

After several brief observations about animal studies, Dr. Cravioto continues.

The results obtained in regard to food utilization as a function of physical activity are shown in table 3. As may be seen the mean efficiency of food utilization, expressed as grams of food per gram of gained body weight in a time period of 32 days, was significantly higher in the active animals. The data clearly shows that at all levels of intake studied physical inactivity reduced the efficiency of food utilization. The greatest difference between the inactive and active groups was present at food intakes equivalent to 73% and 49% of normal.

FOOD'S THREE DIMENSIONS

Since early malnutrition may result

in suboptimal functioning at later ages, it appears as necessary to consider that food is something more than nutrients and energy, and feeding is something more than the ingestion of nutrients and energy. Within the context of the human species food and feeding play a role along several dimensions. The first one, which may be called a physiological dimension, has as a unit of measurement the nutrient and its function is to provide chemical substances for growth, maintenance and metabolic regulation.

The second dimension of food may be considered as psychophysical. Its unit of measurement would be the foodstuff, which through its organoleptic characteristics would provide the organism with a variety of stimuli such as texture, color, aroma, flavor, temperature. In this context a foodstuff presented at the table as two different kitchen preparations having the same nutrient and caloric value would, in fact, appear as if two different foods were offered.

Finally, the third food dimension may be considered as psychosocial in nature. Its unit of measurement would be the meal time. The functions of food in this context are, on the one hand, to aid in symbol formation through the value family and society attach to food as a form of reward or punishment, as an identifying characteristic of an ethnic or subcultural group and so on. On the other hand, the meal time provides opportunities to demonstrate, clarify and practice role and status at the family and at the community level. Who is waited on first? Who sits at the place of honor at the table? Who is served the choice bits? This is how this food dimension is expressed.

It seems easy to visualize that food deprivation in infants and young children represents not only a shortage of nutrients necessary for the increase in body mass but also a deprivation of sensory stimuli and of social experiences. Is it surprising that children who suffered food deprivation in early life show at later ages a lower mental, physical and social performance as compared to those who were not deprived? For the young child, deprivation of food automatically becomes deprivation of chemical substances and deprivation of sensory and social stimuli.

With all the above information in mind, we have attempted to evaluate the effect of added stimulation during the rehabilitation from malnutrition suffered at a very early age. We have studied 36 severely malnourished children, all below six months of age at the moment of admission to a nutrition ward.[39] When admitted all the children showed signs of deceleration of growth and development with weights and heights comparable to those of a normal newborn or at the most to a child two months of age. The level of development in the less severe cases was estimated as equivalent to 50 percent of the mean expected for that age. Immediately after all infectious processes and acute electrolytic disturbances had been corrected, the children were randomly divided into two groups: one with systematic stimulation and another without added stimulation. The behavioral development of both groups was evaluated periodically. The initial design of the study included only two groups of children, one with a program of systematic cognoscitive, emotional and language stimulation and another without stimulation beyond the one found in a normal hospital ward. However, it later became apparent that some children in the latter group instead of showing apathy, lack of movements and expression characteristic of severe malnutrition, were active, smiled and often demanded, through facial expressions and movements of their hands and bodies, interaction with anybody who was nearby. The ward personnel could not resist the charm of these children, who for this reason received more stimulation although not in a systematic fashion nor for specific types of behavior, than the children "without stimulation." We call this third group self-stimulated to emphasize the fact that the children themselves started this interaction.

REHABILITATION'S FOUR STEPS

The program of systematic stimulation included the following aspects: first, learning of a reproducible model of mother-child interaction by a psychologist and the nurses of the day and afternoon shifts in the ward. This model is based on the scales proposed by Ainsworth, Bell and Stayton to evaluate the mother-child transactions during the first year of life.

Second, the microenvironment of the stimulated children was made up to give a high score when evaluated with the home stimulation inventory designed by Betty Caldwell.

Third, based on the record of performance of each child in the Gesell and Uzgiris-McHunt developmental scales a program of individual stimulation in which the psychologist and nurses acted as substitute mothers, inducing the child to acquire the next step in behavior in each of the different scales.

Fourth, the only reward given to the children and the personnel was social reinforcement. Undesirable behavior was not reinforced.

In order to express the improvement in performance over the nutrition rehabilitation period, data for each child were plotted against days in the program. The shape of the curves suggested that the relationships could be represented by a series of linear functions. Data were therefore fitted to algebraic expressions of the form $Y = a + bx$. In this equation Y represents the performance calculated as days of specific behavior, i.e., the age at which a normal infant would give the score obtained in the tested infant; x is the number of days in the program, and the terms a (intercept) and b (slope of the curve) are empirical constants determined by the data. The constant b was estimated by the least-squares method for each group of infants and for each field of behavior, and represents the increment of performance over time.

As may be seen in table 4, the slopes in all four developmental areas studied were systematically above 1.0 in the stimulated group and below 1.0 in the non-stimulated group. The self-stimulated infants placed at an intermediate level with slopes greater than 1.0 (catching-up) in

TABLE 4

Mean Values of Slopes for the Regression Mental Development (Days Equivalent) and Days of Treatment, Obtained in Infants Less Than Six Months of Age Recovering from Severe Malnutrition.

Group	Motor	Adaptive	Language	Social-Personal
Stimulated	1.20 ± 0.24	1.22 ± 0.26	1.12 ± 0.19	1.19 ± 0.24
Self-Stimulated	1.15 ± 0.12	1.14 ± 0.24	0.97 ± 0.10	1.12 ± 0.17
Non-Stimulated	0.83 ± 0.22	0.79 ± 0.22	0.80 ± 0.24	0.78 ± 0.19

the motor, adaptive and social-personal behaviors. In language skills these infants did not attain catch-up values.

The distribution of the slope values obtained during nutrition rehabilitation is presented in figures 3 to 6. It may be noticed that in each area of behavior studied the stimulated group has the greatest proportion of catch-up cases, the non-stimulated group the lowest proportion and the self-stimulated infants close to but above the non-stimulated group. It seems of interest to signal out that for psychomotor development the self-stimulated group performed at the same level as the stimulated group while for language development the proportion of self-stimulated infants who were catching up (slopes greater than 1.0) was as small as that obtained in infants not systematically stimulated.

The results, therefore, indicate that the addition to the dietary management of a program of systematic stimulation given within the context of a good mother-child interaction brings the majority of nutritionally rehabilitated infants (7 to 9 out of every 10) back to normal age-expected levels of performance on the Gessell Scales of Development. As a contrast, only 3 of every 10 infants who received the dietary and medical treatment without systematic stimulation reached the levels of performance accepted as normal.

Preliminary follow-up data on these children seem to indicate that those infants whose mothers learned to carry on the program of systematic stimulation at home, and whose attitudes were changed in order for them to take an active, engaging and satisfying interactive role with their infants, have continued to present normal performance levels at each age tested. Mental scores and physical measurements appear as independent of whether or not stimulation was provided during their hospital stay.

The study by Yatkin and McLaren[40] was also related to the effect of added stimulation during initial recovery. Two groups of severely malnourished children were evaluated during recovery with the Griffith's scale. One of these groups, paired by age and sex, was placed in an environment with paintings, drawings, toys and music, and in which the nurses played and sang with the children establishing affective relationships. The non-stimulated group remained in a ward of similar size but without colors, toys or music. The medical and dietetical treatment was the same for both groups. The initial difference in mental development was not significantly different. With treatment both groups increased their levels of mental performance in a significant and almost parallel way. Only at the end of the observation period of four months did the stimulated group show more elevated quotients mostly due to a low level of performance in the non-stimulated group. Both groups remained with values much lower than expected for their age with the interesting finding that, as with the Mexican children, the biggest deficit occurred in the area of language and communication.

Three to four years after being discharged from the hospital the children were reexamined. Two more groups were included to compare the mental performance of the children with and without stimulation with their healthy siblings and with another control group of healthy children of the same low socioeconomic class.

Mental performance was measured with the Stanford-Binet intelligence test. The children who recovered from malnutrition showed significantly lower intellectual quotients than their siblings and healthy children of the same social class. The children who had received stimulation during the period of hospitalization had lower levels of performance than the group without stimulation. McLaren et al. considered that this low performance of the children previously stimulated could be related to their belonging to the lowest socioeconomic conditions.

By including in their study a fifth group of children with malnutrition not severe enough to require hospitalization, these authors found that admittance to a hospital plays a minimal part in the reduction of mental performance.

Dr. Cravioto cites confirming studies and resumes.

FOOD NOT ONLY INSULT

Fortunately, the study of malnutrition as a possible cause of suboptimal mental development has shifted from the simplistic intent of considering the nutritional factor as the only cause of the low performance and distorted behavior shown by survivors of malnutrition. At present, the effort of most researchers is directed towards the quantification of the various factors along, or better still in interactive combinations, to obtain a clear perspective of the role played by each factor and their eventual control through appropriate intervention.

The findings of all the studies men-

Figure 3. Distribution of slope values of motor development/days of treatment of infants aged less than six months receiving or not systematic stimulation during recovery from severe malnutrition.

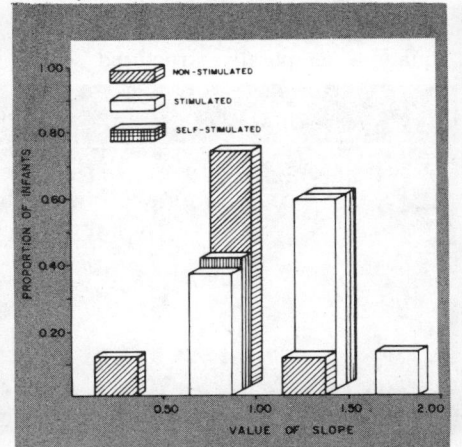

Figure 4. Distribution of slope values of adaptive development/days of treatment of infants aged less than six months receiving or not systematic stimulation during recovery from severe malnutrition.

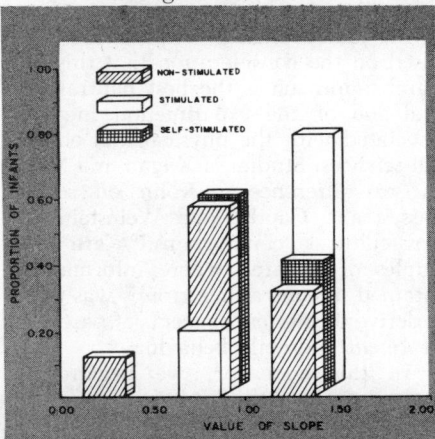

Figure 5. Distribution of slope values of language development/days of treatment of infants aged less than six months receiving or not systematic stimulation during recovery from severe clinical malnutrition.

tioned *(and included in the bibliography, ed.)* show the importance of non-nutritional variables to promote a better development of children living under conditions of deprivation, and the necessity to transform these findings into techniques to be included in community programs, with the main objective of providing systematic stimulation to infants at high risk of developing severe malnutrition, diminishing the negative effects on mental development and performance caused by this syndrome. Intervention through a non-nutritional variable can help to provide families and communities, where malnutrition is highly prevalent, with an alternative for the protection of the intellectual equipment of children living in a marginal economy that is very difficult to change under the present social inequality.

One aspect of particular concern in our studies, vis-a-vis the aim of defining malnutrition in terms of the degree of impairment of biological function associated with distinct degrees of nutritional deficiency, has been the consideration of the particular brain functions or mechanisms which may be differentially affected by the nutritional insult. This consideration was based on our knowledge that injuries of the brain only rarely produce alteration of all functions. The rule is to have a gradient going from functions one hundred percent impaired to functions totally intact.

When the research design for the longitudinal study was established, it was decided that one of the strategies for this assessment would be the comparison of the rates of acquisition of certain functions among groups of children with different risks of malnutrition. The study of contrasting groups as a strategy for identifying determinants of behavior was based on the consideration that this research approach is the best naturalistic analogue of the experimental method associated with the physical and chemical sciences. Studies of Kagan and Moss on sex differences,[57] Kohn on social class,[58] and Caudill and Weinstein on cross-cultural comparisons,[59] are examples of research where information obtained in contrasting groups was used to derive theoretical concepts of parental treatment and child behavior.

In this endeavor, we began the analysis selecting the level of adequacy in the visual-kinesthetic and in the auditory-visual intersensory modalities as indicators of brain development. This takes into consideration that the emergence of complex adaptive capacities seems to be underlaid by the growth of increasing liaison and interdependence among the separate sense systems,[60-62] and that the basic mechanism involved in the formation of conditioned responses (i.e., primary learning) is probably the effective establishment and patterning of intersensory organization.[63, 64] Another reason for using intersensory competence as an indicator of neurointegrative development stemmed from the work of Birch and Lefford.[65] They demonstrated that adequacy of intersensory interrelations improves in an age-specific manner, giving developmental curves as regular as those obtained for age and weight, or age and length.

SPECIFIC TECHNIQUES

Visual-kinesthetic competence was explored by a method of equivalence in the perception of geometric forms. The kinesthetic sense modality used was the sensory inputs obtained through passive arm movement. Such motion entails sensory input from the wrist, elbow, and shoulder joints, and from the arm and shoulder muscles, as its principal components. In the test, kinesthetic information is provided by placing the child's preferred arm behind a screen, and, with the arm out of sight, moving it passively through a path tracing a geometric form.

The specific technique used for studying equivalent relationships among the visual, and kinesthetic sense modalities was the recognition of geometrical forms. A pair comparison technique was utilized, a form presented to one sensory system was compared with equal and different forms randomly presented in another sensory system.

Auditory-visual integrative competence was measured as the ability to equate a temporally structured set of auditory stimuli with a spatially distributed set of visual ones. The specific demand made was the identification of a visual dot pattern that corresponded to the patterning of a rhythmic auditory stimulus. All subjects were tested individually in a quiet room, alone with the examiner. Judgments were scored right or wrong. No reinforcement was given.

The analysis of these two primary mechanisms underlying cognitive growth focused on a comparison of the levels of performance attained at successive ages (66, 73, 78, and 86 months) by the group of survivors of severe malnutrition and two groups of children selected from the same birth cohort who were never diagnosed as severely malnourished. One comparison group was matched at birth for sex, gestational age, season of birth, body weight, total body length, and organization of the central nervous system as determined by the Gesell

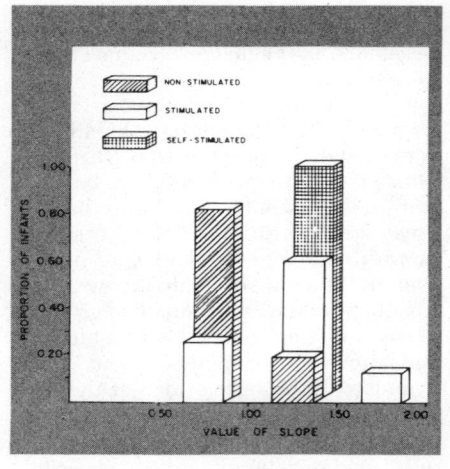

Figure 6. Distribution of slope values of social-personal development/days of treatment of infants aged less than six months receiving or not systematic stimulation during recovery from severe malnutrition.

TABLE 5
Proportions of 73-Month-Old Children Showing 25 or Less Errors in Visual-Kinesthetic Competence. ("Land of the White Dust")

Groups	Proportion of Children with ≤ 25	Errors
MALNOUR	0.529	5 of 10
SIMSTIM	0.823	8 of 10
SIMSIZE	1.000	10 of 10

X^2 Proportions = 28.87; Df = 2; $P < 0.05$
(MALNOUR + SIMSTIM) VS. SIMSIZE = 8.51; Df = 1; $P < 0.05$
MALNOUR VS. SIMSTIM = 20.36; Df = 1; $P < 0.05$

method. The second comparison group included children, full-term and healthy at delivery, who were matched for sex and total scores on home stimulation with the survivors of severe malnutrition. None of the other features of the macroenvironment, including per capita income, main source of income, percentage of total expenditures devoted to food procurement, and family size, nor the biological, educational, and health characteristics of the parents, were different in the three groups of children studied.

The mean number of errors in judging non-identical forms presented simultaneously to the visual and kinesthetic sensory modalities decreased as the child matured, both in survivors of severe malnutrition and in controls for size at birth. The patterns of improvement in performance exhibited by both groups approximated the form of a growth function, with a marked difference in the value of the intercept and in the age at which asymptotic values were attained. The control group reached the asymptote by age 78 months, but it is not yet reached at age 86 months in the survivors of severe malnutrition.

SUSPICIONS CONFIRMED

Not only were mean number of errors greater in the survivors, the variability at all ages studied also was greater. Survivors of malnutrition performed at a significantly lower level of competence at all ages. The data clearly indicate the delay in development of intersensory organization present in these children, right from the first age studied.

For the development of auditory-visual intersensory integration, the level of competence also was markedly inferior for the survivors of severe malnutrition at all ages tested. For example at age 73 months, it was striking that not a single survivor made at least one correct judgment. On the other hand, the proportion of control children scoring higher than 0 was three out of ten, with one of every ten controls reaching a 5 point score. At 78 months of age, while six out of every ten survivors still had scores of either 0 or 1 correct response, the proportion of so poor performers in the control group was only three out of ten. This same pattern was observed when the children reached 86 months of age. The proportion of very poor performers (scores of 0 or 1) among the controls was about one-half of the proportion found in the survivors of severe malnutrition. At the other end of the distribution, while not a single survivor gave more than 4 correct judgments, one of every ten control children reached a 6 to 7 level.

The longitudinal data thus confirm the previous cross-sectional studies that suggested a delayed intersensory integration development in survivors from severe clinical performances at ages 73 and 78 months were selected for analysis of the kinesthetic-visual task, comparing children with and without antecedents of severe clinical malnutrition matched for scores on total home stimulation.

Taking a cut-off point at 25 errors, table 5 shows the proportion of children attaining this or a lower value. As may be seen, there is a clear gradient of competence among the three groups of children, with the controls for size at birth placed at the highest level, the malnourished at the bottom, and the children matched for home stimulation with the survivors at an intermediate level of competence. A Chi-Square Test of proportions indicates that these figures are significantly different at the 0.05 level of statistical confidence.

At 78 months of age, if one takes a cut-off point at 16 errors, survivors of malnutrition, controls for home stimulation, and controls for size at birth exhibit a gradient of performance in kinesthetic-visual ability similar to that seen for the 73-month-old group. Children without antecedents of severe malnutrition and with higher scores on home stimulation placed first, followed by children without antecedents of malnutrition, and, finally, by the survivors of malnutrition who are malnourished.

NO PLACE LIKE HOME

As was mentioned above, survivors of severe malnutrition and controls differed not only in the nutritional antecedent, but also in the amount and quality of the stimulation available in their homes. Thus, since on the one hand the antecedent of severe malnutrition was significantly associated with diminished home stimulation, and on the other hand survivors of severe malnutrition showed a significant delay in both kinesthetic-visual and auditory-visual competences, it seemed logical to try to separate the possible effects of the nutritional and the non-nutritional variable. Our attempt to do so was through the inclusion of a control group of children who were never diagnosed as suffering from severe malnutrition, but whose total scores on home stimulation were equal to the scores of the survivors, both before and after severe clinical malnutrition.

In considering errors it is clear that, for growth functions, the examination of group differences can best be explored after the period of chance performance and before performance reaches the asymptotic level, when the function has completed its growth and does not increment with age; accordingly, the worst performers. Differences among the three groups are statistically significant at the level of confidence of 0.05.

The picture for the development of auditory-visual intersensory integration is markedly different than that obtained for the kinesthetic-visual task, when survivors of severe malnutrition are compared with children having the same low scores on home stimulation but without the antecedent of malnutrition.

At all ages considered, Chi-Square tests of proportions make evident the lack of difference between children with and without antecedents of severe malnutrition matched for total scores on home stimulation (table 6).

The results of the previous cross-

TABLE 6

Auditory-Visual Integration Proportion of Children Making Not Less Than 4 Correct Judgments at 78 Months of Age. ("Land of the White Dust")

Groups	Proportion of Children with 4 or More Correct Judgments	
MALNOUR	0.277	3 of 10
SIMSTIM	0.176	2 of 10
SIMSIZE	0.666	6 of 10

X^2 Proportions = 10.95; Df = 2; P < 0.05
(MALNOUR + SIMSTIM) VS. SIMSIZE = 10.55; Df = 1; P < 0.05
MALNOUR VS. SIMSTIM = 0.40; Df = 1; P > 0.05

sectional studies on kinesthetic-visual intersensory integration are thus in agreement with our data from the longitudinal study, in the sense that the antecedent of severe malnutrition independently of the characteristics of the stimulation available at home, is *per se* strongly associated with the levels of competence in the kinesthetic-visual task. Since the quality and quantity of the stimulation available at home also showed a significant correlation with the intersensory task, the developmental lag observed in survivors of malnutrition appears to be the result of the effects of earlier malnutrition in association with certain microenvironmental factors related to child care.

WHOLE NEW PICTURE EMERGES

The findings in relation to auditory-visual integration give a totally different picture. When the difference in home stimulation between survivors of severe malnutrition and control children was cancelled out, the performance of the survivors was at the same level observed in control children with low scores in stimulation. The disappearance of the developmental lag in the survivors, points to a strong association between stimulation available in the home and competence in auditory-visual integration, and to a lack of association between a previous history of severe malnutrition and auditory-visual competence.

The importance of sorting out specific mental abilities as a function of macro- and microenvironmental factors that would exert a more powerful influence on them is obvious from both practical and theoretical viewpoints. From the nutritional side the planner and the policy-maker must know what to expect in terms of both prevention and rehabilitation of mental sequelae to be accomplished by intervention programs.

The past 20 years have witnessed our efforts to answer some pragmatic questions. The first has been our contribution to document that decelerations in physical growth and biochemical composition are associated with lags in mental development in survivors of severe malnutrition. The second, that by modification of non-nutritional variables plus correction of the nutritional deficiency, the mental lags found in survivors of severe clinical malnutrition, even when suffered at an early age (before six months of age) and of long duration, two-thirds or more of the life of the infant, are reversible. And third, that some basic neurointegrative functions, related to primary learning, and to the acquisition of basic academic skills such as reading and writing, are differentially modulated in their development; nutrition playing a major role in some brain functions and stimulation playing the main influence in another set of functions.

It has taken us 20 years to come to our present situation in tackling the problem of malnutrition, mental development, learning and behavior. From studies of the child we have moved to epidemiological considerations about the agent, the host and the environment, particularly the microenvironment. We are beginning to tease out the different outcomes related to nutritional insult either alone or in combination with other non-nutritional components of the environment of the malnourished child. Finally, we are just moving into the problem of scientifically defining the development sequence at which quantitative estimated levels of nutritional deficiency may interfere with emerging functions to give either delayed or disordered development.

Twenty years is quite a bit of time. "If somebody believes that acquisition of knowledge is expensive, ask him/her to think about the cost of ignorance."

REFERENCES

1. Frenk, S., Metcoff, J., Gomez, F., Ramos-Galvan, R., Cravioto, J. and Antonowicz, I., 1957. "Intracellular Composition and Homeostatic Mechanisms in Chronic Severe Malnutrition. II-Tissue Composition". Pediatrics 20: 105.
2. Gomez, F., Ramos-Galvan, R., Frenk, S., Cravioto, J. and Chavez, R., 1956. "Mortality in Second and Third Degree Malnutrition". J. Trop Pediat. 2: 77.
3. Aguilar, R., 1944. "Estudios Sobre Avitaminosis y Perturbaciones del Crecimiento en Niños Hipoalimentados". Gaceta Médica de México 75: 26.
4. Ramos-Galván, R., Cravioto, J., Gutiérrez, G., Gómez, F. y Frenk, S., 1958. "Operación Zacatepec. III. Comparación de un Método Indirecto y otro Directo, en la Evaluación del Estado de Nutrición de los Niños de una Comunidad Rural". Bol. Méd. Hosp. Infant. (Méx.) 15: 855.
5. Cravioto, J., 1962. "Appraisal of the Effect of Nutrition on Biochemical Maturation". Am. J. Clin. Nutrition 11: 484.
6. Cravioto, J. and Robles, B. "The Influence of Protein Calorie Malnutrition on Psychological Test Behavior". Proc. Swedish Nutrition Foundation. A Symposium on Mild-Moderate Forms of Protein-Calorie Malnutrition. Bastad and Gothemburg, pp. 115, August 1962.
7. Cravioto, J., 1963. "Application of Newer Knowledge of Nutrition on Physical and Mental Growth and Development". Am. J. Publ. Hlth. 53: 1803.
8. Cravioto, J. y Robles, B., 1966. "Evolution of Adaptative and Motor Behavior During Rehabilitation from Kwashiorkor". Am. J. Orthoypsychiat. 35: 449.
9. Pollitt, E. and Granoff, D., 1967. "Mental and Motor Development of Peruvian Children Treated for Severe Malnutrition". Revista Interamericana de Psicología, 1: 93.
10. Monckeberg, F. "Effect of Early Marasmic Malnutrition on Subsequent Physical and Psychological Development". *In:* Scrimshaw, N.E., and Gordon, J.E. (Eds.) Malnutrition, Learning and Behavior, MIT Press, Cambridge, Mass., pp. 269, 1968.
11. Chase, P.H. and Martin, H.P., 1970. "Undernutrition and Child Development". New Engl. J. Med. 282: 933.
12. Barrera-Moncada, G. "Estudios Sobre el Crecimiento y Desarrollo Psicológico del Síndrome Pluricarencial (kwashiorkor)". Caracas, Venezuela, Editora Grafos, 1963.
13. Marcondes, E., Lefevre, A.B. and Machado, D.V., 1969. "Desenvolvimiento Neuropsicomotor de Crianca Desnutrida". Revista Brasileira de Psiquiatría 3: 173.
14. Kardonsky, V., Alvarado, M., Undurraga, O., Manterola, A. and Segure, T. "Desarrollo Intelectual y Físico en el Niño Desnutrido". Unpublished manuscript. University of Chile, Department of Psychology, 1971.
15. Botha-Antoun, E., Babayan, S. and Harfouche, J.E., 1966. "Intellectual Development Relating to Nutritional Status". J. Trop Pediat. 14: 112.
16. Yatkin, U.S. and McLaren, D.S., 1970. "The Behavioral Development of Infants Recovering from Severe Malnutrition". J. Ment. Defic. Res. 14: 25.
17. Hoorverg, J. and Standfield, P. "The Influence of Malnutrition on Psychologic and Neurologic Development". Preliminary Communication. *In:* Panamerican Health Organization (ed.) Nutrition. The Nervous System and Behavior. Scientific Publication 251, 1972.
18. Nwuga, V.C.B., 1977. "Effect of Severe Kwashiorkor on Intellectual Development Among Nigerian Children". Am. J. of Clinical Nutrition, 30: 1423.
19. Guillén-Alvarez, G. "Influence of Severe Marasmic Malnutrition in Early Infancy on Mental Development at School Age". *In:* Wienner Medizinischen Akademic (ed.). Proceedings XII International Congress of Pediatrics, Wien, Austria, 1971.
20. Guthrie, H.A., Guthrie, G.M. and Tayag, A., 1969. "Nutritional status and intellectual performance in a rural Philippine community". Philippine J. of Nutr. 22: 2.
21. Champakam, S., Srikantia, S.G. and Gopalan, C., 1968. "Kwashiorkor and mental development". Amer. J. Clin. Nutr. 21: 844.
22. Liang, P.H., Hie, T.T., Jan, O.H. and Giok, L.T., 1967. "Evaluation of mental development in relation to nutrition". Amer. J. Clin. Nutr. 20: 1290.
23. Cabak, V. and Najdavic, R., 1965. "Effect of undernutrition in early life on physical and mental development". Arch. Dis. Child. 40: 532.
24. Hertzig, M.E., Birch, H.G., Richardson, S.A. and Tizard, J., 1972. "Intellectual Levels of School Age Children Severely Malnourished During the First Two Years of Life". Pediatrics 49: 814.
25. Birch, H.G., Piñeiro, C., Alcalde, E., Toca, T. and Cravioto, J., 1971. "Relation of kwashiorkor in early childhood and intelligence at school age". Pediat. Res. 5: 579.
26. Cravioto, J. and DeLicardie, E.R., 1973. "Environmental Correlates of Severe Clinical Malnutrition and Language Development in Survivors from Kwashiorkor or Marasmus". Bol. Ofna. Sanitaria Panamericana (English Edition) 7: 50.
27. Caldwell, B.M., 1967. "Descriptive Evaluations of Child Development and of Developmental Settings". Pediatrics 40: 46.

28. Cravioto, J. and DeLicardie, E.R. "Mother-Infant Relationship prior to the Development of Clinical Severe Malnutrition in the Child". *In:* White, P.L. and Selvey, N. (eds.) Proceedings VI-Western Hemisphere Nutrition Congress Acton Mass. Publishing Science Group Inc., pp. 126, 1975.
29. Srikantia, S.G. and Sastry, C.Y. "Effect of Maternal Atributes on Malnutrition in Children". Proc. First Asian Congress of Nutrition. India, pp. 584-591, 1972.
30. Matrínez, P.D., Ramos Galván, R. y de la Fuente, R., 1951. "Los Factores Ambientales en la Pelagra de los Niños de México". Bol. Méd. Hosp. Infant. (Méx.) *6:* 743.
31. Cravioto, J., Birch, H.G., DeLicardie, E.R. y Rosales, L., 1967. "The Ecology of Infant Weight Gain in a Preindustrial Society". Acta Paediat. Scand. *56:* 71.
32. Caldwell, B.M. and Hersher, L., 1964. "Mother-Infant Interaction During the First Year of Life". Merrill-Palmer Quart. *10:* 119.
33. Pollitt, E., 1973. "Behavior of Infant in Causation of Nutritional Marasmus". American Journal of Clinical Nutrition. *26:* 264.
34. Bell, R.W., 1971. "Stimulus of Parent or Caretaker by Offspring". Develop. Psychol. *4:* 63.
35. Caldwell, B.M., Hersher, L., Bipton, E.L., Richmond, J.B., Stern, G.G., Eddy, E.D. and Rothman, A., 1963. "Mother-Infant Interaction in Monomatric and Polymatric Families". Am. J. Orthopsychiat. *33:* 653.
36. Sears, R.R., 1951. "A Theoretical Framework for Personality and Social Behavior". Am. Psychologist *6:* 476.
37. Cravioto, J. and DeLicardie, E.R., 1974. "Size at Birth and Preschool Severe Malnutrition". Acta Paediat. Scand. *63:* 577.
38. Viteri, F. "Efecto de la inactividad sobre el crecimiento de ratas alimentadas con una dieta adecuada a niveles de ingestión calórica normal y restringidos". *En: Nuevos Conceptos Sobre Viejos Aspectos de la Desnutrición.* Acad. Mex. Pediatría (eds.) México, pp. 207-229, 1973.
39. Cravioto, J. and Arrieta, R. "The Effect of Added Systematic Stimulation on The Mental Recovery of Severely Malnourished Infants Less Than Six-Months Old". The Pediatrician, 1981 (in press).
40. Yatkin, U.S. and McLaren, D.S., 1970. "The Behavioral Development of Infants Recovering From Severe Malnutrition". Journal of Mental Deficiency Research *14:* 25.
41. Klein, R.E., Lester, B.M., Yarbrough, C. and Habitch, J.P. "On Malnutrition and Development: Some Preliminary Findings". Proc. IX International Congress of Nutrition, México, 1972.
42. Richardson, S.A., 1976. "The Relation of Severe Malnutrition in Infancy to the Intelligence of School Children With Differing Life Histories". Pediatric Res. *10:* 57.
43. Klein, P.S., Forber, G.B. and Nader, P.R., 1975. "Effects of Starvation in Infancy (Pyloric Stenosis) on Subsequent Learning Abilities". Pediatrics *87:* 8.
44. Berlung, G. and Rabo, E., 1974. "A Long-Term Follow-up Investigation of Patients With Hypertrophic Pyloric Stenosis—With Special Reference to the Physical and Mental Development". Acta Paediat. Scand *62:* 306.
45. DeLicardie, E.R., Vega, L., Birch, H.G. and Cravioto, J., 1971. "The Effect of Weight Loss From Birth to Fifteen Days on Growth and Development in the First Year". Biology of the Neonate *17:* 249.
46. Lloyd-Still, J.D., Hurwitz, I., Wolff, P.H. and Schwachaman, H., 1974. "Intellectual Development After Malnutrition in Infancy". Pediatrics *54:* 306.
47. Winick, M., Meyer, K.K. and Harris, R.C., 1975. "Malnutrition and Environmental Enrichment by Early Adoption". Science *190:* 1173.
48. Barnes, R.H. "Behavioral Changes Caused by Malnutrition in The Rat and the Pig". *In:* D.C. Glass (ed) Environmental Influences New York: Rockefeller University Press and Rusell Sage Foundation, 1968.
49. Barnes, R.H., Moore, A.V. and Pond, W.G., 1970. "Behavioral Abnormalities in Young Adult Pigs Caused by Malnutrition in Early Life". Journal of Nutrition *100:* 145.
50. Frankova, S. and Barnes, R.H., 1968. "Effect of Malnutrition in Early Life on Avoidance Conditioning and Behavior of Adult Rats". Journal of Nutrition *96:* 485.
51. Levistky, D.V. and Barnes, R.H., 1972. "Nutritional and Environmental Interactions in the Behavioral Development of the Rat: Long-Term Effects". Science *176:* 68.
52. Levistky, D.V. and Barnes, R.H. "Malnutrition and Animal Behavior" In: Kallen, D.J. (ed) Nutrition, Development and Social Behavior. Washington, D.C. USGPO: Publication No. NIH73-242, 1973.
53. Morgan, B.L.G. and Winick, M., 1980. "Effects of Environmental Stimulation on Brain N-Acetylneuraminic Acid Content and Behavior". Journal of Nutrition *110:* 425.
54. Morgan, B.L.G. and Winick, M., 1980. "Effects of Administration of N-Acetylneuraminic Acid (NANA) on Brain NANA Content and Behavior". Journal of Nutrition *110:* 416.
55. Castilla, L., Cravioto, A. and Cravioto, J., 1979. "Efectos a Corto Plazo de la Interacción Estimulación-Desnutrición Sobre el Desarrollo Bioquímico del Sistema Nervioso Central". Gac. Méd. Mex. *115:* 225-233.
56. Dobbing, J. "Vulnerable Periods in Brain Growth and Somatic Growth". *In:* The Biology of Human Fetal Growth. Roberts, D.F., and Thomson, A.M. (eds.) London: Taylor and Francis, 1976.
57. Kagan, J. and Moss, H.A. "Birth to Maturity". New York. John Wiley and Sons, 1962.
58. Kohn, M.L., 1963. "Social Class and Parent-Child Relationships: An Interpretation". Am. J. Sociol. *68:* 471.
59. Caudill, W. and Weinstein, H., 1969. "Maternal Care and Infant Behavior in Japan and America". Psychiatry *32:* 12.
60. Maier, N.R.F. and Schneirla, T.C. "Principles of Animal Behavior". McGraw-Hill, New York, 1935.
61. Birch, H.G. "Comparative Psychology". *In* Areas of Psychology, F. Marcuse, ed., Harper, New York, pp. 446, 1954.
62. Voronin, L.G. and Guselnikov, V., 1963. "On the phylogenesis of internal mechanisms of the analytic and synthetic activity of the brain". Pavlov Journal of Higher Nervous Activity *13:* 193.
63. Birch, H.G. and Bitterman, M.E., 1949. "Reinforcement and learning: the process of sensory integration". Psychological Review *56:* 292.
64. Birch, H.G. and Bitterman, M.E., 1951. "Sensory integration and cognitive theory". Psychological Review *58:* 335.
65. Birch, H.G. and Lefford, A., 1963. "Intersensory Development in Children". Monographs of the Society for Research in Child Development, Serial 89, Vol. 28 *(5):* 1.

MENTAL HEALTH

Nutritional Demands Imposed by Stress

by National Dairy Council

SUMMARY

Stress is defined as "the nonspecific response of the body to any demand." The response to both psychological (e.g., emotional tension or anxiety) and physical (e.g., injury, operation, trauma, infection, burns, and environmental extremes of temperature) stressors involves a number of adaptive neuroendocrine and metabolic adjustments. The resulting hormonal milieu can influence nutritional processes and increase the needs of tissues for specific nutrients. There are several factors which contribute to an individual's response to stress. Of importance is the pre-stress nutritional status of the individual. The well-nourished person, as opposed to the individual with marginal nutrient reserves, is better able to cope with the nutritional demands imposed by stress. For usual stresses encountered in daily living, nutrient intakes in excess of the Recommended Dietary Allowances (RDA) are unnecessary. In contrast, if the specific stress is of sufficient intensity and duration, the associated hypermetabolism and hypercatabolism significantly reduce the body's endogenous stores of energy. In terms of specific nutrients, stress-related requirements of energy and protein have received the most attention. Mild trauma will elevate energy requirements only slightly, whereas, in major thermal injury, energy needs may be increased by 40% to 125%. Stress-related changes in protein metabolism correlate closely with those of energy metabolism, with weight loss and increased nitrogen excretion being the major indicators of catabolism. If the individual becomes nutritionally depleted during stressful illness, skeletal muscle is unable to provide sufficient amino acids to meet energy demands. Nutritional support is advantageous in terms of preventing rapid wastage of body nutrients, but resolution of the source of stress itself is the chief means of returning the hypermetabolic state to normal. While the metabolism of vitamins, minerals, and electrolytes is altered during stressful illness, there are few indications that stress per se warrants an increase in any of these nutrients in excess of the RDA. Nutrient requirements are largely unchanged during adaptation to cold exposure, mainly because of improved protective clothing and dwellings which markedly reduce body heat loss. In contrast, with extreme heat exposure energy and protein requirements are elevated, particularly when physical work is being performed. Optimal nutritional management of the individual under moderate to severe stress of any kind demands continuous nutritional evaluation and, where appropriate, nutritional support.

Selye (1), who first formulated the concept of stress in 1936, now defines it as "the nonspecific response of the body to any demand." Nonspecific in its causation, stress alters the normal steady state (homeostasis) or challenges the adaptive capacity of the organism (1,2). The condition can be either positive (eustress) or negative (distress)—the stress of creative successful work can be invigorating; the stress of failure or disease can be detrimental (1). Stress is a complex process involving an interaction between psychological and physiological systems (1,3). Stress of an emotional origin appears to be an individual phenomenon. One person, for example, may feel "stressed" when required to perform a distasteful task; this same task may not be perceived as stressful to another individual. The response to physical stress (fever, operation, trauma) is less individual, varying with the degree of stress and the nutritional status of the individual.

From *Dairy Council Digest*, Vol. 51, No. 6, November-December 1980, pp. 31-35. Copyright 1980, National Dairy Council. Reprinted with permission.

This *Digest* discusses the body's response to stress (particularly severe distress) in terms of neuroendocrine and metabolic changes, and the nutritional demands imposed by stressors of a psychological or emotional origin (e.g., nervous tension) or of a physical nature (e.g., injury, operation, trauma, infections, burns, and environmental extremes of temperature). Nutrition and stress interact as follows: (1) a nutritional deprivation itself can produce a stress response; (2) the state of nutrition is a conditioning factor, determining an individual's response to a stressor; and (3) stress can lead to or aggravate nutritional deficiencies (1,2,4,5). Stini (6), reviewing human adaptability to nutritional stress from an evolutionary perspective, shows that man's response to stress increases the utilization of nutrients. If dietary intake is inadequate to meet nutrient requirements for a prolonged period, the body's ability to adapt to severe stress may eventually be limited.

NEUROENDOCRINE AND METABOLIC RESPONSE TO STRESS

Response to stressors (both psychological and physical) is expressed physiologically by a number of neuroendocrine mediated adjustments which are essential for survival (1,3). This response of the body to stress is described as the "flight or fright mechanism," the "alarm reaction," or the "general adaptation syndrome" (1,2,7,8). Although the causation is nonspecific, the pattern of the stress response occurs in a precise sequence. A triphasic course of stress response involving the following steps has been described: (1) an initial alarm reaction during which physiological responses to hormonal release are depressed and resistance falls below normal; (2) a stage during which resistance rises above normal, stress hormones are elevated, and metabolic reactions increase — this heightened level of preparedness or resistance cannot be maintained; and (3) a stage of exhaustion when adaptation energy is depleted (1,7). The different patterns of metabolism at different times during a stressful episode influence the individual's nutritional requirements.

There appears to be some differences in the neuroendocrine and neurochemical response to specific stressors (9,10). Lenox et al (9), for example, found that plasma hormones and brain neurochemical systems in rats responded differently to two different stressors: cold exposure and forced immobilization. Likewise, Beisel (10) has reviewed the endocrine response to stress of infection in man and compared this to the non-septic stress response. The degree of exposure to the stressor also influences the neuroendocrine and metabolic response (10). If the stressor is short-lived, the changes in stress hormone levels will be transient and unlikely to induce a catabolic response. If, on the other hand, the stressor is intense or applied for an extended period of time, changes in the hormonal system can lead to a catabolic state such as nitrogen wasting (10). Lastly, all persons do not react equally to the same stressor due to conditioning factors (7).

Recognizing that the above factors can modify the stress response, the following are some of the kinds of neuroendocrine changes brought about by various stressors and the effects on key metabolic pathways (1,7,8,11-18). Although precise signals which initiate a hypermetabolic response (i.e., increased metabolic rate) to stress are unknown, several lines of evidence point to the role of the central nervous system (15). A wide variety of stressors stimulate the hypothalamus from where impulses proceed to the anterior pituitary for mobilization of adrenocorticotropic hormone (ACTH). ACTH, carried via the vascular system, acts directly on the adrenal glands increasing the release of corticoids (glucocorticoids and mineral corticoids) and catecholamines (norepinephrine and epinephrine). These circulating hormones elicit a variety of physiological effects. The outpouring of glucocorticoids from the adrenal cortex leads to glycogenolysis, gluconeogenesis (the process of conversion of carbon fragments from amino acids and lactic acid into glucose), amino acid mobilization, and lipolysis.

Catecholamines, referred to as the hormones of stress, appear to be the dominant modulators of metabolic activity and are responsible for the post-traumatic hypermetabolic response to stress (11,15). They alter organ blood flow, suppress insulin release and stimulate glucagon, and create a hormonal environment favoring gluconeogenesis and lipolysis (11,15,17,18). The glucagon released exerts its effect primarily on the liver, signalling it to release glucose during a state of blood glucose need. This hormone amplifies the metabolic response to stress, but is not the primary cause of the response.

Both catecholamines and glucocorticoids antagonize the action of insulin, the key anabolic hormone which promotes storage of metabolic fuels within cells (15,17,18). It is the insulin to glucagon ratio that governs the metabolic alterations observed under stress. A high glucagon to insulin ratio results in mobilization of storage fuels and body wasting. Conversely, when insulin is increased relative to glucagon, energy storage, decreased gluconeogenesis, increased protein biosynthesis, and decreased urea nitrogen excretion occurs (15).

In addition to ACTH, growth hormone and prolactin, two other anterior pituitary hormones, are highly stress-responsive, blood levels being elevated following various stresses (15). It is known that growth hormone is catabolic in terms of fat and carbohydrate storage, anabolic with respect to protein (15,17). Newer research on the release of other hormones such as prostaglandins will undoubtedly further unravel the scope of hormonal participation in the stress response.

As discussed below, the multiple changes in hormonal release in response to acute stressful stimuli influence nutritional processes and the needs of tissues for specific nutrients (19). It is likely that almost any kind of stress can upset nutritional balance (20). In fact, Dubos (20) suggests that the range of stresses capable of leading to nutritional pathology is more far reaching than commonly appreciated.

NUTRITIONAL DEMANDS OF STRESS

The nutritional significance of stress is largely unknown (1). In general, the nutrient requirements of the stressed individual are influenced by previous nutritional status, the nature, frequency, intensity, and duration of the stressor, and the amount and type of nutrients lost from the body (1,19). Certainly the well-nourished person, as opposed to the individual with marginal nutrient reserves, is better able to cope with the nutritional demands imposed by stress (1,5). Differences between individuals in terms of their adaptation to a given stressor preclude specific guidelines covering all stress situations. Hence, the critical need for identification of persons under severe stress cannot be overestimated. Hospital malnutrition may be an example of failure to recognize the stress-related nutritional demands associated with illness (21).

For usual stresses encountered in daily living (i.e., stresses which result in transient increases in urinary nitrogen excretion), the Food and Nutrition Board, NAS-NRC advises that nutrient intakes in excess of those indicated in the Recommended Dietary Allowances (RDA) are unnecessary (4). In contrast, more severe stress which elicits a physiologic hypercatabolic response increases the body's requirements for essential nutrients (4).

Psychological or Emotional Stress. Emotional stress, such as tension and anxiety, is one of the most common forms of stress in industrially developed countries. What constitutes this type of stress involves the way an individual perceives a situation (22). Most likely, emotional stress is multifactorial rather than singular in origin. As with other forms of stress, emotional stress results in adaptive hormonal and metabolic responses. In most cases, unconscious modes of adaptation are operative with little apparent effect of the stress per se on the individual's life (22). Of concern is the overwhelming psychological stress which taxes the body's protective mechanisms (1). Some medical evidence indicates a causal relationship between emotional stress (both acute and chronic) and "diseases of adaptation"—cardiovascular disease, hypertension, stomach ulcers, and cancer (1,2,7,15,23-27). For instance, an individual with a so-called Type A behavior pattern, characterized by excessive competitive drive, preoccupation with deadlines, chronic impatience, and a strong sense of time urgency and work orientation, is said to be susceptible to increased risk of coronary heart disease (24). However, stress is only one factor in these multicausal "diseases of adaptation" (1).

In terms of nutrition, abnormal eating behavior such as adherence to food faddism and weight reduction schemes, both of which can result in anorexia nervosa, and compulsive overeating leading to obesity or impeding weight loss, often is associated with psychological stress (1,2,28). Fear, anxiety, and tension increase energy expenditure (i.e., increase metabolic rate), thus the emotional response of a seriously ill person may further contribute to the already increased energy requirements of the disease process (12,15). Emotional stress also may interfere with fat digestion—emotional states influence the rate of chylomicron clearance from the blood (20). This is significant with regard to certain diseases related to fat metabolism. Changes in the sodium content of human milk also have been attributed to acute emotional stress or trauma of the lactating mother (29).

Large doses of vitamin C (two grams or more for adults) are advocated as beneficial in various conditions of stress, including emotional stress (30-32). In fact, countless multivitamin "stress" products are advertised to increase resistance to stress and for treatment of alleged nutrient deficiencies associated with stress (33). However, to date, objective scientific evidence indicating that stress per se warrants an increase in any vitamin in amounts substantially above the RDA is lacking (34).

Stress of Injury, Operation, Trauma, Infections, and Burns. Much attention has been given to the hypermetabolic response and the nutritional sequela of stressors such as injury (15-18,35,36), operation (15,19,37,38), trauma (14,15,39-41), burns (11,13,15,42-44), and infection (10,15,17,45-48). Teleologically, this hypermetabolic state may be considered a normal condition of the body's capacity to survive—the body furnishes substrates from its own tissues during a period of forced inactivity and nutrient shortages following a stressful event (10,17,38). While it is generally agreed that the nutritional requirements of the acutely stressed individual differ quantitatively rather than qualitatively from those of subjects under usual stresses, there is yet uncertainty regarding how specific nutrient requirements are affected by these stress conditions (38,47). Most of the research in this area concerns stress-related energy and protein needs.

The neuroendocrine response of stress results in increased energy expenditure (4). During stressful events, metabolic processes must be re-established to protect the body's internal environment from change. This requires energy (19,41). The magnitude of the hypermetabolic response is influenced by a number of factors including the pre-stress nutritional status of the individual, the age of the subject, and the severity and duration of the stressor (35). The average adult requires a basal energy intake of approximately 1400-1800 kcal/day (41). Mild trauma associated with a relatively uncomplicated surgical procedure elevates energy requirements by less than 10% above normal levels; after multiple fractures or skeletal injuries, resting metabolic expenditure (RME) may be increased by 10%-30%; in the patient with severe infection or sepsis, RME may be elevated by 20%-50% (12,15,35,45,47). But the most devastating energy drain is that related to major thermal injuries (i.e., third degree burns) where energy requirements are increased by 40% to 125% (15,35,38,42,46). If sepsis supervenes on this thermal stress, energy expenditure is further increased (15,42-46). It is common for patients with extensive thermal injuries to require 4,000-8,000 kcal energy per day to remain in energy balance (37,39,41,43). This hypermetabolic state correlates best with the extent of the burn, and energy expenditure returns to normal when the skin surface is healed (43).

As food intake usually is diminished in acutely stressed individuals, endogenous sources of energy become increasingly important (41). The better the nutritional state of the individual prior to the stressful insult, the greater the endogenous stores of energy (41). Immediately after injury, the initial energy requirements are supplied by carbohydrate stores (muscle and liver glycogen). The body's glycogen reserve, however, is exhausted within 24 hours at which point energy must be provided by protein and fat stores (17,35,41). Endogenous amino acids from the breakdown of skeletal muscle protein constitute an important source of energy in the catabolic phase of the stress response (35). If the stressful insult is prolonged, massive tissue wasting and weight loss ensue.

Knowledge of the patient's energy requirements under different stress conditions is necessary for selection of appropriate nutritional supportive therapy (39). Methods to estimate energy intake under a number of clinical situations are available (15,42). Nutrient intake can be administered via oral feeding, tube feeding, or intravenous alimentation (35). While energy replacement is advantageous in terms of preventing or lessening tissue breakdown, the hypermetabolism will not be corrected by providing exogenous energy. This only can be accomplished with resolution of the stress.

Alterations in protein metabolism correlate closely with energy metabolism (45,46). Stress of injury, operation, trauma, burns, and infection is characterized by a glucocorticoid-induced catabolism of protein, resulting in overall negative nitrogen balance (15,18,36,45). Indeed, increased nitrogen excretion is viewed as the hallmark of acute hypercatabolism (i.e., tissue loss) associated with stress.

Protein dynamics during stress have been reviewed by Wannemacher (49) and Blackburn and O'Keefe (50). The negative nitrogen balance (i.e., increased urinary nitrogen excretion) of severe trauma is the result of skeletal muscle protein breakdown which supplies amino acids to the liver for the production of new glucose (i.e., gluconeogenesis) to meet the increased demands for energy. Skeletal muscle contains 40% of total body protein and is one of the major contributors of amino acids during stressful illness (49). Loss of protein-containing tissue, mediated through increased hormonal secretion, is the body's defense mechanism for dealing with acute stress (16). Unlike starvation where protein synthesis is reduced and the rate of protein degradation is largely unchanged, the catabolic response associated with stress is characterized by a greater rate of protein degradation than protein synthesis, resulting in a net loss of body protein (15,41,48,49). Urinary nitrogen excretion is related to the severity and duration of the stress (15,36,49). After seven days of a stressful illness, skeletal muscle can lose 25%-30% of its protein content (49). Poor nutritional intake can accentuate protein catabolism. As the catabolic state subsides with resolution of the disease or with wound healing, for example, urinary nitrogen excretion returns to baseline levels (12,15,36,49,50).

While stress elicits an overall catabolic reponse with respect to protein, protein synthesis also is involved in a number of stress-induced processes (49). In injury, severe burns, major operations, and infection, there is a marked increase in the production of acute-phase proteins, the synthesis of which is related to the severity of the illness and the cause of stress (10,49). Thus, protein catabolism during stress has purposes other than simply providing precursors for gluconeogenesis, namely furnishing amino acids for the synthesis of acutely needed blood proteins, structural proteins, and enzymes (18).

If the patient becomes nutritionally depleted during stressful illness, skeletal muscle is unable to provide sufficient amino acids to meet energy demands, thus to avoid this situation nutritional support is indicated (49). Nitrogen balance can be significantly improved in the immediate post-trauma period by provision of appropriate nutrients, usually a protein intake of 15%-20% of total energy (44,49). Blackburn and Bistrian (18) emphasize the importance of integrating nutritional support with the metabolic environment associated with recovery from injury. For example, exogenous protein should be given only when the metabolic environment is conducive to net protein utilization (18). Increased nitrogen intake at the peak of acute stress only leads to greater urea synthesis and excretion, whereas in convalescence, standard hyperalimentation with increased protein, glucose, and insulin regimes can be used to promote restoration of body cell mass (46,50). Adequate protein intake is essential to prevent rapid wasting of protein stores during periods of stressful illness. However, like energy, the hypercatabolic response of stress only can be arrested by effective treatment of the source of the stress itself (11,18).

Little information is available concerning stress-related demands on vitamins, minerals, and electrolytes (47,48). Undoubtedly, a deficiency of these nutrients would interfere with stress-related metabolic processes. Several investigators (10,12,15,35,47) have reported that during moderate to severe stress increased urinary losses of zinc, copper, magnesium, and calcium are evident. Altered blood levels of several nutrients (e.g., vitamin A, ascorbic acid, zinc, iron) and retention of sodium and water also are a significant part of the metabolic response to stress (10,17,35,41). Correction of manifest deficiencies of these nutrients is indicated. However, there is less quantitative information on which to base dietary recommendations for these nutrients under stressful situations than exists for energy and protein (47). Optimal nutritional management of the individual under moderate to severe stress involves assessment of nutritional status, selection of the appropriate feeding regimen, and regular evaluation of the adequacy of nutritional intake (15,16,18).

Stress Associated with Environmental Extremes. The question of whether nutrient requirements are altered during adaptation to climatic extremes has been reviewed by Consolazio and Schnakenberg (51) and Petrasek (52). Man protects himself against drastic changes in ambient temperature by making adjustments in clothing and dwellings, and to a much lesser extent, in endogenous heat production by metabolic processes to maintain body temperature (4,53).

There appears to be a lack of agreement regarding the claim that man, when exposed to cold, increases basal metabolic rate by 2%-5% to generate more heat and maintain the body's core temperature (12,15). Likewise, data on the role of non-shivering thermogenesis as an adaptive mechanism operating in humans on exposure to cold is inconclusive (15). The nutritional status of the subject is important, however, in terms of adaptation to environmental temperature extremes (12). Malnourished individuals and those with increased body fat exhibit a decreased metabolic response to cold (12,52,53). Yet, persons with increased body fat have greater total body insulation (53). Energy, as well as other nutrient requirements, are largely unchanged during exposure to a cold environment, except when strenuous work is being performed in which case nutrient needs are increased (15,51,52). This lack of change in nutrient requirements on exposure to cold alone emphasizes the dominating role of improved clothing and dwellings which markedly reduce heat loss (52).

On exposure to a hot environmental temperature, sweating is a main mechanism of physical thermoregulation (52). Nutrient requirements are elevated during adaptation to an extremely hot environment ($>37°C$) with energy and protein requirements increased in relation to the higher ambient temperature and to the amount of physical work performed (51,52). Evidence supporting a greater need for carbohydrate and fat is less conclusive (52). Regulation of fluid intake and anticipation of mineral and electrolyte losses (e.g., calcium, iron, sodium, and potassium) is particularly important in hot environments and when physical work (e.g., running) is performed (52). It has been suggested, but not uniformly upheld, that vitamin C requirements in excess of the RDA are induced by stress associated with elevated environmental temperature (4,52).

ACKNOWLEDGMENTS: National Dairy Council assumes the responsibility for writing and editing this publication. However, we would like to acknowledge the help and suggestions of the following reviewers in its preparation: M. MacBurney, R.D.,M.S., Coordinating Dietitian, Nutrition Support Service, The Brigham and Women's Hospital, Boston, Mass.; and R. Manickam, M.D., Assistant to H. Selye, and H. Selye, M.D.,PhD., D. Sc., President, International Institute of Stress, Montreal, Quebec, Canada.

REFERENCES

1. Selye, H. *The Stress Of Life*. New York: McGraw-Hill Book Co., 1976.
2. Racy, J. Ariz. Med. *37*: 352, 1980.
3. Burchfield, S.R. Psychosom.Med. *41*: 661, 1979.
4. Food and Nutrition Board. *Recommended Dietary Allowances, Ninth Revised Edition*. Washington, D.C.: National Academy of Sciences, National Research Council, 1980.
5. Council on Scientific Affairs, American Medical Association. JAMA *242*: 2335, 1979.
6. Stini, W.A. In: *Nutrition, Food, And Man*. Pearson, P.B., and J.R. Greenwell (Eds). Tucson, Arizona: The Univ. of Arizona Press, 1980, pp 124-140.
7. Tache, J., H. Selye, and S.B. Day (Eds). *Cancer, Stress, and Death*. New York: Plenum Med. Book Co., 1979.
8. Wilmore, D.W. Surg. Clin. North Am. *56*: 999, 1976.
9. Lenox, R.H., G.J. Kant, G.R. Sessions, L.L. Pennington, E.H. Mougey, and J.L. Meyerhoff. Neuroendocrinology *30*: 300, 1980.
10. Beisel, W.R. In: *Nutrient Requirements in Adolescence*. McKigney, J.I., and H.N. Munro (Eds). Cambridge, Mass: The MIT Press, 1976, pp 257-278.
11. Wilmore, D.W., J.M. Long, A.D. Mason, Jr., R.W. Skreen, and B.A. Pruitt, Jr. Ann. Surg. *180*: 653, 1974.
12. Wilmore, D.W. Clin.Plast. Surg. *1*: 603, 1974.
13. Wilmore, D.W., J.W. Taylor, E.W. Hander, A.D. Mason, Jr., and B.A. Pruitt, Jr. In: *Metabolism and the Response to Injury*. Wilkinson, A.W., and D. Cuthbertson (Eds). London: Pitman Medical, 1976, pp 274-286.
14. Wilmore, D.W. Clin. Endocrinol. Metab. *5*: 731, 1976.
15. Wilmore, D.W. *The Metabolic Management of the Critically Ill*. New York: Plenum Med. Book Co., 1977.
16. Kaminski, M.V., Jr., R.P. Ruggiero, and C.B. Mills. J.Fla.Med. Assoc. *66*: 390, 1979.
17. Kaminski, M.V., Jr., and H.A. Neufeld. In: *Nutrition in Transition. Proceedings Western Hemisphere Nutrition Congress V*. White, P.L., and N. Selvey (Eds). Chicago: Am. Medical Assoc., 1978, pp 210-219.
18. Blackburn, G.L., and B.R. Bistrian. Surg.Clin. North Am. *56*: 1195, 1976.
19. Navia, J.M., and L. Menaker. Dent.Clin. North Am. *20*: 549, 1976.
20. Dubos, R. Am.J.Clin.Nutr. *32*: 2623, 1979.
21. Butterworth, C.E., Jr. JAMA *230*: 879, 1974.
22. Vaillant, G.E. Am.J.Med. *67*: 732, 1979.
23. Valek, J., and E. Kuhn. Psychother. Psychosom. *18*: 275, 1970.

24. Friedman, M., and R.H. Rosenman. *Type A Behavior And Your Heart.* New York: Alfred A. Knopf, 1974.
25. Report of the Committee on Stress, Strain and Heart Disease. Circulation 55: 1, 1977.
26. Kaplan, N.M. J.Hum. Stress *Sept*: 29, 1978.
27. Leff, D.N. Med. World News *March 24*: 74, 1975.
28. Strain, G.W., and J.J. Strain. Int. J. Obesity 3: 167, 1979.
29. Sevy, S. Am.J.Dis. Child *122*: 459, 1971.
30. Pauling, L. Proc. Natl. Acad. Sci. 67: 1643, 1970.
31. Stone, Y. *The Healing Factor: Vitamin C Against Disease.* New York: Grosset & Dunlap, 1972.
32. Pauling, L. Proc. Natl. Acad. Sci. 71: 4442, 1974.
33. Jukes, T.H. In: *Nutrition, Metabolic and Clinical Applications.* Hodges, R.E. (Ed). New York: Plenum Press, 1979, p 260.
34. Herbert, V. Arch. Intern. Med. *140*: 173, 1980.
35. Walker, W.F. World Rev. Nutr. Diet *19*: 173, 1974.
36. Schiller, W.R., C.L. Long, and W.S. Blakemore. Surg. Gynecol. Obstet. *149*: 561, 1979.
37. Bresner, M. J. Oral Surg. *35*: 200, 1977.
38. Elwyn, D.H. Crit. Care Med. 8: 9, 1980.
39. Clowes, G.H.A., Jr. R.I. Med. J. *58*: 106, 1975.
40. Clowes, G.H.A., Jr., T.F. O'Donnell, G.L. Blackburn, and T.N. Maki. Surg. Clin. North Am. *56*: 1169, 1976.
41. Wieman, T.J. Heart Lung 7: 278, 1978.
42. Curreri, P.W., D. Richmond, J. Marvin, and C.R. Baxter. J.Am.Diet. Assoc. 65: 415, 1974.
43. Bartlett, R.H., P.A. Allyn, T. Medley, and N. Wetmore. Arch. Surg. *112*: 974, 1977.
44. Shenkin, A., M. Neuhauser, J. Bergstrom, L. Chao, E. Vinnars, J. Larsson, S.O. Liljedahl, B. Schildt, and P. Furst. Am.J.Clin.Nutr. *33*: 2119, 1980.
45. Kinney, J.M. Acta Anaesth. Scand. *55*: 15, 1974.
46. Long, C.L. Am.J.Clin.Nutr. *30*: 1301, 1977.
47. Scrimshaw, N.S. Am.J.Clin.Nutr. *30*: 1536, 1977.
48. Nichols, B.L. South.Med.J. *71*: 705, 1978.
49. Wannemacher, R.W., Jr. In: *Nutrition in Transition. Proceedings Western Hemisphere Nutrition Congress V.* White, P.L., and N. Selvey (Eds). Chicago: Am. Medical Assoc., 1978, pp 202-209.
50. Blackburn, G.L., and S.J.D. O'Keefe. In: *Nutrition in Transition. Proceedings Western Hemisphere Nutrition Congress V.* White, P.L., and N. Selvey (Eds). Chicago: Am. Med. Assoc., 1978, pp 220-227.
51. Consolazio, C.F., and D.D. Schnakenberg. Fed.Proc. *36*: 1673, 1977.
52. Petrasek, R. Prog.Fd.Nutr.Sci. 2: 505, 1978.
53. Buskirk, E.R. In: *Environmental Stress: Individual Human Adaptations.* Folinsbee, L.J., J.A. Wagner, J.F. Borgia, B.L. Drinkwater, J.A. Gliner, and J.F. Bedi (Eds). New York: Academic Press, 1978, pp 249-266.

GERIATRIC NEEDS

Nutrition in The Aged

by Robert C. Young, M.D., and John P. Blass, M.D., Ph.D.

As people age, they tend to need fewer calories because their basal metabolism and activity levels decline. In contrast, they continue to need as much protein, vitamins, and minerals as ever. Thus, their optimal diet should have a higher concentration of protein and essential minerals and vitamins than that of younger individuals. Many factors work against this need, however, and the dietary intake in the elderly is often of poor quality.

Physical disabilities may interfere with adequate nutrient intake by interfering with the purchase, preparation, and ingestion of food. Such disabilities include not only such conditions as cardiovascular disease, stroke, arthritis, and poor dentition.

The changes in acuity of the special senses with age tend to cause decreased nutrient intake. Decreased sense of taste or smell may lessen the palatability of food. Poor hearing can interfere with the social aspects of meals. Impaired vision may disrupt shopping for food and food preparation, as well as its enjoyment.

Depression and dementia

Psychiatric illness is prevalent in the elderly and this has an influence on food intake. Apathy and anorexia are common symptoms of depressive illness in aged patients. Depression in this age group too often is undiagnosed or misdiagnosed as dementia. In patients with dementia, the impact of intellectual development on nutrition must be considered. The possibility of alcoholism and other drug dependencies must also be kept in mind.

Social isolation often leads to indifference about food and to reliance on quickly prepared foods of high simple carbohydrate content. It would be wise to counsel such patients about the importance of regularly scheduled meals, even when eating alone.

Economic hardship is prevalent among the elderly and this clearly has nutritional consequences. Many older persons who do not spend their limited funds on the most nutritious foods might benefit from advice in this area. Sometimes, food choices stemming from individual habit or culture may need to be modified. Certainly the elderly need to be made aware of food stamps and other government programs.

The Myth of Extreme Longevity

They were too good to be true... those reports of very old people in the Himalayas, Caucasus, and Andes mountains whose vigorous, healthy life well past age 100 was attributed to physical activity, contented minds, and sparse, low-fat diets.

All three groups most intensively studied—the Hunzakuts of northern Pakistan, the Vilcabambians of Equador, and the Abkhazians of the Georgian Caucasus—were indeed exceptionally active, working as peasant farmers in a harsh environment.

They also shared another characteristic: they tended to be vague about their ages, and tried to please researchers seeking evidence of extreme old age. Subsequent investigators, demanding proof of age, concluded that these people did have many healthy older members, but few if any were over age 100.

The Muslim Hunzakuts subsist largely on grains and dried apricots and rarely eat meat or dairy products. The Vilcabambians also eat an essentially vegetarian diet, but use alcohol and sugar liberally.

The Georgians eat large amounts of meat and animal fats, dairy foods (not just yogurt!), sweets, and wine, as well as vegetables.

So there is no 'wonder diet' promoting longevity—but fewer calories and more exercise may help.

A dietary history is a worthwhile part of evaluation of the geriatric patients. This history might best be obtained by a dietitian or knowledgeable interviewer.

Vitamin deficiencies

Dietary vitamin deficiencies, especially vitamins B_6 and B_{12}, niacin, folate, thiamin, and ascorbate have been documented in both institutionalized and non-institutionalized elderly patients.

The significance of any 'subclinical' deficiency is not

clear. Some nutritionists argue that supplemental vitamin therapy in the elderly is less costly than the equivalent dietary change.

Oral supplements, however, do not always eliminate deficiencies in elderly patients. This may result from malabsorption or drug interference, or of failure to take the daily supplements. Under these circumstances, proper diet or parenteral supplementation may be the better routes.

Dietary deficiencies of iron and calcium are common in the elderly. Hypochromic microcytic anemia is more prevalent in this age group than in younger adults. Osteoporosis, particularly a problem of elderly women, may be exacerbated by dietary deficiencies of calcium and vitamin D.

Effects of drugs

The elderly are major consumers of both prescription and non-prescription drugs. These can affect nutritional status in a variety of ways. For example, anticholinergic drugs decrease salivation and this can produce dysphagia. Idiosyncratic and reversible impairments of taste are associated with the use of such drugs as L-dopa and allopurinol. Anorexia can be produced by digitalis, and interference with nutrient metabolism or absorption occurs with ergot alkaloids. All drugs taken by an elderly patient, including self-prescribed over-the-counter drugs, should be reviewed frequently to avoid the risks of polypharmacy.

Therapeutic diets are valuable in theory but often are unpalatable in practice. Sodium restriction is notoriously hard to implement, even though it is a valuable first line of defense in hypertension and heart disease. Indeed, many Americans eat too much salt for optimal health. However, salt can add to the taste of food, particularly for older people whose taste organs are partly atrophied. Using salt or salt substitutes may increase the palatability, of the diets for such persons.

Conflicting demands

In nutrition, as in other areas of clinical medicine, one necessarily balances conflicting demands. Sick people often need medicines or diets that can interfere with their nutrient usage. Confused or unhappy people often have trouble maintaining a healthy dietary intake, even with the best of care. Svanborg and associates in Sweden found that 4 of 23 patients in their superbly run geriatric ward were clinically undernourished, even though they had been presented with carefully prepared optimal meals.

Furthermore, adequate basic scientific information needs to be gathered on how age, illness, and genetic factors alter nutritional demands. Such information will help practicing physicians balance their patients' changing needs and thus provide better care.

Recommended reading

Busse EW et al: Nutrition of the elderly. *Postgrad Med* 63:117, 1978.

Baker H et al: Oral versus intramuscular vitamin supplementation for hypovitaminosis in the elderly. *J Am Ger Soc* 28:42, 1980.

Baker H et al: Vitamin profiles in elderly persons living at home or in nursing homes vs. profiles in healthy young subjects. *J Am Ger Soc* 27:444, 1979.

Krehl WA: The influence of nutritional environment on aging. *Geriatrics* 29:65, 1974.

Granerus AK, Philip I, Svanborg A: Intake of calories and nutrients in hospitalized geriatric patients, in Carlson LA (ed) *Nutrition in Old Age*, Uppsala, Almqvist and Wiksell, 1972, p. 134.

Vitamin Deficiencies in Older People

While the RDA for energy decreases with age, the RDA for vitamins remains relatively constant. Meeting these recommendations places elderly persons in a dilemma: they must lower caloric intake without decreasing vitamin intake. And nutritionists believe that a diet containing less than 2,000 calories is probably deficient in vitamins.

For this and other reasons—low income, poor appetite, social isolation—the elderly are particularly vulnerable to gradual depletion of body vitamin stores as a result of poor dietary habits.

Yet, clinical signs of a specific deficiency are rare. Much more commonly are nonspecific symptoms, such as malaise, irritability or somnolence, loss of appetite and weight, and impairment of physiological and physical performance socially or at work.

The AMA Council on Food and Nutrition has suggested that an adequate diet can supply all nutrients essential for maintenance of health in a normal individual —but some authorities have stated that the elderly as a group may not be 'normal' in light of their high incidence of chronic illness.

An alternative approach is dietary supplementation with complete multivitamin preparations at RDA levels (*Postgrad Med* 63:155, 1978). In most elderly persons with vitamin deficiencies, this will restore blood levels and enzyme activity to normal. About the only exception are elderly persons with vitamin B_{12} deficiency resulting from lack of intrinsic factor.

Dietary supplementation with multivitamins costs less than would the foods required to correct vitamin deficiency—an economic consideration of particular interest to the elderly poor. And most investigators feel that the benefits of multivitamin supplementation greatly outweigh any possible complications of their use.

Fats and the Elderly

Because the death rate from atherosclerosis is much greater in the aged population, it has been customary to recommend that older people reduce their intake of dietary fats, especially saturated fats. As yet, there are no studies to evaluate the prescription of fat-modifying or cholesterol-lowering diets for persons over age 65 (*Nutrition & the M.D.*, April, 1979).

Although the energy requirements of the elderly are considerably less than those of younger people of the same sex, one of the most common nutritional deficiencies in the elderly population remains inadequate energy intake. One reason for this is the decreased intake of dietary fat by older people. However, any decrease in fat intake is usually compensated by an increase in carbohydrate intake.

Dietary fats enhance the satiety value of food. In addition, fats improve the flavor of many foods, making them more appetizing and appealing.

Dietary fats serve as carriers for the fat-soluble vitamins A, D, E, and K and provide essential fatty acids for the body. These functions can be fulfilled by a diet containing as little as 15 to 25 gms of fat per day. Eggs are an inexpensive, well-accepted source not only of fats but also of high biologic value protein that is easily digested. Eggs are, however, high in cholesterol.

Modification or restriction of dietary fat intake is necessary when fat malabsorption is present. Decreased fat absorption in the elderly has been related to reduced digestive capacity occurring with age or may be a consequence of drug therapy, gastrointestinal surgery, or alimentary tract disease.

Protein Needs of the Aged

Aging is accompanied by changes in both the amount and distribution of body protein. The decreased amount of body protein has been documented by measuring whole-body potassium levels as an index of protein content. Data from postmortem studies show that most of this loss is due to decreased skeletal muscle mass.

As a percentage of total body protein, the amount of muscle decreases from 45% in a young adult to 27% in a person over age 70. Similarly, the amount of protein in liver decreases from 3% in a young adult to 2% in an elderly person.

The rate of whole-body protein turnover falls as a young person approaches adulthood and then continues to decline slowly during the adult years. In addition, with advancing age, muscle provides a progressively decreasing proportion of total protein metabolism. Munro and Young (*Postgrad Med* 63:143, 1978) found that muscle protein accounted for about 27% of whole-body protein breakdown in young men but for only 20% in elderly men.

Based on available information, it appears highly questionable that the elderly require less protein than younger subjects. It is advisable to assure a protein intake of at least a gram per kilogram of body weight.

Results of the Ten State Nutrition Survey indicated that protein intakes among the elderly usually met or exceeded the RDA. It should be noted, though, that numerous factors modify the nutrient needs of all individuals. Infection, trauma, and disease may all be more prevalent in the elderly and these increase their need for both protein and other nutrients.

Recommended Dietary Allowances for Older People

The current guidelines for estimating nutritional adequacy —the RDA—have established recommended intake levels for 17 essential nutrients from infancy through 'age 50+'. However, the increasing proportion of the population over age 65 has led to more interest in the accuracy of such nutritional guidelines for the elderly.

Information about the effects of aging on non-calorie nutrient requirements is accumulating, but is still inadequate. Currently the need for nutrients does not seem to be appreciably altered by increasing age. The nutritional deficiencies that do occur— most commonly iron, calcium, vitamins A and C, thiamin and riboflavin— are most likely related to low food intake or inappropriate food selection, or possibly to altered absorption.

The 1980 RDA publication indicates the *energy* needs of the elderly population decreases. Basically, energy (calorie) requirements reflect resting metabolic rate (RMR), physical activity, and body size or lean body mass ... and with increasing age, these parameters all decline. In addition, the elderly are more subject to chronic and degenerative diseases that limit activity and alter body functions.

For these reasons, the energy requirements in the 1980 RDA have been adjusted downward to compensate for the lessened activity that occurs with age. The RDA separates the mature adult, engaged in *light* physical activity, into three age categories: 23-50 years, 51-75 years, and 76+ years.

Reduction in metabolic rate and activity is reflected in the 51-75 age group by a decrease of 300 kcal/day for men, 200 kcal/day for women, compared to the 23-50 age group. In the 76+ age group, there is a further decrease of 350 kcal/day for men, and 200 kcal/day for women.

Nutrition Programs for the Elderly

The social problems of many elderly Americans which may lead to malnutrition—low income, lack of transportation, inadequate food preparation facilities, and inability to afford dental care, among others—have prompted federal, state, and local agencies to mandate food programs for the aged.

The federal Older Americans Act of 1965 was amended in 1972 to grant states money to provide senior citizens with nutritionally adequate, low-cost meals. Although all persons over 59 years of age are eligible, the primary focus is given to minorities, people with low incomes, and extremely old individuals.

Title III programs

Formerly known as Title VII, the current Title III legislation makes one hot noon meal available five days a week, supplying a third of the RDA. The meal includes 3 oz. meat or equivalent two half-cup servings of vegetables and fruits (one rich in vitamin A, the other in vitamin C), one serving of bread or alternate, 8 oz milk or calcium equivalent, and one serving of dessert.

During fiscal year 1980, federal appropriations for Title III programs were $270 million for meals served in local centers where social and other needs are met, and also $50 million for home-delivered meals. Funding assists with food purchasing and preparation, facilities, and transportation for persons otherwise unable to participate.

Other services

Low-income senior citizens may also obtain food stamps through the Department of Agriculture Food Stamp Program. These are redeemable for a variety of foods at local grocery stores. Proposed federal legislation in 1981 will increase the availability of home-delivered foods, especially those that require simple preparation for homebound elderly people.

Social service agencies

Social work agencies can provide information to guide elderly patients to appropriate nutrition resources in the community, such as Title III meal centers or Meals-On-Wheels programs. On physician referral, Home Health Services (offered through local private and public organizations) provide home health aides to assist older people with shopping, housekeeping, and food preparation.

In addition, some cities have instituted telephone hotlines and 'reassurance' numbers where older Americans can call for aid in acquiring, handling, preparing, and serving food.

Benefits

Results of studies show that, since 1972, these nutrition programs have improved nutritional status of the elderly, especially those with iron-deficiency anemia and vitamin A and C deficiencies.

The principal need for the medical professional is to direct the aged patient to local agencies where help can be found. Usually, local social service agencies are best informed about government, church, and civic organizations that offer support services for the aged.

Constipation in the Aged

With increasing age, the tone of the intestinal smooth muscles diminishes and the activity of the intestinal tract lessens. The result is one of the major banes of growing old—chronic constipation.

This condition not only causes discomfort but also can lead to serious consequences in older patients. Fecal impaction can cause anal fissures, intestinal obstruction or urinary retention. Straining at stool may create sudden severe circulatory changes in the aged.

Other causes

Sometimes constipation can be attributed to faulty bowel habits (most often a chronic failure to heed the urge to defecate) or to inadequate exercise (necessary both to maintain the strength and tone of the abdominal muscles and to promote large bowel propulsion).

When evaluating a patient with constipation, it is also necessary to review any medicines that he or she may be taking. Codeine, morphine, and other narcotics all are constipating, as are papaverine and iron preparations such as ferrous sulfate. With a prolonged history of constipation, check for hypothyroidism.

Constipation (or undue concern over bowel function) often leads to excessive use of laxatives and purgatives; the frequent passage of watery stools may in turn cause fluid and potassium depletion and secondarily may lead to muscle weakness and mental apathy. Often patients depend on at weakness and mental apathy. Often patients depend on a bedtime laxative and sometimes it is not possible to convince them to forego this. Still, the dosage should be kept minimal, and perhaps a stool softener (such as powdered psyllium seed) can be substituted for a cathartic drug.

Dietary management

The diet for elderly persons troubled with constipation should include those foods that provide sufficient fiber to stimulate peristalsis: wholegrain breads, cereals, and raw fruits and vegetables. Raw vegetables are better accepted when served in ground, shredded, or blenderized forms. Fresh fruits are more readily eaten when peeled, sliced, or cubed.

A high fluid intake (ideally, the equivalent of six to eight glasses of liquid a day) can be maintained by beverages such as juices, milk, and milk-based drinks, by soups, and by other foods with a high water content, such as ice cream, sherbet, and gelatin.

Some cautions

The elderly person who begins to eat large amounts of bran cereals, should be advised to increase fluid consumption. Similarly, a constipated person who has been accustomed for years to a low-residue diet should not suddenly begin to consume an excessive amount of vegetables; the colon cannot be expected to adjust itself rapidly to such abrupt changes in its contents.

Prune juice remains a valuable food to alleviate constipation, due to its content of diphenylisatin, a natural laxative. However, diabetic patients must be cautioned about its high carbohydrate content; just 2 oz of prune juice is a fruit exchange in the diabetic exchange system, equivalent to 4 oz of orange juice or half a grapefruit. Also, prune juice is rich in potassium and should be taken with caution by patients with renal failure.

The dietary management of constipation should consist of a varied diet that is high in nutrient density, rich in fiber, and abundant in fluids. When possible, this should be accompanied by an increase in physical activity and exercise.

Nutrition Therapy for Hypertension

Since hypertension is a chronic disease requiring lifelong therapy, many physicians advocate a nonpharmacologic approach. Alternative therapies include diet, exercise, and a variety of behavioral techniques.

There is no convincing evidence that behavioral modification has a prolonged antihypertensive effect. Isotonic exercise reduces blood pressure a few millimeters but cannot be relied on as definitive antihypertensive therapy. Physical training can only be an adjunct to antihypertensive drug therapy.

Effects of diet

Data on the effectiveness of nutritional therapy for hypertension are much more convincing. One report shows that 85% of patients with diastolic blood pressures of 90 to 104 mm Hg will have those pressures reduced to less than 90 mm Hg on a 75-mEq sodium diet (*Hypertension Update*, Health Learning Systems, 1980). Sodium restriction also enhances drug therapy, permitting smaller antihypertensive drug dosages.

Two other reports have shown that weight loss in the range of 20-30 lbs reduces blood pressure (sometimes to normal levels) in hypertensive patients who are overtly obese (*N Engl J Med* 298:1, 1978; *Q J Med* 23:331, 1954).

The Chicago Coronary Prevention Evaluation Program showed that long-term improvements in eating and exercise habits yielding moderate sustained weight loss seemed to prevent hypertension in hypertensive-prone persons and to control established 'mild' hypertension (*JAMA* 243:1819, 1980).

The compliance problem

Dr. Ray Gifford cautions that adherence to dietary regimens is a more formidable obstacle than is adherence to pharmacologic regimens (*Mayo Clin Proc* 55:651, 1980). Many patients will not accept the changes in lifestyle imposed by dietary restrictions of sodium and/or calories.

Young people with mild hypertension—for whom dietary therapy has the most to offer as a substitute for lifetime drug treatment—have the most difficulty following a diet. The activities of many adolescents and young adults are closely linked to fast-foods and convenience foods, and only the most motivated will make an effort to adhere to a sodium-or calorie-restricted diet.

Cautions and contraindications

Before electing to try nutritional management of hypertension as a substitute for drug treatment, Dr. Gifford cautions that the physician and the patient should agree that if the diastolic blood pressure does not reach an established goal within six months, drug therapy will be added to the regimen.

Nonpharmacologic therapy is ill-advised for patients with diastolic blood pressures higher than 104 mm Hg and for patients who already have evidence of cardiovascular complications, regardless of their blood pressure.

New approaches

Although the focus of current research has been on reduction of sodium intake, recent work by Langford et al indicates that it is the relation between sodium and potassium intake that is the key to the development of hypertension. There is some preliminary evidence that increased potassium intake may decrease the risk of hypertension.

Despite the lack of well-controlled studies supporting the antihypertensive effects of behavioral modification techniques, research also continues on the use of yoga, transcendental meditation, biofeedback, and other lifestyle changes by patients with hypertension.

GERIATRIC NEEDS

Psychosocial Forces that Affect Nutrition and Food Choices

by Annette B. Natow, Ph.D., R.D., and Jo-Ann Heslin, M.A., R.D.

Every ninth American is a member of the group called the elderly; eleven percent of the total population is aged sixty-five and over. Every day, approximately 5,000 Americans celebrate their sixty-fifth birthday and approximately 3,600 people over sixty-five die. This result is a net increase of 1,400 aged Americans daily, or one-half million per year. Population projections suggest that by the year 2020, there will be 33 million aged.

Soon it will be necessary to divide this group into subgroups—young-old, middle-old, and very old. As more people reach age sixty-five, the proportion of middle-old and very-old grows. Over two million Americans are eighty-five years of age or older. In the past, if requested, a birthday greeting would be sent from the White House to any American celebrating his eightieth (or later) birthday, Recently, the qualifying age was raised to 100 (returned to age 80 at the time of publication), and in 1976 Social Security records listed 10,690 people aged 100 or more. This is remarkable, since the average life expectancy was forty-nine years in 1900.

Babies born in 1977 will live to an average of seventy-three; this is 68.7 years for males and 76.5 years for females[1]. The increase in life expectancy since 1900 has been achieved through a decrease in infant mortality and infectious diseases that strike the young. Less success has been realized in the battle against chronic disorders and diseases of the elderly such as cancer. Until major medical breakthroughs are made against cardiovascular disease, cancer, and other chronic conditions of the aged, the biblical lifespan of "three score and ten" will not change significantly.

As a result of the longer life expectancy of females, which has not yet been fully explained, most older Americans are women. The average for the total sixty-five-plus population is 146 women for every 100 men; in the eighty-five-plus group, there are 217 women for every 100 men. The vast majority (70 percent) of all women over seventy-five are widows who generally live alone on very meager incomes[2]. Still, when questioned as to choice of living arrangements, over one-half of all widows would rather live alone than be dependent on a relative or friend[3].

Widowers generally fare much worse living alone than do widows. Widowers are usually unprepared to take care of themselves. The remarriage rate for older widowers is higher, as many widowers find the married state to be more comfortable than single life[3].

The vast majority of the aged are satisfied with life, are happy, and lead meaningful existences[4]. This is contrary to the stereotyped view of the older person who is lonely, unhappy, and constantly complaining. Still, many elderly are economically deprived. Income is reduced at retirement and often this lowered income is not adequate to meet basic needs. One seventh (or 3.3 million) of the elderly have incomes below the official 1975 poverty threshold ($3,417 for older couples and $2,720 for older individuals), with elderly women and members of minorities overrepresented in this group[5]. Persons living on fixed incomes are hit hard by inflation. The elderly have few opportunities for improvement of personal income because of "mandatory retirement" and age-discriminatory hiring practices. In a recent survey, 37 percent of those retired said they did not stop working by choice[4].

The limited income of elderly individuals is constantly threatened by ever-increasing healthcare expenditures. In 1976, per capita health care for each older American averaged 3.5 times that spent for each person under sixty-five. The elderly 11 percent of the population incurs 29 percent of the total health care expenditures in the country[2]. Medicare covers less than half of these expenses. Older people see physicians one and one-half times as often, and have about twice as many hospital stays, as do younger people. Also, the hospital stays of the elderly tend to last twice as long as those of younger people. Yet, when questioned, 82 percent of the elderly reported no hospitalization in the previous year and 69 percent reported their health as being good to excellent[4]. Only 5 percent of the noninstitutionalized aged are housebound and only slightly over 1 percent are bedridden[2].

The myriad of psychosocial forces that affect the elderly are impossible to describe totally. The following section will deal, for the most part, with those factors that put the elderly at risk for nutritional problems. (See Figure 10-1 for a list of factors influencing nutritional status.) Those elderly who face the greatest risks are the 15 percent who are economically deprived. An additional 2.2 million elderly are "near-poor," falling into the low income population group. Collectively, the poor and near-poor number 5.5 million, or one-fourth of all persons aged sixty-five and older[5].

The psychosocial problems faced by these elderly—substandard housing, limited income, inadequate transportation, and social isolation—are problems that may strike any age group. These are common maladies of socioeconomically deprived minorities. It is tempting to consider the aged as a

---

From *Geriatric Nutrition* by Annette Natow and Jo-Ann Heslin, pp. 197-224. Copyright 1980, CBI Publishing Company, Inc. Reprinted with permission.

A. Physical
1. Dental problems
2. Excretion problems (constipation, incontinence)
3. Physical weakness (e.g., generalized arteriosclerosis or arthritis with joint stiffness making eating painful)
4. Lack of physical activity
5. Loss of sensation (smell, taste)
6. Chronic disease
7. Lactose intolerance
8. Drug interference (anorexia)
9. Reduced digestive capacity

B. Psychological
1. Emotional depression
2. Anorexia
3. Personal taste preference
4. Lifetime eating habits
5. Lack of socialization with meals

C. Social
1. Financial constrictions
2. Inconvenience of food preparation for one person
3. Inability to adapt to unfamiliar surroundings (hospital or nursing home)
4. Erroneous dietary beliefs
5. Subsequently to "fad nutritional" claims

FIGURE 10-1 Physical and psychosocial factors influencing the nutritional status of the elderly.

Source: Dialogues in Nutrition, Vol. 2, No. 3, "Nutritional Problems of the Elderly," Health Learning Systems Inc., Brookfield, New Jersey, 07003.

minority group. They resemble other minority groups in that they suffer from prejudice, discrimination, and deprivation. Yet, they were not born into this "minority" of deprived aged and they have little sense of group identity or political unity[6]. The elderly may form a *statistical* minority, yet they have few common identifying characteristics except advanced age, a few wrinkles, and greying hair. Herein lies the problem: the aged cannot be readily classified nor can many generalizations be easily drawn about them.

One generalization that may be drawn, however, is that many elderly are subjected to specific nutritional problems. Before intervention techniques are instituted to deal with these nutritional problems, three things must be considered[7].

1. Differences between the young and old from a therapeutic standpoint.
2. Specific age/sex/ethnic/economic differences among members of the older group.
3. Individual differences apart from ethnic/cultural/economic group association.

In short, before intervention is attempted, the elderly person's entire life experience must be considered because it may be just that experience that has created the existing problem or may be a complicating factor.

THE MEANING OF FOOD

Before any nutritional problems can be corrected, the meaning of food and the importance of food habits for that particular person must be understood.

Food is power or security, a symbol of prestige and status, an overture of hospitality and friendship, and an outlet for emotions[8]. Most people tend to define food culturally and not on the basis of the nutritional value of particular items. Food habits are learned. They are a way for a particular culture to exert a standardizing influence on the behavior of an individual in the group so that the group comes to have common eating patterns. Food habits are established early in life and are resistant to change[9]. Familiar food and food patterns represent security to the elderly and provide a link to the past that is a source of comfort. The elderly use food to communicate and an astute health professional can translate their messages. It is important to listen carefully when an elderly person explains likes and dislikes. The elderly person has every right to expect his wishes to be respected.

For the elderly, breakfast is the most enthusiastically received and completely eaten meal of the day. Therefore, this meal, more so than lunch or dinner, should be tailored to the likes and dislikes of the person. During times of anxiety, foods that were given during infancy and childhood may provide comfort. Milk, cooked cereal, and pureed items are often requested. When a person is stressed, anxious, or confused, regression is common and may be reflected in his selection of foods. At other times, these items will be rejected because the older person does not want to be "babied"[10,11].

Nursing home staff members can often predict an emotional episode in a patient by simply observing the foods that are or are not eaten. Increased plate waste often reflects increased emotional stress. Some patients refuse to eat anything and complain bitterly about food preparation or service during a period of unhappiness. As the emotional upset subsides, normal consumption patterns return[12].

For the institutionalized elderly as well as those who are living independently, cultural and traditional patterns of eating will affect food preferences. There have been few published studies of specific food taboos or food preferences among the aged in the United States, but health professionals who have worked with groups of ethnic elderly have made numerous observations worth noting[13].

The United States has long been divided into geographical areas that are identified with certain foods. Presentation of and encouragement to use "down home" food may foster reminiscences, which are considered psychologically important in the aged's adjustment to the final stage of the life cycle[3].

A large proportion of today's elderly were raised in a "culture of poverty" because of their rural or immigrant origins. Many may still be existing at an economic level far below the standard of living enjoyed by others. Therefore, foods associated with status—bakery items and convenience foods—may be preferred and foods identified with poverty, such as beans, may be rejected, regardless of their nutritional value.

Social scientists have also identified *age-appropriate behavior* in older persons which can affect food choices[13]. Older people, particularly older women, are often preoccupied with the health of their bodies. Whether the dysfunction or malfunction is real, imagined, or exaggerated, it will influence food selection and rejection. Digestive upsets, constipation, "poor" blood, and fatigue are often attributed to, and/or "treated" by certain foods.

Educational background is of little significance in the dietary habits of the elderly. Cultural origins and social class are better indicators. This unexpected result is related to the fact that the vast majority of the current generation over 65 had no more than eight years of formal education (and even this being of varying quality). Few received science education and none received nutrition education since nutrition science was in its youth when these people were in theirs. Their nutrition knowledge was acquired as folk myth through family and community association, with more recent information coming through the media[13]. Their lack of basic knowledge may be one reason why they are often subject to faddist notions as they may be unable to differentiate between reliable and unreliable data.

Neighborhoods in transition may interrupt eating habits of the elderly, particularly the low-income urban dweller. Nutritional crises can be precipitated when storeowners vacate, leaving aged residents in familiar but suddenly hostile neighborhoods. Where will the Jewish widow get her meat after the Kosher butcher closes his store? The Italian neighborhood that endures a wave of Puerto Rican immigration leaves little that is familiar to the aged Italians that remain[13]. When customary foods are no longer available and the person feels culturally isolated, food choices are often reduced to readily available bread, starches, and nonnutritious liquids (coffee, tea).

Frequently, the aged, caught in neighborhood decline, may be uprooted and forced to live with their acculturated American children and grandchildren. Antagonism for old-country ways on the part of children and grandchildren often results in withdrawal and exaggerated emphasis on the old ways on the part of the elderly person. Frequently, the defensive grandparent refuses to eat or participate in family meals.

It can be speculated that much of the behavior that ultimately leads to confinement of the aged in a chronic care facility is related to conflict over food and eating. Many nursing home administrators have heard a family say, "He just won't eat!" Assisting families to understand, tolerate, and support the defensive use of food by the aged may reduce the need for institutional care and in some cases may even allow the institutionalized elder to be discharged and reintegrated into the family[14].

Religious beliefs are strong in this country, particularly among the elderly who frequently firmly adhere to religious food practices[13]. An aged Catholic may still insist on "meatless" Fridays even though this practice is no longer required by his church. An elderly Jew may find a cheeseburger offensive as a lunchtime selection; although he may not actively follow the strictest observance of the dietary laws, mixing meat and milk products at the same meal may be unacceptable. Food taboos, fast periods, and holidays are important religious observances that help give structure and meaning to the lives of many people, including the elderly.

Practices of folk medicine may seem absurd to health practitioners but the aged may have great faith in home remedies. The Mexican-Americans and many Latin-Americans often subscribe to the hot-cold theory of disease[13,15,16]. Health is conceived as a state of balance; illness is the result of an imbalance. Foods, herbs, and medications are classified as wet or dry and hot or cold. They are used therapeutically in varying combinations to restore the body's natural balance which manifests itself as somewhat wet and warm. Cold-classified illnesses are treated with "hot" medications and foods, while hot illnesses are treated with "cool" substances. Many chronic disorders are attributed to a chill or eating excessive amounts of cold-classified foods. Arthritis is cold-classified. People who believe in the hot-cold classification and who suffer from arthritis usually will not eat orange juice, bananas, raisins, and other cold-classified foods. If an elderly arthritic patient is prescribed a diuretic and told to eat potassium-rich foods (bananas, orange juice, raisins, dried fruit) to maintain potassium balance, he generally will not follow the physician's orders. If the physician is aware of the patient's folk medicine belief, he could prescribe potassium in the form of a salt substitute or in a liquid form to be taken daily. If the physician is unaware of the patient's views, treatment may be undermined by the patient's self-manipulated diet. The hot-cold classification influences the way a patient adheres to the therapeutic regimens for hypertension, colds, ulcers, constipation, and gastrointestinal problems as well as for arthritis.

SOCIOLOGY OF NUTRITION

Old age is often a time of loss—physical, economic, and social. Food and eating are intensely social functions for the aged. Thus, sociological factors cannot be overlooked when assessing the elderly for nutritional status.

Poor nutritional status is the direct result of improper food selection, but improper food selection may be caused more by a *social* problem than a *health* problem[17]. Poor nutritional status has been correlated with economic impoverishment, poor education, and *social isolation*[10,14]. Any combination of these three factors may be associated with malnutrition in the elderly.

Many elderly persons find themselves socially isolated. A brief discussion of the two forms of social isolation follows.

Isolates

Isolates are people who live alone by choice[3]. They may experience loneliness but they are socially adjusted. Many isolates have been "loners" most of their lives. Others have lost spouses and/or friends but choose to remain independent rather than seek a roommate or live with family.

There are more residentially isolated older women than older men. This is because women live longer than men. Those women who married usually married older men, who predeceased them. Also there are fewer chances for an older women to remarry because of the unequal sex distribution among the aged. Furthermore, women tend to be more capable than men of caring for themselves and for a home, due to their life experience[3].

Even though socially adjusted, isolates may suffer from poor nutrition simply because they are not motivated to shop, cook, and eat by themselves[18].

Desolates

Desolates are those who live alone, though not by choice[3]. These people come to live alone because of the scattering and death of relatives and friends. Each loss of a companion necessitates a rearrangement of lifestyle. If the losses are many, or rapid in succession, there are no substitutes with whom the person can form a meaningful relationship. With no replacement for family, an elderly person may soon find no people with whom friendships may be developed. The emotional upset due to lack of association with other people may manifest itself as actual pain, somatic complaint, or constant recapitulation of the past.

The desolate aged often appear eccentric[4]. Their age precludes a future, their present has little or no meaning, so they cling to the past. Grief may be a constant companion of the desolate and takes the form of chronic depression[19]. Subgroups of the aged population most at risk for desolation are women and blacks, seventy-five years old and over[3].

Other Forms of Adjustment to Old Age

In many urban settings, the environment can have a negative effect on nutritional status. Many elderly do not have the economic, physical, or psychological resources to travel the streets. Public transportation is costly, and may be inaccessible and unadapted to those with limited mobility. Most elderly persons living in urban areas have some fear of theft and violence. Consequently, they may remain locked in their apartment or home, severely restricting shopping trips, and thus drastically altering their diets both in quantity and quality[20].

Undernutrition and malnutrition can also be related to behavior status. Extreme irritability, moodiness, anxiety, and depression can lead to an inability to make proper food choices resulting in a poor nutritional state[12].

Social and psychological differences between aged men and aged women have been reported[21]. These differences need to be understood by anyone assessing nutritional needs. In response to the changes associated with aging, many women display high levels of psychological stress. Loneliness is prevalent among older women. They tend to display higher levels of anxiety, depression, and sensitivity to criticism than younger women. Even though older women usually report their retirement as "voluntary" rather than "mandatory," sociological data shows that women enjoy retirement less than men and take a longer time to adjust to it.

Men are not as likely as women to respond to aging by becoming psychologically stressed. Among older, working class men, aging brings about an acceptable disengagement, a lessened involvement with friends and organizations. Most working class men report that they enjoy retirement. They are the "rocking chair people" who find more pleasure passively observing society than actively entering into it. They feel they have earned this time to relax and be peaceful. Yet, older men eat more meals away from home than older women, making eating one of their major social events. Older men are also willing to spend more money on weekly groceries than older women, regardless of their earnings. Conversely, women spend less on weekly groceries and this amount goes down proportionately as income increases. Thus, having adequate funds to purchase food does not automatically ensure an adequate intake[18].

It has been argued that the aforementioned sex differences are due to a tendency for women to be more willing and to find it more appropriate than men to admit that they have problems[21]. Culturally, men are assigned the capable, caretaker role, therefore older men feel it is a sign of weakness to admit to problems.

The preceding information is a compilation of conclusions drawn by varied professionals—sociologists, psychologists, gerontologists, home economists, social workers, physicians, nutritionists, and others—who have worked with the aged. The nature of this material is such that it does not easily lend itself to controlled studies. However, this observational data is believed to be of value in interpreting sociological factors affecting nutritional status of the aged.

FOOD AS A POSITIVE SOCIAL FACTOR

Eating with others is an important part of life's experiences, contributing to one's sense of belonging. Part of the goal of any nutrition program for the elderly should be to keep participants socially active and psychologically healthy as well as adequately nourished[22].

In 1969, the Senate Select Committee on Nutrition and Human Needs held hearings on "Nutrition and the Aged." Commissioner John Martin of the Administration on Aging (AoA) testified. Throughout his testimony he repeatedly emphasized that malnutrition and undernutrition of older citizens must be considered in the context of interrelated economic, social, physiologic, and psychologic elements[22]. Sensitivity to these interrelated factors must be reflected in nutrition programs for the aged.

Congregate Dining

All nutrition and feeding programs established under the Older Americans Act take into account the total living conditions of the older people who are served. The Older Americans Act supported pilot projects that developed methods and techniques that not only improved the participants' diets, but also enhanced their self-esteem and self-reliance. The success of the initial demonstration projects led to the enactment, in March 1972, of the Title VII Nutrition Program for the Elderly[22].

Title VII funds aid nutrition projects that provide the elderly at least one hot meal per day plus supportive services designed to improve the quality of their lives. The project is based in a community setting which provides congregate dining for individuals sixty years and older and their spouses of any age[23]. These centers are most effective when established near the homes of the elderly or convenient to public transportation[22]. In inner-city locations, elderly living within walking distance are most likely to use the center. Projects have been set up in schools, community centers, public housing facilities, senior citizen centers, homes for the aged, and in church basements.

Whenever possible, meals are prepared in project kitchens. When adequate kitchen facilities are unavailable, meals are purchased from commercial sources. Arrangements can be made to purchase meals from a school, home for the aged, or a commercial caterer. Purchased meals are usually delivered to the site, in bulk, and subsequently portioned into individual servings. Some sites have tested the feasibility of prepackaged meals, delivered to the site in insulated individual trays[22].

Most typically, the noon meal is the one offered to the participants, but some breakfast and a few dinner projects also exist. The meals may be served one day a week, or as frequently as six days a week, depending on the scope and resources available to the project. However, projects funded by Title VII must provide one hot meal a day, at least five days a week, to qualify for subsidies[23].

Participants pay something for their meals. This avoids offending those elderly who would be uncomfortable accepting charity. Participants regard this as a service which they are buying, and therefore avail themselves of it without any lost pride. Cost of the meal is usually a function of one's ability to pay. No one is refused participation because of inability to pay[23]. In 1977, the most recent year for which statistics are available, the cost to produce a typical meal (food and nonfood) was $2.56.

Many nutrition projects use the aged participants in the meal program to help cook, set up, and serve. They may be employed full- or part-time or serve as volunteers. This increased involvement and the opportunity to earn money contributes to self-esteem and social adjustment of the participants. Most project directors enjoy the employment of senior participants since they prove to be capable and reliable employees who come with a lifetime of experience and abilities. The authors know of one case of a retired chef who was a recluse after the death of his wife until he became a cook at a senior citizen center. He went on to work, train employees, and supervise kitchen operations until his death.

Meals in all projects are planned to meet one-third of the Recommended Dietary Allowances as defined for people over age fifty-one[22]. The contribution of this one meal to the total daily intake was recently evaluated[23]. Food records showed that those eating at the meal site consumed more calories, protein, and calcium than nonparticipants and participants who did not eat at the site on the day of the record. A larger proportion of those who eat meals at nutrition sites have diets that rate good to excellent as compared to nonparticipants. Measures of "life satisfaction" and "psychological well-being" increased with the length of participation in the program.

It has been suggested that meals should be planned to provide greater than one-third of the Recommended Dietary Allowances. If a meal were planned to provide 70 percent of the individual's nutrient allowance and the person came to the program every day, one-half of the weekly nutrient needs could be obtained. Participation three times a week would ensure one-third of weekly allowances[23].

A major task of the nutrition project is to reach the socially isolated elderly in the community who most need this service. These people may need special inducements to participate[22]. Older citizens already involved in the program are most effective in recruiting other people of their age group. A sample home-delivered meal can help acquaint the uninitiated with the services and persuade them to join the group. Outreach groups, such as visiting nurses, can be helpful in acquainting the socially isolated with available services. Many centers provide transportation for those elderly who need it, and this naturally boosts participation. In 1978 there were 1,047 Nutrition Program projects serving over 383,000 meals daily. Despite the continued proliferation of programs, only a fraction of the eligible elderly have access to such a program.

Home-Delivered Meals

Delivery of meals to the homes of the handicapped and aged was one of the earliest types of feeding programs to be established. "Meals on wheels" began in England in 1939. Philadelphia became the first city in the United States to organize a "meals on wheels" program, in 1954. Currently, 15 percent of all meals served under the Title VII program are home-delivered meals to housebound elderly[24]. In addition to the federally funded Title VII "meals on wheels" programs, there are state, county, and privately operated programs as well.

Home-delivered meals provide at least one-third of the Recommended Dietary Allowances and may be adapted to suit restricted diets and, in some instances, provide Kosher meals. In addition to meeting nutritional needs, home-delivered meals help meet the social needs of the aged as well. Many meal recipients have no visitors except the volunteer deliverer who comes daily or five times a week. The volunteer provides social contact and often becomes friends with the aged recipient. In the case of temporary disability, the positive social contact resulting from the "meals on wheels" program may interest the older person in joining the congregate meals program at a local site. In the case of chronic disability, home-delivered meals may enable the individual to continue living independently and forestall institutionalization.

Many programs attempt to serve more than one meal daily. They deliver a hot lunch and leave a light supper that is cold or needs only simple heating, such as a canned main dish. Other programs deliver a hot dinner and leave sandwiches for the following day's lunch.

In order to close the significant service gaps that exist in congregate dining and home-delivered meals programs the National Aeronautics and Space Administration (NASA) was asked to use its food technology to develop a convenient, economical, shelf-stable meal system for the homebound elderly[25]. The meals were to be pleasant tasting, easily transportable, shelf-stable, and require few utensils and minimal skills to prepare. If successful, this meal system could be used when congregate or home-delivered meals are not available.

A test of the NASA program in Texas showed very favorable results, with 77 percent of the participants reporting that they "liked the program very much"[26]. The system consists of a complete meal, including main dish, fruit, vegetable, dessert, and beverage packed in one box. The meals are made up of canned, dehydrated, and freeze-dried foods, eliminating the need for refrigeration. Seven meal boxes, a week's supply, are then packed into a larger carton for delivery to the participant's home. The larger box weighed ten pounds or less when fully packed and was designed so that the mail might be used as a means of delivery in outreach areas.

The pilot project confirmed that the NASA meal system was feasible from the standpoint of user acceptability, nutritional adequacy, and cost. The meals are not yet available from retail stores but can be directly mail-ordered from a food manufacturer in Oregon. (Oregon Freeze Dry Foods, Inc., Albany, Oregon, has developed *Easy Meal* under their Mountain House label.)

Institutional Care

An elderly person with a chronic illness or degenerative disease may spend weeks, months, or the remainder of his life in a healthcare facility. Loss of independent living is a devastating event that may manifest itself in depression and anger with staff, relatives, and friends feeling the brunt of these emotions. Many individuals withdraw from personal interaction, some so completely that they may attempt suicide. For many, the regulated, routinized, impersonal environment of the healthcare facility is more like a prison than their "home"[19].

There are varying types of facilities available to the aged—*medically-oriented nursing homes,* for those who require professional round-the-clock medical supervision; *health-related facilities* for ambulatory patients who need minimal medical care but who require a caretaker for activities of daily living; and *housing facilities or proprietary homes* for those who need housekeeping and food service but are otherwise independent. No elderly person should ever be placed in a facility with *more* care provided than they need since this will often make them more dependent on others than is necessary.

It has been reported that female nursing home residents who are dissatisfied with their lives also have poor appetites[11]. They showed lower-than-normal caloric-nutrient intakes for all nutrients except ascorbic acid. If emotions are able to affect attitudes toward meals, they will thus ultimately affect general health.

Little research has been done to document the therapeutic value of a dining room in geriatric living facilities, but staff observations point toward positive effects[27]. Mealtimes become a high point in the day. Residents dress rather than spend the day in robe and slippers when a community meal is taking place. Socialization activities may evolve around meals with residents congregating in living areas for an hour or more before mealtime, waiting for the dining room to "open." Less meal-skipping and reduced plate waste have also been reported when common dining rooms are used. Complaints about food are common in all healthcare facilities but tend to occur less frequently in facilities that use dining room meal service.

Complaints regarding food service can be handled in a manner to encourage participation in group feeding. Setting up a resident's food committee to answer complaints has proven to be effective. If members of the dietary staff are present in the dining room at mealtime to answer questions and converse with residents, meals are more positively accepted. Homestyle or waitress service reduces plate waste when compared to preportioned tray service. Even disoriented residents who observed other people eating became more aware of their surroundings and in some cases began to participate in self-feeding[27]. In one reported case, the dietary supervisor established kitchen tours to prove that food was prepared on-site in a clean, well-equipped kitchen with quality food products. After most of the residents had seen the kitchen, food service complaints fell off markedly.

Geriatric Daycare

A newer concept in care for the elderly is day care, which is far less expensive than institutional care. A 1975 survey estimated that between 14 and 25 percent of all institutionalized elderly are in facilities providing more care than needed[28].

Under day care plans, participants spend the day in a program designed to serve the elderly through social and physical rehabilitation, dietary counseling, and recreational services. The participants return home at night.

All day care facilities provide a minimum of one meal a day, supplying at least one-third of the Recommended Dietary Allowances. Many programs also offer a mid-morning and mid-afternoon snack. If the day care center is located within a longterm care facility, day care participants can eat in a congregate dining room and may even be provided with individually modified diets.

Home aides may provide a type of day care in the person's home which is less structured than the aforementioned[29]. These aides help the older person perform tasks he would do for himself if he were able. Tasks include housecleaning, meal planning and preparation, grocery shopping, assisting with personal care and exercising, and reading to, and writing for the older person. Home aides are often used when an aged person has returned home after hospitalization to reduce further institutionalization during the recuperation phase of illness. Experience with this type of day care seems to indicate that it is most useful and effective for women and non-stroke patients. Men are probably less adaptive to this type of care since they have had little experience directing someone else to do homemaking tasks.

MENTAL DISORDERS

There is a wide range of disordered behavior that is frequently lumped under the category of "senility"[19]. Organic disorders as well as functional disorders occur in old age and both can affect a person's health and nutritional status.

The two main causes of chronic organic brain syndrome are senile deterioration and cerebral arteriosclerosis. Organic disorders are most frequently seen in nursing home patients. Some estimate 55 to 80 percent of all such patients have these disorders[30]. Cerebral arteriosclerosis usually starts before age sixty-five and is often referred to as the "small stroke syndrome," leaving residual damage ranging from slight to severe. Senile deterioration is an insidious process which occurs in later life and causes patchy sclerosing of brain tissue. Both conditions result in irreversible brain damage.

Depression, a functional disorder, is often viewed as a characteristic of senescence or is confused with organic disorders and consequently overlooked[19]. If a patient is ill, depression may be assumed to be part of the reaction to illness. Conversely, it may be the depression that caused the illness. It has been shown that a great number of significant life changes within a given year correlate well with a major health change the following year[31]. Loss of a spouse is the most devastating event that can occur, with widowers coping less effectively than widows. A cluster of life changes (loss of spouse, adjustment to living alone, change of residence) often immediately precedes an illness. Death, rather than coming on unpredictably in life, may follow a major life crisis[32].

Death due to depression is a real occurrence, as evidenced by the high rate of suicide among depressed, elderly, white males[33]. Depression in elderly males often reflects itself in self-aggressive, self-destructive actions. Elderly depressed women become more emotionally detached and attempt manipulative behavior. Attempted suicides by elderly women are often for manipulative rather than self-destructive purposes.

Depression in the elderly must be recognized and treated in order to stop the downward spiral of the individual's clinical state[12]. If neglected, a vicious cycle can be established and lead to apathy, isolation, poor nutrition, neglect of physical health, further depression symptomatology, and, eventually, death.

The incidence of depression in persons over age sixty-five is 8-15 percent in the general population and up to 50 percent in nursing home patient populations[12]. Most of these depressed aged also show some negative symptoms such as insomnia, anorexia, and weight loss and some behavioral disturbances such as isolation, apathy, compulsive or hostile behavior[19].

Depression frequently causes anorexia with subsequent weight loss resulting in a state of undernutrition. Undernutrition is an inadequate intake of food or an incorrect choice of food, or both. This food deprivation exaggerates the depressive behavior and may lead to a clouding of consciousness and a general state of confusion and disorientation. If allowed to proceed uninterrupted, it will lead to starvation and death[12].

Undernutrition caused by depression can be associated with many factors such as grief, social isolation, alcoholism, psychosis, poverty, and poor state of health[12].

Grief may be a constant companion to the elderly. Even people who have successfully "rolled with the punches" throughout life discover that old age can deal blows too cruel and swift to overcome. Chronic grief takes on the form of chronic depression. The elderly person often feels cheated and will often manifest these feelings in delusions about robberies or thefts. The aged begin to hold on to food and priceless objects and may insist on having them ever-present, carrying them from place to place in shopping bags. This clinging to inanimate objects is understandable in light of the ever-increasing losses the elderly person experiences. Food may be hoarded rather than eaten, and this may result in undernutrition which is clearly undesirable[14].

Depression can be causative in alcohol abuse. Elderly alcoholics are often undernourished. They will normally spend money on alcohol while neglecting food. When food is eaten, it often is of the high carbohydrate-high calorie variety resulting in minimal intakes of protein, vitamins, and minerals[12].

The psychotic elderly may refuse to eat because of delusions that the food is poisoned or crawling with insects. Hallucinations of voices may also caution against eating[9].

Overnutrition can be a direct result of depression. To cope with grief, loneliness, and feelings of helplessness, some elderly eat to reduce their anxiety and obtain comfort[12]. Some elderly eat excessively to induce sleep. Even the impoverished aged can become overweight. These people are in a paradoxical situation. They are overweight and undernourished at the same time. They often purchase "comforting" foods (candy, cake, desserts) that are high in calories but low in nutrients, leaving them deficient in protein, vitamins, and minerals. The resultant overweight condition may put the elderly at greater risk for the development of cardiovascular disease and diabetes, both of which have significant mortality rates among the aged.

PHYSICAL DISABILITIES

Since illness and physical impairment increase with age, so, predictably, does disability and limitation of activity. Of all persons sixty-five and over living outside of an institution, 85 percent reported at least one chronic disease and approximately 50 percent reported limitation in normal activity due to chronic health conditions[31].

Malnutrition and undernutrition of the elderly handicapped are major problems that must be solved[34,35,36,37,38]. Preparing, serving, and eating meals can be a major chore for the older homemaker who is handicapped. Arthritis, partial paralysis, impaired vision, and other physical conditions can make the activities of daily living unpleasant endurance events. Still, a handicap should not signal the end of independent living. When a person has a disabling physical condition, tasks must be simplified and wasted motions eliminated. One should let dishes drain dry instead of wiping them, use precut onions, peppers, and vegetables and other foods to eliminate peeling, chopping, and slicing. One should also adapt favorite recipes for convenience foods that require less physical energy to prepare and eliminate all unnecessary lifting. Instead of sliding, one should roll objects on a wheeled cart. Every task must be reduced to its essential motions[35].

Easy-open packages and flip-top cans are of no convenience to an arthritic person with limited strength or joint movement. The arthritic homemaker will tire easily and should plan activities in small sessions. One should never start a job that cannot be stopped in the middle for a rest. It makes sense to sit while doing kitchen work and use only light-weight utensils[35]. For mixing and stirring, large spoons are more easily held and reduce the stress on the hands that comes from grasping a small object. The arthritic person must learn to use the whole hand rather than just fingers to perform many tasks. Stirring can be accomplished by holding the handle of a spoon or fork between the flat palms of two hands. The heels of the hands can be used to apply pressure to package seals, such as on a milk container, to open them[35].

A stroke or surgery may result in the loss of the use of part or all of one arm. If the cause is hemiplegia—paralysis of one side of the body—this may be accompanied by loss of perception and a decreased power of quick mental recall. People with such losses must be taught to turn their heads to compensate for their visual field limitations. These people have lost sight on one side of the visual field and if they do not turn their heads to scan the entire countertop occasionally, things can be overlooked. In food preparation, an ingredient may be omitted because it cannot be seen.

To better understand this handicap, hold your hand up and out alongside your face. Now look down; on one side there will be peripheral vision but on the other side, the one that is blocked, vision is limited only to that which is immediately in front of the line of vision. Side vision is not possible without turning the head.

When a stroke results in aphasia (partial or full loss of the power of expression by speech, writing, or signs, or loss of comprehension of spoken or written language) the person must be taught to plan activities and repeat them over and over again. Easy-to-prepare foods and one-dish meals must be used. Keeping the preparation procedures the same for each meal helps to avoid confusion and frustration.

Hemiplegia makes relearning mealtime tasks difficult, causing the loss of the ability to stabilize food, a pot, or bowl while cooking[38]. New ways of keeping food or utensils from moving or sliding must be learned. The weak arm may be able to help if it is given some support. Holding it in a sling reduces the fatigue of holding the arm up and allows the hands and fingers to hold items. A cutting board with two stainless steel nails hammered through can secure food for cutting or peeling. A wet facecloth or spongecloth under a bowl can anchor it so it will not spin during mixing. Knees can help hold packages as they are opened or unwrapped. The knee-grasp technique works well for almost all packages other than glass screw-top jars. However, jars can be opened with one hand by putting the jar in a drawer, leaning the hip against the drawer to hold the jar securely, and twisting the top off with the free arm. Kitchen tongs work better than a fork or spoon for turning or lifting food during cooking. It is useful to place a heat-proof pad on the counter next to the range. To remove a pot from the range, it can be slid from the range to the counter to avoid lifting. It is easy to use a pitcher to fill an empty pot already on the range or have an extra-long hose attached to the sink sprayer arm, so the pot can be filled directly from the faucet. As with the arthritic patient, lightweight utensils will be the easiest and safest to use[35].

The only time an elderly person will benefit from the use of heavy utensils is when a person suffers from incoordination such as that found in Parkinson's disease[35,38]. This older patient will need to have a great deal of patience in order to complete even the simplest task. The weight of a heavy utensil will help to control excessive motion. Double-handle construction will allow one to grasp and move utensils more securely. Using many of the stabilizing techniques of a hemiplegic and resting both elbows on the counter surface during work will allow for more control.

An older person confined to a wheelchair may find the ordinary home kitchen full of architectural barriers[36]. It may be impossible to maneuver around opened cabinet doors, counters may be too high, faucets too far away to reach, burners on the range are at eye level, a clumsy and dangerous height. Architectural changes will need to be made before this person can live independently again. Today, some of the cost of training, rehabilitating, and purchasing equipment for the handicapped can be provided through local and state departments of vocational rehabilitation. Homemaking is the largest single occupation of the physically handicapped and since 1955 the disabled homemaker has qualified for state and federal funds[38].

SELF-HELP EATING DEVICES

Mealtime is more pleasant and enjoyable when a person can

feed himself independently and without embarrassment. Feeding aids may be useful in assuring the independence of the older person who is having trouble handling regular utensils[34,35].

A built-up handle on a standard eating utensil may be all that is needed to provide a secure grasp for impaired hands. Utensils of this special type can be purchased or a regular eating utensil can be adapted by slipping a foam rubber curler over the handle. The foam surface of the curler increases friction and aids in the maintenance of a steady grasp. These curlers are inexpensive and available in drug and variety stores. Handles may be angled or bent to compensate for limited motion, and a collar or band may be attached to the end of the handle which fits over the person's hand to help prevent the utensil from being dropped.

Plastic and metal plate guards and plates with rims enable the person to pick up his food by first pushing it against the raised edge. A suction cup or sponge cloth under the plate can keep the dish in place while the person is eating.

A spouted cup, extended straws, and pedestal cup can aid in drinking liquids. A two-handled drinking cup is especially useful for older persons with incoordination. Stretch terry cloth glass covers designed for use on cold drink glasses provide a secure grasp when holding a glass. These are available where picnic supplies are sold or can be hand-knit or crocheted. To hold a straw steady and in place, a pen dip can be attached to a cup, and the straw threaded through where the pen was originally held[27]. The *spork*, a combination of fork and spoon, often serrated down one edge, can replace three utensils for a person who has the use of only one hand.

The elderly blind can make use of many of these feeding aids. The lipped plate on which food is placed in a prescribed clockwise fashion is often used to train the blind to feed themselves.

It is important to remember that the ability to feed oneself is a most important factor in feeling independent. It is uncomfortable, humiliating, and embarrassing for an older person to be fed, and every effort should be made to encourage self-feeding. When necessary, eating devices should be provided and the person taught to use them effectively[27,35].

REFERENCES

1. The graying of every 10th American or every 9th American, taken from *Part I Development in aging: 1977*. Washington: US Government Printing Office, 1978.
2. Harris, C.S. *Fact book on aging: A profile of America's older population*. National Council. Aging, Inc. 1828 L Street, N.W., Washington, D.C., 1978.
3. Troll, L.E., 1971. Eating and aging. *J. Am. Diet Assoc.* 59:456.
4. Harris, L., Pres., Louis Harris and Associates, 1974. Who the senior citizens really are. Speech presented at Annual Meeting of National Council on the Aging, Oct. 2, 1974, Detroit, Michigan.
5. Fowles, D.G., 1977. Income and poverty among the elderly. *CNI Weekly Newsletter* 8(24):4.
6. Palmore, E., 1978. Are the aged a minority group? *J. Amer. Geriatrics Soc.* 26(6):214.
7. Brotman, H.B., March, 1972. The fastest growing minority: The aging. *Family Economics Review*, p. 10.
8. Chappelle, M., 1972. The language of food. *Amer. J. of Nursing* 72(7):1294.
9. Todhunter, E.N., 1972. Food is more than nutrients. *Food and Nutrition News* 43(6-7):1.
10. Sherwood, S., October, 1973. Sociology of food and eating: Implications for action for the elderly. *Am. J. Clin. Nutri.* 26:108.
11. Harrill, I., Erbes, C. and Schwartz, C., 1976. Observations on food acceptance by elderly women. *Gerontologist* 16(4):349.
12. Garetz, F.K., 1976. Breaking the dangerous cycle of depression and faulty nutrition. *Geriatrics* 33:73.
13. Howell, S.C. and Loeb, M.B., 1969. Nutrition and aging, chapter III, culture, myths and food, preferences among aged. *Gerontologist* 9(3):66.
14. Weinberg, J., April, 1972. Psychologic implications of the nutritional needs of the elderly. *J. Am. Diet Assoc.* 60:293.
15. Currier, R.L., 1966. The hot-cold syndrome and symbolic balance in Mexican and Spanish-American folk medicine. *Ethnol.* 5:251.
16. Harwood, A., 1971. The hot-cold theory of disease implications for treatment of Puerto Rican patients. *J. Amer. Med. Assoc.* 216(7):1153.
17. Hanson, G., 1978. Considering "social nutrition" in assessing geriatric nutrition. *Geriatrics* 33:49.
18. Brown, E.L., 1976. Factors influencing food choices and intake. *Geriatrics* 31:89.
19. Epstein, L.J., 1976. Symposium on age differentiation in depressive illness, depression in the elderly. *Journal of Gerontology* 31(3):278.
20. Bengtson, V.L. and Haber, D. Social forces and aging individuals: An overview. In *Nursing and the aged*, ed. I. M. Burnside. New York: McGraw-Hill Book Co., 1976.
21. Atchley, R.C., 1976. Selected social and psychological differences between men and women in later life. *J. of Gerontology* 31(2):204.
22. Pelcovits, J., 1971. Nutrition for older Americans. *J. Amer. Dietetic Assoc.* 58(1):17.
23. Kohrs, M.B., O'Hanlon, P. and Eklund, D., 1978. Title VII—nutrition program for the elderly. *J. Amer. Dietetic Assoc.* 72:487.
24. Lawmakers plan new funding for the elderly, 1978. *Institutions* 82(4).
25. Delicious hot meals without cooking, 1978. *Food Engineering* 50:ef-22.
26. Rhodes, L., 1977. NASA food technology, a method for meeting the nutritional needs of the elderly. *The Gerontologist* 17(4):333.
27. Rankin, G., 1975. The therapeutic value of a dining room program in a geriatric setting. *J. Gerontological Nursing* 1(3):5.
28. O'Brien, C.L., 1977. Exploring geriatric day care: An alternative to institutionalization. *J. of Gerontological Nursing* 3(5):26.
29. Neilson, M., et al., 1972. Older persons after hospitalization: A controlled study of home aide service. *Amer. J. of Public Health* 62(8):1094.
30. Schwab, M., 1973. Caring for the aged. *Amer. J. Nursing* 73(12):2049.
31. Shanas, E. and Maddox, G.L. Aging, health and the organization of health resources. In *Handbook of the psychology of the aging*, eds. J.E. Birren and J.E. Schaie. New York: Van Nostrand Reinhold Co., 1977.
32. Rahe, R.H., McKean, J.D. and Arthur, R.J., 1967. A longitudinal study of life change and illness patterns. *J. Psychosomatic Research* 10:355.
33. Latorre, R.A. and McLeod, E., 1978. Machiavellianism and clinical depression in a geriatric sample. *J. Clin. Psychology* 34(3):659.
34. Klinger, J.L., Frieden, F.H. and Sullivan, R.A. *Mealtime manual for the aged and handicapped*, New York: Essandes Special Editions, Simon and Schuster, Inc., 1970.
35. Klinger, J.L., 1978. Mealtime manual for people with disabilities and the aging. Camden, New Jersey: Campbell Soup Corp.
36. Agan, T., et al., 1977. Adjusting the environment for the elderly and the handicapped. *J. Home Economics* 69(5):18.
37. Green, K.B., 1978. Coping daily with the handicapped and the elderly. *J. Home Economics* 70(40):15.
38. Rusk, H.A., 1970. Nutrition in the fourth phase of medical care. *Nutrition Today* 5:24.

OTHER REFERENCES

Kuhn, M., 1978. Insight on aging. *J. Home Economics* 70(40):18.
Lee, R.J., 1976. Self images of the elderly. *Nursing Clinics of North America* 11(1):119.
Lewis, C. *Nutrition: Nutritional consideration for the elderly*. Philadelphia: F.A. Davis Company, 1978.
Montgomery, J.E., 1978. Quality of life for the aging, home economics role. *J. Home Economics* 70(40):12.

GERIATRIC NEEDS

Nutrition and Aging: Some Unanswered Questions

by Richard S. Rivlin, M.D.

The population of the United States 65 years of age and older is expected to double in number between 1960 and the year 2000, growing from 16.7 million to an estimated 31.8 million people.[1] At a time when both the number and proportion of older persons in the population are increasing rapidly, it is appropriate to review what questions need to be resolved before we can understand the nutritional needs of this group. Any recommendations made will require implementation by the elderly themselves, and the first question to be asked is how best to maintain a long-term interest in eating.

That the elderly do not eat adequately seems clear from a number of reports. In a recent analysis of several surveys,[2] it was concluded that a substantial segment of the elderly population as a whole, perhaps as high as 50 percent, is consuming less than two-thirds of the currently recommended dietary allowances for several important nutrients. These key nutrients include calcium, iron, thiamine, riboflavin, niacin, vitamin A and vitamin C. Caloric intake itself has been noted to be below the recommended level in many of these persons.

In other evaluations of the nutritional status of the elderly, the intake of calcium and total calories,[3] and of calcium, vitamin A and thiamine[4] were found most frequently to be deficient. In interpreting data of this kind, one should bear in mind that the validity of recommended dietary allowances for the elderly must depend upon further research specifically in this age group.

These investigations show in general that the elderly persons most frequently consuming inadequate diets are female, poor and black, as well as those persons residing in adult institutions. Nevertheless, poverty *per se* does not seem to explain the entire pattern of nutritional inadequacies in the elderly, and the role of other factors needs to be considered.

Sensory Deprivation. Increasing evidence has been obtained, particularly among the poor, that the elderly become isolated both physically and emotionally, a situation that would be intensified by the development of sensory deprivation. In 1975, of all females 65 to 74 years of age, 33 percent were living alone, and of those women older than 75 years of age, 41 percent were living alone.[5] The progressive impairment of vision with aging is well known, making labels difficult to read and the use of appliances increasingly dangerous. Decrease in pupil size, reduction in transparency of the lens and increase in the thickening of the lens and capsule all combine to diminish greatly the light that reaches the retina.

Reduced hearing also results in progressive reduction in stimuli received.

Taste and Smell. A form of sensory deprivation in the elderly that has been recognized more recently is that of loss of taste and smell abilities. The possible role that impairment of these chemical senses may play in governing food intake and selection in the elderly is just beginning to be appreciated. With aging comes an elevation in the detection and recognition thresholds for a large variety of taste stimuli.[6] Elderly persons have particular difficulty in experiencing mixtures of taste and stimuli, even familiar food items. Loss of taste acuity with aging does not occur abruptly but rather appears to develop gradually throughout the lifetime.

In elderly subjects, major defects of smell sensations also occur frequently. Mean recognition thresholds for some food odors, including cheese, orange, chocolate and bacon, were observed[7] to be at least 11 times higher in patients 65 years of age and older than in a group of students in their 20s. This relative inability of elderly subjects to identify common unseasoned blended foods is shown in Table 1. Each subject was blindfolded and asked first to smell and then to taste a series of food items. The percentage of correct identifications was markedly lower in the older than in the younger group.

Why are taste and smell sensations impaired with aging? The mechanisms are likely to be multiple. The number of taste buds per papilla and probably the total number of papillae decline with aging.[8] Infections in the oral cavity, poor hygiene and diminished rates of salivary flow are likely to contribute to difficulty in taste and smell perception in the elderly. Other causes need to be determined.

The key question that needs answering here is the extent to which losses of taste and smell abilities are potential factors in limiting food intake in general and in the elderly in particular. If favorite items of food no longer provide their customary satisfaction, will the elderly lose motivation to eat? Some authorities have suggested[9] that the taste defects described in elderly individuals may have been exaggerated by inadequate testing procedures. In any event, research needs to be directed towards evaluating the clinical significance of alterations in taste and smell capabilities with aging, and towards preventing further deterioration. The attempt to improve taste abilities for salt and sugar among elderly persons by administration of dietary zinc supplements unfortunately has been disappointing,[10] and other approaches should be made.

Tooth and Bone Loss. Another factor that may limit food selection in the elderly is loss of teeth. An estimated 50 percent of all persons have become edentulous by age 65, and 66 percent

---

From *The American Journal of Medicine*, Vol. 71, September 1981, pp. 337-340. Copyright 1981, Technical Publishing, a company of the Dun & Bradstreet Corp. Reprinted with permission.

by age 75. A major cause of loss of teeth is periodontal disease, and it has been suggested that periodontal disease, in turn, may be associated with, and perhaps an early manifestation of, generalized osteoporosis.[11]

TABLE 1   Percentage of Subjects Correctly Identifying Each of the Blended Foods

Food Substance	Elderly Subjects* (%)	College Students† (%)
Apple	55	81
Banana	24	41
Lemon	24	52
Pear	33	41
Pineapple	37	70
Strawberry	33	78
Walnut	21	33
Broccoli	0	30
Cabbage	7	4
Carrot	7	63
Celery	24	59
Corn	38	67
Cucumber	0	7

NOTE: Data abbreviated from Schiffman.[7]
* Ages from 67 to 93.
† Ages from 18 to 22.

Is osteoporosis a nutritional disorder? Several considerations suggest that nutritional factors may play important roles in its development, and possibly also in its prevention and treatment. The intake of calcium in older individuals is often inadequate, as noted before. Even if elderly subjects were to achieve the levels of dietary calcium currently recommended for adults in the United States population, namely 800 mg per day, these are unlikely to be high enough to retard bone loss. Levels of 1,000 to 1,200 mg per day may be required to prevent negative calcium balance.[12]

The dietary intake of calcium should probably not be considered alone but rather in relation to that of phosphate, as suggested by LaFlamme and Jowsey.[13] Bone loss has been induced by a high-phosphate diet in several species of experimental animals. In dogs fed a high-phosphate diet, the rate of bone resorption in the ulna was doubled, while that of bone formation was cut in half. In the iliac crest, the rate of bone resorption was increased even more by a high-phosphate diet, but that of bone formation was unaffected.[13] Thus, the loss of bone after a high-phosphate diet results predominantly, and perhaps exclusively, from increased rates of resorption. The possible relevance of these findings to clinical osteoporosis is that the typical American diet has a very high ratio of phosphate to calcium, due to the high amounts of phosphate in processed foods, such as flour, macaroni, rice and potatoes.[11]

A nutritional factor that is currently undergoing evaluation is fluoride. This element will increase bone mass[14] but it is not clear whether bone strength is also increased, as under certain circumstances bone mineralization is impaired and resorption increased. These abnormalities may be prevented to some degree by increased calcium intake.[15] The patients most likely to benefit from fluoride need to be determined simply and rapidly.

Nutritional considerations in osteoporosis must also include the potential damage that may result from megavitamin use. This deplorable practice is widespread and is of particular concern because of the intriguing report that vitamin A in large doses will accelerate the bone loss of aging.[14] Confirmation and extension of this finding would provide further reasons for restricting the long-term use of high doses of vitamins.

Other questions concern defining the appropriate dietary protein intake for elderly individuals, as recent evidence indicates its particular relevance for calcium balance. Physicians have often tacitly assumed that a high-protein diet is greatly beneficial to health. The findings of Schuette, Zemel, and Linkswiler[16] that high dietary protein increases calcium excretion suggests a risk of these diets for older persons, particularly when calcium intake is marginal or inadequate. These findings were recently confirmed by another group,[17] but not all investigators are agreed.[18] The problem clearly deserves further study.

Although the etiology of osteoporosis is complex with involvement of parathyroid hormone, calcitonin and other humoral agents, vitamin D, inactivity, genetics and many other factors,[19] we need to ask whether appropriate attention to nutritional factors is not an important step towards prevention and treatment. It is encouraging that in a group of elderly women with osteoporosis, bone density was increased by the combination of calcium-rich foods and a calcium supplement given during a six-month period.[20] It is entirely unknown, however, whether improvement of bone status generally will be of specific benefit in terms of preservation of teeth.

Calories and Lifespan. The evidence to date suggest that the elderly frequently eat inadequately and inappropriately, but defining their needs precisely based on present knowledge is not a simple matter. A pressing question, in fact, is whether too much emphasis has been placed upon urging consumption of sufficient calories rather than upon encouraging caloric restriction.

Fascinating longitudinal studies in rats indicate that there is a prolonged survival of those animals which have a relatively small lean body mass in early adulthood.[21] There is now increasing evidence in several species and under a variety of experimental conditions that, simply by restricting calories, lifespan is significantly prolonged. This effect has been known since 1917 from the work of Osborn, Mendel and Ferry[22] and has been extensively confirmed and expanded subsequently. In a more recent report by Ross,[23] the increment in prolongation of lifespan was inversely related in a linear fashion to the decrement in caloric consumption by animals which were individually caged and permitted to eat ad libitum throughout their lifetimes.

Furthermore, caloric restriction in experimental animals retards the development of respiratory diseases, neoplasms, and cardiovascualr and renal diseases.[24] It is particularly noteworthy that lifetime caloric restriction results in a substantial decrease in the overall incidence of tumors. This phenomenon has been of great interest to investigators, and it has been proposed that the tumor-inhibition effects of undernutrition may have an immunologic basis.[25] Dietary deficits of specific nutrients, such as zinc[25] and riboflavin,[26] will also retard the development of tumors in experimental animals.

The now numerous observations in experimental animals, that caloric restriction results in substantial prolongation of the lifespan and also appears to delay the emergence of certain diseases of aging, certainly points to the possible potential benefits of eating less. We need to ask how relevant these studies are for man. There is little doubt that obesity is associated with an increased mortality rate, particularly when it develops during early or middle life rather than in old age.[27]

It is apparent that many questions remain unanswered concerning the optimal nutritional needs of the elderly. The data base upon which recommendations are currently being made is totally inadequate and needs to be expanded greatly if any of these questions are to be answered.

REFERENCES

1. United States Department of Commerce. Bureau of the Census: Statistical Abstract of the United States. 100th ed. Washington, D.C. 1979.
2. Beauchene RE, Davis TA: The nutritional status of the aged in the U.S.A. Age 1979; 2: 23.
3. O'Hanlon PD, Kohrs MB: Dietary studies of older Americans. AM J Clin Nutr 1978; 31: 1257.
4. Yearick ES, Wang MSL, Pisias SJ: Nutritional status of the elderly: Dietary and biochemical findings. J Gerentol 1980; 35: 663.
5. United States Department of Commerce. Bureau of the Census: Current Population Reports Special Studies. Series P-23, No. 59, 1976, p 48.
6. Cooper RM, Bilach I, Zubek JP: The effect of age on taste sensitivity. J Gerontol 1959; 14: 56.
7. Schiffman S: Food recognition by the elderly. J Gerontol 1977; 32: 586.
8. Arey LB, Tremaine MJ, Monzingo FL: The numerical and topographical relation of taste buds to human circumvallate papillae throughout the life span. Anat Rec 1935; 64:9.
9. Grzegorczyk PB, Jones SW, Mistretta CM: Age related differences in salt-taste acuity. J. Gerontol 1979; 34: 834.
10. Greger JL, Geissler AH: Effect of zinc supplementation on taste acuity of the aged. Am J Clin Nutr 1978; 31: 633.
11. Lutwak L: Periodontal disease. In: Winick M, ed. Nutrition and aging. John Wiley & Sons: New York, 1976: 145.
12. Recker RR, Saville PD, Heaney RP: The effect of estrogens and calcium carbonate on bone loss in postmenopausal women. Ann Intern Med 1977; 87: 649.
13. LaFlamme GH, Jowsey J: Bone and soft-tissue changes with oral phosphate supplements. J Clin Invest 1973; 51: 2834.
14. Avioli LV: What to do with "postmenopausal osteoporosis"? Am J Med 1978; 65: 881.
15. Riggs BL, Hodgson SF, Hoffman DL, et al.: Treatment of primary osteoporosis with fluoride and calcium. JAMA 1980; 242: 446.
16. Schuette SA, Zemel MB, Linkswiler HM: Studies on the mechanism of protein-induced hypercalciuria in older men and women. J Nutr 1980; 110: 305.
17. Licata AA, Bou E, Bartter FC, West F: Acute effects of dietary protein on calcium metabolism in patients with osteoporosis. J Gerontol 1981; 1: 14.
18. Spencer H, Kramer L, DeBartolo M, et al.: Further studies on the effect of high protein diet on calcium metabolism in man. Fed Proc 1981; 40: 885
19. Whedon GD: Recent advances in management of osteoporosis. Adv Exper Med Biol 1980; 128: 597.
20. Lee CJ, Lawler GS, Johnson GH: Effects of supplementation of the diets with calcium and calcium-rich foods on bone density of elderly females with osteoporosis. Am J Clin Nutr 1981; 34: 819.
21. Lesser GT, Deutsch S, Markofsky J: Aging in the rat: Longitudinal and cross-sectional studies of body composition. Am J Physiol 1973; 225: 1472.
22. Osborne TB, Mendel LB, Ferry EL: The effect of retardation of growth upon the breeding period of duration of life in rats. Science 1917; 45: 294.
23. Ross MH: Length of life and caloric intake. Am J Clin Nutr 1972; 25: 834.
24. Sacher GA: Life table and modification of life prolongation. In: Finch CE, Hayflick L, eds. Handbook of the biology of aging. 1972; 25: 834. Van Nostrand Reinhold Co.: New York, 1977: 582.
25. Good RA, Fernandes G, West A: Nutrition, immunity and cancer — A review. Part 1. Influence of protein-calorie malnutrition and zinc deficiency on immunity. Clin Bull 1979; 9:3.
26. Rivlin RS: Riboflavin and cancer: a review. Cancer Res 1973; 33: 1977.
27. Chapman JM, Coulson AH, Clark VA, et al.: The differential effect of serum cholesterol, blood pressure and weight on the incidence of myocardial infarction and angina pectoris. J Chronic Dis 1971; 23: 631.

PART 4
RESOURCES FOR FURTHER INFORMATION

Today, the field of food and nutrition is so complex that no sourcebook can be considered truly complete. However, it can refer the reader to other places for further information on specific aspects of food and nutrition.

Possibly the first place to look for additional information are libraries that have collections devoted to food and nutrition and related topics. Marquis Academic Media has researched specialized libraries and determined those that have heavy concentrations in one or more specific fields of food, food science, agriculture, dietetics, biochemistry, or some other aspect of nutrition.

Following the list of libraries is a directory of approximately 750 major food-related associations. Also in part 4 is a list of schools that offer courses of study in food and nutrition and related areas are included, along with the names of appropriate department chairpersons.

For those researching grants and foundations, there is a section devoted to grant support programs that provides detailed information on approximately 100 separate grants. Magazines in the field are also presented, along with the publishing opportunities available to those interested in professional journals. Finally, book publishers are listed as yet another place to discover further information on a specific area of food and nutrition.

Libraries Specializing in Agriculture, Food and Nutrition Volumes

by *Marquis Academic Media*

No reference book can be complete without listing sources of further information. Presented here are more than 200 libraries across the country that specialize in agriculture, food, and nutrition topics.

Libraries are alphabetized by the name of the company or university they are associated with, not by the specific name of the library. If more than one library is associated with a university, the group of libraries are alphabetized first by the name of the university and then by the specific name of the library. Each listing includes the name of the library, the address, the telephone number, the name of a person to contact for further information, and the library's special concentrations in food and nutrition.

An asterisk following the name of a library indicates that the information in the entry was staff-compiled. All other libraries responded to a questionnaire sent by Marquis Academic Media to verify the information. Some libraries have requested that they not be listed.

A

ABRAHAM BALDWIN AGRICULTURAL COLLEGE
Library
ABAC Station
Tifton, GA 31793
912-386-3223

Contact: Mary Emma Henderson, Librarian
Special Emphasis:
334 titles on agriculture and home economics.

AGRICULTURE CANADA, LIBRARIES DIVISION
Sir John Carling Bldg.
Room 245
Ottawa, Ontario K1A OC5, Canada
613-995-7851

Contact: Mrs. M. L. Morton, Director, Libraries Division
Special Emphasis:
Agriculture and related sciences, nutrition, and food production.

AGRICULTURE CANADA RESEARCH STATION
Fredericton Library
Fredericton, New Brunswick
E3B 4Z7, Canada
506-452-3260

Contact: Donald B. Gammon, Area Coordinator
Special Emphasis:
Agriculture, particularly potatoes, animal nutrition, and the impact of agricultural chemicals on the environment.

AGRICULTURE CANADA, RESEARCH STATION
Harrow Library
Harrow, Ontario N0R 1GO, Canada
519-738-2251

Contact: E. Champagne, Librarian
Special Emphasis:
3,000 volumes on agriculture and related topics.

AGRICULTURE CANADA, RESEARCH STATION
Lacombe Library
Lacombe, Alberta T0C 1SO, Canada

Contact: Dr. D. E. Walden, Director, Lacombe Research Station
Special Emphasis:
Agriculture and nutrition.

AGRICULTURE CANADA, RESEARCH STATION
Lethbridge Library
Lethbridge, Alberta T1J 4B1, Canada
403-327-4561

Contact: John P. Miska, Area Coordinator
Special Emphasis:
4,000 volumes and more than 20,000 government documents and issues of series covering agriculture, biochemistry, microbiology, chemistry, crop entomology, animal parasitology, animal science, plant science and plant pathology, soil science, agricultural economics, food science and agricultural administration.

AGRICULTURE CANADA RESEARCH STATION*
Library
Ottawa, Ontario K1A OC6, Canada

Contact: Mrs. Y. Belanger

AGRICULTURE CANADA,

RESEARCH STATION
Saskatoon Library
107 Science Crescent
Saskatoon, Saskatchewan
  S7N 0X2, Canada
306-343-8214

Contact: Marlene Glen, Librarian
Special Emphasis:
  Agriculture, particularly oilseeds, forage crops, and cereals.

AMERICAN DIETETIC ASSOCIATION*
LuLu G. Graves Memorial Library
430 N. Michigan Ave.
Chicago, IL 60611
312-822-0330

Special Emphasis:
  Food chemistry, nutrition, foods and food values, and diet therapy.

AMERICAN INSTITUTE OF BAKING
Library
1213 Bakers Way
Manhattan, KS 66502
913-537-4750

Contact: Ruth Emerson, Librarian
Special Emphasis:
  7,000 volumes on nutrition, food chemistry, baking science and technology.

ANDERSON CLAYTON FOODS
W. L. Clayton Research Center
Technical Information Services
3333 N. Central Expy.
Richardson, TX 75080
214-231-6121

Contact: Irmgarde Martin, Supervisor, Information Services
Special Emphasis:
  2,000 volumes covering food chemistry, food processing, and edible fats and oils.

AMSTAR CORPORATION*
Research and Development
  Library
266 Kent Ave.
Brooklyn, NY 11211
212-387-6800

Contact: Joseph X. Cavano, Information Specialist
Special Emphasis:
  Food technology, sugar technology, chemical engineering, and analytical chemistry.

APPLIED SCIENCE LABORATORIES, INC.*
Library
Box 440
State College, PA 16801
814-238-2406

Special Emphasis: Lipids.

ARCHER DANIELS MIDLAND CO.
Research Library
4666 Faries Pkwy.
Decatur, IL 62526
217-424-5397

Contact: Richard E. Wallace, Manager Information Services
Special Emphasis:
  6,000 books plus journals and patents covering nutrition, fats and oils, grains, food technology, and chemistry.

ARMOUR FOOD COMPANY & ARMOUR-DIAL, INC.
Research Center Library
15101 N. Scottsdale Rd.
Scottsdale, AZ 85260
602-998-6120

Contact: Lorraine Nesvig, Librarian
Special Emphasis:
  300 volumes covering nutrition and food.

B

BORDEN, INC.
Research Centre Library
600 N. Franklin St.
Syracuse, NY 13205
315-474-8526

Contact: Carol F. Taylor, Librarian
Special Emphasis:
  1,200 volumes on food and food products, food patents, and dairy technology.

BEECH-NUT FOODS CORPORATION
Technical Library
Church St.
Canajoharie, NY 13317
518-673-3251

Contact: Stephanie Price, Librarian
Special Emphasis:
  Food processing and analysis.

C

CPC INTERNATIONAL
Best Foods Research Center
Information Services
1120 Commerce Ave.
Box 1534
Union, NJ 07083
201-688-9000

Contact: Anne M. Troop, Manager, Information Center
Special Emphasis:
  5,000 volumes on nutrition, food analysis, food technology, and food microbiology.

CPC INTERNATIONAL
Moffet Technical Library
Box 345
Argo, IL 60501
312-458-2000

Contact: Joy-Louise Caruso, Manager, Information Services
Special Emphasis:
  Food chemistry and chemical engineering.

CALIFORNIA POLYTECHNIC STATE UNIVERSITY*
University Library
San Luis Obispo, CA 93407
805-546-2345

Contact: Dr. Norman D. Alexander, Director
Special Emphasis:
  Agriculture and home economics.

CAMPBELL INSTITUTE FOR FOOD RESEARCH*
Basic Research and Product
  Development Library
Campbell Place
Camden, NJ 08101
609-964-4000

Special Emphasis:
  Home Economics, food technology, nutrition, and biochemistry.

CAMPBELL TAGGART, INC.*
Research Division-Library
6211 Lemmon Avenue
Dallas, TX 75221
214-358-9211

Contact: Betty Webb, Librarian
Special Emphasis:
  Food technology and processing, nutrition, and cereal chemistry.

CANADIAN CANNERS, LIMITED
Research Center Library
1101 Walker's Line
Burlington, Ontario L7N 2G4, Canada
416-335-9700

Contact: Gisela Smithson, Technical Librarian
Special Emphasis:
Food science: International codex, nutrition, waste water technology and microbiology.

CARGILL, INC.
Information Center
Box 9300
Minneapolis, MN 55440
612-475-6498

Contact: Julia Peterson, Manager
Special Emphasis:
Agricultural and food products, biochemistry, animal feeding and nutrition, and analytical chemistry.

CARNATION RESEARCH LABORATORIES LIBRARY
8015 Van Nuys Blvd.
Van Nuys, CA 91412
213-787-7820

Contact: Kathryn A. Stewart, Librarian
Special Emphasis:
Food science and nutrition.

CARROLL COUNTY FARM MUSEUM*
Landon Burns Memorial Library
500 S. Center St.
Westminster, MD 21157
301-491-4361

Contact: Cindy Hofferberth, Director
Special Emphasis:
Agriculture.

CENTRAL SOYA COMPANY, INC.
Food Research Library
1300 Ft. Wayne National Bank Bldg.
Ft. Worth, IN 46802
219-489-1511

Contact: Margaret Campbell, Librarian
Special Emphasis:
8,000 volumes on food and nutrition, food chemistry, fats and oils, proteins, and soybeans.

CLEMSON UNIVERSITY*
Robert Muldrow Cooper Library
Clemson, SC 29631

Contact: J. W. Gordon Gourlay, Director
Special Emphasis:
Agriculture.

COCA-COLA COMPANY*
Citrus Research & Development Technical Library
Orange Street, Box 550
Plymouth, FL 32768
305-886-1568

Contact: Patricia Waite, Librarian
Special Emphasis:
Food technology and chemistry.

COCA-COLA COMPANY
Technical Information Services
Box 1734
Atlanta, GA 30301
404-898-2008

Contact: Bernard Prudhomme, Manager
Special Emphasis:
Food technology, nutrition and beverages.

COMPLEXE SCIENTIFIQUE DU QUEBEC
Service de Documentation et de Bibliotheque
2700 Einstein C*I*I*
Ste Foy, Quebec G1P 3W8, Canada
418-643-9730

Contact: M. Michael Levesque, Director
Special Emphasis:
3,500 volumes covering agriculture.

CORN REFINERS ASSOCIATION, INC.
Corn Industries Research Foundation Library
1001 Connecticut Ave., NW
Washington, DC 20036
202-331-1634

Contact: Kyd D. Brenner, Director of Public Affairs
Special Emphasis:
Library for use of Association staff only.

CORNELL UNIVERSITY*
Film Library
Judd Falls Rd.
Ithaca, NY 14853
607-256-2091

Contact: Julia M. Fletcher, Film Librarian

Special Emphasis:
Food and nutrition and agriculture.

CORNELL UNIVERSITY
Hotel Administration Library
Statler Hall
Ithaca, NY 14853
607-256-3673

Contact: Margaret J. Oaksford, Librarian
Special Emphasis:
Over 1,000 volumes on food and food chemistry, foodservice, and the food industry.

CORNELL UNIVERSITY
Albert R. Mann Library
Ithaca, NY 14853
607-256-2285

Contact: Jan Kennedy Olsen, Librarian
Special Emphasis:
7,500 volumes covering nutrition, food science, and agriculture.

CORNELL UNIVERSITY
New York State Agricultural Experiment Station Library
Geneva, NY 14456
315-787-2214

Contact: Gail L. Hyde, Librarian
Special Emphasis:
2,700 volumes covering food science, agriculture and enology.

D

DAWE'S LABORATORIES, INC.
Technical and Agricultural Libraries
450 State St.
Chicago Heights, IL 60411
312-757-6000

Contact: Dorothy Corriveau, Librarian
Special Emphasis:
Animal nutrition.

DEERE & COMPANY
Library
John Deere Road
Moline, IL 61265
309-752-4442

Contact: Betty Hagberg, Manager
Special Emphasis:
Agriculture.

388 RESOURCES FOR FURTHER INFORMATION

DEKALB AGRESEARCH, INC.*
Corn Research Center-Library
Sycamore Road
Dekalb, IL 60115
815-758-3461

Contact: Dr. Charles F. Kurll, Vice-President
Special Emphasis:
Agriculture and related subjects.

DELAWARE VALLEY COLLEGE OF SCIENCE AND AGRICULTURE
Joseph Krauskopf Memorial Library
Doylestown, PA 18901
215-345-1500

Contact: Constance R. Shook, Head Librarian
Special Emphasis:
500 volumes covering the food industry and nutrition.

DOANE AGRICULTURAL SERVICE, INC.*
Information Center
8900 Manchester Road
St. Louis, MO 63144
314-968-1000

Contact: James P. Wiesemeyer, Manager
Special Emphasis:
Agriculture.

JOSEPH F. DRAKE MEMORIAL LEARNING RESOURCES CENTER
Alabama A & M University
Normal, AL 35762
205-859-7309

Contact: Birdie O. Weir, Director
Special Emphasis:
4,000 volumes covering agriculture, food science and technology, and nutrition.

DREXEL UNIVERSITY LIBRARIES
Science & Technology Department
32nd & Chestnut Streets
Philadelphia, PA 19104
215-895-2765

Contact: William L. Page, Science Librarian
Special Emphasis:
1,100 volumes covering food and nutrition.

DYNAPOL*
Library

1454 Page Mill Rd.
Palo Alto, CA 94304
415-493-5611

Contact: Joan L. Fuller, Library Supervisor
Special Emphasis:
Organic chemistry, food chemicals, microbiology, and toxicology.

E

ECONOMICS LABORATORY, INC.*
Information Center
Osborn Bldg.
St. Paul, MN 55102
612-224-4678

Contact: Dona M. Bradt, Librarian
Special Emphasis:
Dairy and food processing technology.

F

FAIRVIEW COLLEGE
Library
Box 3000
Fairview, Alberta T0H 1LO, Canada
403-835-2213

Contact: Olive V. Lancaster, Librarian
Special Emphasis:
Agriculture and animal nutrition.

FARMERS UNION CENTRAL EXCHANGE, INC.*
Information Center
Box 43089
South St. Paul, MN 55075
612-451-5133

Contact: Margaret Ludvigsen, Manager, Information Services
Special Emphasis:
Agriculture and related areas.

FOOD, CHEMICAL AND RESEARCH, LABORATORIES, INC.*
Library
4900 9th Ave., NW
Seattle, WA 98107
206-783-4700

Special Emphasis:
Food analysis, bacteriology, and organic chemistry.

FOREMOST-McKEESON, INC.
Library

Box 2277
Dublin, CA 94566
415-828-1440

Contact: Joan La Manna, Librarian
Special Emphasis:
Food technology.

FORT VALLEY STATE COLLEGE
Henry Alexander Hunt Memorial Library
Fort Valley, GA 31030
912-825-6342

Contact: Dorothy M. Haith, Director, Learning Resources Center
Special Emphasis:
465 volumes on agriculture, home economics, education and science.

G

GENERAL FOODS CORPORATION
Maxwell House Division
Research Department Library
1125 Hudson St.
Hoboken, NJ 07030
201-420-3309

Contact: Anne Marie Civinskas, Librarian
Special Emphasis:
Over 1,000 volumes covering food technology, coffee processing, and chemical engineering.

GENERAL FOODS CORPORATION
Technical Center
Research Information Systems Center
White Plains, NY 10625
914-631-6400

Contact: Louis Weinstein, Supervisor, Information Services
Special Emphasis:
Nutrition, food technology, and biochemistry.

GENERAL MILLS, INC.
James Ford Bell Technical Center Library
9000 Plymouth Ave., NW
Minneapolis, MN 55427
612-540-3463

Contact: Dr. Curtis H. Hallstrom, Manager, Technical Information Service
Special Emphasis:
4,000 volumes covering food and chemical research.

GENERAL MILLS, INC.
General Office Library
9200 Wayzata Blvd.
Minneapolis, MN 55426
612-540-3536

Contact: Duane R. Day, Librarian
Special Emphasis:
1,000 volumes covering food.

**GEORGIA AGRICULTURAL
EXPERIMENT STATION LIBRARY**
University of Georgia
Experiment, GA 30212
404-228-7238

Contact: Carole Ledford, Librarian
Special Emphasis:
5,000 volumes covering agriculture and related sciences.

**GEORGIA COASTAL PLAIN
EXPERIMENT STATION LIBRARY**
University of Georgia
Tifton, GA 31794
404-386-3447

Contact: Emory Cheek, Library Associate
Special Emphasis:
Limited volumes on agricultural research.

GERBER PRODUCTS COMPANY
Corporate Library
445 S. State
Fremont, MI 49412
616-928-2631

Contact: Sherrie Anderson, Corporate Librarian
Special Emphasis:
4,500 volumes covering infant nutrition, food processing, agriculture, microbiology, and chemistry.

**W. R. GRACE AND COMPANY,
AGRICULTURAL CHEMICALS GROUP**
Planning Services Library
PO Box 277
100 N. Main Bldg.
Memphis, TN 38101
901-522-2385

Contact: Carolyn Wilhite, Librarian
Special Emphasis:
250 volumes on agriculture and animal nutrition.

H

**HEALTH AND WELFARE CANADA
HEALTH PROTECTION BRAHCH**
Regional Library
1001 Quest Blvd., St. Laurent, CH. 321
Longueuil, Quebec J4K 1C7, Canada
514-283-5472

Contact: Eleanora Ferenczy, Regional Librarian
Special Emphasis:
500 volumes covering nutrition, food and drugs, cosmetics, forensic chemistry, and microbiology.

**HEALTH AND WELFARE CANADA,
HEALTH PROTECTION BRANCH**
Banting Research Centre Library
Tunney's Pasture
Ottawa, Ontario K1A OL2, Canada
613-593-6535

Contact: Ms. M. McConnell, Head
Special Emphasis:
1,500 volumes on food science and nutrition research.

**HEALTH AND WELFARE CANADA,
HEALTH PROTECTION BRANCH**
Ontario Regional Library
2301 Midland Ave.
Scarborough, Ontario M1P 4R7, Canada
416-291-4231

Contact: S. Brockhurst, Library Technician
Special Emphasis:
Food analysis, food processing, and sanitation.

**HEALTH AND WELFARE CANADA
HEALTH PROTECTION BRANCH***
Regional Library
1001 W. Pender St.
Vancouver British Columbia
V6E 2M7, Canada
604-666-3147

Special Emphasis:
Food analysis, microbiology, pesticides, and food inspection

H. J. HEINZ COMPANY LIBRARY
PO Box 57
Pittsburgh, PA 15230
412-237-5948

Special Emphasis:
6,000 volumes covering agriculture, food processing and engineering, and nutrition.

HUNT-WESSON FOODS
Information Center M.S. 506
1645 W. Valencia Dr.
Fullerton, CA 92634
714-680-2158

Contact: Joy Hastings, Manager Information Center
Special Emphasis:
2,300 volumes covering food and nutrition, chemistry, microbiology, food packaging, food science and technology.

I

IRI RESEARCH INSTITUTE, INC.
Library
1 Rockefeller Plaza
Room 1401
New York, NY 10020
212-581-1942

Contact: Jerome F. Harrington, President
Special Emphasis:
Agricultural research and development in the areas of food and field crops, pastures, livestock, roadside revegetation, soils, and food technology.

ITT CONTINENTAL BAKING CO.
Research Laboratories Library
PO Box 731
Rye, NY 10580
914-967-4747

Contact: Jocelyn Rosen, Information Scientist
Special Emphasis:
1,200 volumes covering nutrition, food technology, food analysis and cereal chemistry.

IMASCO FOODS LIMITED
Library
4945 Ontari St. East
Montreal, Quebec H1V 1M2, Canada
514-255-2811

Contact: Louise Pichet, Library Technician
Special Emphasis:
1,000 volumes covering food and nutrition.

INDUSTRIAL GRAIN PRODUCTS, LTD.*
Research & Development Library
PO Box 6089
Montreal, Quebec H3C 3H1, Canada
514-866-7961

Contact: Muriel Henri, Librarian
Special Emphasis:
Nutrition, microbiology, and grain products research.

INSTITUT DE TECHNOLOGIE AGRICOLE
Research Library
Lapocatiere, G0R 1Z0, Canada
418-856-1110

Contact: Rene-Daniel Langlois
Special Emphasis:
Agriculture.

INSTITUTE OF AGRICULTURAL SCIENCES LIBRARY
University of Alaska
Box AE
Palmer, AK 99645
907-745-3257

Contact: Winston M. Laughlin, Soil Scientist
Special Emphasis:
Agriculture, soil science, chemistry, and plant pathology.

INTERNATIONAL FOOD POLICY RESEARCH INSTITUTE
Library
1776 Massachusets Ave., NW
Washington, DC 20036
202-862-5614

Contact: Patricia W. Klosky, Librarian
Special Emphasis:
Food policy and research, agricultural economics, trade, food production, and consumption.

INTERNATIONAL MINERALS & CHEMICALS CORPORATION
Research & Development Library
PO Box 207
Terre Haute, IN 47808
812-232-0121

Contact: Ruth Smedlund, Librarian
Special Emphasis:
Agriculture, fertilizers, microbiology, and nutrition.

IOWA STATE UNIVERSITY LIBRARY
Ames, IA 50011
515-294-1442

Contact: Warren B. Kuhn, Dean of Library Services
Special Emphasis:
1.4 million volumes on human and animal food nutrition, world food problems, and food service and management, with special emphasis on the agricultural and biological sciences.

K

KALSEC, INC.*
Library
3711 W. Main
Kalamazoo, MI 49005
616-349-9711

Contact: Mary Sager, Librarian
Special Emphasis:
Food technology.

KANSAS STATE UNIVERSITY
Farrell Library
Manhattan, KS 66506
913-532-6516

Contact: Brice Hobrock, Dean of Libraries
Special Emphasis:
6,000 volumes covering agriculture and home economics, plus 2,000 general and historical cook books.

KANSAS STATE UNIVERSITY*
Food and Feed Grain Institute
Swanson Memorial Library
Manhattan, KS 66506

Contact: Dr. Charles Deyoe
Special Emphasis:
Food technology, nutrition, biochemistry, cereal chemistry, and milling and feed technology.

KELLOGG COMPANY*
Research Department Library
235 Porter St.
Battle Creek, MI 49016
616-966-2291

Contact: Emily Weingartz, Information Specialist
Special Emphasis:
Nutrition, food science, food technology, microbiology, and chemistry.

KEMPTVILLE COLLEGE OF AGRICULTURAL TECHNOLOGY
Library
Kemptville, Ontario K0G 1JO, Canada
613-258-3411

Contact: A. Meikle, Librarian
Special Emphasis:
1,500 volumes covering home economics and agriculture.

KRAFT, INC.
Business Research Center
Kraft Court
Glenview, IL 60025
312-998-2951

Contact: Dorothy Schmidt, Coordinator
Special Emphasis:
200 volumes on food.

KRAFT, INC.
Research and Development Library
801 Waukegan Rd.
Glenview, IL 60025
312-998-3749

Contact: Helen Pettway, Librarian
Special Emphasis:
4,000 volumes covering nutrition, microbiology, food technology, and dairy science.

KRAUSE MILLING COMPANY
Technical Library
4222 W. Burnham St.
Milwaukee, WI 53215
414-355-7500

Contact: Pamela A. Tweed, Librarian
Special Emphasis:
1,000 agricultural volumes.

L

LIFE SAVERS, INC.*
Research and Development Division
Technical Information Center
Port Chester, NY 10573
914-937-3200

Contact: Rita D. Reade, Librarian
Special Emphasis:
Infant nutrition, food processing, and analytical methodology.

LIPTON, INC.*
Research Library
800 Sylvan Ave.
Englewood Cliffs, NJ 07632
201-567-8000

Contact: Gloria M. Bernstein, Manager, Information Services

Special Emphasis:
Food technology and tea.

ARTHUR D. LITTLE, INC.*
Research Library
15 Acorn Pk.
Cambridge, MA 02140
617-864-5770

Contact: Ann J. Wolpert, Head Librarian
Special Emphasis:
Food and agriculture.

M

MASSACHUSETTS INSTITUTE OF TECHNOLOGY
Department of Food & Nutrition Services
Reading Room, RM 20A-213
Cambridge, MA 02139
617-253-7994

Contact: Margaret Mubiromusoke, Librarian
Special Emphasis:
International nutrition.

MASSACHUSETTS INSTITUTE OF TECHNOLOGY
Science Library
Room 14S-100
Cambridge, MA 02139
617-253-5680

Contact: Irma Y. Johnson, Science Librarian
Special Emphasis:
Nutrition and food sciences, biochemistry, and biology.

McGAW LABORATORIES*
Technical Library
Box 11887
Santa Ana, CA 92711
714-754-2066

Contact: Judy Labovitz, Group Leader
Special Emphasis:
Nutrition, biochemistry, and chemistry.

McGILL UNIVERSITY
MacDonald Campus Library
Baton Bldg.
21, 111 Lakeshore Rd.
Ste. Anne De Bellevue, Quebec
H9X 1CO, Canada
514-457-2000

Contact: Janet Finlayson, Librarian
Special Emphasis:
2,500 monographs and volumes covering food science and agriculture.

McKINNON, ALLEN & ASSOCIATES, LTD.
Research Library
631 42nd Ave., SE
Calgary, Alberta T2G 1Y7, Canada
403-243-4345

Contact: Janice Lore, Librarian
Special Emphasis:
Agricultural consulting.

MEALS FOR MILLIONS
Freedom From Hunger Foundation Resource Center
PO Box 2000
Davis, CA 95616
916-758-6200

Contact: Patricia Butzer Larson, Director
Special Emphasis:
Small-scale food processing and nutrition education for developing countries.

MERCK & CO., INC.*
Literature and Information Services
Kelco Division
8355 Aero Dr.
San Diego, CA 92123
714-292-4900

Contact: Ann A. Jenkins, Administrator
Special Emphasis:
Industrial applications of polysaccharides, biochemistry, chemistry, microbiology, and food.

MICHIGAN STATE UNIVERSITY
Animal Industries Reference Room
208 Anthony Hall
East Lansing, MI 48824
517-355-8483

Contact: Marilyn J. DeYoung, Branch Librarian
Special Emphasis:
1,000 volumes covering nutrition, food science, animal sciences, and animal nutrition.

MICHIGAN STATE UNIVERSITY
Department of Agriculture Library
1615 S. Harrison Rd.
East Lansing, MI 48823
517-373-6410

Contact: Kathleen E. Callahan, Library Assistant
Special Emphasis:
Food and dairy products analysis, agriculture, and liquor and wines.

MINISTERE DE L'AGRICULTURE
des Pecheries et de l'Alimentation
Centre de Documentation
200-A, Chemin Ste-Foy, 1er etage
Quebec, Quebec G1R 4X6, Canada
418-643-2428

Contact: M. Audette, Centre de Documentation
Special Emphasis:
500 volumes.

MINISTRY OF AGRICULTURE*
Business Library
Nootka Court
808 Douglas
Victoria, British Columbia
V8W 2Z7, Canada
604-387-5121

Contact: R. Sera, Head, Information Services
Special Emphasis:
Agriculture.

MOBAY CHEMICAL CORPORATION
Agricultural Chemicals Division Library
Box 4913
Kansas City, MO 64120
816-242-2236

Contact: Cheryl A. Postlewait, Librarian
Special Emphasis:
5,000 serials and monographs on agriculture.

MONSANTO COMPANY
Information Center
800 N. Lindbergh Blvd.
Box 7090
St. Louis, MO 63177
314-694-4778

Contact: William A. Wilkinson, Manager
Special Emphasis:
Agriculture.

RESOURCES FOR FURTHER INFORMATION

MOUNT SAINT VINCENT UNIVERSITY
Library
Halifax, Nova Scotia
B3M 2J6, Canada
902-443-4450

Contact: L. Bianchini, Head Librarian
Special Emphasis:
1,000 volumes covering food, microbiology and food chemistry, experimental foods, nutrition, and meal food production management, and food services administration.

N

NABISCO FOODS, INC.
Research Center Library
2111 Route 208
Fair Lawn, NJ 07410
201-797-6800

Contact: Sonia D. Meurer, Librarian
Special Emphasis:
1,800 volumes covering food, nutrition, and chemistry.

NATIONAL DAIRY COUNCIL
Library
6300 N. River Rd.
Rosemont, IL 60018
312-696-1020

Contact: Diana Culbertson, Librarian
Special Emphasis:
6,000 monographs and 300 journal subscriptions on human nutrition, dairy foods, and nutrition education.

NATIONAL DIGESTIVE DISEASES EDUCATION AND INFORMATION CLEARINGHOUSE
1555 Wilson Blvd.
Roslyn, VA 22209
301-496-9707

Contact: Billie B. Mackey, Director
Special Emphasis:
The Clearinghouse provides a central point for the provision and exchange of information for professional organizations, foundations, and voluntary health organizations involved with health and disease.

NATIONAL INSTITUTE OF ARTHRITIS, DIABETES, AND DIGESTIVE AND KIDNEY DISEASES
Office of Health Research Reports
Bethesda, MD 20205
301-496-3583

Contact: Elizabeth H. Singer, Public Affairs Officer
Special Emphasis:
Clinical and lab research dealing with metabolic diseases, including diabetes, digestive diseases, nutrition and toxicology.

NATIONAL INSTITUTE OF ARTHRITIS, METABOLISM AND DIGESTIVE DISEASES*
Office of Scientific & Technical Reports
Bethesda, MD 20014
301-496-3583

Contact: Victor Wartofsky, Chief
Special Emphasis:
Clinical and lab research dealing with metabolic diseases including diabetes, digestive diseases, nutrition, and toxicology.

NATIONAL LIVESTOCK AND MEAT BOARD
Library
444 N. Michigan Ave.
Chicago, IL 60611
312-467-5520

Contact: William D. Siarny Jr., Information Center Director
Special Emphasis:
4,000 books and 6,000 periodicals on nutrition, meat, food economics, and education.

NEW BRUNSWICK RESEARCH AND PRODUCTIVITY COUNCIL*
Library
PO Box 6000
Fredericton, New Brunswick
E3B 5HL, Canada
506-455-8994

Contact: April James, Librarian
Special Emphasis:
Food science.

NORTH CAROLINA STATE UNIVERSITY
D. H. Hill Library
Box 5007
Raliegh, NC 27650
919-737-2843

Contact: Isaac T. Littleton, Director
Special Emphasis:
1,200 volumes covering agriculture, food science, nutrition, dairy products, poultry, and swine.

NORTHRIDGE LIBRARY*
Public Health Collection
California State University
1811 Nordhoff St.
Northridge, CA 91330
213-885-2283

Contact: Barbara Magnuson, Science Librarian
Special Emphasis:
Nutrition and health education.

NOVA SCOTIA AGRICULTURAL COLLEGE*
Library
Cox Institute
Truro, Nova Scotia B2N 5E3, Canada
902-895-1571

Contact: B. S. Sodhi, Librarian
Special Emphasis:
Agriculture.

NUTRILITE PRODUCTS, INC.
Research Library
5600 Beach Blvd.
Buena Park, CA 90620
714-521-3900

Contact: Jacqeuline McCoy, Librarian
Special Emphasis:
Agriculture, nutrition and cosmetics.

O

OHIO STATE AGRICULTURAL RESEARCH AND DEVELOPMENT CENTER
Library
Wooster, OH 44691
216-264-1021

Contact: Constance J. Britton, Librarian
Special Emphasis:
2,000 volumes covering sciences related to agricultural research.

OHIO STATE UNIVERSITY
Agriculture Library
2120 Fyffe Rd.
Columbus, OH 43210
614-422-6125

Contact: Susan Emerson, Head Librarian
Special Emphasis:
Food technology, dairy science, agriculture, and animal science.

OKLAHOMA STATE UNIVERSITY
Biological Sciences Division
University Library
Stillwater, OK 74074
405-624-6309

Contact: Shelia Johnson, Biological Science Librarian
Special Emphasis:
10,000 volumes covering agriculture, institution administration and management, foods and food science.

OLDS COLLEGE
Learning Resources Centre
Olds, Alberta TOM 1PO, Canada
403-226-8240

Contact: Garry M. Grisak, College Librarian
Special Emphasis:
23,000 volumes covering agriculture.

OREGON STATE UNIVERSITY
William Jasper Kerr Library
Corvallis, OR 97331
503-754-3411

Contact: Rodney K. Waldron, Director of Libraries
Special Emphasis:
10,000 volumes covering agriculture, nutrition, and home economics.

OSCAR MAYER FOODS CORP.
Research and Development Library
Box 7188
Madison, WI 53707
608-241-3311

Contact: Thomas R. Whitemarsh, Research Librarian
Special Emphasis:
1,500 volumes covering meat science, food science and technology, nutrition and meat cookery.

P

PEAVEY COMPANY
Corporate Information Center
11 Peavey Rd.
Chaska, MN 55318
612-448-3113

Contact: Pearl Hunt-McCain, Librarian
Special Emphasis:
8,000 volumes covering food.

PENNSYLVANIA STATE UNIVERSITY
Life Science Library
E205 Pattee
University Park, PA 16802
814-865-7056

Contact: Keith Roe, Head Librarian
Special Emphasis:
60,000 volumes covering temperate zone agriculture, agronomy, dairy and animal science, food science, horticulture, plant pathology, poultry science, and nutrition.

PET INCORPORATED
Corporate Information Center
Box 392
St. Louis, MO 63166
314-622-6134

Contact: Laurence R. Walton, Corporate Librarian
Special Emphasis:
10,000 volumes covering food science, food technology, nutrition and dairy science.

PILLSBURY COMPANY
Technical Information Center
311 2nd St., SE
Minneapolis, MN 55414
612-330-4750

Contact: James B. Tchobanoff, Manager
Special Emphasis:
6,300 volumes covering food science and technology and cereal chemistry.

PRAIRIE VIEW A & M COLLEGE OF TEXAS*
W. R. Banks Library
3rd St., Box T
Prairie View, TX 77445
713-857-3311

Contact: Frank Francis Jr., Head Librarian
Special Emphasis:
Agriculture and home economics.

PRICE-POTTENGER NUTRITION FOUNDATION LIBRARY*
5622 Dartford Way
San Diego, CA 92120
714-583-7450

Contact: Patricia Connolly
Special Emphasis:
Nutrition, agrobiology, and health.

PROCTER & GAMBLE COMPANY OF CANADA, LTD.*
Product Development Library
PO Box 589, Burlington St., E.
Hamilton, Ontario L8N 3L5, Canada
416-545-1121

Contact: Marie Dawson, Librarian
Special Emphasis:
Food products and fats and oils.

PURDUE UNIVERSITY
Biochemistry Library
Biochemistry Building
West Lafayette, IN 47907
317-494-1621

Contact: Martha J. Bailey, Life Sciences Librarian
Special Emphasis:
100 volumes on carbohydrate chemistry and biochemistry.

R

RALSTON PURINA COMPANY*
Library
Checkerboard Square
St. Louis, MO 63188
314-982-2150

Contact: Loretta Lemee, Librarian
Special Emphasis:
Nutrition, animal and human, food processing, and food sanitation.

R. J. REYNOLDS TOBACCO CO.
Science Information Library
Chestnut at Belews St.
Winston-Salem, NC 27102
919-748-2481

Contact: Dr. Frank G. Colby, Associate Director of Scientific Issues
Special Emphasis:
Agriculture, food, chemistry, tobacco, and bioscience.

RIDGETOWN COLLEGE OF AGRICULTURAL TECHNOLOGY
Library
Ridgetown, Ontario NOP 2CO, Canada
519-674-5456

Contact: I. R. Roadhouse
Special Emphasis:
120 volumes covering agriculture.

ROSS LABORATORIES
Library
625 Cleveland Ave.

Columbus, OH 43216
614-227-3503

Contact: Linda Mitro Hopkins, Manager, Library
Special Emphasis:
Nutrition and food technology.

S

SASKATCHEWAN WHEAT POOL
Reference Library
2625 Victoria Ave.
Regina, Saskatchewan
S4P 2Y6, Canada
306-569-4480

Contact: A. D. McLeod, Research Director
Special Emphasis:
Agriculture and cooperatives.

SCHWARZ SERVICES INTERNATIONAL
Library
95 Commerce Rd.
Stamford, CT 06904
203-324-3019

Contact: Mary Altomari, Librarian
Special Emphasis:
Analytical chemistry, food, fermentation, and brewing.

SCOTIA-FUNDY REGIONAL LIBRARY
Fisheries & Oceans
PO Box 550
Halifax, Nova Scotia B3J 2S7, Canada
902-426-3972

Contact: Anna Oxley, Regional Librarian
Special Emphasis:
Food technology, fisheries, and environmental control.

SOCIETY FOR NUTRITION EDUCATION RESOURCE CENTER
1736 Franklin St., 9th Fl.
Oakland, CA 94612
415-548-1363

Contact: Carolyn Franklin, Librarian
Special Emphasis:
1,500 volumes plus 400 periodicals and curricula covering weight control, obesity, pregnancy, and nutrition.

SOUTH DAKOTA STATE UNIVERISTY
Hilton M. Briggs Library

Brookings, SD 57007
605-688-5106

Contact: Dr. Leon Raney, Dean of Libraries
Special Emphasis:
3,000 volumes covering agriculture, plant pathology, home economics, and nursing. (The library is a depository for U.S. government publications in agriculture, health, and related fields.)

STALEY MANUFACTURING CO.
Research Library
2200 E. Eldorado St.
Decatur, IL 62525
217-423-4411

Contact: Ann M. Siedman, Technical Librarian
Special Emphasis:
450 books and journals on corn products, soybean products, fats and oils, carbohydrates, and sweeteners.

STANDARD BRANDS, INC.
Fleischmann Laboratories Library
Betts Ave.
Stamford, CT 06904
203-348-6401

Contact: Melanie C. Sze, Librarian
Special Emphasis:
Nutrition, food science, and technology.

STANFORD UNIVERSITY*
Food Research Institute Library
Stanford, CA 94305
415-497-3943

Contact: Charles C. Milford, Librarian
Special Emphasis:
Agriculture and food supply.

STAUFFER CHEMICAL COMPANY
Eastern Research Center Research Library
Dobbs Ferry, NY 10522
914-693-1200

Contact: Muriel Hogg, Senior Librarian
Special Emphasis:
196 titles on foods and food chemistry.

STAUFFER CHEMICAL COMPANY*
Mountain View Research Center Library
Box 760

Mountain View, CA 94042
408-739-0511

Contact: Adrienne Louise Lohr, Librarian
Special Emphasis:
Agriculture and weed science.

SUGAR ASSOCIATION, INC.
Library
1511 K St., NW
Washington, DC 20005
202-628-0189

Contact: Margaret E. Simon, Librarian
Special Emphasis:
1,500 volumes covering food technology, nutrition, and sugar.

SUNKIST GROWERS, INC.
Research Library
760 E. Sunkist St.
Ontario, CA 91761
714-983-9811

Contact: Martha C. Nemeth, Technical Librarian
Special Emphasis:
Chemistry-organic, analytical and food; citrus and citrus products technology.

SUNY
Agricultural and Technical College at Alfred
Walter C. Hinkle Memorial Library
Alfred, NY 14802
607-871-6363

Contact: Barry Lash, Head Librarian
Special Emphasis:
1,500 volumes covering agriculture, food, and nutrition.

SUNY
Agricultural and Technical College at Cobleskill
Jared van Wagenen Jr., Learning Resource Center
Cobleskill, NY 12043
518-234-5841

Contact: Eleanor M. Carter, Director
Special Emphasis:
5,000 volumes covering agriculture, food service, and food and nutrition.

SUNY
Agricultural and Technical College at Delhi

Library
Delhi, NY 13753
607-746-4107

Contact: Herbert J. Sorgen, Librarian
Special Emphasis:
Agriculture.

SUNY
Agricultural and Technical College at Farmingdale
Thomas D. Greenley Library
Melville Rd.
Farmingdale, NY 11735
516-420-2011

Contact: Sylvia S. Ewen, Chief Librarian
Special Emphasis:
Agriculture.

SUNY
Agricultural and Technical College at Morrisville
Library
Morrisville, NY 13408
315-684-7055

Contact: Michael Gieryic, Head Librarian
Special Emphasis:
Food processing, agriculture and food service.

SUNY
College at Oneonta
James M. Milne Library
Oneonta, KY 13820
607-431-2723

Contact: Richard D. Johnson, Director of Libraries
Special Emphasis:
7,400 volumes covering home economics.

SWIFT AND COMPANY
Research and Development Information Center
1919 Swift Dr.
Oak Brook, IL 60521
312-325-9320

Contact: Marcus Bornfleth, Head, Information Center
Special Emphasis:
29,000 volumes and 6,000 series and monographs covering food, nutrition, fats and oils, microbiology, and biochemistry.

T

TENNESSEE STATE DEPARTMENT OF AGRICULTURE*
Lou Wallace Library
Ellington Agriculture Center
Melrose Station Box 46027
Nashville, TN 37204
615-741-1456

Contact: Elizabeth B. Clarke
Special Emphasis:
Agriculture.

TEXAS A & M UNIVERSITY
Science Technology Division
Sterling G. Evans Library
College Station, TX 77843
713-845-1451

Contact: Katherine M. Jackson, Head, Reference Division
Special Emphasis:
3,000 volumes on agriculture.

TRAVENOL LABORATORIES, INC.*
Library
6301 Lincoln Ave.
Morton Grove, IL 60053
312-965-4700

Contact: Lois A. Bey, Manager, Information Center
Special Emphasis:
Microbiology, enzymes, and food technology.

U

UNDERWOOD COMPANY
Library
1 Red Devil Lane
Westwood, MA 02090
617-329-5300

Contact: Lee Miller-Hartnett, Librarian
Special Emphasis:
2,000 volumes plus periodicals covering the administration, operation, and science of food processing.

UNION CARBIDE CORPORATION
Films-Packaging Division
Technical Library
6733 W. 65th St.
Chicago, IL 60638
312-496-4286

Contact: Nijole K. Pupius, Technical Division

Special Emphasis:
600 volumes on food and organic chemistry.

UNITED FARM WORKERS, AFL-CIO
I. C. Library
La Paz
Keene, CA 93531
805-822-5571

Contact: Peter Gines Velasco, Director
Special Emphasis:
Agriculture, agricultural research, food industry, and economics.

U.S. ARMY
Natick Research and Development Laboratories
Technical Library
Natick, MA 01760
617-633-4248

Contact: Eugene G. Beary, Librarian
Special Emphasis:
2,000 volumes covering food sciences, food engineering, and nutrition.

UNITED STATES DEPARTMENT OF AGRICULTURE
(Science and Education Administration)
Eastern Regional Research Laboratory Library
600 East Mermaid Lane
Philadelphia, PA 19118
215-233-6602

Contact: Wendy H. Kramer, Administrative Librarian
Special Emphasis:
40,000 volumes and 500 serials covering food, dairy products, chemistry, biochemistry, fats and oils, proteins, meats, post harvest research, microbiology, and food processing.

UNITED STATES DEPARTMENT OF AGRICULTURE
Human Nutrition Information Service
10301 Baltimore Blvd.
Beltsville, MD 20705
301-344-3719

Contact: Robyn Frank, Acting Duty Administrator
Special Emphasis:
Human nutrition research, nutrition education, food service management, and food preparation;

also 25,000 agricola database references.

UNITED STATES DEPARTMENT OF AGRICULTURE
National Agricultural Library
10301 Baltimore Blvd.
Beltsville, MD 20705
301-344-3778

Contact: Richard A. Farley, Director
Special Emphasis:
1.7 million volumes covering agriculture, agricultural engineering, plant sciences, chemistry, biology, food and nutrition, soils and fertilizers, and animal industry.

UNITED STATES DEPARTMENT OF AGRICULTURE
(Science and Education Administration)
Richard B. Russell Agricultural Research Center
Southern Region
Box 5677
College Station Rd.
Athens, GA 30604
404-546-3314

Contact: Jean K. Martin, Librarian
Special Emphasis:
Agriculture, chemistry, biology, and environmental engineering.

UNITED STATES DEPARTMENT OF AGRICULTURE
Snake River Conservation Research Center
(Agricultural Research Service)
Library
Route 1, Box 186
Kimberly, ID 83341
208-423-5582

Contact: Aartje Smith, Librarian
Special Emphasis:
Agriculture, plant and crop science, and soil science.

UNITED STATES DEPARTMENT OF AGRICULTURE
(Science and Education Administration)
Southern Regional Research Center
Box 19687
New Orleans, LA 70179
504-589-7072

Contact: Dorothy B. Skau, Librarian
Special Emphasis:
Food processing, vegetable fats and oils, and plant sciences.

UNITED STATES DEPARTMENT OF AGRICULTURE
(Agricultural Research Service)
Western Regional Research Centre Library
Berkeley, CA 94710
415-486-3351

Contact: Rena Schonburn, Librarian
Special Emphasis:
Food technology, chemistry, cereals, fruits and vegetables field crops, and nutrition.

U.S. FISH & WILDLIFE SERVICE
Tunison Laboratory of Fish Nutrition Library
28 Gracie Rd.
Cortland, NY 13045
607-753-9391

Contact: Gary L. Rumsey, Director
Special Emphasis:
General nutrition and fish nutrition.

U.S. FOOD & DRUG ADMINISTRATION
Bureau of Foods Library
200 C St., SW
Washington, DC 20204
202-245-1235

Contact: Milton E. Stephenson, Librarian
Special Emphasis:
Chemistry, biology, and food technology.

U.S. FOOD & DRUG ADMINISTRATION*
Los Angeles District Library
1521 W. Pico Blvd.
Los Angeles, CA 90015
213-688-3788

Contact: John J. Stamp, Chemist
Special Emphasis:
Food technology, food and drug law, chemistry, and microbiology.

UNIVERSAL FOODS CORPORATION
Technical Information Center
6143 N. 60th St.
Milwaukee, WI 53218
414-271-6755

Contact: Aileen Mundstock, Technical Information, Specialist
Special Emphasis:
4,000 volumes covering technical research in the fermentation industry, biotechnology, microbiology, food engineering, and food quality control.

UNIVERSITE DE MONTREAL*
Biologie-Bibliotheque
C.P. 6128, Succursale A
Montreal, Quebec H3C 3J7, Canada
514-343-6801

Special Emphasis:
Nutrition and dietetics.

UNIVERSITY OF ALBERTA
Science Library
Edmonton, Alberta T6G 2J8, Canada
403-432-3785

Contact: Margo Young, Head
Special Emphasis:
Agriculture and home economics.

UNIVERSITY OF BRITISH COLUMBIA
Macmillan Forestry/Agriculture Library
2357 Main Mall
Vancouver, British Columbia
V6T 2A2, Canada
604-228-3445

Contact: Mary W. Macaree, Head
Special Emphasis:
Agriculture.

UNIVERSITY OF CALIFORNIA RIVERSIDE
Bio-Agricultural Library
Riverside, CA 92521
714-787-3238

Contact: Isabel Stirling, Head Librarian
Special Emphasis:
Citrus and vegetable crops, plant sciences, soil sciences, agricultural engineering, biochemistry, biology, and biomedical sciences.

UNIVERSITY OF CALIFORNIA
General Library
Davis, CA 95616
916-752-2110

Contact: Bernard Kreissman, University Librarian
Special Emphasis:
Agriculture, food, and the food industry.

UNIVERSITY OF CALIFORNIA
San Joaquin Valley Agricultural Research Center
9240 S. Riverbend Ave.
Parlier, CA 93648
209-646-2794

Contact: Andrew S. Deal, Director
Special Emphasis:
Vegetable crops, water science, biological control, agronomy, entomology, and nematology.

UNIVERSITY OF CALIFORNIA, BERKELEY
Natural Resources Library
40 Giannini Hall
Berkeley, CA 94720
415-642-4493

Contact: Lois Farrell, Head
Special Emphasis:
15,000 volumes covering agriculture, food and nutrition, and natural resources.

UNIVERSITY OF CHICAGO
Bio-Medical Libraries
Regenstein Library, B-5
1100 East 57th St.
Chicago, IL 60637
312-753-3441

Contact: Christa M. Modschiedler, Bio-Medical Librarian
Special Emphasis:
Human and animal nutrition.

UNIVERSITY OF CONNECTICUT
Library
Storrs, CT 06268
203-486-2219

Contact: John W. Jensen, Head, Reference Department; Carol Stocking, Head, Government Publications Department
Special Emphasis:
A depository for U.S. government publications, including extensive collections from the Department of Agriculture, National Institute of Health, and HEW; publications from the State Agricultural Experiment Station, the World Health Organization, and the Food and Agriculture Organization of the UN.

UNIVERSITY OF DELAWARE, NEWARK
Agricultural Library
Agricultural Hall
Newark, DE 19711
302-738-2530

Contact: Frederick B. Getze, Senior Assistant Librarian

Special Emphasis:
Agriculture, animal nutrition, and related areas in chemistry and engineering.

UNIVERISTY OF FLORIDA*
Agricultural Research & Education Belle-Glade Library
Institute of Food & Agricultural Sciences
Drawer A
Belle Glade, FL 33430
305-996-3062

Special Emphasis:
Soil science, crops science, agriculture, rice, long vegetables fibers, sugarcane, and animal science.

UNIVERSITY OF FLORIDA*
Hume Library
Institute of Food & Agricultural Sciences
McCarty Hall
Gainesville, FL 32611
904-392-1934

Contact: Albert C. Strickland, Librarian
Special Emphasis:
Agriculture, botany, animal science, and biological science.

UNIVERSITY OF GEORGIA
Science Library
Athens, GA 30602
404-542-4535

Contact: Virginia Benjamin, Public Service Librarian
Special Emphasis:
Agriculture and home economics.

UNIVERSITY OF GUELPH
McLaughlin Library
Guelph, Ontario N1G 2W1, Canada
519-824-4120

Contact: Margaret L. Beckman, Chief Librarian
Special Emphasis:
Agriculture, family studies, consumer studies, and food science.

UNIVERSITY OF IDAHO
Science & Technology Library
Moscow, ID 83843
208-885-6235

Contact: Donna M. Hanson, Science Librarian

Special Emphasis:
2,300 monographic and bound volumes on food and nutrition, especially agriculture and the biological sciences.

UNIVERSITY OF ILLINOIS*
Agriculture Library
226 Mumford Hall
Urbana, IL 61801
217-333-4216

Contact: John W. Beecher, Librarian
Special Emphasis:
Animal science, agricultural engineering, food science, and technology.

UNIVERSITY OF ILLINOIS
Home Economics Library
905 S. Goodwin Ave.
Urbana, IL 61801
217-333-0748

Contact: Barbara Swain, Librarian
Special Emphasis:
Food science, home economics, and foods and nutrition.

UNIVERSITY OF KENTUCKY
Agriculture Library
Agricultural Science Center N.
Lexington, KY 40506
606-258-2758

Contact: Antoinette P. Powell, Librarian
Special Emphasis:
Food technology and animal nutrition.

UNIVERSITY OF MANITOBA
University Libraries
Winnipeg, Manitoba R3T 2N2, Canada
204-474-9457

Contact: Judith Harper, Head Agriculture Library
Special Emphasis:
4,800 monographs and serials covering nutrition and food science.

UNIVERSITY OF MINNESOTA
Hormel Institute Library
801 16th Ave., NE
Austin, MN 55912
507-433-8804

Contact: Jacqueline Budde, Librarian

Special Emphasis:
Lipid chemistry, lipid biochemistry, and lipid microbiology.

UNIVERSITY OF MINNESOTA, ST. PAUL
Central Library
1984 Buford Ave.
St. Paul, MN 55108
612-373-0904

Contact: Richard Rohrer, Director
Special Emphasis:
Home economics education, biological sciences, food science and nutrition.

UNIVERSITY OF MINNESOTA TECHNICAL COLLEGE
Learning Resources Center
Waseca, MN 56093
507-835-1000

Contact: Kathryn Rynders, Librarian
Special Emphasis:
3,000 volumes covering food technology and the food industry.

UNIVERSITY OF NEBRASKA
C.Y. Thompson Library
East Campus
Lincoln, NE 68583
402-472-2802

Contact: Lyle Schreiner, Librarian
Special Emphasis:
2,500 volumes covering nutrition, agriculture, and home economics.

UNIVERSITY OF NEVADA, RENO
Life and Health Sciences Library
Fleischmann College of Agriculture Bldg.
Reno, NV 89557
702-784-6616

Contact: Anne Amaral, Librarian
Special Emphasis:
300 books on nutrition and agriculture.

UNIVERSITY OF NEW HAMPSHIRE
Biological Sciences Library
Kendall Hall
Durham, NH 03824
603-862-1018

Contact: Lloyd H. Heidgerd, Branch Librarian
Special Emphasis:
650 volumes on agriculture, animal science, and human nutrition.

UNIVERSITY OF PUERTO RICO
Agricultural Experiment Station
Library, Box H
Rio Piedras, PR 00928
809-767-9705

Contact: Joan P. Hayes, Librarian
Special Emphasis:
Agriculture and food technology.

UNIVERSITY OF PUERTO RICO*
Mayaguez Campus Library
Mayaguez, PR 00708
809-832-4040

Contact: Miguel Angel Optiz, Director
Special Emphasis:
Agriculture.

UNIVERSITY OF TENNESSEE
Agriculture-Veterinary Medicine Library
Veterinary Medicine Bldg., Room A-113
Knoxville, TN 37916
615-974-7338

Contact: Don W. Jett, Librarian
Special Emphasis:
7,000 volumes covering food and nutrition; 90,000 volumes, including USDA publications on agriculture and veterinary medicine.

UNIVERSITY OF TORONTO
Science and Medicine Library
7 Kings College Circle
Toronto, Ontario M5S 1A5, Canada
416-978-2284

Contact: G. Heaton, Head
Special Emphasis:
Food sciences, nutrition, and general health sciences.

UNIVERSITY OF WISCONSIN, MADISON
Steenbock Memorial Library
Madison, WI 53706
608-262-9990

Contact: Daisy T. Wu, Director
Special Emphasis:
3,100 volumes on nutrition, food processing and manufacture, foods and food supply, institutional cookery, and food service; a depository for U.S. Department of Agriculture Publications.

UNIVERSITY OF WISCONSIN, MENOMONIE*
Pierce Library
Media Retrieval Services
Menomonie, WI 54751
715-232-1184

Contact: John J. Jax, Director
Special Emphasis:
Home economics.

UNIVERSITY OF WISCONSIN, STEVENS POINT
James H. Albertson Center for Learning Resources
Stevens Point, WI 54481
715-346-2540

Contact: 400 titles on home economics.

V

VANDERBILT UNIVERSITY
Medical Center Library
Nashville, TN 37232
615-322-2292

Contact: T. Mark Hodges, Director
Special Emphasis:
800 volumes covering nutrition.

VIRGINIA POLYTECHNIC INSTITUTE AND STATE UNIVERSITY
Carol M. Newman Library
Blacksburg, VA 24061
703-951-5593

Contact: H. G. Bechanan, Director of Library
Special Emphasis:
Agriculture, human nutrition and foods, food science and technology, and biochemistry and nutrition.

W

WASCANA INSTITUTE OF APPLIED ARTS & SCIENCES
Resource & Information Center
4635 Wascana Pkwy. Box 556
Regina, Saskatchewan
S4P 5X1, Canada
306-565-4321

Contact: Pran Vohra, Supervisor and Chief Librarian
Special Emphasis:
Agriculture.

WASHINGTON STATE UNIVERSITY
Science and Engineering Library
Pullman, WA 99164
509-335-2671

Contact: Elizabeth P. Roberts, Head
Special Emphasis:
17,500 volumes covering agriculture, nutrition, biochemistry, food chemistry, food bacteriology, applied nutrition, and foodservice management.

WEST TEXAS STATE UNIVERSITY*
Cornette Library
Box 748, W.T. Sta.
Canyon, TX 79016
806-656-2761

Contact: Frank M. Blackburn, University Librarian
Special Emphasis:
Agriculture.

WEST VIRGINIA UNIVERSITY
Evansdale Library
Campus Library
Morgantown, WV 26506
304-293-5039

Contact: Harold Shill, Librarian
Special Emphasis:
2,000 volumes covering agriculture, engineering, forestry, and family resources.

WESTERN WISCONSIN TECHNICAL INSTITUTE*
Library
6th & Vine Sts.
LaCrosse, WI 54601
608-785-9412

Contact: Mrs. Thuan T. Tran, Head Librarian
Special Emphasis:
Agriculture and home economics.

WESTRECO, INC.
(Subsidiary of Libby, McNeill & Libby)
Technical Information Center
Boardman Road
New Milford, CT 06776

Contact: Jean Trapani, Manager, Information Services
Special Emphasis:
2,000 volumes on food technology, analytical chemical, tin corrosion with organic matter, and pineapple growing.

WHIRLPOOL CORPORATION*
Information Center
Monte Rd.
Benton Harbor, MI 49022
616-926-5323

Contact: Clifford L. Tierney, Manager
Special Emphasis:
Food technology.

WILSON & COMPANY, INC.
Research Library
4545 Lincoln Blvd.
Oklahoma City, OK 73105
405-525-4781

Contact: Sandra Garrison, Librarian
Special Emphasis:
Food science.

WORLD HUNGER EDUCATION SERVICE
Library
2000 P St., NW
Suite 205
Washington, DC 20036
202-223-2995

Contact: Dr. Patricia L. Kutzner, Executive Director
Special Emphasis:
World food problems, agricultural policy, and appropriate technology.

Food and Nutrition Related Associations in the United States

by *Marquis Academic Media*

This section lists approximately 750 associations that represent one or more food-related groups. A questionnaire asked each group to verify its name, address, telephone number, the name of a person to contact, as well as to explain membership and purpose. Not all respondents provided information for each category, however. (A number of associations did not state their purpose or provide information about membership.) Information about groups that did not respond to the questionnaire was tabulated by the staff and is so indicated by an asterisk.

In alphabetizing this section, articles, prepositions, and conjunctions were not considered. Abbreviations, such as U.S., are listed as if they were spelled out. Geographic names composed of two separate words, for example, New York, are treated as two words.

A

AGRIBUSINESS COUNCIL
345 East 46th St.
New York, NY 10017
212-682-2730

Contact: Kenneth M. Mueller, President
Membership: 80 Corporate members.
Purpose: To help relieve the world food problem through involvement of agribusiness companies in development of agricultural sectors in the emerging economies.

AGRICULTURAL RESEARCH INSTITUTE
2100 Pennsylvania Avenue, NW
No. 835
Washington, DC 20037
202-659-2517

Contact: Paul T. Truitt, Executive Vice-President

AGRICULTURAL TRADE COUNCIL*
750 13th Street, SE
Washington, DC 20003
202-544-6823

Contact: Peter T. Nelsen, President

AGRICULTURE COUNCIL OF AMERICA
1625 Eye St., NW, Suite 708
Washington, DC 20006
202-466-3100

Contact: Allen Paul, President
Purpose: To advance the interests of the agricultural sector of the U.S. economy.

AGRISERVICES FOUNDATION*
648 West Sierra Avenue
Clovis, CA 93612
209-299-2263

Contact: Dr. Marion Eugene Ensminger, President

AGRI-SILVICULTURE INSTITUTE
PO Box 4166
Palm Springs, CA 92263
714-327-2639

Contact: Paul J. Marks, President
Membership: Restricted to those who have a strong interest in trees and afforestation.

Purpose: To disseminate information on tree crops and their economic value for afforestation of denuded and desert lands.

ALABAMA DAIRY PRODUCTS ASSOCIATION*
200 South Lawrence St.
Montgomery, AL 36104
205-263-9804

Contact: Curtis Springer, General Counsel

ALABAMA PEANUT PRODUCERS ASSOCIATION
PO Box 1282
Dothan, AL 36302
205-792-6482

Contact: Heyward Carroll, Secretary
Purpose: To promote of peanuts and peanut products in research, promotion, and education.

ALL STAR DAIRY ASSOCIATION, INC.
PO Box 428
Lexington, KY 40585
606-255-3644

Contact: John D. Utterback, Founder
Membership: 150 dairy and ice cream companies.
Purpose: An organization of dairy and and ice cream companies joined to promote more economical and efficient operations.

ALMOND BOARD OF CALIFORNIA
PO Box 15920
Sacramento, CA 95852
916-929-6506

Contact: Emil M. Loe, Manager
Purpose: Administer federal marketing order for almonds.

ALUMINUM FOIL CONTAINER MANUFACTURERS ASSOCIATION*
PO Box J
Walworth, WI 53184
414-275-6838

Contact: Paul Uetzmann

AMERICAN AGRICULTURAL ECONOMICS ASSOCIATION
Department of Economics
Iowa State University
Ames, IA 50011
515-294-8700

Contact: Sydney C. James, Secretary-Treasurer
Purpose: To further the development of systematic knowledge of agricultural economics.

AMERICAN AGRICULTURE MARKETING ASSOCIATION
225 Touhy
Park Ridge, IL 60068
312-399-5700

Contact: Robert R. Coleman, Manager

AMERICAN AGRI-WOMEN*
PO Box 424
Buffalo, OK 73834

Contact: Joan Adams, President

AMERICAN ANGUS ASSOCIATION
3201 Frederick Blvd.
St. Joseph, MO 64501
816-233-3101

Contact: Richard L. Spader, Executive Vice-President

Membership: 36,362 members in five categories.
Purpose: Maintain the purity of the Angus breed, promote it, and provide records of identity.

AMERICAN ANOREXIA NERVOSA ASSOCIATION
133 Cedar Lane
Teaneck, NJ 17666
201-836-1800

Contact: Estelle Binn Miller, M.S.W., Executive Director
Purpose: To provide services and programs for interested persons; to aid in the education, research, cure, and prevention of anorexia nervosa.

AMERICAN ASSOCIATION OF CEREAL CHEMISTS
(Milling & Baking Division)
c/o Peavey Company
PO Box 629
Commerce City, CO 80037
303-289-6141

Contact: George K. Minor, Chairman
Membership: 3,800.
Purpose: To promote the cereal industry; to offer symposiums and technical conferences to benefit flour millers, cereal chemists, mix manufacturers, and the allied industry.

AMERICAN ASSOCIATION OF FEED MICROSCOPISTS
1118 Apple Dr.
Mechanicsburg, PA 17055
717-766-6039

Contact: Janet Windsor, Secretary-Treasurer
Purpose: To advance the science, methods, and techniques of feed microscopy.

AMERICAN ASSOCIATION OF MEAT PROCESSORS
224 East High St.
PO Box 269
Elizabethtown, PA 17022
717-367-1168

Contact: Stephen F. Krut, Executive Director
Membership: 1,500 small processing plants and suppliers to the industry.
Purpose: To further and protect the interest of small meat processing businesses and provide information.

AMERICAN ASSOCIATION OF MEDICAL MILK COMMISSIONS, INC.*
PO Box 554
Alpharetta, GA 30201
404-475-6701

Contact: J. L. Hopping, Secretary-Treasurer

AMERICAN ASSOCIATION OF TEACHER EDUCATORS IN AGRICULTURE*
102 Morrill Hall,
North Dakota State University
Fargo, ND 58105
701-237-7436

Contact: Vernon D. Luft, Secretary

AMERICAN BAKERS ASSOCIATION*
2020 K Street, NW, Suite 850
Washington, DC 20006
202-296-5800

Contact: Robert Wager, President

AMERICAN BANTAM ASSOCIATION*
PO Box 610
North Amherst, MA 01059
413-549-0442

Contact: Fred P. Jeffrey, Secretary

AMERICAN BEEFALO ASSOCIATION
116 Executive Park
Louisville, KY 40207
502-897-1650

Contact: George E. O'Connor, Executive Director
Membership: 960 active beefalo breeders internationally, with eight U.S. state/regional chapters.
Purpose: To promote, develop, improve, and register the American beefalo breed.

AMERICAN BLACK MAINE-ANJOU ASSOCIATION*
4310 Central Expressway, Suite 200
Dallas, TX 75206
214-827-2980

Contact: Charles Lankford, Executive Secretary

AMERICAN BLONDE d'AQUITAINE ASSOCIATION

Route B Box 230
Grand View, ID 83624
208-834-2244

Contact: Gerald Cunningham, Secretary
Membership: 340.
Purpose: Registration and promotion of Blonde d'Aquitaine cattle.

AMERICAN BLUE CHEESE ASSOCIATION*
110 North Franklin Street
Chicago, IL 60606
312-263-2733

Contact: R. F. Anderson, Treasurer

AMERICAN BOARD OF NUTRITION*
9650 Rockville Pike
Bethesda, MD 20014
301-530-7110

AMERICAN BRAHMAN BREEDERS ASSOCIATION
1313 LaConcha Lane
Houston, TX 77064
713-795-4444

Contact: Wendell Schronk, Executive Vice-President
Purpose: To collect, record and preserve the pedigrees of Brahman cattle; to promote acceptance and utilization of Brahman cattle; to aid in the genetic improvement of the breed.

AMERICAN BUFFALO ASSOCIATION
PO Box 965
Cody, WY 82414
307-582-4895

Contact: Sandy Snider, Executive Secretary
Membership: 500.
Purpose: To promote conservation of buffalo and recognition and use of buffalo products.

AMERICAN BUTTER INSTITUTE*
110 N. Franklin Street
Chicago, IL 60606
312-263-2733

Contact: Robert F. Anderson, Treasurer

AMERICAN CATFISH MARKETING ASSOCIATION
PO Box 1609
Jackson, MS 39205
601-353-7916

Contact: Henry Williams
Membership: Major processors of catfish in the United States.

AMERICAN CELIAC SOCIETY
45 Gifford Ave.
Jersey City, NJ 07304
201-432-1207

Contact: Anita Garrow, Chairwoman
Purpose: To inform members about following a gluten-free diet and locating gluten-free specialty foods; to encourage retailers to make such products available; to provide educational programs and publications.

AMERICAN CHIANINA ASSOCIATION*
PO Box 159
Blue Springs, MO 64015
816-229-1944

Contact: Jack Barr, Chief Executive Officer

AMERICAN COCA RESEARCH INSTITUTE
(An Affiliate of the Chocolate Manufacturers Association of the U.S.)
7900 Westpark Drive
Suite 514
McLean, VA 22102
703-790-5011

Contact: Richard T. O'Connell
Purpose: To advance all phases of cacao culture; to collect and disseminate scientific information relating to the growing, handling, and distribution of cacao plants; to support with grants-in-aid cacao studies and research.

AMERICAN COLLEGE OF NUTRITION
100 Manhatten Ave. #1606
Union City, NJ 07087
201-855-3518

Contact: Dr. Mildred S. Seelig, President
Membership: 450.
Purpose: To foster and encourage nutrition education; to stimulate exchange of information on nutrition; to encourage research.

AMERICAN CORN MILLERS FEDERATION
6707 Old Dominion Dr.
McLean, VA 22101
703-821-3025

Contact: Robert D. Fondahn, President
Membership: Any person, firm, or corporation engaged in the manufacture of dry milled corn products.
Purpose: To contribute to the growth of the industry; to broaden the uses and knowledge of the product; to conduct studies and engage in research.

AMERICAN CORRECTIONAL FOOD SERVICE ASSOCIATION
277 East 6100 South
Salt Lake, UT 84107
801-268-3000

Contact: Marvin C. Zitting, National Coordinator
Membership: Persons interested in food service serving adult and youth correctional facilities.
Purpose: Education and certification meetings and seminars; publication of a newsletter.

AMERICAN COUNCIL OF APPLIED CLINICAL NUTRITION*
PO Box 28224
4678 Parc Orleans
St. Louis, MO 63132
314-291-5466

Contact: Clarence T. Smith, Ph.D., President

AMERICAN CULINARY FEDERATION
PO Box 3466
St. Augustine, FL 32084
904-824-4336

Contact: L. Edwin Brown, Executive Director
Membership: 10,000 members in 125 chapters.
Purpose: Professional, educational, and fraternal organization of chefs dedicated to the industry and prestige of the culinary arts.

RESOURCES FOR FURTHER INFORMATION

AMERICAN CULTURED DAIRY PRODUCTS INSTITUTE*
910 17th Street, NW
Washington, DC 20006
202-223-1931

Contact: John Speer, Jr., Executive Vice-President & Treasurer

AMERICAN DAIRY ASSOCIATION
6300 North River Rd.
Rosemont, IL 60018
312-696-1880

Contact: Barry D. Pfouts, Executive Vice-President,
Membership: Dairy farmers.
Purpose: Commodity promotion organization.

AMERICAN DAIRY ASSOCIATION OF ILLINOIS*
1 West Front Street
El Paso, IL 61738
309-527-4095

Contact: James Kurtz, Manager

AMERICAN DAIRY SCIENCE ASSOCIATION*
309 West Clark Street
Champaign, IL 61820
217-356-3182

Contact: Claude Cruse, Executive Secretary

AMERICAN DEXTER CATTLE ASSOCIATION
707 W. Water St.
Decorah, IA 52101
319-735-5772

Contact: Daisy Moore, Executive Secretary-Treasurer
Membership: 135.
Purpose: To protect the breed; to register only purebred animals.

AMERICAN DIETETIC ASSOCIATION
430 North Michigan Ave.
Chicago, IL 60611
312-280-5000

Contact: James L. Breeling, Executive Director
Membership: 44,329.

AMERICAN DRY MILK INSTITUTE
130 N. Franklin St.
Chicago, IL 60606
312-782-4888

Contact: Warren S. Clark, Jr., Ph.D., Executive Director
Membership: Corporate manufacturers or reprocessors of dry milk products; allied supply and service industries
Purpose: To maintain high standards of product quality; to expand the utilization of dry milks through research and education; to maintain liaison with government agencies; to promote industry development and growth; to assure a sound relationship with consumers.

AMERICAN EGG BOARD
1460 Renaissance
Park Ridge, IL 60068
312-296-7044

Contact: Louis B. Raffel, President
Membership: 18 egg producers and 18 alternate members.
Purpose: To provide informative and accurate nutrition and consumer education information through promotion, advertising, and research of eggs and egg products.

AMERICAN FARM BUREAU RESEARCH FOUNDATION
225 Touhy
Park Ridge, IL 60068
312-399-5700

Contact: John Datt, Secretary

AMERICAN FEED MANUFACTURERS ASSOCIATION
1701 North Fort Myer Dr.
Arlington, VA 22209
703-524-0810

Contact: Oakley M. Ray, President
Membership: 700 formula feed manufacturers and related firms.
Purpose: To represent the business, legislative, and management interests of feed industry firms.

AMERICAN FISH FARMERS FEDERATION*
PO Box 158
Lonoke, AR 72086
501-676-2800

Contact: Jim Malone, President

AMERICAN FISHERIES SOCIETY
5410 Grosvenor Lane
Bethesda, MD 20814
301-897-8616

Contact: Carl R. Sullivan, Executive Director
Membership: 8,000.

AMERICAN FROZEN FOOD INSTITUTE
1700 Old Meadow Rd., Suite 100
McLean, VA 22102
703-821-0770

Contact: Thomas B. House, President
Membership: 500.
Purpose: Representation of the frozen food processing industry; promotion of frozen foods; research and technical services.

AMERICAN GELBVIEH ASSOCIATION
Livestock Exchange Bldg.
Suite 311
Denver, CO 80216
303-623-4461

Contact: Daryl Loeppke, Executive Director
Membership: 1,000.
Purpose: To register and keep records on Gelbvieh cattle; to promote the use of Gelbvieh cattle in the American beef industry.

AMERICAN GUERNSEY CATTLE CLUB
70 Main St.
Peterborough, NH 03458
603-924-3344

Contact: Bernard M. Heisner, Secretary-Treasurer
Membership: 1,600.
Purpose: Registration and promotion of purebred Guernsey cattle.

AMERICAN INSTITUTE OF BAKING
1213 Bakers Way
Manhattan, KS 66502
913-537-4750

Contact: Dr. William Hoover, President
Membership: Companies in baking and allied industries.
Purpose: To promote the cause of education in nutrition and in the science and art of baking, bakery management, and allied skills.

404 RESOURCES FOR FURTHER INFORMATION

AMERICAN INSTITUTE OF CROP ECOLOGY*
809 Dale Drive
Silver Spring, MD 20910
301-589-4185

Contact: R. Manning, Secretary-Treasurer

AMERICAN INSTITUTE OF FISHERY RESEARCH BIOLOGISTS*
1226 Skyline Drive
Edmonds, WA 98020
206-774-1798

Contact: F. Heward Bell, Secretary-Treasurer

AMERICAN INSTITUTE OF FOOD DISTRIBUTION, INC.
28-06 Broadway
Fairlawn, NJ 07410
201-791-5570

Contact: Roy Harrison
Membership: 2,400, including growers, food processors, brokers, wholesalers, retailers, food industry suppliers, food service buyers, advertising agencies, consulting and research organizations, and government agencies.
Purpose: A non-profit reporting association to keep members accurately informed.

AMERICAN INSTITUTE OF NUTRITION
9650 Rockville Pike
Bethesda, MD 20814
301-530-7050

Contact: M. Milner, Executive Officer
Membership: 2,100 Nutrition Scientists.
Purpose: To develop and extend knowledge of nutrition.

AMERICAN INSTITUTIONS FOOD SERVICE ASSOCIATION
PO Box 155
Midvale, UT 84047
801-571-2300

Contact: Alfred M. Richardson, President
Purpose: An association that concentrates its efforts on food service education.

AMERICAN INTERNATIONAL CHAROLAIS ASSOCIATION
1610 Old Spanish Trail
Houston, TX 77054
713-797-9211

Contact: Joe Garrett, Executive Vice-President

AMERICAN JERSEY CATTLE CLUB*
2105-J South Hamilton Road
Columbus, OH 43227
614-861-3636

Contact: James F. Cavanaugh, Executive Secretary

AMERICAN JUNIOR HEREFORD ASSOCIATION
PO Box 4059
Kansas City, MO 64101
816-842-3757

Contact: Loren C. Jackson, Department Head
Membership: 9,500.
Purpose: Education, promotion and leadership development in the beef and agriculture industries.

AMERICAN JUNIOR SHORTHORN ASSOCIATION*
8288 Hascall Street
Omaha, NE 68124
402-393-7200

Contact: Alan K. Sears, Jr., Activities Director

AMERICAN LOGISTICS ASSOCIATION*
5205 Leesburg Pike
Suite 1213
Falls Church, VA 22041
703-998-5400

Contact: William Lazrus

AMERICAN MAINE-ANJOU ASSOCIATION
564 Livestock Exchange Bldg.
Kansas City, MO 64102
816-474-9555

Contact: Steve Bernhard, Executive Secretary
Membership: 1,700.
Purpose: Register and promote the breed of Maine-Anjou cattle in the U.S.

AMERICAN MEAT INSTITUTE
PO Box 3556
Washington, DC 20007
703-841-2400

Contact: C. Manley Molpus, President
Membership: 300 people or corporations engaged in slaughtering livestock, processing meat, manufacturing sausage and cooked prepared meats, and canning meat products.
Purpose: To create a regulatory, legislative, and consumer environment in which the meat packing and processing industry can operate efficiently and profitably.

AMERICAN MEAT SCIENCE ASSOCIATION*
444 N. Michigan Ave.
Chicago, IL 60611
312-467-5520

Contact: H. Kenneth Johnson

AMERICAN MILKING SHORTHORN SOCIETY
1722-JJ S. Glenstone Ave.
Springfield, MO 65804
417-887-6525

Contact: Marvin L. Kruse, Executive Secretary
Purpose: A member service organization which maintains a registry office and publishes a monthly journal.

AMERICAN MURRAY GREY ASSOCIATION
1222 North 27th St., Suite 218
Billings, MT 59101
406-248-1266

Contact: Joan T. Turnquist, Executive Director
Purpose: To maintain a national beef breed registry; to promote beef.

AMERICAN MUSHROOM INSTITUTE
PO Box 373
Kennet Square, PA 19348
215-388-7806

Contact: Jack Kooker, Executive Director
Membership: Mushroom growers and those associated with industry.
Purpose: Trade association.

AMERICAN NATIONAL COWBELLES
5420 South Quebec St.
PO Box 3881
Englewood, CO 80155
303-694-0313

Contact: Lynne Selig, Executive Vice-President
Membership: 12,000 individuals, 60,000 total with affiliates.
Purpose: Functions as the voice of women in the cattle industry, aiming to disseminate factual information on their product.

AMERICAN NORMANDE ASSOCIATION
PO Box 350
Kearny, MO 64060
816-635-5722

Contact: Jay C. Swisher, President
Purpose: To register and promote Normande cattle.

AMERICAN PARTRIDGE PLYMOUTH ROCK CLUB*
PO Box 207
Franklin, VA 23851
804-562-2646

Contact: Thomas I. Darden, President

AMERICAN PEANUT RESEARCH AND EDUCATION SOCIETY
PO Box 755
Yoakum, TX 77995
512-293-6326

Contact: Donald H. Smith, Executive Secretary-Treasurer
Membership: 700.
Purpose: To participate in cooperative program planning among research and industry personnel; to periodically review research and extension programs, with appropriate recommendations for revision; to transmit and exchange information through the annual meeting and the Society's publications.

AMERICAN POLLED HEREFORD ASSOCIATION
4700 East 63rd St.
Kansas City, MO 64130
816-333-7731

Contact: Dr. T. D. Rich, President
Membership: 40,000.
Purpose: To record ancestry, promote the breed, and provide education, leadership, and aid in the genetic advancement of the breed.

AMERICAN POLLED SHORTHORN SOCIETY*
PO Box 156
Virginia, IL 62691

Contact: Darryl Rahn, Secretary

AMERICAN POMOLOGICAL SOCIETY
103 Tyson Bldg.
University Park, PA 16802
814-863-2198

Contact: Dr. Loren D. Tukey, Business Manager
Purpose: Devoted to fruit variety improvement through breeding and testing.

AMERICAN POULTRY ASSOCIATION
Box 351, RD 4
Troy, NY 12180
518-286-1818

Contact: Bertha L. Traver, Secretary-Treasurer
Membership: 2,500.
Purpose: To promote and protect the standard bred poultry industry in all phases.

AMERICAN PRODUCERS ITALIAN TYPE CHEESE ASSOCIATION*
c/o S & R Cheese Corp.
PO Box 268
Plymouth, WI 53073
800-558-5888

Contact: Joseph Sartori, President

AMERICAN RABBIT BREEDERS ASSOCIATION*
Box 426 New National Bldg.
1925 South Main
Bloomington, IL 61701
309-827-6623

Contact: Edward L. Peifer, Jr., Secretary

AMERICAN RED BRANGUS ASSOCIATION
PO Box 1326
Austin, TX 78767
512-345-2625

Contact: Mike Levi, President
Membership: 582.
Purpose: A voluntary, non-profit livestock association providing for the registration, preservation of purity, and improvement in breeding of Red Brangus cattle.

AMERICAN RED POLL ASSOCIATION
PO Box 35519
Louisville, KY 40232
502-367-2772

Contact: John G. Nemeth, Secretary-Treasurer
Purpose: To promote the breeding, importing, and improving of Red Poll cattle; to keep records of all breeding and transfers of Red Poll cattle; to issue certificates of pedigree and ownership of the cattle.

AMERICAN ROMAGNOLA ASSOCIATION*
PO Box 13548
Houston, TX 77019
713-522-5141

Contact: Robert L. Waltrip, President

AMERICAN SCHOOL FOOD SERVICE ASSOCIATION
4101 East Iliff Ave.
Denver, CO 80222
303-757-8555

Contact: Mrs. Margaretta S. Plewes, Interim Executive Director
Membership: 60,000.
Purpose: To serve members by providing a professional trade journal, certification, and dissemination of information.

AMERICAN SCOTCH HIGHLAND BREEDERS ASSOCIATION
PO Box 5747
LaFayette, IN 47903
317-474-0524

Contact: Gloria Allen, Secretary-Treasurer
Membership: 355.
Purpose: To collect, verify, preserve, and publish pedigrees of Scotch Highland cattle; to protect validity of and promote interest in Scotch Highland cattle.

AMERICAN SEED RESEARCH FOUNDATION
Executive Bldg., Suite 964
1030 15th St., NW
Washington, DC 20005
202-223-4080

Contact: Harold D. Loden, Executive Secretary-Treasurer
Purpose: Organized for the purpose of supporting research on seeds.

AMERICAN SHEEP PRODUCERS COUNCIL*
200 Clayton Street
Denver, CO 80206
303-399-8130

Contact: Richard D. Biglin, Executive Director

AMERICAN SHORTHORN ASSOCIATION*
8288 Hascall Street
Omaha, NE 68124
402-393-7200

Contact: James W. Shirley, Executive Secretary-Treasurer

AMERICAN SHRIMP CANNERS AND PROCESSORS ASSOCIATION
PO Box 50774
New Orleans, LA 70114
504-368-1571

Contact: William D. Chauvin, Executive Director
Membership: 25 companies, mostly from Gulf states.
Purpose: To monitor governmental regulations of shrimp processing; to promote the use and consumption of shrimp and shrimp products; to conduct research to improve quality and methods.

AMERICAN SILKIE BANTAM CLUB*
2221 Blue Ridge Blvd.
Independence, MO 64052
816-254-8389

Contact: Mabel R. Witherell, Secretary

AMERICAN SIMMENTAL ASSOCIATION
1 Simmental Way
Bozeman, MT 59715
406-587-4531

Contact: Earl B. Peterson, Executive Vice-President
Membership: 15,000.
Purpose: To maintain the records and herdbook for all registered Simmental cattle.

AMERICAN SOCIETY OF AGRICULTURAL CONSULTANTS*
8301 Greensboro Drive
Suite 470
McLean, VA 22102
703-356-2455

Contact: Frank Frazier, Executive Vice-President

AMERICAN SOCIETY OF AGRICULTURAL ENGINEERS
2950 Niles Rd.
St. Joseph, MI 49085
616-429-0300

Contact: J. L. Butt, P.E., Executive Vice-President
Membership: 9,000 engineers and 2,000 graduate and undergraduate students.
Purpose: To provide professional and technical services to food and other agricultural engineers.

AMERICAN SOCIETY OF AGRONOMY
(Crop Science Society of America, Soil Science Society of America)
677 S. Segoe Rd.
Mdison, WI 53711
608-274-1212

Contact: David M. Kral, Acting Executive Vice-President
Membership: 12,000
Purpose: To promote research in and disseminate information about the agronomic sciences; to foster high standards in crops and soil education; to encourage the professional improvement of member scientists; to cooperate with other organizations to develop methods of managing natural resources.

AMERICAN SOCIETY OF ANIMAL SCIENCE
Dept. of Animal Science
University of Nebraska
Lincoln, NE 68583
402-472-3571

Contact: Irvin T. Omtvedt, Secretary-Treasurer
Membership: 4,029 professionals and 1,193 student affiliates.
Purpose: To promote more effective research and advancements of the profession; to disseminate information, foster high standards of education, and cooperate with similar organizations.

AMERICAN SOCIETY OF BAKERY ENGINEERS*
2 North Riverside Plaza
Room 1921
Chicago, IL 60606
312-332-2246

Contact: R. A. Fisher, Secretary-Treasurer

AMERICAN SOCIETY OF BREWING CHEMISTS
3340 Pilot Knob Rd.
St. Paul, MN 55121
612-454-7250

Contact: Raymond Tarleton, Executive Secretary
Purpose: To develop standard methods of analysis for raw materials, supplies, and products of brewing, malting, and related industries; to disseminate scientific information.

AMERICAN SOCIETY FOR CLINICAL NUTRITION*
9650 Rockville Pike
Bethesda, MD 20014
301-530-7110

Contact: G. M. Knight, Executive Officer

AMERICAN SOCIETY OF ENOLOGISTS
PO Box 411
Davis, CA 95617
916-752-0835

Contact: Lyndie M. Thomas, Business Manager
Membership: 3,000.
Purpose: To encourage and support research in enology or viticulture and to provide a forum for the dissemination of such research.

AMERICAN SOCIETY FOR HOSPITAL FOOD SERVICE ADMINISTRATORS

American Hospital Association
840 North Lake Shore Dr.
Chicago, IL 606011
312-280-6417

Contact: Mary R. DeMarco, R.D., Society Director
Membership: 2,100.
Purpose: To foster continuing education and development of management skills.

AMERICAN SOCIETY FOR PARENTERAL AND ENTERAL NUTRITION*
1025 Vermont Avenue
Suite 810
Washington, DC 20005
202-638-5881

Contact: Karen Knight, Executive Director

AMERICAN SOCIETY FOR QUALITY CONTROL*
161 West Wisconsin Ave.
Milwaukee, WI 53203
414-272-8575

Contact: Wayne Kost

AMERICAN SOCIETY OF SAFETY ENGINEERS*
850 Busse Highway
Park Ridge, IL 60068
312-692-4121

Contact: James L. Faltinek

AMERICAN SOCIETY OF SUGAR BEET TECHNOLOGISTS
PO Box 1546
Ft. Collins, CO 80522
303-482-8250

Contact: James H. Fisher, Secretary-Treasurer
Membership: Those interested in the advancement of knowledge concerning sugar beet production.
Purpose: To foster all phases of sugar beet and beet sugar research; to disseminate the resulting knowledge and cooperate with other similar organizations.

AMERICAN SOYBEAN ASSOCIATION
PO Box 27300
St. Louis, MO 63141
314-432-1600

Contact: Kenneth L. Bader, Executive Officer
Membership: 20,000.
Purpose: To increase the profits of soybean farmers.

AMERICAN SPICE TRADE ASSOCIATION, INC.
PO Box 1267
Englewood Cliffs, NJ 07632
201-568-2163

Contact: Thomas F. Burns
Purpose: To deal with intra-industry problems of management.

AMERICAN SUGAR CANE LEAGUE OF THE U.S.A.*
416 Whitney Bldg.
New Orleans, LA 70130
504-525-3956

Contact: R. Charles Hodson, Jr., Vice-President

AMERICAN SUGARBEET GROWERS ASSOCIATION*
1156 15th Street NW
No. 1019
Washington, DC 20005
202-833-2398

Contact: Richard W. Blake, Executive Vice-President

AMERICAN TARENTAISE ASSOCIATION
c/o ABBR, 123 Airport Rd.
Ames, IA 50010
515-233-3699

Contact: Jim Glenn, Office Manager

AMERICAN WINE SOCIETY
3006 Latte Rd.
Rochester, NY 14612
716-225-7613

Contact: Angel E. Nardone, Executive Secretary
Membership: People interested in wine making, wine appreciation, and grape growing.
Purpose: A non-profit organization devoted to educating its members and the general public about all aspects of wine.

AMERICAN WIRE CLOTH INSTITUTE*
800 3rd Avenue
New York, NY 10022
212-838-1004

Contact: Peter Miranda

AMERIFAX CATTLE ASSOCIATION
PO Box 149
Hastings, NE 68901
402-463-5289

Contact: John A. Quirk, President
Membership: 100.
Purpose: To maintain herdbook for Amerifax breed of cattle and promote the Amerifax breed.

ANIMAL NUTRITION RESEARCH COUNCIL
c/o Diversified Laboratories, Inc.
3251 Old Lee Highway
Alexandria, VA 22030
202-245-3042

Contact: Roger L. Garrett, Ph.D., Secretary-Treasurer
Membership: Scientists in the fields of animal nutrition, human nutrition, biochemistry, physiology, or nutrient assay.
Purpose: To stimulate interest in research in animal nutrition; to plan and administer projects; to promote collaboration in research.

ANKINA BREEDERS*
5803 Oakes Rd.
Clayton, OH 45315
513-837-4128

Contact: James K. Davis, Ph.D., President

APRICOT PRODUCERS OF CALIFORNIA
1762 Holmes St.
Livermore, CA 94550
415-447-7660

Contact: Les Rose, Vice-President, Operations
Membership: 350.
Purpose: A bargaining association for apricot growers.

ARKANSAS DAIRY PRODUCTS ASSOCIATION
PO Box 4187
Little Rock, AR 72214
501-565-1551

Contact: Floyd R. Smith, Executive Director

Membership: 70.
Purpose: To promote the dairy industry in Arkansas.

ASSOCIATED INDEPENDENT DAIRIES OF AMERICA
PO Box 53
Riverside, CA 92502
714-783-0111

Contact: Richard Shehadey
Purpose: Represents independent milk processors in public relations and group purchasing.

ASSOCIATED NEW YORK STATE FOOD PROCESSORS, INC.*
900 Jefferson Rd.
Rochester, NY 14623
716-424-1803

Contact: John C. Hemingway

ASSOCIATED PIMENTO CANNERS*
111 W. Taylor St.
Griffin, GA 30224
404-227-2803

Contact: Mildred Sawyer

ASSOCIATION OF AMERICAN FEED CONTROL OFFICIALS
c/o Texas Feed & Fertilizer Control Service
Box 3160
College Station, TX 77841
713-845-1121

Contact: Barbara J. Sims, Secretary
Membership: State and federal regulatory officials responsible for enforcing laws governing commercial feeds.
Purpose: To promote uniformity in regulating the commodity.

ASSOCIATION OF AMERICAN FERTILIZER CONTROL OFFICIALS
Division of Reg. SVCS
University of Kentucky
Lexington, KY 40546
317-749-2391

Contact: David L. Terry, Secretary
Membership: Fertilizer control officials in U.S. and Canada.
Purpose: To promote uniformity in fertilizer regulation.

ASSOCIATION OF AMERICAN VINTNERS*
Box 84
Watkins Glen, NY 14891
607-535-4144

Contact: J. William Moffett, Administrative Director

ASSOCIATION FOR DRESSINGS AND SAUCES
5775 Peachtree-Dunwoody Rd.
Suite 500-D
Atlanta, GA 30342
404-252-3663

Contact: R. H. Kellen, President
Memberhip: Manufacturers of salad dressing and sauce products.
Purpose: To promote the interests of the salad dressing and sauce industry; to increase the use of dressings and related products.

ASSOCIATION OF FOOD AND DRUG OFFICIALS*
75 Davis
Providence, RI 02908
401-277-2833

Contact: Fred Slino

ASSOCIATION OF FOOD INDUSTRIES
115 Broadway
Room 1117
New York, NY 10006
212-267-4244

Contact: Richard J. Sullivan, Executive Vice-President

ASSOCIATION OF MANUFACTURERS OF CONFECTIONARY AND CHOCOLATE*
PO Box 68
Mineola, NY 11501
202-872-1488

Contact: Fred Janssen, Administrator

ASSOCIATION OF NEW ENGLAND MILK DEALERS, INC.
18 Lyman St.
Westboro, MA 01581
617-366-1342

Contact: Harold Mikoleit, Executive Director

ASSOCIATION OF OFFICIAL ANALYTICAL CHEMISTS
1111 North 19th St., Suite 210
Arlington, VA 22209
703-522-3032

Contact: David MacLean, Executive Director
Membership: Local, state, or national government agencies, corporations, and governmental or individual scientists.
Purpose: To provide government agencies and industry in all countries with analytical methods that have undergone interlaboratory study to determine compliance research and quality control for products of interest to public health and safety.

ASSOCIATION OF OFFICIAL SEED ANALYSTS*
Mississippi State University
PO Box 5425
Mississippi State, MS 39762
601-325-5130

Contact: Dr. Charles C. Baskin, Secretary-Treasurer

ASSOCIATION OF OPERATIVE MILLERS
127 West 10th St., Suite 939
Kansas City, MO 64105
816-421-6628

Contact: Wayne D. Stahl, Executive Vice-President
Purpose: A professional organization dedicated to the advancement of technology in the flour milling, cereal, and seed processing industries.

ASSOCIATION OF SEAFOOD IMPORTERS
10 Harbor Park Dr.
Port Washington, NY 11050
516-621-5900

Contact: Joel Kolen, President

ASSOCIATION OF STATE AND TERRITORIAL PUBLIC HEALTH NUTRITION DIRECTORS*
c/o Association of State and Territorial Health Officials
1015 15th Street NW
Washington, DC 20005
202-789-1044

Contact: George K. Degnon

ASSOCIATION OF U.S. UNIVERSITY DIRECTORS OF INTERNATIONAL AGRICULTURAL PROGRAMS
210 Agricultural Hall
University of Nebraska
Lincoln, NE 68583

Contact: Robert W. Kleis, President
Membership: 150.
Purpose: To facilitate informative university programs in international agriculture; to encourage scientific and educational programs directed at modernization of world agriculture; to provide liaison between U.S. Colleges of agriculture and government agencies, Congress, private industry groups, and international agencies.

ATLANTIC SALMON ASSOCIATION*
1434 Catherine Street West
Suite 109
Montreal, Quebec H3G 1R4, Canada
514-866-6668

Contact: David M. Lank, President

ATLANTIC SEA RUN SALMON*
State of Maine Bldg.
34 Idaho Avenue
Bangor, ME 04401
207-947-8627

Contact: Glenn H. Manuel, Chairman

ATLANTIC STATES MARINE FISHERIES COMMISSION*
1717 Massachusetts Ave., NW
Suite 703
Washington, DC 20036
202-387-5330

Contact: Irwin M. Alperin, Executive Director

AVOCADO GROWERS BARGAINING COUNCIL*
PO Box 151
Fallbrook, CA 92028
714-728-6004

Contact: Allen Chaikin, Secretary

AYRSHIRE BREEDERS ASSOCIATION*
Brandon, VT 05733
802-247-5774

Contact: J. D. Dodds, Executive Secretary

B

BAKERS ASSOCIATION OF THE CAROLINAS*
PO Box 157
Rockingham, NC 28379
919-997-2215

Contact: Mary Stanley, Secretary

BAKERS COUNCIL OF THE CAROLINAS
PO Box 5141
Columbia, SC 29250
803-799-0388

Contact: Harlan Stout, Executive Vice-President
Membership: Wholesale and larger retail bakeries.
Purpose: For the mutual uplift of its members and the baking industry in general, and to raise the standards of the industry.

BAKERY COUNCIL OF CANADA
130 Bloor St. West
Suite 1101
Toronto Ontario M5S 2X7, Canada

Contact: Charles Tisdall, Managing Director
Membership: Large and small wholesale and retail bakers and suppliers to the baking industry.
Purpose: To protect, promote, and enchance Canada's baking industry.

BAKERY EQUIPMENT MANUFACTURERS ASSOCIATION*
521 5th Ave.
New York, NY 10017
212-687-9071

Contact: Raymond Walter, Secretary-Treasurer

BAKERY PRODUCTION CLUB OF BC*
3450 Vanness Ave.
Vancouver, British Columbia
V5R 5A9, Canada

Contact: Stan Hill, President

BAKING INDUSTRY SANITATION STANDARDS COMMITTEE
521 5th Ave.
New York, NY 10017
212-687-9071

Contact: Raymond Walter, Secretary-Treasurer
Purpose: Development of sanitation standards for the baking industry.

BARZONA BREEDERS ASSOCIATION OF AMERICA
PO Box 631
Prescott, AZ 86302
602-445-5150

Contact: Doug Bard, President
Purpose: To provide a registry of purebred and percentage Barzona cattle and to promote the continued improvement of the breed.

BASS RESEARCH FOUNDATION*
PO Box 99
Starkville, MS 39759
601-323-3131

Contact: Walter Stubbe, Executive Director

BEEFMASTER BREEDERS UNIVERSAL*
GPM South Tower
800 NW Loop 410
San Antonio, TX 78216
512-341-1277

Contact: Gene Kuykendall, Executive Vice-President

BEET SUGAR DEVELOPMENT FOUNDATION
PO Box 1545
1311 South College Ave.
Fort Collins, CO 80522
303-482-8250

Contact: James H. Fisher, Secretary
Membership: Sugarbeet processing companies.
Purpose: Research and education arm for member companies.

BELTED GALLOWAY SOCIETY
PO Box 5
Summitville, OH 43962
216-223-1963

410 RESOURCES FOR FURTHER INFORMATION

Contact: Meda McCord, Secretary
Membership: 94.
Purpose: To promote the breed.

BISCUIT & CRACKER DISTRIBUTORS ASSOCIATION*
111 East Wacker Drive
Chicago, IL 60601
312-644-6610

Contact: Barbara Chalik, Executive Director

BISCUIT AND CRACKER MANUFACTURERS ASSOCIATION
1660 L St., NW
Washington, DC 20036
202-223-3127

Contact: Joseph M. Creed, President and General Counsel
Membership: National and international trade association of cookie and cracker manufacturers.
Purpose: To develop the industry by stimulating the increased consumption of products; to support research and education in the science and technology of baking; to promote improved quality of products.

BLUE ANCHOR, INC.*
PO Box 15498
Sacramento, CA 95813
916-929-3050

Contact: Walter M. Tindell, President

BOARD OF TRADE OF THE CITY OF CHICAGO
141 West Jackson Blvd.
Chicago, IL 60604
312-435-3600

Contact: Robert K. Wilmouth, President
Membership: 1,402 full members, 1,154 conditional associate members.
Purpose: Provides a marketplace for agricultural and other futures.

BOARD OF TRADE OF KANSAS CITY MISSOURI
4800 Main St., Suite 274
Kansas City, MO 64112
816-753-7500

Contact: W. N. Vernon III, Executive Vice-President

Membership: 219.
Purpose: To move grain from the farm to consumers all over the U.S. and the world.

BOARD OF TRADE OF THE WHOLESALE SEAFOOD MERCHANTS
7 Dey St.
New York, NY 10007
212-732-4340

Contact: Dennis F. Ryan, Executive Secretary

BREAD FOR THE WORLD*
32 Union Square East
New York, NY 10003
212-260-7000

Contact: Simon Arthur, Executive Director
Purpose: To end hunger in the United States and to promote a U.S. food policy committed to world food security and rural development as proposed by the World Food Conference

BROKER MANAGEMENT COUNCIL
117 Miramar Ave.
Biloxi, MS 39530
601-374-6537

Contact: Norman E. Bess, Executive Director
Membership: Limited to one selected foodservice brokerage in each regional marketing area of the U.S.
Purpose: To facilitate communication at the executive management level and disseminate information.

BROWN SWISS CATTLE BREEDERS ASSOCIATION OF THE U.S.A.
Box 1038
800 Pleasant St.
Beloit, WI 53511
608-365-4474

Contact: George W. Opperman, Executive Secretary-Treasurer
Membership: 1,200.
Purpose: To maintain accurate and permanent records of ancestry and production of registered Brown Swiss cattle in the United States.

C

CALAVO GROWERS OF CALIFORNIA
4833 Everett Ave.
Vernon, CA 90058
213-587-4291

Contact: P. K. Smith, President
Membership: 2,600.
Purpose: Packs and markets its members' avocados for the fresh market and processes avocado products.

CALIFORNIA ALMOND GROWERS EXCHANGE
18th & C Sts.
Sacramento, CA 95808
916-442-0771

Contact: Walter Payne, Vice-President, Marketing
Purpose: To process and market the almonds produced on member orchards.

CALIFORNIA APRICOT ADVISORY BOARD
1280 Boulevard Way, Suite 107
Walnut Creek, CA 94595
415-937-3660

Contact: Jack M. Hestilow, Manager
Membership: All California apricot Growers.
Purpose: To disseminate information about apricots with the goal of increasing the demand for the product.

CALIFORNIA ARTICHOKE ADVISORY BOARD
PO Box 747
Castroville, CA 95012
408-633-4411

Contact: Lloyd R. Stolich, Manager
Membership: 38.
Purpose: Public relations for the artichoke industry.

CALIFORNIA CANNING PEACH ASSOCIATION
PO Box 7001
Lafayette, CA 94549
415-284-9171

Contact: Ronald A. Schuler
Membership: 650 growers.
Purpose: To negotiate prices and market members' tonnage to

canners; to represent members in industry matters and government relations.

CALIFORNIA CHEESE & BUTTER ASSOCIATION
24 Cazneau Ave.
Sausalito, CA 94965
415-331-2616

Contact: Douglas Johnstone, President
Membership: Manufacturers, distributors, and brokers of cheese and butter.
Purpose: To bring together the cheese and butter segment of the California dairy industry.

CALIFORNIA CANNING PEAR ASSOCIATION*
100 Bush Street
Room 514
San Francisco, CA 94104
415-982-3076

Contact: Cameron Girton

CALIFORNIA DAIRY INDUSTRIES ASSOCIATION
PO Box 255463
Sacramento, CA 95865
916-489-1391

Contact: Pat Dolan, Secretary-Treasurer
Membership: 800.
Purpose: To stimulate interest and study aimed at self-improvement, to promote educational activities; to participate in any activities that contribute to the advancement of the dairy industry.

CALIFORNIA DATE ADMINISTRATIVE COMMITTEE*
81-855 Highway III
Room 2-G
Indio, CA 92201
714-347-4510

Contact: Anne Ezell, Manager

CALIFORNIA DRIED FIG ADVISORY BOARD
PO Box 709
Fresno, CA 93712
209-264-5011

Contact: Ron Klamm, Manager
Membership: All dried fig producers and processors in California.
Purpose: Promotion, research, and quality control.

CALIFORNIA DRIED FRUIT EXPORT ASSOCIATION
PO Box 270-A
303 Brokaw Rd.
Santa Clara, CA 95050
408-727-9302

Contact: Frank A. Mosebar, Secretary-Treasurer
Membership: Dried fruit and tree nut processors and exporters.
Purpose: Engages in export trade in dried fruits and tree nuts and aids the export members.

CALIFORNIA DRY BEAN ADVISORY BOARD
531-D North Alta Ave.
Dinuba, CA 93618
209-591-4866

Contact: Jerry Munson, Manager
Purpose: To advise the California director of Food & Agriculture on matters pertaining to the research and marketing of California dry beans.

CALIFORNIA FIG INSTITUTE
PO Box 709
Fresno, CA 93728
209-264-5011

Contact: Ron Klamm, Managing Director
Membership: 125 dried fig producers.
Purpose: To promote the general welfare of the California fig industry; to engage in research and some promotional activities.

CALIFORNIA FREESTONE PEACH ASSOCIATION
1704 Herndon Rd.,
Ceres, CA 95307
209-538-2372

Contact: Sharon M. Cole, Representative
Membership: 170.
Purpose: To help members place their freestone peaches with a processor and bargain with processor for an equitable price for the fruit; to represent members in industry activities and government relations.

CALIFORNIA GRAPE AND TREE FRUIT LEAGUE*
1630 East Shaw Avenue
Suite 150
Fresno, CA 93710
209-226-6330

Contact: Thomas J. Hale, President

CALIFORNIA HONEY ADVISORY BOARD
PO Box 32
Whittier, CA 90608
213-698-5210

Contact: Marilyn J. Kiser, Manager
Membership: Operated under California Dept. of Food and Agriculture.
Purpose: Educational promotion of extracted honey.

CALIFORNIA ICEBERG LETTUCE COMMISSION
PO Box 3354
Monterey, CA 93940
408-625-2944

Contact: Wade A. Whitfield, General Manager
Membership: All shippers of Iceberg lettuce in California.
Purpose: To develop and execute publicity programs and all types of promotion programs for increasing the consumption of Iceberg lettuce.

CALIFORNIA MACADAMIA SOCIETY
PO Box 666
Fallbrook, CA 92028

Contact: Cynthia Cooper, Secretary
Membership: 500.
Purpose: To disseminate information to interested persons about the macadamia culture, from tree purchase to processing and marketing the nuts.

CALIFORNIA MILK ADVISORY BOARD
PO Box 4680
Modesto, CA 95352
209-521-1060

Contact: Chandler Meloy, Director of Communication Services
Membership: All the dairy farmers in the state of California.
Purpose: Building milk sales for dairymen through advertising, merchandising, research, and public relations.

CALIFORNIA OLIVE ASSOCIATION
c/o California League of Food Processors

1007 L Street
Sacramento, CA 95814
916-444-9260

Contact: Gary Oberti, President

CALIFORNIA PISTACHIO COMMISSION
5118 East Clinton, Suite 107
Fresno, CA 93737
209-252-3345

Contact: Robert C. Gross, President
Membership: All producing pistachio growers, processors, related equipment manufacturers, and researchers in the state.
Purpose: In addition to advertising and promotion, the commission provides the industry with reports and conducts field and market research.

CALIFORNIA PRUNE ADVISORY BOARD*
World Trade Center
Room 103
San Francisco, CA 94111
415-986-1452

Contact: F. W. Davis

CALIFORNIA RAISIN ADVISORY BOARD
PO Box 5335
Fresno, CA 93755
209-224-7010

Contact: Jean Burkhart, Director of Home Economics and Consumer Services

CALIFORNIA RARE FRUIT GROWERS
Fullerton Arboretum
California State University
Fullerton, CA 92634
714-526-7198

Contact: Pat Sawyer, President
Membership: 650.
Purpose: To introduce and distribute new fruits; to select superior varieties of established fruits; to exchange seeds, cuttings, and scion wood; to conduct research on hardiness, propagation, and growing requirements in California conditions.

CALIFORNIA STRAWBERRY ADVISORY BOARD
PO Box 269
Watsonville, CA 95076
408-724-1301

Contact: David R. Riggs, Executive Director
Membership: California strawberry growers, shippers, and processors.
Purpose: To conduct agricultural research and develop markets for fresh and processed strawberries.

CALORIE CONTROL COUNCIL
5775 Peachtree-Dunwoody Rd.
Suite 500-D
Atlanta, GA 30342
404-252-3663

Contact: Robert H. Kellen, President
Purpose: To provide an effective channel of communication between the calorie control food industry and governmental regulatory bodies; to promote the industry and foster industry knowledge through educational programs and scientific research.

CAN MANUFACTURERS INSTITUTE*
1625 Massachusetts Ave., NW
Washington, DC 20036
202-232-4677

Contact: J. Michael Dunn

CANADIAN FOOD PROCESSORS ASSOCIATION
130 Rue Albert, Suite 1409
Ottawa, Ontario K1P 5G4, Canada
613-233-4049

Contact: Elmer T. Banting, Executive Vice-President
Membership: Canadian firms engaged in the canning, freezing, and dehydrating of fruits and vegetables, and in the production of allied products.
Purpose: To represent the members at the national and international level; to monitor governmental regulations; to assist in the development of the industry.

CANDY BROKERS ASSOCIATION OF AMERICA*
8636 Curtis Ave.
Alexandria, VA 22309
703-360-5023

Contact: C. M. McMillan

CANDY, CHOCOLATE AND CONFECTIONERY INSTITUTE
1701 Lake Ave.
Suite 260
Glenview, IL 60025
312-724-6120

Contact: Alfred V. Heilman, Executive Director

CANNED SALMON INSTITUTE*
1600 S. Jackson St.
Seattle, WA 98144
206-323-3540

Contact: Larry Kaner

CANNERS LEAGUE OF CALIFORNIA*
1007 L Street
Sacramento, CA 95814
916-444-9260

Contact: Lawrence K. Taber

CAROLINA RETAIL BAKERS ASSOCIATION*
c/o Florence Cake Box
Florence Mall
Florence, SC 29501
803-662-1217

Contact: Marge Cheek, Secretary

CENTER FOR SCIENCE IN THE PUBLIC INTEREST
1755 S St., NW
Washington, DC 20009
202-332-9110

Contact: Michael P. Jackson, Ph.D., Executive Director
Membership: 33,000.
Purpose: A consumer advocacy, educational group which produces health information materials, monitors government activities, and seeks to improve programs and practices related to food, diet, nutrition, health, science, and technology.

CENTRAL MINNESOTA DAIRYMEN & CREAMERY OPERATORS ASSOCIATION
PO Box 80
Starbuck, MN 56381
612-239-2226

Contact: Gene G. Watnaas, Secretary
Membership: Creamery operators and dairymen from Minnesota.
Purpose: To promote the dairy industry.

CENTRAL OHIO DAIRY FOODS ASSOCIATES
Ohio State University
Dept. Food Science and Nuitrition
Columbus, OH 43210
614-422-6281

Contact: J. P. Kenyon, Corresponding Secretary
Membership: 40-50 members associated with the dairy food industry.
Purpose: Continuing education for the dairy food industry.

CENTRAL WISCONSIN CHEESEMAKERS & BUTTERMAKERS ASSOCIATION
Route 2
Colby, WI 54421
715-223-2874

Contact: Terry Eggebrecht, Secretary-Treasurer
Membership: 75 central Wisconsin cheesemakers & buttermakers.
Purpose: To promote dairy products.

CEREAL INSTITUTE INC.*
1111 Plaza Drive
Suite 720
Schaumburg, IL 60195
312-843-1880

Contact: Dr. Eugene B. Hayden

CERTIFIED COLOR MANUFACTURERS ASSOCIATION*
900 17th Ave., NW
Suite 600
Washington, DC 20006
202-452-1300

Contact: Daniel R. Thompson

CERTIFIED MILK PRODUCERS ASSOCIATION OF AMERICA
Manlius-Chittenango Rd.
Chittenango, NY 13027
315-682-9833

Contact: Daniel F. Gates, Secretary
Membership: Farms producing Certified Milk.
Purpose: To promote members' business interests; to improve the quality and distribution of Certified Milk.

CHAR-SWISS BREEDERS ASSOCIATION
407 Chambers St.
Marlin, TX 76661
817-883-6045

Contact: G. T. Fairbairn, Secretary-Treasurer

CHEESE IMPORTERS ASSOCIATION OF AMERICA, INC.
460 Park Ave.
New York, NY 10022
212-753-7500

Contact: Robert Fromer
Membership: 155.

CHEFS DE CUISINE ASSOCIATION OF AMERICA
Paramount Hotel, Suite 325
235 West 46th St.
New York, NY 10036
212-245-7173

Contact: Joseph J. Melz, President
Membership: 300.
Purpose: To promote and uphold culinary excellence; to promote youth to join the profession by supporting culinary schools with scholarship funds; to assist and support culinary exhibits and functions.

CHEMICAL MANUFACTURERS ASSOCIATION
2501 M St., NW
Washington, DC 20037
202-887-1100

Contact: Robert A. Roland, President
Membership: 200.
Purpose: To promote of the interests of the chemical manufacturing industry.

CHERRY GROWERS & INDUSTRIES FOUNDATION*
1005 Tieton Drive
Yakima, WA 98902
509-453-4837

Contact: Ken Severn

THE CHILDREN'S FOUNDATION*
1420 New York Ave., NW
Suite 800
Washington, DC 20005
202-347-3300

Contact: Barbara Bode, President

CHOCOLATE MANUFACTURERS ASSOCIATION OF THE USA
7900 Westpark Dr., Suite 514
McLean, VA 22102
703-790-5011

Contact: Richard T. O'Connell
Purpose: To engage in research to improve manufacturing procedures and techniques; to participate in public relations programs; to engage in government relations activities affecting the industry.

CINCINNATI BOARD OF TRADE*
5675 Killy Rd.
Harrison, OH 45030
513-367-4518

Contact: James A. Cornelius, President

CLING PEACH ADVISORY BOARD
PO Box 7111
San Francisco, CA 94120
415-541-0100

Contact: Allen H. Burgi
Membership: A quasi-state agency working under the director of food and agriculture, state of California.
Purpose: To promote and merchandise canned cling peaches and canned fruit cocktail.

THE COCOA MERCHANTS ASSOCIATION OF AMERICA, INC.
PO Box 5476
Grand Central Station
New York, NY 10163
212-883-9522

Contact: Johann J. Scheu, President

Membership: Importers of cocoa beans and products, chocolate manufacturers and foreign trade houses, and banks and carriers serving the cocoa trade as associate members.
Purpose: To foster the trade in cocoa beans and products; to provide arbitration facilities for the amicable settling of controversies; to fight abuses.

COFFEE, SUGAR AND COCOA EXCHANGE*
Four World Trade Center
8th Floor
New York, NY 10048
212-938-2800

Contact: Bennett J. Corn, President

COLORADO MEAT DEALERS ASSOCIATION
789 Sherman St.
#380
Denver, CO 80203
303-837-1280

Contact: Roger Gifford
Membership: 140.
Purpose: To promote the meat industry in Colorado.

COLUMBIA NATIONAL FISHERIES RESEARCH LABORATORY
Fish and Wildlife Service
US Department of the Interior
Route #1
Columbia, MO 65201
314-875-5399

Contact: Dr. Richard Schoettger, Director

COMMERCIAL REFRIGERATOR MANUFACTURERS ASSOCIATION
1101 Connecticut Ave., NW
Washington, DC 20036
202-857-1145

Contact: Robert T. Chancler, Executive Director
Membership: Manufacturers of commercial refrigeration equipment for food stores and their suppliers.
Purpose: To develop commercial refrigeration standards; to address federal, state and local regulations affecting commercial refrigeration.

COMMITTEE TO ASSURE THE AVAILABILITY OF CASEIN*
1700 Pennsylvania Ave., NW
Suite 670
Washington, DC 20006
202-298-6134

Contact: Larry Umiauf, Chairman

COMMUNITY NUTRITION INSTITUTE
1146 19th St., NW
Washington, DC 20036
202-833-1730

Contact: Rod Leonard, Executive Director
Purpose: Specializes in food and nutrition issues and is an active advocate of consumer issues; provides training and technical assistance to agencies at the federal, state, and local levels.

COMMUNITY SYSTEMS FOUNDATION
1130 Hill St.
Ann Arbor, MI 48104
313-761-1357

Contact: Naomi Gottlieb, Executive Officer
Purpose: Dedicated to improving the quality of life through applied research and direct assistance to communities by helping them to help themselves.

CONCORD GRAPE ASSOCIATION
5775 Peachtree-Dunwoody Rd.
Suite 500-D
Atlanta, GA 30342
404-252-3663

Contact: Robert H. Kellen, President
Purpose: To conduct cooperative activities which will promote the best interests and welfare of the Concord grape industry.

CONNECTICUT ASSOCIATION OF DAIRY & FOOD SANITARIANS*
State Office Bldg.
Hartford, CT 96115
203-566-2874

CONNECTICUT BAKERS ASSOCIATION
85 Belcher Rd.
Wethersfield, CT 06109
203-529-1984

Contact: Lee Silva, Executive Secretary
Membership: 225.
Purpose: To develop of the baking industry by increasing the use of commercially baked products.

CONNECTICUT MEAT PACKERS-PROCESSORS ASSOCIATION*
c/o Connecticut Packing Co.
335 Cottage Grove Rd.
Bloomfield, CT 06002
203-242-5521

Contact: Robert Cherlin

CONNECTICUT MILK DEALERS ASSOCIATION
PO Box 5296
Hamden, CT 06518
203-281-1528

Contact: Michael Marcus, President
Purpose: Represents trade associations of the dairy industry on regulatory, legislative, and other matters affecting the membership.

CONSUMER FEDERATION OF AMERICA
1012 14th St., NW, Suite 901
Washington, DC 20005
202-737-3732

Contact: Stephen J. Brobeck, Executive Director

CONSUMER UNION OF UNITED STATES
256 Washington St.
Mount Vernon, NY 10550
914-644-6400

Contact: Monte Florman, Technical Director
Membership: Several million subscribers to Consumer Reports magazine.
Purpose: To provide information and counsel to consumers on a broad spectrum of topics.

CONSUMERS OPPOSED TO INFLATION IN THE NECESSITIES*
2000 P Street, NW
Suite 413
Washington, DC 20036

Contact: Roger Hickey, Director

CONSUMERS RESEARCH
Bowerstown Rd.
PO Box 168
Washington, NJ 07882
201-689-3300

Contact: F. J. Schlink, Technical Director
Purpose: Dedicated to service of the consumer

COOKIE & SNACK BAKERS ASSOCIATION*
c/o Bishop Baking Co.
PO Box 69
Cleveland, TN 37311
615-472-1561

Contact: Craig Parrish, Secretary

CORN REFINERS ASSOCIATION, INC.
1001 Connecticut Ave., NW
Washington, DC 20036
202-331-1634

Contact: Robert C. Liebnow

COUNCIL FOR AGRICULTURAL SCIENCE AND TECHNOLOGY
250 Memorial Union
Ames, IA 50011
515-294-2036

Contact: Charles A. Black, Executive Vice-President
Membership: 25 food and agricultural science societies are the controlling members; approximately 4,500 members.
Purpose: To advance the understanding and use of food and agricultural science and technology in the public interest.

COUNCIL OF FOOD PROCESSORS ASSOCIATION EXECUTIVES
1133 20th St., NW
Washington, DC 20036
202-331-5941

Contact: Claudia R. Fuquay, Secretary

COUNCIL FOR RESPONSIBLE NUTRITION
1707 N St., NW
Washington, DC 20036
202-872-1488

Contact: Robert K. Fredericks, President
Membership: Manufacturers, distributors, and ingredient suppliers of nutritional supplements and products.
Purpose: Dedicated to enhancing the health of the U.S. population through responsible nutrition, including the use of nutrient supplementation.

COUNCIL ON SOIL TESTING AND PLANT ANALYSIS
University of Georgia
Dept. of Horticulture
Athens, GA 30602
404-542-2471

Contact: Dr. J. Benton Jones Jr., Secretary-Treasurer
Membership: Researchers, consultants, students, and laboratory operators.
Purpose: To promote uniform testing, stimulate research, disseminate information, and provide a forum and information clearinghouse.

CRANBERRY INSTITUTE*
PO Box N
29 Rockland Trust Bldg.
Duxbury, MA 02332
617-934-5666

Contact: Orrin G. Colley, President

CROP*
28606 Phillips Street
Elkhart, IN 46514
219-264-3102

Contact: Ronald E. Stenning, Director

CROP QUALITY COUNCIL*
PO Box 15047
Minneapolis, MN 55415
612-333-5237

Contact: Vance V. Goodfellow, President

CROP SCIENCE SOCIETY OF AMERICA*
677 South Segoe Rd.
Madison, WI 53711
608-274-1212

Contact: Matthias Stelly, Executive Vice-President

D

DAIRIES FEDERATION OF MINNESOTA*
3824-47 Avenue South
Minneapolis, MN 55406
612-724-8079

Contact: R. J. Godin, President

DAIRY COUNCIL, INC.*
6820 Hawthorn Park Drive
Indianapolis, IN 46201
317-842-3060

Contact: Nancy Rainey, Executive Director

DAIRY COUNCIL, INC.
12450 N. Washington
Thornton, CO 80241
303-451-7711

Contact: Ruth Bowling, Program Director
Membership: Serving dairy industry members in Colorado and Wyoming.
Purpose: Dissemination of information.

DAIRY COUNCIL OF ARIZONA
2008 South Hardy Dr.
Tempe, AZ 85282
602-968-7814

Contact: Ernest Cornwall, Administrator
Membership: The dairymen of Arizona.
Purpose: A nonprofit nutrition organization supported by dairymen of Arizona; an affiliated unit of National Dairy Council dedicated to promoting good nutrition and health.

DAIRY COUNCIL OF CALIFORNIA
2775 Cottage Way, Suite 19
Sacramento, CA 95825
916-445-8790

Contact: Cynthia Carson, Manager
Purpose: Provides nutrition education and communications programs designed to inform people how to make daily food choices using the four food groups.

DAIRY COUNCIL OF MICHIGAN
30600 Telegraph Rd.
Suite 3380
Birmingham, MI 48010

Contact: Carolyn Shafer, Executive Director
Purpose: To contribute to the achievement of optimal health by providing leadership in nutrition education based on the concept of a balanced diet.

DAIRY COUNCIL OF NORTHERN INDIANA*
501 N. Main Street
South Bend, IN 46601
219-232-8171

Contact: Marcella Ellett, Executive Director

DAIRY COUNCIL OF SOUTH DAKOTA
619 Fifth Ave.
Brookings, SD 57006
605-692-4812

Contact: Beth Alderson, Program Director
Purpose: To promote optimal health through leadership in nutrition education.

DAIRY COUNCIL OF UTAH
1213 East 21st South
Salt Lake City, UT 84106
801-487-9976

Contact: Jo Anne Criddle, Program Director
Purpose: Resource center for nutrition education materials, films, and programs.

DAIRY & FOOD INDUSTRIES SUPPLY ASSOCIATION
6245 Executive Blvd.
Rockville, MD 20852
301-984-1444

Contact: Fred J. Greiner, Executive Vice-President

DAIRY FOODS FOUNDATION OF NORTHEASTERN OHIO & DAIRY & NUTRITION COUNCIL MIDEAST*
6155 Rockside Road
Independence, OH 44131
216-447-1012

Contact: Raymond Hromco, Executive Secretary

DAIRY INDUSTRY COMMITTEE*
5530 Wisconsin Ave.
Washington, DC 20015
301-652-4420

Contact: Fred J. Greiner, Chairman

DAIRY INSTITUTE OF CALIFORNIA*
11th & L Bldg., Suite 718
Sacramento, CA 95814
916-441-6921

Contact: Larry Maes, Executive Director

DAIRY PROCESSORS, INC.*
2015 Rice Street
St. Paul, MN 55113
612-488-0261

Contact: Cliff Markuson, Executive Director

DAIRY PRODUCTS ASSOCIATION OF KENTUCKY, INC.*
136 St. Matthews Ave.
Louisville, KY 40207
502-896-1377

Contact: Glenn Cross, Executive Secretary

DAIRY PRODUCTS INSTITUTE OF TEXAS*
1006 Perry Brooks Bldg.
Austin, TX 78701
512-472-7231

Contact: Glenn Brown, Executive Vice-President

DAIRY RESEARCH, INC.
6300 River Rd.
Rosemont, IL 60018
312-696-1870

Contact: Ray Mykleby, Executive Vice-President
Membership: Dairy farmers throughout the U.S.
Purpose: To support and fund basic and applied research and development activities relating to milk production, processing, and marketing.

DAIRY SHRINE
c/o Midwest Breeders Cooperative
Shawano, WI 54166
715-526-2141

Contact: James M. Leuenberger, Secretary
Membership: Includes dairy cattle breeders, scientists, industrialists, and students from all fields.
Purpose: Primarily to stimulate, inspire, educate, and record the development of dairying in the U.S.

DAIRY SOCIETY INT'L, INC.
3008 McKinley St., NW
Washington, DC 20015
202-363-3359

Contact: George W. Weigold, Managing Director
Membership: Individuals, companies, and cooperatives interested in the dairy industry.
Purpose: To enhance health and economic progress by encouraging the development of the dairy industry.

DAIRY TRAINING AND MERCHANDISING INSTITUTE*
910 17th Street NW
Washington, DC 20006
202-296-4250

Contact: John F. Speer, Jr., President

DAIRYLEA COOPERATIVE*
One Blue Hill Plaza
Pearl River, NY 10965
914-627-3131

Contact: Clyde E. Rutherford, President

DAIRYMEN'S SERVICE ASSOCIATION
Box 53
Riverside, CA 92502
714-783-0111

Contact: Paul Coram, Secretary-Manager
Purpose: Represents milk processors and distributors in various regulatory matters.

DEEP SOUTH RETAIL BAKERS ASSOCIATION*
4037 Jefferson Highway
New Orleans, LA 70113
504-837-0190

Contact: David Haydel, Board Chairman

DEHYDRATED AND CONVENIENCE FOODS COUNCIL*
PO Box 801
Healdsburg, CA 95448
707-433-1864

Contact: W. R. Lucius, Executive Secretary

DENMARK CHEESE ASSOCIATION
570 Taxter Rd.
Elmsford, NY 10523
914-592-5277

Contact: Jorgen Kolding, Managing Director
Purpose: To heighten consumer and trade awareness of Danish cheese products.

DIAMOND WALNUT GROWERS
PO Box 1727
1050 S. Diamond St.
Stockton, CA 95201
209-466-4851

Contact: Frank R. Light, President
Membership: 2,706.
Purpose: Non-profit farmer cooperative which processes and markets its members' production of walnuts and pecans.

DISTILLERS FEED RESEARCH COUNCIL
208 Airpark Dr.
PO Box 75153
Cincinnati, OH 45275
606-371-1360

Contact: William N. Isgrigg, Executive Director

DRIED FIG ADVISORY BOARD
PO Box 709
Fresno, CA 93728
209-264-5011

Contact: Ron Klamm, Manager
Membership: 125 fig producers and 4 fig processors.
Purpose: Quality control, inspection, research, and promotional activities.

DRIED FRUIT ASSOCIATION OF CALIFORNIA
PO Box 270-A
Santa Clara, CA 95052
408-727-9302

Contact: Frank A. Mosebar, Executive Vice-President
Membership: Dried fruit and tree nut handlers in California.
Purpose: To promote better understanding between growers and processors; to encourage sound trade practices.

DUTCH BELTED CATTLE ASSOCIATION OF AMERICA*
Box 358
Highland County
Venus, FL 33960

Contact: James H. Hendrie, Secretary-Treasurer

E

EARTHWORK/CENTER FOR RURAL STUDIES
3410 19th St.
San Francisco, CA 94110
612-377-5686

Contact: Mark Ritchie, Director
Purpose: Information on food and agriculture issues.

EASTERN FROSTED FOODS ASSOCIATION, INC.*
95 E. Valley Stream Blvd.
Valley Stream, NY 11580
516-825-6673

Contact: Margaret Clamser

EASTERN MICHIGAN RETAIL BAKERS*
c/o Hamilton's Pastry Shop
117 East Main Street
Midland, MI 48640
517-832-8190

Contact: Ray Hamilton, President

ENID BOARD OF TRADE*
PO Box 1747
2309 North 10th
Enid, OK 73701
405-233-1528

Contact: Joe Neal Hampton, Secretary-Treasurer

EVAPORATED MILK ASSOCIATION
PO Box 188
Rockville, MD 20850
301-424-2150

Contact: Dr. J. C. Flake, Executive Vice-President

F

FARMERS AND MANUFACTURERS BEET SUGAR ASSOCIATION*
470 Plaza N
Saginaw, MI 48603
517-792-1531

Contact: Perc A. Reeve, Executive Vice-President

FATS AND PROTEINS RESEARCH FOUNDATION, INC.
2720 Des Plaines Ave.
Des Plaines, IL 60018
312-827-0139

Contact: David L. Gilcrest, President
Membership: Companies involved in the rendering industry.
Purpose: Initiates and conducts research activities oriented toward developing new and expanded uses for animal by-products and related materials.

FATTY ACID PRODUCERS COUNCIL
475 Park Ave. S.
New York, NY 10016
212-725-1262

Contact: Theodore E. Brenner, President
Membership: Producers of fatty acids.

FEDERATED PECAN GROWERS ASSOCIATION OF THE U.S.
PO Drawer AX
University Station
Baton Rouge, LA 70803
504-388-2222

Contact: Earl Puls

FEINGOLD ASSOCIATION OF THE UNITED STATES
Drawer AG
Holtsville, NY 11742

Contact: Jane Hersey, President
Purpose: To assist parents of hyperactive children through parent-to-parent sharing programs and educational activities. The association uses a dietary program developed by Dr. Ben F. Feingold.

FISHERY COUNCIL*
118 South Street
New York, NY 10038
212-962-1608

Contact: Robert Smith

FLAVOR AND EXTRACT MANUFACTURERS ASSOCIATION OF THE USA, INC.*
900 17th Street NW
Washington, DC 20006
202-452-1300

Contact: Daniel R. Thompson
Membership: 114.

FLEXIBLE PACKING ASSOCIATION
1090 Vermont Ave., NW
Suite 500
Washington, DC 20003
202-842-3880

Contact: Richard Lillquist, President
Membership: Manufacturers of flexible packaging converted products and raw materials or equipment for the industry.
Purpose: To provide an industry fact-gathering organization which helps members.

FLORIDA BAKERS CLUB
PO Box 7450
Hollywood, FL 33021
305-987-0214

Contact: H. M. Jaeger, Secretary-Treasurer
Membership: 200 active and retired bakers in the U.S.
Purpose: To bring into closer relationship bakers and others allied to the baking industry.

FLORIDA CITRUS MUTUAL
PO Box 89
Lakeland, FL 33802
813-682-1111

Contact: Bobby F. McKown, Executive Vice-President
Membership: 13,240 Florida citrus growers.
Purpose: To achieve cooperation in securing appropriate state and federal legislation affecting the Florida citrus industry; to disseminate information.

FLORIDA CITRUS NURSERYMEN'S ASSOCIATION
700 Experiment Station Rd.
Lake Alfred, FL 33850
813-956-1151

Contact: Dr. William S. Castle, Secretary
Membership: 90.
Purpose: To promote the interests of citrus nurserymen; to aid the production, distribution, and sale of citrus nursery stock and related products; to address legislative matters.

FLORIDA CITRUS PROCESSORS ASSOCIATION
PO Box 780
Winter Haven, FL 33880
813-293-4171

Contact: Warren E. Savant, Executive Vice-President
Membership: 40 citrus processing firms in Florida.
Purpose: To represent the membership before USDA, FDA, and state regulatory and legislative bodies; to work toward product improvement.

FLORIDA DAIRY PRODUCTS ASSOCIATION*
Suite 314
Bradshaw Bldg.
Orlando, FL 32801
305-849-0581

Contact: Joseph Antink, President

FLORIDA DEPARTMENT OF CITRUS
Box 148
Lakeland, FL 33802
813-682-0171

Contact: William F. Jones, Public/Industry Relations Director
Membership: 12 members of the Florida Citrus Commission, appointed by the governor.
Purpose: Conducts commodity advertising and promotional programs; scientific, market, and economic research.

FLORIDA FRUIT & VEGETABLE ASSOCIATION
PO Box 20155
Orlando, FL 32814
305-894-1351

Contact: James T. Duncan, Executive Vice-President & General Manager
Membership: Growers of fruits, vegetables, and sugar cane in Florida.
Purpose: An agricultural trade and service organization

FLORIDA LIME AND AVOCADO ADMINISTRATIVE COMMITTEES
18710 SW 28th St.
Homestead, FL 33030
305-248-0848

Contact: Charles Walker, Executive Vice-President
Membership: Supported by all growers of Florida limes and avocados.
Purpose: To regulate grade and maturity standards, container standards; to fund production and marketing research projects.

FLORIDA LYCHEE GROWERS ASSOCIATION*
PO Box 9491
Winter Haven, FL 33880
813-294-4445

Contact: Bill Ross, Secretary

FLORIDA MEAT PACKERS ASSOCIATION
c/o ABC Research Corporation
3437 SW 24th Ave.
Gainesville, FL 32601
904-372-0436

Contact: Dr. William Brown

FLORIDA PEANUT PRODUCERS ASSOCIATION*
PO Box 447
Graceville, FL 32440
904-263-6130

Contact: Stuart Jones

FOOD DEFENSE FUND*
National Press Bldg.
Suite 930

Washington, DC 20045
202-638-7517

Contact: James L. Maxwell, Chairman

**FOOD DISTRIBUTION
RESEARCH SOCIETY***
Ohio State University
2120 Fyffe Rd.
Columbus, OH 43210

Contact: Vern A. Vandemark, Secretary-Treasurer

FOOD & DRUG LAW INSTITUTE
1200 New Hampshire Ave., NW
Suite 380
Washington, DC 20036
202-833-1601

Contact: Gary L. Yingling
Membership: 140 companies or law firms that are related to the food, drug, cosmetic, or medical device industries.
Purpose: To develop a better understanding of food and drug laws, regulations, and technology; to make the public more aware of the quality of protection provided by industry, government, and other concerned groups.

FOOD FOR THE HUNGRY, INC.
7729 East Greenway Rd.
Scottsdale, AZ 85260
602-998-3100

Contact: Larry Ward, President
Purpose: Relief, information, and developmental education.

**FOOD INDUSTRIES SUPPLIERS
ASSOCIATION***
PO Box 1242
Caldwell, ID 83605
208-454-0523

Contact: Fred King

**FOOD INDUSTRY ASSOCIATION
EXECUTIVES**
6909 Northeast Dr.
Austin, TX 78723
512-928-1696

Contact: Kay L. Knapp, CAE, Executive Director
Membership: Retail grocer trade associations; national, state, and local manufacturers, suppliers, and educators.
Purpose: Communication link in the food industry; research and education in association management; legislative action.

FOOD MARKETING INSTITUTE
1750 K St., NW
Washington, DC 20006
202-452-8444

Contact: Robert O. Aders, President
Membership: 1,000 retail supermarket and grocery wholesale companies operating stores in the U.S. and overseas.
Purpose: Research, education, and public affairs.

FOOD AND NUTRITION BOARD
2101 Constitution Ave., NW
Washington, DC 20418
202-389-6366

Contact: Myrtle L. Brown, Ph.D., Executive Secretary

**FOOD PROCESSING MACHINERY
& SUPPLIES ASSOCIATION**
1828 L St., NW
Suite 700
Washington, DC 20036
202-833-1790

Contact: W. Dewey Clower
Membership: 500.
Purpose: To help members market their products.

**THE FOOD PROCESSORS
INSTITUTE**
1133 20th St., NW
Washington, DC 20036
202-857-0980

Contact: Jill P. Strachan, Ph.D., Executive Director
Purpose: An educational and training organization affiliated with the National Food Processors Association.

**FOOD RESEARCH AND ACTION
CENTER**
2011 Eye St., NW
Suite 700
Washington, DC 20006
202-452-8250

Contact: Nancy Amidei, Director
Membership: Attorneys, nutritionists, lobbyists, and organizers.
Purpose: To alleviate hunger and malnutrition in the United States through litigation and supportive legal services, legislative and administrative advocacy, and public education.

FOOD SANITATION INSTITUTE*
1701 Drew Street
Clearwater, FL 33515
813-446-1674

Contact: Harold C. Rowe

**FOODSERVICE CONSULTANTS
SOCIETY INTERNATIONAL**
13227 8th Ave., NW
Seattle, WA 98177
206-362-7780

Contact: C. Russell Nickel, Executive Director
Membership: More than 350 designers of commercial food facilities for hotels, restaurants, airlines, schools, hospitals, etc., in the U.S. and overseas.
Purpose: To assist members to become more knowledgeable in their professions.

**FOODSERVICE EQUIPMENT
DISTRIBUTORS ASSOCIATION**
332 S. Michigan Ave., Suite 1558
Chicago, IL 60604
312-427-9605

Contact: William Englehaupt, Executive Director
Membership: Distributors/dealers of foodservice equipment and supplies.
Purpose: To provide usual association services for members and to act as a source of information for others in the industry.

**FOODSERVICE
FROZEN FOOD ASSOCIATION
OF NEW ENGLAND**
PO Box 115
Acton, MA 01720
617-263-1171

Contact: Angelika R. Ensins, Executive Director
Membership: Brokers, packers, distributors, retail chains, and food service operators.

Purpose: To coordinate and enhance frozen foods within the industry.

FOODSERVICE & LODGING INSTITUTE*
1919 Pennsylvania Ave.
Suite 504
Washington, DC 20006
202-659-9060

Contact: William G. Giery

FOREIGN-TYPE CHEESEMAKERS ASSOCIATION*
1211 17th Ave.
Monroe, WI 53566
608-325-2507

Contact: John Dahman, Secretary

FORT WORTH GRAIN EXCHANGE*
2707 Decatur Avenue
Ft. Worth, TX 76106
817-626-8213

Contact: C. G. Mathews, Secretary

FOUNDATION FOR AMERICAN AGRICULTURE PROGRAM OF THE FARM FOUNDATION*
Orange Bldg.
1616 H Street NW
Washington, DC 20005
202-628-1321

Contact: C. Dana Bennett

FOUNDATION BEEFMASTER ASSOCIATION*
200 Livestock Exchange Bldg.
4701 Marion
Denver, CO 80216
303-825-3019

Contact: Walter H. Rice, Jr., Executive Secretary

FROZEN ONION RING PACKERS COUNCIL*
1700 Old Meadow Rd.
Suite 100
McLean, VA 22102
703-821-0770

Contact: Francis G. Williams

FUTURE FARMERS OF AMERICA
National FFA Center
Box 15160
Alexandria, VA 22309
703-360-3600

Contact: Byron F. Rawls, National Advisor

G

GALLOWAY CATTLE SOCIETY OF AMERICA*
Box 70-A
Hennepin, IL 61327
815-925-7144

Contact: Patricia A. Morine, Secretary-Treasurer

GELATIN MANUFACTURERS INSTITUTE OF AMERICA*
516 5th Ave.
Room 507
New York, NY 10036
212-575-1234

Contact: J. Alleavitch, Secretary-Treasurer

GEORGIA DAIRY PRODUCTS ASSOCIATION*
PO Box 801
Macon, GA 31202
912-746-1588

Contact: Jill Duvall, Administrator

GEORGIA INDEPENDENT MEAT PACKERS AND PROCESSORS ASSOCIATION*
PO Box 801
Macon, GA 31202
912-743-8612

Contact: Joe W. Andrews, Jr.

GEORGIA PEANUT COMMISSION
PO Box 967
110 East 4th St.
Tifton, GA 31794
912-386-3470

Contact: J. Tyron Spearman, Coordinator
Membership: 16,000.
Purpose: To promote peanuts and peanut products.

GLASS PACKAGING INSTITUTE*
2000 L Street NW
Suite 815
Washington, DC 20036
202-782-1280

Contact: Gunter Rohland

THE GLUTAMATE ASSOCIATION — U.S.
5775 Peachtree-Dunwoody Rd.,
Suite 500-D
Atlanta, GA 30342
404-252-3663

Contact: Robert H. Kellen, President
Membership: Manufacturers, national marketers, and processed food users of glutamic acid and its salts, including monosodium glutamate.
Purpose: To serve as an information clearinghouse on the application, efficacy, history, and safety of glutamic acid and its salts.

GRAHAM CENTER*
Route 3, Box 95
Wadesboro, NC 28170
704-851-9346

Contact: Kathryn J. Waller, Executive Director

GRAIN SORGHUM PRODUCERS ASSOCIATION*
1708-A 15th Street
Lubbock, TX 79401
806-763-4425

Contact: Elbert Harp, Executive Director

GREATER PITTSBURGH DAIRY INDUSTRY ASSOCIATION*
813 Investment Bldg.
Pittsburgh, PA 15222
412-471-2747

Contact: C. J. Milroth, Executive Director

GREATER SOUTHWEST RETAIL BAKERS ASSOCIATION
312 North Standard
Longview, TX 75604
214-759-3915

Contact: M. W. Bass Jr., Secretary

GREEN OLIVE TRADE ASSOCIATION*
325 14th Street
Carlstadt, NJ 07072
201-935-0233

Contact: Edward Culleton

RESOURCES FOR FURTHER INFORMATION 421

GROCERY MANUFACTURERS OF AMERICA, INC.
1010 Wisconsin Ave., NW, Suite 800
Washington, DC 20007
202-337-9400

Contact: George W. Koch, President

GULF AND CARIBBEAN FISHERIN GULF AND CARIBBEAN FISHERIES INSTITUTE
Rosenstiel School of Marine and Atmospheric Science
University of Miami
4600 Rickenbacker
Miami, FL 33149
305-350-7533

Contact: James B. Higman, Executive Director
Membership: Sportsmen, scientists, fishery administrators, industrial and government representatives.
Purpose: To better understand current fishery science and trends in fishery policy conservation, waste treatment, etc.; to exchange ideas on new approaches to fishery research, management and conservation; to provide technical training for fishermen and technicians.

H

HAWAIIAN SUGAR PLANTERS ASSOCIATION
PO Box 1057
Aiea, HI 96701
808-487-5561

Contact: D. J. Heinz, Vice-President
Membership: Producers and processors of sugarcane in Hawaii
Purpose: To maintain, advance, improve and protect the sugar industry in Hawaii; to support the development of agriculture in general.

HERB TRADE ASSOCIATION
4302 Airport Rd.
Austin, TX 78722
512-454-8628

Contact: Mark Blumenthal, Director of Public Relations
Membership: Members of the herb industry who produce and sell herbs and herbal products.
Purpose: To develop responsible information regarding the use of herbs and herbal products through *Herb News* magazine.

HOLLAND CHEESE EXPORTERS ASSOCIATION
45 Rockefeller Plaza
New York, NY 10020
212-265-1512

Contact: Frans Donselmann, Marketing Manager
Purpose: Promotion of cheeses imported from Holland.

HOLSTEIN-FRIESIAN ASSOCIATION OF AMERICA*
PO Box 808
Brattleboro, VT 05301
802-254-4551

Contact: Zane V. Akins, Executive Secretary

HONEY INDUSTRY COUNCIL OF AMERICA, INC.
217 Hillside Dr.
Navasota, TX 77868
713-825-2124

Contact: Jonathan W. White, Ph.D., Executive Secretary
Purpose: To promote cooperation among the segments of the beekeeping industry.

HOP GROWERS OF AMERICA*
504 North Naches Ave.
Suite 5
Yakima, WA 98901
509-453-4749

Contact: Bill Harris, Manager

HOSPITAL FOOD DIRECTORS ASSOCIATION
4115 Barnett St.
Philadelphia, PA 19135

Contact: William J. Glickman, President
Membership: Food service directors, assistants, and dieticians of local area hospitals and nursing homes.
Purpose: Communication and distribution of pertinent management and diet rules and regulations needed to direct a dietary department.

HOSPITAL, INSTITUTION, AND EDUCATIONAL FOOD SERVICE SOCIETY
4410 West Roosevelt Rd.
Hillside, IL 60162
312-449-2770

Contact: Jean Denwood, Executive Director
Membership: Dietetic assistants and technicians.
Purpose: Maintaining a higher level of competency and quality in the dietary the departments of health care facilities.

I

IDAHO MILK PROCESSORS ASSOCIATION*
PO Box 3083
University Station
Moscow, ID 83843
208-885-6455

Contact: John Montoure, Secretary-Treasurer

IDAHO POTATO COMMISSION*
PO Box 1068
Boise, ID 83701
208-344-8519

Contact: G. C. Randall

ILLINOIS BAKERS ASSOCIATION
PO Box 384
Decatur, IL 62525
217-423-7585

Contact: Rotha Dickey, Secretary-Treasurer
Membership: 70.

INDEPENDENT BAKERS ASSOCIATION
PO Box 3731
Washington, DC 20007
202-223-2325

Contact: Robert N. Pyle, President
Membership: 300 wholesale bakery independents.
Purpose: To represent the nation's independent bakers in Washington.

INDIANA ASSOCIATION OF SANITARIANS
1330 West Michigan St.
Indianapolis, IN 46206
812-824-4135

Contact: Kevin Burk, President
Membership: 261.
Purpose: To distribute educational materials and further professionalism among members.

INDIANA BAKERS ASSOCIATION*
9934 E. Fall Creek Road
Indianapolis, IN 46256
317-259-7551

Contact: Oliver Schnieders, Executive Secretary

INDIANA FOOD PROCESSORS ASSOCIATION
2120 North Meridan St.
Indianapolis, IN 46202
317-924-5106

Contact: Warren Spangle, Executive Vice-President

INDIANA MEAT PACKERS & PROCESSORS ASSOCIATION, INC.
2120 N. Meridan St.
Indianapolis, IN 46202
317-924-5106

Contact: Warren Spangle, Executive Vice-President

INFANT FORMULA COUNCIL
5775 Peachtree-Dunwoody Rd.
Suite 500-D
Atlanta, GA 30342
404-252-3663

Contact: R. H. Kellen
Membership: Manufacturers of infant formula in the United States.
Purpose: To support scientific research; collect and disseminate information; provide information on legislative matters.

INSTITUTE FOR FOOD AND DEVELOPMENT POLICY
2588 Mission St.
San Francisco, CA 94110
415-648-6090

Contact: Patricia Bergeron, Assistant, Media Outreach
Purpose: A research, documentation, and education center that focuses on world hunger and development issues.

INSTITUTE OF FOOD TECHNOLOGISTS
221 North LaSalle St., Suite 2120
Chicago, IL 60601
312-782-8482

Contact: Calvert L. Willey, Executive Director
Membership: 20,000.
Purpose: To promote the application of science and engineering to the production of food.

INSTITUTE OF SHORTENING & EDIBLE OILS, INC.*
1750 New York Avenue NW
Washington, DC 20006
202-296-7960

Contact: William W. Goodrich

INTER-AMERICAN TROPICAL TUNA COMMISSION
c/o Scripps Institution of Oceanography
LaJolla, CA 92037
714-453-2820

Contact: James Joseph, Ph.D., Director
Purpose: To study the biology of the tunas and related species and to recommend appropriate conservation measures.

INTERNATIONAL APPLE INSTITUTE AND NATIONAL APPLE MONTH, INC.
6707 Old Dominion Dr.
Suite 210
McLean, VA 22101
703-442-8850

Contact: Fred P. Corey, Director of Market Development
Membership: Apple growers; fresh fruit and processed product manufacturers and marketers.
Purpose: To provide information services for the industry; to conduct consumer education and public relations programs on behalf of the industry.

INTERNATIONAL ASSOCIATION OF AGRICULTURAL ECONOMICS
1211 West 22nd St.
Oak Brook, IL 60521
312-986-9393

Contact: Dr. R. J. Hildreth, Secretary
Purpose: To foster the application of agricultural economics in the improvement of the economic and social conditions of rural people.

INTERNATIONAL ASSOCIATION OF MILK, FOOD & ENVIRONMENTAL SANITARIANS
PO Box 701
Ames, IA 50010
515-232-6699

Contact: Earl O. Wright, Executive Secretary
Purpose: To improve the professional status of the sanitarian; to develop uniform and proper methods of supervision of dairy farms, milk and milk product plants; to encourage sanitary production methods; to disseminate information and assist members in their technical work.

INTERNATIONAL BRAFORD ASSOCIATION*
PO Box 1030
Ft. Pierce, FL 33450
305-461-6321

Contact: Alto Adams, Jr., President

INTERNATIONAL BRANGUS BREEDERS ASSOCIATION
9500 Tioga
San Antonio, TX 78230
512-696-8231

Contact: J. D. Morrow, Executive Vice-President

INTERNATIONAL CASTOR OIL ASSOCIATION*
Route 30, RFD
West Pawlet, VT 05775
802-645-0167

Contact: Matt F. Antonovich, Secretary-Treasurer

INTERNATIONAL CHEESE & DELI ASSOCIATION, INC.
PO Box 5528
Madison, WI 53705
608-238-7908

Contact: W. T. Reese, Executive Director
Purpose: To sponsor an annual convention to benefit its members; to promote the cheese and deli food industry; to disseminate information.

INTERNATIONAL CHEFS ASSOCIATION
(American Culinary Federation)
ACE Big-Apple Chapter
GPO Box 1889

New York, NY 10116
201-825-8455

Contact: Helmut Hamann, President
Membership: 225 chefs and associated members.
Purpose: To advance in the culinary field; to learn about new products on the market; to promote education in the foodservice.

INTERNATIONAL COLLEGE OF APPLIED NUTRITION
PO Box 386
LaHabra, CA 90631
213-697-4576

Contact: Mrs. Harold Stone, Executive Secretary
Membership: 1,200 professionals.
Purpose: To maintain and promote the highest standards in nutritional education; to stimulate and encourage research in nutritional aspects of disease; to conduct courses in nutrition.

INTERNATIONAL COMMITTEE FOR THE ANTHROPOLOGY OF FOOD AND FOOD HABITS*
c/o Wilson Museum
Castine, ME 04421

Contact: Margaret L. Arnott, President

INTERNATIONAL CORNISH BANTAM BREEDERS' ASSOCIATION*
Route 2
Borden, IN 47106

Contact: Ray Farmer, Secretary

INTERNATIONAL DWARF FRUIT TREES ASSOCIATION
Department of Horticulture
Michigan State University
East Lansing, MI 48824
517-355-5200

Contact: Robert F. Carlson, Executive Secretary
Membership: 1,600.
Purpose: To promote an understanding of the nature and use of dwarf fruit trees through dissemination of information; to expand knowledge in the industry by encouraging continued research efforts.

INTERNATIONAL FEDERATION OF AGRICULTURAL PRODUCERS
PO Box 28316, Central Station
Washington, DC 20005

Contact: M. P. Cracknell, Secretary-General
Membership: National-level representative farm organizations from 50 countries.
Purpose: To represent farmers interests at the international level; to provide a forum for meetings of the world's farmers; to organize development programs for farm organization members in developing countries; to supply information about matters of concern to farmers and their organizations.

INTERNATIONAL FOOD ADDITIVES COUNCIL
5775 Peachtree-Dunwoody Rd.
Suite 500-D
Atlanta, GA 30342
404-252-3663

Contact: Robert H. Kellen, President
Membership: Manufacturers and processed food users of food additives.
Purpose: To provide and encourage communication about food additives; to serve as an information resource; to conduct and monitor research.

INTERNATIONAL FOOD SERVICES EXECUTIVES ASSOCIATION
111 East Wacker Dr., Suite 600
Chicago, IL 60601
312-644-6610

Contact: Barbara Chalik, Executive Vice-President
Membership: Management personnel in all aspects of the foodservice industry.
Purpose: Dedicated to raising foodservice industry standards, educating members, and recognizing member achievements.

INTERNATIONAL FOODSERVICE DISTRIBUTORS ASSOCIATION
(Division of National-American Wholesale Grocers Association)
51 Madison Ave.
New York, NY 10010
212-532-8899

Contact: Patt Patterson, Acting Executive Director
Membership: 250 food wholesalers.

Purpose: To provide government representation in Washington; to disseminate information to foodservice distributors.

INTERNATIONAL FOODSERVICE EDITORIAL COUNCIL
82 Osborne Lane
East Hampton, NY 11937
516-324-2880

Contact: Betty Bastion, Membership Director
Membership: Editors, educators, publicists, and consultants in the foodservice industry.
Purpose: Dedicated to the advancement of institutional food through the interchange of ideas.

INTERNATIONAL FOODSERVICE MANUFACTURERS ASSOCIATION
875 N. Michigan Ave.
Suite 3460
Chicago, IL 60611
312-944-3838

Contact: Michael J. Licata, President
Membership: 300 manufacturers of foods, food products, and foodservice equipment; companies which service the industry; foodservice brokers and manufacturers' agents.
Purpose: To promote and improve the industry; to disseminate research data and information; to preserve a healthy foodservice business climate; to cooperate with industry trade associations and government bodies.

INTERNATIONAL FROZEN FOOD ASSOCIATION
1700 Old Meadow Rd., Suite 100
McLean, VA 22102
703-821-0770

Contact: Thomas B. House, Director-General
Membership: Processors and brokers of frozen foods.
Purpose: To advance the frozen food industry worldwide; to serve as a clearinghouse for commercial, technical, and legislative information concerning frozen foods.

INTERNATIONAL ILLAWARRA ASSOCIATION
1722-JJ S. Glenstone Ave.
Springfield, MO 65804
417-887-6526

Contact: Marvin L. Kruse, Executive Secretary
Membership: Owners of Illawarra cattle and others interested in promoting the cattle.
Purpose: A member service organization which maintains a registry office and publishes a journal.

INTERNATIONAL JELLY & PRESERVE ASSOCIATION
5775 Peachtree-Dunwoody Rd.
Suite 500-D
404-252-3663

Contact: R. H. Kellen, Executive Vice-President
Membership: Manufacturers of fruit spreads and suppliers to the industry.
Purpose: To initiate and foster standards of excellence of product and service; to cooperate with federal, state and municipal authorities in promoting uniformity of laws, rules, and regulations affecting the industry.

INTERNATIONAL MAPLE SYRUP INSTITUTE
743 Grosvenor
Montreal, Quebec H3Y 2S9, Canada
514-486-8895

Contact: Claude Tardif, Executive Manager
Membership: 12,000 maple syrup producers and equipment suppliers in Canada and the United States.
Purpose: To promote and protect the market for maple syrup products.

INTERNATIONAL NATURAL SAUSAGE CASING ASSOCIATION*
710 North Rush Street
Chicago, IL 60611
312-664-7800

Contact: Lucille Lampman, Executive Secretary

INTERNATIONAL NORTH PACIFIC FISHERIES COMMISSION
6640 NW Marine Dr.
Vancouver, British Columbia
V6T 1X2, Canada
604-228-1128

Contact: C. R. Forrester, Executive Director
Purpose: To promote and coordinate scientific studies relating to the fishery resources of the North Pacific Ocean; to conserve fishery resources.

INTERNATIONAL PACIFIC HALIBUT COMMISSION
PO Box 5509, University Station
Seattle, WA 98105
206-634-1838

Contact: Dr. Donald A. McCaughran, Director
Purpose: To conduct scientific studies; to propose annual regulations for the halibut fishery to the U.S and Canadian governments.

INTERNATIONAL PACIFIC SALMON FISHERIES COMMISSION
PO Box 30
New Westiminster, British Columbia
V3L 4X9, Canada
604-521-3771

Contact: A. C. Cooper, Director
Purpose: For the protection, preservation, and extension of the sockeye and pink salmon fisheries in the Frazer River system.

INTERSTATE PRODUCERS LIVESTOCK ASSOCIATION*
1705 West Luthy Drive
Peoria, IL 61615
309-691-5360

Contact: Glenn A. Burmeister, General Manager

INTERNATIONAL SOCIETY OF SUGAR CANE TECHNOLOGISTS
PO Box 1057
Aiea, HI 96701
808-487-5561

Contact: Daniel J. Dougherty, Custodian
Membership: Technologists involved in the production of sugar cane.
Purpose: To promote the technical discussion of field and factory problems of the industry.

INTERRELIGIOUS TASKFORCE ON U.S. FOOD POLICY
110 Maryland Ave., NE
Washington, DC 20002
202-543-2800

Contact: George A. Chauncey, Chairman
Purpose: To advocate and help the religious community advocate a morally responsible U.S. food policy.

INTERSTATE PRODUCERS LIVESTOCK ASSOCIATION
1705 W. Luthy Drive
Peoria, IL 61615
309-691-5300

Contact: Glenn A. Burmeister, General Manager

IOWA ASSOCIATION OF MILK, FOOD & ENVIRONMENTAL SANITARIANS
4010 University Ave.
Des Moines, IA 50311
515-281-4937

Contact: H. E. Hansen, Secretary-Treasurer
Membership: 125.
Purpose: To assist members in their technical work and development; to disseminate information; to work with other professional groups in advancing public health.

IOWA DAIRY COUNCIL, INC.*
101 NE Trilein Drive
Ankeny, IA 50021
515-964-0696

Contact: Mary Kleinschmit, Program Director

IOWA DAIRY FOODS ASSOCIATION
1805 74th St.
Des Moines, IA 50322
515-276-3302

Contact: John Brockway, Executive Vice-President
Membership: Iowa processors of bottled milk, cottage cheese, and ice cream products.
Purpose: To serve as liaison between producer-processor and the consumer as well as state or federal agencies.

IOWA-NEBRASKA FOOD PROCESSORS*
c/o Morton House Kitchens
1001 7th Corso
Nebraska City, NE 68410
402-873-6671

Contact: Mary Ann Lutz

K

KANSAS BAKERS ASSOCIATION*
c/o Ketterman's Bakers
2607 East Douglas
Wichita, KS 67211
316-682-5161

Contact: Russ Ketterman, President

KENTUCKY MEAT PROCESSORS ASSOCIATION*
c/o Dept. of Animal Sciences
Agri Science Blvd., South
Room 205
University of Kentucky
Lexington, KY 40506
606-257-3821

Contact: W. Y. Varney

KENTUCKY RETAIL BAKERS ASSOCIATION*
c/o Wahlieb's Bakery
3711 Klondike Lane
Louisville, KY 40220
502-451-4458

Contact: Owl Wahlieb

KEYSTONE ASSOCIATION OF ICE CREAM MANUFACTURERS*
RD & Box 376
Shavertown, PA 18708
717-696-2429

Contact: Robert Lawhorn, Assistant Secretary-Treasurer

L

LEAFY GREENS COUNCIL*
Two North Riverside Plaza
Chicago, IL 60606
312-726-6926

Contact: Robert W. Strube, President

LEAGUE FOR INTERNATIONAL FOOD EDUCATION*
915 15th Street NW
Room 915
Washington, DC 20005
202-331-1658

Contact: Carol I. Waslien, Ph.D., Executive Officer

LEMON ADMINISTRATIVE COMMITTEE*
117 West 9th Street
Room 905
Los Angeles, CA 90015
213-624-3403

Contact: David A. Beavers, Manager

LIVESTOCK CONSERVATION INSTITUTE
239 Livestock Exchange Bldg.
South Saint Paul, MN 55075
612-457-0132

Contact: Neal Black, President
Membership: Livestock industry organizations and companies and others.
Purpose: To reduce losses of livestock resulting from disease, parasites, and mishandling.

LIVESTOCK MARKETING ASSOCIATION*
4900 Oak
Kansas City, MO 64112
816-531-2235

Contact: C. T. Sanders, General Manager

LIVESTOCK MERCHANDISING INSTITUTE
301 East Armour Blvd.
Kansas City, MO 64111
816-531-2235

Contact: James L. Fries, Executive Director
Membership: 1,000 trustees.
Purpose: To help maintain equitable and stable profits for the livestock industry.

LOS ANGELES GRAIN EXCHANGE*
9690 Telstar Avenue
Suite 226
El Monte, CA 91731
213-443-9432

Contact: Donna Brown, Secretary

LOUISIANA DAIRY PRODUCTS ASSOCIATION*
PO Box 1006
Baton Rouge, LA 70821
504-343-8801

Contact: Gerald Simmons, Executive Director

LOUISIANA SUGAR EXCHANGE*
415 Whitney Bldg.
New Orleans, LA 70130
504-525-7503

Contact: G. R. Price, Executive Secretary

M

MAINE DAIRY & NUTRITION COUNCIL
State House Station #97
State Office Bldg.
Augusta, ME 04333
207-289-3621

Contact: Wayne L. Thurston, Program Director

MAINE INDEPENDENT MEAT PACKERS ASSOCIATION
PO Box 3927
Portland, ME 04104
207-772-5411

Contact: J. G. Kelly, Jr., Secretary/Treasurer
Membership: Meat packers and processors and their suppliers.
Purpose: To support the industry in Maine; to keep members informed about regulations, etc.

MAINE LOBSTERMEN'S ASSOCIATION*
Box 128
Stonington, ME 04681
207-367-2409

Contact: Edward Blackmore, President

MAINE POTATO COUNCIL
744 Main St.
Suite #1
Presque Isle, ME 04769
207-769-2711

Contact: Dorothy P. Kelly
Purpose: Provides potato producers with information on legislation, new products, etc.

MAINE SARDINE COUNCIL*
470 N. Main Street
Brewer, ME 04412
207-989-2180

Contact: James L. Warren

426 RESOURCES FOR FURTHER INFORMATION

MAINE SARDINE PACKERS ASSOCIATION*
PO Box 337
Brewer, ME 04412
207-989-2180

Contact: James L. Warren, Executive Secretary-Treasurer

MARASCHINO CHERRY & GLACE FRUIT PROCESSORS
115 Broadway, Room 1117
New York, NY 10006
212-267-4244

Contact: Richard Sullivan

MARKY CATTLE ASSOCIATION*
PO Box 342
Atlanta, TX 75551
214-796-4882

Contact: Bill Carter, President

MASSACHUSETTS RETAIL BAKERS ASSOCIATION
c/o Swanson's Bakery
918 Massachusetts Ave.
Arlington, MA 02174

Contact: Gus Swanson
Membership: Retail bakers and allied suppliers.
Purpose: To work together for the continued growth of the retail baking industry.

MASTER DAIRIES, INC.
2346 S. Lynhurst
PO Box 41297
Indianapolis, IN 46297
317-243-3511

Contact: Thad Hundertmark, Executive Vice-President

THE MATERIAL HANDLING INSTITUTE*
1326 Freeport Road
Pittsburgh, PA 15238
412-782-1624

Contact: Thomas W. Shea

MEALS FOR MILLIONS/FREEDOM FROM HUNGER FOUNDATION
815 2nd Ave.
New York, NY 10017
212-986-4170

Contact: Peter J. Davies, Jr., President
Membership: 35,000 donors.
Purpose: To help developing communities in 10 countries, including the U.S., to solve their food problems with special emphasis on nutritional needs of infants, children, pregnant and lactating women, and the elderly.

MEAT IMPORTERS COUNCIL OF AMERICA*
1901 North Fort Myer Drive
Arlington, VA 22209
703-522-1910

Contact: William C. Morrison Executive Director

MEAT INDUSTRY SUPPLIERS ASSOCIATION
1919 Penn Avenue, NW, #300
Washington, DC 20006
202-872-1990

Contact: Leif Oxaal, President
Membership: Companies providing supplies and services to the meat, poultry, and seafood processing industries.
Purpose: To promote more effective marketing and to improve trade.

MEAT MACHINERY MANUFACTURERS INSTITUTE
1919 Penn Avenue, NW, #300
Washington, DC 20006
202-872-1900

Contact: Leif Oxaal, Executive Director
Membership: Manufacturers of meat processing and packaging machinery.

METROPLEX INDEPENDENT RETAIL BAKERS ASSOCIATION*
700 West Hickory
Denton, TX 76201
817-387-6712

Contact: Don Davis, Treasurer

METROPOLITAN DAIRY INSTITUTE*
22 East 40th Street
New York, NY 10016
212-679-8408

Contact: Howard Tisch

MICHIGAN APPLE COMMITTEE
2726 East Michigan Ave.
Lansing, MI 48912
517-372-0102

Contact: Mark Arney, Manager
Purpose: To enhance the economic standing of the Michigan apple producer through advertising, promotion, and public relations.

MICHIGAN ASSOCIATION OF CHERRY PRODUCERS
Riverview Center
Suite 410
678 Front St., NW
Grand Rapids, MI 49504
616-454-6196

Contact: Tom Martin, President
Membership: 1,600 growers of cherries in western Michigan.
Purpose: To enchance and expand the use of cherries in the marketing and consumer environment; to maintain productive quality and supply through research.

MICHIGAN CANNERS & FREEZERS ASSOCIATION
Box 35
Shelby, MI 49455
616-861-4481

Contact: E. G. Van Sickle, Secretary

MICHIGAN DAIRY FOODS ASSOCIATION
748 North Cedar St.
Lansing, MI 48906
517-484-3417

Contact: Frank Koval, Executive Director
Membership: Dairy food processors in Michigan.
Purpose: Education and information.

MICHIGAN MEAT ASSOCIATION
507 Young Ave.
Muskegon, MI 49441
616-759-7459

Contact: B. T. Sullivan, Executive Secretary

MIDWEST DAIRY PRODUCTS ASSOCIATION, INC.
5610 Crawfordsville Rd., Suite 1104
Indianapolis, IN 46224
317-243-9341

Contact: Peter Holm, Executive Vice-President
Purpose: To provide and protect the dairy processing industry.

MIDWESTERN FROZEN FOOD ASSOCIATION
333 North Michigan Ave., Suite 800
Chicago, IL 60601
312-332-1601

Contact: James Alexander, Executive Director
Membership: A full spectrum of related areas.
Purpose: To support efforts towards improved methods of processing, distribution, and marketing of quality frozen foods.

MILK DISTRIBUTORS ASSOCIATION OF THE PHILADELPHIA AREA, INC.
333 West State St.
Trenton, NJ 08618
609-394-5362

Contact: Dan Wettkin Jr., President
Membership: Those companies that process and distribute most of the milk consumed in the greater Philadelphia area.

MILK INDUSTRY FOUNDATION*
910 17th Street, NW
Washington, DC 20006
202-296-4250

Contact: John Speer, Jr., Executive Vice-President

MILLERS NATIONAL FEDERATION*
1776 F Street, NW
Washington, DC 20006
202-783-4900

Contact: W. E. Swegle, President

MINNESOTA BAKERS ASSOCIATION*
301 First National Bank Bldg.
Wayzata, MN 55391
612-475-0711

Contact: Ralph Turtinen, Executive Vice-President

MINNESOTA SANITARIANS ASSOCIATION*
c/o Dairy Quality Control Institute, Inc.
2353 Rice Street
St. Paul, MN 55113
612-484-7269

Contact: Roy Ginn, Secretary-Treasurer

MISSISSIPPI DAIRY PRODUCTS ASSOCIATION
PO Drawer AX
Mississippi State, MS 39762
601-325-2330

Contact: Edward W. Custer, Executive Secretary
Membership: Dairy processing plants in Mississippi and plants in other states doing business in Mississippi.
Purpose: To promote and advance the dairy industry in Mississippi; to conduct research; to disseminate information.

MISSISSIPPI MEAT PACKERS ASSOCIATION
PO Drawer 5228
Mississippi State, MS 39762
601-325-2802

Contact: Robert Rogers, Executive Secretary
Membership: Meat packers and processors in Mississippi as well as suppliers of equipment and services to the industry.
Purpose: To have an organized group to respond to important issues concerning the industry.

MISSOURI ASSOCIATION OF MILK, FOOD & ENVIRONMENTAL HEALTH
State Building
PO Box 570
Jefferson City, MO 65102
314-751-2713

Contact: Dr. Erwin Gadd, Secretary-Treasurer
Membership: 300.
Purpose: Reviews and consults with industry on public health issues; serves as quality compliance officers in food and drug work for government agencies.

MISSOURI BAKERS ASSOCIATION*
523 South 127th Street
Omaha, NE 68154
402-333-5301

Contact: Louis O'Konski, Secretary

MISSOURI BUTTER & CHEESE INSTITUTE*
3 Overbrook Drive
Kirksville, MO 63501
816-665-2034

Contact: Dale Gardner, Secretary-Treasurer

MISSOURI MEAT PACKERS ASSOCIATION*
706 Chestnut Street
Suite 814
St. Louis, MO 63101
314-241-8907

Contact: John Faust

MISSOURI MILK, FOOD & ENVIRONMENTAL HEALTH ASSOCIATION
State Bldg., PO Box 570
Jefferson City, MO 65102
314-751-2713

Contact: Mr. Erwin Gadd, Secretary
Membership: 200 environmental sanitarians and related industry people.
Purpose: To educate membership and consult with industry on public health issues; to serve as quality compliance officers in food and drug work for government agencies.

MOBILE INDUSTRIAL CATERERS ASSOCIATION*
4676 Admiralty Way, S 522
Marina Del Rey, CA 90291
213-822-4540

Contact: Joseph J. Merlo, Executive Director

MONTANA DAIRYMEN'S ASSOCIATION*
PO Box 593
Helena, MT 59624
406-442-1440

Contact: Alfred Dougherty, Counsel

MUSHROOM GROWERS ASSOCIATION*
18 South Water Market
Chicago, IL 60608
312-421-7088

Contact: Charles A. Evans, President

N

NATIONAL AGRICULTURAL CHEMICALS ASSOCIATION
1155 15th St., NW
Washington, DC 20005
202-296-1585

Contact: Jack D. Early, President
Membership: National trade association representing the producers and formulators of crop protection chemicals.
Purpose: To stimulate research to improve the quality of pest control materials and techniques; to encourage safer and more efficient methods of application of crop protection chemicals; to cooperate with state and federal agencies, other groups to further scientific pest control strategies; to assist in the development of regulatory controls.

NATIONAL AGRICULTURAL MARKETING OFFICIALS
NASDA National Food and Agriculture Exposition
1616 H St., NW
Washington, DC 20006
202-628-1566

Contact: Sidney C. Miller, Secretary-Treasurer
Membership: Heads of state agencies responsible for service work in the marketing of agricultural products; people working with or interested in marketing problems related to food or farm products.
Purpose: To improve the marketing, handling, storage, processing, transportation, and distribution of agricultural products; to collect and disseminate marketing information.

NATIONAL AGRICULTURAL PLASTICS ASSOCIATION*
Vegetable Research Farm
R-5, University of Maryland
Salisbury, MD 21801
301-742-8788

Contact: Franklin D. Schales, Executive Secretary

NATIONAL AMERICAN INDIAN CATTLEMEN'S ASSOCIATION*
1660 S. Albion St., Suite 918
Denver, CO 80222
303-759-5379

Contact: Don Buckley, Executive Director

NATIONAL AMERICAN WHOLESALE GROCERS' ASSOCIATION*
51 Madison Avenue
New York, NY 10010
212-532-8899

Contact: Gerald E. Peck

NATIONAL ASSOCIATION OF ANIMAL BREEDERS
PO Box 1033
Columbia, MO 65205
314-445-4406

Contact: William M. Durfey, Executive Vice-President
Purpose: To unite those individuals and organizations engaged in the artificial insemination of cattle and other livestock; to promote the interests of the members.

NATIONAL ASSOCIATION OF ANOREXIA NERVOSA AND ASSOCIATED DISORDERS
PO Box 271
Highland Park, IL 60035
312-831-3438

Contact: Vivian Meehan, President
Membership: Health professionals and lay members concerned with eating disorders.
Purpose: To seek to understand and alleviate the problem of eating disorders, especially anorexia nervosa and bulimia.

NATIONAL ASSOCIATION OF CONCESSIONARIES*
35 E. Wacker Drive
Chicago, IL 60601
312-236-3858

Contact: Charles A. Winans, Executive Director

NATIONAL ASSOCIATION OF CONVENIENCE STORES
Three Skyline Place
Suite 809
5201 Leesburg Pike
Falls Church, VA 22041
703-578-1800

Contact: Harry C. Hunter, Executive Director

NATIONAL ASSOCIATION OF FARMER ELECTED COMMITTEEMEN*
Pine Lawn Farms
Newman, IL 61942
217-837-2533

Contact: Ray Wax, Secretary

NATIONAL ASSOCIATION OF FOOD EQUIPMENT MANUFACTURERS
111 E. Wacker Dr.
Chicago, IL 60601
312-644-6610

Contact: William W. Carpenter, Executive Vice-President
Membership: 450.
Purpose: To cooperate with government regulatory agencies in furthering the industry; to encourage private enterprise; to improve education and communication in the industry.

NATIONAL ASSOCIATION OF FRUIT, FLAVORS AND SYRUPS
PO Box 337
Lake Success, NY 11042
516-328-3120

Contact: Walter B. Jacobsen
Membership: 120 food manufacturers and ingredient suppliers.
Purpose: To protect industry interests.

NATIONAL ASSOCIATION OF GREENHOUSE VEGETABLE GROWERS*
6500 Pearl Road
Cleveland, OH 44130
216-885-4761

Contact: Lois Jones, Secretary-Treasurer

NATIONAL ASSOCIATION OF HORSERADISH PACKERS
West Towers, Suite 603
West Des Moines, IA 50265
515-225-0212

Contact: John S. McLaren, Executive Secretary
Purpose: Activities vary depending on members' needs.

RESOURCES FOR FURTHER INFORMATION   429

NATIONAL ASSOCIATION OF ICE CREAM VENDORS
5600 Brookwood Terrace
Nashville, TN 37205
615-356-4240

Contact: Joe E. Maxwell, Executive Director

NATIONAL ASSOCIATION OF MARGARINE MANUFACTURERS
1625 I St., NW
Suite 1024A
Washington, DC 20006
202-785-3232

Contact: Siert F. Riepma

NATIONAL ASSOCIATION OF MEAT PURVEYORS
8365-B Greensboro Dr.
McLean, VA 22102
703-827-5754

Contact: G. Robert Smith, Executive Vice-President
Membership: 400 firms who sell meat and meat based products to hotels, restaurants, and institutions.
Purpose: To provide educational servides to members, including seminars, conventions, and publications; to monitor government actions; to assist members to be better business people.

NATIONAL ASSOCIATION OF THE PET INDUSTRY*
431 Chauncey St.
Brooklyn, NY 11233
212-455-8220

Contact: Mrs. Jay Winter, Secretary

NATIONAL ASSOCIATION OF PRODUCE MARKET MANAGERS*
Box 13504
Columbia State Farmers Market
Columbia, SC 29201
803-758-3325

Contact: George Bell, Editor

NATIONAL ASSOCIATON OF RETAIL GROCERS
PO Box 17208
Washington, DC 20016
703-860-3300

Contact: Frank D. Register
Membership: 40,000.

Purpose: To provide retailer employee training programs; to provide members and consumers with educational programs and information, including pr releases, publications, and media interviews; to set standards for ground meat products.

NATIONAL ASSOCIATION OF SPECIALTY FOOD AND CONFECTION BROKERS
2030 Condolea Dr.
Leawood, KS 66209
913-648-7715

Contact: George F. Kopf, Secretary
Membership: 85.
Purpose: To represent specialty foods and confections.

NATIONAL ASSOCIATION FOR THE SPECIALITY FOOD TRADE, INC.
1270 Avenue of the Americas
New York, NY 10020
212-586-7313

Contact: Jean Frame, Terrence McGovern, Executive Directors
Membership: 450 domestic manufacturers, importers, and distributors of gourmet foods, fine confections, wine and cooking accessories.
Purpose: Sponsors two trade shows each year.

NATIONAL ASSOCIATION OF SUPERVISORS OF AGRICULTURAL EDUCATION
State Dept. of Education
State Education Bldg., 502D
Little Rock, AR 72201

Contact: Robert Crawley, President

NATIONAL ASSOCIATION OF VOCATIONAL HOME ECONOMICS TEACHERS*
Box 36
Park City, KY 42160
502-749-3131

Contact: Suzanne H. Waldrop, President

NATIONAL ASSOCIATION OF WHEAT GROWERS*
415 2nd St., NW
Suite 300
Washington, DC 20002
202-547-7800

Contact: Carl Schwensen, Executive Vice-President

NATIONAL BAKERY SUPPLIERS ASSOCIATION
c/o Markel Hill & Byerley
1625 K St., NW
Suite 505
Washington, DC 20006
202-628-5530

Contact: Wayne Hill, Legal Counsel

NATIONAL BROILER COUNCIL
The Madison Bldg.
1155 15th St., NW
Washington, DC 20005
202-296-2622

Contact: George B. Watts, President
Purpose: Trade association representing the U.S. poultry industry in matters of legislation, regulatory agencies, and consumer education.

NATIONAL BUFFALO ASSOCIATION
Box 706
Custer, SD 57730
605-673-2073

Contact: Judi Hebbring, Executive Director
Membership: 400 buffalo producers, retailers of related products, meat processors, collectors and historians.
Purpose: To encourage the propagation of the buffalo and promote its products.

NATIONAL CANDY WHOLESALERS ASSOCIATION*
1430 K St., NW
Washington, DC 20005
202-393-6733

Contact: Ray Foley, Executive Vice-President

NATIONAL CAPON COUNCIL*
2 N. Riverside Plaza
Suite 2329
Chicago, IL 60606
312-726-6926

Contact: Marc Nichols, President

NATIONAL CATTLEMENS ASSOCIATION
PO Box 569

1001 Lincoln Street
Denver, CO 80203
303-861-1904

Contact: W. T. Berry Jr., Executive Vice-President

NATIONAL CHEESE INSTITUTE*
110 North Franklin Street
Chicago, IL 60606
312-263-2733

Contact: Robert F. Anderson

NATIONAL CHERRY GROWERS & INDUSTRIES FOUNDATION, INC.*
1105 NW 31st Street
Corvallis, OR 97330
503-753-8508

Contact: Robert F. Cain

NATIONAL COFFEE SERVICE ASSOCIATION
1000 Vermont Ave., NW
Washington, DC 20005
202-628-4634

Contact: Kathleen Lynott, Executive Secretary
Membership: 500 office coffee service operator companies and suppliers to the industry.
Purpose: To bring a quality product to the workplace; to provide a unified voice to the office coffee service industry.

NATIONAL CONFECTIONERY SALESMEN'S ASSOCIATION OF AMERICA
5 Jupiter St.
New Monmouth, NJ 07748
201-671-3435

Contact: John T. Mullarkey, Executive Secretary
Membership: Candy manufacturers and brokers, associates who store and transport confectionery products, salesmen of confectioners machinery and supplies.
Purpose: To promote and protect the welfare of members; to cooperate with other candy associations; to collect and report information on employment in the industry; to correct any disagreeable aspects of the industry; to insure that inductees meet all requirements of the Candy Hall of Fame.

NATIONAL CORN GROWERS ASSOCIATION
818 18th St., NW
Suite 645
Washington, DC 20006
202-233-6296

Contact: Michael L. Hall, Chief Executive Officer
Membership: 15,000.
Purpose: To promote the general welfare of the U.S. corn farmer by maintaining and developing a domestic corn production program and a price and income support program.

NATIONAL COTTONSEED PRODUCTS ASSOCIATION
PO Box 12023
Memphis, TN 38112
901-324-4417

Contact: Kenneth O. Lewis, Executive Vice-President
Membership: Processors, chemists, brokers, dealers, and refiners of cottonseed oil.
Purpose: To interface with federal agencies; to maintain and present applicable industry data.

NATIONAL COUNCIL OF FARMER COOPERATIVES
1800 Massachusetts Ave., NW
Washington, DC 20036
202-659-1525

Contact: Kenneth D. Naden, President
Membership: Represents about 90% of the 6,400 farm cooperatives in the U.S. with a combined membership of 2,000,000 farmers.
Purpose: Lobbying arm for U.S. farmer cooperatives.

NATIONAL DAIRY COUNCIL
6300 River Rd.
Rosemont, IL 60018
312-696-1020

Contact: M. F. Brink, Ph.D., President
Purpose: To achieve optimal health through leadership in a nutrition research and nutrition education program based on a balanced diet with includes milk and milk products.

NATIONAL DRY BEAN COUNCIL*
PO Box 247
Crows Landing, CA 95313
202-466-2804

Contact: Paul Bracken, President

NATIONAL DUCKLING COUNCIL*
2 N. Riverside Plaza
Suite 2329
Chicago, IL 60606
312-726-6926

Contact: Nelson D. Houck, President

NATIONAL EXTENSION HOMEMAKERS COUNCIL
Route 2, Box 3070
Vale, OR 97918
503-473-2619

Contact: Majorie Griffin, President
Membership: 500,000.
Purpose: To improve the quality of family living through education of the homemaker/mother.

NATIONAL FAMILY FARM COALITION*
918 F St., NW
Washington, DC 20004
202-638-6848

Contact: Catherine Lerza, Director

NATIONAL FARM COALITION*
201 S. 7th St.
Columbia, MO 65201
314-874-5430

Contact: Edward Andersen, Chairman

NATIONAL FEDERATION OF FISHERMAN
2424 Pennsylvania Ave., NW
Suite 516
Washington, DC 20037
202-554-3272

Contact: Lucy Sloan, Executive Director
Purpose: To represent commercial fishermen before Congress and the executive branch of government.

NATIONAL FEED INGREDIENTS ASSOCIATION*
1 Corporate Place
Suite 360
Des Moines, IA 50265
515-225-9611

Contact: Marvin L. Vinsand, Executive Vice-President

NATIONAL FISHERIES INSTITUTE
1101 Connecticut Ave., NW
Suite 700
Washington, DC 20036
202-857-1110

Contact: Lee Weddig, Executive Vice-President
Membership: 1,000 firms.
Purpose: To advance the welfare of the industry; to increase the consumption of fish and seafood in the U.S.; to represent the interests of the industry to the government.

NATIONAL FOOD BROKERS ASSOCIATION
1916 M St., NW
Washington, DC 20036
202-331-9120

Contact: Mark Singer
Membership: 2,500.
Purpose: To improve business conditions for brokers and for the benefit of the food industry.

NATIONAL FOOD AND CONSERVATION THROUGH SWINE, INC.
RR4, Box 397
Fox Run Road
Sewell, NJ 08080
609-468-5447

Contact: Ronnie Polen, Secretary-Treasurer
Membership: Feeders, breeders, brokers, and ecologists.
Purpose: To get more licensed processed food waste feeders so that more raw material can be processed and fed properly; to seek new and improved methods for handling and processing the raw product.

NATIONAL FOOD DISTRIBUTORS ASSOCIATION
111 E. Wacker Dr.
Chicago, IL 60601
312-655-6610

Contact: Maxine Couture, Executive Assistant
Membership: Specialty food manufacturers and food distributors.
Purpose: To promote the use of specialty food distributors; to establish better relations with retail and institutional trade; to establish high quality standards for products and service; to promote industry research and development.

NATIONAL FOOD PROCESSORS ASSOCIATION
1133 20th St., NW
Washington, DC 20036
202-331-5900

Contact: Charles Carey.
Membership: Processors of fruits, vegetables, meat, fish, and specialty products; suppliers to the canning, freezing, and preserving industry.
Purpose: To conduct research and technical work; to carry out legislative and regulatory liaison; to develop member publications and communications.

NATIONAL FOODSERVICE ASSOCIATION
PO Box 1932
Columbus, OH 43216
614-263-3346

Contact: Robert R. Williams, Executive Vice-President

NATIONAL FROZEN FOOD ASSOCIATION, INC.
PO Box 398
Hershey, PA 17033
717-534-1601

Contact: Richard C. Funk, President
Membership: Companies involved in frozen food processing, sales, distribution, and storage.
Purpose: To promote the use and sales of frozen foods through research and promotional programs.

NATIONAL FROZEN PIZZA INSTITUTE*
1700 Old Meadow Road
Suite 100
McLean, VA 22102

Contact: Frank G. Williams

NATIONAL GRAIN AND FEED ASSOCIATION*
PO Box 28328
Washington, DC 20005
202-783-2024

Contact: Alvin E. Oliver, Executive Vice-President

NATIONAL HAY ASSOCIATION*
PO Box 1059
Jackson, MI 49204
517-782-2688

Contact: Harry D. Gates, Jr., Executive Secretary

NATIONAL HONEY PACKERS & DEALERS ASSOCIATION
1515 5th Street
Snohomish, WA 98290
206-568-4459

Contact: Howard Graff

NATIONAL HOT DOG AND SAUSAGE COUNCIL
400 West Madison St.
Chicago, IL 60606
312-454-1242

Contact: Frances Altman, Executive Secretary
Purpose: To generate consumer awareness of the wide variety of sausage products.

NATIONAL ICE CREAM MIX ASSOCIATION
5610 Crawfordsville Rd.
Suite 1104
Indianapolis, IN 46224
317-243-9342

Contact: Wald Hol, Executive Director
Membership: Milkshake, ice cream mix, and related products processing companies.

NATIONAL ICE CREAM RETAILERS ASSOCIATION INC.
5600 Brookwood Terrace
Nashville, TN 37205
615-356-4244

Contact: Joe Maxwell, Executive Director

NATIONAL INDEPENDENT DAIRY FOODS ASSOCIATION
1625 K St., NW
Suite 1206
Washington, DC 20006
202-393-6010

Contact: D. A. Randall, Executive Vice-President
Membership: Independent dairy foods processors in the U.S.
Purpose: To promote dairy food processors' interests; to monitor and influence regulatory policies.

NATIONAL INDEPENDENT POULTRY AND FOOD DISTRIBUTORS ASSOCIATION
2310 Highway 80 West
Suite A, Room 202
Jackson, MS 39204
601-354-0355

Contact: Charles H. Carpenter, Executive Director
Membership: Independent distributors, processor/distributors, brokers, marketing specialists, and processors of poultry, supply, transportation, and affiliated companies.
Purpose: To promote the progress, markets, and development of poultry and food distribution through collection and dissemination of trade statistics, cooperation with government officials, and other necessary activities.

NATIONAL INSTITUTE FOR THE FOODSERVICE INDUSTRY
20 North Wacker Dr.
Chicago, IL 60606
312-782-1703

Contact: Chester G. Hall, Ph.D., Executive Vice-President
Membership: Non-membership foundation supported by restaurateurs, foodservice manufacturers, wholesalers and distributors.
Purpose: To advance professionalism in foodservice management through education.

NATIONAL INSTITUTE OF OILSEED PRODUCTS
111 Sutter St.
San Francisco, CA 94104
415-392-5718

Contact: Robert L. Moon, Executive Secretary
Membership: 250 buyers, sellers, processors and manufacturers of vegetable oil and related products.
Purpose: To promote the general welfare of members.

NATIONAL INSTITUTIONAL FOOD DISTRIBUTOR ASSOCIATES*
PO Box 19936
Atlanta, GA 30325
404-952-0871

Contact: Timothy I. Mahanay, President

NATIONAL JUICE PRODUCTS ASSOCIATION*
512 Florida Ave.
Tampa, FL 33601
813-229-1089

Contact: David Kerr, General Counsel

NATIONAL KRAUT PACKERS ASSOCIATION*
108½ E. Main Street
PO Box 31
St. Charles, IL 60174
312-584-8950

Contact: William R. Moore

NATIONAL LAMB FEEDERS ASSOCIATION*
Box 578
Menard, TX 76859
915-396-4521

Contact: Jamie Kothmann, President

NATIONAL LAND FOR PEOPLE
2348 N. Cornelia
Fresno, CA 93711
209-233-4727

Contact: George Ballis, Executive Director
Purpose: Small farm support organization for lobbying, educating, and developing alternative marketing systems.

NATIONAL LIVESTOCK EXCHANGE
c/o Coburn, Endsley & Sedwick
2577 Kentucky Ave.
Indianapolis, IN 46241
317-243-9366

Contact: Jim Henry, President
Membership: Indianapolis, Peoria, and Memphis livestock exchanges.
Purpose: To promote the central market concept of selling livestock.

NATIONAL LIVESTOCK & MEAT BOARD*
444 North Michigan Ave.
Chicago, IL 60611
312-467-5520

Contact: John Huston

NATIONAL LIVESTOCK PRODUCERS ASSOCIATION
307 Livestock Exchange Bldg.
Denver, CO 80216
303-623-2098

Contact: Darrell D. Hipes, Executive Vice-President & General Manager
Membership: 12 member marketing agencies, 6 credit corporations.
Purpose: A livestock marketing cooperative that finances livestock operations.

NATIONAL MEAT ASSOCIATION
734 15th St., NW
Suite 800
Washington, DC 20005
202-347-1000

Contact: John G. Mohay, President
Membership: Slaughterers of cattle, hogs, and sheep and manufacturers of processed meats.
Purpose: To protect and further the legislative interests of the independent segment of the meat packing industry.

NATIONAL MEAT CANNERS ASSOCIATION
PO Box 3556
Washington, DC 20007
703-841-2400

Contact: A. Dewey Bond, Executive Secretary

NATIONAL MILK PRODUCERS FEDERATION
30 F St., NW
Washington, DC 20001
202-393-8151

Contact: Patrick Healy, Secretary
Membership: Dairy Cooperatives
Purpose: To provide a legislative voice to dairy coops and its farmer members.

NATIONAL NUTRITION CONSORTIUM, INC.
24 3rd St., NE
Suite 200
Washington, DC 20002
202-547-4819

Contact: Betty B. Blouin, M.S., R.D., Administrative Officer
Membership: Professional associations.

Purpose: To provide information to members on government activities; to act as a liaison between public policy makers and nutrition professionals.

NATIONAL NUTRITIONAL FOODS ASSOCIATION*
7727 S. Painter Avenue
Whittier, CA 90602
213-945-2669

Contact: Ron Weiner

NATIONAL ONION ASSOCIATION
5701 East Evans Ave.
Suite 26
Denver, CO 80222
303-756-1581

Contact: Roger N. Foerch, Executive Vice-President
Membership: 400.
Purpose: An informational, lobbying, and promotional organization.

NATURAL ORGANIC FARMERS ASSOCIATION*
PO Box 86
Greensboro Bend, VT 05842
802-525-4459

Contact: Samuel Kaymen, Educational Counsel

NATIONAL PASTA ASSOCIATION
PO Box 1008
Palatine, IL 60067
312-358-1022

Contact: Robert M. Green, Executive Director
Membership: 42 pasta manufacturers (active members) and 40 suppliers (associate members).
Purpose: To promote the development and use of pasta and related products; to provide programs and services for members.

NATIONAL PEACH COUNCIL
PO Box 1085
Martinsburg, WV 25401
304-267-6024

Contact: Lillie E. Hoover, Executive Director
Membership: Peach growers and state peach groups; associate members include allied industries such as chemical and machinery companies and nurseries.
Purpose: Promotion and legislative activities to benefit the peach industry.

NATIONAL PEANUT COUNCIL
1000 16th St., NW
Suite 700
Washington, DC 20036
202-775-0450

Contact: Perry A. Russ, President
Membership: Peanut farmers, shellers, processors, brokers, manufacturers, and allied support trades.
Purpose: To improve the quality, utilization and marketing of peanuts and peanut products through research activities, sales and promotional campaigns, and cooperation with other associations and companies.

NATIONAL PECAN SHELLERS AND PROCESSORS ASSOCIATION*
c/o Smith Bucklin & Associates, Inc.
111 E. Wacker Drive
Chicago, IL 60601
312-644-6610

Contact: Henry A. Bucklin, Executive Secretary

NATIONAL PEST CONTROL ASSOCIATION*
8150 Leesburg Pike
Suite 1100
Vienna, VA 22180
703-790-8300

Contact: Jefferson D. Keith, CAE, Executive Vice-President

NATIONAL PORK PRODUCERS COUNCIL
PO Box 10383
Des Moines, IA 50306
515-223-2600

Contact: Linda Welch, Director, Consumer Communications
Membership: 110,000 pork producers.
Purpose: To improve or increase the quality, production, distribution, and sales of pork and pork products.

NATIONAL POTATO COUNCIL
12075 E. 45th Ave.
Suite 301
Denver, CO 80231
303-373-5639

Contact: Dan Hall, Executive Director
Membership: 14,000 growers.
Purpose: To promote the welfare of U.S. potato growers.

NATIONAL POTATO PROMOTION BOARD
1385 S. Colorado Blvd., #512
Denver, CO 80222
303-758-7783

Contact: Robert L. Mercer, Executive Vice-President
Membership: Potato producers with 5 acres or more of production.
Purpose: To educate consumers on the nutritional benefits of potatoes; to increase potato consumption and develop new markets.

NATIONAL POULTRY IMPROVEMENT PLAN
USDA, Alphis-VS, BARC East
Bldg. 265
Beltsville, MD 20705
301-344-2227

Contact: Raymond D. Schar, Senior Coordinator

NATIONAL PREPARED FROZEN FOOD PROCESSORS ASSOCIATION*
95 E. Velley Stream Blvd.
Valley Stream, NY 11580
516-825-6673

Contact: Margaret Clamser

NATIONAL PRETZEL BAKERS INSTITUTE
800 New Holland Ave.
PO Box 1433
Lancaster, PA 17603
717-394-3108

Contact: Michele D. Madonna, Executive Secretary
Membership: Pretzel bakers.
Purpose: To promote the pretzel industry through legislative monitoring and public relations activities; to act as a liaison among members.

NATIONAL RESTAURANT ASSOCIATION*
311 1st St., NW
Washington, DC 20001
202-638-6100

Contact: Robert Neville

NATIONAL RED CHERRY INSTITUTE
678 Front St., NW
Suite 140
Grand Rapids, MI 49504
616-454-6196

Contact: Tom Martin, President
Membership: 4,000 growers in Michigan, New York, Wisconsin, and Pennsylvania.
Purpose: To promote and enhance the use of cherries; to inform and educate.

NATIONAL RICE GROWERS ASSOCIATION*
Route 1, Box 166
Branch, LA 70516

Contact: Grant Link, President

NATIONAL SAFFLOWER COUNCIL*
111 Sutter Street
Suite 1436
San Francisco, CA 94104
415-392-5718

Contact: Robert L. Moon, Executive Secretary

NATIONAL SHELLFISHERIES ASSOCIATION, INC.
Pacific Biological Station
PO Box 100
Nanaimo, British Columbia
V9R 5K6, Canada

Contact: Dr. Victor Burrell, President
Membership: Scientists, management officials, and industry members.
Purpose: To encourage scientific investigation; to develop sound management principles for shellfish production, safety, quality, and conservation through research and educational programs.

NATIONAL SHRIMP BREADERS AND PROCESSORS ASSOCIATION*
Fulton Federal Bldg., 10th Floor
Atlanta, GA 30303
404-577-5100

Contact: Rod Rodemich

NATIONAL SHRIMP CONGRESS*
1320 19th St., NW
Washington, DC 20036
202-785-2130

Contact: William Nelson Utz

NATIONAL SINGLE SERVICE FOOD ASSOCIATION
5775 Peachtree-Dunwoody Rd.
Suite 500-D
Atlanta, GA 30342
404-252-3663

Contact: Robert H. Kellen, President
Membership: Manufacturers and packagers of single service food and beverages for the food service industry.
Purpose: To provide industry representation and liaison; to develop industry programs; to encourage high standards of manufacturing and marketing among industry members.

NATIONAL SOCIETY OF LIVESTOCK RECORD ASSOCIATION
210 Utah Ave.
West Plains, MO 65775
417-256-8259

Contact: Harold Boucher, Secretary
Membership: Livestock registry associations.
Purpose: To advance the interests of the general livestock industry and of the member registry associations.

NATIONAL SOYBEAN CROP IMPROVEMENT COUNCIL*
211 S. Race Street
Urbana, IL 61801
217-367-0412

Contact: Robert W. Judd, Managing Director

NATIONAL SOYBEAN PROCESSORS ASSOCIATION
1800 M St., NW
Washington, DC 20036
202-452-8040

Contact: Sheldon J. Hauck
Membership: Processors, consumers and refiners of soybean meal and oil.
Purpose: To promote and and increase production of soybeans and soybean products through development of equitable trading rules and research activities; to promote the sale of soybean products internationally; to educate the public to the benefits of soybean products.

NATIONAL SUGAR BROKERS ASSOCIATION*
One World Trade Center
Suite 5011
New York, NY 10048
212-938-0990

Contact: F. E. Wallace, Executive Secretary

NATIONAL SUNFLOWER ASSOCIATION
PO Box 2533
Bismark, ND 58502
701-224-3019

Contact: Judi Adams, R.D., Marketing Consultant
Membership: Sunflower producers, processors, exporters, and seed companies.
Purpose: To increase the domestic and world markets for sunflower products; to serve as a clearing house for research and nutrition information.

NATIONAL TURKEY FEDERATION
Reston International Center
11800 Sunrise Valley Drive
Reston, VA 22091
703-860-0120

Contact: G. L. Walts, Executive Vice-President

NATIONAL VOCATIONAL AGRICULTURAL TEACHERS' ASSOCIATION*
PO Box 15051
Alexandria, VA 22309
703-780-1862

Contact: Sam Stenzel, Executive Director

NEBRASKA BAKERS ASSOCIATION
PO Box 37718
Millard, NE 68137
402-330-2424

Contact: Chuck Skoumal, Secretary

NEBRASKA CHEESE ASSOCIATION
Dodge, NB 68633
402-693-2231

Contact: Don Wadzinski, Secretary

NEBRASKA DAIRY INDUSTRIES ASSOCIATION
116 Filley Hall
E. Campus, UN-L
Lincoln, NE 68583
402-472-2912

Contact: T. A. Evans, Executive Secretary
Membership: Dairy processing plants, producer cooperatives, and companies supplying services/or equipment.
Purpose: To encourage legislation or programs that will promote the industry; to promote fellowship among members; to cooperate with federal and state government agencies with regard to programs affecting the industry; to improve the dairy industry and products supplied to the public.

NEW ENGLAND ASSOCIATION OF ICE CREAM MANUFACTURERS*
c/o H. P. Hood & Sons
56 Roland St.
Boston, MA 02129
617-242-0600

Contact: Robert Doe

NEW ENGLAND BAKERS ASSOCIATION
38 Robin Circle
Stoughton, MA 02072
617-344-5881

Contact: Joseph Keene, Secretary-Treasurer
Membership: 176.
Purpose: To promote fellowship and to further the image of the industry.

NEW ENGLAND DAIRY & FOOD COUNCIL*
1034 Commonwealth Ave.
Boston, MA 02215
617-734-6750

Contact: Edith Syrjala, Executive Director

NEW ENGLAND FISH EXCHANGE
Administration Bldg.
Boston Fish Pier
Boston, MA 02210
617-542-9040

Contact: Robert G. Dunn, President
Membership: 30.
Purpose: To auction fish from boats to wholesale fish dealers in Boston.

NEW ENGLAND ICE CREAM RESTAURANT ASSOCIATION
45 Carlton Rd.
Belmont, MA 02078
617-484-2187

Contact: E. A. Blakelock, Executive Secretary
Membership: Retail ice cream and sandwich shops; ice cream restaurants.
Purpose: To promote good food and service in sandwich shops, restaurants, and ice cream shops.

NEW HAMPSHIRE MILK DEALERS ASSOCIATION*
c/o Weeks Concord, Inc.
328 N. State Street
Concord, NH 03301
603-225-3379

Contact: John Weeks, Jr., Secretary

NEW JERSEY ASPARAGUS INDUSTRY COUNCIL
New Jersey Department of Agriculture, CN 330
Trenton, NJ 08625
609-292-8853

Contact: Mary Anne Guender, Manager

NEW JERSEY BAKERS BOARD OF TRADE*
1597 Ratzer Road
Wayne, NJ 07470
201-942-2075

Contact: Francis Dietch, Executive Secretary

NEW JERSEY MILK INDUSTRY ASSOCIATION
333 West State St.
Trenton, NJ 08618
609-396-4597

Contact: Dan Wettlin Jr., President

NEW YORK ASSOCIATION OF MANUFACTURING RETAIL BAKERS*
PO Box 68, Main Station
Yonkers, NY 10702
914-961-6460

Contact: Walter Michel, Secretary
Membership: 300.
Purpose: To further the retail bakers trade; to conduct educational workshops and exhibits; to provide scholarships to young people who want to become bakers.

NEW YORK CANDY CLUB
235 West End Ave.
New York, NY 10023
212-799-0194

Contact: Henry Nadel, Executive Secretary.
Membership: 119 confectionary brokers and salesmen.
Purpose: To encourage ethical business standards; to sponsor, sell and merchandise quality products; to cooperate with other associations.

NEW YORK COCOA CLEARING ASSOCIATION*
4 World Trade Center
New York, NY 10048
212-839-9143

Contact: S. L. Branson, Treasurer

NEW YORK STATE ASSOCIATION OF MILK AND FOOD SANITARIANS
11 Stocking Hall
Cornell University
Ithaca, NY 14853
607-256-3027

Contact: David Bandler, Interim Secretary
Membership: 750 milk cooperatives, dairy and food processing plants, control laboratories, regulatory agencies, colleges, food distribution companies, dairy and food supply and equipment dealers, institutional caterers, and restaurant management companies.
Purpose: To promote greater uniformity in food regulations; to keep informed about the sanitary, nutritional, and progressive aspects of the total food industry.

NEW YORK STATE CHEESE MANUFACTURER'S ASSOCIATION, INC.
11 Stocking Hall
Cornell University
Ithaca, NY 14853
607-256-3027

Contact: David Bandler, Technical Advisor
Membership: Manufacturers of cheese, suppliers of materials for the manufacture, storage, and distribution of cheese, and brokers or sales agents associated with the business operations of the industry.
Purpose: To encourage, assist, advise and aid its members in the making of New York state cheese; to promote the sale of cheese manufactured in New York; to improve and control the quality of cheese made by its members.

NEW YORK STATE DAIRY FOODS, INC.*
41 State Street
Albany, NY 12207
518-434-6516

Contact: Edmund Towle, Executive Vice-President

NEW YORK STATE FRUIT TESTING COOPERATIVE ASSOCIATION
Geneva, NY 14456
315-787-2205

Contact: John M. Kasper, Manager
Membership: 5,000
Purpose: To grow, test, and report on merits of new fruits.

NORTH AMERICAN BLUEBERRY COUNCIL
PO Box 166
Marmora, NJ 08223
609-399-1559

Contact: Myrtle L. Ruch, Secretary-Manager
Purpose: To promote blueberries throughout the world; to provide educational materials on blueberries.

NORTH AMERICAN LIMOUSIN FOUNDATION
100 Livestock Exchange Bldg.
Denver, CO 80216
303-623-6544

Contact: Greg Martin, Executive Vice-President
Membership: 25,000.
Purpose: To promote limousin beef cattle and keep the ancestral and performance records on the breed.

NORTH AMERICAN POULTRY COOPERATIVE ASSOCIATION
3 Worth St.
New York, NY 10013
212-966-0340

Contact: Berwyn B. Gehgan, General Manager
Purpose: Sales agency for eggs and egg products.

NORTH ATLANTIC SEAFOOD ASSOCIATION
1220 Huron Rd.
Cleveland, OH 44115
216-781-6400

Contact: Patrick Ginley, Marketing Chairman
Membership: Major fishery producers of Canada, Denmark, Iceland, and Norway.
Purpose: To create awareness and interest in North Atlantic fish in particular and fish in general.

NORTH CAROLINA DAIRY PRODUCTS ASSOCIATION
505 Oberlin Road
PO Box 10506
Raleigh, NC 27605
919-833-2850

Contact: John E. Johnson, Executive Vice-President
Membership: A trade organization of dairy product processors in North Carolina.
Purpose: To promote the general welfare of the dairy industry in North Carolina through cooperation with government and civic agencies, development of new dairy products, educational meetings, and publication of educational information; to propose industry policies and codes of ethics.

NORTH CAROLINA MEAT PACKERS ASSOCIATION
c/o Inform, Inc.
222 Northgate Mall
Durham, NC 27701
919-286-7717

Contact: Barbara Short, Executive Secretary
Purpose: To promote the welfare of its members; to encourage the development of the meat packing industry in North Carolina; to collect and disseminate information in order to improve the quality of products and the work of the industry.

NORTH CAROLINA PEANUT GROWERS ASSOCIATION
109 S. Main St.
Rocky Mount, NC 27801
919-446-8060

Contact: Norfleet L. Sugg, Executive Secretary
Membership: Peanut producers in North Carolina.
Purpose: To promote the increased consumption of North Carolina grown peanuts through promotion, education, legislation, and research.

NORTH CENTRAL CHEESE INDUSTRIES ASSOCIATION
PO Box 80113
St. Paul, MN 55108

Contact: E. A. Zottola, Secretary-Treasurer
Membership: Manufacturers, processors, and wholesalers of cheese.

NORTH CENTRAL TEXAS FOOD INDUSTRY ASSOCIATION
1515 Mockingbird Lane
Suite 113
Dallas, TX 75235
214-630-2139

Contact: Daisy Fern Nelson, Executive Director
Membership: 500.
Purpose: To promote the retail food industry.

NORTH DAKOTA BAKERS ASSOCIATION*
c/o Wally's Fairway Foods
155 East 12th Street
Grafton, ND 58237
701-352-0770

Contact: Robert Paulsen, President

NORTH DAKOTA CHEESEMAKERS ASSOCIATION*
Box 327
Lakota, ND 58344
701-247-2801

Contact: Glen Knetter, President

NORTH DAKOTA DAIRY INDUSTRIES
c/o Peterson Cremery
Williston, ND 58801
701-572-6971

Contact: Jerry Peterson, President
Membership: North Dakota creameries and milk plants.

NORTHEAST DAIRY COOPERATIVE FEDERATION*
428 S. Warren St.
Syracuse, NY 13202
315-474-6581

Contact: Robert C. Forsythe, General Manager

NORTHEAST DAIRY PRACTICES COUNCIL
141 Riley-Robb Hall
Cornell University
Ithaca, NY 14853
607-256-5433

Contact: Richard March, Executive Secretary
Purpose: To develop and disseminate educational guidelines for the dairy industry; to provide mutual assistance among the northeastern states in adopting improved procedures for the production of milk and dairy products.

NORTHEAST ICE CREAM ASSOCIATION, INC.
1474 Route 23
PO Box 1816
Wayne, NJ 07470
201-694-3308

Contact: R. W. Shafer, Executive Secretary

NORTHEASTERN WISCONSIN CHEESEMAKERS & BUTTERMAKERS ASSOCIATION
Route 1, Box 313
Shawano, WI 54166
715-526-5558

Contact: Dale Hodkiewicz, President
Membership: All dairy plants in northeastern Wisconsin.
Purpose: To promote dairy products; to exchange information with members on how to improve products.

NORTHERN NUT GROWERS ASSOCIATION
c/o Niagara College
PO Box 340
St. Catharines, Ontario L2R 6V6, Canada

Contact: R. D. Campbell, Secretary
Membership: 2,500 horticultural professionals, teachers, institutions, corporations, food processors, farmers, investors, hobbyists, and gardners.
Purpose: To promote an interest in nut bearing plants; to conduct scientific research into their breeding and culture; to disseminate information regarding the growing, breeding, processing, storing, and marketing of nut crops.

NORTHWEST ATLANTIC FISHERIES ORGANIZATION
PO Box 638
Dartmouth, Nova Scotia
B27 3V9, Canada
902-469-9105

Contact: Captain J. C. Esteves Cardoso, Executive Secretary
Membership: International, including Canada, the European economic community, Japan, etc.
Purpose: To investigate, protect, and conserve the fishery resources of the Northwest Atlantic.

NORTHWEST CHERRY BRINERS*
1105 NW 31st Street
Corvallis, OR 97330
503-753-8508

Contact: Robert Cain

NORTHWEST DRIED FRUIT EXPORT ASSOCIATION*
PO Box 23126
Tigard, OR 97223
503-639-3118

Contact: D. J. Duncan, Secretary

NORTHWEST FISHERIES ASSOCIATION
2208 SW Market St.
Seattle, WA 98107
Suite 210C
206-789-6197

Contact: Stephen L. Chase, Executive Director
Membership: 79 firms in Washington state and Alaska.
Purpose: Trade association of seafood processors.

NORTHWEST FOOD PROCESSORS ASSOCIATION*
2828 SW Corbett
Suite 229
Portland, OR 97201
503-226-2848

Contact: David A. Pahl

NORTHWEST HORTICULTURAL COUNCIL
PO Box 570
002 Larson Bldg.
Yakima, WA 98907
509-453-3193

Contact: Christian Schlect, President
Purpose: To work on problems involving transportation, international trade, and national legislation affecting the tree fruit industries of Washington and Oregon.

NORTHWEST PACKERS INDUSTRIAL RELATIONS ASSOCIATION, INC.
9414 SW Barbur Blvd., 2C
Portland, OR 97219
503-245-7261

Contact: Gary Barnes, President
Membership: Food processing companies located in Oregon and Washington.
Purpose: To provide labor and industrial relations services to members.

NUTRITION FOUNDATION, INC.
Office of Education & Public Affairs
888 17th St., NW
Washington, DC 20006
202-872-0778

Contact: Richard Stalvey, Vice-President
Membership: 50 food and food related companies.
Purpose: A non-profit organization dedicated to the advancement of nutrition knowledge and its effective application for the improvement of mankind's health and welfare.

NUTRITION TODAY SOCIETY
PO Box 1829
703 Giddings Ave.
Annapolis, MD 21404
301-267-8616

Contact: Cortez F. Enloe, Jr., Executive Vice-President

Membership: Health professionals, laymen interested in nutrition, libraries, and students in the fields of agriculture, biochemistry, food technology, medicine, home economics, nutrition, denistry, etc.

O

OHIO DAIRY PRODUCTS ASSOCIATION, INC.
1429 King Ave.
Columbus, OH 43212
614-486-6000

Contact: Donald L. Buckley, Executive Vice-President
Membership: Manufacturers, processors, and distributors of dairy and food products.
Purpose: To undertake and engage in activities which will advance the efficiency and business standards of the dairy industry.

OHIO FOOD PROCESSORS ASSOCIATION
PO Box 312
Worthington, OH 43085
604-885-6045

Contact: Wilbur A. Gould, Executive Vice-President
Membership: Food processors in Ohio.
Purpose: To act as a vehicle for exchange of ideas on the industry problems of Ohio food processors.

OHIO SWISS CHEESE ASSOCIATION*
116 Factory Street
Box 445
Sugar Creek, OH 44681
216-852-2311

Contact: Robert Ramseyer, President

OIL TRADES ASSOCIATION OF NEW YORK*
225 W. 34th Street
Suite 1202
New York, NY 10122
212-695-1385

Contact: William R. Wilcox, Secretary

OKLAHOMA DAIRY PRODUCTS INSTITUTE*
Office 14, 129 NW 44th St.
Oklahoma City, OK 73118
405-525-0292

Contact: Thomas Ashinhurst, Executive Director

OLIVE OIL ASSOCIATION OF AMERICA, INC.
115 Broadway, Room 117
New York, NY 10006
212-267-4244

Contact: Richard Sullivan, Executive Vice-President

ONTARIO FOOD PROCESSORS ASSOCIATION
2395 Cawthra Rd.
Suite 1
Mississauga, Ontario L5A 2W8, Canada
416-276-6727

Contact: E. L. Chudleigh, Executive Vice-President

Purpose: To serve members' needs including assistance in dealing with the government and with suppliers; to inform members of industry developments.

OREGON ASSOCIATION OF MILK, FOOD AND ENVIRONMENTAL SANITARIANS
Oregon State University
Wiegand Hall, Room 240
Corvallis, OR 97331
503-754-3463

Contact: Floyd Bodyfelt, Secretary-Treasurer
Membership: Milk and food sanitarians, regulatory officials, dairy and food industry quality control personnel, sanitation supply and equipment companies.
Purpose: To provide educational programs for the membership.

OREGON DAIRY COUNCIL
10505 SW Barbur Blvd.
Portland, OR 97219
503-229-5033

Contact: Charlene Moore, Executive Director
Membership: Oregon dairy producers and processors.
Purpose: To provide educational materials and consultation on nutrition to teachers, health professionals, and community leaders; to encourage use of milk and milk products.

OREGON DAIRY INDUSTRIES
Oregon State University
Food Science & Technology
Wiegand Mall, Room 100
Corvallis, OR 97331
503-754-3131

Contact: Mary K. Moran, Executive Secretary
Membership: Northwest Dairy processing plants and their suppliers.
Purpose: To conduct an annual technical seminar and dairy product evaluation; to finance scholarship for a food science student; to sponsor judging team in annual dairy judging competition.

OREGON RETAIL BAKERS ASSOCIATION*
5605 NE Portland Ave.
West Linn, OR 97068
503-655-7575

Contact: Bill Murray, President

OZARK FOOD PROCESSORS ASSOCIATION*
Route 11
Fayetteville, AR 72701
501-442-9421

Contact: A. A. Kattan

P

PACIFIC COAST CANNED PEAR SERVICE*
300 Elliott Ave. West
Seattle, WA 98119
206-284-8383

Contact: Frederick D. Sprague, Promotion Director

PACIFIC COAST OYSTER GROWERS ASSOCIATION
270 S. Hanford St.
Seattle, WA 98134
206-625-1481

Contact: W. Arnold Waring, President
Membership: Commercial farmers of oysters, clams, and mussels.
Purpose: To represent the industry in federal, state, and local government.

RESOURCES FOR FURTHER INFORMATION

PACIFIC NORTHWEST GRAIN AND FEED ASSOCIATION*
200 SW Market St., No. 770
Portland, OR 97201
503-227-0234

Contact: Don W. Munkers, Executive Vice-President

PACIFIC SEAFOOD PROCESSORS ASSOCIATION
1620 S. Jackson St.
Seattle, WA 98144
206-328-1205

Contact: W. V. Yonker, Executive Vice-President

PACKAGED ICE ASSOCIATION*
111 East Wacker Drive
Suite 600
Chicago, IL 60601
312-644-6610

Contact: Michael C. Rippey, Executive Director

PACKING INSTITUTE USA*
2000 K St., NW
Washington, DC 20006
202-331-8181

Contact: Claude S. Breeden, Jr.

PEANUT BUTTER AND NUT PROCESSORS ASSOCIATION
5101 Wisconsin Ave.
Suite 504
Washington, DC 20016
202-966-7888

Contact: James E. Mack, Managing Director
Membership: Packers, manufacturers and processors of peanut and tree nuts; suppliers of industry goods and services.
Purpose: To inform the industry; to represent the industry with the government, the media, the public, and other industries; to protect the business interests of the industry.

PENNSYLVANIA ASSOCIATION OF MILK DEALERS, INC.*
100 Walnut Street
Harrisburg, PA 17101
717-238-1738

Contact: H. R. Geisinger, Executive Vice-President

PACIFIC COAST CANNED PEAR SERVICE*
300 Elliott Ave. West
Seattle, WA 98119
206-284-8383

Contact: Frederick D. Sprague, Promotion Director

PACIFIC COAST OYSTER GROWERS ASSOCIATION
270 S. Hanford St.
Seattle, WA 98134
206-625-1481

Contact: W. Arnold Waring, President
Membership: Commercial farmers of oysters, clams, and mussels.
Purpose: To represent the industry in federal, state, and local government.

PACIFIC NORTHWEST GRAIN AND FEED ASSOCIATION*
200 S.W. Market St., No. 700
Portland, OR 97201
503-227-0234

Contact: Don W. Munkers, Executive Vice-President

PACIFIC SEAFOOD PROCESSORS ASSOCIATION
1620 S. Jackson St.
Seattle, WA 98144
206-328-1205

Contact: W. V. Yonker, Executive Vice-President

PACKAGED ICE ASSOCIATION*
111 E. Wacker Dr., Suite 600
Chicago, IL 60601
312-644-6610

Contact: Michael C. Rippey, Executive Director

PACKAGING INSTITUTE USA*
2000 K St., NW
Washington, DC 20006
202-331-8181

Contact: Claude S. Breeden, Jr.

PEANUT BUTTER AND NUT PROCESSING ASSOCIATION
5101 Wisconsin Ave., Suite 504
Washington, DC 20016
202-966-7888

Contact: James E. Mack, Managing Director
Membership: Packers, manufacturers and processors of peanut and tree nuts; suppliers of industry goods and services.
Purpose: To inform the industry; to represent the industry with the government, the media, the public, and other industries; to protect the business interests of the industry.

PENNSYLVANIA ASSOCIATION OF MILK DEALERS, INC.*
100 Walnut Street
Harrisburg, PA 17101
717-238-1738

Contact: H. R. Geisinger, Executive Vice-President

PENNSYLVANIA BAKERS ASSOCIATION
407 N. Front St.
Harrisburg, PA 17101
717-236-7949

Contact: Robert Maurer, Executive Vice-President & Legal Council
Membership: Large and small retail and wholesale bakers in Pennsylvania.
Purpose: To act as a spokesperson for the baking industry; to monitor governmental regulations; to disseminate information; to promote and protect baking industry interests throughout Pennsylvania.

PENNSYLVANIA FOOD PROCESSORS ASSOCIATION
22 S. 3rd St.
Harrisburg, PA 17101
717-238-1252

Contact: Rocco V. Pugliese, Executive Director
Purpose: To promote cooperation among all food processors; to encourage protective and favorable legislation; to encourage processing of high grade foods; to reform any abuses in the industry.

PERFORMANCE REGISTRY INTERNATIONAL
c/o BF Livestock Company
Fairland, OK 74343
918-676-3266

Contact: Glenn Butts, Manager

Purpose: To record and encourage accurate records of the performance and production of beef cattle; to cooperate with breeder associations in the promotion of more profitable cattle; to encourage the use of high quality breeding stock.

PERMANENT WARE INSTITUTE*
334 S. Main St.
Dayton, OH 45402
513-461-1794

Contact: John Fanning, President

PET FOOD INSTITUTE
1101 Connecticut Ave., NW
Washington, DC 20036
202-857-1120

Contact: Duane Ekedahl
Membership: Dog and cat food manufacturers.
Purpose: To represent manufacturers with respect to governmental agencies; to gather and disseminate information to the industry, public and private agencies, and technical and professional societies; to stimulate growth of the industry.

PICKLE PACKERS INTERNATIONAL, INC.*
PO Box 31
St. Charles, IL 60174
312-584-8950

Contact: William R. Moore

PINEAPPLE GROWERS ASSOCIATION OF HAWAII*
1902 Financial Place of Pacific
Honolulu, HI 96813
808-531-5395

Contact: John T. Tolan

PIONEER DAIRYMEN'S CLUB OF AMERICA
6543 U.S. Highway 12
Eau Claire, WI 54701
715-835-5809

Contact: Joseph Schwebach, President
Membership: 343 members.
Purpose: To socialize and to disseminate information to members.

THE PLAN
PO Box 872
Santa Cruz, CA 95061
408-429-3020

Contact: Clayton L. Olson, President
Purpose: A non-profit organization promoting the establishment of community foods tree nurseries and the planning of public-access food trees.

PLASTIC CONTAINER MANUFACTURERS INSTITUTE, INC.*
54 Apple St.
Tinton Falls, NJ 07724
201-741-3800

Contact: Richard Hartung, Executive Director

POPCORN INSTITUTE*
1 Illinois Center
111 E. Wacker Dr.
Chicago, IL 60601
312-644-6610

Contact: William E. Smith, Executive Director

POTATO ASSOCIATION OF AMERICA*
c/o University of Maine
114 Deering Hall
Orono, ME 04469
207-581-2771

Contact: Hugh Murphy

THE POTATO BOARD
1385 S. Colorado Blvd.
Room 512
Denver, CO 80222
303-758-7783

Contact: Robert L. Mercer
Membership: Potato producers and allied industries.
Purpose: To promote the potato as a nutritious, tasty and economical vegetable; to improve the financial position of producers and allied industry people by promotion and development of markets for potatoes.

POTATO CHIP/SNACK FOOD ASSOCIATION
1735 Jefferson Davis Hwy.
Suite 915
Arlington, VA 22202
703-920-4805

Contact: Lawrence D. Burch, Executive Vice-President
Membership: 536 snack manufacturers and suppliers.
Purpose: Lobbying, research and training.

POTOMAC STATES BAKERS ASSOCIATION
7400 York Rd.
Townson, MD 21204
301-828-8410

Contact: William Devilbiss, Treasurer
Membership: Bakers and suppliers in Delaware, Maryland, D.C., Virginia and West Virginia.
Purpose: To promote the good of the industry; to form a strong industry voice.

POULTRY BREEDERS OF AMERICA
1456 Church
Decatur, GA 30030
404-377-6465

Contact: Harold Ford, Secretary-Treasurer
Membership: Companies engaged in the genetic development and marketing of various breeds of chickens.
Purpose: To further the development of more productive animals for eggs, frying chickens, and turkeys.

POULTRY & EGG INSTITUTE OF AMERICA*
1815 North Lynn St.
Suite 801
Arlington, VA 22209
816-361-5775

Contact: Lee Campbell

POULTRY SCIENCE ASSOCIATION*
309 W. Clark St.
Champaign, IL 61820
217-356-3182

Contact: Claude Cruse, Business Manager
Membership: 3,500 members including professionals, university students, and library subscribers.
Purpose: To advance knowledge and technology in poultry science.

PRICE-POTTENGER NUTRITION FOUNDATION

PO Box 2614
LaMessa, CA 92041
714-582-4168

Contact: Mrs. Pat Connolly, Curator
Membership: 950.
Purpose: Publishes nutrition research and a quarterly journal; distributes films, slides, and books.

PROCESS EQUIPMENT MANUFACTURERS ASSOCIATION
PO Box 8745
Kansas City, MO 64114
913-642-3114

Contact: Art Parchen, Executive Director
Membership: 70 member companies in the chemical, environmental, food, pulp and paper, mining and liquid-solids separation and processing fields.
Purpose: To provide a management forum for the discussion of common problems in the various process industries.

PROCESSED APPLES INSTITUTE
5775 Peachtree-Dunwood Rd.
Suite 500-D
Atlanta, GA 30342
404-252-3663

Contact: R. H. Kellen, President
Membership: Processors of apples in the U.S. and Canada; suppliers of goods or services to the processed apple industry.
Purpose: To improve business conditions; to encourage the industry to better serve the interests of consumers.

PRODUCE MARKETING ASSOCIATION
700 Barksdale Plaza
Newark, DE 19711
302-738-7100

Contact: Robert L. Carey, Executive Vice-President
Membership: Growers, shippers, wholesalers, retailers, and packers of produce and flowers.
Purpose: To provide leadership in marketing; to advance the industry; to foster better communications among the membership.

PUREBRED DAIRY CATTLE ASSOCIATION*

PO Box 126
Peterborough, NH 03458
603-924-3344

Contact: Iring E. Nichols, Secretary-Treasurer

Q

QUALITY CHEKD DAIRY PRODUCTS ASSOCIATION
201 E. Ogden Ave.
Hinsdale, IL 60521
312-235-0660

Contact: Mel W. Rapp, Director
Membership: 84 fluid milk and ice cream plants.
Purpose: To provide assistance to members in marketing, production, quality assurance, purchasing, and packaging.

R

RARE FRUIT COUNCIL INT'L., INC.
Museum of Science
13609 Old Cutler Rd.
Miami, FL 33158
305-238-1360

Contact: Frank Smathers, Jr., President
Purpose: To collect and disseminate information on cultural requirements and propagating techniques; to encourage plant breeding and bring into bearing tropical fruits that haven't previously been fruited in the local area; to promote interest in tropical fruit; to promote interest in rare tropical fruits.

RED ANGUS ASSOCIATION OF AMERICA*
Box 776
Denton, TX 76201
817-387-3502

Contact: Lyle V. Springer, Executive Director

REFRIGERATION RESEARCH FOUNDATION
7315 Wisconsin Ave.
Bethesda, MD 20814
301-652-5674

Contact: Richard M. Powell, Executive Director

RETAIL BAKERS OF AMERICA
Presidential Bldg.
Suite 250
6525 Belcrest Rd.
Hyattsville, MD 20782
301-277-0990

Contact: Richard C. Gohla, Executive Vice-President
Membership: Retail bakers and allied companies.
Purpose: To improve the relationship with the consuming public; to encourage the production of high quality, healthful bakery goods; to foster closer cooperation among American bakers; to represent the baking industry in its relations with government.

RETAIL BAKERS OF SOUTHERN CALIFORNIA*
c/o Wisateria Bake Shop
3887 E. Sierra Madre Blvd.
Pasadena, CA 91107
213-355-3332

Contact: Mike Sample, President

RETAIL MASTER BAKERS ASSOCIATION OF WESTERN PENNSYLVANIA
160 Clearview Ave.
Pittsburgh, PA 15229
412-931-3436

Contact: Jack Kort, Correspondence Secretary
Membership: 103 baker members, and 32 allied members.
Purpose: To improve the quality or retail baking and to promote the industry as a whole; to exchange ideas on successful techniques.

RHODE ISLAND MASTER BAKERS*
c/o DeLouise Bakery
1251 S. Chalkstone
Providence, RI 02908
401-351-5826

Contact: Anthony DeLouise, Board Chairman

RICE MILLERS ASSOCIATION*
Crystal Plaza One
Suite 808
2001 Jefferson Davis Highway
Arlington, VA 22202
703-920-1281

Contact: J. Stephen Gabbert, Executive Vice-President

ROCHESTER MILK DEALERS, INC.*
35 N. Washington Street
Rochester, NY 14614
716-232-6798

Contact: Louis Spinelli, President

ROCKY MOUNTAIN FOOD PROCESSORS ASSOCIATION*
800 Continental Bank Bldg.
Salt Lake City, UT 84101
801-531-8900

Contact: M. Byron Fisher

S

SALMON INSTITUTE*
c/o Evans Pacific Inc.
300 Elliott Ave., West
Seattle, WA 98119
206-284-8383

Contact: Larry Kaner, Chairman

SANTA CLARA COUNTY FOOD PROCESSORS ASSOCIATION
c/o California League of Food Processors
1007 L St.
Sacramento, CA 95814
916-444-9260

Contact: F. A. Davey, President

SANTA GERTRUDIS BREEDERS INTERNATIONAL
PO Box 1257
Kingsville, TX 78363
512-592-9357

Contact: Bill Warren, Executive Vice-President
Membership: 4,000.
Purpose: To maintain the records of the association; to provide leadership directed to the improvement of the Santa Gertrudis breed.

SELENIUM-TELLURIUM DEVELOPMENT ASSOCIATION
PO Box 3096
Darien, CT 06820
203-655-0470

Contact: M. S. Bell, President
Membership: 11 major producers of copper and other non-ferrous metals.
Purpose: To disseminate information about selenium and tellurium and to sponsor research projects leading to the greater utilization of these elements.

SHELLFISH INSTITUTE OF NORTH AMERICA*
400 N. Capital St.
Suite 323
Washington, DC 20001
202-783-2800

Contact: Josh Lanier

SINGLE SERVICE INSTITUTE
1025 Connecticut Ave., NW, #1015
202-347-0020

Contact: Joseph W. Bow, Executive Vice-President

SOCIETY FOR THE ADVANCEMENT OF FOOD SERVICE RESEARCH*
628 Anderson Ave.
Ft. Wayne, IN 46805
219-424-8462

Contact: Helen M. Spencer, Executive Secretary

SOCIETY OF FLAVOR CHEMISTS*
c/o Arthur D. Little
15 Acorn Park
Cambridge, MA 02140
617-864-5770

Contact: Lynne Wheeler, Secretary

SOCIETY FOR FOODSERVICE MANAGEMENT
310 West Liberty St.
Louisville, KY 40202
502-583-3783

Contact: Phillip Cooke, Executive Director
Membership: Those who maintain or operate employee foodservice and vending facilities.
Purpose: To provide opportunity for members to exchange ideas and information; to develop more economical methods of providing high quality, economical food and service; to keep the membership informed of pertinent governmental regulations and scientific advances; to assist members in solving specific operating problems; to promote employee foodservice programs as a contribution to better company/employee relations; to develop and encourage high standards among management personnel serving the industry.

SOCIETY FOR THE PROTECTION OF THE UNBORN THROUGH NUTRITION
17 N. Wabash, Suite 603
Chicago, IL 60602
312-332-2334

Contact: Jay Hodin, Executive Director
Purpose: Provides educational and other services designed to safeguard maternal/fetal and newborn health from malnutrition-induced complications; maintains a prenatal nutrition hotline.

SOCIETY OF SOFT DRINK TECHNOLOGISTS
1101 16th St., NW
Washington, DC 20036
202-833-2450

Contact: Harry E. Korab, Secretary-Treasurer
Membership: 850.
Purpose: To promote the application of science and technology to the soft drink industry; to enhance the promotion, development, and dissemination of soft drink technology; to encourage research and technical programs.

SOIL AND HEALTH SOCIETY
33 E. Minor St.
Emmaus, PA 18049
215-967-5171

Contact: Dr. Mark Schwartz, Executive Director
Membership: 3,500.
Purpose: To support research in health, diet, organic agriculture, and related areas of natural living.

SOIL SCIENCE SOCIETY OF AMERICA*
677 South Segoe Road
Madison, WI 53711
608-274-1212

Contact: Matthias Stelly, Executive Vice-President

RESOURCES FOR FURTHER INFORMATION 443

SOUTH DAKOTA BAKERS ASSOCIATION*
PO Box 144
Mitchell, SD 57301
605-996-6671

Contact: Marty Pemrick, Secretary

SOUTH DAKOTA STATE DAIRY ASSOCIATION
South Dakota State University
Dairy Science Department
Brookings, SD 57007
605-688-5420

Contact: Shirley Seas, Executive Secretary
Membership: Dairy product processing plants in South Dakota.
Purpose: To promote cooperative work among plants on legislation, problems, and regulations affecting the industry.

SOUTHEAST MASTER RETAIL BAKERS ASSOCIATION*
c/o Cakes, Cakes, Cakes, Inc.
Castle Park Shop Center
Valdosta, GA 31601
912-242-6142

Contact: Lillian Wilson, Secretary

SOUTHEAST UNITED DAIRY INDUSTRY ASSOCIATION, INC.*
1575 Phoenix Blvd.
Suite 1
Atlanta, GA 30349
404-996-6085

Contact: Gil Morgan, Executive Vice-President

SOUTHEASTERN FISHERIES ASSOCIATION*
124 W. Jefferson
Tallahassee, FL 32301
904-224-0612

Contact: Robert P. Jones

SOUTHEASTERN FOOD PROCESSORS ASSOCIATION
PO Box 73
111 W. Taylor St.
Griffin, GA 30224
404-227-2803

Contact: Albert Bloodworth, Jr., Secretary-Treasurer

Membership: Food processors in the southeastern U.S.
Purpose: To promote cooperation among members; to keep abreast of federal and state legislation affecting the industry.

SOUTHEASTERN PEANUT ASSOCIATION*
PO Box 1746
Albany, GA 31702
912-888-2508

Contact: John W. Greene

SOUTHEASTERN PECAN GROWERS ASSOCIATION*
1104 Friar Tuck Road
Starkville, MS 39759
601-323-5873

Contact: Mrs. Chesley Hines

SOUTHEASTERN POULTRY AND EGG ASSOCIATION
1456 Church St.
Decatur, GA 30030
404-377-6465

Contact: Harold E. Ford, Executive Vice-President
Membership: Producers of poultry products and allied industries.
Purpose: To identify and address the needs of the industry; to fund research; to conduct seminars and sponsor trade shows; to improve the production and welfare of the breeder.

SOUTHEASTERN WISCONSIN CHEESE ASSOCIATION
Route 1
St. Cloud, WI 53079
414-922-5374

Contact: Art Loehr, Secretary-Treasurer
Membership: 75.
Purpose: To promote the cheese industry.

SOUTHERN ASSOCIATION OF AGRICULTURAL SCIENTISTS
PO Box 1522
Tifton, GA 31794
912-382-7044

Contact: Donna J. Littrell, Secretary-Treasurer

Membership: Scientists from southern states.
Purpose: To share research.

SOUTHERN ASSOCIATION OF DAIRY FOOD MANUFACTURERS, INC.
PO Box 10506
Raliegh, NC 27605
919-834-8719

Contact: John E. Johnson, Executive Secretary-Treasurer
Membership: A trade association of dairy product processors in 14 southeastern states and the District of Columbia.
Purpose: To promote the production, processing, storage, distribution and sale of milk and dairy products; to foster high standards in the industry; to improve members' business; to promote and support government policies which promote the industry; to obtain and furnish data on the industry.

SOUTHERN BAKERS ASSOCIATION*
2970 Peachtree Road, NW
Atlanta, GA 30305
404-237-1849

Contact: James Stroupe

SOUTHERN FROZEN FOOD ASSOCIATION*
Fulton Federal Bldg.
Atlanta, GA 30303
404-577-5100

Contact: Mary Smith

SOUTHERN PEANUT WAREHOUSEMEN'S ASSOCIATION
PO Box 3706
Albany, GA 31706
912-883-2072

Contact: C. F. Harpole, Executive Director
Purpose: Education and information.

SOUTHWESTERN PEANUT GROWERS ASSOCIATION*
PO Box 338
Gorman, TX 76454
817-734-2222

Contact: Ross Wilson

SOUTHWESTERN PEANUT SHELLERS ASSOCIATION*
10 Duncannan Court
Dallas, TX 75225
214-692-3332

Contact: Sydney C. Reagan, Advisor

SOY PROTEIN COUNCIL
1800 M St., NW
Washington, DC 20036
202-467-6610

Contact: Sheldon J. Hauck, Executive Vice-President
Membership: Firms that process and sell vegetable proteins or food products containing vegetable proteins.
Purpose: To build awareness of the nutritional properties of commercially available vegetable proteins; to participate in formulating U.S. nutrition goals and policies; to assist government agencies, the public, and the food processing industry in understanding the role and use of vegetable protein; to promote food regulations that encourage maximum use of vegetable proteins.

SOYCRAFTERS ASSOCIATION OF NORTH AMERICA*
Sunrise Farm
100 Health Rd.
Colrain, MA 01340
413-624-5591

Contact: Richard Leviton, Executive Director

SUGAR ASSOCIATION, INC.
1511 K St., NW
Washington, DC 20005
202-628-0189

Contact: J. R. O'Connell Jr., President
Membership: Various segments of the U.S. sugar producing industry.
Purpose: A public information and education arm of the sugar industry.

SUN-DIAMOND GROWERS OF CALIFORNIA
1050 S. Diamond St.
Stockton, GA 95205
209-466-4851

Contact: Frank R. Light, President
Membership: 5,682.
Purpose: Non-profit cooperative which markets members' products.

SUN-MAID GROWERS OF CALIFORNIA*
13525 S. Bethel Ave.
Kingsburg, CA 93631

Contact: F. R. Light, President

SWITZERLAND CHEESE ASSOCIATION
444 Madison Ave.
New York, NY 10022
212-751-3690

Contact: Heinz P. Hofer, Manager
Membership: Farmers, cheesemakers and cheese exporters of natural Switzerland cheese.
Purpose: Trade association for Switzerland cheese.

T

TENNESSEE BAKERS ASSOCIATION*
609 Skyview Drive
Nashville, TN 37206
615-227-4668

Contact: R. L. Pettigrew, Secretary-Treasurer

TENNESSEE DAIRY PRODUCTS ASSOCIATION
Room 202
1719 W. End Ave.
Nashville, TN 37204
615-269-3236

Contact: T. H. Rose, Executive Secretary
Membership: 90% of the dairy industry in Tennessee.
Purpose: To promote dairy products.

TENNESSEE INDEPENDENT MEAT PACKERS ASSOCIATION
221 Graeme Dr.
Nashville, TN 37214
615-883-4583

Contact: Fred C. Powell, Executive Director
Membership: 29 packers/processors, 42 suppliers/servicers.
Purpose: To survey unfavorable state legislative activities; to maintain liaison with other meat packing associations; to give members an opportunity to exchange information and keep them advised of industry developments.

TEXAS ENVIRONMENTAL HEALTH ASSOCIATION
PO Box 187
Grand Prairie, TX 75051
214-263-5221

Contact: Burl Cockrell, R.S., Executive Secretary
Membership: Professional environmentalists, sanitarians, engineers, public health inspectors, associate public and industry physicians, veterinarians, and others interested in environmental health work.
Purpose: To be informed and work together to keep Texas healthy.

TEXAS FOOD PROCESSORS ASSOCIATION, INC.
PO Box 341
College Station, TX 77841
713-845-7023

Contact: Al Wagner

TEXAS LONGHORN BREEDERS ASSOCIATON OF AMERICA
3701 Airport Freeway
Ft. Worth, TX 76111
817-831-4377

Contact: J. Patrick Buchen, Executive Director
Membership: 2,000.
Purpose: To register and promote purebred Texas longhorn cattle; to educate the general public about the breed.

TEXAS SHRIMP ASSOCIATION
403 Vaughn Bldg.
Austin, TX 78701
512-476-8446

Contact: Ralph Rayburn, Executive Director
Membership: Shrimp harvestors operating primarily in the Gulf of Mexico.
Purpose: To insure product quality and maintain awareness of environmental matters; to improve government relations and provide information services.

TEXAS AND SOUTHWESTERN CATTLE RAISERS ASSOCIATION*
1301 W. 7th Street
Ft. Worth, TX 76102
817-332-7064

Contact: Don C. King, Secretary-General Manager

TOMATO GENETICS COOPERATIVE
Department of Horticulture
Purdue University
West LaFayette, IN 47907

Contact: E. C. Tigchelaar, Executive Officer
Membership: 400 international scientists.
Purpose: To promote the exchange of information and stocks in the area of tomato genetics and breeding.

TOP FARMERS OF AMERICAN ASSOCIATION*
225 E. Michigan
Milwaukee, WI 53202
414-276-6600

Contact: Cliff Ganschow, President

TUNA RESEARCH FOUNDATION*
1101 17th St., NW
Suite 603
Washington, DC 20036
202-296-4630

Contact: John P. Mulligan

U

UNITED DAIRY/ALLIED PURCHASING
Box 1249
Mason City, IA 50401
800-247-5956

Contact: R. E. Gildner, Executive Vice-President
Membership: 600 dairies, ice cream companies, and soft drink bottlers.
Purpose: Cooperative buying of equipment, ingredients, services, and supplies.

UNITED DAIRY INDUSTRY ASSOCIATION*
6300 N. River Road
Rosemont, IL 60018
312-696-1860

Contact: John W. Sliter, Executive Vice-President

UNITED EGG PRODUCERS*
3951 Snapfinger Parkway
Suite 580
Decatur, GA 30035
404-288-6700

Contact: Albert E. Pope, President

UNITED FRESH FRUIT & VEGETABLE ASSOCIATION
727 N. Washington St.
Alexandria, VA 22314
703-836-3410

Contact: John D. Nelson Jr., Vice-President
Membership: 2,500 growers, shippers, brokers, sales agents, wholesalers, retailers, and industry suppliers.
Purpose: To increase the sale and consumption of all fresh fruits and vegetables.

UNITED SOFT SERVE & FAST FOODS ASSOCIATION*
9934 Fall Creek Blvd.
Indianapolis, IN 46256
317-259-7551

Contact: O. J. Schneiders

UNITED STATES ANIMAL HEALTH ASSOCIATION
6924 Lakeside Ave.
Suite 205
Richmond, VA 23228
804-266-3275

Contact: J. C. Shook, Secretary
Membership: 1,200.
Purpose: To study and disseminate information on animal health science and milk and meat hygiene; to unify laws, regulations, and policies pertaining to milk and meat hygiene; to prevent transmissible animal diseases; to coordinate efforts among various animal regulatory organizations.

UNITED STATES BEET SUGAR ASSOCIATION
1156 15th St., NW
Suite 1019
Washington, DC 20005
202-296-4820

Contact: David C. Carter, President

UNITED STATES DURUM GROWERS ASSOCIATION
Heart of the Durum Country
Devils Lake, ND 58301
701-622-2079

Contact: L. A. Braunagel, Secretary
Membership: 2,200.
Purpose: To support agronomic research; to promote favorable production legislation; to expand consumption and to increase production; to review marketing methods and lower shipping costs.

US FEED GRAINS COUNCIL
1575 Eye St., NW
Suite 1000
Washington, DC 20005
202-789-0789

Contact: Darwin E. Stolte, President
Membership: Agribusiness and feed grain producer representatives.
Purpose: To stimulate the growth of overseas demand for surplus U.S. corn, sorghum, and barley.

UNITED STATES MEAT EXPORT FEDERATION*
7200 Stapleton Plaza
3333 Quebec Street
Denver, CO 80207
303-399-7151

Contact: Alan R. Middaugh, President

U.S. NATIONAL FRUIT EXPORT COUNCIL*
1133 20th St., NW
Washington, DC 20036
202-331-5900

Contact: Leonard K. Lobred, Secretary-Treasurer

U.S. TROUT FARMERS ASSOCIATION*
PO Box 171
Lake Ozark, MO 65049
314-365-2478

Contact: Tim Pilkington

U.S. WHEAT ASSOCIATES
1575 Eye St., NW
Suite 200
Washington, DC 20005
202-789-2110

Contact: Winston Wilson
Purpose: To establish, expand, and maintain markets throughout the world for all classes of wheat grown in the U.S.

UPPER PENINSULA DAIRY MANUFACTURERS ASSOCIATION*
4315 3rd Street
Menominee, MI 49858
906-863-5016

Contact: Mrs. C. Vocke, Executive Secretary

UTAH CATTLEMEN'S ASSOCIATION
150 S. 6th E.
Suite 10B
Salt Lake City, UT 84102
801-355-5748

Contact: Michael R. Sibbett, Executive Director
Membership: Western states cattle ranchers, associated feeders, and livestock markets.
Purpose: To promote and protect the cattle industry; to improve the quality of beef; to encourage and establish good marketing principles; to represent members in government.

V

VANILLA BEAN ASSOCIATION OF AMERICA*
47-22 Pearson Place
Long Island City, NY 11101
212-392-7800

Contact: Paul H. Manheimer, Treasurer

VANILLA INFORMATION BUREAU
Empire State Bldg.
Suite 634
New York, NY 10118
212-563-2670

Contact: Marshall W. Neale

VERMONT DAIRY INDUSTRY ASSOCIATION
University of Vermont
Burlington, VT 05405
802-656-2070

Contact: H. V. Atherton, Secretary-Treasurer
Membership: 250.
Purpose: To work for the welfare of the dairy industry.

VERMONT MAPLE INDUSTRY COUNCIL
Morrill Hall
University of Vermont
Burlington, VT 05405
802-656-2990

Contact: Donald McFeeters, Secretary-Treasurer
Membership: Maple processors and manufacturers and their allied industries.
Purpose: To promote cooperation among producers, packers, retailers, consumers, and equipment manufacturers; to study and solve problems of the industry.

VINEGAR INSTITUTE
5775 Peachtree-Dunwoody Rd.
Suite 500-D
Atlanta, GA 30342
404-252-3663

Contact: Larry Davenport, Executive Director
Purpose: To promote the interests of the vinegar industry; to increase the use of vinegar; to act as a voice for the industry in governmental and public relations matters; to keep members informed of research and legislation affecting the industry.

VINIFERA WINE GROWERS ASSOCIATION
Box P
The Plains, VA 22171
703-754-8564

Contact: R. de Treville Lawrence, Sr., President and Editor
Purpose: To produce a journal which informs and assists the home wine grower and maker.

VIRGINIA BAKERS ASSOCIATION
102 Twin Lake Ln.
Richmond, VA 23229
804-288-7683

Contact: George Nolde, Secretary-Treasurer
Purpose: To promote, foster, and encourage ethical standards relative to legislation that would affect the baking industry; to evaluate labor problems in the industry.

VIRGINIA FOOD PROCESSORS ASSOCIATION, INC.
1307 Palmer Dr.
Blacksburg, VA 24060
703-552-1453

Contact: Jane C. Cooler

VIRGINIA PEANUT GROWERS ASSOCIATION
PO Box 149
Capron, VA 23829
804-658-4573

Contact: Russell Schools, Executive Secretary

VIRGINIA POULTRY BREEDERS CLUB*
PO Box 207
Franklin, VA 23851
804-562-2646

Contact: Thomas I. Darden, Secretary-Treasurer

VIRGINIA-CAROLINA PEANUT ASSOCIATION*
PO Box 499
Suffolk, VA 23434
804-539-2100

Contact: W. Randolph Carter

W

WASHINGTON STATE APPLE COMMISSION
PO Box 18
Wenatchee, WA 98801
509-662-2123

Contact: Joe Brownlow, Manager
Membership: All apple growers in Washington.
Purpose: Advertising, promotion, and market development.

WATER & WASTEWATER EQUIPMENT MANUFACTURERS ASSOCIATION*
7900 Westpark Dr.
Suite 102
McLean, VA 22102
703-893-1520

Contact: Rick Harroun

WELSH BLACK CATTLE ASSOCIATION*
Route 1
Wahkon, MN 56386
612-767-3478

Contact: Max L. Allen, Secretary

WEST VIRGINIA BAKERS ASSOCIATION*
407 Cypress Dr.
Charleston, WV 26306
304-925-4674

Contact: W. Myron Eberly, Executive Secretary

WEST VIRGINIA DAIRY PRODUCTS*
West Virginia University
Agricultural Science Bldg.
Room 1504
Morgantown, WV 26506
304-293-2429

Contact: Paul Smith, Secretary-Treasurer

WESTERN GROWERS ASSOCIATION*
PO Box 2130
Newport Beach, CA 92663
714-641-5000

Contact: Daryl Arnold

WESTERN MICHIGAN RETAIL BAKERS
c/o Royal Dutch Bakery
3940 30th St.
Grandville, MI 49418
616-534-7041

Contact: Mart Steenstra, Treasurer
Membership: Bakers and suppliers in western Michigan.
Purpose: To keep bakers in western Michigan up to date on new and different products.

WESTERN STATES MEAT ASSOCIATION
88 1st St., Suite 201
San Francisco, CA 94105
415-982-2466

Contact: Rosemary M. Mucklow, Executive Vice-President & General Manager
Membership: Meat packers, slaughters, processors, sausagemakers, jobbers, and purveyors.
Purpose: A nonprofit trade association.

WHEAT FLOUR INSTITUTE
600 Maryland Ave., SW
Suite 305W
Washington, DC 20024
202-484-2200

Contact: C. Joan Reynolds, Director

WHEY PRODUCTS INSTITUTE
130 N. Franklin St.
Chicago, IL 60606
312-782-5455

Contact: Warren S. Clark, Jr.
Membership: Manufactuers and suppliers.
Purpose: To stimulate and conduct research for educating the public; to promote the utilization of whey products; to disseminate information.

WHITE PARK CATTLE ASSOCIATION
419 N. Water St.
Madrid, IA 50156
515-795-2013

Contact: Roy D. Adkisson, President
Membership: 141.
Purpose: To collect, verify, record, preserve, and publish pedigrees of White Park cattle; to promote interest in and publish information about the breed; to conduct breeding classes at shows and fairs.

WINE INSTITUTE*
165 Post Street
San Francisco, CA 94108
415-986-0878

Contact: John A. DeLuca, President

WISCONSIN BAKERS ASSOCIATION
161 W. Wisconsin Ave.
Room 510
Milwaukee, WI 53203
414-289-0669

Contact: Joseph Pipp, Executive Secretary
Purpose: To promote and protect the welfare of its members through improvement of bakery hygiene, industry promotion, legislative proposals, and public relations activities.

WISCONSIN CANNERS & FREEZERS ASSOCIATION*
PO Box 1297
Madison, WI 53701
608-255-9946

Contact: Alvin H. Randall

WISCONSIN CHEESE MAKERS ASSOCIATION
115 W. Main St.
Madison, WI 53703
608-255-2027

Contact: James E. Tillison, Executive Director
Membership: Cheese makers, plants, processors, wholesalers, distributors, and suppliers to the dairy industry.
Purpose: Trade association for the dairy industry, representing the nation's cheese makers and dairy industry in state and national lobbying.

WISCONSIN DAIRY PRODUCTS ASSOCIATION
2805 E. Washington Ave.
Madison, WI 53704
608-241-4973

Contact: Norm Maier, Executive Director
Membership: Cooperations, cooperatives, and proprietary plants.
Purpose: To represent members in formulating local, state, and federal laws and regulations affecting the industry; to protect the interests of consumers; to promote the use of milk and dairy products; to gather and provide information to members.

WISCONSIN GIFT CHEESE ASSOCIATION*
PO Box 26
Mt. Horeb, WI 53572
608-437-8600

Contact: Dean Roth, Executive Secretary

WISCONSIN SWISS & LIMBURGER CHEESE PRODUCERS ASSOCIATION*
1209 17th Ave.
Monroe, WI 53566
608-325-2507

Contact: Richard McKnight, President

WORLD HUNGER EDUCATION SERVICE*
2000 P St., NW
Suite 205
Washington, DC 20036
202-223-2995

Contact: Dr. Patricia L. Kutzner, Executive Director

WORLD HUNGER YEAR*
350 Broadway
Suite 209
New York, NY 10013
212-226-2714

Contact: Martin H. Rogol, Executive Director

WORLD POULTRY SCIENCE ASSOCIATION, USA BRANCH
U.S. Department of Agriculture
APHIS-VS
Beltsville, MD 20705
301-344-2227

Contact: Raymond D. Schar, Secretary-Treasurer
Membership: Scientists students, and lay people interested in the industry.
Purpose: To promote and exchange knowledge on all aspects of the poultry industry in the U.S. and overseas.

Colleges and Universities Offering Accredited Courses in Agriculture, Food, and Nutrition

by *Marquis Academic Media*

Two-year and four-year institutions of higher education in the United States and Canada that feature departments for all aspects of food—agriculture, nutrition, food technology, dietetics, etc.—are listed in this section. Institutions in the United States are identified primarily by member, candidate, or applicant accreditation status with one or more of the accrediting agencies that belong to the Council on Postsecondary Accreditation. (The key to accrediting agencies follows the listing of all schools). These nongovernmental voluntary agencies establish criteria, evaluate institutions at their request, and extend their approval to those whose purposes, resourses, and performance entitle them to the confidence of the educational community and the public. Institutions listed here are empowered to grant at least an Associate degree in the Arts (A.A.). Proprietary schools are listed if they have achieved junior college status with at least one accrediting agency.

Canadian institutions do not have a national accreditation program. Instead, each school holds a provincial charter that, in conjunction with membership in the Association of Universities and Colleges of Canada, constitutes the closest equivalent to accreditation.

Each complete entry provides the reader with a composite picture of the institution by supplying its address, phone number, year founded, affiliation or control, student body, and calendar system, along with accreditation information and the names of the chairpersons or departments that offer courses in food and nutrition and/or related areas.

In the listings, one asterisk indicates that the school did not supply updated information in 1981; two asterisks indicate the school did not supply updated information during 1980.

ALABAMA

ALABAMA AGRICULTURAL & MECHANICAL UNIVERSITY
Huntsville, AL 35762
205-859-7011

Founded 1875
Type 4-year
Control .... State
Calendar System .... Semester

Academic Dean
Dr. Winfred Thomas .... Sch of Agri, Envl Sci & Home Econ

Department and Division Heads
Dr. Prince Preyer .... Agribusiness Education
Dr. Gopal R. Sunki ...... Food Sciences & Technology
Ann Warren .... Foods & Nutrition

ALABAMA LUTHERAN ACADEMY & COLLEGE**
1804 Green Street
Selma, AL 36701
205-872-3053

Founded 1922
Type 2-year
Affiliation .... Lutheran Church-Missouri Synod
Accreditation .... SACS Cand 1977

Department Chairman
Gracie Hollins .... Home Economics

AUBURN UNIVERSITY
Auburn, AL 36830
205-826-4000

Founded 1856
Type 4-year
Control .... State
Calendar System .... Quarter
Accreditation .... SACS 1922/1973

Academic Dean
Ruth Galbraith .... Home Economics

Department Chairman
Bessie D. Fick .... Nutrition & Foods

JACKSONVILLE STATE UNIVERSITY
North Pelham Road
Jacksonville, AL 36265
205-435-9820

Founded 1883
Type .... 4-year, Graduate
Control .... State
Calendar System .... Semester
Accreditation .... SACS 1935/1972

Department Head
Louise R. Clark .... Home Economics

JUDSON COLLEGE
Marion, AL 36756
205-683-6161

Founded 1838
Type 4-year
Affiliation .... Southern Baptist
Accreditation .... SACS 1925/1973

Department Chairman
Margaret Putnam .... Home Economics

SAMFORD UNIVERSITY
800 Lakeshore Drive
Birmingham, AL 35229
205-870-2011

Founded 1841
Type .... 2-, 4-year, Graduate
Affiliation .... Alabama Baptist State Convention
Calendar System 4-1-4
Accreditation .... SACS 1975, NCATE, NLN, AALS, ABA, NASA

Department Chairman
Marion Ferguson .... Home Economics

UNIVERSITY OF ALABAMA
Rose Administration Building
University Boulevard
University, AL 35486

Founded 1831
Type .... 4-year, Graduate
Control .... State
Calendar System .... Semester
Accreditation .... SACS 1974

Academic Dean
Mary A. Crenshaw .... Sch of Home Economics

Department Chairperson
Vera Wall .... Food, Nutrition & Inst Mgmt

UNIVERSITY OF MONTEVALLO
Calkins Hall
Montevallo, AL 35115
205-665-2521

Founded 1896
Type .... 4-year, Graduate
Control .... State
Calendar System .... Semester
Accreditation .... SACS 1980

Department Head
Sara A. Bagby .... Home Economics

UNIVERSITY OF NORTH ALABAMA
Florence, AL 35632
205-766-4100

Founded 1872
Type .... 4-year, Graduate
Control .... State
Calendar System .... Semester
Accreditation .... SACS 1934/1971

Department Chairman
Florine K. Rasch .... Home Economics

* School did not supply update for this edition
** School did not supply update for this edition or for previous edition

ARIZONA

ARIZONA STATE UNIVERSITY
Tempe, AZ 85281
602-965-9011

Founded 1885
Type . . . . 4-year, Graduate
Control . . . . State
Calendar System . . . . Semester
Accreditation . . . . NCA 1931/1973
Department Chairmen
Richard R. Chalquest . . . . Agriculture
Helene M. Hoover . . . . Home Economics

ARIZONA WESTERN COLLEGE
P.O. Box 929
Yuma, AZ 85364
602-726-1000

Founded 1961
Type 2-year
Control . . . . State & Local
Calendar System . . . . Semester
Accreditation . . . . NCA 1978
Department Chairman
Esther Howe . . . . Home Economics

GLENDALE COMMUNITY COLLEGE
6000 West Olive Avenue
Glendale, AZ 85301
602-934-2211

Founded 1965
Type 2-year
Control . . . . State & Local
Calendar System . . . . Semester
Accreditation . . . . NCA 1967/1977
Department Chairman
Rosa Poling . . . . Home Economics

MESA COMMUNITY COLLEGE
1833 West Southern Avenue
Mesa, AZ 85202
602-833-1261

Founded 1965
Type 2-year
Control . . . . State & Local
Calendar System . . . . Semester
Accreditation . . . . NCA 1977
Department Chairman
Jo Wilson . . . . Home Economics

PHOENIX COLLEGE**
1202 West Thomas Road
Phoenix, AZ 85013
602-264-2492

Founded 1920
Type 2-year
Control . . . . State & Local
Calendar System . . . . Semester
Accreditation . . . . NCA 1926/1977
Department Chairman
Peggy Hartnell . . . . Food Services
Home Economics

NAVAJO COMMUNITY COLLEGE
Tsaile, AZ 86556
602-724-3311

Founded 1968
Type 2-year
Control . . . . Navajo Tribe
Calendar System . . . . Semester
Accreditation . . . . NCA 1976
Department Chairperson - Shiprock Campus
Kado Holiday . . . . Agriculture

UNIVERSITY OF ARIZONA
Tucson, AZ 85721
602-626-0111

Founded 1885
Type . . . . 4-year, Graduate
Control . . . . State
Calendar System . . . . Semester
Accreditation . . . . NCA 1917/1970
Academic Officer
Bartley Cardon . . . . Dean, Coll of Agriculture
Robert R. Rice . . . . Dir Sch of Home Economics

ARKANSAS

ARKANSAS STATE UNIVERSITY
State University, AR 72467
501-972-2100

Founded 1909
Type . . . . 4-year, Graduate
Control . . . . State
Calendar System . . . . Semester
Accreditation . . . . . . NCA 1928/1973, NASM, NLN 1970
AACSB, NCATE
Academic Dean
George A. Berger . . . . Agriculture

ARKANSAS TECH UNIVERSITY
Russellville, AR 72801
501-968-0237

Founded 1909
Type 2-, 4-year
Control . . . . State
Calendar System . . . . Semester
Accreditation . . . . . . NCA 1930/1981; NASM 1961/1981;
NCATE 1961/1981; AMA-CAHEA/MA 1981;
AMA-CAHEA/MRA 1980
Department Chairman
Kenneth Pippin . . . . Agriculture

HENDERSON STATE UNIVERSITY
Arkadelphia, AR 71923
501-246-5511

Founded 1890
Type 2-, 4-year
Control . . . . State
Calendar System . . . . Semester
Accreditation . . . . NCA 1934/1972
Department Chairman
Evelyn Good . . . . Home Economics

OUACHITA BAPTIST UNIVERSITY
OBU Box 753
Arkadelphia, AR 71923
501-246-4531

Founded 1886
Type 4-year
Control . . . . Private
Calendar System . . . . Semester
Accreditation . . . . NCA 1980
Department Chairman
Joyce Morehead . . . . Home Economics

SOUTHERN ARKANSAS UNIVERSITY
Magnolia, AR 71753
501-234-5120

Founded 1909
Type . . . . 4-year, Graduate
Control . . . . State
Calendary System . . . . Semester
Accreditation . . . . NCA 1929/1974
Department Chairman
John T. Attebery . . . . Agriculture

UNIVERSITY OF ARKANSAS, FAYETTEVILLE
Fayetteville, AR 72701
501-575-2000

Founded 1871
Type . . . . 2-, 4-year, Graduate
Control . . . . State
Calendar System . . . . Semester
Accreditation . . . . NCA 1924/1976
Academic Dean
Glenn W. Hardy . . . . Agriculture
Home Economics

UNIVERSITY OF ARKANSAS AT MONTICELLO
Monticello, AR 71655
501-367-6811

Founded 1909
Type 4-year
Control . . . . State
Calendar System . . . . Semester
Accreditation . . . . NCA 1980
Department Chairman
Gerald Brown . . . . Agriculture

UNIVERSITY OF ARKANSAS AT PINE BLUFF*
Pine Bluff, AR 71601
501-541-6500

Founded 1873
Type 4-year
Control . . . . State
Calendar System . . . . Semester
Accreditation . . . . NCA 1950/1976
Academic Dean
Sellers J. Parker . . . . Agriculture & Technology

UNIVERSITY OF CENTRAL ARKANSAS
Conway, AR 72032
501-329-2931

Founded 1907
Type 4-, 5-year
Control . . . . State
Calendar System . . . . Semester
Accreditation . . . . NCA 1931/1980
Department Chairman
Sue Thompson . . . . Home Economics

CALIFORNIA

BAKERSFIELD COLLEGE
1801 Panorama Drive
Bakersfield, CA 93305
805-395-4011

Founded 1913
Type 2-year
Control . . . . State & Local
Calendar System . . . . Semester
Accreditation . . . . WASC 1975/1978
Department Chairman
Lloyd Hokit . . . . Agriculture

BUTTE COLLEGE*
Pentz & Clark Roads
Oroville, CA 95965
916-895-2484

Founded 1966
Type 2-year
Control . . . . State & Local
Calendar System . . . . Quarter
Accreditation . . . . WASC 1972/1975
Division Chairperson
Frank E. Hutchinson . . . . Agriculture

CALIFORNIA STATE UNIVERSITY, CHICO
First & Normal Streets
Chico, CA 95929
916-895-6116

Founded 1887
Type . . . . 4-year, Graduate
Control . . . . State
Calendar System . . . . Semester
Accreditation . . . . WASC 1949/1979
Academic Dean
Lucas Calpouzos . . . . Agriculture
Home Economics

* School did not supply update for this edition
** School did not supply update for this edition or for previous edition

RESOURCES FOR FURTHER INFORMATION 451

CALIFORNIA STATE UNIVERSITY, FRESNO
Fresno, CA 93740
209-487-9011

Founded 1911
Type 4-year
Control .... State
Calendar System .... Semester
Accreditation .... WASC 1949/1979

Academic Dean
Charles M. Smallwood .... Agriculture
                                      Home Economics

CALIFORNIA STATE UNIVERSITY, LONG BEACH
1250 Bellflower Boulevard
Long Beach, CA 90840
213-498-4111

Founded 1949
Type .... 4-year, Graduate
Control .... State
Calendar System .... Semester
Accreditation .... WASC 1957/1977

Department Chairperson
Bonnie Rader .... Home Economics

CALIFORNIA STATE UNIVERSITY, LOS ANGELES
5151 State University Drive
Los Angeles, CA 90032
213-224-0111

Founded 1947
Type 4-year
Control .... State
Calendar System .... Quarter
Accreditation .... WASC 1954/1980

Department Chairman
Winona Brooks .... Home Economics

CALIFORNIA STATE UNIVERSITY, NORTHRIDGE
18111 Nordhoff Street
Northridge, CA 91330
213-885-1200

Founded 1958
Type .... 4-year, Graduate
Control .... State
Calendar System .... Semester
Accreditation .... WASC 1958/1980

Department Chairperson
Marjory Joseph .... Home Economics

CALIFORNIA STATE UNIVERSITY, SACRAMENTO
600 Jay Street
Sacramento, CA 95819
916-454-6301

Founded 1947
Type .... 4-year, Graduate
Control .... State
Calendar System .... Semester
Accreditation .... WASC 1951/1975

Department Chairperson
Cecilia D. Gray .... Home Economics

HUMBOLDT STATE UNIVERSITY
Arcata, CA 95521
707-826-3011

Founded 1913
Type .... 4-year, Graduate
Control .... State
Calendar System .... Quarter
Accreditation .... WASC 1970

Department Chairman
Emilla Tschanz .... Home Economics

SAN FRANCISCO STATE UNIVERSITY**
1600 Holloway Avenue
San Francisco, CA 94132
415-469-2141

Founded 1899
Type .... 4-year, Graduate
Control .... State
Calendar System .... Semester
Accreditation .... WASC 1949/1977

Department Chairman
Mai Nygren .... Home Economics

SAN JOSE STATE UNIVERSITY
Washington Square
San Jose, CA 95192
408-277-3456

Founded 1857
Type 4-year
Control .... State
Calendar System .... Semester
Accreditation .... WASC 1949/1979

Department Chairman
Sybil Weir (interim) .... Home Economics

CALIFORNIA POLYTECHNIC STATE UNIVERSITY, POMONA
3801 West Temple Avenue
Pomona, CA 91768
714-598-4592

Founded 1938
Type .... 4-year, Graduate
Control .... State
Calendar System .... Quarter
Accreditation .... WASC 1979

Academic Dean
Allen C. Christensen (acting) .... Agriculture

Department Chairmen
Floyd V. Matthews .... Agricultural Engineering
Ruby Beilby .... Foods, Nutrition & Home Econ

CALIFORNIA POLYTECHNIC STATE UNIVERSITY, SAN LUIS OBISPO
San Luis Obispo, CA 93407
805-546-0111

Founded 1901
Type 4-year
Control .... State
Calendar System .... Quarter
Accreditation .... WASC 1951/1975

Academic Dean
Howard C. Brown .... Agri & Natural Resources

Associate Dean
John W. West .... Agri & Natural Resources

Academic Department Heads
Davis S. Hatcher .... Agricultural Engineering
Robert D. Vance .... Food Science

CHRISTIAN HERITAGE COLLEGE
2100 Greenfield Drive
El Cajon, CA 92021
714-440-3043

Founded 1970
Type 4-year
Affiliation .... Independent Baptist
Calendar System .... Modular
Accreditation .... WASC Cand 1976

Academic Department Head
Patricia Ennis .... Home Economics

ORANGE COAST COLLEGE
2701 Fairview Road
Costa Mesa, CA 92626
714-556-5651

Founded 1948
Type 2-year
Control .... State & Local
Calendar System .... Semester
Accreditation .... WASC 1954/1974

Department Chairman
Gary James .... Agri & Biological Sciences

COLLEGE OF THE DESERT
43-500 Monterey Avenue
Palm Desert, CA 92260
714-346-8041

Founded 1958
Type 2-year
Control .... State & Local
Calendar System .... Semester
Accreditation .... WASC 1962/1977

Department Chairman
Elizabeth Lawson .... Home Economics

CONTRA COSTA COLLEGE**
2600 Mission Bell Drive
San Pablo, CA 94806
415-235-7800

Founded 1948
Type 2-year
Control .... Local
Calendar System .... Semester
Accreditation .... WASC 1952/1979

Department Head
Lucille Barcroft .... Home Economics

LOMA LINDA UNIVERSITY
Loma Linda Campus
Loma Linda, CA 92350
714-796-3741

La Sierra Campus
Riverside, CA 92515
714-785-2022

Founded 1905
Type .... 2-, 4-year, Graduate
Affiliation .... Seventh-day Adventist
Calendar System .... Quarter
Accreditation .... WASC 1937/1980

Department Chairman
John E. Carr .... Agriculture

AMERICAN RIVER COLLEGE*
4700 College Oak Drive
Sacramento, CA 95841
916-484-8011

Founded 1955
Type 2-year
Control .... State & Local
Calendar System .... Semester
Accreditation .... WASC 1959/1979

Assistant Dean
James Leavitt .... Home Economics

MERCED COLLEGE
3600 M Street
Merced, CA 95340
209-723-4321

Founded 1962
Type 2-year
Control .... State & Local
Calendar System .... Semester
Accreditation .... WASC 1964/1978

Division Chairman
Ken Heupel .... Agriculture

FULLERTON COLLEGE
321 E. Chapman Ave.
Fullerton, CA 92634
714-871-8000

Founded 1913
Type 2-year
Control .... State & Local
Calendar System .... Semester
Accreditation .... WASC 1977

Division Chairperson
Karen Lindstrom-Titus .... Home Economics

PACIFIC UNION COLLEGE
Angwin, CA 94508
707-965-6011

Founded 1882
Type .... 2-, 4-year, Graduate
Affiliation .... Seventh Day Adventist
Calendar System .... Quarter
Accreditation .... WASC 1951/1978

* School did not supply update for this edition
** School did not supply update for this edition or for previous edition

RESOURCES FOR FURTHER INFORMATION

Department Chairman
Ralph Wood............... Agriculture & Animal Sci.
Esther Ambs.................... Home Economics

POINT LOMA COLLEGE
3900 Lomaland Drive
San Diego, CA 92106
714-222-6474

Founded................................. 1902
Type....................................... 4-year
Affiliation................... Church of the Nazarene
Calendar System........................... Quarter
Accreditation.................. WASC 1949/1980
Department Chairman
Sandy Foster..................... Home Economics

SAN DIEGO MESA COLLEGE
7250 Mesa College Drive
San Diego, CA 92111
714-279-2300

Founded................................. 1962
Type....................................... 2-year
Control........................... State & Local
Calendar System.......................... Semester
Accreditation.......................... WASC 1974
Department Chairman
Andre Rouelle........... Food Services Occupations

CITY COLLEGE OF SAN FRANCISCO
50 Phelan Avenue
San Francisco, CA 94112
415-239-3300

Founded................................. 1935
Type....................................... 2-year
Control........................... State & Local
Calendar System.......................... Semester
Accreditation.................. WASC 1952/1972
Program Coordinator
Sandra Nager..................... Home Economics

SANTA MONICA COLLEGE**
1900 Pico Boulevard
Santa Monica, CA 90405
213-450-5150

Founded................................. 1929
Type....................................... 2-year
Control........................... State & Local
Calendar System.......................... Semester
Accreditation.................. WASC 1952/1976
Department Chairman
Grace Berry...................... Home Economics

SANTA ROSA JUNIOR COLLEGE
1501 Mendocino Avenue
Santa Rosa, CA 95401
707-527-4011

Founded................................. 1918
Type....................................... 2-year
Control........................... State & Local
Calendar System.......................... Semester
Accreditation.................. WASC 1952/1976
Department Chairmen
Steve Olson......................... Agriculture
Betty Blauw...................... Home Economics

SHASTA COLLEGE
1065 North Old Oregon Trail
Redding, CA 96001
916-241-3523

Founded................................. 1949
Type....................................... 2-year
Control........................... State & Local
Calendar System.......................... Semester
Accreditation.................. WASC 1952/1974
Division Director
Bill Burrows......................... Agriculture
                                Natural Resources

STANFORD UNIVERSITY
Stanford, CA 94305
415-497-2300

Founded................................. 1885
Type............................. 4-year, Graduate
Control.................................. Private
Calendar System........................... Quarter
Accreditation.................. WASC 1949/1981
Department Chairman
Walter P. Falcon........... Food Research Institute

UNIVERSITY OF CALIFORNIA, BERKELEY
Berkeley, CA 94720
415-642-6000

Founded................................. 1868
Type............................. 4-year, Graduate
Control.................................... State
Calendar System........................... Quarter
Accreditation.................. WASC 1949/1980
Department Chairperson
D.H. Calloway................. Nutritional Sciences

UNIVERSITY OF CALIFORNIA, DAVIS
Davis, CA 95616
916-752-1011

Founded................................. 1905
Type....................................... 4-year
Control.................................... State
Calendar System........................... Quarter
Accreditation.................. WASC 1954/1972
Academic Dean
Charles E. Hess........... Agricultural & Environ Sci
B.S. Schweigert........ Food Science & Technology

UNIVERSITY OF CALIFORNIA, RIVERSIDE
P.O. Box 112
Riverside, CA 92502
714-787-1012

Founded................................. 1907
Type............................. 4-year, Graduate
Control.................................... State
Calendar System........................... Quarter
Accreditation.................. WASC 1956/1978
Academic Dean
W. Mack Dugger.......... Natural & Agricultural Sci

VICTOR VALLEY COLLEGE
18244 Bear Valley Road
P.O. Drawer OO
Victorville, CA 92392
714-245-4271

Founded................................. 1961
Type....................................... 2-year
Control.................................... Local
Calendar System.......................... Semester
Accreditation.................. WASC 1963/1977
Department Chairmen
Robert Adams........................ Agriculture
Richard Smith...................... Food Service
Jo Ann Kroencke................. Home Economics

WEST HILLS COLLEGE
300 Cherry Lane
Coalinga, CA 93210
209-935-0801

Founded................................. 1932
Type....................................... 2-year
Control........................... State & Local
Calendar System.......................... Semester
Accreditation.................. WASC 1952/1978
Division Chairman
Tom Mora................. Agriculture Technology

WHITTIER COLLEGE
13406 Philadelphia Street
Whittier, CA 90608
213-693-0771

Founded................................. 1901

Type....................................... 4-year
Control.................................. Private
Calendar System............................. 4-1-4
Accreditation.................. WASC 1949/1980
Department Chairman
Frances Hoffmann................ Home Economics

MODESTO JUNIOR COLLEGE
College Avenue
Modesto, CA 95350
209-526-2000

Founded................................. 1921
Type....................................... 2-year
Control........................... State & Local
Calendar System.......................... Semester
Accreditation.................. WASC 1952/1978
Department Chairmen
Dr. Stanley Hodges........... Agriculture & Biol Scis
Jeanne Palmie......... Home Econs & Trade/Tech Ed

COLORADO

COLORADO STATE UNIVERSITY*
Fort Collins, CO 80523
303-491-6211

Founded................................. 1870
Type...................................... State
Control....................... 4-year, Graduate
Calendar System................ Modified Semester
Accreditation................... NCA 1925/1974
Academic Deans
Donal D. Johnson.............. Agriculture Sciences
Helen McHugh.................... Home Economics

NORTHEASTERN JUNIOR COLLEGE
Sterling, CO 80751
303-522-6600

Founded................................. 1941
Type....................................... 2-year
Control........................... State & Local
Calendar System........................... Quarter
Accreditation................... NCA 1964/1974
Division Chairman
Jim Piper............................ Agriculture

UNIVERSITY OF NORTHERN COLORADO
Greeley, CO 80639
303-351-1890

Founded................................. 1889
Type....................................... 4-year
Control.................................... State
Calendar System........................... Quarter
Accreditation........... NCA 1916/1975; NCATE 1965
Department Chairman
Marilyn Burns.................... Home Economics

CONNECTICUT

UNIVERSITY OF CONNECTICUT
Storrs, CT 06268
203-486-2000

Founded................................. 1881
Type............................. 4-year, Graduate
Control.................................... State
Calendar System.......................... Semester
Accreditation................... NEA 1931/1977
Academic Dean
Robert G. Ryder................. Home Economics

DELAWARE

DELAWARE STATE COLLEGE
Dover, DE 19901
302-678-4901

Founded................................. 1891

---
* School did not supply update for this edition
** School did not supply update for this edition or for previous edition

Type...4-year
Control..State
Calendar System........................Semester
Accreditation............................MSA 1972
Department Chairmen
Ulysses S. Washington...Agriculture & Nat Resources
Eva W. Adams....................Home Economics

UNIVERSITY OF DELAWARE
Newark, DE 19711
302-738-2000

Founded......................................1833
Type...............................4-year, Graduate
Control...............................State Assisted
Calendar System........................Semester
Accreditation............................MSA 1972
Department Chairmen
Ernest N. Scarborough.......Agriculture Engineering
Raymond C. Smith....Agriculture & Food Economics
Daniel F. Farkas....Food Science & Human Nutrition

DISTRICT OF COLUMBIA

GALLAUDET COLLEGE
7th and Florida Avenue, NE
Washington, DC 20002
202-651-5065

Founded......................................1864
Type...4-year
Control.......................................Private
Calendar System........................Semester
Accreditation........................MSA 1957/1977
Department Chairman
Kay Oman......................Home Economics

HOWARD UNIVERSITY
2400 6th Street, NW
Washington, DC 20059
202-636-6100

Founded......................................1867
Type...............................4-year, Graduate
Control.......................................Private
Calendar System........................Semester
Accreditation........................MSA 1921/1978
Department Chairman
Christine Weaver...................Clinical Nutrition

**UNIVERSITY OF THE DISTRICT
OF COLUMBIA***
4200 Connecticut Avenue, NW
Washington, DC 20008
202-282-7550

Founded......................................1975
Type..........................2-, 4-year, Graduate
Control............................District of Columbia
Calendar System........................Semester
Accreditation............................MSA 1979
Academic Deans
Joshua Kearney......................Food Science
Virginia Moore...................Home Economics

FLORIDA

OKALOOSA-WALTON JUNIOR COLLEGE
100 College Boulevard
Niceville, FL 32578
904-678-5111

Founded......................................1963
Type...2-year
Control...............................State & Local
Calendar System........................Semester
Accreditation........................SACS 1965/1971
Department Chair
Flora Conger......................Home Economics

PENSACOLA JUNIOR COLLEGE
1000 College Boulevard
Pensacola, FL 32504

904-476-5410

Founded......................................1948
Type...2-year
Control...............................State & Local
Calendar System........................Semester
Accreditation...................................SACS
Department Head
Peggy Morrison...................Home Economics

FLORIDA INTERNATIONAL UNIVERSITY
Tamiami Campus
Tamiami Trail
Miami, FL 33199
305-552-2000
Bay Vista Campus
Biscayne Boulevard at NE 151 Street
Miami, FL 33181
305-940-5700

Founded......................................1965
Type...4-year
Control..State
Calendar System........................Semester
Accreditation............................SACS 1974
Department Chairperson
Betty Morrow.....................Home Economics

FLORIDA STATE UNIVERSITY
Tallahassee, FL 32306
904-644-2525

Founded......................................1857
Type...4-year
Control..State
Calendar System........................Semester
Accreditation........................SACS 1915/1972
Academic Dean
Margaret A. Sitton..........Coll of Home Economics
Department & Program Chairmen
Natholyn Harris....................Food & Nutrition
Jane White.............Home Economics Education

UNIVERSITY OF FLORIDA
Gainesville, FL 32611
904-392-1311

Founded......................................1853
Type...4-year
Control..State
Calendar System........................Semester
Accreditation............................SACS 1971
Academic Dean
Gerald Zachariah......................Agriculture
Department Chairmen
Carl Beeman..........Agricultural & Extension Educ
Rush Choate...............Agricultural Engineering
J.R. Kirk................................Food Science
L. Polopolus...........Food & Resource Economics

GEORGIA

BERRY COLLEGE
Mount Berry, GA 30149
404-232-5374

Founded......................................1902
Type...............................4-year, Graduate
Control.......................................Private
Calendar System........................Quarter
Accreditation........................SACS 1957/1979
Department Heads
Clayton C. O'Mary.....................Agriculture
Catherine McDonald..............Home Economics

MORRIS BROWN COLLEGE*
643 Hunter Street, SW
Atlanta, GA 30314
404-525-7831

Founded......................................1881
Type...4-year
Affiliation..................African Meth Episcopal
Calendar System........................Semester
Accreditation........................SACS 1941/1979

Department Chairman
Jean Cooper........Home Econs & Restaurant Mgmt

UNIVERSITY OF GEORGIA
Athens, GA 30602
404-542-3030

Founded......................................1785
Type...............................4-year, Graduate
Control..State
Calendar System........................Quarter
Accreditation........................SACS 1971/1981
Department Chairmen
Robert H. Brown..........Agricultural Engineering
John Powers.........................Food Science

ABRAHAM BALDWIN AGRICULTURAL COLLEGE
Tifton, GA 31793
912-386-3236

Founded......................................1908
Type...2-year
Control..State
Calendar System........................Quarter
Accreditation........................SACS 1953/1975
Division Head
Frank S. McCain..........Agriculture, HE & Forestry

FT. VALLEY STATE COLLEGE
State College Drive
Fort Valley, GA 31030
912-825-6315

Founded......................................1895
Type...4-year
Control..State
Calendar System........................Quarter
Accreditation...............NCATE 1972; SACS 1969
Division Head
James I. Kirkwood.....................Agriculture
Dorothy B. Conteh................Home Economics

GEORGIA COLLEGE
Milledgeville, GA 31061
912-453-4444

Founded......................................1889
Type...............................4-year, Graduate
Control..State
Calendar System........................Quarter
Accreditation........................SACS 1925/1973
Department Chairman
Therry N. Deal....................Home Economics

GEORGIA SOUTHERN COLLEGE
Statesboro, GA 30460
912-681-5611

Founded......................................1906
Type...4-year
Control..State
Calendar System........................Quarter
Accreditation........................SACS 1935/1973
Department Chairman
Betty Lane.......................Home Economics

SAVANNAH STATE COLLEGE*
Savannah, GA 31404
912-356-2240

Founded......................................1890
Type...4-year
Control..State
Calendar System........................Quarter
Accreditation...SACS 1971; NCATE 1971; ECPD 1973
Department & Division Head
Diane Wagner.....................Home Economics

HAWAII

UNIVERSITY OF HAWAII AT MANOA
Honolulu, HI 96822
808-948-8111

---

* School did not supply update for this edition
** School did not supply update for this edition or for previous edition

Founded 1907
Type .... 4-year, Graduate
Control .... State
Calendar System .... Semester
Accreditation .... WASC 1952/1980

Department Chairmen
Barry Brennan (acting) ..... Agricultural Biochemistry
Chauncey Ching .. Agriculture & Resource Economics
M. Ray Smith .... Agricultural Engineering
Robert Van Reen .... Food & Nutritional Sciences
                                    Food Science & Technology
Elnora Huyck .... Home Economics

IDAHO

BOISE STATE UNIVERSITY
1910 University Drive
Boise, ID 83725
208-385-1011

Founded 1932
Type 2-, 4-year
Control .... State
Calendar System .... Semester
Accreditation .... NWA 1941/1974

Department Chairman
Elaine Long .... Home Economics

COLLEGE OF SOUTHERN IDAHO
PO Box 1238
Twin Falls, ID 83301
208-733-9554

Founded 1965
Type 2-year
Control .... State & Local
Calendar System .... Semester
Accreditation .... NWA 1968/1974

Department Chairman
Paul Wetter .... Agriculture & Animal Science

**EASTERN IDAHO VOCATIONAL-
TECHNICAL SCHOOL**
2299 East 17th Street
Idaho Falls, ID 83401
208-524-3000

Founded 1970
Type .... Vocational-Technical
Control .... State
Calendar System .... 5 terms
Accreditation .... NWA Cand

Department Head
Robert Welker .... Agriculture

RICKS COLLEGE
Rexburg, ID 83440
208-356-2011

Founded 1888
Type 2-year
Control .... Latter-day Saints (Mormon)
Calendar System .... Semester
Accreditation .... NWA 1936/1979

Department Chairman
Marlene Hatton .... Home Economics

UNIVERSITY OF IDAHO
Moscow, ID 83843
208-885-6111

Founded 1889
Type 4-year
Control .... State
Calendar System .... Semester
Accreditation .... NWA 1918/1974

Academic Dean
Raymond Miller .... Coll of Agriculture

Department Chairmen
Douglas Pals .... Agricultural Education
Delbert W. Fitzsimmons ..... Agricultural Engineering
Gladys Phelan .... Home Economics

ILLINOIS

BRADLEY UNIVERSITY
1501 West Bradley Avenue
Peoria, IL 61625
309-676-7611

Founded 1897
Type 4-year
Control .... Private
Calendar System .... Semester
Accreditation .... NCA 1913/1971

Department Head
Dr. Doris Wilson .... Home Economics

CARL SANDBURG COLLEGE
2232 South Lake Storey Road
PO Box 1407
Galesburg, IL 61401
309-344-2518

Founded 1966
Type 2-year
Control .... State
Calendar System .... Quarter
Accreditation .... NCA 1974/1981

Division Head
Don Crist .... Agriculture

CHICAGO STATE UNIVERSITY
Ninety-Fifth Street at King Drive
Chicago, IL 60628
312-995-2000

Founded 1867
Type 4-year
Control .... State
Calendar System .... Trimester
Accreditation .... NCA 1941/1977; NCATE

Department Chairperson
Rhea Shields .... Home Economics

EASTERN ILLINOIS UNIVERSITY
Charleston, IL 61920
217-581-2021

Founded 1895
Type 4-year
Control .... State
Calendar System .... Semester
Accreditation .... NCA 1915/1975

Department Chairman
Barbara Owens (acting) .... Home Economics

ILLINOIS CENTRAL COLLEGE
East Peoria, IL 61635
309-694-5011

Founded 1966
Type 2-year
Control .... State & Local
Calendar System .... Semester
Accreditation .... NCA 1972

Department Chairman
William Martinie .... Agriculture

ILLINOIS STATE UNIVERSITY
Normal, IL 61761
309-438-5677

Founded 1857
Type .... 4-year, Graduate
Control .... State
Calendar System .... Semester
Accreditation .... NCA 1913/1978

Department Chairpersons
George Forgey .... Agriculture
Bessie Hackett .... Home Economics

JOLIET JUNIOR COLLEGE
1216 Houbolt Avenue
Joliet, IL 60436
815-729-9020

Founded 1901
Type 2-year
Control .... Local
Calendar System .... Semester
Accreditation .... NCA 1917/1977

Department Chairman
Stanley Kosiba .... Agriculture

KISHWAUKEE COLLEGE
Malta, IL 60150
815-825-2086

Founded 1967
Type 2-year
Control .... State & Local
Calendar System .... Semester
Accreditation .... NCA 1974/1979

Department Chairman
Rollan Bonneau .... Agriculture

LAKELAND COLLEGE
U.S. 45 South
Mattoon, IL 61938
217-235-3131

Founded 1966
Type 2-year
Control .... State
Calendar System .... Quarter
Accreditation .... NCA 1973/1978

Division Chairman
Thomas Reedy .... Agriculture & Life Science

NORTHERN ILLINOIS UNIVERSITY
DeKalb, IL 60115
815-753-1000

Founded 1895
Type .... 4-year, Graduate
Control .... State
Calendar System .... Semester
Accreditation .... NCA 1974

Department Chairman
B.J. Johnston .... Home Economics

OLIVET NAZARENE COLLEGE
Kankakee, IL 60901
815-939-5011

Founded 1907
Type .... 2-, 4-year, Graduate
Affiliation .... Nazarene
Calendar System .... Semester
Accreditation .... NCA 1956/1975

Department Chairman
Rubalee Wickland .... Home Economics

ROSARY COLLEGE
7900 West Division Street
River Forest, IL 60305
312-366-2490

Founded 1901
Type .... 4-year, Graduate
Affiliation .... Roman Catholic
Calendar System .... Semester
Accreditation .... NCA 1919/1975

Department Chairman
Sr. Diona McNichols .... Home Economics

SHAWNEE COLLEGE**
Shawnee College Road
Ullin, IL 62992
618-634-2242

Founded 1967
Type 2-year
Control .... Independent
Calendar System .... Semester
Accreditation .... NCA 1974/1977

Department Chairman
Luther H. Hilterbrand .... Agri & Animal Science

**SOUTHERN ILLINOIS UNIVERSITY
AT CARBONDALE**
Carbondale, IL 62901
618-453-2121

* School did not supply update for this edition
** School did not supply update for this edition or for previous edition

RESOURCES FOR FURTHER INFORMATION

Founded 1869
Type. .... 4-year, Graduate, Profl
Control .... State
Calendar System. .... Semester
Accreditation. ... NCA 1969/1979; NASA; AACSB; APA;
ADA; ECPD; FID; SAF; ABSFE; ACEJ;
ABA; LCME; NASM; APTA; ASL-HA; CSWE;
NCATE 1977

Division/Department Head
Thomas R. Stitt. .... Agricultural Education

**UNIVERSITY OF ILLINOIS
URBANA-CHAMPAIGN**
Urbana, IL 61801
217-333-1000

Founded 1867
Type. .... 4-year, Graduate
Control .... State
Calendar System. .... Semester
Accreditation. .... NCA 1913/1969

Department Heads
Roger R. Yoerger. .... Agricultural Engineering
Arthur J. Siedler. .... Food Science
L. Ross Hackler. .... Food & Nutrition

WESTERN ILLINOIS UNIVERSITY
900 West Adams
Macomb, IL 61455
309-295-1414

Founded 1899
Type. .... 4-year, Graduate
Control .... State
Calendar System. .... Semester
Accreditation. .... NCA 1971/1981

Department Chairman
Nargis Sheikh. .... Home Economics

INDIANA

BALL STATE UNIVERSITY
2000 University Avenue
Muncie, IN 47306
317-289-1241

Founded 1918
Type. .... 2-, 4-year, Graduate
Control .... State
Calendar System. .... Quarter
Accreditation. .... NCA 1925/1974

Department Chairman
Helen Smith. .... Home Economics

GOSHEN COLLEGE
1700 South Main
Goshen, IN 46526
219-533-3161

Founded 1894
Type. 4-year
Affiliation. .... Mennonite
Calendar System. .... Trimester
Accreditation. .... NCA 1941/1975

Department Chairperson
Catherine Mumaw. .... Home Economics

INDIANA STATE UNIVERSITY
Terre Haute, IN 47809
812-232-6311

Founded 1865
Type. .... 4-year, Graduate
Control .... State
Calendar System. .... Semester
Accreditation. .... NCA 1915/1980

Department Chairman
Beverly Fowler. .... Home Economics

MANCHESTER COLLEGE
604 College Avenue
North Manchester, IN 46962
219-982-2141

Founded 1889
Type. 4-year
Control .... Church of the Brethren
Calendar System. 4-1-4
Accreditation. ...... NCA 1932/1973; NASM 1968/1973;
NCATE 1964/1973; CSWE 1977

Department Chairman
Brenda F. Sands. .... Home Economics

PURDUE UNIVERSITY
West Lafayette, IN 47907
317-494-8211

Founded 1869
Type. .... 2-, 4-year, Graduate
Control .... State
Calendar System. .... Semester
Accreditation. ... NCA 1913/1980; NLN; ASHA; AACSB;
ACS; APA; ABET; FAA; FID; SAF; ASLA;
ACPE; NCATE; AVA; ACCE; AALAC

Academic Dean
Bernard J. Liska. .... Sch Agriculture

Department Heads
Gerald W. Isaacs. .... Agricultural Engineering
Richard P. Abernathy. .... Foods & Nutrition

SAINT MARY-OF-THE-WOODS COLLEGE
Saint Mary-of-the-Woods, IN 47876
812-535-4141

Founded 1840
Type. 4-year
Affiliation. .... Roman Catholic
Calendar System. .... Semester
Accreditation. .... NCA 1919/1972

Department Chairman
Donna Palky. .... Home Economics

VALPARAISO UNIVERSITY
Valparaiso, IN 46383
219-464-5000

Founded 1859
Type. .... 4-year, Graduate
Affiliation. .... Lutheran Church-Missouri Synod
Calendar System. .... Semester
Accreditation. .... NCA 1929/1978

Department Chairman
E. Lucile Shabowich. .... Home Economics

IOWA

CENTRAL UNIVERSITY OF IOWA
812 University
Pella, IA 50219
515-628-4151

Founded 1853
Type. 4-year
Affiliation. .... Reformed Church in America
Calendar System. 3-3
Accreditation. .... NCA 1942/1974

Department Chairman
Mina M. Baker. .... Home Economics

MUSCATINE COMMUNITY COLLEGE
152 Colorado Street
Muscatine, IA 52761
319-263-8250

Founded 1929
Type. 2-year
Control .... State
Calendar System. .... Semester
Accreditation. .... NCA 1967/1977

Department Chairperson
Gary Apel. .... Agriculture

HAWKEYE INSTITUTE OF TECHNOLOGY
Box 8015
1501 East Orange Road
Waterloo, IA 50704
319-296-2320

Founded 1966
Type. .... State
Control 2-year
Calendar System. .... Quarter
Accreditation. .... NCA 1975/1980

Department Chairman
Virgil W. Christensen. ..... Agric & Natural Resources

IOWA LAKES COMMUNITY COLLEGE
101 North Sixth Street
Estherville, IA 51334
712-362-2601

Type. 2-year
Control. .... State & Local
Calendar System. .... Quarter
Accreditation. .... NCA 1976

Department Chairman
Robert J. Ford. .... Agriculture

**IOWA STATE UNIVERSITY OF
SCIENCE & TECHNOLOGY**
Ames, IA 50011
515-294-4111

Founded 1858
Type. .... 2-, 4-year, Graduate
Control .... State
Calendar System. .... Semester
Accreditation. .... NCA 1916/1976

Academic Dean
L.R. Kolmer. .... Coll of Agriculture

Department Chairmen
Howard P. Johnson. .... Agricultural Engineering
Jacqueline Dupont. .... Food & Nutrition
William W. Marion. .... Food Technology
R.P. Hughes. .... Home Economics Education

NORTH IOWA AREA COMMUNITY COLLEGE
500 College Drive
Mason City, IA 50401
515-423-1264

Founded 1918
Type. 2-year
Control .... Local
Calendar System. .... Semester
Accreditation. .... NCA 1968/1974

Division Chairman
Dean Nerdig. .... Agriculture

NORTHEAST IOWA TECHNICAL INSTITUTE*
Box 400
Calmar, IA 52132
391-562-3263

Founded 1966
Type. 2-year
Control. .... State & Local
Calendar System. .... Quarter
Accreditation. .... NCA 1977

Department Chairperson
Doyle Gorden. .... Agriculture

UNIVERSITY OF IOWA
Iowa City, IA 52242
319-353-2121

Founded 1847
Type. .... 4-year, Graduate
Control .... State
Calendar System. .... Semester
Accreditation. .... NCA 1913/1978; NASM; AACSB;
ADA; NCATE; ECPD; ABA; AMA-AAMC; NLN; ACPE;
ALA; CSWE; ACS; APA; ASHA

Department Chairman
Sara C. Wolfson. .... Home Economics

UNIVERSITY OF NORTHERN IOWA
Cedar Falls, IA 50613
319-273-2311

Founded 1876
Type. .... 4-year, Graduate
Control .... State
Calendar System. .... Semester

---

* School did not supply update for this edition
** School did not supply update for this edition or for previous edition

RESOURCES FOR FURTHER INFORMATION

Accreditation............... NCA 1971; NCATE 1973; NCA Doctoral 1978; ACS 1972; AHEA 1976; CSWE 1978; NASM 1942/69; ASLHA 1978; AAM 1976

Department Head
Mary Franken (acting)............. Home Economics

WESTMAR COLLEGE
1002 Third Avenue, SE
LeMars, IA 51031
712-546-7081

Founded 1890
Type...................................... 4-year
Affiliation...................... United Methodist
Calendar System..................... 14-2-14
Accreditation..................... NCA 1953/1975

Department Chairman
Janice Heckroth................. Home Economics

KANSAS

BAKER UNIVERSITY
606 Eighth Street
Baldwin, KS 66006
913-594-6451

Founded 1858
Type...................................... 4-year
Affiliation...................... United Methodist
Calendar System......................... 4-1-4
Accreditation................................. NCA

Department Chairman
Jan Brummell................... Home Economics

BENEDICTINE COLLEGE
Atchison, KS 66002
913-367-6110

Founded 1858
Type...................................... 4-year
Affiliation...................... Roman Catholic
Calendar System......................... 4-4-1
Accreditation......... NCA 1973/1978; NCATE; NASM

Department Chairman
Sr. Norma Honz.................. Home Economics

BETHEL COLLEGE
North Newton, KS 67117
316-238-2500

Founded 1887
Type...................................... 4-year
Affiliation............................. Mennonite
Calendar System......................... 4-1-4
Accreditation..................... NCA 1938/1979

Department Chairmen
Fremont Regier...................... Agriculture
Marjorie Warta................. Home Economics

FORT HAYS STATE UNIVERSITY
Hays, KS 67601
913-628-4000

Founded 1902
Type...................................... 4-year
Control....................................... State
Calendar System...................... Semester
Accreditation......... NCA 1915/1972; NCATE 1972; NASM 1968; NLN 1973

Department Chairman
W.W. Harris......................... Agriculture
June Krebs (acting)............... Home Economics

GARDEN CITY COMMUNITY JUNIOR COLLEGE
801 Campus Drive
PO Box 977
Garden City, KS 67846
316-276-7611

Type...................................... 2-year
Control....................................... Local
Calendar System...................... Semester
Accreditation..................... NCA 1975/1980

Department Chairman
Ira J. Mann........................ Agriculture

KANSAS STATE UNIVERSITY
Manhattan, KS 66506
913-532-6011

Founded 1863
Type.. State
Control..................................... 4-year
Calendar System...................... Semester
Accreditation.......................... NCA 1972
John Dunbar......................... Agriculture

Department Chairmen
Gus Fairbanks............. Agricultural Engineering
Jane Bowers................... Foods & Nutrition

MCPHERSON COLLEGE
1600 East Euclid Street
McPherson, KS 67460
316-241-0731

Founded 1887
Type...................................... 4-year
Affiliation.................. Church of the Brethren
Calendar System......................... 4-1-4
Accreditation..................... NCA 1921/1978

Department Chairperson
Connie Nichols.................. Home Economics

PITTSBURG STATE UNIVERSITY
Pittsburg, KS 66762
316-231-7000

Founded 1903
Type.. State
Control..................................... 4-year
Calendar System...................... Semester
Accreditation..................... NCA 1922/1973

Department Chairperson
Sue G. Hippensteel.............. Home Economics

SAINT MARY COLLEGE
4100 South 4th Street Trafficway
Leavenworth, KS 66048
931-682-5151

Founded 1923
Type...................................... 4-year
Affiliation...................... Roman Catholic
Calendar System....................... 14-4-14
Accreditation..................... NCA 1928/1977

Department Chairman
Sr. Dorothy Harvat............... Home Economics

WASHBURN UNIVERSITY OF TOPEKA
1700 College
Topeka, KS 66621
913-295-6300

Founded 1865
Type...................................... 4-year
Control.................................. Municipal
Calendar System...................... Semester
Accreditation..................... NCA 1913/1975

Department Chairman
Jennifer Cobb................... Home Economics

KENTUCKY

BEREA COLLEGE
College Post Office
Berea, KY 40404
606-986-9341

Founded 1855
Type...................................... 4-year
Control..................................... Private
Calendar System......................... 4-1-4
Accreditation..................... SACS 1926/1974

Department Chairmen
Dr. Robert Johnstone................. Agriculture
Marjorie Hylton................. Home Economics

EASTERN KENTUCKY UNIVERSITY
Lancaster Avenue
Richmond, KY 40475
606-622-0111

Founded 1906
Type...................... 2-, 4-year, Graduate
Control....................................... State
Calendar System...................... Semester
Accreditation.................... SACS 1928/1975

Department Chairmen
Dwight Barkley...................... Agriculture
Betty Powers.................... Home Economics

GEORGETOWN COLLEGE
Jackson Street
Georgetown, KY 40324
502-863-8011

Founded 1829
Type............................ 4-year, Graduate
Affiliation.................... Southern Baptist
Calendar System...................... Semester
Accreditation.................... SACS 1919/1972

Department Chairman
Elinor C. Hay.................... Home Economics

KENTUCKY STATE UNIVERSITY
East Main Street
Frankfort, KY 40601
502-564-2550

Founded 1886
Type............................ 4-year, Graduate
Control....................................... State
Calendar System...................... Semester
Accreditation......... SACS 1935/1978; NCATE 1975; NLN 1973

Department Chairman
Ruth King...................... Home Economics

MOREHEAD STATE UNIVERSITY
Morehead, KY 40351
606-783-2221

Founded 1922
Type............................ 4-year, Graduate
Control....................................... State
Calendar System...................... Semester
Accreditation.... SACS 1930/1980; NCATE 1969/1980; NASM 1965/1980; AVMA 1977/1980; CSWE 1977

Department Heads
(vacant)............................. Agriculture
Charlotte Bennett................ Home Economics

MURRAY STATE UNIVERSITY
Murray, KY 42071
502-762-3011

Founded 1922
Type............................ 4-year, Graduate
Control....................................... State
Calendar System...................... Semester
Accreditation.......................... SACS 1972

Department Chairmen
Charles Chaney (acting)............... Agriculture
Alice Koenecke.................. Home Economics

UNIVERSITY OF KENTUCKY
Lexington, KY 40506
606-258-9000

Founded 1865
Type...................................... 4-year
Control....................................... State
Calendar System...................... Semester
Accreditation.................... SACS 1915/1971

Academic Deans
Charles E. Barnhart.................. Agriculture
Marjorie S. Stewart............... Home Economics

Department Chairmen
John N. Walker............. Agricultural Engineering
Harold Binkley............... Agriculture Education

UNIVERSITY OF LOUISVILLE*
Belknap Campus
Louisville, KY 40208
502-588-5555

Founded 1798
Type............................ 4-year, Graduate

* School did not supply update for this edition
** School did not supply update for this edition or for previous edition

Control... State
Calendar System......................... Semester
Accreditation..... SACS 1915/1976; AMA-AAMC; APA;
AALS; ADA; CSWE; ECPD; NASM; NCATE;
ABA; ACS; NLN; AAALAC

Department Chairman
Clark F. Wood (acting)............. Home Economics

WESTERN KENTUCKY UNIVERSITY
College Heights
Bowling Green, KY 42101
502-745-0111

Founded...................................... 1906
Type... State
Control...................................... 4-year
Calendar System......................... Semester
Accreditation......... SACS 1926/1973; NCATE; NLN;
ECPD; NLN; ADA

Department Chairmen
Leonard D. Brown..................... Agriculture
William A. Floyd......... Home Econ & Family Living

LOUISIANA

GRAMBLIN STATE UNIVERSITY
OF LOUISIANA
Grambling, LA 71245
318-247-6941

Founded...................................... 1901
Type.............................. 4-year, Graduate
Control...................................... State
Calendar System......................... Semester
Accreditation......... SACS 1949/1980; NCATE 1979

Department Chairman
Dr. Geraldine Anderson............ Home Economics

LOUISIANA STATE UNIVERSITY
AT BATON ROUGE
Baton Rouge, LA 70803
504-388-5011

Founded...................................... 1860
Type.............................. 4-year, Graduate
Control...................................... State
Calendar System......................... Semester
Accreditation........................... SACS 1972

Department Chairmen
William H. Brown........... Agricultural Engineering
Auttis M. Mullins..................... Food Science
Neva F. Olson..................... Home Economics

LOUISIANA TECH UNIVERSITY
Ruston, LA 71272
318-257-3785

Founded...................................... 1894
Type.............................. 4-year, Graduate
Control...................................... State
Calendar System......................... Quarter
Accreditation........................ SACS 1927/1972

Department Chairman
J.W.D. Robbins............. Agricultural Engineering

MCNEESE STATE UNIVERSITY
Ryan Street
Lake Charles, LA 70609
318-477-2520

Founded...................................... 1939
Type..................... 4-year, Graduate, Prof
Control...................................... State
Calendar System......................... Semester
Accreditation........................ SACS 1954/1975

Department Chairmen
Harold Aymond......................... Agriculture
Barbara D. Coatney............... Home Economics

NICHOLLS STATE UNIVERSITY**
Nicholls University Station
Thibodaux, LA 70301
504-446-8111

Founded...................................... 1948

Type................................. 2-, 4-year
Control...................................... State
Calendar System......................... Semester
Accreditation........................ SACS 1964/1974

Department Chairmen
Carroll J. Falcon..................... Agriculture
Margaret V. Jolley............... Home Economics

NORTHEAST LOUISIANA UNIVERSITY
700 University Avenue
Monroe, LA 71209
318-372-2011

Founded...................................... 1931
Type.............................. 4-year, Graduate
Control...................................... State
Calendar System......................... Semester
Accreditation........................ SACS 1955/1978

Department Heads
James L. Cason....................... Agriculture
Marianna M. Kapp................ Home Economics

SOUTHEASTERN LOUISIANA UNIVERSITY
University Station
Hammond, LA 70402
504-549-2000

Founded...................................... 1925
Type.............................. 4-year, Graduate
Control...................................... State
Calendar System......................... Semester
Accreditation........................ SACS 1946/1973

Department Chairmen
Addison D. Owings.................... Agriculture
Rebecca Raburn................... Home Economics

SOUTHERN UNIVERSITY & AGRICULTURAL
& MECHANICAL COLLEGE
Southern Branch Post Office
Baton Rouge, LA 70813
504-771-4500, 771-2011

Founded...................................... 1880
Type.............................. 4-year, Graduate
Control...................................... State
Calendar System......................... Semester
Accreditation........................ SACS 1937/1980

Academic Deans
Leroy Davis........................... Agriculture
Eula D. Masingale............... Home Economics

Department Chairperson
Bernestine McGee............... Food & Nutrition

UNIVERSITY OF SOUTHWESTERN LOUISIANA
East University Avenue
Lafayette, LA 70504
318-264-6000

Founded...................................... 1898
Type........................... 2-, 4-year, Graduate
Control...................................... State
Calendar System......................... Semester
Accreditation........................ SACS 1925/1980

Department Heads
Stephen Langlinais....... Agricultural Engineering
Miriam S. Gurman............... Home Economics

MAINE

UNIVERSITY OF MAINE AT FARMINGTON
86 Main Street
Farmington, ME 04938
207-778-3501

Founded...................................... 1864
Type... 4-year
Control...................................... State
Calendar System......................... Semester
Accreditation.......... NEA 1971/1976; NCATE 1971

Department Chairman
Virginia T. Morrell...... Home Economics & Dietetics

UNIVERSITY OF MAINE AT ORONO
Orono, Maine 04469
207-581-1110

Founded...................................... 1865
Type.............................. 4-year, Graduate
Control...................................... State
Calendar System......................... Semester
Accreditation........................ NEA 1929/1977

Department Chairmen
Norman Smith............ Agricultural Engineering
Elizabeth Barden..................... Food Science

MARYLAND

COLUMBIA UNION COLLEGE**
7600 Flower Avenue
Takoma Park, MD 20012
301-270-9200

Founded......................................1904
Type................................. 2-, 4-year
Affiliation................... Seventh-Day Adventist
Calendar System......................... Trimester
Accreditation........................ MSA 1942/1971

Department Chairman
Margaret E. Wright............... Home Economics

HOOD COLLEGE
Rosemont Avenue
Frederick, MD 21701
301-663-3131

Founded...................................... 1893
Type... 4-year
Control...................................... Private
Calendar System......................... Semester
Accreditation........................ MSA 1922/1973

Department Chairperson
Donna Cowan................... Home Economics

MORGAN STATE UNIVERSITY*
Cold Spring Lane and Hillen Road
Baltimore, MD 21239
301-444-3200

Founded...................................... 1867
Type.............................. 4-year, Graduate
Control...................................... State
Calendar System......................... Semester
Accreditation........................ MSA 1925/1978

Department Chairperson
Herma Williams................. Home Economics

UNIVERSITY OF MARYLAND
COLLEGE PARK CAMPUS
College Park, MD 20742
301-454-0100

Founded...................................... 1807
Type.............................. 4-year, Graduate
Control...................................... State
Calendar System......................... Semester
Accreditation........................ MSA 1921/1976

Academic Dean
Earl H. Brown.................... Coll of Agriculture

UNIVERSITY OF MARYLAND
EASTERN SHORE
Princess Anne, MD 21853
301-651-2200

Founded...................................... 1886
Type.............................. 4-year, Graduate
Control...................................... State
Calendar System......................... Semester
Accreditation........................ MSA 1937/1976

Department Chairman
F. Harrell Smith....................... Agriculture

MASSACHUSETTS

ATLANTIC UNION COLLEGE
South Lancaster, MA 01561
617-365-4561

* School did not supply update for this edition
** School did not supply update for this edition or for previous edition

Type.. 2-, 4-year
Affiliation.................... Seventh-day Adventist
Calendar System........................... Semester
Accreditation........................... NEA 1978

Department Chairman
Sharlene Tessler................. Home Economics

FRAMINGHAM STATE COLLEGE
100 State Street
Framingham, MA 01701
617-620-1220

Founded 1839
Type... 4-year
Control.. State
Calendar System........................... Semester
Accreditation................ NEA 1950/1974; NCATE

Department Chairman
Joan Broadcorens.............. Home Economics

SIMMONS COLLEGE
300 The Fenway
Boston, MA 02115
617-738-2000

Founded 1899
Type... 4-year
Control...................................... Private
Calendar System........................... Semester
Accreditation........... NEA 1929/1969; ALA; CSWE;
AMA-AAMC; APTA

Department Chairman
Patricia Kreutler....................... Nutrition

UNIVERSITY OF MASSACHUSETTS AMHERST
Whitmore Administration Building
Amherst, MA 01003
413-545-0111

Founded 1863
Type........................... 2-, 4-year, Graduate
Control.. State
Calendar System........................... Semester
Accreditation........................ NEA 1932/1979

Academic Dean
James B. Kring (acting).... Food & Natural Resources

Department Chairmen
Joe T. Clayton....... Food & Agricultural Engineering
R. Glenn Brown............ Food Science & Nutrition

MICHIGAN

ADRIAN COLLEGE
110 South Madison Street
Adrian, MI 49221
517-265-5161

Founded 1859
Type... 4-year
Affiliation................................. Methodist
Calendar System........................... Semester
Accreditation............ NCA 1958/1979; NCATE 1979

Department Chairman
Rosalie M. Warrick............... Home Economics

ANDREWS UNIVERSITY
Berrien Springs, MI 49104
616-471-7771

Founded 1874
Type............................... 4-year, Graduate
Affiliation.................... Seventh-day Adventist
Calendar System............................ Quarter
Accreditation.......... NCA 1922/1972; NCATE; ACS;
NASM; NLN; CSWE; ASCP; ADA; ATS

Department Chairmen
Bernard C. Anderson.................... Agriculture
Fonda L. Chaffee................. Home Economics

CENTRAL MICHIGAN UNIVERSITY
Mount Pleasant, MI 48859
517-774-3151

Founded 1892
Type............................... 4-year, Graduate
Control.. State
Calendar System........................... Semester
Accreditation................ NCA 1915/1973; NCATE

Department Chairperson
Janis Voege...................... Home Economics

EASTERN MICHIGAN UNIVERSITY
Ypsilanti, MI 48197
313-487-1849

Founded 1849
Type............................... 4-year, Graduate
Control.. State
Calendar System........................... Trimester
Accreditation........................ NCA 1915/1976

Department Chairman
Billie Louise Sands............... Home Economics

MADONNA COLLEGE
36600 Schoolcraft Road
Livonia, MI 48150
313-591-5000

Founded 1947
Type... 4-year
Affiliation......................... Roman Catholic
Calendar System........................... Semester
Accreditation........................ NCA 1959/1978

Division of Natural Sciences & Mathematics
Sr. Mary Bridget..... Home Economics, Dietetic Tech

MERCY COLLEGE OF DETROIT
8200 West Outer Drive
Detroit, MI 48219
313-592-6000

Founded 1941
Type... 4-year
Affiliation................ Religious Sisters of Mercy
Calendar System........................... Semester
Accreditation........................ NCA 1951/1980

Department Chairperson
Barbara MacDonald............... Home Economics

MICHIGAN STATE UNIVERSITY
East Lansing, MI 48824
517-355-1855

Founded 1855
Type............................... 4-year, Graduate
Control.. State
Calendar System............................ Quarter
Accreditation........................ NCA 1965/1975

Academic Dean
James H. Anderson........ Agri & Natural Resources

WESTERN MICHIGAN UNIVERSITY
Kalamazoo, MI 49008
616-383-1600

Founded 1903
Type... 4-year
Control.. State
Calendar System........................... Trimester
Accreditation........................ NCA 1915/1971

Department Chairmen
Lee O. Baker.......................... Agriculture
Sue S. Coates.................... Home Economics

MINNESOTA

COLLEGE OF ST. CATHERINE
2004 Randolph Avenue
St. Paul, MN 55105
612-690-6000

Founded 1905
Type... 4-year
Affiliation......................... Roman Catholic
Calendar System............................. 4-1-4
Accreditation............................. NCA 1974

Department Chairman
Sr. Catherine Mary Stensrud....... Home Economics

COLLEGE OF ST. SCHOLASTICA
1200 Kenwood Avenue
Duluth, MN 55811
218-723-6000

Founded 1912
Type... 4-year
Affiliation......................... Roman Catholic
Calendar System............................ Quarter
Accreditation........................ NCA 1931/1973

Department Chairman
Sr. Johnette Maher................ Home Economics

CONCORDIA COLLEGE
Moorhead, MN 56560
218-299-4321

Founded 1891
Type... 4-year
Affiliation..................... American Lutheran
Calendar System........................... Semester
Accreditation........................ NCA 1927/1974

Department Chairman
Winnie Sandal.................... Home Economics

MANKATO STATE UNIVERSITY
South Road and Ellis Avenue
Mankato, MN 56001
507-389-1111

Founded 1867
Type... 4-year
Control.. State
Calendar System............................ Quarter
Accreditation........... NCA 1916/1976; NCATE 1954

Department Chairperson
Ruth McNeal..................... Home Economics

ST. OLAF COLLEGE
Northfield, MN 55057
507-663-2222

Founded 1874
Type... 4-year
Affiliation..................... American Lutheran
Calendar System............................. 4-1-4
Accreditation................ NCA 1915/1973; NCATE

Department Chairman
George Holt...................... Home Economics

UNIVERSITY OF MINNESOTA
Minneapolis, MN 55455
612-373-2851

Founded 1851
Type........................... 2-, 4-year, Graduate
Control.. State
Calendar System............................ Quarter
Accreditation............................. NCA 1977

Academic Dean
James F. Tammen................ Coll of Agriculture

Department Chairmen
Arnold Flikke............. Agricultural Engineering
Elwood Caldwell........... Food Science & Nutrition

UNIVERSITY OF MINNESOTA TECHNICAL COLLEGE, WASECA
Waseca, MN 56093
507-835-1000

Founded 1969
Type... 2-year
Control.. State
Calendar System............................ Quarter
Accreditation........................ NCA 1975/1978

Academic Coordinators
Byron Harrison............. Agricultural Production
William Coleman........ Food Industry & Technology

MISSISSIPPI

BELHAVEN COLLEGE
Jackson, MS 39202
601-352-0013

---

* School did not supply update for this edition
** School did not supply update for this edition or for previous edition

Founded..1883
Type..4-year
Affiliation................................Presbyterian
Calendar System.........................Semester
Accreditation.............SACS 1946/1976; NASM

Department Chairman
Mary Parker Harmon................Home Economics

BLUE MOUNTAIN COLLEGE
Box 338
Blue Mountain, MS 38610
601-685-5711

Founded..1873
Type..4-year
Affiliation...........................Southern Baptist
Calendar System.........................Semester
Accreditation........................SACS 1927/1981

Department Chairman
Candace Carrie....................Home Economics

DELTA STATE UNIVERSITY
Kethley Hall
Cleveland, MS 38733
601-846-6664

Founded..1924
Type................................4-year, Graduate
Control..State
Calendar System.........................Semester
Accreditation.............SACS 1930/1973; ACTE 1929

Department Chairman
Sarah R. Jordan...................Home Economics

HINDS JUNIOR COLLEGE
Raymond, MS 39154
601-857-5261

Founded..1917
Type..2-year
Control.................................State & Local
Calendar System.........................Semester
Accreditation........................SACS 1928/1974

Department Chairmen
Thad Owens............................Agriculture
Robbie Dukes......................Home Economics

HOLMES JUNIOR COLLEGE**
Goodman, MS 39079
601-472-2312

Founded..1925
Type..2-year
Control.................................State & Local
Calendar System.........................Semester
Accreditation........................SACS 1934/1974

Department Chairman
O.A. Cleveland.........................Agriculture

ITAWAMBA JUNIOR COLLEGE
Fulton, MS 38843
601-862-3101

Founded..1948
Type..2-year
Control.................................State & Local
Calendar System.........................Semester
Accreditation........................SACS 1955/1976

Department Chairmen
Charles Stone..........................Agriculture
Karen McFerring...................Home Economics

MISSISSIPPI STATE UNIVERSITY
Mississippi State, MS 39762
601-325-3221

Founded..1878
Type................................4-year, Graduate
Control..State
Calendar System.........................Semester
Accreditation........................SACS 1926/1972

Department Chairmen
William R. Fox........Agrl & Biological Engineering
Jean K. Snyder....................Home Economics

NORTHEAST MISSISSIPPI JUNIOR COLLEGE
Cunningham Boulevard
Booneville, MS 38829
601-728-7751

Founded..1941
Type..2-year
Control.................................State & Local
Calendar System.........................Semester
Accreditation........................SACS 1956/1980

Department Chairmen
W.D. Clifton............Agriculture & Animal Science
Barbara McCoy....................Home Economics

NORTHWEST MISSISSIPPI JUNIOR COLLEGE**
Senatobia, MS 38668
601-562-5262

DeSoto Center
Southaven, MS 38668
601-342-1570

Founded..1927
Type..2-year
Control.................................State & Local
Calendar System.........................Semester
Accreditation........................SACS 1953/1976

Department Chairman
Allen Holiday..........................Agriculture

UNIVERSITY OF MISSISSIPPI, OXFORD CAMPUS
University, MS 38677
601-232-7111

Founded..1848
Type................................4-year, Graduate
Control..State
Calendar System.........................Semester
Accreditation........................SACS 1895/1978

Department Chairman
Willie Wilson Price (acting).........Home Economics

UNIVERSITY OF SOUTHERN MISSISSIPPI
Southern Station, Box 1
Hattiesburg, MS 39041
601-266-7311

Founded..1910
Type...........................2-, 4-year, Graduate
Control..State
Calendar System.........................Semester
Accreditation........................SACS 1929/1974

Department Chairman
(vacant).................Home Economics Education

WILLIAM CAREY COLLEGE
Tuscan Avenue
Hattiesburg, MS 39041
601-582-5051

Founded..1906
Type......................................4-year Graduate
Affiliation...........................Southern Baptist
Calendar System.........................Semester
Accreditation........................SACS 1958/1978

Department Chairman
Evelyn McClure....................Home Economics

MISSOURI

CROWDER COLLEGE
Neosho, MO 64850
417-541-3223

Founded..1963
Type..2-year
Control.................................State & Local
Calendar System.........................Semester
Accreditation.................................NCA 1977

Department Chairman
Hugh Hardie...........Agriculture & Animal Science

DRURY COLLEGE
900 North Benton Avenue
Springfield, MO 65802
417-865-8731

Founded..1873
Type................................4-year, Graduate
Control..Private
Calendar System..............................4-1-4
Accreditation........................NCA 1915/1976

Department Chairman
Eleanor Beck......................Home Economics

EAST CENTRAL MISSOURI JUNIOR COLLEGE
Union, MO 63084
314-583-5193

Founded..1968
Type..2-year
Control..Local
Calendar System.........................Semester
Accreditation.................................NCA 1976

Department Chairperson
Hugh D. Hardie.........................Agriculture

FONTBONNE COLLEGE
6800 Wydown Boulevard
St. Louis, MO 63105
314-862-3456

Founded..1923
Type..4-year
Affiliation........................Roman Catholic
Calendar System.........................Semester
Accreditation.....NCA 1926/1981; NCATE 1968/1981;
NASM; AHEA

Deparment Chairman
Sr. Mary Carol Anth................Home Economics

MISSOURI WESTERN STATE COLLEGE
4525 Downs Drive
St. Joseph, MO 64507
816-271-4000

Founded..1915
Type..4-year
Control..State
Calendar System.........................Semester
Accreditation......NCA 1975/1980; NCATE 1973/1979

Department Chairperson
Glen Johnson..........................Agriculture

NORTHEAST MISSOURI STATE UNIVERSITY
Kirksville, MO 63501
816-785-4000

Founded..1867
Type................................4-year, Graduate
Control..State
Calendar System.........................Semester
Accreditation.................................NCA 1975

Department Chairman
Lydia Inman......................Home Economics

ST. LOUIS UNIVERSITY
221 North Grand Boulevard
St. Louis, MO 63103
314-535-3300

Type...........................2-, 4-year, Graduate
Affiliation........................Roman Catholic
Calendar System.........................Semester
Accreditation........................NCA 1916/1972

Department Chairman
Audrey M. Wattler.........................Dietetics

THE SCHOOL OF THE OZARKS
Point Lookout, MO 65726
417-334-6411

Founded..1906
Type..4-year
Affiliation....................Interdenominational
Calendar System..........................Trimester
Accreditation...........NCA 1961/1971; NASM 1976;
NCATE 1978/1980

Department Chairmen
Marvin E. Oetting......................Agriculture
Delores H. Stanford................Home Economics

* School did not supply update for this edition
** School did not supply update for this edition or for previous edition

460 RESOURCES FOR FURTHER INFORMATION

SOUTHEAST MISSOURI STATE UNIVERSITY
Cape Girardeau, MO 63701
314-651-2000

Founded 1873
Type .... 2-, 4-year, Graduate
Control .... State
Calendar System .... Semester
Accreditation .... NCA 1915/1973

College of Applied Arts & Sciences
Dr. William Meyer .... Agriculture
Grace Hoover .... Home Economics

SOUTHWEST MISSOURI STATE UNIVERSITY
901 South National
Springfield, MO 65802
417-836-5000

Founded 1905
Type .... 4-year, Graduate
Control .... State
Calendar System .... Semester
Accreditation .... NCA 1915/1976

Department Chairmen
Anson Elliot .... Agriculture
Jacquelyn E. Ledbetter .... Food Science

TRENTON JUNIOR COLLEGE**
1301 Main Street
Trenton, MO 64683
816-359-3948

Founded 1925
Type 2-year
Control .... Local
Calendar System .... Other
Accreditation 3IC

Department Chairman
Don Claycomb .... Agriculture & Animal Science

UNIVERSITY OF MISSOURI, COLUMBIA
Columbia, MO 65211
314-882-2121

Founded 1839
Type .... 4-year, Graduate
Control .... State
Calendar System .... Semester
Accreditation .... NCA 1913/1975

Academic Deans
Max Lennon .... Agriculture
Bea Litherland .... Home Economics

Department Chairpersons
C. LeRoy Day .... Agricultural Engineering
H. Donald Naumann .... Food Science & Nutrition
Richard Dowdy ...... Human Nutrition, Foods & Food
                                     Systems Management

MONTANA

MONTANA STATE UNIVERSITY
Montana Hall
Bozeman, MT 59717
406-994-0211

Founded 1893
Type .... 4-year, Graduate
Control .... State
Calendar System .... Quarter
Accreditation .... NWA 1932/1980

Department Chairmen
William Larsen .... Agricultural Engineering
Margaret Briggs .... Home Economics

NORTHERN MONTANA COLLEGE
PO Box 751
Havre, MT 59501
406-265-7821

Founded 1929
Type 4-year
Control .... State
Calendar System .... Quarter
Accreditation .... NWA 1972/1977; NCATE 1972

Department Chairman
David W. Watkins .... Agriculture

UNIVERSITY OF MONTANA
Missoula, MT 59812
406-243-0211

Founded 1893
Type .... 4-year, Graduate
Control .... State
Calendar System .... Quarter
Accreditation .... NWA 1932/1978

Department Chairperson
Sara Steensland .... Home Economics

NEBRASKA

KEARNEY STATE COLLEGE
905 West 25th Street
Kearney, NE 68847
308-236-4141

Type .... 4-year, Graduate
Control .... State
Calendar System .... Semester
Accreditation .... NCA 1916/1974; NCATE; NASM

Department Chairman
Wilma Larsen .... Home Economics

NORTHEAST TECHNICAL COMMUNITY COLLEGE
801 East Benjamin
Norfolk, NE 68701
402-371-2020

Founded 1973
Type 2-year
Control .... State & Local
Calendar System .... Semester
Accreditation .... NCA 1979

Department Chairman
Charles Pohlman .... Agriculture

UNIVERSITY OF NEBRASKA AT LINCOLN
14th and R Streets
Lincoln, NE 68588
402-472-7211

Founded 1869
Type 4-year
Control .... State
Calendar System .... Semester
Accreditation .... NCA 1913/1977

Academic Deans
Ted E. Hartung .... Coll of Agriculture
Hazel M. Anthony .... Coll of Home Economics

Department Chairmen
W.E. Splinter .... Agricultural Engineering
Lloyd Bullerman (acting) .... Food Science & Tech
Hazel M. Fox .... Human Nutrition
                                 Food Services Management

UNIVERSITY OF NEBRASKA MEDICAL CENTER
42nd and Dewey Avenue
Omaha, NE 68105
402-541-4000

Founded 1869
Type .... 2-, 4-year, Graduate, Profl
Control .... State
Calendar System .... Semester
Accreditation .... NCA 1913/1977

Division Director
Jack L. Smith, Ph.D ...... Medical Nutrition Education

NEVADA

UNIVERSITY OF NEVADA, RENO
Reno, NV 89557
702-784-1110

Founded 1874
Type .... 4-year, Graduate
Control .... State
Calendar System .... Semester
Accreditation .... NWA 1938/1978

Academic Deans
Dale W. Bohmont .... Agriculture
Donna Beth Downer .... Home Economics

Department Chairman
Gordon L. Myer .... Agriculture

NEW HAMPSHIRE

RIVIER COLLEGE
410 Main Street
Nashua, NH 03060
603-888-1311

Founded 1933
Control .... Private
Calendar System 4-4
Accreditation .... NEA 1948/1977

Department Chairman
Sr. Rita Ritchotte .... Home Economics

UNIVERSITY OF NEW HAMPSHIRE
Durham, NH 03824
603-862-1234

Founded 1866
Type .... 4-year, Graduate
Control .... State
Calendar System .... Semester
Accreditation .... NEA 1929/1973

Academic Dean
Kurt C. Feltner .... Coll of Life Sci & Agri

Department Chairman
Henry Thompson .... Home Economics

NEW JERSEY

COLLEGE OF SAINT ELIZABETH
Convent Station, NJ 07961
201-539-1600

Founded 1899
Type 4-year
Control .... Private
Calendar System .... Semester
Accreditation .... MSA 1921/1974

Department Chairman
Sr. Anita Richard Heilenday .... Home Economics

GLASSBORO STATE COLLEGE
Glassboro, NJ 08028
609-445-5000

Founded 1923
Type .... 4-year, Graduate
Control .... State
Calendar System 4-1-4
Accreditation .... NCATE 1967/1977; MSA 1979

Department Chairperson
Doris Palzer .... Home Economics

MONTCLAIR STATE COLLEGE
Valley Road
Upper Montclair, NJ 07043
201-893-4211

Founded 1908
Type .... 4-year, Graduate
Control .... State
Calendar System .... Semester
Accreditation .... MSA 1937/1977

Department Chairman
Lois Guthrie .... Home Economics

NEW MEXICO

NEW MEXICO STATE UNIVERSITY MAIN CAMPUS
PO Box 3AA
Las Cruces, NM 88003
505-646-0111

---

* School did not supply update for this edition
** School did not supply update for this edition or for previous edition

Founded 1888
Type........................ 2-, 4-year, Graduate
Control .... State
Calendar System......................... Semester
Accreditation...................... NCA 1926/1978
Joe A. Richardson................. Dir Agri Institute
William P. Stephens............. Dir NM Dept of Agri
Academic Dean
L.S. Pope........... Coll of Agri & Home Economics
Department Chairmen
George H. Abernathy........ Agriculture Engineering
Mercedes Hoskins (acting)......... Home Economics

UNIVERSITY OF NEW MEXICO
Albuquerque, NM 87131
505-277-0111

Founded 1889
Type....................................... 4-year
Control .... State
Calendar System......................... Semester
Accreditation...................... NCA 1922/1979
Department Chairman
Richard M. Smith................. Home Economics

WESTERN NEW MEXICO UNIVERSITY*
College Avenue
Silver City, NM 88061
505-538-6317

Founded 1893
Type..................................... 2-, 4-year
Control .... State
Calendar System......................... Semester
Accreditation...................... NCA 1926/1975
Department Chairman
Barbara Johnson................. Home Economics

NEW YORK

BROOKLYN COLLEGE OF THE CITY UNIVERSITY OF NEW YORK
Bedford Avenue & Avenue H
Brooklyn, NY 11210
212-780-5485

Founded 1930
Type....................................... 4-year
Control .... State & Local
Calendar System......................... Semester
Accreditation...................... MSA 1933/1975
Department Chairman
Chrysie Costantakos............. Home Economics
                                            Consumer Studies

QUEENS COLLEGE
65-30 Kissena Boulevard
Flushing, NY 11367
212-520-7000

Founded 1937
Type............................... 4-year, Graduate
Control .... State & Local
Calendar System......................... Semester
Accreditation...................... MSA 1941/1976
Department Chairman
Phyllis G. Tortota................. Home Economics

CORNELL UNIVERSITY
Ithaca, NY 14853
607-256-1000

Founded 1865
Type............................... 4-year, Graduate
Control .... Private
Calendar System......................... Semester
Accreditation...................... MSA 1921/1980
Academic Dean
David Call............. Coll of Agriculture & Life Sci
Academic Director
Malden C. Nesheim........ Div of Nutritional Science

NEW YORK STATE COLLEGE OF AGRICULTURE & LIFE SCIENCES AT CORNELL UNIVERSITY
Ithaca, NY 14853
607-256-2241

Founded 1865
Type............................... 4-year, Graduate
Control .... State
Calendar System......................... Semester
Accreditation...................... MSA 1921/1980
J. Robert Cooke..................... Dir Instruction

MARYMOUNT COLLEGE
Tarrytown, NY 10591
914-631-3200

Founded 1907
Type....................................... 4-year
Control .... Private
Calendar System.......................... 4-1-4
Accreditation...................... MSA 1927/1975
Department Chairman
Renee Paulantonio............... Home Economics

PAUL SMITH'S COLLEGE OF ARTS & SCIENCES
Paul Smiths, NY 12970
518-327-6227

Founded 1946
Type....................................... 2-year
Control .... Private
Calendar System......................... Semester
Accreditation........................... MSA 1977
Department Chairman
Frances M. Peroni......................... Foods

SUNY COLLEGE AT ONEONTA
Oneonta, NY 13820
607-431-3500

Founded 1889
Type............................... 4-year, Graduate
Control .... State
Calendar System......................... Semester
Accreditation..... MSA (Renewed) 1973; NCATE; ACS
Department Chairman
Elsa A. McMullen................. Home Economics

SUNY COLLEGE AT PLATTSBURGH
Plattsburgh, NY 12901
518-564-2000

Founded 1889
Type....................................... 4-year
Control .... State
Calendar System......................... Semester
Accreditation.......... NLN; MSA 1952/1972; NCATE;
                        ACS; NYS Board of Regents
Department Chairman
Dr. Marilyn Chase................. Home Economics

SUNY AGRICULTURAL & TECHNICAL COLLEGE ALFRED
Alfred, NY 14802
607-871-6111

Founded 1908
Type....................................... 2-year
Control .... State
Calendar System......................... Semester
Accreditation...................... MSA 1952/1981
Department Chairman
Walter H. Wietgrefe............. Agriculture Industry

SUNY AGRICULTURAL & TECHNICAL COLLEGE CANTON
Canton, NY 13617
315-386-7011

Founded 1906
Type....................................... 2-year
Control .... State
Calendar System......................... Semester
Accreditation........................... MSA 1971
Academic Dean
H. David Chamberlain..... Division of Agri & Life Scis

Academic Department Chairperson
Edwin Smith............................ Agriculture

SUNY AGRICULTURAL & TECHNICAL COLLEGE COBLESKILL
Cobleskill, NY 12043
518-234-5011

Founded 1916
Type....................................... 2-year
Control .... State
Calendar System......................... Semester
Accreditation...................... MSA 1952/1971
Division Chairman
Robert Wingert............ Agri & Natural Resources
Department Chairman
Kenneth Olcott............ Agricultural Engineering

SUNY AGRICULTURAL & TECHNICAL COLLEGE DELHI
Main Street
Delhi, NY 13753
607-746-4111

Founded 1913
Type....................................... 2-year
Control .... State
Calendar System......................... Semester
Accreditation.................. MSA/CHE 1952/1972
Division Chairman
(vacant)................. Agriculture & Life Sciences

SUNY AGRICULTURAL & TECHNICAL COLLEGE FARMINGDALE
Rt. 110 & Melville Road
Farmingdale, NY 11735
516-420-2000

Founded 1912
Type....................................... 2-year
Control .... State
Calendar System......................... Semester
Accreditation........................... MSA 1971
Academic Dean
E. Garcia........... Engineering & Agricultural Tech

SUNY AGRICULTURAL & TECHNICAL COLLEGE MORRISVILLE
Morrisville, NY 13408
315-684-7000

Type....................................... 2-year
Control .... State
Calendar System......................... Semester
Accreditation...................... MSA 1952/1972
Division Chairperson
Donald F. Jones....................... Agriculture

NORTH CAROLINA

BENNETT COLLEGE
Greensboro, NC 27420
919-273-4431

Founded 1873
Type....................................... 4-year
Affiliation...................... United Methodist
Calendar System......................... Semester
Accreditation........................... SACS 1979
Department Chairman
Louise G. Streat................. Home Economics

CAMPBELL UNIVERSITY
PO Box 127
Buie's Creek, NC 27506
919-893-4111

Founded 1887
Type....................................... 4-year
Affiliation................. N.C. Baptist Convention
Calendar System......................... Semester
Accreditation........................... SACS 1970
Department Chairman
Lenore D. Tuck................. Home Economics

* School did not supply update for this edition
** School did not supply update for this edition **or** for previous edition

RESOURCES FOR FURTHER INFORMATION

MARS HILL COLLEGE
Mars Hill, NC 28754
704-689-1141

Founded 1856
Type 2-, 4-year
Affiliation .... N.C. Baptist State Convention
Calendar System 4-1-4
Accreditation .... SACS 1967/1971; NASM
Department Chairman
Winona D. Bierbaum .... Home Economics

MEREDITH COLLEGE
Hillsborough Street
Raleigh, NC 27611
919-833-6461

Founded 1891
Type 4-year
Affiliation .... Baptist
Calendar System .... Semester
Accreditation .... SACS 1921/1980
Department Chairman
Marilyn Stuber .... Home Economics

DAVIDSON COUNTY COMMUNITY COLLEGE
PO Box 1287
Lexington, NC 27292
704-249-8186

Founded 1958
Type 2-year
Control .... State & Local
Calendar System .... Quarter
Accreditation .... SACS 1969/1972
Department Chairman
William H. Adams .... Agricultural Technology

SOUTHEASTERN COMMUNITY COLLEGE
PO Box 151
Whiteville, NC 28472
919-642-7141

Type 2-year
Control .... State & Local
Calendar System .... Quarter
Accreditation .... SACS 1967/1972
Department Chairman
Al Phillips .... Agriculture Science

WAYNE COMMUNITY COLLEGE
Caller Box 8002
Goldsboro, NC 27530
919-735-5151

Founded 1957
Type 2-year
Control .... State & Local
Calendar System .... Quarter
Accreditation .... SACS 1970/1974
Department Chairman
Robert Goodman .... Agriculture & Natural Resources

CENTRAL CAROLINA TECHNICAL COLLEGE
1105 Kelly Drive
Sanford, NC 27330
919-775-5401

Founded 1962
Type 2-year
Control .... State & Local
Calendar System .... Quarter
Accreditation .... SACS 1969/1976
Department Chairman
Joe Parson .... Agricultural Science

HAYWOOD TECHNICAL COLLEGE
Freedlander Drive
Clyde, NC 28721
704-626-2821

Founded 1965
Type 2-year
Control .... State & Local
Calendar System .... Quarter
Accreditation .... SACS 1973

Department Chairman
Doug Staigut .... Agriculture & Biological Sciences

PITT COMMUNITY COLLEGE
PO Drawer 7007
Greenville, NC 27834
919-756-3130

Founded 1961
Type 2-year
Control .... State
Calendar System .... Quarter
Accreditation .... SACS 1969/1973
Department Chairperson
William H. Moore .... Agriculture Science

SAMPSON TECHNICAL COLLEGE
PO Drawer 318
Clinton, NC 28328
919-592-8081

Founded 1965
Type 2-year
Control .... State
Calendar System .... Quarter
Accreditation .... SACS 1977
Department Chairman
Gregory Jackson .... Agriculture Science

SALEM COLLEGE
PO Box 10548, Salem Station
Winston-Salem, NC 27108
919-721-2600

Founded 1772
Type 4-year
Affiliation .... Moravian
Calendar System 4-1-4
Accreditation .... SACS 1922/1970
Department Chairman
Margaret P. Snow .... Home Economics

UNIVERSITY OF NORTH CAROLINA AT CHAPEL HILL
South Building
Chapel Hill, NC 27514
919-933-2211

Founded 1789
Type 4-year
Control .... State
Calendar System .... Semester
Accreditation .... SACS 1974
Department Chairman, School of Public Health
Joseph C. Edozien .... Nutrition

UNIVERSITY OF NORTH CAROLINA AT GREENSBORO
1000 Spring Garden Street
Greensboro, NC 27412

Founded 1892
Type .... 2-, 4-year, Graduate
Control .... State
Calendar System .... Semester
Accreditation .... SACS 1972
Department Chairmen
Lucille Wakefield .... Food, Nutrition
                                Food Service Management
Mildred Johnson .... Home Economic Education

APPALACHIAN STATE UNIVERSITY**
Boone, NC 28608
704-262-2000

Founded 1899
Type .... 4-year, Graduate
Control .... State
Calendar System .... Semester
Accreditation .... SACS 1942/1972
Department Chairman
Josephine Foster .... Home Economics

EAST CAROLINA UNIVERSITY
East Fifth Street
Greenville, NC 27834

919-757-6131

Founded 1907
Type .... 4-year, Graduate
Control .... State
Calendar System .... Semester
Accreditation .... SACS 1927/1973
Academic Dean
Eugenia Zallen .... Home Economics

NORTH CAROLINA AGRICULTURAL & TECHNICAL STATE UNIVERSITY
312 North Dudley Street
Greensboro, NC 27411
919-379-7500

Founded 1891
Type .... 4-year, Graduate
Control .... State
Calendar System .... Semester
Accreditation .... SACS 1970
Academic Dean
B.C. Webb .... School of Agriculture
Department Chairmen
Arthur P. Bell .... Agriculture Education
Harold Mazyck .... Home Economics

NORTH CAROLINA CENTRAL UNIVERSITY
1805 Fayetteville Street
Durham, NC 27707
919-683-6000

Founded 1910
Type .... 4-year, Graduate, J.D.
Control .... State
Calendar System .... Semester
Accreditation .... SACS 1979; ABA 1978; ALA 1981;
                    NCATE 1981; Nt'l League of Nursing 1971
Department Chairman
Beverly Nichols .... Home Economics

NORTH CAROLINA STATE UNIVERSITY
Raleigh, NC 27650
919-737-2011

Founded 1887
Type .... 2-, 4-year, Graduate
Control .... State
Calendar System .... Semester
Accreditation .... SACS 1973
Academic Dean
James E. Legates .... Agriculture & Life Sciences
Department Chairmen
F.J. Hassler .... Biological & Agricultural Engineering
D.R. Lineback .... Food Science

PEMBROKE STATE UNIVERSITY
Pembroke, NC 28372
919-521-4214

Founded 1887
Type 4-year
Control .... State
Calendar System .... Semester
Accreditation .... SACS 1980
Department Chairman
Anne M. Elam .... Home Economics

WESTERN CAROLINA UNIVERSITY
Cullowhee, NC 28723
704-227-7211

Founded 1889
Type 4-year
Control .... State
Calendar System .... Semester
Accreditation .... SACS 1946/1975
Department Chairman
Wilma Cosper .... Home Economics

* School did not supply update for this edition
** School did not supply update for this edition or for previous edition

NORTH DAKOTA

NORTH DAKOTA STATE UNIVERSITY
State University Station
Fargo, ND 58105
701-237-8011

Founded...1890
Type..State
Control..2-, 4-year
Calendar System...............................Quarter
Accreditation........................NCA 1915/1976

Academic Deans
H.R. Lund.......................Coll of Agriculture
Jacqueline H. Voss........Coll of Home Economics

Department Chairman
Clayton N. Haugse......Agriculture & Animal Science

UNIVERSITY OF NORTH DAKOTA
Grand Forks, ND 58201
701-777-2011

Founded...1883
Type................................2-, 4-year, Graduate
Control..State
Calendar System.............................Semester
Accreditation........................NCA 1913/1974

Department Chairman
Mabel Curry.........................Home Economics

OHIO

ASHLAND COLLEGE
401 College Avenue
Ashland, OH 44805
419-289-4142

Founded...1878
Type................................2-, 4-year, Graduate
Affiliation............................Brethren Church
Calendar System.............................Semester
Accreditation....................................NCA 1979

Division Chairman
Margery McBurny...................Home Economics

BALDWIN-WALLACE COLLEGE
Administration Building
275 Eastland Road
Berea, OH 44017
216-826-2900

Founded...1845
Type..4-year
Affiliation......................................Methodist
Calendar System................................Quarter
Accreditation..........NCA 1933/1978; NCATE 1979;
                                    NASM 1977; ACS

Department Chairman
Bette Schaffner....................Home Economics

BLUFFTON COLLEGE
Bluffton, OH 45817
419-353-8015

Founded...1899
Type..4-year
Control..Mennonite
Calendar System...................................1-3-3-2
Accreditation....................................NCA 1979

Department Chairman
Barbara Stettler..Home Economics, Food & Nutrition

BOWLING GREEN STATE UNIVERSITY
East Wooster Street
Bowling Green, OH 43403
419-372-2531

Founded...1910
Type..4-year
Control..State
Calendar System...............................Quarter
Accreditation........................NCA 1916/1973

Department Chairman
Ronald Russell......................Home Economics

CASE WESTERN RESERVE UNIVERSITY
2040 Adelbert Road
Cleveland, OH 44106
216-368-4344

Founded...1826
Type..4-year
Control..Private
Calendar System.............................Semester
Accreditation........................NCA 1913/1975

School of Medicine Department Chairman
Janice N. Neville............................Nutrition

COLLEGE OF MT. ST. JOSEPH ON THE OHIO
Delhi Pike and Neeb Road
Mount St. Joseph, OH 45051
513-244-4200

Founded...1920
Type..2-, 4-year
Calendar System.............................Semester
Accreditation........................NCA 1932/1979

Department Chairman
Loretta Flanagan........Home Economics & Dietetics

KENT STATE UNIVERSITY, MAIN CAMPUS
Kent, OH 44242
216-672-2121

Founded...1910
Type................................2-, 4-year, Graduate
Control..State
Calendar System.............................Semester
Accreditation...NCA 1974; NCATE; NASM, ACS; ALA;
               NAAB; AACSB; ACEJ; APA; ASHA;
                            ABESPA; NASA; NLN

Department Chairman
Karen Arms (acting)..............Home Economics

MIAMI UNIVERSITY
Oxford, OH 45056
513-529-2161

Founded...1809
Type................................2-, 4-year, Graduate
Control..State
Calendar System.............................Semester
Accreditation........................NCA 1913/1975

Department Chairman
Jane L. Rees........................Home Economics
                                    Consumer Services

NOTRE DAME COLLEGE OF OHIO
4545 College Road
Cleveland, OH 44121
216-381-1680

Founded...1922
Type..4-year
Affiliation..........................Roman Catholic
Calendar System...................................4-1-4
Accreditation........................NCA 1931/1980

Department Chairman
Sr. Mary St. Martha..............Home Economics

OHIO DOMINICAN COLLEGE
1216 Sunbury Road
Columbus, OH 43219
614-253-2741

Founded...1911
Type..4-year
Affiliation..........................Roman Catholic
Calendar System.............................Semester
Accreditation........................NCA 1934/1978

Department Chairman
Karen Rohr..........................Home Economics

OHIO STATE UNIVERSITY, MAIN CAMPUS
190 North Oval Mall
Columbus, OH 43210
614-422-6446

Founded...1870
Type................................2-, 4-year, Graduate
Control..State
Calendar System...............................Quarter
Accreditation........................NCA 1913/1976

Academic Dean
Roy M. Kottman......Agriculture & Home Economics

Academic Director
Francille M. Firebaugh...School of Home Economics

Department, Academic Faculties, Division Directors
J. Robert Warmbrod............Agriculture Education
Gordon L. Nelson..............Agriculture Engineering
Dan D. Garrison.......Agriculture Technical Institute
T. Kristofferson............Food Science & Nutrition
Joan E. Gritzmascher....Home Economics Education
Virginia Vivian.........Human Nutrition & Food Mgmt

UNIVERSITY OF AKRON
302 East Buchtel Avenue
Akron, OH 44325
216-375-7111

Founded...1870
Type..................................4-year, Graduate
Control..State
Calendar System.............................Semester
Accreditation........................NCA 1914/1977

Department Head
Mary C. Rainey......................Home Economics
                                         Family Ecology

UNIVERSITY OF DAYTON
300 College Park Avenue
Dayton, OH 45469
513-229-0123

Founded...1850
Type.....................................2-year, Graduate
Affiliation..........................Roman Catholic
Calendar System........................Early Semester
Accreditation........................NCA 1928/1978

Department Chairman
Julie A. Palmert....................Home Economics

URSULINE COLLEGE
2550 Lander Road
Cleveland, OH 44124
216-449-4200

Founded...1871
Type..4-year
Affiliation..........................Roman Catholic
Calendar System.............................Semester
Accreditation..........NCA 1931/1971; NLN 1951/1979

Department Chairman
Sr. Monica Marie....................Home Economics

YOUNGSTOWN STATE UNIVERSITY
410 Wick Avenue
Youngstown, OH 44555
216-746-3000

Founded...1908
Type................................2-, 4-year, Graduate
Control..State
Calendar System...............................Quarter
Accreditation........................NCA 1945/1978

Department Chairman
Mary J. Beaubien...................Home Economics

OKLAHOMA

CAMERON UNIVERSITY
Lawton, OK 73505
405-248-2200

Founded...1907
Type..4-year
Control..State
Calendar System.............................Semester
Accreditation....................................NCA 1973

Department Heads
David Martin...............................Agriculture
Dr. Grace Githens....................Home Economics

* School did not supply update for this edition
** School did not supply update for this edition or for previous edition

464 RESOURCES FOR FURTHER INFORMATION

CENTRAL STATE UNIVERSITY
100 North University Drive
Edmond, OK 73034

Founded 1890
Type................................ 4-year, Graduate
Control..................................... State
Calendar System........................... Semester
Accreditation........ NCA 1921/1979; NLN 1954/1978; NCATE 1954/1979

Academic Department Head
Virginia Lamb..................... Home Economics

CONNORS STATE COLLEGE OF AGRICULTURE & APPLIED SCIENCE
Box 398
Warner, OK 74469
918-463-2931

Founded 1908
Type... 2-year
Control..................................... State
Calendar System........................... Semester
Accreditation................................. NCA 1973

Division Chairman
Dr. Gary Updyke........ Dean of Agriculture & Tech Ed

Department Chairmen
Gary Harding........... Agriculture & Animal Science
Linda M. Frances.................. Home Economics

EASTERN OKLAHOMA STATE COLLEGE
Wilburton, OK 74578
918-465-2361

Type... 2-year
Control..................................... State
Calendar System........................... Semester
Accreditation......................... NCA 1954/1976

Division Head
Forrest Hamilton..... Agriculture & Home Economics

LANGSTON UNIVERSITY
PO Box 907
Langston, OK 73050
405-466-2281

Founded 1897
Type..................................... 2-, 4-year
Control..................................... State
Calendar System........................... Semester
Accreditation........... NCA 1948/1977; NCATE 1965

Department Chairmen
Richmond Kinnard..................... Agriculture
Dr. Willa Combs.................. Home Economics

MURRAY STATE COLLEGE
Tishomingo, OK 73460
405-371-2371

Founded 1908
Type... 2-year
Control..................................... State
Calendar System........................... Semester
Accreditation......................... NCA 1964/1974

Division Chairman
Jerry Barbee......................... Agriculture

Department Chairman
Jerry Barbee......................... Agriculture

NORTHEASTERN OKLAHOMA A & M COLLEGE
2nd and I Street, NE
Miami, OK 74354
918-542-8441

Founded 1919
Type... 2-year
Control..................................... State
Calendar System........................... Semester
Accreditation......................... NCA 1950/1977

Department Chairman
Harry Synar..................... Agriculture & Farm

OKLAHOMA PANHANDLE STATE UNIVERSITY
Box 430
Goodwell, OK 73939
405-349-2637

Founded 1909
Type... 4-year
Control..................................... State
Calendar System........................... Semester
Accreditation......................... NCA 1957/1975

Department Chairman
Jerry J. Martin......................... Agriculture
Sandy Latham.................... Home Economics

OKLAHOMA STATE UNIVERSITY OF AGRICULTURE & APPLIED SCIENCE
Stillwater, OK 74078
405-624-6384

Founded 1890
Type............................. 2-, 4-year, Graduate
Control..................................... State
Calendar System........................... Semester
Accreditation......................... NCA 1916/1976

Academic Deans
C.B. Browning........................ Agriculture
Beverly Crabtree................. Home Economics

Department Chairpersons
H. Robert Terry............. Agricultural Education
C.T. Haan.................. Agricultural Engineering
Esther A. Winterfeldt.... Food, Nutrition & Inst Admin
D. Elaine Jorgenson..... Home Economics Education

SOUTHEASTERN OKLAHOMA STATE UNIVERSITY
Station A
Durant, OK 74701
405-924-0121

Founded 1909
Type................................ 4-year, Graduate
Control..................................... State
Calendar System........................... Semester
Accreditation......... NCA 1972/1974; NCATE; AACTE

Department Chairperson
Kathleen Meadows................. Home Economics

SOUTHWESTERN OKLAHOMA STATE UNIVERSITY
Weatherford, OK 73096
405-772-6611

Founded 1901
Type................................ 4-year, Graduate
Control..................................... State
Calendar System........................... Semester
Accreditation......................... NCA 1922/1971

Department Chairman
Helen B. Brown................... Home Economics

UNIVERSITY OF OKLAHOMA
Norman, OK 73019
405-325-0311

Founded 1890
Type............................. 2-, 4-year, Graduate
Control..................................... State
Calendar System........................... Semester
Accreditation......................... NCA 1913/1972

School Director
Dortha Killian (acting).............. Home Economics

UNIVERSITY OF SCIENCE & ARTS OF OKLAHOMA
17th and Grand Avenue
Chickasha, OK 73018
405-224-3140

Founded 1908
Type... 4-year
Control..................................... State
Calendar System........................... Trimester
Accreditation......................... NCA 1920/1977

Department Chairman
Dr. Irene Clements................ Home Economics

OREGON

CLACKAMAS COMMUNITY COLLEGE
19600 South Molalla Avenue
Oregon City, OR 97045
503-656-2631

Founded 1966
Type... 2-year
Control............................... State & Local
Calendar System........................... Quarter
Accreditation......................... NWA 1971/1976

Assistant Dean
George Warren.... Agriculture & Industrial Education

Department Chairpersons
David Myers......................... Agriculture
Carolyn Knutson... Home Economics & Human Servs

CLATSOP COMMUNITY COLLEGE
16th and Jerome
Astoria, OR 97103
503-324-0910

Founded 1962
Type... 2-year
Control............................... State & Local
Calendar System........................... Quarter
Accreditation......................... NWA 1965/1971

Department Chairman
Reed Stucki........... Agriculture & Animal Science

LANE COMMUNITY COLLEGE
4000 East 30th Avenue
Eugene, OR 97405
503-747-4501

Founded 1964
Type... 2-year
Control............................... State & Local
Calendar System........................... Quarter
Accreditation......................... NWA 1968/1974

Department Head
Judith Dresser................... Home Economics

LINFIELD COLLEGE
McMinnville, OR 97128
503-472-4121

Founded 1849
Type... 4-year
Affiliation......... American Baptist Churches, USA
Calendar System........................... Semester
Accreditation......................... NWA 1928/1978

Department Chairman
Bonnie Meyer.................... Home Economics

OREGON STATE UNIVERSITY
15th and Jefferson
Corvallis, OR 97331
503-754-0123

Founded 1868
Type................................ 4-year, Graduate
Control..................................... State
Calendar System........................... Quarter
Accreditation......................... NWA 1924/1978

Academic Directors
Ernest J. Briskey.............. School of Agriculture
Betty E. Hawthorne...... School of Home Economics

Academic Department Heads
John Oades................... Agriculture Education
D.E. Kirk (acting)............. Agriculture Engineering
Ludwig M. Eisgruber..... Agri & Resource Economics
Margy L. Woodburn................ Food & Nutrition
Paul E. Kifer......... Food Science & Technology
Sylvia L. Lea........... Home Economics Education

PORTLAND COMMUNITY COLLEGE
12000 SW 49th Avenue
Portland, OR 97219
503-244-6111

Founded 1961
Type... 2-year
Control..................................... Local
Calendar System........................... Quarter
Accreditation.................. NWA 1929/177; NLN

Department Chairmen
John Wirth.................. Agriculture/Landscape
Commery Warrell............... Home Economics

* School did not supply update for this edition
** School did not supply update for this edition or for previous edition

RESOURCES FOR FURTHER INFORMATION 465

TREASURE VALLEY COMMUNITY COLLEGE
650 College Boulevard
Ontario, OR 97914
503-889-6493

Founded 1962
Type 2-year
Control .... State
Calendar System .... Quarter
Accreditation .... NWA 1966/1980
Department Chairman
Roger Findley .... Agriculture

PENNSYLVANIA

ALBRIGHT COLLEGE
13th and Exeter Streets
Reading, PA 19604
215-921-2381

Founded 1856
Type 4-year
Affiliation .... United Methodist
Calendar System 4-1-5
Accreditation .... MSA 1926/1973; NLN 1975
Department Chairman
Kathy Novak .... Home Economics

**DELAWARE VALLEY COLLEGE OF
SCIENCE & AGRICULTURE**
Route 202 and New Britain Road
Doylestown, PA 18901
215-345-1500

Founded 1896
Type 4-year
Control .... Private
Calendar System .... Semester
Accreditation .... MSA 1962/1973
Department Chairman
Richard M. Dommel .... Food Industry

INDIANA UNIVERSITY OF PENNSYLVANIA
Indiana, PA 15705
412-357-2100

Founded 1875
Type 4-year
Control .... State
Calendar System .... Semester
Accreditation ..... MSA 1941/1973; NCATE 1955/1975;
AMA-AACM; ACS; NLN; ACEJ; NASA; AACSB;
ACS; ASHA; NASM
Academic Dean
M. Kathleen Jones .... Sch Home Econ
Department Chairpersons
Ronald Simpkins .... Food & Nutrition
Alma K. Kazmer .... Home Economics Education

MERCYHURST COLLEGE
501 East 38th Street
Erie, PA 16546
814-864-0681

Founded 1926
Type 4-year
Affiliation .... Roman Catholic
Accreditation .... MSA 1965/1975
Department Chairman
Mary Ann Dowdell .... Foods & Nutrition

PENNSYLVANIA STATE UNIVERSITY
University Park, PA 16802
814-865-4700

Founded 1855
Type .... 2-, 4-year, Graduate
Control .... State
Calendar System .... Four 10-week terms
Accreditation .... MSA 1921/1976
Academic Dean
James M. Beattie .... College of Agriculture

**PENNSYLVANIA STATE UNIVERSITY
WILKES-BARRE CAMPUS**
PO Box 1830
Wilkes-Barre, PA 18708
717-675-2171

Founded 1916
Type 2-year
Control .... State
Calendar System .... Trimester
Accreditation .... MSA/CHE 1974/1976
Department Chairman
Thaddeus Olszewski .... Agriculture

SETON HILL COLLEGE
Greensburg, PA 15601
412-834-2200

Founded 1883
Type 4-year
Affiliation .... Roman Catholic
Calendar System .... Semester
Accreditation .... MSA 1921/1972
Department Chairman
Patricia Kooser .... Home Economics

VILLA MARIA COLLEGE
Erie, PA 16505
814-838-1966

Founded 1925
Type 4-year
Affiliation .... Roman Catholic
Calendar System .... Semester
Accreditation .... MSA 1980; NLN 1979;
CSWE 1979; ADA 1979
Department Chairmen
Dawna Mughal .... Dietetics
Dr. Suzanne Loss .... Home Economics

RHODE ISLAND

UNIVERSITY OF RHODE ISLAND
Kingston, RI 02881
401-792-1000

Founded 1888
Type .... 2-, 4-year, Graduate
Control .... Public
Calendar System .... Semester
Accreditation ..... NEA 1930/1977; AAU; AACSB; ACS;
ADA; ECPD; NASM; NLN; ACPE; APA
Department Chairman
James Bergan .... Food Science & Technology

SOUTH CAROLINA

ANDERSON COLLEGE*
316 Boulevard
Anderson, SC 29621
803-226-6181

Founded 1911
Type 2-year
Affiliation .... Southern Baptist
Calendar System .... Semester
Accreditation .... SACS 1959/1970
Department Chairman
Mary Martin .... Home Economics

BOB JONES UNIVERSITY
Wade Hampton Boulevard
Greenville, SC 29614
803-242-5100

Founded 1927
Control .... Private
Calendar System .... Semester
Accreditation .... State
Department Chairman
Karis Kohli .... Home Economics

CLEMSON UNIVERSITY
PO Box 992
Clemson, SC 29631
803-656-3311

Founded 1889
Type .... 2-, 4-year, Graduate
Control .... State
Calendar System .... Early Semester
Accreditation .... SACS 1927/1972
Department Heads
B.K. Webb .... Agriculture Engineering
J.H. Rodgers (acting) .... Agriculture Education
W.P. Williams, Jr .... Food Science

ERSKINE COLLEGE
Due West, SC 29639
803-379-2131

Founded 1839
Type 4-year
Affiliation .... Associated Reformed Presbyterian
Calendar System 4-1-4
Accreditation .... SACS 1925/1972
Department Head
Hazel Haddon .... Home Economics

SOUTH DAKOTA

MITCHELL VOCATIONAL-TECHNICAL SCHOOL
821 North Capitol
Mitchell, SD 57301
605-996-6671

Founded 1968
Type 1-, 2-year
Control .... Local
Calendar System .... Quarter
Accreditation .... NCA 1980
Department Head
Loren Kasten .... Agriculture

OGLALA SIOUX COMMUNITY COLLEGE
PO Box 439
Kyle, SD 57752
605-455-2321

Founded 1971
Type 2-year
Control .... Local-Oglala Sioux Tribe
Calendar System .... Semester
Accreditation .... NCA Cand 1979
Department Director
Mohamed Salih .... Agriculture

SOUTH DAKOTA STATE UNIVERSITY
University Station
Brookings, SD 57007
605-688-4111

Founded 1881
Type .... 4-year, Graduate
Control .... State
Calendar System .... Semester
Accreditation .... NCA 1920/1978
Academic Deans
Delwyn D. Dearborn .... Agriculture & Bio Scis
Ardyce Gilbert .... Home Economics
Department Heads
Dennis L. Moe .... Agricultural Engineering
Edna P. Anderson .... Home Economics Education

TENNESSEE

CARSON-NEWMAN COLLEGE
Russell Avenue
Box 552
Jefferson City, TN 37760
615-475-9061

Founded 1851
Type 4-year
Affiliation .... Southern Baptist
Calendar System .... Semester

* School did not supply update for this edition
** School did not supply update for this edition or for previous edition

466 RESOURCES FOR FURTHER INFORMATION

Accreditation.......................SACS 1927/1972
Department Chairman
Kitty R. Coffey.....................Home Economics

DAVID LIPSCOMB COLLEGE
Nashville, TN 37203
615-385-3855

Founded............................1891
Type...............................4-year
Affiliation........................Church of Christ
Calendar System....................Quarter
Accreditation......................SACS 1954/1975
Department Chairman
Eva B. Redmon......................Home Economics

FREED-HARDEMAN COLLEGE
158 East Main Street
Henderson, TN 38340
901-989-4611

Founded............................1869
Type...............................4-year
Affiliation........................Church of Christ
Calendar System....................Semester
Accreditation......................SACS 1956/1976
Department Chairman
Carolyn J. Townsley...Home & Consumer Economics

AUSTIN PEAY STATE UNIVERSITY
College Street
Clarksville, TN 37040
605-648-7011

Founded............................1927
Type...............................2-, 4-year, Graduate
Control............................State
Calendar System....................Quarter
Accreditation.........SACS 1948/1973; NASM 1964; NCATE 1963
Department Head
Dr. Gaines Hunt....................Agriculture

EAST TENNESSEE STATE UNIVERSITY*
Johnson City, TN 37601
615-929-4112

Founded............................1911
Type...............................2-, 4-year, Graduate
Control............................State
Calendar System....................Quarter
Accreditation......................SACS 1927/1972
Department Chairman
Sue Mays...........................Home Economics

MIDDLE TENNESSEE STATE UNIVERSITY
Murfreesboro, TN 37132
615-898-2622

Founded............................1911
Type...............................2-, 4-year, Graduate
Control............................State
Calendar System....................Semester
Accreditation......................SACS 1928/1974
Department Chairmen
Harley Foutch..........Agriculture & Animal Science
Hattie Arthur......................Home Economics

TENNESSEE STATE UNIVERSITY
3500 Centennial Boulevard
Nashville, TN 37203
615-320-3131
Downtown Campus
10th Avenue, North at Charlotte
Nashville, TN 37203
615-251-1441

Founded............................1912
Type...............................2-, 4-year, Graduate
Control............................State
Calendar System....................Semester
Accreditation.......SACS 1946/1979; CSWE; NCATE; NASM; ECPD; ADA; NLN
Academic Dean
Roland Norman......Sch of Agri & Home Economics
Department Chairperson
Mary H. Greer......................Home Economics

TENNESSEE TECHNOLOGICAL UNIVERSITY
Cookeville, TN 38501
615-528-3101

Founded............................1915
Type...............................4-year, Graduate
Calendar System....................Quarter
Accreditation......................SACS 1939/1974
Academic Dean
Sumner Griffin.....................Sch of Agriculture
Department Chairman
Mary Below.........................Home Economics

JACKSON STATE COMMUNITY COLLEGE
North Parkway East
Jackson, TN 38301
901-424-3520

Founded............................1965
Type...............................2-year
Control............................State
Calendar System....................Quarter
Accreditation......................SACS 1969/1973
Department Chairman
James Harris.......................Agriculture

SHELBY STATE COMMUNITY COLLEGE
PO Box 40568
Memphis, TN 38104
901-528-6700

Founded............................1970
Type...............................2-year
Control............................State
Calendar System....................Quarter
Accreditation......................SACS 1974
Department Chairperson
F. Cleo Long..Nutrition, Dietetics & Food Serv Admin

UNIVERSITY OF TENNESSEE AT CHATTANOOGA
Chattanooga, TN 37402
615-755-4011

Founded............................1886
Type...............................4-year, Graduate
Control............................State
Calendar System....................Semester
Accreditation.........SACS 1910/1971; NCATE; ACS; ECPD; NCSWE; NLN
Department Chairman
Mary Jo Cochran....................Home Economics

UNIVERSITY OF TENNESSEE, KNOXVILLE
527 Andy Holt Tower
Knoxville, TN 37916
615-974-3288

Founded............................1794
Type...............................2-, 4-year, Graduate
Control............................State
Calendar System....................Quarter
Accreditation......................SACS 1897/1971
Academic Deans
O. Glenn Hall......................Agriculture
Nancy Belck........................Home Economics
Department Chairmen
Carroll J. Southards..............Agricultural Biology
Houston Luttrell..............Agricultural Engineering
R.E. Beaucene............Food Science, Nutrition & Food Systems Administration
J.T. Miles................Food Technology & Science

UNIVERSITY OF TENNESSEE AT MARTIN
Martin, TN 38238
901-587-7000

Founded............................1927
Type...............................2-, 4-year, Graduate
Control............................State
Calendar System....................Quarter
Accreditation......................SACS 1951/1971
Academic Deans
Harold J. Smith....................Agriculture
Ronald Fannin......................Home Economics

TEXAS

ABILENE CHRISTIAN UNIVERSITY
Campus Court
Abilene, TX 79699
915-677-1911

Founded............................1906
Type...............................2-, 4-year, Graduate
Control............................Private
Calendar System....................Semester
Accreditation......................SACS 1951/1981
Department Chairmen
Bryan E. Brokaw....................Agriculture
Donice Kelly.......................Home Economics

AMARILLO COLLEGE
2201 South Washington Street
PO Box 447
Amarillo, TX 79178
806-376-5111

Founded............................1929
Type...............................2-year
Control............................State & Local
Calendar System....................Semester
Accreditation......................SACS 1933/1972
Department Chairman
Zuma S. Austin.....................Home Economics

ANGELO STATE UNIVERSITY
2601 West Avenue North
San Angelo, TX 76901
915-942-2131

Founded............................1928
Type...............................2-, 4-year, Graduate
Control............................State
Calendar System....................Semester
Accreditation......................SACS 1967/1971
Academic Department
G. Leon Holland....................Agriculture

BAYLOR UNIVERSITY
Waco, TX 76798
817-755-1011

Founded............................1845
Type...............................4-year, Graduate
Affiliation........................Southern Baptist
Calendar System....................Semester
Accreditation......................SACS 1914/1974
Department Chairman
Dorothy W. McAlister...............Home Economics

COOKE COUNTY COLLEGE
PO Box 815
Gainesville, TX 76240
817-668-7731

Founded............................1924
Type...............................2-year
Control............................State & Local
Calendar System....................Semester
Accreditation......................SACS 1961/1971
Department Chairman
T.J. Davidson......................Agriculture

EAST TEXAS STATE UNIVERSITY
Commerce TX 75428
214-886-5000

Founded............................1889
Type...............................4-year, Graduate
Control............................State
Calendar System....................Semester
Accreditation......................SACS 1925/1972
Department Chairman
Charley Jones..........Agriculture & Animal Science

LAMAR UNIVERSITY
Lamar University Station
Beaumont, TX 77710
713-838-7011

* School did not supply update for this edition
** School did not supply update for this edition or for previous edition

RESOURCES FOR FURTHER INFORMATION

Founded 1923
Type .... 2-, 4-year, Graduate
Control .... State
Calendar System .... Semester
Accreditation .... SACS 1955/1977
Department Head
Virginia Anderson .... Home Economics

LAREDO JUNIOR COLLEGE
West Washington Street
Laredo, TX 78040
512-722-0521

Founded 1946
Type 2-year
Control .... State & Local
Calendar System .... Semester
Accreditation .... SACS 1957/1978
Department Chairman
Martha Haslam .... Home Economics

LUBBOCK CHRISTIAN COLLEGE*
5601 W 19th
Lubbock, TX 79407
806-792-3221

Founded 1957
Type 2-, 4-year
Affiliation .... Church of Christ
Calendar System .... Semester
Accreditation .... SACS 1972/1977
Department Chairmen
Rodney Blackwood .... Agriculture
Eupha Skillman .... Home Economics

ODESSA COLLEGE
201 West University
Odessa, TX 79762
915-337-5381

Founded 1946
Type 2-year
Control .... State & Local
Calendar System .... Semester
Accreditation .... SACS 1952/1972
Department Chairman
Mary Joyce Harding .... Home Economics

SAM HOUSTON STATE UNIVERSITY
Huntsville, TX 77341
713-294-1013

Founded 1879
Type 4-year
Control .... State
Calendar System .... Semester
Accreditation .... SACS 1925/1979
Department Chairpersons
David G. Moorman .... Agriculture
Mattie B. Medford .... Home Economics

**SAN JACINTO JUNIOR COLLEGE
CENTRAL CAMPUS**
Pasadena, TX 77505
713-479-1501

Founded 1960
Type 2-year
Control .... State & Local
Calendar System .... Semester
Accreditation .... SACS 1963/1970
Division Chairman
Ella Parker .... Home Economics

**SAN JACINTO JUNIOR COLLEGE
NORTH CAMPUS**
5800 Uvalde Road
Houston, TX 77049
713-458-4050

Founded 1974
Type 2-year
Control .... State & Local
Calendar System .... Semester
Accreditation .... SACS 1976
Department Chair
Linda Young .... Home Economics

SOUTH PLAINS COLLEGE
1401 College Avenue
Levelland, TX 79336
806-894-9611

Founded 1957
Type 2-year
Accreditation .... SACS 1963/1973
Department Chairperson
James Carroll .... Agri/Applied Sci & Tech

SOUTHWEST TEXAS STATE UNIVERSITY
San Marcos, TX 78666
512-245-2121

Founded 1899
Type 4-year
Control .... State
Calendar System .... Semester
Accreditation .... SACS 1925/1979
Department Heads
Joan Terry .... Home Economics
Roy V. Miller Jr. .... Agriculture

SOUTHWESTERN ADVENTIST COLLEGE
Keene, TX 76059
817-645-3921

Founded 1894
Type 4-year
Affiliation .... Seventh-day Adventist
Calendar System .... Early Semester
Accreditation .... SACS 1970/1974
Department Chairman
Marie Redwine .... Home Economics

STEPHEN F. AUSTIN STATE UNIVERSITY
Austin Building, North Street
Nacogdoches, TX 75962
713-569-2011

Founded 1923
Type .... 4-year, Graduate
Control .... State
Calendar System .... Semester
Accreditation .... SACS 1927/1971
Department Chairmen
Thomas J. Stanly .... Agriculture & Animal Science
Gloria Durr .... Home Economics

TEXAS A & I UNIVERSITY
West Santa Gertrudis Avenue
PO Box 101
Kingsville, TX 78363
512-595-2111

Founded 1925
Type 4-year
Control .... State
Calendar System .... Semester
Accreditation .... SACS 1933/1973
Academic Dean
Charles DeYoung .... Coll of Agriculture
Department Chairman
Eugene Jekel .... Agriculture Education
Marilyn Sampley .... Home Economics

TEXAS A & M UNIVERSITY
College Station TX 77843
713-845-4331

Founded 1876
Type .... 4-year, Graduate, Profl
Calendar System .... Semester
Accreditation .... SACS 1924/1973
Academic Dean
H.O. Kunkel .... Coll of Agriculture
Department Chairmen
Edward A. Hilerl .... Agricultural Engineering
Earl H. Knebel .... Agricultural Education

TARLETON STATE UNIVERSITY
Tarleton Station
Stephenville, TX 76402
817-968-9000

Founded 1899

Type .... 2-, 4-year, Graduate
Control .... State
Calendar System .... Semester
Accreditation .... SACS 1926/1980; NCATE 1980
Department Chairmen
Billy F. Irick .... Agricultural Education
Weldon H. Newton .... Agriculture
Dolly I. Thiem .... Home Economics

TEXAS CHRISTIAN UNIVERSITY
Sadler Hall
PO Box 30570A
Forth Worth, TX 76129
817-921-7000

Founded 1873
Type .... 4-year, Graduate
Control .... Private
Calendar System .... Semester
Accreditation .... SACS 1922/1971
Department Chairman
Nell B. Robinson .... Home Economics

TEXAS SOUTHERN UNIVERSITY**
3201 Wheeler Avenue
Houston, TX 77004
713-527-7011

Founded 1947
Type 4-year
Calendar System .... Semester
Accreditation .... SACS 1948/1970; AACSB;
                                      ACPE; NCATE
Department Chairman
Janie W. Cotton .... Home Economics

TEXAS TECH UNIVERSITY**
West Broadway
PO Box 4349
Lubbock, TX 79409
806-742-2011

Founded 1923
Type .... 4-year, Graduate
Control .... State
Calendar System .... Semester
Accreditation .... SACS 1928/1973
Academic Affairs
Dr. Samuel E. Curl .... Coll of Agricultural Sci
Dr. Donald Longworth ...... Coll of Home Economics
Department Chairmen
Dr. Jerry Stockton .... Agricultural Education
Dr. Marvin Dvoracek .... Agricultural Engineering
Dr. Charles Morr .... Food & Nutrition
Dr. Camille G. Bell .... Home Economics Education

UNIVERSITY OF TEXAS AT AUSTIN
U.T. Station
Austin, TX 78712
512-471-1233

Founded 1883
Type .... 4-year, Graduate
Control .... State
Calendar System .... Semester
Accreditation .... SACS 1901/1976
Department Chairman
Mary E. Durrett .... Home Economics

WEST TEXAS STATE UNIVERSITY
Canyon, TX 79016
806-656-0111

Founded 1909
Type .... 4-year, Graduate
Control .... State
Calendar System .... Semester
Accreditation .... SACS 1925/1974
Academic Dean
James T. Thompson .... Agriculture

WHARTON COUNTY JUNIOR COLLEGE
911 Boling Highway
Wharton, TX 77488
713-532-4560

Founded 1946

* School did not supply update for this edition
** School did not supply update for this edition or for previous edition

Type..................................... 2-year
Control............................ State & Local
Calendar System........................ Semester
Accreditation................. SACS 1956/1980
Department Chairman
Charles Nunnally..................... Agriculture

UTAH

BRIGHAM YOUNG UNIVERSITY
Provo, Utah 84602
801-378-1211

Founded................................... 1875
Type..................................... 4-year
Affiliation............. Church of Jesus Christ
of Latter-Day Saints
Calendar System......................... 4-4-2-2
Accreditation...................... NASC 1976
Academic Dean and Director
A. Lester Allen............. Biological & Agri Scis
Department Chairmen
Clayton S. Huber........... Food Science & Nutrition
Carol Ellsworth.................. Home Economics

SNOW COLLEGE
Ephraim, UT 84627
801-283-4021

Founded................................... 1888
Type..................................... 2-year
Control................................... State
Calendar System........................ Quarter
Accreditation.................. NWA 1953/1972
Department Chairman
Jack Anderson...................... Agriculture

UTAH STATE UNIVERSITY
Logan, UT 84322
801-750-1000

Founded................................... 1890
Type......................... 4-year, Graduate
Control................................... State
Calendar System........................ Quarter
Accreditation.................. NWA 1968/1978
Academic Dean
Doyle J. Matthews.................. Agriculture
Academic Department or Division Heads
College of Agriculture
Gilbert A. Long.............. Agricultural Education
Carl A. Ernstrom.......... Nutrition & Food Sciences
College of Family Life
Carol A. Bocan..... Home Economics & Consumer Ed
Carl A. Ernstrom.......... Nutrition & Food Sciences

VERMONT

**UNIVERSITY OF VERMONT &
STATE AGRICULTURAL COLLEGE**
85 South Prospect Street
Burlington, VT 05401
802-656-3480

Founded................................... 1791
Type..................... 2-, 4-year, Graduate
Control................................... State
Calendar System........................ Semester
Accreditation................. NEASC 1972/1979
Academic Dean
Robert O. Sinclair.................. Agriculture
Department Chairpersons
Fred C. Webster............. Agri & Resources Econ
Marilyn Osborn......... Home Economics Education
Eleanor D. Schlenker....... Human Nutrition & Foods

VERMONT TECHNICAL COLLEGE
Randolph Center, VT 05061
802-728-3391

Founded................................... 1957
Type..................................... 2-year
Control................................... State

Calendar System........................ Semester
Accreditation................. NEA 1970; ABET
Department Head
Robert C. Brown..................... Agriculture

VIRGINIA

BRIDGEWATER COLLEGE
Bridgewater, VA 22812
703-828-2501

Founded................................... 1880
Type..................................... 4-year
Control........ Independent (Church of the Brethren)
Calendar System......................... 3-3-1-3
Accreditation................. SACS 1925/1981
Department Chairman
Anna Mae Myers.................. Home Economics

EASTERN MENNONITE COLLEGE
1200 Park Road
Harrisonburg, VA 22801
703-433-2771

Founded................................... 1917
Type..................................... 4-year
Affiliation..................... Mennonite Church
Calendar System........................ Trimester
Accreditation................. SACS 1959/1980
Department Chairman
Doris Bomberger.................. Home Economics

JAMES MADISON UNIVERSITY
Harrisonburg, VA 22807
703-433-6211

Founded................................... 1908
Type......................... 4-year, Graduate
Control................................... State
Calendar System........................ Semester
Accreditation................. SACS 1927/1972
Department Head
Dr. Dorothy Rowe.................. Home Economics

NORFOLK STATE UNIVERSITY
2401 Corpew Avenue
Norfolk, VA 23504
804-623-8600

Founded................................... 1935
Type..................................... 4-year
Control................................... State
Calendar System........................ Semester
Accreditation................. SACS 1967/1977
Department Chairman
Lillian P. Wright.................. Home Economics

RADFORD UNIVERSITY
University Station
Radford, VA 24142
703-731-5000

Founded................................... 1910
Type..................................... 4-year
Control................................... State
Calendar System........................ Semester
Accreditation.... SACS 1928/1972; NCATE 1961/1971;
NLN 1976; NASM 1977; CSWE 1976
Department Chairman
Roslyn M. Lester.................. Home Economics

LORD FAIRFAX COMMUNITY COLLEGE
PO Box 47
Middletown, VA 22645
703-869-1120

Founded................................... 1969
Type..................................... 2-year
Control................................... State
Calendar System........................ Quarter
Accreditation................. SACS 1972/1976
Division Chairman
Ronald L. Ludwick.................. Agricultural &
Natural Resources

**VIRGINIA POLYTECHNIC INSTITUTE
& STATE UNIVERSITY (VIRGINIA TECH)**
Blacksburg, VA 24061
703-961-6000

Founded................................... 1872
Type..................................... 4-year
Control................................... State
Calendar System........................ Quarter
Accreditation................. SACS 1923/1977
Academic Dean
James R. Nichols......... Agriculture & Life Sciences
S. J. Ritchey..................... Home Economics
Department Chairmen
G. Gene Haugh............ Agricultural Engineering
Richard V. Lechowich.... Food Science & Technology
Ryland Webb............. Human Nutrition & Foods

VIRGINIA STATE UNIVERSITY
Petersburg, VA 23803
804-520-5000

Founded................................... 1882
Type..................... 2-, 4-year, Graduate
Control................................... State
Calendar System........................ Semester
Accreditation................. SACS 1933/1978
Academic Dean
Dr. Beverly B. Archer....... Agriculture & Applied Scis

WASHINGTON

CENTRAL WASHINGTON UNIVERSITY
Ellensburg, WA 98926
509-963-1111

Founded................................... 1890
Type..................................... 4-year
Control................................... State
Calendar System........................ Quarter
Accreditation.......... NWA 1979; NCATE 1954/1979
Department Chairman
Luther Baker..................... Home Economics

EASTERN WASHINGTON UNIVERSITY
Cheney, WA 99004
509-235-6221

Founded................................... 1882
Type......................... 4-year, Graduate
Control................................... State
Calendar System........................ Quarter
Accreditation.......... NWA 1968; NCATE; AASCB;
NASC 1919/1978
Department Chair
Beverly Schaad................... Home Economics

UNIVERSITY OF PUGET SOUND
1500 North Warner
Tacoma, WA 98416
206-756-3100

Founded................................... 1888
Type......................... 4-year, Graduate
Affiliation........................ Methodist
Calendar System......................... 4-1-4
Accreditation.. NWA 1923/1979; AMA; AOTA; NACTE;
NASM; NCATE; ABA; ACS; AALS; APTA
Department Head
Amy Sinclair........................... Nutrition

WALLA WALLA COLLEGE
College Place, WA 99324
509-527-2121

Founded................................... 1892
Type......................... 4-year, Graduate
Affiliation............... Seventh-day Adventists
Calendar System........................ Quarter
Accreditation.......... NWA 1932/1972; NASM; NLN
Department Chairman
June Bishop..................... Home Economics

* School did not supply update for this edition
** School did not supply update for this edition or for previous edition

RESOURCES FOR FURTHER INFORMATION

WASHINGTON STATE UNIVERSITY
Pullman, WA 99164
509-335-3564

Founded 1890
Type .... 4-year, Graduate
Control .... State
Calendar System .... Semester
Accreditation .... NWA 1918/1980

Academic Deans
Dr. John S. Robins .... Agriculture
Dr. Alberta Hill .... Home Economics

Department Chairmen
Dr. Larry G. King .... Agricultural Engineering
Dr. Larry A. Branen ...... Food Science & Technology
Mrs. Margaret Hard ...... Home Economics Research
Dr. Dean C. Fletcher .... Human Nutrition & Foods

WESTERN WASHINGTON UNIVERSITY
Bellingham, WA 98225
206-676-3000

Founded 1899
Type 4-year
Control .... State
Calendar System .... Quarter
Accreditation ..... NWA 1973/1978; NCATE 1968/1978; ACS

Department Chairman
Roscoe L. Buckland .... Home Economics

WEST VIRGINIA

MARSHALL UNIVERSITY
Huntington, WV 25701
304-696-3170

Founded 1837
Type .... 2-, 4-year, Graduate
Control .... State
Calendar System .... Semester
Accreditation .... NCA 1928/1976

Department Chairman
Carole Vickers .... Home Economics

WEST VIRGINIA STATE COLLEGE
Institute, WV 25112
304-766-3000

Founded 1891
Type 2-, 4-year
Control .... State
Calendar System .... Semester
Accreditation .... NCA 1927/1978; NCATE 1963; ACS 1971; CSWE

Department Chairman
Lina S. Kelley .... Home Economics

WEST VIRGINIA WESLEYAN COLLEGE
Buckhannon, WV 26201
304-473-7011

Founded 1890
Type .... 4-year, Graduate
Affiliation .... Methodist
Calendar System 4-1-4
Accreditation .... NCA 1927/1975; NLN; NASM

Department Chairman
Lillian Halverson .... Home Economics

WISCONSIN

BLACKHAWK TECHNICAL INSTITUTE
Route 3, Prairie Road
Janesville, WI 53545
608-756-4121

Founded 1968
Type 2-year
Control .... State & Local
Calendar System .... Semester
Accreditation .... NCA 1978

Department Chairmen
William Johnson .... Agriculture
Gladys Olson .... Home Economics

CARDINAL STRITCH COLLEGE
6801 North Yates Road
Milwaukee, WI 53217
414-352-5400

Founded 1937
Type .... 2-, 4-year, Graduate
Affiliation .... Roman Catholic
Calendar System .... Semester
Accreditation ...... NCA 1953/1973; NCATE 1966/1975

Department Chairman
Sr. Claudine Heintz .... Home Economics

DISTRICT ONE TECHNICAL INSTITUTE
EAU CLAIRE
Eau Claire, WI 54701
715-836-3900

Founded 1912
Type 2-year
Control .... State & Local
Calendar System .... Semester
Accreditation .... NCA 1973/1978

Academic Coordinator
James Anderson .... Agriculture

FOX VALLEY TECHNICAL INSTITUTE
1825 North Bluemound Drive
PO Box 2277
Appleton, WI 54913
414-739-8831

Founded 1967
Type 2-year
Control .... Local
Calendar System .... Open Entry
Accreditation .... NCA 1979

Department Supervisors
Merlin Gentz .... Agriculture
Robert Martin .... Home & Consumer Scis

GATEWAY TECHNICAL INSTITUTE
District Office & Kenosha Campus
3520 30th Avenue
Kenosha, WI 53141
414-656-6900

Founded 1911
Type 2-year
Control .... Local
Calendar System .... Semester
Accreditation .... NCA 1970

Division Heads
Lloyd Larson & Harold Sahakian .... Agriculture

LAKESHORE TECHNICAL INSTITUTE
1290 North Avenue
Cleveland, WI 53015
414-693-8211

Founded 1912
Type 2-year
Control .... Local
Calendar System .... Semester
Accreditation .... NCA 1977

Division Supervisors
James Ferries .... Agriculture
Antoinette Pontar .... Home Economics

MADISON AREA TECHNICAL COLLEGE
211 North Carroll Street
Madison, WI 53703
608-266-5050

Founded 1912
Type 2-year
Control .... State & Local
Calendar System .... Semester
Accreditation .... NCA 1969/1973

Division Chairman
Phyliss Schwebke .... Home Economics

MID-STATE TECHNICAL INSTITUTE
500 32nd Street North
Wisconsin Rapids, WI 54494
715-423-5650

Founded 1967
Type 2-year
Control .... State & Local
Calendar System .... Semester
Accreditation .... NCA 1972

Department Chairmen
Ronald Elmhorst .... Agriculture
Eldean Walling .... Home Economics

MORAINE PARK TECHNICAL INSTITUTE
FOND DU LAC
235 North National Avenue
Fond du Lac, WI 54935
414-922-8611

Founded 1967
Type 2-year
Control .... District
Calendar System .... Terms
Accreditation .... NCA 1975/1978; NLN

Division Chairpersons
Wayne Koene .... Agri-Biotechnology
Dr. Jean Fleming .... Home Economics

MOUNT MARY COLLEGE
2900 North Menomonee River Pkwy
Milwaukee, WI 53222
414-258-4810

Founded 1913
Type 4-year
Affiliation .... Roman Catholic
Calendar System .... Semester
Accreditation .... NCA 1962/1973; NCATE; AMA; CSWE; ADA

Department Head
Sr. Juliana Wieser .... Home Economics

NORTH CENTRAL TECHNICAL INSTITUTE*
1000 Schofield Avenue
Wausau, WI 54401
715-675-3331

Founded 1911
Type 2-year
Control .... Local
Calendar System .... Semester
Accreditation .... NCA 1970/1978

Department Chairman
Reuben Roehl .... Agriculture Education

NORTHEAST WISCONSIN TECHNICAL INSTITUTE**
2740 West Mason Street
Green Bay, WI 54303
414-497-3125

Founded 1913
Type 2-year
Control .... State & Local
Calendar System .... Semester
Accreditation .... NCA 1976

Academic Coordinator
Donald Jaworski .... Agriculture
Nannette Hoppe .... Home Economics

SOUTHWEST WISCONSIN VOCATIONAL-TECHNICAL INSTITUTE*
Bronson Boulevard
Fennimore, WI 53805
608-822-3262

Founded 1967
Type 2-year
Control .... State & Local
Calendar System .... Semester
Accreditation .... NCA 1976

Division Chairman
Diane Barton .... Home Economics

* School did not supply update for this edition
** School did not supply update for this edition or for previous edition

RESOURCES FOR FURTHER INFORMATION

UNIVERSITY OF WISCONSIN
MADISON
Madison, WI 53706
608-262-1234

Founded 1849
Type .... 2-, 4-year, Graduate
Control .... State
Calendar System .... Semester
Accreditation .... NCA 1913/1979

Academic Dean
Leo M. Walsh .... Coll of Agri & Life Scis

UNIVERSITY OF WISCONSIN
PLATTEVILLE
West Main
Platteville, WI 53818
608-342-1234

Founded 1866
Type 4-year
Control .... State
Calendar System .... Semester
Accreditation ..... NCA 1951/1977; NCATE 1958/1963;
ABET 1968/1974; ACS 1973; NAIT 1980

Academic Dean
Charles DeNure .... College of Agriculture

Department Chairmen
Milton Shute .... Agricultural Engineering
William Hoffman .... Agricultural Sciences

UNIVERSITY OF WISCONSIN
RIVER FALLS
410 South Third Street
River Falls, WI 54022
715-425-3913

Founded 1874
Type 4-year
Control .... State
Calendar System .... Quarter
Accreditation .... NCA 1935/1978; NCATE

Academic Officer
Roger Swanson (acting) .... Dean Coll of Agri

Department Chairmen
Marvin D. Thompson .... Agricultural Education
Charles Jones .... Agricultural Engineering
& Technology
Dean Henderson .... Animal & Food Sciences

UNIVERSITY OF WISCONSIN
STEVENS POINT
2100 Main Street
Stevens Point, WI 54481
715-346-0123

Founded 1893
Type 4-year
Control .... State
Calendar System .... Semester
Accreditation .... NCA 1981

Department Chairman
Mary Jo Czaplewski .... Home Economics

UNIVERSITY OF WISCONSIN
STOUT
Menomonie, WI 54751
715-232-0123

Founded 1893
Type 4-year
Control .... State
Calendar System .... Semester
Accreditation .... NCA 1928/1976; NCATE

Academic Dean
J. Anthony Samenfink .... Sch of Home Economics

Department Chairman
Anita Wilson .... Food & Nutrition

UNIVERSITY OF WISCONSIN
EXTENSION
432 North Lake Street
Madison, WI 53706
608-262-3786

Founded 1891
Control .... State

Calendar System .... Continuous

Program Area Chairperson
Donald R. Peterson .... Agriculture

VITERBO COLLEGE
815 South 9th Street
La Crosse, WI 54601
608-784-0040

Founded 1890
Type 4-year
Affiliation .... Roman Catholic
Calendar System .... Semester
Accreditation .... NCA 1954/1969; ACTE;
ADA; NLN

Department Chairman
Sabra Mumford .... Home Economics

WESTERN WISCONSIN TECHNICAL INSTITUTE
Sixth and Vine Streets
La Crosse, WI 54601
608-785-9200

Founded 1912
Type 2-year
Control .... State & Local
Calendar System .... Quarter
Accreditation .... NCA 1972

Division Chairmen
Walter Weihrouch .... Agriculture
Barbara J. Walter .... Home Economics

WISCONSIN INDIANHEAD VOCATIONAL,
TECHNICAL & ADULT EDUCATION DISTRICT
PO Box B
Shell Lake, WI 54871
715-468-2815

Founded 1968
Type 2-year
Control .... Local
Calendar System .... Semester
Accreditation .... NCA 1979

Coordinators
Albert Schultz .... Agriculture
Renee Ramsay .... Home Economics

WISCONSIN INDIANHEAD TECHNICAL INSTITUTE
NEW RICHMOND
1019 South Knowles Avenue
New Richmond, WI 54017
715-246-6561

Founded 1967
Type 2-year
Control .... Local
Calendar System .... Semester
Accreditation .... NCA 1979

Department Supervisor
Gary Douglas .... Agriculture

WISCONSIN INDIANHEAD TECHNICAL INSTITUTE
RICE LAKE*
1900 College Drive
Rice Lake, WI 54868
715-234-7082

Founded 1941
Type 2-year
Control .... Local
Calendar System .... Semester
Accreditation .... NCA 1979

Department Supervisor
Al Schultz .... Agriculture

WYOMING

UNIVERSITY OF WYOMING
Box 3434, University Station
Laramie, WY 82071
307-766-1121

Founded 1886
Type .... 4-year, Graduate
Control .... State

Calendar System .... Semester
Accreditation .... NCA 1923/1980

Academic Dean
Harold J. Tuma .... Agriculture

Division Head
Lois Hughes .... Home Economics

Department Chairman
Clarence F. Becker .... Agricultural Engineering

UNITED STATES OUTLYING AREAS

GUAM

UNIVERSITY OF GUAM
Box EK
Agana, Guam 96910
749-2177

Founded 1952
Type 2-, 4-year
Control .... State
Calendar System .... Semester
Accreditation .... WASC 1963/1978

Academic Dean
Wilfred Leon Guerrero .... Coll of Agri & Life Sciences

PUERTO RICO

UNIVERSITY OF PUERTO RICO
RIO PIEDRAS CAMPUS
Rio Piedras, PR 00931
809-764-0000

Founded 1903
Type .... 4-year, Graduate
Control .... State
Calendar System .... Semester
Accreditation ... MSA 1946/1975; NAAB; NCATE; ABA;
AALS; ACS; CSWE; AIP; CRE

Department or Division Head
Education
Lillian Colon de Reguero (acting) ... Home Economics

UNIVERSITY OF PUERTO RICO
MAYAGUEZ CAMPUS
College Station
Mayaguez, PR 00708
809-832-4040

Founded 1911
Type 2-, 4-year
Control .... State
Calendar System .... Semester
Accreditation .... MSA 1946/1974; ABET 1980

Academic Deans
Alejandro Ayala .... Agricultural Sciences
Pedro Melendez ... Assoc Dean Faculty of Agriculture

Department Chairman
Jose A. Villamil .... Agricultural Education

CANADA

ALBERTA

FAIRVIEW COLLEGE
Box 3000
Fairview, Alberta T0H 1L0
405-835-2213

Founded 1951
Type 1-, 2-year
Control .... Provincial
Calendar System .... Semester

Department Chairman
(vacant) .... Agriculture Technologies

---

* School did not supply update for this edition
** School did not supply update for this edition or for previous edition

RESOURCES FOR FURTHER INFORMATION

OLDS COLLEGE
Olds, Alberta T0M 1P0
403-556-8281

Founded 1913
Type 1-, 2-year
Control .... Public
Calendar System .... Semester
Department Chairman
Denis Kennedy .... Agricultural Production

UNIVERSITY OF ALBERTA
Edmonton, Alberta T6G 2E1
403-432-3112

Founded 1906
Type .... 4-year, Graduate
Control .... Provincial
Dean of Faculty
J.P. Bowland .... Agriculture & Forestry
D. Badir .... Home Economics

BRITISH COLUMBIA

UNIVERSITY OF BRITISH COLUMIA
2075 Wesbrook Mall
Vancouver, British Columbia V6T 1W5
604-228-2211

Founded 1915
Type 4-year
Control .... Public
Calendar System .... Year
Academic Dean
Dr. W.D. Kitts .... Agricultural Sciences

MANITOBA

ASSINIBOINE COMMUNITY COLLEGE
1430 Victoria Avenue East
PO Box 935
Brandon, Manitoba R7A 5Z9
204-725-4530

Founded 1961
Type 2-year
Control .... Provincial
Calendar System .... Tri-Semester
Department Chairperson
W. Wight .... Agrcultural Training

UNIVERSITY OF MANITOBA
Winnipeg, Manitoba R3T 2N2
204-474-8880

Founded 1877
Type .... 4-year, Graduate
Control .... Provincial
Calendar System .... Session
Department Chairmen
G.E. Laliberte .... Agricultural Engineering
E.D. Murray .... Food Science
N.A.M. Eskin .... Foods & Nutrition

NOVA SCOTIA

ACADIA UNIVERSITY
Wolfville, Nova Scotia B0P 1X0
902-542-2201

Founded 1838
Type .... 4-year, Graduate
Academic Dean
Virginia Campbell .... Sch of Home Economics

MOUNT SAINT VINCENT UNIVERSITY
166 Bedford Highway
Halifax, Nova Scotia B3M 2J6
902-443-4450

Founded 1925

Type .... 3-, 4-year, Graduate
Control .... Private
Calendar System .... Academic Year
Department Chairman
Dr. Marilyn McDowell .... Home Economics

NOVA SCOTIA AGRICULTURAL COLLEGE
College Road
Truro, Nova Scotia B2N 5E3
902-895-1571

Founded 1905
Type 2-, 3-year
Control .... Provincial
Department Chairman
James Adams .... Agricultural Engineering

ST. FRANCIS XAVIER UNIVERSITY
Antigonish, Nova Scotia B2G 1C0
902-863-3300

Founded 1853
Department Chairman
Helen T. Aboud .... Home Economics

ONTARIO

BRESCIA COLLEGE
1285 Western Road
London, Ontario N6G 1H2
519-432-8353

Founded 1919
Type 3-, 4-year
Control .... Private
Department Chairman
Dr. Patricia Giovannetti .... Home Economics

**GEORGE BROWN COLLEGE OF APPLIED
ARTS & TECHNOLOGY**
PO Box 1015, Station B
Toronto 2B, Ontario M5T 2T9
416-967-1212

Founded 1967
Control .... Provincial
Academic Dean
M. Kerman .... Food Technology

**KEMPTVILLE COLLEGE OF AGRICULTURAL
TECHNOLOGY**
Kemptville, Ontario K0G 1J0

Founded 1971
Type 2-year
Control .... Provincial
Calendar System .... Annual
Department Chairmen
J.H. Clark .... Agricultural Engineering
R.I. Shaver .... Food

**RIDGETOWN COLLEGE OF AGRICULTURAL
TECHNOLOGY**
Ridgetown, Ontario N0P 2C0
519-674-5456

Founded 1922
Type 2-year
Control .... Provincial
Calendar System .... Trimester
Department Chairman
R.V. Jung .... Agricultural Engineering

RYERSON POLYTECHNICAL INSTITUTE
50 Gould Street
Toronto, Ontario M5B 1E8
416-595-5000

Founded 1948
Type 4-year
Control .... Provincial
Calendar System .... Semester

Department Chairman
J. Welsh (acting) .... Food, Nutrition

UNIVERSITY OF GUELPH
Guelph, Ontario N1G 2W1
519-824-4120

Founded 1964
Control .... Provincial
Calendar System .... Trimester
Director
W.R. Usborne .... Food Science

UNIVERSITY OF OTTAWA
Ottawa, Ontario K1N 6N5
613-231-3311

Founded 1848
Type .... 4-year, Graduate
Control .... Private
Calendar System .... Semester & Trimester
Department Chairman
Nicole Begin-Heick .... Nutrition

UNIVERSITY OF WINDSOR
Sunset Avenue
Windsor, Ontario N9B 3P4
519-253-4232

Founded 1857
Control .... Independent
Calendar System .... Annual
Department Chairman
N. Hall .... Home Economics

PRINCE EDWARD ISLAND

UNIVERSITY OF PRINCE EDWARD ISLAND
Charlottetown, Prince Edward Island C1A 4P3
902-892-4121

Founded 1969
Type 4-year
Control .... Public
Department Chairman
Estelle Reddin .... Home Economics

QUEBEC

MCGILL UNIVERSITY
845 Sherbrooke Street West
Montreal, Quebec H3A 2T5
514-392-4311

Founded 1821
Type 3-year
Control .... Provincial
Academic Dean
L.E. Lloyd .... Agriculture
School Director
S.M. Weber .... Food Science

SASKATCHEWAN

UNIVERSITY OF SASKATCHEWAN
Saskatoon, Saskatchewan S7N 0W0
306-343-2100

Founded 1907
Type .... 4-year, Graduate
Control .... Provincial
Calendar System .... 3 sessions
Academic Deans
J.A. Brown .... College of Agriculture
Dr. T.J. Abernathy ...... College of Home Economics
Academic Director
J.R. Peters .... School of Agriculture
College of Agriculture
J.A. Brown .... Dean
Dr. E.S. Humbert .... Dairy & Food Science

* School did not supply update for this edition
** School did not supply update for this edition or for previous edition

Key to accrediting agency acronyms

AABC	American Association of Bible Colleges
AACSB	American Assembly of Collegiate Schools of Business
AADS	American Association of Dental Schools
AALAC	American Association for Accreditation of Laboratory Animal Care
AALS	Association of American Law Schools
AAM	American Association of Museums
AANA	American Association of Nurse Anesthetists
AARTS	Association of Advanced Rabbinical and Talmudic Schools
AATS	Association of Theological Schools
ABA	American Bar Association
ABESPA	American Board of Examiners in Speech Pathology & Audiology
ABET	Accrediting Board of Engineering and and Technology
ABFSE	American Board of Funeral Service Education
ACBS	Accrediting Commission for Business Schools
ACC	Association of Chiropractic Colleges
ACCE	American Council for Construction Education
ACCJC	Accrediting Commission for Community and Junior Colleges
ACEJ	American Council on Education for Journalism
ACHA	American College Health Association
ACP	American College of Physicians
ACPE	American Council on Pharmaceutical Education
ACS	American Chemical Society
ACTE	American Council for Teacher Education
ACU	Association of Commonwealth Universities
ADA	American Dental Association Council on Dental Education
AHEA	American Home Economics Association
AICS	Association of Independent Colleges and Schools
AIP	American Institute of Physics
ALA	American Library Association Committee on Accreditation
AMA-AAMC	American Medical Association-Association of American Medical Colleges Joint Council on Medical Education
AMA-CAHEA/MA	American Medical Association, Committee on Allied Health Education and Accreditation, Medical Assistant
AMA-CAHEA/MRA	American Medical Association, Committee on Allied Health Education and Accreditation, Medical Records Administrator
AMC	American Medical Colleges
AOA	American Osteopathic Association, Office of Education
AOPA	American Optometric Association, Council on Education
AOTA	American Occupational Therapy Association
APA	American Psychological Association
APOD	American Podiatry Association, Council on Podiatry Education
APTA	American Physical Therapy Association
ASCP	American Society of Clinical Pathologists
ASHA	American Speech and Hearing Association
ASLA	American Society of Landscape Architects
ASLHA	American Speech-Language-Hearing Association
ATS	Association of Theological Seminaries
AUCC	Association of Universities and Colleges of Canada
AVA	American Veterinary Association, Council on Education
AVMA	American Veterinary Medical Association
CCE	Council on Chiropractic Education
CHE	Council on Education for Public Health
CODE	Commission on Dental Education
CRE	Council on Rehabilitation Education
CSWE	Council on Social Work Education
ECPD	Engineers Council for Professional Development
FAA	Federal Aviation Administration
FIDER	Foundation for Interior Design Education Research
ICC	Interstate Certification Compact
ICCC	International Council on Christian Churches
IFT	Institute of Food Technologies, Educational Committee
ISBE	Illinois State Board of Education
LCME	Liaison Committee on Medical Education
MAA	Middle Atlantic Association of Colleges of Business Administration
MSA	Middle States Association of Colleges and Secondary Schools
NAAB	National Architectural Accrediting Board
NAPNES	National Association for Practical Nurse Education and Service
NASA	National Association of Schools of Art
NASC	Northwest Association of Schools and Colleges
NASM	National Association of Schools of Music
NAST	National Association of Schools of Theatre
NATTS	National Association of Trade and

RESOURCES FOR FURTHER INFORMATION 473

NCA	North Central Association of Colleges and Schools	SABI	Southern Association of Bible Institutes, Bible Colleges and Bible Seminaries
NCATE	National Council for Accreditation of Teacher Education	SACS	Southern Association of Colleges and Schools
NEA	New England Association of Colleges and Schools	SAF	Society of American Foresters
NHSC	National Home Study Council	SCCE	Pontifical Faculty, Sacred Congregation for Catholic Education
NLN	National League of Nursing		
NSRA	National Shorthand Reporters Association	3IC	Three institution credit acceptance accreditation
NUCEA	National University Continuing Education Association	WASC	Western Association of Schools and Colleges
NWA	Northwest Association of Secondary Technical Schools		
			and Higher Schools

Grant Support Programs in Food Science, Agriculture, and Nutrition

by *Marquis Academic Media*

To assist readers interested in obtaining information on the grant support programs of government agencies, public and private foundations, corporations, community trusts, unions, educational and professional associations, and special interest organizations, the staff isolated data data from the *Annual Register of Grant Support, 1981-82*. Only those programs that awarded grants in agriculture, food science, and nutrition were selected.

Each complete program description in this alphabetical listing contains details on the type, purpose, and duration of the grant; the amount of funding available for each award and the entire program or all programs of the organization; eligibility requirements; number of applicants and recipients in the most recent year for which statistics are available; application instructions and deadline; personnel for the funding organization, as well as its address, founding date, and telephone number; data concerning the organization's areas of interest, cooperative funding programs, and consulting or volunteer services; and other pertinent information and special stipulations.

Essential programs in the *Register* for which no updated information was returned are included either as they appeared in the previous annual edition, or compiled entirely through secondary research. These entries are designated for the user by an asterisk following the name of the funding organization.

A

ADMINISTRATION FOR CHILDREN, YOUTH, AND FAMILIES*
Department of Health and Human Services
P.O. Box 1182
Washington, DC 20013
202-755-7782

Name of program:
Project Head Start
Type: Grants for comprehensive programs focused primarily upon children from low-income families who have not reached the age of compulsory school attendance. Supported projects should involve: (1) Comprehensive health (including medical and dental examinations), nutritional, social, psychological, educational and mental health services. (2) Appropriate activities to encourage, and provide opportunities for, participation of parents and effective use of provided services. (3) Other pertinent training, technical assistance, evaluation and follow-through activities.
Year program started: 1965
Purpose: To provide children from low-income families with such comprehensive health, nutrition, educational, social, and other services as will aid the children to attain their full potential.
Legal basis: Title V, Part A of the "Economic Opportunity Act of 1964," as amended.
Eligibility: Community Action Agencies, public and private nonprofit organizations or institutions of higher education are eligible to apply. However, the actual operation of a Head Start program may be delegated to an organization qualified to and capable of operating such a program.
Financial data: Federal funds may not exceed 80 percent of total project costs except in very poor communities where grantees may be relieved of all or part of the non-federal share.
Total amount of support: $735,000,000 federal appropriation for the fiscal year 1980.
Number of applicants most recent year: 1,262
Application information: Applicants for a Head Start grant should contact the HHS regional office in their area. Parents wishing to enroll their children should consult the local Community Action Agency or other public assistance agencies.
Duration: Grant awards are normally for one year in length.
Deadline: 150 days prior to planned operation.

ADMINISTRATION ON AGING OFFICE OF HUMAN DEVELOPMENT SERVICES
Department of Health and Human Services
330 Independence Ave., S.W.
Washington, DC 20201
202-245-0827

Founded: July 1965
Name of program:
Programs for the Aging
Type: Formula grants and projects used for the benefit of older persons. Programs could include establishing and maintaining area agencies on aging, planning and coordinating special programs for the aging, training of personnel to work on behalf of the elderly, research programs, model projects for the aging in high priority areas of states,

nutrition projects advocacy and long-term care.
Purpose: To serve older persons, especially low income and minority older persons. To provide assistance to states and area organizations for support of programs for older persons. To support training, research, and special demonstration programs for older persons.
Legal basis: Older Americans Act of 1965, Public Law 89-73, as amended by Public Laws 90-42, 91-69, 92-258, 93-29, 93-351, 94-135, 95-65, and 95-478.
Eligibility: All states and territories with approved state plans for formula grants, public or private agencies for projects.
Financial data: Programs are funded on federal and state matching rates with a consideration of the population 60-plus.
Amount of support per award: Average award for area planning $1,660,714 and $304,196 for social services. Average award for research and development is $100,000. Average award for nutrition is $3,314,732. Average award for model projects is $100,000. Award range for training is $23,000 to $240,000.
Application information: For formula grants, state plans are required to be submitted by the governor on a prescribed state plan format. Application forms for project grants are available from state agencies or regional offices.
Duration: Funds are awarded annually for formula and project grants.
Address inquiries to: Administration on Aging at above address.

ADRENAL METABOLIC RESEARCH SOCIETY OF THE HYPOGLYCEMIA FOUNDATION, INC.
153 Pawling Ave.
Troy, NY 12180
518-272-7154

Founded: Foundation founded in 1956; Fund in 1969.
Areas of interest: Hypoglycemia, adrenal dysfunction, nutrition.
Consulting or volunteer services: Both are offered.
Name of program.
  John W. Tintera, M.D. Memorial Fund
Year program started: 1969
Purpose: To acknowledge outstanding work in the field of endocrinology, nutrition, and metabolism.
Legal basis: Nonprofit, tax-exempt membership corporation chartered in the State of New York.
Financial data: No amount is specified, but is at the discretion of the board of directors.
Application information: By nomination only, at the discretion of the board of directors.
Officers and directors, 1978:
  Marilyn Hamilton Light, President and Executive Director
  Clair L. Pepperd, Vice President
  Lillian Schwartz Hilliard, Secretary
  Edward W. Light, Treasurer
  Rev. Chaudoin Callaway
  Elaine C. Grimm
  Rebecca H. Pratt

AGENCY FOR INTERNATIONAL DEVELOPMENT*
U.S. International Development Cooperative Agency
Washington, DC 20523
703-235-9011

Founded: 1961
Name of program:
  Centrally Funded Research Program
Type: Contracts addressing worldwide research problems relating to developing countries in the field of agriculture, forestry, fisheries, population, health, nutrition, education, development administration, science and technology, institutional development, and economics.
Year program started: 1961
Purpose: To promote research focusing on critical problems affecting the lives of the majority of people living in developing countries.
Legal basis: Foreign Assistance Act of 1961, as amended, and Public Law 93-189.
Eligibility: Program contracts are through institutions only, and must demonstrate a high degree of relevance to the problems of developing countries.
Financial data: Contracts vary in amount, depending upon the needs and nature of the request.
Total amount of support: $12,000,000 for the fiscal year 1977.
Application information: Further information can be obtained, on request, from the address below.
Duration: Varies.
Officers:
  Miloslav Rechcigl, Jr., Chief, Research and Methodology Division
Address inquiries to:
  Dr. M. Rechcigl, Jr.
  Agency for International Development
  DS/PO, Room 214E, RPC
  Washington, DC 20523

AMERICA THE BEAUTIFUL FUND
Shoreham Building
Washington, DC 20016
202-638-1649

Founded: 1965
Areas of interest: Architecture, history, museums and libraries, creative and performing arts, cultural relations, aged, children and youth, community development and services, construction and facilities, rural development, conservation, agriculture, and land resources.
Type: Advisory services, recognition awards, training sessions, and "seed" grants available to innovative community projects to enrich the quality of the natural, historic, and man-made environment.
Consulting or volunteer services: Available to develop workable community programs, provide professional level technical skills, arrange problem solving information exchanges between communities.
Year program started: 1965
Purpose: To assist and encourage realistic grassroots efforts to improve community life, rescue and revive American cultural and historical sites and traditions and develop community self-reliance.
Legal basis: IRS, New York Charities.
Eligibility: Local projects to protect, enhance or restore a community landmark or tradition that have broad-scale participation by a significant number of people and can be given an immediate try-out or testing period.
Financial data: "Seed" grants of up to $1,000 available plus equivalent in advisory services, educational materials, and workshops and technical assistance.
Amount of support per award: $500 average.
Total amount of support: $309,000 for the year 1980.
Matching fund requirements: "Seed" grants require matching funds or services.
Number of applicants most recent year: 1,000

Number of awards: 125 for the year ending June 1980.
Duration: One year, nonrenewable.
Deadline: June 30.
Board of Trustees:
  Nash Castro
  Henry Cowan
  Molly Hageboeck
  Mary Hemingway
  Peter Jamison
  Francis Kennedy
  Josh Peterfreund
  Richard Pough
  Gerd Stern
  James Sullivan
Officers:
  Alan Gussow, President
  Nash Castro, Vice President
  Charles Hobson, Vice President
  Paul B. Dowling, Secretary
  James Sullivan, Treasurer
Address inquiries to:
  P.B. Dowling, Executive Director
  America the Beautiful Fund
  219 Shoreham Building
  Washington, DC 20005

THE AMERICAN DIETETIC ASSOCIATION
430 North Michigan Ave.
Chicago, IL 60611
312-280-5000

Founded: 1917
Names of programs:
  1. *Mary C. Zahasky Memorial Awards*
  2. *Graduate Fellowships, Scholarships and Awards (Category A)*
  3. *Internship Scholarships (Category B)*
  4. *Undergraduate/Coordinated Undergraduate Scholarships (Category C)*
  5. *Dietetic Technician Scholarships (Category D)*
  6. *Sunkist Growers' Essay Competition*
Type: Scholarships, fellowships, short-term educational awards, and essay competition in the field of dietetics and nutrition.
Year program started: 1941
Purpose: Progress in the educational and scientific advancement of dietetics.
Eligibility: *Zahasky Awards:* These are short-term educational programs (seminars, workshops, etc.) for registered dietitians to widen, renew, and elaborate their professional development. *Scholarships (Category A):* Membership in The American Dietetic Association, status as a dietetic intern or senior in a coordinated undergraduate program, or admission or present pursuit of a program of graduate study, intention to practice in the field of dietetics, and U.S. citizenship. *Scholarships (Category B):* Acceptance by an accredited dietetic internship (application for scholarship may be made in advance of dietetic internship appointment; however, appointment must be confirmed by the time scholarship recipients are chosen in May), need for financial assistance, promise of being a valuable, contributing member of the profession, and U.S. citizenship. *Scholarships (Category C):* Completion of the academic requirements in an accredited college or university for standing as a junior in a curriculum of foods and nutrition, institution management, or the equivalent (NOTE: Application is made in the junior year; the award is given for study in the senior year), demonstration of financial need, and U.S. citizenship. *Scholarships (Category D):* Must be in first year of study in an ADA approved dietetic technician program (if selected, the scholarship is applicable for study during the second year), show promise of making a substantial contribution as a dietetic technician, show evidence of leadership and academic ability, and U.S. citizenship. *Sunkist Growers' Essay Competition:* This competition has been extended to its 18th year to encourage dietetic interns, senior in coordinated undergraduate programs, and members of ADA to report, in writing, effective programs of diet therapy. Sunkist Growers is offering annual awards for worthy descriptions (case histories) of effective dietary care of patients with special emphasis on the role of diet in the patient's progress.
Financial data: Zahasky Awards are made from the income of this endowment fund. Three monetary awards, a first prize of $150 and two awards of $100 each, will be made in the Sunkist Growers' Essay Contest. Each winner will also receive a copy of the bicentennial volume of James Lind's "Treatise on Scurvy", a classic in nutrition.
Application information: Scholarship applications may be requested from The Awards, Scholarships and Loan Fund Committee at the address above, from November 1, 1981 through January 15, 1982 for the Graduate, Undergraduate/CUP and Dietetic Technician Categories; and from November 1, 1981 through January 31, 1982 for the Intern Category. Due to the time required for processing, NO APPLICATIONS WILL BE SENT AFTER THESE DATES. Applications for all scholarships must reach Headquarters Office by February 15, 1982.
Special note for scholarships: When requesting applications, please specify which category: A—Graduate, B—Intern, C—Undergraduate/CUP or D—Dietetic Technician. You may apply for only one category. Deadline for essay competition is May 1.

AMERICAN HOME ECONOMICS ASSOCIATION FOUNDATION
2010 Massachusetts Ave., N.W.
Washington, DC 20036
202-862-8300

Founded: 1963
Areas of interest: Home economics and related subject matter.
Names of programs:
  1. *Ellen H. Richards Memorial Fund*
  2. *Freda A. DeKnight Fund*
  3. *Marie Dye Fund*
  4. *Ella H. McNaughton Fund*
  5. *AHEA Foundation General Fellowships Fund*
  6. *Ethel L. Parker Fund*
  7. *Flemmie P. Kittrell Fund*
  8. *Carley-Canoyer-Cutler Fund*
  9. *HEIH Section-Twin Cities HEIH Fund*
  10. *American Council of Life Insurance Fund*
  11. *International Fellowship Fund*
  12. *Marion K. Piper Fund*
  13. *Kappa Omicron Phi/Hettie Margaret Anthony Fund*
  14. *Inez Eleanor Radell Fund*
  15. *Virginia HEA Projects Grants*
  16. *National Porkettes Fellowship Fund*
  17. *Ruth O'Brien Project Grants*
  18. *Kraft Nutrition Grants*
Type: Fellowships offered to AHEA members, to minorities in the United States and to persons from developing countries for graduate study. The foundation shall be operated exclusively for scientific, educational, and charitable purposes. The particular business and objects of the foundation (as stated in the certificate of incorporation) shall be to encourage in the broadest and most liberal manner, not for profit but exclusively for educational,

scientific or charitable purposes, the advancement of home economics in all of its aspects; the promotion of education, study and scientific research in all fields relating to home economics and the support for such study and research by others in all other endeavors relating to dissemination of information concerning home economics, thereby fostering the public well-being. The foundation shall solicit funds from donors, and it shall disperse its assets only to individuals and educational and scientific organizations having purposes consonant with those of the foundation and whose work supports these objectives and purposes.
Legal basis: Nonprofit 501(c)(3)
Eligibility: Varies. Information on request.
Amount of support per award: $1,000-$5,000.
Number of applicants most recent year: Fellowships 103, 1982. Grants 12, 1981.
Number of awards: 14 fellowships in 1981; 6 grants in 1981.
Application information: Application forms available.
Duration: One year.
Deadline: Fellowships, January 15; Grants, November 15. Award announcement date within two months of deadlines.
Officers:
  Dr. Elizabeth W. Crandall, President
  Mrs. Mary Ellen McFarland, President-Elect
  Dr. Lois Lund, Treasurer
  Miss Mercedes Bates, Immediate Past President
  Ruth Hoeflin, AHEA President-Elect
  Mrs. Lois B. Rupert, Foundation State Representative
  Ms. Louise Young, Chairman, Deferred Giving/Estate Planning Committee
  Mrs. Naomi R. Koehler, Chairman, Foundation Grants/Corporate Giving Committee
  Dr. Helen LeBaron Hilton, Chairman, Membership Giving Committee
  Donald McDowell, At-Large Trustee
  Dr. Alice Morrow, At-Large Trustee
  Dr. Kinsey B. Green, Executive Director
  Glenn Craig, At-Large Trustee
Address inquiries to:
  Staff Liaison
  American Home Economics Association Foundation
Deadline: January 15.

AMERICAN HOME ECONOMICS ASSOCIATION FOUNDATION
2010 Massachusetts Ave., N.W.
Washington, DC 20036

Founded: 1962
Name of program:
  International Fellowships of the A.H.E.A.F.
Type: Graduate or advanced undergraduate fellowships for international students for study in the areas of home economics: child development, family economics, home management, foods and nutrition, clothing and textiles, housing, household equipment, and teacher education.
Eligibility: Applicants must be able to read and speak English sufficiently well to make study in the U.S. profitable, must be interested in home economics, and must have a strong interest in contributing to the development of home economics in their own countries.
Financial data: Approximately three to six fellowships ranging in value from $1,000 to $3,500 (tuition/fees equal to $500 minimum are remitted by cooperating colleges). Travel costs are not covered, but eligible scholars may apply for Fulbright Travel Grants.
Application information: Applications and information can be obtained from the address above.
Duration: Fellowships are tenable at approved institutions for one academic year in the United States.
Deadline: January 15.
Officers:
  Elizabeth Crandall, President
  Kinsey Green, Executive Director
Address Inquiries to:
  Staff Liaison-Fellowships

AMERICAN HOME ECONOMICS ASSOCIATION FOUNDATION
2010 Massachusetts Ave., N.W.
Washington, DC 20036

Founded: 1962
Name of program:
  National Fellowships of the A.H.E.A.F.
Type: Graduate fellowships in the area of home economics.
Eligibility: Applicants must be members of the American Home Economics Association and must have completed at least 1 year of professional home economics experience by the beginning of the academic year for which the award is granted and must show clearly defined plans for full-time graduate study during the time the award is held.
Financial data: Approximately five fellowships are awarded each year varying in value from $2,500 to $1,000 per award.
Application information: Applications and information may be obtained from the address above.
Duration: One academic year.
Deadline: January 15.
Officers:
  Elizabeth Crandall, President
  Kinsey Green, Executive Director
Address inquiries to:
  Staff Liaison-Fellowships

AMERICAN INSTITUTE OF BAKING
1213 Bakers Way
Manhattan, KS 66502
913-537-4750

Founded: 1919
Areas of interest: Research and education in baking, cereal science, food plant sanitation, and nutrition.
Name of program:
  Course in Baking Science and Technology
Type: Partial tuition scholarships for the course.
Year program started: August, 1952.
Purpose: To build new talent into the baking industry at an advanced level.
Legal basis: Non-profit corporation, tax-exempt (501(c)(3).
Eligibility: Applicants are judged by a scholarship committee.
Amount of support per award: $1,000.
Total amount of support: $12,000.
Matching fund requirements: $3,300 living expense and partial tuition.
Number of applicants most recent year: 65.
Number of awards: 12 per year.
Application information: Transcripts and letters of recommendation required.
Duration: Indefinite.
Deadline: December 1 and June 1, with announcement December 10 and June 10 respectively.
Executive Committee:
  J. Allen Baird
  Langdon S. Flowers
  Ernest B. Hueter
  John A. Kleutsch
  Philip W. Orth
  Curtis J. Patterson
  Morton I. Sosland
  Dr. William J. Hoover, Ex-Officio

Officers:
Langdon S. Flowers, Chairman
J. Allen Baird, Vice Chairman
Dr. William J. Hoover, President
Paul Klover, Treasurer
Sharon Forst, Assistant Secretary
Address inquiries to:
The Registrar
Special stipulations: Scholarships are awarded only for the Baking Science and Technology course of The American Institute of Baking.

AMERICAN INSTITUTE OF COOPERATION
1800 Massachusetts Ave., N.W.
Suite 508
Washington, DC 20036
202-296-6825

Founded: 1926 (National Association of Agriculture Cooperatives).
Names of programs:
1. *AIC Edwin G. Nourse Doctoral Award*
2. *AIC Master's Thesis Awards*
3. *AIC Undergraduate Term Paper Awards*

Type: Awards for the top doctoral dissertation, the two best master's theses, and five undergraduate term papers that deal directly with economic or social issues that affect operations of U.S. agricultural cooperatives.
Year program started: 1968 and 1975-76 respectively.
Eligibility: Graduate and undergraduate students in economics, agricultural economics, rural sociology, extension, education, journalism, and business in universities and colleges in the United States are invited to submit their entries.
Amount of support per award: Edwin G. Nourse Doctoral Award, $1,000. Master's Theses awards, $600 and $400. Five undergraduate awards of $100 each.
Application information: Entries for the three graduate awards should be completed in the 15-month period January 1-March 31 and undergraduate awards in the period September 1-June 1 immediately preceding submission.
Deadline: Graduate, April 15; Undergraduate, June 15.
Officers:
Owen K. Hallberg, President

AMERICAN MEAT INSTITUTE FOUNDATION
P.O. Box 3556
Washington, DC 20007
703-841-2400

Areas of interest: Meat science and technology.
Type: Project grants.
Purpose: To develop new basic knowledge to aid in meat quality improvements.
Legal basis: Nonprofit corporation.
Eligibility: University or college staff are eligible for grants.
Amount of support per award: $3,000 to $10,000 annually.
Total amount of support: $90,000 for the year 1980-81.
Cooperative funding programs: Occasionally.
Number of applicants most recent year: 29.
Number of awards: Six for the year
Application information: A research proposal is required.
Duration: One year, renewable.
Address inquiries to:
Dr. Forrest Dryden
Acting Director of Scientific Affairs

THE AMERICAN-SCANDINAVIAN FOUNDATION
127 East 73rd St.
New York, NY 10021
212-879-9779

Founded: 1910
Name of program:
The George C. Marshall Memorial Fund in Denmark
Type: Awards for (1) a professional study program lasting normally a minimum of three months, open to candidates in all fields (e.g., farming, labor organization, trade, merchandising, social work, design), or (2) graduate or undergraduate research in supervised Danish study programs of one academic year's duration.
Year program started: 1967
Purpose: To enable young Americans to study in Denmark, or to undertake special training or observation in their fields.
Legal basis: Nonprofit educational institution qualifying under statutes 501(c)(3), 509(a)(1), and 170(c)(2) of the IRS code.
Eligibility: Applicants must be U.S. citizens under 40 years of age. Graduate and undergraduate students may apply. Other factors being equal, preference will be given to younger candidates who have not previously studied in Denmark. In certain fields (e.g., literature) a working knowledge of Danish will be required; in others, a knowledge of Danish, while desirable, may not be necessary.
Financial data: Grants for the maximum twelve months will not exceed approximately $6,000 toward all expenses, including international travel. Grants for programs of shorter duration will be correspondingly lower.
Number of awards: 15-20 for the year 1981-82.
Application information: Applications may be obtained from the Exchange Division at the address above. In all cases candidates must present realistic, well-outlined programs including, where appropriate, correspondence with educators or professionals in Denmark, in which they demonstrate the merit of undertaking their project in Denmark. Applicants in design, architecture, music, etc., should be prepared to submit samples of their work for evaluation. Final decisions made by Marshall Fund Board in Copenhagen.
Duration: 3-12 months.
Deadline: November 1.
Address inquiries to:
Exchange Division

AMERICAN SOCIETY OF ENOLOGISTS
P.O. Box 411
Davis, CA 95617
916-752-0385

Founded: 1950
Areas of interest: A scientific society of enologists, viticulturists, and others in the fields of wine and grape production, promoting technical advancement and integrated research in science and industry.
Name of program:
American Society of Enologists Scholarships
Type: Scholarships for undergraduate or graduate students enrolled in enology or viticulture or in a curriculum which emphasizes a science basic to the wine and grape industry, and who intend to pursue a career in the wine or grape industry after graduation from college or university.
Eligibility: High school seniors, undergraduates, and graduate students may apply who have been accepted at an accredited college or university in the United States, are

enrolled in an appropriate field of study, are U.S. citizens, and demonstrate financial need and scholastic achievement.
Financial data: At least two scholarships (if satisfactory applicants are available) are to be awarded annually.
Amount of support per award: $1,500 per academic year.
Number of applicants most recent year: 12.
Number of awards: Five for the year 1979-80.
Application information: For application forms, contact the Secretary-Treasurer at the address above.
Duration: One academic year; renewable in open competition.
Deadline: March 15, with announcement May 15.
Address inquiries to:
Secretary-Treasurer

ARCA FOUNDATION
1425 21st St., N.W.
Washington, D.C. 20036
202-484-8871

Founded: 1952
Type: At present, the focus of the Arca Foundation is on intermediate or appropriate technology programs. The emphasis in this area is on alternative energy projects and small-scale farming programs, particularly concerned about program activity that is related to local community development projects and activities.
Eligibility: Institutions, organizations and groups are eligible to apply.
Amount of support per award: $5,000 to $25,000.
Total amount of support: $400,000 for the year 1979-80.
Number of applicants most recent year: 800.
Number of awards: 25 for years 179-80.
Application information: A brief letter and summary of project is required.
Duration: One year or the program period with possibility of renewal.
Deadline: October 15 and April 15 of each year.
Directors:
Smith Bagley, President
Anne B. Grant, Vice President
Hyman L. Battle, Jr., Secretary-Treasurer
Susan S. Bloom
Nancy S. Reynolds, Director
Jane Lehman, Director
Robert H. Levi, Director

Russell H. Long, Director
Address Inquiries to:
Margery Tabankin
Executive Director

ASSOCIATION OF OFFICIAL ANALYTICAL CHEMISTS
1111 N. 19th St.,
Suite 210
Arlington, VA 22209
703-522-3032

Founded: 1884
Name of program:
The Harvey W. Wiley Scholarship Award
Type: A scholarship for an undergraduate college student majoring in a subject of concern to the A.O.A.C. (chemistry, microbiology, pharmacology, etc.).
Year program started: 1966
Purpose: To encourage students to pursue careers in areas important to agriculture and public health.
Eligibility: The awardee should be a "B" average or better student ready for his last two years of undergraduate study, and be planning graduate study or proposing to work in an area important to public health or agriculture. He must have good character and need financial assistance to complete his education.
Financial data: $1,000 given at the rate of $500 per year.
Total amount of support: $500 for the year 1981.
Number of applicants most recent year: 10.
Number of awards: One for the year 1981.
Application information: Applications should be made to the individual listed below.
Duration: Two years.
Deadline: May 1 of the year the award is to be made.
Officers: David B. MacLean, Executive Director
Address inquiries to:
Kathleen Fominaya
Program Assistant

ASSOCIATION OF OFFICIAL ANALYTICAL CHEMISTS
1111 N. 19th St.
Suite 210
Arlington, VA 22209
703-522-3032

Founded: 1884

Name of program:
Harvey W. Wiley Award for the Development of Analytical Methods
Type: An award given annually to the scientist, or group of scientists, who has made outstanding contributions to the development and establishment of methods of analysis of those materials—foods, vitamins, food additives, color additives, pesticides, drugs, cosmetics, plants, feeds, fertilizers, forensic materials, and contaminants of food, water, air, or soil—for which provision is made in Official Methods of Analysis of the Association of Official Analytical Chemists
Year program started: 1957
Purpose: To emphasize the role of the scientist in protecting the consumer and the quality of his environment in a broad sense, including but not limited to protecting the consumer against unsafe, filthy, or decomposed food, unsafe or ineffective drugs, and unsafe cosmetics; against drugs, foods including additives, feeds, and fertilizers that fall below established standards or deviate from the statement on the label; against economic cheats and certain hazardous products; and against contaminants in the environment.
Eligibility: Nominees must have made outstanding contributions to analytical methodology for materials important to agriculture and public health.
Financial data: One award of $750 per year.
Total amount of support: $750 for the year 1981.
Number of applicants most recent year: 30.
Number of awards: One for the year 1981.
Application information: Application should be made to the individual listed below.
Duration: One year.
Deadline: April 1 of each year.
Officers:
David B. MacLean, Executive Director
Address inquiries to:
Kathleen Fominaya
Program Assistant

ASSOCIATION OF UNIVERSITIES AND COLLEGES OF CANADA
151 Slater St.
Ottawa, Ontario K1P 5N1 Canada
613-563-3502

Areas of interest: The fellowship will be awarded to the candidate studying subjects relating to agricultural credit systems.
Name of program:
Farm Credit Corporation Fiftieth Anniversary Fellowship
Purpose: In recognition of Canada's need for highly-trained, professionally-qualified men and women in the field of agriculture, the Farm Credit Corporation is establishing a fellowship to encourage research in the field of agricultural credit.
Eligibility: Candidates must be Canadian citizens or have held permanent resident status for one year prior to submitting application. Candidates must be graduates of a Canadian university or college with important previous exposure to agriculture. Fellowship holder may not hold concurrently any other awards in excess of total value of $3,500. On completion of the fellowship, one copy of the approved thesis must be sent to the Awards Office, AUCC, who will in turn forward it to the Farm Credit Corporation. The candidate may be an employee or a former employee of the Farm Credit Corporation. The fellowship would start any time during the next fiscal year following the date of acceptance.
Amount of support per award: At the master's level, each fellowship will consist of an annual contribution of $7,000 to the fellow whereas at the Doctorate level, $10,000 will be disbursed annually. Only tuition fees not exceeding $3,000 will be paid by the donor upon presentation of bills and/or receipts. In addition, married fellows will receive a supplementary allocation of $2,000 if the spouse accompanies the fellow. If the fellow were to study away from his/her residence, one return trip, economy class, would be paid from the fellow's residence to the university at which the successful candidate would be studying. However, if the fellow were married, a sum of $2,000 maximum would be paid per couple traveling, economy class. It is to be noted that during the last year of the Master's Program, the fellow would receive $6,000 of the total $7,000 disbursement, the remaining sum would only be paid upon the presentation and approval of the thesis. Similarly, at the Doctorate level, $9,000 would be paid for each of the two last years, the remaining $2,000 would then be disbursed upon presentation and approval of the thesis.
Number of awards: Not more than one person can be on fellowship during any fiscal year starting April 1. Tenable at any university, college or institution recognized by the AUCC.
Duration: *Master's:* The award is tenable for the duration of a two-year program provided the progress is satisfactory and approved by the supervisor. *Doctorate:* The award is tenable for the duration of a three-year program provided the progress is satisfactory and approved by the supervisor. *Note:* In unusual circumstances, a maximum extension of six months would be allowed to complete the study. The winning candidate at the master's level would not be eligible for the doctorate fellowship.
Deadline: February 1.
Application information: For further information and application forms write to the Awards Officer, Canadian Awards Division, at the address above.

ASSOCIATION OF UNIVERSITIES AND COLLEGES OF CANADA
151 Slater St.
Ottawa, Ontario, K1P 5N1 Canada
613-563-3502

Name of program:
Belgian Government Fellowships
Type: Fellowships for study and research at the postgraduate level in the fields of fine arts, art education, mathematics, chemistry, biology, zoology, botany, geology, physical geography, applied science, medicine, veterinary medicine, pharmacy, agronomy, social sciences including political science and economics; law, philology, history, philosophy, psychology and teaching. Scholarships are tenable at Universite Libre de Bruxelles, Universite Catholique de Louvain, Universite de Mons, Universite de Liege, Faculte de sciences agronomiques de l'Etat a Gembloux, University of Gent, University of Brussels, University Centre Antwerp, Ecole d'interpretes internationaux de l'Universite de l'Etat a Mons, Royal Academy of Fine Arts, Royal Conservatory of Music, Brussels, National Institute of Fine Arts, Antwerp, National Institute of Architecture and Urbanism, Antwerp.
Eligibility: Candidates must have a good knowledge of French or Dutch for specialized work and either of these or English for other work. Candidates must be Canadian citizens who are graduates of a Canadian university or college that is a member or affiliated to a member of the AUCC. Candidates must be under 35 years of age by April 20th in year of competition. There is no age limit for research awards. Applicants in Fine Arts, Music and Architecture must provide examples of their work with their application. For specifications and further information, contact address listed above.
Financial data: Study awards: 14,000-17,000 B.F. monthly, depending on the nature of the studies and the degrees or other qualifications held by the candidate. Research awards: 17,000 B.F. monthly. Awards include travel both ways, reimbursement of fees for courses and examinations, insurance against accidents and illness for the holder of an award and his/her family, reimbursement for necessary books and materials up to 6,000 B.F. per academic year and government intervention in the cost of printing a thesis (10,000-20,000 B.F.).
Number of applicants most recent year: 35.
Number of awards: Five.
Application information: Further information and application forms are available form the address listed above.
Duration: Study awards: one academic year with possibility of renewal. Research awards: 1-6 months.
Deadline: October 31.
Address inquiries to:
Director, International Programs

AUSCOTT, PTY, LIMITED
5 Gaesham St.
Sydney, New South Wales, Australia 2000

Name of program:
Postgraduate Scholarship in Agriculture
Type: Scholarships to graduates in agriculture from Australian universities.
Year program started: 1970
Eligibility: Candidates must have completed studies for their first degree within five years of making application.

Financial data: Scholarships are awarded every other year when vacant. Award covers the cost of return fare, tuition fees, a book allowance of $100 (Australian) and an incidental allowance of $550 (Australian) per year.
Amount of support per award: Consider as a guide the amount $3,650 (Australian) for Australian scholar plus travel, books, fees and allowance for incidental expenditures.
Application information: Applications and information are available from the registrars of any Australian university, or from the address listed above.
Duration: Scholarships are tenable at approved educational institutions in the United States, usually for two years.
Deadline: Applications must be received before February 28, in the year the scholarship is offered.
Address inquiries to:
  The Secretary
  Auscott Postgraduate Scholarship Committee

B

BUREAU OF INDIAN AFFAIRS
1951 Constitution Ave., N.W.
Washington, DC 20245
202-343-5875

Name of program:
  Indian Loans—Economic Development
Type: Loans for business, industry, agriculture, rehabilitation, education, and for relending by tribes and Indian organizations to members of such organizations; assistance to obtain financing from private and governmental sources.
Legal basis: Indian Financing Act of 1974.
Eligibility: Federally recognized Indians, Alaska natives, tribes, and Indian organizations on or near reservations are eligible.
Amount of support per award: Range of $1,000 to over $1,000,000: $100,000 average.
Total amount of support: $11,000,000 estimated for fiscal year 1981.
Application information: Applications must be initiated at the local, usually agency, level.
Deadline: None.
Address inquiries to:
  Division of Financial Assistance

C

THE CANADIAN DIETETIC ASSOCIATION*
7 Pleasant Blvd.
Suite 214
Toronto, Ontario M4T 1K2 Canada
416-925-2225

Founded: 1935
Areas of interest: Dietetics and nutrition.
Type: Awards for graduate study.
Year program started: 1966
Legal basis: Incorporated under Canada Corporations Act.
Eligibility: Membership in the Association is required.
Amount of support per award: One award of $1,500; two awards of $500.
Total amount of support: $5,500 for all awards for the year 1980-81.
Number of applicants most recent year: 10 for all awards.
Number of awards: Six for the year 1980-81.
Application information: Completed application form, statement of purpose for graduate study, academic transcript, and four recommendations are required.
Deadline: February 15, with announcement in June.
Officers, Board of Directors:
  Doreen N. Johnson, President
  Alice Wilson, Vice President
  Sister Roberta Freeman, President-Elect
  Mrs. Lorraine Van Allen, Secretary
  Mrs. Helen Macklin, Treasurer
Address inquiries to:
  Awards Committee

CANADIAN HOME ECONOMICS ASSOCIATION
151 Slater St.
Suite 203
Ottowa, Ontario K1P 5H3 Canada
613-232-9791

Founded: 1939
Areas of interest: Clothing and textiles, foods and nutrition, family life and home management, home economics education.
Names of programs:
  1. *Carnation Company Incentive Award*
  2. *Mary A. Clarke Scholarship*
  3. *Silver Jubilee Scholarship*
  4. *Ruth Binnie Scholarship*
Type: Scholarships to help students to continue with graduate work in home economics and related areas.
Year program started: 1972
Eligibility: Candidate must possess an undergraduate degree in home economics, with proven ability to do superior work.
Amount of support per award: Carnation Incentive Award, $500; Clarke, $2,000; Silver Jubilee, $2,000; Binnie, $3,500.
Total amount of support: $11,500 for the year 1980.
Cooperative funding programs: Carnation Company Incentive Award funding is donated by Carnation Company.
Number of awards: One in each category, except two Binnie Scholarships, for the year 1980.
Application information: Application forms may be obtained from the address above.
Duration: One year, nonrenewable.
Deadline: December 31.
Officers:
  Dr. Elizabeth Feniak, Past President
  May Maskow, President
  Linda McKay, Vice President
  Margaret Murray, Secretary
  Ellen Boynton, Treasurer

THE CHEMICAL INSTITUTE OF CANADA
151 Slater St.
Suite 906
Ottawa, Ontario, Canada K1P 5H3
613-233-5623

Founded: 1945
Name of program:
  The Ogilvie Flour Mills—Kenneth Armstrong Fellowship
Type: Fellowships for graduate study in fields comprising or related to physical biochemistry, colloidal chemistry of biological materials, or natural product chemistry. Particular systems of greatest interest would include proteins, carbohydrates, lipids, and enzymes.
Year program started: 1961
Eligibility: Graduates of Canadian universities who are enrolled in a master's or doctoral program in chemistry, biochemistry, or chemical engineering at a Canadian university or other institution accredited for postgraduate work are eligible.
Financial data: The stipend for each year is $5,000. In addition, $1,000 is paid to the institution at which the work is performed.
Total amount of support: $12,000 for the year 1979.
Number of applicants most recent

year: 18.
Number of awards: Two for the year ending June 1980.
Application information: Applications must be made on the prescribed form, which is available upon request from the address above. A statement of the student's acceptance at a qualified institution, a transcript of academic record, and a statement from a qualified person on the applicant's ability to carry out research must be sent with the completed application.
Duration: Fellowships are tenable for a period of 12 months, commencing on October 1. Renewal applications are possible for a second year toward the master's degree and for a second year toward the doctorate.
Deadline: Applications must be submitted no later than November 15 of the year preceding the fellowship tenure.
Selection Committee:
  G. Auger
  C. T. Bishop
  H. Favre
  B. Shelton
Executive Director:
  T. H. Glynn Michael
Address inquiries to:
  Executive Director

THE CLARK FOUNDATION
6116 N. Central Expressway
Suite 304
Dallas, TX 75206
214-361-7498

Founded: 1951
Areas of interest: Creative and performing arts, elementary through higher education and educational research, law and order, medical research, agriculture, land resources, teenage drug abuse program and mental retardation.
Name of program:
  The Clark Foundation Scholarship Program
Type: One-year scholarship assistance to selected high school graduates who have successfully competed in academic events, are in the upper quarter of their respective graduating classes, and require financial assistance.
Year program started: 1967
Purpose: To encourage and assist worthy and needy selected high school graduates who have successfully competed in academic events, are in the upper quarter of their respective graduating classes, and require financial assistance.
Eligibility: Any student in the Dallas Independent School District, and for statewide eligibility, The Texas Interscholastic League, who meets the eligibility requirements and competes in the academic contests may apply. Applicants must submit their applications to either the Principal of the high school they attend in the Dallas Independent School District or the designated counselor for the Clark Program. In the State, applications must be submitted to the Texas Interscholastic League, Austin, Texas.
Financial data: Amount of all scholarship awards is $1,000 and for one year only. No renewables.
Total amount of support: $125,000.
Number of applicants most recent year: Approximately 356.
Number of awards: 125.
Application information: Applications are accepted only through the Dallas Independent School District and The Texas Interscholastic League.
Duration: One year, nonrenewable.
Deadline: May 30 of each year.
Trustees:
  David J. Henry
  Walter Kerbel
  DeWitt Weaver
Officers:
  Walter Kerbel, Executive Secretary
Address inquiries to:
  Walter Kerbel

COLUMBIA UNIVERSITY
College of Physicians and Surgeons
701 W. 168th St.
New York, NY 10032
212-579-2500

Founded: 1754
Name of program:
  The Louisa Gross Horwitz Prize
Type: An annual prize designed to honor a major scientific contribution in basic research to the fields of biology or biochemistry.
Year program started: 1967
Purpose: To honor extraordinarily noteworthy research in biology or biochemistry.
Eligibility: The prize is open to anyone in basic research in the fields of biology or biochemistry.
Amount of support per award: Varies with endowed income.
Number of awards: One for each year ending in December. May be shared.
Application information: Anyone may make a nomination. A 500-word description of the research is required and should be written on a form available from the above address. Information and nomination forms are mailed annually to an extensive list of possible nominators.
Duration: The prize is awarded annually.
Chairman:
  I. Bernard Weinstein, M.D.
Address inquiries to:
  I. Bernard Weinstein, M.D., Chairman
  Louisa Gross Horwitz Prize Committee

COMMUNITY SERVICES ADMINISTRATION
Office of Community Action
Community Food and Nutrition Program
1200 19th St., N.W.
Washington, DC 20506
202-632-6694

Name of program:
  Community Food and Nutrition Program
Type: Project grants; training. Funds may be used in a variety of ways to supplement, extend and broaden other food programs and to provide, on an emergency basis, foodstuffs to low-income families/individuals in order to counteract conditions of starvation and malnutrition.
Purpose: To help communities counteract the conditions of hunger and malnutrition among the poor.
Legal basis: Economic Opportunity Act of 1964 as amended, Title II, Section 222(a)(1); Public Law 95-568; 42 U.S.C. 2809; 92 Stat. 2426.
Eligibility: Community action agencies, state and local governments, public and private nonprofit agencies that meet CSA's general eligibility criteria, Indian tribal councils, migrant and seasonal farmworker organizations are eligible to apply.
Financial data: Funding decisions are reviewed at the national level.
Amount of support per award: $5,000 to $300,000; $42,000 average.
Total amount of support: $28,645,000 for fiscal year 1979; $28,000,000 estimated for fiscal year 1980; $26 million estimated for fiscal year 1981.
Matching fund requirements: No nonfederal share.
Application information: Application materials are available upon request to the address above.
Duration: 12-24 months.

Deadline: Contact the agency.
Address inquiries to:
Marshall Boarman
Community Food and Nutrition Program

CONSERVATION AND RESEARCH FOUNDATION
P.O. Box 1445
Connecticut College
New London, CT 06320
203-873-8514

Founded: 1953
Areas of interest: Conservation, education, environmental law, earth sciences, agriculture and land resources, biology, environmental technology.
Name of program:
Environmental Awards
Type: Projects and activities in the environmental field, especially those not eligible for support from conventional sources, are funded through grants and contracts. Fellowships are awarded occasionally for very special programs.
Year program started: 1953
Purpose: To promote the conservation of the earth's natural resources and deepen understanding of the intricate relationship between man and the environment that supports him.
Eligibility: Individuals and institutions are eligible to apply.
Amount of support per award: $500 to $5,500 for the year 1980.
Total amount of support: $12,000 for the year 1980.
Number of applicants most recent year: 144.
Number of awards: Seven for the year ending December 1980.
Application information: A letter of inquiry should be sent to the President at the address above.
Duration: Unrestricted and renewable.
Deadline: None.
Trustees and officers:
Richard H. Goodwin, President
John R. Johnston, Treasurer & Clerk
Mary G. Wetzel, Secretary
Winslow Briggs, Trustee
Wallace D. Bowman, Trustee
Belton A. Copp, Trustee
Frederick Kavanagh, Trustee
Hubert W. Vogelmann, Trustee
Alexander T. Wilson, Trustee
Address inquiries to:
Richard H. Goodwin, President

CORN INDUSTRIES RESEARCH FOUNDATION, INC.
Division of Corn Refiners Association, Inc.
1001 Connecticut Ave., N.W.
Washington, DC 20036
202-331-1634

Founded: 1932
Areas of Interest: Analytical chemistry, biochemistry, engineering, environmental science, enzymology, nutrition (animal and human), organic chemistry, physical chemistry, and other disciplines as they relate to corn, corn wet-milling, and the products derived from corn by the corn wet-milling process (starch, corn syrup, dextrose, corn oil, corn gluten meal, and feed).
Type: Fellowships, technical investigations, contract research, and research grants.
Year program started: 1933
Purpose: To conduct industry-wide programs or research, technical service, and public information. To further public welfare, to further the welfare of the industry, and to contribute to the advancement of science.
Legal basis: Nonprofit corporation.
Amount of support per award: Variable.
Total amount of support: Variable.
Matching fund requirements: None.
Number of applicants most recent year: 50, all programs.
Number of awards: Five for the year 1978.
Application information: Research form must be submitted.
Duration: One year, January 1 to December 31; renewable.
Deadline: April 15, with notification December 15.
Officers:
Robert C. Liebenow, President
Address inquiries to:
Director of Scientific Activities

D

DEPARTMENT OF HEALTH & HUMAN SERVICES
Office of Human Development Services
Administration for Native Americans
330 Independence Ave., S.W.
Washington, DC 20201
202-426-3960

Founded: 1974
Areas of interest: General community programming, training and technical assistance and research, demonstration and evaluation.
Name of program:
Native American Programs
Type: Grants may be used for such purposes as, but not limited to: projects aimed at increasing the capabilities of Indian tribes to take over services now provided by non-Indian controlled organizations; projects designed to meet the nutritional and emergency medical needs of Native Americans and to provide other needed services to promote individual and family self-sufficiency; providing for the establishment and operation of urban centers serving Indian people living off-reservation; providing for self-help and community economic development efforts.
Joint funding: This program is considered suitable for joint funding with closely related federal financial assistance programs in accordance with the provision of OMB Circular No. A-111. For programs that are not identified as suitable for joint funding, applicant may consult the headquarters or field office of the appropriate funding agency for further information on statutory or other restrictions involved.
Year program started: Transferred from OEO to HEW in FY 1974.
Purpose: To promote the goal of economic and social self-sufficiency for American Indians, native Hawaiians, and Alaskan natives.
Legal basis: 42 U.S.C. 2991 et seq.; Title VIII, Community Services Act of 1974, Public Law 93-644. Extended through September 30, 1981 by P.L. 95-568.
Eligibility: Governing bodies of Indian tribes, Alaska native villages, and regional corporations, and other public or private nonprofit agencies.
Financial data: Tribal grants range from $40,000 to $5,250,000 with $125,000 average; Urban grants range from $40,000 to $200,000 with $80,000 average.
Total amount of support: $33,800,000 estimated for FY 1982; $33,800,000 available for 1981.
Matching fund requirements: Formula and matching requirements general rules: 20 percent in nonfederal contributions. Waiver for this matching share may be obtained if grantee meets criteria which are published in 45 CFR 1336.52.
Cooperative funding programs: Not applicable to grants.
Number of applicants most recent

year: 262 applications received in FY 1980.
Number of awards: 211 grant awards made in FY 1980.
Application information: Nonprofit organizations that have not previously received HDS program support must submit proof of nonprofit status. Preapplication coordination: Applicants are required to submit program plans to clearinghouse in accordance with Part I of OMB Circular A-95 (Revised). Federally recognized tribes are exempt from submitting plans to state clearinghouses but are encouraged by the Administration for Native Americans to do so. Information regarding the availability of grant funds will be published from time to time in the Federal Register as Program Announcements, which will provide details on program objectives for which applications are being solicited and other application requirements. Applicants whether applying for new or continuation grants are required to submit plans to clearinghouses on the same basis as stated above. The Administration for Native Americans will provide each applicant agency with the appropriate forms for applying for federal assistance and instructions for preparation of application for grants from Human Development Services programs. Applications for urban Indian programs should be submitted to the HEW Regional Offices. All other applications should be submitted to HDS Grants Management Branch, Department of Health and Human Services, HHS North Building, Room 1740, 330 Independence Ave., S.W., Washington, DC 20201. This program is subject to provisions of OMB Circular No. A-110.
Duration: Duration of support and renewal possibilities will be indicated in the Program Announcement in the Federal Register.
Deadline: Deadlines for receipt of applications for potential new grantees will be shown in the Program Announcement. Grantees applying for continuation support may do so within their project period. Formal funding request for continuation (renewal) grants should be received in HDS Grants Management Branch 90 days prior to anticipated approval date (project period end.) Award announcement date will be made by letter from Commissioner for the Administration for Native Americans.
Officers:
Richard Schweiker, Secretary of Health and Human Services
Arabella Martinez, Assistant Secretary for Human Development Services, Health, Education and Welfare
A. David Lester, Commissioner, Administration for Native Americans, Human Development Services, Health, Education and Welfare
Address inquiries to:
For program information and statistics: Director, Policy Planning and Budget Division Administration for Native Americans. (Contact person for this update).
*****Please note:** General areas of interest: (1) General Community Programming (providing for core administration, and local priority social services programs). (2) Training and Technical Assistance (by contract to provide man days to grantees for assistance in management, financial, personnel and planning activities). (c) Research, Demonstration, and Evaluation (identification of gaps in services for Native Americans, evaluation of Native American programs in effect, review and research impact, implications and possible applications of previous research in Native American projects in the last decade).

F

FARM FOUNDATION
1211 W. 22nd St.
Oak Brook, IL 60521

Founded: 1933
Name of program:
Extension Graduate Training Fellowships
Type: Extension Graduate Training Fellowships for study in the fields of social sciences and educational administration and methodology with emphasis on courses in agricultural economics, rural sociology, psychology, political science, and agricultural geography.
Year program started: 1947
Purpose: To stimulate further training in study courses of value in extension work.
Eligibility: Agricultural extension workers in the United States may apply. Priority is given to administrators and supervisory personnel. Applicants must be recommended by their extension directors and accepted by the university selected as the training center.
Financial data: Approximately eight fellowships are awarded annually. Value of the fellowship varies, depending on need and the period of study, with maximum of $4,000 for nine months. Payments are made monthly.
Total amount of support: $19,000 for the year 1980-81.
Application information: Applications and information are available from the address given above.
Duration: Fellowships are tenable at selected universities in the United States for one quarter, one semester, or nine months. Fellowships may be renewed by resubmitting applications.
Deadline: March 1.
Trustees:
W. R. Peirson, Chairmain of the Board
Joseph P. Sullivan, Vice Chairman of the Board
Richard E. Albrecht, Chairman, Executive Committee
And 26 additional Trustees
Officers:
R. J. Hildreth, Managing Director
Address inquiries to:
Managing Director

FATS AND PROTEINS RESEARCH FOUNDATION, INC.
2720 Des Plaines Ave.
Des Plaines, IL 60018
312-827-0139

Founded: 1962
Areas of interest: Chemistry, agriculture, nutrition, biology, industrial technology and manufacturing, environmental technology.
Type: Grants-in-aid and contracts for research projects pertaining to new and expanded uses for inedible and edible animal and poultry fats and proteins; processing of animal by-products.
Purpose: To promote scientific and technological research into new and expanded uses for fats and proteins from animal by-products and processing technology.

Eligibility: Colleges, universities, and research institutes with appropriate interests and capabilities are eligible to apply.
Financial data: Awards vary in amount, depending upon the needs and nature of the request.
Total amount of support: $572,000 for the year 1980.
Application information: Prospective applicants should submit a brief outline of the proposed project (including background information, objectives, scope and mode of approach) along with a statement of the required budget and a brief biographical sketch of personnel to be involved in the research.
Duration: Varies.
Deadline: Applications may be submitted at any time and are considered on an individual basis.
Directors:
George Theobald Sr., Chairman
Charles Tocalino, Vice Chairman
Jack R. Barensfeld, Secretary-Treasurer
David L. Gilcrest, Executive Director
Werner R. Boehme, Technical Director
Eleanor S. Beckley, Assistant Secretary-Treasurer

FEDERATION OF AMERICAN SOCIETIES FOR EXPERIMENTAL BIOLOGY
9650 Rockville Pike
Bethesda, MD 20014
301-530-7090

Name of program:
3M Life Sciences Award, administered by FASEB
Sponsor: 3M Company
Type: Award for research studies in the life sciences that have made significant contributions to the health and welfare of mankind.
Eligibility: Nominees must be members of FASEB Societies.
Amount of support per award: $5,000 to the awardee; an additional $1,500 for travel funds for three additional scientists; $10,000 to the parent institution to support the awardee's research and travel.
Application information: Nominations must be made by members of FASEB Societies.
Deadline: November 1.
Address inquiries to:
3M Award Nominating Committee
Attention: Mrs. Ann Nixon

G

GEORGETOWN UNIVERSITY*
Department of Chemistry
Washington, DC 20057
202-625-4065

Founded: 1789
Name of program:
Doctoral Program in Chemistry
Type: University Fellowships to enable graduate students to earn Ph.D. degree in chemistry (inorganic, organic, analytical, physical or theoretical chemistry, or biochemistry).
Year program started: 1924
Eligibility: Fellowships are open to nationals of any country, and a bachelor's degree or the equivalent is required.
Financial data: The fellowship provides a $6,500 award, plus $4,670 worth of free tuition for 12 months.
Amount of support per award: $11,170 per 12-month fellowship.
Number of applicants most recent year: 155.
Number of awards: 17 for the year 1980-81.
Application information: Application information may be obtained from the address above.
Duration: Nine months to a year.
Deadline: Applications will be accepted at any time, but preferably before March 1.
Directors:
Louis Baker, Chairman & Professor
Vaclav Horak, Professor
Joseph Earley, Professor
Soma Kumar, Professor
Michael Pope, Professor
Daniel Martire, Professor
Charles Hammer, Associate Professor
Robert deLevie, Professor
Delanson Crist, Associate Professor
Richard Bates, Associate Professor
Officers:
Jacinto Steinhardt, Emeritus Professor
Daniel W. Armstrong, Assistant Professor
Richard G. Weiss, Assistant Professor
David C. Yang, Assistant Professor
Edwin Becker, Professorial Lecturer
G. William Milne, Professorial Lecturer
Walter L. Zielinski, Lecturer

H

THE HONOR SOCIETY OF PHI KAPPA PHI
P.O. Box 16000
Louisiana State University
Baton Rouge, LA 70893
504-388-4917

Founded: 1897
Areas of interest: Phi Kappa Phi recognizes scholastic excellence in all academic fields—from agriculture through zoology.
Name of program:
Graduate Fellowships
Type: Fellowships for the first year of graduate or professional school.
Year program started: 1932
Purpose: To stimulate members of Phi Kappa Phi to go to graduate or professional school.
Legal basis: Incorporated in Michigan, May 20, 1972; authorized to operate in Louisiana, September 1978. Tax-exempt under IRS 501(c)(3).
Eligibility: Applicant must maintain high scholastic standing and be recommended by a chapter of Phi Kappa Phi.
Financial data: Recipient may not accept another fellowship simultaneously, but may accept tuition waivers and scholarships.
Amount of support per award: $3,000.
Matching fund requirements: None.
Cooperative funding programs: Awards made through Phi Kappa Phi Foundation, a companion organization to the Society.
Number of applicants most recent year: 121.
Number of awards: 40 for the year 1980-81.
Application information: Further information is available from a chapter secretary or from the national office.
Duration: One academic year, nonrenewable.
Deadline: March 1, with announcement April 1.
Board of Directors:
James T. Barrs, Vice President, Eastern Region
George W. Bright, Vice President, East Central Region
Albert L. Fisher, President
Ray Newton, Vice President, Western Region
Elizabeth Ann Halley, Regent
Albertine Krohn, Past President
Ilona Herlinger, National Vice President
John J. McDow, President Elect

Arthur A. Rezny, Vice President, West Central Region
George L. Robertson, Executive Director
Stephen W. White, Editor
Roger R. Yoerger, Director of Fellowships

Address inquiries to: Application forms must be submitted to chapter secretary or chapter selection committee.

I

INSTITUTE OF FOOD TECHNOLOGISTS
221 North LaSalle St.
Suite 2120
Chicago, IL 60601
312-782-8424

Founded: 1939
Name of program:
IFT Fellowship and Scholarship Program
Type: 23 graduate fellowships to support advanced study in the field of food technology; 55 scholarships to encourage undergraduate enrollment in food science and technology.
Year program started: 1950
Purpose: To extend and improve knowledge concerning the application of modern science and engineering to the manufacture and distribution of food.
Eligibility: Qualified individuals with above-average interest in research are eligible for fellowship support. During tenure of the fellowship award, applicants must be enrolled in a United States or Canadian educational institution that is doing fundamental research in food science. Scholarship applicants must be students with exceptionally high scholastic ability who must be enrolled in an IFT approved school at the effective date of the scholarship.
Financial data: Fellowship winners may not accept more than $7,500 in nonservice awards, including the IFT Fellowship award.
Amount of support per award:
Fellowships carry stipends of $1,000, $1,250, $5,000 and $6,000.
Scholarships are $500 and $1,000.
Application information: Official application materials are available from the department head of an educational institution offering an IFT approved program in food science and technology, or upon request to the Institute at the address above. Completed applications must be submitted directly to the department head who will forward them to the Institute.
Duration: Fellowships and scholarships provide one year of support with renewals possible upon reapplication.
Deadline: Applications must be submitted by February 1, February 15, and March 1 for study to be undertaken during the following academic year.

THE INTERNATIONAL ATLANTIC SALMON FOUNDATION
P.O. Box 429
St. Andrews, New Brunswick
Canada E0G 2X0
506-529-3818

Founded: 1968
Areas of interest: Conservation of Atlantic salmon and aquatic resources through programs in education, research, and management.
Name of program:
IASF Fellowships
Type: Fellowships for advanced study or research in fields concerning Atlantic salmon.
Year program started: 1974
Purpose: To allow persons involved in Atlantic salmon biology, management, or related fields to pursue programs of higher education, or to develop new ideas of benefit to salmon.
Legal basis: Tax-exempt, nonprofit organization.
Eligibility: Applicant must be a North American resident, generally having an undergraduate degree or experience in the field.
Amount of support per award: $1,000-$3,000.
Total amount of support: $3,000 for the year 1979.
Number of applicants most recent year: 18.
Number of awards: 2 for the year 1980.
Application information: Further information can be obtained from the Canadian address above.
Duration: 1 year, renewal unlikely.
Deadline: End of February, with announcement in April.
Address inquiries to:
Mrs. Lee Sochasky
Program Coordinator

THE INTERNATIONAL ATLANTIC SALMON FOUNDATION
P.O. Box 429
St. Andrews, New Brunswick
Canada E0G 2X0
506-529-3818

Founded: 1968
Areas of interest: Conservation of Atlantic salmon and aquatic resources through programs in education, research, and management.
Name of program:
IASF Grants
Type: Flexible granting program. Awards in the past have been given for research projects, conferences, book publishing, lecture series, and equipment purchases.
Year program started: 1969
Purpose: To promote wise management of Atlantic salmon and the aquatic environment through support of programs in education research, management, and international cooperation.
Legal basis: Tax-exempt, nonprofit organization.
Amount of support per award: Past range of $50-$12,000.
Total amount of support: Up to $15,000 in 1978.
Number of applicants most recent year: 8.
Number of awards: 2 for the year 1980.
Application information: Further information may be obtained from the Canadian address above.
Duration: Varies, as do renewal possibilities.
Deadline: None.
Address inquiries to:
Dr. W. M. Carter, Executive Director
*Please note: Grant requests are received throughout the year from sources in North America and abroad and are evaluated individually.

INTERNATIONAL AGRICULTURAL CENTRE
P.O. Box 88
6700 AB Wageningen, Netherlands
08370-19040

Founded: 1951
Name of program:
International Agricultural Centre Fellowship
Type: Fellowships to enable nationals from industrialized countries to follow a program of study, in the Netherlands, in agricultural science in the widest sense.

Year program started: 1951
Purpose: Furthering international contact in agricultural sciences by creating possibilities for study for promising scientists.
Eligibility: In general, the program is for nationals of industrialized countries who are 25 years of age or older, possess at least a B.S. degree, and have experience in their particular field of study.
Financial data: Fellowship includes full room and board, book allowance and health insurance, plus cash allowance of Dfl. 18 per day. Travel costs to and from country of origin are not paid.
Number of applicants most recent year: 70.
Number of awards: 40 for the year ending December 1980.
Application information: Official application forms are available upon request from the address above.
Duration: 2 weeks to 6 months, with a possibility for extension.
Deadline: Minimum 3 months in advance of program dates.

INTERNATIONAL CENTRE FOR AGRICULTURAL EDUCATION (CIEA)
Mattenhofstrasse 5
CH-3003 Berne (Switzerland)
(031) 61 26 19

Founded: 1956
Areas of interest: Agriculture education and international studies; technical assistance; women's studies; community development and services; rural development; secondary, adult, and vocational education; educational research; communications.
Name of program:
International Course on Vocational Education and Teaching in Agriculture
Type: International cooperation on the improvement of agricultural education and teaching on the secondary level. Organization of courses (in even numbered years) and excursions.
Year program started: 1958
Purpose: Recycling.
Legal basis: Swiss federal legislation. Newest by-law; August 15, 1973.
Eligibility: Directors, professors, and teachers with several years of experience in the field of agricultural teaching from any country are eligible to apply. Courses are in English, French, and German. Open to candidates of both industrial and developing countries.
Financial data: Grants for participants from developing countries according to the means available.
Amount of support per award: Either the total cost of the course and board and traveling expenses, or part of it, depending on the needs of the recipient.
Number of applicants most recent year: 100-120.
Number of awards: 40-60 for the year ending August 1980.
Application information: Application information is available on request from the address above.
Duration: Four weeks (July to August), nonrenewable.
Deadline: Applications must be returned by May 31.
Organizing Committee:
Dr. W. Thomann, President
W. Greminger, Director of the Course
Dr. M. Bachmann
B. Beuret
R. Kaser
R. Morgenthaler
P. Niklaus
O. Raemy
Dr. A. Wehrli
Address inquiries to:
Secretariat of the CIEA

INTERNATIONAL FOOD SERVICE EXECUTIVES ASSOCIATION, INC.
111 East Wacker Dr.
Suite 600
Chicago, IL 60601
312-644-6610

Founded: 1901
Areas of interest: An educational and fraternal organization of proprietors, managers, stewards, caterers, dietitians, purchasing agents of hotels, clubs, restaurants, cafeterias, institutions, dining cars, steamships, and airlines.
Names of programs:
1. *IFSEA Scholarship*
2. *Statler Scholarship*
3. *Worthy Goal Scholarship*
Type: Tuition scholarships.
Year program started: 1939
Purpose: To give needed assistance to qualified young people in furthering their careers in the food service field.
Legal basis: Tax-exempt nonprofit.
Eligibility: All applications must be submitted through a chartered local branch of IFSEA. Post-high school applicants are eligible.
Amount of support per award: $200 to $500.
Total amount of support: $100,000 for the year 1980.
Number of applicants most recent year: 280 for the year 1980.
Number of awards: 250 for the year 1980.
Application information: All applicants must be screened at the branch level. Applications must include transcript of grades, letter of acceptance from the school of the student's choice, and three letters of recommendation.
Duration: Annual; renewable.
Deadline: March 1; IFSEA and Worthy Goal scholarships are announced in April and May, the Statler in August.
Trustees, Worthy Goal Foundation:
John Ceruti
Gil Wiggins
Neil Goodman
1978-1979 Board of Directors:
Neil Goodman, International President
Beverly Lowe, 1st Vice President
Michael Mavros, 2nd Vice President
Steven Chen, International Treasurer and Central Region Vice President
Jerry Rubenstein, International Secretary and Eastern Region Vice President
Richard Dixon, Southern Region Vice President
James Salerno, Western Region Vice President
Thomas Berndt and Isadore Goldscher, Eastern Region Directors
Rosemary Bass, Central Region Director
David Hassler, Southern Region Director
Dieter Gonzales, Western Region Director
Milton Vallen, Immediate Past President
Barbara Chalik, Executive Vice President
Address inquiries to:
Barbara Chalik
Executive Vice President
*****Please note:** IFSEA and Worthy Goal winners are selected by Regional Scholarship Committees at the regional conferences in the spring. All applications then are referred to Statler for further grants.

K

KAPPA OMICRON PHI, INC.
National Home Economics Honor Society

1411 Lafayette Parkway
Williamsport, PA 17701
717-323-7641

Founded: 1922
Areas of interest: Home economics.
Name of program:
  Kappa Omicron Phi/Hettie Margaret Anthony Fellowship
Type: Fellowship awarded to home economics major for graduate study at master's or doctoral level.
Year program started: 1969-70
Purpose: To further the best interests of home economics by recognizing and encouraging scholastic excellence.
Legal basis: Nonprofit corporation.
Eligibility: Applicants must meet the requirements of the AHEA Fellowships Committee.
Financial data: The committee reserves the right to reconsider an award if the recipient receives a similar award for the same academic year.
Amount of support per award: $2,000 per year.
Cooperative funding programs:
  American Home Economics Association Foundation.
Number of awards: 1 annually.
Application information: Secure applications from the AHEA Fellowships Staff Liaison at the address below.
Duration: One academic year, nonrenewable.
Deadline: January 15; awards are made in March; the official announcement is made at the Annual AHEA Meeting in June.
Officers until August 1980:
  Dr. Alice Koenecke, President
  Dr. Patsy R. Alexander, Vice President/Program
  Dr. Blanche Wise, Vice President/Finance
  Mrs. Mary Ann Cessna, Secretary
  Mrs. Betty J. Church, Conclave Manager
  Vicki Varner, Student Representative
  Kathryn Buhmann, Student Representative
  Rita Marie Schneider, *Distaff* Editor
  Dr. Dorothy I. Mitstifer, Executive Secretary, Central Office

W. K. KELLOG FOUNDATION
400 North Ave.
Battle Creek, MI 49016
616-965-1221

Founded: 1930
Type: Grants for experimental or pioneering projects to improve professional education and services in the areas of medicine, hospital care, nursing, dentistry, education and agriculture. Primary interest is in projects concerned with the application of knowledge rather than basic research alone. Support is not available for endowments, development campaigns, capital facilities, conferences, research, or publications and is seldom provided for the operational phases of established programs.
Year program started: 1930
Purpose: To narrow the gap between the creation of knowledge and its use for the public good by supporting nonpartisan, educational, agricultural, and health activities in the public interest.
Eligibility: Qualified tax-exempt nonprofit institutions and agencies with appropriate interests are eligible to apply.
Financial data: Grants vary in amount, depending upon the needs and nature of the requests.
Total amount of support: $47,670,993 for the fiscal year ending August 31, 1980.
Number of awards: 530 program payments including 279 new commitments for the year ending August 31, 1981.
Application information: No official application forms are issued. Prospective applicants should, as a first step, submit a brief letter or memorandum which includes a statement of the basic problem and plans for its solution, an outline of project objectives and proposed operational procedures, a description of available personnel and financial resources and an estimate of project duration and cost. If necessary, applicants may then be requested to develop a more detailed proposal. This initial letter of inquiry should be directed to the Secretary of the Foundation, at the address above.
Trustees:
  A. H. Aymond
  William N. Hubbard, Jr.
  Dorothy A. Johnson
  Russell G. Mawby
  Andrew Pattullo
  Fred Sherriff
  John O. Snook
  Durward B. Varner
  Jonathon T. Walton

CHARLES F. KETTERING FOUNDATION
5335 Far Hills Ave.
Suite 300
Dayton, OH 45429
513-434-7300

Founded: 1927
Areas of interest: Elementary and secondary education, international relations, urban leadership and governance, scientific research of factors relating to food plant productivity.
Type: Mission-oriented research organization with four principal program areas: education, science and technology, international affairs, and urban affairs.
Purpose: To develop prototype solutions to selected critical social issues. Emphasis is placed upon collaborative, interdisciplinary research programs. Descriptions of current missions can be obtained by writing to the Foundation.
Legal basis: Section 501(c)(3), Organizations—Private Operating Foundation.
Eligibility: The majority of projects undertaken by the Foundation are initiated by its staff to fulfill specific program area missions. Given its mission orientation, the Foundation is able to respond favorably only to a very small percentage of unsolicited grant proposals. Grants are given only to support projects designed as part of the Foundation's missions. No grants to individuals.
Total amount of support: $5,993,794 total program spending for the fiscal year ending August 31, 1980. Total assets as of August 31, 1980: $77,693,210.
Address inquiries to:
  Mrs. Carol A. Farquhar
  Grants Coordinator

N

NATIONAL CENTER ON CHILD ABUSE AND NEGLECT
Children's Bureau, Administration for Children, Youth, and Families
P.O. Box 1182
Washington, DC 20013
202-755-0587

Founded: 1974
Areas of interest: American Indian studies, black studies, Chicano studies; children and youth, community development and

services, delinquency and crime prevention, rural development (availability of services); elementary and secondary education, higher education, adult and vocational education; agencies, hospitals and clinics, medical education and training, nursing, psychiatry and mental health, medical care and rehabilitation, public health; law; pediatrics, psychiatry; home economics.

Consulting or volunteer services: The center has, both at the national and regional level, training and technical assistance activities that are intended to enhance the skills of practitioners engaged in treatment or prevention, and to provide technical assistance to policy makers and program managers in the field.

Name of program:
Child Abuse and Neglect Prevention, Identification and Treatment

Type: This is a federally funded activity that provides an information clearinghouse on child abuse and neglect programs and research; makes grants to or enters into contracts with public organizations or private nonprofit organizations for demonstration programs and projects or the conduct of research related to child abuse and neglect; and makes direct grants to those states that have satisfied certain conditions stipulated in Public Law 93-247. Please see note below concerning the Center's current status.

Year program started: 1974

Purpose: To assist state, local, and voluntary agencies and organizations to strengthen their capacities to prevent child abuse and neglect; identify abused and neglected children; and provide necessary ameliorative services to them and their families.

Legal basis: P.L. 93-247, as amended. 45 CFR Subtitle B, part 1340.

Eligibility: Grants for demonstration programs or projects and research projects may be made to public agencies or private nonprofit organizations. Grants are made directly to states found to be eligible. Technical assistance is presently being provided under contract by firms or organizations possessing appropriate capabilities.

Financial data: Pertinent information is provided with all announcements concerning grant applications.

Amount of support per award: Varies, ranging from $30,000 to $300,000. Average research and demonstration grant, $166,000.

Total amount of support: $22,069,000 for the year 1976.

Number of awards: 108 for the year ending June 1980.

Application information: Standard grant application forms provided by the Center must be used. Complete instructions and necessary forms are issued with each announcement or solicitation.

Duration: Normally 2 to 3 years.

Deadline: As provided in announcement.

Address inquiries to:
Director (See address above.)

*****Special stipulations:** Grant announcements and/or requests for proposals substantially reflect the program priorities of the Center and are of a magnitude which essentially equals the funds budgeted for the program.

*****Please note:** The authorization for the National Center currently expires in fiscal year 1981. The future status of P.L 93-247 is being debated by the Congress and the issues being discussed have significant impact on future funding authority. Currently, the National Center has committed its fiscal year 1981 funds to continue the research and demonstration programs initiated during previous fiscal years and to begin new projects. Please inquire concerning the status of this program before applying.

NATIONAL DAIRY COUNCIL
6300 North River Rd.
Rosemont, IL 60018
312-696-1020

Founded: 1915

Areas of interest: Human nutrition research, nutrition education through health professionals and teachers, dentistry and dental health, medical education and training, elementary and secondary education, educational research, general practitioner training.

Consulting or volunteer services: The Council acts on occasion as nutrition consultant regarding the use of dairy products in human diet. Also on staff are specialists in nutrition education from kindergarten through high school.

Name of program:
Nutrition Research Grant-in-Aid Program

Type: Grants-in-aid to facilitate research already in progress, provide assistance in undertaking a research effort, or develop a new approach to an existing situation in animal and human nutrition research. Supported projects must concern some aspect of the need for, or utilization of, the proteins, fats, carbohydrates, minerals or vitamins found in or added to products made from milk or some human disease or disturbance suggested as being related to or alleviated by the consumption of dairy foods.

Year program started: 1941

Purpose: To encourage investigations directed toward evaluating the total nutritional value of milk and dairy foods in the human diet and their proper role in improving growth and development and maintainng good health.

Eligibility: Qualified investigators associated with accredited institutions of higher learning in the United States are eligible for support. Applicants must hold a Ph.D., M.D., D.D.S., D.V.M. or equivalent degree.

Financial data: Grants vary in amount, depending upon the needs and nature of the request. Funds are not available for alteration of facilities or purchase of permanent equipment.

Amount of support per award: $15,000-$20,000 average.

Total amount of support: $530,000 for the year 1981.

Matching fund requirements: Not required, but preferred.

Cooperative funding programs: If research interests of two or more additional organizations coincide, cooperative projects are preferred to enhance efficiency of funds utilized and to benefit the researcher through a broader base of support.

Number of applicants most recent year: 50.

Number of awards: 33 as of January 1981.

Application information: A preliminary letter of intent (6 copies) should be submitted to the Director, Div. of Nutrition Research, containing a brief statement of proposed objectives, experimental procedures, estimated total time and budget requirements and significance of the proposed study to the dairy industry. Also a curriculum vitae should be included for all investigators. The letter of intent will be reviewed by the N.D.C. Nutrition Research Advisory Committee and a decision will be made as to whether a formal application will be requested using the official N.D.C. Grant Application Form.

Duration: Initial support is for one year with the possibility of renewal for the additional years necessary to complete a project.

Deadline: Applications must be received by May 1 of the year preceding that for which support is requested.

Address inquiries to:
Dr. E. W. Speckmann,
Director of Nutrition Research

NATIONAL ENVIRONMENTAL HEALTH ASSOCIATION
1200 Lincoln
Suite 704
Denver, CO 80203
303-861-9090

Founded: 1937

Areas of interest: The attainment of optimum human health through the control of environmental hazards. Categories include general environmental health; injury prevention and occupational health; air, land, and water quality; environmental management; institutional environmental health and safety; food sanitation.

Consulting or volunteer services: Services rendered to: H.E.W, E.P.A., A.I.D., National Health Council, A.S.A.H.P., A.P.H.A., C.L.E.H.A., N.S.P.I.

Name of program:
Undergraduate Scholarship Program

Type: Scholarships restricted to the field of environmental health science and available only to attend colleges with an accredited curriculum. One of the four awards is restricted to Wisconsin.

Year program started: 1970

Purpose: To further the upgrading of and to guide the nation's education of professional environmentalists.

Legal basis: Nonprofit.

Eligibility: Applications must be for the junior level to apply and consideration will be given those intent upon pursuit of an environmental health career. Applicable only to schools accredited by the National Environmental Health Association. Applicants must have a grade point average of 3.00 or better on a 4.00 scale and must demonstrate financial need.

Amount of support per award: $500 annually for each of 4 grants.

Total amount of support: $2,000 for the year 1980.

Number of awards: 4 for the year 1980.

Application information: Candidate must supply name, address, scholastic honors, grade point average, proposed research project (a short abstract of the paper must be attached), marital status, number of dependents, parents' names, parents' address and occupation, other sources of income and amount, special plans regarding the future, and references.

Duration: Annual.

Deadline: January 31, with notification April 1.

Address inquiries to:
Lawrence J. Krone, Ph.D., R.S.
Executive Director

*****Please note:** The scholarship applicants are reviewed by a scholarship committee and the awards are based on their determination.

NATIONAL HEALTH AND MEDICAL RESEARCH COUNCIL*
P.O. Box 100
Woden, Canberra A.C.T. 2606
Australia
NL 062 (STD 891555)

Founded: 1936

Name of programs:
1. *Applied Health Sciences Fellowships*
2. *C.J. Martin Research Fellowships*
3. *Public Health Traveling Fellowships*
4. *Research Project Grants*

Type: Fellowships in a broad range of health topics to assist appropriately qualified younger persons, within a definite period of time, to acquire research skills through study and observation, in approved research and teaching institutions both in Australia and overseas. The fellowships provide an opportunity especially for training in research methods and their application to medicine, through collaboration with acknowledged experts in overseas and local laboratories and institutions. Areas of research might include biostatistics, clinical aspects of surgery, clinical pharmacology, demography, economics and evaluation of health care or health services, epidemiology, genetics, human nutrition, psychiatry, psychology, or other areas where the applicant has an aptitude and interest in applied research, a specific study plan, affiliation with an overseas investigator or institution for the study, and reasonable prospects of a responsible position in Australia on completion of the fellowship.

Eligibility: Graduates in all relevant fields are eligible. Preference will be given to persons who already have research experience and are seeking advanced study not available in Australia.

Financial data: The stipend shall be determined on the basis of qualifications, experience, and status of the applicant and relative to the place of tenure.

Total amount of support: Approximately $60,000 for the year 1978.

Number of applicants most recent year: 32.

Number of awards: 9.

Application information: Applications and further information are available from the administrative officers of universities, hospitals, and research institutions, or from the address listed above.

Duration: The fellowships are normally awarded for a period of three years, of which the first two are to be spent overseas and the third in Australia. A fellow shall take up the fellowship not later than March 31 of the year of the award, except with special permission of the Chairman of the Council.

Deadline: February 28.

Council:
Gwyn Howells, Chairman
N. A. Andersen
A. J. Bloomfield
Mrs. D. E. H. Cavaye
L. W. Cox
D. de Souza, Secretary
R. G. Edwards
J. A. Hancock
T. H. Hurley
P. I. Korner
B. Kynaston
W. A. Langsford
G. L. Lipton
J. Ludbrook
J. R. Macintyre
N. J. McCarthy
B. P. McCloskey
R. G. McEwin
J. C. McNulty
B. W. Neal
P. R. Patrick

W. J. Simmonds
R. H. Thorp
P. S. Woodruff

Officers:
Gwyn Howells, Chairman and Director-General
D. de Souza, Secretary and First Assistant Director-General
Garry James, Assistant Director-General
Clive Colochoon, Chief Executive Officer

Address inquiries to:
The Secretary

NATIONAL INSTITUTE FOR THE FOODSERVICE INDUSTRY
20 North Wacker Dr.
Suite 2620
Chicago, IL 60606
312-782-1703

Names of programs:
1. *NIFI-Heinz Scholarships and Fellowships*
2. *IFMA Golden Plate Scholarship Awards*
3. *NRA/NIFI Teacher Work-Study Grants*

Type: Funds for foodservice management students. Seven Senior College Awards, and three Junior/Community College Awards supported by the H.J. Heinz Company Foundation.
One hundred IFMA awards to college and graduate school students, supported by the International Foodservice Manufacturers Association (IFMA) Educational Foundation.
Thirty grants Teacher Work Study supported by the National Restaurant Association: (NRA).

Eligibility: Scholarship competition is open to students of foodservice management (Hotel-Restaurant Management, Institutional Foodservice Management, Dietetics, etc.). Students also must have full-time status and expect to attend school for the full academic year starting with the fall term of the academic year. Judged on basis of motivation toward an industry career, academic records, and financial need.

Amount of support per award: NIFI-HEINZ Scholarships: Seven Senior College Awards, $2,600 each over 2 years; three Junior/Community College Awards, $1,900 each over 2 years. GOLDEN PLATE Scholarships: For Junior/Community College, Senior College, and Graduate Students, 100 awards, $600 each for one year. NIFI-HEINZ Graduate Degree Fellowships: One fellowship, $2,000; one fellowship, $1,200; five fellowships, $1,000 each. NRA-NIFI Teacher Work Study Grants; 30 grants for $1,500 each.

Number of awards: See "Type" above.

Application information: Applications are available from program or department directors/chairman of the school the student is attending in addition to Director of Financial Aid, or write directly to NIFI.

Duration: Varies.
Deadline: April 1.
Address inquiries to:
Scholarship Coordinator

NATIONAL INSTITUTE OF ARTHRITIS, METABOLISM, AND DIGESTIVE DISEASES
National Institutes of Health
Bethesda, MD 20205
301-496-3583

Name of program:
Diabetes

Type: The Diabetes Research Program provides grant support for a wide range of fundamental and clinical studies related to the etiology, pathogenesis, prevention, diagnosis, treatment, and cure of diabetes mellitus and its complications. Specific areas of research interest encompass the structure/function of the pancreatic hormones and related peptides and enzymes, including biosynthesis, secretion, and mechanisms of metabolism; and nutritional interrelationships including obesity. Other opportunities for research include studies of the genetic nature of diabetes and identification of specific markers which characterize individuals predisposed to diabetes; studies to assess immunological and infectious factors as they relate to diabetes; and studies related to nutrition, metabolic regulation, and hormone synthesis/secretion/action with respect to the pathobiology of diabetes mellitus and its sequelae. Other areas of particular interest include islet cell transplantation, insulin delivery systems and glucose sensors, behavioral research epidemiologic studies, and diabetes-related conferences.

Legal basis: Public Health Act, Sections 301(d), 433, 472.

Eligibility: Individuals and public and nonprofit institutions are eligible for research grants. Research contracts are awarded to public commercial/industrial, hospital, nonprofit, and educational institutions. For special manpower awards, recipients must be U.S. citizens, or have been admitted to the U.S. for permanent residence.

Amount of support per award: Range of research grants, $5,000 to $1,600,000; $94,000 average. Range of contracts, $5,200 to $1,230,000; $297,000 average. Range of National Research Service Postdoctoral Awards, $8,000 to $184,000; $46,000 average.

Total amount of support: $62,861,000 estimated for FY 1980.

Number of awards: 395 research grants, 12 contracts and 94 NRSAs estimated for fiscal year 1980.

Duration: Up to five years for research grants; one to five years for contracts; individual fellowships awarded for one to three years.

Deadline: Varies.

NATIONAL INSTITUTE OF ARTHRITIS, METABOLISM, AND DIGESTIVE DISEASES
National Institutes of Health
Bethesda, MD 20205
301-496-1333

Name of program:
Digestive Diseases

Type: Project grants to support basic laboratory research and clinical investigations extramurally and to provide postdoctoral biomedical training opportunities for individuals interested in research in digestive diseases which include
(1) esophageal, gastric, and colonic diseases including research on structure and function of the esophagus, stomach, and colon and diseases such as reflux esophagitis, ulcers; functional bowel disease; inflammatory bowel diseases;
(2) intestinal and pancreatic diseases including research on structure and function of these organs as well as diseases such as malabsorption syndrome, sprue, diarrhea, acute and chronic pancreatitis, Z-E syndrome, pancreatic transplantation, GI hormones; (3) liver and biliary tract diseases including research on structure and function of these organs as well as diseases such as portal hypertension, toxic liver disorders, chronic hepatitis,

cirrhosis, Wilson's disease, jaundice, Dubin-Johnson syndrome, haptic encephalopathy, fatty liver, Reye's syndrome, transplantation, cholestasis, pigment and cholesterol gallstones.

Amount of support per award: Range of research grants, $7,850 to $1,350,000; $92,000 average. Range of contracts, $12,000 to $1,000,000; $281,000 average. Range of National Research Service Postdoctoral Awards, $11,000 to $150,000; $41,000 average.

Total amount of support: $37,243,000 estimated for fiscal year 1980.

Number of awards: 359 research grants, 6 contracts and 73 NRSAs estimated for fiscal year 1980.

NATIONAL INSTITUTE OF ARTHRITIS, METABOLISM, AND DIGESTIVE DISEASES
National Institutes of Health
Bethesda, MD 20205
301-496-3583

Name of program:
Metabolic Diseases

Type: This program provides support for investigator-initiated research into enzymatic mechanisms and their regulation, biological transport, and membrane structure as they relate to understanding the etiology, pathogenesis, and treatment of acquired or inborn errors of metabolism. The program supports research in normal and abnormal carbohydrate, fat, amino acid, urea, pyrimindine, and purine metabolism; synthesis and biosynthesis of chemicals and proteins; and studies of protein structure as they pertain to elucidation of pathometabolic processes. Aminoacidopathies, hyperuricemias, organic acidurias, urea cycle disorders, and mucopolysacchari doses constitute research areas of major programmatic interest. Areas of emphasis in inborn errors of metabolism include diagnostic techniques and enzyme replacement therapy, as well as study of isozymes and defective enzymes involved in these diseases.

Legal basis: Public Health Service Act, Sections 301(d), 433,472.

Eligibility: Individuals and public and nonprofit institutions are eligible for research grants. Research contracts are awarded to public commercial/industrial, hospital, nonprofit, and educational instititutions. For special manpower awards, recipients must be U.S. citizens, or have been admitted to the U.S. for permanent residence.

Amount of support per award: Range of research grants, $7,000 to $981,000; $81,000 average. No contracts awarded. Range of National Research Service Postdoctoral Awards, $9,600 to $116,000; $21,000 average.

Total amount of support: $32,234,000 estimated for fiscal year 1980.

Number of awards: 445 research grants, no contracts and 59 NRSAs estimated for fiscal year 1980.

Duration: Up to five years for research grants, one to five years for contracts; individual fellowships awarded for one to three years.

Deadline: Varies.

NATIONAL INSTITUTE OF ARTHRITIS, METABOLISM, AND DIGESTIVE DISEASES
National Institutes of Health
Bethesda, MD 20205
301-496-1333

Name of program:
Nutrition

Type: Project grants and research grants to support basic laboratory research, clinical investigators, and behavioral studies extramurally, and to provide postdoctoral biomedical and clinical research training for individuals interested in nutrition. Of concern are studies of the normal requirements and function of vitamins, minerals, proteins and amino acids, fats and fatty acids, and carbohydrates in nutrition, and their relationships to the varied diseases and disordered states of metabolism. Related areas of support include digestion, absorption and transcomposition, obesity and its consequences, dietary fiber, trace minerals, toxicity of nutrients, and therapeutic diets. International collaborative research relates to iron deficiency anemias, malabsorption, nutrition and infection, and factors affecting nutritional requirements.

Amount of support per award: Range of research grants $15,000 to $663,000; $86,000 average. Range of National Research Service Postdoctoral Awards, $14,000 to $191,000; $37,000 average.

Total amount of support: $14,745,000 for fiscal year 1980.

Number of awards: 168 research awards, one contract and 27 NRSAs estimated for fiscal year 1980.

NATIONAL INSTITUTE OF DENTAL RESEARCH
National Institutes of Health
Bethesda, MD 20205
301-496-4000

Founded: 1948

Name of program:
Dental Research Grants

Type: Grants made to individual investigators for the support of clinical and nonclinical research projects bearing on oral health conditions.

Year program started: 1948

Purpose: To develop methods of preventing and treating oral diseases and conditions through research related to dental caries, periodontal diseases, craniofacial anomalies, soft tissue diseases, restorative materials, pain control, mineralization, salivary secretions, and nutrition.

Legal basis: Public Health Service Act as amended, Section 301(c); 42 CFR 61; 42 U.S.C. 288a.

Eligibility: Scientists at universities, hospitals, laboratories, and other public or nonprofit institutions. Applications are competitively rated on the basis of scientific merit and grants must be approved by the National Advisory Dental Research Council.

Financial data: Grant funds may be used for salaries of professional and nonprofessional personnel, equipment, supplies, travel, other approved expenditures, and indirect costs.

Amount of support per award: Variable.

Total amount of support: $42,842,166 for the year 1980.

Number of applicants most recent year: 880 competing and noncompeting for year 1980. Includes 371 new applications.

Number of awards: 522 for the year ending 1980. Includes 119 new awards for $4,911,000.

Application information: Request application form PHS-398 from the office listed above.

Duration: Variable, usually three years.

Deadline: New grants: March 1, July 1, and November 1; Renewals: February 1, June 1, and October 1.

Address inquiries to:
Richard L. Christiansen, D.D.S., Ph.D. (Address above)

NATIONAL INSTITUTE OF DENTAL RESEARCH
National Institutes of Health
Bethesda, MD 20205
301-496-4000

Founded: 1948
Name of program:
Individual Postdoctoral Fellowships for National Research Service Award
Type: Awards made to individual applicants selected through national competition for research training in specified health and health-related areas.
Year program started: 1974
Purpose: To develop individuals for careers in research related to dental caries, periodontal diseases, soft tissue diseases, craniofacial anomalies, restorative materials, pain control, mineralization, salivary secretions, and nutrition.
Legal basis: Public Health Service Act as amended, Section 301(c); 42 CFR 61; 42 U.S.C. 288a.
Eligibility: Applicants must be citizens or noncitizen nationals of the United States and have a Ph.D., M.D., D.D.S., D.O., D.V.M. or equivalent degree prior to the beginning date of the proposed fellowship.
Financial data: Stipend level based on number of years of postdoctoral experience. Allowances for tuition, fees, health insurance, supplies, equipment, and related expenses. No allowance for dependents.
Amount of support per award: The new stipend levels are $13,380 to $5,718,780 up to $5,000 per 12 months for institutional allowances.
Total amount of support: $1,137,030 for the year 1980.
Number of applicants most recent year: 85 for the year 1980.
Number of awards: 64 for the year 1980.
Application information: Request application from the office listed below.
Duration: One, two or three years.
Deadline: February 1, June 1, and October 1.
Address inquiries to:
Special Assistant for Research Manpower

NATIONAL INSTITUTE OF DENTAL RESEARCH
National Institutes of Health
Bethesda, MD 20205
301-496-4000

Founded: 1948
Name of program:
Institutional Grants for National Research Service Award
Type: Grants made to institutions for a number of research training fellowships in areas indicated in the NIH Guide for Grants and Contracts Vol. 6, No. 20, November 14, 1977.
Year program started: 1974
Purpose: To enable nonprofit institutions to develop research training opportunities for individuals interested in careers in research related to dental caries, periodontal diseases, soft tissue diseases, craniofacial anomalies, restorative materials, pain control, salivary secretions, and nutrition.
Legal basis: Public Health Service Act as amended Section 1, Public Law 93-348.
Eligibility: Applications may be submitted by domestic private, public, and nonprofit or government institutions. The sponsoring institution must be able to develop suitable staff and facilities. Institutional directors will be responsible for selection, appointment of fellows, and overall direction of the proposed training program.
Financial data: Stipends and allowances for each fellow plus institutional allowances for staff support and other expenses. Stipend level based on number of years of postdoctoral experience. No allowance for dependents.
Amount of support per award: Stipends of $13,380 to $18,780 per fellow. Allowances up to 8 percent of direct costs for overhead and an institutional allowance of up to $3,000 per predoctoral trainee and $5,000 per postdoctoral trainee per year may be requested for research supplies, equipment, staff travel, salaries and other expenses essential to the program. In addition trainee costs, such as tuition and fees, and trainee travel may be requested.
Total amount of support: $2,725,101 for the year 1980.
Number of applicants most recent year: 34 for the year 1980.
Number of awards: 27 for the year 1980.

NATIONAL INSTITUTE OF DENTAL RESEARCH
National Institutes of Health
Bethesda, MD 20205
301-496-4000

Founded: 1948
Areas of interest: Research in cariology, mineralization, craniofacial anomalies, nutrition, dental pain control, periodontal diseases, restorative materials, salivary secretions, soft tissue diseases, and selected behavioral studies.
Name of program:
New Investigator Research Award
Type: Special grants made to new investigators selected through national competition for clinical and nonclinical research projects related to oral health.
Purpose: To help scientists with promising research careers in the oral health field to bridge the gap from training status to established investigators; to facilitate funding for relatively inexperienced scientists with meritorious research plans in their initial efforts as independent scientists.
Legal basis: Public Health Service Act Title III Section 301(c).
Eligibility: New investigators at domestic universities, hospitals, laboratories, or other public or nonprofit institutions. Applicants who have not previously been principal investigators on PHS-supported research projects, and have not had more than five years of research experience after completion of formal training. Ordinarily, applicants should have a doctorate degree or its equivalent.
Financial data: Grant funds may be used for the salary of the principal investigator, for technical support, supplies, publication costs, limited equipment and necessary travel.
Amount of support per award: Direct costs of up to $107,500 for three years of support and up to $37,500 for any one year may be requested. Up to $25,000 salary for the principal investigator may be requested; this amount should be commensurate with project time and effort, and consistent with the institution's salary level for professionals of equivalent rank.
Total amount of support: $1,560,374 for the year 1979.
Number of applicants most recent year: 82 for the year 1979 (includes 35 noncompeting applications).
Number of awards: 60 for the year 1979 (includes 25 new awards).
Application information: Request

application form PHS-398 from the office listed below.
Duration: Three years, renewable as regular grants.
Deadline: New grants: March 1, July 1, and November 1. Renewals: February 1, June 1, and October 1.
Address inquiries to:
Dr. George Hausch
National Institute of Dental Research
NIH-Westwood Bldg., Room 509
5333 Westbard Ave.
Bethesda, MD 20205
301-496-7748

NATIONAL INSTITUTE OF DENTAL RESEARCH
National Institute of Health
Bethesda, MD 20205
301-496-4000

Founded: 1948
Areas of interest: Research in cariology, mineralization, craniofacial anomalies, nutrition, dental pain control, periodontal diseases, restorative materials, salivary secretions, soft tissue diseases, and selected behavioral studies.
Name of program:
Short-term Research Training for Students in Health Professional Schools.
Type: Grants made to health professional schools to support short-term research training for discrete periods up to three months in specified health and health-related areas. Trainees are not subject to payback provisions.
Year program started: 1979
Purpose: To expose talented students in health professional schools to the opportunities offered by a research career. The program is designed to ameliorate the future shortage of clinical investigators by attracting highly qualified professional students into biomedical and behavioral research careers.
Legal basis: Amendment (November, 1978) to the National Research Service Award Act, Public Law 95-622
Eligibility: (1) *Applicant Institutions:* Domestic nonprofit private or public schools of medicine, osteopathy, dentistry, veterinary medicine, optometry, pharmacy, and podiatry may apply for these grants. The applicant institutions must have the staff and facilities required for the proposed program. Each grant must provide for no fewer than four, nor more than 32 student-trainees. Only one application per health professional school will be accepted.
(2) *Trainees:* The training institution will be responsible for the selection and appointment of trainees. Trainees must have succesfully completed at least one semester at an accredited school of medicine, osteopathy, dentistry, veterinary medicine, optometry, pharmacy or podiatry prior to participating in the program. Trainees must be citizens or noncitizen nationals of the United States NRSA awards cannot be used to support courses which are required for the M.D., D.O., D.D.S., D.V.M., or other similar professional degrees.
Financial data: Stipends plus institutional allowances are available.
Amount of support per award: Stipend support of $420 per month per trainee, with no payback requirement. Costs of up to $250 per month per trainee may be requested for applicable institutional expenses. Indirect costs may be requested at 8 percent of total allowable direct costs or actual rate, whichever is less.
Number of applicants most recent year: 21 for the year 1980.
Number of awards: 10 for the year 1980.
Application information: Request application from the office listed below.
Duration: Five years.
Deadline: May 1.
Address inquiries to:
Chief, Dental Research Centers and Special Programs
National Institute of Dental Research
NIH-Westwood Bldg., Room 509
5333 Westbard Ave.
Bethesda, MD 20205
301-496-7748

NATIONAL LIVE STOCK AND MEAT BOARD
444 N Michigan Ave.
Chicago, IL 60611
312-467-5520

Founded: 1922
Name of program:
Nutrition Research in Meat
Type: Research contracts and grants-in-aid for experimental projects in the area of health and nutrition as related to meat or nutrients present in meat.
Year program started: 1923
Purpose: To gain further knowledge of the value of meat in our diets.
Eligibility: Qualified nonprofit organizations with appropriate interests are eligible to apply.
Financial data: Awards vary in amount, ranging from $5,000 to $18,000 and seldom exceeding $12,000. Total grant expenditures vary from $100,000 to $200,000 per year.
Application information: Official application materials are available upon request to the Director of Nutrition Research at the above address, after it has been established that the proposal would be of mutual interest.
Duration: Support is provided for one year with the possibility of renewal if continued investigations appear to be warranted.
Deadline: Applications must be received by March 1 for awards to be announced in August.
Address inquiries to:
Director, Nutrition Research

NATIONAL MARINE FISHERIES SERVICE
F/CMI Page Building No. 2
Room 105
Washington, DC 20235
202-634-7454

Name of program:
Anadromous Fish Conservation Act
Type: Funds can be used for spawning area improvement, installment of fishways, construction of fish protection devices and hatcheries, and research to improve management and increase anadromous fish resources, and to conduct emergency studies on striped bass. Funds cannot be used for law enforcement, public relations, or construction of facilities and vessels, the primary purpose of which is to commercially harvest, handle, and process fishery products. In addition, funds cannot be used for projects in the Columbia River Basin.
Year program started: 1966
Purpose: To cooperate with the states and other nonfederal interests in the conservation, development, and enhancement of the Nation's anadromous fish and those in the Great Lakes and Lake Champlain (re. Amendment approved 10-17-78, Public Law 95-464) that ascend streams to spawn.
Legal basis: Anadromous Fish Conservation Act of 1965, Public Law 89-304 as amended; 16 U.S.C. 757a.F;

Reorganization Plan No. 4, 1970.
Eligibility: Any interested person or organization may propose a cooperative undertaking. However, all proposals must be coordinated with the State Fishery agency having responsibility for the resource to be affected by the proposal.
Amount of support per award: Approx. $34,500 (average).
Total amount of support: $2,500,000 for fiscal year 1980.
Matching fund requirements: Federal share not to exceed 50 percent; two or more states maximum 66⅔ percent.
Number of applicants most recent year: 21 states and 5 other nonfederal interests.
Number of awards: 58 for the year September 30, 1979.
Application information: A description of work to be accomplished including objectives and needs, expected results and benefits, approach, cost location, and time required for completion must be submitted.
Duration: One to three years, nonrenewable. However, an approved on-going project can be extended by submission of an amendment document.
Deadline: 30 days in advance of desired effective date.
Address inquiries to:
Regional Directors, National Marine Fisheries Service
Gloucester, MA 01930;
St. Petersburg, FL 33702;
Terminal Island, CA 90731;
Seattle, WA 98109;
Juneau, AK 99801
*Please note: Program is jointly administered with U.S. Fish and Wildlife Service, Department of the Interior.

NATIONAL NUTRITION CONSORTIUM, INC.
1635 P. St., N.W.
Suite 1
Washington, DC 20036
202-234-7760

Founded: 1973
Areas of interest: Food, nutrition, dietetics.
Name of program:
NNC Fellowship Program
Type: Fellowship for graduate students in fields related to nutrition, health, and food science. Candidates are selected to work with the Consortium staff on specific projects and ongoing programs. The students gain experience in nutrition policy development, government organization, and the operations of professional food, dietetic, and nutrition societies. They prepare a report on their experiences for their academic committee and participate in graduate seminars of universities in the Washington area.
Year program started: 1979
Legal basis: 501(c)(3).
Eligibility: Candidates for Ph.D., Ed.D., or M.D. degrees who are specializing in nutrition and whose universities accredit a one-semester experience are eligible.
Financial data: A monthly stipend is offered.
Number of awards: New in 1979.
Application information: Application forms are available on request.
Duration: Six months.
Deadline: March 10 and September 10.
Executive officer:
Mahlon A. Burnette III, Ph.D.
Address inquiries to:
Dr. Mahlon A. Burnette III

NATIONAL RESEARCH COUNCIL
Associateship Office (JH/608-D5)
2101 Constitution Ave., N.W.
Washington, DC 20418
202-389-6554

Name of program:
NRC—United States Army Natick Research and Development Command Resident Research Associateships
Type: Regular and senior associateships at the doctoral level for research in biochemistry, bioengineering, biomass conversion, biophysics, food and nutrition, food technology, microbiology, photochemistry, pollution abatement, psychology, and textiles to be conducted at the Army Natick Laboratories, Natick, Massachusetts.
Purpose: To provide investigators of unusual ability and promise with an opportunity for direct exchange of ideas and knowledge, and for advanced research in association with experienced scientists and engineers, and to contribute to the general research effort of the federal laboratories.
Eligibility: United States citizens and foreign nationals who hold the Ph.D. or Sc.D. degree (or will have completed the requirements for such a degree before entering upon an associateship) are eligible to apply. Applicants for senior associateships must have held the doctorate at least five years at the time of application and have secured scientific recognition through publication and other accomplishments.
Financial data: Associates at the recent postdoctoral level normally receive stipends at the rate of $22,400 per year. An appropriately higher stipend will be set for senior awardees. Travel and relocation allowances are also available.
Application information: Official application materials are available upon request to the address above. Inquiries should be received by January 5 and should specify the federal organization of interest.
Duration: Associateships are tenable for one year. Seniors may request shorter tenures. Renewals may be possible.
Deadline: Applications must be postmarked no later than January 15 for awards to be announced in April.
Officers:
J.C. McKee, Director of Associateships
Harold W. Lucien, Associate Director of Associateships

NATIONAL RESEARCH COUNCIL
Associateship Office (JH 608-D5)
2101 Constitution Ave., N.W.
Washington, DC 20418
202-389-6554

Name of program:
NRC—Armed Forces Radiobiology Research Institute Resident Research Associateships
Type: Regular and senior resident research associateships at the doctoral level, tenable at the Armed Forces Radiobiology Research Institute, Bethesda, Maryland, for advanced research and study in behavioral sciences, biochemistry, experimental hematology, physiology, and radiobiology.
Eligibility: Postdoctoral associateships are awarded to persons who have held the doctorate less than five years. Senior associateships are available to scientists and engineers of demonstrated accomplishment who have held the doctorate five years or more at the time of application. Both United States citizens and foreign nationals are eligible.
Financial data: Associates at the recent postdoctoral level receive

stipends of $22,400 per year at the present time. An appropriately higher stipend will be set for senior awardees. Travel and relocation allowances are also available.
Application information: Application materials and detailed information may be requested from the address above from October 1 to January 5. Inquiries must specify the federal organization of interest.
Duration: Associates are normally appointed for one year; however, tenures of less than a year may be considered for senior associates. Renewals may be possible.
Deadline: Applications must be postmarked by January 15. Awards are normally made in April.
Officers:
J.C. McKee, Director of Associateships
Harold W. Lucien, Associate Director of Associateships

NATIONAL RESEARCH COUNCIL
Associateship Office (JH 606-Q)
2101 Constitution Avenue, N.W.
Washington, DC 20418
202-389-6554

Name of program:
NRC—Naval Medical Research and Development Command Research Associateships
Type: Postdoctoral and senior resident research associateships, *tenable in the laboratories and research centers of the Naval Medical Research and Development Command,* for advanced research and study in aerospace medicine, biochemistry, biomechanics, biophysics and radiation biology, physiology, human engineering, immunology, metabolism, microbiology-communicable diseases, parasitology, behavioral sciences, experimental dentistry and medicine, vision and visual perception, psychoacoustics, and underwater medicine.
Eligibility: Postdoctoral appointments are made on a competitive basis to scientists and engineers who have held the doctorate less than five years. Senior Associateships are for persons of demonstrated accomplishment who have held the doctorate five years or more at time of application. Awards are open to United States citizens and foreign nationals.
Financial data: Postdoctoral Associateships carry stipends of $22,400 a year at present. An appropriately higher stipend will be set for senior awardees. Travel and relocation allowances are available.
Application information: Application materials and detailed information may be requested from the address above from October 1 to January 5. Inquiries must specify the federal organization of interest.
Deadline: Applications must be postmarked by January 15. Awards are normally made in April.
Officers:
J.C. McKee, Director of Associateships
Harold W. Lucien, Associate Director of Associateships

NATIONAL RESEARCH COUNCIL
Associateship Office (JH 608-D5)
2101 Constitution Ave., N.W.
Washington, DC 20418
202-389-6554

Name of program:
NRC—Walter Reed Army Institute of Research Resident Research Associateships
Type: Postdoctoral and senior resident research associateships, tenable at the Walter Reed Army Institute of Research, Washington, DC, and Fort Detrick, MD (U.S. Army Medical Research Institute of Infectious Diseases), for advanced research and study in biochemistry, communicable diseases, microbiology, immunology, neuropsychiatry, and endocrine and cellular physiology, molecular virology, nutritional immunology, toxicology (bacterial) and viral immunology.
Eligibility: Regular postdoctoral associateships are awarded on a competitive basis to persons who have held the doctorate less than five years. Senior associateships are available to scientists and engineers of demonstrated accomplishment who have held the doctorate five years or more at the time of application. Both United States citizens and foreign nationals are eligible.
Financial data: Associateships at the recent postdoctoral level carry stipends of $22,400 per year at the present time. An appropriately higher stipend will be set for senior awardees. Travel and relocation allowances are available.
Application information: Application materials and detailed information may be requested from the address above from October 1 to January 5. Inquiries must specify the federal organization of interest.
Duration: Associates are normally appointed for one year; however, shorter tenures may be considered for senior associates. Renewals may be possible.
Deadline: Applications must be postmarked by January 15. Awards are normally announced in March.
Officers:
J.C. McKee, Director of Associateships
Harold W. Lucien, Associate Director of Associateships

NATURAL SCIENCES AND ENGINEERING RESEARCH COUNCIL OF CANADA
Ottawa, Ontario K1A OR6, Canada
613-993-2454/1930

Name of program:
Postgraduate Scholarships
Purpose: To assist students in undertaking graduate study and research leading to advanced degrees in the fields of astronomy, biology, chemistry, physics, computing and information science, engineering, earth sciences, marine science, mathematics, psychology, space research, and multidisciplines (e.g. forestry, kinesiology, food science, agriculture).
Eligibility: Candidates must be Canadian citizens or landed immigrants residing in Canada.
Amount of support per award: In 1980-81, each scholarship provided $9,350 per year plus travel allowances.
Duration: Maximum support is normally four years.
Deadline: December 1, with announcement by the end of March.
Address inquiries to:
Scholarships Officer

NATURAL SCIENCES AND ENGINEERING RESEARCH COUNCIL OF CANADA
Ottawa, Ontario K1A OR6, Canada
613-993-9630/9631

Areas of interest: Physical sciences, life sciences, engineering.
Name of program:
Strategic Grants
Type: Operating or equipment grants to individuals and groups to encourage researchers in Canadian

universities to make greater contributions than in the past toward the understanding or solution of problems in certain identified areas of Canadian concern.

Eligibility: Applicants must be eligible to hold an NSERC operating grant and undertake research projects in one of the following areas: communications, energy, environmental toxicology, food and agriculture, oceans. An "open" category has been added where NSERC invites universities to submit a limited number of proposals in areas of national concern other than the five specified areas mentioned previously.

Amount of support per award: Varies, depending on the proposal.
Duration: One, two, or three years.
Deadline: May 1, with announcement in October.
Address inquiries to:
Associate Awards Officer
(Strategic Grants)

O

OFFICE OF EDUCATION
400 Maryland Ave.
Donohoe Building, Room 1628
Washington, DC 20202
202-426-9303

Name of program:
Consumers' Education Program
Type: Contracts and grants to eligible applicants to initiate and expand consumer education in elementary and secondary schools, higher education institutions, and communities. Awards also support projects to develop, disseminate, and evaluate new and improved consumer education curriculums; to train educational and public service personnel, community and labor leaders, and government employees in consumer education, as well as to conduct activities for the general public. Areas included are basic economics of the marketplace; legal rights, redress, and consumer laws; financial management and credit; the human and civic services, health, welfare, police, and fire; energy use and public utilities; major purchases, such as food, housing, and insurance; special problems, such as advertising and product safety, federal assistance; and consumer representation.
Year program started: 1976
Purpose: To help individuals make informed, rational decisions about consumer transactions.
Type: Education Amendments of 1978, Public Law 95-561.
Eligibility: Institutions of higher education, state and local education agencies, libraries, and other public and private nonprofit agencies, organizations, and institutions may apply.
Financial data: The amount of funds available under this program is $3,617,000 with approximately $2,600,000 going for grant awards and the balance for procurement contracts. It is estimated that a total of approximately 50 new grants were awarded during fiscal year 1981. The average grant is expected to be about $45,000, though no minimum or maximum amounts have been predetermined.
Number of applicants most recent year: From 713 applications submitted in 1980, all were eligible and were reviewed.
Number of awards: 59 grant awards for the year 1980.
Application information: Application materials are available on request.
Deadline: Not determined yet but possibly late April.
Officer:
Dustin W. Wilson, Jr.
Address inquiries to:
Director
Consumers' Education Program

OMICRON NU SOCIETY, INC.
Human Ecology Building
Michigan State University
East Lansing, MI 48824
517-339-3324

Founded: 1912
Areas of interest: Home economics.
Name of program:
International Fellowship and Research Fellowship
Type: Fellowship for graduate study in related fields.
Purpose: To promote research and graduate study in areas related to the well-being of individuals and families throughout the world.
Legal basis: Nonprofit corporation, 501(c)(3) status.
Eligibility: Students are eligible who enrolled in a Master's (international) or Ph.D. program at a university with a strong research program, who show interest and competency in research, and evidence of potential for leadership.
Amount of support per award: $3,000.
Total amount of support: $3,000 research and $3,000 international for the year 1982-83.
Number of applicants most recent year: 26.
Number of awards: One for the year 1981-82; two for the year 1982-83.
Application information: Candidate must submit an application form, transcripts, and three letters of recommendation.
Duration: One academic year, renewal not guaranteed.
Deadline: January 15, with announcement April 15.
Officers:
Judy Oppert, Chairman
Fellowship Committee
Dr. Rosalie King, President
Omicron Nu
Address inquiries to:
Eileen C. Maddex
Executive Director
P.O. Box 247
Haslett, MI 48840

R

RALSTON PURINA COMPANY
Checkerboard Square
St. Louis, MO 63188
314-982-3210

Founded: 1894
Name of program:
Additional Education Programs
Type: *High School Work-Study Program*—Each year high school seniors from St. Louis public schools attend classes during the morning at Checkerboard Square. In the afternoon they work in a variety of clerical and laboratory jobs. The program is administered by the Equal Opportunity Affairs Department.
Kansas State University Feed Technology Scholarship—A specific $650 scholarship is offered to worthy students of Kansas State University's Department of Grain Science and Industry. One new four-year award is offered annually with four awards continually available. The program is designed primarily for outstanding feed technology students who demonstrate a particularly strong financial need.
Purpose: To strengthen existing educational institutions which have demonstrated long-term excellence in business and agricultural

curriculums. It is hoped that individual recipients will make a greater contribution to their profession and to society.
Amount of support per award: Varies.
Application information: Program details and application forms may be obtained by writing the individual listed below.
Address inquiries to:
George H. Kyd, Chairman of the Donations Committee

RALSTON PURINA COMPANY
Checkerboard Square Plaza
St. Louis, MO 63188
314-982-3210

Founded: 1894
Name of program:
Food Science Fellowship Program
Type: Fellowship to assist in the training of qualified personnel for future leadership in the field of food science.
Year program started: 1971
Purpose: To strengthen existing educational institutions that have demonstrated long-term excellence in business and agricultural curriculums. It is hoped that individual recipients will make a greater contribution to their profession and to society.
Eligibility: An individual who has pursued an undergraduate program with a food science orientation will be eligible. The applicant will be expected to plan M.S. or Ph.D. programs at institutions with faculty in specific departments of food science or food technology. Graduate degree need *not* be officially described as a food science degree.
Amount of support per award: $5,600 per year.
Number of awards: Six annually.
Application information: For further information contact the committee below.
Duration: The fellowship may be renewed only twice for a total tenure not to exceed three years.
Deadline: For deadline information contact the committee below.
Address inquiries to:
Ralston Purina Food Science Graduate Fellowship Committee
c/o Mr. George H. Kyd

RALSTON PURINA COMPANY
Checkerboard Square
St. Louis, MO 63188
314-982-3210

Founded: 1894
Name of program:
Ralston Purina Scholarship
Type: Scholarship award for an incoming junior or senior who is an outstanding student in the College of Agriculture at a land grant college. The selection committee is asked to consider undergraduate students majoring in a field closely associated with the Ralston Purina industry.
Eligibility: Recipient must qualify as follows: scholastic rank in upper 25 percent of class; leadership evidenced by participation in special activities; character, moral firmness, and vigor in all relationships; extracurricular activities plus a good citizenship record, sincerity of purpose in choosing the agricultural field; financial need clearly demonstrated.
Financial data: One annual $650 scholarship for land grant institutions in each state plus one in Puerto Rico and three Canadian colleges (Macdonald, Ontario Agricultural, and Laval).
Application information: Students should apply to their respective scholarship committees at the beginning of the spring semester of their junior year in college.
Duration: A student may receive this award only once.
Address inquiries to:
George H. Kyd, Chairman of the Donations Committee

RALSTON PURINA COMPANY
Checkerboard Square Plaza
St. Louis, MO 63188
314-982-3210

Founded: 1894
Name of program:
Research Fellowship in Animal Science
Type: Research fellowships in nutrition and physiology as they apply to animal, dairy and poultry science to assist in the training of exceptional personnel for leadership in the science of livestock and poultry production.
Year program started: 1949
Purpose: To recognize and further develop meritorious students in the hope that they will make a greater contribution to their field in particular and society in general.
Eligibility: Students qualified for graduate study in a Canadian or United States agricultural college are eligible to apply.
Amount of support per award: $5,600 per year.
Number of awards: Six annually.
Application information: Official application materials are available upon request to the committee at the address above.
Duration: Fellowships provide for one year of advanced study; renewable annually for maximum tenure of three years.
Deadline: For deadline information contact the address above.
Address inquiries to:
Ralston Purina Research Fellowship Committee
c/o Mr. George H. Kyd

THE WINTHROP ROCKEFELLER FOUNDATION
308 E 8th St.
Little Rock, AR 72202
501-376-6854

Founded: 1974
Areas of interest: Education, human services, energy and environment, agriculture and economic development, public policy formulation.
Purpose: To improve the quality of life for Arkansans.
Legal basis: Tax-exempt, private foundation.
Eligibility: Tax-exempt organizations in Arkansas. No grants to individuals.
Amount of support per award: Grants range to $100,000.
Total amount of support: $1,299,000 for the year 1980.
Matching fund requirements: Depends on project. Usually encouraged, but not required.
Number of applicants most recent year: 301.
Number of awards: 33 regular grants and 29 discretionary grants, (of $1,000 or less) for the year 1980.
Application information: A letter, telephone call, or visit to the foundation can begin the application process. Formal application procedures are included in the foundation's annual report, but should not be used until preliminary contact has been made with the Foundation staff.
Duration: No grants awarded on a continuing basis. No general support grants.
Deadline: None, announcements quarterly.
Board of directors:
John T. Meriwether, Vice Chairman

Henry L. McHenry, Vice Chairman
A. Baer Jr.
James D. Bernstein
Wiley A. Branton
Marion Burton
Patricia D. Jacobs
Max Milam
Winthrop Paul Rockefeller
Robert Shults

Staff:
Thomas C. McRae, President
Bob J. Nash, Vice President
Leland P. Gordon Jr., Vice President
Sandra Boatright, Secretary/Treasurer
Denise Felton, Secretary

Address inquiries to:
Thomas C. McRae, President

*Special stipulations:
Grants limited to Arkansans.

T

THE TRASHER RESEARCH FUND
50 E N Temple
7th Floor
Salt Lake City, UT 84150
801-531-3386

Founded: 1977
Areas of interest: All grants must be child health related. Priority will be given to research and demonstration projects in the areas of health information and technology transfer, health promotion/disease prevention, infectious diseases, nutrition, and general biomedical.
Type: Primary focus is on project grants. Conferences, workshops, and research fellowships may also be considered.
Year program started: 1977
Purpose: To support child health related projects that will bless the world's children.
Legal basis: Tax-exempt private organization.
Eligibility: Applications are accepted from nonprofit institutions and organizations and private individuals.
Financial data: Grants are generally made on a one- to three-year basis.
Amount of support per award: $30,000 maximum per year.
Total amount of support: Approximately $1,000,000.
Matching fund requirements: None.
Number of applicants most recent year: 50.
Number of awards: 20.
Application information: Initial inquiries should be made in the form of a concise prospectus that provides statements on the purpose and significance of the proposed project; a summary of the project design and methodology; a budget description; a proposed time frame; the qualifications of the institution or organization; a curriculum vitae of the principal investigator(s). Prospectus and summary should not exceed five single-spaced pages.
Duration: No grants awarded on a continuing basis.
Deadline: None. Awards announced quarterly in March, June, September, and December.

Executive Committee:
Victor L. Brown, Chairman
H. Burke Peterson
J. Richard Clarke
E. W. "Al" Thrasher
Janath R. Cannon
Richard P. Lindsay, Ph.D.
James O. Mason, M.D., Ph.D.

Officers:
Isaac C. Ferguson, Ph.D., Executive Director
Robert M. Briem, Executive Assistant

Address inquiries to:
Isaac C. Ferguson, Ph.D.
Executive Director

TUPPERWARE HOME PARTIES
P.O. Box 2353
Orlando, FL 32802
305-847-3111

Founded: 1951
Areas of interest: Home economics, journalism.
Name of program:
National Newspaper Food Editors Internship
Type: Ten-week summer internship under the supervision of a major daily newspaper food editor and receives a maximum grant of $2,000. Two new grants of $500 for each of two runner-up winners have been established to encourage allied study-research, or attendance at professional conventions in journalism or home economics.
Year program started: 1972
Purpose: To encourage careers in newspaper food editing for undergraduates majoring in journalism or home economics.
Eligibility: Candidate must be a junior or senior majoring in journalism or home economics and attending an accredited college or university.
Amount of support per award: $2,000 maximum for ten week summer internship. Two grants of $500 for each of two runner-up winners.
Number of awards: Three for the year 1981.
Application information: Contact the individual listed below for further information. One entry per applicant.
Duration: Ten weeks in the summer.
Deadline: April 1, with announcement after May 15.
Address inquiries to:
Mrs. Tina Engleman
Director Educational Services
Tupperware Home Parties
P.O. Box 2353
Orlando, FL 32802

U

UNIVERSITY OF CALIFORNIA
School of Public Health
Berkeley, CA 94720

Name of program:
Master's of Public Health Program for American Indians
Type: Graduate degree program for Native Americans interested in careers in public health: hospital administration, health administration and planning, laboratory sciences, health education, environmental health sciences, epidemiology, nutrition, alcohol and substance abuse, and others.
Year program started: 1971
Eligibility: Students must be American Indian or Alaskan Native and must have a bachelor's degree.
Number of awards: 152 students from 56 tribal groups in 24 states since 1971.
Application information: Further information is available on request.
Duration: 21-24 months, depending upon specialization chosen by student, with three to six months spent in field placement situations.
Address inquiries to:
Elaine Walbroek
Director
MPH Program for American Indians

USDA FOOD AND NUTRITION SERVICE
14th St. & Independence Ave., S.W.
Washington, DC 20250
202-447-8130, School Programs;
202-447-8211, Child Care and Summer Programs

Founded: August 1969; prior to that, agency programs were part of

Consumer and Marketing Service.
Names of programs:
1. *School Programs*
2. *Child-Care and Summer Programs*

Type: Grants for the support of food service in schools and child-care institutions to improve child nutrition. Support is available through the:
(1) National School Lunch Program, (2) Food Service Equipment Assistance Program, (3) School Breakfast Program, (4) Child Care Food Program (5) Summer Food Service Program for Children, (6) Special Milk Program.

Year program started: 1946 (National School Lunch Program)

Purpose: To help safeguard the health and well-being of the nation's children and to encourage the domestic consumption of nutritious agricultural commodities and other foods.

Legal basis: The National School Lunch Act, as amended, and the Child Nutrition Act of 1966, as amended.

Eligibility: All public and nonprofit private schools of high school grade or under and licensed public or nonprofit private residential child-care institutions are eligible to participate in the National School Lunch and School Breakfast Programs.

The Special Milk Program is made available to public and nonprofit schools of high school grade and under, as well as nonprofit child-care institutions such as nursery schools, child-care centers, settlement houses, and summer camps.

The Child Care Food Program is designed to assist public or private, nonprofit institutions providing licensed or approved day care services where children are not maintained in permanent residence. Programs must also be tax-exempt under section 501(c)(3) of the Internal Revenue code of 1954, or moving toward tax-exempt status.

The Summer Food Service Program for Children is designed to assist nonresidential public or private, nonprofit institutions or residential public or private nonprofit summer camps that develop a summer food program providing food service to children similar to the School Lunch and School Breakfast Programs. This program is also available to children on school vacations in areas operating under a continuous school calendar.

The Food Service Equipment Assistance Program is designed to assist schools drawing attendance from areas in which poor economic conditions exist with equipment, other than land or buildings, for the storage, preparation, transportation, and serving of food to enable such schools to establish, maintain, and expand school food service programs.

Financial data: Schools or service institutions in these programs receive USDA donated foods and payment for each meal served as determined by their state agency or Food and Nutrition Service Regional Office where applicable, as well as technical advice on food service operations.

Rate of food assistance for lunches served in the School Lunch Program and for lunches and suppers served in the Child Care Food Program is adjusted annually based on changes in the Price Index for Food Used in Schools and Institutions computed from the Bureau of Labor Statistics Producers Price Index. The rate prescribed for January 1, 1981-June 30, 1981 is 13.50 cents per lunch and supper.

Rates of cash assistance are adjusted annually based on changes in the Consumer Price Index. Average rates for the period January 1-June 30, 1981 are 16 cents for all lunches and an additional 83.50 cents for all free lunches and 63.50 cents for reduced price lunches served to eligible needy children.

In the School Breakfast Program, Federal average rates of cash assistance for January and June 1981 are 14.75 cents for all breakfasts and an additional 37.25 cents and 27.75 cents for free and reduced price breakfast respectively.

In the Child Care Food Program, Federal rates of cash assistance for January-June 1981 are 18.50 cents for all lunches and suppers; 14.75 cents for all breakfasts; and 4.5 cents for all snacks served to children.

An additional 63.50 cents for all lunches and suppers; 27.75 cents for breakfasts; and a set 20.25 for snacks served to children from families whose incomes meet the family size income standards established by the state for reduced price school meals.

An additional 83.50 cents for lunches and suppers; 37.25 cents for breakfasts; and a set 27.50 cents for snacks served free.

In the Summer Food Service Program for Children, Federal funds are given to eligible institutions for the costs involved in obtaining, preparing, and serving food under this program (including administrative costs and rental of office space and equipment).

Participants in the Special Milk Program receive partial or full payment for the cost of each half-pint of milk served, depending on the need of children served.

The Food Service Equipment Assistance Program authorizes up to 75 percent of the purchase cost or rental value of food service equipment required to initiate or expand food service in eligible schools. However, eligible schools and institutions determined to be especially needy, with and without food service, may receive 100 percent funding.

Matching fund requirements: For requirements, contact the address above.

Total amount of support: $3,100,000,000 for the year 1980.

Number of awards: Approximately 94,000 schools and 42,000 child-care outlets.

Application information: Official application materials are available upon request to state educational agencies. In states where education agencies do not administer the programs for nonprofit private schools, such applicants should contact the appropriate Food and Nutrition Service Regional Office of the Department of Agriculture.

W

WHITEHALL FOUNDATION, INC.
310 Royal Poinciana Plaza
Palm Beach, FL 33480
305-655-4474

Founded: 1937
Areas of interest: Biology and agricultural economics.
Type: Research grants. No clinical or behavioral work.
Purpose: To support research in the fields of biology and agricultural economics.
Legal basis: Nonprofit organization.
Financial data: Grants vary in amount.
Amount of support per award: $15,000

to $35,000 average.
Total amount of support: $1,116,947 for the year October 1979—September 1980.
Number of applicants most recent year: 75 for the year 1976.
Number of awards: 12 new awards in 1980.
Application information: Applications are submitted in the form of a proposal which will be evaluated in terms of project objectives, feasibility of execution, qualifications of applicant. Required format is available on request.
Duration: Three years; renewal possible on evaluation of previous work.
Deadline: February for April voting session; August for October voting session.
Officers:
  James A. Moffett, President-Treasurer
  Laurel T. Baker, Assistant Treasurer, Secretary
  J. Wright Rumbough Jr., Vice President
  Warren S. Adams, Vice President
  Kenneth S. Beall, Jr.
  Mrs. Helen M. Brooks
  Van Vechten Burger
  George M. Moffett 2d.

THE WOMAN'S NATIONAL FARM AND GARDEN ASSOCIATION
c/o Mrs. Elmer Braun
13 Davis Dr.
Saginaw, MI 48602

Founded: 1914
Name of program:
  Sara Tyson Memorial Fellowships
Type: Fellowships for study in the fields of horticulture, agriculture, and allied subjects.
Year program started: 1928
Purpose: To encourage better living around the world.
Eligibility: Applicant must be a college graduate. Special consideration will be given to financial need and an excellent scholastic record.
Amount of support per award: $500.
Number of applicants most recent year: Three.
Number of awards: Four for the year ending April 1, 1979.
Application information: There are no application forms. A letter of application should be sent to the Chairman of the Committee.
Trustees:
  Boston Deposit and Trust Company

Officers:
  Miss Ruth Gray, President
  Mrs. C. D. MacPherson, Vice President
  Mrs. C. F. Kirshler Jr., Treasurer
  Miss Aileen Maury, Recording Secretary
  Mrs. William Slattery, Corresponding Secretary
Address inquiries to:
  Mrs. Elmer Braun
  13 Davis Dr.
  Saginaw, MI 48602

Magazines Covering Food and Nutrition

by *Magazine Industry Market Place 1982*

This section offers an alphabetical listing of North American magazines that feature food and nutrition topics from agricultural aspects to food science, and from foodservice distribution to biochemistry for medical and dental doctors. The list is based on data from *Magazine Industry Market Place 1982*.

Each listing includes the name, address, and telephone number of the periodical, along with the name of at least one person to contact. In addition, the staff of Marquis Academic Media isolated the key description of each magazine's audience for food and nutrition related topics. However, cookbook and/or recipe information was excluded.

A

AGRI FINANCE
Century Communications, Inc.
5520-G Touhy Ave.
Skokie, IL 60077
312-676-4060

Contact: Philip C. Miller, Publisher
Purpose: Edited for professional financing and managing farms for agriculture.

AGRI MARKETING
Century Communications, Inc.
5520-G Touhy Ave.
Skokie, IL 60077
312-676-4060

Contact: Philip C. Miller, Publisher
Purpose: Serves those involved in marketing and communications in agribusiness.

AGRICHEMICAL AGE
California Farmer Publishing Co.
83 Stevenson St.
San Francisco, CA 94105
415-495-3340

Contact: Jack. T. Pickett, Publisher
Purpose: Geared to agrichemical professionals including dealers, custom and aerial applicators, licensed advisers and consultants. Emphasis on technical and field use information.

AGRICULTURAL EDUCATION
Agricultural Ed Magazine, Inc.
Mississippi State University
Mississippi State, MS 39762

Contact: Jasper S. Lee, Editor-in-Chief
Purpose: Professional articles on agricultural education; for agriculture teachers, libraries, educators.

AGWAY COOPERATOR
Agway, Inc.
Box 4933
Syracuse, NY 13221
315-477-6488

Contact: James E. Hurley, Editor
Purpose: Features information about farmer cooperative services of Agway. Includes articles on feed, seed, fertilizers and general farm supplies and marketing services for Northeastern farmers.

AIRLINE & TRAVEL FOOD SERVICE
International Publishing Co.
665 LaVilla Dr.
Miami Springs, FL 33166
305-887-1701

Contact: Alex Morton, Publisher
Purpose: Articles pertinent to airline, cruise ship and railroad food executives, ship suppliers, caterers, duty free operators and vendors, onboard entertainment. Formerly *Airline Food & Flight Service.*

AMERICAN AGRICULTURIST & THE RURAL NEW YORKER
American Agriculturist, Inc.
Box 369
DeWitt Bldg.
Ithaca, NY 14850
607-273-3507

Contact: Albert Hoefer, Jr., General Manager
Purpose: Material to help farmers make a better living and have a better life;

Based on material reprinted from *Magazine Industry Market Place 1982*, with permission of the R. R. Bowker Company. Copyright 1981 by Xerox Corporation.

for commercial farmers and the agribusiness community in the Northeast.

AMERICAN BEE JOURNAL
Dadant & Sons, Inc.
Hamilton, IL 62341
217-847-3324

Contact: Joe M. Graham, Managing Editor
Purpose: Directed to hobbyists, professionals and scientific community covering all aspects of beekeeping and honey production.

AMERICAN FRUIT GROWER
Meister Publishing Co.
37841 Euclid Ave.
Willoughby, OH 44094
216-942-2000

Contact: Richard T. Meister, President and Editor
Purpose: All phases of commercial vertically integrated fruit operations; new equipment and state grower news; grower marketing efforts; for commercial fruit and nut growers, small fruit and citrus producers.

AMERICAN JOURNAL OF CLINICAL NUTRITION
American Society for Clinical Nutrition
9650 Rockville Pike
Bethesda, MD 20014
301-530-7027

Contact: T.B. Van Itallie, Editor-in-Chief
Purpose: For physicians and scientists interested in human nutrition. Includes reports of original research, nutrition surveys, perspectives in nutrition, diet therapy, book reviews.

ANIMAL NUTRITION & HEALTH
California Farmer Publishing Co.
83 Stevenson St.
San Francisco, CA 94105
415-495-3340

Contact: Jack T. Pickett, Publisher
Purpose: Trade magazine for nutrition/health specialists including feed animal veterinarians, livestock and poultry nutritionists, consultants, extension specialists, fieldmen, dealers and feeding operations.

AQUACULTURE MAGAZINE
Briggs & Associates
620 E Sixth St.
Little Rock, AR 77203
501-376-1921

Contact: Porter Briggs, Publisher and Editor-in-Chief
Purpose: Instructive and technical articles for those involved in the field of aquaculture. Formerly *The Commercial Fish Farmer & Aquaculture News, The Catfish Farmer, Fish Farming Industries & American Fish Farmer & World Aquaculture News.*

B

BAKERY PRODUCTION & MARKETING
Gorman Publishing Co.
5725 E River Rd.
Chicago, IL 60631
312-693-3200

Contact: Bill Donohue, Publisher
Purpose: For wholesale, retail and in-store bakeries; emphasis on management techniques, new products and general industry news.

BAKING INDUSTRY
Putman Publishing Co.
301 E Erie St.
Chicago, IL 60611
312-644-2020

Contact: Laurie A. Gorton, Publishing Director and Editor

BEEF
The Webb Co.
Webb Publications Div.
1999 Shepard Rd.
St. Paul, MN 55116
612-690-7452

Contact: Stuart J. Legaard, Publisher
Purpose: Production information including animal health, nutrition, equipment design, research, breeding, news events, legislative problems and market outlook; for cow-calf and stocker operators and feeders.

BEEF IMPROVEMENT NEWS
The Outlook Co.
417 Main St.
Box 1127, ISU Sta.
Ames, IA 50010
515-232-2051

Contact: Angus Stone, Publisher
Purpose: Performance programs, management practices, health, nutrition, environment, genetics and marketing for Midwest cow/calf industry. Formerly *IBIA News.*

BETTER NUTRITION
Syndicate Magazines, Inc.
6 E 43 St.
New York, NY 10017
212-949-0800

Contact: J.T. Schwartz, L.D. Solomon, Publishers
Purpose: A magazine about health food; contains articles on health, diet, nutrition, ecology.

BEVERAGE INDUSTRY
Magazines For Industry, Inc.
747 Third Ave.
New York, NY 10017
212-838-7778

Contact: Don Gussow, Chairperson, Editor-in-Chief
Purpose: Marketing and technological news and features on all aspects of the soft drink, beer, wine, bottled water and juice markets. Formerly *Soft Drink Industry.*

BEVERAGE WORLD
Keller International Publishing Corp.
150 Great Neck Rd.
Great Neck, NY 11021
516-829-9210

Contact: Gerald Keller, Publisher and Advertising Manager
Purpose: For multi-product beverage industry execuitves; reports on marketing, manufacturing, packaging and new developments. Formerly *Soft Drinks.*

BLAIR & KETCHUM'S COUNTRY JOURNAL
Country Journal Publishing Co.
205 Main St.
Brattleboro, VT 05301
802-257-1321

Contact: William S. Blair, Publisher
Purpose: Practical articles about gardening, raising livestock, alternative sources of energy, recreational and cultural activities and other aspects of country life, primarily for the active rural homeowner. Regular columns cover

RESOURCES FOR FURTHER INFORMATION

the problems and rewards of country living.

BUCKEYE FARM NEWS
Ohio Farm Bureau Federation
Box 479
35 E Chestnut St.
Columbus, OH 43216
614-225-8905

Contact: Sam Cashman, Editor-in-Chief
Purpose: General farm magazine which covers agricultural issues.

BULLETIN OF ENVIRONMENTAL CONTAMINATION & TOXICOLOGY
Springer-Verlag New York, Inc.
175 Fifth Ave.
New York, NY 10010
212-477-8200

Contact: Yutaka Iwata, Editor-in-Chief
Purpose: Publishes significant advances, discoveries and methodology in the fields of air, soil, water and food contamination and pollution.

C

CANDY & SNACK INDUSTRY
Magazines For Industry, Inc.
747 Third Ave.
New York, NY 10017
212-838-7778

Contact: Don Gussow, Chairperson and Editor-in-Chief
Purpose: Management publication covers company operations, meetings and conventions and new ingredients and equipment.

THE CATTLEMAN
Texas & Southwestern Cattle Raisers Association
1301 W Seventh St.
Ft. Worth, TX 76102
817-332-7155

Contact: Dale Segraves, Editor-in-Chief
Purpose: Magazine for beef cattle industry and cattlemen in the Southwest.

CHAIN STORE AGE EXECUTIVE
Lebhar-Friedman, Inc.
425 Park Ave.
New York, NY 10022

212-371-9400

Contact: Ellis Rowland, Publication Director
Purpose: Magazine for headquarters executives of retail chains, shopping center developers, store planners and construction and equipment specifiers.

CHAIN STORE AGE SUPERMARKETS
Lebhar-Friedman, Inc.
425 Park Ave.
New York, NY 10022
212-371-9400

Contact: Arnold D. Friedman, Publisher
Purpose: Reports buying and sales trends to chain, cooperative, voluntary and wholesaler headquarters executives and stores.

CHEMTECH
American Chemical Society
48 Maple St.
Summit, NJ 07901
201-273-4923

Contact: Benjamin J. Luberoff, Editor
Purpose: For chemists, engineers and executives in the chemical industry; articles cover chemical technology, engineering energy, materials, food, fabrics, biologically active materials, economics, management and government regulations.

COMMODITIES MAGAZINE
Commodities Magazine, Inc.
219 Parkade
Cedar Falls, IA 50613
319-277-6341

Contact: Merrill Oster, Publisher
Purpose: Articles on national and international factors and people influencing price changes in commodities and techniques used to trade the market.

COMMODITY JOURNAL
American Association of Commodity Traders
10 Park St.
Concord, NH 03301
603-224-2376

Contact: Arthur N. Economou, Editor-in-Chief
Purpose: To aid and educate members and readers in the field of commodity spot markets, contracts, options, farming and food marketing; for traders, investors and hedgers.

CONSUMER GUIDE
Publications International Ltd.
3841 W Oakton St.
Skokie, IL 60076
312-676-3470

Contact: Louis Weber, Publisher
Purpose: Consumer information product evaluation test reports and discount prices on cars, stereo, tape and photo equipment; analysis and recommendation of diets, health and exercise programs and prescribed and over-the-counter drugs.

CONSUMER LIFE
The Webb Co.
1999 Shepard Rd.
St. Paul, MN 55116
612-690-7238

Contact: Peter Muzzy, Publisher
Purpose: Information on how to stretch house, landscape, remodeling, automibile, food and entertainment budgets, with emphasis on direct-response purchasing. Standing features include Tips from Consumers, Get it Free, Consumer Beware and New Products.

CONSUMERS DIGEST
Consumers Digest, Inc.
5705 N Lincoln Ave.
Chicago, IL 60659
312-275-3590

Contact: Arthur Weber, Publisher
Purpose: Informative consumer publication, advises best buys and prices on products and services, includes health, education, finance, food, nutrition, taxes, insurance, travel, investments.

COOPERATIVE FARMER
Southern States Cooperative, Inc.
Box 26234
Richmond, VA 23260
804-281-1317

Contact: Don R. Tindall, Editor
Purpose: Agriculture news and trends, research, how-to; cooperative agriculture reports; for members of Southern States Cooperative,

agricultural college students and vocational workers.

D

DAIRY GOAT JOURNAL
Dairy Goat Journal Publishing Corp.
14415 N 73 St.
Scottsdale, AZ 85260
602-991-4628

Contact: Kent Leach, Publisher
Purpose: For persons interested in dairy goats; basic how-to articles and occasional scientific articles. Advertisements of breeders and commercial firms. Veterinary column, coming events, classified ads, editorial material, photos.

DAIRY HERD MANAGEMENT
Miller Publishing Co.
Box 67
2501 Wayzata Blvd.
Minneapolis, MN 55440
612-374-5200

Contact: George Ashfield, Editorial Director
Purpose: Case histories, current research, new techniques and products, news, animal health and nutrition and government activities; for operators of large dairy farms.

DAIRY RECORD MAGAZINE
Gorman Publishing Co.
5725 E River Rd.
Chicago, IL 60631
312-693-3200

Contact: Dave Coulter, Publisher
Purpose: National news and features of the dairy processing industry.

DIABETES CARE
American Diabetes Association
2 Park Ave.
New York, NY 10016
212-683-7444

Contact: Jay S. Skyler, MD, Editor-in-Chief
Purpose: Clinical journal for health care team aimed at improving care of patients with diabetes and containing research advances, reviews, diagnosis.

DIABETES FORECAST
American Diabetes Association, Inc.
2 Park Ave.
New York, NY 10016
212-683-7444

Contact: Harold Rifkin, MD, Editor-in-Chief
Purpose: Factual information about the care and nature of diabetes for those with the disease. Contains news of the latest research developments.

DIABETES: THE JOURNAL OF THE AMERICAN DIABETES ASSOCIATION
American Diabetes Association
2 Park Ave.
New York, NY 10016
212-683-7444

Contact: Daniel W. Foster, MD, Editor-in-Chief
Purpose: For physicians and those in scientific fields concerned with diabetes and related endocrine and metabolic disorders.

DIALYSIS & TRANSPLANTATION
Creative Age Publications
12849 Magnolia Blvd.
North Hollywood, CA 91607
213-980-4184

Contact: Deborah Carver, Co-Publisher
Purpose: Articles of interest to dialysis and transplant physicians, nurses, technicians, administrators, nutritionists and social workers.

F

FAMILY HEALTH
Family Media, Inc.
149 Fifth Ave.
New York, NY 10010
212-677-0870

Contact: Robert E. Riordan, President and Publisher
Purpose: Deals with better health in daily living, covering food and nutrition, prenatal, baby and child care, preventive medicine, practical self-help, diet and exercise, beauty and good grooming.

FARM EQUIPMENT
Johnson Hill Press, Inc.
1233 Janesville Ave.
Fort Atkinson, WI 53538
414-563-6388; 800-558-9537

Contact: James Rank, Publisher
Purpose: Covers new products, technology and services of interest to farm equipment dealers, wholesalers and manufacturers.

FARM INDUSTRY NEWS
The Webb Co.
1999 Shepard Rd.
St. Paul, MN 55116
612-690-7293

Contact: Robert Moraczewski, General Manager and Editor-in-Chief
Purpose: Contains product news, how to be a better buyer for high income manager-farmers in the midwestern states.

FARM JOURNAL
230 W Washington Sq.
Philadelphia, PA 19105
215-574-1200

Contact: Dale E. Smith, President and Publisher
Purpose: Articles on management for maximizing profits, of interest to the businessperson farmer. Editorial version each farmer receives depends upon crops grown and livestock raised.

FARM WEEKLY
Sioux City Newspapers, Inc.
Box 118
Sixth and Pavonia
Sioux City, IA 51102
712-279-5028

Contact: Larry Myhre, Editor
Purpose: New farming methods, reports from agricultural experiment stations and universities, 4-H and FFA reports, livestock and grain market reports, homemaking and legislative reports; for Iowa, Minnesota, Nebraska and South Dakota farm and city readers.

THE FARMER
The Webb Co.
Webb Publications Div.
1999 Shepard Rd.
St. Paul, MN 55116
612-690-7361

Contact: Bert O. Lund, Publisher

Purpose: Crop and livestock management, farm business and home, market and legislative reports, new product review; for Minnesota and North and South Dakota crop and livestock farmers and ranchers.

FARMER'S DIGEST
Farmer's Digest, Inc.
2645 Maple Hill La.
Brookfield, WI 53005
414-782-1570, 5525

Contact: H. Lee Schwanz, Publisher
Purpose: Digest-sized magazine for farmers. Contains current information on all phases of agriculture including beef, hog, dairy and field crops.

THE FARMER-STOCKMAN
The Farmer-Stockman Publishing Co.
Box 25125
Oklahoma City, OK 73125
405-231-3341

Contact: Jack Blakeney, Publisher
Purpose: Informational articles on production and marketing of farm and livestock products.

FARMFUTURES
ACI, Inc.
225 E Michigan
Milwaukee, WI 53202
414-278-7676

Contact: Paul Hermberg, Publisher
Purpose: Provides economic information to guide business decisions; commodity market outlook, economic climate, future planning guides, for operating business managers of large farm and ranch units.

FARMLAND NEWS
Farmland Industries, Inc.
Box 7305
3315 N Oak
Kansas City, MO 64116
816-459-6000

Contact: Frank Whitsitt, Editor
Purpose: Farm news, living and management from cooperative viewpoint; information on legislative action affecting farming and cooperatives; for predominantly rural audience. Formerly *Cooperative Consumer*.

FEED & GRAIN TIMES
Johnson Hill Press, Inc.
1233 Janesville Ave.
Fort Atkinson, WI 53538
414-563-6388; 800-558-9537

Contact: Al Paulson, Publisher
Purpose: Covers new product services and technology of interest to grain and feed processors, terminal elevator managers and fertilizer/chemical dealers.

FEEDSTUFFS
The Miller Publishing Co.
Box 67
2501 Wayzata Blvd.
Minneapolis, MN 55440
612-374-5200

Contact: George Gates, Publisher
Purpose: For those involved in feed production and distribution and animal feeding; features animal nutrition and health, feed production, transportation, handling and storage and industry news.

THE FISHERMEN'S NEWS
The Fishermen's News, Inc.
C-3 Bldg., Rm. 110
Fishermen's Terminal
Seattle, WA 98119
206-282-7545

Contact: Walter M. Kisner, Jr., Publisher
Purpose: Trade journal for the commercial fishing industry of the Pacific Coast from Bristol Bay to San Diego.

FOOD & DRUG PACKAGING
Magazines For Industry, Inc.
747 Third Ave.
New York, NY 10017
212-838-7778

Contact: Don Gussow, Chairperson and Editor-in-Chief
Purpose: For food, drug and medical manufacturers who package their goods; focuses on packaging, machinery, technique and other news of interest.

FOOD ENGINEERING
Chilton Co.
Chilton Way
Radnor, PA 19089
215-687-8200

Contact: Thomas R. Stillman, Publisher
Purpose: Magazine for food and beverage manufacturing management. Contains articles on processing developments, plant management, marketplace events and issues and fabricated food technology.

FOOD MONITOR
World Hunger Year, Inc.
150 Broadway, No. 209
New York, NY 10013
212-226-2714

Contact: Jack Clark, Editor-in-Chief
Purpose: Concerned with issues of food, land and hunger; provides information, analysis and action on these issues; of interest to consumers, activists, human rights workers, policymakers and co-op members.

FOOD PLANT IDEAS
Lairwood Publications
731 Hennepin Ave.
Minneapolis, MN 55403
612-333-0471

Contact: Jerry A. Machalek, Publisher
Purpose: Contains news of equipment ingredients, packaging, supplies and materials used by the food processing, manufacturing and allied industries, such as drugs, cosmetics and tobacco.

FOOD PROCESSING
Putman Publishing Co.
301 E Erie St.
Chicago, IL 60611
312-644-2020

Contact: John Cappelletti, President
Purpose: Magazine serves executive and operating management in food processing industry. Articles describe new products and developments.

FOOD PRODUCT DEVELOPMENT
Magazines For Industry, Inc.
747 Third Ave.
New York, NY 10017
212-838-7778

Contact: Don Gussow, Chairperson and Editor-in-Chief
Purpose: Responds to the interests of the food industry, particularly

product development, ingredients and quality assurance.

FOOD PRODUCTION/MANAGEMENT
Canning Trade, Inc.
2619 Maryland Ave.
Baltimore, MD 21218
301-467-3338

Contact: Arthur I. Judge, II, Editor
Purpose: For managers, salesmen and production people in the canning, glasspacking and frozen food industry; articles on management, production and distribution.

FOOD SERVICE MARKETING
EIP, Inc.
2132 Fordem Ave.
Madison, WI 53701
608-244-3528

Contact: Philip L. Rane, Publisher
Purpose: Management, marketing, food, equipment, design and decor for commercial and institutional food service operations.

FOOD TRADE NEWS
Best Met Publishing Co.
119 Sibley Ave.
Ardmore, PA 19003
215-642-7040

Contact: Robert J. Johnson, Publisher
Purpose: Contains news affecting persons distributing and selling food at retail. News stories cover the impact of legislation on the area, store openings, promotions, mergers, personnel changes, achievements, financial reports and coming events.

FOODSERVICE EQUIPMENT SPECIALIST
Cahners Publishing Co.
5 S Wabash Ave.
Chicago, IL 60603
312-372-6880

Contact: David S Wexler, Publisher
Purpose: Trade magazine for foodservice equipment specialists and supply and design professionals.

FOODSERVICE PRODUCT NEWS
Young/Conway Publications, Inc.
342 Madison Ave.
New York, NY 10017
212-986-4119

Contact: Arthur T. Conway, Publisher
Purpose: For operators of restaurants and institutional food services; features new products, services and literature. Formerly *Food & Equipment Product News.*

FORECAST FOR HOME ECONOMICS
Scholastic, Inc.
50 W 44 St.
New York, NY 10036
212-944-7700

Contact: Steven C. Swett, Publisher
Purpose: Serves the professional home economist teaching in elementary and secondary schools, colleges and universities, home demonstration work and through home service classes in other businesses. Formerly *Practical Forecast.*

THE FURROW
Deere & Co.
John Deere Rd.
Moline, IL 61265
309-752-4872

Contact: Ralph Reynolds, Editor-in-Chief
Purpose: Farmers throughout the world, plus agricultural influencers.

G

GROCERY COMMUNICATIONS
Gro Com Group
Box 311
Barrington, RI 02806
401-245-4896

Contact: Brad McDowell, Publisher, Editor-in-Chief
Purpose: Trade publication covers news, promotions, broker-update and highlights the major changes in the food industry.

GROCERY DISTRIBUTION MAGAZINE
Market Publications
39 S LaSalle St.
Chicago, IL 60603
312-263-1057

Contact: Richard W. Mulville, Publisher and Editor-in-Chief
Purpose: A magazine of physical distribution and plant development for the food industry, circulated to executives whose job functions deal with distribution transportation.

H

HEALTH SCIENCE
The American Natural Hygiene Society, Inc.
695 Brooklawn Ave.
Bridgeport, CT 06604
203-366-6229

Contact: Jack Dunn Trop, Editor-in-Chief
Purpose: News and articles on whole food, exercise, ecology, organic gardening, relaxation and techniques for changing habits.

HEALTHWAYS MAGAZINE
American Chiropractic Association, Inc.
2200 Grand Ave.
Des Moines, IA 50312
515-243-1121

Contact: Tracy Mullen, Editor
Purpose: A general health magazine for lay persons; contains articles on proper nutrition, exercise, the importance of the environment, related developments in health and science and general topics.

HOARD'S DAIRYMAN
W.D. Hoard & Sons
28 Milwaukee Ave., W
Fort Atkinson, WI 53538
414-563-5551

Contact: W.D. Knox, Editor-in-Chief
Purpose: Provides farming information for the American dairyman.

HOOSIER FARMER
Indiana Farm Bureau, Inc.
130 E Washington St.
Indianapolis, IN 46204
317-631-8331, ext. 1421

Contact: Clark Q. Lewis, Managing Editor
Purpose: Agricultural problems and farm policy, commodities, farm women, new crop varieties, marketing and new farming methods; for Indiana farmers.

INTERNATIONAL HARVESTER FARM FORUM
International Harvester Co.
401 N Michigan Ave.
Chicago, IL 60611
312-836-2000

Contact: Michael Homberg, Editor
Purpose: A general interest farm and ranch magazine distributed by dealers. Emphasizes mechanization and other modern farming and ranching practices.

IRRIGATION AGE
The Webb Co.
1999 Shepard Rd.
St. Paul, MN 55116
612-690-7203, 7377

Contact: Bob Snyder, Publisher
Purpose: For farmers practicing irrigation and volume producers located in areas under irrigation development.

J

JOURNAL OF AMERICAN DIETETIC ASSOCIATION
The American Dietetic Association
430 N Michigan Ave.
Chicago, IL 60611
312-280-5000

Contact: Dorothea F. Turner, Editor-in-Chief
Purpose: For dietitians and nutritionists; reports on research trends and recent developments in the food and nutrition fields.

JOURNAL OF CARBOHYDRATES-NUCLEOSIDES-NUCLEOTIDES
Marcel Dekker Journals
270 Madison Ave.
New York, NY 10016
212-889-9595

Contact: Robert E. Harmon, Editor-in-Chief
Purpose: Articles on all aspects of basic and applied chemical and biological research on carbohydrates, nucleosides and nucleotides, stressing new methodology and reagents in general use. For an international audience.

JOURNAL OF CYCLIC NUCLEOTIDE RESEARCH
Raven Press
1140 Ave. of the Americas
New York, NY 10036
212-575-0335

Contact: Alan Edelson, Publisher
Purpose: Reviews and current research for biochemists, pharmacologists, physiologists and endocrinologists.

JOURNAL OF FOOD PROTECTION
International Association of Milk, Food and Environmental Sanitarians, Inc.
Box 701
Ames, IA 50010
515-232-6699

Contact: Elmer H. Marth, Editor-in-Chief
Purpose: Research related to all levels of food processing and production; review papers, field topics for governmental regulatory agency personnel, educators, and industry personnel.

JOURNAL OF FOOD SCIENCE
Institute of Food Technologists
221 N LaSalle St.
Chicago, IL 60601
312-782-8424

Contact: C.L. Willey, Publisher
Purpose: Research in food science and technology. Formerly *Food Research*.

THE JOURNAL OF FUTURES MARKETS
John Wiley & Sons
605 Third Ave.
New York, NY 10158
212-850-6570

Contact: Allan Wittman, Publisher
Purpose: Articles deal with financial futures, commodity forecasting techniques, corporate hedging strategies, tax and accounting implications of hedging, analysis of commodity trading systems, commodity portfolio optimization, trading in futures markets. For traders, brokers, investment advisors, chief economists, money managers, portfolio managers.

JOURNAL OF HOME ECONOMICS
American Home Economics Association
2010 Massachusetts Ave., NW
Washington, DC 20036
202-862-8300; 800-424-8080

Contact: Kinsey B. Green, Executive Director
Purpose: Articles cover various aspects of home economics: child and family, house and home, food and furnishing.

JOURNAL OF NUTRITION
American Institute of Nutrition
Department of Food Science & Human Nutrition
Gainesville, FL 32611
904-392-2559

Contact: James S. Dinning, Editor-in-Chief
Purpose: Scientific papers submitted by researchers active in the nutrition field.

JOURNAL OF NUTRITION EDUCATION
Society for Nutrition Education
2140 Shattuck Ave.
Suite 1110
Berkeley, CA 94704
415-548-1363

Contact: Susan M. Oace, Editor
Purpose: Designed to stimulate interest and research in applied nutritional sciences and to disseminate information to educators and others concerned with positive nutrition practices and policies.

JOURNAL OF STUDIES ON ALCOHOL
Rutgers Center of Alcohol Studies
Box 969
Piscataway, NJ 08854
201-932-3510

Contact: Timothy G. Coffey, Editor-in-Chief
Purpose: Research findings in physiology, biochemistry, psychiatry, psychology, sociology, economics, statistics, education, law and other fields; abstracts of reports on alcohol studies; book reviews, abstracts, bibliography and indexes. Formerly *Quarterly Journal of Studies on Alcohol*.

JOURNAL OF THE ASSOCIATION OF OFFICIAL ANALYTICAL CHEMISTS
Association of Official Analytical Chemists
1111 N 19 St.
Suite 210
Arlington, VA 22209
703-522-3032

Contact: Helen L. Reynolds
Purpose: Association magazine that carries research articles and reports of the development, validation and interpretation of analytical methods for agricultural commodities, food, drugs, cosmetics, colors, the environment and other areas that affect the public and are subject to government regulation.

JOURNAL OF THE MILKING SHORTHORN AND ILLAWARRA BREEDS
American Milking Shorthorn Society
1722-JJ S Glenstone
Springfield, MO 65804
417-887-6525

Contact: Janet Beavers, Editor-in-Chief
Purpose: Breed, editorial and sale information, breed programs, advertising of cattle and farm products and show information; for Milking Shorthorn breeders. Formerly *Milking Shorthorn Journal*.

L

LET'S LIVE
Oxford Industries, Inc.
444 N Larchmont Blvd.
Los Angeles, CA 90004
213-469-3901

Contact: Mrs. W.J. Basset, President and Publisher
Purpose: Natural living magazine covers nutrition, diet, longevity, health foods, physical fitness, organic gardening and environmental protection.

LIFE & HEALTH
Review & Herald Publishing Association
6856 Eastern Ave., NW
Washington, DC 20012
202-723-3700

Contact: Joyce McClintock, Editor
Purpose: Family health magazine features articles on prevention of disease, food and nutrition, exercise, aging, mental health, dental health, health care, home and family, hobbies and recreation.

LIFE SCIENCES
Pergamon Press, Inc.
Maxwell House, Fairview Park
Elmsford, NY 10523
914-592-7700

Contact: R. Bressler, MD, Editor-in-Chief
Purpose: Concerns general and molecular biology, biochemistry, physiology and pharmacology. Aims to link research workers in many life science disciplines with workers in their own fields and related areas.

LIVESTOCK
Crow Publications, Inc.
Drawer 17F
Denver, CO 80217
303-623-2800

Contact: Richard A. Crow, President
Purpose: Ranch management, marketing, investment, animal health, feeds, sanitation, new equipment; for livestock producers, feedlot operators and horsemen in the 17 western states.

N

NATIONAL FISHERMAN
Journal Publications
21 Elm St.
Camden, ME 04843
207-236-4342

Contact: David P. Jackson, Publisher
Purpose: Trade journal for domestic commercial fishing industry, with secondary coverage for professional and amateur boatbuilder. Formerly *Maine Coast Fisherman*.

THE NATIONAL FUTURE FARMER
Future Farmers of America
Box 15130
Alexandria, VA 22309
703-360-3600

Contact: Wilson W. Carnes, Editor-in-Chief
Purpose: For members of Future Farmers of America and students of vocational agriculture; FFA news, technical agriculture, and general youth interest.

NATIONAL HOG FARMER
The Webb Co.
Webb Publications Div.
1999 Shepard Rd.
St. Paul, MN 55116
612-690-7452

Contact: Stuart J. Legaard, Publisher
Purpose: Management practices, production and marketing, industry development, trends in breeding, processing and retailing; for commercial producers marketing more than 200 hogs per year.

THE NEW FARM
Rodale Press, Inc.
33 E Minor St.
Emmaus, PA 18049
215-683-3111

Contact: John Haberern, Publisher
Purpose: Geared to the needs and interests of independent family farmers concerned with the health of their land and the quality of the food it produces. Editorial emphasis is directed toward helping the small farmer survive in a world of spiraling energy and equipment costs.

NUTRITION HEALTH REVIEW
Vegetus Publications
143 Madison Ave.
New York, NY 10016
212-679-3590

Contact: Frank Ray Rifkin, Publisher
Purpose: Vegetarian-oriented articles, medical news, nutrition, psychology and food-preparation information.

NUTRITION REVIEWS
The Nutrition Foundation
Dept. of Biochemistry
St. Louis University School of Medicine
St. Louis, MO 63104
314-664-9800, ext. 131

Contact: Robert E. Olson, Editor-in-Chief
Purpose: Articles and interpretive summaries of clinical and experimental research in biochemistry, food science, public health, toxicology, dentistry,

pediatrics, internal medicine, gastroenterology, other clinical specialties and related sciences; special reports on government actions.

NUTRITION TODAY
Nutrition Today Society
Box 1829
703 Giddings Ave.
Annapolis, MD 21404
301-267-8616

Contact: Cortez Enloe Jr., MD, Publisher and Editor
Purpose: For members of the Nutrition Today Society; articles and information dedicated to the dissemination of knowledge about nutrition.

NUTRITIONAL SUPPORT SERVICES
Creative Age Publications
12849 Magnolia Blvd.
North Hollywood, CA 91607
213-980-4184

Contact: Deborah Carver, Co-Publisher
Purpose: Editorial content covers patient assessment, determination and application of therapy, use of equipment and formulation, preparation of substrates, continuing education processes, home training, system comparison.

O

OBESITY & BARIATRIC MEDICINE
American Society of Bariatric Physicians, Inc.
5200 S Quebec St., No. 300
Englewood, CO 80111
303-779-4833

Contact: W.L. Asher, MD, Editor-in-Chief
Purpose: For clinicians and researchers who have a special interest in the study and treatment of obesity.

P

PRACTICAL GASTROENTEROLOGY
Pharmaceutical Communications, Inc.
42-15 Crescent St.
Long Island City, NY 11101
212-937-4283

Contact: Thomas R. Jones, Publisher
Purpose: Articles concerning the diagnosis, therapy and management of patients with digestive disorders and the nutritional requirements of patients whose needs are not met by conventional feeding. For primary care physicians.

PRAIRIE FARMER
Prairie Farmer Publishing Co.
2001 Spring Rd.
Oak Brook, IL 60521
312-323-3800

Contact: Richard E. Albrecht, Publisher
Purpose: Primarily technical articles on crop and livestock production, aimed at commercial farm operators.

PREVENTION
Rodale Press, Inc.
33 E Minor St.
Emmaus, PA 18049
215-967-5171

Contact: Marshall Ackerman, Publisher
Purpose: Focuses on health and personal fitness. Covers natural foods, nutritional supplements, medical treatments, exercise and contemporary lifestyle.

PREVENTIVE MEDICINE
Academic Press, Inc.
111 Fifth Ave.
New York, NY 10003
212-741-6800

Contact: Ernst L. Wynder, MD Editor-in-Chief
Purpose: Scientific journal dealing with all aspects of prevention including cancer, heart disease, stroke, infectious diseases; screening, health education and planning, health economics.

PROCESSED PREPARED FOOD
Gorman Publishing Co.
5725 E River Rd.
Chicago, IL 60631
312-693-3200

Contact: Harry Stagnito, Publisher
Purpose: In-plant features, product news, news and special reports for executives and department heads of processed food companies. Formerly *Canner Packer*.

PROGRESSIVE FARMER
820 Shades Creek Pkwy.
Birmingham, AL 35202
205-870-4440

Contact: Eugene Butler, Chairperson of the Board
Purpose: Contains localized subject matter for the South and Southwest; articles on farming, farm management, machinery, crops, livestock and farm life.

PROGRESSIVE GROCER
Div. of Maclean Hunter Media, Inc.
708 Third Ave.
New York, NY 10017
212-490-1000

Contact: John W. Skeels, President
Purpose: For executives in the retail grocery industry; features articles on consumer trends, merchandising and other areas of current interest.

R

RESTAURANT BUSINESS
Bill Communications, Inc.
633 Third Ave.
New York, NY 10017
212-986-4800

Contact: Jeffrey P. Berlind
Purpose: For food-service managers; features news on management skills, personnel and products.

RESTAURANT HOSPITALITY
Penton IPC, Inc.
1111 Chester Ave.
Cleveland, OH 44114
216-696-7000

Contact: Shelden Jones, Publishing Director
Purpose: Written to assist commercial food service operators in their business.

RESTAURANTS & INSTITUTIONS
Cahners Publishing Co.
Div. of Reed Publishing Corp.
5 S Wabash Ave.
Chicago, IL 60603
312-372-6880

Contact: David S. Wexler, Publisher

Purpose: For buyers and specifiers in chain and independent food service and lodging establishments; features articles on operations, purchasing, administration, design, decor, maintenance, merchandising and personnel. Formerly *Institutions/Volume Feeding; Institutions.*

ROHM & HAAS REPORTER
Rohm & Haas Co.
Independence Mall W
Philadelphia, PA 19105
215-592-3262

Contact: Benjamin D. Allen, Editor-in-Chief
Purpose: Articles deal with the way agricultural and industrial chemical and plastics are used worldwide.

S

SERVICE WORLD INTERNATIONAL
Cahners Publishing Co.
Div. of Reed Holdings, Inc.
265 E 42 St.
New York, NY 10017
212-949-4377, 4378, 4379

Contact: Fergus McKeever, Publisher
Purpose: International hotel, food service and tourism industries' supply publication covers tourism development and investment, hotel/resort and catering complexes, international market trends and air and surface carrier advances.

SOYBEAN DIGEST
American Soybean Assocation
Box 27300
777 Craig Rd.
St. Louis, MO 63141
314-432-1600

Contact: Grant Mangold, Editor-in-Chief
Purpose: Provides the top soybean growers in the US with management information designed to help them produce and market soybeans profitably.

SUCCESSFUL FARMING
Meredith Corp.
1716 Locust St.
Des Moines, IA 50336
515-284-2011

Contact: Jim Cornick, Publisher
Purpose: Covers all areas of farming, including livestock, crops, soils, machinery, buildings, economics and management.

SUPERMARKET BUSINESS
Fieldmark Media, Inc.
25 W 43 St.
New York, NY 10036
212-354-5169

Contact: Jeffrey A. Schaeffer, Publisher
Purpose: Covers important issues, trends and developments for the supermarket business community. Each monthly issue includes material concerning operations, general merchandise and HaBA, equipment and services, perishables and gorcery products. Formerly *Supermarketing.*

SUPERMARKET NEWS
Fairchild Publications
7 E 12 St.
New York, NY 10003
212-741-4000

Contact: Ernest B. Obermeyer, Publisher
Purpose: For supermarket executives, owners and managers; features promotion and general industry news.

V

VEGETARIAN TIMES
Vegetarian Times, Inc.
124 N Austin
Oak Park, IL 60302
312-848-8120

Contact: Paul Barret Obis, Publisher and Editor-in-Chief
Purpose: The nation's only vegetarian periodical not associated with an organization.

W

WALLACE'S FARMER
Wallace Homestead Co.
1912 Grand Ave.
Des Moines, IA 50305
515-243-6181

Contact: Richard Albrecht, President
Purpose: Covers livestock and crop production and information on tax and estate planning.

WEIGHT WATCHERS MAGAZINE
American/Harlequin in arrangement with W/W Twentyfirst Corp.
575 Lexington Ave.
New York, NY 10022
212-888-9166

Contact: Alan Goldberg, Publisher
Purpose: Magazine devoted to weight control, grooming and fashion.

WINES & VINES
The Hiaring Co.
703 Market St.
San Francisco, CA 94103
415-392-1146

Contact: Philip Hiaring, Publisher, Editor-in-Chief and Managing Editor
Purpose: Focuses on wine grape growing and wine making.

Publishing Opportunities in Food and Nutrition

by *Marquis Academic Media*

This section of part 4 includes only those periodicals that represent real publishing opportunities and accept submissions in English on food, food science, agriculture, and nutrition topics. Not listed are publications of abstracting services, periodicals that are direct translations from foreign journals, or periodicals prepared by an in-house staff.

Periodicals listed include professional journals, technical journals, and publications produced by business firms, unions, or associations. The editors or publishers of these journals completed questionnaires that requested manuscript requirements, details of author payment, and copyright information, as well as an editorial description of the journal, the languages of publication, and circulation figures. An asterisk following the title of the periodical indicates that no updated information was returned by the editor or publisher. In these cases, the staff of Marquis Academic Media updated the information as much as possible.

A

ACA JOURNAL OF CHIROPRACTIC
American Chiropractic Association
2200 Grand
Des Moines, IA 50312
515-243-1121

Subscription data: Previous title *National Chiropractic Journal.* First published in 1930.
Issues and rates: Monthly. 6 articles per average issue. Circulation 13,303. Annual rate: $10.00
Sponsoring organization: American Chiropractic Association, Inc.
Editorial description: Emphasizes the premise that the relationship between structure and function in the human body is a significant health factor, and promotes the advancement of the philosophy, science and art of chiropractic.
Audience: Professional
Manuscript information
Subject field(s): Research papers, book reviews, features dealing with neurology, nutrition, orthopedics, sports injuries, physical therapy, and roentgenology, medical legislation, insurance, etc.
Manuscript requirements: Style guide sent upon request. Submit 2 copies, double-spaced, with a 125-word summary, and brief biography.
Author information and reprints: No payment. Simultaneous submission not permitted. Copyright held by publication. Reprints available at cost.
Disposition of manuscript: Acknowledged within 1 week; decision in 1 month; published 3-12 months after acceptance. Rejections returned, with SASE.
Submit to: Jerry Marsengill, Editor

ADDICTIVE BEHAVIORS*
An International Journal
Pergamon Press Inc.
Fairview Park
Maxwell House
Elmsford, New York 10523
University of Mississippi Medical Center
Jackson, MS 39216

Subscription data: First published in 1975.
Issues and rates: Quarterly. 12 articles per average issue. Circulation 1,000. Annual rates: $30.00
Editorial description: Publishes original research, theoretical papers, and critical reviews in the area of substance abuse. Sound experimental design, combined with objective assessment procedures is a requisite.
Audience: Professional.
Manuscript information
Subject field(s): Alcoholism, drug abuse, obesity, smoking.
Manuscript requirements: APA style. Submit 3 copies, and a 100 word abstract, all double-spaced.
Author information and reprints: No payment. Simultaneous submission not permitted. Copyright held by publication. Reprints available.
Disposition of manuscript: Acknowledged with 2 weeks; decision in 3 months; published 8 months after acceptance. Rejections returned, with criticism.
Submit to: Dr. Peter M. Miller, Editor
Dept. of Behavioral Medicine
Hilton Head Hospital
Hilton Head, SC 29928
803-785-6122

AFRICAN ENVIRONMENT
Environmental Studies and Regional Planning Bulletin
PO Box 3370
Dakar, Senegal
21-60-27, 94 22-42-29

Subscription data: Previous title *Envirnoment in Africa.* First published in 1974.
Issues and rates: Quarterly. 5 articles per average issue. Circulation 2,200. Annual rate: $20.00
Sponsoring organization: ENDA
Managing editors: Jacques Bugmcourt, and Liberty Mhlanga
Editorial description: Mss. which are relevant to problems of environment and development in Africa and the Third World; short notes, work reports, and book reviews.
Audience: Thos concerned with the Third World.
Manuscript information
Subject field(s): Urban planning, rural development, conservation, geography, appropriate technology, self-reliant development, human settelements, nutrition, agriculture.
Manuscript requirements: Preferred length 10-15 pages. Submit 2 copies, double-spaced, with a brief biographical sketch of author. Accepted in French or English.
Author information and reprints: No payment. Simultaneous submission is permitted. Copyright held by publication. Reproduction allowed for non-commercial use, with knowledge of publisher.
Disposition of manuscript: Acknowledged immediately; decision in 3 weeks; publishing time varies.
Submit to: Heike Fofane
Editorial Secretary

AGRICULTURAL EDUCATION
PO Drawer AV
Miss. State, MS 39762
601-325-3326

Subscription data: First published in 1927.
Issues and rates: Monthly. 15 articles per average issue. Circulation 8,050. Annual rate: $5.00
Editorial description: Directed toward the improvement of agricultural education and reports ideas and happenings in the field.
Audience: Academic.
Manuscript information
Manuscript requirements: Style guide sent upon request. Preferred length 6 pp., typewritten, double-spaced. Submit 1 copy.
Author information and reprints: No payment. Simultaneous submission not permitted. Copyright held by journal.
Disposition of manuscript: Acknowledged in 1 week; decision and published in 1-6 months after acceptance. Rejections returned.
Submit to: Jasper S. Lee
Editor

AGRICULTURAL ENGINEERING MAGAZINE
2950 Niles Road
St. Joseph, MI 49085
616-429-0300

Subscription data: First published in 1921.
Issues and rates: Published monthly. Articles per average issue. 5. Paid circulation 12,000; 1,500 controlled. Annual rate(s): $16.00; Foreign $16.00 (surface mail; request rate for air mail); Members $8.00
Sponsoring organization: American Society of Agricultural Engineers.
Editorial description: Focuses on agricultural progress through mechanization, including national and international issues which interact with that progress.
Audience: Agricultural engineers, agribusiness, educators, extension services.
Manuscript information
Subject field(s): Imaginative solutions to problems of agriculture and of food and feed handling.
Manuscript requirements: GPO. Length depends on content. Submit 2 copies, in English only. No abstracts required.
Author information and reprints: Query letter of 500 words on proposed article content required. No payment. Simultaneous submission not permitted. Publication holds exclusive rights after acceptance. Copyright held by publication. Author must obtain written permission to reprint. Reprints available; cost available from Publications Department.
Disposition of manuscript: Receipt is not acknowledged. Decision within 3 months; publishing date depends on content. Rejected manuscript is returned, with reasons for rejection only, with SASE or if return postage is supplied by author.
Submit to: Marianna Pratt
Managing Editor

AGRICULTURAL HISTORY
University of California, Davis
Davis, CA 95616
916-752-3046

Subscription data: First published in 1927.
Issues and rates: Published quarterly. Articles per average issue: 6. Circulation 1,480. Annual rate(s): $15.00; Institutions $28.00.
Sponsoring organization: Agricultural History Society.
Editorial description: A medium for the publication of research and documents pertaining to the history of agriculture in all its phases, and as a clearinghouse for information of interest and value to workers in the field.
Audience: Academic, business, government.
Manuscript information
Subject field(s): History, economics, geography, land use and tenure, ecology, biology, botany, genetics, agricultural technology and political science as they relate to agriculture.
Manuscript requirements: See latest issue for style requirements. Preferred length 10-12 pages. Submit 2 copies. Typewritten, double-spaced; all charts, graphs, and photographs to be camera ready. Return postage requested.
Author information and reprints: No payment. Simultaneous submission not permitted. Periodical holds exclusive rights after acceptance. Copyright held by publication. Reprints available, 25 gratis, additional at cost.
Disposition of manuscript: Receipt acknowledged. Decision in 3-6 months. Published 6-12 months after acceptance. Rejected manuscript is returned, criticized.
Submit to: James H. Shideler
Editor

AGRICULTURAL HISTORY REVIEW
British Agricultural History Society
Museum of English Rural Life
The University, Whiteknights
Reading, Berks., England

Subscription data: First published in 1953.
Issues and rates: Published semi-

annually. Articles per average issue: 5. Circulation 1,800. Annual rate(s): 5.00.

Sponsoring organization: British Agricultural History Society.

Editorial description: Publishes new research and views on agricultural history, including land use techniques, farm structure, landownership, agricultural finance, and marketing, and rural society. Articles dealing with periods other than the 19th century are preferred.

Audience: Historical, academic.

Manuscript information

Manuscript requirements: Style sheet sent on request. Preferred lenght 8,000 words maximum. Submit 1 copy.

Author information and reprints: Payment in 25 reprints. Simultaneous submission is permitted. Copyright held by author. Reprints available at cost. Query letter advisable.

Disposition of manuscript: Receipt acknowledged. Decision in 2 months. Published 18 months after acceptance. Rejected manuscript is returned, with SASE.

Submit to: Prof. G.E. Mingay
Editor
Rutherford College
University of Kent
Canterbury, Kent, England CT2 7NX
Canterbury 66822 (Telephone number)

AGRICULTURAL WATER MANAGEMENT
An International Journal
Elsevier Scientific Publishing Co.
PO Box 211
Amsterdam, The Netherlands
020-580-3911

Subscription data: First published in 1976.

Issues and rates: Quarterly. 8 articles per average issue. Annual rate: Dfl. 143.00.

Managing Editor: Dr. J. Wesseling, Wageneningen

Editorial description: Deals with both research on and management of water in world agriculture.

Audience: Agronomists, agricultural engineers, agricultural hydrologists.

Manuscript information

Subject field(s): Crop irrigation and drainage; ground and surface water management; water technology.

Manuscript requirements: Style guide sent upon request and printed in journal. Length depends on quality of content. Submit 3 copies, with bibliography and abstract of 400 words max. All double-spaced.

Author information and reprints: 50 reprints free; additional at cost. Simultaneous submission not permitted. Copyright held by journal. No page charges.

Disposition of manuscript: Acknowledged within 4 weeks; decision in 2-3 months; published 3-6 months after acceptance. Rejections returned, criticized.

Submit to: Editorial Secretariat
Agricultural Water Management
PO Box 330
1000 A-H Amsterdam, The Netherlands

AGRICULTURE AND ENVIRONMENT
International Journal for Scientific Research or the Relationships of Agriculture, and Food production plus the Biosphere
Elsevier Scientific Publishing Co.
PO Box 211
Amsterdam, The Netherlands
020-515-9222

Subscription data: First published in 1974.

Issues and rates: Quarterly. 6 articles per average issue. Annual rate: Dfl. 138.

Managing editor: Dr. T.L.V. Ulbricht, London, England.

Editorial description: An international journal considering agriculture in terms of its effects on and interrelationships with the environment.

Manuscript information

Subject field(s): Relationships between any field of plant and animal production, forestry, environmental health and management.

Manuscript requirements: Style guide sent upon request; printed in journal as well. Submit 3 copies, abstract of 400 words max., all double-spaced in English.

Author information and reprints: 50 reprints free. Simultaneous submission not permitted. Copyright held by publication. Additional reprints available at cost.

Disposition of manuscript: Acknowledged within 1 week; decision in 2-3 months; published 3-6 months after acceptance. Rejections returned, criticized.

Submit to: Editorial Secretariat
Agriculture and Environment
PO Box 330
1000 A-H Amsterdam, The Netherlands

AGROLOGIST
151 Slater Street
Suite 907
Ottawa, Ontario, K1P 5H4
613-232-9459

Subscription data: Previously entitled *A1C Review, Agricultural Institute Review*. First published in 1934.

Issues and rates: Quarterly. 6 articles per average issue. Circulation 8,000. Annual rate: $6.00.

Sponsoring organization: Agricultural Institute of Canada.

Editorial description: Contains articles on trends and developments in agriculture in Canada and internationally.

Audience: Professional.

Manuscript information

Manuscript requirements: Canadian Government Style Manual for Writers and Editors. Preferred length 1,000 words. Submit 2 copies.

Author information and reprints: $100.00 per article. Simultaneous submission is permitted. Copyright held by publication. Reprints available, at cost. Query letter advisable.

Disposition of manuscript: Receipt acknowledged. Decision in 6-8 weeks. Published 6 months after acceptance. Rejected manuscript is returned, with SASE.

Submit to: John Watts
Editor

ALTERNATIVE/APPROPRIATE TECHNOLOGIES IN AGRICULTURE
55 Garihat Road
PO Box 10210
Calcutta, 700019 India
47-4872

Subscription data: First published in 1980.

Issues and rates: Quarterly. 4 articles per average issue. Circulation 1,700. Annual rate. RS. 250, U.S. $50, 25.

Editorial description: Started as a sequel to agriculture checklist for all units connected with agriculture as an industry or as science. Unlike other journals in the field, it will not limit itself to items bringing profit to agro-industrial units only. It will limit itself to a one-way saturation unrelated to the needs of both the developed and the developing world. It will not limit itself to being used as "invisible researcher" and "technological gatekeeper" in academic disciplines and technology transfers.

Manuscript information

Manuscript requirements: Preferred length 10,000 words. Submit 2 copies with an abstract.

Author information and reprints: No payment. Simultaneous submission not permitted. Copyright held by author. Reprints available; 25 free, additional at cost.

Disposition of manuscript: Acknowledged within 30 days; decision in 90 days; published about 6 months after acceptance. Rejections returned if author supplies return postage.

Submit to: Dr. K.K. Roy
Editor

AMERICAN ASSOCIATION OF TEACHER EDUCATORS IN AGRICULTURE. JOURNAL
PO Drawer AV
Mississippi State, MS 39762
601-325-4734

Subscription data: First published in 1961.

Issues and rates: Published three times per year. Articles per average issue: 4-5. Paid circulation averages 300. Annual rate(s): $10.00; Foreign $15.00.

Sponsoring organization: American Association of Teacher Educators in Agriculture.

Editorial description: Contains articles on developments, innovations, and trends in teacher education in agriculture.

Audience: Academic.

Manuscript information

Subject field(s): Vocational and agricultural education, vocational guidance, research, teacher education.

Manuscript requirements: See latest issue for style requirements. Preferred length 900-3000 words; 3-10 pages. Submit 1 copy. Abstract not required. Ms. should be accompanied by footnotes and references. Author's name, title and position should appear.

Author information and reprints: No payment. Author given 2 copies of issue. Simultaneous submission is not permitted. Periodical holds exclusive manuscript rights after acceptance. Copyright held by publication. Reprints not available. Query letter not necessary.

Disposition of manuscript: Receipt of manuscript is acknowledged. Decision in 6-8 weeks. Published 6-12 months after acceptance. Rejected manuscript is returned, criticized, if return postage is supplied by author.

Submit to: Ronald A. Brown
Editor

AMERICAN GERIATRICS SOCIETY JOURNAL
10 Columbus Circle
New York, NY 10019
212-582-1333

Subscription data: First published in 1953.

Issues and rates: Monthly. 8 articles per average issue. Annual rate: $25.00.

Sponsoring organization: American Geriatrics Society.

Editorial description: Accepts original papers in all aspects of clinical and laboratory geriatric medicine.

Audience: Professional.

Manuscript information

Subject field(s): Studies of the causes, prevention and treatment of diseases of the aging; nutrition; mental hygiene; rehabilitation; pertinent animal investigations; social and related problems; case reports, review articles, books.

Manuscript requirements: Style guide available upon request. Submit 1 original copy and a duplicate, all double-spaced; tables, charts, on separate pages. Include an abstract not to exceed 250 words, and author information on title sheet.

Author information and reprints: No payment; excess page charges. Simultaneous submission not permitted. Copyright held by publication. Reprints available at cost.

Disposition of manuscript: Acknowledged promptly; decision varies; published 6 months after acceptance. Rejections returned, sometimes criticized.

Submit to: Paul B. Beeson, M.D.
Editor-in-Chief

AMERICAN JOURNAL OF AGRICULTURAL ECONOMICS
Department of Agricultural and Applied Economics
University of Minnesota
St. Paul, MN 55108
612-376-3560

Subscription data: Previous title *Journal of Farm Economics,* until 1968. First published in 1919.

Issues and rates: 5 issues per year. 10 articles per average issue. Circulation 7,000. Annual rate: $25.00.

Sponsoring organization: American Agricultural Economics Association.

Editorial description: Articles on all topics of economics dealing with agriculture, natural resources, rural affairs, etc.

Audience: Professional economists.

Manuscript information

Subject field(s): Economics of agriculture, natural resources, rural affairs, resource use, food policy, trade, development, etc.

Manuscript requirements: Style guide on inside cover of issue. Preferred length 12-15 pages. Submit 2 copies, typewritten, double-spaced, with an abstract.

Author information and reprints: Payment by author to publication of $40 per printed page. Simultaneous submission not permitted. Copyright held by journal. Reprint available at cost.

Disposition of manuscript: Acknowledged within 10 days; decision in 3 months; published 5-7 months after acceptance. Rejections returned, criticized.

Submit to: James P. Houck
Dept. of Agriculture and Applied Economics
University of Minnesota
St. Paul, MN 55108
612-376-3560

AMERICAN JOURNAL OF CLINICAL NUTRITION*
American Society for Clinical Nutrition
9650 Rockville Pike
Bethesda, MD 20014
301-530-7111

Subscription data: First published in 1952.

Issues and rates: Published monthly. Articles per average issue: 25. Paid circulation 4,400. Annual rate(s): $30.00

Sponsoring organization: American Society for Clinical Nutrition, American Institute of Nutrition, Clinical Division.

Editorial description: Contains concise

reports of original research in experimental and clinical nutrition; papers dealing with nutrient, trace element, and energy metabolsim and requirements; reports of scientific meetings; editorials; letters to the editor; perspectives in nutrition; papers dealing with economics and nutritional programs; and nutrition education.

Audience: Professional.

Manuscript information

Subject field(s): Nutrition, as related to health and disease, biochemistry; gastroenterology; diet therapy; microbiology, as related to digestion; nutrition programs.

Manuscript requirements: See latest issue for style requirements. Submit 3 copies, with abstract.

Author information and reprints: No payment. Simultaneous submission is not permitted. Periodical holds exclusive rights after acceptance. Copyright held by publication. Reprints available, at cost. Query letter beforehand necessary.

Disposition of manuscript: Receipt of manuscript is acknowledged. Decision in 2-4 months. Published 4-6 months after acceptance. Rejected manuscript is returned, criticized.

Submit to: Robert H. Herman, M.D.
Editor
Department of Medicine
Letterman Army Institute of Research
San Francisco, CA 94129
415-561-4147

AMERICAN JOURNAL OF GASTROENTEROLOGY
299 Broadway
New York, NY 10007
212-227-7590

Subscription data: Previously entitled *She Review of Gastroenterology*. First published in 1934.

Issues and rates: Published monthly. Articles per average issue: 10-12. Circulation 3,150. Annual rate(s): $30.00; Foreign $45.00.

Sponsoring organization: American College of Gastroenterology.

Managing Editor: Daniel Weiss

Editorial description: Contains material on digestive diseases.

Audience: Professional, medical.

Manuscript information

Manuscript requirements: See latest issue for style requirements. Submit 2 copies and abstract.

Author information and reprints: No payment. Author given 2 copies of issue in which article appears. Simultaneous submission is not permitted. Periodical holds exclusive rights after acceptance. Copyright held by American College of Gastroenterology. Reprints available, cost varies. Query letter not necessary.

Disposition of manuscript: Receipt of manuscript is acknowledged. Decision in 2 months. Published 9 months after acceptance. Rejected manuscript is returned, not criticized.

Submit to: Arthur E. Lindner, M.D. Editor-in-Chief

AMERICAN JOURNAL OF PUBLIC HEALTH
1015 15th Street, NW
Washington, DC 20015
202-789-5600

Subscription data: First published in 1911.

Issues and rates: Monthly. Average number of articles per issue 12. Circulation 35,000. Annual rate(s): Domestic $40.00; Foreign $48.00.

Sponsoring organization: American Public Health Association.

Managing editor: William H. McBeath, M.D., MPH.

Editorial description: The Journal publishes original, significant articles covering current aspects of public health, including original research and evaluation studies, program evaluation of broad interest, and descriptive analytic of methodological papers, new and unusual developments in public health, or preliminary findings of significant investigations.

Audience: Health professionals, academics, government officials (health).

Manuscript information

Subject field(s): Health planning, dental health, environment epidemiology, food and nutrition, gerontological health, health administration, injury control/EMS, international health, laboratory, maternal and child health, medical care, mental health, occupational health, podiatric health, population, health education, public health nursing, radiological health, school health, social work, statistics, veterinary public health, vision care, alcohol/drug problems, health law, bioethics.

Manuscript requirements: Style sheet sent on request. Also published in the Journal in January, April, July, and October of each year. Preferred length 4,500 words per article, 1,000-1,500 words Public Health Brief. Submit 3 copies in English. Abstract required of 250 words per article; 75 words Public Health Brief. All manuscripts should be double-spaced, on side of paper, tables on separate sheets, references in sequential order and numbered. No query letter required from author.

Author information and reprints: No payment. Simultaneous submission is not permitted. Periodical holds exclusive rights after acceptance. Copyright held by publication with author having residual rights. Reprints available in quantities of 100, ordered with galleys.

Disposition of manuscript: Receipt of manuscript is acknowledged upon receipt. Peer reviewed, decision in 2 months. Published 3-6 months after acceptance. Rejected manuscript returned, criticized.

Submit to: Aflred Yankaer, M.D., MDH, Editor

ANIMAL FEED SCIENCE AND TECHNOLOGY
An International Journal
Elsevier Scientific Publishing Co.
PO Box 211
Amsterdam, The Netherlands
020-515-9222

Subscription data: First published in 1976.

Issues and rates: Quarterly. 8 articles per average issue. Annual rate: Dfl. 148.00, postage included.

Managing editor: Dr. J.F.D. Greenhalgh, Aberdeen.

Editorial description: Brings together scientific papers concerned with research on animal feeds.

Audience: Crop and animal scientists, feed manufacturers.

Manuscript information

Subject field(s): Evaluation of nutritive value of feed; feed conservation and processing; feed formulation and manufacturing; quality control, etc.

Manuscript requirements: Style guide sent upon request and printed in journal. Length depends upon quality. Submit 3 copies, with a

bibliography and abstract of 400 words max. All double-spaced, in English.
Author information and reprints: 50 reprints free, additional at cost. Simultaneous submission not permitted. Copyright held by journal.
Disposition of manuscript: Acknowledged within 1 week; decision in 2-3 months; published 3-6 months after acceptance. Rejections returned.
Submit to: Editorial Secretariat
Animal Feed Science and Technology
PO Box 330
1000 AH Amsterdam, The Netherlands

ANIMAL PRODUCTION
Journal of the British Society of Animal Production
Longman Group Ltd.
43/45 Annandale Street
Edinburgh, Scotland EH7 4AT
031-557-2454

Subscription data: First published in 1959.
Issues and rates: Published bi-monthly. Articles per average issue: 17. Paid circulation averages 2400. Annual rate(s): 41.00; $106.00.
Sponsoring organization: British Society of Animal Production.
Senior editor: Dr. J.A.F. Rook
Editorial description: Contains original research articles in the field of animal science and related disciplines.
Audience: Research & extension workers.
Manuscript information
Subject field(s): Animal science and all related disciplines.
Manuscript requirements: Style booklet sent on request. Brevity is encouraged. Submit 3 copies, with abstract. In English only.
Author information and reprints: No payment. Simultaneous submission is not permitted. Copyright held by publication. Reprints available at cost.
Disposition of manuscript: Receipt of manuscript is acknowledged. Decision 1-2 months. Published 6-8 months after acceptance. Rejected manuscript is returned, criticized.
Submit to: Dr. P.D. Wilson
Assistant Editor
Hannah Research Institute
Ayr Scotland KA6 5HL
Prestwick (0292) 76103

ANNALS OF APPLIED BIOLOGY
National Vegetable Research Station
Wellesbourne, Warwick, U.K. CV 35 9EF
(0789) 84 03 82

Subscription data: First published 1914.
Issues and rates: 9 issues per year. 20 articles per average issue. Circulation 2,450. Annual rate: 68. 75 with Supplement.
Sponsoring organization: Associaton of Applied Biologists.
Managing editor: G.A. Wheatley
Editorial description: Scientific papers describing original work on a wide range of applied biological topics. Principally concerned with agricultural, horticultural, ornamental and silvicultural crop protection and production research.
Audience: Research, advisory/extension workers.
Manuscript information
Subject field(s): Applied biology; pests and disease biology; pesticides; host-plant resistance to pests and diseases; plant breeding; crop nutrition; plant physiology; agronomy; post-harvest biology, etc.
Manuscript requirements: Style guide sent upon request. Preferred length 8,000 words max. Submit 2 copies, double-spaced, with a summeary at the beginning.
Author information and reprints: No payment. Simultaneous submission not permitted. Intellectual copyright held by author. Reprints available, 25 free, additional at cost.
Disposition of manuscript: Acknowledged within 1 week; decision in 8-12 weeks; published 16-18 weeks after acceptance. Rejections returned.
Submit to: The Secretary

ANNALS OF NUTRITION AND METABOLISM
European Journal of Nutrition, Metabolic Diseases and Dietetics
S. Karger AG
PO Box, CH-4009
Basel, Switzerland
061-390880

Subscription data: Previously entitled *Nutrition and Metabolism.*
Issues and rates: Published bimonthly. One annual volume with 6 issues. Average issue contains 10 articles. Circulation 1,200. Annual rate(s): SFr. 190.00; approx. $108.00 per volume.
Main editor: N. Zollner, Munich
Editorial description: In an expanding field, researchers confront the classic problems of malnutrition and the more recent quest for an optimal nutrition guideline. Collaterally, the progess of clinical medicine, particularly in genetics and epidemiology, has posed new questions. This journal, now European based, covers essential basic and clinical research reflecting modern biochemical techniques, in vivo and invitro, as well as the establishment of reliable studies in man.
Manuscript information
Manuscript requirements: Style sheet sent on request. See latest issue for style requirements. Preferred length 6 printed pages at 3,800 characters. Submit 2 copies and abstract, with 3-9 key words.
Author information and reprints: No payment. Simultaneous submission is not permitted. Periodical holds exclusive rights after acceptance. Copyright held by publication. Reprints available at cost. Charge for additional printed pages.
Disposition of manuscript: Receipt acknowledged. Rejected manuscript is returned, critized.
Submit to: Publisher

APPROPRIATE TECHNOLOGY
Intermediate Technology Publications, Ltd.
9 King Street
London WC2E 8HN, England

Subscription data: First published in 1973.
Issues and rates: Quarterly. 13 articles per average issue. Circulation 4,000. Annual rates: $20.00 Institutions; $15.00. Individuals.
Editorial description: Book reviews, notes, and news. Intermediate and appropriate technologies suitable for use by people in the third world, i.e., low-cost, indigenous, self-help construction. Emphasis is firmly on the practical side, rather than the theoretical. Steers clear of politics.
Audience: Mostly third world countries.
Manuscript information
Subject field(s): Agriculture, nutrition, wood and metal working, aquaculture, water and irrigation techniques, building construction, solar energy, small scale power

sources, etc.
Manuscript requirements: Preferred length 1,500-2,000 words. Submit 3 copies, double-spaced in clear, simple English suitable for comprehension for laymen. Illustrations to be black & white glossies, or line drawings clearly captioned. Include author's name and address, relevant experience in subject.
Author information and reprints: An honorarium of 10-15 is available. Simultaneous submission is permitted, with notification. Copyright held by journal. Reprints available at cost.
Disposition of manuscript: Acknowledged within 2 weeks; decision in 2-6 weeks; published 3-6 months after acceptance. Rejections returned.
Submit to: Frank Solomon
Editor & Publisher

AQUACULTURE
Elsevier Scientific Publishing Company
PO Box 211, Jan van Galenstraat 335
Amsterdam, The Netherlands
020-515-9222

Subscription data: First published in 1972.
Issues and rates: Monthly. (3 vols. per year) 8 articles per average issue. Annual rate(s): Dfl. 375.00 ($152.95).
Managing editor: C.E. Nash, Washington, USA; S.J. De Groot, Ijmuiden.
Editorial description: An international journal devoted to research on the exploration and improvement of all aquatic food resources, both floristic and faunistic, from freshwater, brackish and marine environments, related directly or indirectly to human consumption.
Audience: Professional, research, academic.
Manuscript information
Subject field(s): Exploration of new food resources; breed improvement; culture methods; all with emphasis on aquatic fauna.
Manuscript requirements: See latest issue for style requirements. Style sheet sent on request. Preferred length depends on quality of content. Submit 3 copies, abstract max. 400 words. Everything double-spaced.
Author information and reprints: Payment in 50 reprints. Simultaneous submission not permitted. Copyright held by publication. Reprints in excess of 50 at quoted cost. Query letter advisable.
Disposition of manuscript: Receipt acknowledged. Decision in 2 months. Published 3-4 months after acceptance. Rejected manuscript is returned.

Authors in the Americas and Japan, China, Southeast Asia and Australasia submit to:
Dr. C.E. Nash
Karmer, Chin e Mayo, Inc.
1917 First Avenue
Seattle, WA 98101
USA Institute
Makapuu Point
Waimanalo, HI 96795

ARCHIVES OF BIOCHEMISTRY AND BIOPHYSICS
Academic Press, Inc.
111 Fifth Avenue
New York, NY 10003

Subscription data: First published in 1942.
Issues and rates: 14 per year. Annual rate(s): $448.00 (U.S.A.); $520.00 (outside U.S.A.).
Editorial description: An international journal dedicated to the dissemination of fundamental knowledge in all areas of biochemistry and biophysics.
Manuscript information
Manuscript requirements: See latest issue for style requirements. Submit 3 copies. Abstract of 50-200 words.
Author information and reprints: Simultaneous submission not permitted. Copyright held by publication, fifty gratis reprints provided; additional reprints may be purchased.
Disposition of manuscript: Receipt acknowledged. Rejected manuscript is returned, criticized.
Submit to: Editorial Office
111 Fifth Avenue
New York, NY 10003

ASSOCIATION OF OFFICIAL ANALYTICAL CHEMISTS JOURNAL
Box 540
Benjamin Franklin Station
Washington, DC 20044
202-245-1526

Subscription data: Previously entitled *Journal of the Association of Official Agricultural Chemists.* First published in 1915.
Issues and rates: Published bi-monthly. Articles per average issue: 45. Circulation 4,515. Annual rate(s): $62.00; Foreign $70.00.
Sponsoring organization: Association of Official Analytical Chemists.
Editorial description: Publishes chemical and biological assay methods for foods, drugs, agricultural products, beverages, cosmetics, coloring materials and pesticides. Also covers the official transactions of the Association.
Manuscript information
Subject field(s): Analytical methodology in fertilizers, feeds, foods, pesticides, drugs, cosmetics, hazardous substances; forensic scienes; colors.
Manuscript requirements: Style sheet sent on request. Preferred length 10-20 pages. Submit 3 copies, with abstract.
Author information and reprints: No payment. Simultaneous submission is not permitted. Copyright held by publication. Reprints available; cost on sliding scale. Query letter desirable if subject area is in question.
Disposition of manuscript: Receipt acknowledged. Decision in 8-10 weeks. Published within 6 months after acceptance. Rejected manuscript is returned, criticized.
Submit to: Helen L. Reynolds
Editor
Special stipulations: All manuscripts subject to technical review by 2 members of peer group.

B

BIOCHEMICAL JOURNAL*
The Biochemical Society
Warwick Court
London WC1R 5DP, England
01-405-4918

Subscription data: First published in 1906.
Issues and rates: Published semi-monthly. Articles per average issue: 24. Circulation 5,000. Annual rate(s): $320.00.
Sponsoring organization: The Biochemical Society.
Managing editor: J.T. Dingle

Editorial description: Contains full-length papers and short communications describing original research work in all fields of biochemistry.
Audience: Research workers and students.
Manuscript information
Manuscript requirements: See "Instructions to Authors" in January 1 issue. Preferred length for papers: none; short communications: 2,400 words maximum. Submit 1 copy for papers; 2 for short communications. Include abstract.
Author information and reprints: No payment. Simultaneous submission not permitted. Copyright held by publication. Reprints available, 50 free.
Disposition of manuscript:
Receipt acknowledged. Decision in 5 weeks for papers and 2 weeks for short communications. Published 26 and 10 weeks respectively after acceptance. Rejected manuscript is returned, criticized.
Submit to: John David Killip
Editorial Secretary

BIOCHEMISTRY
American Chemical Society
1155 16th Street, NW
Washington, DC 20036

Subscription data:
Issues and rates: Bi-weekly. Circulation 6,000. Annual rate(s): $168.00.
Sponsoring organization: American Chemical Society.
Editorial description: Publishes results of original research in all areas of biochemistry. Emphasis is given to the relationship among chemistry, biochemistry and the other biological sciences.
Manuscript information
Subject field(s): Enzymes, proteins, carbohydrates, lipids, nucleic acids and their metabolism, genetics and protein synthesis.
Manuscript requirements: ACS. Submit 3 copies.
Author information and reprints: No payment. Simultaneous submission is not permitted. Periodical holds exclusive rights after acceptance. Copyright held by the Society. Reprints available at cost.
Disposition of manuscript:

Receipt acknowledged. Decision in 2 months. Published 3 months after acceptance. Rejected manuscript is returned, criticized.
Submit to: Hans Neurath
Editor
University of Washington
Seattle, WA 98195

BIOORGANIC CHEMISTRY
An International Journal
Academic Press, Inc.
111 Fifth Avenue
New York, NY 10003

Subscription data: First published in 1971.
Issues and rates: Published quarterly. Articles per average issue: 10. Annual rate(s): $37.50; Foreign $41.50.
Editorial description: Publishes accounts of research on the organic and physical organic chemistry of biological or biologically related reactions.
Manuscript information
Subject field(s): Enzyme reactions; biogenetic-type organic synthesis; molecular structure and the behavior of enzymes; enzyme models; prebiotic and evolutionary organic chemistry; chemistry of biopolymers; molecular pharmacology.
Manuscript requirements: See latest issue for style requirements. Style sheet sent on request. Submit 3 copies, with abstract. Drawings and formulas other than routine must be of a quality suitable for direct reproduction.
Author information and reprints: No payment. Simultaneous submission permitted, but not encouraged. Periodical holds exclusive rights after acceptance. Copyright held by publication. Reprints availabe, 50 free.
Disposition of manuscript:
Receipt acknowledged. Decision in 1-2 months. Published 3 months after acceptance. Rejected manuscript is returned, criticized.
Submit to: Eugene E. van Tamelen
Editor
Department of Chemistry
Stanford University
Stanford, CA 94305
415-497-3507

C

CANADIAN HOME ECONOMICS JOURNAL
Canadian Home Economics Association
151 Slater Street, Ste. 203
Ottawa K1P 5H3, Canada
613-232-9791

Subscription data:
Issues and rates: Published quarterly. Articles per average issue: 12-15. Annual rate(s): Canada $12.00; U.S. or foreign, $13.50.
Sponsoring organization: Canadian Home Economics Association.
Editorial description: A professional journal of interest to home economists and others interested in individuals and families.
Manuscript information
Subject field(s): Foods, textiles, consumer trends and studies, family life education, human ecology, metric conversion, housing, education, extension.
Manuscript requirements: Guide for authors available on request. Submit 3 copies in English or French. Include 100-150 word abstract. Double-spaced typescript with author's name, title, bibliography.
Author information and reprints: No payment. Simultaneous submission permitted with permission of journal. Reprints available.
Disposition of manuscript:
Receipt acknowledged. Decision in 1 month. Published 3-6 months after acceptance. Rejected manuscript is returned.
Submit to: Betty Mullen
Editor
20 Marlboro Road
Edmonton, Alberta T6J 2C6, Canada
403-434-0711
416-492-5250

CANADIAN INSTITUTE OF FOOD SCIENCE AND TECHNOLOGY. JOURNAL
Journal de L'Institut Canadien de Science et Technologie Alimentaire
Department of Food Science
University of Guelph
Guelph, Ontario, Canada
519-824-4120 ext. 3878

Subscription data: First published in 1968.

Issues and rates: Published quarterly. Articles per average issue: 15. Circulation 3,000. Annual rate(s): Canadian $65.00; Non-member $65.00; U.S. $55.00.
Sponsoring organization: Canadian Institute of Food Science and Technology.
Managing editor: F.R. van de Voort
Editorial description: Publishes scientific papers in the field of food science and technology; reviews of current interest and news concerning the Institute.
Audience: Food scientists and food technologists.
Manuscript information
Subject field(s): Food science, food technology, nutritional value of foods, food quality.
Manuscript requirements: Council of Biology Edtiors style manual. Preferred length 10-15 typed pages. Submit 3 copies, with abstract. Mss accepted in English & French.
Author information and reprints: Payment by author or his institution to publication of $40 per page. Simultaneous submission not permitted. Copyright held by Pergamon Press. Reprints available.
Disposition of manuscript: Receipt acknowledged. Decision in 1-3 months. Published 4-6 months after acceptance. Rejected manuscript is returned, criticized.
Submit to: F.R. van de Voort
Editor

CANADIAN JOURNAL OF ANIMAL SCIENCE
151 Slater Street
Suite 907
Ottawa, Ontario K1P 5H4 Canada
613-232-9459

Subscription data: Previously entitled *Canadian Journal of Agricultural Science,* 1953-1956; *Scientific Agriculture,* 1920-1952.
Issues and rates: Quarterly. 20-30 articles per average issue. Circulation 1,300. Annual rate: $26.00.
Sponsoring organization: Agricultural Institute of Canada; Canadian Society of Animal Science.
Editorial description: Contains articles relating to scientific research in breeding, genetics, meats, physiology, ruminant nutrition, non ruminant nutrition, and related subjects.

Manuscript information
Manuscript requirements: See latest issue for style requirements. Style sheet sent on request. Preferred length up to 20 printed pages. Submit 3 copies, and a resume of not more than 200 words.
Author information and reprints: Payment of $25.00 per page. Simultaneous submission not permitted. Periodical holds exclusive rights after acceptance. Copyright held by publication. Reprints available at cost.
Disposition of manuscript: Receipt acknowledged. Decision in 1-6 months. Published 4-6 months after acceptance. Rejected manuscript is returned, criticized.
Submit to: Dr. L.P. Milligan
Editor
Department of Animal Science
University of Alberta
Edmonton, Alta. T6G 2P5
403-432-3232

CANADIAN JOURNAL OF BIOCHEMISTRY
National Research Council of Canada
100 Sussex Drive
Ottawa, K1A OR6 Canada
613-993-0362

Subscription data: First published in 1964.
Issues and rates: Published monthly. Articles per average issue: 12. Circulation 2,600. Annual rate(s): $16.00; Institutions $55.00.
Sponsoring organization: National Research Council of Canada.
Managing editor: Gabrielle Adams
Editorial description: Contains papers on the results of original scientific research in any branch of biochemistry and cell biology also special issues in selected areas.
Audience: Research biochemists.
Manuscript information
Subject field(s): Amino acid chemistry and metabolism, carbohydrate chemistry, cell biology (biochemical aspects), clinical biochemistry, hormone action, control of carbohydrate and lipid metabolsim, enzymology, immunochemistry, lipid chemistry and biosynthesis, microbial metabolism, neurochemistry, nucleic acid chemistry, nucleic acid metabolism, nutrition and metabolism.
Manuscript requirements: Style sheet sent on request. Mss. accepted in English and French. Preferred length under 30 pages. Submit 3 copies and abstract.
Author information and reprints: No payment. Simultaneous submission is not permitted. Periodical holds exclusive rights after acceptance. Copyright held by publication. Reprints available only at time of publication; cost is dependent on length.
Disposition of manuscript: Receipt acknowledged. Decision in 3 months. Published 3 months after acceptance. Rejected manuscript is returned, criticized.
Submit to: J. Gordin Kaplan, M. Kates
Editors
Canadian Journal of Biochemistry
Faculty of Science and Engineering
University of Ottawa
Ottawa, K1N 6N5 Canada
613-231-6560
Special stipulations: We publish special issues periodically on specific fields.

CANADIAN JOURNAL OF SOIL SCIENCE
151 Slater Street
Suite 907
Ottawa, K1P 5H4 Canada
613-232-9459

Subscription data: Previously entitled *Canadian Journal of Agricultural Science.* First published in 1920.
Issues and rates: Published quarterly. Articles per average issue: 15. Circulation 1,500. Annual rate(s): Foreign $33.00.
Sponsoring organization: Canadian Society of Soil Science.
Editorial description: Research in soil science, soil analysis, and the relationship of soil to crops.
Audience: Professional agronomists.
Manuscript information
Manuscript requirements: See latest issue for style requirements. Style sheet sent on request. Submit 3 copies and abstract of not more than 200 words. Mss accepted in English and French.
Author information and reprints: Payment to publication by author of current page charge plus costs for illustrations, tables, and translations of abstracts. Simultaneous submission is not permitted. Copyright held by publications. Reprints available at various prices.

Disposition of manuscript:
Receipt acknowledged. Published 3-6 months after acceptance. Rejected manuscript is returned.
Submit to: Current editor as listed in recent copy of publication. Editorship changes every three years.

CARBOHYDRATE RESEARCH
An International Journal
Elsevier Scientific Publishing Company
PO Box 211, Jan van Galenstraat 335
Amsterdam, The Netherlands
020-515-9222

Subscription data: First published in 1965.
Issues and rates: Published monthly. Articles per average issue: 30. Annual rate(s): Dfl. 665.00 plus postage.
Editorial description: Publishes reports of original research in carbohydrate chemistry and biochemistry; preliminary research and book reviews.
Audience: Professional, academic, industrial.
Manuscript information
Subject field(s): Sugars and their derivatives; chemical synthesis; structures and stereochemistry; reactions and their mechanisms; isolation of natural products; action of enzymes; immunochemistry; biology; pharmacology; and technological aspects.
Manuscript requirements: Style sheet sent on request. No fixed length. Submit copies. Mss accepted in English, French and German. Submit original figures with ms. Full papers should include an abstract of 80-200 words.
Author information and reprints: Payment in 50 reprints only. Additional available at cost. Simultaneous submission is not permitted. Periodical holds exclusive rights after acceptance. Copyright held by publication.
Disposition of manuscript: Receipt acknowledged. Decision in 1 month. Published 3 months after acceptance. Rejections returned, with return postage paid by publication.
Submit to: Regional editors:
D. Horton
Department of Chemistry
140 West 18th Avenue
The Ohio State University
Columbus, OH 43210

R. Stuart Tipson
10303 Parkwood Drive
Kensington, MD 20795
R.W. Jeanloz
Laboratory for Carbohydrate Research
Massachusetts General Hospital
Boston, MA 02114

COMMUNICATIONS IN SOIL SCIENCE & PLANT ANALYSIS
Department of Horticulture
University of Georgia
Athens, GA 30602
404-542-2471

Subscription data: First published in 1970.
Issues and rates: Monthly. 10 articles per average issue. Circulation 700; 20 controlled. Annual rates: Individuals $76; Institutions $152; Foreign Individuals $96.40; Foreign Institutions $175.40.
Sponsoring organization: Marcel Dekker
Managing editor: Iris Accardino
Editorial description: Provides rapid publication of articles on soil science and crop production, particularly in the areas of mineral content of soils and plants and of plant nutrition.
Audience: Agricultural scientists.
Manuscript information
Subject field(s): Soil fertility and plant nutrition related to crop production with particular reference to soil testing and plant analysis.
Manuscript requirements: Style sheet sent on request. Preferred length 8-20 pages. Submit 2 double-spaced copies in English only.
Author information and reprints: Query letter requirements available on request, or see back cover of journal. No payment. Simultaneous submission not permitted. Periodical holds exclusive manuscript rights after acceptance. Copyright held by publication. Reprints available in lots of 100; cost varies with length.
Disposition of manuscript: Acknowledged within 1 week; decision in 1-2 months; published 4-6 months after acceptance. Rejections returned with reasons for rejection only.
Submit to: J. Benton Jones, Jr.
Executive Editor

CROPS AND SOILS MAGAZINE
American Society of Agronomy
677 South Segoe Road
Madison, WI 53711
608-274-1212

Subscription data: First published in 1948. Previous titles *What's New in Crops and Soils*, 1948-1958, *Crops and Soils* through 1966.
Issues and rates: 9 issues per year. 3-4 features, 23 shorts per average issue. Circulation 23,000. Annual rate: $7.00.
Sponsoring organization: American Society of Agronomy.
Editorial description: Written in a semi-popular style, it takes information from Society journals and elsewhere and presents it to an audience of farmers, farm managers, extension personnel, agribusiness executives.
Manuscript information
Subject field(s): Practical results of agricultural (especially, but not exclusively) research; crop management techniques; soil management; environmental information; new crops; new uses for old crops, etc.
Manuscript requirements: Style guide sent upon request. Preferred length 2,000-4,000 words. Submit 2 copies, double-spaced, abstract not necessary. Query letter helpful, not mandatory.
Author information and reprints: Payment of $15-$45 for features; none for shorts. Simultaneous submission not permitted. Copyright of entire issue held by American Society of Agronomy. Copyright of individual articles within issue subject to the Copyright Law. Reprints available at low cost.
Disposition of manuscript: Acknowledged immediately; decision in 1-2 months; published 2-6 months after acceptance. Unsolicited mms. not returned unless accompanied by S.A.S.E.
Submit to: William R. Luellen
Editor

D

DESALINATION
An International Journal on the Science and Technology of Desalination and Water Purification
Elsevier/Excerpta Medica/North Holland
PO Box 211
Amsterdam, The Netherlands

Subscription data: First published in 1966.
Issues and rates: Published bimonthly. Articles per average issue: 8. Annual rate(s): Institutions $102.30 per volume.
Editorial description: Covers the broad area of water purification, pollution control, deslaination techniques as applied to food, chemical, drugs and mettalurgy.
Audience: Desalination researchers and engineers.
Manuscript information
Manuscript requirements: See latest issue for style requirements. Submit 2 copies. Abstract not to exceed 100 words.
Author information and reprints: No payment. Simultaneous submission is permitted. Periodical holds exclusive rights after acceptance. Copyright held by publication. Reprints available at cost. Query letter advisable.
Disposition of manuscript: Receipt acknowledged. Decision in 2 weeks. Published 4 months after acceptance. Rejected manuscript is returned.
Submit to: Miriam Balaban
Editor
PO Box 4122
Jerusalem, Israel

DEVELOPMENTAL NEUROSCIENCE
S. Karger AG
PO Box
CH-4009 Basel, Switzerland
061-39 08 80

Subscription data: First published in 1978.
Issues and rates: Bimonthly. 6 articles per average issue. Circulation 800. Annual rates: Sfr. 154.00; $88.00 per volume.
Main editors: E. Giacobini, Storrs; A. Vernadakis, Denver.
Editorial description: Contains articles focused on the various aspects of the developing nervous system, ranging from the primitive nervous systems to *in vitro* growth of neural cells to the human brain.
Audience: Professional.
Manuscript information
Subject field(s): Environmental factors such as drugs, radiation, nutrition; cell differentiation, synapse formation, neurotransmitters, effects of drugs and nutrition, etc.
Manuscript requirements: Style sheet sent upon request. See also latest issue. Preferred length 10 pages. Submit 2 copies and an abstact with 3-9 key words. Mss. accepted in English.
Author information and reprints: No payment. Simultaneous submission not permitted. Copyright held by publication. Reprints available at cost. Charges for additional printed pages.
Disposition of manuscript: Receipt acknowledged. Rejections returned, with criticism.
Submit to: Dr. Antonia Vernadakis
Departments of Psychiatry and Pharmacology
University of Colorado
School of Medicine
4200 East Ninth Street
Denver, CO 80220

Dr. Ezio Giacobini
Laboratory of Neuro-Psychopharmacology
Department of Biobehavioral Sciences
University of Connecticut
U-154
Storrs, CT 06268

DIABETES FORECAST
American Diabetes Association
2 Park Avenue
New York, NY 10016
212-683-7444

Subscription data: First published in 1948.
Issues and rates: Bimonthly. 8 articles per average issue plus regular features. Circulation 140,000. Annual rates: $6.00.
Sponsoring organization: American Diabetes Association, Inc.
Editorial description: Furnishes those with diabetes, and their families, with informative, up-to-the-minute articles on current research, relevant health care, nutrition, and coping with the problems faced in daily life.
Manuscript information
Manuscript requirements: Preferred length 1,000 words. Submit 1 copy.
Author information and reprints: No payment. Simultaneous submission not permitted. Copyright held by the Assocation. Reprints available.
Disposition of manuscript: Receipt sometimes acknowledged; decision and publishing times vary.
Submit to: Ricki Rusting
Managing Editor

E

EASTERN AFRICA JOURNAL OF RURAL DEVELOPMENT
Makerere University
Box 7062
Kampala, Uganda
56931

Subscription data: Previous title *East African Journal of Rural Development.* First published in 1967.
Issues and rates: Annual. 14 articles per average issue. Circulation 1,000; 50 controlled.
Editorial description: Primary focus of the journal is eastern Africa, but articles concerned with the economiics of food and agriculture throughout the developing world are also considered.
Audience: Researchers, academics, teachers, professional economists, and other social scientists, agricultural scientists, policy makers and planners with an interest in the problems of agriculture and rural development in developing countries.
Manuscript information
Subject field(s): General agricultural economics, production economics, farm management economics, agricultural marketing, agricultural finance, development economics, development planning, agricultural policy, econometrics and any other economics subject relating to food and agriculture.
Manuscript requirements: Preferred length 25 pages maximum. Submit 2 copies, double-spaced throughout.
Author information and reprints: Payment with 5 reprints only. Simultaneous submission not permitted. Copyright held by publication. Reprints not available.
Disposition of manuscript: Acknowledged within 30 days; decision in 1-3 months; published 6-12 months after acceptance.
Submit to: Jossy R. Bibangamra
Editor

EASTERN GRAPE GROWER & WINERY NEWS MAGAZINE
Box 329
Watkins Glen, NY 14891
607-535-7133

Subscription data:
Issues and rates: Published 7 times a year. 6-7 articles per average issue. Circulation 2,500; 2,000 controlled. Annual rates: Domestic and Canada $8.50 surface mail, $16 airmail; Foreign $15 surface mail, $35 airmail.
Sponsoring organization: Eastern Grape Grower, Inc.
Managing editor: Richard Figiel
Editorial description: Trade magazine of the eastern (North America) wine and grape industry. Issues contain reports of industry events and occurrences plus articles on winery management and vineyard practices.
Audience: Grape growers, winery personnel, university researchers in wine and grapes, and others interested in the industry.
Manuscript information
Subject field(s): See editorial description above, and inquire before submitting.
Manuscript requirements: Inquire about length. Submit 1 copy.
Author information and reprints: State subject, proposed length, and qualifications for writing in query letter. Publication occasionally pays per article. Simultaneous submission not permitted. Periodical holds exclusive manuscript rights after acceptance. Copyright negotiable. Reprints available on request.
Disposition of manuscript: Receipt acknowledge; decision in 2 weeks; published 2 months after acceptance. Rejections returned with return postage.

ECOLOGY OF FOOD AND NUTRITION
An International Journal
171 Ashley Avenue
Charleston SC 29402
803-792-2411, ext. 50

Subscription data: First published in 1972.
Issues and rates: Bimonthly. 8 articles per average issue. Annual rates: Individuals $29.50; Institutions $76.50.
Sponsoring organization: Gordon and Breach Science Publishers.
Editorial description: An international journal of the nutritional sciences with a particular emphasis on foods and their utilization in the nutritional needs of mankind, but also extending to nonfood contributions to obesity and leanness malnutrition, vitamin requirements, and mineral needs. The scope is broad, and the content wide, so that cultural prohibitions, traditional usages, marketing and transport problems, additives and food quality are also areas for consideration. The journal also has ecological perspective and includes contributions by ecologists in general and human ecologists in particular.
Audience: Students and scientists in fields of nutrition, anthropology, clinical medicine, human behavior.
Manuscript information
Subject field(s): Food industry and criticisms; food technology; food contaminants and purity standards; nutritional sciences; nutrition and behavior, human geography, disease, physical fitness, pregnancy, age and ecology.
Manuscript requirements: Style sheet sent on request. Preferred length 7,500 words. Submit 3 copies, with key words, title page. Mss. should be in English only and should be accompanied by an abstract of 150 words or less.
Author information and reprints: Author pays publication $10.50 per page. Simultaneous submission not permitted. Periodical holds exclusive manuscript rights after acceptance. Copyright held by publication. Reprints available in units of $100; $10.50 per page.
Disposition of manuscript: Acknowledged within 2 weeks; decision in 6 weeks; published 4-12 months after acceptance. Rejections returned and criticized.
Submit to: John R.K. Robson, M.D. Editor

ENVIRONMENTAL NUTRITION NEWSLETTER
A Consumer's Guide to Survival
52 Riverside Drive, Suite 15-A
New York, NY 10024
212-595-0345

Subscription data: First published in 1977.
Issues and rates: Published 10 times a year. 5-6 articles per average issue. Annual rates: Domestic $18.00; Canada $20.00.
Sponsoring organization: Environmental Nutrition Inc.
Managing editor: Virginia Tan, R.D.
Editorial description: The newsletter is essentially a digest covering all aspects of food and nutrition. It runs articles on current topics of concern and controversy; nutritive values of food; weight loss tips; consumer information and lableing, additives, etc.; as well as reviewing publications on food and nutrition. The newsletter tries to be fair and objective while, at the same time, indicating where we feel the weight of evidence falls.
Audience: Consumers and professionals dealing with consumers.
Manuscript information
Subject field(s): Food and nutrition, diets for specific nutritional problems.
Manuscript requirements: Style sheet sent on request. Preferred length 800-1,000 words. Submit 1 copy. Manuscript in English, clear and readable. Abstract not required. Also give author's background information.
Submit to: Editor

ENZYME
Metabolism, Experimental and Clinical Enzymology
S. Karger AG
PO Box
CH-4009 Basel, Switzerland
061-390880

Subscription data: First published in 1961.
Issues and rates: Bimonthly. Articles per average issue. 5-6. Circulation 700. Annual rate(s): SFr. 252.00; Foreign $144.00.
Editors: J. Frei, Lausanne; W.E. Knox, Boston; O. Greengard, New York; J.P. Colombo, Bern; O. Sperling, Petah Tikra.
Editorial description: Contains articles on the biological and medical problems of enzymology with direct emphasis on the pathophysiological rather than the biochemical aspects of enzymology.
Manuscript information
Manuscript requirements: Style sheet sent on request. Preferred length 6 printed pages at 3,800 characters. Submit 3 copies, with abstract and a list of 3-9 key words. Mss. accepted in English.
Author information and reprints: No payment. Simultaneous submission is not permitted. Copyright held by publication. Reprints available at cost. Charge for additional printed pages.

Disposition of manuscript:
Receipt acknowledged. Rejected manuscript is returned, criticized.
Submit to: Dr. J.P. Colombo
Chemisches Zentrallabor
Inselspital
CH-3010 Bern, Switzerland

Dr. W. Eugene Knox
185 Pilgrim Road
Boston, MA 02215

F

FAMILY PERSPECTIVE
Brigham Young University
2234 SFLC
Provo, UT 84602
801-377-1211, ext. 3914

Subscription data: First published in 1966.
Issues and rates: Quarterly. 6 articles per average issue. Annual rate: $7.00.
Sponsoring organization: Brigham Young University, College of Family, Home and Social Sciences.
Editorial description: Deals with issues that impact on the family including not only family realtions, organizations, education, but also related to nutrition, housing, clothing, resource management, etc.
Audience: Professional.
Manuscript information
Subject field(s): Home economics, food science and nutrition, child development, clothing and textiles, interior environment, etc.
Manuscript requirements: Style guide sent upon request. Preferred length c. 15 pp. Submit 3 copies, with an abstract of 100 words or less.
Author information and reprints: No payment. Simultaneous submission not permitted. Copyright held by journal.
Disposition of manuscript:
Acknowledged within 1 week; decision in 60-90 days; published within 6 months. Rejections returned, with SASE.
Submit to: Dr. Ruth E. Brasher
Editor

FEDERATION OF AMERICAN SOCIETIES FOR EXPERMINTAL BIOLOGY. PROCEEDINGS
9650 Rockville Pike
Bethesda, MD 20014
301-530-7100

Subscription data: First published in 1942.
Issues and rates: Published monthly. Articles per averages issue: 25. Circulation 18,000. Rate(s): Members $10.00; Nonmembers (personal) $50.00; Institutional $65.00; Students $25.00; Single issue $9.00. Postage differentials: Foreign $10.00; Canada and Mexico $6.00.
Sponsoring organization: Federation of American Societies for Experimental Biology.
Editorial description: Publishes critical papers in the field of experimental biology. Also considers papers in the area of scientific public affairs.
Audience: Biomedical experimenters.
Manuscript information
Subject field(s): Biology, physiology, biochemistry, pharmacology, pathology, nutrition, immunology, science news.
Manuscript requirements: See latest issue for style requirements. Preferred length 5 printed pages. Submit 3 copies, with abstract.
Author information and reprints: No payment. Simultaneous submission not permitted. Periodical holds exclusive rights after acceptance. Copyright held by publication. Reprints available at cost. Query letter is preferred beforehand.
Disposition of manuscript:
Receipt acknowledged. Decision in 2 months. Published 3 months after acceptance. Rejected manuscript is returned, criticized.
Submit to: Karl F. Heumann
Executive Editor

FIELD CROPS RESEARCH
Elsevier Scientific Publishing Co.
PO Box 211
Amsterdam, The Netherlands
020-515-9222

Subscription data: First published in 1977.
Issues and rates: Quarterly. 7 articles per average issue. Annual rate. Dfl. 158.
Managing editor: Prof. J.R. McWilliams, Armidale, Australia.
Editorial description: Publishes papers concerned with biological and physical research on field crops in the areas of crop agronomy, improvement, physiology, ecology, protection, soil and water management, and farming systems.
Manuscript information
Manuscript requirements: Style guide sent upon request; see also inside back cover. Submit 3 copies, abstract of 400 words max., all double-spaced in English.
Author information and reprints: 50 reprints free. Additional reprints available at cost. Simultaneous submission not permitted. Copyright held by publication.
Disposition of manuscript:
Acknowledged within 1 week; decision in 2-3 months; published 3-6 months after acceptance. Rejections returned, criticized.
Submit to: Editorial Secretariat
Field Corps Research
PO Box 330
1000AH Amsterdam, The Netherlands

FOOD RESEARCH INSTITUTE STUDIES
Stanford University
Stanford, CA 94305
415-497-4160

Subscription data: Previous title *Food Research Institute Studies in Agricultural Economics, Trade, and Development.* First published in 1960.
Issues and rates: 3 per year. 5-6 articles per average issue. Annual rates: $15.00.
Sponsoring organization: Stanford University, Food Research Institute.
Editorial description: Includes a long series of studies of commodities futures markets, food and agricultural economies of tropical Africa and Latin America, agricultural productivity and policy, international trade in basic commodities, and a considerable range of topics in the general area of agricultural economics.
Audience: Professional.
Manuscript information
Subject field(s): Economics of agriculture, consumption, production; commodity prices and markets; international trade problems and prices; financial development; demographic studies.
Manuscript requirements: Style guide sent upon request. Submit 2 copies.
Author information and reprints:
Payment with 50 free reprints only. Simultaneoius submission not permitted. Copyright held by the Food Research Institute.
Disposition of manuscript:
Receipt is acknowledged within 2 weeks; decision in 1-2 months;

publishing time varies. Rejections returned, with SASE.
Submit to: Walter P. Falcon
Editor

FOOD TECHNOLOGY
221 North LaSalle Street
Chicago, IL 60601
312-782-8425

Subscription data: First published in 1947.
Issues and rates: Published monthly. Articles per average issue: 10. Circulation 20,000. Annual rate(s): $40.00; Foreign $45.00.
Editorial description: Features articles that are designed to aid professional food technologists, scientists, engineers, executives and educators solve their technological and management problems in the entire chain of producing wholesome foods. News departments cover the food industry and news of the Institute of Food Technologists.
Manuscript information
Subject field(s): Product development, processing and engineering, nutrition, packaging, pollution control, quality assurance, food safety, marketing, food laws and regulations, advertising, distribution, laboratory methods.
Manuscript requirements: Style sheet sent on request. Preferred length maximum of 15 pages. Submit 3 copies.
Author information and reprints: No payment. Simultaneous submission not permitted. Periodical holds exclusive rights after acceptance. Copyright held by publication. Reprints available at cost.
Disposition of manuscript:
Receipt of manuscript is acknowledged. Decision in 1 month. Published 3 months after acceptance. Rejected manuscript is returned, criticized.
Submit to: John B. Klis
Editor and Director of Publications

FUTURE SURVEY
World Future Society
4916 St. Elmo Avenue
Washington, DC 20014
301-656-8274

Subscription data: First published in 1979.
Issues and rates: Published monthly. Paid circulation 5,000; 50 controlled. Annual rate(s): Individuals $28.00; Institutions $40.00.
Sponsoring organization: World Future Society.
Editorial description: Monthly abstract of recently published books, articles and reports concerning forecasts, trends and policy proposals.
Audience: Academic teachers, researchers, planners, policy makers.
Manuscript information
Subject field(s): World futures, international economics, defense and disarmament, energy, environment and resources, food and agriculture, economic policy, cities and housing, transportation, communications, crime and justice, health, science and technology and politics and administration.
Manuscript requirements: Submit manuscripts in English only.
Submit to: Michael Marien
Editor
5413 Webster Road
LaFayette, NY 13084
Special stipulations: Submitted material must be published; periodical is an abstract journal of public affairs affording an opportunity for miniaturized republishing.

G

GEODERMA*
An Internationa Journal of Soil Science
Elsevier Scientific Publishing Company
PO Box 211, 1000 AE
Amsterdam, The Netherlands

Subscription data: First published in 1967.
Issues and rates: Published bimonthly. Annual rate(s): Dfl 120.00.
Editorial description: The entire field of soil research.
Audience: Soil scientists, chemists, colleges, libraries.
Manuscript information
Subject field(s): Soil testing, agricultural chemistry, fertilizer, land development.
Manuscript requirements: Style sheet sent on request. Submit 3 copies with abstract.
Author information and reprints:
Payment in 50 reprints only. Simultaneous submission not permitted. Periodical holds exclusive rights after acceptance. Copyright held by publication. Reprints available at cost.
Disposition of manuscript:
Receipt of manuscript is acknowledged. Decision in 6 weeks. Published 6 months after acceptance. Rejected manuscript is returned.
Submit to: R.W. Simonson
Editor

H

HEALTH EDUCATION
American Alliance for Health, Physical Education and Recreation
1201 16th Street, NW
Washington, DC 20036
202-833-5551

Subscription data: Previous title *School Health Review* first published in 1969.
Issues and rates: Published bimonthly. 12 articles per average issue. Circulation 11,000. Annual rates: $25.00.
Sponsoring organization: American Alliance for Health, Physical Education and Recreation.
Editorial description: Contains articles of concern to health educators at all levels of education, from early childhood through adult education and public health programs.
Audience: Teachers and administrators.
Manuscript information
Subject field(s): Any subject field or topic of interest to health educators: philosophy, curriculum, methodology, research, in a variety of specific areas such as nutrition, values clarification, sex education, mental health, etc.
Manuscript requirements: Preferred length: 8-10 typewritten, double-spaced pages. Submit 2 copies. A 200 word abstract is desirable.
Author information and reprints: No payment. Simultaneous submission is not permitted. Publication holds exclusive rights between acceptance and publication. Copyright held by publication. Permission is granted for author to use material in a book of his own. Reprints not available.
Disposition of manuscript:
Receipt acknowledged within 5 days; decision in 3 months; published in 6 months.
Submit to: Patricia Galagan Hurley
Managing Editor

HISTORY OF AGRICULTURE
International Association for History of Agriculture
55 Gariahat Road
PO Box 10210
Calcutta-700019, Indian
47-4872

Subscription data: First published in 1973.
Issues and rates: Quarterly. 4 articles per average issue. Circulation 1,700. Annual rate: R 180.00; Foreign $25.00.
Sponsoring organization: International Association for History of Agriculture.
Editorial description: Seeks to provide a channel of communication for a world-wide network of people interested in establishing an agricultural historiography of a high standard of scholarship. It aims to integrate the research of all epochs of agriculture, all aspects of agricultural development, and agricultural institutions.
Manuscript information
Subject field(s): Agricultural history in its whole international range of cultural, scientific, and social implications.
Manuscript requirements: Preferred length 10,000 words. Submit 2 copies, with an abstract.
Author information and reprints: No payment. Simultaneous submission not permitted. Copyright held by author. Reprints available, 25 free, additional at cost.
Disposition of manuscript:
Acknowledged within 30 days; decision in 90 days; published c. 6 months after acceptance. Rejections returned, if author supplies postage.
Submit to: Dr. K.K. Roy
Editor

HOME ECONOMICS RESEARCH JOURNAL
2010 Massachusetts Avenue
Washington, DC 20036
202-862-8386

Subscription data: First published in 1972.
Issues and rates: Quarterly. 10 articles per averge issue. Circulation 2,000; 20 controlled. Annual rates: Individuals $35; Members $25.
Sponsoring organization: American Home Economics Association.
Editorial description: Instituted to report the latest research in all areas of home economics, the journal has stated goals of providing a forum for research and of becoming an instrument for further development of research in the profession.
Audience: Researchers, graduate instructors, graduate students, and professionals.
Manuscript information
Subject field(s): All areas of home economics research.
Manuscript requirements: Style sheet sent on request. Submit 3 copies with a concise summary of 100-200 words. For more details, see Guide for Authors published in the journal each year.
Author information and reprints: Author pays publication $35 per page. Simultaneous submission not permitted. Periodical holds exclusive manuscript rights after acceptance. Copyright held by publication. Unlimited reprints available from an independent reprint service.
Disposition of manuscript:
Receipt acknowledged; decision in 6 months; published 6 months after acceptance. Rejections returned and criticized with SASE.
Submit to: Dr. S.J. Ritchey, Dr. Rebecca Lovingood
Editors
College of Home Economics
Virginia Polytechnic Institute and State University
Blacksburg, VA 24061
703-961-6779

I

INSECTICIDE AND ACARICIDE TESTS
4603 Calvert Road
College Park, MD 20740
301-864-1334

Subscription data: First published in 1975.
Issues and rates: Annual. 300 reports per average issue. Circulation 1,000. Annual rates: Domestic $13.25; Foreign $15.25.
Sponsoring organization: Entomoligcal Society of America.
Managing editor: Lorraine S. Gilbert
Editorial description: Disseminates annual research reports, data on minor crop use, and progress on candidate pesticides.
Audience: Researchers, extension people and agricultural-chemical industry.
Manuscript information
Subject field(s): Pest management in fruit, nut, vegetable, cereal, and ornamental crops; forestry; stored products; urban and industrial areas; materials available for testing; materials under trial.
Manuscript requirements: "Guidelines for Preparing Reports" available on request and in previous volume. Submit 3 copies. Articles published in abstract/table form.
Author information and reprints: No query letter required. No payment. Simultaneous submission permitted.
Disposition of manuscript:
Receipt acknowledged; decision in 2 months; published 6 months after acceptance. Rejections returned and criticized.
Submit to: Editor

INTERNATIONAL ACADEMY OF PREVENTIVE MEDICINE. JOURNAL
10409 Town & Country Way
Houston, TX 77024
713-468-7851

Subscription data: First published in 1974.
Issues and rates: Semi-annual. 8-12 articles per average issue. Circulation c. 2,000. Annual rates: $12.00.
Sponsoring organization: Internatinal Academy of Preventive Medicine.
Editor: Dr. Leon R. Pomeroy.
Editorial description: Contains articles of interest to professionals regarding any facet of preventive medicine, medical nutrition, and health maintenance.
Audience: Health care professional at doctoral level.
Manuscript information
Subject field(s): Medicine/Dentistry; oriented to the prevention of disease or maintenance of health.
Manuscript requirements: Style guide sent upon request. Preferred length 2,000 words maximum. Submit 1 copy.
Author information and reprints: No payment. Simultaneous submission is permitted, but prefer exclusivity. Copyright held by publication. Reprints available.
Disposition of manuscript:
Receipt is acknowledged within 15 days; decision 3-6 months; published 6 months after acceptance. Rejections returned.
Submit to: Joseph A. Nowell
Executive Director

INTERNATIONAL JOURNAL OF PEPTIDE AND PROTEIN RESEARCH
Munksgaard International Publishers
35 Norre Sogade
DK-1370 Copenhagen K, Denmark
(01) 12 70 30

Subscription data: Previously entitled *International Journal of Protein Research*. First published in 1969.
Issues and rates: Monthly except June and December. Average issue contains 12 articles. Paid circulation averages 1,000. Annual rate(s): Dkr. 690 plus Dkr. 44 postage; Foreign $139.50.
Editorial description: Contains original papers concerning peptides and proteins and their basic elements from every conceivable angle, such as chemical, physico-chemical, physiological, including experimental and theoretical work.
Manuscript information
Subject field(s): Peptides, proteins, amino acids.
Manuscript requirements: See latest issue for style requirements. Preferred length 20 printed pages maximum. Submit 3 copies and abstract.
Author information and reprints: No payment. Simultaneous submission is not permitted. Periodical holds exclusive rights after acceptance. Copyright held by author. Query letter not necessary.
Disposition of manuscript: Receipt of manuscript is acknowledged. Decision in 6 weeks. Published 4-5 months after acceptance. Rejected manuscript is returned, criticized.
Submit to: Prof. Choh Hao LI
University of California
Room 1088, HSW
San Francisco, CA 94143

J

JOURNAL OF AGRICULTURAL AND FOOD CHEMISTRY
American Chemical Society
1155 16th Street, NW
Washington, DC 20036

Subscription data: First published in 1953.
Issues and rates: Published bimonthly. Articles per average issue: 40. Paid circulation 5,000. Annual rate(s): Members $16.00; Foreign members $21.00; Nonmembers $64.00; Foreign nonmembers $69.00.
Sponsoring organization: American Chemical Society.
Editorial description: Publishes articles in a broad multidisciplinary area concerned with the chemistry of all aspects of agriculture and food.
Manuscript information
Subject field(s): Chemistry of composition of food and farm feeds, pesticides, plant growth regulators; photochemistry.
Manuscript requirements: See "Guide for Authors," published in first issue of each volume. Submit 3 copies, double-spaced. Abstract of 100-150 words required, with 1-paragraph summary.
Author information and reprints: Payment by author to publication of $40 per page. Periodical holds exclusive rights after acceptance. Copyright held by publication. Reprints are available.
Disposition of manuscript: Receipt is acknowledged. Rejected manuscript is returned, criticized.
Submit to: K.I. Biggs
Managing Editor

JOURNAL OF AGRICULTURAL SCIENCE
Cambridge University Press
32 East 57th Street
New York, NY 10022

Subscription data: First published in 1905.
Issues and rates: Six times per year. 32 articles per average issue. Annual rate: $235.00.
Editorial description: Concise papers reporting original experimental data or methods or new analyses of already existing data, in any aspect of agricultural science.
Audience: Researchers and scientist.
Manuscript information
Manuscript requirements: See latest issue for style requirements. Submit 2 copies, with a brief abstract which indicates the experiments described, the main resutls and important conclusions. A simple direct style of writing, avoiding unnecessary repetition and circumlocution, is preferred.
Author information and reprints: Payment in 25 reprints only. Simultaneous submission not permitted. Periodical holds exclusive rights after acceptance. Copyright held by publication. Query letter is not necessary, but advisable.
Disposition of manuscript: Receipt acknowledged; decision in 1 month; published 6 months after acceptance.
Submit to: Sir James Beament
Editor
Dept. of Applied Biology
Pembroke Street
Cambridge CB2 3DX, U.K.

JOURNAL OF APPLIED NUTRITION
International College of Applied Nutrition
Box 386
La Habra, CA 90631
213-697-4576

Subscription data: First published in 1949.
Issues and rates: Published semi-annually. Articles per average issue: 4-7. Circulation 3,500. Annual rate(s): $12.00.
Sponsoring organization: International College of Applied Nutrition.
Editorial description: Provides current, factual, scientific information on the inter-relationship of food, health, and life. Presents the highest standards in nutritional education: medical, dental, and nutritional practice, and research in nutrition.
Manuscript information
Subject field(s): All phases of nutritional research.
Manuscript requirements: See latest issue for style requirements. Submit 2 copies, typewritten, double-spaced; Abstract.
Author information and reprints: No payment. Simultaneous submission not permitted. Copyright held by publication. Reprints available, cost upon request.
Disposition of manuscript: Receipt acknowledged. Decision in 1 month. Rejected manuscript is returned, with SASE.
Submit to: M. Taher Fouad, Ph.D.
Editor-in-Chief

JOURNAL OF CARBOHYDRATES-NUCLEO-SIDES-NUCLEOTIDES
An International Forum for Rapid Communication
Marcel Dekker, Inc.
270 Madison Avenue
New York, NY 10016
212-490-7700

Subscription data: First published

in 1974.
Issues and rates: Published bimonthly. Articles per average issue: 8. Circulation 1,025. Annual rate(s): $56.50; Institutions $113.00.
Editorial description: Deals with the chemistry of carbohydrates, nucleosides, and nucleotides and their biological activities.
Audience: Organic chemists, biochemists, and biologists.
Manuscript information
Subject field(s): Chemistry, biochemistry, and biological chemistry.
Manuscript requirements: No specific style guide. Preferred length 8-30 pages. Submit original and 2 copies, with a summary of research, accomplishments, result obtained and any desired conclusion.
Author information and reprints: Simultaneous submission not permitted. Copyright held by publication. Reprints available at cost.
Disposition of manuscript: Receipt acknowledged. Decision in 2-3 weeks. Published 3 months after acceptance. Rejected manuscript is returned with SASE.
Submit to: Dr. Robert E. Harmon
Executive Editor
Department of Chemistry
Western Michigan University
Kalamazoo, MI 49001
616-383-6211

JOURNAL OF CONSUMER RESEARCH
University of Illinois
Chicago Circle
PO Box 6905
Chicago, IL 60680
312-996-5312

Subscription data: First published in June 1974.
Issues and rates: Quarterly. 12 articles per average issue. Circulation 3,650. Annual rate: $42.00.
Sponsoring organization: American Association for Public Opinion Research, American Anthropological Association, American Economic Association, American Home Economics Association, American Marketing Association, American Psychological Association, Association for Consumer Research, Institute of Management Science, International Communication Association.
Managing editor: Audrey Young.

Editorial description: An interdisciplinary journal publishing articles on consumer behavior from the viewpoint of the various social sciences.
Manuscript information
Subject field(s): Communications, economics, home economics, marketing, political science, psychology, sociology, statistics, management sciences.
Manuscript requirements: Style guide sent upon request. Preferred length 20-40 pages. Submit 4 copies, double-spaced, including references, footnotes, with a short abstrct of 50 words or less.
Author information and reprints: No payment. Simultaneous submission not permitted. Copyright held by publication. Reprints available at cost.
Disposition of manuscript: Acknowledged within 14 days; decision in 6 months; published in 3 months or less after acceptance. Rejections returned, with SASE.
Submit to: Robert Ferber
Editor

JOURNAL OF DEVELOPING AREAS
Western Illinois University
Macomb, IL 61455
309-298-1108

Subscription data: First published in 1966.
Issues and rates: Published quarterly. Articles per average issue: 5. Circulation 1,550. Annual rate(s): $15.00; Institutions $20.00.
Editorial description: Contains articles, bibliography section, news and notes, book review section, editorial comment. International scope, interdisciplinary with the intention of stimulating the descriptive, theoretical, and comparative study of regional development, past and present; promoting fuller understanding of man's relationship to the developmental process.
Manuscript information
Subject field(s): Economics, political science, sociology, geography, international business, agriculture, anthropology, history, literature, education, law.
Manuscript requirements: Chicago. Preferred length 5,000-9,000 words; 20-30 pages. Submit 3 copies. Keep tabular material to a minimum. All figures professionally prepared and in camera-ready form. Author's name and affiliation on the title page only. Everything typewritten, double-spaced. Abstract optional.
Author information and reprints: No payment. Author given 2 copies of the issue and 50 offprints. Simultaneous submission is permitted if editor is notified. Periodical holds exclusive rights after acceptance. Copyright held by publication.
Disposition of manuscript: Receipt is acknowledged. Decision in 2-4 months. Published 1 year after acceptance. Rejected manuscript is returned, criticized, with SASE.
Submit to: Nicholas C. Pano
General Editor

JOURNAL OF ENVIRONMENTAL HEALTH
1200 Lincoln Street
No. 704
Denver, CO 80203
303-861-9090

Subscription data: Previously entitled *The Sanitarian*. First published in 1983.
Issues and rates: Bimonthly. 6 articles per average issue. Circulation 6,250. Annual rate: $25.00; Foreign $30.00 plus $20.00 foreign airmail.
Sponsoring organization: National Environmental Health Association.
Managing editor: Lawrence J. Krone, Ph.D.
Editorial description: Contains professional articles about environmental sanitation problems and solutions, professional development, organization activities, research, and various timely topics.
Audience: Local, state and federal health and environmental personnel; those employed by institutions and industry.
Manuscript information
Subject field(s): Sanitation, food sanitation, potable water supply, housing, planning, solid waste disposal, air pollution control, hospital sanitation, noise, waste water disposal, radiation, radiological health, vector control, transportation, land use, recreation.
Manuscript requirements: Style sheet sent on request. Preferred length 5,000 words; 20 pages maximum. Submit 3 copies. Double-spaced, 1 inch all around margin, 2 inches top of first page. Abstract 150 words at

beginning. Title page required.
Author information and reprints: No payment. Simultaneous submission is not permitted. Periodical holds exclusive rights after acceptance. Copyright held by author. Reprints available, at cost, 100 copies minimum.
Disposition of manuscript: Receipt of manuscript is acknowledged within 2 weeks. Decision in 2 months. Published 2-6 months after acceptance. Rejected manuscript is returned, criticized.
Submit to: Ida Frances Marshall
Editor-in-Chief
Special stipulations: Material prepared by or for commercial firms must not be slanted commercially, but written so the material is beneficial to professional environmental control personnel. Brand names should not be used.

JOURNAL OF FOOD PROTECTION
PO Box 701
Ames, IA 50010
515-232-6699

Subscription data: Previous titles *Journal of Milk Technology, Journal of Milk and Food Technology.* First published in 1973.
Issues and rates: Monthly. 12-15 articles per average issue. Circulation 4,000. Annual rate: $25.00.
Sponsoring organization: International Association of Milk, Food, and Environmental Sanitarians.
Managing editor: Earl O. Wright
Editorial description: Contains research, review, and technical articles on food safety, food and dairy hygiene (sanitation), and food and dairy science and technology.
Audience: Public health officials, researchers, academics.
Manuscript information
Manuscript requirements: Style guide sent upon request. Preferred length 10-15 pp. for research papers; 4-5 pp. for notes; as required for review papers and technical articles. Submit 2 copies.
Author information and reprints: Payment of $35.00 per page for research mss. only. Simultaneous submission not permitted. Copyright held by publication. Reprints available at cost.
Disposition of manuscript: Receipt acknowledged; decision in 4-6 weeks; published 5-7 months after acceptance. Rejections returned, with criticism.
Submit to: Elmer H. Marth
Editor
Department of Food Sciences
University of Wisconsin
Madison, WI 53706
608-263-2004

JOURNAL OF FOOD SCIENCE
221 North LaSalle Street
Chicago, IL 60601
312-782-8424

Subscription data: Previously titled *Food Research.* First published in 1936.
Issues and rates: 6 times per year. Articles per averge issue: 55. Paid circulation averages 10,000. Annual rate(s): $45.00; Foreign $50.00.
Sponsoring organization: Institute of Food Technologists.
Managing editor: Bernard Schukraft.
Editorial description: Publishes papers which report the results of original research related to foods. It contains two major sections: Basic Science and Applied Science and Engineering.
Audience: Professional.
Manuscript information
Subject field(s): Basic food science, applied food science, food engineering.
Manuscript requirements: Style sheet sent on request. Submit 3 copies. Abstract, see style guide.
Author information and reprints: Payment by author or his institution to publication of $50 per page, unless such payment would be a hardship. Simultaneous submission is not permitted. Periodical holds exclusive rights after acceptance. Copyright held by publication. Reprints available at cost.
Disposition of manuscript: Receipt of manuscript is acknowledged. Decision in 2 months. Published 8 months after acceptance. Rejected manuscript is returned, criticized.
Submit to: Dr. Aaron E. Wasserman, IFT Scientific Editor
PO Box 6197
Philadelphia, PA 19115
215-934-6581

JOURNAL OF NUTRITION EDUCATION
Dept. of Nutritional Science
University of California
Berkeley, CA 94720
415-642-8137

Subscription data: First published in 1969.
Issues and rates: Published quarterly. Articles per average issue: 7-9. Circulation 11,000. Annual rate(s): Individuals $20.00; Institutions $25.00.
Sponsoring organization: Society for Nutrition Education.
Editorial description: Contains research articles, critiques, reviews, and features relevant to nutrition education to help the nutrition educator to be more effective in communicating with students, patients, colleagues, or the lay public.
Manuscript information
Subject field(s): Background data affecting nutrition education, nutrition education methods, evaluation of nutrition education, food behavior, nutrition policy.
Manuscript requirements: Style sheet sent upon request. Preferred length up to 15 pages typewritten, double-spaced. Submit original and 4 copies. Abstract of up to 150 words discussing content and findings.
Author information and reprints: No payment. Simultaneous submission not permitted. Copyright held by publication. Reprints available at cost. All mss. are reviewed for significance and soundness by a panel of expert reviewers. Occasional supplements published if funding is obtained by author.
Disposition of manuscript: Receipt acknowledged. Decision in 2 months. Published 6-12 months after acceptance. Rejected manuscript is returned, criticized.
Submit to: Susan M. Oace
Editor

JOURNAL OF PLANT NUTRITION
Department of Horticulture
University of Georgia
Athens, GA 30602
404-542-2471

Subscription data: First published in 1979.
Issues and rates: Published 10 times per year. Articles per average issue: 10. Paid circulation 250; 20 controlled. Annual rate(s): Individuals $60.75; Foreign individuals $80.65; Institutions $121.50; Foreign

institutions $141.00.
Sponsoring organization: Marcel Dekker.
Managing editor: Iris Accordino
Editorial description: Provides rapid publication of important findings from original research on plant mineral nutrition, including influence of both the currently known essential elements as well as those which are considered nonessential. Also accepts review papers of past and current literature.
Audience: Researchers studying plant nutrition.

Manuscript information

Manuscript requirements: Style guide sent on request. Preferred length 8-20 pages. Submit 2 copies, in English only, double-spaced. No abstract required.
Author information and reprints: No payment. Simultaneous submission not permitted. Periodical holds exclusive rights after acceptance. Copyright held by publication. Reprints available in lots of 100; cost varies with page number.
Disposition of manuscript: Receipt is acknowledged immediately. Decision within 1-2 months; published 4-6 months after acceptance. Rejected manuscript is returned, with reasons for rejection only.
Submit to: J. Benton Jones, Jr. Executive Editor

JOURNAL OF SCHOOL HEALTH
American School Health Association
PO Box 708
Kent, OH 44240
216-678-1601

Subscription data: First published in 1931.
Issues and rates: Published monthly except June and July. Articles per average issue: 10. Paid circulation averages 10,000. Annual rate(s): $30.00; Foreign $33.00; Institutions $25.00.
Sponsoring organization: American School Health Association.
Editorial description: Publishes articles on timely subjects of interest to school health professionals, school physicians, school nurses, health educators, psychologists and other members of the school health team.
Audience: Professional, academic.

Manuscript information
Subject field(s): Alcohol, health careers, community health, dental education, drug education, environmental ehalth, exceptional children, family life, sex education, first aid and society, growth and development, learning disabilities, mental health, nutrition, philosophy, smoking, vision, etc.
Manuscript requirements: Style sheet sent on request. AMA. Preferred length 10 pages. Submit 3 copies. Abstract not necessary, but preferred.
Author information and reprints: Payment: 2 copies of issue only. Simultaneous submission not permitted. Periodical holds exclusive rights after acceptance. Copyright held by publication. Query letter is not necessary, but advisable.
Disposition of manuscript: Receipt of manuscript is acknowledged. Decision in 6-8 weeks. Published 3 months after acceptance. Rejected manuscript is returned, with SASE. Reasons for rejections only.
Submit to: Gay E. Groomes Editor

JOURNAL OF SOIL SCIENCE
Department of Soil Science
The University
Reading RG1 5AQ, U.K.

Subscription data: First published in 1949.
Issues and rates: Quarterly. 15 articles per average issue. Circulation 2,000. Annual rates: 27.00.
Editorial description: Containes articles on soil chemistry, physics, biology, pedology, and management.

Manuscript information

Manuscript requirements: No special style guide. Submit 2 copies, double-spaced, and an abstract of up to 150 words.
Author information and reprints: No payment. Simultaneous submission not permitted. Copyright held by publication. Reprints available.
Disposition of manuscript: Acknowledged within 2 weeks; decision in 2 months; published 6 months after acceptance. Rejections returned.
Submit to: Prof. A. Wild Honorary Editor

JOURNAL OF THE AMERICAN DIETETIC ASSOCATION
430 North Michigan Avenue
Chicago, IL 60611
312-280-5018

Subscription data: First published in 1925.
Issues and rates: Published monthly. Articles per average issue: 7-11. Circulation 50,000. Annual rate(s): $27.50; Foreign $33.50.
Sponsoring organization: The American Dietetic Association.
Managing editor: Dolores E. Henning
Editorial description: Publishes reports of original research and other papers covering the broad aspects of dietetics, including nutrition and diet therapy, community nutrition, education and training, and administration.

Manuscript information

Manuscript requirements: Style sheet sent on request. Preferred length 12 to 14 pages. Submit 4 copies. Abstract not to exceed 90 words.
Author information and reprints: No payment. Simultaneous submission is not permitted. Periodical holds exclusive rights after acceptance. Copyright held by publication. Reprints available, cost varies.
Disposition of manuscript: Receipt of manuscript is acknowledged. Refereed journal. Decision in 3 months. Rejected manuscript is returned.
Submit to: Dorothea F. Turner, R.D. Editor

JOURNAL OF THE AMERICAN OIL CHEMISTS' SOCIETY
508 South Sixth Street
Champaign, IL 61820
217-359-2344

Subscription data: Previously entitled *Oil & Soap*. First published in 1923.
Issues and rates: Published monthly. Articles per average issue: 8-10. Circulation 6,650. Annual rate(s): $50.00.
Managing editor: James Lyon.
Editorial description: Contains original papers and timely review of physical, chemical and processing data and methods for fats, waxes and related products such as fatty acids; information on fat derivatives, detergents, paints, proteins and oilseed products; symposia sometimes published as a unit.

Manuscript information

Manuscript requirements: AIBS style

guide. Submit 3 copies, with abstract.
Author information and reprints: Payment by author or his institution to publication of $55 per page. Simultaneous submission not permitted. Copyright transfer required. Reprints available, cost varies with length.
Disposition of manuscript: Receipt acknowledged. Decision in 1-2 months. Published 2-3 months after acceptance. Rejected manuscript is returned, criticized.
Submit to: A.R. Baldwin
Editor
Cargill, Inc.
PO Box 9300
Minneapolis, MN 55440
612-475-6238

JOURNAL OF THE SCIENCE OF FOOD & AGRICULTURE*
Society of Chemical Industry
14 Belgrave Square
London SW1X 8PS, England

Subscription data:
Issues and rates: Monthly. 16 articles per average issue. Circulation 1,800. Annual rate: $150.00.
Sponsoring organization: The Society of Chemical Industry.
Editorial description: Contains research papers in any subject related to food or agriculture.
Audience: Professional, academic.
Manuscript information
Subject field(s): Any scientific field related to food or agriculture.
Manuscript requirements: See latest issue for style requirements. Submit 3 copies.
Author information and reprints: Payment in 25 reprints only. Simultaneous submission not permitted. Copyright held by publication until 6 months after publication. Reprints available at cost.
Disposition of manuscript: Receipt acknowledged. Decision in 2 months. Published 6 months after acceptance. Rejected manuscript is returned, criticized, if requested.
Submit to: Editorial Secretary

L

LIPIDS
508 South Sixth Street
Champaign, IL 61820
217-359-2344

Subscription data: First published in 1965.
Issues and rates: Articles per average issue: 8-14. Circulation 2,000. Annual rate(s): $50.00, Foreign $54.00.
Sponsoring organization: American Oil Chemists' Society.
Managing editor: James Lyon
Editorial description: Contains significant original findings of physical, chemical, biochemical, pharmacological and physiological characteristics of lipids, lipoproteins and other lipid complexes. Includes methods for identification, qualitative and quantitative analysis, and other forms of characterization of these substances. Reviews on timely topics will be published occassionally.
Manuscript information
Manuscript requirements: AIBS. Submit 4 copies and abstract.
Author information and reprints: Payment by author or his institution to publication at $55 per page. Simultaneous submission is not permitted. Periodical holds exclusive rights afater acceptance. Copyright held by publication. Reprints available, cost varies with length. Query letter not necessary.
Disposition of manuscript: Receipt of manuscript is acknowledged. Decision in 1-2 months. Published 2-3 months after acceptance. Rejected manuscript is returned, criticized.
Submit to: Ralph T. Holman
Editor
The Hormel Institute
801 16th Avenue, NE
Austin, MN 55912
507-433-8804

LIVESTOCK PRODUCTION SCIENCE
Elsevier Scientific Publishing Company
PO Box 211, Jan van Galenstraat
Amsterdam, The Netherlands

Subscription data: First published in 1974.
Issues and rates: Published bimonthly. Articles per average issue: 8. Annual rate(s): Dfl. 203.00.
Sponsoring organization: European Association for Animal Production.
Editorial description: A medium for the publication of original research studies and comprehensive reviews in the field of livestock production and the exchange of current views.
Audience: Researchers, livestock production managers.
Manuscript information
Subject field(s): Animal production; breeding; housing, feeding, management, reproduction, health, advisory activities; product quality, technical and economic aspects, etc.
Manuscript requirements: See latest issue for style requirements. Style sheet sent on request. Submit 3 copies and 3 abstracts, one in English, French, and German not to exceed 200 words.
Author information and reprints: Authors receive 50 reprints free. Simultaneous submission not permitted. Periodical holds exclusive rights after acceptance. Copyright held by publication. Reprints available at cost.
Disposition of manuscript: Receipt acknowledged. Decision in 2 months. Published c. 6 months after acceptance. Rejected manuscript is returned, criticized.
Submit to: H. de Boer
Editor
Postbus 501
3700 A.M. Zeist, The Netherlands

M

MINERAL AND ELECTROLYTE METABOLISM
S. Karger AG
PO Box
CH-4009 Basel, Switzerland
(061) 39 08 80

Subscription data: First published in 1978.
Issues and rates: Monthly. 9 articles per average issue. Annual rates: Sfr. 168.00; $96.00 per volume.
Main editor: S.G. Massry, Los Angeles
Editorial description: A forum for endocrine, nephrology, and metabolism topics, it contains articles encompassing the normal physiology and diseases of minerals and electrolytes.
Audience: Professional.
Manuscript information
Subject field(s): Vitamin D, parathyroid hormone, bone physiology and disease, renal osteodystrophy, soft tissue calcification, nutrition, and disorders of trace metals, etc.
Manuscript requirements: Style sheet

sent upon request or see latest issue. Submit 3 copies. Preferred length 6 printed pages at 3,800 letters. Include an abstract, with 3-9 key words. Mss. accepted in English.

Author information and reprints: No payment. Simultaneous submission not permitted. Copyright held by publication. Reprints available at cost. Charge for additional printed pages.

Disposition of manuscript: Receipt acknowledged; decision in 1 month; published 4-5 months after acceptance. Rejections returned, criticized.

Submit to: Dr. Shaul G. Massry
University of Southern California
School of Medicine
2025 Tonal Avenue
Los Angeles, CA 90033

N

NATIONAL ASSOCIATION OF COLLEGES AND TEACHERS OF AGRICULTURE. JOURNAL
NACTA Journal
Secretary-Treasurer
Sam Houston State University
PO Box 2088
Huntsville, TX 77340
713-295-6211

Subscription data: First published in 1957.

Issues and rates: Published quarterly. Circulation averages 1,200 controlled. Annual rate(s): Members $15.00; Institutions $8.00.

Sponsoring organization: National Association of Colleges and Teachers of Agriculture.

Editorial description: Directed toward the professional advancement of the college teacher of agriculture, its total offering includes something for every college teacher regardless of the size of his institution and subject matter.

Audience: Academic.

Manuscript information

Subject field(s): All aspects of the teaching of college agriculture: methods, problems, philosophy, and rewards.

Manuscript requirements: See latest issue for style requirements. Preferred length 3,000 words typescript. Submit 4 copies.

Author information and reprints: Payment in 5 copies of the issue only. Simultaneous submission is permitted. Periodical does not hold exclusive rights after acceptance. Not copyrighted. Reprints available at cost. Query letter is not necessary, but advisable.

Disposition of manuscript: Receipt of manuscript is acknowledged. Published 12 months after acceptance. Rejected manuscript is returned with return postage paid by publication.

Submit to: Dr. Jack C. Everly
Editor
Office of Instructional Resources
University of Illinois
608 West Vermont
Urbana, IL 61801
217-333-3690

NATURAL LIFE
PO Box 640
Jarvis, Ontario NOA 1J0 Canada

Subscription data: First published in 1976.

Issues and rates: Quarterly. 5 articels per average issue. Circulation 35,000. Annual rate: $8.

Sponsoring organization: Natural Dynamics, Inc.

Managing editor: Wendy Priesnitz

Editorial description: Ecological, down-to-eart, health-oriented, holistic, how-to articles: gardening without pesticides, alternate energy, natural healing, natural foods preparation, natural child rearing.

Manuscript information

Manuscript requirements: Preferred length 1,000 words.

Author information and reprints: Query letter required before submitting ms. Payment of $10-$50. Simultaneous submission not permitted. All rights purchased by publication.

Disposition of manuscript: Receipt acknowledged with SASE. Rejections returned with SASE.

Submit to: Editor

NEW OUTLOOK: THE MIDDLE EAST MONTHLY*
8 Karl Netter
Tel Aviv, Israel
(03) 292-2435

Subscription data: First published in 1957.

Issues and rates: 8 issue per year. 20 articles per average issue. Circulation 4,500. Annual rate: IL 60.00; U.S. $24.00.

Sponsoring organization: Jewish-Arab Institute, Givat Haviva.

Managing editors: Simha Flapan, David Shaham.

Editorial description: Dedicated to the search for peace in the Middle East and to cooperation and development of all the area's peoples. Contains articles of all viewpoints in politics, philosophy, sociology, psychology, agriculture, economics, etc.

Audience: University level, etc.

Manuscript information

Manuscript requirements: Preferred length 3,000 words max. Submit 1 copy, with a short author biography (1-2 sentences). Accepted in English.

Author information and reprints: Payment considered, if requested. Normally, none. Simultaneous submission permitted in other languages only. Copyright held by journal. Reprints available, at cost.

Disposition of manuscript: Decision in 1 month; time to publishing varies. Rejections returned, if author supplies postage.

Submit to: The Editor

NEWSLETTER OF PARENTING
803 Church Street
Honesdale, PA 18431
717-253-1080

Subscription data: First published in 1978.

Issues and rates: Published monthly. Articles per average issue: 14. Paid circulation 4,000. Annual rate(s): $5.00.

Sponsoring organization: Highlights for Children, Inc.

Editorial description: Contains material of interest to parents of children, from infancy through age eight, on child development, child rearing, parenting concerns.

Audience: High-school educated parents without background in child development.

Manuscript information

Subject field(s): Child development, child rearing, discipline, nutrition, school concerns, sibling relationships, adoption.

Manuscript requirements: Style guide sent on request. Preferred length 500-1,200 words. Submit 1 copy. Abstract not required.

Author information and reprints: Payment by publication to author of up to $100 per article. Simultaneous submission is not permitted. Periodical holds exclusive rights after acceptance. Copyright held by publication; author generally given right to reprint material. Reprints not available, but author may request additional copies.

Disposition of manuscript: Receipt is not acknowledged. Decision within 6-8 weeks; published 3-12 months after acceptance. Rejected manuscript is returned, not criticized, with SASE or if return postage is supplied by author.

Submit to: Catherine Johnson
Editorial Coordinator

NUTRITION PLANNING
PO Box 8080
Ann Arbor, MI 48104
313-761-1357

Subscription data: First published in 1978.
Issues and rates: Published quarterly. Articles per average issue: 120. Paid circulation 900; 500 controlled. Annual rate(s): $45.00; Foreign $55.00.
Sponsoring organization: Community Systems Foundation.
Editorial description: An international journal of abstracts about food and nutrition policy, planning and programs.
Audience: Planners, policy makers, practitioners, project personnel, researchers, students and others interested in nutrition.

Manuscript information

Subject field(s): Planning process, methodology and analysis; consequences of malnutrition; nutritional status assessment; nutritional education and home-centered activities; public health and curative measures; food processing and distribution; agriculture; economics; social and cultural aspects; comprehensive programs.
Author information and reprints: No payment. Simultaneous submission is permitted. Periodical does not hold exclusive rights after acceptance. Copyright held by publication. Reprints are not available.
Disposition of manuscript: Rejected manuscript is not returned.
Submit to: Naomi Gottlieb
Business Manager

NUTRITION TODAY MAGAZINE
PO Box 1829
703 Giddings Avenue
Annapolis, MD 21404

Subscription data: Formerly entitled *Nutrition Today*. First published in 1966.
Issues and rates: Published bimonthly. Articles per average issue: 3. Annual rate(s): $14.75; Students $7.40; Foreign $16.75.
Editorial description: Articles for health professionals, students, and enlightened laymen on all fields relating to nutrition.

Manuscript information

Subject field(s): Nutrition and allied fields: medicine, dentistry, dietetics, food service, home economics, biochemistry, paramedicine, agriculture, and technology.
Manuscript requirements: GPO, NYT. Submit 1 copy. Abstract not necessary.
Author information and reprints: Payment varies. Simultaneous submission not permitted. Periodical holds exclusive rights after acceptance. Copyright held by publication. Reprints available on order. Query letter necessary.
Disposition of manuscript: Receipt of manuscript is acknowledged. Decision in 60 dyas. Published 3-6 months after acceptance. Rejected manuscript is returned.
Submit to: Cortez F. Enloe, Jr., M.D.
Editor and Publisher

O

OECOLOGIA
Springer-Verlag
175 Fifth Avenue
New York, NY 10010
212-673-2660

Subscription data:
Issues and rates: Annual rate(s): DM 180 per volume.
Sponsoring organization: International Association for Ecology (Intecol).
Editor: Prof. Hermann Remmert.
Editorial description: Publishes original contributions and short communications dealing with the ecology of all organisms.

Manuscript information

Subject field(s): Autecology, physiological ecology, population dynamics, production biology, demography, epidemiology, behavioral ecology, food cycles, theoretical ecology, including population genetics.
Manuscript requirements: See latest issue for style requirements. Preferred length 10,000 words; maximum 20 pages. Submit 2 copies, and a summary of the main points.
Author information and reprints: Payment of 75 offprints only. Simultaneous submission not permitted. Periodical holds exclusive rights after acceptance. Copyright held by publisher.
Submit to: Member of the Editorial Board according to the appropriate subject matter listed on cover of latest issue.

P

PEDIATRICS*
Official Publication of The American Academy of Pediatrics, Inc.
1801 Hinman
Evanston, IL 60201
312-869-4255

Subscription data:
Issues and rates: Published monthly. Circulation 22,000. Annual rate(s): $17.00, Foreing $24.00.
Sponsoring organization: American Academy of Pediatrics, Inc.
Editorial description: Edited for the pediatrician and those concerned with child health and development. Each issue contains papers on original research and special feature or review articles in the field of pediatrics as broadly defined.

Manuscript information

Subject field(s): Premature and newborn, infant diseases and immunology, nutrition, metabolism, pediatric practice, heart and blood vessel, endocrinology, neurology and psychiatry, respiratory tract, surgery, genito-urinary tract, orthopedics, allergy, tumors, drugs.
Manuscript requirements: See latest issue for style requirements. Submit 2 copies.
Author information and reprints: Simultaneous submission not permitted. Periodical holds exclusive rights after acceptance. Copyright held by publication. Reprints available.
Disposition of manuscript: Receipt of manuscript is acknowledged. Decision in 30 days. Published 90-180 days after

acceptance. Rejected manuscript is returned, criticized.
Submit to: Dr. Jerold F. Lucey
Editor-in-Chief
Mary Fletcher Hospital
Burlington, VT 05401

PEPTIDES
An International Journal
PO Box 426
Fayetteville, NY 13066
315-463-0182

Subscription data: First published in 1980.
Issues and rates: Quarterly. 15 articles per average issue. Circulation 600. Annual rates: Individuals $25.00; Institutions $100.00; Foreign Institutions $110.00.
Sponsoring organization: ANKHO International, Inc.
Editorial description: Publishes original reports of systematic studies on the chemistry, biochemistry, neurochemistry, endocrinology, gastroenterology, physiology, and the neuroligical and behavioral effects of the peptides.
Audience: Academic, professional.
Manuscript information
Subject field(s): Peptide research.
Manuscript requirements: Style instructions on inside back cover of journal. Submit 3 copies. Manuscript in English. Abstract not to exceed 170 words.
Author information and reprints: Payment in 25 reprints. Simultaneous submission is not permitted. Publication holds exclusive manuscript rights between acceptance of article and publication date. Copyright held by publication. Reprints available; requested through author, ordered in lots of 50 only.
Disposition of manuscript: Manuscript acknowledged. Decision within 4 weeks. Publication within 90 dyas. Rejected manuscript returned; criticized with reasons for rejection only.
Submit to: Abba J. Kastin
Editor-in-Chief
Veterans Administration Medical Center
1601 Perdido Street
New Orleans, LA 70146
504-568-0811

PESTICIDE SCIENCE*
Society of Chemical Industry
14 Belgrave Square
London SW1X 8PS, England
(01) 235-3681

Subscription data: First published in 1970.
Issues and rates: Published bimonthly. Articles per average issue: 15. Circulation 900. Annual rate(s): $105.00.
Sponsoring organization: Society of Chemical Industry.
Editorial description: Original investigations concerning the use of insecticides, fungicides, herbicides, and growth substances as well as other methods for the control of pests, diseases and weeds.
Manuscript information
Manuscript requirements: Style sheet sent on request. Submit 3 copies. Abstract not necessary.
Author information and reprints: Payment in 25 reprints only. Simultaneous submission not permitted. Copyright held by publication. Reprints available at cost.
Disposition of manuscript: Receipt acknowledged. Rejected manuscript is returned.
Submit to: The Editor

THE POINTER
Heldref Publications
400 Albemarle Street, NW
Washington, DC 20016
202-362-6445

Subscription data: First published in 1956.
Issues and rates: 3 per year, 12 articles per average issue. Circulation 650. Annual rates: $15.00.
Sponsoring organization: Heldref Publications.
Managing editor: Nancy Graham.
Editorial description: Contains classroom ideas for teachers of handicapped children; suggestions for parents on how to help handicapped children at home and how to coordinate home activities with school activities.
Audience: Special teachers and parents of handicapped.
Manuscript information
Subject field(s): Reading projects, nutrition and health, math teaching, vocational training, preschools, adaptation of existing items for use by handicapped, etc.
Manuscript requirements: APA.
Preferred length 1500-3000 words. Submit 3 copies, double-spaced.
Author information and reprints: Payment of complimentary copy of journal. Simultaneous submission not permitted. Copyright held by publication.
Disposition of manuscript: Receipt acknowledged within 3 months; decision in 3-6 months; published 4 months after acceptance. Rejections returned, sometimes criticized.
Submit to: Dr. Stanley A. Fagen
Executive Editor
l605 Lemontree Lane
Silver Spring, MD 20904

S

SCIENCE OF THE TOTAL ENVIRONMENT
Elsevier Scientific Publishing Company
PO Box 330
1000A E Amsterdam, The Netherlands
515-9222

Subscription data: First published in 1972.
Issues and rates: Monthly. Articles per average issue: 8. Annual rate(s): Dfl. 512.
Editorial description: An international journal for scientific research into the environment and its relationship with man. Particular emphasis is placed on applied environmental chemistry.
Audience: Specialists, academic, industrial, governmental.
Manuscript information
Subject field(s): Applications of techniques of chemistry and biochemistry to environmental problems; air, water, soil pollution and human nutrition; medicine; environmental planning and policy.
Manuscript requirements: See latest issue for style requirements. Style sheet sent on request. Submit 2 copies. Abstract not to exceed 200 words.
Author information and reprints: Payment in 50 reprints. Simultaneous submission not permitted. Copyright held by publication. Reprints available at cost.
Disposition of manuscript: Receipt acknowledged. Decision in 2 weeks. Published 5 months after acceptance. Rejected manuscript is returned.

Submit to: Dr. I.C. Smith
c/o Solar Energy Research Institute
1617 Cole Boulevard
Golden, CO 80401, U.S.A.

SOCIAL AND ECONOMIC STUDIES*
Institute of Social and Economic Research
University of the West Indies
Mona
Kingston 7, Jamaica

Subscription data: First published in 1953.

Issues and rates: Published quarterly. Articles per average issue: 5. Annual rate(s): $6.00.

Editorial description: A journal devoted to the publication of research and discussion on agricultural, anthropoligical, demographic, economic, educational, monetary, political and sociological questions with emphasis on the problems of the developing territories, particularly those in the Carribean.

Manuscript information

Manuscript requirements: See latest issue for style requirements. Submit 3 copies, with abstract.

Author information and reprints: Payment in 25 reprints. Simultaneous submission not permitted. Copyright held by publication. Reprints available at cost.

Disposition of manuscript: Receipt acknowledged. Decision in 3 months. Published 6-12 months after acceptance. Rejected manuscript is returned.

Submit to: Vaughan Lewis
Editor

SOIL SCIENCE
428 East Preston Street
Baltimore, MD 21202
301-528-4116

Subscription data: First published in 1916.

Issues and rates: Monthly. 10 articles per average issue. Circulation 2,700. Annual rate: $23.00.

Sponsoring organization: Rutgers University.

Editorial description: Contains original scientific articles on soil science from all parts of the world.

Manuscript information

Manuscript requirements: See latest issue for style requirements. Submit 2 copies, with an abstract.

Author information and reprints: Payment by author or his institution to publication. $45.00 per page for all pages over 6. Simultaneous submission not permitted. Periodical holds exclusive rights after acceptance. Copyright held by publication. Reprints available.

Disposition of manuscript: Receipt acknowledged. Decision in 3 months. Published 1 year after acceptance. Rejected manuscript is returned.

Submit to: Lowell A. Douglas
Editor
Dept. of Soils and Crops
Rutgers University
New Brunswick, NJ 08903
201-932-9800 1773

T

THE NEW PHYSICIAN
American Medical Student Association
14650 Lee Road
PO Box 131
Chantilly, VA 22021
703-968-7920

Subscription data: First published in 1952.

Issues and rates: Monthly, except combined July/August issue. Circulation 75,000. Annual rate(s): $12.00.

Sponsoring organization: American Medical Student Association.

Editorial description: Examines issues of critical concern to physicians-in-training. Also publishes basic clinical features on nutrition, clinical pharmacology, family practice, etc., and features innovative columns on humanistic medicine, sexual medicine, and medico-legal issues.

Manuscript information

Manuscript requirements: See latest issue for style requirements. Preferred length 2,000 words. Submit 2 copies.

Author information and reprints: Payment only for solicited manuscripts. Simultaneous submission permitted. Copyright held by publication. Reprints available.

Disposition of manuscript: Receipt acknowledged. Decision in 8 weeks. Published 3-6 months after acceptance. Rejected manuscript is returned only on request.

Submit to: Todd Dankmeyer
Editor

Book Publishers of Food and Nutrition

by *Literary Market Place 1982*

This section features an alphabetical presentation of U.S. and Canadian book and micro publishers that specialize in food and nutrition publications. The list is based on data from *Litarary Market Place 1982*.

Each listing includes the name, address, and telephone number of the publisher, along with the name of at least one person to contact. In addition, the staff isolated the key description of each book publisher's emphasis on specific food and nutrition related topics. Publishers of cookbooks were not listed, unless they also published books in other food and nutrition areas.

A

A & W PUBLISHERS, INC.
95 Madison Ave.
New York, NY 10016
212-725-4970

Contact: Lawrence D. Alexander, President
Food area: Home economics.

AVI PUBLISHING CO.
Box 831
Westport, CT 06881
203-226-0738

Contact: Wilfred W. Tressler, President
Food area: Food science and technology, nutrition, agriculture, food service and health.

ANDERSON WORLD, INC.
Affiliate of Runner's World Magazine Co.
1400 Stierlin Rd.
Mountain View, CA 94043
415-965-8777

Contact: Bob Anderson, President
Food area: How-to trade editions on diet.

AND/OR PRESS, INC.
Box 2246
Berkeley, CA 94702
415-849-2665

Contact: Jim Schreiber, Executive Editor
Food area: Health and nutrition.

ANN ARBOR SCIENCE PUBLISHERS, INC.
Subs. of Butterworth Publishers, Inc.
Box 1425
Ann Arbor, MI 48106
313-761-5010

Contact: Edward E. Lewis, President
Food area: Food, agriculture, biochemical at professional and graduate levels.

AUTUMN PRESS PUBLISHERS
1318 Beacon St.
Brookline, MA 02146
617-738-5680

Contact: M. Nahum Stiskin, President
Food area: Natural foods.

B

BENNETT PUBLISHING CO.
809 W Detweiller Dr.
Peoria, IL 61615
309-691-4454

Contact: Richard H. Simpson, Chairman of the Board
Food area: Textbooks: home economics.

BETTER HOMES & GARDENS BOOKS
Imprint of Meredith Book Publishing Group, Meredith Corp.
17th at Locust St.
Des Moines, IA 50336
5115-284-9011

Contact: Gerald M. Knox, Editor
Food area: Food.

Based on material reprinted from *Literary Market Place 1982* with permission on the R. R. Bowker Company. Copyright 1981 by Xerox Corporation.

RESOURCES FOR FURTHER INFORMATION

BIOSIS (BIOSCIENCES INFORMATION SERVICE)
Professional Services Div.
2100 Arch St.
Philadelphia, PA 19103
215-568-4016

Contact: H. Edward Kennedy, Executive Director
Food area: *Biological Abstracts:* Twice-monthly secondary publication for the biological and biomedical sciences; access to 170,000 research reports, mostly from journals; microfilm edition (from 1927); microfiche 1970-1974 (Vols. 51-58); paper cumulative indexes semi-annually.
 Microfilm Indexes to Biological Abstracts, 1927-1959 (Vols. 1-33): Annual cumulations; 5-year cumulative indexes for 1959-1964 (Vols. 34-45); 1965-1969 (Vols. 46-50); 1970-1974 (Vols. 51-58); 1975-1979 (Vols 59-68).
 Biological Abstracts/RRM (Reports, Reviews, Meetings), from 1980: Twice-monthly secondary publication for the biological and biomedical sciences. Succeeds *BioResearch Index* (1967-1979); covers 130,000 items mostly from conferences and reviews; paper cumulative indexes semi-annually.

BULL PUBLISHING CO.
Box 208
Palo Alto, CA 94302
415-322-2855

Contact: David C. Bull, President
Food area: Nutrition and health care, weight loss.

C

CBI PUBLISHING CO, INC.
Member of International Thomson Organization; Affiliate of Science Books International, Inc.
51 Sleeper St.
Boston, MA 02210
617-426-2224

Contact: Mike A. Tucker, President
Food area: Food service.

CHRONICLE BOOKS
Div. of Chronicle Publishing Co.
870 Market St.
San Francisco, CA 94102
415-777-7240

Contact: Larry L. Smith, General Manager
Food area: Food.

CLAY PUBLISHING CO., LTD.
Bewdley, ON K0L 1E0, Canada
416-797-2281

Contact: Charlotte Clay, Publisher and Editor
Purpose: Animal husbandry.

COMPACT PUBLICATIONS, INC.
3014 Willow La.
Hollywood, FL 33021
305-983-6464

Contact: Donald L. Lessne, President
Food area: Diet, Health and nutrition.

COMPCARE PUBLICATIONS
Div. of Comprehensive Care Corp.
2415 Annapolis La.
Minneapolis, MN 55441
800-328-3330

Contact: Diane DuCharme, Editor-in-Chief
Food area: Specializes in the areas of alcoholism/weight control.

D

GREEY DE PENCIER PUBLICATIONS LTD.
59 Front St. E
Toronto, ON M5E 1B3, Canada
416-364-3333

Contact: Michael de Pencier
Food area: Home Economics.

THE DONNING CO/PUBLISHERS
5041 Admiral Wright Rd.
Virginia Beach, VA 23462
804-499-0589

Contact: Robert S. Friedman, President
Food area: Home economics.

E

THE EAST WOODS PRESS
820 E Boulevard
Charlotte, NC 28203
704-334-0897

Contact: Sally McMillan, Editor
Food area: Health and nutrition.

F

FAIRCHILD BOOKS & VISUALS
Div. of Fairchild Publications, a div. of Capital Cities Media, Inc.
7 E 12 St.
New York, NY 10003

Contact: Edward B. Gold, Book Division Manager
Food area: Home economics.

FOOD & NUTRITION PRESS, INC.
265 Post Rd. W
Westport, CT 06880
203-227-6596

Contact: John J. O'Neil, President
Food area: College and secondary textbooks and reference books in food science and nutrition and related fields.

THE FRANKLIN INSTITUTE PRESS
Affiliate of the Franklin Institute
Box 2266
Philadelphia, PA 19103
215-448-1551

Contact: Julia S. Hough, Director
Food area: Books and periodicals in problem solving, biomedical and energy fields.

C.J. FROMPOVICH PUBLICATIONS
RD 1, Chestnut Rd.
Coopersburg, PA 18036
215-346-8461

Contact: Catherine J. Frompovich, Editor-in-Chief
Food area: Publications and educational materials on natural nutrition together with self-help publications.

H

HAWKES PUBLISHING, INC.
3775 S Fifth W
Salt Lake City, UT 84115
801-262-5555

Contact: John D. Hawkes, President
Food area: Food storage.

RESOURCES FOR FURTHER INFORMATION

HERMAN PUBLISHING, INC.
45 Newbury St.
Boston, MA 02116
617-536-5810

Contact: Sanford M. Herman, President
Food area: Food service, home economics.

I

THE INTERSTATE PRINTERS & PUBLISHERS, INC.
19 N Jackson St.
Danville, IL 61832
217-446-0500

Contact: Russell L. Guin, Chairman of the Board
Food area: Elementary, secondary and college textbooks in agriculture and agribusiness, home economics.

IOWA STATE UNIVERSITY PRESS
Ames, IA 50010
515-294-5280

Contact: James Schwartz, President
Food area: Professional and college works in agriculture, home economics.

L

LAKEWOOD BOOKS
Subs. of Lakewood Publications, Inc.
1070 Kapp Dr.
Clearwater, FL 33515
813-461-1585

Contact: Thomas Stephens, President
Food area: Diet.

LEBHAR-FRIEDMAN BOOKS
Subs. of Lebhar-Friedman, Inc.
425 Park Ave.
New York, NY 10022
212-371-9400

Contact: A.D. Friedman, Chairman of the Board
Food area: Retailing, food service and distribution.

M

MCKNIGHT PUBLISHING CO.
Bloomington, IL 61701
309-663-1341

Contact: William McKnight III, Chairman of the Board
Food area: Home economics.

N

NATIONAL BOOK CO.
Div. of Educational Research Associates
333 SW Park Ave.
Portland, OR 97205
503-228-6345

Contact: C. Theo Yerian, Chairman of the Board
Food area: Individualized instruction programs, home economics.

NEWCASTLE PUBLISHING CO., INC.
13419 Saticoy St.
North Hollywood, CA 91605
213-873-3191

Contact: Alfred Saunders, President
Food area: Nutrition.

NOYES DATA CORP.
Mill Rd. & Grand Ave.
Park Ridge, NJ 07656
201-391-8484

Contact: Robert Noyes, Chairman, President and Publisher
Food area: Food.

O

THE ORYX PRESS
2214 N Central at Encanto
Phoenix, AZ 85004
602-254-6156

Contact: Phyllis B. Steckler, President
Food area: Micropublishing: *Bibliography of Agriculture Retrospective on Microfiche: 1970-1978.*

P

PAPERJACKS LTD.
330 Steelcase Rd.
Markham, ON L3R 2M1, Canada
416-495-1261

Contact: Jack Stoddart, President
Food area: Canadian Farm and Home Almanac.

THE PENNSYLVANIA STATE UNIVERSITY PRESS
215 Wagner Bldg.
University Park, PA 16802
814-865-1327

Contact: Chris W. Kentera, Director
Food area: Agriculture.

PHOENIX PUBLISHING
Canaan, NH 03471
603-523-9901; 9902

Contact: A.L. Morris, Adrian A. Paradis, Partners
Food area: Home economics.

R

REIMAN PUBLICATIONS, INC.
Box 643
Milwaukee, WI 53201
414-423-0100

Contact: Roy J. Reiman, President
Food area: Agriculture, foods.

STACKPOLE BOOKS
Affiliate of Commonwealth Communications Services
Box 1831
Cameron and Kelker Sts.
Harrisburg, PA 17105
717-234-5091

Contact: Henry A. Hamel, President
Food area: Food.

STRAWBERRY HILL PRESS
2594 15 Ave.
San Francisco, CA 94127
415-664-8112; 228-6888

Contact: Jean-Louis Brindamour, President
Food area: Health and nutrition.

T

TAYLOR & NG
400 Valley Dr.
Brisbane, CA 94005
415-467-2600

Contact: Win Ng, Chairman of the Board
Food area: Home economics.

TEXAS A&M UNIVERSITY PRESS
Drawer C
College Station, TX 77843
713-845-1436

Contact: Lloyd G. Lyman, Director
Food area: Agriculture.

TIMBER PRESS
Box 1631
Beaverton, OR 97075
503-292-2606

Contact: Richard Abel
Food area: Agriculture.

TIME-LIFE BOOKS, INC.
Subs. of Time, Inc.
Alexandria, VA 22314
703-960-5000

Contact: John D. McSweeney, Chairman of the Board
Food area: Food.

U

UNIPUB
A Xerox Publishing Group Co; Div. of R.R. Bowker Co.
345 Park Ave. S
New York, NY 10010
212-686-4707

Contact: Wayne S. Kerwood, President
Food area: U.S. distribution agency for international organizations including: Commonwealth Agriculture Bureaux (CAB); Food & Agriculture Organization of the UN (FAO); International Institute of Refrigeration (IIR); International Rice Research Institute (IRRI); Centre for Agricultural Publishing & Documentation (PUDOC).

UNIVERSITY OF NEBRASKA PRESS
901 N 17 St.
Lincoln, NE 68588
402-472-3581

Contact: David H. Gilbert, Director
Food area: Agriculture.

UNIVERSITY OF THE TREES PRESS
Box 644
Boulder Creek, CA 95006
408-338-2161

Contact: Christopher Hills, Chairman of the Board
Food area: New foods.

UPDATA PUBLICATIONS, INC.
1756 Westwood Blvd.
Los Angeles, CA 90024
213-829-5090; 474-5900

Contact: Herbert Sclar, President
Food area: Micropublishers in all formats. U.S. Dept. of Agriculture; all U.S. Dept. of Agriculture documents from inception to date; all U.S. National Marine Fisheries Service (NOAA) and its predecessors 1871-ongoing.

W

WESTVIEW PRESS, INC.
5500 Central Ave.
Boulder, CO 80301
303-444-3541

Contact: Maurice B. Mitchell, Chairman of the Board
Food area: Agricultural science and agricultural engineering.

WOODBRIDGE PRESS PUBLISHING CO.
Box 6189
Santa Barbara, CA 93111
805-965-7039

Contact: Howard B. Weeks, President
Food area: Nutrition, home economics.

INDEX

A

Abraham, Sidney, 75-84
Absorption
  of drugs, 328-29
  of nutrients, 332-33
Acceptable risk. *See* Risk/benefit analysis
Acetylcholine, 89
Acne
  healing of, and zinc, 106
  and use of fluorine, 107
Acrodermatitis enteropathica (AE), 126
Acrylonitrile, banning of, under Delaney clause, 27
Adams, Catherine F., 40-68
Addiction Research Foundation (Ontario, Canada), 174
Additives, foods, 23, 24, 27, 160
  coloring as, 29, 31, 120
  and hyperactivity, 207, 331
  and risk/benefit analysis, 30-31
  and sodium nitrate, 263
Adenosine triphosphate (ATP), 246
  uses of, 72
Adequate and safe intakes. *See* Estimated adequate and safe intakes
Adipose tissue cellularity, and obesity, 72-73
Adolescence
  athletes in, 235, 240
  dietary practices in, 234-37
  need for zinc in, 126
  nutrition and common diseases in, 236-37
  nutrition needs during, 170, 236
  Recommended Dietary Allowances (RDAs) for, 236
  underweight in, 238-40
Adolescent pregnancy
  health implications of, 241
  nutrient needs during, 126, 241, 242
  prepregnancy weight and gain during, 241-42
  Recommended Dietary Allowances (RDAs) during, 241
  sociological implications of, 241
  vegetarianism during, 234, 242
Adrenal cortical tumors, 307
Adrenal medullary tumors, 307
Adrenocortico-steroids, use of, in cancer treatment, 344
Adrenocorticotropic hormone (ACTH), 363
Adrianycin cardiotoxicity, 347
Afferent loop syndrome, 343
Aflatoxin, 29
Aged/Aging
  adjustment of, to old age, 376
  and bone loss, 381-82
  and caloric intake, 382-83
  and congregate dining, 3, 376-77
  constipation for, 371
  effect of psychosocial forces on nutrition of, 373-80
  fat intake of, 370
  and geriatric daycare, 378
  health problems of, 343-44
  home-delivered meals for, 377
  host-defense system breakdown of, 214-15
  hypertension in, 371-72
  and institutional care, 377-78
  isolation of, 375
  meaning of food for, 374-75
  mental disorders of, 378-79
  nutrition needs of, 171, 368-72, 381-83
  nutritional programs for, 3, 370-71
  physical disabilities of, 379
  protein needs of, 370
  Recommended Dietary Allowances (RDAs) for, 329, 370, 377
  and sensory deprivation, 381
  and smell, 381
  sodium restriction for, 369
  and taste, 381
  and tooth loss, 381-82
  and use of self-help eating devices by, 379-80
  vitamin deficiencies in, 369
  for women, 171
Agriculture, changes in, and trace minerals, 102
Ahrens, Edward H., Jr., 282
Akgun, Suat, 316-18
Akyroyd, W. R., 169-70
Alarm reaction, 363
Alcohol
  consumption of
    for the aged, 378-79
    and diabetes, 326-27
    for athletes, 255
  effect of, on appetite, 332
  and fat, cholesterol and sodium intake, 76
  in human milk composition, 179
  and hypertension, 310
  ingestion of, during pregnancy, 185-89
  need for moderation in diet, 4
  and undernutrition, 269
Alkali disease, 123
Alkaline phosphatase, 126
Allopurinol, effect of, on taste, 369
Amebiasis, 183

American Academy of Pediatrics Committee on Nutrition, 149-52
American College of Obstetricians and Gynecologists, 173
American Diabetes Association (ADA), 156-57
American Dietetic Association, 204-13, 250-56
American Federation of State, County and Municipal Employees, 23
American Federation of Teachers, 23
American Health Foundation (AHF), 161, 163
American Heart Association (AHA), 280
American Meat Institute, 25
American Medical Association (AMA), 4, 6, 13, 120, 173, 369
American Medical News, 6-7
American Medical Student Association, 23
American Waterworks Association, 117
Ames, Bruce, 93
Amino acid dopa, 330
Amino acids
  effect of, on immunologic function, 219
  metabolism disorders, 208
  mobilization of, 363
Aminopterin, 188
Amitriptyline, 331
Amphetamines, effect of, on appetite, 331
Anderson, J. W., 324-25
Anderson, T. W., 104
Andriamycin, 347
Anemia
  and cancer, 340-41
  hemolytic, 183, 241, 333
  hyperchromic microcytic, 369
  iron deficiency, 31, 96, 105, 169, 205, 206, 236, 334, 335
  megaloblastic, 178, 335
  pernicious, 88
  sports, 248
Anesthesia, and obesity, 70
Anorexia nervosa, 176, 207, 214, 219, 240, 331, 332, 338
  in the aged, 368, 378
  and cancer, 338-339
  causes of, 364-66, 369
  drug-induced, 331-32
  treatment of, 331
Antabuse, 330
Antacids, 333
Antibiotics, 87, 333
Anticancer drugs, 182
Anticholinergic drugs, 369
Anticonvulsant therapy, 206-7
Antigraphy, 13-14

INDEX

Antihistamines
 effect on appetite, 331
 role of, in heat exhaustion, 260
 vitamin C as natural, 89
Antihypertensive medications, 307, 308-9
Antimicrobials, 182-83
Antineoplastic drugs, 331-32
Antioxidants
 role of, in cancer etiology, 273
 role of vitamin E in protection, 100
Antithyroid drugs, 183
Antitumor therapy, 241
Anxiety, and nutrition, 364-66
Apathy, in elderly toward diet, 368
Aphasia, 379
Apoprotein, 296
Appendicitis, and dietary fiber, 146
Appetite
 in adolescent, 234-37
 in aged, 368, 376
 as component of eating behaviors, 9
 disorders of, 9, 126
 effects of drugs on, 330-31
 suppressants of 73, 331
Arky, Ronald A., 157
Arsenic, 30, 110
Arteriosclerosis, 149, 288
Arthritis, 9, 379
Artificial coloring, 29, 31, 120
Aryl hydrocarbon hydroxylase (AHH),
 role of, in cancer etiology, 274
Ascorbate, deficiencies of, in aged, 368
Ascorbic Acid, 89, 91, 92, 346
 amount available for consumption, per capita per day, 22
 average intake for infants, 194
 and chemotherapy, 346-47
 in composition of human milk, 178
 deficiencies of, 249, 334, 370, 381
 effect of, on immunologic function, 217
 and iron, 95-96, 105, 111
 in national food supply, 19, 20, 21
 need for, 85, 86, 366
 neutralization of PCBs, 86
 Recommended Dietary Allowances (RDAs) for 36
 and recovery after surgery, 86
 and stress, 364-66
Aspartame, usage of, 159, 162
Aspirin, use of, and iron, 105
Asthma, treatment of, 122, 331
Atabrine, 27
Atarax, 331
Atherosclerosis, 140, 280, 281, 289, 292-93, 307, 370
 and diet, 12-15, 269
 and dietary fiber, 145
 reversal of, through use of Pritikin diet, 12-15
Athetosis, 208
Athletes
 adolescent, 235, 240
 carbohydrates in diet, 257
 dietary recommendations for, 252-55
 nutrition for, 245-46, 257-58, 259-61
Atkinson, Stephanie A., 177-80
Atomic absorption spectrometry, 110, 125
Autosomal recessive syndromes, 8

B

Baby blues, 88-89
Bacteria, oral, and dental caries, 312
Balanced diet, 86
Basic four food groups, 16-18
Bayley, Nancy, 354
Beard, Howard, 93
Beckman Glucose Analyzer, 316, 320
Beer belly, 326
Behavior modification, and obesity, 73, 250, 269
Beissel, W. R., 216-21

Benzodiazepines, 331
Bergland, Bob, 3
Beriberi, 85, 269
Bertrand's mathematical model, 33
Betacarotene, 86-87
Beverage industry, use of sweeteners by, 154-55
Beverages, nutritive values of some, 67
BHA, role of, in cancer etiology, 273
BHT, 273
Bile acids
 relationship between diet, neutral steroids and, 264
 role of, in cancer etiology, 273
Bioflavinoids, 92
Biologic dose-responsive curve, 34
Biotin, 89
 adequate and safe intake for, 33, 36
Bixler, William, 24
Black, Thomas N., 175
Bladder cancer
 relative risk of, 271
 and use of saccharin, 163
Blankenhorn, David H., 14
Blass, John P., 368-72
Blind loop syndrome, 340, 341
Blood cholesterol. See Cholesterol, serum
Blood pressure. See Hypertension
Bollenback, Norris, 154-155
Bone phosphatase, 126
Book publishers, food and nutrition, 536-39
Borderline hypertension, 141
Boric acid poisoning, 334
Bottle feeding, 170
Botulism, 26
Bowel cancer
 correlation between, and fat consumption, 272-73
 risk of, 272
Bowles, Watson A., Jr., 181-84
Brain neurotransmitters, and control of eating, 71
Bread, use of food additives in, 31
Breast cancer, 263, 265
Breast cysts, and use of vitamin E, 92
Breast feeding, 170, 180
 effects of medications on infant, 181-82
 See also Milk composition, human
Brewer's yeast, 106
Brickey, Carolyn, 23
Bromocriptine, effect of, on lactation, 182
Bronchopulmonary dysplasia, 100, 334
Brown sugar, 155
Bulking agents, and appetite, 332
Bureau of Foods, 175
Burg, Alan W., 174
Burkitt, D. P., 144
Burns, healing of, and zinc, 106
Butterworth, C. E., 278-79
Butyric acids, 290

C

Cadmium, 110
 effect of, on iron, 105
 and need for zinc, 106
 and pollution, 102
Caffeine, 166, 175
 average daily consumption of, 174
 effects of, 175-76
 and fatty acid mobilization, 255
 and generally recognized as safe (GRAS) list, 30
 history of useage, 172
 prevention of dehydration for athletes, 258
 recommendation on usage, 174
 safety of, 172-74
 and thiamine, 87
Calcidiol, 97-98
Calcitonin, 340

Calcium, 109
 amount available for consumption, per capita per day, 22
 average intake for infants, 198, 199
 compounding of, with phytates, 107
 deficiencies of
  in adolescent pregnancy, 241
  in aged, 369, 370, 381
  and fluorine, 107
  in human milk composition, 179
  in interaction of, with protein, 111-12
  in national food supply, 19, 20, 21
 need for, 103
 and phosphorus, 104
 Recommended Dietary Allowances (RDAs) for, 36
 role of vitamin D in absorption of, 92
Calcium carbimide, 330
Calcium pangamate, 93
Caldwell, Betty, 354, 356
Calorie Control Council, 159
Calories
 amount available for consumption, per capita per day, 22
 definition of, 41
 intake level
  for aged, 382-83
  for infants, 196, 197
 from sugar consumption, 153-54
Calories-plus-nutrients foods, 252-53
Calorigenic agents,
 as treatment of obesity, 73
Cancer, 243
 animal studies on, 273
 and dietary fiber, 145-46, 149
 epidemiologic studies on, 270-73
 food as factor in etiology of, 269-77
 incidence of, 339
 mortality from, and cholesterol intake, 284
 nutrition
  problems caused by, 338-42
  problems caused by treatment of, 266, 342-44
  relationship between diet and, 6, 75, 262-68, 273-75, 278-79
 nutrition therapy in patient, 344-45
 and obesity, 70
 and stress, 364-66
 and use of saccharin, 163, 263
Cancer cachexia, 266, 338
Capric acids, 290
Caproic acids, 290
Caprylic acids, 290
Carbamazepine, 328
Carbenicillin, 333
Carbo loading, 87
Carbohydrate loading, 254, 258
Carbohydrates
 amounts available for consumption, per capita per day, 22
 for athletes, 257
 metabolism of, 316-18
  disorders of, 208
 in national food supply, 19, 20, 21
Carbonic anhydrase, 125
Carboxypeptidase A, 125
Carcinogenesis, 262, 263-64
Carcinogenic absorption, 274
Carcinogens
 nitrosamines as, 263
 risk levels of, 27-29
 saccharin as, 23, 24, 25, 30, 156, 159-65
Cardiac glycosides, and appetite, 332
Cardiovascular disease. See Coronary heart disease
Carpenter's syndrome, 205
Carroll, Catherine, 164-65
Carroll, Margaret D., 75-84
Carruth, B. R., 241-42
Carruthers, S. G., 307-11
Castelli, William, 14, 15, 288

Catecholamines, 363
Celebral palsy, feeding children with, 208
Celiac syndrome, 340
Cellulose, 147, 149
Center for Science in the Public Interest, 23, 173
Central nervous system, effect of monosodium glutamate (MSG) on, 136-37
Cerebral arteriosclerosis, 378
Cerebrovascular disease, and obesity, 70
Chapel, Frank, 13
Check, William A., 93-94
Chelating agents, 332
Chemoprevention, 346
Chemotherapy
  effect of, on diet, 266, 331-32, 344
  interactions of vitamins with, 346-49
Chen, W-J L., 324-25
Chicago Coronary Prevention Evaluation Program, 309
Chicago School Children Study, 308
Chicken. See Poultry and poultry products
Child Care Food Program (CCFP), 222, 225
Child Nutrition Amendments (1978), 225
Childbirth, and obesity, 70
Children
  nutrient needs of, 126, 204-5
  nutritional problems of, 205-6
  and role of dietary fiber, 149-52
  and selected salted snacks, 228-33
  usual food patterns of, 150
  use of caffeine by, 173
  use of monosodium glumate (MSG) by, 136
Chinese restaurant syndrome, 137-38, 141
Chloramphenicol, 182
Chlordiazepoxide, 331
Chloride, adequate and safe intake for, 33, 36
Chlorine, use of, to purify drinking water, 120
Chlorpromazine, 331
Chlorpropamide, 330, 331
Cholecalciferol, 289, 346
Cholecystokinin, and control of eating, 71
Cholesterol, dietary, 280
  avoidance of, 3
  and cancer mortality, 284
  debate over effects of, 287-88
  in diet of persons 1-74 years, 80
  effect of, on mortality rate, 14-15
  essential need for, 290-91
  mean daily intake and percent of provided by major food groups, 81
  and noncardiovascular mortality, 285-86
  recommended daily consumption of, 281
  and saturated fat, 289-91
Cholesterol, serum
  and dietary fiber, 144, 146
  and use of saccharin, 164
Cholestyramine, 288, 343
Choline, 89
Chromium, 106, 109, 110
  adequate and safe intake for, 33, 35, 36
  deficiency in, 111
  energy ratio of foods, 114, 115
  and glucose metabolism, 113
Chronic kidney disease, 307
Chronic selenium toxicity, 123
Cimetidine, 332
Cirrhosis, 333
  and zinc metabolism, 125
Cis-diammine-chloroplatinum, 347
Citrovorum factor, 334, 347
Citrus products
  as source of absorbic acid, 19
Cleft lip and/or palate disorders in children, 208
Climatic extremes
  stress associated with, 366
  effect of vitamin C, 89
Clofibrate, 288
Coalition for Safe Food, 23
  opposition of, to Food Safety Amendments of 1981, 24
Coarctation of the aorta, 307
Cobalamin. See Vitamin B¹²
Cobalt, 108
Cobe, Patricia, 257-58
Coffee. See Caffeine
Coffee nerves, 87
Cohen's syndrome, 205
Colds, effect of Vitamin C on, 89
Colitis, ulcerative, 147, 236
Collagen synthesis, 125
Collagenase, 126
Colleges and universities offering accredited courses in agriculture, food and nutrition, 449-73
Collier, Durward R., 116-18
Collins, Thomas F., 172-73, 175
Colman, Neville, 93-94
Colon cancer, 149, 264-65, 273
Colors, artificial, 29, 31, 120
Community Nutrition Institute, 23
Congenital glutathione synthetase deficiency, 100
Congenital heart disease, feeding children with, 209-10
Congenital hypertrophic pyloric stenosis, genetic basis of, 9
Conn's syndrome, 307
Constipation
  in the aged, 371
  and dietary fiber, 144-45
Consumers Union, 280-84
Contraceptive pill. See Oral contraceptives
Cooking ware, interaction of foods with, 112-13
Copper, 106, 109
  adequate and safe intake for, 33, 34-35, 114
  deficiency, 333
  density of, in foods, 114
  dependency of, on dietary concentration of molybdenum and sulfur, 34
  depletion of
    in cancer patient, 342
  effect of fiber on utilization of, 151-52
  in human milk composition, 179
  and zinc, 106
Cori cycle, 339
Corn sirups, 154-55
Cornelia de Lange's syndrome, 205
Coronary heart disease, 243
  and diet, 6, 12-15, 75, 280-84
  and dietary fiber, 145, 149
  and lipoproteins, 296
  and magnesium, 104
  and obesity, 3, 69, 70
  and physical fitness, 250
  relationship of employment status for women, 298-306
  research on, 292-94
  risk factors related to, 26
  and sodium restriction, 369
  and stress, 364-66
  and use of saccharin, 164
Corticosteroids, 332
Cortisol, and control of eating, 71
Cortisone, and Vitamin C, 89
Cottonmouth, 249
Council for Agricultural Science and Technology, 28
Crapo, Phyllis A., 319-23
Cravioto, J., 350-61
Crohn's disease, 236
Cuprous iodine, 128
Cyanide, need for in foods, 30
Cyanocobalmin, in human milk, 178
Cyclamate
  banning of, 30
  usage of, 159, 161-62
Cyclophosphamide, 182

Cycloserine, 334
Cyproheptadine hydrochloride, 331
Cystic fibrosis, feeding children with, 210
Cystine, 219
Cystinuria, 332
Czarnecki, Susanne K., 295-97

D

Dahl-sensitive strain, 308
Daily food guide, 16-18
Dairy products, 103
  and fat, cholesterol and sodium intake, 76, 78
  iodine content of, 120
  nutritive values of, 42-45
Darby William, 93, 94
Darby William J., 132-34
Darby, William S., 168-71
Daro, August, 104
Davidson, John, 156, 157
Daycare, for the aged, 378
DDT, residues of, in food, 26
Degenerative disease, and diet, 12-15
Dehydration, 245, 246, 246-47, 253, 258, 260
Delaney amendment, 23, 24, 27
DeLuca, Hector F., 97-98
Dementia, impact of intellectual development on nutrition, 368
Dental caries, 205, 206, 243
  in adolescence, 237
  and control of carcinogenic bacteria, 315
  and diet, 4, 153, 312
  and fluorine, 35, 107, 116-18
  and oral bacteria, 312
  and protection of the teeth, 314
  and Streptococcus mutans, 312-13
  susceptibility to, 9
Depakene, 206
Dephytinizing, 111
Depression, in the aged, 368, 378-79
Desolates, nutrition of, 375
Developmental disabilities, effect of, on child nutrition, 206-10
Dexedrine, 206
Dextroamphetamine, 206, 331
Dextrose, 155
Diabesity, 243
Diabetes, 12-15, 243
  and diet, 12-15, 317
  and dietary fiber, 146, 324-25
  effect of alcohol consumption on, 326-27
  genetic basis of, 9
  and obesity, 3, 157
  and physical fitness, 250
Diazepam, 183, 206, 331
Diet
  and dental caries, 4, 153, 312, 314-15
  and disease, 6, 12-15
  and heart disease, 280-84
  and obesity, 9, 73, 317
  relationship between nutrition, cancer and, 262-68
Dietary cholesterol. See Cholesterol, dietary
Dietary fiber. See Fiber, dietary
Dietary Goals for the United States, 3
Dietary guidelines
  Considerations for new, 16-18
  USDA-DHHS, 3-4
Dietary Guidelines for Americans, 133
Diet-heart theory, 280-81
  complicating factors, 283
  experimental evidence for, 281-82
  grounds for skepticism, 282-83
  support for, 281
Diethylnitrosamine, 348
Diethylpyrocarbonate, banning of, 27
Diethylstilbestrol (DES), in food, 28
Digitalis, 369

Digitalis cachexia, 331-32
Digoxin, 328
Dilantin, 206
Dimethylglycine hydrochloride (DMG), 93-94
DiPalma, Joseph R., 346-49
Diphenylhydantoin, 206, 334
Diphenylisatin, 371
Disease, relationship between nutrition and, 210-11, 269-70
Disulfiram, 330
Disulfiram reactions, 330
Diverticular disease, 325
Diverticulosis, and dietary fiber, 145-149
Doisy, Richard, 106
Dole, Robert, 24
Dopamine, 330
Dowager's hump, 103
Doxorubicin, 347
D-Penicillamine, 332
Drugs
 absorption of, 328-39
 abuse of, in pregnancy, 188
 and adolescent nutrition, 239
 and composition of human milk, 179, 205
 effects of food on, 328-34
 effects of, on lactating mother and infant, 181-84
 and nutrition in aged, 369
 role of, in mineral depletion, 333-34
 and vitamins, 334-35
 and weight control, 331
Drug subculture, 239
Dumping syndrome, 343
Durabolin, 331
Dysphagia, 369
Dysplasia, 279

E

Early Periodic Screening, 211
Ectrodactyly, 172, 175
EDDI, overuse of, 122
Eggs
 consumption of, 31
 and fat, cholesterol and sodium intake, 76, 80, 283-84
 nutritive values of, 45
Elavil, 331
Elderly. See Aged
Electrolytes, stress-related demands on, 366
Employment status and employment related behaviors to incidence of coronary heart disease in women, 298-306
Encephalopathy, 307
Endometrial cancer, 279
Endometrium, and obesity, 263-64
Energy balance throughout the life cycle, 69-74
Energy Intake, Recommended, and Mean Heights and Weights, 37
 and obesity, 8, 71-72
Enteral feeding, 209
Environment, role of, in cancer, 271
Equivalents by volume and weight, 40
Ergogenic supplements, 254-55
Ergonovine maleate, effect of, on lactation, 182
Ergot alkaloids, effect of, on nutrient metabolism, 369
Ergot derivatives, effect of, on lactation, 182
Ergotrate, 182
Erogenic dietary aids, 245, 249
Ertel, Norman H., 316-18
Erythrosine, 120
Esophagectomy, 343
Estimated adequate and safe intakes, 33-34, 113
 of biotin, 33, 36

of chloride, 33, 36
of chromium, 33, 35, 36
of copper, 33, 34-35, 114
of fluoride, 34, 35, 36, 114
of fluorne, 33
of manganese, 33, 34, 35, 36, 114
of molybdenum, 33, 35, 37, 114
obstacles to implementation of 37-38
of panthothenic acid, 33, 36
of potassium, 33, 36, 254
of selenium, 33, 35, 36, 114
of sodium, 4, 33, 36, 253-54
Ethacrynic acid, 333
Ethanol, 188, 329
Ethoxyquin, role of, in cancer etiology, 273
Ethylenediamine dihydroiodide (EDDI), 120
Exercise
 calories burned per minute, 258
 energy cost of, 246
 and nutrition, 250-56
 relationship to physical condition, 252
 as treatment of obesity, 73
Expanded Food and Nutrition Education Program, 211
Extopic hormones, 340-41
Exudative diathesis, 123

F

Fad diets, 239, 245, 248-49, 364-66
Fasting, for athletes, 258
Fat and fat intake, 76, 78
 amount available for consumption, per capita per day, 22
 avoidance of, 3
 in composition of human milk, 178
 consumption of, in elderly, 370
 in diet of persons 1-74 years, 75, 77-80
 digestion of, and tension, 364-66
 hard or soft, 284
 in national food supply, 19, 20, 21
 nutritive values of, 45-46
Fatigue, use of Vitamin B^{12} to cure, 88
FD&C Red No. 2, 29
FD&C Red No. 3, 120
FD&C Yellow No. 5, 31
Federal Older Americans Act (1965), 370, 376
Federal Trade Commission (FTC), 3
Federation of American Societies for Experimental Biology (FASEB), 4, 30, 153, 157, 173, 176
Federation of Homemakers, 23
Feeding problems, in children, 207-8
Feingold Associates, 23
Feinlieb, Manning, 298-306
Female. See Women
Fenfluramine, 331
Fenner, Louise, 128-31
Ferguson, S. K., 324-25
Fetal alcohol syndrome, 166, 185-89
Fetal malnutrition, 204
Fetus, effect of monosodium glumate (MSG) on, 136
Fiber, crude,
 comparison of dietary fiber and, 145, 149
Fiber, dietary, 4
 as not a single entity, 258
 for athletes, 258
 benefits from, 144-46, 149-50
 comparison of crude fiber and, 145, 149
 content of foods, 151
 definition of, 144
 dietary recommendations of, 147
 and disease prevention, 149
 food sources of, 147
 impact of, on glucose metabolism of persons with diabetes, 324-25
 recommendations on, 150-51
 role of, in cancer etiology, 273-74
 too much, 146-47

Fish, 119
 and fat, cholesterol and sodium intake, 76
 nutritive values of, 47
Flagyl, 182-83, 347
Flavor enhancers, 30, 263
Flight or fright syndrome, 363
Fluoridation
 dental and medical benefits of, 116-17
 process of, and fluorine, 116
 safety of, 117
Fluoride
 adequate and safe intake of, 34, 35, 36, 114
 deficiencies of, in aged, 382
 and dental caries, 206, 314
 need for supplementary, for infants, 202-3
Fluorine, 107, 110
 adequate and safe intake for, 33
 dental and medical benefits of, 116-17
 and dental caries, 116-18
 in human milk composition, 179
 safety of, 117
Fluorouracil therapy, 348
Flush reactions, 330
Flushing, 88
Folacin
 deficiency, 206-7, 241, 334
 depletion, 335
 Recommended Dietary Allowances (RDAs) of, 36
Folate, 88-89, 91
 deficiencies of, in aged, 368
 metabolism, 241
Folic acid, 278
 in composition of human milk, 178
 deficiency of, and immunologic functions, 216, 217
Folk medicine, meaning of, to aged, 375
Food(s)
 adverse drug reactions caused by, 329, 30
 dimensions of, 355-56
 effects of, on drug absorption and bioavailability, 328-29
 as factor in etiology of cancer, 269-77
 interaction of cooking ware with, 112-13
 needed increase in supply of, 31-32
 nutritive values of, 40-68
 as positive social factor for aged, 376-78
 psychological aspects of, 259-60
 regulatory mechanisms for control of intake, 71-72
 and risks of death, 26-27
Food additives, 23, 24, 27, 160
 and coloring, 29, 31, 120
 and hyperactivity, 207, 331
 and the risk/benefit concept, 30
 and sodium nitrates, 263
Food and Beverage Trades Department, 23
Food and Drug Administration (FDA), 3, 159, 163, 164, 175-76
Food energy. See Calories
Food faddism, 239, 245, 248-49, 364-66
Food groups, contribution of major, to national food supply, 20
Food and nutrition-related associations in the U.S., 400-48
Food and Nutrition Service (FNS), 222-27
Food Safety Amendments of 1981, 23
Food for Sport (Smith), 258
Food Stamps, 211, 371
Food technologists, 275
Food, Drug and Cosmetic Act (1955), 24, 41, 142
Food Additives amendment to, 23, 24, 27, 160
Foot rot, 120
Forbes, Allan L., 140-43

544 INDEX

Forbes, Gilbert B., 8-9
Formon, Samuel J., 180, 191
Four food groups, 16-18
Fragile sites and somatic mutations
  concept of, 279
Framingham (Massachusetts) Heart Study,
  14, 70, 243, 280, 285, 288, 298
Fratalli, Victor, 157
Friends of the Earth, 23
Fructose, 155, 156-58, 314, 316-23
Fructose intolerance, 208
Fruits and fruit products
  and fat, cholesterol and sodium
    intake, 76
  nutritive values of, 50-54
  servings per day from inverse
    pyramid food guide, 17
Furadantin, 183
Furazolidone, 330
Furosemide, 333

G

Galactose, 208
Galactosemia, 9, 208
Gall bladder disease, and obesity,
  3, 69, 70
Gamma carboxyglutamic acid (Gla), 347-48
Ganglioneuroblastoma, 340
Gardner, Sherwin, 25
Gastrectomy, 343
Gastric bypass, as treatment of obesity, 73
Gastric emptying, 254
Gastro-colic fistulas, 340
Gastrojejunal anastamosis, 344
Gavage study, 176
General adaptation syndrome, 363
Generally recognized as safe (GRAS)
  list, 30
  and caffeine, 173
  and monosodium glutamate (MSG), 138
  and saccharine, 160
  and salt intake, 132-33
  and sodium, 128, 129
Gesell Scales of Development, 356, 357
Giardiasis, 183
Glucagon, 71, 363
Glucocorticoids, 331, 333, 363
Gluconeogenesis, 339, 363, 365
Glucose, 155, 324-25
Glutathione perosidase, 123
Glycogen loading, 245, 247-48, 254, 259
Glycogen, role of vitamin E in
  improved storage of, 92
Glycogen storage disease, 208
Glycogenolysis, 363
Glycosuria, 317, 344
Goiter, 107, 119, 120, 122, 128
Goodrich, William, 25
Gore, Robert, 24
Gori, Gio B., 269-77
Gottlieb, William, 85-92, 102-9
Gout, 70, 246
Goyan, Jere E., 161, 163, 174
Grains and grain products
  and fat, cholesterol and
    sodium intake, 76, 78
  nutritive values of, 54-61
  servings per day from inverse
    pyramid food guide, 17
Grant support programs in food science,
  agriculture, and nutrition, 474-501
GRAS list. See Generally recognized as
  safe (GRAS) list
Grass staggers, 102
Grassley, Charles, 24
Gray, Fred, 154, 155
Gray, George, 175
Greeley, Sharon, 125-27
Griseofulvin, 328-29, 330
Grocery Manufacturers of America, 25

Gross, Ludwik, 107
Growth hormone, 71, 363
Guar gum, and appetite, 332
Gynecomastia, 99, 182

H

Haas, Ellen, 23
Hackler, Tim, 287-88
Handicapped children, nutritional
  problems of, 206-10
Harper, Alfred E., 6, 7
Harpinden caliper, 238
Hartnup's disease, 208
Hashimoto's thyroiditis, 122
Hatch Act, 23-25
Hatch, Orrin, 23
Hausman, Patricia, 12-15
Hayakawa, S. I., 25
Hayes, Arthur Hull, Jr., 24, 160, 161, 162
Haynes, Suzanne G., 298-306
Head Start, 211
Healthy People, 3, 133
Heart disease. See Coronary heart disease
Heartbook (American Heart Association), 289
Heat exhaustion, 260
Heatstroke, 104-5
Height-weight tables, use of, to
  determine whether athlete is under or
  over weight, 260
Heinz Infant Feeding Study, 177
Helms, Jesse, A., 24
Heme iron, 95, 105
Hemicellulose, 149
Hemiplegia, 379
Hemochromatosis, 31
Hemolytic anemia, 183, 241, 333
Hemorrhagic stroke, 307
Hemorrhoids, and need for bioflavonoids, 92
Henkin, Robert, 103
Hepatic resection, 344
Herbert, Victor, 93, 94
Heroin, effect of vitamin C on, 89
Heslin, Jo-Ann, 373-80
Hiatal hernia, and dietary fiber, 146
High blood pressure. See Hypertension
High Performance Diet, 258
High-density lipoproteins (HDLs), 283,
  287, 290, 292
High-fructose corn syrup (HFCS), use of,
  and higher carbohydrate level, 19-20
Histidinemia, 208
Hodgkins disease, 330, 339, 342
Home Health Services for aged, 371
Homocystinuria, 208
Honey, 155
Honolulu Heart Study, 285
Hookworm, 170
Hoover, Robert, 160-61, 163
Hormones
  and control of eating, 71
  role of, in cancer etiology, 274
Horvitz, Norman, 10-11
Host defenses, benefits and problems of
  marginal malnutrition on, 215
Hot-cold theory of disease, 375
Huddleston, Walter, 24
Hull, Peter Barton, 25
Human milk composition. See Milk
  composition, human
Human performance, role of nutrition in,
  245-49
Human research, and obesity, 8-9
Humoral satiety signals, 71
Hunger, as component of eating
  behavior, 9
Hursh, Laurence, 259-61
Hyaluronidase, 347
Hydralazine, 328
Hydrochlorothiazide, 328
Hydroxyzine hydrochloride, 331

Hyperactivity, 207, 331
Hyperalimentation, 365
Hypercalcemia, 333
Hypercalciuria, 333
Hypercellular obesity, 72-73
Hypercholesterolemia, 217, 219
Hyperlipoproteinemias, 296
Hyperoxaluria, 343
Hyperphagic agents, 331
Hyperplasis, 344
Hyperplastic obesity, 72-73
Hypertension, 99, 243
  animal model for, 308
  borderline, 141
  dietary control of, 142-43, 269,
    308-11, 371-72
  effect of, on mortality, 14-15
  and obesity, 3, 69, 70, 309
  and salt intake, 6, 133, 307-8
  and sodium intake, 129, 140, 369
  and stress, 364-66
Hyperthyroidism, treatment of, 122
Hypertonic solutions, 254
Hypertriglyceridemia, 322
Hypertrophic obesity, 72-73
Hyperuricemia, 246
Hypervalinemia, 208
Hypervitaminosis A, 346
Hypoalbuminemia, 340-41
Hypocholesterolemic effect, 149
Hypoglobulinemia, 340
Hypoglycemia, 188, 326, 330, 343
Hypoglycemic agents, 331
Hypoglycemic reactions, 330
Hypogonadal dwarfism, 106, 126
Hypokalemia, 309, 333
Hypomagnesemia, 325
Hypoparathyroidism, 98
Hypophagic agents, 331
Hypophosphatemia, effect of, on
  breast-fed infant, 183
Hypothyroidism, 119, 371
Hypovitaminoses, 334-35
Hyprchromic microcytic anemia, 369

I

Idiopathic scoliosis, genetic basis of, 9
Ikeda, Kikunae, 135
Imipramine, 206
Imipramine HCl, 239
Immune system dysfunction, 216
Immunity
  effects of malnutrition on humoral, 214
  malnutrition and mucosal, 214-15
  nutritional suppression of cellular, 215
Immuno-deficiency, 214
Infancy
  effect of medications on, 181-84
  iodine intake of, 119-20
  nutrition during, 169-70, 190-201, 204
  obesity in, 203
Inflammatory bowel diseases, in
  adolescence, 236
Inositol, 89
INQ (Index of Nutrient Quality), 235
Insomnia, and magnesium, 104
Institute of Food Technologists' Expert
  Panel on Food Safety and Nutrition,
  26-32, 135-39, 144-48
Insulin
  and chromium, 106
  and control of eating, 71
Intestinal resection, 343-44
Iodine, 107, 109, 119-22
  Recommended Dietary Allowances
    (RDAs) for, 36
  sources of, in adult diet, 121
  use of, to purify drinking water, 120
Iodine 131, effect of, on breast-fed infant, 183
Iodophors, 120, 122

Iron, 95, 105, 109
 and absorbic acid, 95-96, 111
 amount available for consumption, per capita per day, 22
 availability of, for absorption, 34
 calculation of available dietary, 38
 compounding of, with phytates, 107
 deficiencies in, 333-34
  in adolescent pregnancy, 241
  in aged, 369, 370, 381
 food values for, 41
 in human milk composition, 179
 intake for infants, 191, 200-201, 202
 in national food supply, 19-21
 Recommended Dietary Allowances (RDAs) for, 36, 111
  for women, 170
Iron deficiency, 113
 effect of, on breast-fed infant, 183
 effect of, on immunologic functions, 216, 219
Iron deficiency anemia, 31, 96, 106, 169, 205, 206, 236, 334, 335
Irritable bowel syndrome, and dietary fiber, 149
Isocarboxazid, 329
Isolates, nutrition of, 375
Isoniazid, 334
Isovaleric acidemia, 208
IUD, and need for bioflavonoids, 92

J

Jacobson, Michael, 25, 163-65
James, Thomas N., 284, 292-94
Jaw wiring, as treatment of obesity, 73
Jejuno-colic fistulas, 340
Jejunoileal bypass, as treatment of obesity, 73
Jepson, Roger W., 24
Johnson, Guy H., 190-201
Journal of the American Medical Association (JAMA), 13
Jowsey, Jennifer, 103
Junk foods, 234-35

K

Karnel, William B., 288
Karounos, D., 324-25
Katz, Harold, 10
Kaufmann, William, 87
Kennedy, Ted, 25
Keshan disease, 123, 124
Ketoacidosis, 327
Ketosis, 246, 327
Keys, Ancel, 281
Kidney stones, and magnesium, 104
Kidneys
 cancer of, 263-64
 and hypertension, 307
Knochel, James, 104
Kolterman, Orville G., 319-23
Korbut, Olga, 86
Korsakoff syndrome, 188
Krebs, Ernst, Sr., and Jr., 93
Kritchevsky, David, 295-97
Kummerow, Fred A., 289-91
Kwashiorkor, 169, 214, 351

L

L-dopa, effect of, on taste, 369
L-prostacyclin, 288
La Leche League International, Inc., 182
Lebeling, nutrition, 130, 142, 143
Lactating mothers
 effect of medications on, 181-84
 See also Breast feeding; Milk composition, human
Lacto-ovo-vegetarians, 234
Lactose, 9, 155
Laetrile, 87, 93, 267
Lange caliper, 238
Lateral hypothalamus, and control of eating, 71
Laurence-Moon-Biedl syndrome, 205
Laxatives, 371
Lead, 110
 effect of, on iron, 105
 and need for calcium, 103
 and need for zinc, 106
 and pollution, 102
Learning, effect of nutrition on, 350-61
Lecithin, 89
Lecos, Chris W., 153-55, 156-58, 159-62, 172-74
Legumes (dry), nuts, seeds, and related products and fat, cholesterol and sodium intake, 76
 nutritive values of, 61
Leucine-sensitive hypoglycemia, 208
Leucovorin, 346
Leukemia, 333, 339
Levodopa, 334
Levulose, 155
Levy, Robert I., 13
Lexander, Orville A., 123-24
Libraries specializing in agriculture, food and nutrition volumes, 385-99
Librium, 331
Lignin, 149
Limited nutritional value, 235
Linoleic acid, 75, 79, 290,
Lipids
 effect of, on immunologic function, 219-20
 influence of saccharin on metabolism of, 164-65
Lipolysis, 363
Lipoproteinemias, typing of, 296
Lipoproteins, 243
 characteristics of hyperlipoproteinemias, 296
 and heart disease, 296
 separation of the various, 295-96
Lithium, effect of, on breast-fed infant, 183
Liver disease, and obesity, 70
Localized nutrient deficiency, concept of, 278-79
Longevity, myth of, and diet, 368
Low density lipoproteins (LDLs), 283, 287, 290, 295
Luxury foods, servings per day from inverse pyramid food guide, 17
Lymphocytopenia, 340
Lymphoid tissue atrophy, 216
Lymphoma, 340
Lynch, Sean R., 95-96

M

Macho syndrome, 239
Machta, Phyllis, 12-15
Macrocrystalline nitrofurantoin, 328
Macrodantin, 183
Magazines covering food and nutrition, 502-11
Magnesium, 102, 104, 109
 amount available for consumption per capita per day, 22
 compounding of, with phytates, 107
 deficiency, 333
 depletion, 342
  in cancer patient, 343-44
 effect of fiber on utilization of 151-52
 effect of, on immunologic function, 219
 and fluorine, 107
 in human milk composition, 179
 in national food supply, 19-21
 Recommended Dietary Allowances (RDAs) for, 36
Malabsorption, in cancer patient, 343-44
Malnutrition, 204, 240
 in adolescence, 238-40
 in the aged, 378-79
 benefits and problems of marginal, on host defenses, 215
 and cancer, 262, 344-45
 and disease, 214
 effect of, on humoral immunity, 214
 effect of, on mental development, 269, 350-61
 effect of, on pregnancy, 187-88
 identification of, 210
 and mass media, 353-54
 and mucosal immunity, 214-15
Maltitol, 155
Mandibulectomy, 343
Manganese, 107, 109
 adequate and safe intake for, 33, 34, 35, 36, 114
 in human milk consumption, 179
Mannitol, 155-56
Mantel-Bryan concept of virtual food safety, 29
Maple syrup urine disease, 208
Marasmus, 214
Marijuana, effect of, on breast-fed infant, 183
Markasis, Pericles, 107
Marplan, 329
Marston, Ruth M., 19-22
Mass media, and malnutrition, 353-54
Mastitis, 120
Maternal Behavior Profile, 354
Mathandrosterolone, 331
Maturity-onset diabetes, and obesity, 69, 70
McCollum, E. V., 132
McGovern, George, 6, 129
McMichael, Robert, 346-49
Meals on Wheels programs, 371, 377
Meat and meat products
 and fat, cholesterol and sodium intake, 76, 77-78
 nutritive values of, 47-49
Medications. *See* Drugs
Medium-chain triglyceriders (MCT), 343
Megaloblastic anemia, 178, 335
Megavitamin therapy
 for the aged, 382
 for cancer, 266-67, 346-49
Mellaril, 206
Memory, effect of vitamin B^6 on, 88
Menstruation
 and need for bioflavonoids, 92
 and vitamin A, 86-87
Mental development, effect of nutrition on, 350-61
Meprobamate, 331
Merrill, Richard A., 24
Mertz, Walter, 33-39, 110-15
Metabolic disease, hereditary control of, 208
Metalloproteins, 125
Metaprolol, 329
Methergine, 182
Methimazole, 183
Methionine, 219
Methodone, 183
Methotrexate, 331-34, 346-48
Methyl cellulose, and appetite, 332
Methyldopa hypersensitivity, 333
Methylergonovine, 182
Methylmalonia aciduria, 208
Methylphenidate, 206, 331
Methylphenidate HCl, 239
Metoprolol, 328

Metronidazol, 347
Metronidazole, 182-83, 330
Meyer, H., 238-40
Microwaves, effect of, on folates, 88-89
Mid-arm circumference (MAC), 238
Mid-arm muscle circumference (MAMC), 238
Milk and milk products
 consumption of, by athletes, 249
 See also Dairy products
Milk composition, human drugs in, 205
 effect of normal psychological factors on, 177
 effect of premature birth on, 179-80
 environmental factors
  maternal dietary intake, 177-79
  maternal drug ingestion, 179
  maternal ingestion of contaminants, 179
 factors affecting human, 177
Milk fever, 102
Milk sugar, 155
Miller, Roger W., 140-43
Miner's cramps, 133
Minerals
 in composition of human milk, 179
 depletion of
  role of drugs in 333-34
 level of, in cancer patients, 342
 status of, and dietary fiber, 324-25
 stress-related demands on, 366
 See also specific
Molybdenum, 108, 110
 adequate and safe intake of, 33, 35, 36, 37, 114
Monoamine oxidase inhibitor drugs, 329-30
Monosodium glutamate (MSG), 130, 135-36, 138, 141
 acute and chronic toxicity studies, 136
 and the "Chinese restaurant syndrome," 137-38
 effect of, on central nervous system, 136-37
 effect of, on fetus and young children, 136
 and generally recognized as safe (GRAS) list, 138
 regulatory status of, 138
 safety of, 137
Mono-unsaturated fats, 75, 280
Monte, Tom, 12-15
Morgan, K. S., 228-33
Mormons, risk of cancer among, 272
Mouth blindness, 266
Multiple Risk Factor Intervention Trial (MRFIT), 14
Muscle cramps, and need for calcium, 103
Muscle mass, role of exercise in increasing, 246
Musculoskeletal disorders, and obesity, 70
Myasthenia gravis, 107
Myelomeningocele, 205
 feeding children with, 210

N

Nardil, 206, 329
National Academy of Sciences (NAS), 3, 4, 159, 160, 166
National Aeronautics and Space Administration (NASA), 377
National Cancer Institute (NCI), 29, 163
National Coffee Association, 174
National Consumer League, 23
National Council of Senior Citizens, 23
National Dairy Council, 69-74, 222-27, 245-49, 262-68, 362-67
National food supply
 contribution of major food groups to, 20
 nutrient content of, 19-22
National Health, Lung and Blood Institute (NHLBI), 13, 142, 284, 285
National Health and Nutrition Examination Survey (NHANES) I, 75
National Institutes of Health (NIH), 4, 14, 285-86
National Nutrition Consortium Board, 4
National Research Council (NRC), 3, 6, 166, 191, 287, 292-93
National School Lunch Act, 225
National School Lunch Program (NSLP), 222, 223-24
National Soft Drink Association, 24-25
Natow, Annette B., 373-80
Natural toxicants
 in food substances, 29-30
 and the risk/benefit concept, 29-30
NCBR (Nutrient Calorie Benefit Ratio), 235
Neoplastic tissues, radiosensitivity of, 347
Neuromotor feeding problems, 207
Neutral steroids, relationship between diet, bile acids, and, 264
Neutropenia, 182
Newborn
 feeding problems of, in intensive care unit, 208-9
 goiter in, 122
 See also Infants
Newman, G., 169
Niacin, 20, 87-88, 90, 346
 amount available for consumption, per capita per day, 22
 average intake for infants, 192, 193
 deficiencies
  in aged, 368, 381
  in cancer patient, 348
 food values for, 41
 in national food supply, 19, 20, 21
 Recommended Dietary Allowances (RDAs) for, 36
Niacinamide, 88
Nickle, 110
Nickles, Don, 24
Nicotine acid, 288
Nicotinic acid, 88, 178
Nilevar, 331
Nitrite
 need for in foods, 30, 263
 safety of 25, 263
Nitrofurantoin, 183, 328
Nitrosamines, 263
Nolan, William, 288
Noncardiovascular mortality, and cholesterol, 285-86
Nonheme iron, 38, 95-96, 105
Norepinephrine, 71, 330
Norethandrolone, 331
Nucleotidyltransferases, 126
Nursing. See Breast feeding; Lactating mothers
Nutri/System Weight Loss Medical Centers, success of, 10-11
Nutrition Policy Issues, 3-5
 guidelines for Americans, 3
Nutrients
 amount available for consumption per capita per day, 22
 contribution of major food groups to supplies of 20-21
 effects of drugs on absorption of, 332-33
 interactions with drugs, 206-7
Nutrition
 and the aged, 368-72, 381-83
 and cancer, 266-67, 278-79, 344-45
 effect of psychosocial forces on, 373-80
 effect of, on stimulation, mental development, and learning, 350-61
 and human performance, 245-49
 and hypertension, 307-11
 and immunity, 214-15
 and physical fitness, 250-56
 relationship between diet, cancer and, 262-68, 274
 relationship between disease and, 269-70
 relationship of, to woman's health, 168-71
 role of excess or deficient, in cancer etiology, 274
 as science, 85
 sociology of 375-76
 and stress, 364-66
Nutrition and Cancer, 278
Nutrition education, 4, 7, 269
Nutrition and the M.D., 234-40
Nutritional counseling, 204
Nutritional labeling, 130, 142, 143
Nutritional muscular dystrophy, 123
Nyad, Diana 89

O

Obesity, 243
 and adipose tissue cellularity, 72-73
 in adolescence, 236-37
 in the aged, 379
 and cancer, 263-64
 in children, 205-6
 and compulsive overeating, 364-66
 consequences of, 70-71
 in diet, 9, 317
 and dietary fiber, 149
 and energy intake and expenditure, 71-72
 as genetic disease, 8-9
 and hypertension, 309
 importance of control, 6-7
 incidence of, 69-70
 in infancy, 203
 linkage of, to disease, 3, 69
 multifactorial etiology of, 71-73
 and nutrition, 269
 treatment of, 10-11, 73, 331
 types of, 72-73
Obligatory energy expenditure, 72
Offals, as source of vitamin A, 19
Olefsky, Jerrold M., 319-23
Oleic acid, 79-80, 290
Olson, Robert E., 6, 7, 100
O'Malley, L., 324-25
100-fold safety factor, 29
Oral contraceptives
 and deficiency of vitamin B⁶, 86
 effect of, on human milk composition, 178
 effect of, on lactation, 182
 use of, and nutritional chantes, 334-35
Oral glucose tolerance testing (OGTT), 316
Organ meats, 123
Orthomolecular psychiartry, 207
Orthomolecular therapy, 346-47
Orthotuluensulfonamide (OTS), 160
Oski, F. A., 99
Osteoarthritis, 70
Osteomalacia, 333
Osteoporosis, 98, 103, 382
Ovellette, E. M., 185-89
Overnutrition. See obesity
Oxytocin, 179

P

PABA (Para-aminobenzoic acid), 89
Palmitic acid, 290
Pancreatectomy, 344
Pancreatic cholera, 340
Pancreatic insufficiency, 210, 344
Pancytopenia, 181
Pangamic acid, 87, 93-94, 267

Panthothenic acid, 89, 91
  adequate and safe intake for, 33, 36
  in composition of human milk, 178
  effect of deficiency in, on
    immunologic function, 217
Pape, Stuart, 25
Parakeratosis, 125
Parkinson's disease, 379
Parnate, 329
Pauling, Linus, 85
PCBs (Polychorinated biphenyls)
  in human milk composition, 179
  neutralization of, by vitamins A
    and C, 86
PCM (protein-calorie malnutrition), 169
Pectin, 145, 147, 149
Pediatrics, 180
Pellagra, 85, 87
Penicillamine, 333, 334
Penicillin, 333
Pennington, Jean A. T., 16-18
Peptic ulcers, 239
Periactin, 331
Peripheral vascular disease, 70
Pernicious anemia, 88
Pharmacological agents, and obesity, 73
Phenelzine, 206, 329
Phenobarbital, 206, 334
Phenothiazine, 207, 331
Phenylalanine, 208, 219
Phenylketonuria (PKU), 208
Pheochromocytoma, 307, 340
Phlebitis, and dietary fiber, 146
Phosphate depletion syndrome, 333
Phosphates, effect of, on iron, 105
Phospholipid, 290, 295
Phosphorus, 104, 109
  amount available for consumption,
    per capita per day, 22
  average intake for infants, 198, 199
  in human milk composition, 179
  interaction of, with protein, 111-12
  in national food supply, 19, 20, 21
  Recommended Dietary Allowances
    (RDAs) for, 36
Phosphorus-calcium ratio, 104
Phyridoxal phosphate, 347
Physical fitness. See Exercise
Phytate, 126
  and compounds of zinc, calcium,
    magnesium, and iron, 107
Pickles, nutritive values of some, 67
Pill. See Oral contraceptives
Pines, Wayne, 163
PL 92-433, 225
PL 93-326, 226
PL 93-150, 226
PL 94-105, 223, 225, 226
PL 95-166, 225, 227
PL 95-627, 226
PL 96-499, 225, 226
Placental transfer, 136
Polyunsaturated fats, 75, 280
Polyunsaturated fatty acids (PUFAs),
  219, 289
Polyvinyl chloride, banning of, 27
Pondimin, 331
Pork, as source of thiamin, 19
Postpartum blues, 88
Potassium, 104-5, 109
  adequate and safe intake for, 33,
    36, 254
  depletion, 333
    in cancer patients, 342
  need for, 103, 235
  and nutrition labeling, 130
  and sodium, 104-5
Potassium iodine, 128
Poultry and poultry products
  and fat, cholesterol and sodium
    intake, 76
  nutritive values of, 49-50

Prader-Willi's syndrome, 205
Prednisolone, 182
Preeclampsia, 104, 241
Pre-event meal, 247, 255, 259
Pregnancy, 126
  and need for vitamin B^6, 88
  nutrition needs of women during,
    170-71
  and obesity, 70
  and use of caffeine, 172, 174
  See also Adolescent pregnancy
Premature birth, effect of, on human
  milk composition, 179-80
Premature infants, feeding problems of,
  208-9
Pritikin diet, 12-15
Pritikin Program for Diet and
  Exercise, 13
Pritikin, Nathan, 12-15
Procarbazine, 330
Project Methuselah, 99
Prolactin, and stress, 363
Propionic acidemia, 208
Propoxygphene, 328
Propranolol, 329, 329
Propylithiouracil, 183
Prostaglandins, 363
Protease inhibitors in cancer
  etiology, 273
Protein
  amount available for consumption,
    per capita per day, 22
  average intake for infants, 196, 197
  in composition of human milk, 178
  deficiency of
    and adolescent pregnancy, 241
    and alcohol, 332
  for athletes, 235, 246, 257, 258
  interaction of, with minerals, 111-12
  metabolism of, and stress, 365
  in national food supply, 19-21
  needs of aged for, 370
  and osteoporosis, 103
  as percentage of caloric intake, 251
  Recommended Dietary Allowances
    (RDAs) for, 36
  servings per day from inverse
    pyramid food guide, 17

Protein biosynthesis, 363
Prothrombin, 347-48
Pseudo-Cushing syndrome, 179
Psychiatric illness, influence of, on
  food intake, 368
Psychoactive drugs, use of, during
  pregnancy, 187
Psychosocial factors
  and control of eating, 71-72
  effect of, on nutrition, 373-80
Psychotropic drugs
  effect of, on appetite, 331
  effect of, on breast-fed infant, 183
Psyllium seed, 371
Publishing opportunities in food and
  nutrition, 512-35. See also Book
  publishers
Puerto Rico Heart Study, 285
Pulmonary embolism, 99
Pulmonary impairment, and obesity, 70
Purvis, George A., 190-201
Pyridoxine, 88, 90, 346
  and chemotherapy, 347
  in composition of human milk, 178
  deficiency of
    in adolescent pregnancy, 241
    effect of, on immunologic functions,
      216, 217
  effect of, on lactation, 182
  and magnesium, 104
  metabolism of, 334
  pharmacologic doses of, 207

Q

Quayle, Dan, 24

R

Radiation therapy, effect of, on
  nutrition status of patient, 342-43
Radioimmune assays, 346
Radiopharmaceuticals, 183
Radiotherapy, effect of, on diet, 266
Rapeseed oil controversy, 293
Raw sugar, 155
Recommended Dietary Allowances (RDAs)
  in adolescence, 236
  during adolescent pregnancy, 241
  for the aged, 369, 370, 377
  for ascorbic acid, 36
  for calcium, 36
  dynamic nature of, 33
  for folacin, 36
  for iodine, 36
  for iron, 36, 111
  for magnesium, 36
  for niacin, 36
  for phosphorus, 36
  for protein, 36
  relationship to physical
    conditioning program, 251-52
  for riboflavin, 36
  and stress, 364-66
  for thiamin, 36
  for vitamin A, 36
  for vitamin D, 36
  for vitamin E, 36
  for zinc, 126
Red cell glutathione reducatase assay, 335
Renal artery stenosis, 307
Renal disease, 70, 307
Renal osteodystrophy, 98
Respiratory distress syndrome, 334
Resting metabolic expenditure (RME), 365
Retinoid deficiency, 346
Rheumatoid arthritis, 332
Riboflavin, 87, 90, 328, 346
  amount available for consumption,
    per capita per day, 22
  average intake for infants, 192, 193
  in composition of human milk, 178
  deficiencies in, 334, 335
    in adolescent pregnancy, 241
    in aged, 370, 381
    in cancer patient, 348
  effect of, on antibiotics and
    tranquilizers, 87
  food values for, 41
  in national food supply, 19, 20, 21
  Recommended Dietary Allowances
    (RDAs) for, 36
  use of, in treatment of boric acid
    poisoning, 334
Riboflavin-5-Phosphate, 328
Richardson, Martha, 40-68
Richmond, Julius, 282
Rickets, 85, 178, 202, 205, 269
Risk-benefit analysis, application of,
  to food, 24, 26-32
Ritalin, 206, 207
Rivlin, R. S., 381-83
Roberts, Howard, 25
Roberts, Hyman, J., 99-101
Roe, Daphne A., 328-37
Rogers, Paul, 25
Rorie, James, 175
Rosett, Henry L., 185-89

S

Saccharin, 319

ban on 23-25, 30
and cancer, 163, 263
future of, 156
and generally recognized as safe (GRAS) list, 160
influence on lipid metabolism of, 164-65
safety of, 163-65
usage of, 159-61
Saccharin Study and Labeling Act (1977), 160
Safe intakes. *See* Estimated adequate and safe intakes
Sage, Paul, 93
Salt Institute, 129
Salt tablets, 254, 258, 260
Salt, dietary
  acute depletion of, 133
  addition of iodine to, 119, 128
  appetite for, 132
  composition of, 128
  controversy on intake limitation, 133
  differences between sodium and, 128-29
  estimates of intake, 132-33
  and generally recognized as safe (GRAS) list, 132-33
  history of, 132
  and hypertension, 6, 133, 307-10
  physiological requirements for, 132
  recommendations for restricting in processed foods, 130
  substitutes for, 130-31
  toxicity of excessive, 133
  uses of, 128
  See also Sodium
Salted snack foods, impact of, on diet of children, 228-33
Sandstead, Harold H., 125-27
Saturated fat and fatty acids
  age patterns of consumption of, 78-79
  avoidance of, 3
  and cholesterol, 289-91
  essential need for, 289-90
  intake of, 75
  role of, in cardiovascular disease, 280
Schachtele, C. R., 312-15
Schistosomisis, 170
Schizophrenia, as mistaken for pellagra, 87
Schoenberger, James, 284
School Breakfast Program (SBP), 222, 224
School lunch program, beginning of, 3
Schrauzer, Gerald, 107
Schroeder, Henry, 102, 103
Schweiker, Richard S. HHS Secretary, 160,
Scientific study, anatomy of, 175-76
Scurvy, 9, 269
Seafood, 47, 76, 123, 283-84
Seatangle, 135
Selenium, 107, 108, 109, 110, 123
  adequate and safe intake for, 33, 35, 36, 114
  biochemical role of, 123
  dietary intakes of, 124
  dietary requirements for, 124
  dietary scources of, 123-24
  effect of, on immunologic function, 219
  and human health, 123, 124
  relationship between vitamin E and, 123
  role of, in cancer etiology, 273
Seligsohn, Mel, 23-25
Senate Select Committee on Nutrition and Human Needs, 3, 6, 129-30, 307, 376
Senile deterioration, 378
Senility, 378
Senior citizens. *See* Aged/aging
Sepsis, 365
Serotonin, 71, 88
Serum cholesterol. *See* Cholesterol, serum

Seventh-Day Adventists
  intake of saturated fat/cholesterol of, and heart disease 282
  risk of cancer among, 263, 272
Sexual maturation, and need for zinc, 106
Shellfish
  and fat, cholesterol and sodium intake, 76, 283-84
  nutrititive values of, 47
Shils, Maurice E., 338-45
Short bowl syndrome, 332
Sieling, B., 324-25
Silicon, 108, 110
Silverman, Richard, 25
Simon, Sir John, 169
Sipping study, 176
Skinfold measurements, use of, to determine body fat level, 251
Smith, Nathan, 258
Smoking
  during pregnancy, 187, 188
  effect of, on mortality rate, 14-15
  and need for vitamin C, 92
  and relative risk of cancer, 270, 271
Snack foods, impact of selected salted, 228-33
Snacking, in adolescence, 234
Sodium, 105, 109
  adequate and safe intake for, 4, 33, 36, 253-54
  avoidance of too much, in diet, 4
  depletion of
    in cancer patient, 342
  diuretics and potassium deficiency, 105
  and generally recognized as safe (GRAS) list, 128, 129
  as a health problem, 140
  intake, 80-82
    for children, 231
    for diet of persons 1-74 years, 80-82
    for infants, 191, 198, 199
  need for, by adolescent athlete, 235
  need to modify consumption of, 140-43
  and nutrition labeling, 130
  and potassium, 104-5
  restriction of, for elderly, 369
Sodium ascorbate, 141
Sodium benzoate, 130
Sodium bicarbonate, 130
Sodium chloride. *See* Sodium
Sodium nitrate, 130
  banning of, 263
Sodium phosphate, 130
Soft drinks, caffeine in, 172, 174
Solanine, need for in foods, 30
Sorbitol, 155, 156, 157, 316-18
Soups, nutritive values of some, 67-68
Spasticity, 208
Special Milk Program (SMP), 222, 224-25
Special Supplemental Food Programs for Women, Infants, and Children (WIC), 3, 204, 211, 222, 225-26
Spironolactone, 328, 333
Sports anemia, 248
Spritz, Norman, 287
Stamler, Jeremiah, 15
Starch, need for, in diet, 4
Staver, Sari, 10-11
Steatorrhea, 340-343
Steroids
  effect of, on appetite, 331
  vitamin D as, 97
Stimulation, effect of nutrition on, 350-61
Stomach cancer, incidence of, in U.S., 271
Streptococcus mutans, and dental caries, 312-13, 315
Stress
  definition of, 362
  effect of, on adolescent nutrition, 239
  neuroendocrine and metabolic response to, 363-64

nutritional demands of, 364-66
and vitamin A, 86-87
Stroke Belt, 107
Substances, testing of, 29
Sucaryl, 159
Sucrose, 155, 316. *See also* Sugar and sweets
Sugar and sweets
  avoidance of too much, in diet, 4
  concern over usage of, 153-55
  and fat, cholesterol and sodium intake, 76
  history of usage, 153
  in infant foods, 190
  intake of, and dental caries, 269, 314-15
  and need for chromium, 106
  nutritive values of, 62
  role of, in diet, 153-55
  types of, 155
Sulfonylurea tolbutamide, 331
Summer Food Service Program for Children (SFSPC), 222, 225
Supermarket obesity, 71
Supplemental Food Program for Women Infants and Children (WIC), 3, 204, 211, 222, 225-26
Surgeon General, 3, 4, 129
Surgery
  for cancer, 343-44
  as treatment of obesity, 70, 73
Synthetic colors, in foods, 29, 30, 31, 120

T

Tapazole, 183
Taste disorders, and zinc deficiency, 126
Taylor, Flora, 119-22
Technetium 99, 183
Teenagers. *See* Adolescence
Teeth, loss of, and aging, 381-82
  See also Dental caries
Temperature extremes
  effect of vitamin C on control of, 89
  stress associated with, 366
Tension, and nutrition, 364-66
Testosterone, 331
Tetrachlorethylene, 330
Tetrahydrocannabinol 14C, 183
Thermogenesis, and stress, 366
Thiamin/Thiamine, 87, 90, 346
  amount available for consumption, per capita per day, 22
  average intake for infants, 192
  in composition of human milk, 178
  deficiencies of
    in aged 368, 370, 381
    and alcohol, 332
    in cancer patient, 348
    in pregnancy, 188
  food values for, 41
  in national food supply, 19, 20, 21
  need for 85
  Recommended Dietary Allowances (RDAs) for, 36
Thiazides, 308-9, 333
Thioridazine, 206
Thorazine, 331
Threonine, 219
Thromboembolism, 100
Thrombophlebitis, 99
Thrombosis, and dietary fiber, 146
Thrombotic stroke, 307
Thurmond, Strom, 24
Thymidine, 168
Thymidylate synthetase, 334
Thyroid gland, 119, 128
Thyroid hormone, 107
Tin, 110
Title III programs, 370-71
Title VII Nutrition Program for the Elderly, 370, 376-77
Tocopherols, 99
Tofranil, 206

INDEX

Total Diet Study (TDS),
    inclusion of iodine in, 119
Total invert suger, 155
Toward Healthful Diets (Food and
    Nutrition Board), 3, 6, 133
Tower, John G., 24
Toxicants, natural, 29-30. *See also*
    Carcinogens
Trace element-controlled isolator
    system, 110
Trace elements and minerals, 110-15
    absorption of, and protein, 112
    body's need for, 102-3
    effect of deficiency in, on pregnancy, 188
    and food, 111
    interactions among, 111
    level of, in cancer patients, 342
    See also specific minerals
Tranquilizers
    magnesium as, 104
    and riboflavin, 87
Tranylcypromine, 329, 330
Triamterene, 333
Triceps skinfold, 238, 251
Triceps skinfold thickness (TSF), 238
Trichloroethylene, 27, 29
Trichomoniasis, 183
Tricyclic antidepressants, and
    appetite, 331
Tricyclic neuroleptic drugs, 207
Triglyceride, 295
Tryptophan, 219
Tumorigenesis, 262, 264
Turbinado sugar, 155
Twiggy syndrome, 239
Twin studies, and obesity, 9
Tyramine reactions, 329-30
Tyrosine, 219
Tyrosinosis, 208

U

Ulcerative colitis, 147, 236
Ulcers peptic, 239
    and stress, 364-66
Ullman, Robert, 94
Undernutrition. *See* Malnutrition
United Food and Commerical Workers, 23
U.S. Department of Agriculture (USDA),
    3, 7, 31-32
U.S. Department of Health and Human
    Services, 166
U.S. nutritional status study, 3
Universities. *See* Colleges
Urea cycle defects, 208
Uzgiris-McHunt Development Scale, 356

V

Vaisrub, Samuel, 287
Valine, 219
Valium, 183, 206, 331
Valproic acid, 206
Vanadium, 108, 110
Varicose veins, and need for
    bioflavonoids, 92
Vegetable and vegetable products
    and fat, cholesterol and sodium
        intake, 76
    nutritive values of, 63-66
    servings per day from inverse
        pyramid food guide, 17
Vegetarianism
    in adolescent pregnancy, 234, 242
    and the athlete, 257
    and dietary fiber, 325
    and need for vitamin B^{12}, 88
    relationship to hypertension, 310
Ventromedial hypothalamus, and control
    of eating, 71
Verner-Morrison syndrome, 340
Very low density lipoproteins (VLDL), 290, 296
Vincristine, 182

Viral oncogenesis, 279
Vistaril, 331
Vitamin A, 86-87, 90
    amount available for consumption,
        per capita per day, 22
    average intake for infants, 194-95
    deficiencies of, 249
        in adolescent pregnancy, 241
        in aged, 370, 381
        and immunologic functions, 216-17
    in human milk composition, 178
    interaction of, with chemotherapy, 346
    in national food supply, 19, 20, 21
    neutrilization of PCB, 86
    Recommended Dietary Allowances
        (RDAs) for, 36
    role of, in inhibiting carcinogens, 264
    use of, in megavitamin therapy for
        aged, 382
Vitamin B^1. *See* Thiamin/Thiamine
Vitamin B^2. *See* Riboflavin
Vitamin B^3. *See* Niacin
Vitamin B^6. *See* Pyridoxine
Vitamin B^{12}, 88, 90
    amount available for consumption,
        per capita per day, 22
    in breast-fed infant, 183
    in composition of human milk, 178
    deficiencies of
        in adolescent pregnancy, 242
        in aged, 368
    interaction of, with chemotherapy, 347
    in national food supply, 19, 20, 21
Vitamin B^{15}, 93
Vitamin B^{17}, 87
Vitamin C. *See* Ascorbic acid
Vitamin D, 91, 92, 97
    cellular and molecular mechanism
        of action of calcitriol, 98
    in composition of human milk, 178
    deficiency in, 249
    diseases related to, 98
    metabolism of, 97-98
    need for supplementary, for infants, 202
    Recommened Dietary Allowances
        (RDAs) for, 36
Vitamin D-resistant rickets, 98
Vitamin D^3, 97-98, 289
Vitamin E, 91, 92, 99-101
    clinical disorders attributed to, 99
    deficiency in, 249
    effect of, on immunologic function, 217
    for athletes, 86
    interaction of, with chemotherapy, 347
    and pollution, 86
    Recommended Dietary Allowances
        (RDAs) for, 36
    relationship between selenium and, 123
    role of, in cancer etiology, 264, 273
    and self-medication, 99
    use of, in prevention of
        bronchopulmonar dysplasia in
        infants, 334
Vitamin K
    adequate and safe intake for, 33, 36
    deficiency of, in infants, 183
    interaction of, with chemotherapy,
        347-48
    need for, 334
    use of in cancer treatment, 340
Vitamins
    in composition of human milk, 178-79
    deficiencies of
        in aged, 368-69
        and pregnancy, 188
    and drugs, 334-35
    interactions of, with chemotherapy, 346-49
    level of, in cancer patients, 341-42
    pharmacologic doses of, 207
    status of, and dietary fiber, 324-25
    stress-related demands on, 366
    supplements of, for athletes, 258

W

Wallace, Robert D., 190-201
Water discipline, for athletes, 260
Watkins, Anna, 164-65
Watson, R. R., 214-15
Weight loss centers, success of, 10-11
Weight, maintenance of ideal, 3
Weight reduction
    and athletics, 248
    and dietary fiber, 146
    and disease prevention, 6
    and hypertension, 309-10
    and sodium intake, 129
    See also Obesity
Welsh, John J., 175
Welsh, Susan O., 19-22
Western Electric Study, 282
White House Conference on Food,
    Nutrition and Heath, 3
White muscle disease, 123
White, Philip L., 6
WIC. *See* Supplemental Food Program
    for Women, Infants, and Children (WIC)
Widowers/widows. *See* Aged
Wiley, Harvey W., 159
Williams, Roger, 89, 104
Wilson's disease, 332
Winston, Mary, 13
Winter, Robert J. 326-27
Wisconsin Alumni Research Foundation, 160
Wissler, Robert, 14
Women
    need for calcium, 103
    need for iron, 170
    need for vitamin B^6, 88
    nutritional ages of, 168-71
    relationship of employment status of,
        to incidence of coronary heart disease,
        298-306
Woodruff, C. W., 202-3
World Health Organization (WHO), 117, 126

X

Xerostomia, 207, 266
Xylitol, 155, 156, 157, 314, 316-18

Y

Young, Robert C., 368-72

Z

Zinc, 106-7, 109
    adolescent pregnancy, 241
    and alcohol, 332
    effect of, on immunologic
        functions, 216, 219
    animal versus vegetable sources of, 111
    compounding of, with phytates, 107
    content of U.S. food supply, per
        capita per day civilian consumption, 21
    contributions of, by major food
        groups, 20
    and copper, 106
    deficiency of, 168, 333
    depletion of, in cancer patient, 342
    effect of fiber on utilization of, 151-52
    functions of, 125-26
    in human milk composition, 179
    level of nutriture, 125
    in national food supply, 20-21
    need for, 103
    populations potentially at risk, 126
    Recommended Dietary Allowances
        (RDAs) for, 20-21, 36, 126
    and recovery after surgery, 86
    women's need for, 171
Zollinger-Ellison syndrome, 340
Zorinsky, Edward, 24

KIRTLEY LIBRARY
COLUMBIA COLLEGE
COLUMBIA, MO 65216